Lecture Notes in Computer Science 13849

The series Lecture Notes in Computer Science (LNCS), including its subseries Lecture Notes in Artificial Intelligence (LNAI) and Lecture Notes in Bioinformatics (LNBI), has established itself as a medium for the publication of new developments in computer science and information technology research, teaching, and education.

LNCS enjoys close cooperation with the computer science R & D community, the series counts many renowned academics among its volume editors and paper authors, and collaborates with prestigious societies. Its mission is to serve this international community by providing an invaluable service, mainly focused on the publication of conference and workshop proceedings and postproceedings. LNCS commenced publication in 1973.

Seung-Hyun Seo · Hwajeong Seo
Editors

Information Security and Cryptology – ICISC 2022

25th International Conference, ICISC 2022
Seoul, South Korea, November 30 – December 2, 2022
Revised Selected Papers

Springer

Editors
Seung-Hyun Seo
Hanyang University
Ansan, Korea (Republic of)

Hwajeong Seo
Hansung University
Seoul, Korea (Republic of)

ISSN 0302-9743 ISSN 1611-3349 (electronic)
Lecture Notes in Computer Science
ISBN 978-3-031-29370-2 ISBN 978-3-031-29371-9 (eBook)
https://doi.org/10.1007/978-3-031-29371-9

This Springer imprint is published by the registered company Springer Nature Switzerland AG
The registered company address is: Gewerbestrasse 11, 6330 Cham, Switzerland

Preface

The 25th International Conference on Information Security and Cryptology (ICISC 2022) was held from November 30 – December 2, 2022. This year's conference was hosted by the KIISC (Korea Institute of Information Security and Cryptology) and NSR (National Security Research Institute).

The aim of this conference is to provide an international forum for the latest results of research, development, and applications within the field of information security and cryptology. This year, we received 69 submissions and were able to accept 24 papers at the conference. The challenging review and selection processes were successfully conducted by program committee (PC) members and external reviewers via the EasyChair review system. For transparency, it is worth noting that each paper underwent a blind review by at least three PC members. For the LNCS post-proceedings, the authors of selected papers had a few weeks to prepare their final versions, based on the comments received from the reviewers.

The conference featured two invited talks, given by Elisa Bertino and Matthias J. Kannwischer. We thank the invited speakers for their kind acceptance and valuable presentations. We would like to thank all authors who submitted their papers to ICISC 2022, as well as all PC members. It was a truly wonderful experience to work with such talented and hardworking researchers. We also appreciate the external reviewers for assisting the PC members. Finally, we would like to thank all attendees for their active participation and the organizing members who successfully managed this conference. We look forward to seeing you again at next year's ICISC.

November 2022

Seung-Hyun Seo
HwaJeong Seo

December 2022

Seung-Hyun Seo
Hwajeong Seo

Organization

General Chairs

Hyojin Choi	NSR, Korea
Okyeon Yi	Kookmin University, Korea

Organizing Chairs

ChangHoon Lee	Seoul National University of Science and Technology, Korea
HeeSeok Kim	Korea University, Korea

Program Chairs

Seung-Hyun Seo	Hanyang University, Korea
HwaJeong Seo	Hansung University, Korea

Program Committee

Dongguk Han	Kookmin University, Korea
Kwangsu Lee	Sejong University, Korea
Munkyu Lee	Inha University, Korea
Jooyoung Lee	KAIST, Korea
Hyungtae Lee	Chungang University, Korea
Dongyoung Roh	National Security Research Institute, Korea
SeogChung Seo	Kookmin University, Korea
Jaehong Seo	Hanyang University, Korea
Jihye Kim	Kookmin University, Korea
Changmin Lee	Korea Institute for Advanced Study, Korea
Jongsung Kim	Kookmin University, Korea
Aaram Yun	Ewha Womans University, Korea
Taekyoung Youn	DanKook University, Korea
Jungyeon Hwang	Sungshin Women's University, Korea
Minhye Seo	Duksung Women's University, Korea
Suhri Kim	Sungshin Women's University, Korea

Dohyun Kim	Catholic University of Pusan, Korea
Seongmin Kim	Sungshin Women's University, Korea
Haehyun Cho	Soongsil University, Korea
Myungseo Park	Kangnam University, Korea
Dongyoung Koo	Hansung University, Korea
Hyojin Jo	Soongsil University, Korea
Wonsuk Choi	Hansung University, Korea
Taehwan Park	National Security Research Institute, Korea
Daehee Jang	Sungshin Women's University, Korea
Yeonjoon Lee	Hanyang University, Korea
Jonghwan Park	Sangmyung University, Korea
Seungkwang Lee	Dankook University, Korea
Ben Lee Wai Kong	Gachon University, Korea
Wenling Wu	Institute of Software Chinese Academy of Sciences, China
Zhenfu Cao	East China Normal University (ECNU), China
Swee-Huay Heng	Multimedia University, Malaysia
Toshihiro Yamauchi	Okayama University, Japan
Jiqiang Lu	Beihang University, China
Joonsang Baek	University of Wollongong, Australia
Josef Pieprzyk	CSIRO, Australia
Katsuyuki Okeya	Hitachi High-Tech Corporation, Japan
Keita Emura	National Institute of Information and Communications Technology (NICT), Japan
Bimal Roy	Indian Statistical Institute, India
Dongseong Kim	University of Queensland, Australia
Donghoon Chang	IIIT-Delhi, India
Hung-Min Sun	National Tsing Hua University, Taiwan
Iraklis Leontiadis	Inpher, USA
Baodong Qin	Xi'an University of Posts and Telecommunications, China
Fuchun Guo	University of Wollongong, Australia
Xinyi Huang	Fujian Normal University, China
Olivier Sanders	Orange Labs, France
Sherman S. M. Chow	Chinese University of Hong Kong, China
Daniel Slamanig	AIT Austrian Institute of Technology, Austria
Yahya Hassanzadeh	Dapper Labs, Canada
Jonathan Bootle	IBM Research, USA
Sanaz Taheri-Boshrooyeh	Status Research and Development, Switzerland
Reza Azarderakhsh	Florida Atlantic University, USA
Anubhab Baksi	Nanyang Technological University, Singapore

Contents

Cryptanalysis

Cyber Security

Applied Cryptography

Cryptanalysis

See-In-The-Middle Attacks on Blockciphers ARIA and DEFAULT

Jonghyun Park[1(✉)] and Jongsung Kim[1,2]

[1] Department of Financial Information Security, Kookmin University, Seoul, Republic of Korea
{mmo330,jskim}@kookmin.ac.kr

[2] Department of Information Security, Cryptology, and Mathematics, Kookmin University, Seoul, Republic of Korea

Abstract. See-In-The-Middle (SITM) is an analysis technique that utilizes side-channel information for differential cryptanalysis. The SITM attack exploits side-channel leakage in the middle round of blockcipher implementations. The blockcipher ARIA proposed at ICISC 2003 is a Korean national standard, and the blockcipher DEFAULT proposed at Asiacrypt 2021 offers proctection against differential fault analysis. In this study, we propose SITM attacks on the ARIA-128, 192, 256 and DEFAULT. Consequently, it is demonstrated that for these blockciphe r based on look-up-table implementations and no masking technique SITM attacks are possible with practical attack complexities.

Keywords: ARIA · DEFAULT · Side-channel analysis · Differential cryptanalysis · SITM

1 Introduction

Differential cryptanalysis is a representative mathematics-based cryptographic analysis technique [5]. Side-channel analysis is a powerful attack technique against cryptographic implementations [7]. Many methods have been proposed to utilize various types of side-channel information such as power consumption and electromagnetic emissions of devices for attacks [1,8]. These techniques are used to evaluate the security of cipher algorithms and they represent an essential security criterion that must be fulfilled in the cryptographic design process.

The side-channel assisted differential plaintext attack (SCADPA) proposed at DATE 2018 is an analysis technique that utilizes side-channel information for differential analysis [6]. While SCADPA targets only bit-permutation based blockciphers, the see-in-the-middle (SITM) technique proposed at TCHES 2020

This work was supported by Institute for Information & communications Technology Promotion (IITP) grant funded by the Korea government (MSIT) (No. 2017-0-00520, Development of SCR-Friendly Symmetric Key Cryptosystem and Its Application Modes).

S.-H. Seo and H. Seo (Eds.): ICISC 2022, LNCS 13849, pp. 3–16, 2023.
https://doi.org/10.1007/978-3-031-29371-9_1

has been extended to target substitution-permutation network (SPN) blockciphers [4]. The SITM analysis technique utilizes the power trace information of blockciphers in which partial rounds are not implemented with masking techniques for differential cryptanalysis. By using this attack, it is possible to determine the appropriate number of rounds by applying the partial first or higher-order masking technique when implementing the blockcipher, and this can reduce the cost of the masking technique. Currently, the AES, SKINNY, and PRESENT attacks with SITM techniques have been presented [4,10,11].

Contributions

In this paper, we present the results of SITM attacks against the blockciphers ARIA-128, 192, 256 and DEFAULT. The targets of these attacks are look-up-table (LUT) implementation based blockciphers. The results demonstrate that these LUT implementation based blockciphers to which no masking technique is applied are susceptible to SITM attacks with practical attack complexities. Our associated attack complexities are summarized in Table 1. In this table, depth refers to a round position for measuring a power trace through side-channel observation. These attacks are the first SITM attacks against ARIA and DEFAULT.

Table 1. Summary of SITM attack complexities on ARIA and DEFAULT

Blockcipher	Key#	Depth	Data	Time	Memory	Ref
ARIA	128	2, 3 4, 5	$2^{15.12}$	$2^{15.12}$	$2^{10.02}$	Section 3
	192	2, 3 4, 5	$2^{15.12}$	$2^{15.12}$	$2^{10.02}$	Section 3
	256	2, 3 4, 5	$2^{15.12}$	$2^{15.12}$	$2^{10.02}$	Sect. 3
DEFAULT	128	3	2^{10}	2^{10}	2^{15}	Section 4

Key# is the key size and the unit of memory is byte.

2 Background

2.1 BlockCipher ARIA

ARIA proposed at ICISC 2003 is a Korean national standard [9]. ARIA encrypts a 128-bit plaintext by using a 128-, 192-, or 256-bit masterkey (MK) and processes 12, 14, and 16 rounds, respectively. For convenience, we label the bytes in the ARIA state column-wise from left to right, as follows:

$$\begin{bmatrix} 0 & 4 & 8 & 12 \\ 1 & 5 & 9 & 13 \\ 2 & 6 & 10 & 14 \\ 3 & 7 & 11 & 15 \end{bmatrix}.$$

The round function of ARIA is composed of substitution layer (SL), diffusion layer (DL), and addroundkey (ARK). In the SL, an 8-bit S-box is applied to the 128-bit state, and four types of S-boxes are used. There are two types of SL, and they are used alternately in different rounds. DL multiplies the 16×16 binary matrix with the input data (Figs. 1 and 2).

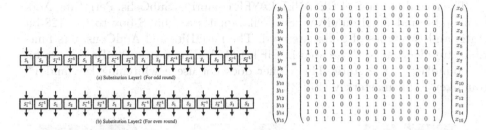

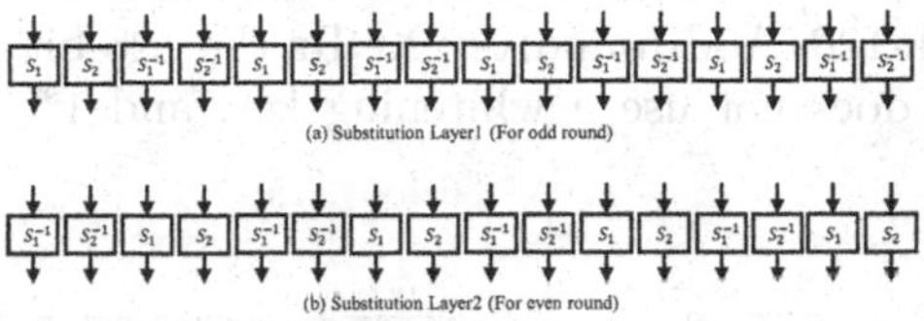

Fig. 1. Substitution layer of the ARIA

$$\begin{pmatrix} y_0 \\ y_1 \\ y_2 \\ y_3 \\ y_4 \\ y_5 \\ y_6 \\ y_7 \\ y_8 \\ y_9 \\ y_{10} \\ y_{11} \\ y_{12} \\ y_{13} \\ y_{14} \\ y_{15} \end{pmatrix} = \begin{pmatrix}
0&0&0&1&1&0&1&0&1&1&0&0&0&1&1&0 \\
0&0&1&0&0&1&0&1&1&1&0&0&1&0&0&1 \\
0&1&0&0&1&0&1&0&0&0&1&1&1&0&0&1 \\
1&0&0&0&0&1&0&1&0&0&1&1&0&1&1&0 \\
1&0&1&0&0&1&0&0&1&0&0&1&0&0&1&1 \\
0&1&0&1&1&0&0&0&0&1&1&0&0&0&1&1 \\
1&0&1&0&0&0&0&1&0&1&1&0&1&1&0&0 \\
0&1&0&1&0&0&1&0&1&0&0&1&1&1&0&0 \\
1&1&0&0&1&0&0&1&0&0&1&0&0&1&0&1 \\
1&1&0&0&0&1&1&0&0&0&0&1&1&0&1&0 \\
0&0&1&1&0&1&1&0&1&0&0&0&0&1&0&1 \\
0&0&1&1&1&0&0&1&0&1&0&0&1&0&1&0 \\
0&1&1&0&0&0&1&1&0&1&0&1&1&0&0&0 \\
1&0&0&1&0&0&1&1&1&0&1&0&0&1&0&0 \\
1&0&0&1&1&1&0&0&0&1&0&1&0&0&1&0 \\
0&1&1&0&1&1&0&0&1&0&1&0&0&0&0&1
\end{pmatrix} \cdot \begin{pmatrix} x_0 \\ x_1 \\ x_2 \\ x_3 \\ x_4 \\ x_5 \\ x_6 \\ x_7 \\ x_8 \\ x_9 \\ x_{10} \\ x_{11} \\ x_{12} \\ x_{13} \\ x_{14} \\ x_{15} \end{pmatrix}$$

Fig. 2. Diffusion layer of the ARIA

ARK XORs the ith roundkey k_i to the state. ARIA uses the whitening key. The key schedule of the ARIA comprises the initialization part and the roundkey generation part. In the initialization part, a 3-round feistel cipher is used. The feistel cipher is identical to the 3-round ARIA except for the roundkey. This cipher uses a fixed constant instead of a roundkey as follow.

- C1 = 0x517CC1B727220A94FE13ABE8fA9A6EE0
- C2 = 0x6DB14ACC9E21C820FF28B1D5EF5DE2B0
- C3 = 0xDB92371D2126E9700324977504E8C90E

During the feistel cipher encryption process, $W_0 \sim W_3$ are generated. We denote the odd round be F_o, the even round be F_e and the ith byte of key as key[i]. The detailed key schedule of the ARIA-128 is as follows:

1. key = masterkey || 0^{128}
2. $CK_1 = $ C1, $CK_2 = $ C2, $CK_3 = $ C3.
3. KL = key[0..15], KR = key[16..31]
4. $W_0 = $ KL
5. $W_1 = F_o(W_0, CK_1) \oplus$ KR
6. $W_2 = F_e(W_1, CK_2) \oplus W_0$
7. $W_3 = F_o(W_2, CK_3) \oplus W_1$
   - $k_0 = W_0 \oplus (W_1 \ggg 19)$, $k_1 = W_1 \oplus (W_2 \ggg 19)$
   - $k_2 = W_2 \oplus (W_3 \ggg 19)$, $k_3 = W_3 \oplus (W_0 \ggg 19)$

We describe the generation process of these roundkeys because only $k_0 \sim k_3$ are used for key recovery. The key schedule of ARIA-192, 256 is similar to the above. Please refer to [9] for details.

2.2 BlockCipher DEFAULT

DEFAULT proposed at Asiacrypt 2021 offers protection against differential fault analysis [2], and it is similar to GIFT-128 [3], except for S-box. DEFAULT encrypts a 128-bit plaintext by using a 128-bit masterkey and processes 80 rounds. This cipher has a sandwich structure composed of DEFAULT-LAYER and DEFAULT-CORE.

The round function of DEFAULT-LAYER comprises SubCells, PermBits, AddConstants, and AddRoundKey. SubCells applies a 4-bit S-box to the 128-bit state, and two types of S-box are used. The PermBits and AddConstants functions are identical to those used in GIFT-128. AddRoundKey XORs the 128-bit i^{th} roundkey to the state. This cipher does not use a whitening key, and 1st roundkey is the masterkey (Fig. 3).

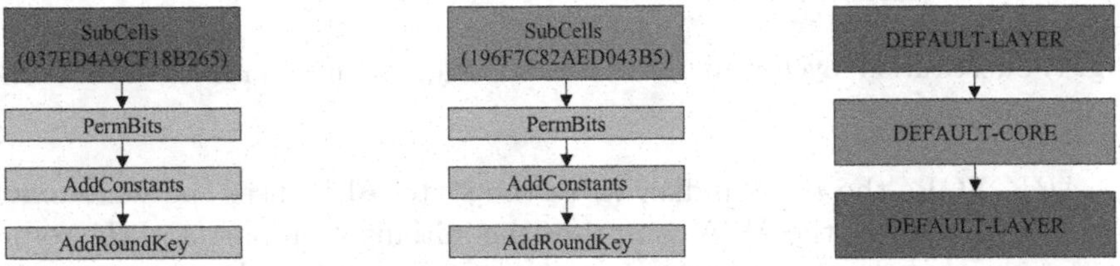

(a) Round Function of DEFAULT-LAYER (b) Round Function of DEFAULT-CORE (c) Structure of DEFAULT

Fig. 3. Structure of DEFAULT

DEFAULT-CORE is similar to DEFAULT-LAYER, except for the S-box and number of rounds. The number of rounds in DEFAULT-LAYER is 28, and whereas that in DEFAULT-CORE is 24.

- DEFAULT-LAYER
  S-box = [0x0, 0x3, 0x7, 0xE, 0xD, 0x4, 0xA, 0x9, 0xC, 0xF, 0x1, 0x8, 0xB, 0x2, 0x6, 0x5].
- DEFAULT-CORE
  S-box = [0x1, 0x9, 0x6, 0xF, 0x7, 0xC, 0x8, 0x2, 0xA, 0xE, 0xD, 0x0, 0x4, 0x3, 0xB, 0x5].

Because we do not use a key schedule in key-recovery, we omit a description of this. Please refer to [2] for details.

2.3 SITM Overview

An SITM attack uses differences in the power traces generated during the encryption process to filter plaintext pairs and utilize them for differential cryptanalysis. The following definitions are used in the description of SITM.

- Power trace:
  flow of power from a device equipped with a cryptographic function.

– Difference trace:
  difference between two power traces.
– Differential trail:
  expected trail through which a specific difference propagates when different plaintexts are encrypted.
– Differential pattern:
  differential trails.
– Active S-box:
  S-box with non-zero input difference on differential trail (or pattern).
– Non-active S-box:
  S-box with zero input difference on differential trail (or pattern).

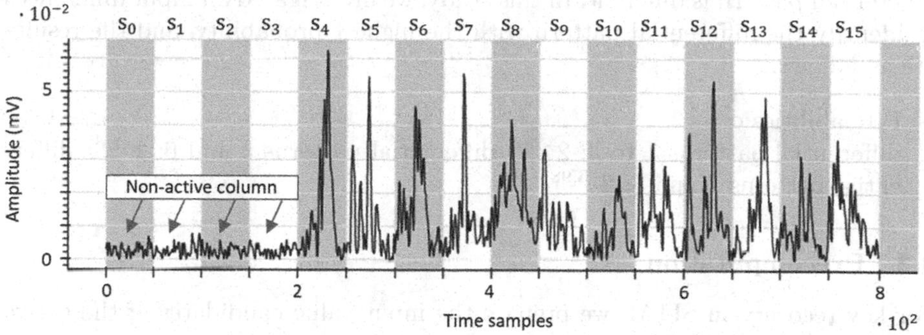

Fig. 4. Example of difference trace in AES SubBytes operation

An SITM attack uses the difference trace generated during the encryption of different plaintext pairs as the key idea. Assume that different plaintext pairs have gathered the power traces generated during encryption. It can be predicted that if the input values match each other during S-box operation at the same location, the two power traces are similar. If not, the two power traces are different. This principle can be used to select plaintext pairs that satisfy the differential trail (or pattern) expected by the attacker. Figure 4 is a graph of difference trace generated from the AES SubBytes operation used in [10]. The logic in which the non-active S-box is clearly visible in the Fig. 4 is used for SITM attacks. The secret key can be recovered by utilizing the selected plaintext and differential transition. The detailed key-recovery process is described in Sects. 3 and 4.

3 SITM Attacks on ARIA

3.1 ARIA Differential Patterns

We used Eight differential patterns for the attack. These patterns are depicted in Fig. 5. For differential patterns, it is probable that two active bytes have the same difference after the SL_1 operation. We proceed with the following steps to find the differential pattern with the optimal probability.

1) For two different S-boxes, find all pairs of input differences in which the possible candidates for output differences match each other.
2) For each pair of input differences satisfying the above, all the probabilities of differential trails whose output differences coincide with each other after the SL_1 operation are summed.
3) The input difference pair with the highest probability is used for the differential pattern.

If these 2 active bytes are identical, the state after DL_1 operation must comprise 6 active bytes. This is because the branch number of DL is 8. These cases are summarized in Table 2.

Because SL applies different S-boxes to each state row, the probability of each differential pattern is different. In this study, we investigated all input differences to identify the differential pattern with the highest probability, and the results are as follows.

- Probabilities of
  differential patterns 1 to 4: $2^{-7.64}$ differential patterns 5 and 6: $2^{-7.62}$ differential patterns 7 and 8: $2^{-6.98}$

3.2 Precomputation

For key-recovery in SITM, we prepare the input value candidates of the active byte positions in SL_1 as follows.

1. Calculate the differential distribution table (DDT) for four types of S-boxes used in SL.

Table 2. DL operation from 2 active bytes to 6 active bytes.

No	Input difference	Output difference
1	00 00 00 01	00 00 01 00
	00 00 00 00	00 00 01 01
	00 00 00 00	01 00 00 00
	00 01 00 00	01 01 00 00
2	00 00 00 02	00 00 02 00
	00 00 00 00	00 00 02 02
	00 00 00 00	02 00 00 00
	00 02 00 00	02 02 00 00
⋮	⋮	⋮
255	00 00 00 FF	00 00 FF 00
	00 00 00 00	00 00 FF FF
	00 00 00 00	FF 00 00 00
	00 FF 00 00	FF FF 00 00

2. By using each DDT, find the output difference where the input difference 0x90 and 0x25 can be the same difference after the SL_1 operation.
3. Store all the input values of the input differences for the output differences found. Let these values be In_{List}.

The other differential patterns can be used to obtain In_{List} through a similar process. For each of the patterns, the number of In_{List} is different as follows.

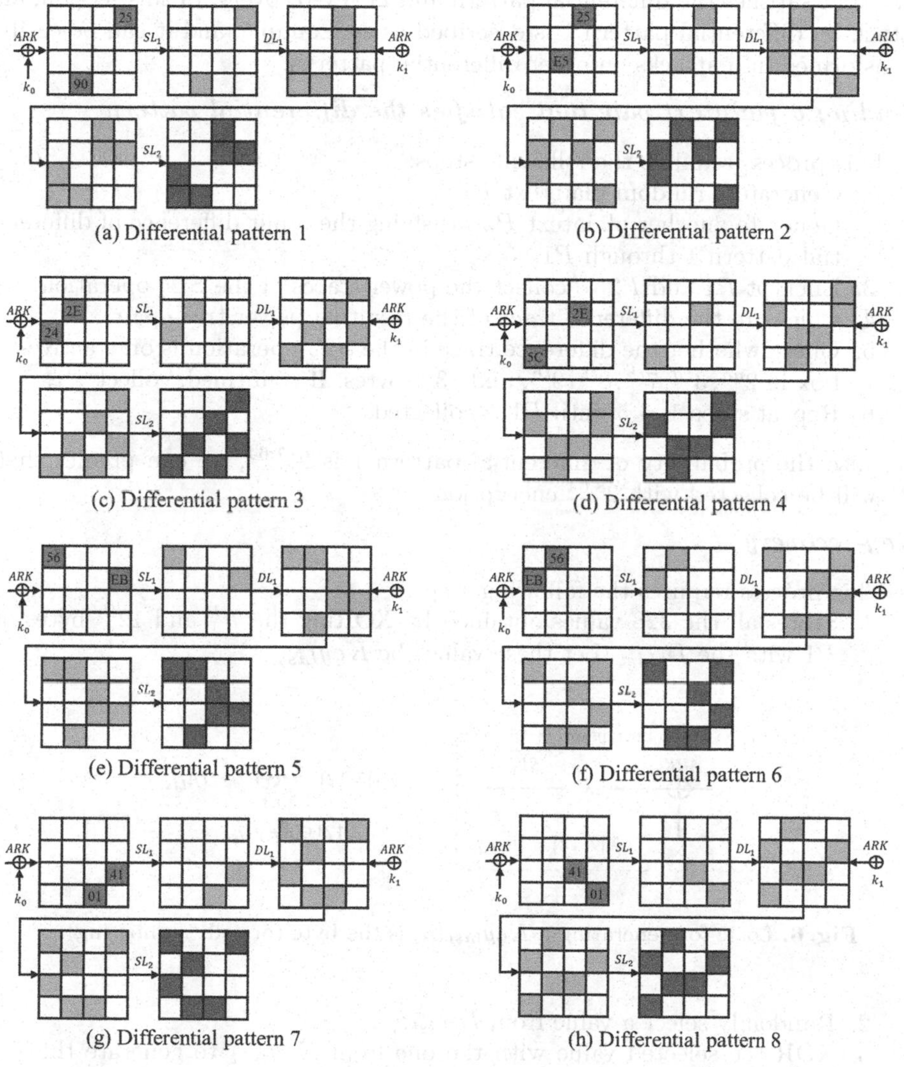

Fig. 5. Eight differential patterns of ARIA (For each pattern, the green bytes denote specific differences, yellow bytes denote equal differences, red bytes denote truncated differences, and all colored bytes denote non-zero differences).

- The numbers of In_{List} for
  differential patterns 1 to 4: 328
  differential patterns 5 and 6: 332
  differential patterns 7 and 8: 520

3.3 SITM Application

The proposed SITM attack is divided into two processes: 1) finding a plaintext pair that satisfies the differential pattern and 2) key-recovery. In this section, an attack on differential pattern 1 is described as an example, and it can be easily transformed into attacks on other differential patterns.

Finding a plaintext pair that satisfies the differential pattern

- This process requires the following steps:
  1. Generate a random plaintext $P1$
  2. Generate another plaintext $P2$ satisfying the input difference of differential pattern 1 through $P1$.
  3. Encrypt $P1$ and $P2$ to collect the power traces of the SL_2 operation.
  4. Calculate the difference trace of the resulting power trace pair.
  5. Check whether the difference trace in the SL_2 operation is only active-S-box in $2^{nd}, 3^{rd}, 7^{th}, 8^{th}, 9^{th}$, and 13th bytes. If confirmed, collect $P1$.
  6. Repeat steps 1 $\sim$ 5 until $P1$ is collected.

Because the probability of differential pattern 1 is $2^{-7.64}$, we can predict that $P1$ will be collected with $2^{8.64}$ encryption.

Key-recovery

- This process requires the following steps:
  1. Stores all the 328 values obtained by XORing the 7th and 12th bytes of $P1$ with the In_{List}. Let these values be Key_{List}.

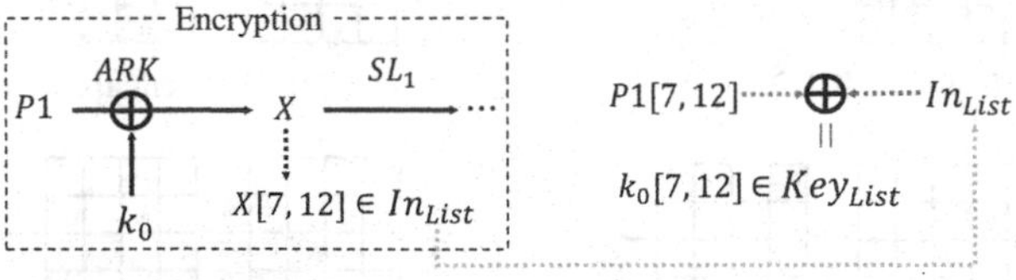

Fig. 6. Logic for generating a Key_{List}([i] is the byte (or cell) numbering).

  2. Randomly select a value from In_{List}.
  3. XOR the selected value with the one from Key_{List} to generate the 7th and 12th bytes of plaintext $P1$. Let the used key candidate be key_u.
  4. Generate random but fixed values for remaining bytes of plaintext $P1$.
  5. Generate another plaintext $P2$ that satisfies the input difference of differential pattern 1 through $P1$.

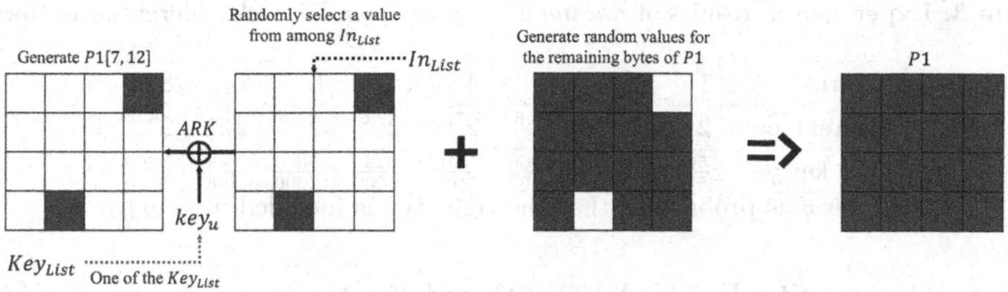

Fig. 7. Process for generating plaintext $P1$.

6. Check whether the difference trace in the SL_2 operation is only active S-box in $2^{nd}, 3^{rd}, 7^{th}, 8^{th}, 9^{th}$, and 13th bytes. If confirmed, collect key_u.
7. Repeat step 1 $\sim$ 6 until key_u is collected by using the other Key_{List} (Figs. 6 and 7).

The 7th and 12th bytes of the value that $P1$ and k_0 are XORed with are included in In_{List} by differential transition. Therefore, the right key is included in key_{List}. Consequently, the 7th and 12th bytes of k_0 can be recovered by the above process.

All bytes of k_0 can be recovered through a similar attack process by using the remaining differential patterns. After recovering k_0, we can repeat the attack to recover k_1 by choosing plaintexts that have pairwise differential patterns beginning from DL_1 and observe leakage in round 3. With this method, it is possible to recover $k_0 \sim k_3$. If the masterkey recovery method described [12] is used, the ARIA masterkey can be recovered only with $k_0 \sim k_3$, and this applies to ARIA-128, 192, and 256.

1. $A = k_0 \oplus (k_1 \ggg 19) = W_0 \oplus (W_2 \ggg 38)$
2. $B = k_2 \oplus (k_3 \ggg 19) = W_2 \oplus (W_0 \ggg 38)$
3. $A \oplus (B \ggg 38) = W_0 \oplus (W_0 \ggg 76)$

If we guess the most significant 2-bits of $W_0 \oplus (W_0 \ggg 76)$ as 0 or 1, we get 4 candidates for W_0. W_0 can be used to obtain W_1 according to the key schedule logic. By using W_0 and W_1, we can get the masterkeys of ARIA-128, 192, and 256.

Experiment. We experimented with the *finding a plaintext pair* process 5000 times, assuming that there is a side channel tool to observe the power trace. From this experimental result, we obtain the average number of plaintexts used for each differential pattern and the probability that the right key is included in key_{List} generated with collected plaintexts. Table 3 is the result of the experiment.

Table 3. Experimental results of *finding a plaintext pair* for each differential pattern.

Pattern	1	2	3	4	5	6	7	8
Plaintext pair	$2^{7.64}$	$2^{7.66}$	$2^{7.63}$	$2^{7.63}$	$2^{7.64}$	$2^{7.6}$	$2^{6.95}$	$2^{6.94}$
Right key#	$\frac{5000}{5000}$	$\frac{5000}{5000}$	$\frac{5000}{5000}$	$\frac{5000}{5000}$	$\frac{5000}{5000}$	$\frac{5000}{5000}$	$\frac{5000}{5000}$	$\frac{5000}{5000}$

Right key# is probability that the right key is included in key_{List}.

Attack Complexity. For ARIA-128, 192, and 256, the attack requires $4 \times \{4 \times 2 \times (2^{7.64} + 328) + 2 \times 2 \times (2^{7.62} + 332 + 2^{6.98} + 520)\} \approx 2^{15.12}$ plaintexts, the memory space of $2 \times 520 \approx 2^{10.02}$-bytes to store the 2-byte key candidates, the time complexity of $2^{15.12}$ and side-channel observation in rounds $2 \sim 5$.

4 SITM Attack on DEFAULT

4.1 DEFAULT Differential Trails

We used the eight differential trails shown in Fig. 8 for the attack. Each differential trail, consists of truncated differential trails and differential trails. Because DEFAULT-LAYER does not use the whitening key, if the 128-bit value before 1st round AddRoundKey is determined, the plaintext can be generated through partial decryption. Our attack randomly generates a 128-bit value before the 1st

Table 4. DDT of S-box used in DEFAULT-LAYER.

Input difference	Out difference															
	0	1	2	3	4	5	6	7	8	9	A	B	C	D	E	F
0	16	0	0	0	0	0	0	0	0	0	0	0	0	0	0	0
1	0	0	0	8	0	0	0	0	0	8	0	0	0	0	0	0
2	0	0	0	0	0	0	0	8	0	0	0	0	0	8	0	0
3	0	0	0	0	8	0	0	0	0	0	0	0	0	0	8	0
4	0	0	0	0	0	0	0	8	0	0	0	0	0	8	0	0
5	0	0	0	0	8	0	0	0	0	0	0	0	0	0	8	0
6	0	0	0	0	0	0	0	0	0	0	16	0	0	0	0	0
7	0	0	0	8	0	0	0	0	0	8	0	0	0	0	0	0
8	0	0	0	0	0	0	8	0	0	0	0	0	8	0	0	0
9	0	0	0	0	0	0	0	0	0	0	0	0	0	0	0	16
A	0	8	0	0	0	0	0	0	0	0	0	8	0	0	0	0
B	0	0	8	0	0	0	0	0	8	0	0	0	0	0	0	0
C	0	8	0	0	0	0	0	0	0	0	0	8	0	0	0	0
D	0	0	8	0	0	0	0	0	8	0	0	0	0	0	0	0
E	0	0	0	0	0	0	8	0	0	0	0	0	8	0	0	0
F	0	0	0	0	0	16	0	0	0	0	0	0	0	0	0	0

round AddRoundKey, and therefore the truncated differential trail depends on that value. Differential trails have a probability of 2^{-4} that the number of active S-boxes is 1 after the 2nd round operation. In addition to the input differences 0x3, 0xB, 0xA, and 0xB, other input differences can be used in the attack without changing the probability and differential trails, and the differences can be easily obtained from the DDT (Table 4).

4.2 Precomputation

For key recovery in SITM, we prepare input the value candidates of the active cell positions in 2nd round SubCells. The process of preparing input value candidates for a differential trail is as follows.

1. Calculate the DDT for the S-box used in SubCells.
2. Store all input values such that input differences 0x3, 0xB, 0xA, and 0xB become output differences 0x4, 0x2, 0x1, and 0x8 after SubCells operation. Let these values be In_{List}.

The number of In_{List} for the differential trails is 2^{12}.

4.3 SITM Application

Our SITM attack process is divided into two processes: 1) finding four plaintext pairs that satisfy the differential trail; and 2) key-recovery. This section describes the attack on a differential trail 1 in Fig. 8 as an example, which can easily be transformed into attacks on other differential trails.

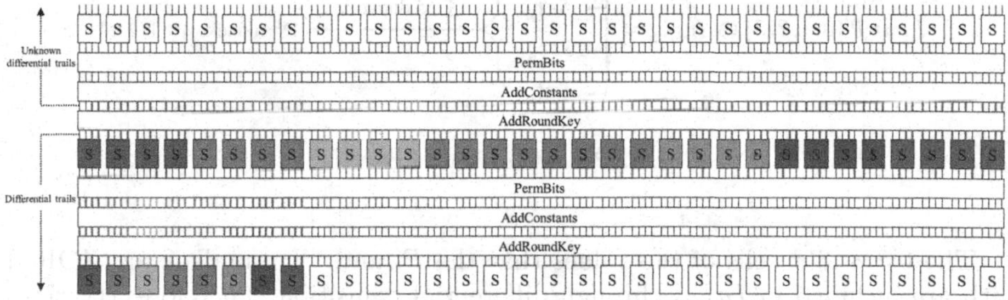

Fig. 8. Eight differential trails of DEFAULT with probability 2^{-4} (Each differential trail is indicated by a different color, and from left to right are differential trailx 1 to 8).

Finding Four Plaintext Pairs that Satisfy the Differential Trail

- This process requires the following steps:
  1. Generate a 128-bit random value before the 1st round AddRoundKey. Let this value be P'.
  2. Partially decrypt P' to convert it into plaintext $P1$.
  3. Generate another plaintext $P2$ that satisfies the input difference of the differential trail through $P1$.
  4. Encrypt $P1$ and $P2$ to collect the power traces of the 3rd round SubCells operation.
  5. Calculate the difference trace for the power trace pair.
  6. Check whether the difference trace in the 3rd round SubCells operation is only active-S-box in the 0th cells. If confirmed, collect P'.
  7. Repeat steps $1 \sim 6$ untill four P' are collected. Each time a P' is collected, the input difference of the differential trail must be changed.

Because the probability of the differential trail is 2^{-4}, we can predict that four P' will be collected in 2^7 encryption.

Key-recovery

- This process requires the following steps:
  1. For each P', store all 2^{12} values obtained by XORing the $0^{th} \sim 3^{rd}$ cells of P' with In_{List}. Let the values stored in the four P' be $Set_1 \sim Set_4$.
  2. Find duplicate elements in $Set_1 \sim Set_4$ (Fig. 9).

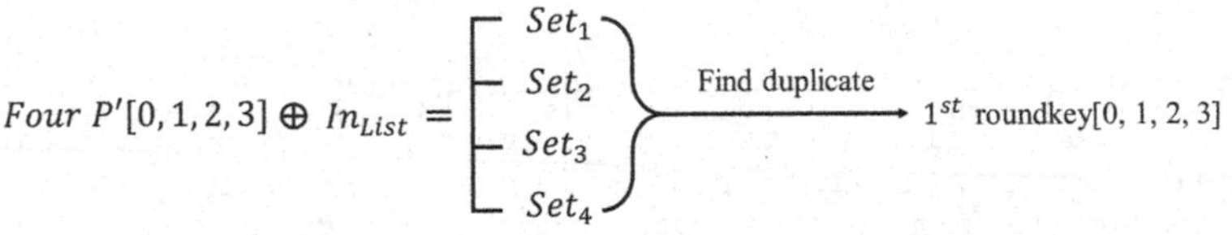

Fig. 9. Process of key-recovery.

The $0^{th} \sim 3^{rd}$ cells of the values that the P' and 1st roundkey are XORed with are included in In_{List} through differential transition. Therefore, the right key is included in Set_i. The Set_i is a subset of size 2^{12} of the full set of size 2^{16}. Therefore, when these sets are intersected, it can be predicted that the number of key candidates will decrease to $2^{16-4-4-4-4} = 1$. Consequently, the $0^{th} \sim 3^{rd}$ cells of 1st roundkey can be recovered by the above process. The entire cell of the 1st roundkey can be recovered through a similar attack process by using the remaining differential trails, and the 1st roundkey is masterkey.

Experiment We experimented with the *finding four plaintext pairs* process 5000 times, assuming that there is a side channel tool to observe the power trace. From this experimental result, we obtain the average number of plaintexts used for

Table 5. Experimental results of *finding four plaintext pairs* for each differential trail.

Trail	1	2	3	4	5	6	7	8
Plaintext pairs	$2^{5.99}$	$2^{6.0}$	$2^{6.0}$	$2^{5.99}$	$2^{6.00}$	$2^{5.99}$	$2^{6.0}$	$2^{6.0}$
Right key#	$\frac{5000}{5000}$	$\frac{5000}{5000}$	$\frac{5000}{5000}$	$\frac{5000}{5000}$	$\frac{5000}{5000}$	$\frac{5000}{5000}$	$\frac{5000}{5000}$	$\frac{5000}{5000}$

Right key# is probability that the right key is included in key_{List}.

each differential trail and the probability that the right key is included in key_{List} generated with collected plaintexts. Table 5 is the result of the experiment.

Attack Complexity. For DEFAULT, the attack requires $8 \times 2 \times 4 \times (2^4) = 2^{10}$ plaintexts, the memory space of $4 \times 2 \times 4096 = 2^{15}$-bytes to store the four 2-byte key candidates, the time complexity of 2^{10}, and side-channel observation in round 3.

5 Conclusion

In this study, we performed SITM attacks against the Korean blockcipher ARIA-128, 192, and 256 with practical attack complexity. To counter these attack, ARIA should be applied with at least a 4-round partial masking implementation.

Moreover, we performed an SITM attack against the blockcipher DEFAULT with practical attack complexity. To counter this attack, DEFAULT should be applied with at least a 6-round partial masking implementation.

In conclusion, an SITM attack is a strong attack against LUT implementation based blockciphers, and implementation using the bitslice technique or masking technique, instead of LUT, is necessary to counter.

References

1. Agrawal, D., Archambeault, B., Rao, J.R., Rohatgi, P.: The EM side—channel(s). In: Kaliski, B.S., Koç, K., Paar, C. (eds.) CHES 2002. LNCS, vol. 2523, pp. 29–45. Springer, Heidelberg (2003). https://doi.org/10.1007/3-540-36400-5_4
2. Baksi, A., Bhasin, S., Breier, J., Khairallah, M., Peyrin, T., Sarkar, S., Sim, S.M.: DEFAULT: cipher level resistance against differential fault attack. In: Tibouchi, M., Wang, H. (eds.) ASIACRYPT 2021. LNCS, vol. 13091, pp. 124–156. Springer, Cham (2021). https://doi.org/10.1007/978-3-030-92075-3_5
3. Banik, S., Pandey, S.K., Peyrin, T., Sasaki, Yu., Sim, S.M., Todo, Y.: GIFT: a small present. In: Fischer, W., Homma, N. (eds.) CHES 2017. LNCS, vol. 10529, pp. 321–345. Springer, Cham (2017). https://doi.org/10.1007/978-3-319-66787-4_16
4. Bhasin, S., Breier, J., Hou, X., Jap, D., Poussier, R., Sim, S.M.: SITM: see-in-the-middle side-channel assisted middle round differential cryptanalysis on SPN block ciphers. CHES **2020**, 95–122 (2020)
5. Biham, E., Shamir, A.: Differential cryptanalysis of the data encryption standard. Springer Science & Business Media (2012)

6. Breier, J., Jap, D., Bhasin, S.: SCADPA: side-channel assisted differential-plaintext attack on bit permutation based ciphers. In: 2018 Design, Automation & Test in Europe Conference & Exhibition, DATE 2018, Dresden, Germany, 19–23 March, 2018, pp. 1129–1134. IEEE (2018)
7. Kocher, P.C.: Timing attacks on implementations of Diffie-Hellman, RSA, DSS, and other systems. In: Koblitz, N. (ed.) CRYPTO 1996. LNCS, vol. 1109, pp. 104–113. Springer, Heidelberg (1996). https://doi.org/10.1007/3-540-68697-5_9
8. Kocher, P., Jaffe, J., Jun, B.: Differential power analysis. In: Wiener, M. (ed.) CRYPTO 1999. LNCS, vol. 1666, pp. 388–397. Springer, Heidelberg (1999). https://doi.org/10.1007/3-540-48405-1_25
9. Kwon, D., Kim, J., Park, S., Sung, S.H., Sohn, Y., Song, J.H., Yeom, Y., Yoon, E.-J., Lee, S., Lee, J., Chee, S., Han, D., Hong, J.: New block cipher: ARIA. In: Lim, J.-I., Lee, D.-H. (eds.) ICISC 2003. LNCS, vol. 2971, pp. 432–445. Springer, Heidelberg (2004). https://doi.org/10.1007/978-3-540-24691-6_32
10. Park, J., Kim, H., Kim, J.: Improved see-in-the-middle attacks on aes. In: International Conference on Information Security and Cryptology, pp. 271–279. Springer (2022)
11. Park, J., Kim, H., Kim, J.: Improved sitm attack on the present blockcipher. J. Korea Inst. Inf. Secur. Cryptol. **32**(2), 155–162 (2022)
12. Seo, J., Kim, C., Ha, J., Moon, S., Park, I.: Differential power analysis attack of a block cipher aria. J. Korea Inst. Inf. Secur. Cryptology **15**(1), 99–107 (2005)

Implicit Key-Stretching Security of Encryption Schemes

Jannis Bossert[1], Eik List[2(✉)], and Stefan Lucks[3]

[1] Independent researcher, Weimar, Germany
[2] Nanyang-Technological University, Singapore, Singapore
eik.list@ntu.edu.sg
[3] Bauhaus-Universität Weimar, Weimar, Germany
stefan.lucks@uni-weimar.de

Abstract. When keys are small or parts thereof leak, key-recovery attacks on symmetric-key primitives still pose a plausible threat. Key stretching is one well-known means to throttle potential adversaries, where stretching a key by s bit means that a key-recovery attack has to perform $\min\{2^{k-1}, 2^{k-\lambda+s-1}\}$ operations on average for λ bit information leakage. However, typical explicit key stretching requires also the defender to pay for the stretch operations.

The usual assumption is that a surrounding encryption scheme does not increase the key-recovery security of its internal primitives. This work challenges this assumption by considering the structure of popular encryption schemes. In particular, message lengths may be non-negligible in settings such as full-disk encryption or archiving, where the adversary can obtain only long messages. Surprisingly, the question of whether a surrounding encryption scheme has only a negligible impact on key recovery seems to have remained uninvestigated. Therefore, it is interesting to study if "implicit" key stretching may come for free as an inherent property of popular schemes.

We define an encryption scheme as "fully key-stretching-secure" if an adversary that sees plaintext-ciphertext pairs of at least m blocks each must perform at least m primitive calls for testing a key candidate. Using a similar definition of affine modes as Chakraborti et al. in JMC 2018, we systematically explore common encryption schemes with respect to their key-stretching security. In total, we consider five classes of (1) online, (2) SIV-like, (3) parallelizable two-pass (EME-like), (4) sequential two-pass (CMC-like), and (5) three-pass (HCTR-like) encryption schemes. By modeling them as affine modes, we can identify all considered encryption schemes key-stretching-insecure, i.e., one needs only $O(1)$ primitive calls for testing a key candidate. However, for the insecure schemes from types (4) and (5), namely for EME-, CMC-, and HCTR-like schemes, we propose minor tweaks to ensure full key-stretching security.

Keywords: Symmetric-key cryptography · Provable security · Encryption

S.-H. Seo and H. Seo (Eds.): ICISC 2022, LNCS 13849, pp. 17–40, 2023.
https://doi.org/10.1007/978-3-031-29371-9_2

1 Introduction

Key Recovery and Message Lengths. In symmetric-key cryptography, key-recovery attacks on primitives are a research topic of their own. Besides time-memory-data trade-offs, cryptanalysis on round-based primitives aims to identify non-ideal properties in the primitive that can be used for key-recovery attacks thereafter. For higher-level schemes that employ keyed primitives, the implicit assumption is that no key-recovery attacks on the primitive better than exhaustive search with the best known time-memory-data trade-offs exist. Thus, schemes are usually not expected to add any further security in this regard.

Explicit Key Stretching. Key-derivation functions are cryptographic primitives for deriving cryptographic keys from potentially low-entropy secrets. By guaranteeing a high time-memory-data product, they can stretch an initial seed K_0 of only k' bit of entropy to a key K of $k = |K|$-bit entropy. A simple way is to iterate a function $K_i \leftarrow F^i(K_{i-1})$ for m iterations to have $K = K_m$, for computing $C \leftarrow E_K(M)$. In this manner, the naive memoryless key recovery needs $\min\{2^k, m \cdot 2^{k'}\}$ primitive calls. Though, this process also throttles the legitimate seed owner when deriving the key. Thus, it appears desirable to identify further entropy-stretching means that do not throttle the owner.

Message Lengths. Using already present long messages may be one possible means. Some settings restrict messages (or message segments) to a non-negligible minimal length. For example, Full-Disk Encryption schemes typically process fixed-sized chunks of data whose lengths are fixed to multiples of 512 or 4096 bytes each. Optical-Transport Networks (OTNs) use longer message frames of 64 kiB [27], which corresponds to 2^{12} AES blocks. Moreover, long-term archive backup frames usually consist of (multi-)MiByte-size chunks. In such settings, the minimum length has not been considered a security-enhancing factor yet. Thus, it is interesting to evaluate if a significant minimal length could increase the security of a scheme.

In addition to settings that enforce a minimal message length by a surrounding standard, the sender and receiver can simply choose longer messages. While active adversaries could naturally decide to introduce shorter messages, known-plaintext attacks are often preferable over their chosen plain- and ciphertexts counterparts, for an adversary might want to remain passive and undetected, can only receive but not send, or is otherwise thwarted from choosing inputs, e.g. by further means of authentication. Then, it must resort to a known-plaintext attack and is limited to exploiting message material obtained from eavesdropping. In all these settings, whenever the minimum lengths of observed materials are non-negligible, a study of its effect on key recovery is worth an evaluation.

Attack Model. Imagine a key-recovery attack on an encryption scheme Π. An adversary observes or queries q plaintext-ciphertext pairs (M^i, C^i), where each message $M^i = (M^i_1, \ldots, M^i_{m^i})$ consists of a minimal number of $m = \min\{m^1, \ldots, m^q\}$ blocks each. It may obtain additional information, e.g. in the form of $\lambda \leq k$ bits of leakage from the employed secret keys. The adversary's goal is to recover the key, which requires the ability to map at least parts from one of the plaintexts M^i to parts of its corresponding ciphertext C^i. Given a plaintext-ciphertext pair for a keyed secure black-box primitive and λ bits of effective information about the secret key, a key recovery should succeed in $O(2^{k-\lambda})$ operations and require half of that number of primitive computations on average. The surrounding cryptographic scheme may add complexity, i.e., may increase the adversary's computational effort for testing keys. If the amount of necessary computations approaches $m \cdot 2^{k-\lambda}$, we say that Π provides $\log_2(m)$ bits of *implicit key stretching.*

Contribution. This work introduces *implicit key stretching* as a robustness property of cryptographic schemes. Since the property is equivalent to a lower bound on the number of blocks to be processed for a cipher for an m-block message, we use a query complexity as a measure for the number of necessary primitive calls for obtaining a relation for filtering key candidate. We call a transcript of plaintext-ciphertext queries m-block-minimal if all plain- and ciphertexts consist of at least m blocks. We say that a scheme provides *full implicit key stretching* if at least m primitive computations must be performed for each key candidate. After showing why it must be trivial for online schemes, we study well-known existing encryption, authenticated encryption, and tweakable enciphering schemes that we categorize as:

- SIV-like constructions: Deoxys-II [15], Farfalle [4], and SIV [24],
- EME-like constructions, i.e., parallelizable two-pass encryption schemes: AEZ [13], EME [10,12], and EME* [8,9],
- CMC-like constructions, i.e., sequential two-pass encryption schemes: CMC [11], and the two-pass construction that reversed the block order in the middle layer from the paper "Turning Online Ciphers Off" [2], that we call TOCO as an hommage to the paper, and
- HCTR-like constructions: HCTR [28], PIV [26], and RIV [1].

Before our study of existing schemes, we developed some intuitive assumptions on full implicit key stretching:

- For online schemes, it is impossible to achieve.
- For schemes that combine two layers of an online scheme with a mixing layer in the middle, it depends on the middle layer whether they can achieve full implicit key stretching or not.
- CMC- and EME-like schemes provide it due to their middle layers.
- Three-pass schemes can achieve full implicit key stretching.

Given those initial assumptions, we studied the schemes above to identify their security in terms of our notion and the pivotal properties. From our model, we can derive several results. We could confirm our former two assumptions, i.e., the impossibility of full implicit key stretching as a property of online schemes.

Table 1. Comparison of existing schemes and here-proposed schemes with minor modifications. •/– = Feature is present/absent. Dependency for messages of $\geq m$ blocks.

	2-pass							3-pass			This work					
Aspect	AEZ	CMC	Deoxys-II	EME	Farfalle	SIV	TOCO	HCTR	PIV	RIV	CMC′	EME′	HCTR′	PIV′	RIV′	TOCO′
Redundancy	•	–	•	–	•	•	•	–	–	•	–	–	–	–	•	•
Parallelizeable	•	–	•	•	•	•	–	•	•	•	–	•	•	•	•	–
Primitive-query complexity	4	4	2	4	2	2	4	2	2	2	$O(m)$					

For two-pass schemes, we illustrate that CMC-like schemes can possess full implicit key stretching. The sequential nature of each encryption pass of two-pass schemes is necessary (although not sufficient), with a special middle layer.

Interestingly, our assumption that CMC and EME-like schemes would provide full implicit key stretching was contradicted. Moreover, our fourth intuition was falsified: we show that all considered HCTR-like schemes have small constant implicit key stretching due to their usage of an encryption scheme with an efficiently invertible primitive. However, we demonstrate that they can possess both full parallelizability and full implicit key stretching if their middle layer uses a non-efficiently invertible function instead of a permutation. We propose to salvage some well-known three-pass HCTR-like schemes from minimal modifications. Moreover, we illustrate how to add a sufficient middle layer to CMC, a nonlinear middle layer to EME, and half of a middle layer to AEZ to achieve full implicit key stretching. Table 1 summarizes our results, where we denote slightly modified schemes by an apostrophe, i.e., EME′is the modified variant of EME.

Outline. In the following, we detail the notions and the setting we consider. Thereupon, we study existing modes concerning whether or not they implicitly stretch the primitive key. We show that the additional complexity that the mode adds to key recovery is at best a small multiple for most of them in Sect. 4. We derive variants of the previous modes we considered with full implicit key stretching and reevaluate their properties in Sect. 5. We discuss and conclude in Sect. 6.

2 Preliminaries

2.1 General Notations

We will use lowercase letters x, y for indices and integers, uppercase letters X, Y for binary strings and functions, calligraphic uppercase letters $\mathcal{X}, \mathcal{Y}$ for sets and spaces, and bold letters $\mathbf{A}$ for matrices (and, abusing the notation a little to be consistent to the quasi-standard notation, also bold letters for adversaries). We write $\mathbb{F}_2$ for the finite field of characteristic 2 and $\mathbb{F}_2^n$ for an n-element vector of elements in $\mathbb{F}_2$, or bit strings. We will use $\mathbb{F}_2^n$ and $\{0, 1\}^n$ interchangeably in this paper. $X \| Y$ denotes the concatenation of binary strings X and Y, and $X \oplus Y$ for their bitwise XOR, that is, addition in $\mathbb{F}_2$. We indicate the length of X in bits by $|X|$ and write X_i for the i-th block. Moreover, for nonnegative integers $x < 2^n$, we use $\langle x \rangle \in \mathbb{F}_2^n$ for their encoding as an n-bit string. We denote by $X_1, \ldots, X_m \twoheadleftarrow \mathcal{X}$ that $X_1, \ldots, X_m$ are chosen uniformly at random from the set $\mathcal{X}$. We define $\mathsf{Func}(\mathcal{X}, \mathcal{Y})$ for the set of all functions $F : \mathcal{X} \to \mathcal{Y}$, $\mathsf{Perm}(\mathcal{X})$ for the set of all permutations $\pi : \mathcal{X} \to \mathcal{X}$, and $\widetilde{\mathsf{Perm}}(\mathcal{T}, \mathcal{X})$ for the set of tweakable permutations $\widetilde{\pi} : \mathcal{T} \times \mathcal{X} \to \mathcal{X}$ over $\mathcal{X}$ with tweak space $\mathcal{T}$.

Primitive. For a block space $\mathcal{X}$ and a vector of values $X = (X_1, \ldots, X_j) \in \mathcal{X}^j$ for any non-negative integer j, we define by $(X_1, \ldots, X_j) \xleftarrow{\mathcal{X}} X$ the injective splitting of X into blocks $X_i \in \mathcal{X}$ for all i. For $m \in \mathbb{N}$, $\mathcal{X}^{\leq m} =^{\text{def}} \bigcup_{i=0}^{m} \mathcal{X}^i$. For $q \in \mathbb{N}$, we define $[q] =^{\text{def}} \{1, \ldots, q\}$ and $[0..q] =^{\text{def}} \{0, \ldots, q\}$.

A block cipher is a family of functions $E : \mathcal{K} \times \mathcal{X} \to \mathcal{X}$ such that for each key $K \in \mathcal{K}$, $E_K(\cdot)$ is a permutation over a block space $\mathcal{X}$. A tweakable block cipher $\widetilde{E} : \mathcal{K} \times \mathcal{T} \times \mathcal{X} \to \mathcal{X}$ adds a tweak, i.e., for each key $K \in \mathcal{K}$ and tweak $T \in \mathcal{T}$, $\widetilde{E}_K^T(\cdot)$ is a permutation over a block space $\mathcal{X}$. We define $\mathsf{BlockCipher}(\mathcal{K}, \mathcal{X})$ as the set of all block ciphers $E : \mathcal{K} \times \mathcal{X} \to \mathcal{X}$ and $\mathsf{TBlockCipher}(\mathcal{K}, \mathcal{T}, \mathcal{X})$ as the set of all tweakable block ciphers $\widetilde{E} : \mathcal{K} \times \mathcal{T} \times \mathcal{X} \to \mathcal{X}$. In this work, a block is an element of $\mathcal{X} = \mathbb{F}_2^n$. An m-block-message $M = (M_1, \ldots, M_m)$ is an m-tuple $M \in \mathcal{X}^m$. We write $M_{i..j} = (M_i, M_{i+1}, \ldots, M_j)$ as a subsequent set of blocks.

Moreover, we write matrices as $\mathbf{A}$ with r rows and c columns of elements from $\mathcal{B}$, $\mathbf{A}_{i,j}$ for the element at Row i and Column j, and $\mathbf{A}_{i,*}$ and $\mathbf{A}_{*,j}$ for the i-th row and the j-th column, respectively. For $i \in \{0, \ldots, r-1\}$, we call $\mathbf{L}_i$ the shift matrix by i rows, where $\mathbf{L}_{j,k} = \delta_{j,k+i}$, where $\delta_{j,k}$ is the Kronecker delta. Moreover, we define the half-diagonal matrix $\mathbf{HD}$ where $\mathbf{HD}_{r,c} = 1$ if and only if $c = \lfloor (r+1)/2 \rfloor$ and 0 otherwise. For a vector $X = (X_i, \ldots, X_x)$, we denote by $\mathsf{wt}(X) = |\{X_i : X_i \neq 0\}|$ the number of non-zero entries of X.

2.2 Online Ciphers

Let $F \in \mathsf{Func}(\mathcal{X}^m, \mathcal{Y}^r)$. For $i \leq r$, we define $F^{(i)} : \mathcal{X}^m, \mathcal{Y}^i$ to return the first i elements of the result of F. That means for all inputs $X = (X_1, \ldots, X_m) \in \mathcal{X}^m$ and $Y = (Y_1, \ldots, Y_r) = F(M)$, $F^{(i)}(M) = (Y_1, \ldots, Y_i)$.

Definition 1 (Online Function [3]). *Let n, m be positive integers. Let $F : \mathcal{X}^m \to \mathcal{X}^m$ be length-preserving. We call F online if there exists a function $G : \mathcal{X}^m \to \mathcal{X}$ such that for every $M \in \mathcal{X}^m$ and every $i \leq m$, it holds that $F^{(i)}(M) = G(M_1, \ldots, M_i)$. A keyed function $F : \mathcal{K} \times \mathcal{X}^m \to \mathcal{X}^m$ is called online if F_K is online for all $K \in \mathcal{K}$.*

Definition 2 (Online Permutation [3]). *Let F be an online function. Fix $M_{1..i-1} = (M_1, \ldots, M_{i-1}) \in \mathcal{X}^{i-1}$. We define $P^F_{M_{1..i-1}}(M_i) =^{def} F^{(i)}(M_1, \ldots, M_{i-1}, M_i)$ for all $M_i \in \mathcal{X}$. F is an online permutation for $i \geq 1$ and all $M_{1..i} \in \mathcal{X}^{i-1}$ if $P^F_{M_{1..i-1}}$ is a permutation over $\mathcal{X}$. We use $\mathsf{OPerm}(\mathcal{X}^m)$ as the set of all online permutations over $\mathcal{X}^m$.*

Definition 3 (Online Cipher [3]**).** *Let P and F be as above. An online cipher* $\Pi = (\mathcal{E}, \mathcal{D})$ *for* $\mathcal{E} : \mathcal{K} \times \mathcal{X}^{\leq m} \to \mathcal{X}^{\leq m}$ *is a length-preserving cipher such that for all* $i \leq m$*, all* $M = (M_1, \ldots, M_{i-1}) \in \mathcal{X}^{i-1}$*,* $M_i \in \mathcal{X}$*, and* $K \in \mathcal{K}$*, it holds that*

$$\mathcal{E}_K(M_1, \ldots, M_i) = \left(P^{F_K}(M_1), P^{F_K}_{M_1}(M_2), \ldots, P^{F_K}_{M_{1..i-1}}(M_i)\right).$$

We call a cipher Π offline if Π is not online. We define $\mathsf{OCipher}(\mathcal{K}, \mathcal{X})$ for the set of all online ciphers with a non-empty key set or space $\mathcal{K}$ that operates on blocks of space $\mathcal{X}$. Note that ciphers can be "almost" online, e.g. *online-but-last* [2], where for each $M = (M_1, \ldots, M_m) \in \mathcal{X}^m$, the cipher is online for all computations to M_{m-1} but not for the processing of M_m. Analogously, one can define *online-but-first*, where for each $M = (M_1, \ldots, M_m) \in \mathcal{X}^m$, the cipher is online for all computations from M_2 through M_m, but not for processing M_1.

By non-efficiently invertible functions, we mean exponentially hard-to-invert functions in the sense of [7]. Thus, we assume that no probabilistic polynomial-time algorithm $\mathbf{A}$ has significant advantage in inverting them.

3 Model

3.1 Affine Modes

Our definitions of affine modes are based on those by [6]. Let $E : \mathcal{K} \times \mathcal{B} \to \mathcal{B}$ be a keyed permutation. We model the encryption schemes $\Pi[E_K] = (\widehat{\mathcal{E}}[E_K], \widehat{\mathcal{D}}[E_K])$ that we consider as alternating sequences of affine layers $\mathbf{A}_i$ and nonlinear keyed encryption modes $\mathcal{E}_i$. Chakraborti et al. defined the layers $\mathcal{E}_i : \mathcal{B}^{\leq m} \to \mathcal{B}^{\leq m}$ as ECB modes, i.e., given inputs $X \in \mathcal{B}^m$, each encryption layer $\mathcal{E}_i$ encrypts $Y_i = E_K(X_i)$ for $i \in [m]$, where we assume arbitrary nonnegative integers m. This choice allows us to later determine the number of nonlinear computations by the number of blocks that must be computed over all layers $\mathcal{E}_i$. This follows the model by Chakraborti et al. [6].

Note that this model does not cover all possible constructions: online ciphers [3] can be more complex. The i-th call to the primitive may depend on all inputs to and outputs from the previous calls; one can also use the input to the primitive as a tweak. We consider an extended model later, where we add tweaks to the individual encryption passes and assume tweakable primitives.

Our goal is similar to that of the work by Chakraborti et al., i.e., to find the number of nonlinear computations where attacks are possible in terms of calls to E_K. We differ in the definition of what we call an attack, or rather a key-filter condition. Similar to their work, we model Π as

$$\mathbf{A}_r \circ \mathcal{E}_{r-1} \circ \mathbf{A}_{r-1} \circ \cdots \circ \mathcal{E}_1 \circ \mathbf{A}_1 .$$

The number of encryption modes in the model of schemes represents the number of passes. We will focus on single-, two-, and three-pass modes, represented by

$$\mathbf{A}_2 \circ \mathcal{E}_1 \circ \mathbf{A}_1 ,$$
$$\mathbf{A}_3 \circ \mathcal{E}_2 \circ \mathbf{A}_2 \circ \mathcal{E}_1 \circ \mathbf{A}_1 , \text{ and}$$
$$\mathbf{A}_4 \circ \mathcal{E}_3 \circ \mathbf{A}_3 \circ \mathcal{E}_2 \circ \mathbf{A}_2 \circ \mathcal{E}_1 \circ \mathbf{A}_1 ,$$

respectively. Here, the affine layers $\mathbf{A}_i$ produce the inputs to layer $\mathcal{E}_i$. The final affine layer yields the ciphertext output. We denote by U_i and V_i the inputs to and outputs from $\mathcal{E}_1$, i.e., $V_i = E_K(U_i)$; by W_i and X_i the inputs to and outputs from $\mathcal{E}_2$, $X_i = E_K(W_i)$; and by Y_i and Z_i the inputs to and outputs from $\mathcal{E}_3$: $Z_i = E_K(Y_i)$. We define the encryption layers $\mathcal{E}_i \circ \mathbf{A}_i$ as online ciphers: they are allowed to use previous outputs from $\mathcal{E}$ of the layer, which is necessary to model modes such as CBC. Though, we define that they cannot use encryptions of later blocks.

Restrictions. While we can try to use as general definitions as possible, overly broad definitions may produce many instances with invalid or non-decryptable data flows, e.g., that U_i in encryption direction may depend on V_i, although $V_i = E_K(U_i)$ demands that U_i is defined before. Therefore, we focus on subsets of plausible bijective constructions. We use the following notations:

- All-zero submatrices are denoted by $\mathbf{0}$.
- Non-strictly lower triangular submatrices use a single underline.
- Strictly lower triangular submatrices use a double underline.

Single-pass Modes are represented as

$$\begin{bmatrix} U \\ C \end{bmatrix} = \begin{bmatrix} \mathbf{A}_1^M & \underline{\underline{\mathbf{A}_1^V}} & \mathbf{A}_1^L \\ \mathbf{A}_2^M & \underline{\overline{\mathbf{A}_2^V}} & \mathbf{A}_2^L \end{bmatrix} \cdot [M\ V\ L]^\top ,$$

where the submatrices $\mathbf{A}_1^M$, $\mathbf{A}_1^V$, $\mathbf{A}_1^L$ define the mappings of M, V, L to U, respectively, and the second row the similar mappings to C. Thus, $\mathbf{A}_1, \mathbf{A}_2 \in \mathcal{B}^{m \times (2m+\kappa)}$, where κ is the number of words of the vector L. Similarly as Chakraborti et al., we say that $L = (K, \langle 1 \rangle)$ contains a key-derived value for keyed linear computations as well as a constant entry $\langle 1 \rangle \in \mathcal{B}$ so that the modes are affine. The modes must be decryptable uniquely. We defer the analogous definitions of the decryption models for one through three passes to Appendix B.

Two-pass Modes are modeled as

$$\begin{bmatrix} U \\ W \\ C \end{bmatrix} = \begin{bmatrix} \mathbf{A}_1^M & \underline{\underline{\mathbf{A}_1^V}} & \mathbf{0} & \mathbf{A}_1^L \\ \mathbf{A}_2^M & \overline{\mathbf{A}_2^V} & \mathbf{0} & \mathbf{A}_2^L \\ \mathbf{0} & \mathbf{A}_3^V & \underline{\mathbf{A}_3^X} & \mathbf{A}_3^L \end{bmatrix} \cdot [M\ V\ X\ L]^\top$$

We suggest a clearer equivalent representation, where we split $\mathbf{A}_3^V = \mathbf{A}_3^W \cdot \mathbf{A}_2^V$:

$$\begin{bmatrix} U \\ W \\ C \end{bmatrix} = \begin{bmatrix} \mathbf{A}_1^M & \underline{\underline{\mathbf{A}_1^V}} & \mathbf{0} & \mathbf{0} & \mathbf{A}_1^L \\ \mathbf{A}_2^M & \overline{\mathbf{A}_2^V} & \mathbf{0} & \mathbf{0} & \mathbf{A}_2^L \\ \mathbf{0} & \mathbf{0} & \mathbf{A}_3^W & \underline{\mathbf{A}_3^X} & \mathbf{A}_3^L \end{bmatrix} \cdot [M\ V\ W\ X\ L]^\top .$$

Three-pass Modes extend the model by denoting $X_i = E_K(W_i)$, $Y = \mathbf{A}_3 \cdot (M, V, X, K)^\top$, $Z_i = E_K(Y_i)$, and $C = \mathbf{A}_4 \cdot (M, V, X, Z, K)^\top$. Thus, we define our model, where we already suggest a more readable representation that splits $\mathbf{A}_3^V$ into $\mathbf{A}_3^W \cdot \mathbf{A}_2^V$ and $\mathbf{A}_4^X$ into $\mathbf{A}_4^Y \cdot \mathbf{A}_3^X$:

$$\begin{bmatrix} U \\ W \\ Y \\ C \end{bmatrix} = \begin{bmatrix} \mathbf{A}_1^M & \underline{\underline{\mathbf{A}_1^V}} & \mathbf{0} & \mathbf{0} & \mathbf{0} & \mathbf{0} & \mathbf{A}_1^L \\ \mathbf{A}_2^M & \overline{\mathbf{A}_2^V} & \mathbf{0} & \mathbf{0} & \mathbf{0} & \mathbf{0} & \mathbf{A}_2^L \\ \mathbf{0} & \mathbf{0} & \mathbf{A}_3^W & \mathbf{A}_3^X & \mathbf{0} & \mathbf{A}_3^Z & \mathbf{A}_3^L \\ \mathbf{0} & \mathbf{0} & \mathbf{0} & \mathbf{0} & \mathbf{A}_4^Y & \underline{\mathbf{A}_4^Z} & \mathbf{A}_4^L \end{bmatrix} \cdot [M\, V\, W\, X\, Y\, Z\, L]^\top .$$

3.2 Rationale of Restrictions

In the following, we define two sets of restrictions.

Generic Restrictions. The definitions of single-, two-, and three-pass modes above already contain a preliminary set of restrictions, similar to those in [6]:

- The submatrices $\mathbf{A}_1^X$, $\mathbf{A}_2^X$, $\mathbf{A}_1^W$, $\mathbf{A}_2^W$, $\mathbf{A}_i^M$, $\mathbf{A}_i^V$, for all $i \geq 3$, are $\mathbf{0}$.
- For any modes, $\mathbf{A}_1^V$ is strictly lower triangular.
- For single-, two-, and three-pass modes, $\mathbf{A}_2^V$, $\mathbf{A}_3^X$, and $\mathbf{A}_4^Z$ are non-strictly lower triangular. In general, the matrix that maps the outputs of the final encryption layer to the ciphertext is non-strictly lower triangular.

Restrictions for Compositions from Online Ciphers. Moreover, we add a second set of restrictions for constructions that are composed of online encryption layers, in the spirit of [2,6]. This means, that

- For single-pass modes, the entire mode, $\mathbf{A}_2 \circ \mathcal{E}_1 \circ \mathbf{A}_1$, is an online cipher.
- For two-pass modes, $\mathbf{A}_3 \circ \mathcal{E}_2$ and $\mathcal{E}_1 \circ \mathbf{A}_1$ are online ciphers each.
- For three-pass modes, $\mathbf{A}_4 \circ \mathcal{E}_3$, $\mathcal{E}_2$, and $\mathcal{E}_1 \circ \mathbf{A}_1$ are online ciphers each.

Then, we employ the following restrictions for compositions from online ciphers, where we represent single-, two- and three-pass modes by

$$\begin{bmatrix} U \\ C \end{bmatrix} = \begin{bmatrix} \underline{\mathbf{A}_1^M} & \underline{\underline{\mathbf{A}_1^V}} & \mathbf{A}_1^L \\ \underline{\mathbf{A}_2^M} & \underline{\overline{\mathbf{A}_2^V}} & \mathbf{A}_2^L \end{bmatrix} \cdot [M\, V\, L]^\top ,$$

$$\begin{bmatrix} U \\ W \\ C \end{bmatrix} = \begin{bmatrix} \underline{\mathbf{A}_1^M} & \underline{\underline{\mathbf{A}_1^V}} & \mathbf{0} & \mathbf{0} & \mathbf{A}_1^L \\ \mathbf{A}_2^M & \overline{\mathbf{A}_2^V} & \mathbf{0} & \mathbf{0} & \mathbf{A}_2^L \\ \mathbf{0} & \mathbf{0} & \underline{\mathbf{A}_3^W} & \underline{\mathbf{A}_3^X} & \mathbf{A}_3^L \end{bmatrix} \cdot [M\, V\, W\, X\, L]^\top \quad \text{and,}$$

$$\begin{bmatrix} U \\ W \\ Y \\ C \end{bmatrix} = \begin{bmatrix} \underline{\mathbf{A}_1^M} & \underline{\underline{\mathbf{A}_1^V}} & \mathbf{0} & \mathbf{0} & \mathbf{0} & \mathbf{0} & \mathbf{A}_1^L \\ \mathbf{A}_2^M & \overline{\mathbf{A}_2^V} & \mathbf{0} & \mathbf{0} & \mathbf{0} & \mathbf{0} & \mathbf{A}_2^L \\ \mathbf{0} & \mathbf{0} & \mathbf{A}_3^W & \mathbf{A}_3^X & \mathbf{0} & \underline{\underline{\mathbf{A}_3^Z}} & \mathbf{A}_3^L \\ \mathbf{0} & \mathbf{0} & \mathbf{0} & \mathbf{0} & \underline{\mathbf{A}_4^Y} & \underline{\overline{\mathbf{A}_4^Z}} & \mathbf{A}_4^L \end{bmatrix} \cdot [M V W X Y Z L]^\top ,$$

respectively. The decryption definitions and restrictions follow naturally. Our models, with indicated restrictions, are visualized in Fig. 5.

3.3 Number of Nonlinear Computations

To obtain a key filter, an adversary tries to find an overdetermined equation system. Thus, the task is to formulate the system so to find an overdetermined subset of equations, given the knowns M, C, the known current key candidate K, and values derived from K in the vector L. Let $\widehat{U}, \widehat{W}, \widehat{Y}$ denote the reduced rows of U, W, Y Then, we find the number of primitive computations by the weight of $\mathsf{wt}(U)$ in the equation system in single-, by $\mathsf{wt}(U) + \mathsf{wt}(W)$ in two- and by $\mathsf{wt}(U) + \mathsf{wt}(W) + \mathsf{wt}(Y)$ in three-pass schemes. Given an encryption scheme $\Pi[E_K]$, $\mathsf{q_c}$ denotes an upper bound of the *query complexity*, i.e., the maximal number of primitive computations E_K induced by an equation system.

4 Analysis of Modes

This section shows that online, SIV-like, CMC-like, EME-like, and HCTR-like schemes lack full implicit key stretching; for the former two construction types, it is impossible to achieve. Throughout this section, we assume that $\Pi[E_K]$ is an encryption scheme based on a block cipher $E \in \mathsf{BlockCipher}(\mathcal{K}, \mathcal{B})$, where $\mathcal{K}$ and $\mathcal{B}$ are a key and a block space, respectively, and $K \twoheadleftarrow \mathcal{K}$ is a secret key. An adversary is given a transcript $\tau = \{\mathcal{M}, \mathcal{C}\}$, consisting of a set of $q \geq 1$ messages $\mathcal{M} = \{M^i\}_{i \in [q]}$ and a set of their corresponding ciphertexts $\mathcal{C} = \{C^i : C^i \in \mathcal{B}^{\geq m}\}_{i \in [q]}$ where $C^i = \Pi[E_K](M^i)$ for all $i \in [q]$. $\Pi[E_K]$ is an encryption scheme based on a block cipher E with a secret key $K \twoheadleftarrow \mathcal{K}$. We call τ m-block-minimal if $M^i, C^i \in \mathcal{B}^{\geq m}$ for all $i \in [q]$ and positive integer m.

4.1 Online Schemes

Theorem 1. *Let $\Pi[E_K] \in$ OCipher$(\mathcal{K}, \mathcal{B})$ be an online cipher and τ an m-block-minimal transcript for $\Pi[E_K]$. Then, we can build an equation system with query complexity* $\mathsf{q_c}(\Pi[E_K]) = O(1)$.

Proof. For any multi-block plaintext-ciphertext pair (M, C) of $M = (M_1, \ldots, M_m)$, $C = (C_1, \ldots, C_m) \in \mathcal{B}^m$ where $C = \Pi[E]_K(M)$, it holds by definition of an online cipher that C_1 depends only on a constant amount of primitive output blocks $V_1, \ldots, V_c$ for some constant $c \geq 1$. Thus, $\mathsf{q_c}(\Pi) = O(1)$. □

As a direct consequence of Theorem 1, schemes such as GCM [17], OCB [16,23], OTR [19], or Duplex [5] cannot possess implicit key stretching beyond constant query complexity. However, they can achieve limited key stretching when used as higher-level schemes. Some schemes employ an online cipher for their encryption that operates on a different block size than the internal primitive. For example, OTR uses a two-round Feistel network with double blocks for encryption. Thus, it employs a block cipher $E \in \mathsf{BlockCipher}(\mathcal{K}, \mathcal{B})$ on a block space that is half of that of its online cipher $\mathcal{X} = \mathcal{B}^2$. This can be a wrapped online cipher $\widehat{\Pi} = (\widehat{\mathcal{E}}, \widehat{\mathcal{D}})$ such as **CHAIN** [14] that operates on potentially large segment spaces $\mathcal{X}$, whereas each segment is processed individually by an offline cipher $\Pi = (\mathcal{E}, \mathcal{D})$ with primitives that operate on smaller block spaces $\mathcal{B}$. The minimal number of primitive calls for obtaining a key-filter relation in $\widehat{\Pi}$ is then upper bounded by the minimal number of primitive calls in Π.

4.2 Schemes with PRP-Based Counter Mode

The following filter is probably well-known, but may not have been formulated as such. We state it here only for the sake of self-containment. Its relevance stems from the widespread use of the counter mode in two- or three-pass encryption and authenticated encryption schemes, such as SIV or HCTR. There, it usually takes an additional secret (a pseudorandom secret initial value $IV \in \mathcal{IV}$ from a space $\mathcal{IV}$) as an input and employs a block cipher E as before. Let $\mathcal{I} \subseteq \mathbb{N}_0$ be an index space. Then, $\mathsf{CTR}[E_K]^{IV}(M)$ encrypts as

$$\begin{bmatrix} U \\ C \end{bmatrix} = \begin{bmatrix} \mathbf{0} & \mathbf{0} & \mathbf{A}_1^L \\ \mathbf{1} & \mathbf{1} & \mathbf{0} \end{bmatrix} \cdot \begin{bmatrix} M & V & L \end{bmatrix}^\top, \quad \mathbf{A}_1^L = \begin{bmatrix} 1 & 1 & 1 & \cdots & 1 \\ 0 & 1 & 2 & \cdots & m-1 \end{bmatrix}^\top, \text{ and } L = (IV, \langle 1 \rangle).$$

Theorem 2 (Differential Filter of CTR Mode). Let $\mathsf{CTR}[E_K]$ denote the counter mode above. Given a transcript τ with any message-ciphertext pair of at least two blocks, $\mathsf{q_c}(\mathsf{CTR}[E_K]) \leq 2$.

Proof. Consider the reduced equation system with $M = (M_1, M_2)$ and $C = (C_1, C_2)$. Given M, C, and the current candidate for K, the adversary can compute $U_1 = E_K^{-1}(M_1 \oplus C_1)$ and $U_2 = E_K^{-1}(M_2 \oplus C_2)$, and obtains an $|IV|$-bit key-filter from the equation system

$$\begin{bmatrix} 0 \\ 0 \end{bmatrix} = \begin{bmatrix} 1 & 0 & 1 & 0 \\ 0 & 1 & 1 & 1 \end{bmatrix} \cdot \begin{bmatrix} U_1 & U_2 & IV & 1 \end{bmatrix}^\top.$$

□

The query complexity for counter-based schemes with invertible primitives, such as Farfalle, HCTR, PIV, RIV, or SIV, is limited to two.

4.3 EME-like Schemes

In the following, we study EME-like schemes, e.g., EME$^+$EME*, EME2, or AEZ. Such schemes $\widehat{\Pi} = (\widehat{\mathcal{E}}, \widehat{\mathcal{D}})$ are composed of two passes of an online cipher $\Pi = (\mathcal{E}, \mathcal{D})$ based on a primitive E_K and $\mathbf{A}_2$. The online cipher is a variant of OCB.

Though, EME-like schemes possess a middle layer with at least one nonlinear call. As a result, we model them as three pass schemes with an incomplete central encryption layer $\mathcal{E}_2$. Given $M = (M_1, \ldots, M_m)$, we model the encryption as

$$\begin{bmatrix} U \\ W \\ Y \\ C \end{bmatrix} = \begin{bmatrix} \mathbf{1} & \mathbf{0} & \mathbf{0} & \mathbf{0} & \mathbf{0} & \mathbf{0} & \mathbf{A}_1^L \\ \mathbf{0} & \mathbf{A}_2^V & \mathbf{0} & \mathbf{0} & \mathbf{0} & \mathbf{0} & \mathbf{A}_2^L \\ \mathbf{0} & \mathbf{0} & \mathbf{A}_3^W & \mathbf{A}_3^X & \mathbf{0} & \mathbf{0} & \mathbf{0} \\ \mathbf{0} & \mathbf{0} & \mathbf{0} & \mathbf{0} & \mathbf{0} & \mathbf{1} & \mathbf{A}_4^L \end{bmatrix} \cdot \begin{bmatrix} M & V & W & X & Y & Z & L \end{bmatrix}^\top$$

with

$$\mathbf{A}_1^L = \mathbf{A}_4^L = \begin{bmatrix} 1\,2 \cdots 2^{m-1} \\ 0\,0 \cdots \quad 0 \end{bmatrix}^\top ,$$

$$\mathbf{A}_2^V = \begin{bmatrix} 1 \cdots 1 \\ 0 \cdots 0 \\ \vdots \ddots \vdots \\ 0 \cdots 0 \end{bmatrix}, \quad \mathbf{A}_3^V = \begin{bmatrix} 0\,0\,0 \cdots 0 \\ 0\,1\,0 \cdots 0 \\ \vdots\,\vdots\,\vdots \ddots \vdots \\ 0\,0\,0 \cdots 1 \end{bmatrix}, \quad \mathbf{A}_3^W = \mathbf{A}_3^X = \begin{bmatrix} 0 & 0 \cdots 0 \\ 2 & 0 \cdots 0 \\ \vdots & \vdots \ddots \vdots \\ 2^{m-1} & 0 \cdots 0 \end{bmatrix}.$$

Here, two neighboring non-initial (EME) and non-final (AEZ) blocks can be used to construct an efficient filter with four nonlinear computations. Figures 1a and 1b show the computations in EME and AEZ for necessary filters (the arrows indicate computations).

Theorem 3. *Let $\widehat{\Pi}[\Pi[E_K]] = (\widehat{\mathcal{E}}[\mathcal{E}[E_K]], \widehat{\mathcal{D}}[\mathcal{E}[E_K]])$ be an EME-like scheme as defined above with an online cipher $\Pi = (\mathcal{E}, \mathcal{D})$. Given an m-block-minimal transcript τ, it holds that $\mathsf{q_c}(\widehat{\Pi}[E_K]) \leq 4$.*

Proof. For EME-like schemes, we can denote the offset in the middle layer and assume it to be an n-bit secret value L independent from K. Note that this strictly renders the attack harder for the adversary since it can compute L, given M, C, and K from $m+1$ computations of $E_K(\cdot)$. But our goal is to show that we can spare those $m+1$ calls to E_K. We can define the computation of non-initial blocks C_i from M_i and L, for some $i \geq 2$, as:

$$\begin{bmatrix} U_{2..m} \\ Y_{2..m} \\ C_{2..m} \end{bmatrix} = \begin{bmatrix} \mathbf{1\,0\,0\,0} & \mathbf{0} \\ \mathbf{0\,1\,0\,0} & \mathbf{A}_3^L \\ \mathbf{0\,0\,0\,1} & \mathbf{A}_4^L \end{bmatrix} \cdot \left[M_{2..m}\; V_{2..m}\; Y_{2..m}\; Z_{2..m}\; L\right]^\top ,$$

where $\mathbf{A}_3^L = \left[2\; 2^2 \ldots 2^{m-1}\right]^\top \cdot L$. We can reduce the equation system by considering any subset of disjoint indices $i, j \in [m]$ and obtain the equation system

$$Y_i = E_K^i(M_i) + 2^{i-1}L = D_K^i(C_i) \quad \text{and} \quad Y_j = E_K^j(M_j) + 2^{j-1}L = D_K^j(C_j),$$

which leads to the filter relation

$$(2^{i-1})^{-1} \cdot (E_K^i(M_i) + D_K^i(C_i)) \stackrel{?}{=} (2^{j-1})^{-1} \cdot (E_K^j(M_j) + D_K^j(C_j)).$$

This holds with probability one for the correct key candidate K, but with negligible probability, for sufficiently large $|\mathcal{B}|$, otherwise. Hence, a filter can be tested with four (parallelizable) primitive computations. □

A similar distinguisher can be given for AEZ. Similar to EME, we can also model AEZ as a three-pass mode with an encryption layer in the middle, represented by a vector L:

$$\begin{bmatrix} U \\ W \\ Y \\ C \end{bmatrix} = \begin{bmatrix} \mathbf{A}_1^M & \mathbf{A}_1^V & \mathbf{0\,0} & \mathbf{0} & \mathbf{0} \\ \mathbf{1} & \mathbf{1} & \mathbf{0\,0} & \mathbf{0} & \mathbf{0} \\ \mathbf{0} & \mathbf{0} & \mathbf{1\,0} & \mathbf{A}_3^Z & \mathbf{A}_3^L \\ \mathbf{0} & \mathbf{0} & \mathbf{0\,0} & \mathbf{1} & \mathbf{0} \end{bmatrix} \cdot \left[M\; V\; W\; X\; Z\; L\right]^\top ,$$

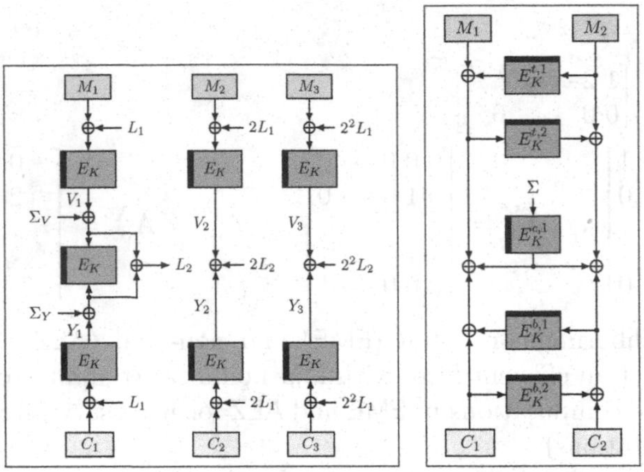

(a) EME. (b) AEZ.

Fig. 1. Two non-initial blocks in the en- and decryption of EME can be used for a key filter with four primitive calls. It holds that $\Sigma_V = \bigoplus_{i=2}^{m} V_i$ and $\Sigma_Y = \bigoplus_{i=2}^{m} Y_i$. For AEZ, a similar filter can be constructed from a non-final double block.

where $\mathbf{A}_1^M$ is the exchange matrix, $\mathbf{A}_1^V = \mathbf{A}_3^Z = \mathbf{S}_1$ (the lower shift matrix by 1 row down), and $\mathbf{A}_3^L = \mathbf{HD}$, i.e., the half-diagonal matrix. While AEZ introduces $m/2$ additional nonlinear computations in the middle layer, reusing the middle layer's results opens an attack angle for an efficient key-candidate filter with only four nonlinear computations.

Theorem 4. *Let $\widehat{\Pi}[E_K] = (\widehat{\mathcal{E}}[E_K], \widehat{\mathcal{D}}[E_K])$ be AEZ. Given an m-block-minimal transcript τ, it holds that $\mathsf{q_c}(\widehat{\Pi}[E_K]) \leq 4$.*

Proof. We consider a non-final full double block, e.g., (M_1, M_2) that is mapped to (C_1, C_2), for any message-ciphertext pair (M, C). An adversary can compute

$$V_1 = E_K^{t,1}(M_2) + M_1 \qquad V_2 = E_K^{t,2}(V_1) + M_2$$
$$W_1 = E_K^{b,1}(W_2) + C_1 + L \qquad W_2 = E_K^{b,2}(C_1) + C_2 + L\,,$$

and obtains

$$(E_K^{t,1}(M_2) + M_1) + (E_K^{b,1}(E_K^{b,2}(C_1) + C_2) + C_1)$$
$$\stackrel{?}{=} (E_K^{t,2}(E_K^{t,1}(M_2) + M_1) + M_2) + (E_K^{b,2}(C_1) + C_2)\,,$$

which holds with probability one for the correct key candidate K, but only with negligible probability otherwise. Thus, the filter differs in the sense that AEZ has a nonlinear middle layer.

Algorithm 1. Filters for schemes with small $\mathsf{q_c}$.

function $F_{\text{OTR}}[E]_{K^i}(M_1, M_2, C_1, C_2)$
  $Y_1 \leftarrow M_1 \oplus C_1$
  $X_1^i \leftarrow E_{K^i}^{-1}(Y_1)$
  $Y_2 \leftarrow M_2 \oplus C_2$
  $X_2^i \leftarrow E_{K^i}^{-1}(Y_2)$
  return $X_1^i \oplus C_2 \stackrel{?}{=} X_2^i \oplus M_1$

function $F_{\text{EME}}[E]_{K^i}(M_2, M_3, C_2, C_3)$
  $L \leftarrow E_{K^i}(0)$
  $X_1^i \leftarrow E_{K^i}(M_2 \oplus 2L) \oplus E_{K^i}^{-1}(C_2 \oplus 2L)$
  $X_2^i \leftarrow E_{K^i}(M_3 \oplus 4L) \oplus E_{K^i}^{-1}(C_3 \oplus 4L)$
  return $2X_1^i \stackrel{?}{=} X_2^i (\rightarrow 2 \cdot 2M \stackrel{?}{=} 4M)$

function $F_{\text{TOCO}}[\widetilde{E}]_{K^i}(M_1, M_2, C_{m-1}, C_m)$
  $X_1^i \leftarrow \widetilde{E}_{K^i}^{0,0}(M_1)$
  $X_2^i \leftarrow \widetilde{E}_{K^i}^{M_1, X_1^i}(M_2)$
  $Y_{m-1}^i \leftarrow X_2^i$
  $Y_m^i \leftarrow (\widetilde{E}_K^{Y_{m-1}^i, C_{m-1}})^{-1}(C_m)$
  return $Y_m^i \stackrel{?}{=} X_1^i$

function $F_{\text{OCB}}[E]_{K^i}(N, M_1, C_1)$
  $\Delta \leftarrow E_{K^i}(N)$
  return $C_1 \stackrel{?}{=} E_{K^i}(M_1 \oplus 2\Delta) \oplus 2\Delta$

function $F_{\text{SIV}}[E]_{K^i}(IV, M_1, C_1)$
  $Y_1 \leftarrow M_1 \oplus C_1$
  return $E_{K^i}(IV) \stackrel{?}{=} Y_1$

function $F_{\text{HCTR}}[E]_{K^i}(M_1, M_2, C_1, C_2)$
  $Y_1 \leftarrow M_1 \oplus C_1$
  $Y_2 \leftarrow M_2 \oplus C_2$
  $X_1^i \leftarrow E_{K^i}^{-1}(Y_1)$
  $X_2^i \leftarrow E_{K^i}^{-1}(Y_2)$
  return $X_1^i \oplus X_2^i \stackrel{?}{=} 1$

function $F_{\text{AEZ}}[E]_{K^i}(M_1, M_2, C_1, C_2)$
  $X_2 \leftarrow E_{K^i}^{t,1}(M_1) \oplus M_2$
  $X_1 \leftarrow E_{K^i}^{t,2}(X_2) \oplus M_1$
  $Y_2 \leftarrow E_{K^i}^{b,2}(C_1) \oplus C_2$
  $Y_1 \leftarrow E_{K^i}^{b,1}(Y_2) \oplus C_1$
  return $X_1 \oplus Y_1 \stackrel{?}{=} X_2 \oplus Y_2$

4.4 SIV-like Schemes

Two-pass modes with only a single online encryption pass – i.e., a single online layer that maps M to C and vice versa – can stretch the key implicitly only as much as an online cipher can. This holds for all SIV-like schemes, such as Deoxys-II, Farfalle, and (naturally) also for SIV. Such modes can be described as shown in Fig. 2b:

1. First, the message is processed by a PRF F: $IV \leftarrow F_{K_1}(M)$.
2. IV is used for encrypting $C_R \leftarrow \mathcal{E}_{K_2}^{IV}(M_R)$ in an online cipher $\mathcal{E}$.
3. Finally, any invertible transformation is used to derive $C_L \leftarrow E_{K_3}(IV)$.

Note that E_{K_3} may be the identity map, as is the case for SIV or Deoxys-II. The final transformation must be invertible since decryption could not reconstruct the IV otherwise. E_{K_3} must not use the major part of the plaintext or ciphertext since the scheme would consist of three passes otherwise.

We can model length-extending schemes like SIV as affine modes by adding a value S to the output vector. Thus, $IV \leftarrow E_K(S)$, and $L = (IV, 1)$. In the following, we consider the combination of CBC-MAC with CTR mode:

$$\begin{bmatrix} U \\ S \\ W \\ C \end{bmatrix} = \begin{bmatrix} \mathbf{1} & \mathbf{A}_1^V & \mathbf{0} & \mathbf{0} & \mathbf{0} \\ \mathbf{0} & (1, \ldots, 1) & \mathbf{0} & \mathbf{0} & \mathbf{0} \\ \mathbf{0} & \mathbf{0} & \mathbf{1} & \mathbf{0} & \mathbf{A}_3^L \\ \mathbf{1} & \mathbf{0} & \mathbf{0} & \mathbf{1} & \mathbf{0} \end{bmatrix} \cdot [M \; V \; W \; X \; L]^\top ,$$

where

$$\mathbf{A}_1^V = \begin{bmatrix} 0 & \cdots & 0 & 0 \\ 1 & \cdots & 0 & 0 \\ \vdots & \ddots & \vdots & \vdots \\ 0 & \cdots & 1 & 0 \end{bmatrix} \quad \text{and} \quad \mathbf{A}_3^L = \begin{bmatrix} 1 & 1 & \cdots & 1 \\ 0 & 1 & \cdots & m-1 \end{bmatrix}^\top .$$

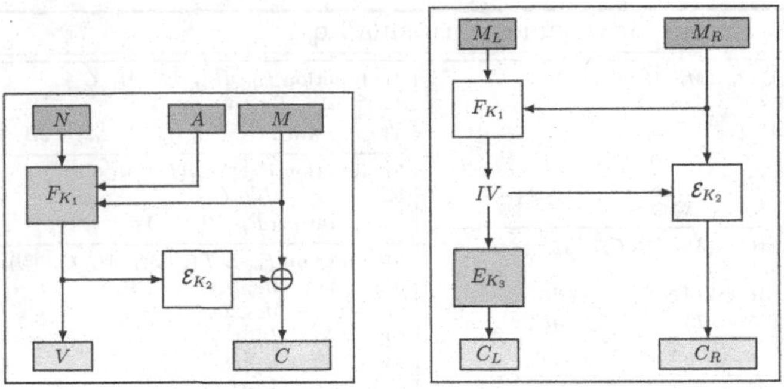

(a) SIV. (b) Generic two-pass modes.

Fig. 2. **Left:** Schematic illustration of SIV-like schemes. **Right:** Illustration of generalized two-pass modes, which cannot achieve full block-wise dependency.

Theorem 5. *Let $\widehat{\Pi}[E_K] = (\widehat{\mathcal{E}}, \widehat{\mathcal{D}})$ be a SIV-like two-pass encryption scheme. Given an m-block-minimal transcript τ, there exists a positive integer m such that $\mathsf{q_c}(\widehat{\Pi}[E_K]) = O(1)$.*

Proof. Choose any plaintext-ciphertext tuple (M, C) from τ. In decryption direction, there must exist a constant c_1 such that the computation of a candidate of IV depends on only c_1 primitive calls, here, those in C_L. Since $\mathcal{E}_{K_2}$ is online, the first block depends on only IV and a set of c_2 primitive inputs to compute C_1 from M_1 and IV. Thus, the claim follows. □

Remark 1. Theorem 5 also implies that the generic compositions of Encrypt-then-MAC, Encrypt-and-MAC, and MAC-then-Encrypt cannot provide implicit key stretching with an online encryption scheme in our model. Moreover, a similar statement follows for all schemes from [20]. Since those schemes release the encryption of M, they would have to make the IV depend on the full message or the full ciphertext in both encryption and decryption direction otherwise.

4.5 Constructions from Two Passes of Online Ciphers

Andreeva et al. [2] studied the security of ciphers composed of multiple stacked layers of online ciphers. Assume a secure online cipher $\Pi[\widetilde{E}_K] \in \mathsf{OCipher}(\mathcal{K}, \mathcal{B})$ with $\widetilde{E} \in \mathsf{TBlockCipher}(\mathcal{K}, \mathcal{T}, \mathcal{B})$, $\mathcal{T} = \mathcal{B}^2$, and $K \twoheadleftarrow \mathcal{K}$. While there exist various secure sequential online ciphers from a TBC, we use $\mathsf{TC2}$ [25] for description.

The Generic Single-Pass Online Cipher. We can model the generic single-pass online cipher as an affine mode by introducing an additional vector $T_1 = (T_{1,1}, \ldots, T_{1,m})$, where $T_{1,i}$ represents the tweak in the i-th primitive call; the subscript one denotes the first encryption pass for generalizing to multi-pass modes later. For the generic scheme, we employ a two-part tweak $T_{1,1} = (T_{1,1,1}, \ldots, T_{1,m,1})$ and $T_{1,2} = (T_{1,1,2}, \ldots, T_{1,m,2})$ to address the potential that both inputs and outputs may be processed independently by the primitive. We define

$$\begin{bmatrix} U \\ T_{1,1} \\ T_{1,2} \\ C \end{bmatrix} = \underbrace{\begin{bmatrix} \mathbf{A}_1^M & \mathbf{A}_1^V & \mathbf{A}_1^L \\ \hline \mathbf{T}_{1,1}^M & \mathbf{T}_{1,1}^V & \mathbf{T}_{1,1}^L \\ \hline \mathbf{T}_{1,2}^M & \mathbf{T}_{1,2}^V & \mathbf{T}_{1,2}^L \\ \hline \mathbf{A}_2^M & \mathbf{A}_2^V & \mathbf{A}_2^L \end{bmatrix}}_{\mathbf{M}} \cdot [M\ V\ L]^\top, \quad \text{with} \quad \mathbf{M} = \begin{bmatrix} 1\,0\,0 \\ 1\,0\,0 \\ 0\,1\,0 \\ 0\,1\,0 \end{bmatrix} \quad \text{for TC2.}$$

The Generic Two-Pass Cipher. For the generic two-pass construction, $\mathcal{E}_1 \circ \mathbf{A}_1$ and $\mathbf{A}_3 \circ \mathcal{E}_2$ are online ciphers. The two-pass scheme follows the description in Sect. 3.1 but adds vectors $T_{2,1}$ and $T_{2,1}$ for the second encryption pass

$$\begin{bmatrix} U \\ T_{1,1} \\ T_{1,2} \\ W \\ T_{2,1} \\ T_{2,2} \\ C \end{bmatrix} = \begin{bmatrix} \mathbf{A}_1^M & \mathbf{A}_1^V & \mathbf{0} & \mathbf{0} & \mathbf{A}_1^L \\ \mathbf{T}_{1,1}^M & \mathbf{T}_{1,1}^V & \mathbf{0} & \mathbf{0} & \mathbf{T}_{1,1}^L \\ \mathbf{T}_{1,2}^M & \mathbf{T}_{1,2}^V & \mathbf{0} & \mathbf{0} & \mathbf{T}_{1,2}^L \\ \mathbf{A}_2^M & \mathbf{A}_2^V & \mathbf{0} & \mathbf{0} & \mathbf{A}_2^L \\ \mathbf{0} & \mathbf{0} & \mathbf{T}_{2,1}^W & \mathbf{T}_{2,1}^X & \mathbf{T}_{2,1}^L \\ \mathbf{0} & \mathbf{0} & \mathbf{T}_{2,2}^W & \mathbf{T}_{2,2}^X & \mathbf{T}_{2,2}^L \\ \mathbf{0} & \mathbf{0} & \mathbf{A}_3^W & \mathbf{A}_3^X & \mathbf{A}_3^L \end{bmatrix} \cdot [M\ V\ W\ X\ L]^\top .$$

We define $\mathbf{A}_2^V$ as the exchange matrix and $\mathbf{A}_2^M = \mathbf{A}_2^L = \mathbf{0}$. Thus, $W_i = V_{m+1-i}$ for $i \in [m]$. We call this construction TOCO as a reference to the paper title of [2] and will show briefly that and why it lacks full implicit key stretching.

4.6 Attack on the Generic Two-Pass Construction

Theorem 6. *Let $\Pi[\widetilde{E}_K] \in \mathsf{OCipher}(\mathcal{K}, \mathcal{B})$. Let $\mathbf{A}_2$ be the exchange matrix and $\widehat{\Pi}[\Pi[\widetilde{E}_K]] = (\widehat{\mathcal{E}}, \widehat{\mathcal{D}})$ with $\mathbf{A}_2$ denote the TOCO construction. Then, given an m-block-minimal transcript τ for arbitrary $m \geq 2$, it holds that $\mathsf{q_c}(\widehat{\Pi}) \leq 3$.*

Proof. For $m = 1$, the filter is trivial and needs only two calls to compute from M_1 to C_1 or vice versa. Given a current key candidate K as well as any plaintext-ciphertext pair (M, C) of $m \geq 2$ blocks, the adversary can compute

$$W_m = \widetilde{E}_K^{T_{1,1,0}, T_{1,2,0}}(M_1), \quad \text{and} \quad W_{m-1} = \widetilde{E}_K^{M_1, W_m}(M_2)$$

and test on $C_m \stackrel{?}{=} \widetilde{E}_K^{W_{m-1}, C_{m-1}}(W_m)$, which holds for the correct K but only with probability about $|\mathcal{B}|^{-1}$ otherwise. □

The same key-recovery filter also applies to a variant of TOCO with three passes of an online cipher Π, where both $\mathbf{A}_2$ and $\mathbf{A}_3$ are exchange matrices. We call this construction TOCO3. Though, this filter is not extendable to four or more passes.

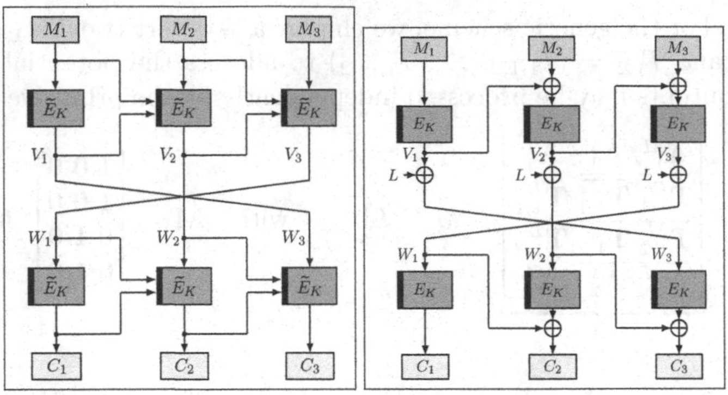

(a) TOCO. (b) CMC.

Fig. 3. Encryption with TOCO and CMC, for $m = 3$ message blocks each. For CMC, it holds that $L = 2(V_1 \oplus V_m) = 2(W_1 \oplus W_m)$.

Theorem 7. *Let $\widehat{\Pi}[\Pi[\widetilde{E}_K]] = (\widehat{\mathcal{E}}[\mathcal{E}[\widetilde{E}_K]], \widehat{\mathcal{D}}[\mathcal{E}[\widetilde{E}_K]])$ denote the TOCO3 construction and let $\mathbf{A}_2$ and $\mathbf{A}_3$ be exchange matrices. Then, given an m-block-minimal transcript τ, it holds that $\mathsf{q_c}(\widehat{\Pi}) \leq 5$.*

Proof. Again, the filter is trivial for $m = 1$ and needs only three calls to compute from M_1 to C_1 or vice versa. For $m \geq 2$, given a current key candidate K as well as any plaintext-ciphertext pair (M, C), the adversary can compute

$$W_m = \widetilde{E}_K^{T_{1,1,0}, T_{1,2,0}}(M_1), \quad W_{m-1} = \widetilde{E}_K^{M_1, V_1}(M_2),$$
$$X_m = Y_1 = \widetilde{D}_K^{T_{3,1,0}, T_{3,2,0}}(C_1), \quad X_{m-1} = Y_2 = \widetilde{D}_K^{Y_1, C_1}(C_2),$$

and can test on $X_m \stackrel{?}{=} \widetilde{E}_K^{W_{m-1}, X_{m-1}}(W_m)$, which holds for the correct K but only with probability about $|\mathcal{B}|^{-1}$ otherwise. □

4.7 CMC-Like Constructions

CMC consists of two mirrored passes of CBC with an affine layer $\mathbf{A}_2$ that adds $2(V_1 + V_m)$ to each block. Nevertheless, the stronger middle layer does not strengthen the scheme by stretching the key.

Theorem 8. *Let $\Pi[E_K] = (\mathcal{E}, \mathcal{D})$ denote CMC. Then, given an m-block-minimal transcript τ for arbitrary $m \geq 2$, it holds that $\mathsf{q_c}(\widehat{\Pi}) \leq 3$.*

Proof. Again, the key-candidate filter is trivial for $m = 1$ and needs only two calls to compute from M_1 to C_1 or vice versa. For $m \geq 2$ blocks and given a current key candidate K as well as any plaintext-ciphertext pair (M, C), the adversary can compute

$$V_1 = E_K(M_1), \quad V_2 = E_K(M_2 + V_1), \quad \text{and} \quad W_1 = E_K^{-1}(C_1).$$

Algorithm 2. TOCO′, CMC′, and EME′with full implicit key stretching.

11: **function** TOCO′$[\widetilde{E}]_K(M,C)$	31: **function** CMC′$[E]_K(M,C)$	51: **function** EME′$[E]_K(M,C)$
12: $(M_1,\ldots,M_m) \xleftarrow{\mathcal{X}} M$	32: $(M_1,\ldots,M_m) \xleftarrow{\mathcal{X}} M$	52: $(M_1,\ldots,M_m) \xleftarrow{\mathcal{X}} M$
13: $T_1 \leftarrow (0^n, 0^n)$	33: $V_0 \leftarrow 0$	53: **for** $i \leftarrow 1..m$ **do**
14: **for** $i \leftarrow 1..m$ **do**	34: **for** $i \leftarrow 1..m$ **do**	54: $U_i \leftarrow 2^{i-1}L_1 \oplus M_i$
15: $X_i \leftarrow \widetilde{E}_{K_i}^{T_i}(M_i)$	35: $U_i \leftarrow M_i \oplus V_{i-1}$	55: $V_i \leftarrow E_K(U_i)$
16: $T_{i+1} \leftarrow (M_i, X_i)$	36: $V_i \leftarrow E_K(U_i)$	56: $\Sigma_V \leftarrow \bigoplus_{i=2}^m V_i$
17: $U \leftarrow 2(X_1 \oplus X_m)$	37: $W \leftarrow \mathbf{A}_2^V \cdot V$	57: $W_1 \leftarrow V_1 \oplus \Sigma_V$
18: **for** $i \leftarrow 1..m$ **do**	38: $W_0 \leftarrow 0$	58: $X_1 \leftarrow E_K(W_1)$
19: $Y_i \leftarrow X_i \oplus U$	39: **for** $i \leftarrow 1..m$ **do**	59: $L_2 \leftarrow W_1 \oplus X_1$
20: $Z_i \leftarrow Y_{m+1-i}$	40: $X_i \leftarrow E_K(W_i)$	60: $\Sigma_Y \leftarrow \bigoplus_{i=2}^m Y_i$
21: $T_1 \leftarrow (0^n, 0^n)$	41: $C_i \leftarrow X_i + W_{i-1}$	61: $Y_1 \leftarrow X_1 \oplus \Sigma_Y$
22: **for** $i \leftarrow 1..m$ **do**	42: **return** $(C_1 \| \cdots \| C_m)$	62: **for** $i \leftarrow 1..m$ **do**
23: $C_i \leftarrow \widetilde{E}_{K_i}^{T_i}(Z_i)$		63: **if** $i \geq 2$ **then**
24: $T_{i+1} \leftarrow (Z_i, C_i)$		64: $Y_i \leftarrow V_i \oplus 2^{i-1}L_2$
25: **return** $(C_1 \| \cdots \| C_m)$		65: $Z_i \leftarrow E_K(Y_i)$
		66: $C_i \leftarrow 2^{i-1}L_1 \oplus Z_i$
		67: **return** $(C_1 \| \cdots \| C_m)$

Then, it can rewrite $W_1 = V_m + 2V_1 + 2V_m = 2V_1 + 3V_m$, such that $V_m = 3^{-1}(W_1 + 2V_1)$, which allows it to derive

$$W_m = 3V_1 + 2V_m \quad \text{and} \quad W_{m-1} = V_2 + 2V_1 + 2V_m,$$

and to test if $C_m \overset{?}{=} E_K(W_m) + W_{m-1}$, which always holds for the correct K but only with negligible probability otherwise for sufficiently large $|\mathcal{B}|$.   □

5 Minimal Modifications for Full Implicit Key Stretching

Two passes can suffice to obtain full block-wise dependency. We show that no sequential encryption passes are necessary as long as the middle layer is MDS. Since full implicit key stretching can benefit also three-pass modes, we can try to achieve it for HCTR-like schemes in this section. Those schemes lacked full implicit key stretching only due to their use of counter mode with invertible primitives. We will try to improve it with minimal modifications. In general, we denote the modified schemes by an apostrophe appended to their names, e.g., EME is modified to EME′.

5.1 Adding Full Implicit Key Stretching to Two-Pass Modes

For two passes, the efficient key filters depend on the intermediate layer $\mathbf{A}_2$. We will show that an MDS matrix as $\mathbf{A}_2$ will suffice to provide full implicit key stretching for the generic construction from two passes of an online cipher $\Pi[\widetilde{E}_K]$. In the following, we will show a key filter similar to that on TOCO.

We show briefly that the filter is made inapplicable by an MDS matrix for $\mathbf{A}_2$ instead, leading to full implicit key stretching - even if we replace the encryption passes $\mathcal{E}_1 \circ \mathbf{A}_1$ and $\mathbf{A}_3 \circ \mathcal{E}_2$ as ΘCB3 layers each, with all independent alls to $\widetilde{E}_K^i$. Thus, $\mathbf{A}_1$ maps $U_i = M_i$ and $\mathbf{A}_3$ is defined so that $C_i = X_i$ for all $i \in [m]$. The same property follows clearly for CMC as well as for an arbitrary (stronger) two-pass online cipher with an MDS matrix as a middle layer. Thus, we illustrate that the property is caused by the middle layer and not the complexity of the encryption passes.

Theorem 9. *Let $\widehat{\Pi}[\widetilde{E}_K] = (\widehat{\mathcal{E}}, \widehat{\mathcal{D}})$ denote the generic construction from two passes of an online cipher $\Pi[\widetilde{E}_K] = (\mathcal{E}, \mathcal{D})$ as above. Let $\mathbf{A}_2^M = \mathbf{A}_2^L = \mathbf{0}$ and let $\mathbf{A}_2^V$ be MDS and non-singular. Given an m-block-minimal transcript τ, it holds that $\mathsf{q_c}(\widehat{\Pi}) = m + 1$.*

Proof. To show that the bound in Theorem 9 is tight, we consider two statements: (1) there exists no key filter with $\leq m$ primitive calls, and (2) $m+1$ calls suffice. Both statements follow from the MDS property of $\mathbf{A}_2^V$. In the following, we denote its coefficients in Row r and Column c as $a_{r,c}$. For any $i \in [m]$, it holds that $W_i =^{\text{def}} \sum_{j=1} a_{i,j} V_j$. Since $\mathbf{A}_2^V$ is MDS, the equation system of any W_i yields no solution if any of the values V_j are unknown, which shows the first statement. Hence, an overdetermined equation system for any W_i needs to compute all values $V_j = E_K(M_j)$, for all $j \in [m]$, as well as $W_i = E_K^{-1}(C_i)$. It is also possible to derive a similar equation system with different blocks chosen as inputs and outputs which needs one primitive call for each $j \in [m]$ and an index i, such that W_i and V_i are both contained. Since this key filter uses exactly $m+1$ primitive calls, it shows the second statement. Theorem 9 follows. □

Theorem 9 implies that CMC' and TOCO' – that replace only their previous $\mathbf{A}_2^V$ with an arbitrary MDS matrix compared to CMC and TOCO, respectively – provide $\mathsf{q_c}(m + 1)$, i.e. full implicit key stretching. An MDS matrix needs to be efficient and easily extendable. One extendable instance for arbitrary non-negative integer m is the Vandermonde matrix for a generator $\alpha \in \mathcal{B}$. We call the constructions of EME, CMC, and TOCO that replace their matrix $\mathbf{A}_2^V$ by the Vandermonde matrix as EME', CMC', and TOCO'.

We emphasize that a mode with only r passes block-wise-operating independent STPRPs with an MDS matrix in between would not be a secure SPRP. This structure is an r-round SPN, which is vulnerable to yoyo or mixture attacks, and the here-proposed minimal modified variants, e.g., EME'or CMC' must therefore include chaining between message blocks.

5.2 Keystream Generator as a Middle Mode of Three Passes

HCTR-like schemes lacked full implicit key stretching since their internal counter modes were invertible. Thus, even under an unknown IV, two primitive outputs could be decrypted to test on a linear relation. As a countermeasure, we suggest a PRG whose outputs are indistinguishable from random and that is secure against key-recovery attacks. Then, HCTR-like schemes can benefit from a secret IV that is used as the key in the PRG. We model such schemes as shown in Fig. 4:

1. In the first pass, the full message is used to compute an initial value $IV \leftarrow \widetilde{\mathcal{E}}_{K_1}^{M_R}(M_L)$. This pass must be invertible if M_L is non-empty. If M_L is empty, it can also be a not efficiently invertible PRF F.

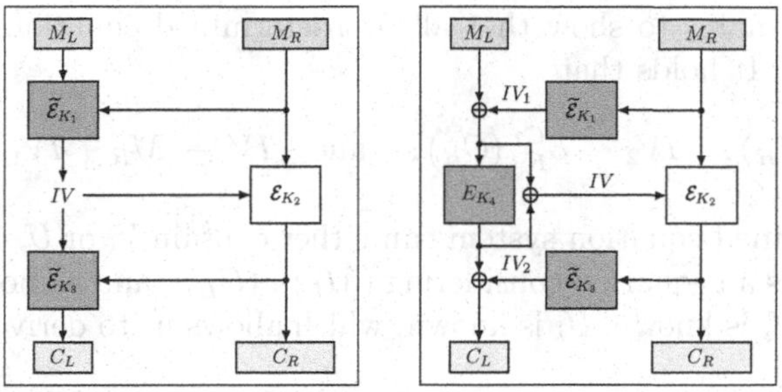

Fig. 4. Left: PIV as an example of HCTR-like scheme with invertible transformations $\widetilde{\mathcal{E}}_{K_1}$ and $\widetilde{\mathcal{E}}_{K_3}$. **Right:** HCTR as an example of for a scheme with $\widetilde{\mathcal{E}}_{K_1}$ and $\widetilde{\mathcal{E}}_{K_3}$ that yield the IV from additions $M_L + IV_1$ or $C_L + IV_2$.

2. IV is used for encrypting $C_R \leftarrow \widetilde{\mathcal{E}}_{K_2}(G(IV, i)) \oplus M_R$ in a keystream generator $\mathcal{E}$. We denote the keystream as $Y = (Y_1, \ldots, Y_r) \leftarrow \widetilde{\mathcal{E}}_{K_2}(IV)$.
3. Finally, any invertible transformation is used to derive $C_L \leftarrow \widetilde{\mathcal{E}}_{K_3}^{C_R}(IV)$.

Theorem 10 (Theorem 5 in [21]). *Let $H = (H_1, \ldots, H_d)$ be a vector of d polynomials in $M = (M_1, \ldots, M_m)$ and K over some field $\mathbb{F}$ that can be computed by s multiplications. If $m \geq 2(s - r) + 1$ with $r \leq d$, then, there exist distinct X, X' elements of $\mathbb{F}^r$ and $\Delta \in \mathbb{F}$ such that*

$$\Pr_{K \twoheadleftarrow \mathcal{K}} [H_K(X') + \delta = H_K(X)] \geq |\mathbb{F}|^{-r}.$$

Thus, to obtain d almost universal hash output blocks $H_i \in \mathcal{B}$ on messages $M \in \mathcal{B}^m$, at least $(d-1)+m/2$ key-dependent multiplications are necessary. For $d = 1$, $m/2$ is thus minimal.

Theorem 11. *Let $K \twoheadleftarrow \mathcal{K}$ and $F : \mathcal{K} \to \mathcal{B} \to \mathcal{B}$ be a non-efficiently invertible function. Let $\widehat{\Pi}[\mathsf{CTR}[F_K]] = (\widehat{\mathcal{E}}, \widehat{\mathcal{D}})$ be as above with $\widetilde{\mathcal{E}}_1$ and $\widetilde{\mathcal{E}}_3$ being universal in $\mathcal{B}$. Given an m-block-minimal transcript τ, it holds that $\mathsf{q_c}(\widehat{\Pi}[E_K]) \geq m/2$.*

Note that the universality assumptions of $\widetilde{\mathcal{E}}_1$ and $\widetilde{\mathcal{E}}_3$ are standard, and necessarily fulfilled by all HCTR-like schemes.

Proof. The proof consists of three steps: (1) All overdetermined equation systems that serve as a key filter allow deriving IV or $IV_1 + IV_2$ linearly. Hence, an overdetermined equation system that is the equivalent of every key filter needs knowledge of IV or $IV_1 + IV_2$. (2) Deriving the IV needs $m/2$ key-dependent multiplications or primitive calls. (3) Obtaining an overdetermined equation system needs either one additional nonlinear call in $\widetilde{\mathcal{E}}_2$, or $m/2$ additional nonlinear computations in $\widetilde{\mathcal{E}}_{K_3}$. First, we replace $\mathsf{CTR}[F_K]$ by a random function $\rho \twoheadleftarrow \mathsf{Func}(\mathcal{B}, \mathcal{B})$ The advantage is upper bounded by the maximal PRF advantage against $\mathsf{CTR}[F_K]$ for $K \twoheadleftarrow \mathcal{K}$.

Step (1). It remains to show that all overdetermined equation systems allow deriving the IV. It holds that

$$IV_1 \leftarrow \widetilde{\mathcal{E}}_{K_1}^{M_L}(M_R), \quad IV_2 \leftarrow \widetilde{\mathcal{E}}_{K_3}^{C_L}(C_R), \quad \text{and} \quad IV \leftarrow M_R + IV_1 = C_R + IV_2 .$$

The overdetermined equation system can either contain V_i or U_i in $\widetilde{\mathcal{E}}_{K_2}(IV)$. In this case, there is an equation considering $(M_L)_i$, $(C_L)_i$, and a known V_i that can be matched. If V_i is known, U_i is known, which allows us to derive IV efficiently from $F_i^{-1}(IV)$.

Otherwise, there must be an overdetermined equation system solely with M_R, C_R, and the knowledge of $IV_1 + IV_2$. If either IV_1 or IV_2 are known, IV can be computed from them. Then, our claim would follow. Since the computation of IV_1 and IV_2 are independent of each other and use distinct keys, the computation of $IV_1 + IV_2$ would need strictly more key-dependent multiplications or primitive calls than each computation of either of IV_1 or IV_2.

Step (2). There are three ways of deriving the IV: computing $IV \leftarrow \widetilde{\mathcal{E}}_{K_1}^{M_R}(M_L)$, computing $IV \leftarrow \widetilde{\mathcal{D}}_{K_3}^{C_R}(C_L)$, or deriving it inside $\widetilde{\mathcal{E}}_{K_2}$. Since the computation of IV is universal by assumption, Theorem 10 ensures that their computations in $\widetilde{\mathcal{E}}_{K_1}$ or in $\widetilde{\mathcal{D}}_{K_3}$ need at least $m/2$ key-dependent multiplications or primitive calls. Since $\mathcal{G}$ is an ideal PRG, the advantage of computing IV from $\widetilde{\mathcal{E}}_{K_2}$ is zero.

Step (3). Given the IV from either $\widetilde{\mathcal{E}}_{K_1}$ or $\widetilde{\mathcal{D}}_{K_3}$, each output in $\widetilde{\mathcal{E}}_{K_2}$ needs at least one primitive call to encrypt any message block or decrypt any ciphertext block. Our claim follows then from the individual proof steps. □

Consequently, an HCTR-like scheme can employ a variant of Counter mode instantiated with a PRF and a secret IV. Such a variant can be as simple as AES in Davies-Meyer mode or AES-PRF [18], which encrypts 128-bit message blocks as efficiently as the AES and provides close to $O(q/2^n)$ security. Alternatively, Counter-in-Tweak [22] also provides an n-bit-secure PRF from a tweakable block cipher when used with a $2n$-bit IV as input.

6 Conclusion

Implicit key stretching can be satisfied by offline encryption schemes besides their core security goals. This work proposed it as a property that can help throttle passive attacks based on known plaintext-ciphertext pairs. We introduce full implicit key stretching as a property that helps analyze it from a simple affine-mode representation. We see large-file archive backups and file-disk encryption as exemplary settings where messages may have substantial minimal lengths. Nevertheless, more applications of implicit key stretching may exist.

We could show that online schemes can provide only constant implicit key stretching. Moreover, modes with two passes of a secure online cipher around a mixing layer can provide full implicit key stretching with the help of an MDS layer between both encryptions, at the price of implementation drawbacks.

As part of a remedy, we could show that three passes can provide full implicit key stretching if the input is processed in full in the wrapping layer, independent of a high level of parallelization or not. Existing three-pass modes such as HCTR, PIV, or RIV can add it by a minor modification: the middle layer of a counter mode based on a permutation is replaced by one that employs a PRF or an already available tweakable block cipher instead.

Acknowledgements. We are highly thankful to the reviewers of CT-RSA 2022 and ICISC 2022 for their fruitful comments. This research was funded by DFG Grant LU 608/9-1.

A Encryption-Model Visualization

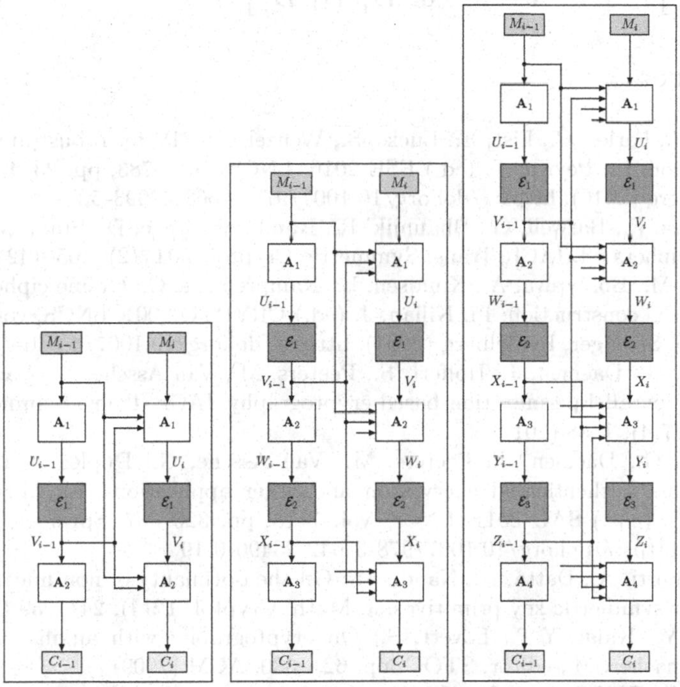

(a) Single-pass modes. (b) Two-pass modes. (c) Three-pass modes.

Fig. 5. Models for single-, two-, and three-pass modes. Arrows without an input indicate that our models are restricted to plausible variants.

B Decryption Representations

For single-pass modes, we define the decryption model as

$$\begin{bmatrix} V \\ M \end{bmatrix} = \begin{bmatrix} \mathbf{D}_1^M & \mathbf{D}_1^V & \mathbf{D}_1^L \\ \mathbf{D}_2^M & \mathbf{D}_2^V & \mathbf{D}_2^L \end{bmatrix} \cdot [C\ U\ L]^\top .$$

For two-pass schemes, the decryption can be represented as

$$\begin{bmatrix} X \\ V \\ M \end{bmatrix} = \begin{bmatrix} \mathbf{D}_1^C & \mathbf{D}_1^W & \mathbf{0} & \mathbf{0} & \mathbf{D}_1^L \\ \mathbf{D}_2^C & \mathbf{D}_2^W & \mathbf{0} & \mathbf{0} & \mathbf{D}_2^L \\ \mathbf{0} & \mathbf{0} & \mathbf{D}_3^V & \mathbf{D}_3^U & \mathbf{D}_3^L \end{bmatrix} \cdot [C\ W\ V\ U\ L]^\top .$$

For three passes, the decryption is represented as

$$\begin{bmatrix} Z \\ X \\ V \\ M \end{bmatrix} = \begin{bmatrix} \mathbf{D}_1^C & \mathbf{D}_1^Y & \mathbf{0} & \mathbf{0} & \mathbf{0} & \mathbf{0} & \mathbf{D}_1^L \\ \mathbf{D}_2^C & \mathbf{D}_2^Y & \mathbf{0} & \mathbf{0} & \mathbf{0} & \mathbf{0} & \mathbf{D}_2^L \\ \mathbf{0} & \mathbf{0} & \mathbf{D}_3^X & \mathbf{D}_3^W & \mathbf{0} & \mathbf{D}_3^U & \mathbf{D}_3^L \\ \mathbf{0} & \mathbf{0} & \mathbf{0} & \mathbf{0} & \mathbf{D}_4^Y & \mathbf{D}_4^U & \mathbf{D}_4^L \end{bmatrix} \cdot [C\ Y\ X\ W\ VU\ L]^\top .$$

References

1. Abed, F., Forler, C., List, E., Lucks, S., Wenzel, J.: RIV for robust authenticated encryption. In: Peyrin, T. (ed.) FSE 2016. LNCS, vol. 9783, pp. 23–42. Springer, Heidelberg (2016). https://doi.org/10.1007/978-3-662-52993-5_2
2. Andreeva, E., Barwell, G., Bhaumik, R., Nandi, M., Page, D., Stam, M.: Turning online ciphers off. IACR Trans. Symmetric Cryptol. **2017**(2), 105–142 (2017)
3. Bellare, M., Boldyreva, A., Knudsen, L., Namprempre, C.: Online ciphers and the Hash-CBC construction. In: Kilian, J. (ed.) CRYPTO 2001. LNCS, vol. 2139, pp. 292–309. Springer, Heidelberg (2001). https://doi.org/10.1007/3-540-44647-8_18
4. Bertoni, G., Daemen, J., Hoffert, S., Peeters, M., Van Assche, G., Van Keer, R.: Farfalle: parallel permutation-based cryptography. IACR Trans. Symmetric Cryptol. **2017**(4), 1–38 (2017)
5. Bertoni, G., Daemen, J., Peeters, M., Van Assche, G.: Duplexing the sponge: single-pass authenticated encryption and other applications. In: Miri, A., Vaudenay, S. (eds.) SAC 2011. LNCS, vol. 7118, pp. 320–337. Springer, Heidelberg (2012). https://doi.org/10.1007/978-3-642-28496-0_19
6. Chakraborti, A., Datta, N., Nandi, M.: On the optimality of non-linear computations for symmetric key primitives. J. Math. Cryptol. **12**(4), 241–259 (2018)
7. Dodis, Y., Kalai, Y.T., Lovett, S.: On cryptography with auxiliary input. In: Mitzenmacher, M., editor, STOC, pp. 621–630. ACM (2009)
8. Halevi, S.: EME*: extending EME to handle arbitrary-length messages with associated data. In: Canteaut, A., Viswanathan, K. (eds.) INDOCRYPT 2004. LNCS, vol. 3348, pp. 315–327. Springer, Heidelberg (2004). https://doi.org/10.1007/978-3-540-30556-9_25
9. Halevi, S.: EME*: extending EME to handle arbitrary-length messages with associated data. IACR Cryptol. ePrint Arch. **2004**, 125 (2004)
10. Halevi, S., Rogaway, P.: A parallelizable enciphering mode. IACR Cryptol. ePrint Arch. **2003**, 147 (2003)

11. Halevi, S., Rogaway, P.: A tweakable enciphering mode. In: Boneh, D. (ed.) CRYPTO 2003. LNCS, vol. 2729, pp. 482–499. Springer, Heidelberg (2003). https://doi.org/10.1007/978-3-540-45146-4_28
12. Halevi, S., Rogaway, P.: A parallelizable enciphering mode. In: Okamoto, T. (ed.) CT-RSA 2004. LNCS, vol. 2964, pp. 292–304. Springer, Heidelberg (2004). https://doi.org/10.1007/978-3-540-24660-2_23
13. Hoang, V.T., Krovetz, T., Rogaway, P.: Robust authenticated-encryption AEZ and the problem that it solves. In: Oswald, E., Fischlin, M. (eds.) EUROCRYPT 2015. LNCS, vol. 9056, pp. 15–44. Springer, Heidelberg (2015). https://doi.org/10.1007/978-3-662-46800-5_2
14. Hoang, V.T., Reyhanitabar, R., Rogaway, P., Vizár, D.: Online authenticated-encryption and its nonce-reuse misuse-resistance. In: Gennaro, R., Robshaw, M. (eds.) CRYPTO 2015. LNCS, vol. 9215, pp. 493–517. Springer, Heidelberg (2015). https://doi.org/10.1007/978-3-662-47989-6_24
15. Jean, J., Nikolić, I., Peyrin, T.: Deoxys v1.41. Third-round submission to the CAESAR competition; Deoxys-II became finalist, 12 Oct 2016
16. Krovetz, T., Rogaway, P.: The software performance of authenticated-encryption modes. In: Joux, A. (ed.) FSE 2011. LNCS, vol. 6733, pp. 306–327. Springer, Heidelberg (2011). https://doi.org/10.1007/978-3-642-21702-9_18
17. McGrew, D.A., Viega, J.: The security and performance of the Galois/Counter Mode (GCM) of operation. In: Canteaut, A., Viswanathan, K. (eds.) INDOCRYPT 2004. LNCS, vol. 3348, pp. 343–355. Springer, Heidelberg (2004). https://doi.org/10.1007/978-3-540-30556-9_27
18. Mennink, B., Neves, S.: Optimal PRFs from blockcipher designs. IACR Trans. Symmetric Cryptol. **2017**(3), 228–252 (2017)
19. Minematsu, K.: Parallelizable rate-1 authenticated encryption from pseudorandom functions. In: Nguyen, P.Q., Oswald, E. (eds.) EUROCRYPT 2014. LNCS, vol. 8441, pp. 275–292. Springer, Heidelberg (2014). https://doi.org/10.1007/978-3-642-55220-5_16
20. Namprempre, C., Rogaway, P., Shrimpton, T.: Reconsidering generic composition. In: Nguyen, P.Q., Oswald, E. (eds.) EUROCRYPT 2014. LNCS, vol. 8441, pp. 257–274. Springer, Heidelberg (2014). https://doi.org/10.1007/978-3-642-55220-5_15
21. Nandi, M.: On the minimum number of multiplications necessary for universal hash functions. In: Cid, C., Rechberger, C. (eds.) FSE 2014. LNCS, vol. 8540, pp. 489–508. Springer, Heidelberg (2015). https://doi.org/10.1007/978-3-662-46706-0_25
22. Peyrin, T., Seurin, Y.: Counter-in-Tweak: authenticated encryption modes for tweakable block ciphers. In: Robshaw, M., Katz, J. (eds.) CRYPTO 2016. LNCS, vol. 9814, pp. 33–63. Springer, Heidelberg (2016). https://doi.org/10.1007/978-3-662-53018-4_2
23. Rogaway, P.: Efficient instantiations of tweakable blockciphers and refinements to modes OCB and PMAC. In: Lee, P.J. (ed.) ASIACRYPT 2004. LNCS, vol. 3329, pp. 16–31. Springer, Heidelberg (2004). https://doi.org/10.1007/978-3-540-30539-2_2
24. Rogaway, P., Shrimpton, T.: A provable-security treatment of the key-wrap problem. In: Vaudenay, S. (ed.) EUROCRYPT 2006. LNCS, vol. 4004, pp. 373–390. Springer, Heidelberg (2006). https://doi.org/10.1007/11761679_23
25. Rogaway, P., Zhang, H.: Online ciphers from tweakable blockciphers. In: Kiayias, A. (ed.) CT-RSA 2011. LNCS, vol. 6558, pp. 237–249. Springer, Heidelberg (2011). https://doi.org/10.1007/978-3-642-19074-2_16

26. Shrimpton, T., Terashima, R.S.: A modular framework for building variable-input-length tweakable ciphers. In: Sako, K., Sarkar, P. (eds.) ASIACRYPT 2013. LNCS, vol. 8269, pp. 405–423. Springer, Heidelberg (2013). https://doi.org/10.1007/978-3-642-42033-7_21
27. International Telecommunication Union. ITU Recommendation G.709/Y.1331 (06/20). Technical report, International Telecommunication Union, 06 Jun 2020
28. Wang, P., Feng, D., Wu, W.: HCTR: a variable-input-length enciphering mode. In: Feng, D., Lin, D., Yung, M. (eds.) CISC 2005. LNCS, vol. 3822, pp. 175–188. Springer, Heidelberg (2005). https://doi.org/10.1007/11599548_15

Related-Key Differential Cryptanalysis of GMiMC Used in Post-Quantum Signatures

Shiyao Chen[1(✉)], Chun Guo[3,4], Jian Guo[2], Li Liu[3,4], Meiqin Wang[3,4,5], Puwen Wei[3,4,5], and Zeyu Xu[3,4]

[1] Strategic Centre for Research in Privacy-Preserving Technologies and Systems, Nanyang Technological University, Singapore, Singapore
shiyao.chen@ntu.edu.sg

[2] Division of Mathematical Sciences, School of Physical and Mathematical Sciences, Nanyang Technological University, Singapore, Singapore
guojian@ntu.edu.sg

[3] School of Cyber Science and Technology, Shandong University, Qingdao, China
{chun.guo,mqwang,pwei}@sdu.edu.cn, {sdu_liuli,xuzeyu}@mail.sdu.edu.cn

[4] Key Laboratory of Cryptologic Technology and Information Security, Ministry of Education, Shandong University, Qingdao, China

[5] Quan Cheng Laboratory, Jinan, China

Abstract. With the urgency of the threat imposed by quantum computers, there is a strong interest in making the signature schemes quantum resistant. As the promising candidates to ensure post-quantum security, symmetric-key primitives, in particular the recent MPC/FHE/ZK-friendly hash functions or block ciphers, are providing another choice to build efficient and secure signature schemes that do not rely on any assumed hard problems. However, considering the intended use cases, many of these novel ciphers for advanced cryptographic protocols do not claim the related-key security.

In this paper, we initiate the study of the ignored related-key security of GMiMC proposed by Albrecht *et al.* at ESORICS 2019, some versions of which are optimized and designed to be used in post-quantum secure signatures. By investigating the potential threats of related-key attacks for GMiMC intended to be deployed as the underlying building block in post-quantum signature schemes, we then construct two kinds of iterative related-key differentials, from which not only do we explore its security margin against related-key attacks, but also collision attacks on its key space can be performed. For example, for GMiMC instance that beats the smallest signature size obtainable using LowMC, we can find its key collision using only about 2^{10} key pairs. It worths noting that our current key collision attack is only applicable when the adversarial power is sufficiently strong (e.g., in the so-called multi-user setting), and it does not threaten the one-wayness of GMiMC. Furthermore, from the experiments of our related-key differentials, it can be observed that the differential clustering effect of GMiMC differs in both aspects: the choice of the finite field $\mathbb{F}$ being $\mathbb{F}_p$ or $\mathbb{F}_2^n$, and the size of the finite field $\mathbb{F}$.

S.-H. Seo and H. Seo (Eds.): ICISC 2022, LNCS 13849, pp. 41–60, 2023.
https://doi.org/10.1007/978-3-031-29371-9_3

Keywords: Related-key differential cryptanalysis · Post-quantum signature · Collision attack · GMiMC

1 Introduction

Quantum cryptanalysis has become an important topic in recent years, for example, Shor's algorithm [24] breaking the security of public-key cryptosystems RSA and ECC, and Simon's algorithm [25] promoting symmetric-key cryptanalysis on multiple systems [17,20,21]. Consequently, the design of cryptographic primitives that remains secure against quantum attacks has attracted more and more attentions. This has led to the NIST Post-Quantum Cryptography standardization project [13], and its candidates to be standardized have been announced recently.[1]

To achieve the post-quantum security, building secure and efficient signature schemes from symmetric-key primitives rather than relying on structured hardness assumptions is becoming an interesting and promising direction. For instances, one of NIST post-quantum cryptography candidates—SPHINCS$^+$ [6] is a stateless hash-based signature scheme, and one of NIST Round 3 submissions—Picnic [11] is a signature scheme whose security is based on the one-wayness of a block cipher and the pseudo-random properties of an extensible hash function. When deriving post-quantum security from symmetric-key primitives, the recent developments of advanced cryptographic protocols, such as Multiparty Computation (MPC), Fully Homomorphic Encryption (FHE) and Zero-Knowledge proof (ZK), opens up new directions of designing novel MPC/FHE/ZK-friendly symmetric-key ciphers as alternatives to AES and SHA-3, with LowMC [4], MiMC [3] and its variants GMiMC [1], and Rescue [5] as notable examples. Following the traditional statistical cryptanalysis, many of these novel symmetric-key primitives are shown to be with sound security against statistical cryptanalytic attacks. However, they remain relatively new and less extensively studied. Considering the intended use cases, it is worth noting that *most of these MPC/FHE/ZK-friendly symmetric-key primitives explicitly do not claim the security in related-key models* [8,18]. Under the related-key setting, it assumes that an attacker has the ability to manipulate the key, which is always more powerful than traditional single-key differential cryptanalysis [9]. However, these newly symmetric-key ciphers are gradually used as the underlying building blocks in a wide range of purposes to ensure the post-quantum security, it is still necessary to study the resistance against related-key differential attacks of these primitives in detail, which might be ignored for the original intended applications.

Contributions. On one hand, we investigate the potential threats of the related-key attacks for `GMiMC-erf`[2] when deployed as PRP/PRFs in the post-

[1] https://csrc.nist.gov/projects/post-quantum-cryptography/selected-algorithms-2022.

[2] One of GMiMC variants with expanding round functions.

quantum signature schemes, which is the recommended version of GMiMC and aims at competing with LowMC in post-quantum signature applications.

- For one-way function use case in Picnic digital signature scheme [12], traditional statistical attacks do not apply to this low-data scenario, while our related-key attacks still work with the limited data access and will pose some potential threats if there are many users, such as the multi-user setting.[3] It should be noted that this does not threaten the one-wayness of `GMiMC-erf`.
- For hash function use case in Enhanced Privacy ID (EPID) signatures built only from symmetric-key primitives presented by Boneh *et al.* [10], it requires the underlying PRF with full-data security and collision resistance on its key space, which can be attributed to the resistance of `GMiMC-erf` against related-key attacks and are directly related to the security of key revocation strategy of the resulting EPID schemes.

We then construct two kinds of iterative related-key differentials to explore the security margin of `GMiMC-erf` under related-key setting, which are provided in Table 1. What calls for the attention is that our proposed related-key differentials are also constructed for collision attacks, it means that the output differences of our distinguishers must be zero, which are more demanding than the previous single-key truncated differentials [1, 7] and supposed to be bounded by the birthday bound.

Table 1. Comparisons of different bounds of differential distinguishers of `GMiMC-erf`.

Attack setting	The bound of number of rounds	The probability bound of a random permutation	Resource
Single-key differential	$1+t+\lceil\frac{n(t^2+t)}{2(n-1)}\rceil^{\star}$	2^{-nt}	[1]
	t^2-t-2	$2^{-n(t-2)}$	[7]
Related-key collision	$\lfloor\frac{t}{4}\rfloor\cdot(t+1)$	$2^{-\frac{nt}{2}\dagger}$	Sect. 3.2
	$(2+\lfloor\frac{t}{2}-3\rfloor\cdot t)$	$2^{-\frac{nt}{2}\dagger}$	Sect. 3.3

⋆ `GMiMC-erf` is a generalized Feistel block cipher with number of branches t and the state of each branch belonging to a finite filed $\mathbb{F}$, where $n=\lceil\log_2|\mathbb{F}|\rceil$. Thus, the block size of `GMiMC-erf` is $N=nt$. More detailed description of `GMiMC-erf` will be given in Sect. 2.

† This is the birthday bound for the collision attack, and we defer the detailed discussion in Sect. 3.1.

On the other hand, to verify these two related-key differentials, the experiments for both `GMiMC-erf` instantiations over $\mathbb{F}_p$ with the odd characteristic and $\mathbb{F}_2^n$ are performed, that is with any given x, we can easily find the key collision

[3] In this paper, when discussing a Picnic-style signature, we consider that its underlying symmetric-key primitive LowMC is replaced with GMiMC, which is designed to compete with LowMC in some ZK use-cases.

(sk_0, sk_1) such that $\texttt{GMiMC-erf}(sk_0, x) = \texttt{GMiMC-erf}(sk_1, x)$ with only about 2^7 (over $\mathbb{F}_p$) and 2^{10} (over $\mathbb{F}_2^n$) key pairs. From all these experiment results, we have two observations: 1) the smaller finite field we choose to instantiate `GMiMC-erf`, the stronger differential clustering effect it can be observed for our proposed related-key differentials; 2) when instantiating `GMiMC-erf` over small finite field to achieve the smaller signature size, it is better to choose instances over $\mathbb{F}_2^n$ due to the intractable differential clustering effect for smaller $\mathbb{F}_p$. All these observations we hope can facilitate the related design and cryptanalysis in the future.

Organization. The rest of the paper is organized as follows. Section 2 gives the preliminaries of GMiMC, differential cryptanalysis and its extension under related-key setting. In Sect. 3, the potential threats of related-key attacks in post-quantum signature applications are discussed, and followed by constructing two kinds of iterative related-key differentials. The experiments of these two differentials are provided in Sect. 4. Finally, we conclude the paper in Sect. 5.

2 Preliminaries

2.1 Specifications of GMiMC

GMiMC is a family of symmetric-key primitives proposed by Albrecht *et al.* [1] based on several generalized Feistel networks and power maps $S(x) := x^d$, which can be used as hash functions or block ciphers. In this paper, we focus on the variant `GMiMC-erf` with expanding round function, as depicted in Fig. 1, which is the recommended variant from both aspects of security and performance.

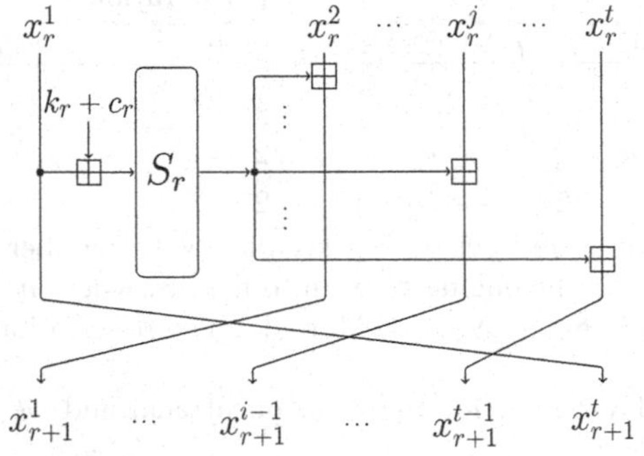

Fig. 1. The round function of `GMiMC-erf`.

Throughout this paper, for `GMiMC-erf` operating over a finite field $\mathbb{F}$, it can be instantiated over $\mathbb{F}_p$ of odd characteristic or $\mathbb{F}_2^n$. It also should be noted that the addition operator is used to represent the addition ($\mathbb{F}_p$) or the XOR ($\mathbb{F}_2^n$) if not specified. We let $n = \lceil \log_2 |\mathbb{F}| \rceil$ denote the branch size in bits where $|\cdot|$ is the cardinality of a given set, then the block size of `GMiMC-erf` can be denoted by

$N = nt$, where t is the number of branches and the branches are numbered from 1 to t from left to right. For example, as shown in Fig. 1, the state of Branch 1 and round r (starting from 1) of `GMiMC-erf` is represented by x_r^1 where $x_r^1 \in \mathbb{F}$. As for the key schedule, there are two cases for the master key K with the key size in bits $\log_2 |K|$: the *univariate case* has $n = \log_2 |K|$ and the *multivariate case* has $N = \log_2 |K|$, we focus on the latter case because `GMiMC-erf` is intended to be used as block ciphers in post-quantum signature applications, which will be detailed discussed in Sect. 4.

Number of rounds of `GMiMC-erf`: For full-data scenario, the designers [2, Table 2] take $R_{TD} \geq 1 + t + \lceil (t^2 + t) \times \frac{n}{2(n-1)} \rceil$ rounds to provide the resistance against truncated differential attacks for multivariate case under single-key setting. This bound then has been broken and extended to $t(t-2)$ rounds by Beyne *et al.* [7]. For low-data scenario, an attacker has limited data access, that is given only one or two known plaintext-ciphertext pairs for the cryptanalysis, thus designers mainly consider Greatest Common Divisors (GCD) and Gröbner Basis attacks, the number of rounds to provide security is

$$R_G \geq \lceil 1.262 \cdot n - 4 \cdot \log_3(n) \rceil + 3t + 3.$$

As can be observed, for large n, $R_{TD} \approx \frac{(t+1)^2}{2}$. For small n, $R_G \approx 3t + 3$. In the rest of the paper, the concrete instance of `GMiMC-erf` will be represented by `GMiMC-erf`(n, t) or `GMiMC-erf`(n, t, R) where R is the total number of rounds. For more details, we refer the reader to full version of GMiMC design paper [2].

2.2 Differential Cryptanalysis

Differential cryptanalysis [9] and its variants are the most widely used techniques to analyze symmetric-key primitives. The differential probability of the function F over $\mathbb{F}_2^m$ is defined by

$$DP(\Delta P, \Delta C) = \frac{|x : F(x) \oplus F(x \oplus \Delta P) = \Delta C|}{2^m},$$

where $\Delta P \in \mathbb{F}_2^m, \Delta C \in \mathbb{F}_2^m$ and $x \in \mathbb{F}_2^m$. Naturally, the differential probability of the function F over $\mathbb{F}_p^t$ can be generalized as below

$$DP(\Delta P, \Delta C) = \frac{|x : F(x) - F(x - \Delta P) = \Delta C|}{p^t},$$

where $\Delta P \in \mathbb{F}_p^t, \Delta C \in \mathbb{F}_p^t$ and $x \in \mathbb{F}_p^t$. The XOR difference is simply replaced by the subtraction difference for $\mathbb{F}_p^t$. It is well known that $S(x) := x^3$ is an Almost Perfect Non-linear function (APN) [23], thus the optimal differential probability of S over a finite field $\mathbb{F}$ is bounded by $\frac{2}{|\mathbb{F}|}$.

Roughly speaking, one first needs to find a differential trail $\Delta P \to \Delta C$ with high probability to attack a target function F, such as distinguish attack, collision attack or key-recovery attack.

Related-Key differential cryptanalysis: Related-key attacks [8,18] are variations of differential cryptanalysis, which usually outperform the conventional single-key differential attacks due to attackers' additional ability to manipulate the keys. More specifically, under the related-key setting, one can introduce the difference ΔK of the master key K into the key schedule and find a high probability related-key differential trail $(\Delta P, \Delta K) \rightarrow \Delta C$ for attacks.

Despite that the presence of related-keys is a strong assumption, it *can* be fulfilled in block cipher-based modes or protocols, which may rekey the block cipher with related-keys. For example, it has given rise to a forgery attack on 3-DES-based RMAC [19].

3 Related-Key Differentials Cryptanalysis on GMiMC-erf

In this section, we try to explore the security margin of GMiMC-erf against related-key differential attacks when used as the underlying symmetric-key primitives in post-quantum signatures.

3.1 Potential Threats of Related-Key Differential Attacks in Post-Quantum Signature Applications

As has been mentioned in GMiMC design paper [2, Section 7.3], there are two intended applications when deployed in some previous post-quantum signatures:

- One-way function (low-data scenario): such as Picnic [12].
- Collision resistant hash function (full-data scenario): such as group signature [10].

For one-way function usage, only one or two plaintext-ciphertext pairs per key of $f(k, x) = y$ is visible to an adversary, the security of the signature scheme is derived from the underlying symmetric-key primitives f. It should be noted that our related-key attacks can be also applied to this low-data scenario. For a given x, one can find two different keys (k, k') such that $f(k', x) = f(k, x)$. Despite that this does not threaten the one-wayness of f instantiated by GMiMC-erf when used in the signature scheme [12], we hope to find more potential applications for this kind of collision attack in the future, such as the possible multi-user setting.

For collision resistant hash function usage requiring full-data security, it has to consider traditional statistical attacks that usually needs a large amount of data. Compared to the sponge construction adopted in [14], Boneh *et al.* [10] proposed applying a lower-cost Davies-Meyer (DM) construction with low multiplicative complexity ciphers to obtain a hash function with a fixed message length, depicted in Fig. 2, that is $f(k, x) = E(k, x) + x$. The resulting scheme relies on a PRF f, which is collision resistant on its keyspace. This collision resistant property of $f(k, x)$ can be attributed to the related-key security under a fixed known plaintext x, which is important to the feature of the key revocation of the resulting EPID signatures [10]. To be specific, if f is not secure against collision attacks on its keyspace, one can firstly prepare two different secret keys sk_0 and sk_1, such that $f(sk_0, c) = f(sk_1, c)$ for a given challenge c obtained from the manager, as shown in Fig. 3. Based on this collision attack, an adversary can still pretend to be a valid user even if sk_0 is revoked by the manager, by using sk_1 to sign on behalf of the group without being detected, which can break the revocation strategy of the group signature scheme. For more details, we refer the reader to [10].

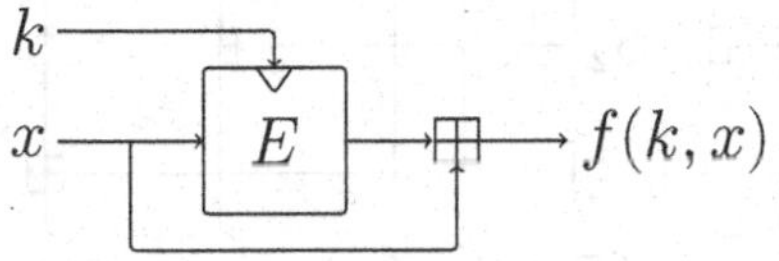

Fig. 2. Davies-Meyer construction with block cipher E.

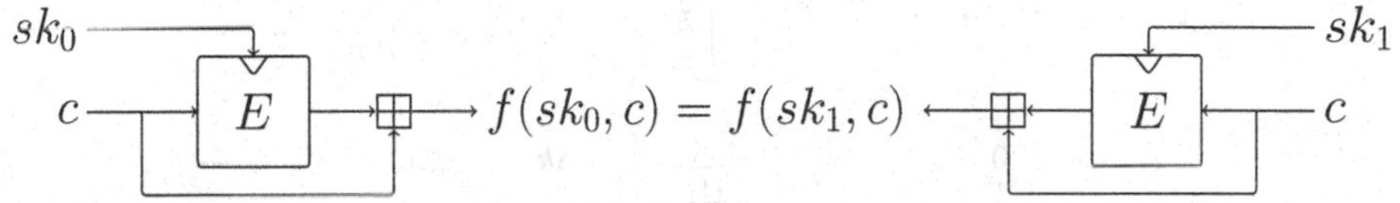

Fig. 3. Collision attack of f on its keyspace.

The designers of LowMC and GMiMC both *do not claim the security in related-key models.* However, according the intended use cases discussed above, special attention still should be paid to the resistance against related-key differential attacks with all zero input/output differences and non-zero key difference. We note that the probability bound here for the related-key distinguisher is $2^{-\frac{\log_2 |K|}{2}} = 2^{-\frac{N}{2}}$ due to the birthday bound of this kind of key collision attack. In the following, we will construct two different related-key differentials for `GMiMC-erf`.

3.2 $(t + 1)$-round Iterative Related-Key Differential

We first construct a $(t + 1)$-round related-key differential with the same input and output differences, as depicted in Fig. 4, which can be iterated for more

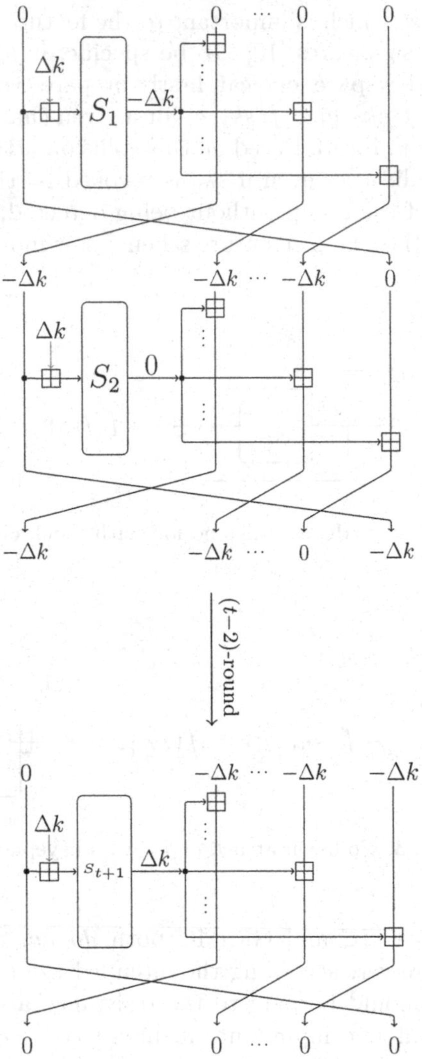

Fig. 4. $(t+1)$-round related-key differential of GMiMC-erf.

rounds. For each round, it will activate two S-boxes but requires the same subkey difference, and we will dicuss how to find such key schedule in Sect. 4 later. This $(t+1)$-round related-key differential trail consists of following three parts:

- **First round:** the input and output differences of the S-box are Δk and $-\Delta k$ respectively, that is $\Delta k \xrightarrow{S_1} -\Delta k$.
- **Middle** $(t-2)$ **rounds:** the input difference of the S-box will be cancelled to zero difference due to the same subkey difference.

- **Last round:** the input and output differences of the S-box are Δk and Δk respectively, that is $\Delta k \xrightarrow{S_{t+1}} \Delta k$.

The differential probability of this $(t+1)$-round iterative related-key characteristic are determined by the S-boxes of the first and last round. For `GMiMC-erf` over $\mathbb{F}_p$, the probability is at least $\frac{2}{p^2}$ for valid differential propagations.[4] For `GMiMC-erf` over $\mathbb{F}_2^n$, the probability is $2^{-2(n-1)}$. Assume that we can iterate this characteristic for s_1 times at most, considering the birthday bound $(\frac{1}{p})^{\frac{t}{2}}$ or $2^{-\frac{t}{2}n}$, then it has $s_1 = \lfloor \frac{t}{4} \frac{\log \frac{1}{p}}{\log \frac{\sqrt{2}}{p}} \rfloor$ or $s_1 = \lfloor \frac{t}{4} \rfloor$. Thus, the bounds of total number of rounds of the related-key differential trail are $\lfloor \frac{t}{4} \frac{\log \frac{1}{p}}{\log \frac{\sqrt{2}}{p}} \rfloor \cdot (t+1)$ for `GMiMC-erf` over $\mathbb{F}_p$ and $\lfloor \frac{t}{4} \rfloor \cdot (t+1)$ for `GMiMC-erf` over $\mathbb{F}_2^n$. As for the real probability of this iterative differential trail, the following two factors should also be taken into consideration:

- The choice of Δk. We need to choose the difference Δk that can pass to Δk and $-\Delta k$ according to the DDT of S-box over $\mathbb{F}_p$ or $\mathbb{F}_2^n$.
- The clustering effect. The clustering effect may have great influences on the estimation of the differential probability, which has been found for many ciphers [15,22,27] and used to enhance the probability of the distinguisher for attacks. The differential clustering effect of `GMiMC-erf` will be exhibited by the experiments of these related-key differentials in next section.

3.3 *t*-round Iterative Related-Key Differential

Now we present a t-round related-key differential, as depicted in Fig. 5, which is circled with blue rectangle and similar to the iterative single-key differential constructed in [7]. It begins with first two rounds (circled with green rectangle) with all zero input difference and output difference $(\Delta k_{1,2}, \cdots, \Delta k_{1,2}, \Delta k_2, \Delta k_1)$, where $\Delta k_{1,2} = \Delta k_1 + \Delta k_2 = \Delta k_0$. This has probability $\frac{1}{p}$ or 2^{-n} and aims to cancel the following $(t-2)$-round input differences of the S-box, then this t-round iterative differential trail consists of two parts as below:

- **First** $(t-2)$ **rounds:** the input and output differences of the S-box are both zero due to $\Delta k_{0,1,2} = \Delta k_0 + \Delta k_1 + \Delta k_2 = 0$.
- **Last two rounds:** the output differences of the S-boxes of the last two rounds are Δk_3 and Δk_4 respectively. In order to iterate this t-round truncate differential, the output difference should be $(\Delta k_{1,2}, \cdots, \Delta k_{1,2}, *, *)$ where $*$ is the unknown difference.

[4] It is well known that the cubic function is Almost Perfect Non-linear (APN), then probability is bounded above by $2/|\mathbb{F}_p|$.

For the first prepared two rounds, it has probability $\frac{1}{p}$ or 2^{-n} as $\Delta k_{0,1,2} = 0$. For the first $(t-2)$-round of this iterative trail, it does not produce any active S-boxes. For the last two rounds, it has probability $\frac{1}{p}$ or 2^{-n} due to the iterative condition $\Delta k_{3,4} = \Delta k_3 + \Delta k_4 = 0$. Besides, when the whole distinguisher ends with this t-round trail with all zero output differences, it must guarantee that $\Delta k_{2,4} = \Delta k_2 + \Delta k_4 = 0$ and $\Delta k_{1,3} = \Delta k_1 + \Delta k_3 = 0$, which has probability $\frac{1}{p^2}$ or 2^{-2n}. So, we can iterate this t-round differential for $s_2 = \lfloor \frac{t}{2} - 3 \rfloor$ times at most, considering the birthday bound $(\frac{1}{p})^{1+s_1+2} \geq (\frac{1}{p})^{\frac{t}{2}}$ or $2^{-(1+s_2+2)n} \geq 2^{-\frac{t}{2}n}$, and this kind of t-round iterative related-key differential can be bounded by $(2 + \lfloor \frac{t}{2} - 3 \rfloor \cdot t)$ rounds of `GMiMC-erf`.

4 Experiments of Related-Key Differentials of `GMiMC-erf`

Before provding the experiment results of two related-key differential distinguishers presented above, we first discuss how to find a key schedule that meets the demands of GMiMC design and guarantees the same subkey differences for each round.

When used as block ciphers in these post-quantum signature applications, GMiMC works with the multivariate case, that is $\log_2 |K| = N = t \times n$. Let k_i be the subkey of round i, then the master key $K = k_0 \parallel k_1 \parallel \cdots \parallel k_{t-1}$. Let M be a $t \times t$ matrix with elements in $\mathbb{F}_{2^n}$ or $\mathbb{F}_p$. For each $1 \leq i \leq \lceil R/t \rceil$ where R is the total number of rounds, it has

$$[k_{i\times t} \parallel k_{i\times t+1} \parallel \cdots \parallel k_{i\times t+(t-1)}]^T = M \times [k_{(i-1)\times t} \parallel \cdots \parallel k_{(i-1)\times t+(t-1)}]^T.$$

The designers require the invertible matrix M to satisfy the following condition:

- for each $1 \leq i \leq \lceil R/t \rceil$, it has

$$M^i[j,l] \equiv \underbrace{M \times M \times \cdots \times M}_{i\text{-th times}}[j,l] \neq 0,$$

  for all $0 \leq j, l < t$, where $M[j,l]$ denotes the entry in row j and the column l of the matrix M.

This condition requires that *the number of zeros in matrices M to $M^{\lceil R/t \rceil}$ should be as few as possible, preferably no zero coefficients.* However, the designers of GMiMC [2] do not provide a specific method to generate such matrices.

Now we consider the condition of iterative related-key differential presented above, it loads the master key differences with $\Delta K = (\Delta k, \cdots, \Delta k)$ and expects the same output differences after updating by the matrix M as below,

$$M \times \begin{pmatrix} \Delta k \\ \Delta k \\ \vdots \\ \Delta k \end{pmatrix} = \begin{pmatrix} m_{0,0} & m_{0,1} & \cdots & m_{0,t-1} \\ m_{1,0} & m_{1,1} & \cdots & m_{1,t-1} \\ \vdots & \vdots & \ddots & \vdots \\ m_{t-1,0} & m_{t-1,1} & \cdots & m_{t-1,t-1} \end{pmatrix} \times \begin{pmatrix} \Delta k \\ \Delta k \\ \vdots \\ \Delta k \end{pmatrix} = \begin{pmatrix} \Delta k \\ \Delta k \\ \vdots \\ \Delta k \end{pmatrix}.$$

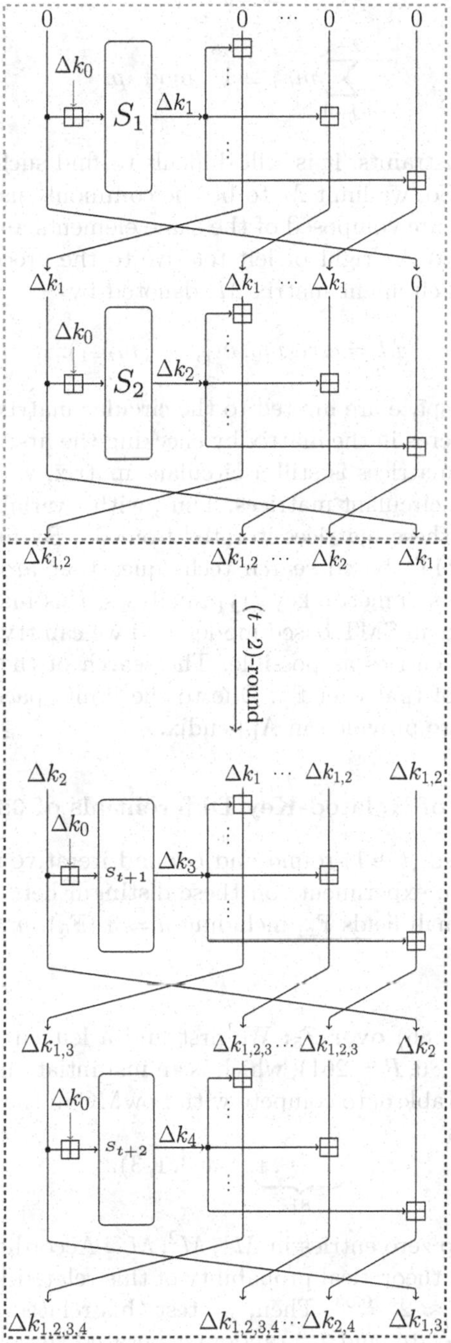

Fig. 5. t-round related-key differential of `GMiMC-erf`.

Thus for each $0 \le l \le t-1$, it has $\sum_{j=0}^{t-1} m_{l,j} \times \Delta k \equiv \Delta k \mod p$, that is

$$\sum_{j=0}^{t-1} m_{l,j} \equiv 1 \mod p.$$

With only such t constraints, it is still difficult to find such matrices M in the whole matrix space. So, we limit M to be the commonly used *circulant matrix*, where all row vectors are composed of the same elements and each row vector is rotated one element to the right or left relative to the preceding row. Here, we only consider the left circulant matrix M, denoted by

$$M = circ(m_0, m_1, \cdots, m_{t-1}).$$

As our target search space are limited to the circular matrix, it is easy to determine the number of zeros in the matrix by checking the first row. Also, the product of two circulant matrices is still a circulant matrix, which means that M^2, M^3 to $M^{\lceil R/t \rceil}$ are all circulant matrices. Thus, with t variables $(m_0, \cdots, m_{t-1})$, we can represent all these matrices iterated from M. By utilizing Satisfiability Modulo Theories (SMT) based search techniques that are already convenient tools at hand for the symmetric-key cryptanalysts, this matrix search problem can be translated into an SMT based model, and we can try to find these matrices with as few zero entries as possible. The search of the matrix M over $\mathbb{F}_2^n$ bears the similarity of that over $\mathbb{F}_p$. Due to the limit space, the details of our SMT based models are provided in Appendix.

4.1 Experiments of Related-Key Differentials of GMiMC-erf over $\mathbb{F}_p$

Based on the proposed $(t+1)$-round and t-round iterative related-key differential trails, we perform experiments on these distinguishers for some GMiMC-erf instantiations over small fields $\mathbb{F}_p$, including $n = 3$ ($\mathbb{F}_5$), $n = 5$ ($\mathbb{F}_{17}$) and $n = 6$ ($\mathbb{F}_{41}$).

GMiMC-erf$(n = 3, t = 86)$ over $\mathbb{F}_5$: We first find a left circulant matrix M for GMiMC-erf$(n = 3, t = 86, R = 261)$, which is an instantiation over $\mathbb{F}_p$ provided in the design paper [2, Table 6] to compete with LowMC in the context of ZKB++. The first row of M is

$$(\underbrace{1, \cdots, 1}_{81}, 4, 4, 3, 1, 3),$$

by which there are no zero entries in M^1, M^2, M^3. According to the estimation given in Sect. 3.2, the theoretical probability of this related-key differential characteristic is $(\frac{1}{5} \times \frac{2}{5})^3 \approx 2^{-10.93}$. Then, we test this related-key differential trail with input $x = (0, \cdots, 0)$[5] and 2^{16} random generated key pairs with the master

[5] Other choice of x has the similar results.

key difference $\Delta K = (1, \cdots, 1)$, and 591 collisions are found. Thus, the experimental probability of this trail is $2^{-6.79}$. Some other number of rounds of this iterative $(t+1)$-round related-key differential and t-round related-key differential are also tested, listed in Table 2. It should be noted that we adopt the same matrix M presented above for different rounds of $\texttt{GMiMC-erf}(n = 3, t = 86)$ over $\mathbb{F}_5$, because the searching space of the SMT based search model becomes large with the number of rounds growing, which makes the search inefficient. Also, the found matrix M for $R = 261$ is already good enough, in terms of the number of nonzero entries of these circulant matrices iterated from M.

From the experiments of $\texttt{GMiMC-erf}(n = 3, t = 86)$ over $\mathbb{F}_5$, it can be observed that the experimental probability of $(t+1)$-round iterative related-key trail obviously deviates from the theoretical estimation with the number of rounds growing, which shows a very strong differential clustering effect of this related-key differential for higher number of rounds. And we provide our codes of the experiments at https://www.dropbox.com/sh/kxex7rqw440zes4/AAC1omTjoPoM5B8Ka19ErmjZa?dl=0, which are performed by the tool SAGE [26] with version 8.8.

Table 2. Experiments of $\texttt{GMiMC-erf}(n = 3, t = 86)$ over $\mathbb{F}_5$.

Types	Rounds	Theoretical Probility	Experimental Probility
$(t+1)$-round iterative with $\Delta K = (1, \cdots, 1)$	87	$\frac{2}{25} \approx 2^{-3.64\dagger}$	$2^{-3.66}$
	174*	$(\frac{2}{25})^2 \approx 2^{-7.29}$	$2^{-5.01}$
	261	$(\frac{2}{25})^3 \approx 2^{-10.93}$	$2^{-6.79}$
	348	$(\frac{2}{25})^4 \approx 2^{-14.58}$	$2^{-8.36}$
	435	$(\frac{2}{25})^5 \approx 2^{-18.22}$	$2^{-9.48}$
	522	$(\frac{2}{25})^6 \approx 2^{-21.86}$	$2^{-11.00}$
	609	$(\frac{2}{25})^7 \approx 2^{-25.51}$	$2^{-12.43}$
	696	$(\frac{2}{25})^8 \approx 2^{-29.15}$	$2^{-13.09}$
	783	$(\frac{2}{25})^9 \approx 2^{-32.79}$	$2^{-15.39}$
	870	$(\frac{2}{25})^{10} \approx 2^{-36.44}$	$2^{-15.61}$
	957	$(\frac{2}{25})^{11} \approx 2^{-40.08}$	$2^{-16.83}$
t-round iterative with $\Delta K = (1, \cdots, 1)$	88	$(\frac{1}{5})^3 \approx 2^{-6.97}$	$2^{-5.19}$
	174*	$(\frac{1}{5})^4 \approx 2^{-9.29}$	$2^{-5.01}$
	260	$(\frac{1}{5})^5 \approx 2^{-11.61}$	$2^{-7.77}$
	346	$(\frac{1}{5})^6 \approx 2^{-13.93}$	$2^{-11.25}$
	432	$(\frac{1}{5})^7 \approx 2^{-16.25}$	$2^{-14.00}$

† For cubic function over $\mathbb{F}_5$, $\Delta k = 1$ passes to $\Delta k = 1$ with probability $\frac{2}{5}$ and $\Delta k = 1$ passes to $-\Delta k = -1$ with probability $\frac{1}{5}$.

⋆ These two 174-round trails are the same when iterating two times and with the same master key difference. This is similar for the results thereafter.

$\texttt{GMiMC-erf}(n = 5, t = 52)$ over $\mathbb{F}_{17}$: The first row of matrix M we found for $\texttt{GMiMC-erf}(n = 5, t = 52, R = 159)$ is

$$(13, 2, 5, 3, 2, 10, 8, 9, 13, 2, 14, 15, 10, 2, 14, 2, 7, 2, 4, 5, 6, 7, 11, 16, 3, 1, 4, 9, 7,$$

Table 3. Experiments of GMiMC-erf$(n = 5, t = 52)$ over $\mathbb{F}_{17}$.

Types	Rounds	Theoretical Probility	Experimental Probility
$(t+1)$-round iterative with $\Delta K = (1, \cdots, 1)$	53	$(\frac{2}{17})^2 \approx 2^{-6.17}$	$2^{-6.19}$
	106	$(\frac{2}{17})^4 \approx 2^{-12.35}$	$2^{-11.64}$
	159	$(\frac{2}{17})^6 \approx 2^{-18.52}$	$2^{-17.14}$
t-round iterative with $\Delta K = (1, \cdots, 1)$	54	$(\frac{1}{17})^3 \approx 2^{-12.26}$	$2^{-13.30}$
	106	$(\frac{1}{17})^4 \approx 2^{-16.35}$	$2^{-11.64}$
	158	$(\frac{1}{17})^5 \approx 2^{-20.44}$	$2^{-19.00}$

$$16, 16, 16, 16, 16, 16, 16, 16, 16, 16, 16, 16, 16, 16, 16, 16, 5, 11, 16, 3, 2, 8, 4).$$

The experiment results of $(t+1)$-round and t-round related-key differentials are provided in Table 3. Considering the feasible runtime when choosing larger finite field, we limit the trail to be iterated three times at most. From the results of these iterative related-key differentials for GMiMC-erf$(n = 5, t = 52)$ over $\mathbb{F}_{17}$, it can be observed that the differential clustering effect seems not as strong as that of GMiMC-erf$(n = 3, t = 86)$ over $\mathbb{F}_5$.

Table 4. Experiments of GMiMC-erf$(n = 6, t = 43)$ over $\mathbb{F}_{41}$.

Types	Rounds	Theoretical Probility	Experimental Probility
$(t+1)$-round iterative with $\Delta K = (10, \cdots, 10)$	44	$(\frac{2}{41})^2 \approx 2^{-8.72}$	$2^{-8.71}$
	88	$(\frac{2}{41})^4 \approx 2^{-17.43}$	$2^{-17.19}$
	132	$(\frac{2}{41})^6 \approx 2^{-26.15}$	$2^{-25.19}$
t-round iterative with $\Delta K = (10, \cdots, 10)$	45	$(\frac{1}{41})^3 \approx 2^{-16.07}$	$2^{-15.83}$
	88	$(\frac{1}{41})^4 \approx 2^{-21.43}$	$2^{-17.19}$
	131	$(\frac{1}{41})^5 \approx 2^{-26.79}$	$2^{-26.19}$

GMiMC-erf$(n = 6, t = 43)$ over $\mathbb{F}_{41}$: The first row of matrix M we found for GMiMC-erf$(n = 6, t = 43, R = 132)$ is

$$(6, 14, 28, 12, 5, 10, 30, 30, 19, 21, 8, 14, 18, 32, 38, 25, 37, 29, 31, 33, 20,$$

$$25, 9, 25, 39, 33, 40, 40, 40, 40, 40, 40, 40, 12, 40, 2, 3, 1, 1, 2, 3, 1, 8).$$

The experiments of $(t+1)$-round and t-round related-key differentials are performed with the master key difference $\Delta K = (10, \cdots, 10)$, which are provided in Table 4. Despite the limited number of rounds, it can be observed that the clustering effect of these related-key differentials seems not significant for GMiMC-erf over $\mathbb{F}_{41}$ when compared to the instantiations over $\mathbb{F}_5$ and $\mathbb{F}_{17}$.

4.2 Experiments of Related-Key Differentials of GMiMC-erf over $\mathbb{F}_2^n$

To compare with the experiments over $\mathbb{F}_p$ presented above, we also verify these related-key differentials for GMiMC-erf over $\mathbb{F}_2^n$.

Table 5. Experiments of GMiMC-erf$(n = 3, t = 86)$ over $\mathbb{F}_2^3$.

Types	Rounds	Theoretical Probility	Experimental Probility
$(t+1)$-round iterative with $\Delta K = (1, \cdots, 1)$	87	$(\frac{2}{2^3})^2 = 2^{-4}$	$2^{-4.04}$
	174*	$(\frac{2}{2^3})^4 = 2^{-8}$	$2^{-8.00}$
	261	$(\frac{2}{2^3})^6 = 2^{-12}$	$2^{-10.19}$
	348	$(\frac{2}{2^3})^8 = 2^{-16}$	$2^{-14.41}$
	435	$(\frac{2}{2^3})^{10} = 2^{-20}$	$2^{-16.68}$
t-round iterative with $\Delta K = (3, \cdots, 3)$	88	$(\frac{1}{2^3})^3 = 2^{-9}$	$2^{-7.11}$
	174*	$(\frac{1}{2^3})^4 = 2^{-12}$	$2^{-10.42}$
	260	$(\frac{1}{2^3})^5 = 2^{-15}$	$2^{-12.49}$
	346	$(\frac{1}{2^3})^6 = 2^{-18}$	$2^{-15.19}$
	432	$(\frac{1}{2^3})^7 = 2^{-21}$	$2^{-18.09}$

⋆ These two 174-round trails are different due to the different master key differences.

GMiMC-erf$(n = 3, t = 86)$ over $\mathbb{F}_2^3$: The irreducible polynomial of the instantiation over $\mathbb{F}_2^3$ is set to be $x^3 \oplus x \oplus 1$[6], then we find M for GMiMC-erf$(n = 3, t = 86, R = 261)$ over $\mathbb{F}_2^3$, which is an instantiation over $\mathbb{F}_2^n$ in the design paper and even achieves smaller signature size than the previous smallest size obtainable using LowMC in Picnic. The first row of M is

$$(5, 5, 4, 6, 2, 1, 3, 5, 1, 4, 3, 5, 1, 5, 6, 1, 5, 5, 4, 5, 3, 1, 7, 6, 2, 1, 2, 1, 4,$$
$$5, 1, 5, 2, 6, 2, 2, 5, 3, 1, 4, 3, 2, 6, 4, 7, 3, 7, 2, 5, 2, 5, 1, 4, 1, 1, 4, 1, 6,$$
$$1, 6, 3, 1, 6, 3, 1, 2, 1, 7, 4, 6, 6, 7, 4, 2, 3, 2, 5, 5, 4, 7, 5, 6, 1, 6, 2, 4).$$

The experiments of $(t+1)$-round and t-round related-key differentials are performed with the master key differences $\Delta K = (1, \cdots, 1)$ and $\Delta K = (3, \cdots, 3)$ respectively, which are provided in Table 5. From the results of GMiMC-erf$(n = 3, t = 86)$ over $\mathbb{F}_2^3$, it also shows a differential clustering effect for both $(t+1)$-round and t-round related-key differentials, but which is not as strong as that of GMiMC-erf$(n = 3, t = 86)$ over $\mathbb{F}_5$.

[6] This is the default choice for GF(2^3) in software tool SAGE [26] that we perform the experiments in this paper. Other choice of irreducible polynomials has the similar results.

Table 6. Experiments of GMiMC-erf$(n = 5, t = 52)$ over $\mathbb{F}_2^5$.

Types	Rounds	Theoretical Probility	Experimental Probility
$(t+1)$-round iterative with $\Delta K = (3, \cdots, 3)$	53	$(\frac{2}{2^5})^2 = 2^{-8}$	$2^{-8.00}$
	106	$(\frac{2}{2^5})^4 = 2^{-16}$	$2^{-15.75}$
	159	$(\frac{2}{2^5})^6 = 2^{-24}$	$2^{-22.83}$
t-round iterative with $\Delta K = (9, \cdots, 9)$	54	$(\frac{1}{2^5})^3 = 2^{-15}$	$2^{-14.83}$
	106	$(\frac{1}{2^5})^4 = 2^{-20}$	$2^{-20.00}$
	158	$(\frac{1}{2^5})^5 = 2^{-25}$	$2^{-24.42}$

GMiMC-erf$(n = 5, t = 52)$ over $\mathbb{F}_2^5$: Similarly, the irreducible polynomial of the instantiation over $\mathbb{F}_2^5$ is set to be $x^5 \oplus x^2 \oplus 1$, then we find M for GMiMC-erf$(n = 5, t = 52, R = 159)$ over $\mathbb{F}_2^5$, the first row of which is

$$(14, 6, 14, 13, 15, 15, 14, 10, 5, 6, 15, 14, 6, 7, 15, 14, 10, 15, 6, 19, 15, 10, 15, 3, 3, 14,$$

$$15, 14, 6, 12, 12, 15, 7, 15, 7, 14, 8, 9, 1, 12, 15, 10, 4, 13, 14, 18, 13, 6, 4, 7, 15, 10).$$

The experiments of $(t + 1)$-round and t-round related-key differentials are performed with the master key differences $\Delta K = (3, \cdots, 3)$ and $\Delta K = (9, \cdots, 9)$ respectively, which are provided in Table 6. From the results of GMiMC-erf$(n = 5, t = 52)$ over $\mathbb{F}_2^5$, the experimental probability of these two kinds of iterative related-key differentials matches the theoretical estimation.

Remark: According to all experiments of GMiMC-erf over $\mathbb{F}_p$ and $\mathbb{F}_2^n$ presented above, it can be concluded that the smaller finite field we choose to instantiate the cipher, the stronger differential clustering effect we can observe for these iterative related-key differentials of GMiMC-erf. However, if pursuing small view size is the primary goal in the target application, GMiMC-erf instances over $\mathbb{F}_2^n$ seem to be better than the comparable parameterizations over $\mathbb{F}_p$, not only because the performance is better in terms of the signature size, but also the differential clustering effect seems intractable for instantiations over smaller $\mathbb{F}_p$, such as $\mathbb{F}_5$. It also should be noted that our experiments presented above are still limited in terms of the number of rounds and the number of differential trails, thus more comprehensive studies theoretical evaluating method of differential clustering effect over $\mathbb{F}_p$ are expected in the future.

5 Conclusion

In this paper, we have studied the security of GMiMC against the related-key differential cryptanalysis. By investigating the potential threats of related-key attacks of GMiMC-erf when used as the PRP/PRF in the post-quantum signature applications, we constructed two kinds of iterative related-key differentials, by which not only did we explore the security margin of GMiMC-erf against related-key attacks, but also collision attacks on its key space could be performed. We then utilized the distinguisher to find key collision of GMiMC-erf instance that is intended to compete with LowMC in Picnic signature schemes, with only about 2^{10} key pairs. Furthermore, interesting differences in the clustering effect of our proposed related-key differentials of GMiMC-erf between $\mathbb{F}_p$ and $\mathbb{F}_2^n$ are observed.

Acknowledgements. This research is supported by the National Research Foundation, Singapore under its Strategic Capability Research Centres Funding Initiative, the Nanyang Technological University in Singapore under Start-up Grant 04INS000397C230, and Ministry of Education in Singapore under Grants RG91/20 and MOE2019-T2-1-060, the National Key Research and Development Program of China (Grant No. 2018YFA0704702), the National Natural Science Foundation of China (Grant No. 62032014), the Major Basic Research Project of Natural Science Foundation of Shandong Province, China (Grant No. ZR202010220025), the National Key R&D Program of China (Grant No. 2022YFB2701700), Shandong Provincial Natural Science Foundation (Grant No. ZR2020MF053) and the National Natural Science Foundation of China (Grant No. 62002202). Any opinions, findings and conclusions or recommendations expressed in this material are those of the author(s) and do not reflect the views of National Research Foundation, Singapore.

Appendix SMT based Search Model of Matrix M in the Key Schedule of GMiMC

In this paper, we use STP [16] solver to perform the search of the matrix, which is a constraint solver (or SMT solver) aimed at solving constraints of bitvectors and arrays. In the following, we describe our SMT based search models by using CVC language[7], which is the default input language of STP. And our codes of generating the SMT based search model of matrix M over $\mathbb{F}_p$ and $\mathbb{F}_2^n$ are provided at https://www.dropbox.com/sh/kxex7rqw440zes4/AAC1omTjoPoM5B8Ka19ErmjZa?dl=0.

The model of searching M over $\mathbb{F}_p$: Each variable in SMT based model can be expressed by a bitvector, that is, a variable $m_0 \in \mathbb{F}_p$ in the circulant matrix M can be represented by using $n = \lceil \log_2 p \rceil$ bits. An example of a non-zero variable $m_0 \in \mathbb{F}_5$ is:

```
m0 : BITVECTOR(3);
ASSERT(NOT(m1 = 0bin000));
ASSERT(BVLT(m1, 0bin101));
```

[7] Please refer to the brief introduction via https://github.com/stp/stp/blob/ee83ef70ffeb386575f7452095b52406894b0489/docs/cvc-input-language.rst.

As M is a left circulant matrix, for matrix M^i $(2 \leq i)$, the variable $M^i[1,l]$ in the first row can be recursively expressed by

$$M^i[1,l] \equiv \sum_{j=1}^{t-1} (M^{i-1}[1,j] \times m_{(l+j) \mod t}) \mod p,$$

where $0 \leq j, l \leq t-1$. This relationship can be described by using the predicates: BVPLUS, BVMULT and BVMOD in CVC language. Then, the number of zero entries of these $t \times \lceil R/t \rceil$ variables is counted as an objective function to minimize during the search. Once we obtain a solution of M, it has to be checked whether it is invertible. If not, this solution should be excluded from the search model, and repeat the process until we find a proper one.

The model of searching M over $\mathbb{F}_2^n$: Similar to the model over $\mathbb{F}_2^n$, a variable $m_0 \in \mathbb{F}_2^n$ in the circulant matrix M can be represented by using n bits. An example of non-zero variable $m_0 \in \mathbb{F}_2^3$ is:

```
m0 : BITVECTOR(3);
ASSERT(NOT(m1 = 0bin000));
```

In the same way, the variable $M^i[1,l]$ in the first row can be recursively expressed by

$$M^i[1,l] \equiv \sum_{j=1}^{t-1} M^{i-1}[1,j] \times m_{(l+j) \mod t},$$

where $0 \leq j, l \leq t-1$. Note that the addition here for $\mathbb{F}_2^n$ is the XOR operation, the multiplication operation here is the field multiplication operation that needs the corresponding irreducible polynomial. By using the predicate BVXOR in CVC language, we can describe polynomial multiplication and modular polynomial operations by the SMT based model. Then, it follows the similar search process of that over $\mathbb{F}_p$ presented above.

References

1. Albrecht, M.R., et al.: Feistel structures for MPC, and more. In: Sako, K., Schneider, S., Ryan, P.Y.A. (eds.) ESORICS 2019. LNCS, vol. 11736, pp. 151–171. Springer, Cham (2019). https://doi.org/10.1007/978-3-030-29962-0_8
2. Albrecht, M.R., et al.: Feistel structures for MPC, and more. IACR Cryptol. ePrint Arch, p. 397 (2019). https://eprint.iacr.org/2019/397
3. Albrecht, M., Grassi, L., Rechberger, C., Roy, A., Tiessen, T.: MiMC: efficient encryption and cryptographic hashing with minimal multiplicative complexity. In: Cheon, J.H., Takagi, T. (eds.) ASIACRYPT 2016. LNCS, vol. 10031, pp. 191–219. Springer, Heidelberg (2016). https://doi.org/10.1007/978-3-662-53887-6_7
4. Albrecht, M.R., Rechberger, C., Schneider, T., Tiessen, T., Zohner, M.: Ciphers for MPC and FHE. In: Oswald, E., Fischlin, M. (eds.) EUROCRYPT 2015. LNCS, vol. 9056, pp. 430–454. Springer, Heidelberg (2015). https://doi.org/10.1007/978-3-662-46800-5_17

5. Aly, A., Ashur, T., Ben-Sasson, E., Dhooghe, S., Szepieniec, A.: Design of symmetric-key primitives for advanced cryptographic protocols. IACR Trans. Symmetric Cryptol. **2020**(3), 1–45 (2020). https://doi.org/10.13154/tosc.v2020.i3.1-45
6. Aumasson, J.P., et al.: SPHINCS$^+$. In: Submission to NIST Post-Quantum Cryptography project (2020). https://sphincs.org/data/sphincs+-round3-specification.pdf
7. Beyne, T., et al.: Out of oddity – new cryptanalytic techniques against symmetric primitives optimized for integrity proof systems. In: Micciancio, D., Ristenpart, T. (eds.) CRYPTO 2020. LNCS, vol. 12172, pp. 299–328. Springer, Cham (2020). https://doi.org/10.1007/978-3-030-56877-1_11
8. Biham, E.: New types of cryptanalytic attacks using related keys. J. Crypt. **7**(4), 229–246 (1994). https://doi.org/10.1007/BF00203965
9. Biham, E., Shamir, A.: Differential cryptanalysis of DES-like cryptosystems. J. Crypt. **4**(1), 3–72 (1991). https://doi.org/10.1007/BF00630563
10. Boneh, D., Eskandarian, S., Fisch, B.: Post-quantum EPID signatures from symmetric primitives. In: Matsui, M. (ed.) CT-RSA 2019. LNCS, vol. 11405, pp. 251–271. Springer, Cham (2019). https://doi.org/10.1007/978-3-030-12612-4_13
11. Chase, M., et al.: The picnic signature scheme. In: Submission to NIST Post-Quantum Cryptography Project (2020). https://github.com/microsoft/Picnic/blob/master/spec/design-v2.2.pdf
12. Chase, M., et al.: Post-quantum zero-knowledge and signatures from symmetric-key primitives. In: Proceedings of the 2017 ACM SIGSAC Conference on Computer and Communications Security, CCS 2017, pp. 1825–1842 (2017). https://doi.org/10.1145/3133956.3133997
13. Chen, L., et al.: Report on post-quantum cryptography, vol. 12. US Department of Commerce, National Institute of Standards and Technology (2016)
14. Derler, D., Ramacher, S., Slamanig, D.: Post-quantum zero-knowledge proofs for accumulators with applications to ring signatures from symmetric-key primitives. In: Lange, T., Steinwandt, R. (eds.) PQCrypto 2018. LNCS, vol. 10786, pp. 419–440. Springer, Cham (2018). https://doi.org/10.1007/978-3-319-79063-3_20
15. Eichlseder, M., Kales, D.: Clustering related-tweak characteristics: application to MANTIS-6. IACR Trans. Symmetric Cryptol. **2018**(2), 111–132 (2018). https://doi.org/10.13154/tosc.v2018.i2.111-132
16. Ganesh, V., Dill, D.L.: A decision procedure for bit-vectors and arrays. In: Computer Aided Verification, 19th International Conference, CAV 2007, pp. 519–531 (2007). https://doi.org/10.1007/978-3-540-73368-3_52
17. Kaplan, M., Leurent, G., Leverrier, A., Naya-Plasencia, M.: Breaking symmetric cryptosystems using quantum period finding. In: Robshaw, M., Katz, J. (eds.) CRYPTO 2016. LNCS, vol. 9815, pp. 207–237. Springer, Heidelberg (2016). https://doi.org/10.1007/978-3-662-53008-5_8
18. Knudsen, L.R.: Cryptanalysis of LOKI. In: Imai, H., Rivest, R.L., Matsumoto, T. (eds.) ASIACRYPT 1991. LNCS, vol. 739, pp. 22–35. Springer, Heidelberg (1993). https://doi.org/10.1007/3-540-57332-1_2
19. Knudsen, L.R., Kohno, T.: Analysis of RMAC. In: Johansson, T. (ed.) FSE 2003. LNCS, vol. 2887, pp. 182–191. Springer, Heidelberg (2003). https://doi.org/10.1007/978-3-540-39887-5_14
20. Kuwakado, H., Morii, M.: Security on the quantum-type even-mansour cipher. In: Proceedings of the International Symposium on Information Theory and its Applications, ISITA 2012, Honolulu, HI, USA, October 28–31(2012), pp. 312–316, 2012. https://ieeexplore.ieee.org/document/6400943/

21. Leander, G., May, A.: Grover meets Simon – quantumly attacking the FX-construction. In: Takagi, T., Peyrin, T. (eds.) ASIACRYPT 2017. LNCS, vol. 10625, pp. 161–178. Springer, Cham (2017). https://doi.org/10.1007/978-3-319-70697-9_6
22. Leurent, G., Pernot, C., Schrottenloher, A.: Clustering effect in Simon and Simeck. In: Tibouchi, M., Wang, H. (eds.) ASIACRYPT 2021. LNCS, vol. 13090, pp. 272–302. Springer, Cham (2021). https://doi.org/10.1007/978-3-030-92062-3_10
23. Nyberg, K., Knudsen, L.R.: Provable security against differential cryptanalysis. In: Brickell, E.F. (ed.) CRYPTO 1992. LNCS, vol. 740, pp. 566–574. Springer, Heidelberg (1993). https://doi.org/10.1007/3-540-48071-4_41
24. Shor, P.W.: Algorithms for quantum computation: discrete logarithms and factoring. In: 35th Annual Symposium on Foundations of Computer Science, Santa Fe, New Mexico, USA, 20–22 November 1994, pp. 124–134 (1994). https://doi.org/10.1109/SFCS.1994.365700
25. Simon, D.R.: On the power of quantum computation. In: 35th Annual Symposium on Foundations of Computer Science, Santa Fe, New Mexico, USA, 20–22 November 1994, pp. 116–123 (1994). https://doi.org/10.1109/SFCS.1994.365701
26. The Sage Developers: SageMath, the Sage mathematics software system (Version 8.8). https://www.sagemath.org
27. Wang, M., Sun, Y., Tischhauser, E., Preneel, B.: A model for structure attacks, with applications to PRESENT and serpent. In: Canteaut, A. (ed.) FSE 2012. LNCS, vol. 7549, pp. 49–68. Springer, Heidelberg (2012). https://doi.org/10.1007/978-3-642-34047-5_4

Impossible Differential Cryptanalysis on Reduced-Round PRINCEcore

Li Zhang[1,2], Wenling Wu[1,2(✉)], and Yongxia Mao[1,2]

[1] Trusted Computing and Information Assurance Laboratory, Institute of Software Chinese Academy of Sciences, Beijing 100190, China
{zhangli2021,wenling,yongxia2018}@iscas.ac.cn

[2] University of Chinese Academy of Sciences, Beijing 100049, China

Abstract. The area of lightweight cryptography, i.e., ciphers with particularly low implementation costs, has drawn considerable attention over the last few years. PRINCE is a lightweight block cipher proposed by J. Borghoff et al. at ASIACRYPT 2012. In 2017, Ding et al. constructed a 4-round truncated impossible differential distinguisher. They treat S-boxes as ideal ones that any nonzero input difference could produce any nonzero output difference. Obviously, this is not true for the S-boxes in the real block ciphers. In this paper, after investigating the properties of both the S-box and the linear layer of PRINCE, we construct two types of 5-round impossible differential distinguishers. Then we exhibit two types of key-recovery attacks on 9 out of 12 rounds of PRINCEcore. The corresponding data complexities are $2^{53.3}$ and $2^{56.1}$ chosen plaintexts, respectively. Our results are the best impossible differential cryptanalysis on PRINCE as far as we know to date, and our attacks meet the security claims of the designers.

Keywords: Lightweight cryptography · PRINCE · Impossible differentials · Distinguisher · S-box

1 Introduction

With the development of mobile communications and the Internet of Things, communication security has received extensive attention. Many corresponding applications should be supported by cryptographic techniques, such as smart homes, intelligent transportation, etc. However, the contradiction between mass information encryption and limited resource processing has become increasingly prominent, and most of these devices work in unreliable environments, such as the smart sensors used in the Internet of things. In such a case, how to protect data security is an essential issue. In order to use a minimum of resources to provide the required security in some extreme applications, some designers proposed the concept of lightweight block cipher, which can guarantee privacy and occupy fewer resources than the classic block cipher at the same time. Several lightweight block ciphers have been proposed in the last decade, such as PRESENT [1], SIMON [2] and SKINNY [3].

S.-H. Seo and H. Seo (Eds.): ICISC 2022, LNCS 13849, pp. 61–77, 2023.
https://doi.org/10.1007/978-3-031-29371-9_4

PRINCE [4], proposed by J. Borghoff et al., is a low-latency block cipher. In order to reduce the latency in hardware implementation, the designers employ the FX structure [5] and a property called α-reflection [6]. Based on the FX construction, a 12-round core cipher, called PRINCEcore is used to hold the major encryption process. There are already many cryptanalytic results on PRINCEcore. In [7], Jean et al. gave Integral attacks on 4, 5, and 6-round PRINCEcore. In [8], Zhao et al. found the 5-round and 6-round truncated differential distinguishers and presented an attack on 7-round PRINCEcore. In [9], Ding et al. constructed a 4-round impossible differential distinguisher. Based on the distinguisher, they launched impossible differential attacks on the 6-round and 7-round PRINCEcore. In [10], Ding et al. further presented an impossible differential attack on the 8-round of PRINCEcore. In [11], the authors proposed a new technique named key-dependent sieve, which was applied to attack on 8-round of PRINCEcore. In [12], Farzaneh et al. presented an independent-biclique attack on the full version of PRINCEcore.

Impossible differentials is one of the effective methods for evaluating the security of block ciphers, which was independently proposed by Knudsen [13] and Biham [14], and had successfully attacked many block ciphers, such as AES [15], Camellia [16], LBlock [17]. Impossible differentials are typically constructed by the miss-in-the-middle method, i.e., by tracing differences between inputs and outputs in the encryption and decryption directions. If there are contradictions in the middle, it is possible to find the impossible differential. Among these impossible differentials, truncated impossible differentials [18] attract much attention. However, they do not take advantage of the properties of the non-linear substitution layer (e.g., S-box), their target is not the concrete cipher, but the "structure" [19]. A concrete cipher should consider both S-box and key schedule, but the mechanism by which the key schedule affects differential propagation is unclear. In [20,21], they show that there do not exist such impossible truncated differentials covering more than four rounds for AES with the S-box considered and the key schedule omitted. If the differential property of the S-boxes is considered, more and longer impossible differential distinguishers might be discovered.

Our Contributions. Firstly, we study the differential distribution table of the S-box which stores the input/output differences and the corresponding values. Then we find the property of M' operation. The property shows that, for the input and output states of M' operations, if the output states are fixed, the set of values for the input state are determined. Based on these properties, two types of 5-round impossible differential distinguishers of PRINCE are constructed, including a distinguisher with only one active nibble for input-output difference and a distinguisher with only one active nibble for input difference and two active nibbles for output difference. Finally, we use them to launch impossible differential attacks on 9-round PRINCEcore, respectively.

Table 1 summarizes our results compared with some major previous results on PRINCEcore under single-key model. The rest of the paper is organized as follows. The necessary preliminaries and a brief description of PRINCE are visited in Sect. 2. Section 3 identifies some properties of PRINCE. In Sect. 4, we construct two types of 5-round impossible differential distinguishers of PRINCE. Impossible differential attacks on 9-round PRINCEcore are proposed in Sect. 5. We conclude the paper in Sect. 6.

Table 1. Summary of the attacks on PRINCEcore in the single-key model.

Technique	Rounds	Data	Time	Memory	Source
Integral	4	2^4	2^8	2^4	[7]
Integral	5	$2^{6.3}$	2^{21}	2^8	[7]
Integral	6	2^{16}	2^{30}	2^{16}	[7]
Impossible differential	6	$2^{42.6}$	2^{43}	2^{30}	[9]
Truncated differential	6	2^{48}	$2^{56.26}$	2^{48}	[12]
Truncated differential	7	2^{50}	$2^{48.2}$	$2^{22.6}$	[8]
Impossible differential	7	2^{56}	$2^{53.8}$	2^{43}	[9]
MITM	8	2^{53}	2^{53}	2^{28}	[11]
Impossible differential	8	2^{60}	$2^{62.26}$	2^{45}	[10]
Impossible differential†	9	$2^{53.3}$	$2^{63.91}$	$2^{51.02}$	Section 5.1
Impossible differential†	9	$2^{56.1}$	$2^{50.68}$	$2^{36.3}$	Section 5.2
Biclique	12	2^{40}	$2^{62.72}$	2^8	[12]

†: The details of the S-box are considered.

2 Preliminaries

2.1 Notations

$\oplus$:	Bit-wise XOR
X_i:	The $(i+1)$-th nibble of the state X
X^i/Y^i:	The input/output state of the $(i+1)$-th round
$\triangle X$:	The XOR difference of two values, i.e., $\triangle X = X \oplus X'$
$wt(X)$:	The hamming weight of the state X
$X^i_{col(j)}$:	The $(j+1)$-th column of X^i
$k_1[i]$:	The $(i+1)$-th nibble of k_1
$\triangle X^i$:	The $(i+1)$-th round difference of the state
$D^{i,j}_a$:	a 4×4 matrix over the finite fields F_2^4 which all the positions are 0 except the position (i,j) equals a

2.2 Brief Description of PRINCE

PRINCE is a block cipher with block-length of 64-bit and key-length of 128-bit. The 128-bit key is split into two 64-bit keys, i.e., $k = k_0||k_1$. k_0 and k_0' are used as the input and output whitening keys respectively, where $k'_0 = (k_0 \ggg 1) \oplus (k_0 \gg 63)$. And k_1 is used as the identical round-key of its internal function PRINCEcore as illustrated in Fig. 1.

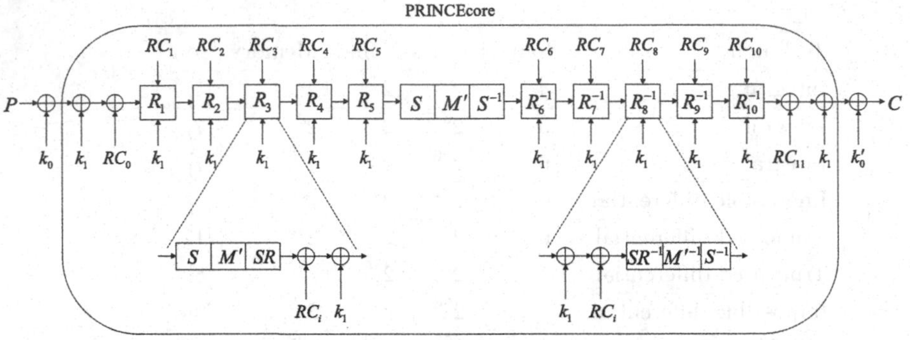

Fig. 1. Encryption process of PRINCE

PRINCEcore is a 12-round SPN block cipher. We take the state as a 4×4 nibble matrix, and the matrix is indexed by

$$\begin{pmatrix} 0\,4\,8\,c \\ 1\,5\,9\,d \\ 2\,6\,a\,e \\ 3\,7\,b\,f \end{pmatrix} \quad or\ 0123|4567|89ab|cdef.$$

Each round of PRINCEcore consists of an S-box layer (S), a linear layer (M), a round-constant addition (RC), and a round-key addition (AK). The details of the round function $R^i = AK \circ RC \circ M \circ S$ are as follows:

(1) **S-box Layer** (S). The S-box is a single 4-bit to 4-bit S-box which is applied 16 times in parallel, and it is shown in Table 2.

Table 2. The S-box of PRINCE

x	0	1	2	3	4	5	6	7	8	9	A	B	C	D	E	F
$S(x)$	B	F	3	2	A	C	9	1	6	7	8	0	E	5	D	4

(2) **Linear Layer** (M). The linear layer is defined as $M = SR \circ M'$, where M' is a matrix multiplication that has a branch number of four and SR is a shifting-row permutation. In fact, M' acts as a diagonal matrix multiplication denoted as $M' = diag(\hat{M}_0, \hat{M}_1, \hat{M}_1, \hat{M}_0)$, in which $\hat{M}_0$ and $\hat{M}_1$ are 16×16 matrices. If we take the state as a 4×4 nibble matrix, the

four columns of a state are multiplied with $\hat{M_0}$ or $\hat{M_1}$, respectively. The structures of $\hat{M_0}$ and $\hat{M_1}$ are defined as below.

$$\hat{M_0} = \begin{pmatrix} M_0\, M_1\, M_2\, M_3 \\ M_1\, M_2\, M_3\, M_0 \\ M_2\, M_3\, M_0\, M_1 \\ M_3\, M_0\, M_1\, M_2 \end{pmatrix}, \hat{M_1} = \begin{pmatrix} M_1\, M_2\, M_3\, M_0 \\ M_2\, M_3\, M_0\, M_1 \\ M_3\, M_0\, M_1\, M_2 \\ M_0\, M_1\, M_2\, M_3 \end{pmatrix},$$

where

$$M_0 = \begin{pmatrix} 0\,0\,0\,0 \\ 0\,1\,0\,0 \\ 0\,0\,1\,0 \\ 0\,0\,0\,1 \end{pmatrix}, M_1 = \begin{pmatrix} 1\,0\,0\,0 \\ 0\,0\,0\,0 \\ 0\,0\,1\,0 \\ 0\,0\,0\,1 \end{pmatrix}, M_2 = \begin{pmatrix} 1\,0\,0\,0 \\ 0\,1\,0\,0 \\ 0\,0\,0\,0 \\ 0\,0\,0\,1 \end{pmatrix}, M_3 = \begin{pmatrix} 1\,0\,0\,0 \\ 0\,1\,0\,0 \\ 0\,0\,1\,0 \\ 0\,0\,0\,0 \end{pmatrix}.$$

(3) **Round-key addition** (AK).The 64-bit state is XORed with the subkey k_1.
(4) **Round-constant addition** (RC). The round constants satisfy the condition $RC_i \oplus RC_{11-i} = \alpha$ for $0 \leq i \leq 11$, where α is a specific constant. It allows PRINCE to decrypt a ciphertext by simply encrypting it with the key $k_0||k_1 \oplus \alpha$. This is the so-called α-reflection property.

Denote the 5-round PRINCE as

$$R^5 = R^{-1} \circ S^{-1} \circ M' \circ S \circ R^1 \circ R^1,$$

where $R^1 = SR \circ M' \circ S, R^{-1} = S^{-1} \circ M'^{-1} \circ SR^{-1}$. Since we are only considering differences, we can leave out AddKey (AK) and constant addition (RC) for sake of clarity.

2.3 Impossible Differential Cryptanalysis

Definition 1. *For an iterative block cipher algorithm, let α_0 be the difference $\triangle X$ of plaintext X and X', and α_r be the corresponding difference $\triangle Y$ of ciphertext Y and Y'. If $P(\triangle Y = \alpha_r \mid \triangle X = \alpha_0) = 0$, $\alpha_0 \overset{r}{\nrightarrow} \alpha_r$ is a r-round impossible differential.*

Under the miss-in-the-middle technique, there are generally two kinds of contradictions. For simplicity, we denote them as "direct contradiction" and "indirect contradiction".

For direct contradiction, the distinguisher is constructed based on two truncated differentials from the directions of encryption and decryption with direct contradiction. For example, in [9,10], the distinguisher does not consider the real difference value but only finds the direct contradiction by whether the difference is active.

For indirect contradiction, the contradiction is discovered by secondary calculation. In this case, the direct contradiction is nonexistent and some uncertain difference of the internal states can be calculated with certain ones to make a contradiction. For uncertain differences, we can use the difference property of

S-box to traverse all possible differences, and then put them into set 1, 2. If set 1 and set 2 have no intersection, then the contradiction is true. The complexity is high due to the need to traverse all possible differences. In order to solve this problem, we use quicksort and dichotomy for difference collision, which greatly reduces the complexity.

3 The Properties of the S-box and the Linear Layer

In this section, firstly, we need to investigate some details about the S-box of PRINCE. Table 3 shows the input/output differences and the number of corresponding input pairs of the S-box. When the input and output differences of the S-box are known, the values of the corresponding input/output pairs can be obtained by looking up DDT. Secondly, since M' is constructed by $\hat{M}_0$ and $\hat{M}_1$, we study the properties of $\hat{M}_0$ and $\hat{M}_1$ instead of M'. Due to the linearity of $\hat{M}_0$, the analysis of its input and output differences can be regarded as the analysis of its input and output text. We give the properties of S and M' below.

Definition 2. *(Difference Distribution Table) Let S be a function from F_2^n to F_2^n. The difference distribution table (DDT) is a two-dimensional table defined by*

$$DDT(\alpha, \beta) = \#\{x \in F_2^n : S(x) \oplus S(x + \alpha) = \beta\},$$

where $\alpha, \beta \in F_2^n$.

Table 3. DDT of PRINCE's 4-bit S-box.

	0	1	2	3	4	5	6	7	8	9	a	b	c	d	e	f
0	16	0	0	0	0	0	0	0	0	0	0	0	0	0	0	0
1	0	4	0	0	2	0	2	0	4	2	0	2	0	0	0	0
2	0	2	0	4	0	0	0	2	2	0	0	0	0	4	2	0
3	0	0	0	0	0	2	2	0	2	2	2	2	2	0	0	2
4	0	2	2	4	2	2	0	0	2	0	2	0	0	0	0	0
5	0	0	2	2	0	2	0	2	0	2	0	2	2	2	0	0
6	0	0	2	2	0	2	2	0	0	2	0	2	0	0	4	0
7	0	0	2	0	0	0	2	0	2	0	4	0	0	2	2	2
8	0	0	2	0	4	2	0	0	2	2	0	2	0	2	0	0
9	0	0	2	2	0	0	0	0	0	2	2	0	4	2	0	2
a	0	0	0	2	2	4	0	4	2	0	0	0	0	0	0	2
b	0	2	0	0	4	0	0	2	0	0	0	2	2	0	2	2
c	0	4	0	0	0	2	2	0	0	0	2	2	2	0	2	0
d	0	2	0	0	0	0	0	2	0	4	2	0	0	2	2	2
e	0	0	2	0	0	0	4	2	0	0	0	2	2	2	0	2
f	0	0	2	0	2	0	2	2	0	0	2	0	2	0	2	2

Definition 3. *Define* $DDT_{out}(\alpha) = \{\beta | \exists\ x \in F_2^4, s.t.\ S(x) \oplus S(x \oplus \alpha) = \beta\}$, *then we have* $DDT_{out}(0x1) = \{0x1, 0x4, 0x6, 0x8, 0x9, 0xb\}$.

Definition 4. *Define* $DDT_{in}(\beta) = \{\alpha | \exists\ x \in F_2^4, s.t.\ S(x) \oplus S(x \oplus \alpha) = \beta\}$, *then we have* $DDT_{in}(0x1) = \{0x1, 0x2, 0x4, 0xb, 0xc, 0xd\}$.

Property 1. Let $\hat{M_0}$ be a function from $(F_2^4)^4$ to $(F_2^4)^4$. When the input difference $X_{col(0)}$ has A active nibbles and the output difference $Y_{col(0)}$ has B active nibbles, we can determine the number of input differences that satisfy this condition, namely,

$$Num_{AB} = \#\{X_{col(0)} \in (F_2^4)^4 : wt(X_{col(0)}) = A, wt(Y_{col(0)}) = B\}, \quad (1)$$

where $Y_{col(0)} = \hat{M_0}(X_{col(0)})$ and $A, B \in \{0, 1, 2, 3, 4\}$.

We use $wt(X_{col(j)})$ and $wt(Y_{col(j)})$ to demonstrate the number of active nibbles for the input and output difference of the $(j+1)$-th column, respectively. Since M' can be viewed as four 16×16 bitmatrix multiplications in four columns of the state respectively. The first and fourth columns of the state are multiplied by $\hat{M_0}$, while the other two columns are multiplied by $\hat{M_1}$. For the linear layer $\hat{M_0}$ and $\hat{M_1}$, although they are different in the order of rows, they have the same property which can be proved similarly. Then we can get the number of input differences that satisfy Eq. (1) through the linear layer M'. As shown in Table 4, where $i, j \in \{0, 1, 2, 3\}$, we give the quantitative relation between input-output differences through the linear layer M' (regarding the state as a 4×4 nibble matrix).

Table 4. The quantitative relationship between input states and output states of M'

$wt(X_{col(j)})$	$wt(Y_{col(j)})$				
	0	1	2	3	4
0	1	0	0	0	0
1	0	0	0	16	44
2	0	0	28	256	1066
3	0	16	256	2848	10380
4	0	44	1066	10380	39135

4 Impossible Differential Distinguishers of PRINCE

Currently, the longest impossible differential distinguisher is four rounds, and it is constructed through the direct contradiction of the miss-in-the-middle technique. In order to get a longer distinguisher, we want to find indirect contradictions in the intermediate states. In this section, we present two types of 5-round impossible differential distinguishers of PRINCE by using the properties of the S-box and the linear layer in Sect. 3.

In the first type of impossible differential distinguisher, each input difference $\triangle X$ and the output difference $\triangle Y$ has only one active nibble. Then we need to test $2^4 \cdot 2^4$ nibble positions. Also, we need to iterate through all possible values of $F_{2^4}/\{0\}$ for each byte. Then, there are $2^4 \cdot 2^4 \cdot (2^4-1)^2 = 57600$ candidate input-output difference pairs. Among them, 56392 candidate pairs satisfy the 5-round impossible differential distinguisher, and 1208 candidate pairs are not. See GitHub for all distinguishers[1].

Example of the First Type of Distinguishers

One of the 56392 5-round impossible differential distinguishers of PRINCE is

$$0x1000|0000|0000|0000 \overset{R^5}{\nrightarrow} 0x1000|0000|0000|0000.$$

We manually verify the above example of impossible differential distinguisher of PRINCE. It is completely different from the previous impossible differential distinguishers in that the impossible differentials are detected by considering the details of the S-box.

Proposition 1. *Let* $R^1 = SR \circ M' \circ S$*, the input difference* $D^{0,0}_{0x1}$ *can propagate to at least one of the output differences of* $SR \circ M'(D^{0,0}_{0x1}), SR \circ M'(D^{0,0}_{0x4}), SR \circ M'(D^{0,0}_{0x6}), SR \circ M'(D^{0,0}_{0x8}), SR \circ M'(D^{0,0}_{0x9})$ *and* $SR \circ M'(D^{0,0}_{0xb})$ *through* R^1.

Proposition 2. *Let* $G = M' \circ S \circ R^1$*, since considering the details of the S-box, when the input difference* $\triangle X^0 = D^{0,0}_{0x1}$ *propagate to the output difference* $\triangle W^1$ *through* G*, there are 7370 output differences, which we put into the set* H *and classify them into seven classes by the hamming weight, as shown in Table 5.*

Table 5. The output differences of the set H

$wt(\triangle W^1)$	Number	$wt(\triangle W^1)$	Number
16	1704	12	139
15	2852	11	333
14	1574	10	333
13	317	9	118

Theorem 1. *For a 5-round PRINCE with an* M' *layer in the middle. The input difference* $0x1000|0000|0000|0000$ *cannot propagate to the output difference* $0x1000|0000|0000|0000$ *after 5 rounds of PRINCE by considering all the details of the S-box.*

Proof. In Fig. 2, the input difference is propagated in forwards by 3 rounds, and the output difference is propagated in backwards by 2 rounds.

[1] https://github.com/ZLAa-oss/PRINCE.git.

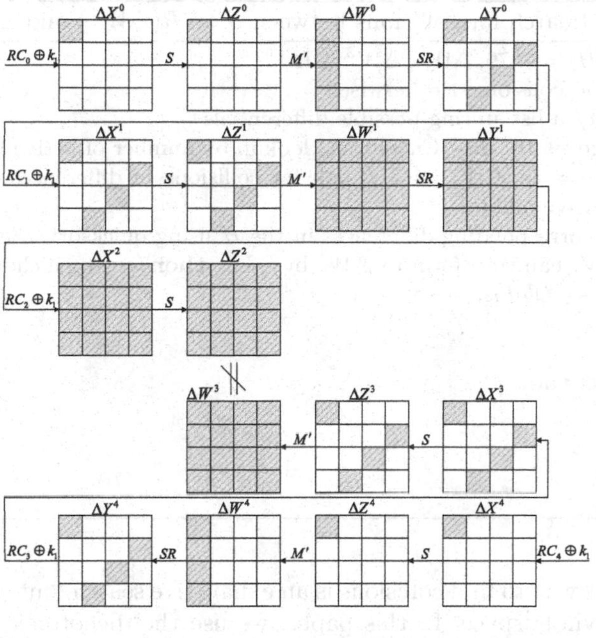

Fig. 2. 5-round impossible differential distinguisher of PRINCEcore

1. As shown in the encryption direction of Fig. 2, for the input difference $\triangle X^0 = D^{0,0}_{0x1}$, it can propagate to one of the following six differences through R^1.

$$\begin{pmatrix} 0x1 & 0 & 0 & 0 \\ 0 & 0 & 0 & 0x1 \\ 0 & 0 & 0x1 & 0 \\ 0 & 0 & 0 & 0 \end{pmatrix}, \begin{pmatrix} 0x4 & 0 & 0 & 0 \\ 0 & 0 & 0 & 0 \\ 0 & 0 & 0x4 & 0 \\ 0 & 0x4 & 0 & 0 \end{pmatrix}, \begin{pmatrix} 0 & 0 & 0 & 0 \\ 0 & 0 & 0 & 0x8 \\ 0 & 0 & 0x8 & 0 \\ 0 & 0x8 & 0 & 0 \end{pmatrix},$$

$$\begin{pmatrix} 0x6 & 0 & 0 & 0 \\ 0 & 0 & 0 & 0x2 \\ 0 & 0 & 0x4 & 0 \\ 0 & 0x6 & 0 & 0 \end{pmatrix}, \begin{pmatrix} 0x1 & 0 & 0 & 0 \\ 0 & 0 & 0 & 0x9 \\ 0 & 0 & 0x9 & 0 \\ 0 & 0x8 & 0 & 0 \end{pmatrix}, \begin{pmatrix} 0x3 & 0 & 0 & 0 \\ 0 & 0 & 0 & 0xb \\ 0 & 0 & 0x9 & 0 \\ 0 & 0xa & 0 & 0 \end{pmatrix}.$$

2. As shown in the decryption direction of Fig. 2, since PRINCE possesses the similarity of encryption and decryption, $\triangle W^3 = \triangle W^1$. The output difference $\triangle X^4 = D^{0,0}_{0x1}$ can propagate to one of the above six differences through R^1. At the same time, all possible differences of $\triangle W^3$ are in Table 5.
3. A key question is whether any difference $\triangle W^1 \in H$ cannot propagate to any difference $\triangle W^3 \in H$ though $S \circ SR$, namely, $\triangle W^1 \overset{S \circ SR}{\nrightarrow} \triangle W^3$. Therefore, we only need to find the indirect contradiction between $S \circ SR(\triangle W^1)$ and $\triangle W^3 \in H$ to prove that the 5-round impossible differential distinguisher is valid.

   In this paper, we use the combination of classification search and dichotomy to find collisions, as shown in Algorithm 1. The source codes are available in https://github.com/ZLAa-oss/PRINCE.git.

Algorithm 1. Search for collisions between $S \circ SR(\triangle W^1)$ and $\triangle W^3$

Input: Set $H, |H| = 7370, \triangle W^1, \triangle W^3 \in H$
Output: 1 for no colision, -1 otherwise.

ObjList=[ ];// a list storing possible differentials
for i in range $(9, 16)$ **do**//Categorical lookup by number of active bytes
    $wt(\triangle W_1) = wt(\triangle W_3) = i$//Look for collisions in differences with the same number of active nibbles
    Sort the corresponding differences in the H using quicksort//See Table 5
    if all $\triangle W_1$ can transform to $\triangle W_3$ by S-box **then**//using dichotomy
        $\triangle W_3 \rightarrow ObjList$
    end if
end for
if $ObjList = \varnothing$ **then**
    return 1
else
    return -1
end if

The most direct way to find collisions is an exhaustive search, but the complexity is almost the whole space. In this paper, we use the dichotomy to reduce the complexity and take only two days to run all nibble positions and all nibble values. Finally, we prove that $\triangle W^1 \overset{S \circ SR}{\nrightarrow} \triangle W^3$ is impossible differentials of the S-boxes.

All in all, the input difference $0x1000|0000|0000|0000$ cannot propagate to the output difference $0x1000|0000|0000|0000$ after 5 rounds of PRINCE by considering all the details of the S-box.

In the second type of impossible differential distinguisher, the input difference $\triangle X$ has one active nibble and the output difference $\triangle Y$ has only two active nibble. The 5-round impossible differential distinguishers of PRINCE is

$$0x1000|0000|0000|0000 \overset{R^5}{\nrightarrow} 000x10|0000|0000x1|0000.$$

Theorem 2. *For a 5-round PRINCE with an M' layer in the middle. The input difference* $0x1000|0000|0000|0000$ *cannot propagate to the output difference* $0x1000|0000|0000|0000$ *after 5 rounds of PRINCE by considering all the details of the S-box.*

The proof is similar to Theorem 1, and we ignore it. The 5-round impossible differential distinguisher of PRINCEcore is shown in Fig. 3.

5 Impossible Differential Attack on 9-Round PRINCEcore

In this section, we show impossible differential attacks on 9-round PRINCEcore using the 5-round impossible differential distinguishers presented in Sect. 4.

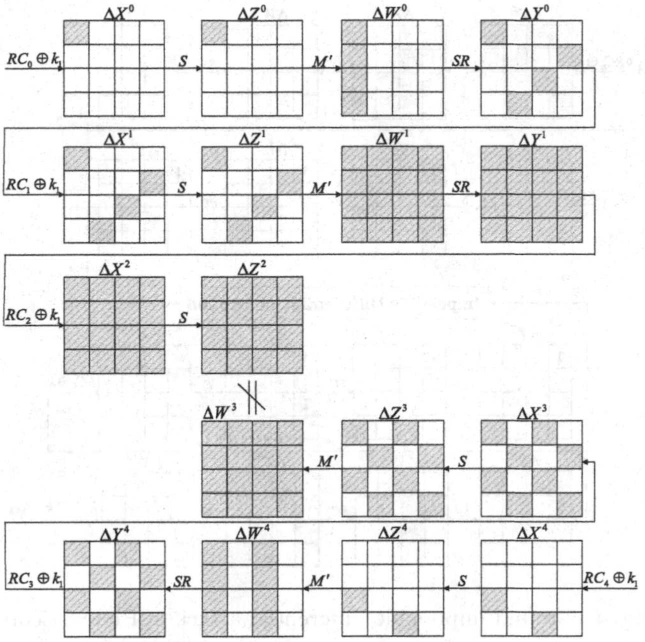

Fig. 3. 5-round impossible differential distinguisher of PRINCEcore

5.1 The First Key Recovery Attack on PRINCEcore

We utilized a 5-round impossible differential distinguisher in Theorem 1 with two rounds extended at the top and the bottom to attack the 9-round PRINCEcore. The procedure of this attack is as follows, and see also Fig. 4.

(1) Precomputation

According to Table 4, when each column of $\triangle W^0$ has only one active nibble, the corresponding $\triangle Z^0$ has at least three active nibbles in the same column. And the number of $\triangle Z^0$ is $(16+44)^3 \approx 2^{17.7}$, so the number of possible input pairs in $\triangle X^1$ is at least $2^{17.7}$. For the $2^{17.7}$ input pairs, we compute all the possible values of the 12 nibbles and store them in a hash table.

(2) Data Collection

Take 2^N structure of plaintexts, and each takes all the possible $2^{17.7}$ values in the hash table of $\triangle X^0_{col(0,1,2)}$ with a fixed value of $\triangle X^0_{col(3)}$. We can generate approximately $2^{34.4}$ plaintext pairs for each structure. Select pairs whose ciphertext difference $\triangle X^8$ is zero in $\triangle X^8_{col(3)}$. We expect to have $2^{N+34.4} \times 2^{-16} = 2^{N+18.4}$ pairs on average.

(3) Key Recovery

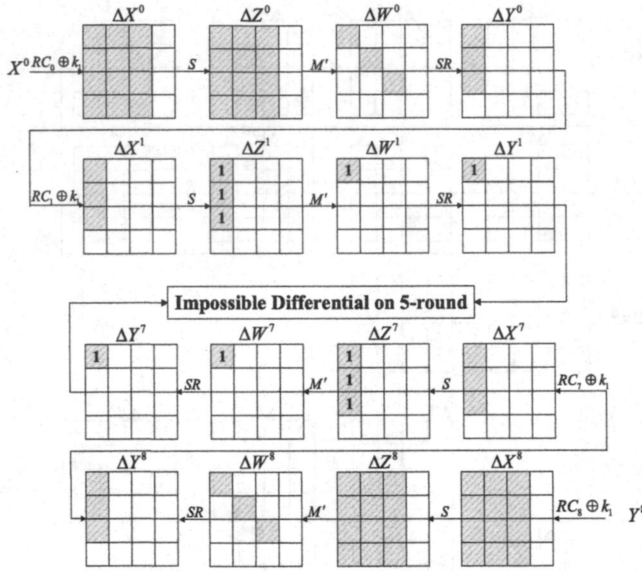

Fig. 4. 9-round impossible differential attack of PRINCEcore

Step 1: Guess the values of $k_1[0-2]$ and partially encrypt the corresponding nibbles in X^0. Choose pairs whose differences $\triangle W^1_{col(0)} = (0x1, 0, 0, 0)^T$ after M' operation. In this step, we expect to have $2^{N+18.4} \times 2^{-8} = 2^{N+10.4}$ pairs. The probability of this step is 2^{-8}. According to Definition 4, when the output difference is $0x1$, there are six input differences. Then there are $6^3 \approx 2^8$ possible differences of X^1.

Step 2: For every $k_1[0-2]$ guessed in step 1, we guess the values of $k_1[3]$. Partially decrypt the associated nibbles in Y^8. Choose pairs whose differences $\triangle W^8_{col(0)}$ after M' operation are non-zero at one nibble and zero at the other three nibbles. In this step, we expect to have $2^{N+10.4} \times 2^{-12} \times 3 = 2^{N+0.4}$ pairs. The probability of having one active nibble is 2^{-12}, and we have three choices to locate the active nibbles.

Step 3: Guess the values of $k_1[4-7]$ and partially decrypt the corresponding nibbles in Y^8. Choose pairs whose difference $\triangle W^8_{col(1)}$ after M' operation is non-zero at one nibble and zero at the other three nibbles. In this step, we expect to have $2^{N+0.4} \times 2^{-12} \times 2 = 2^{N-10.6}$ pairs. $2^{-12} \times 2$ is the probability of having one active nibble, and we have two choices to locate the active nibbles. (to avoid active nibbles in every column after the SR operation).

Step 4: Guess the values of $k_1[8-11]$ and partially decrypt the corresponding nibbles in Y^8. Choose pairs whose difference $\triangle W^8_{col(2)}$ after M' operation is non-zero at one nibble and zero at the other three nibbles. In this step, we expect to have $2^{N-10.6} \times 2^{-12} = 2^{N-22.6}$ pairs. 2^{-12} is the probability of having one active nibble, and there is only one choice for the location of this nibble because it is required to be in the same column as the active nibble mentioned in steps 2 and 3 after the SR operation.

Step 5: For every $k_1[0-2]$ guessed in step 1, partially decrypt the associated nibbles in Y_7. Check pairs whose difference $\triangle W^7_{col(0)} = (0x1, 0, 0, 0)$ after M' operation. If this condition is satisfied, the corresponding data pairs meet the 5-round impossible difference distinguisher, and the guessed key is wrong. We discard the corresponding $k_1[0-11]$ from the list of all the 2^{48} possible partial values of k_1. The probability of this step is 2^{-8}.

(4) Attack Complexity

In this attack, we guess the possible 2^{48} bits of k_1. After testing the $2^{N-22.6}$ remaining pairs, the probability that a wrong 48 bits key guess of $k_1[0-11]$ remains is $(2^{48}-1) \times (1-2^{-8})^{2^{N-22.6}}$. To single out the correct key, we must guarantee $N \geq 35.6$. Consequently, the data complexity of the attack is $2^{35.6+17.7} = 2^{53.3}$ chosen plaintexts.

The time complexity of our attack consists of three parts. Step 1 requires $2 \times 2^{12} \times 2^{N+18.4} = 2^{67}$ encryptions. Step 2 requires $2 \times 2^{16} \times 2^{N+10.4} = 2^{63}$ decryptions. Step 3 requires $2 \times 2^{16} \times 2^{N+0.4} = 2^{53}$ decryptions. And Step 4 requires $2 \times 2^{16} \times 2^{N-10.6} = 2^{42}$ decryptions. Consequently, the overall time complexity of the attack is $(2^{67} + 2^{63} + 2^{53} + 2^{42})/9 \approx 2^{63.91}$ full encryptions. We can obtain the remain 2^{16} of k_1 by exhaustive search with 2^{16} encryptions, so $2^{63.91} + 2^{16} \approx 2^{63.91}$ 9-round encryptions are required to recover the whole k_1.

The memory occupied by the attack consists of two main parts. Firstly, we need to store 2^{48} bits, i.e., 2^{45} bytes memory. Secondly, $2^{N+18.4}/8 = 2^{51}$ bytes of memory are needed to store the pairs remaining after data collection. Accordingly, $2^{45} + 2^{51} \approx 2^{51.02}$ bytes of memory are necessary to launch the attack.

5.2 The Second Key Recovery Attack on PRINCEcore

We propose a 9-round impossible differential attack by adding two rounds on top and the bottom of the 5-round distinguisher in Theorem 2, as shown in Fig. 5. The specific attack steps are as follows.

(1) Precomputation

According to Table 4, when each column of $\triangle W^0$ has only one active nibble, the corresponding $\triangle Z^0$ has at least three active nibbles in the same column. And the number of $\triangle Z^0$ is $(16+44)^3 \approx 2^{17.7}$, so the number of possible input pairs in $\triangle X^1$ is at least $2^{17.7}$. For the $2^{17.7}$ input pairs, we compute all the possible values of the 12 nibbles and store them in a hash table.

(2) Data Collection

Take 2^N structure of plaintexts, and each takes all the possible $2^{17.7}$ values in the hash table of $\triangle X^0_{col(0,1,2)}$ with a fixed value of $\triangle X^0_{col(3)}$. We can generate approximately $2^{34.4}$ plaintext pairs for each structure. Select pairs whose ciphertext difference $\triangle X^8$ is zero in $\triangle X^8_{col(3)}$. We expect to have $2^{N+34.4} \times 2^{-32} = 2^{N+2.4}$ pairs on average.

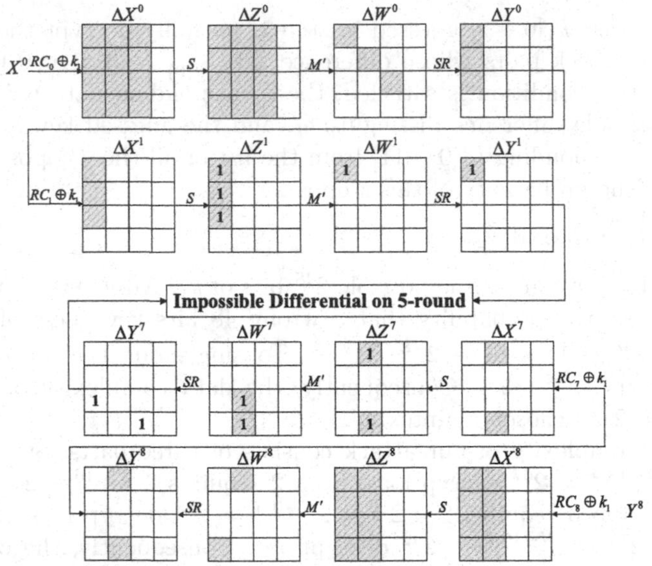

Fig. 5. 9-round impossible differential attack of PRINCEcore

(3) Key Recovery

Step 1: Guess the values of $k_1[0-2]$ and partially encrypt the corresponding nibbles in X^0. Choose pairs whose differences $\triangle W^1_{col(0)} = (0x1, 0, 0, 0)^T$ after M' operation. In this step, we expect to have $2^{N+2.4} \times 2^{-8} = 2^{N-6.4}$ pairs. The probability of this step is 2^{-8}. According to Definition 4, when the output difference is $0x1$, there are six input differences. Then there are $6^3 \approx 2^8$ possible differences of X^1.

Step 2: For every $k_1[0-2]$ guessed in step 1, we guess the values of $k_1[3]$. Partially decrypt the associated nibbles in Y^8. Choose pairs whose differences $\triangle W^8_{col(0)}$ after M' operation are non-zero at one nibble and zero at the other three nibbles. In this step, we expect to have $2^{N-6.4} \times 2^{-12} \times 2 = 2^{N-17.4}$ pairs. The probability of having one active nibble is 2^{-12}, and we have three choices to locate the active nibbles.

Step 3: Guess the values of $k_1[4-7]$ and partially decrypt the associated nibbles in Y^8. Choose pairs whose difference $\triangle W^8_{col(1)}$ after M' operation is non-zero at one nibble and zero at the other three nibbles. In this step, we expect to have $2^{N-17.4} \times 2^{-12} = 2^{N-29.4}$ pairs. 2^{-12} is the probability of having one active nibble, and we have one choice to locate the active nibbles. (to avoid active nibbles in every column after the SR operation).

Step 4: For every $k_1[4-7]$ guessed in step 3, partially decrypt the associated nibbles in Y_7. Check pairs whose difference $\Delta W^7_{col(0)} = (0, 0, 0x1, 0x1)^T$ after M' operation. If this condition is satisfied, the corresponding data pairs meet the 5-round impossible difference distinguisher, and the guessed key is wrong. We discard the corresponding $k_1[0-7]$ from the list of all the 2^{32} possible partial values of k_1. The probability of this step is $2^{-5.2}$. According to Definition 4, when the output difference is $0x1$, there are six input differences. Then there are $6^2 \approx 2^{5.2}$ possible differences of X^1.

(4) Attack Complexity

In this attack, we guess the possible 2^{32} bits of k_1. After testing the $2^{N-29.4}$ remaining pairs, the probability that a wrong 32 bits key guess of $k_1[0-7]$ remains is $(2^{32}-1)\times(1-2^{-5.2})^{2^{N-29.4}}$. To single out the correct key, we must guarantee $N \geq 38.4$. Consequently, the data complexity of the attack is $2^{38.4+17.7} = 2^{56.1}$ chosen plaintexts.

The time complexity of our attack consists of three parts. Step 1 requires $2 \times 2^{12} \times 2^{N+2.4} = 2^{53.8}$ encryptions. Step 2 requires $2 \times 2^{16} \times 2^{N-6.4} = 2^{49}$ decryptions. Step 3 requires $2 \times 2^{16} \times 2^{N-17.4} = 2^{38}$ decryptions. Consequently, the overall time complexity of the attack is $(2^{53.8} + 2^{49} + 2^{38})/9 \approx 2^{50.68}$ full encryptions. We can obtain the remaining 2^{32} of k_1 by exhaustive search with 2^{32} encryptions, so $2^{50.68} + 2^{32} \approx 2^{50.68}$ 9-round encryptions are required to recover the whole k_1.

The memory occupied by the attack consists of two main parts. Firstly, we need to store 2^{32} bits, i.e., 2^{29} bytes memory. Secondly, $2^{N+2.4}/8 = 2^{36.3}$ bytes of memory are needed to store the pairs remaining after data collection. Accordingly, $2^{29} + 2^{36.3} \approx 2^{36.3}$ bytes of memory are necessary to launch the attack.

6 Conclusion

The work of this paper starts from the designer's viewpoint, giving more accurate impossible differential cryptanalysis for PRINCE by considering the details of the S-box. Compared to the cryptanalysis of the SPN structure, our results are closer to the attacks on the concrete cipher.

We solve the impractical situation that an exhaustive search traverses the whole space by classifying the difference and adding dichotomy to make the difference through S-box realize collision. It is worth mentioning that although the two types of distinguishers have the same number of rounds, the complexity required to recover the key is different when the input and output differences are different. In addition, our results can be generalized to other lightweight block ciphers for finding longer impossible differential distinguishers with considering the details of the S-box.

In the future, the only chance of finding longer impossible differentials distinguisher for PRINCE, is restricted by this paper to the situation where the key schedule must be considered, which is a problem worth further investigating.

Acknowledgements. This work is supported by the National Natural Science Foundation of China (No. 62072445). We thank the anonymous reviewers for their valuable comments and suggestions.

References

1. Bogdanov, A., et al.: PRESENT: an ultra-lightweight block cipher. In: Paillier, P., Verbauwhede, I. (eds.) CHES 2007. LNCS, vol. 4727, pp. 450–466. Springer, Heidelberg (2007). https://doi.org/10.1007/978-3-540-74735-2_31
2. Beaulieu, R., Shors, D., Smith, J., et al.: The Simon and Speck lightweight block ciphers. In: Proceedings of the 52nd Annual Design Automation Conference, San Francisco, CA, USA, 7–11 June 2015, pp. 175: 1–175: 6 (2015). https://doi.org/10.1145/2744769.2747946
3. Banik, S., et al.: Midori: a block cipher for low energy. In: Iwata, T., Cheon, J.H. (eds.) ASIACRYPT 2015. LNCS, vol. 9453, pp. 411–436. Springer, Heidelberg (2015). https://doi.org/10.1007/978-3-662-48800-3_17
4. Borghoff, J., et al.: PRINCE – a low-latency block cipher for pervasive computing applications. In: Wang, X., Sako, K. (eds.) ASIACRYPT 2012. LNCS, vol. 7658, pp. 208–225. Springer, Heidelberg (2012). https://doi.org/10.1007/978-3-642-34961-4_14
5. Kilian, J., Rogaway, P.: How to protect DES against exhaustive key search (an analysis of DESX). J. Cryptol. **14**(1), 17–35 (2000). https://doi.org/10.1007/s001450010015
6. Soleimany, H., et al.: Reflection cryptanalysis of PRINCE-like ciphers. In: Moriai, S. (ed.) FSE 2013. LNCS, vol. 8424, pp. 71–91. Springer, Heidelberg (2014). https://doi.org/10.1007/978-3-662-43933-3_5
7. Jean, J., Nikolić, I., Peyrin, T., Wang, L., Wu, S.: Security analysis of PRINCE. In: Moriai, S. (ed.) FSE 2013. LNCS, vol. 8424, pp. 92–111. Springer, Heidelberg (2014). https://doi.org/10.1007/978-3-662-43933-3_6
8. Zhao, G., Sun, B., Li, C., et al.: Truncated differential cryptanalysis of PRINCE. Secur. Commun. Netw. **8**(16), 2875–2887 (2015). https://doi.org/10.1002/sec.1213
9. Ding, Y.L., Zhao, J.Y., Li, L.B., et al.: Impossible differential analysis on round-reduced prince. J. Inf. Sci. Eng. **33**(4), 1041–1053 (2017)
10. Ding, Y., Jia, K., Wang, A., Shi, Y.: Impossible differential analysis on 8-round PRINCE. In: Liu, Q., Liu, X., Li, L., Zhou, H., Zhao, H.-H. (eds.) Proceedings of the 9th International Conference on Computer Engineering and Networks. AISC, vol. 1143, pp. 383–395. Springer, Singapore (2021). https://doi.org/10.1007/978-981-15-3753-0_37
11. Li, L., Jia, K., Wang, X.: Improved meet-in-the-middle attacks on AES-192 and PRINCE. In: IACR Cryptology ePrint Archive 2013/573 (2013)
12. Farzaneh, A., Eik, L., Stefan, L.: On the security of the core of prince against biclique and differential cryptanalysis. In: IACR Cryptology ePrint Archive 2012/712 (2012)
13. Knudsen, L.: DEAL-a 128-bit block cipher. Complexity **258**(2), 216 (1998)
14. Biham, E., Biryukov, A., Shamir, A.: Cryptanalysis of skipjack reduced to 31 rounds using impossible differentials. In: Stern, J. (ed.) EUROCRYPT 1999. LNCS, vol. 1592, pp. 12–23. Springer, Heidelberg (1999). https://doi.org/10.1007/3-540-48910-X_2

15. Daemen, J., Rijmen, V.: The Design of Rijndael: AES - The Advanced Encryption Standard. Information Security and Cryptography, Springer, Heidelberg (2002). https://doi.org/10.1007/978-3-662-04722-4
16. Aoki, K., et al.: *Camellia*: a 128-bit block cipher suitable for multiple platforms—design and analysis. In: Stinson, D.R., Tavares, S. (eds.) SAC 2000. LNCS, vol. 2012, pp. 39–56. Springer, Heidelberg (2001). https://doi.org/10.1007/3-540-44983-3_4
17. Wu, W., Zhang, L.: LBlock: a lightweight block cipher. In: Lopez, J., Tsudik, G. (eds.) ACNS 2011. LNCS, vol. 6715, pp. 327–344. Springer, Heidelberg (2011). https://doi.org/10.1007/978-3-642-21554-4_19
18. Kanda, M., Matsumoto, T.: Security of camellia against truncated differential cryptanalysis. In: Matsui, M. (ed.) FSE 2001. LNCS, vol. 2355, pp. 286–299. Springer, Heidelberg (2002). https://doi.org/10.1007/3-540-45473-X_24
19. Sun, B., et al.: Links among impossible differential, integral and zero correlation linear cryptanalysis. In: Gennaro, R., Robshaw, M. (eds.) CRYPTO 2015. LNCS, vol. 9215, pp. 95–115. Springer, Heidelberg (2015). https://doi.org/10.1007/978-3-662-47989-6_5
20. Wang, Q., Jin, C.: Upper bound of the length of truncated impossible differentials for AES. Des. Codes Crypt. **86**(7), 1541–1552 (2017). https://doi.org/10.1007/s10623-017-0411-z
21. Wang, Q., Jin, C.: More accurate results on the provable security of AES against impossible differential cryptanalysis. Des. Codes Crypt. **87**(12), 3001–3018 (2019). https://doi.org/10.1007/s10623-019-00660-7

Cyber Security

Towards Constructing Consistent Pattern Strength Meters with User's Visual Perception

Leo Hyun Park[1], Eunbi Hwang[1], Donggun Lee[2], and Taekyoung Kwon[1](✉)

[1] Yonsei University, Seoul, South Korea
{dofi,ebhwang95,c15336,taekyoung}@yonsei.ac.kr
[2] Ministry of National Defense, Seoul, South Korea

Abstract. Pattern lock strength meters designed for securing Android devices are inconsistent in their metering, e.g., assigning higher scores to weaker patterns. In this paper, we raise this inconsistency problem by analyzing five existing pattern strength meters. We reveal that they commonly miss some important visual features and even assign erroneous weights to features. As a preliminary study toward a consistent pattern strength meter in the future, we design a rigorous user study to identify the visual features of a pattern that correspond to real-world users' criteria to score the strength of the pattern. We conducted an online survey for 3,851 users to collect reliable labels for 625 patterns. The statistical result of the user study sheds light on a pattern strength meter that reflects the user's visual perception with various visual features.

Keywords: Pattern lock · Pattern strength meter · Shoulder surfing attack

1 Introduction

Android pattern lock, which is one of the authentication methods used to protect a smartphone, originates from the earlier recall-based systems such as Draw-A-Secret (DAS) [18] and Pass-Go [30]. A pattern lock user draws a pattern shape on 3 × 3 grid in a touchscreen and enrolls it. When unlocking the smartphone, the user only needs to draw the enrolled pattern. As a graphical password, pattern lock utilizes the fact that graphical information is easier to be remembered by humans than text information [5,28]. It is also preferred by users because of its good error recovery [37]. Although the recent trend is using a biometric authentication that has been developed newly, in this case, users should adopt the pattern lock or PIN as a secondary authentication method.

Android pattern lock is one of the most common authentication methods for smartphone [16,21]. It is reported in a previous study that about 40% of Android users are using the pattern lock [35]. Furthermore, in our user study, we found that 35.91% of Android smartphone users are currently using the pattern lock,

S.-H. Seo and H. Seo (Eds.): ICISC 2022, LNCS 13849, pp. 81–99, 2023.
https://doi.org/10.1007/978-3-031-29371-9_5

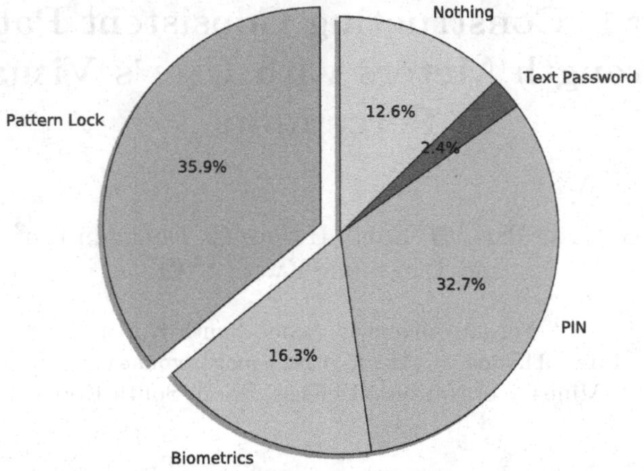

Fig. 1. Proportion of current authentication method usage of survey participants

which accounts for the most among authentication schemes (see Fig. 1). Users who have experience using the pattern lock comprised 93.35% of all participants. This indicates that Android pattern lock still influences heavily protecting users' smartphones.

Despite a number of smartphone users using Android pattern lock, a variety of security issues with the pattern lock have been raised. Theoretically, the possible number of unique patterns in Android pattern lock is 389,112. It is a tremendous amount but actual pattern usage differs from the theory. Users commonly use simple and usable but insecure patterns. This decreases the number of patterns that an attacker should consider and makes the pattern lock vulnerable to the guessing attack [27,32]. Moreover, as a simple pattern is easier to be remembered by both user and attacker, it is easily exposed to the shoulder-surfing attack [36]. Because the shoulder-surfing attack does not need any prior knowledge about the pattern lock, it is more dangerous considering that anyone near the user can perform the attack. Therefore, there needs equipment that leads users to choose more complex and secure patterns to prevent two types of attacks on the pattern lock.

From decades ago, there have been a lot of studies about password strength meters as equipment to increase the security of user's text password [13]. Against the brute-force attack [13,14], the dictionary attack [8,9,13,19,33,34,39], and the guessing attack [9], those existing works applied features such as Markov model and entropy to their meters. The text password strength meters are deployed on websites, encouraging users to choose more secure passwords [34]. Inspired by the case of the text password, there have been several studies about a pattern strength meter to prevent shoulder-surfing attack and guessing attack [2,6,27,29,32]. They extracted various features based on their own criteria, designed a metric to measure the strength of a pattern, and performed user studies to confirm the validity of their meters. They commonly concluded that pattern strength meters can help choose more secure patterns. However, all of the existing pattern strength meters have an inconsistency problem. In other words, they have the possibilities that they estimate a simple pattern that is vulnerable to attacks complex. Likewise, they might estimate a complex pattern that is robust to attacks simple. Their inconsistencies can cause a fatal defect that they can recommend a vulnerable pattern to users. Due to this reason, the existing pattern strength meters are premature to be applied to public users.

In this paper, we conduct a preliminary study toward consistent pattern strength meters. We first summarize five existing pattern strength meters [2,6,27,29,32] and identify the reason for their inconsistency problem. They commonly miss some important features and assign improper weight values to used features. Furthermore, they designed their meters from the subjective perspective of authors, not the real-world users' perspective. We claim that features relevant to users' visual perception should be applied as much as possible to the strength metering to solve the problem. In this respect, we raise a fundamental question: visual features of patterns correspond with the perception of real-world users? We perform a large-scale online survey subjected to 3,851 android users to answer the question. In this process, various feature values of patterns were measured and a clustering algorithm was applied to select 1,000 survey patterns. Through the statistical analysis of the survey result, we obtained reliable strength scores of 625 patterns among 1,000 patterns. Our study result implies that a future pattern strength meter based on abundant features and their proper weights can clearly explain how human recognizes a pattern and scores the strength of the pattern. In summary, this paper makes the following contributions:

- We raise the inconsistency problem of the existing five pattern strength meters through several pattern examples that are misestimated. We identify that the reason for their problem is the lack of used features and improper feature weights due to the subjective perspective.
- We perform a large-scale online survey for 3,851 android users (Sect. 3). Unlike previous studies, 100 of our survey participants who responded to one pattern can give the ground truth of the strength of the pattern. We also obtain reliable strength scores of 625 patterns through statistical analysis.
- Further, we discuss solutions to resolve the problems and to measure an accurate pattern strength (Sect. 4). We define requirements for a consistent pattern strength meter. We also discuss how the survey result can be utilized to construct the strength meter.

2 Pattern Strength Meters

Despite of efforts of the previous works, the existing pattern strength meters have an inconsistency in measuring the strength of a pattern. In other words, they are possible to judge a weak pattern to be strong and a strong pattern to be weak. This can lead to a serious problem in that those meters guide users to choose weak patterns. In this section, we introduce the existing five pattern strength meters [2,6,27,29,32], analyzing their inconsistency.

We first analyze an error caused by a single pattern meter. Figure 2 shows error patterns that we found the existing meters measure erroneously. In Figs. 2(a), (b), (d), and (e), the right pattern generally looks simpler than the left one for human, but each meter concludes that the right pattern is much more complex than the left one. In Figs. 2(c), the right pattern generally looks more complex than the right one, but the Sun meter estimates similar complexities for both patterns. We repeatedly sorted 389,112 patterns in ascending orders of the five meters. We then extracted the Nth strong pattern in each existing meter to identify erroneous patterns.

2.1 Existing Pattern Strength Meters

Uellenbeck Meter. Uellenbeck et al. [32] measured the security of a pattern against the guessing attack, based on the hidden Markov model. Their pattern strength metric based on an n-gram Markov model can be defined as follows.

$$P(c_1, ..., c_m) = P(c_1, ..., c_{n-1}) \cdot \prod_{i=n}^{m} P(c_i | c_{i-n+1}, ..., c_{i-1}) \quad (1)$$

In the above equation, c_n indicates a 3-gram pattern sequence token, $P(c_1, ..., c_{n-1})$ indicates an initial probability, and $P(c_n | c_1, ..., c_{n-1})$ indicates a transition probability. They collected user patterns of hundreds of participants in the user study to collect the probability of each token.

It is more real to utilize probabilities from the usage distribution of real-world users, but it is impossible to investigate the usage distribution of all 389,112 patterns and all users. We, therefore, implemented their meter, defining the probability that the current dot moves to another dot as the transition probability. From now on, we call Uellenbeck's meter *the Markov meter* in this paper.

The major error we can find from the Markov model is that the security measurement relies heavily on the number of dots in a pattern. This metric can reflect the security against the guessing attack but cannot reflect the security against the shoulder-surfing attack. In Fig. 2(a), the complexity ranking of the right pattern in the Markov meter is higher than the left one. The right pattern seems less secure than the left one because of the lack of features such as cross point, the direction of segments, and the angle of segments. However, the Markov meter does not consider those features and over-estimated the right pattern.

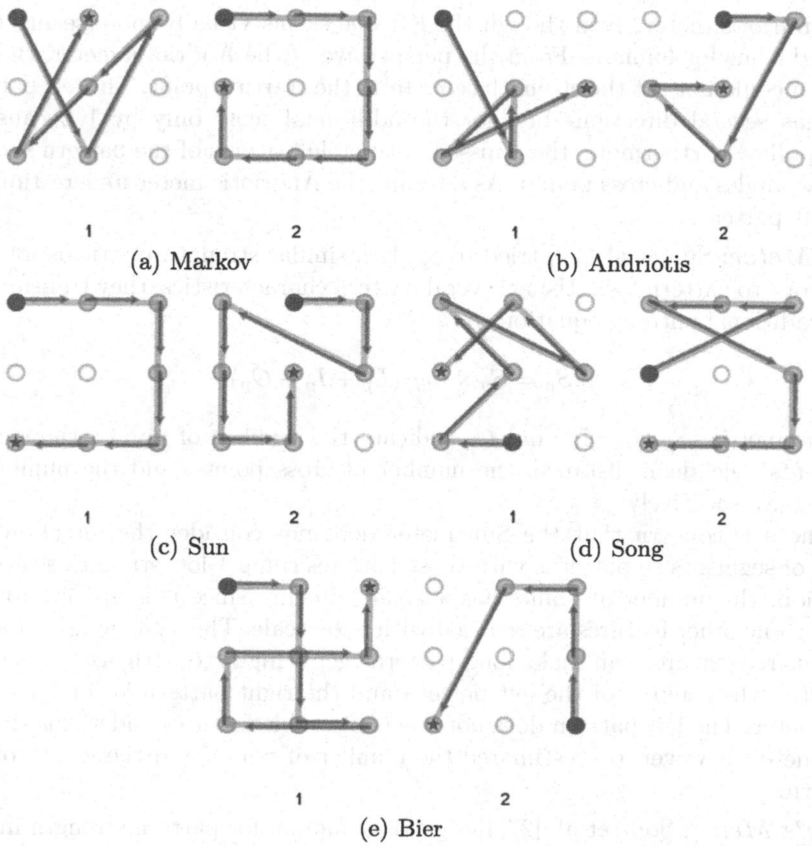

Fig. 2. Error patterns caused by existing single pattern strength meters. Each meter estimated the much larger strength score of the right pattern than the left one except for the Sun meter. Sun meter estimated similar strength scores for both patterns. The circle in the pattern denotes the starting point, and the asterisk in the pattern denotes the endpoint.

***Andriotis Meter*:** Andriotis et al. [2] utilized five pattern features and defined conditions for each feature to increase a security score. The score increase condition x_i is as follows. 1) x_1 is 1 if the starting point is not upper left, otherwise, it is 0. 2) x_2 is $|P| - 5$ where $|P|$ is length of the pattern if $|P| >= 6$, otherwise, it is 0. 3) x_3 is 1 if the number of turns is more than or equal to 2, otherwise, it is 0. 4) x_4 is the number of knight moves. 5) x_5 is the number of overlaps. The final pattern score θ is defined with

$$\theta = \sum_{i=1}^{5} x_i. \tag{2}$$

Figure 2(b) illustrates an example of the error of the Andriotis meter. In this figure, the ranking of the left pattern and that of the right pattern is identical in the Andriotis meter, even though the left one seems visually more secure than the right one for humans. From the perspective of the Andriotis meter, the left pattern could not get the strength score from the starting point. The left pattern also has several directions but got the additional score only by 1 because of their policy. Furthermore, they missed noticeable features of the pattern such as narrow angles and cross points. As a result, the Andriotis meter underestimated the left pattern.

***Sun Meter*:** Sun et al. [29] tried to apply a similar strength metric as for text password to pattern lock. Using several pattern characteristics, they transformed the traditional entropy equation to

$$PS_p = S_p \times log_2(L_p + I_p + O_p) \tag{3}$$

In this metric, S_p, L_p, I_p, and O_p indicate the number of points, the sum of segments' euclidean distance, the number of cross points, and the number of overlaps, respectively.

There is concern that the Sun meter does not consider the direction and angle of segments so patterns with those features can get low strength scores. In addition, the number of points has a great influence since it is applied to true value while other features are reduced with a log scale. The same weights for the other three features can make long patterns get a high strength score easily. In Fig. 2(c), the ranking of the left pattern and the right pattern is similar in the Sun meter. The left pattern does not have noticeable features and seems simple. Sun meter, however, overestimated the number of points and the length of the pattern.

***Song's Meter*:** Song et al. [27] designed a function for pattern strength meter, which is combined from three pattern features considering both guessing attack and shoulder-surfing attack.

$$M_P = 0.81 \times \frac{L_P}{15} + 0.04 \times N_P + 0.15 \times \frac{min(I_P, 5)}{5} \tag{4}$$

They extracted a feature that had not been extracted by other existing approaches before. L_P is sum of segments' vertical and horizontal length, N_P is the ratio of non-repeated sub-patterns, and I_P is the number of intersections. The repetition of the same segments makes a pattern seem simple to users and increases guessability. The weights of the three features were initialized to 0.33 in common. They updated their weights as the above equation through a user study.

They assigned a too-large weight to the pattern length but a small weight to the sub-pattern feature. In Fig. 2(d), the ranking of the left pattern is lower than the right pattern in Song meter, while the left pattern seems more complex for humans. Song meter over-estimated the right pattern since they assigned a large weight to euclidean distance. They also underestimated the left pattern and reduced its ranking improperly since they missed narrow angles of segments of the pattern.

Bier's Meter: Bier et al. [6] concentrated on the directional feature of segments. Their pattern strength metric is as below

$$m(P_0, d_1 d_2 ... d_k) = (1 - p(P_0))(1 - \alpha^k)\frac{1}{3k}\sum_{i=1}^{s(k)} w(d_i). \tag{5}$$

Given k segments, d_i indicates ith segment. $p(P_0)$, α, $w(d_i)$ indicate weights for starting point, the sensitivity of the number of points, and ith segment, respectively. They assigned larger weights for diagonal segments than vertical and horizontal segments.

Bier meter is missing important features such as euclidean distance, cross points, overlap, and angle of segments. In Fig. 2(e), the ranking of the left pattern is lower than the right pattern in the Bier meter. The left pattern was underestimated even though its many turns and overlap increase the complexity. Bier meter also over-estimated knight move of the right pattern, increasing its ranking unnecessarily.

2.2 Common Problem of Pattern Strength Meters

We additionally found the common error cases from the five existing meters. We could identify their common problem from those cases. Figure 3 depicts two patterns that the five meters commonly under-estimated or over-estimated. In Fig. 3(a), compared with the right pattern, the left pattern seems much more complex. This example represents that the existing meters commonly overlook the angle and density of the left pattern. Meanwhile, in Fig. 3(b) illustrates an opposite example. In this figure, compared with the left pattern, the right pattern seems much simpler. We can conclude that the existing meters overly concentrated on pattern features such as the length, and the number of points.

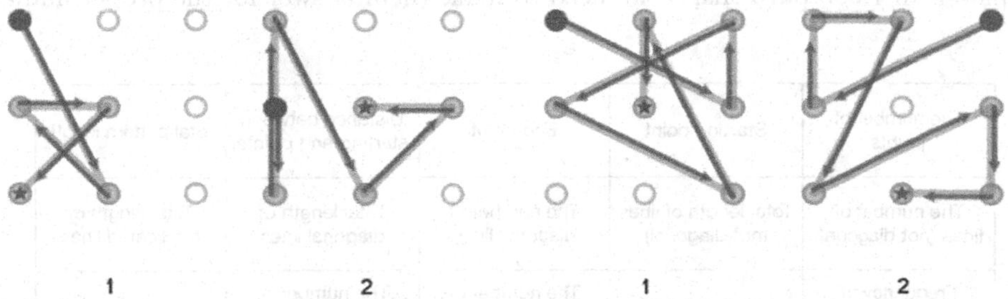

(a) Under estimated pattern (left) (b) Over estimated pattern (right)

Fig. 3. Common error patterns caused by five existing pattern strength meters. All of the existing meters estimated the smaller strength score of the left pattern of (a) than the right one. In addition, they estimated the larger strength score of the right pattern of (b) than the left one.

3 Our Study

In this section, we perform a user study based on a survey to identify whether the strength scores of patterns measured by visual features correspond with those of real-world users. In the following subsections, we explain how we designed, performed, and analyzed the survey and also explain how we created the pattern strength scores.

3.1 Survey Pattern Selection

The ideal approach is collecting labels of patterns as many as possible from real-world users. However, it is impossible to ask for all of 389,112 patterns to users. We need to choose a part of those patterns to be included in the training dataset. The chosen patterns should be able to represent other patterns and create objective data. If patterns have more points and become more complex, people may not be able to answer their accurate strengths. For this reason, we use patterns whose number of points does not exceed six for this user study. We found that 34,792 patterns satisfy this criterion. We still have too many patterns to be considered so we grouped similar patterns among them into clusters.

We utilized scikit-learn [24], the Python-based open source machine learning library, for pattern clustering. We used kmeans++ among the available algorithms. We used 29 visual features, which are extractable from a pattern itself, in Fig. 4 for clustering. Each feature has a different scale so feature values are normalized from 0 to 1 by the min/max scaler. Intersections make lines of a pattern more densely such that the pattern gets more complex. Therefore, we increased the weight of the intersection ten times because we thought that intersections have significant importance to pattern strength.

We chose representative patterns (i.e. centroids), that will be displayed to respondents in the survey, from 1,000 clusters. It is difficult for a respondent to answer all 1,000 patterns, so we need to make them answer for the proper num-

The number of points	Starting point	End point	Distance between starting/end points	Total pattern length
The number of lines (not diagonal)	Total length of lines (not diagonal)	The number of diagonal lines	Total length of diagonal lines	Total length of duplicated lines
Frequency of vectors (total 16 directions)	The number of cross points	The number of overlapped lines (not diagonal)	The number of overlapped lines (diagonal)	

Fig. 4. A total of 29 visual features used for pattern clustering. For the frequency of vectors (left bottom in the figure), each direction of vectors is an independent feature.

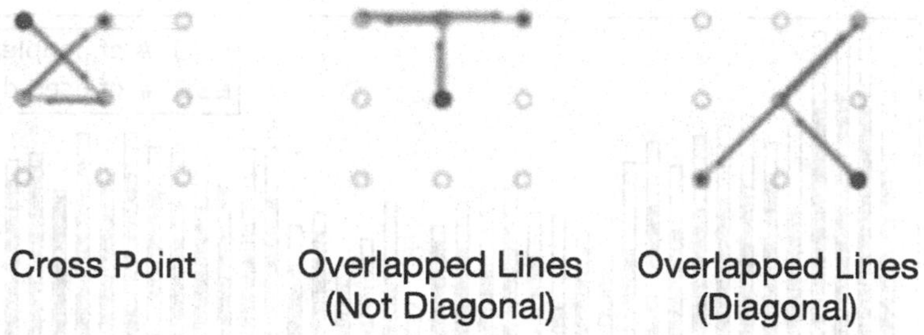

Fig. 5. Example patterns that describe an intersection (i.e., cross point) and overlapped lines

ber of patterns to obtain an objective answer. Therefore, we created 40 survey groups, limiting the number of patterns a respondent can answer to 25. There are simple (i.e. weak) patterns and complex (i.e. secure) patterns among the chosen patterns. For respondents to answer from a weak pattern to a secure pattern, we created five temporary pattern complexity groups and let the respondents answer for all complexity groups. The respondents are asked to answer five patterns for each complexity group.

We sorted 1,000 patterns based on our own criteria to determine which complexity group they belong to. We considered that any features that have a large value significantly affect the pattern strength, so we sorted the patterns in ascending order of feature values. The order of the priority of features is the number of unique directions, the sum of intersections and overlaps, the number of points, intersections, overlaps, and the total euclidean length. Patterns are firstly sorted in ascending order of the number of directions. When two patterns have the same value, the pattern with the smaller sum of intersections and overlaps, which is the next priority feature, is considered simpler than the other. We divided the sorted patterns into five groups of the same size, then assigned the first 200 patterns into complexity group 1 and the last 200 patterns into complexity group 5.

3.2 Survey Design

We have 40 survey groups through the result of clustering. 25 patterns are assigned to each survey group. We set 100 respondents for each survey group and we planned to recruit a total of 4,000 respondents. We expected that 100 samples of a pattern are enough to derive the ground-truth of the strength score. The respondents were limited to Android smartphone users located in the United States. We used Amazon Mechanical Turk where we can accommodate a lot of participants to request our surveys. The questionnaire design for each survey group is identical to each other but the only difference is in the shape of the patterns. To display the pattern shape, we printed a point sequence of a pattern as an image. One questionnaire contains two main survey sections. Both survey

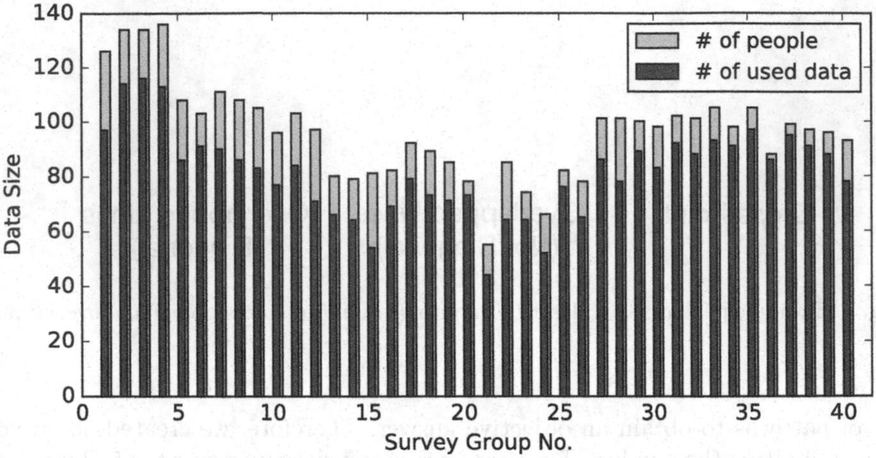

Fig. 6. The number of participants and used data size for each survey group of user study

sections are used to calculate the label of a pattern. The organization of a survey is as follows.

Survey Section 1 consists of five questions. Each question is related to one complexity group and shows five patterns in the group. Respondents should watch the patterns and answer the complexity ranking of the patterns. The ranking of patterns in one question must be different from each other. In this survey section, we want to identify the detailed differences in scores among patterns in the same complexity group.

Survey Section 2 consists of 25 questions. Each question shows a pattern and respondents should answer the objective complexity score, ranging from one to five, of the pattern. Score one means the pattern is the weakest, and score five means the pattern is the most secure. In this section, five questions are assigned for each complexity group. We want to identify the objective score in this section, that is not related to complexity groups. It is possible for the same respondent to make bias by answering the same pattern in both sections. Therefore, we deployed Section 1 patterns of the even survey group in Section 2 of the odd survey group. In the same way, we deployed Section 1 patterns of the odd survey group in Section 2 of the even survey group.

A total of 3,851 respondents were recruited as the result of 40 survey groups. A lot of respondents participated in the initial phase of survey groups, but their participation became slow such that some groups could not recruit over 100 respondents. There were a variety of the age of respondents, ranging from teenagers to 60s, and their education level. The survey group that recruited the most respondents had 136 respondents, and the group that recruited the least respondents had 55 respondents. On average, each survey group recruited 96.275 respondents.

We did not use all of the respondent's data. As the label of training patterns must be measured by the reliable labeling method, we used only the reliable ones among all data. We regarded the data of respondents who gave an answer that makes no sense as noise and rejected them. For instance, some respondents answered the most complex pattern as the simplest, and vice versa. We also rejected the data of randomly answered respondents. The number of respondents and used samples are illustrated in Fig. 6. The number of total used samples for labeling was 3,257 over 40 survey groups. The survey group with the most samples had 116 samples, and the group with the least samples had 44 samples. On average, each survey group had 81.425 samples.

3.3 Strength Score Measurement

In this step, we measure the strength score of the patterns used in the survey. Although we utilize both survey sections to determine the strength of a pattern, they have different purposes and structures. In this respect, we obtain scores of a pattern using different methods for each survey section and then combine two scores. Survey Sect. 1 results in the relative score of a pattern compared to the other four patterns in the same complexity group. For the conversion from a relative score to the absolute value, a score range of five complexity groups should be defined. Therefore, we first analyze the result of survey Sect. 2 to define their range. Fortunately, we identified that there is a statistical difference among pattern complexity groups so we can consider those groups are separated. However, we cannot assure that the grouping result is definitely objective. In the real world, the most complex pattern in the Nth group may be more complex than the simplest one in the N+1th group. For this reason, we permit overlap of the range of two complexity groups to some degree.

We calculated the objective score of Sect. 2 by averaging the responses of all respondents who answered in the same pattern. The score range of each complexity group is determined by the minimum/maximum Sect. 2 scores in the group. Same as Sect. 2, we calculated the Sect. 1 score by averaging all responses of a pattern. The scale of the Sect. 1 score changes when the relative Sect. 1 score is converted to the objective score. Given a pattern P, its complexity group G, its Sect. 2 score S^2, and its relative Sect. 1 score S^1, the equation to obtain the objective Sect. 1 score $S_P^{1'}$ is defined as

$$S_P^{1'} = \frac{(max(S_G^2) - min(S_G^2))}{4} \times (S_p^1 - 1) + min(S_G^2). \tag{6}$$

$mim(S_G^2)$ and $max(S_G^2)$ means the minimum and maximum score of G. $\frac{(max(S_G^2)-min(S_G^2))}{4}$ means the interval between two adjacent objective scores. The relative score 1 of Sect. 1 is converted to the objective score $min(S_G^2)$. The relative score 5 of Sect. 1 is converted to $max(S_G^2)$. The relative score 2, 3, and 4 is converted to objective scores based on the score interval of G. In conclusion, the equation of combining Sect. 1 score $S_P^{1'}$ and Sect. 2 score S_P^2 to measure the

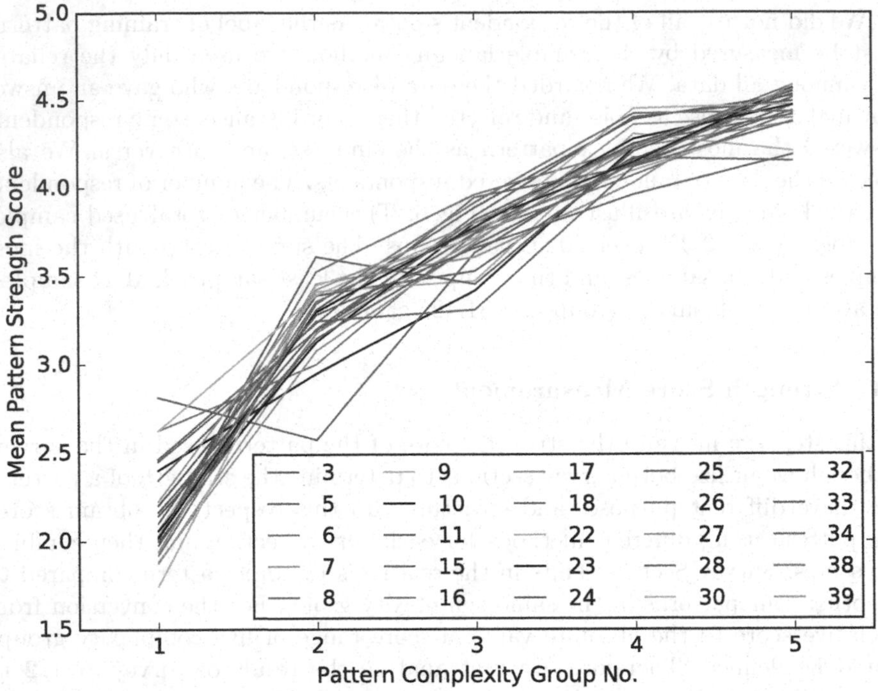

Fig. 7. Mean pattern strength score of pattern complexity groups of user study. Each color of line describes a survey group number.

pattern strength label L_p of a pattern P is defined as

$$L_P = \sqrt{(S_P^{1'})^2 + (S_P^2)^2}. \tag{7}$$

3.4 Survey Results

We make sure that the five complexity groups over 40 independent survey groups match people's perspectives and that the difference in scores between the complexity groups is significant. If our grouping contains an error, it leads to an error in the design of the questionnaire and the survey results become difficult to analyze. We confirmed this by conducting a statistical analysis based on Mixed Factorial ANOVA. We eliminated 15 survey groups during the statistical test, we only labeled the strength scores of patterns in the remaining 25 survey groups.

The normality which is the basic assumption of ANOVA analysis was established with more than 30 survey groups. The homogeneity which is another basic assumption of ANOVA analysis wasn't established since the sample sizes of some surveys were too small or too large to satisfy homogeneity of variance. The 1st, 2nd, 12th, 13th, 14th, 21st, 29th, 31st, and 35th survey groups made this problem, so we excluded those survey groups to satisfy homogeneity of variance.

Table 1. Within-Subjects effect test

Source	Type3 sum of square	Degree of freedom	Mean square	F value	P value
Pattern group	6348.427	3.681	1724.597	4661.218	.000
Pattern*Survey group	276.939	88.347	3.129	8.456	.000
Error (Pattern group)	2699.420	7295.954	.370		

Table 2. Within-Subjects contrast test

Source	Type3 sum of square	Degree of freedom	Mean square	F value	P value
Pattern group	5917.302	1	5917.302	12680.546	.000
Pattern *Survey group	71.927	24	2.997	6.422	.000
Error (Pattern group)	924.889	2982	.467		

Levene's test of equality of error variance showed no difference in all pattern groups based on median (p-value > 0.05). Meanwhile, as there was a significant mean difference among the remaining 31 survey groups (p-value < 0.025), we identified that the 4th, 19th, 20th, 36th, 37th, and 40th survey groups had a large difference in mean among groups by conducting LSD post-analysis that is sensitive to the average difference. We removed the results of these survey groups and made the remaining survey groups have no mean difference (p-value > 0.05).

Mixed Factorial ANOVA analysis suggested that the pattern complexity group did not satisfy the sphericity which is the basic assumption of Mixed Factorial ANOVA (p-value < 0.05). Nevertheless, we assumed that the sphericity was ensured because the Greenhouse-Geissser value was close to 1. Table 1 showed that the mean difference among pattern complexity groups was significant (p-value > 0.05). Also, from Table 2, which is the result of the contrast test, we found that the difference was significant in linear models (p-value < 0.05). As shown in Fig. 7, the complexity of the pattern group is upward. Therefore, through the survey result, we identified survey groups that have no difference from other groups and confirmed that there is a linear upward difference among pattern complexity groups. In addition, we also found that the pattern complexity of those patterns measured by our approach follows the visual perception of real-world users.

4 Discussion

Through the analysis of error cases of the existing pattern strength meters identified in Sect. 2, we define their two main problems. First, each of them is missing at least one visual feature which affects the safety of a pattern. The strength of text passwords can be represented by simple features. On the other hand, the strength of patterns must be represented with more complex visual features. We showed that, in Sect. 2, incorporating used and missing features of existing meters can reenact the criteria of real-world users to evaluate patterns. For more accurate metering, we can consider further features such as Markov model [32], repeating sub-patterns [27], or the angle of two lines.

The second problem of existing pattern strength meters is that they assigned wrong weights to their features due to the intervention of the author's subjective perspective. Song et al. [27] adopted a machine learning model, but its weights of features were initialized by the author. Even though the strength of our survey patterns was accurately derived, we cannot manually measure the strength of all existing patterns. Therefore, we suggest the strength of a pattern should be measured by the machine learning model alone rather than by applying someone's opinion to assign accurate weights for various features. Deep learning is a promising solution to extract latent features. DNN consists of layers with neurons. Each neuron of different layers are connected by weights and biases (i.e., parameters). The topology of DNN can be designed freely. A sophisticated DNN can solve a difficult problem such as a non-linear problem. We believe that DNN can extract the latent features from the perspective of a human.

Meanwhile, the machine learning model requires a ground-truth for training. The strength scores of 625 survey patterns are a reliable ground-truth because they were measured by multiple users and evaluated by the statistical test. If we deploy a regression model, the model learns the appropriate weights of features from the label of survey patterns. The model then calculates the strength of the remaining patterns with feature values of the patterns and weight parameters of the model.

5 Related Work

5.1 Security of Android Pattern Lock

Android pattern lock has a security issue in that users prefer to use only a few pattern spaces to draw actual patterns within the theoretical limits of pattern space [2,32]. There is a trade-off between security and usability according to the complexity of lock patterns [29]. However, users tend to select the simple pattern which is easily stolen and replicated for usability rather than security. Various types of attacks targeted to android pattern lock have been proposed, such as guessing attacks [3,10,27], shoulder surfing attacks [22,31], a smudge attacks [4], a video-based attack [41,42], and a thermal attack [1]. Such attacks have a common ground that they are performed via a leakage of pattern shapes [25], where simple patterns are more vulnerable to those attacks. In this study, we focused on guessing attack and shoulder-surfing attack which are more feasible in real-world.

Some previous works proposed some modifications of existing schemes including pattern lock to prevent the leakage of graphical passwords [11,17,38,43]. They focused on an increment of resistance against only one specific attack. However, they could not deal with other attacks they do not consider while more than two attacks that target the Android pattern lock can coexist in the real world. Moreover, in general, they could not guarantee a significant improvement in security or they reduced the usability of their schemes.

As the essential motivation of attacks on graphical authentication is to crack the shape of private passwords, the behavior-based authentication leveraged not only private passwords but also user behavior collected by embedded sensors in a smartphone to prevent those attacks [7,12,15,23,26,40]. Especially, Ku et al. [20] applied the behavioral approach to android pattern lock. They turned a private pattern into a public one by displaying the pattern to multiple users. They used only user's behavior information to distinguish users. As a consequence, they could remove existing threats on the traditional android pattern lock. However, this system is still hard to be accepted by public users who are firmly using android pattern lock which.

5.2 Password Strength Meter

One of the methods to offer a secure password authentication system for users is maintaining the current scheme and recommending for them to use secure passwords [19]. Text password policies had been studied to create passwords that are robust against guessing attack. Policies were created based on LUDS formulation that counts lower and uppercase letters, digits, and symbols while the policies depend on different websites using passwords as an authentication method [19,39]. However, the LUDS formulation had problems of usability and ineffectiveness against guessing attack [39].

To resolve this problem, studies about password meters have begun [34]. Ur et al. [33] implemented a meter that scores a password by combining various heuristics related to a neural network and created data-based text feedback. Castelluccia et al. [9] implemented an adaptive password strength meter (APSM) that estimates password strength using the Markov model. It was accurate on the guessability of a password and robustness against other attack models. Some studies proved that password meters are helpful for password creation [14,33]. Users who utilize a password meter create longer passwords than those who do not utilize the meter, and passwords created with help of the meter displaying a visual bar are slower to be cracked than those without the meter [14,34].

5.3 Pattern Strength Meter

There are five previous studies that are most relevant to our work [2,6,27,29,32]. They developed pattern strength meters that improve the security of android pattern lock by assessing the strength score of a pattern and encouraging users to use secure patterns. Uellenbeck et al. [32] utilized the Markov model to measure the guessability of a pattern. Although they did not consider shoulder-surfing attack, we included Markov probability in our feature set because we consider guessing attack as well as shoulder-surfing attack. The other four studies focused on security against shoulder-surfing attack. They established their metrics to calculate the visual complexity of a pattern. Various numerical features such as starting point, length, directions, cross points, and overlaps were included in their metrics. They have two main problems that cause inconsistency in pattern metering. First, they included only few features in their metrics so they could not fully reflect the user's visual perception. As a solution for the first problem, we combined most of their features into our feature set and also included new features (i.e., angles). Second, except Song et al. [27], they assigned the wrong weights to their features because of their subjectivity. Song et al. [27] initialized feature weights and updated their weights by regression. However, they collected a label of a pattern from a limited number of users. As a result, their labels could not represent the ground-truth and they assigned wrong weights to features as well. We collected reliable strength scores of patterns, from large-scale user survey, that can also be used for training a further strength meter as the labels.

6 Conclusion

As smartphone contains users' private data more than before and android pattern lock becomes a target of various attacks, the need for novel equipment that protects the smartphone from those attacks is continuously increasing. We proposed a novel pattern strength meter that reflects the user's visual perception, overcomes the inconsistency problem of existing pattern strength meters and eventually encourages users to create more secure patterns. Based on various visual features of a pattern, the proposed pattern strength meter can score the accurate robustness of a pattern against a guessing attack and a shoulder-surfing attack. We performed a large-scale online survey of android users. From the survey, we could obtain the ground-truth of the user's perspective about a pattern and identified that complexities of patterns measured by our features follow the visual perception of real-world users. We are considering future work on the pattern strength meter with some improvements toward the ground-truth of the strengths of all patterns.

Acknowledgements. This work was supported by the National Research Foundation of Korea (NRF) grant funded by the Korea government (MSIT) (No. NRF-2019R1A2C1088802).

References

1. Abdelrahman, Y., Khamis, M., Schneegass, S., Alt, F.: Stay Cool! Understanding thermal attacks on mobile-based user authentication. In: Conference on Human Factors in Computing Systems, pp. 3751–3763. CHI 2017, ACM, USA (2017). https://doi.org/10.1145/3025453.3025461. http://doi.acm.org/10.1145/3025453.3025461
2. Andriotis, P., Tryfonas, T., Oikonomou, G.: Complexity metrics and user strength perceptions of the pattern-lock graphical authentication method. In: Tryfonas, T., Askoxylakis, I. (eds.) HAS 2014. LNCS, vol. 8533, pp. 115–126. Springer, Cham (2014). https://doi.org/10.1007/978-3-319-07620-1_11
3. Aviv, A.J., Budzitowski, D., Kuber, R.: Is Bigger better? comparing user-generated passwords on 3x3 vs. 4x4 grid sizes for android's pattern unlock. In: Annual Computer Security Applications Conference, pp. 301–310. ACSAC 2015. ACM (2015)
4. Aviv, A.J., Gibson, K., Mossop, E., Blaze, M., Smith, J.M.: Smudge attacks on smartphone touch screens. In: Workshop on Offensive Technologies, pp. 1–7. WOOT 2010. USENIX (2010)
5. Biddle, R., Chiasson, S., Van Oorschot, P.C.: Graphical passwords: learning from the first twelve years. ACM Comput. Surv. (CSUR) **44**(4), 19 (2012)
6. Bier, A., Kapczyński, A., Sroczyński, Z.: Pattern lock evaluation framework for mobile devices: human perception of the pattern strength measure. In: Gruca, A., Czachórski, T., Harezlak, K., Kozielski, S., Piotrowska, A. (eds.) ICMMI 2017. AISC, vol. 659, pp. 33–42. Springer, Cham (2018). https://doi.org/10.1007/978-3-319-67792-7_4
7. Buriro, A., Crispo, B., DelFrari, F., Wrona, K.: Hold and sign: a novel behavioral biometrics for smartphone user authentication. In: the Security and Privacy Workshops, pp. 276–285. SPW 2016. IEEE (2016)
8. Burr, W., Dodson, D., Polk, W.: Electronic authentication guideline. Tech. rep, National Institute of Standards and Technology (2004)
9. Castelluccia, C., Dürmuth, M., Perito, D.: Adaptive password-strength meters from Markov models. In: NDSS (2012)
10. Cha, S., Kwag, S., Kim, H., Huh, J.H.: Boosting the guessing attack performance on android lock patterns with smudge attacks. In: Asia Conference on Computer and Communications Security, pp. 313–326. AsiaCCS 2017. ACM (2017)
11. Cho, G., Huh, J.H., Cho, J., Oh, S., Song, Y., Kim, H.: SysPal: system-guided pattern locks for android. In: Symposium on Security and Privacy, pp. 338–356. S & P 2017. IEEE (2017)
12. Crawford, H., Ahmadzadeh, E.: Authentication on the go: assessing the effect of movement on mobile device keystroke dynamics. In: Symposium on Usable Privacy and Security, pp. 163–173. SOUPS 2017. USENIX (2017)
13. De Carnavalet, X.D.C., Mannan, M., et al.: From very weak to very strong: analyzing password-strength meters. In: NDSS, vol.14, pp. 23–26 (2014)
14. Egelman, S., Sotirakopoulos, A., Muslukhov, I., Beznosov, K., Herley, C.: Does my password go up to eleven?: the impact of password meters on password selection. In: Proceedings of the SIGCHI Conference on Human Factors in Computing Systems, pp. 2379–2388. ACM (2013)
15. Frank, M., Biedert, R., Ma, E., Martinovic, I., Song, D.: Touchalytics: On the Applicability of Touchscreen Input as a Behavioral Biometric for Continuous Authentication. IEEE Trans. Inf. Forensics Secur. **8**(1), 136–148 (2013)
16. Harbach, M., De Luca, A., Egelman, S.: The anatomy of smartphone unlocking: a field study of android lock screens. In: Proceedings of the 2016 CHI Conference on Human Factors in Computing Systems, pp. 4806–4817. ACM (2016)

17. Higashikawa, S., Kosugi, T., Kitajima, S., Mambo, M.: Shoulder-surfing resistant authentication using pass pattern of pattern lock. IEICE Trans. Inf. Syst. **101**(1), 45–52 (2018)
18. Jermyn, I., Mayer, A., Monrose, F., Reiter, M.K., Rubin, A.D.: The design and analysis of graphical passwords. In: 8th Usenix Security Symposium. USENIX (1999)
19. Komanduri, S., Shay, R., Cranor, L.F., Herley, C., Schechter, S.: Telepathwords: preventing weak passwords by reading users' minds. In: 23rd {USENIX} Security Symposium ({USENIX} Security 14), pp. 591–606 (2014)
20. Ku, Y., Park, L.H., Shin, S., Kwon, T.: Draw it as shown: behavioral pattern lock for mobile user authentication. IEEE Access **7**, 69363–69378 (2019)
21. Kunda, D., Chishimba, M.: A survey of android mobile phone authentication schemes. Mobile Netw. Appl. **26**, 2558–2566 (2018)
22. Lashkari, A.H., Farmand, S., Zakaria, D., Bin, O., Saleh, D., et al.: shoulder surfing attack in graphical password authentication. arXiv preprint arXiv:0912.0951 (2009)
23. Li, L., Zhao, X., Xue, G.: Unobservable re-authentication for smartphones. In: Network and Distributed System Security Symposium, NDSS 2013 (2013)
24. Pedregosa, F., et al.: Scikit-learn: Machine learning in Python. J. Mach. Learn. Res. **12**, 2825–2830 (2011)
25. Rao, V.V., Chakravarthy, A.: Analysis and bypassing of pattern lock in android smartphone. In: 2016 IEEE International Conference on Computational Intelligence and Computing Research (ICCIC), pp. 1–3. IEEE (2016)
26. Sitová, Z., et al.: HMOG: new behavioral biometric features for continuous authentication of smartphone users. IEEE Trans. Inf. Forensics Secur. **11**(5), 877–892 (2016)
27. Song, Y., Cho, G., Oh, S., Kim, H., Huh, J.H.: On the effectiveness of pattern lock strength meters: measuring the strength of real world pattern locks. In: Proceedings of the 33rd Annual ACM Conference on Human Factors in Computing Systems, pp. 2343–2352. ACM (2015)
28. Standing, L., Conezio, J., Haber, R.N.: Perception and memory for pictures: single-trial learning of 2500 visual stimuli. Psychonomic Sci. **19**(2), 73–74 (1970)
29. Sun, C., Wang, Y., Zheng, J.: Dissecting pattern unlock: the effect of pattern strength meter on pattern selection. J. Inf. Secur. Appl. **19**(4–5), 308–320 (2014)
30. Tao, H., Adams, C.: Pass-go: a proposal to improve the usability of graphical passwords. IJ Netw. Secur. **7**(2), 273–292 (2008)
31. Tari, F., Ozok, A., Holden, S.H.: A Comparison of perceived and real shoulder-surfing risks between alphanumeric and graphical passwords. In: Symposium on Usable Privacy and Security, pp. 56–66. SOUPS 2006. ACM (2006)
32. Uellenbeck, S., Dürmuth, M., Wolf, C., Holz, T.: Quantifying the security of graphical passwords: the case of android unlock patterns. In: Proceedings of the 2013 ACM SIGSAC Conference on Computer & Communications Security, pp. 161–172. ACM (2013)
33. Ur, B., et al.: Design and evaluation of a data-driven password meter. In: Proceedings of the 2017 CHI Conference on Human Factors in Computing Systems, pp. 3775–3786. ACM (2017)
34. Ur, B., et al.: How does your password measure up? the effect of strength meters on password creation. In: Presented as part of the 21st {USENIX} Security Symposium ({USENIX} Security 12), pp. 65–80 (2012)
35. Van Bruggen, D.: Studying the impact of security awareness efforts on user behavior, Ph. D. thesis, University of Notre Dame (2014)

36. Von Zezschwitz, E., De Luca, A., Janssen, P., Hussmann, H.: Easy to draw, but hard to trace?: on the observability of grid-based (un) lock patterns. In: Conference on Human Factors in Computing Systems, pp. 2339–2342. CHI 2015. ACM (2015)
37. Von Zezschwitz, E., Dunphy, P., De Luca, A.: Patterns in the wild: a field study of the usability of pattern and pin-based authentication on mobile devices. In: Proceedings of the 15th International Conference on Human-computer Interaction With Mobile Devices and Services, pp. 261–270. ACM (2013)
38. Von Zezschwitz, E., Koslow, A., De Luca, A., Hussmann, H.: Making Graphic-based Authentication Secure against Smudge Attacks. In: Proceedings International Conference on Intelligent User Interfaces, pp. 277–286. IUI 2013. ACM (2013)
39. Wheeler, D.L.: zxcvbn: Low-budget password strength estimation. In: 25th {USENIX} Security Symposium ({USENIX} Security 16), pp. 157–173 (2016)
40. Xu, H., Zhou, Y., Lyu, M.R.: Towards continuous and passive authentication via touch biometrics: an experimental study on smartphones. In: Symposium on Usable Privacy and Security. SOUPS 2014, vol. 14, pp. 187–198 (2014)
41. Ye, G., et al.: Cracking android pattern lock in five attempts. In: Network and Distributed System Security Symposium, NDSS 2017 (2017)
42. Ye, G., et al.: A video-based attack for android pattern lock. ACM Trans. Privacy Secur. (TOPS) **21**(4), 19 (2018)
43. Zakaria, N.H., Griffiths, D., Brostoff, S., Yan, J.: Shoulder surfing defence for recall-based graphical passwords. In: Symposium on Usable Privacy and Security, p. 6. SOUPS 2011. ACM (2011)

Exploring Encrypted Keyboards to Defeat Client-Side Scanning in End-to-End Encryption Systems

Mashari Alatawi(✉) and Nitesh Saxena

Texas A&M University, College Station, TX 77843, USA
{mashari,nsaxena}@tamu.edu

Abstract. End-to-End Encryption (E2EE) aims to make all messages impossible to read by anyone except you and your intended recipient(s). Many well-known and widely used Instant-Messaging (IM) applications (such as Signal, WhatsApp, Apple's iMessage, and Telegram) claim to provide an E2EE functionality. However, a recent technique called client-side scanning (CSS), which could be implemented by these IM applications, makes these E2EE claims grandiose and hollow promises. The CSS is a technology that scans all sending and receiving messages from one end to the other, including text, images, audio, and video files. Some in industry and government now advocate this CSS technology to combat the growth of malicious child pornography, terrorism, and other illicit communication. Even though combating the spread of illegal and morally objectionable content is a laudable effort, it may open further backdoors that impact the user's privacy and security. Therefore, it is not end-to-end encryption when there are censorship mechanisms and backdoors in end-to-end encrypted applications. In this paper, we shed light on this hugely problematic issue by introducing an encrypted keyboard that works as a system keyboard and can be enabled on the user's phone device as a default system keyboard. Therefore, it works on every application on the user's phone device when the user is asked to enter some data. To avoid the CSS system, users can use this encrypted keyboard to encrypt and decrypt their messages locally on their phone devices when sending and receiving them via IM applications. We first design and implement our encrypted keyboard as a custom keyboard application, and then we evaluate the effectiveness and security of our encrypted keyboard. Our study results show that our encrypted keyboard can successfully encrypt and decrypt all sending and receiving messages through IM applications, and therefore, it can successfully defeat the CSS technology in end-to-end encrypted systems. We also show that our encrypted keyboard can be used to add another layer of E2EE functionality on top of the existing E2EE functionality implemented by many end-to-end encrypted applications.

Keywords: End-to-end encryption · Encrypted keyboard · IM security · Client-side scanning

S.-H. Seo and H. Seo (Eds.): ICISC 2022, LNCS 13849, pp. 100–123, 2023.
https://doi.org/10.1007/978-3-031-29371-9_6

1 Introduction

Smartphones are becoming increasingly important in today's society as more people rely on them for daily communication. Due to this widespread use of smartphones, many applications are continuously being developed to meet people's needs and facilitate their text, audio, and video communications. However, people today are concerned about the security and privacy of their communications due to government surveillance programs and law enforcement agencies, which have pushed them to worry about their online activities and sharing sensitive information. As a consequence of these concerns, many Instant-Messaging (IM) applications have been developed to address these issues by providing secure messaging solutions through a method known as End-to-End Encryption (E2EE) which protects conversations from any third party. However, these IM applications, which claim to provide an E2EE feature, are vulnerable to Man-in-the-Middle (MitM) attacks, either by compromising the service providers or by using another form of attack.

Furthermore, the E2EE functionality has been plagued by a recent attack called *client-side scanning*, *endpoint filtering*, or *local processing*, which breaks the E2EE feature claimed by IM applications [20]. In this client-side scanning (CSS) system, an end-to-end encrypted application performs a scan against any text, image, audio, or video in the message before encrypting the message and sending it to the intended recipient. If the CSS system in the end-to-end encrypted application finds any matching item, it will prevent the user from sending the message or reporting any matching item to government censorship or law enforcement authorities. It is a laudable effort when end-to-end encrypted applications tend to use the CSS technique to prevent child exploitation imagery (CEI), thwart terrorism, or provide copyright protection. However, this will lead to open another door for further censorship mechanisms and build further backdoors that impact the user's privacy. Having such CSS technology in end-to-end encrypted applications could be abused by many attackers. Thus, it might be causing more threats to the user's privacy than protecting objectionable content. People are now worried that the Meta company is listening in on their WhatsApp conversations, which are supposed to be encrypted from end to end, to show them ads that are more relevant to them [3]. Recently, the Apple company has also proposed its CSS system to fight child sexual abuse materials (CSAMs) over the Internet [28]. It uses a database of known CSAM image hashes maintained by child safety organizations and reports any matching image to law enforcement agencies. This database is nothing but a set of hashes whereby each image is converted into a different unique numeric representation. A hash function, which is a computer function that maps data of arbitrary size to fixed-size values called hash values, converts such an image into a small hash value, and only that hash value is converted into that image. Also, it has come out that the Federal Bureau of Investigation (FBI) and its international partners secretly ran an encrypted messaging app called *Anom* to spy on and collect tens of millions of messages from *Anom* users [22]. Their goal was to monitor organized crime on a global scale by looking over the shoulders of organized criminals as they talked to each other. The revealed parts of the code showed that the exchanged messages were secretly duplicated and sent to a third party (which is the FBI and its law enforcement partners) that was hidden from the users' contact lists. Therefore, from a security perspective, that is not an E2EE functionality when having these censorship mechanisms and backdoors in end-to-end encrypted applications. The end-to-end encrypted applications should provide the E2EE feature in such a way that the exchanging of messages is known only to the sender and the intended recipient. No third party, not even the service provider, should be privy to any message content exchanged between the sender and the intended recipient.

In this paper, we introduce an encrypted keyboard to address this issue facing the E2EE functionality implemented by IM applications. This encrypted keyboard is a system keyboard that the user can enable on his phone device and therefore use to encrypt or decrypt a message. Many IM applications implement the CSS system and still advertise that they provide the E2EE feature. They may argue that the CSS mechanism will just occur right before and after the encryption and decryption of messages while keeping the promise of providing the E2EE functionality to take place between two endpoints. However, this will be a hollow promise, and there will not be an E2EE anymore since the service provider is sitting on both endpoints and watching over the user's shoulder to filter all sending and receiving messages. The goal of our encrypted keyboard is to encrypt multimedia data (including text, image, audio and video) locally on the user's phone before the user puts them into any IM app (like WhatsApp) and then decrypt them when they reach the other end. Our encrypted keyboard on the user's phone device will ensure that any CSS system implemented by an IM application will be prevented. Our approach not only protects against CSS technologies but also strengthens the E2EE feature used by current end-to-end encrypted applications by implementing it twice.

Contributions: Our contributions are as follows:

- **Encrypted Keyboard for Preventing Client-Side Scanning:** We introduce our encrypted keyboard, built as a system keyboard, that can effectively prevent CSS technologies in many end-to-end encrypted systems. Our encrypted keyboard can be enabled on the user's phone device as a primary keyboard; therefore, it works on every application on the user's phone device that requires inputs from the user. We believe that our encrypted keyboard can provide a great solution to secure users' messages from filtering techniques and other surveillance mechanisms that technology companies may use.
- **Design and Implementation of the Encrypted Keyboard:** We design an encrypted keyboard that follows a similar layout to one of the most popular keyboard layouts, such as a QWERTY English keyboard. Our implementation consists of a custom keyboard application that allows users to encrypt and decrypt their data locally on their phone devices. It also allows users to display the decrypted data on the custom keyboard's interface. This custom keyboard application can be installed on the users' phones like any other application. Users can then enable this custom keyboard as the default system keyboard

on their phone devices and, therefore, can use it to encrypt data locally on their phone devices before entering them into IM applications. It also works locally on users' phones to decrypt data that were encrypted and sent to them through IM apps.

- **Evaluating the Encrypted Keyboard for Effectiveness and Security:** We evaluate the effectiveness of our encrypted keyboard by testing its ability to encrypt and decrypt the user's data. Here we focus only on the ability to defeat such a CSS system by encrypting and decrypting the user's data locally on his phone device. We show that our encrypted keyboard can not only allow users to encrypt their data locally on their phone devices but is also able to decrypt their encrypted data locally on their phone devices. We also establish that our encrypted keyboard can encrypt and decrypt the user's data before or after exchanging them through IM applications. Our results show that our encrypted keyboard can be effective against CSS technologies by encrypting and decrypting users' data locally on their phone devices. Our encrypted keyboard may also be used to enhance the security of E2EE functionality implemented by many end-to-end encrypted applications by adding an extra layer of E2EE functionality on top of their E2EE functionality.

2 Background

Secure messaging applications aim to provide private communications in such a way that sensitive information is hidden from anyone who is not a part of these communications. This can be done through an E2EE functionality, which ensures that all private messages are only viewable by the sender and the intended recipient. Due to the Snowden revelations about widespread government surveillance in 2013, people were concerned about their security and privacy in online communications [24]. Therefore, IM and Voice over IP (VoIP) applications began integrating E2EE security features to make communication more secure. Several IM and VoIP applications, including WhatsApp [11], Telegram [8], Signal [6], Viber [10], and Skype [7], have adopted the E2EE protocol to protect all private communications in recent years. Although many IM and VoIP applications claim to implement the E2EE protocol to secure private communications, they vary in their goals, ambiguous security claims, threat models, usability, and adoption properties [31,37].

Furthermore, several end-to-end encrypted applications may implement the CSS technology to scan messages just before they are sent from a sender or after they are received by an intended recipient. Using this technology, end-to-end encrypted applications aim to scan and flag any message before transmission, thereby preventing the transmission of any message or item that may contravene legal prohibitions. This could be done by adding a scanning system as a part of the end-to-end encrypted application; in other words, the scanning mechanism could be built into the end-to-end encrypted application such as Signal, WhatsApp, and many others [30]. These applications may use related software to check such a message against a database of problematic content (such as

CSAM images), extremist content, copyright infringement, rumors, or misinformation. This means that if any match has been found, it may block the message or report it to law enforcement authorities. From their perspective, these end-to-end encrypted applications claim that adding such a CSS system can protect against any illegal and morally objectionable content. However, even though this point of view is considered a well-intentioned attempt to help ban such content, it could open many doors to expanding the scope of the CSS system [14]. Backdoors and censorship in end-to-end encrypted applications will break the E2EE feature, even though these applications promise and guarantee their users that their messages will be encrypted between two endpoints and that the CSS system will only scan their messages right before encrypting them or right after decrypting them [20]. The E2EE feature should ensure that a message is only seen by the sender and the recipient. This means that no one else can read the message or scan its content to figure out what it is about.

2.1 Related Work

There has been a vast amount of work studying secure messaging solutions. Borisov et al. [16] proposed a protocol, called "off-the-record messaging", in 2004 for secure online communication. Their protocol was designed to provide perfect forward secrecy and deniable authentication for messages exchanged between two users. It was inspired by the notion of having a private conversation in a room between two people, Alice and Bob. In this scenario, Alice will be confident that no one else outside the room can hear the private conversation between her and Bob. Also, she will be confident that no one, not even Bob, can go to court and blame her by using her words against her. The OTR protocol has been plugged into different IM applications such as Pidgin [2]; however, it has not been adopted widely due to its usability shortcomings [36]. Frosch et al. [21] analyzed the Signal protocol to provide a detailed analysis of its underlying cryptographic protocol and highlight its claimed security features. Similarly, Cohn-Gordon et al. [18] performed a formal security analysis of the Signal protocol as a multi-stage authenticated key exchange protocol. They showed some standard security properties and showed that these properties meet the protocol's security claims. Further, Unger et al. [37] conducted a comprehensive academic survey on secure communication tools in terms of investigating their security, usability, and ease of adoption properties. They systematized these tools and discussed three fundamental issues of secure messaging solutions: trust establishment, conversation security, and transport privacy.

On the other hand, there is prior work that has studied the CSS technology in terms of the security and privacy issues of using this technology. Abelson et al. [14] studied the potential security and privacy risks of utilizing CSS technologies. They argued that these systems could be exploited to open many doors that may impact the privacy and security of communications, even though the initial objective of these systems is solely to prevent the spread of illegal and morally objectionable content. Then, people would struggle to stop the system's expansion and prevent its abuse. Another study by Reis et al. [29] showed that it is possible to scan messages on end-to-end encrypted systems. They explored the idea of using fact-checking to detect misinformation in WhatsApp and proposed an architecture that could be implemented by WhatsApp to detect and flag misinformation on users' devices. This might introduce new system vulnerabilities and effectively violate E2EE's privacy and security guarantees. To address this, we propose an encrypted keyboard that protects end users' devices from CSS technologies, which could be implemented by numerous end-to-end encrypted applications.

There are some encrypted keyboard applications available on the Apple App Store and the Google Play Store, such as Enigma Encryption Keyboard [5] and WhisperKeyboard [12], that aim to provide end-to-end encryption and decryption for text messages. While these applications focus only on encrypting and decrypting text messages, we consider encrypting and decrypting not only text messages but also other multimedia messages (like images, audio, and video) in our encrypted keyboard. We also consider using an automated process to decipher encrypted text messages in our encrypted keyboard, whereas these applications require a user to copy the encrypted text message to the phone's clipboard in order to decipher the encrypted text message, thereby adding extra burden to users every time they want to decode their encrypted text messages.

2.2 Threat Model

As a reminder, the goal of the E2EE functionality is to protect the contents of a message against anyone who is not involved in the private conversation. Therefore, we assume the same threat model as outlined in a comprehensive survey on secure messaging by Unger et al. [37]. The authors stated that the threat model includes the following attackers:

- **Local Adversary:** An (active/passive) attacker who can control local networks on any side of the conversation, such as owners of open wireless access points.
- **Global Adversary:** An (active/passive) attacker who can control many parts of the Internet service (e.g., powerful nation-states or large internet service providers).
- **Service Providers:** All service operators could be considered potential attackers when IM and VoIP applications utilize a centralized infrastructure for distributing public keys and storing or forwarding messages (such as a public-key directory).

However, in this work, we extend our threat model to include the endpoints of end-to-end encrypted applications, since many of these applications could use CSS technology. We assume that the CSS technology is made as a part of an end-to-end encrypted application such as Signal or WhatsApp, which means that it is built into the end-to-end encrypted application. It is possible that these applications perform pre-scanning of the users' messages by sitting on any endpoint and looking over the user's shoulder when he sends a message. Therefore, these

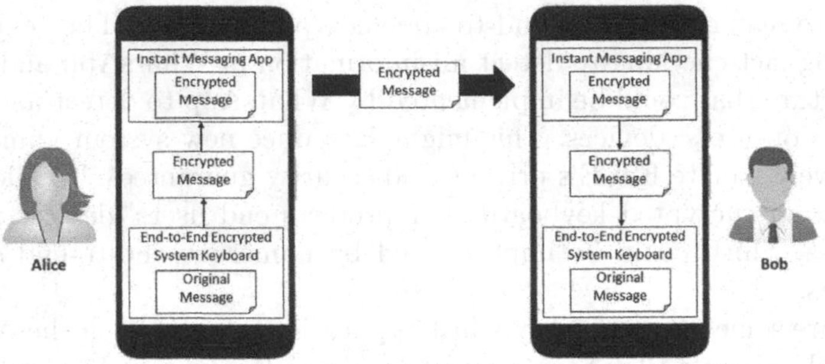

Fig. 1. The architecture of our encrypted keyboard. The sender (Alice) creates a message, encrypts it using the custom keyboard, and then sends it via an instant messaging app. At the other end, the receiver (Bob) gets the encrypted message in the instant messaging app and uses the custom keyboard to decrypt it.

applications should not be trusted by users and should be considered potential adversaries. We assume that the operating system of a phone device is healthy and secure at both endpoints. We also assume that the attacker does not have a deeper access to information on a device. In other words, the attacker only has direct access to a database and files that are associated with the end-to-end encrypted application (e.g., WhatsApp) installed on the user's phone device but does not have internal control of the other parts of the user's phone system, including other applications' data on the user's phone device.

3 Design and Implementation

We designed a system keyboard application using Android Studio to demonstrate the ability to provide a protection mechanism against CSAM image-related techniques, copyright infringement, or any material whose illegality is uncontested. In addition to the CSS technology, our encrypted keyboard aims to provide an extra layer of E2EE security over the existing E2EE functionality implemented by the end-to-end encrypted applications. Our encrypted keyboard architecture is shown in Fig. 1.

3.1 End-to-End Encrypted System Keyboard

We developed an Android application that implements the input method service needed by an Input Method Editor (IME) to get connected to the Android system. Therefore, our encrypted keyboard runs as a system keyboard and creates an input method that allows the user to enter encrypted text into any IM application. In addition to encrypting text, our encrypted keyboard allows the user to encrypt images, audio, and video files locally on his phone device before sending them via any IM application. Another key design component of our encrypted keyboard is to build it as an end-to-end encrypted system, thereby adding another layer of E2EE security on top of the current E2EE functionality implemented by many end-to-end encrypted applications. In order to enable our encrypted keyboard on the user's phone device, the user needs to install our encrypted keyboard application on his phone device and then navigate to the *Language and input* setting in his phone's system settings, where he can select this encrypted keyboard to be the default keyboard on his phone device. The user can then use this encrypted keyboard in any application that requires data entry. The user interface of our encrypted keyboard is depicted in Fig. 2.

We designed five different interfaces for our encrypted keyboard. First, we designed a user interface layout to encrypt/decrypt text and followed a similar layout for one of the most popular keyboard layouts, such as a standard QWERTY English keyboard with an additional numeric keyboard layout (see Figs. 2a and 2b). This user interface layout contains additional elements (i.e., encryption and decryption buttons, an edit text field, etc.) to implement the E2EE functionality. It also contains keys at the bottom of the interface to allow the user to navigate between other user interfaces. Then, we designed an additional three interfaces for encrypting and decrypting other multimedia elements such as images, audio, and video (see Figs. 2c, 2d, and 2e). In each user interface, there is a list that contains all the existing user's images, audio, or video files on his phone device. The user can select any image, audio, or video file from the list and display that image on the image box, play the audio file using audio control buttons, or play the video file using video control buttons on the current keyboard interface. Moreover, in the audio keyboard layout, we added audio recording buttons to allow the user to record voice memos. We put the encryption and decryption buttons at the bottom of these new user interfaces so that the user can encrypt and decrypt his multimedia data on his phone.

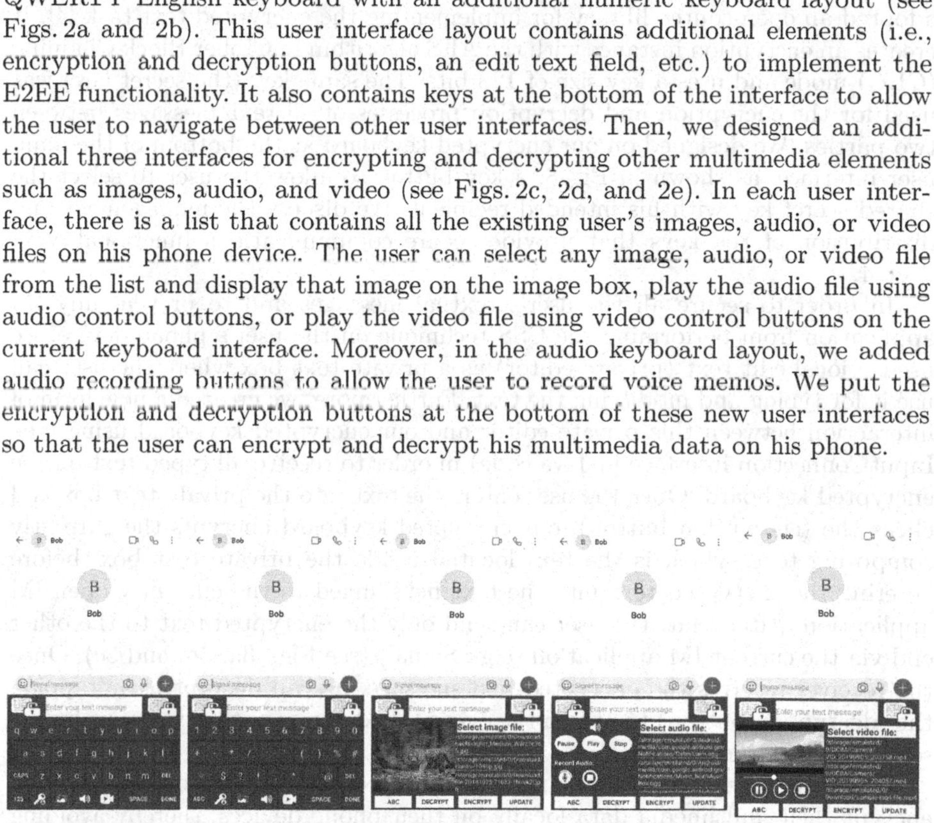

(a) QWERTY keyboard layout (b) Numeric keyboard layout (c) Image keyboard layout (d) Audio keyboard layout (e) Video keyboard layout

Fig. 2. User interface of our encrypted keyboard

3.2 Strong Encryption Algorithm

In order to provide confidentiality to the data, we used the Advanced Encryption Standard (AES) to encrypt and decrypt multimedia data. It is one of the most powerful encryption algorithms that is widely used in many different technology fields and computer systems. It is also one of the most efficient encryption algorithms, and it is considered to be fast and flexible, thereby ensuring the security of data and making it trustworthy for users [13]. AES is one of the symmetric encryption algorithms where both the sender and the receiver have the same key to encrypt and decrypt data. It uses three different key sizes, such as 128, 192, and 256 bits, with a 128-bit block cipher. The details of the encryption and decryption processes of the AES algorithm can be found in [13,19,26]. We adopted an open-source library for implementing the encrypted text task [4]. It creates an encryption instance with the AES algorithm in Cipher Block Chaining (CBC) mode and uses a key size of 128 bits. The same key (the secret key) was used for the encryption and decryption processes of all text messages between two parties. We designed on our encrypted keyboard at the bottom of the main user interface, as shown in Fig. 8, a key button to allow the user to select the shared secret key with his intended recipient. We discuss the management and distribution of the keys that provide secure communications functionality in Sect. 4.

In order to secure all the user's textual messages and to prevent any IM application from performing the CSS technique on the user's phone device, we used a local edit text (private editor) as a private text box where the user can use it for typing and modifying the text. Furthermore, we created a new form of interaction between this private editor and our encrypted keyboard using (the InputConnection interface in Java code) in order to receive all typed text on the encrypted keyboard. Once the user enters the text into the private text box and clicks the (encryption button), our encrypted keyboard encrypts the currently composing text, which is the text located inside the private text box, before entering the encrypted text into the text field linked to the currently open IM application. After that, the user can send only the encrypted text to the other end via the current IM application (e.g., Signal) (see Figs. 3a, 3b, and 3c). Once the receiver receives the encrypted text message, he can decrypt it by tapping the (decryption button) to obtain the original text message that was sent by the sender (see Fig. 3d).

The basic idea underlying using our encrypted keyboard is to allow users to encrypt their multimedia data locally on their phone devices, thereby avoiding any implementation of CSS technologies. Furthermore, we implement an E2EE feature for messages sent from one party of the private conversation to the other. This E2EE feature could be used to enhance the security against attackers listening onto the channel when users exchange their messages over an end-to-end encrypted application (e.g., WhatsApp) since users can encrypt their multimedia data using our encrypted keyboard before inserting them into the end-to-end encrypted application, which will then encrypt them once again using its E2EE functionality. Our encrypted keyboard can guarantee that no messages will be revealed to those attackers even if they can somehow compromise the encrypted messages transmitted by any end-to-end encrypted application. Therefore, when our encrypted keyboard is used in an IM application that also has an E2EE feature, it will add an extra layer of E2EE security.

(a) Alice composes a text for Bob using the private text box.

(b) Alice encrypts her text message to Bob by tapping the encryption key located at the top right corner of the encrypted keyboard.

(c) Alice sends her encrypted text message to Bob.

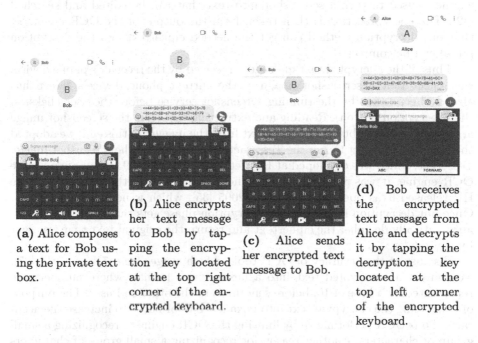

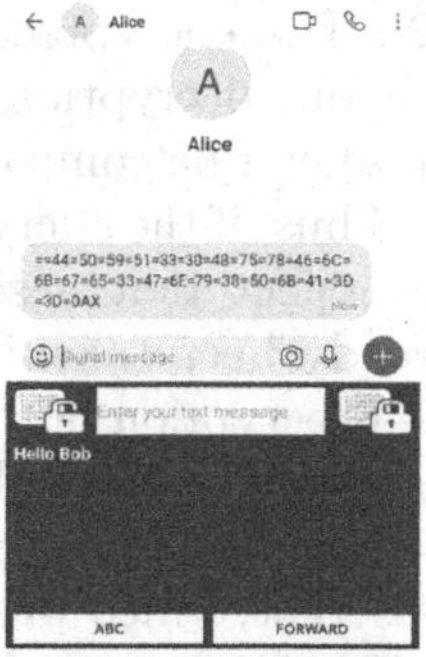

(d) Bob receives the encrypted text message from Alice and decrypts it by tapping the decryption key located at the top left corner of the encrypted keyboard.

Fig. 3. Encryption and decryption of the text message using our encrypted keyboard when the Signal application is used to send and receive the encrypted text message exchanged between Alice and Bob.

3.3 Automated Decryption Process

In our study, we considered the usability aspect in terms of automating the decryption process in order to make it easier to decrypt any encrypted text on the user's phone device. We aim to reduce the burden on the user when he unscrambles encrypted text messages on his phone device. SMASheD [25] utilizes the Android Debug Bridge (ADB) functionality to have access to phone device resources/services. Therefore, we adapted the SMASheD server and pushed it to the phone device to run a screenshot service every second in the background and to store the screenshot image in a file. Our implementation does not store all these screenshot images. Instead, this image file will be overwritten every time a screenshot image is taken, thereby avoiding the consumption of too many resources. Even though many real-world applications can take screenshots and are used daily, our encrypted keyboard is a more trustworthy application because it works as a system keyboard and does not send any images outside the user's phone device during the actual implementation. The screenshot service will keep running in the background until the user decides to stop it or the phone device is switched off. Our goal in running this screenshot service on a phone device is to get the content displayed in the foreground of a phone device's screen to use as an input file for an Optical Character Recognition (OCR) engine. The OCR engine is used to turn a screenshot into text that can be edited and searched [32]. The encrypted text is then taken from the output of the OCR engine so that our decryption method can get the needed ciphertext and the decryption phase can be completed.

Thus, if the encrypted text message is received by the receiver's phone device, we expect that a screenshot image of the current phone device's screen has already been taken by the running screenshot service before the user clicks on the (decryption button). Reading and extracting text from the screenshot image are then needed to obtain the ciphertext from the image. To this end, we adopted the (tess-two) project to run the Tesseract OCR engine on the screenshot image. Tesseract, which was developed at HP between 1984 and 1994, is an open-source OCR engine. It was adjusted and enhanced in 1995 for better accuracy before HP released it as open source in late 2005 [35], which is now available at [9]. Once our decryption method in the decryption phase gets the ciphertext, it will automatically decipher the ciphertext and return the original text that was sent by the sender.

Because of the accuracy of OCR tools, which ranges from 71% to 98% [27], we convert an encrypted text into a hexadecimal format, where numbers are represented by a base of 16, before sending it to the other end user. The purpose of converting the encrypted text into hexadecimal format is to increase the accuracy of our OCR performance by limiting the OCR engine to recognizing a small group of characters. Another reason for recognizing a small group of characters is to avoid any noisy and garbled results that may occur if the OCR engine reads all possible characters. Therefore, we set up a white list for our OCR engine that contains hexadecimal symbols from 0 to 9, corresponding to number values from 0 to 9, and A to F, corresponding to number values from 10 to 15. By converting an encrypted text into a hexadecimal format, we believe that any accuracy issue that might result from our OCR performance can be surmounted.

3.4 Multimedia Support

Not only can our encrypted keyboard encrypt and decrypt text messages, but it can also encrypt and decrypt multimedia messages like images, audio, and video. Figure 4 shows how our encrypted keyboard is used to encrypt and decrypt an image file when an instant messaging app like Signal is used to send and receive the encrypted image file between two end users. The same steps, as shown in Fig. 4, can be done if we want to encrypt and decrypt other multimedia elements (such as audio and video) using the additional user interfaces of our encrypted keyboard associated with audio and video tasks (see Figs. 2d and 2e).

(a) Alice encrypts the image file locally on her phone device by tapping the ENCRYPT button located at the bottom of the encrypted keyboard.

(b) Alice sends the encrypted image file to Bob.

(c) Bob receives the encrypted image file from Alice.

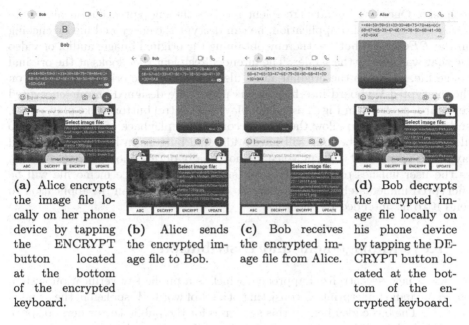

(d) Bob decrypts the encrypted image file locally on his phone device by tapping the DECRYPT button located at the bottom of the encrypted keyboard.

Fig. 4. Encryption and decryption of the image file using our encrypted keyboard when the Signal application is used to send and receive the image file exchanged between Alice and Bob.

Our encrypted keyboard can encrypt and decrypt multimedia data locally on the user's phone device. As shown in Fig. 2a, for the purpose of encrypting and decrypting multimedia elements locally on the user's phone device, the main user interface of our encrypted keyboard has three different keys at the bottom of the interface that allow a user to easily navigate between other interfaces for image, audio, and video tasks. We designed new custom layouts as additional layouts to our main encrypted keyboard layout that allow a user to encrypt and decrypt his multimedia data locally on his phone device (see Figs. 2c, 2d, and 2e). Therefore, the user can prevent any IM application from performing the CSS technique on his phone device, thereby securing all his multimedia messages that may be scanned by an IM application. In our encrypted keyboard application, the AES algorithm in CBC mode was used to encrypt and decrypt multimedia data. We used the same key for the encryption and decryption processes of all multimedia messages that were sent between two end users. The user needs to click on the image, audio, or video key button at the bottom of the main user interface of our encrypted keyboard in order to navigate to the related keyboard interface, and therefore can view an exhaustive list of all existing images, audio, or video files on his phone device. Then, from the long list displayed on his current keyboard interface, he can choose an existing image, audio, or video file and encrypt it by clicking the *ENCRYPT* button. After that, the user can send the encrypted file through an IM application (such as Signal) to the intended recipient. Once the intended recipient receives the encrypted file on his phone device through the IM application, he can decrypt the encrypted file by clicking on the *DECRYPT* button, thereby obtaining the original image, audio, or video file that was sent by the sender. The intended recipient then looks at the original image file, listens to the original audio file, or watches the original video file on the encrypted keyboard interface on his phone. We designed on our encrypted keyboard, as shown in Figs. 2d and 2e, playback control buttons (like play, pause, and stop) in order to allow the user to control the playback of audio and video files. Furthermore, the user will have additional buttons in his audio keyboard layout to record and encrypt voice memos locally on his phone device. As soon as the user finishes recording his voice memo file, the voice memo file will be encrypted immediately, and therefore he can insert it into an IM application to send it to his intended recipient.

4 Keys Management and Distribution

We use a new decentralized approach, which is a public key verification system based on audio fingerprints R consisting of a set of words W spoken in the owner's voice V. The basic idea behind this system is for the public key owners to speak the fingerprint of their static/permanent public keys, and for the receivers to authenticate the validity of the public key by verifying the audio fingerprint. To bind the public key to the owners, the audio fingerprint should be verified at two levels: (1) data integrity and (2) voice integrity. To verify that the fingerprint is valid, receivers should verify that the fingerprint matches the hash of the public key (i.e., data integrity) and that the fingerprint is spoken by the owner (i.e., voice integrity). The integrity of data in this system is verified by an *automatic fingerprint comparison* tool that is built on top of speech transcription [34]. This tool automatically converts the audio fingerprint to text and compares it to the hash of the received public key. The attacker who injects his public key should also inject the fingerprint by generating a matching fingerprint in the user's voice. If the attacker only injects the public key but does not change the fingerprint, the receiver can detect the attack. Also, if the attacker speaks his fingerprint, the receiver can detect the attack since the voice speaking the fingerprint does not match the voice of the owner, even though the fingerprint may match the hash of the public key. This system consists of the following components, as depicted in Fig. 5.

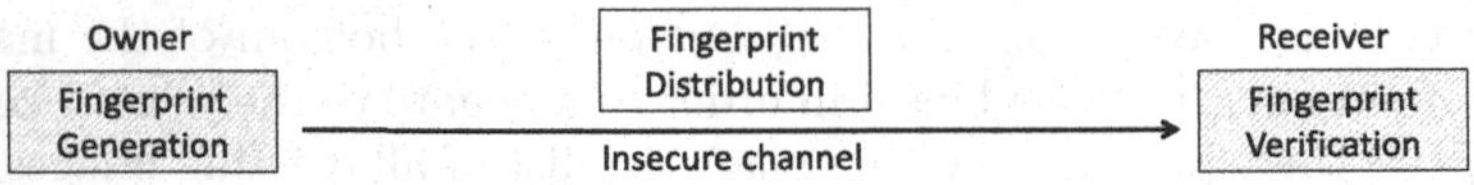

Fig. 5. The main components of keys distribution approach. The fingerprint distribution channel is insecure.

(1) **Fingerprint Generation and Recitation:** Figure 6 shows the process of generating the fingerprint in this system. Here, the hash of the public key is mapped into PGP words [23], following the approach used by ZRTP [1]. The output of the SHA-256 hash is fully mapped to the fingerprint without truncation, resulting in 32 PGP words W. The PGP word list consists of two sets of 256 phonetically distinct words, such that they have an *optimum distinction.* To encode a bit string, each byte is mapped into one word from one of the odd and even word sets. Since the even and odd lists are different, human errors in duplicate reading, swapping words, and omission of words are detected. The user generates the audio fingerprint R by speaking and recording W in their own voice characterized by V. Since this task takes place only once, the user can spend sufficient effort on preparing acceptably high-quality audio, perhaps using home recording devices in a quiet place. The user can also check (pre-evaluate) the results of the transcription to make sure that R would be perceived well at the receiver's side. Any errors during this phase may be corrected by the user by re-recording the fingerprint.

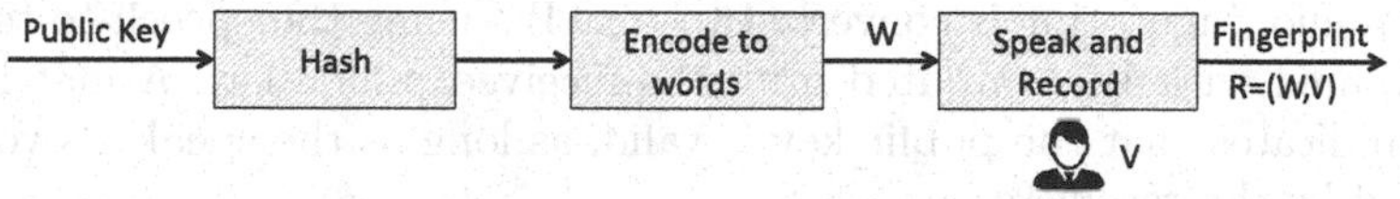

Fig. 6. Generating and reciting the audio fingerprint from the public key

(2) **Fingerprint Distribution:** This new approach is a distributed public key verification system and does not require imposing trust onto centralized third parties (e.g., a certificate authority) and does not require any trusted auxiliary channel (e.g., out-of-band secure channels). It uses the human voice to authenticate users and binds the public keys to owners' identities. Therefore, in this system, the user can share the fingerprint along with the public key on any public platform accessible by the other parties.

(3) **Fingerprint Verification:** Figure 7 shows the process of verifying the fingerprint in this system. This step represents the core novel component of this system, which involves building a fingerprint comparison tool. This tool was built by carefully adapting speaker-independent speech-to-text transcription engines. To bind the public keys to the owners, we rely on the users to verify the public key owners' voice V. The users should have prior knowledge of each other's voices.

This system does not require imposing trust on third parties or a distributed network of trusted users, unlike prior models such as a Public Key Infrastructure (PKI) and web of trust. Each user simply generates a key fingerprint by computing the hash of the public key mapped into PGP words and key owners speak, record, and share the fingerprint with peers (via any out-of-band channel) who can validate the binding between the public key and its owner by:

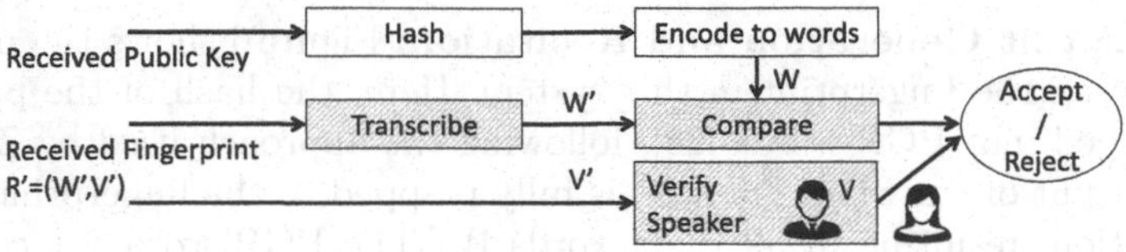

Fig. 7. Verifying the received fingerprint

(1) automatically converting the vocalized fingerprint to the textual fingerprint using speech-to-text technology and comparing it with the hash of the public key, and (2) manually verifying that the voice speaking the vocalized fingerprint corresponds to the public key owner. Therefore, the automated vocalized fingerprint comparison tool was built using speech recognition technology. This new system can benefit from any off-the-shelf transcriber (e.g., Google Cloud Speech-to-Text). The fingerprint comparison tool receives the public key and the audio fingerprint R from the owner. The tool generates the hash of the public key and maps it to the words W, the same as the fingerprint generation tool. The received audio fingerprint is converted to text W' using the speech-to-text tool and compared with W computed from the received public key. A matching W and W' indicates that the public key is valid, as long as the speaker's voice can be verified by the receivers.

Also, as a part of the fingerprint verification process in this system, receivers should identify the public key owners by their voice, a process that the system refers to as speaker verification. Speaker verification is based on the uniqueness of the sound waves produced by a voice. Since the sound waves reflect the vibrations of air, and such vibrations are dependent on the shape of the oral and nasal cavities above the larynx, each individual's voice should produce a different signal. Besides, each person has a different speech behavioral pattern (e.g., speaking style and accent) that gives each person a unique acoustic feature set, reflecting the body anatomy and speaking style. Thus, the human can identify a particular speaker's voice by recognizing the voice features and behavioral patterns. We assume that users know each other in advance and can recognize each other's voices (the same assumption applies to all other applications that rely on audio fingerprints). Possibly, if they do not have prior knowledge of the speaker's voice, they can make a phone call or listen to publicly available voice samples of the owner (e.g., published on social media). Similar approaches, such as the web of trust, could also be used, in which unknown people would be vouched for by other trusted users. In our scenario, this implies that if a receiver named Bob does not know the voice of a user named Alice, he can rely on some trusted mutual friends or trusted introducers who do know Alice. Thus, users would be able to agree on a shared symmetric key to be used for the encryption/decryption processes of all their textual and multimedia messages. This shared symmetric key can be saved on our encrypted keyboard application and used for encryption and decryption when a user wants to communicate securely with an intended recipient (see Fig. 8).

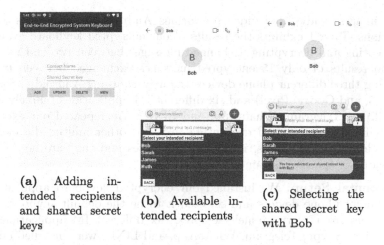

(a) Adding intended recipients and shared secret keys

(b) Available intended recipients

(c) Selecting the shared secret key with Bob

Fig. 8. User interface of using shared secret key

In this system, we assume a model similar to other decentralized trust models for public key verification. In this model, the end users handle the management and distribution of the keys that provide secure communications functionality such as E2EE, decryption, signing, and verification. The end nodes, their devices, and the incorporated tools (including the transcriber, whether performed by a remote service or a localized engine residing on the device) are assumed to be trusted. However, the channel over which the key is distributed may be controlled by the attacker. An attacker can perform a MitM attack to inspect and alter the public key. For example, the attacker can alter an email containing the user's public key to inject an invalid key, or the attacker can compromise the service that holds the public keys and change them as he wishes.

However, we assume that the attacker does not have full control over the distributed fingerprint. That is, the attacker cannot insert the fingerprint of his public key while speaking it in the user's voice. This assumption comes from the fact that every human has a unique voice. We note that the attacker may be able to generate fake fingerprints in the user's voice by synthesizing or replicating the victim's voice. For example, the attacker may collect the isolated words available in the dictionary in the user's voice and merge them to create a fingerprint in the user's voice. However, if the dictionary consists of rarely used words (or fake words) such as PGP words, the attacker perhaps would not be able to create the synthesized voice, as argued in [15], in contrast to a dictionary of frequently used ones such as digits. Moreover, we will discuss voice authentication and the prevention of voice replication and synthesis attacks in Sect. 6.

5 Evaluation

In this section, we will evaluate the effectiveness of our encrypted keyboard application for encrypting and decrypting text and other multimedia elements such as images, audio, and video on various Android phone devices and IM applications. Table 1 exhibits the results of our encrypted keyboard evaluation for encrypting and decrypting exchanged messages between two end users. We show the results of only 15 encrypted messages exchanged between two end users using three different phone devices (namely Samsung Android 4, Samsung Android 5, and Google Pixel) and six different IM applications (namely Signal, Viber, Skype, Telegram, WhatsApp, and LINE). We repeated our exchanged messages for encrypting and decrypting text and other multimedia elements, which yielded similar results, in 60 different cases and they are not reported here because of space constraints.

Experimental Setup: We installed our encrypted keyboard application on three different phone devices and selected it to be the default keyboard on all three devices from every phone's settings. Six different IM applications (i.e., Signal, Viber, Skype, Telegram, WhatsApp, and LINE) were installed on these phone devices to use them for exchanging encrypted textual messages as well as exchanging other encrypted multimedia messages. We created several user accounts on these installed IM applications to utilize them in our experiment. By using these user accounts, each phone device was used either to encrypt textual messages (or other multimedia messages) on one end or to receive the encrypted textual messages (or the encrypted multimedia messages) and decipher them at the other end. We established many communication channels between any two phone devices used in our experiment to evaluate the efficiency of our encrypted keyboard application for encrypting and decrypting textual messages or other multimedia messages. We used our encrypted keyboard enabled on both phone devices to encrypt and decrypt textual messages or other multimedia messages. We also used the installed IM applications on both phone devices to exchange encrypted textual messages (or encrypted multimedia messages) between two end users. We utilized the ADB functionality and the SMASheD platform to push a native service into the */data/local/tmp/* directory on each phone device. By using that, we are running the native service in the background for taking a screenshot of the contents of a phone device's screen every second to make sure that the screenshot image is always obtainable and can be used by the OCR engine as an input file. To ensure the perfect performance of the OCR engine on each phone device, a trained data file for the English language was installed simultaneously with the encrypted keyboard application installation on each phone device.

Observations: To measure the effectiveness of our encrypted keyboard application, we can consider the capability of our encrypted keyboard in terms of encrypting a text, image, audio, or video file on one end and deciphering it on the other end. To observe the ability to encrypt and decrypt textual messages using our encrypted keyboard, we typed a text message using our encrypted keyboard and encrypted it on one phone device (the sender). Then, we sent the encrypted textual message via an IM application (i.e., Signal, Viber, or Skype) to the other phone device (the receiver). Using our encrypted keyboard on the receiver's phone device, we deciphered the encrypted textual message and obtained the plaintext of the original textual message. In addition, to test the effectiveness of our encrypted keyboard application in encrypting and decrypting other multimedia messages, we chose (an image, audio, or video file) and encrypted it on one phone device (the sender). Then, we sent (the encrypted file) over an IM application (i.e., Signal, Viber, Skype, Telegram, WhatsApp, or LINE) to the other phone device (the receiver). By using our encrypted keyboard on the receiver's phone device, we deciphered (the encrypted file) and therefore obtained (the original image, audio, or video file). Subsequently, we displayed the original image file, played the original audio file, or played the original video file on the receiver's phone screen. We repeated these processes (encrypting and decrypting text, images, audio, and video files) many times using three different phone devices and six different IM applications (i.e., Signal, Viber, Skype, Telegram, WhatsApp, and LINE). Thus, we observed the capability of our encrypted keyboard to perform both encryption and decryption of textual messages as well as other multimedia messages on these phone devices and IM applications. The results of the sending and receiving of encrypted textual messages as well as other multimedia messages among three different phone devices are shown in Table 1. A total of six different instant messaging applications were utilized to send and receive encrypted textual messages and other multimedia messages. The results show that our encrypted keyboard can encrypt text, images, audio, and video files on one phone device and decipher them on the other phone device. Therefore, our encrypted keyboard application can easily encrypt and decrypt any text, image, audio, or video file that two end users exchange. This protects the user's data from any CSS technique that an IM application could use.

6 Discussion and Future Work

6.1 Strengths and Limitations of Our Study

We believe that our study has several strengths. Our encrypted keyboard covers all users' messages (textual and multimedia messages) just like in day-to-day messaging system use. This is in contrast to current encrypted keyboard applications (such as Enigma Encryption Keyboard and WhisperKeyboard), which only allow the user to encrypt and decrypt textual messages. Also, our encrypted keyboard automates the decryption process of textual messages, whereas, in current encrypted keyboard applications (such as Enigma Encryption Keyboard and WhisperKeyboard), the user needs to copy and paste the text every time he wants to decrypt such a textual message, which may place a very heavy burden on the user. By using the SMASheD server and an OCR mechanism in the decryption process, it helps to automate the text decryption on our encrypted keyboard and, therefore, unburdens the human user from copying and pasting text on the system keyboard. In the decryption process, we also convert the encrypted text into a hexadecimal format to increase the accuracy of the OCR performance. As a rule of thumb, the accuracy of OCR tools can fluctuate every time the OCR engine reads any selected text, recognizing all possible text characters. Therefore, limiting the number of characters to a small group of characters

Table 1. Evaluation results of our encrypted keyboard for encrypting and decrypting exchanged messages

Message no.	Message type	Encryption status	Sender device	Messaging application medium	Receiver device	Accuracy of OCR engine	Decryption status
1	Text	Successful	Samsung Android 4	Signal	Samsung Android 5	100%	Successful
2	Text	Successful	Google Pixel	Viber	Samsung Android 4	100%	Successful
3	Text	Successful	Samsung Android 5	Skype	Google Pixel	100%	Successful
4	Image	Successful	Google Pixel	Telegram	Samsung Android 5	N/A	Successful
5	Image	Successful	Samsung Android 5	WhatsApp	Samsung Android 4	N/A	Successful
6	Image	Successful	Samsung Android 4	Signal	Google Pixel	N/A	Successful
7	Audio	Successful	Samsung Android 5	LINE	Samsung Android 4	N/A	Successful
8	Audio	Successful	Samsung Android 4	Viber	Google Pixel	N/A	Successful
9	Audio	Successful	Google Pixel	Skype	Samsung Android 5	N/A	Successful
10	Voice memo	Successful	Samsung Android 4	Telegram	Samsung Android 5	N/A	Successful
11	Voice memo	Successful	Google Pixel	WhatsApp	Samsung Android 4	N/A	Successful
12	Voice memo	Successful	Samsung Android 5	Signal	Google Pixel	N/A	Successful
13	Video	Successful	Google Pixel	LINE	Samsung Android 5	N/A	Successful
14	Video	Successful	Samsung Android 5	Viber	Samsung Android 4	N/A	Successful
15	Video	Successful	Samsung Android 4	Skype	Google Pixel	N/A	Successful

like the hexadecimal symbols will improve the accuracy of OCR performance. As shown in Table 1, we achieved 100% accuracy on the OCR performance by converting the encrypted text into a hexadecimal format. We believe that recognizing a small group of characters by the OCR engine is better than recognizing all possible text characters if we consider the accuracy of OCR tools, which fluctuates from 71% to 98% [27]. It helped us reach 100% accuracy in the OCR performance because we recognized only hexadecimal symbols from 0 to 9, and A to F. To automate our decryption process in textual messaging, our decryption process has to perform two tasks. The first task is to run the OCR engine on a screenshot image to obtain an editable and searchable text. Once the text is extracted from the screenshot image, the second task in our decryption process is performed by reading and extracting an encrypted text to decipher it by using the AES algorithm with the same secret key.

In our study, we focused on studying secure messaging by designing an encrypted keyboard that runs on Android phone devices as a system keyboard. As indicated in Sect. 5, we conducted our experiments using only Android phones available in our laboratory. We utilized two older versions and one more recent one. However, we believe that our encrypted keyboard is compatible with every Android phone device, regardless of its version, as it is an Android app that was designed as a system keyboard app. Users can type text on this encrypted keyboard and encrypt it before putting it into an instant messaging application like WhatsApp, Signal, or Viber. Users can then use the IM application to send the encrypted text message to the other intended parties. Likewise, they can use this encrypted keyboard to encrypt other multimedia elements such as images, audio, and video. The main objective of this encrypted keyboard is to prevent any IM application from performing a CSS technique and thereby provide protection for all messages exchanged between end users, including text, images, audio, and video files. By using our encrypted keyboard to encrypt multimedia data before inserting it into instant messaging applications, users can avoid the CSS technique that may be performed by these instant messaging applications when they exchange their messages via these applications. Our encrypted keyboard can also be used to decipher the encrypted multimedia data once the intended recipients receive it in these IM applications. Therefore, our study showed that our encrypted keyboard is a practical and feasible approach that can effectively overcome the CSS technique that could be performed by an IM application (e.g., WhatsApp, Signal, or Viber). However, due to an automated decryption process that relies heavily on a screenshot image of the current phone's screen, we could not have control over the length of the text, especially in long text messages. The phone's screen size (viewport size) is an important factor that needs to be taken into consideration and may affect the process of decrypting encrypted textual messages. Thus, our encrypted keyboard decrypts the encrypted text showing on the current phone's screen, which is based on various screen sizes (viewport sizes) from one phone to another. Further studies should be conducted to cover any length of the text that may exceed the phone's screen size (viewport size) during the automated decryption process of decrypting encrypted textual messages.

6.2 Voice Reordering Attacks

In [33], a "voice reordering" attack was introduced against end-to-end short-spoken text authenticated systems. In the reordering attack, the attacker collects isolated units of the fingerprint (e.g., words or digits) and combines them to create new fingerprints not spoken before. We argue that a reordering attack would be very difficult to pursue if the fingerprint dictionary is sufficiently large. We assume that the dictionary consists of 256 words for even positions and 256 words for odd positions. The easiest attack is to assume that the attacker has obtained "all the words" in the dictionary and has built a data set to create "any desired fingerprint" in the user's voice by mixing and matching the words from this data set. To collect all the words, we should assume that the user has at least 16 ($= 512/32$) unique public keys with no repetitive words in any of them, i.e., the user has 16 public keys mapping to 16 fingerprints $R_i = (W_i, V_i), i \in \{1, ..., 16\}$ (each W_i is a sequence of 32 words w_i, 16 words in even and 16 words in odd positions) such that $\forall\ 0 < i, j \leq 32, w_i = w_j \implies i = j$. The probability of the user having 16 different fingerprints with absolutely no repetitive words (in each fingerprint, and among all fingerprints) can be calculated as the following (multiplying the probability of each textual fingerprint W_i not containing any of the dictionary words used in the $i-1$ preceding fingerprints):

$$
\begin{aligned}
P1 = \frac{(256-0)^{32}}{256^{32}} \times \frac{(256-16)^{32}}{256^{32}} \times \frac{(256-32)^{32}}{256^{32}} \cdots \\
\times \frac{(256-240)^{32}}{256^{32}} = \frac{15!}{16^{16}} = 7.09E-8
\end{aligned}
\qquad (1)
$$

As can be seen, the probability of the attacker collecting all the words in the dictionary (even if we generously assume that the user has 16 different public keys) is very low.

On the other end of this statistic, we can assume that the user has only 1 fingerprint (i.e., 1 public key). Therefore, the attacker has collected a total of 16 words (assuming that the fingerprint does not contain any duplicate words) from each of the even and odd sets. The attacker tries to create a public key such that the words in the attacker's fingerprint match the words used in the user's fingerprint (but perhaps not in the same order). The probability of succeeding in this attack is:

$$P2 = \frac{16^{16}}{256^{32}} = \frac{1}{16^{16}} = 5.42E - 20 \tag{2}$$

Note that in any other situation (i.e., the user having more than 1 and less than 16 unique fingerprints), the attacker has access to only a subset of the dictionary in the user's voice. Therefore, $P3$, which is the probability of creating a fingerprint containing only the spoken words, falls between $P1$ and $P2$, i.e., $P1 < P3 < P2$. Note that increasing the size of the dictionary can also help to reduce the chance of a reordering attack. Finally, if the attacker creates a fingerprint by mixing some of the words from the spoken data set and replacing the rest with synthesized voices, such inconsistency and the use of synthesized voices should be detected (since we expect the user to listen to the audio samples and verify the speaker).

6.3 Attacks on Speech Recognition

A few types of attacks against transcription technology have been proposed recently [17,38]. These attacks generate *audible* samples that are not intelligible to the human user but interpretable by the transcriber. Although these types of attacks may be used against virtual personal assistant applications to run the attacker's commands, we assume that in the public key verification system, the user who listens to the vocalized fingerprint to verify the speaker can detect such suspiciously malformed audible/robotic audio samples and would notice if the content of the vocalized fingerprint is completely different from the fingerprint (e.g., music being played in the background). Inaudible attacks on speech transcription, such as the one proposed in [39], require physical access to the speech transcription device. Besides, such an approach should have knowledge of the hardware characteristics of the speech transcription device and therefore is not relevant to this system and cannot compromise the security of online transcription systems.

7 Conclusions

In this paper, we introduce an encrypted keyboard built as a system keyboard. Our encrypted keyboard can be enabled by users on their phone devices as a default system keyboard in order to use it on every application that prompts users to enter some data. Our encrypted keyboard can offer protection against CSS technologies that might be implemented by a vast number of IM applications. Besides the protection against CSS technologies, our encrypted keyboard can be used to strengthen security against MitM attackers by adding an extra E2EE layer on top of the current E2EE functionality implemented by many end-to-end encrypted applications. Users can use our encrypted keyboard to encrypt their multimedia data locally on their phone devices before exchanging it over an IM application. They can also use our encrypted keyboard to decipher all encrypted multimedia data received from an IM application locally on their phone devices. Our work shows that our encrypted keyboard can successfully encrypt and decrypt all sending and receiving messages through IM applications. Therefore, our encrypted keyboard can prevent any CSS system that might be implemented by an IM application. It can also be used to reinforce the security of E2EE functionality against MitM attacks by providing another E2EE functionality in addition to the current E2EE feature provided by end-to-end encrypted applications. Therefore, users can have a duplicate encryption scheme when they use our encrypted keyboard to encrypt their messages and then exchange them via end-to-end encrypted applications. This duplicate encryption scheme gives our encrypted keyboard a strong defense mechanism against MitM attackers, even if they can somehow compromise the E2EE functionality provided by end-to-end encrypted applications.

Acknowledgment. The authors would like to thank Malihch Shirvanian who contributed to the audio fingerprinting approach.

References

1. The Zfone Project - Frequently Asked Questions (2006). http://zfoneproject.com/faq.html
2. Pidgin (2020). https://pidgin.im/
3. Ads triggered by WhatsApp "end to end encrypted" messages? (2022). https://news.ycombinator.com/item?id=32950204. Accessed 23 Sep 2022
4. Encryption (2022). https://github.com/simbiose/Encryption/
5. Enigma Encryption Keyboard (2022). https://apps.apple.com/us/app/enigma-encryption-keyboard/id971945391?platform=iphone
6. Signal (2022). https://signal.org/
7. Skype (2022). https://www.skype.com/en/
8. Telegram (2022). https://telegram.org/
9. Tesseract-Ocr (2022). https://github.com/tesseract-ocr/
10. Viber (2022). https://www.viber.com/en/
11. WhatsApp (2022). https://www.whatsapp.com/
12. WhisperKeyboard (2022). https://play.google.com/store/apps/details?id=cn.security.kbshrimp
13. Abdullah, A.M., et al.: Advanced encryption standard (aes) algorithm to encrypt and decrypt data. Cryptography Network Secur. **16**, 1–11 (2017). https://www.researchgate.net/publication/317615794_Advanced_Encryption_Standard_AES_Algorithm_to_Encrypt_and_Decrypt_Data

14. Abelson, H., et al.: Bugs in our pockets: The risks of client-side scanning. arXiv preprint arXiv:2110.07450 (2021). https://doi.org/10.48550/arXiv.2110.07450
15. Bai, X., Xing, L., Zhang, N., Wang, X., Liao, X., Li, T., Hu, S.M.: Staying secure and unprepared: Understanding and mitigating the security risks of apple zeroconf. In: 2016 IEEE Symposium on Security and Privacy (SP). pp. 655–674. IEEE (2016). https://doi.org/10.1109/SP.2016.45
16. Borisov, N., Goldberg, I., Brewer, E.: Off-the-record communication, or, why not to use pgp. In: Proceedings of the 2004 ACM Workshop on Privacy in the Electronic Society, pp. 77–84 (2004). https://doi.org/10.1145/1029179.1029200
17. Carlini, N., et al.: Hidden voice commands. In: 25th USENIX security symposium (USENIX security 16), pp. 513–530 (2016). https://www.usenix.org/conference/usenixsecurity16/technical-sessions/presentation/carlini
18. Cohn-Gordon, K., Cremers, C., Dowling, B., Garratt, L., Stebila, D.: A formal security analysis of the signal messaging protocol. J. Cryptology **33**(4), 1914–1983 (2020). https://doi.org/10.1007/s00145-020-09360-1
19. Daemen, J., Rijmen, V.: The advanced encryption standard process. In: The design of Rijndael, pp. 1–8. Springer (2002). doi:https://doi.org/10.1007/978-3-662-04722-4_1
20. ERICA PORTNOY: Why adding client-side scanning breaks end-to-end encryption (2019). https://www.eff.org/deeplinks/2019/11/why-adding-client-side-scanning-breaks-end-end-encryption. Accessed 22 Mar 2022
21. Frosch, T., Mainka, C., Bader, C., Bergsma, F., Schwenk, J., Holz, T.: How secure is textsecure? In: 2016 IEEE European Symposium on Security and Privacy (EuroS&P), pp. 457–472. IEEE (2016). https://doi.org/10.1109/EuroSP.2016.41
22. Joseph Cox: This is the code the fbi used to wiretap the world (2022). https://www.vice.com/en/article/v7veg8/anom-app-source-code-operation-trojan-shield-an0m. Accessed 10 Jul 2022
23. Juola, P.: Whole-word phonetic distances and the pgpfone alphabet. In: Proceeding of Fourth International Conference on Spoken Language Processing, ICSLP'96, vol. 1, pp. 98–101. IEEE (1996). https://doi.org/10.1109/ICSLP.1996.607046
24. MARY MADDEN: Public perceptions of privacy and security in the post-snowden era (2014). https://www.pewresearch.org/internet/2014/11/12/public-privacy-perceptions/. Accessed 27 Mar 2022
25. Mohamed, M., Shrestha, B., Saxena, N.: Smashed: Sniffing and manipulating android sensor data for offensive purposes. IEEE Trans. Inf. Forensics Secur. **12**(4), 901–913 (2016). https://doi.org/10.1109/TIFS.2016.2620278
26. NIST, A.: specification of the advanced encryption standard (aes). Federal Information Processing Standards Publication 197 (2001). https://doi.org/10.6028/NIST.FIPS.197
27. Patel, C., Patel, A., Patel, D.: Optical character recognition by open source ocr tool tesseract: a case study. Int. J. Comput. Appl. **55**(10), 50–56 (2012). https://doi.org/10.5120/8794-2784
28. Paul Rosenzweig: The apple client-side scanning system (2021). https://www.lawfareblog.com/apple-client-side-scanning-system. Accessed 10 Apr 2022
29. Reis, J., Melo, P.d.F., Garimella, K., Benevenuto, F.: Can whatsapp benefit from debunked fact-checked stories to reduce misinformation? arXiv preprint arXiv:2006.02471 (2020). https://doi.org/10.48550/arXiv.2006.02471
30. Rosenzweig, P.: The law and policy of client-side scanning (originally published by lawfare) (2020). https://digitalcommons.wcl.american.edu/research/58

31. Rottermanner, C., Kieseberg, P., Huber, M., Schmiedecker, M., Schrittwieser, S.: Privacy and data protection in smartphone messengers. In: Proceedings of the 17th International Conference on Information Integration and Web-based Applications & Services, pp. 1–10 (2015). https://doi.org/10.1145/2837185.2837202
32. Shinde, A.A., Chougule, D.: Text pre-processing and text segmentation for ocr. Int. J. Comput. Sci. Eng. Technol. **2**(1), 810–812 (2012). https://ijcset.net/docs/Volumes/volume2issue1/ijcset2012020111.pdf
33. Shirvanian, M., Saxena, N.: Wiretapping via mimicry: Short voice imitation man-in-the-middle attacks on crypto phones. In: Proceedings of the 2014 ACM SIGSAC Conference on Computer and Communications Security, pp. 868–879 (2014). https://doi.org/10.1145/2660267.2660274
34. Shirvanian, M., Saxena, N.: Cccp: closed caption crypto phones to resist mitm attacks, human errors and click-through. In: Proceedings of the 2017 ACM SIGSAC Conference on Computer and Communications Security, pp. 1329–1342 (2017). https://doi.org/10.1145/3133956.3134013
35. Smith, R.: An overview of the tesseract ocr engine. In: Ninth international conference on document analysis and recognition (ICDAR 2007), vol. 2, pp. 629–633. IEEE (2007). https://doi.org/10.1109/ICDAR.2007.4376991
36. Stedman, R., Yoshida, K., Goldberg, I.: A user study of off-the-record messaging. In: Proceedings of the 4th Symposium on Usable Privacy and Security, pp. 95–104 (2008). https://doi.org/10.1145/1408664.1408678
37. Unger, N., Dechand, S., Bonneau, J., Fahl, S., Perl, H., Goldberg, I., Smith, M.: Sok: secure messaging. In: 2015 IEEE Symposium on Security and Privacy, pp. 232–249. IEEE (2015). https://doi.org/10.1109/SP.2015.22
38. Vaidya, T., Zhang, Y., Sherr, M., Shields, C.: Cocaine noodles: exploiting the gap between human and machine speech recognition. In: 9th USENIX Workshop on Offensive Technologies (WOOT 15) (2015). https://www.usenix.org/conference/woot15/workshop-program/presentation/vaidya
39. Zhang, G., Yan, C., Ji, X., Zhang, T., Zhang, T., Xu, W.: Dolphinattack: inaudible voice commands. In: Proceedings of the 2017 ACM SIGSAC Conference on Computer and Communications Security, pp. 103–117 (2017). https://doi.org/10.1145/3133956.3134052

Differential Testing of Cryptographic Libraries with Hybrid Fuzzing

Hoyong Jin[1], Dohyeon An[1,2], and Taekyoung Kwon[1](✉)

[1] Graduate School of Information, Yonsei University, Seoul 03722, South Korea
{hoyong2007,overflow,taekyoung}@yonsei.ac.kr
[2] Coinone inc., Seoul 07335, South Korea

Abstract. Differential fuzz testing is a promising technique to detect numerous bugs in cryptographic libraries by providing the same input for different implementations of cryptographic algorithms. Cryptofuzz is an edge-cutting project that supports various libraries in this regard, employing coverage-guided libFuzzer as its back-end core. However, we observe that Cryptofuzz heavily relies on heuristic custom mutation strategies to expand code coverage while fuzzing, compensating for the limited performance of libFuzzer and the overhead of differential fuzzing. In this paper, we show such evidence and then present a novel tweak method to make differential fuzzing perform better with advanced fuzzers rather than the custom mutators overfitted with cryptographic features. Our basic insight is that hybrid fuzzing, which combines fuzzing and concolic execution, could help. We make the front end of Cryptofuzz standalone for differential testing of cryptographic libraries with hybrid fuzzers. We conduct experiments and use AFL and Intriguer for hybrid fuzzing. Our evaluation results show that the proposed method achieves better code coverage independently of the custom mutators and is more effective in bug-finding than Cryptofuzz. Our method generalizes its back end to use any advanced fuzzers for differential testing of cryptographic libraries.

Keywords: Differential fuzzing · Differential testing · Cryptographic library fuzzing · Cryptofuzz · Hybrid fuzzing

1 Introduction

Cryptographic libraries (also called cryptography or briefly crypto libraries) are increasingly widely used by developers to furnish their implementation with various kinds of security features, ranging from individual cryptographic algorithms to full-fledged SSL/TLS protocol suites. Many cryptographic libraries in use today, such as OpenSSL, libgcrypt, and Crypto++, are written in C and C++ code, which means that unfortunately, security-related bugs are inevitable. For instance, many triaged bugs in OpenSSL, 1,168 closed and 526 open at this submission time, are enumerated at OpenSSL's GitHub [24]. Furthermore, due

S.-H. Seo and H. Seo (Eds.): ICISC 2022, LNCS 13849, pp. 124–144, 2023.
https://doi.org/10.1007/978-3-031-29371-9_7

to the complexity of cryptographic algorithms and protocols, there could be *implementation discrepancies* in diverse libraries, producing crucial bugs with wrong output but hardly detectable because of incurring no crash on execution. For example, CVE-2022-1343 [7] reported a flaw in OpenSSL's Online Certificate Status Protocol (OCSP) response that returns a negative number instead of 0 when the signer's certificate verification failed, making a linked application falsely believe the certificate. This implementation discrepancy bug doesn't make a crash but results in the protocol going wrong in using the particular library. Differential fuzz testing, which provides the same test input for different implementations of the same objective, is a promising technique to detect not only syntactic bugs but also semantic bugs in cryptographic libraries, in that sense.

Cryptofuzz is an edge-cutting project for differential fuzzing that supports various cryptographic libraries, including but not limited to OpenSSL, LibreSSL, BoringSSL, Crypto++, cppcrypto, libgcrypt, libsodium, Bitcoin and Monero cryptographic code, Veracrypt cryptographic code, and the Whirlpool reference implementation [5]. To include target libraries in differential fuzzing, Cryptofuzz requires the harness code to call the functions inside each library by linking with the libraries under test. For fuzzing, Cryptofuzz employs LibFuzzer as its back-end core, which is a coverage-guided in-process fuzzer developed by the LLVM project and adds the custom mutator [6] written by considering various cryptographic features on test input. The front-end of Cryptofuzz mainly devotes to detecting implementation discrepancies through differential testing while the back-end dedicates to finding memory bugs as well as expanding code coverage. Indeed, Cryptofuzz reported many bugs discovered successfully in various cryptographic libraries [5]. However, to the best of our knowledge, the performance of Cryptofuzz has not been questioned and studied concerning both end cores.

In this context, (§3) our new observation is intriguing. Firstly, about the front-end of Cryptofuzz, (§3.1) we compare the performance of differential fuzzing and single target fuzzing. We observe there is a substantial overhead in differential fuzzing. Secondly, about the back-end of Cryptofuzz, (§3.2) we compare the performance of Cryptofuzz in two versions, i.e., with and without the custom mutator. We observe that Cryptofuzz heavily relies on the custom mutator to explore complex and narrow paths for fuzzing. Note that the custom mutator code keeps requiring sophisticated manual work considering specific features of cryptographic libraries [6]. Thus, we come up with our fundamental question. *What about adopting more advanced fuzzers with Cryptofuzz rather than the combination of custom mutator and LibFuzzer?* For example, hybrid fuzzers, such as QSYM [32] and Intriguer [4], which combine coverage-guided fuzzing and concolic execution, show significant advancement in exploring complex and narrow paths while fuzzing. However, such advanced fuzzers are designed for fuzzing a single target application only.

In this paper, (§3) we scrutinize the performance of differential fuzzing with Cryptofuzz and show the above observation by experiments. Subsequently, (§4) we present a novel tweak method of differential fuzzing to effectively work with advanced fuzzers. The key idea of our method is to transform Cryptofuzz into a standalone application in a way that (§4.1) accommodates its well-structured harness code and differential fuzzing functionality and (§4.2) conforms to the existing advanced fuzzers targeting a single application. We (§5) implement our system and (§6) evaluate its performance by experiments regarding three research questions about (§6.1) code coverage, (§6.2) bug-finding capability, and (§6.3) differential fuzzing overhead. We use three cryptographic libraries such as OpenSSL, Crypto++, and Libgcrypt in our experiments. Our implementation leverages Cryptofuzz, AFL, and Intriguer but our system design is general in accommodating other advanced fuzzers. For example, (§7) AFL++ can reinvoke the custom mutator if necessary and more advanced fuzzers, such as employing deep learning algorithms, can selectively work with our system.

2 Background

2.1 Cryptofuzz

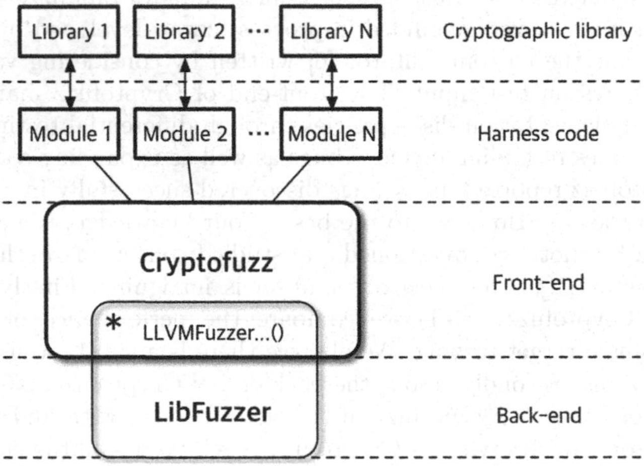

Fig. 1. Structure of Cryptofuzz. * implies the custom mutator inside.

Cryptofuzz [5], a state-of-the-art cryptographic library fuzzer conducting differential fuzzing, is written as the front-end of LibFuzzer. Unlike normal libraries, implementation discrepancies of cryptographic libraries that do not invoke crashes but return abnormal outputs can lead to fatal outcomes. Detecting bugs caused by implementation discrepancies with tools like address sanitizer is difficult because implementation discrepancies do not cause crashes, so it can be seen as normal behavior. Fortunately, cryptography has a standard and implementation convention so that no matter which library is used, the return value of cryptographic library functions must be equal if the same input is given to functions that conduct the same operation. Cryptofuzz utilizes these features of the cryptographic library to perform differential fuzzing. If Cryptofuzz is built with multiple cryptographic libraries, Cryptofuzz gives single input generated by the fuzzer to each target library and checks the return value difference to detect implementation discrepancies. If Cryptofuzz is built with a single cryptographic library, Cryptofuzz conducts single target fuzzing because there are no other libraries to compare.

Fig. 1 describes the structure of Cryptofuzz briefly. Cryptofuzz can be divided into three large portions. The back-end of Cryptofuzz generates input and passes it to the front end of Cryptofuzz. Cryptofuzz uses LibFuzzer as its back-end fuzzing core by default. The front-end of Cryptofuzz contains the main routines of Cryptofuzz that select parts to test such as an encryption scheme or operation based on the input from the back-end fuzzer and pass input to harness code. A difference check which compares results from each harness of multiple libraries is also conducted in the front-end. In addition, the front-end of Cryptofuzz conducts internal consistency testing that compares the results of multiple functions constructed for the same function. The harness of cryptographic libraries which is called a module in Cryptofuzz calls functions in cryptographic libraries with the input given from the front-end to conduct an operation which is selected by the front-end of Cryptofuzz and returns the results. If address sanitizer is included when the target libraries are built, bugs related to memory corruption can also be detectable.

LibFuzzer, the default back-end fuzzer of Cryptofuzz, is a fuzzer that is included in LLVM Project and is widely used for library fuzzing. LibFuzzer is an in-process, coverage-guided fuzzer that passes the input generated in the fuzzing process to the fuzzing entry point function named LLVMFuzzerTestOneInput() as an argument of the function. It repeats the testing process that conducts on the LLVMFuzzerTestOneInput() function to maximize coverage. LibFuzzer provides an option to use multiple workers so that the fuzzing process can use multiple CPU cores easily. However, LibFuzzer which is based on random mutation is not efficient on Cryptofuzz or cryptographic libraries that have narrow and complex paths. LibFuzzer enables to use custom mutator. Cryptofuzz uses a custom mutator [6] that fits on the structure of the front-end of Cryptofuzz to overcome the inefficiency of LibFuzzer.

Cryptofuzz was released in 2019 and has been continuously updated to this day. Currently, it is implemented to perform fuzzing targeting 88 cryptographic libraries and supports the functions for 90 operations, 386 ciphers including AEADs, 98 digests, and more than 110 ECC curves. Until today, Cryptofuzz has discovered over 160 bugs in open-source cryptographic libraries such as OpenSSL, Crypto++, libgcrypt, and relic, proving that Cryptofuzz is effective in detecting bugs in cryptographic libraries.

2.2 Hybrid Fuzzing

Coverage-guided fuzzing [8,9,17] and symbolic execution [3] are the most representative way to find software bugs. Fuzzing that gives a random value to the input of the programs executes the program and classifies it to a bug if a crash occurs. Coverage-guided fuzzing measures the coverage of the program on each input and uses it afterward fuzzing if new code coverage is found. By this method, coverage-guided fuzzing can pass the branches one by one and eventually can test branches that are hard to reach. However, because of the randomly generated inputs used on fuzzing basically, it is still hard to pass the narrow and complex branches. To pass the branch that has 4 bytes constraint, for instance, it needs an average 2^{32} times of random trial. Such branches that are not easily passed cause the fuzzer not to find a new path.

Symbolic execution is a method to analyze which part of the input can execute a specific path of the program. The symbolic executor executes the program not using the concrete value that is utilized in normal execution but using the symbolic value as input. The constraints of each branch can be represented as an expression that contains the symbolic values which are used for the input of the program. The symbolic executor solves this constraint expression with the solver to generate an answer that can satisfy the branch conditions. Using this method, input that can reach the specific path can be generated. However, symbolic execution is too slow compared to normal execution because it has to manage every symbol that is used on the program, and it has a problem that state explosion can occur.

Hybrid fuzzing utilizes fuzzing and symbolic execution complementarily to make up for each shortcoming. Coverage-guided fuzzing has difficulty in making input that can satisfy complex constraints, but symbolic execution can easily generate input by solving these constraints. Symbolic execution has a state explosion problem, but this can be minimized by utilizing symbolic execution only on the path that the fuzzer found. By combining these two methods, hybrid fuzzing can find bugs more efficiently than using each method alone. Driller [27], QSYM [32], and Intriguer [4] on user-level applications, and HFL [15] on Linux kernel, for example, show that hybrid fuzzing is efficient.

3 Motivation

In this section, we describe the motivation of our study by analyzing the overhead of differential fuzzing at the front-end of Cryptofuzz compared to single target fuzzing and the reliance on the custom mutator for fuzzing at the back-end of Cryptofuzz. We explain our findings by experiments. The experimental settings and the target libraries, such as OpenSSL, Crypto++, and libgcrypt, conform to the details described in our evaluation part (§6).

3.1 Overhead of Differential Fuzzing

To analyze the overhead of differential fuzzing, we use Cryptofuzz for fuzzing in two ways: First, we fuzz each of three libraries OpenSSL, Crypto++, and libgcrypt in a single target fuzzing fashion. Second, we conduct differential fuzzing on the three libraries. Our hypothesis is that differential fuzzing results

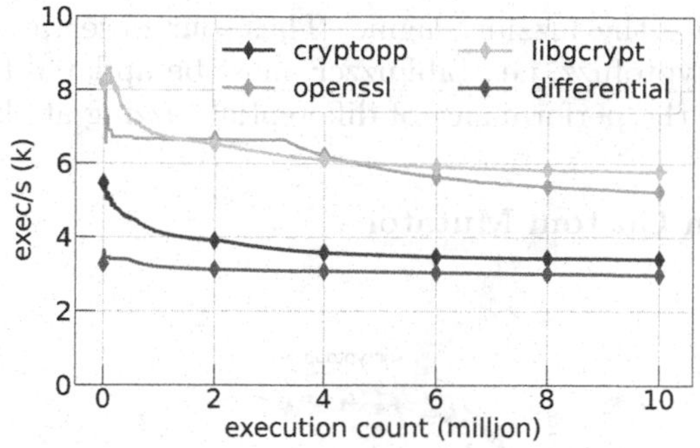

Fig. 2. Throughput comparison of differential fuzzing and single target fuzzing: Cryptofuzz

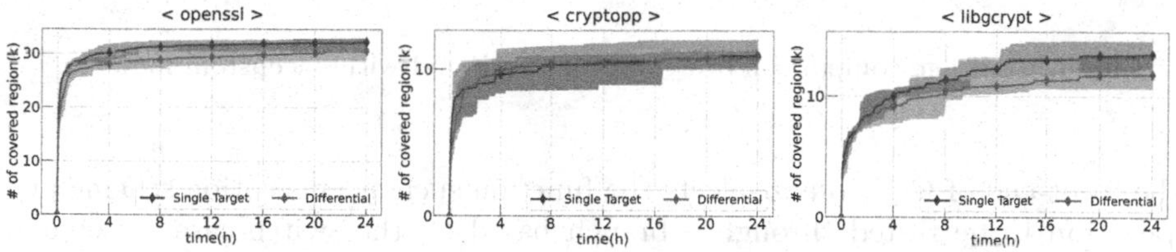

Fig. 3. Coverage comparison of differential fuzzing and single target fuzzing: Cryptofuzz

in lower performance than each single target fuzzing. This is looking straightforward but our intention is to comprehend how large is the overhead, saying, whether it is negligible or not at the current combination of Cryptofuzz. Thus, we measure the throughput of fuzzing and also the code coverage.

Fig. 2 illustrates the fuzzing throughput obtained by the experiment according to the number of executions. In the results of single target fuzzing, Crypto++ showed the lowest throughput. The result of differential fuzzing is even lower than Crypto++ as expected. In particular, in the case of libgcrypt, the execution per time was 94.4% higher than that of differential fuzzing when executed 10 million times, resulting in a very high throughput overhead when differential fuzzing was performed on libgcrypt. Fig. 3 is a graph showing the results of fuzzing for 24 hours as region coverage over time. As with the throughput results, the number of regions tested by differential fuzzing is lower than single target fuzzing. Crypto++ which has the lowest throughput overhead has no significant difference in coverage results, but for libgcypt, which had the largest throughput overhead, single target fuzzing secured up to 37.4% higher coverage.

Our observation at the front-end of Cryptofuzz is that the overhead of differential fuzzing is real and non-negligible. Another observation is that there is a variance in the throughput of each fuzzing and that of differential fuzzing. Despite the lower performance, differential fuzzing is very necessary for cryptographic libraries, and the only way to improve the performance of differential fuzzing is to update the fuzzing engine. Thus, our observation supports that the back-end of Cryptofuzz, i.e., LibFuzzer, must be updated to more advanced fuzzers to improve the performance of differential fuzzing at the front-end.

3.2 Reliance on Custom Mutator

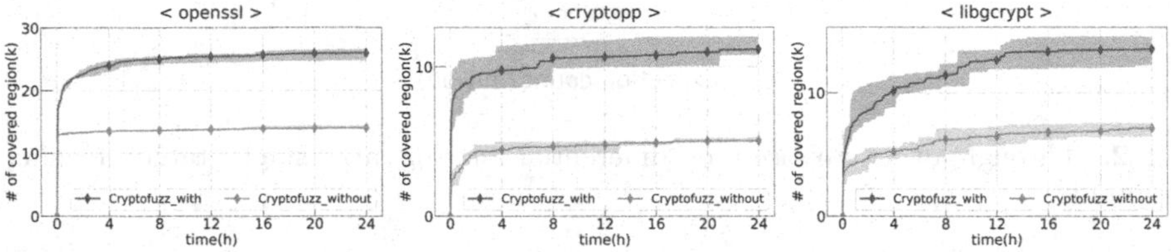

Fig. 4. Coverage comparison of Cryptofuzz with and without custom mutator

The front-end of Cryptofuzz selects the function such as encryption scheme and operation to be tested through a branch based on the switch-case statement. Branches based on the switch-case statement can be reached when a specific offset of the input matches a specific value, so the front-end of the Cryptofuzz mainly consists of a narrow path. The input generated by LibFuzzer, which is the default back-end fuzzer of Cryptofuzz, is a value generated based on randomness, so it is difficult to pass through these narrow paths. Cryptofuzz implements and uses the custom mutator [6] optimized for the front-end of Cryptofuzz to overcome the limitations of LibFuzzer. We confirmed how much the custom mutator of Cryptofuzz overcame the limitations of LibFuzzer through experiments. The experiment compared vanilla Cryptofuzz with Cryptofuzz without a custom mutator and was performed for three libraries: OpenSSL, Crypto++, and libgcrypt.

Fig. 4 represents the coverage results of Cryptofuzz with and without a custom mutator. Cryptofuzz_with and Cryptofuzz_without in the legend of Fig. 4 represent Cryptofuzz using a custom mutator and Cryptofuzz which do not use a custom mutator respectively. Each fuzzing was conducted for 24 hours and repeated 5 times. The results of comparing Cryptofuzz_with with Cryptofuzz_without show that Cryptofuzz which utilized a custom mutator obtained much more coverage. In the five repeated experiments, Cryptofuzz using the custom mutator secured an average of 122%, 95%, and 98% more coverage on libgcrypt, OpenSSL, and Crypto++ respectively. Through this, we confirmed the effect of the custom mutator on performance.

Our observation at the back-end of Cryotofuzz is that the reliance on the custom mutator is substantial in Cryptofuzz to explore complex and narrow paths and expand code coverage. The current custom mutator of Cryptofuzz is written in C++ by the author of Cryptofuzz who knows the structure of Cryptofuzz very well and is composed of over 2000 lines of code [6]. The custom mutation strategies are heuristic and incorporate many details of target libraries. For new users to modify the custom mutator or add new functions to it, the manual analysis of the front-end of Cryptofuzz and the target libraries should precede first. In other words, the custom mutator of Cryptofuzz has the limitation of taking substantial effort and time for analysis and manual work. On the other hand, to explore complex and narrow paths and expand code coverage while fuzzing, hybrid fuzzing is excellent. Hybrid fuzzing, which provides a solver to solve the constraint of branch conditions inside the target, is known to be more advantageous than fuzzing in searching for complex branches because it mathematically calculates and generates an input that can discover a path over the branch. Thus, our observation supports that the back-end of Crytofuzz must be replaced by hybrid fuzzers to avoid or remove the reliance on the custom mutator.

4 Design

In this section, we describe the design of our system. The key idea of our system design is to transform Cryptofuzz, which incorporates the custom mutator and LibFuzzer inside, into a standalone version that removes all of those cumbersome and low-performing components. Fig. 5 illustrates an overview of our system design concept. The so-called Crytofuzz-standalone takes input from outside fuzzers and conducts differential fuzzing on linked libraries. Thus, this generalization of the back-end enables the adoption of hybrid fuzzers.

4.1 Making Cryptofuzz Standalone

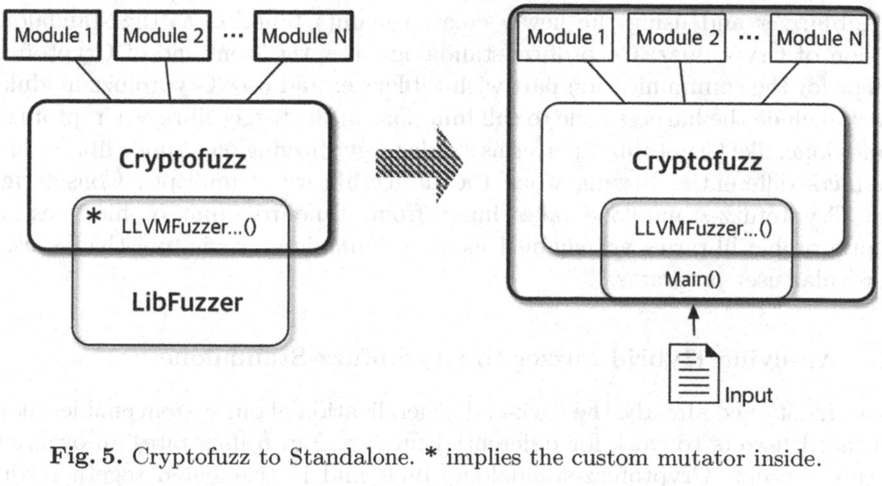

Fig. 5. Cryptofuzz to Standalone. * implies the custom mutator inside.

To make Cryptofuzz standalone, LibFuzzer and LibFuzzer-dependent parts in Cryptofuzz must be removed. In the front-end of Cryptofuzz, there are functions to communicate with LibFuzzer which is the default back-end of Cryptofuzz. LLVMFuzzerInitialize() function initializes options related to fuzzing and loads Cryptofuzz modules in which harness code for fuzzing target library is implemented. After initialize process is done, LLVMFuzzerTestOneInput() function receives input from LibFuzzer and conducts tests according to the structure of the Cryptofuzz front-end. LLVMFuzzerCustomMutator() function is a custom mutator for LibFuzzer which was implemented suitably on the front-end of Cryptofuzz. Likewise, functions that are prefixed *LLVMFuzzer* are made to use on LibFuzzer, and these functions are the root cause that makes Cryptofuzz dependent on LibFuzzer. Therefore, the new main() function has to be constructed to call LLVMFuzzerInitialize(), LLVMFuzzerTestOneInput(), and LLVMFuzzerCustomMutator() which are prefixed *LLVMFuzzer* similar to the main() function of LibFuzzer. Using this new main() function instead of the main() function in LibFuzzer can eliminate the dependencies of Cryptofuzz on LibFuzzer.

In the main() function to be newly constructed, the LLVMFuzzerInitialize() function that initializes the library and loads the module to be fuzzed should be called first when the program starts. The receiving part has to be constructed to receive input from standard input or file after the initializing part. Since the main() function receives the input generated by the back-end dynamic analysis tool, the receiving part can be constructed by selecting a method that is convenient to use the dynamic analysis tool. After receiving the input, the main() function passes it to the LLVMFuzzerTestOneInput() function to test the target. If the dynamic analysis tool used as a back-end supports the use of a custom mutator, the existing LLVMFuzzerCustomMutator() function can be used by modifying it according to the custom mutator format of the corresponding dynamic analysis tool.

Cryptofuzz-standalone was constructed by eliminating the portion that relies on LibFuzzer and using the newly created main() function as the standalone version of Cryptofuzz. Cryptofuzz-standalone uses the front-end of Cryptofuzz except for the communication part with LibFuzzer and uses Cryptofuzz modules which include the harness code to call functions in the target library. Cryptofuzz-standalone, like Cryptofuzz, performs single target fuzzing on a single library and conducts differential fuzzing when the target library is multiple. Considering that Cryptofuzz-standalone takes input from standard input or files, testing cryptographic libraries are enabled using a dynamic analysis tool that is used on regular user programs.

4.2 Applying Hybrid Fuzzer to Cryptofuzz-Standalone

As we mentioned already, the back-end generalization of our system enables more advanced fuzzers to work for differential fuzzing. Fig. 6 illustrates an overview of this concept. Cryptofuzz-standalone, built and instrumented together with linked libraries, runs as a target binary of the hybrid fuzzer, taking test input from the corpus and providing coverage information while fuzzing. We then describe our design decision regarding the hybrid fuzzers.

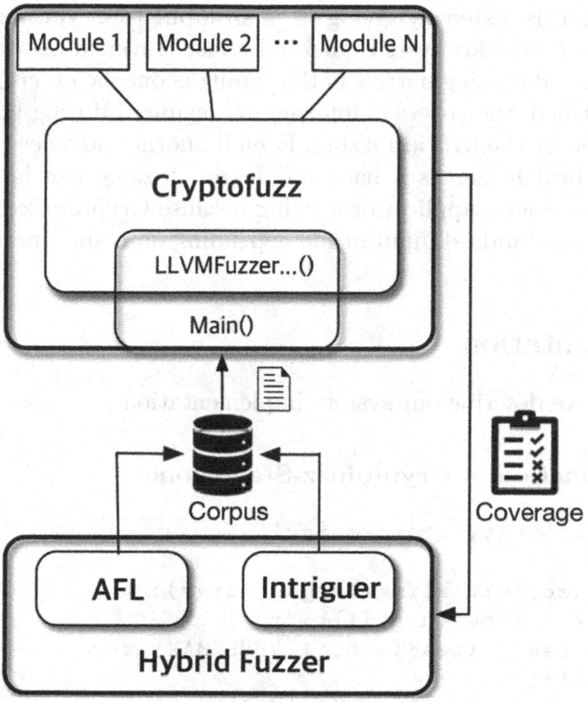

Fig. 6. Overview: Hybrid Fuzzing with Cryptofuzz-standalone

LibFuzzer does not provide a function to perform fuzzing in parallel with other fuzzing instances because it can use multiple workers by itself. In order to use LibFuzzer in parallel with other fuzzing instances, it is necessary to add synchronization tasks manually such as merging the input corpus of each instance periodically. For this reason, LibFuzzer is inconvenient to be used for hybrid fuzzing that needs to continuously synchronize the concolic execution instance and the fuzzing instance. AFL, on the other hand, is basically designed to perform fuzzing by using only one core per instance. When fuzzing is performed in parallel using multiple cores, AFL continuously synchronizes the input queue with other fuzzing instances during fuzzing. Because of these characteristics, AFL is adopted and used as a fuzzing engine in many hybrid fuzzing studies.

The hybrid fuzzer used in this paper uses AFL as the fuzzing engine. In terms of performance, it would also be more advantageous to use AFL in a hybrid fuzzer. According to a fuzzing experiment on OpenSSL, which performs by Fuzzbench [11], a service that evaluates fuzzers for real-world software, AFL can perform well on cryptographic fuzzing compared to LibFuzzer. Intriguer, the state-of-the-art concolic execution engine that showed better performance than QSYM, is used as the concolic execution engine of the hybrid fuzzer.

The AFL instance and the Intriguer instance run in parallel and share the seed by synchronizing the input queue. The seed generated through fuzzing or concolic execution is tested by giving it as an input to Cryptofuzz-standalone. Large amounts of code are tested quickly by fast traversal of wide paths done through fuzzing and passing narrow paths through concolic execution. When the execution is finished, the coverage information acquired during the execution is used as feedback for the hybrid fuzzing. Even if another advanced fuzzer is used instead of a hybrid fuzzer as a back-end fuzzer, fuzzing can be performed in the same way as general application fuzzing because Cryptofuzz-standalone can receive input from standard input or file depending on main function implementation.

5 Implementation

In this section, we describe our system implementation.

5.1 Main Function of Cryptofuzz-Standalone

```
int main(int argc, char **argv)
{
    LLVMFuzzerInitialize(&argc, &argv);
    FILE *f = fopen(argv[1], "rb");
    size_t len = fread(buf, 1, BUF_MAX, f);
    fclose(f);
    LLVMFuzzerTestOneInput(buf, len);
}
```

Code. 1: the main() function getting input from a file

```
int main(int argc, char **argv)
{
  LLVMFuzzerInitialize(&argc, &argv);
  size_t len = read(0, buf, BUF_MAX);
  LLVMFuzzerTestOneInput(buf, len);
}
```

Code. 2: the main() function getting input from the standard input

Cryptofuzz-standalone is inspired by StandaloneFuzzTargetMain.c [18] which is a part of fuzzer in LLVM-Project. StandaloneFuzzTargetMain.c includes the main() function which calls LLVMFuzzerInitialize() when the program starts and tests each input file by passing it to the LLVMFuzzerTestOneInput() function. However, since Cryptofuzz-standalone is designed for fuzzing and concolic execution that only receives one input at a time, we deleted repeated statements to make the execution time caused by comparison for repetition not be wasted. Code. 1 and Code. 2 represent the implementation of the main() function getting input from files and standard input. If the input is received as a file, the file passed as an argument is read when the program is executed and used to test the target by the LLVMFuzzerTestOneInput() function. If the input is received as standard input, one input is received through the read() function and used to test the target by the LLVMFuzzerTestOneInput() function.

```
__AFL_FUZZ_INIT();
int main(int argc, char **argv) {
  #ifdef __AFL_HAVE_MANUAL_CONTROL
  __AFL_INIT();
  #endif
  LLVMFuzzerInitialize(&argc, &argv);
  while (__AFL_LOOP(AFL_REPEAT_CNT)) {
    memset(buf, 0, BUF_SIZE);
    size_t len = read(0, buf, BUF_SIZE);
    LLVMFuzzerTestOneInput(buf, len);
  }
}
```

Code. 3: the main() function for AFL

Intriguer used as a concolic executor does not matter which way Cryptofuzz-standalone receives input from standard input and file, so it does not matter which version is used as the main() function. However, in the case of Cryptofuzz-standalone for using AFL, if the above method is used as it is, the initialization function is repeatedly executed unnecessarily leading to wasting execution time. Therefore, in Code. 3, we build Cryptofuzz-standalone for AFL using AFL persistent mode [10] to repeat the testing process that receives input and tests with the LLVMFuzzerTestOneInput() function without restarting the program. We added some code on the main() function of Cryptofuzz-standalone for AFL persistent mode. The code related to LLVMFuzzerCustomMutator() function is not dealt with separately because AFL does not support custom mutators.

The code of Cryptofuzz that we wrote and modified to construct Cryptofuzz-standalone other than the main() function is as follows. A header file was additionally created to connect the main() function of Cryptofuzz-standalone and functions prefixed *LLVMFuzzer*, The code of the mutator.cpp in Cryptofuzz was partially modified to build normally without LibFuzzer. Also, to build Cryptofuzz-standalone, we have added the code to build in Makefile.

5.2 Hybrid Fuzzing with Cryptofuzz-Standalone

To perform hybrid fuzzing, we need to separately build two versions of Cryptofuzz-standalone for fuzzing and concolic execution. In the case of Cryptofuzz-standalone which is built to use AFL, we need to build it using the compiler named *afl-clang-fast* that performs instrumentation for AFL. When building Cryptofuzz-standalone to use Intriguer, *clang*, the compiler of LLVM-Project, is used, and `-O0`, `-fno-jump-tables` can be used as compile flags to enable the intriguer to perform analysis well. If the dynamic analysis tool to use is not able to build with the clang compiler or if we need to use the GCC compiler to utilize tools such as gcov, we have to replace the clang builtin macros such as `__builtin_rotateright32()` used by Cryptofuzz.

In this study, we used docker to perform hybrid fuzzing using the built Cryptofuzz-standalone. The docker image set for hybrid fuzzing is run as a container according to the number of instances, and the CPU to be used in each instance is fixed using the `-cpuset-cpus` option of the docker. Through this, the CPU core of the fuzzing machine performing hybrid fuzzing can be utilized without waste. The output directory of each fuzzing instance and concolic execution instance running on docker is mounted in the same directory on the host machine with the `-v` option when running docker. The fuzzer instance running on docker and the concolic execution instance can synchronize with each other to perform hybrid fuzzing through this process.

6 Evaluation

We evaluated our approach, to answer the following three research questions.

- **RQ1**: How much is code coverage increased by our method?
- **RQ2**: How effective is our method in terms of bug-finding capabilities?
- **RQ3**: Can our method reduce the overhead of differential fuzzing?

We used three cryptographic libraries in our experiments: OpenSSL v3.0.0, Crypto++ v8.7, and Libgcrypt v1.9.3. Each library was compiled for Cryptofuzz, AFL, and Intriguer. We conducted our experiments on a machine with two MD Ryzen Threadripper PRO 3975WX CPUs and 256GB RAM, running Ubuntu 18.04 LTS. The fuzzers are run inside docker v20.10.7, and the Docker images were created based on Ubuntu 16.04. We used Cryptofuzz from git commit *83d3c0a8212fb4dbb61be90d2dbb5fd7c801900d* for the experiment.

6.1 RQ1: Code Coverage

To answer RQ1, we compared our hybrid approach with Cryptofuzz which not uses a custom mutator. Our approach is to replace the back-end fuzzer by utilizing Cryptofuzz-standalone. In order to compare the exact performance difference due to this technology, we conduct a control experiment in which the custom mutator, a variable that can affect performance, was removed in Cryptofuzz. Fig. 7 shows the code coverage obtained as a result of fuzzing by Cryptofuzz without a custom mutator and our hybrid fuzzer leveraging Cryptofuzz-standalone to three cryptographic libraries, OpenSSL, Crypto++, and Libgcrypt, respectively. Each experiment was conducted for 24 hours, and each fuzzer uses three CPU cores for fuzzing. We repeated the experiments for 5 runs per fuzzer [16]. The solid lines in the Fig. 7 are median, and the shaded region around is the min/max.

As a result of the experiment, Cryptofuzz without a custom mutator achieves lower coverage than our hybrid approach. This is because the inside of cryptographic libraries and the front-end of Cryptofuzz are complex to test through the random-based input generated by LibFuzzer. On the other hand, our approach was able to get much higher coverage because it generates an input that can explore narrow and complex paths through concolic solving during hybrid fuzzing. We confirmed that simply replacing the Cryptofuzz back-end with a better dynamic analysis tool can significantly improve performance.

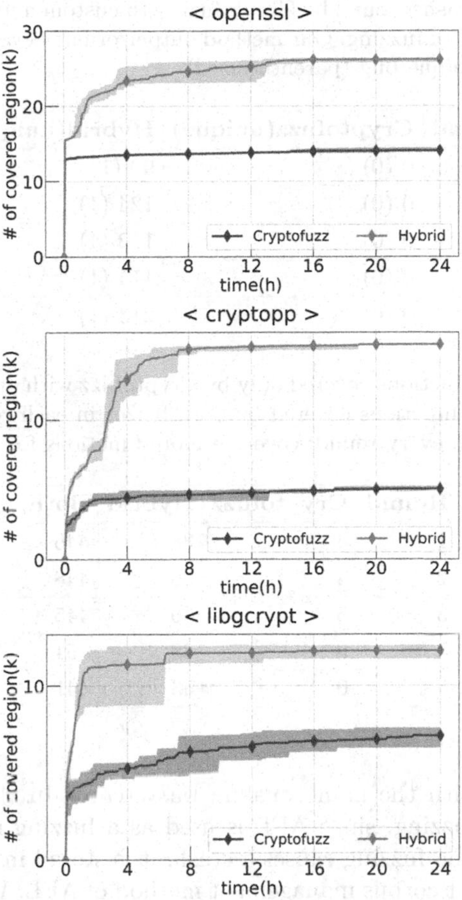

Fig. 7. Coverage comparison of our method (Hybrid) and Cryptofuzz without custom mutator

6.2 RQ2: Bug Discovery Capability

To answer RQ2, the bug-finding experiment was conducted to find the 1-day bug discovered by Cryptofuzz. Since the bug-finding experiment is not an evaluation for the back-end but for the practicality of the fuzzer itself, we compare our hybrid approach with vanilla Cryptofuzz. In the experiment, each fuzzer used 6 CPU cores. Cryptofuzz uses 6 workers, and hybrid fuzzer uses 4 AFL instances and 2 Intriguer instances. The CPU core distribution ratio of the hybrid fuzzer is the same ratio that the typical hybrid fuzzer such as QSYM and Intriguer used.

The criteria for determining that a bug has been detected are as follows. In the case of Cryptofuzz, the name of the input file in the input corpus is stored and managed as a hash value, and in the event of a crash, the file is stored in the form of `crash-`⟨Hash⟩. Therefore, we can determine that Cryptofuzz detected

Table 1. Number of crashes found by Cryptofuzz with custom mutator and our method (Hybrid) in each round of fuzzing. Our method outperforms in every round: discovering many crashes and a unique bug (parenthesized).

Round	Cryptofuzz(unique)	Hybrid(unique)
1	0 (0)	90 (1)
2	0 (0)	124 (1)
3	0 (0)	112 (1)
4	0 (0)	114 (1)
5	0 (0)	213 (1)

Table 2. Number of functions covered only by Cryptofuzz with custom mutator or our method (Hybrid) and functions covered by both fuzzer in each round of fuzzing. Our method outperforms in every round: covering more functions for fuzzing.

Round	Cryptofuzz	Hybrid	Both
1	4	38	446
2	4	36	448
3	5	39	445
4	0	38	451
5	0	43	441

a bug when a file with the name `crash-` was created in the input corpus. In the case of hybrid fuzzing, since AFL is used as a fuzzing engine, if a specific input generated during fuzzing causes a crash, it is stored in the crash directory according to the input corpus management method of AFL. When a file is stored in the crash directory, we then know that the hybrid fuzzer has detected a bug.

The experiment to find a 1-day bug was conducted for 24 hours. To increase the reliability of the experiment results, the experiment is repeated 5 times under the same condition. Table. 1 shows that during 5 repeated experiments, Cryptofuzz did not generate any crash files in the input corpus directory. On the other hand, in the case of hybrid fuzzing, 90 to 213 crash files were generated for one unique bug in all experiments. The unique bug found with hybrid fuzzing is the bug that causes a null pointer to dereference when the modulus is 0 in the BN_mod_exp2_mont() function. It was reported on February 6, 2022, through the issue of the OpenSSL official git [23] and patched on March 2. By this result, we can see that hybrid fuzzing could be more efficient in the same condition compare to Cryptofuzz and has proved that can detect bugs in real-world cryptographic libraries.

We have extracted the function coverage of the results of 1-day bug finding experiments. The number of functions that are covered only by Cryptofuzz or hybrid fuzzer is represented in Table. 2. Cryptofuzz and hybrid fuzzer tested on average 448.8 functions and 485 functions during 5 repeated experiments respectively. During the 5 repeated experiments, the maximum number of functions covered only by Cryptofuzz is 5, and the number of functions covered only by hybrid fuzzer is 38.8 on average. This shows that a hybrid fuzzer can quickly test code that Cryptofuzz cannot easily reach by traveling narrow and complex branches in the Cryptofuzz front-end and cryptographic libraries without a custom mutator. This means that the hybrid fuzzer can quickly reach and test bugs that exist in functions that are difficult to reach by Cryptofuzz, and detect bugs. In summary, in this experiment, a hybrid fuzzer can quickly reach functions that Cryptofuzz cannot easily reach without a custom mutator, allowing more code to be tested, and it detects one unique bug that occurred in OpenSSL showing that the technique proposed in this paper is sufficiently meaningful in terms of bug finding.

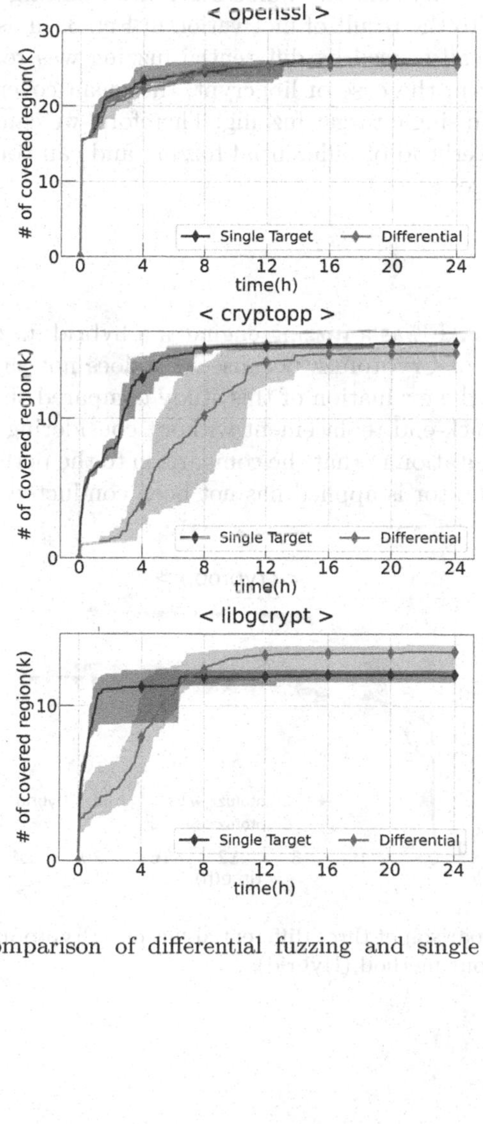

Fig. 8. Coverage comparison of differential fuzzing and single target fuzzing: Our method (Hybrid).

6.3 RQ3: Overhead Reduction

To answer RQ3, we apply our hybrid approach to differential fuzzing and single target fuzzing and evaluate the impact of overhead caused by differential fuzzing. Three libraries, OpenSSL, Crypto++, and libgcrypt, were built simultaneously in Cryptofuzz-standalone to perform differential fuzzing, and built each library separately to perform single target fuzzing. As with RQ1, each experiment was conducted for 24 hours, and each fuzzer uses three CPU cores for fuzzing. The solid line and shaded region in Fig. 8 describe the median and min/max of 5 repeated experiments.

As shown in Fig. 8, the overhead of differential fuzzing is up to 14.6% in Crypto++, and in libgcrypt and OpenSSL, the overhead is up to 1.9%, and 9.8% respectively. The maximum overhead is the result obtained by dividing the best single target coverage and the worst differential fuzzing coverage among 5 replicates. Compare to the result of motivation in Fig. 3, in aspects of coverage, the maximum overhead caused by differential fuzzing was reduced from 37.4% to 14.6%. Especially in the case of libgcrypt, the mean coverage of differential fuzzing is higher than single target fuzzing. Therefore, we can say that our approach reduced the overhead of differential fuzzing and can completely offset the overhead in some cases.

7 Discussion

In this paper, we use AFL as a fuzzing engine of a hybrid fuzzer. We cannot use the custom mutator of Cryptofuzz because AFL does not support customizing mutator. Therefore, the evaluation of this study compared the performance difference due to the back-end replacement without considering the custom mutator, but there is a limitation in that the comparison to the performance difference when the custom mutator is applied has not been conducted.

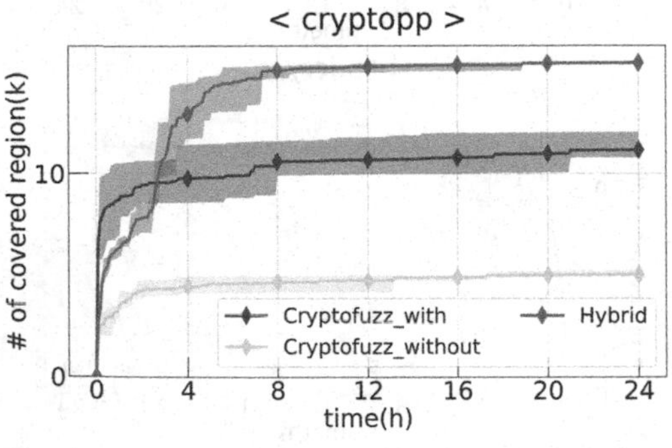

Fig. 9. Coverage comparison of three differential fuzzers: Cryptofuzz with and without custom mutator and our method (Hybrid).

Fig. 9 is a graph showing the results of fuzzing for Crypto++ using a hybrid fuzzer, Cryptofuzz_with with custom mutator, and Cryptofuzz_without which do not use the custom mutator. In this result, the hybrid fuzzing approach that we used earned more coverage for Crypto++ than the others even though it did not use the custom mutator. Considering that the custom mutator has a very large effect on the performance of Cryptofuzz if the custom mutator is also applied to the hybrid fuzzing approach, it is expected to show much better performance than the existing Cryptofuzz.

In a future study, we will perform hybrid fuzzing using a fuzzing engine that supports a custom mutator such as AFL++ [8]. When custom mutator and hybrid fuzzing are used together, the Cryptofuzz front-end can be quickly explored through the custom mutator and explore the deep part of the cryptographic library through concolic execution. It is expected that this method will show better performance. In addition, Cryptofuzz-standalone is designed to be applied to any dynamic analysis tool for user applications, so not only hybrid fuzzing but also advanced fuzzers based on AI technology such as EcoFuzz [31] and NEUZZ [26] can be applied.

8 Related Work

Among the vulnerabilities that occur in the cryptographic library, the percentage of vulnerabilities caused by cryptographic issues and those caused by memory safety issues is only 64.4% [2]. Vulnerabilities due to implementation discrepancy belonging to the remaining 35.6% can lead to fatal issues but are difficult to detect by general methods. In this study, we tried to efficiently detect vulnerabilities due to implementation discrepancy as well as vulnerabilities due to memory issues through differential fuzzing. By applying the advanced fuzzing method to Cryptofuzz, the state-of-the-art cryptographic library differential fuzzer, differential fuzzing can be performed more efficiently.

We utilized the well-structured harness of Cryptofuzz, a state-of-the-art fuzzing project for cryptographic libraries, as a harness for testing cryptographic libraries. Unlike general programs, libraries cannot be executed alone, so fuzzing can be performed only if there is a harness that calls the functions of the library. Therefore, fuzzing research targeting libraries is being studied not only to improve the performance of fuzzing itself but also how to quickly and efficiently create a harness to be used for fuzzing.

In 2019 ACM CCS, Fudge [1] extracts the API call sequence from the open source code that uses the library and automatically extracts the library's harness using this information. Fudge has generated fuzz drivers for numerous libraries, some of which were integrated into OSS-Fuzz [25] fuzzing infrastructure.

In 2020 Usenix Security, FuzzGen [13] infers the interface of the library by analyzing the source code of the whole system statically and generates a harness based on the collected information. This process does not need human interaction and can apply to various libraries. The harness generated by FuzzGen was fuzzed by LibFuzzer and obtained 6.94% more code coverage compared to the manually written harness.

In 2021 NDSS, Winnie [14] does not conduct fuzzing on libraries but generates a harness automatically to bypass GUI code on the Windows binary. Winnie synthesizes harnesses of application based on the sample executions and uses them to test binaries. As a result, Winnie found 61 unique bugs on 32 windows binaries and showed its efficiency.

Differential fuzzing, which is essential when testing cryptographic libraries, is also being studied to improve efficiency or apply it to new domains. In 2019, DifFuzz [21] performed differential fuzzing to find side-channel vulnerabilities. DifFuzz analyzed the two versions of the program and performed directed fuzzing in the direction that the difference in resource consumption increase through resource-guided heuristics. DifFuzz proved its effectiveness by discovering a new vulnerability in the Apache FTP server, a JAVA open-source application.

In 2020 ICSE, HyDiff [22] used a hybrid approach combining two techniques, feedback-directed grey-box fuzzing, and shadow symbolic execution, for differential software analysis. Divergence-driven feedback was used for grey-box fuzzing, and four-way forking was utilized for symbolic execution. HyDiff found the first divergence much faster than the single technique and identified a much larger number of total divergences.

In 2021 OSDI, Fluffy [30] conducted multi-transaction differential fuzzing to find Ethereum consensus bugs. To find the consensus bug, Fluffy ran multi-transaction test cases using multiple existing Ethereum clients. Fluffy showed its excellence by discovering two new exploitable consensus bugs in the Geth Ethereum Client.

9 Conclusion

In this paper, we constructed Crytofuzz-standalone taking input from outside fuzzers and conducting differential fuzzing. As an outside fuzzer, we used a hybrid fuzzing approach using AFL and Intriguer to easily cover the narrow path of the front-end of Cryptofuzz without a custom mutator. We have shown that our method outperforms Cryptofuzz in the terms of obtaining coverage and finding bugs. Furthermore, our method reduced the overhead of differential fuzzing, and in some cases, we have shown the overhead can be completely offset. In the future study, we plan to adopt a hybrid fuzzer in Cryptofuzz-standalone using a fuzzing engine that supports a custom mutator. In addition, we plan to adopt an advanced fuzzer based on AI technology instead of hybrid fuzzers.

Acknowledgement. This work was supported by Institute for Information & communications Technology Planning & Evaluation (IITP) grant funded by the Korea government (MSIT) (No.2018-0-00513, Machine Learning Based Automation of Vulnerability Detection on Unix-based Kernel) in part and by the National Research Foundation of Korea (NRF) grant funded by the Korea government (MSIT) (No. NRF-2019R1A2C1088802) in part.

References

1. Babić, D., et al.: Fudge: fuzz driver generation at scale. In: Proceedings of the 2019 27th ACM Joint Meeting on European Software Engineering Conference and Symposium on the Foundations of Software Engineering (ESEC/FSE 19), pp. 975–985 (2019). https://doi.org/10.1145/3338906.3340456
2. Blessing, J., Specter, MA., Weitzner, DJ.: You Really Shouldn't Roll Your Own Crypto: An Empirical Study of Vulnerabilities in Cryptographic Libraries. In: arXiv preprint arXiv:2107.04940 (2021)
3. Cadar, C., Sen, K.: Symbolic execution for software testing: three decades later. Commun. ACM **56**(2), 82–90 (2013)
4. Cho, M., Kim, S., Kwon, T.: Intriguer: Field-level constraint solving for hybrid fuzzing. In: Proceedings of the 2019 ACM SIGSAC Conference on Computer and Communications Security (CCS 19), pp. 515–530 (2019). https://doi.org/10.1145/3319535.3354249
5. Cryptofuzz. https://github.com/guidovranken/cryptofuzz. 2019 (2022)
6. Cryptofuzz's Matator. https://github.com/guidovranken/cryptofuzz/blob/master/mutator.cpp. (2022)
7. CVE-2022-1343. https://access.redhat.com/security/cve/cve-2022-1343. (2022)
8. Fioraldi, A., Maier, D., Eißfeldt, H., Heuse, M.: AFL++: Combining Incremental Steps of Fuzzing Research. In: 14th USENIX Workshop on Offensive Technologies (WOOT 20) (2020)
9. Google.AFL. https://github.com/google/AFL. 2013 (2022)
10. Google.AFL Persistent mode demo. https://github.com/google/AFL/tree/master/experimental/persistent_demo. (2022)
11. Google.FuzzBench report. https://www.fuzzbench.com/reports/2021-06-02/index.html_openssl_x509-summary (2022)
12. Google.Syzkaller. https://github.com/google/syzkaller. (2022)
13. Ispoglou, K., Austin, D., Mohan, V., Payer, M.: FuzzGen: Automatic Fuzzer Generation. In: 29th USENIX Security Symposium (USENIX Security 20), pp. 2271–2287 (2020)
14. Jung, J., Tong, S., Hu, H., Lim, J., Jin, Y., Kim, T.: Winnie: Fuzzing windows applications with harness synthesis and fast cloning. In: The Network and Distributed System Security Symposium (NDSS 2021), pp. 1–17 (2021)
15. Kim, K., Jeong, DR., Kim, CH., Jang, Y., Shin, I., Lee, B.: HFL: Hybrid Fuzzing on the Linux Kernel. In: The Network and Distributed System Security Symposium (NDSS 2020), pp. 1–17 (2020)
16. Klees, G., Ruef, A., Cooper, B., Wei, S., Hicks, M.: Evaluating fuzz testing. In: Proceedings of the 2018 ACM SIGSAC Conference on Computer and Communications Security (CCS 18), pp. 2123–2138 (2018). https://doi.org/10.1145/3243734.3243804
17. LibFuzzer Docs. https://llvm.org/docs/LibFuzzer.html. (2022)
18. LibFuzzer Standalone. https://github.com/llvm/llvm-project/tree/main/compiler-rt/lib/fuzzer/standalone. (2022)
19. LLVM Project. https://github.com/llvm/llvm-project. (2022)
20. Mera, A., Feng, B., Lu, L., Kirda, E.: DICE: Automatic emulation of dma input channels for dynamic firmware analysis. In: 2021 IEEE Symposium on Security and Privacy (SP), pp. 1938–1954 (2021). https://doi.org/10.1109/SP40001.2021.00018

21. Nilizadeh, S., Noller, Y., Pasareanu, CS. Pasareanu.: DiffFuzz: differential fuzzing for side-channel analysis. In:2019 IEEE/ACM 41st International Conference on Software Engineering (ICSE), pp. 176–187 (2019). https://doi.org/10.1109/ICSE.2019.00034
22. Noller, Y., Păsăreanu, CS., Böhme, M., Sun, Y., Nguyen, HL., Grunske, L.: HyDiff: Hybrid differential software analysis. In: 2020 IEEE/ACM 42nd International Conference on Software Engineering (ICSE), pp. 1273–1285 (2020)
23. OpenSSL 1-day bug: BN_mod_exp2_mont NULL pointer dereference. https://github.com/openssl/openssl/issues/17648. (2022)
24. OpenSSL's Github Issue labeled triaged:bug. https://github.com/openssl/openssl/issues?q=is:issue+is:open+label: triaged:+bug (2022)
25. Serebryany, K.: OSS-Fuzz: Google's continuous fuzzing service for open source software. https://github.com/google/oss-fuzz. (2017). (2022)
26. She, D., Pei, K., Epstein, D., Yang, J., Ray, B., Jana, S.: Neuzz: efficient fuzzing with neural program smoothing. In: 2019 IEEE Symposium on Security and Privacy (SP), pp. 803–817 (2019). https://doi.org/10.1109/SP.2019.00052
27. Stephens, N., et al.: Augmenting fuzzing through selective symbolic execution. In: the Network and Distributed System Security Symposium (NDSS 2016), pp. 1–16 (2016)
28. Wang, D., Zhang, Z., Zhang, H., Qian, Z., Krishnamurthy, SV., Abu-Ghazaleh, N.: SyzVegas: Beating Kernel Fuzzing Odds with Reinforcement Learning. In: 30th USENIX Security Symposium (USENIX Security 21), pp. 2741–2758 (2021)
29. Yang, X., Chen, Y., Eide, E., Regehr, J.: Finding and understanding bugs in C compilers. In: Proceedings of the 32nd ACM SIGPLAN conference on Programming language design and implementation (PLDI 11), pp. 283–194 (2011). https://doi.org/10.1145/1993498.1993532
30. Yang, Y., Kim, T., Chun, BG.: Finding consensus bugs in ethereum via multi-transaction differential fuzzing. In: 15th USENIX Symposium on Operating Systems Design and Implementation (OSDI 21), pp. 349–365 (2021)
31. Yue, T., et al.: EcoFuzz: Adaptive Energy-Saving Greybox Fuzzing as a Variant of the Adversarial Multi-Armed Bandit. In: 29th USENIX Security Symposium (USENIX Security 20), pp. 2307–2324 (2020)
32. Yun, I., Lee, S., Xu, M., Jang, Y., Kim, T.: QSYM: a practical concolic execution engine tailored for hybrid fuzzing. In: 27th USENIX Security Symposium (USENIX Security 18), pp. 745–761 (2018)

Applied Cryptography

Public Key Encryption with Hierarchical Authorized Keyword Search

Zi-Yuan Liu[1,2], Chu-Chieh Chien[1], Yi-Fan Tseng[1], Raylin Tso[1](✉), and Masahiro Mambo[2]

[1] National Chengchi University, Taipei 116016, Taiwan
{zyliu,ge10946,yftseng,raylin}@cs.nccu.edu.tw
[2] Kanazawa University, Kanazawa 920-1192, Japan
mambo@ec.t.kanazawa-u.ac.jp

Abstract. Public key encryption with keyword search (PEKS), which was introduced by Boneh *et al.* at EUROCRYPT' 04, is a breakthrough approach to searching encrypted data under a public key setting. In this cryptographic primitive, senders can generate searchable ciphertexts for specific keywords to be retrieved from a given document; receivers can generate corresponding trapdoors for search by using their private keys. Recently, Jiang *et al.* (ACISP' 16) proposed an improved PEKS scheme called public key encryption with authorized keyword search (PEAKS); this scheme enables authorized users to generate trapdoors for specific sets of keywords even if these users do not have access to the private key. Unfortunately, authorized users cannot delegate this power to other unauthorized users because the authorization in PEAKS is insufficiently flexible; therefore, this scheme is not suitable for enterprise scenarios in general. In this work, we introduce a novel cryptographic primitive called public key encryption with hierarchical authorized keyword search (PEHAKS) to solve this problem. In contrast to PEAKS, the proposed primitive enables authorized users to further hierarchically delegate their power of generating trapdoors to unauthorized users. We formally define the system model of PEHAKS under a multikeyword setting, and the security requirements are designed to withstand attacks in a real scenario. Furthermore, we propose a provably secure scheme using the technique of dual pairing vector spaces and demonstrate that the scheme is secure under the hardness of the n-extended decisional Diffie–Hellman assumption. Therefore, the proposed scheme is secure and can be applied in scenarios that require hierarchical authorization. To the best of the authors' knowledge, no PEKS variant schemes with this property have been previously designed.

Keywords: Authorization · Hierarchical · Multikeyword Search · Public Key Encryption

S.-H. Seo and H. Seo (Eds.): ICISC 2022, LNCS 13849, pp. 147–170, 2023.
https://doi.org/10.1007/978-3-031-29371-9_8

1 Introduction

1.1 Background

Cloud computing is becoming increasingly ubiquitous [8,15,19], with cloud storage services being especially popular [3,21]. Data uploaded to the server can be easily accessed by users at any time and from any place; moreover, the service provider ensures that users have sufficient storage and do not lose data. However, these services are usually provided and managed by an untrusted server. To ensure the privacy of sensitive data, users must encrypt their data before uploading them. Unfortunately, encryption hinders data manipulation. For example, a user searching for a specific file hosted in the cloud must first download all of the encrypted data and locally decrypt it before searching. This method is inefficient and computationally expensive, especially when compared with local storage.

To solve this problem, Boneh *et al.* [4] proposed public key encryption with keyword search (PEKS) to allow users to search encrypted data without decrypting it in a public key setting. Specifically, there are three roles in PEKS: the sender, receiver, and cloud server. The sender first retrieves related keywords from the data and then encrypts not only the data but also related keywords, which are ciphertexts that can be searched by the receiver. Finally, the sender uploads both the encrypted data and the searchable ciphertexts to the cloud server. Consequently, to determine whether encrypted data related to a keyword exists, the receiver can generate a trapdoor for a specific keyword using the receiver's private key. This trapdoor is uploaded to the cloud server that then searches for searchable ciphertexts that match the trapdoor. Finally, the corresponding encrypted data are returned to the receiver.

The scheme of Boneh *et al.*'s [4] is both efficient and elegant; therefore, it has been used as a basis for several subsequently proposed extended PEKS schemes, including schemes that are resistant to keyword guessing attacks [5,12,16] and schemes that support more functions for a greater variety of scenarios [17,18]. However, in normal PEKS schemes, only the receiver's private key can be used to generate a valid trapdoor. In an enterprise scenario, if employees want to generate trapdoors to search encrypted data that have been encrypted using the enterprise's public key, they must access the corresponding private key, which may lead to key abuse.

Public key encryption with authorized keyword search (PEAKS), which was proposed by Jiang *et al.* [9], enables receivers to authorize other users to search encrypted data; users do not need to access a private key to generate a trapdoor. More concretely, an authority holding a private key can authorize a user to generate a trapdoor by giving the user a token associated with a set of keywords $\mathcal{W}$. The authorized user can then adaptively generate a trapdoor for any keyword $w \in \mathcal{W}$. However, authorized users cannot further delegate their power to other users in PEAKS. In actual enterprise scenarios, employees often belong to different departments or are at different organizational levels. If employees at each level could delegate trapdoor generation authority to employees at the next level, not only can the burden on the private key holder be reduced but search policies can also be flexibly tailored to various scenarios.

1.2 Our Contributions

In this work, we first formalize a novel cryptosystem termed public key encryption with hierarchical authorized keyword search (PEHAKS), in which authorized users can further hierarchically delegate their power to unauthorized users. Specifically, the system model of PEHAKS is developed in a multikeyword setting.

An authority can provide the ability to generate trapdoors to users, called authorization; this is done by producing authorization tokens $token_{\mathcal{W}}$ for a set of keywords $\mathcal{W}$. The authorized users can then further delegate their authorization to unauthorized users by generating delegated authorization tokens $token_{\mathcal{W}'}$ for a set of keywords $\mathcal{W}'$ for some $\mathcal{W}' \subseteq \mathcal{W}$. Consequently, let $\mathcal{W}''$ be a set of keywords such that $\mathcal{W}'' \subseteq \mathcal{W}$ and $\mathcal{W}'' \subseteq \mathcal{W}'$, both authorized users and delegated users can generate trapdoors $td_{\mathcal{W}''}$ for the set of keywords $\mathcal{W}''$ by using authorization tokens and delegated authorization tokens, respectively. In addition, let $ct_{\mathcal{W}}$ be a searchable ciphertext related to some set of keywords $\mathcal{W}$ then, if $\mathcal{W}'' \subseteq \mathcal{W}$, the cloud server can search $ct_{\mathcal{W}}$ using $td_{\mathcal{W}''}$.

We also rigorously model a security requirement known as semantic security against chosen keyword attacks (SS-CKA) between a challenger and an adversary to ensure that no adversary can obtain any keyword information from the searchable ciphertext. In addition, based on the dual pairing vector spaces (DPVS) technique [13], we introduce a concrete scheme supporting a multikeyword setting. By leveraging the semi-functional technique [20], we present security proof to show that our scheme is SS-CKA secure if OT.1 and OT.2 assumptions are hard. We also theoretically compare the proposed scheme with the PEAKS scheme of Jiang *et al.* in terms of their properties and computational requirements. To the best of our knowledge, the proposed scheme is the first scheme to allow hierarchical multikeyword searches and delegation for authorization.

1.3 Intuition Behind Our Scheme

Generally, let $\mathcal{W}' \subseteq \mathcal{W}$, $\mathcal{W}'' \subseteq \mathcal{W}$, and $\mathcal{U}$ be a sorted universal keyword space with polynomial large size. In this work, we aim to formulate a scheme that has the following two properties.

1. Support hierarchical delegation from an authorization token (or a delegated authorization token) $token_{\mathcal{W}}$ to a delegated authorization token $token_{\mathcal{W}'}$.
2. Allow a ciphertext $ct_{\mathcal{W}}$ to be searched by a trapdoor $td_{\mathcal{W}''}$.

To realize it, we choose a proper mapping function map in our scheme. This function maps a nonempty set of keywords $\mathcal{W} \subseteq \mathcal{U}$ to a unique ℓ-bit string $\boldsymbol{bit}_{\mathcal{W}}$. The ith bit of $\boldsymbol{bit}_{\mathcal{W}_i}$ is set to 1 if the ith keyword of $\mathcal{U}$ is in $\mathcal{W}$; otherwise, it is set as 0. For example, if $\mathcal{U} := \{\text{Australia, Egypt, Greece, Norway}\}, \mathcal{W} := \{\text{Australia, Greece}\}$, then $\boldsymbol{bit}_{\mathcal{W}} := \mathsf{map}(\mathcal{W}) = 1010$. Hence, each possible set of keywords is presented as a unique string.

Our strategy is to propose methods of generating elements (*i.e.*, authorization tokens, delegated authorization tokens, ciphertexts, and trapdoors) in PEHAKS for various strings such that these elements meet the requirements of the PEHAKS. Concretely, the authorization token for a string (*e.g.*, 1010) can be further transformed to a delegated authorization token for substrings of this string (*e.g.*, 1000 or 0010). A ciphertext for a string (*e.g.*, 1111) can be searched by a trapdoor (which is produced from an authorization token or a delegated authorization token) for a substring (*e.g.*, 0110) of 1111.

To achieve this goal, we adopt the inner-product encryption with generalized key delegation (WKP-IPE) proposed by Abdalla *et al.* [2] as a basic building block of our proposed scheme. We then modify their [2] generic transformation of WKP-IPE to an (anonymous) wildcard identity-based encryption (IBE) scheme with generalized key delegation (WW-IBE). More concretely, we propose three novel encoding functions that map bit strings to patterns, and modify them accordingly. Therefore, the resulting private keys have a hierarchical structure, enabling delegation, and the inner product of the vector representation of the ciphertext and the trapdoor under the specified base are 0. Therefore, with the proposed encoding functions, the resulting (variant) WW-IBE can provide the desired outcomes. After obtaining a variant WW-IBE, the patterns can be considered an identity and we can further apply Abdalla *et al.*'s [1] IBE-to-PEKS transform on the variant WW-IBE. Thus, the first PEHAKS scheme is obtained.

1.4 Paper Organization

The remainder of this paper is organized as follows. We start with formulating the proposed PEHAKS system in Sect. 2, including describing the whole system and defining formal definition as well as the security model. Then, in Sect. 3, we review some preliminaries, including background on the dual pairing vector space and two complexity assumptions. In Sect. 4, we propose a concrete PEHAKS scheme and the corresponding correctness. Furthermore, in Sect. 5, we show the proposed scheme is SS-CKA secure. In Sect. 6, we also provide a theoretical comparison between the proposed scheme and Jiang *et al.*'s scheme [9]. Finally, we summarize this work and provide interesting future work in Sect. 7.

2 Problem Formulation

2.1 System Description

As illustrated in Fig. 1, a PEHAKS system comprises four parties: *Authority*, *Sender*, *Receiver*, and *Server*.

- *Authority*. The authority can authorize users the power of generating trapdoors for search.
- *Sender*. The sender uploads encrypted data and searchable ciphertexts to the server. The searchable ciphertexts, generated using the authority's public key, are related to a set of keywords retrieved from the data.
- *Receiver*. There are two types of receivers—authorized users and delegated users. Authorized users, authorized by the authority, can further delegate authorization for unauthorized users (called delegated users now). These delegated users can also hierarchically delegate their authorization to other unauthorized users. In addition, both authorized users and delegated users can generate a trapdoor for search by using their authorization token and delegated authorization tokens, respectively.
- *Server*. The server determines which searchable ciphertext matches the trapdoor. It then returns the corresponding encrypted data to users.

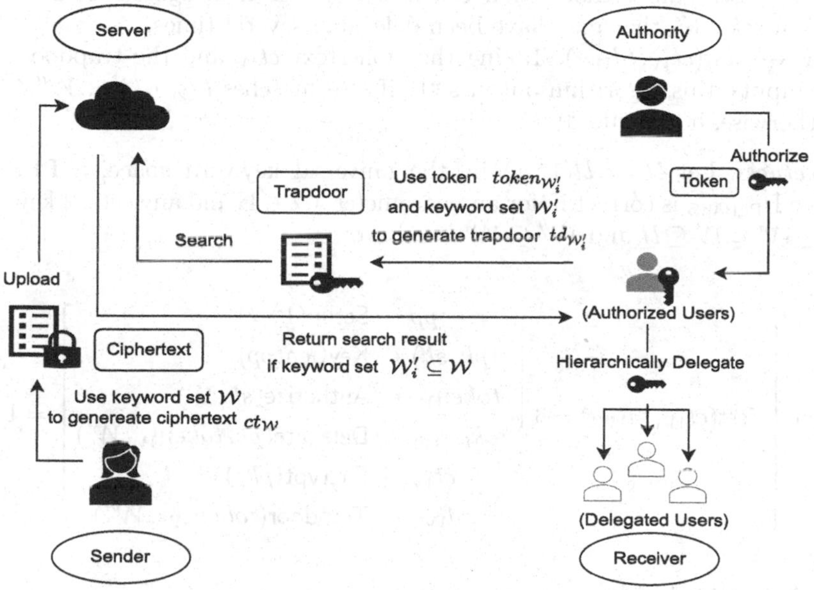

Fig. 1. High-level description of PEHAKS.

2.2 Algorithm Definitions

A PEHAKS Π_{PEHAKS} comprises seven polynomial-time algorithms—Setup, KeyGen, Authorize, Delegate, Encrypt, Trapdoor, and Test—which are described as follows:

- $pp \leftarrow \mathsf{Setup}(1^\lambda, \ell)$. Taking a security parameter λ and the size ℓ of the universal keyword space as inputs, this algorithm outputs a public parameter pp. Note that pp is implicitly included in the following algorithms.
- $(pk, sk) \leftarrow \mathsf{KeyGen}(pp)$. Taking the public parameter pp as inputs, this algorithm generates a public and private key pair (pk, sk).
- $token_{\mathcal{W}} \leftarrow \mathsf{Authorize}(sk, \mathcal{W})$. Taking the private key sk and a set of keywords $\mathcal{W}$ as inputs, this algorithm outputs an authorization token $token_{\mathcal{W}}$ for $\mathcal{W}$.
- $token_{\mathcal{W}'} \leftarrow \mathsf{Delegate}(pk, token_{\mathcal{W}}, \mathcal{W}')$. Taking the public key pk, the authorization (or delegated authorization token) $token_{\mathcal{W}}$, and a set of keywords $\mathcal{W}' \subseteq \mathcal{W}$ as inputs, this algorithm outputs a delegated authorization token $token_{\mathcal{W}'}$ for $\mathcal{W}'$.
- $ct_{\mathcal{W}} \leftarrow \mathsf{Encrypt}(pk, \mathcal{W})$. Taking the public key pk and a set of keywords $\mathcal{W}$ as inputs, this algorithm outputs a ciphertext $ct_{\mathcal{W}}$ for $\mathcal{W}$.
- $td_{\mathcal{W}''} \leftarrow \mathsf{Trapdoor}(token_{\mathcal{W}^*}, \mathcal{W}'')$. Taking an authorization token (or delegated authorization token) $token_{\mathcal{W}^*}$ and a set of keywords $\mathcal{W}'' \subseteq \mathcal{W}^*$ as inputs, this algorithm outputs a trapdoor $td_{\mathcal{W}''}$ for $\mathcal{W}''$. Here, we use $token_{\mathcal{W}^*}$ to represent an authorization token $token_{\mathcal{W}}$ or a delegated authorization token $token_{\mathcal{W}'}$ that may have been delegated several times.
- $1/0 \leftarrow \mathsf{Test}(ct_{\mathcal{W}}, td_{\mathcal{W}''})$. Taking the ciphertext $ct_{\mathcal{W}}$ and the trapdoor $td_{\mathcal{W}''}$ as inputs, this algorithm outputs "1" if $ct_{\mathcal{W}}$ matches $td_{\mathcal{W}''}$ (*i.e.*, $\mathcal{W}'' \subseteq \mathcal{W}$). Otherwise, it outputs "0".

Correctness. Let $\mathcal{U} = \mathcal{U}(1^\lambda, \ell)$ be the universal keyword space, a PEHAKS scheme Π_{PEHAKS} is correct if, for any parameter $\lambda, \ell \in \mathbb{N}$ and any sets of keywords $\mathcal{W}'' \subseteq \mathcal{W}' \subseteq \mathcal{W} \subseteq \mathcal{U}$ and $\mathcal{W}'' \subseteq \mathcal{W}^*$, we have

$$\Pr\left[\mathsf{Test}(ct_{\mathcal{W}}, td_{\mathcal{W}''}) = 1 \;\middle|\; \begin{array}{r} pp \leftarrow \mathsf{Setup}(1^\lambda, \ell) \\ (pk, sk) \leftarrow \mathsf{KeyGen}(pp) \\ token_{\mathcal{W}} \leftarrow \mathsf{Authorize}(sk, \mathcal{W}) \\ token_{\mathcal{W}'} \leftarrow \mathsf{Delegate}(pk, token_{\mathcal{W}}, \mathcal{W}') \\ ct_{\mathcal{W}} \leftarrow \mathsf{Encrypt}(pk, \mathcal{W}) \\ td_{\mathcal{W}''} \leftarrow \mathsf{Trapdoor}(token_{\mathcal{W}^*}, \mathcal{W}'') \end{array}\right] = 1.$$

2.3 Security Model

To ensure that no adversary can obtain any keyword information from ciphertexts, we define a security game termed semantic security against chosen keyword attacks (SS-CKA) for PEHAKS. This game follows the SS-CKA game defined in the work of Jiang *et al.*'s [9], in which a challenger $\mathcal{C}$ and an adversary $\mathcal{A}$ interact.

- **Setup.** $\mathcal{C}$ runs $pp \leftarrow \mathsf{Setup}(1^\lambda, \ell)$ and $(pk, sk) \leftarrow \mathsf{KeyGen}(pp)$ algorithms. $\mathcal{C}$ then sends (pp, pk) to $\mathcal{A}$ and keeps sk secret.
- **Phase 1.** In this phase, $\mathcal{A}$ performs a polynomially bounded number of queries:

- Authorization Query. $\mathcal{A}$ issues a set of keywords $\mathcal{W}$ to $\mathcal{C}$ for this query. $\mathcal{C}$ responds to $\mathcal{A}$ with an authorization token $token_{\mathcal{W}}$ for $\mathcal{W}$.
- Delegation Query. $\mathcal{A}$ issues two sets of keywords $\mathcal{W}', \mathcal{W}$ to $\mathcal{C}$ for this query, where $\mathcal{W}' \subseteq \mathcal{W}$. $\mathcal{C}$ responds to $\mathcal{A}$ with a delegated authorization token $token_{\mathcal{W}'}$ for $\mathcal{W}'$.

- **Challenge.** After $\mathcal{A}$ stops **Phase 1**, $\mathcal{A}$ selects two sets of keywords $(\mathcal{W}_0^*, \mathcal{W}_1^*)$ with the same size as the challenge and sends them to $\mathcal{C}$. $\mathcal{C}$ then randomly chooses a bit $b \xleftarrow{\$} \{0,1\}$ and responds to $\mathcal{A}$ with a challenge ciphertext $ct_{\mathcal{W}_b^*} \leftarrow \mathsf{Encrypt}(pk, \mathcal{W}_b^*)$. Here, the restriction for $\mathcal{A}$ is that $\mathcal{A}$ has never issued any set of keywords $\widetilde{\mathcal{W}}$ for some $\widetilde{\mathcal{W}} \subseteq \mathcal{W}_0^*$ or $\widetilde{\mathcal{W}} \subseteq \mathcal{W}_1^*$ to $\mathcal{C}$ for an authorization query or delegation query to generate a (delegated) authorization token $token_{\widetilde{\mathcal{W}}}$.
- **Phase 2.** $\mathcal{A}$ continues to perform queries as in **Phase 1**. The restriction is that $\mathcal{A}$ cannot issue authorization queries or delegation queries on any set of keywords $\widetilde{\mathcal{W}}$ for some $\widetilde{\mathcal{W}} \subseteq \mathcal{W}_0^*$ or $\widetilde{\mathcal{W}} \subseteq \mathcal{W}_1^*$, and that the size of ($\mathcal{W}_0^*$ and $\mathcal{W}_1^*$) must be the same.
- **Guess.** $\mathcal{A}$ outputs a bit b' as its guess.

The advantage of $\mathcal{A}$ winning this game is defined as

$$\mathsf{Adv}^{\text{SS-CKA}}_{\mathcal{A},\Pi_{\mathsf{PEHAKS}}}(\lambda, \ell) := \left|\Pr[b' = b] - \frac{1}{2}\right|.$$

Definition 1 (SS-CKA Security of PEHAKS). *A PEHAKS scheme* Π_{PEHAKS} *satisfies SS-CKA security if for any probabilistic polynomial time (PPT) adversary* $\mathcal{A}$*, the function* $\mathsf{Adv}^{\text{SS-CKA}}_{\mathcal{A},\Pi_{\mathsf{PEHAKS}}}(\lambda, \ell)$ *is negligible.*

Remark 1. In the system model of Jiang *et al.* [9], each token is associated with a timestamp; if it expires, the token becomes invalid. In addition, to capture the possibility of an invalid token being used by an adversary, they define the security requirement termed "trapdoor existential unforgeability." However, as a similar result can be easily achieved by equipping a concrete scheme with a secure digital signature [7,10], we omit discussing timestamps in our system model. Consequently, we also do not consider trapdoor existential unforgeability because this security requirement can be trivially satisfied if the underlying digital signature scheme satisfies existential unforgeability under chosen message attacks.

3 Preliminaries

3.1 Dual Pairing Vector Spaces (DPVS)

In this subsection, we briefly describe the concept of DPVS introduced by Okamoto and Takashima [13]. We focus on the DPVS over symmetric pairing groups.

Definition 2 (Symmetric Pairing Groups). *Let $(\mathbb{G}, \mathbb{G}_T, N, g, \hat{e})$ be a symmetric pairing groups. Here, $\mathbb{G}$ is an elliptic curve group, and $\mathbb{G}_T$ is a multiplicative subgroup. N is the prime order of $\mathbb{G}$ and $\mathbb{G}_T$, g is a generator of $\mathbb{G}$, and $\hat{e} : \mathbb{G} \times \mathbb{G} \rightarrow \mathbb{G}_T$ is a nondegenerate bilinear pairing operation. In addition, the following three properties should be satisfied:*

- *For all $u, v \in \mathbb{G}$ and $a, b \in \mathbb{Z}_N$, we have $\hat{e}(u^a, v^b) = \hat{e}(u, v)^{ab}$.*
- *$\hat{e}(g, g)$ is a generator of group $\mathbb{G}_T$.*
- *For all $u, v \in \mathbb{G}$, $\hat{e}(u, v)$ can be efficiently computed.*

Now, let $(\mathbb{G}, \mathbb{G}_T, N, g, \hat{e}, \mathbb{V}, \mathbb{A})$ be a DPVS tuple over symmetric pairing, there exist three important properties.

- **Vector space** $\mathbb{V}$: For some $n \in \mathbb{N}$, $\mathbb{V} := \mathbb{G}^n$ is termed a "vector space" containing n-dimensional vectors (*e.g.*, $\boldsymbol{x} = (g^{x_1}, \cdots, g^{x_n}) \in \mathbb{V}$, where $x_1, \cdots, x_n \in \mathbb{Z}_N$).
- **Canonical base** $\mathbb{A}$: The canonical base of $\mathbb{V}$ is defined as $\mathbb{A} := (\boldsymbol{a}_1, \cdots, \boldsymbol{a}_n)$, where $\boldsymbol{a}_i$ is a vector whose elements are all 1 except that the ith element is g (*i.e.*, $\boldsymbol{a}_i = (1, \cdots, 1, g, 1, \cdots, 1)$). Then, $\boldsymbol{x} \in \mathbb{V}$ can be expressed as $(x_1, \cdots, x_n)_{\mathbb{A}}$.
- **Pairing operation**: For $\boldsymbol{x}, \boldsymbol{y} \in \mathbb{V}$, the pairing operation of $\boldsymbol{x}$ and $\boldsymbol{y}$ can be defined as

$$\hat{e}(\boldsymbol{x}, \boldsymbol{y}) := \prod_{i \in [n]} \hat{e}(g^{x_i}, g^{y_i}) = \hat{e}(g, g)^{\sum_{i=1}^{n} x_i \cdot y_i} = \hat{e}(g, g)^{\langle \boldsymbol{x} \cdot \boldsymbol{y} \rangle}.$$

In the following we further introduce a crucial DPVS algorithm that is used in the proposed scheme:

Definition 3 (Dual Orthonormal Bases Generator). *Given a security parameter λ and $n \in \mathbb{N}$, let the general linear group $\mathsf{GL}(n, \mathbb{F}_q)$ be an algorithm that outputs a set of $n \times n$ matrices with entries in the field $\mathbb{F}_q$ whose determinant is nonzero [6]. The random dual orthonormal bases generator* $\mathsf{DOBGen}(1^\lambda, n)$ *operates as follows:*

1. *Generate DPVS parameters as $pp_{\mathbb{V}} := (\mathbb{G}, \mathbb{G}_T, N, g, \hat{e}, \mathbb{V}, \mathbb{A})$ under parameters λ and n.*
2. *Pick $\boldsymbol{R} := (r_{i,j})_{i \in [n], j \in [n]} \xleftarrow{\$} \mathsf{GL}(n, \mathbb{Z}_N)$ and set $\boldsymbol{R}^* := (r^*_{i,j})_{i \in [n], j \in [n]} = (\boldsymbol{R}^\top)^{-1}$.*
3. *Set $\mathbb{B} := (\boldsymbol{b}_i)_{i \in [n]}$ and $\mathbb{B}^* := (\boldsymbol{b}^*_i)_{i \in [n]}$, where $\boldsymbol{b}_i = \sum_{j \in [n]} r_{i,j} \cdot \boldsymbol{a}_j$ and $\boldsymbol{b}^*_i = \sum_{j \in [n]} r^*_{i,j} \cdot \boldsymbol{a}_j$.*
4. *Return a tuple $(pp_{\mathbb{V}}, \mathbb{B}, \mathbb{B}^*)$.*

Here $(\mathbb{B}, \mathbb{B}^*)$ is called a dual orthonormal base of $\mathbb{V}$ with the property that

$$\hat{e}(\boldsymbol{b}_i, \boldsymbol{b}^*_j) := \begin{cases} \hat{e}(g, g) & if i = j; \\ 1 & otherwise. \end{cases}$$

3.2 Complexity Assumptions

We now recall two assumptions (OT.1 and OT.2) introduced by Lewko *et al.* [11] that are used in the security proof of our scheme. Let $(pp_{\mathbb{V}} := (\mathbb{G}, \mathbb{G}_T, N, g, \hat{e}, \mathbb{V}, \mathbb{A}), \mathbb{B} := (\boldsymbol{b}_i)_{i\in[2n+3]}, \mathbb{B}^* := (\boldsymbol{b}_i^*)_{i\in[2n+3]}) \leftarrow \mathsf{DOBGen}(1^\lambda, 2n+3)$, the descriptions of $\mathcal{D}_1$ and $\mathcal{D}_2$ are defined as follows:

Description of $\mathcal{D}_1$	Description of $\mathcal{D}_2$
$\mu, \rho \xleftarrow{\$} \mathbb{Z}_N$	$\mu, \rho, \omega, \iota \xleftarrow{\$} \mathbb{Z}_N$
$\boldsymbol{\mu} := (\mu_1, \cdots, \mu_n) \xleftarrow{\$} \mathbb{Z}_N^n$	$\boldsymbol{\nu} := (\nu_1, \cdots, \nu_n) \xleftarrow{\$} \mathbb{Z}_N^n$
$\boldsymbol{U} := (\boldsymbol{u}_i)_{i\in[n]} := (u_{i,j})_{i\in[n],j\in[n]} \xleftarrow{\$} \mathsf{GL}(n, \mathbb{Z}_N)$	$\boldsymbol{U} := (\boldsymbol{u}_i)_{i\in[n]} := (u_{i,j})_{i\in[n],j\in[n]} \xleftarrow{\$} \mathsf{GL}(n, \mathbb{Z}_N)$
$\hat{\mathbb{B}} := (\boldsymbol{b}_1, \cdots, \boldsymbol{b}_n, \boldsymbol{b}_{2n+1}, \boldsymbol{b}_{2n+3})$	$\hat{\mathbb{B}} := (\boldsymbol{b}_1, \cdots, \boldsymbol{b}_n, \boldsymbol{b}_{2n+1}, \boldsymbol{b}_{2n+3})$
$\hat{\mathbb{B}}^* := (\boldsymbol{b}_1^*, \cdots, \boldsymbol{b}_n^*, \boldsymbol{b}_{2n+1}^*, \boldsymbol{b}_{2n+2}^*)$	$\hat{\mathbb{B}}^* := (\boldsymbol{b}_1^*, \cdots, \boldsymbol{b}_{2n+2}^*)$
$\boldsymbol{e}_0 := (\mu \cdot \boldsymbol{b}_i + \mu_i \cdot \boldsymbol{b}_{2n+3})_{i\in[n]}$	$\boldsymbol{Z} := (\boldsymbol{z}_i)_{i\in[n]} := (z_{i,j})_{i\in[n],j\in[n]} = (\boldsymbol{U}^\top)^{-1}$
$\boldsymbol{e}_1 := (\mu \cdot \boldsymbol{b}_i + \rho \cdot \sum_{j\in[n]} u_{i,j} \cdot \boldsymbol{b}_{n+j} + \mu_i \cdot \boldsymbol{b}_{2n+3})_{i\in[n]}$	$\boldsymbol{e} := (\mu \cdot \boldsymbol{b}_i + \rho \cdot \sum_{j\in[n]} u_{i,j} \cdot \boldsymbol{b}_{n+j})_{i\in[n]}$
$\mathcal{D}_1 := (pp_{\mathbb{V}}, \hat{\mathbb{B}}, \hat{\mathbb{B}}^*)$	$\boldsymbol{h}_0 := (\omega \cdot \boldsymbol{b}_i^* + \nu_i \cdot \boldsymbol{b}_{2n+2}^*)_{i\in[n]}$
	$\boldsymbol{h}_1 := (\omega \cdot \boldsymbol{b}_i^* + \iota \cdot \sum_{j\in[n]} z_{i,j} \cdot \boldsymbol{b}_{n+j}^* + \nu_i \cdot \boldsymbol{b}_{2n+2}^*)_{i\in[n]}$
	$\mathcal{D}_2 := (pp_{\mathbb{V}}, \hat{\mathbb{B}}, \hat{\mathbb{B}}^*, \boldsymbol{e})$

We define the advantage of a PPT algorithm $\mathcal{A}$ for breaking OT.1 assumption to be

$$\mathsf{Adv}_{\mathcal{A}}^{OT.1}(\lambda) := |\Pr[\mathcal{A}(\mathcal{D}_1, \boldsymbol{e}_0) = 1] - \Pr[\mathcal{A}(\mathcal{D}_1, \boldsymbol{e}_1) = 1]|,$$

and the advantage of a PPT algorithm $\mathcal{A}$ for breaking OT.2 assumption to be

$$\mathsf{Adv}_{\mathcal{A}}^{OT.2}(\lambda) := |\Pr[\mathcal{A}(\mathcal{D}_2, \boldsymbol{h}_0) = 1] - \Pr[\mathcal{A}(\mathcal{D}_2, \boldsymbol{h}_1) = 1]|.$$

Definition 4 (OT.1 and OT.2 Assumptions). *We say that OT.1 (resp. OT.2) holds for generator* $\mathsf{DOBGen}(1^\lambda, 2n+3)$ *if for all PPT algorithms* $\mathcal{A}$, $\mathsf{Adv}_{\mathcal{A}}^{OT.1}(\lambda)$ *(resp.* $\mathsf{Adv}_{\mathcal{A}}^{OT.2}(\lambda)$*) is a negligible function of* λ.

Lewko *et al.* showed that the hardnesses of breaking assumptions OT.1 and OT.2 are the same as breaking the n-extended decisional Diffie–Hellman (Lemma 6 and Lemma 7 in [11]). In addition, Okamoto and Takashima further proved that these assumptions can be reduced to decision linear assumption (Lemma 1 and Lemma 2 in [14]).

4 Public Key Encryption with Hierarchical Authorized Keyword Search

In this section, we introduce a concrete PEHAKS scheme. Let $\mathcal{U}$ be a sorted universal keyword space with size ℓ, and let n be the total length of a string representing ℓ (*i.e.*, $n = 2\ell$). The proposed scheme is described as follows:

$\mathsf{Setup}(1^\lambda, \ell) \rightarrow pp$. Given a security parameter λ and the size ℓ of $\mathcal{U}$, this algorithm performs the following steps:

- Choose symmetric pairing groups $(\mathbb{G}, \mathbb{G}_T, N, g, \hat{e})$ as defined in Definition 2.
- Define three encoding functions $\mathsf{Encode}_1, \mathsf{Encode}_2$, and Encode_3 that take an ℓ-bit string $\boldsymbol{bit}$ as input as in Fig. 2.

Function $\mathsf{Encode}_1(\boldsymbol{bit})$	Function $\mathsf{Encode}_2(\boldsymbol{bit})$	Function $\mathsf{Encode}_3(\boldsymbol{bit})$
for $i \in [\ell]$ **do**	**for** $i \in [\ell]$ **do**	**for** $i \in [\ell]$ **do**
if $\boldsymbol{bit}_i = 1$ **then**	**if** $\boldsymbol{bit}_i = 1$ **then**	**if** $\boldsymbol{bit}_i = 1$ **then**
$\boldsymbol{x}_i := (0, 0)$	$\boldsymbol{x}_i := (0, 0)$	$\boldsymbol{x}_i := (1, 1)$
else	**else**	**else**
$\boldsymbol{x}_i := (1, 0)$	$r_i \xleftarrow{\$} \mathbb{Z}_N$	$\boldsymbol{x}_i := (1, 0)$
output $\boldsymbol{x}$	$\boldsymbol{x}_i := (0, r_i)$	**output** $\boldsymbol{x}$
	output $\boldsymbol{x}$	

Fig. 2. Procedure of encoding functions.

- Choose a proper mapping function $\mathsf{map} : \mathcal{W} \to \{0, 1\}^\ell$ that maps a nonempty set of keywords $\mathcal{W} \subseteq \mathcal{U}$ to a unique ℓ-bit string $\boldsymbol{bit}_\mathcal{W}$, where the ith bit of $\boldsymbol{bit}_{\mathcal{W}_i}$ is set to 1 if the ith keyword of $\mathcal{U}$ is in $\mathcal{W}$ and set to 0 otherwise.

Finally, the public parameter is set as

$$pp := (\lambda, \ell, N, g, \hat{e}, \mathbb{G}, \mathbb{G}_T, \mathsf{Encode}_1, \mathsf{Encodes}_2, \mathsf{Encodes}_3, \mathsf{map}).$$

$\mathsf{KeyGen}(pp) \to (pk, sk)$. Given the public parameter pp, this algorithm first runs $(pp_\mathbb{V}, \mathbb{B}, \mathbb{B}^*) \leftarrow \mathsf{DOBGen}(1^\lambda, 2n + 3)$. Then, it sets

$$\hat{\mathbb{B}} := (\boldsymbol{b}_1, \cdots, \boldsymbol{b}_n, \boldsymbol{b}_{2n+1}, \boldsymbol{b}_{2n+3}); \quad \Omega := \hat{e}(g, g).$$

The algorithm outputs the public and private key pair as

$$pk := (pp_\mathbb{V}, \hat{\mathbb{B}}, \Omega); \quad sk := \mathbb{B}^*.$$

$\mathsf{Authorize}(sk, \mathcal{W}) \to token_\mathcal{W}$. Given the private key sk and a nonempty set of keywords $\mathcal{W} \subseteq \mathcal{U}$, this algorithm first performs the following steps:

- Generate an encoding result $\boldsymbol{w} := (\boldsymbol{w}_1, \cdots, \boldsymbol{w}_\ell) \leftarrow \mathsf{Encode}_1(\mathsf{map}(\mathcal{W}))$, where each $\boldsymbol{w}_i \in \{(0, 0), (1, 0)\}$.
- Choose $r, r_1, \cdots, r_\ell \xleftarrow{\$} \mathbb{Z}_N$, compute

$$\boldsymbol{\delta} := (\boldsymbol{\delta}_1, \cdots, \boldsymbol{\delta}_\ell) := (r_1 \cdot \boldsymbol{w}_1, \cdots, r_\ell \cdot \boldsymbol{w}_\ell),$$

and set

$$token^\alpha_\mathcal{W} := (\boldsymbol{\delta}_1, \cdots, \boldsymbol{\delta}_\ell, \mathbf{0}_n, 1, r, 0)_{\mathbb{B}^*} \in \mathbb{G}^{2n+3},$$

where $\mathbf{0}_n$ is an n-dimensional zero vector.

- Define

$$\begin{cases} \mathcal{X} & := \{i \in [\ell] : \boldsymbol{w}_i \neq (0,0)\}; \\ \mathcal{Y} & := \{2i-1, 2i : \exists i \in [\ell] \text{ s.t. } \boldsymbol{w}_i = (0,0)\}. \end{cases}$$

- For each $i \in \mathcal{X}$, choose $s_i, s_{i,1}, \cdots, s_{i,\ell} \xleftarrow{\$} \mathbb{Z}_N$, compute

$$\boldsymbol{\zeta}_i := (\boldsymbol{\zeta}_{i,1}, \cdots, \boldsymbol{\zeta}_{i,\ell}) := (s_{i,1} \cdot \boldsymbol{w}_1, \cdots, s_{i,\ell} \cdot \boldsymbol{w}_\ell),$$

  and set

$$token^{\beta}_{\mathcal{W},i} := (\boldsymbol{\zeta}_{i,1}, \cdots, \boldsymbol{\zeta}_{i,\ell}, \boldsymbol{0}_n, 0, s_i, 0)_{\mathbb{B}^*} \in \mathbb{G}^{2n+3}.$$

- Choose $t \xleftarrow{\$} \mathbb{Z}_N$ and for each $i \in \mathcal{Y}$, runs the following steps:
  - Choose $t_i, t_{i,1}, \cdots, t_{i,\ell} \xleftarrow{\$} \mathbb{Z}_N$, and compute

$$\boldsymbol{\eta}_i := (\boldsymbol{\eta}_{i,1}, \cdots, \boldsymbol{\eta}_{i,\ell}), \text{ where } \boldsymbol{\eta}_{i,j} := \begin{cases} (t,0) & \text{if } j = \lceil \frac{i}{2} \rceil \text{ and } i \text{ is odd;} \\ (0,t) & \text{if } j = \lceil \frac{i}{2} \rceil \text{ and } i \text{ is even;} \\ t_{i,j} \cdot \boldsymbol{w}_j & \text{otherwise.} \end{cases}$$

  - Set

$$token^{\gamma}_{\mathcal{W},i} := (\boldsymbol{\eta}_{i,1}, \cdots, \boldsymbol{\eta}_{i,\ell}, \boldsymbol{0}_n, 0, t_i, 0)_{\mathbb{B}^*} \in \mathbb{G}^{2n+3}.$$

- The authorization token $token_{\mathcal{W}}$ is set as

$$token_{\mathcal{W}} := \left\{ token^{\alpha}_{\mathcal{W}}, \{token^{\beta}_{\mathcal{W},i}\}_{i \in \mathcal{X}}, \{token^{\gamma}_{\mathcal{W},i}\}_{i \in \mathcal{Y}} \right\}.$$

Remark 2. The token, ciphertext, and trapdoor, described as follows, are vectors of length $2n+3$ with base $\mathbb{B}$ or $\mathbb{B}^*$ in the vector space $\mathbb{V}$. The content of these vectors is the vectors obtained by the encoding functions after randomization and concatenation with a specific format.

$\mathsf{Delegate}(pk, token_{\mathcal{W}}, \mathcal{W}') \rightarrow token_{\mathcal{W}'}$. Given the public key pk, a (delegated) authorization token $token_{\mathcal{W}}$, and a nonempty set of keywords $\mathcal{W}' \subseteq \mathcal{W}$, this algorithm is executed as follows:

- Generate $\boldsymbol{w} := (\boldsymbol{w}_1, \cdots, \boldsymbol{w}_\ell) \leftarrow \mathsf{Encode}_1(\mathsf{map}(\mathcal{W}))$ and $\boldsymbol{w}' := (w'_i, \cdots, w'_n) := (\boldsymbol{w}'_1, \cdots, \boldsymbol{w}'_\ell) \leftarrow \mathsf{Encode}_1(\mathsf{map}(\mathcal{W}'))$.
- Define four sets as follows:

$$\begin{cases} \mathcal{X} & := \{i \in [\ell] : \boldsymbol{w}_i \neq (0,0)\}; \\ \mathcal{X}' & := \{i \in [\ell] : \boldsymbol{w}'_i \neq (0,0)\}; \\ \bar{\mathcal{X}} & := \{i \in [\ell] : \boldsymbol{w}_i = (0,0)\}; \\ \mathcal{Y}' & := \{2i-1, 2i : \exists i \in [\ell] \text{ s.t. } \boldsymbol{w}'_i = (0,0)\}. \end{cases}$$

- Choose $r'_1, \cdots, r'_\ell \xleftarrow{\$} \mathbb{Z}_N$ and compute

$$\begin{aligned} token^{\alpha}_{\mathcal{W}'} = token^{\alpha}_{\mathcal{W}} &+ \sum_{i \in \mathcal{X}} r'_i \cdot token^{\beta}_{\mathcal{W},i} \\ &+ \sum_{i \in \bar{\mathcal{X}}} r'_i \cdot (w'_{2i-1} \cdot token^{\gamma}_{\mathcal{W},2i-1} + w'_{2i} \cdot token^{\gamma}_{\mathcal{W},2i}). \end{aligned}$$

- For each $i \in \mathcal{X}'$, choose $s'_{i,1}, \cdots, s'_{i,\ell} \xleftarrow{\$} \mathbb{Z}_N$ and compute

$$\begin{aligned} token^{\beta}_{\mathcal{W}',i} &= \sum_{j \in \mathcal{X}} s'_{i,j} \cdot token^{\beta}_{\mathcal{W},j} \\ &+ \sum_{j \in \bar{\mathcal{X}}} s'_{i,j} \cdot (w'_{2j-1} \cdot token^{\gamma}_{\mathcal{W},2j-1} + w'_{2j} \cdot token^{\gamma}_{\mathcal{W},2j}). \end{aligned}$$

- Choose $t' \xleftarrow{\$} \mathbb{Z}_N$. For each $i \in \mathcal{Y}'$, choose $t'_{i,1}, \cdots, t'_{i,\ell} \xleftarrow{\$} \mathbb{Z}_N$ and compute

$$\begin{aligned} token^{\gamma}_{\mathcal{W}',i} &= t' \cdot token^{\gamma}_{\mathcal{W},i} + \sum_{j \in \mathcal{X}} t'_{i,j} \cdot token^{\beta}_{\mathcal{W},j} \\ &+ \sum_{j \in \bar{\mathcal{X}}} t'_{i,j} \cdot (w'_{2j-1} \cdot token^{\gamma}_{\mathcal{W},2j-1} + w'_{2j} \cdot token^{\gamma}_{\mathcal{W},2j}). \end{aligned}$$

- Output a delegated authorization token

$$token_{\mathcal{W}'} := \left\{ token^{\alpha}_{\mathcal{W}'}, \{token^{\beta}_{\mathcal{W}',i}\}_{i \in \mathcal{X}'}, \{token^{\gamma}_{\mathcal{W}',i}\}_{i \in \mathcal{Y}'} \right\}.$$

$\mathsf{Encrypt}(pk, \mathcal{W}) \rightarrow ct_{\mathcal{W}}$. Given a nonempty set of keywords $\mathcal{W} \subseteq \mathcal{U}$, this algorithm is executed as follows.

- Generate an encoding result $\boldsymbol{w} := (\boldsymbol{w}_1, \cdots, \boldsymbol{w}_\ell) \leftarrow \mathsf{Encode}_2(\mathsf{map}(\mathcal{W}))$.
- Choose $\sigma, q, q_1, \cdots, q_\ell \xleftarrow{\$} \mathbb{Z}_N$ and compute

$$\boldsymbol{\tau} := (\boldsymbol{\tau}_1, \cdots, \boldsymbol{\tau}_\ell) := (q_1 \cdot \boldsymbol{w}_1, \cdots, q_\ell \cdot \boldsymbol{w}_\ell).$$

- Set

$$ct_{\mathcal{W},1} := (\boldsymbol{\tau}_1, \cdots, \boldsymbol{\tau}_\ell, \boldsymbol{0}_n, \sigma, 0, q)_{\mathbb{B}} \in \mathbb{G}^{2n+3}; \quad ct_{\mathcal{W},2} := \Omega^{\sigma} \in \mathbb{G}_T.$$

- Output a ciphertext $ct_{\mathcal{W}} := \{ct_{\mathcal{W},1}, ct_{\mathcal{W},2}\}$.

$\mathsf{Trapdoor}(token_{\mathcal{W}'}, \mathcal{W}'') \rightarrow td_{\mathcal{W}''}$. Given the (delegated) authorization token $token_{\mathcal{W}'}$ and a specific nonempty set of keywords $\mathcal{W}'' \subseteq \mathcal{W}'$, this algorithm is executed as follows:

- Compute $\boldsymbol{w}' := (\boldsymbol{w}'_1, \cdots, \boldsymbol{w}'_\ell) \leftarrow \mathsf{Encode}_1(\mathsf{map}(\mathcal{W}'))$ and $\boldsymbol{w}'' := (w''_i, \cdots, w''_n) := (\boldsymbol{w}''_1, \cdots, \boldsymbol{w}''_\ell) \leftarrow \mathsf{Encode}_3(\mathsf{map}(\mathcal{W}''))$.
- Defines

$$\begin{cases} \mathcal{X} := \{i \in [\ell] : \boldsymbol{w}'_i \neq (0,0)\}; \\ \bar{\mathcal{X}} := \{i \in [\ell] : \boldsymbol{w}'_i = (0,0)\}. \end{cases}$$

– Chooses $r'_1, \cdots, r'_\ell \xleftarrow{\$} \mathbb{Z}_N$ and compute $td_{\mathcal{W}''}$ as follows:

$$\begin{aligned} td_{\mathcal{W}''} &= token^{\alpha}_{\mathcal{W}'} + \sum_{i \in \mathcal{X}} r'_i \cdot token^{\beta}_{\mathcal{W}',i} \\ &\quad + \sum_{i \in \bar{\mathcal{X}}} r'_i \cdot (w''_{2i-1} \cdot token^{\gamma}_{\mathcal{W}',2i-1} + w''_{2i} \cdot token^{\gamma}_{\mathcal{W}',2i}) \\ &= (\delta_1, \cdots, \delta_\ell, \mathbf{0}_n, 1, r, 0)_{\mathbb{B}^*} + \sum_{i \in \mathcal{X}} r'_i \cdot (\zeta_{i,1}, \cdots, \zeta_{i,\ell}, \mathbf{0}_n, 0, s_i, 0)_{\mathbb{B}^*} \\ &\quad + \sum_{i \in \bar{\mathcal{X}}} r'_i \cdot (w''_{2i-1} \cdot (\eta_{2i-1,1}, \cdots, \eta_{2i-1,\ell}, \mathbf{0}_n, 0, t_{2i-1}, 0)_{\mathbb{B}^*} \\ &\quad + w''_{2i} \cdot (\eta_{2i,1}, \cdots, \eta_{2i,\ell}, \mathbf{0}_n, 0, t_{2i}, 0)_{\mathbb{B}^*}). \end{aligned}$$

Because the aforementioned operation yields a linear combination of elements on $\mathbb{B}^*$, $td_{\mathcal{W}''}$ can be represented by $(\delta^{td}_1, \cdots, \delta^{td}_\ell, \mathbf{0}_n, 1, r^{td}, 0)_{\mathbb{B}^*}$ for simplicity, where $\delta^{td}_1, \cdots, \delta^{td}_\ell \in \mathbb{Z}^2_N$ and $r^{td} \in \mathbb{Z}_N$.

– Output a trapdoor

$$td_{\mathcal{W}''} := (\delta^{td}_1, \cdots, \delta^{td}_\ell, \mathbf{0}_n, 1, r^{td}, 0)_{\mathbb{B}^*} \in \mathbb{G}^{2n+3}.$$

$\mathsf{Test}(ct_{\mathcal{W}}, td_{\mathcal{W}''}) \to 1/0$. Given a ciphertext $ct_{\mathcal{W}}$ and a trapdoor $td_{\mathcal{W}''}$, this algorithm outputs 1 if $\hat{e}(ct_{\mathcal{W},1}, td_{\mathcal{W}''}) = ct_{\mathcal{W},2}$ holds, and outputs 0 otherwise.

Correctness. Suppose that a ciphertext $ct_{\mathcal{W}} := (ct_{\mathcal{W},1}, ct_{\mathcal{W},2})$ for $\mathcal{W}$ and a trapdoor $td_{\mathcal{W}''}$ for $\mathcal{W}''$ are produced, where $\mathcal{W}'' \subseteq \mathcal{W}$. Here, $ct_{\mathcal{W},1} := (\tau_1, \cdots, \tau_\ell, \mathbf{0}_n, \sigma, 0, q)_{\mathbb{B}}$, $ct_{\mathcal{W},2} := \Omega^{\sigma}$, and $td_{\mathcal{W}''} := (\delta^{td}_1, \cdots, \delta^{td}_\ell, \mathbf{0}_n, 1, r^{td}, 0)_{\mathbb{B}^*}$. In addition, $\boldsymbol{\tau} := (\tau_1, \cdots, \tau_\ell)$ and $\boldsymbol{\delta} := (\delta_1, \cdots, \delta_\ell)$ are linear combinations of $\boldsymbol{w} \leftarrow \mathsf{Encode}_2(\mathsf{map}(\mathcal{W})$ and $\boldsymbol{w}'' \leftarrow \mathsf{Encode}_1(\mathsf{map}(\mathcal{W}''))$ multiplied by random coefficients, respectively. Therefore, because $\mathcal{W}'' \subseteq \mathcal{W}$, we have $\langle \tau_i, \delta_i \rangle = 0$ for $i = 1, \cdots, \ell$. According to Definition 3, we have

$$\hat{e}(ct_{\mathcal{W},1}, td_{\mathcal{W}''}) = \hat{e}(g,g)^{\sigma + \sum_{i=1}^{\ell} \langle \tau_i, \delta_i \rangle} = \hat{e}(g,g)^{\sigma} = \Omega^{\sigma} = ct_{\mathcal{W},2}.$$

5 Security Proof

In this section, we demonstrate that the following theorem holds.

Theorem 1. *The proposed scheme satisfies SS-CKA if the assumptions OT.1 and OT.2 hold.*

Our strategy for proving the theorem is to define a sequence of games between a PPT adversary $\mathcal{A}$ and a challenger $\mathcal{C}$. The first game is the real SS-CKA game. For the following games, the semi-functional technique introduced by Waters [20] is utilized, and the ciphertexts and tokens given to the adversary are gradually changed to be semi-functional. In the last game, the challenge ciphertext is generated from a random set of keywords instead of the challenge set of keywords. Then, we demonstrate that $\mathcal{A}$ cannot distinguish between any two adjacent games. Therefore, no information about the challenge set of keywords is revealed to the adversary.

We describe three types of semi-functional algorithms and their properties are described as follows:

- Semi-functional ciphertexts. To create a semi-functional ciphertext for a set of keywords $\mathcal{W}$, this algorithm first runs $\mathsf{Encrypt}(pk, \mathcal{W})$ to generate a normal ciphertext $ct_{\mathcal{W}} := \{ct_{\mathcal{W},1}, ct_{\mathcal{W},2}\}$, where $ct_{\mathcal{W},1} := (\boldsymbol{\tau}_1, \cdots, \boldsymbol{\tau}_\ell, \mathbf{0}_n, \sigma, 0, q)_{\mathbb{B}}$ and $ct_{\mathcal{W},2} := \Omega^\sigma$. It then sets $ct^{sf}_{\mathcal{W},1}$ to be identical to $ct_{\mathcal{W},1}$ in all respects except that $ct^{sf}_{\mathcal{W},1}$ is such that the element $\mathbf{0}_n$ in $ct_{\mathcal{W},1}$ is replaced by a random vector $\boldsymbol{v}^{ct} \xleftarrow{\$} \mathbb{Z}_N^n$. That is,
$$ct^{sf}_{\mathcal{W},1} := (\boldsymbol{\tau}_1, \cdots, \boldsymbol{\tau}_\ell, \boldsymbol{v}^{ct}, \sigma, 0, q)_{\mathbb{B}}.$$
In addition, it also sets $ct^{sf}_{\mathcal{W},2} := ct_{\mathcal{W},2}$. Finally, the semi-functional ciphertext for $\mathcal{W}$ is set as
$$ct^{sf}_{\mathcal{W}} := \left\{ct^{sf}_{\mathcal{W},1}, ct^{sf}_{\mathcal{W},2}\right\}.$$
- Semi-functional tokens. To create a semi-functional tokens for a set of keywords $\mathcal{W}$, this algorithm first runs $\mathsf{Authorize}(sk, \mathcal{W})$ algorithm to generate a normal token $token_{\mathcal{W}} := \{token^\alpha_{\mathcal{W}}, \{token^\beta_{\mathcal{W},i}\}_{i\in\mathcal{X}}, \{token^\gamma_{\mathcal{W},i}\}_{i\in\mathcal{Y}}\rangle$, where $token^\alpha_{\mathcal{W}} := (\boldsymbol{\delta}_1, \cdots, \boldsymbol{\delta}_\ell, \mathbf{0}_n, 1, r, 0)_{\mathbb{B}^*}$, $token^\beta_{\mathcal{W},i} := (\boldsymbol{\zeta}_{i,1}, \cdots, \boldsymbol{\zeta}_{i,\ell}, \mathbf{0}_n, 0, s_i, 0)_{\mathbb{B}^*}$, and $token^\gamma_{\mathcal{W},i} := (\boldsymbol{\eta}_{i,1}, \cdots, \boldsymbol{\eta}_{i,\ell}, \mathbf{0}_n, 0, t_i, 0)_{\mathbb{B}^*}$. It also randomly picks vectors $\boldsymbol{v}^\alpha, \{\boldsymbol{v}^\beta_i\}_{i\in\mathcal{X}}, \{\boldsymbol{v}^\gamma_i\}_{i\in\mathcal{Y}} \xleftarrow{\$} \mathbb{Z}_N^n$. It then sets $token^{sf.\alpha}_{\mathcal{W}}$ to be identical to $token^\alpha_{\mathcal{W}}$, $\{token^{sf.\beta}_{\mathcal{W},i}\}_{i\in\mathcal{X}}$ to be identical to $\{token^\beta_{\mathcal{W},i}\}_{i\in\mathcal{X}}$, and $\{token^{sf.\gamma}_{\mathcal{W},i}\}_{i\in\mathcal{Y}}$ to be identical to $\{token^\gamma_{\mathcal{W},i}\}_{i\in\mathcal{Y}}$ with the exception being that in each case, the element $\mathbf{0}_n$ in the former token are replaced by $\boldsymbol{v}^\alpha, \{\boldsymbol{v}^\beta_i\}_{i\in\mathcal{X}}$ and $\{\boldsymbol{v}^\gamma_i\}_{i\in\mathcal{Y}}$, respectively. That is,
$$\begin{cases} token^{sf.\alpha}_{\mathcal{W}} := (\boldsymbol{\delta}_1, \cdots, \boldsymbol{\delta}_\ell, \boldsymbol{v}^\alpha, 1, r, 0)_{\mathbb{B}^*}; \\ token^{sf.\beta}_{\mathcal{W},i} := (\boldsymbol{\zeta}_{i,1}, \cdots, \boldsymbol{\zeta}_{i,\ell}, \boldsymbol{v}^\beta_i, 0, s_i, 0)_{\mathbb{B}^*}; \\ token^{sf.\gamma}_{\mathcal{W},i} := (\boldsymbol{\eta}_{i,1}, \cdots, \boldsymbol{\eta}_{i,\ell}, \boldsymbol{v}^\gamma_i, 0, t_i, 0)_{\mathbb{B}^*}. \end{cases}$$
Finally, the semi-functional token for $\mathcal{W}$ is set as
$$token^{sf}_{\mathcal{W}} := \left\{token^{sf.\alpha}_{\mathcal{W}}, \{token^{sf.\beta}_{\mathcal{W},i}\}_{i\in\mathcal{X}}, \{token^{sf.\gamma}_{\mathcal{W},i}\}_{i\in\mathcal{Y}}\right\}.$$
- Semi-functional trapdoors. A semi-functional trapdoor can be generated by running the $\mathsf{Trapdoor}$ algorithm with a semi-functional token as its input. Thus, the semi-functional trapdoor can be represented as
$$td^{sf}_{\mathcal{W}''} := (\boldsymbol{\delta}^{td}_1, \cdots, \boldsymbol{\delta}^{td}_\ell, \boldsymbol{v}^{td}, 1, r^{td}, 0)_{\mathbb{B}^*},$$
where
$$\boldsymbol{v}^{td} = \boldsymbol{v}^\alpha + \sum_{i\in\mathcal{X}} r'_i \cdot \boldsymbol{v}^\beta_i + \sum_{i\in\bar{\mathcal{X}}} r'_i \cdot (w''_{2i-1} \cdot \boldsymbol{v}^\gamma_{2i-1} + w''_{2i} \cdot \boldsymbol{v}^\gamma_{2i}).$$

The crucial property of the semi-functional elements used in the following security proof is as follows: if the Test algorithm takes a semi-functional ciphertext $ct^{sf}_{\mathcal{W}}$ for $\mathcal{W}$ and a semi-functional trapdoor $td^{sf}_{\mathcal{W}''}$ for $\mathcal{W}''$ as its inputs, it returns 0 with high probability even if $\mathcal{W}'' \subseteq \mathcal{W}$ because

$$\hat{e}(ct^{sf}_{\mathcal{W},1}, td^{sf}_{\mathcal{W}''}) = \hat{e}(g,g)^{\sigma+\sum_{i=1}^{\ell}\langle \tau_i, \delta_i\rangle + \langle v^{ct}, v^{td}\rangle},$$

where $\langle \boldsymbol{v}^{ct}, \boldsymbol{v}^{td}\rangle \neq 0$ since $\boldsymbol{v}^{ct}$ and $\boldsymbol{v}^{td}$ are uniformly and independently distributed with overwhelming probability. If one of the input tokens in Trapdoor algorithm is semi-functional, the generated trapdoor will be semi-functional, because v^{td} can be a uniformly and randomly distributed $\mathbb{Z}_N^n$ element.

Let q denote the total number of queries made by $\mathcal{A}$ in **Phase 1** and **Phase 2**. The sequences of games are defined as follows:

- $\mathbf{Game}_{Real}$: This is the same as the SS-CKA game of PEHAKS.
- $\mathbf{Game}_{Res}$: This game is the same as $\mathbf{Game}_{Real}$ except that $\mathcal{A}$ cannot issue delegation queries in **Phase 1** and **Phase 2**.
- $\mathbf{Game}_0$: This game is the same as $\mathbf{Game}_{Res}$, except that the challenge ciphertext given to $\mathcal{A}$ is semi-functional.
- $\mathbf{Game}_{i,j}$: For $i = 1, \cdots, q$ and $j = 0, \cdots, n+1$, $\mathbf{Game}_{i,j}$ is the same as $\mathbf{Game}_0$ except that the output tokens of the first $i-1$ authorization queries are semi-functional; while the outputs of the remaining $q-i$ authorization queries are normal. For the ith authorization query, only the first j elements are semi-functional and the rest are normal. In addition, for convenience, we also let $\mathbf{Game}_{1,0} := \mathbf{Game}_0$ and $\mathbf{Game}_{i,n+1} := \mathbf{Game}_{i+1,0}$.
- $\mathbf{Game}_{Final}$: This game is the same as $\mathbf{Game}_{q,n+1}$, except that the challenge ciphertext is generated for a random set of keywords instead of the challenge sets of keywords.

In the following, we provide several lemmas to demonstrate that no PPT algorithm can distinguish between any two adjacent games.

Lemma 1. *The probability that there exists an algorithm $\mathcal{A}$ that can distinguish* $\mathbf{Game}_{Real}$ *from* $\mathbf{Game}_{Res}$ *is negligible.*

Proof. Let $\mathcal{W}$ and $\mathcal{W}'$ be two sets of keywords with $\mathcal{W}' \subseteq \mathcal{W}$, and let $token_{\mathcal{W}'}$ be a token for $\mathcal{W}'$. We demonstrate that the probability that $\mathcal{A}$ can distinguish $\mathbf{Game}_{Real}$ from $\mathbf{Game}_{Res}$ is negligible because the probability that $\mathcal{A}$ can determine whether $token_{\mathcal{W}'}$ is generated by Authorize$(sk, \mathcal{W}')$ or by Delegate$(pk, token_{\mathcal{W}}, \mathcal{W}')$ is negligible, where $token_{\mathcal{W}} \leftarrow$ Authorize$(sk, \mathcal{W})$.

Because $\{token^{\beta}_{\mathcal{W},i}\}_{i\in\mathcal{X}}$ in $token_{\mathcal{W}}$ can be regarded as a linear combination of coefficients that are chosen uniformly at random, the distribution of $\{token^{\beta}_{\mathcal{W},i}\}_{i\in\mathcal{X}}$ can be considered to be uniform and random. In addition, $\{token^{\beta}_{\mathcal{W},i}\}_{i\in\mathcal{X}}$ also plays a role in the randomization of the Delegate$(pk, token_{\mathcal{W}}, \mathcal{W}')$ algorithm. Concretely, $token_{\mathcal{W}'}$ can be regarded as the linear combinations of $\{token^{\beta}_{\mathcal{W},i}\}_{i\in\mathcal{X}}$ with coefficients chosen uniformly at random. Therefore, the distribution of $token_{\mathcal{W}'}$ is also uniform and random.

Suppose the element of t used to compute $token_{\mathcal{W}}$ in Authorize is 0, $token_{\mathcal{W}'}$ is then not random because some entries of $\{token^{\gamma}_{\mathcal{W},i}\}_{i\in\mathcal{Y}}$ become 0, and the elements that are chosen in Delegate and that operate on those entries also become 0. Fortunately, the probability of $t = 0$ is $1/N$, which is a negligible number.

In summary, the probability that there exists an algorithm $\mathcal{A}$ that can determine whether $token_{\mathcal{W}'}$ is generated by $\mathsf{Authorize}(sk, \mathcal{W}')$ or by $\mathsf{Delegate}(pk, token_{\mathcal{W}}, \mathcal{W}')$ is negligible. □

Lemma 2. *If an algorithm $\mathcal{A}$ that can distinguish* $\mathbf{Game}_{Res}$ *from* $\mathbf{Game}_0$ *with advantage ϵ exists, then an algorithm $\mathcal{C}$ that can break OT.1 assumption with advantage ϵ necessarily exists.*

Proof. Given an instance $(pp_{\mathbb{V}}, \hat{\mathbb{B}}, \hat{\mathbb{B}}^*, \boldsymbol{e}_\xi := (e_{\xi,1}, \cdots, e_{\xi,n}))$ of OT.1 assumption, $\mathcal{C}$ simulates the following game and interacts with $\mathcal{A}$ to answer whether ξ is 0 or 1.

Setup. $\mathcal{C}$ first generates $pp \leftarrow \mathsf{Setup}(1^\lambda, \ell)$. It then computes $\Omega = \hat{e}(g, g)$ and sets $pk := (pp_{\mathbb{V}}, \hat{\mathbb{B}}, \Omega)$ and $sk := \hat{\mathbb{B}}^*$. Then, $\mathcal{C}$ gives (pp, pk) to $\mathcal{A}$ and keeps sk secret.
Phase 1. To answer the authorization query for any set of keywords, $\mathcal{C}$ generates the corresponding authorization token using sk.
Challenge. $\mathcal{A}$ selects two challenge sets of keywords with the same size $(\mathcal{W}_0^*, \mathcal{W}_1^*)$ and sends them to $\mathcal{C}$. $\mathcal{C}$ randomly chooses $b \xleftarrow{\$} \{0, 1\}$ and generates the encoding result $\boldsymbol{w}^* := (\boldsymbol{w}_1^*, \cdots, \boldsymbol{w}_\ell^*) \leftarrow \mathsf{Encode}_2(\mathsf{map}(\mathcal{W}_b^*))$. Then, $\mathcal{C}$ chooses $\sigma, q_1, \cdots, q_\ell \xleftarrow{\$} \mathbb{Z}_N$ and sets

$$\boldsymbol{\tau}^* := (\tau_1^*, \cdots, \tau_n^*) := (\boldsymbol{\tau}_1^*, \cdots, \boldsymbol{\tau}_\ell^*) := (q_1 \cdot \boldsymbol{w}_1^*, \cdots, q_\ell \cdot \boldsymbol{w}_\ell^*).$$

Furthermore, $\mathcal{C}$ computes

$$ct_{\mathcal{W}_b^*,1} = \sum_{i\in[n]} \tau_i^* \cdot e_{\xi,i} + \sigma \cdot \boldsymbol{b}_{2n+1}; \quad ct_{\mathcal{W}_b^*,2} = \Omega^\sigma.$$

Finally, $\mathcal{C}$ responds to $\mathcal{A}$ with $ct_{\mathcal{W}_b^*} := (ct_{\mathcal{W}_b^*,1}, ct_{\mathcal{W}_b^*,2})$.
Phase 2. $\mathcal{A}$ can perform authorization queries as **Phase 1** with the same restrictions defined in the SS-CKA game.
Guess. Finally, $\mathcal{A}$ outputs a guess b' for b.
Analysis. The **Challenge** phase has two cases:

- If $\xi = 0$, then

$$\boldsymbol{e}_\xi = (\mu \cdot \boldsymbol{b}_i + \mu_i \cdot \boldsymbol{b}_{2n+3})_{i\in[n]}$$

and

$$\begin{aligned} ct_{\mathcal{W}_b^*,1} &= \sum_{i\in[n]} \tau_i^* \cdot e_{\xi,i} + \sigma \cdot \boldsymbol{b}_{2n+1} \\ &= (\mu \cdot \boldsymbol{\tau}_1^*, \cdots, \mu \cdot \boldsymbol{\tau}_\ell^*, \boldsymbol{0}_n, \sigma, 0, \langle \boldsymbol{\tau}^*, \boldsymbol{\mu} \rangle)_{\mathbb{B}} \\ &= (\hat{\boldsymbol{\tau}}_1, \cdots, \hat{\boldsymbol{\tau}}_\ell, \boldsymbol{0}_n, \sigma, 0, q)_{\mathbb{B}}, \end{aligned}$$

where $\hat{\tau}_i = \mu \cdot \tau_i^*$ and $q = \langle \boldsymbol{\tau}^*, \boldsymbol{\mu} \rangle$. Therefore, the challenge ciphertext is distributed as in $\mathbf{Game}_{Res}$.
- If $\xi = 1$, then

$$\boldsymbol{e}_\xi = (\mu \cdot \boldsymbol{b}_i + \rho \cdot \sum_{j \in [n]} u_{i,j} \cdot \boldsymbol{b}_{n+j} + \mu_i \cdot \boldsymbol{b}_{2n+3})_{i \in [n]}$$

and

$$\begin{aligned} ct_{\mathcal{W}_b^*,1} &= \sum_{i \in [n]} \tau_i^* \cdot \boldsymbol{e}_{\xi,i} + \sigma \cdot \boldsymbol{b}_{2n+1} \\ &= (\mu \cdot \tau_1^*, \cdots, \mu \cdot \tau_\ell^*, \rho \cdot \langle \boldsymbol{\tau}^*, \boldsymbol{u}_1 \rangle, \cdots, \rho \cdot \langle \boldsymbol{\tau}^*, \boldsymbol{u}_n \rangle, \sigma, 0, \langle \boldsymbol{\tau}^*, \boldsymbol{\mu} \rangle)_{\mathbb{B}} \\ &= (\hat{\tau}_1, \cdots, \hat{\tau}_\ell, \boldsymbol{v}^{ct}, \sigma, 0, q)_{\mathbb{B}}, \end{aligned}$$

where $\hat{\tau}_i = \mu \cdot \tau_i^*$, $\boldsymbol{v}^{ct} = (v_1^{ct}, \cdots, v_n^{ct})$ with $v_i^{ct} = \rho \cdot \langle \boldsymbol{\tau}^*, \boldsymbol{u}_i \rangle$ and $q = \langle \boldsymbol{\tau}^*, \boldsymbol{\mu} \rangle$. Because $\boldsymbol{\tau}^* \neq \mathbf{0}_n$ and $\boldsymbol{u}_1, \cdots, \boldsymbol{u}_n$ as well as $\boldsymbol{\mu}$ belong to a uniform and independent distribution, the challenge ciphertext is properly distributed as in $\mathbf{Game}_0$.

Therefore, if $\mathcal{A}$ can determine which game it is interacting with, then $\mathcal{C}$ can use $\mathcal{A}$ as a black box to break OT.1 assumption. □

Lemma 3. *If an algorithm $\mathcal{A}$ exists that can distinguish $\mathbf{Game}_{i,k-1}$ from $\mathbf{Game}_{i,k}$ with advantage ϵ, where $i = 1, \cdots, q$ and $k = 1, \cdots, n+1$, then there exists an algorithm $\mathcal{C}$ that can break OT.2 assumption with advantage ϵ.*

Proof. Given an instance $(pp_{\mathbb{V}}, \hat{\mathbb{B}}, \hat{\mathbb{B}}^*, \boldsymbol{e}, \boldsymbol{h}_\xi := (h_{\xi,1}, \cdots, h_{\xi,n}))$ of OT.2 assumption, $\mathcal{C}$ simulates the following game and interacts with $\mathcal{A}$ to answer whether ξ is 1 or 0.

Setup. $\mathcal{C}$ first generates $pp \leftarrow \mathsf{Setup}(1^\lambda, \ell)$. It then computes $\Omega = \hat{e}(g, g)$ and sets $pk := (pp_{\mathbb{V}}, \hat{\mathbb{B}}, \Omega)$ and $sk := \hat{\mathbb{B}}^*$. $\mathcal{C}$ then gives (pp, pk) to $\mathcal{A}$ and keeps sk secret.

Phase 1. $\mathcal{C}$ responses to the first $i-1$ authorization queries with semi-functional tokens generated as described in Theorem 1. The last $q-i$ authorization queries are answered with normal tokens generated identically to those in the Authorize algorithm. For the ith authorization query for a set of keywords $\mathcal{W}$, $\mathcal{C}$ first generates $token_{\mathcal{W}}$ as in $\mathsf{Authorize}(sk, \mathcal{W})$. $\mathcal{C}$ then converts tokens with a sequence less than k in $token_{\mathcal{W}}$ into semi-functional tokens as described in Theorem 1. $\mathcal{C}$ sets kth token of the ith query $token_{\mathcal{W},k}$ of $token_{\mathcal{W}}$ depending on its original type. Specifically,

$$token_{\mathcal{W},k} := \begin{cases} \sum_{i \in [n]} \delta_i \cdot h_{\xi,i} + \boldsymbol{b}_{2n+1}^* & \text{if type is } \alpha; \\ \sum_{i \in [n]} \zeta_i \cdot h_{\xi,i} & \text{if type is } \beta; \\ \sum_{i \in [n]} \eta_i \cdot h_{\xi,i} & \text{if type is } \gamma, \end{cases}$$

where $(\delta_1, \cdots, \delta_n) := (\boldsymbol{\delta}_1, \cdots, \boldsymbol{\delta}_\ell)$, $(\zeta_1, \cdots, \zeta_n) := (\boldsymbol{\zeta}_1, \cdots, \boldsymbol{\zeta}_\ell)$, and $(\eta_1, \cdots, \eta_n) := (\boldsymbol{\eta}_1, \cdots, \boldsymbol{\eta}_\ell)$.

Remark 3. Suppose that $\mathcal{A}$ wants to generate trapdoor $td_{\mathcal{W}}$ by using all $n+1$ parts of $token_{\mathcal{W}}$ in the ith query for the set $\mathcal{W}$, the generated trapdoor $td_{\mathcal{W}}$ differs based on the original type of $token_{\mathcal{W},k}$, the value of ξ, and the elements of the converted $token_{\mathcal{W},k}$, described as follows.

- If the original type of $token_{\mathcal{W},k}$ is α (*i.e.*, $k=1$) and $\xi=0$, then

$$\boldsymbol{h}_{\xi} = (\omega \cdot \boldsymbol{b}_i^* + \nu_i \cdot \boldsymbol{b}_{2n+2}^*)_{i\in[n]}$$

  and

$$\begin{aligned} token_{\mathcal{W},k} &= \sum_{i\in[n]} \delta_i \cdot h_{\xi,i} + \boldsymbol{b}_{2n+1}^* \\ &= (\omega\cdot\boldsymbol{\delta}_1, \cdots, \omega\cdot\boldsymbol{\delta}_{\ell}, \boldsymbol{0}_n, 1, \langle\boldsymbol{\delta},\boldsymbol{\nu}\rangle, 0)_{\mathbb{B}^*} \\ &= (\hat{\boldsymbol{\delta}}_1, \cdots, \hat{\boldsymbol{\delta}}_{\ell}, \boldsymbol{0}_n, 1, r, 0)_{\mathbb{B}^*}, \end{aligned}$$

  where $\hat{\boldsymbol{\delta}}_i = \omega\cdot\boldsymbol{\delta}$ and $r = \langle\boldsymbol{\delta},\boldsymbol{\nu}\rangle$. Therefore, the generated trapdoor $td_{\mathcal{W}}$ is set as

$$\begin{aligned} td_{\mathcal{W}} :=& (\hat{\boldsymbol{\delta}}_1, \cdots, \hat{\boldsymbol{\delta}}_{\ell}, \boldsymbol{0}_n, 1, r, 0)_{\mathbb{B}^*} + \sum_{i\in\mathcal{X}} r_i' \cdot token_{\mathcal{W},i}^{\beta} \\ &+ \sum_{i\in\bar{\mathcal{X}}} r_i' \cdot (w_{2i-1}\cdot token_{\mathcal{W},2i-1}^{\gamma} + w_{2i}\cdot token_{\mathcal{W},2i}^{\gamma}) \\ =& (\hat{\boldsymbol{\delta}}_1, \cdots, \hat{\boldsymbol{\delta}}_{\ell}, \boldsymbol{0}_n, 1, r, 0)_{\mathbb{B}^*} + \sum_{i\in\mathcal{X}} r_i' \cdot (\boldsymbol{\zeta}_{i,1}, \cdots, \boldsymbol{\zeta}_{i,\ell}, \boldsymbol{0}_n, 0, s_i, 0)_{\mathbb{B}^*} \\ &+ \sum_{i\in\bar{\mathcal{X}}} r_i' \cdot (w_{2i-1}'' \cdot (\boldsymbol{\eta}_{2i-1,1}, \cdots, \boldsymbol{\eta}_{2i-1,\ell}, \boldsymbol{0}_n, 0, t_{2i-1}, 0)_{\mathbb{B}^*} \\ &\qquad + w_{2i}'' \cdot (\boldsymbol{\eta}_{2i,1}, \cdots, \boldsymbol{\eta}_{2i,\ell}, \boldsymbol{0}_n, 0, t_{2i}, 0)_{\mathbb{B}^*}) \\ =& (\boldsymbol{\delta}_1^{td}, \cdots, \boldsymbol{\delta}_{\ell}^{td}, \boldsymbol{0}_n, 1, r^{td}, 0)_{\mathbb{B}^*}, \end{aligned}$$

  which is a normal trapdoor.
- If the original type of $token_{\mathcal{W},k}$ is α (*i.e.*, $k=1$) and $\xi=1$, then we have

$$\boldsymbol{h}_{\xi} = (\omega \cdot \boldsymbol{b}_i^* + \iota \cdot \sum_{k\in[n]} z_{i,k} \cdot \boldsymbol{b}_{n+k}^* + \nu_i \cdot \boldsymbol{b}_{2n+2}^*)_{i\in[n]}$$

  and

$$\begin{aligned} token_{\mathcal{W},k} &= \sum_{i\in[n]} \delta_i \cdot h_{\xi,i} + \boldsymbol{b}_{2n+1}^* \\ &= (\omega\cdot\boldsymbol{\delta}_1, \cdots, \omega\cdot\boldsymbol{\delta}_{\ell}, \iota\cdot\langle\boldsymbol{\delta},\boldsymbol{z}_1\rangle, \cdots, \iota\cdot\langle\boldsymbol{\delta},\boldsymbol{z}_n\rangle, 1, \langle\boldsymbol{\delta},\boldsymbol{\nu}\rangle, 0)_{\mathbb{B}^*} \\ &= (\hat{\boldsymbol{\delta}}_1, \cdots, \hat{\boldsymbol{\delta}}_{\ell}, \boldsymbol{v}, 1, r, 0)_{\mathbb{B}^*}, \end{aligned}$$

where $\hat{\delta}_i = \omega \cdot \delta, v = (v_1, \cdots, v_n), (v_i = \iota \cdot \langle \delta, z_i \rangle)_{i \in [n]}, (z_i)_{i \in [n]} = Z$, and $r = \langle \delta, \nu \rangle$. The generated trapdoor $td_{\mathcal{W}}$ is set as

$$\begin{aligned} td_{\mathcal{W}} := & (\hat{\delta}_1, \cdots, \hat{\delta}_\ell, v, 1, r, 0)_{\mathbb{B}^*} + \sum_{i \in \mathcal{X}} r'_i \cdot (\zeta_{i,1}, \cdots, \zeta_{i,\ell}, \mathbf{0}_n, 0, s_i, 0)_{\mathbb{B}^*} \\ & + \sum_{i \in \bar{\mathcal{X}}} r'_i \cdot (w''_{2i-1} \cdot (\eta_{2i-1,1}, \cdots, \eta_{2i-1,\ell}, \mathbf{0}_n, 0, t_{2i-1}, 0)_{\mathbb{B}^*} \\ & + w''_{2i} \cdot (\eta_{2i,1}, \cdots, \eta_{2i,\ell}, \mathbf{0}_n, 0, t_{2i}, 0)_{\mathbb{B}^*}) \\ = & (\delta^{td}_1, \cdots, \delta^{td}_\ell, v^{td}, 1, r^{td}, 0)_{\mathbb{B}^*}. \end{aligned}$$

Because v^{td} in the generated trapdoor $td_{\mathcal{W}}$ is a random vector of $\mathbb{Z}_N^n$ as described in Theorem 1, the generated trapdoor $td_{\mathcal{W}}$ is semi-functional.

- If the original type of $token_{\mathcal{W},k}$ is β, then

$$token_{\mathcal{W},k} = \begin{cases} \sum_{i \in [n]} \zeta_i \cdot h_{0,i} & = (\omega \cdot \zeta_1, \cdots, \omega \cdot \zeta_\ell, \mathbf{0}_n, \langle \zeta, \nu \rangle, 0)_{\mathbb{B}^*} \\ & = (\hat{\zeta}_1, \cdots, \hat{\zeta}_\ell, \mathbf{0}_n, 0, s, 0)_{\mathbb{B}^*}, \text{ if } \xi = 0; \\ \sum_{i \in [n]} \zeta_i \cdot h_{1,i} & = (\omega \cdot \zeta_1, \cdots, \omega \cdot \zeta_\ell, \iota \cdot \langle \zeta, z_1 \rangle, \cdots, \\ & \quad \iota \cdot \langle \zeta, z_n \rangle, 0, \langle \zeta, \nu \rangle, 0)_{\mathbb{B}^*} \\ & = (\hat{\zeta}_1, \cdots, \hat{\zeta}_\ell, v^\beta, 0, s, 0)_{\mathbb{B}^*}, \text{ if } \xi = 1, \end{cases}$$

where $\hat{\zeta}_i = \omega \cdot \zeta, s = \langle \zeta, \nu \rangle, v^\beta = (v^\beta_1, \cdots, v^\beta_n)$, and $(v^\beta_i = \iota \cdot \langle \zeta, z_i \rangle)_{i \in [n]}$. We also note that because $k > 1$, there must be at least one part (*i.e.*, $token_{\mathcal{W},1}$) in $token_{\mathcal{W}}$ that is semi-functional. According to Theorem 1, the generated trapdoor $td_{\mathcal{W}}$ is also semi-functional and is set as $td_{\mathcal{W}} := (\delta^{td}_1, \cdots, \delta^{td}_\ell, v^{td}, 1, r^{td}, 0)_{\mathbb{B}^*}$.

- If the original type of $token_{\mathcal{W},k}$ is γ, then

$$token_{\mathcal{W},k} := \begin{cases} \sum_{i \in [n]} \eta_i \cdot h_{0,i} & = (\omega \cdot \eta_1, \cdots, \omega \cdot \eta_\ell, \mathbf{0}_n, 0, \langle \eta, \nu \rangle, 0)_{\mathbb{B}^*} \\ & = (\hat{\eta}_1, \cdots, \hat{\eta}_\ell, \mathbf{0}_n, 0, t, 0)_{\mathbb{B}^*}, \text{ if } \xi = 0; \\ \sum_{i \in [n]} \eta_i \cdot h_{1,i} & = (\omega \cdot \eta_1, \cdots, \omega \cdot \eta_\ell, \iota \cdot \langle \eta, z_1 \rangle, \cdots, \\ & \quad \iota \cdot \langle \eta, z_n \rangle, 0, \langle \eta, \nu \rangle, 0)_{\mathbb{B}^*} \\ & = (\hat{\eta}_1, \cdots, \hat{\eta}_\ell, v^\gamma, 0, t, 0)_{\mathbb{B}^*}, \text{ if } \xi = 1, \end{cases}$$

where $\hat{\eta}_i = \omega \cdot \eta, t = \langle \eta, \nu \rangle, v^\gamma = (v^\gamma_1, \cdots, v^\gamma_n)$, and $(v^\gamma_i = \iota \cdot \langle \eta, z_i \rangle)_{i \in [n]}$. For the same reason as those for the previous cases, the generated trapdoor $td_{\mathcal{W}}$ is also semi-functional and set as $td_{\mathcal{W}} := (\delta^{td}_1, \cdots, \delta^{td}_\ell, v^{td}, 1, r^{td}, 0)_{\mathbb{B}^*}$.

Challenge. $\mathcal{A}$ selects two challenge sets of keywords with the same size $(\mathcal{W}^*_0, \mathcal{W}^*_1)$ and sends them to $\mathcal{C}$. $\mathcal{C}$ randomly chooses $b \xleftarrow{\$} \{0,1\}$ and generates a encode result $w^* := (w^*_1, \cdots, w^*_\ell) \leftarrow \mathsf{Encode}_2(\mathsf{map}(\mathcal{W}^*_b))$. Then, $\mathcal{C}$ chooses $\sigma, q_1, \cdots, q_\ell \xleftarrow{\$} \mathbb{Z}_N$ and sets

$$\tau^* := (\tau^*_1, \cdots, \tau^*_n) := (\boldsymbol{\tau}^*_1, \cdots, \boldsymbol{\tau}^*_\ell) := (q_1 \cdot w^*_1, \cdots, q_\ell \cdot w^*_\ell).$$

Furthermore, $\mathcal{C}$ computes

$$\begin{aligned} ct_{\mathcal{W}_b^*,1} &= \sum_{i\in[n]} \tau_i^* \cdot \boldsymbol{e}_i + \sigma \cdot \boldsymbol{b}_{2n+1} + q \cdot \boldsymbol{b}_{2n+3} \\ &= (\mu \cdot \boldsymbol{\tau}_1^*, \cdots, \mu \cdot \boldsymbol{\tau}_\ell^*, \rho \cdot \langle \boldsymbol{\tau}^*, \boldsymbol{u}_1 \rangle, \cdots, \rho \cdot \langle \boldsymbol{\tau}^*, \boldsymbol{u}_n \rangle, \sigma, 0, q)_{\mathbb{B}} \\ &= (\hat{\boldsymbol{\tau}}_1, \cdots, \hat{\boldsymbol{\tau}}_\ell, \boldsymbol{v}^{ct}, \sigma, 0, q)_{\mathbb{B}}; \\ ct_{\mathcal{W}_b^*,2} &= \Omega^\sigma, \end{aligned}$$

where $\hat{\boldsymbol{\tau}}_i = \mu \cdot \boldsymbol{\tau}_i^*, \boldsymbol{v}^{ct} = (v_1^{ct}, \cdots, v_n^{ct})$, and $(v_i^{ct} = \rho \cdot \langle \boldsymbol{\tau}^*, \boldsymbol{u}_i \rangle)_{i\in[n]}$.

Phase 2. $\mathcal{A}$ can perform an authorization query as described in **Phase 1** with the same restrictions defined in SS-CKA game.

Guess. Finally, $\mathcal{A}$ outputs a guess b' for b.

Analysis. We now analyze the advantage of $\mathcal{A}$ to determine which game it interacts with. First, we consider the case for $k = 1$. Suppose that $\xi = 0$; the trapdoor $td_{\mathcal{W}}$ generated by $\mathcal{A}$ using all $n+1$ parts of $token_{\mathcal{W}}$ in the ith query for the set $\mathcal{W}$ is then a normal trapdoor. Therefore, the joint distribution of the challenge ciphertext and the generated trapdoor is the same as those in $\mathbf{Game}_{i,0}$. Suppose $\xi = 1$; the generated trapdoor $td_{\mathcal{W}}$ is then semi-functional. Therefore, the joint distributions of the challenge ciphertext and the generated trapdoors in $\mathbf{Game}_{i,0}$ and $\mathbf{Game}_{i,1}$ are the same.

Second, we consider the case for $k = 2, \cdots, n+1$. Regardless of whether of ξ is 0 or 1, the trapdoor $td_{\mathcal{W}}$ generated with $n+1$ parts of $token_{\mathcal{W}}$ in the ith query for set $\mathcal{W}$ is semi-functional. Therefore, for $k = 2, \cdots, n+1$, the joint distributions of the challenge ciphertext and the generated trapdoors in $\mathbf{Game}_{i,k-1}$ and $\mathbf{Game}_{i,k}$ are the same.

In summary, if $\mathcal{A}$ can distinguish between any two adjacent games, then $\mathcal{C}$ can use $\mathcal{A}$ as a black box to break OT.2 assumption. □

Lemma 4. *The view of an algorithm $\mathcal{A}$ in $\mathbf{Game}_{q,n+1}$ is identical to that of $\mathcal{A}$ in $\mathbf{Game}_{Final}$.*

Proof. Given the dual orthonormal bases of $\mathbb{V}$ used in $\mathbf{Game}_{q,n+1}$

$$\begin{cases} \mathbb{B} & := (\boldsymbol{b}_1, \cdots, \boldsymbol{b}_n, \boldsymbol{b}_{n+1}, \cdots, \boldsymbol{b}_{2n}, \boldsymbol{b}_{2n+1}, \boldsymbol{b}_{2n+2}, \boldsymbol{b}_{2n+3}); \\ \mathbb{B}^* & := (\boldsymbol{b}_1^*, \cdots, \boldsymbol{b}_n^*, \boldsymbol{b}_{n+1}^*, \cdots, \boldsymbol{b}_{2n}^*, \boldsymbol{b}_{2n+1}^*, \boldsymbol{b}_{2n+2}^*, \boldsymbol{b}_{2n+3}^*), \end{cases}$$

we construct another dual orthonormal base $(\mathbb{D}, \mathbb{D}^*)$ of $\mathbb{V}$ as follows: First, choose $\boldsymbol{U} := (\boldsymbol{u}_i \xleftarrow{\$} \mathbb{Z}_N^n)_{i\in[n]}$ and $\boldsymbol{m} := (m_i \xleftarrow{\$} \mathbb{Z}_N)_{i\in[n]}$, then define

$$\begin{cases} \mathbb{D} & := (\boldsymbol{b}_1, \cdots, \boldsymbol{b}_n, \boldsymbol{d}_{n+1}, \cdots, \boldsymbol{d}_{2n}, \boldsymbol{b}_{2n+1}, \boldsymbol{b}_{2n+2}, \boldsymbol{b}_{2n+3}); \\ \mathbb{D}^* & := (\boldsymbol{d}_1^*, \cdots, \boldsymbol{d}_n^*, \boldsymbol{b}_{n+1}^*, \cdots, \boldsymbol{b}_{2n}^*, \boldsymbol{d}_{2n+1}^*, \boldsymbol{b}_{2n+2}^*, \boldsymbol{b}_{2n+3}^*), \end{cases}$$

where $(\boldsymbol{d}_{n+i} = \boldsymbol{b}_{n+i} - \sum_{j\in[n]} u_{i,j} \cdot \boldsymbol{b}_j - m_i \cdot \boldsymbol{b}_{2n+1})_{i\in[n]}$, $(\boldsymbol{d}_i^* = \boldsymbol{b}_i^* + \sum_{j\in[n]} u_{i,j} \cdot \boldsymbol{b}_{n+j}^*)_{i\in[n]}$, and $\boldsymbol{d}_{2n+1}^* = \boldsymbol{b}_{2n+1}^* + \sum_{j\in[n]} m_i \cdot \boldsymbol{b}_{n+j}^*$.

Because this transformation preserves the dual orthonormal property, $(\mathbb{D}, \mathbb{D}^*)$ are still dual orthonormal and distributed in the same manner as $(\mathbb{B}, \mathbb{B}^*)$. Furthermore, because $\boldsymbol{b}_{n+1}, \cdots, \boldsymbol{b}_{2n}$ and $\mathbb{B}^*$ are hidden from the adversary, an adversary cannot determine whether tokens or ciphertexts are represented in $(\mathbb{B}, \mathbb{B}^*)$ or in $(\mathbb{D}, \mathbb{D}^*)$ if the adversary can only access the public key information. Therefore, we can rewrite tokens and the challenge ciphertext in $\mathbf{Game}_{q,n+1}$ from the bases $(\mathbb{B}, \mathbb{B}^*)$ to the bases $(\mathbb{D}, \mathbb{D}^*)$.

Now, we rewrite each semi-functional token in $\mathbf{Game}_{q,n+1}$ under base $\mathbb{D}^*$. For example, consider an α-type token:

$$
\begin{aligned}
&token^{sf.\alpha}_{\mathcal{W}} \\
&= (\boldsymbol{\delta}_1, \cdots, \boldsymbol{\delta}_\ell, \boldsymbol{v}^\alpha, 1, r, 0)_{\mathbb{B}^*} \\
&= \sum_{i\in[n]} \delta_i \cdot \boldsymbol{b}^*_i + \sum_{i\in[n]} v_i \cdot \boldsymbol{b}^*_{n+i} + \boldsymbol{b}^*_{2n+1} + r \cdot \boldsymbol{b}^*_{2n+2} \\
&= \sum_{i\in[n]} \delta_i \cdot (\boldsymbol{d}^*_i - \sum_{j\in[n]} u_{i,j} \cdot \boldsymbol{b}^*_{n+j}) \\
&\quad + \sum_{i\in[n]} v_i \cdot \boldsymbol{b}^*_{n+i} + (\boldsymbol{d}^*_{2n+1} - \sum_{j\in[n]} m_i \cdot \boldsymbol{b}^*_{n+j}) + r \cdot \boldsymbol{b}^*_{2n+2} \\
&= \sum_{i\in[n]} \delta_i \cdot \boldsymbol{d}^*_i + \sum_{i\in[n]} (v_i - \langle \boldsymbol{\delta}_i, \boldsymbol{u}_i \rangle - m_i) \cdot \boldsymbol{b}^*_{n+i} + \boldsymbol{d}^*_{2n+1} + r \cdot \boldsymbol{b}^*_{2n+2} \\
&= (\boldsymbol{\delta}_1, \cdots, \boldsymbol{\delta}_\ell, \boldsymbol{v}', 1, r, 0)_{\mathbb{D}^*},
\end{aligned}
$$

where $\boldsymbol{v}' = (v'_1, \cdots, v'_n)$ with $v'_i = v_i - \langle \boldsymbol{\delta}_i, \boldsymbol{u}_i \rangle - m_i$. Here, $\boldsymbol{v}'$ is uniformly distributed. Moreover the challenge ciphertext in $\mathbf{Game}_{q,n+1}$ can also be rewritten under base $\mathbb{D}$ as follows:

$$
\begin{aligned}
&ct_{\mathcal{W}^*_b,1} \\
&= (\boldsymbol{\tau}_1, \cdots, \boldsymbol{\tau}_\ell, \boldsymbol{v}^{ct}, \sigma, 0, q)_{\mathbb{B}} \\
&= \sum_{i\in[n]} \tau_i \cdot \boldsymbol{b}_i + \sum_{i\in[n]} v^{ct}_i \cdot \boldsymbol{b}_{n+i} + \sigma \cdot \boldsymbol{b}_{2n+1} + q \cdot \boldsymbol{b}_{2n+3} \\
&= \sum_{i\in[n]} \tau_i \cdot \boldsymbol{b}_i \\
&\quad + \sum_{i\in[n]} v^{ct}_i \cdot (\boldsymbol{d}_{n+i} + \sum_{j\in[n]} u_{i,j} \cdot \boldsymbol{b}_j + m_i \cdot \boldsymbol{b}_{2n+1}) + \sigma \cdot \boldsymbol{b}_{2n+1} + q \cdot \boldsymbol{b}_{2n+3} \\
&= \sum_{i\in[n]} (\tau_i + \langle \boldsymbol{v}^{ct}, \boldsymbol{u}_i \rangle) \cdot \boldsymbol{b}_i + \sum_{i\in[n]} v^{ct}_i \cdot \boldsymbol{d}_{n+i} + (\sigma \cdot \langle \boldsymbol{v}^{ct}, \boldsymbol{u} \rangle) \cdot \boldsymbol{b}_{2n+1} + q \cdot \boldsymbol{b}_{2n+3} \\
&= (\hat{\boldsymbol{\tau}}_1, \cdots, \hat{\boldsymbol{\tau}}_\ell, \boldsymbol{v}^{ct}, \sigma', 0, q)_{\mathbb{D}},
\end{aligned}
$$

affecting only $\boldsymbol{\tau}$ and σ and where τ and $\sigma' = \sigma \cdot \langle \boldsymbol{v}^{ct}, \boldsymbol{u} \rangle$. Both $\hat{\boldsymbol{\tau}}$ and σ' are independently and uniformly distributed and $ct_{\mathcal{W}^*_b,2}$ is still equal to Ω^σ. After the base transformation, the challenge ciphertext is equivalent to that obtained by generating for a random set of keywords, and the views of an algorithm $\mathcal{A}$ in $\mathbf{Game}_{q,n+1}$ and $\mathbf{Game}_{Final}$ are the same. □

6 Theoretical Comparison

We compare our proposed scheme with the PEAKS scheme of Jiang *et al.* [9] in terms of computational cost, communication cost, and their properties. We use ℓ to denote the size of the set of keywords. With respect to their computational cost (Table 1), five algorithms are considered, the Authorize, Delegate, Encrypt, Trapdoor, and Test algorithms. We focused on four time-consuming operations: modular exponentiation (E), pairing computation (P), modular multiplication (M), and hashing (H). In comparisons of communication cost (Table 2) $|\mathbb{G}|$, $|\mathbb{G}_T|$ and $|\mathbb{Z}_p|$ denote the size of a group element in groups $\mathbb{G}$, $\mathbb{G}_T$, and $\mathbb{Z}_p$ respectively.

Table 1. Computational cost of our scheme and that of Jiang *et al.* [9].

Scheme	Authorize	Delegate	Encrypt	Trapdoor	Test
[9]	$3E + H$	–	$(\ell + 2)E + (\ell - 1)M$	$(2\ell + 1)E + (2\ell - 2)M$	$5P + H$
Ours	$3 * (4\ell + 3)^2 E$	$3 * (4\ell + 3)^2 E$	$((4\ell + 3)^2 + 1)E + P$	$(4\ell + 3)^2 E$	$(4\ell + 3)P$

Table 2. Communication cost of our scheme and that of Jiang *et al.* [9].

Scheme	Public key	Private key	Auth. token	Dele. token	Ciphertext	Trapdoor
[9]	$(3\ell + 3)\lvert\mathbb{G}\rvert$	$\lvert\mathbb{G}\rvert + 4\lvert\mathbb{Z}_p\rvert$	$2\lvert\mathbb{G}\rvert$	-	$3\lvert\mathbb{G}\rvert$	$4\lvert\mathbb{G}\rvert$
Ours	$(2\ell + 3)\lvert\mathbb{G}\rvert + \lvert\mathbb{G}_T\rvert$	$(4\ell + 3)\lvert\mathbb{G}\rvert$	$(2\ell + 1)(4\ell + 3)\lvert\mathbb{G}\rvert$	$(2\ell + 1)(4\ell + 3)\lvert\mathbb{G}\rvert$	$(4\ell + 3)\lvert\mathbb{G}\rvert + \lvert\mathbb{G}_T\rvert$	$(4\ell + 3)\lvert\mathbb{G}\rvert$

Table 3. Properties of our scheme and that of Jiang *et al.* [9].

Scheme	Assumption	Multikeyword search	Token delegation	Hierarchical search
[9]	(n, ℓ)-MSE-DDH	No	No	No
Ours	OT.1 & OT.2	Yes	Yes	Yes

The properties of our scheme and that of Jiang *et al.* are presented in Table 3. With regard to the hardness assumption, Jiang *et al.* [9] relied on the (n, ℓ)-multisequence of exponents Diffie-Hellman ((n, ℓ)-MSE-DDH) assumption; our scheme relies on the OT.1 and OT.2, which can be reduced to decision linear assumption. In addition, our scheme is more flexible than that of Jiang *et al.* [9]. First, our scheme supports multikeyword search; users with direct or delegated authorization can generate trapdoors that are related to a set of keywords $\mathcal{W}''$ to search for ciphertexts related to another set of keywords $\mathcal{W}$ if $\mathcal{W}'' \subseteq \mathcal{W}$. In other words, the proposed scheme supports searching the ciphertext using multiple keywords at a time. Second, our scheme supports token delegation; authorized users can further delegate their tokens, which are related to a set of keywords $\mathcal{W}$, to another set of keywords if $\mathcal{W}' \subseteq \mathcal{W}$. Thus, token delegation is not restricted, and our scheme is more applicable to various real-world scenarios. Finally, because an upper-level user can also generate a trapdoor from his/her token, our scheme naturally provides a hierarchical search function. To the best of our knowledge, other PEKS-derived schemes do not allow for both token delegation and hierarchical search properties.

7 Conclusion and Future Work

In this work, we introduce a novel cryptosystem, called public key encryption with hierarchical authorized keyword search (PEHAKS), to support delegation for authorization over multikeyword search. We formally define the system model and the security requirement. To obtain a concrete construction, we design three encoding functions, modify Abdally *et al.*'s generic transformation, and carefully combine them together. In addition, detailed security proof is also provided to show the proposed scheme is SS-CKA secure under OT.1 and OT.2 assumptions.

Although PEHAKS is useful for various applications, the current scheme has some flaws. Specifically, the computational cost of Test algorithm and the communication cost are linearly related to the size of the set of keywords. In addition, the sizes of all elements depend on the size of the universal keyword space; thus, the scheme can be applied only in a polynomial-size universal keyword space (the existing PEAKS scheme [9] also has this drawback). Hence, increasing the efficiency of the proposed PEHAKS scheme is an open problem that we will investigate in a future study.

Acknowledgments. The authors thank the anonymous reviewers for their insightful suggestions on this work. This research is partially supported by the National Science and Technology Council, Taiwan (ROC), under grant numbers NSTC 109-2221-E-004-011-MY3, NSTC 110-2221-E-004-003-, NSTC 110-2622-8-004-001-, NSTC 111-2218-E-004-001-MBK, and NSTC 111-2221-E-004-005-.

References

1. Abdalla, M.: Searchable encryption revisited: consistency properties, relation to anonymous IBE, and extensions. In: Shoup, V. (ed.) CRYPTO 2005. LNCS, vol. 3621, pp. 205–222. Springer, Heidelberg (2005). https://doi.org/10.1007/11535218_13
2. Abdalla, M., De Caro, A., Phan, D.H.: Generalized key delegation for wildcarded identity-based and inner-product encryption. IEEE Trans. Inf. Forensics Secur. **7**(6), 1695–1706 (2012)
3. Abu-Libdeh, H., Princehouse, L., Weatherspoon, H.: RACS: a case for cloud storage diversity. In: ACM Symposium on Cloud Computing (2010)
4. Boneh, D., Crescenzo, G.D., Ostrovsky, R., Persiano, G.: Public key encryption with keyword search. In: EUROCRYPT (2004)
5. Chen, R., et al.: Server-aided public key encryption with keyword search. IEEE Trans. Inf. Forensics Secur. **11**(12), 2833–2842 (2016)
6. Conway, J.H.: Atlas of Finite Groups: Maximal Subgroups and Ordinary Characters for Simple Groups. Oxford University Press (1985)
7. Goldwasser, S., Micali, S., Rivest, R.L.: A digital signature scheme secure against adaptive chosen-message attacks. SIAM J. Comput. **17**(2), 281–308 (1988)
8. Hayes, B.: Cloud computing (2008)
9. Jiang, P., Mu, Y., Guo, F., Wen, Q.: Public key encryption with authorized keyword search. In: ACISP (2016)
10. Johnson, D., Menezes, A., Vanstone, S.: The elliptic curve digital signature algorithm (ECDSA). Int. J. Inf. Secur. **1**(1), 36–63 (2001)

11. Lewko, A., Okamoto, T., Sahai, A., Takashima, K., Waters, B.: Fully secure functional encryption: attribute-based encryption and (hierarchical) inner product encryption. In: EUROCRYPT (2010)
12. Liu, Z.Y., Tseng, Y.F., Tso, R., Chen, Y.C., Mambo, M.: Identity-certifying authority-aided identity-based searchable encryption framework in cloud systems. IEEE Syst. J. **16**, 4629–4640 (2021)
13. Okamoto, T., Takashima, K.: Hierarchical predicate encryption for inner-products. In: EUROCRYPT (2009)
14. Okamoto, T., Takashima, K.: Fully secure functional encryption with general relations from the decisional linear assumption. In: Rabin, T. (ed.) CRYPTO 2010. LNCS, vol. 6223, pp. 191–208. Springer, Heidelberg (2010). https://doi.org/10.1007/978-3-642-14623-7_11
15. Qian, L., Luo, Z., Du, Y., Guo, L.: Cloud computing: an overview. In: IEEE International Conference on Cloud Computing (2009)
16. Qin, B., Chen, Y., Huang, Q., Liu, X., Zheng, D.: Public-key authenticated encryption with keyword search revisited: Security model and constructions. Inf. Sci. **516**, 515–528 (2020)
17. Wang, J., Chow, S.S.: Omnes pro uno: practical multi-writer encrypted database. In: USENIX Security (2022)
18. Wang, P., Chen, B., Xiang, T., Wang, Z.: Lattice-based public key searchable encryption with fine-grained access control for edge computing. Futur. Gener. Comput. Syst. **127**, 373–383 (2022)
19. Wang, T., Quan, Y., Shen, X.S., Gadekallu, T.R., Wang, W., Dev, K.: A privacy-enhanced retrieval technology for the cloud-assisted internet of things. IEEE Trans. Industrial Inform. **18**, 4981–4989 (2021)
20. Waters, B.: Dual system encryption: realizing fully secure IBE and HIBE under simple assumptions. In: Halevi, S. (ed.) CRYPTO 2009. LNCS, vol. 5677, pp. 619–636. Springer, Heidelberg (2009). https://doi.org/10.1007/978-3-642-03356-8_36
21. Wei, L., et al.: Security and privacy for storage and computation in cloud computing. Inf. Sci. **258**, 371–386 (2014)

Private Evaluation of a Decision Tree Based on Secret Sharing

Mohammad Nabil Ahmed(✉) and Kana Shimizu(✉)

Waseda University, Tokyo, Japan

mnabil.ahmed@asagi.waseda.jp, shimizu.kana@waseda.jp

Abstract. There has been increasing interest in developing privacy-preserving algorithms for evaluating machine learning (ML) models. With the advancement of cloud computing, it is now possible for model owners to host their trained ML models on a cloud server and offer cloud computing solutions on different ML tasks to users (clients). Thus private evaluation of ML models is an attractive area of research as it allows solution providers to protect their propriety ML models and users to protect their sensitive data while using cloud computing solutions. In this work, we propose an algorithm to privately evaluate a decision tree. We examine current state-of-the-art private evaluation protocols and present a solution that is sublinear in tree size and linear in tree depth. The key feature of our proposal is that it is entirely based on secret sharing and thus there are no computational costs associated with heavy cryptographic primitives such as modular exponentiation. We propose a new method to privately index arrays that avoids the use of public/symmetric key cryptosystem, typically associated with private array indexing protocols. The results of our experiments show that our solution has a low communication cost compared to existing methods (lower by a factor of ≈10 in the online phase), and demonstrate a faster runtime at low network latency (such as LAN network). We conclude by suggesting improvement to our protocol and proposing potential areas of future research.

Keywords: Secret sharing · Private decision tree evaluation · Privacy preserving machine learning

1 Introduction

Solutions based on cloud computing have become increasingly popular in recent years. By leveraging the power of cloud computing, technology companies are already offering a diverse range of *services* based on the needs of their customers [1,24,35]. Of particular interest are solutions based on machine learning (ML), as they allow users with limited computational resources to perform tasks using computationally expensive ML models. For instance, an organization may host a pre-trained ML model in its cloud server and offer services to its clients, allowing them to perform a variety of different ML tasks like dataset classification.

S.-H. Seo and H. Seo (Eds.): ICISC 2022, LNCS 13849, pp. 171–194, 2023.
https://doi.org/10.1007/978-3-031-29371-9_9

Classification is a typical example of a supervised machine learning (ML) task, which first involves training a *classifier* and then evaluating the trained classifier on samples from a raw dataset to predict their associated labels. Real-world applications of classification using ML are varied, ranging from spam filtering, credit fraud detection to drug discovery and diagnosing the presence or absence of a disease [25,33,46]. Consider a case where a ML classifier trained by a service provides on one of these datasets is offered as a computing service to its clients.

While this sort of arrangement poses no risk when the client's dataset consists of nonsensitive data, it raises serious *privacy* concerns for datasets with privately identifiable information (PII). For instance, consider the case of a ML model that detects the presence or absence of a disease using clinical data. A client with sensitive data would be unwillingly to use such a model hosted on a cloud server as the client data is sent and thus leaked to the server. An obvious approach to deal with this scenario would be to outsource the ML model to the client but this would mean that confidential information such as the internal structure of the model are potentially leaked to the client, which in turn could be detrimental to the business of cloud service provider. All these point to the fact that there are practical benefits to designing algorithms that evaluate ML based classifiers without leaking any information about the query or the model parameters. A diverse group of ML classifiers are used in practice, from relatively simplistic models such as decision trees (DT) to complex ones such as neural networks. In this work, we primarily focus on a DT classifier as DT models are easy to interpret, they can be explained using boolean logic and are thus the classifier of choice in clinical diagnosis [40].

1.1 Our Contribution

We propose an outsourced two-party protocol between two computing nodes that privately evaluate a DT, where the depth of the tree is publicly known. These nodes which can be considered as servers (or cloud servers), receive an input query and a DT classification model as *secret shares* from a query and tree holder respectively. The computing nodes thus learn neither the query nor the DT model since they operate on shares. Meanwhile, the query holder remains oblivious to the DT parameters, and the tree holder to the input query. The nodes then jointly run a private protocol and output the result as secret shares to the query holder. Thus, *only* the query holder learns the result of classification from the private protocol.

Just as in the case of a plain evaluation of a DT, the number of comparisons in our private protocol is proportional to the depth of the tree. This helps us achieve a round complexity that is linear in tree depth and sublinear in tree size, a feature that is important for designing optimal protocols for not only deep-but-sparse trees but also shallow-but-dense trees. The main contribution of our approach is that the decision tree and the query vector are represented as arrays, we design private protocols on array based tree traversal and query feature selection using random shuffling. This helps us save computational costs associated with public/symmetric key operations of oblivious transfer (OT) based array indexing, as well as communication costs with transmitting the ciphertexts during these operations. Lastly, our entire protocol is based on secret sharing, which helps us avoid computationally expensive cryptographic primitives such as those based on modular exponentiation. As a result, our protocol is suited for scenarios where clients have limited computational resources and bandwidth while also achieving reasonably fast protocol runtime. A high level overview of our private decision tree evaluation protocol (PDTE) is shown in Fig. 1 and a detailed explanation on its implementation is given in Sect. 4.4.

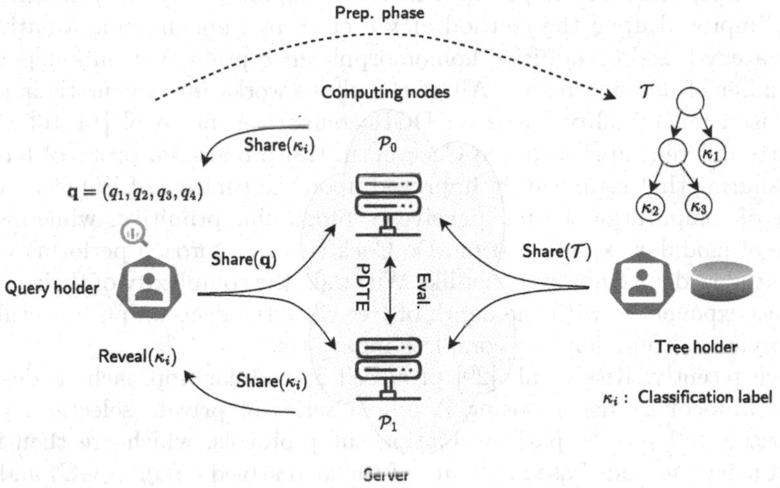

Fig. 1. An overview of our proposed model, a query holder $\mathcal{B}$ evaluates a query $\mathbf{q}$ using a decision tree $\mathcal{T}$ held by tree holder $\mathcal{A}$ such that neither $\mathbf{q}$ nor $\mathcal{T}$ is leaked. The model has a preparation phase, where $\mathcal{A}$ and $\mathcal{B}$ interact to setup a private decision tree evaluation (PDTE) protocol. $\mathcal{T}$ and $\mathbf{q}$ are then secret shared to computing nodes $\mathcal{P}_k$ (server) who run the PDTE protocol. We refer to the this stage of the model as the evaluation phase, and upon the termination of PDTE protocol, $\mathcal{P}_k$ obtain the shares of classification label, κ_i corresponding to $\mathbf{q}$. These are then sent to $\mathcal{B}$ as shares, who reconstructs the actual label from the shares.

2 Related Works

Numerous methods on designing two-party based private decision tree evaluation (PDTE) protocols have been proposed in literature [8,18,29,32,41,42,45], and on a fundamental level all these protocols have a similar idea. Input query features are first mapped to the decision nodes of a tree using a cryptographic primitive such as oblivious transfer (OT). A secure comparison protocol is then run to evaluate a decision function by comparing the query features to the decision node thresholds. Finally, a path evaluation function determines the classification label associated with the query. We now present some of the prior works on designing PDTE protocol in chronological order. Bost et al. [8] proposed a privacy-preserving protocol by modeling the path evaluation a tree as a polynomial function of boolean variables and then evaluating this function using leveled fully homomorphic encryption. Meanwhile, Wu et al. [45] use a path evaluation strategy based on a decision bit string which is then evaluated using additive homomorphic encryption. Despite being more efficient than Bost et al.'s approach due to the use of additive homomorphic encryption, Wu et al.'s method does not perform well for deeply rooted trees (trees with high depth) since it transforms a binary decision tree into a full binary decision tree and thus the complexity of the protocol increases exponentially with depth. Tai et al. [41] improved upon the method of Wu et al. by implementing a path selection strategy based on additive homomorphic encryption that only depends on the number of decision nodes. All of the above works implement their private comparison functionality based on DGK comparison protocol [14–16]. Taking a slightly different approach, De Cock et al. [18] proposed a protocol based on secret sharing that significantly improved upon the runtime of Wu et al. due to the use of computationally inexpensive cryptographic primitives while avoiding the use of modular exponentiation. De Cock et al.'s approach performs well for trees with low depth, however just like Wu et al., the complexity of their protocol increases exponential with the depth of tree since the decision path is evaluated as a polynomial function of a complete binary tree.

More recently, Kiss et al. [29] proposed a modular approach to designing PDTE protocol by decomposing it into a series of private selection, private comparison and private path evaluation sub-protocols, which are then implemented using methods based on state-of-the-art garbled circuits (GC) and additive homomorphic encryption (HE). Just like the prior HE-based approaches, Kiss et al. also use the DGK comparison protocol and make use of single-instruction-multiple-data (SIMD) slots for efficient implementation through parallel processing [7]. As for their GC based comparison protocol, they use Yao's garbled circuit [47,48] along with the optimizations from [4,31,49]. Meanwhile, Tueno et al. [42] proposed a PDTE model with an array based representation of decision tree and a GC based evaluation protocol, while studying the protocol performance on a variety of array indexing methods such as GC+OT, oblivious transfer (OT) and oblivious RAM (ORAM). A key feature of their approach is that the round complexity of the protocol depends on the depth of the tree as opposed to the size of the tree of previous methods. Meanwhile, Zheng et al. [50] proposed a PDTE protocol based on secret sharing that is outsourced to two *cloud* servers. Unlike the prior works that implement private selection using OT, Zheng et al. instead use an indicator matrix created by a DT provider that maps query features to decision node thresholds. This matrix is then secret shared to the cloud servers, who privately select the relevant query features and thresholds for each of the decision node using secure matrix multiplication. Like Tai et al. [41], Zheng et al. also formulate private path evaluation as a path cost problem, but this requires running the private comparison protocol over all the decision nodes, which results in a PDTE protocol that is non-sublinear in tree size unlike

Tueno et al. Lastly, Ma et al. [32] propose a PDTE protocol that is sublinear in tree size, by secret sharing the tree and then evaluating the tree using GC based comparison protocol. Ma et al. show that their protocol outperforms other PDTE protocols that are linear in tree depth, while also outperforming constant round PDTE protocols at higher tree depth. The overall computational complexity of the above protocols compared to our approach is summarized in Table 1, construction of which is inspired from [32].

Table 1. Summary of previous approaches to private decision tree evaluation protocols based on asymptotic complexity of all the participants of the protocol. FHE: Fully homomorphic encryption, DGK: DGK comparison protocol, HE: Additive homomorphic encryption, GC: Garbled circuit, SS: Secret sharing, SKE: Symmetric key encryption/decryption, t : No. of query features, m : No. of decision nodes, l : bit-length, d : Depth of tree, $\bar{t}$: No. of padded query features, $\bar{n}$: No. of depth-padded nodes, $\mathcal{A}$: Tree holder, $\mathcal{B}$: Query holder, $\mathcal{P}_k$: Computational node k.

Method	Primitives	Computational Complexity		Rounds	Leakage
		Server	Client		
Bost et al.	FHE	$\mathcal{O}(ml)$ FHE + $\mathcal{O}(m)$ DGK	$\mathcal{O}(tl) + \mathcal{O}(m)$ DGK	$\mathcal{O}(1)$	m
Cock et al.	SS	$\mathcal{O}(2^d)l$	$\mathcal{O}((t+2^d)l$	$\mathcal{O}(1)$	d
Wu et al.	HE	$\mathcal{O}(2^d)$ DGK + $\mathcal{O}(2^d)$ HE	$\mathcal{O}((t+2^d)l$ HE	$\mathcal{O}(1)$	d, m
Tai et al.	HE	$\mathcal{O}(ml)$ SKE	$\mathcal{O}(m+tl)$ HE+ $\mathcal{O}(m)$ DGK	$\mathcal{O}(1)$	m
Kiss et al. (GGH)	GC + HE	$\mathcal{O}(md)$ HE+ $\mathcal{O}(l(m \log m + t))$ SKE	$\mathcal{O}(m)$ HE+ $\mathcal{O}(l(m \log m + t))$ SKE	$\mathcal{O}(1)$	m
Tueno et al. (OT)	SS + GC	$\mathcal{O}(2^d + dl)$	$\mathcal{O}((t+l)d)$	$\mathcal{O}(d)$	d
Ma et al. (Sparse)	SS + GC	$\mathcal{O}(m + dl)$	$\mathcal{O}((t+l)d) + d$ SKE	$\mathcal{O}(d)$	d, m
		Cloud Server	Provider + Client		
Zheng et al.	SS	$\mathcal{O}(mt) + \mathcal{O}(ml)$	$\mathcal{O}(m) + \mathcal{O}(t)$	$\mathcal{O}(l)$	d, m
		$\mathcal{P}_k$	$\mathcal{A} + \mathcal{B}$		
Ours	SS	$\mathcal{O}(dl)$	$\mathcal{O}(\bar{t}) + \mathcal{O}(\bar{n})$	$\mathcal{O}(d)$	d

3 Preliminaries

Unless stated otherwise, the notations used throughout the paper are adopted based on Table 2.

3.1 Secret Sharing

A linear secret sharing scheme splits an integer $x \in \mathbb{Z}_p$ into n pieces known as *shares* in an arithmetic field $\mathbb{Z}_p$. Any *t-out-of-n* subset of these *arithmetic shares* can then be used to reconstruct the original integer [6,20,27,39]. Our protocols use a 2-*out-of*-2 additive secret sharing scheme which consists of two functions - $\mathsf{Share}(x) \rightarrow [\![x]\!]_0, [\![x]\!]_1$, that splits an integer into shares and $\mathsf{Reveal}([\![x]\!]_0, [\![x]\!]_1) \rightarrow x$, that reconstructs the original integer. We use the notation $[\![x]\!]_k$ to denote the shares of x held by party $\mathcal{P}_k$ and distinguish from its *plain* form x. Hereafter, we use the term *shares* to denote *arithmetic shares.*

Table 2. List of notations used throughout the paper

Symbol	Meaning
$\mathcal{A}$	Tree holder (client)
$\mathcal{B}$	Query holder (client)
$\mathcal{P}_k$	Computing node k (server)
$\mathcal{T}$	Decision tree
d	Depth of decision tree
m	Number of decision nodes in $\mathcal{T}$
n	Number of nodes in tree in $\mathcal{T}$
t	Number of query features
$\mathbf{x}$	Vector with node ids of $\mathcal{T}$. $\mathbf{x} = (x_1, x_2, \dots x_n)$, $x_i \in [1, n]$
λ_i	Level at x_i, $\lambda_i \in [0, d]$
θ_i	Comparison threshold at x_i, $\theta_i \in \mathbb{R}$
ω_i	Feature to be selected at x_i, $\omega_i \in [1, t]$
$\mathbf{v}$	Look-up vector of $\mathcal{T}$. $\mathbf{v} = (v_1, v_2, \dots v_n)$, $v_i \in \mathbb{Z}$
$\mathbf{d}$	Threshold vector of $\mathcal{T}$. $\mathbf{d} = (d_1, d_2, \dots d_n)$, $d_i \in \mathbb{R}$
$\mathbf{t}$	Feature select vector of $\mathcal{T}$. $\mathbf{t} = (t_1, t_2, \dots t_n)$, $t_i \in [1, t]$
$\mathbf{c}$	Class label vector of $\mathcal{T}$. $\mathbf{c} = (c_1, c_2, \dots c_n)$, $c_i \in \mathbb{Z}$
$\mathbf{f}$	Flag vector indicating if *children* are swapped. $\mathbf{f} = (f_1, f_2, \dots f_n)$, $f_i \in \{0, 1\}$
$\mathbf{q}$	Query vector held by $\mathcal{B}$, $\mathbf{q} = (q_1, q_2, \dots q_t)$, $q_i \in \mathbb{R}$
$\mathbf{w}$	Secure feature select vector, $\mathbf{w} = (w_1, w_2, \dots w_n)$, $w_i \in [1, t]$
$[\![z]\!]$	*Secret shares* of z in $\mathbb{Z}_p$, where p is a prime
$\mathbf{z}[i]$	i-th element of vector $\mathbf{z}$, $\mathbf{z}[1]$ corresponds to its first element
$\tilde{\mathbf{z}}$	Randomly shuffled $\mathbf{z}$
$[\![\mathbf{z}]\!]$	$([\![z_1]\!], [\![z_2]\!], \dots [\![z_l]\!])$ vector of shares or bitwise sharing of $z = \sum_{i=1}^{l} 2^{i-1} \cdot z_i$, $z_i \in \{0, 1\}$

3.2 Operations Using Secret Sharing

Addition. Addition using secret sharing can be performed with local computation by simply summing over shares. Let $[\![x]\!]_k, [\![y]\!]_k$ be the shares of integers x and y held by $\mathcal{P}_k$. The operation $x + y$ can be computed locally, with $\mathcal{P}_0$ computing $[\![z]\!]_0 := [\![x]\!]_0 + [\![y]\!]_0$, and $\mathcal{P}_1$ computing $[\![z]\!]_1 := [\![x]\!]_1 + [\![y]\!]_1$, where $[\![z]\!]$ represents the shares of z, such that $z = x + y$. Similarly, multiplication with a scalar c can also be performed locally by computing $[\![z]\!] = c[\![x]\!]$, such that $z = c \cdot x$ since it is just repeated addition.

Multiplication. Multiplication using secret sharing is more complex, and unlike addition cannot be performed without distributed computing. More concretely, multiplication over shares of x, y is defined by $\mathsf{Mult}([\![x]\!], [\![y]\!]) \rightarrow [\![z]\!]$, such that $z = x \cdot y$. Numerous works exist in literature that describe the construction of a Mult protocol [2,17,26,44]. In this work we use the two-party protocol of Beaver which requires only one interactive round using notions from commodity-based cryptography [3]. The key idea of Beaver's protocol is to pre-compute a set correlated randomness known as Beaver's triples (BT) which can then used to perform multiplication. BTs are either generated collaboratively by the two-parties or by a trusted initializer [28,36]. We adopt the trusted initializer setting when implementing the Mult protocol.

Boolean Operations. Boolean operations can be represented using multiplication and thus, boolean operations using secret sharing can be defined using Mult as a sub-protocol. Let a, b be two boolean variables, we define conjunction over boolean shares as $\mathsf{AND}([\![a]\!], [\![b]\!]) := \mathsf{Mult}([\![a]\!], [\![b]\!]) \rightarrow [\![z]\!]$, such that $z = a \wedge b$, disjunction as $\mathsf{OR}([\![a]\!], [\![b]\!] := [\![a]\!] + [\![b]\!] - \mathsf{Mult}([\![a]\!], [\![b]\!])) \rightarrow [\![z]\!]$, such that $z = a \vee b$, and exclusive disjunction as $\mathsf{XOR}([\![a]\!], [\![b]\!] := [\![a]\!] + [\![b]\!] - 2 \cdot \mathsf{Mult}([\![a]\!], [\![b]\!]) \rightarrow [\![z]\!])$, such that $z = a \oplus b$. Meanwhile, $\mathsf{NOT}([\![a]\!])$ can be performed locally - each party simply computes $[\![z]\!] = [\![1]\!] - [\![a]\!]$, where $z = \neg a$. We define a *bitwise* sharing in l-bits as $[\![\mathbf{z}]\!]$ such that $[\![\mathbf{z}]\!] = \{[\![z_1]\!], [\![z_2]\!], \ldots [\![z_l]\!]\}$ and $z_i = \{0, 1\}$.

Comparison. Relational operations are useful for defining many mathematical functions and thus secret sharing based *less-than* comparison protocol is an active area of research [10,13,22,37,38]. Less-than comparison protocols are typically constructed using secure boolean operations and is defined as, $\mathsf{LT}([\![x]\!], [\![y]\!]) \rightarrow [\![z]\!]$ such that $z = 0$ if $(x < y)$, and $z = 1$ otherwise. In this work, we implement Garay et al.'s LT protocol [22] using the improvement suggested by Veugen et al. [43]. Garay et al.'s LT protocol has a round complexity of $\lceil \log p \rceil$ interactive rounds, where $\lceil \log p \rceil$ is the minimum number of bits required to represent the prime, p in arithmetic field, $\mathbb{Z}_p$. Note that we have defined all the above operations (including boolean operations) using arithmetic shares only.

3.3 Security Definition

The protocols presented in this paper are two-party protocols, follow security definitions of two-party computational model introduced in [5,12,23,34] using Universal Composability (UC) framework [9] and adopt the notion of semi-honest security. We assume that one of the parties is corrupted before protocol execution. The corrupted party does not deviate from the protocol but tries to learn as much information as possible from its inputs and the messages exchanged during the protocol. Furthermore, we also assume the presence of a trusted initializer [3,28] that generates all the necessary correlated random prior to the execution of the protocol. Let Π be a protocol behind two-parties performing some ideal functionality $\mathcal{F}$. We say that a protocol is secure in the semi-honest model if there exits an algorithm $\mathcal{S}$ that can simulate its execution given its input and output.

4 Methods

4.1 Problem Setting

We formulate the problem of private evaluation of a decision tree (PDTE) as follows: a tree holder $\mathcal{A}$ possesses a DT model $\mathcal{T}$ of depth d with n nodes, and a query holder $\mathcal{B}$ holds a query vector $\mathbf{q}$ with t features. $\mathcal{B}$ would like to learn the *class label* associated with $\mathbf{q}$ by privately evaluating the classification model held by $\mathcal{A}$. Here the term *private evaluation* implies that $\mathcal{B}$ evaluates $\mathcal{T}$ without learning anything about the internal structure of $\mathcal{T}$ (other than its depth), whereas $\mathcal{A}$ learns nothing about $\mathbf{q}$. To accomplish this we propose an outsourced two-party protocol between two computing nodes, $\mathcal{P}_0$ and $\mathcal{P}_1$ using a 2-*out-of*-2 secret sharing scheme based on a semi-honest security model [23]. $\mathcal{A}$ creates *shares* of $\mathcal{T}$ and $\mathcal{B}$ secret shares of $\mathbf{q}$, which are then distributed to $\mathcal{P}_0$ and $\mathcal{P}_1$. The nodes then participate in a PDTE protocol that evaluates $\mathbf{q}$ on $\mathcal{T}$ and outputs a classification label κ_i, which we denote in plain form by $\mathcal{T}(\mathbf{q}) \rightarrow \kappa_i$. We assume that the depth, d of $\mathcal{T}$ is publicly known, and the protocol reveals no information other than d. A general overview of our protocol is shown in Fig. 1 and in Sect. 4.2 we present the basic data structure corresponding to $\mathcal{T}$.

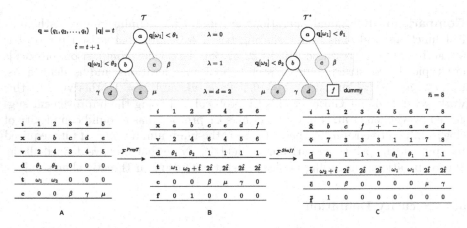

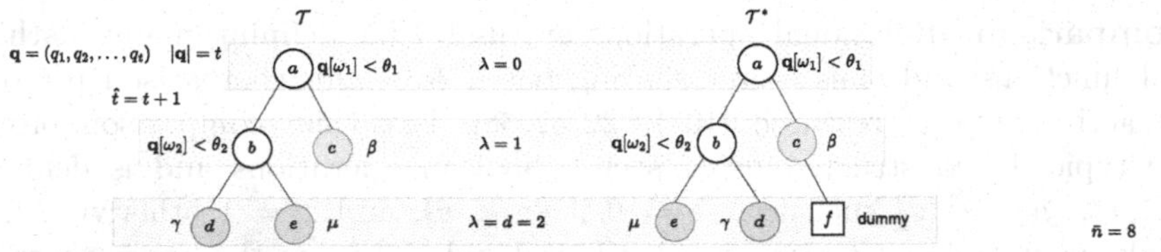

i	1	2	3	4	5
$\mathbf{x}$	a	b	c	d	e
$\mathbf{v}$	2	4	3	4	5
$\mathbf{d}$	θ_1	θ_2	0	0	0
$\mathbf{t}$	ω_1	ω_2	0	0	0
$\mathbf{c}$	0	0	β	γ	μ

A

$\mathcal{F}^{PrepT}$ →

i	1	2	3	4	5	6
$\mathbf{x}$	a	b	c	e	d	f
$\mathbf{v}$	2	4	6	4	5	6
$\mathbf{d}$	θ_1	θ_2	1	1	1	1
$\mathbf{t}$	ω_1	$\omega_2 + \hat{t}$	$2\hat{t}$	$2\hat{t}$	$2\hat{t}$	$2\hat{t}$
$\mathbf{c}$	0	0	β	μ	γ	0
$\mathbf{f}$	0	1	0	0	0	0

B

$\mathcal{F}^{Shuff}$ →

i	1	2	3	4	5	6	7	8
$\tilde{\mathbf{x}}$	b	c	f	+	−	a	e	d
$\tilde{\mathbf{v}}$	7	3	3	3	1	1	7	8
$\tilde{\mathbf{d}}$	θ_2	1	1	1	θ_1	θ_1	1	1
$\tilde{\mathbf{t}}$	$\omega_2 + \hat{t}$	$2\hat{t}$	$2\hat{t}$	$2\hat{t}$	ω_1	ω_1	$2\hat{t}$	$2\hat{t}$
$\tilde{\mathbf{c}}$	0	β	0	0	0	0	μ	γ
$\tilde{\mathbf{f}}$	1	0	0	0	0	0	0	0

C

Fig. 2. The representation of $\mathcal{T}$ using tree arrays $\mathbf{v}, \mathbf{d}, \mathbf{t}, \mathbf{c}$ is shown in A. $\mathcal{T}$ represents the base data structure and $\mathcal{T}^*$ represents the hardened data structure with depth padding and path randomization. Update of $\mathbf{v}, \mathbf{d}, \mathbf{t}, \mathbf{c}$ after applying $\mathcal{F}^{PrepT}$ and output $\mathbf{f}$ is shown in B. Meanwhile, the transformation of $\mathbf{v}, \mathbf{d}, \mathbf{t}, \mathbf{f}, \mathbf{c}$ into $\tilde{\mathbf{v}}, \tilde{\mathbf{d}}, \tilde{\mathbf{t}}, \tilde{\mathbf{f}}, \tilde{\mathbf{c}}$ after using $\mathcal{F}^{Shuff}$ is shown in C. The prepend position of the tree arrays (lines 2–3 of Fig. 4) is indicated using − in $\tilde{\mathbf{x}}$ and the append position (lines 5–6 of Fig. 4) is indicated using +.

4.2 Base Data Structure

Let $\mathcal{T}$ be a decision tree of depth d with n nodes, m of which are decision nodes. Let $\mathbf{x} = (x_1, x_2, \ldots x_n)$ be a vector with the id of all nodes in breadth-first search (BFS) order such that $x_i \in [1, n]$. We assume a binary DT and thus each decision node x_i has two children, a threshold θ_i and a feature ω_i. The remaining $n - m$ nodes with no *children* are called leaf nodes, and have an associated class label κ_i. The level of $\mathcal{T}$ is represented as $\lambda \in [0, d]$ and the level of x_i is specified using λ_i. Suppose $\mathbf{q}$ is a query vector with t attributes. For any decision node x_i, its *child* is selected based on the result of the comparison operation $g(\mathbf{q}[\omega_i], \theta_i) \to \{0,1\}$, where $g = 0$ if $(\mathbf{q}[\omega_i] < \theta_i)$, and $g = 1$ otherwise. The result of the operation, $g \to 0$ selects the *left child* of x_i and $g \to 1$ selects the *right child* of x_i, this is known as path evaluation. Decision tree classification is thus a traversal of decision nodes starting from the root node at $\mathbf{x}[1]$ until reaching a leaf x_l, whereby the classifier outputs κ_l which is the class label associated with x_l.

Look-Up Vector. The key feature of our approach is to represent $\mathcal{T}$ as a combination of array-like data structure and then evaluate the tree by traversing these arrays using a look-up vector. We define a lookup vector, $\mathbf{v} \in \mathbb{Z}^n$ such that $\mathbf{v}$ contains the index of (pointer to) the *left child* in case of decision nodes, and the index of itself in case of non-decision nodes. Since we assume a binary decision tree with node ids in BFS order, the index of the *left child* of x_i is given by $2i$ and the *right child* is given by $2i+1$. Therefore, it is sufficient to store the index of either one of the two *children*, since the index of the *right child* can be derived from the *left child* and vice versa. This is depicted in Fig. 2 A where the *left child* of $\mathbf{x}[1] = a$ is given by $\mathbf{v}[1] = 2$, since $\mathbf{x}[2] = b$ and b is the *left child* of a. Meanwhile, its *right child* is retrieved by computing $\mathbf{v}[1] + 1 = 3$, as $\mathbf{x}[3] = c$ and c is the *right child* of a.

Algorithm 1: $\mathcal{F}^{PrepT}$

Input: $\mathbf{x}, \mathbf{v}, \mathbf{t}, \mathbf{c} \in \mathbb{Z}^n$, $\mathbf{d} \in \mathbb{R}^n$, $\lambda_i \in \mathbb{Z}$
Output: $\mathbf{x}, \mathbf{v}, \mathbf{t}, \mathbf{f}, \mathbf{c} \in \mathbb{Z}^{\bar{n}}$, $\mathbf{d} \in \mathbb{R}^{\bar{n}}$

Define $\mathbf{f} \in \mathbb{Z}^n$
Compute $\lambda_{min} = \min(\lambda_m, \lambda_{m+1}, \ldots \lambda_n)$, where $x_m, x_{m+1}, \ldots x_n$ are leaf nodes
for $1 \le i \le d - \lambda_{min}$ **do**
  Append 0 to $\mathbf{x}, \mathbf{v}, \mathbf{d}, \mathbf{t}, \mathbf{c}, \mathbf{f}$ ▷ Depth padding
  Set $\mathbf{x}[n+i] = n + i$
end
Define $\bar{n} := |\mathbf{x}|$, $\hat{t} := t + 1$
for $1 \le i \le \bar{n}$ **do**
  if *x_i is a decision node* **then**
    Sample $r \xleftarrow{\$} \{0,1\}$
    if $r = 1$ **then**
      Swap $\mathbf{v}[2i]$ with $\mathbf{v}[2i+1]$, $\mathbf{d}[2i]$ with $\mathbf{d}[2i+1]$
      Swap $\mathbf{t}[2i]$ with $\mathbf{t}[2i+1]$, $\mathbf{c}[2i]$ with $\mathbf{c}[2i+1]$ ▷ Compute in parallel
    Update $\mathbf{t}[i] = \omega_i + \lambda_i \hat{t}$
    Set $\mathbf{f}[i] = r$
  else if *x_i is a leaf or dummy node* **then**
    if $\lambda_i < d$ **then**
      Update $\mathbf{t}[i] = \hat{t} + \lambda_i \hat{t}$
      Update $\mathbf{v}[i] = 2i$ ▷ *Left child* of x_i is at $\mathbf{x}[2i]$
    else
      Update $\mathbf{t}[i] = \hat{t} + (d-1)\hat{t}$
      Update $\mathbf{v}[i] = i$ ▷ Only necessary for dummy nodes
    Update $\mathbf{d}[i] = 1$
end

Fig. 3. Implementation of $\mathcal{F}^{PrepT}$ that outputs $\mathbf{f}$ and updates $\mathbf{v}, \mathbf{d}, \mathbf{t}, \mathbf{c}$, see Fig. 2 B for a schematic representation.

Tree Array. The complete structure of $\mathcal{T}$ is represented using three additional vectors denoted by $\mathbf{d}, \mathbf{t}, \mathbf{c}$. Here, $\mathbf{d}$ stores the information corresponding to the *threshold* for all nodes, where $\mathbf{d}[i] := \theta_i$ if x_i is a decision node and $\mathbf{d}[i] := 0$, otherwise. Meanwhile, $\mathbf{t}$ consists of the query feature to be selected at each x_i, that is $\mathbf{t}[i] = \omega_i$ if x_i is a decision node, and $\mathbf{t}[i] = 0$ otherwise. Lastly, $\mathbf{c}$ contains the class labels of leaf nodes, we define $\mathbf{c}[i] := \kappa_i$ if x_i is a leaf node, and $\mathbf{c}[i] = 0$ otherwise. See Fig. 2 A for an illustration, here $\mathbf{d}[2] = \theta_2$ as θ_2 is the threshold associated with b, $\mathbf{t}[3] = 0$ since c is a leaf and $\mathbf{c}[4] = \gamma$ as γ is the class label of d.

4.3 Secure Data Structure

The tree arrays and look-up vector as described above cannot be used in a PDTE protocol as this would reveal information about the decision path and internal structure of $\mathcal{T}$. Therefore we apply an array preprocessing functionality and shuffle the tree arrays to obtain their equivalent secure version which leaks no information other than that which is already known. An implementation of the preprocessing functionality is shown in Fig. 3 where $\mathcal{F}^{PrepT}$ is run on $\mathbf{v}, \mathbf{d}, \mathbf{t}, \mathbf{c}$ to obtain $\mathbf{f}$ and update $\mathbf{v}, \mathbf{d}, \mathbf{t}, \mathbf{c}$. $\mathcal{F}^{PrepT}$ consists of two main steps: depth padding (lines 5–7 in Fig. 3) and path randomization (lines 10–16 in Fig. 3), these steps are discussed in further detail below. After the preprocessing step, the padded arrays are shuffled using $\mathcal{F}^{Shuff}$ as presented in Fig. 4 on the output vectors of $\mathcal{F}^{PrepT}$. An illustration of the preprocessing step is shown in Fig. 2 B and the shuffling step is shown in Fig. 2 C.

Depth Padding. To ensure that all the decision paths evaluate to the same depth, we follow a strategy that is similar to [29] and [32]. This is known as depth padding and our padding strategy involves inserting $d - \lambda_{min}$ dummy nodes for the *whole* tree. Here, λ_{min} is the λ_i for the leaf node that is *closest* to the root of tree. Thus starting from $\lambda_{min} + 1$, each level of tree has a unique dummy node, and each leaf node with $\lambda_i < d$ will point to the dummy node at $\lambda_i + 1$. Dummy and leaf nodes are both assigned the threshold $\theta_i = 1$ and attribute $\omega_i = t + 1 = \hat{t}$. Moreover, the values in $\mathbf{t}$ are shifted by $\lambda_i \hat{t}$, that is $\mathbf{t}[i] = \mathbf{t}[i] + \lambda_i \hat{t}$, except for nodes where $\lambda_i = d$. In this case $\mathbf{t}[i] = \mathbf{t}[i] + (d-1)\hat{t}$ and we elaborate on the rationale behind this in Sect. 4.4. This is shown in Fig. 2 B, where $\mathbf{t}[2] = \omega_2 + \hat{t}$ since $\lambda_i = 1$, and $\mathbf{t}[4] = 2\hat{t}$ since $\mathbf{x}[4] = e$ is a leaf node and thus $\mathbf{t}[4] = \hat{t} + (d-1)\hat{t} = 2\hat{t}$.

Path Randomization. In order to hide the decision path selected during the evaluation of $\mathcal{T}$, the children of all decision nodes are randomly swapped and this information is stored in a flag vector $\mathbf{f}$. As seen in line 11 of Fig. 3, a random number $r \xleftarrow{\$} \{0, 1\}$ is first sampled, and the *left child* of x_i is swapped with its *right child* if $r = 1$. The result of this operation is stored in $\mathbf{f}$ as it necessary for correct path evaluation. The above step randomizes the decision path since the

Algorithm 2: $\mathcal{F}^{Shuff}$

Input: $\mathbf{x}, \mathbf{v}, \mathbf{t}, \mathbf{f}, \mathbf{c} \in \mathbb{Z}^n$, $\mathbf{d} \in \mathbb{R}^n$
Output: $\tilde{\mathbf{x}}, \tilde{\mathbf{v}}, \tilde{\mathbf{t}}, \tilde{\mathbf{f}}, \tilde{\mathbf{c}} \in \mathbb{Z}^n, \tilde{\mathbf{d}} \in \mathbb{R}^n$
1 Define $\tilde{\mathbf{x}} := \mathbf{x}, \tilde{\mathbf{v}} := \mathbf{v}$, $\tilde{\mathbf{d}} := \mathbf{d}$, $\tilde{\mathbf{t}} := \mathbf{t}$, $\tilde{\mathbf{f}} := \mathbf{f}$, $\tilde{\mathbf{c}} := \mathbf{c}$
2 Prepend $\tilde{\mathbf{x}}[1]$ to $\tilde{\mathbf{x}}$, $\tilde{\mathbf{v}}[1]$ to $\tilde{\mathbf{v}}$, $\tilde{\mathbf{d}}[1]$ to $\tilde{\mathbf{d}}$ ▷ Prepend first index
3 Prepend $\tilde{\mathbf{t}}[1]$ to $\tilde{\mathbf{t}}$, $\tilde{\mathbf{f}}[1]$ to $\tilde{\mathbf{f}}$, $\tilde{\mathbf{c}}[1]$ to $\tilde{\mathbf{c}}$ ▷ Compute in parallel
4 **if** $|\tilde{\mathbf{x}}|$ *is* $2k \pm 1$ **then**
5 Append $\tilde{\mathbf{x}}[|\tilde{\mathbf{x}}|]$ to $\tilde{\mathbf{x}}$, $\tilde{\mathbf{v}}[|\tilde{\mathbf{x}}|]$ to $\tilde{\mathbf{v}}$, $\tilde{\mathbf{d}}[|\tilde{\mathbf{x}}|]$ to $\tilde{\mathbf{d}}$ ▷ Append if $|\tilde{\mathbf{x}}|$ is odd
6 Append $\tilde{\mathbf{t}}[|\tilde{\mathbf{x}}|]$ to $\tilde{\mathbf{t}}$, $\tilde{\mathbf{f}}[|\tilde{\mathbf{x}}|]$ to $\tilde{\mathbf{f}}$, $\tilde{\mathbf{c}}[|\tilde{\mathbf{x}}|]$ to $\tilde{\mathbf{c}}$ ▷ Vectors are of equal length
7 Compute $n = \frac{|\tilde{\mathbf{x}}|}{2}$
8 **for** $1 \le i \le n-1$ **do**
9 Sample $j \xleftarrow{\$} [i, n]$
10 Swap $\tilde{\mathbf{x}}[2i]$ with $\tilde{\mathbf{x}}[2j]$, $\tilde{\mathbf{v}}[2i]$ with $\tilde{\mathbf{v}}[2j]$, $\tilde{\mathbf{d}}[2i]$ with $\tilde{\mathbf{d}}[2j]$
11 Swap $\tilde{\mathbf{t}}[2i]$ with $\tilde{\mathbf{t}}[2j]$, $\tilde{\mathbf{f}}[2i]$ with $\tilde{\mathbf{f}}[2j]$, $\tilde{\mathbf{c}}[2i]$ with $\tilde{\mathbf{c}}[2j]$ ▷ Compute in parallel
12 Swap $\tilde{\mathbf{x}}[2i+1]$ with $\tilde{\mathbf{x}}[2j+1]$, $\tilde{\mathbf{v}}[2i+1]$ with $\tilde{\mathbf{v}}[2j+1]$, $\tilde{\mathbf{d}}[2i+1]$ with $\tilde{\mathbf{d}}[2j+1]$
13 Swap $\tilde{\mathbf{t}}[2i+1]$ with $\tilde{\mathbf{t}}[2j+1]$, $\tilde{\mathbf{f}}[2i+1]$ with $\tilde{\mathbf{f}}[2j+1]$, $\tilde{\mathbf{c}}[2i+1]$ with $\tilde{\mathbf{c}}[2j+1]$ ▷ Compute in parallel
14 **end**

Fig. 4. Implementation of $\mathcal{F}^{Shuff}$ that shuffles tree arrays $\mathbf{v}, \mathbf{d}, \mathbf{t}, \mathbf{f}, \mathbf{c}$ pairwise, see Fig. 2 C for a schematic representation.

left and *right child* of decision nodes are randomly flipped. This suggests that the decision path cannot be used to guess which of the two *children* nodes were selected during evaluation. The idea is illustrated in Fig. 2 B, where *children* of $\mathbf{x}[2] = b$ is flipped and thus $\mathbf{f}[2] = 1$.

Level Hiding. Next the level of each node is hidden by obtaining a random permutation of $\mathcal{T}$. We do so by using an approach which we term as *pairwise* shuffling. Here the vectors are randomly shuffled in such a way that the *left* and *right child* of each decision node are always adjacent to each other after shuffling. This is realized using the functionality $\mathcal{F}^{Shuff}$, where $\mathbf{x}, \mathbf{v}, \mathbf{d}, \mathbf{t}, \mathbf{c}, \mathbf{f}$ are randomly shuffled using the Fisher-Yates shuffle algorithm [30] to output $\tilde{\mathbf{x}}, \tilde{\mathbf{v}}, \tilde{\mathbf{d}}, \tilde{\mathbf{t}}, \tilde{\mathbf{c}}, \tilde{\mathbf{f}}$ as demonstrated in Fig. 4. Since the root node has no sibling we duplicate it by prepending the first index (line 2 in Fig. 4). Next if necessary, we pad the vector by appending the last element such that its length is divisible by 2 (even). See Fig. 2 C for an illustration, here $\tilde{\mathbf{v}}$ is updated based on the criteria described in Sect. 4.2. For instance, $\tilde{\mathbf{v}}[1] = 7$ since the *left child* of $\tilde{\mathbf{x}}[1] = b$ is $\tilde{\mathbf{x}}[7] = e$ which is accessed by $\tilde{\mathbf{v}}[7]$. Thus, we have $\tilde{\mathbf{v}}[r] = \mathbf{v}[i]$ and likewise, $\tilde{\mathbf{d}}[r] = \mathbf{d}[i], \tilde{\mathbf{t}}[r] = \mathbf{t}[i], \tilde{\mathbf{c}}[r] = \mathbf{c}[i]$ and $\tilde{\mathbf{f}}[r] = \mathbf{f}[i]$ due to pairwise shuffling.

Tree Traversal. Here we present an overview of how tree traversal is performed using shuffled look-up vector $\tilde{\mathbf{v}}$, given that the index of root node is known. Let us denote the result of the evaluation at each decision node as $e \rightarrow \{0, 1\}$, and denote the position of root node in $\tilde{\mathbf{v}}$ as r. $\mathcal{T}$ can be traversed by recursively accessing $\tilde{\mathbf{v}}$ as follows: $\tilde{\mathbf{v}}[\tilde{\mathbf{v}}[r]+e]$, $\tilde{\mathbf{v}}[[\tilde{\mathbf{v}}[r]+e]+e]$, $\tilde{\mathbf{v}}[\ldots\tilde{\mathbf{v}}[[\tilde{\mathbf{v}}[r]+e]+e]\ldots+e]$. Since elements of $\tilde{\mathbf{v}}$ with decision nodes point to its *left child*, the operation $\tilde{\mathbf{v}}[i]+e$ will access either the *left* or *right child of* x_i. However, the above explanation is simplistic as it is also necessary to invert e by computing $g = e \oplus \tilde{\mathbf{f}}[\tilde{\mathbf{v}}[i]]$, since the *children* of decision nodes are randomly flipped. Thus given that $\tilde{\mathbf{v}}$ is shuffled using $\mathcal{F}^{Shuff}$ and that r is random, recursively accessing $\tilde{\mathbf{v}}[\ldots\tilde{\mathbf{v}}[[\tilde{\mathbf{v}}[r]+g]+g]\ldots+g]$ leaks neither the decision path nor the level of tree. However, this means that $\tilde{\mathbf{v}}$ is only secure for one query, as multiple queries on the same $\tilde{\mathbf{v}}$ would leak information, thereby making it non-secure.

4.4 Secure Evaluation

So far we have described an approach to securely traverse tree arrays. However, a secure evaluation protocol requires secure feature selection through a secure query vector. We implement this by using a query preprocessing functionality $\mathcal{F}^{Prep}$ that outputs a randomly shuffled query vector $\tilde{\mathbf{q}}$ and give the details of its construction below. The key idea behind obtaining $\tilde{\mathbf{q}}$ is that a unique query feature is selected *for each* level of $\mathcal{T}$. Since $\tilde{\mathbf{t}}$ can no longer be used to select features in $\tilde{\mathbf{q}}$, a new protocol Π^{SelQ} is run between $\mathcal{A}$ and $\mathcal{B}$ through which $\mathcal{A}$ obtains a secure query select vector $\tilde{\mathbf{w}}$. This allows for secure feature selection, in other words ω_i is obtained from $\tilde{\mathbf{q}}$ using $\tilde{\mathbf{w}}$ without learning ω_i.

Query Preprocessing. The query vector is preprocessed using $\mathcal{F}^{PrepQ}$ to obtain a shuffled query vector such that a *unique* query feature is accessed at each level of $\mathcal{T}$. This prevents protocol participants from deducing that the same feature has been previously selected and is also our reasoning for shifting each element in $\tilde{\mathbf{t}}$ (see Sect. 4.3). In $\mathcal{F}^{PrepQ}$, we first define $\mathbf{q}' := \mathbf{q}$ and add a new feature $\hat{t} = t+1$ for dummy and leaf nodes by zero padding, such that $\mathbf{q}[\hat{t}] = 0$. Next, the $\hat{t}$ elements of $\mathbf{q}'$ are copied and appended d times to $\mathbf{q}'$, such that $|\mathbf{q}'| = \hat{t}d = \bar{t}$. Thus, accessing $\mathbf{q}'$ through $\tilde{\mathbf{t}}$ selects a unique feature in $\mathbf{q}'$ for each $\lambda < d$ in $\mathcal{T}$, since $\tilde{\mathbf{t}}[i] = \tilde{\mathbf{t}}[i] + \lambda_i\hat{t}$ and $\lambda_i \in [0, d-1]$. To illustrate, consider two decision nodes x_i and x_j with $\omega_i = \omega_j$ and $\lambda_i \neq \lambda_j$, in spite of the fact that $\omega_i = \omega_j$, accessing $\mathbf{q}'$ through $\tilde{\mathbf{t}}$ would correspond to different features in $\tilde{\mathbf{q}}$ since $\lambda_i \neq \lambda_j$. Lastly, in order to hide the selection of features in $\mathbf{q}'$, it is shuffled by some random shuffling algorithm [30] to obtain $\tilde{\mathbf{q}}$. However, this also means that $\tilde{\mathbf{t}}$ cannot be used to select features from $\tilde{\mathbf{q}}$ and thus we define a new protocol to securely select features from $\tilde{\mathbf{q}}$ as we demonstrate below. For an implementation of $\mathcal{F}^{PrepQ}$ see Fig. 5 and refer to Fig. 7 for its schematic representation.

Query Selection. Here, we define a protocol Π^{SelQ} between $\mathcal{A}, \mathcal{B}$ and $\mathcal{P}_k$ that outputs a vector $\tilde{\mathbf{w}}$, which can securely select features from $\tilde{\mathbf{q}}$. The main idea behind the construction of $\tilde{\mathbf{w}}$ is that features selected from $\tilde{\mathbf{q}}$ using $\tilde{\mathbf{w}}$ correspond to the same features in $\mathbf{q}'$ as we demonstrate below. In Π^{SelQ}, $\mathcal{B}$ first computes $\mathbf{h}$ such that $\mathbf{q}'[j] = \tilde{\mathbf{q}}[\mathbf{h}[j]]$ for all $1 \leq j \leq \bar{t}$. Notice that $\mathbf{h}$ can be easily computed since $\mathcal{B}$ knows the permutation of $\tilde{\mathbf{q}}$. Next $\mathcal{B}$ sends $\mathbf{h}$ to $\mathcal{A}$, who constructs $\tilde{\mathbf{w}}$

Algorithm 3: $\mathcal{F}^{PrepQ}$

Input: $\mathbf{q} \in \mathbb{R}^t$
Output: $\mathbf{q}', \tilde{\mathbf{q}} \in \mathbb{R}^{\bar{t}}$
Define $\mathbf{q}' := \mathbf{q}$
Append 0 to $\mathbf{q}'$ ▷ Zero padding
for $1 \leq k \leq d-1$ **do**
  Append $\mathbf{q}$ to $\mathbf{q}'$ ▷ Increases $|\mathbf{q}'|$ to $(t+1)\,d$
end
Define $\tilde{\mathbf{q}} := \mathbf{q}'$, $\bar{t} := (t+1)d$
for $1 \leq i \leq \bar{t}-1$ **do**
  Sample $j \xleftarrow{\$} [i, \bar{t}]$
  Swap $\tilde{\mathbf{q}}[i]$ with $\tilde{\mathbf{q}}[j]$ ▷ Shuffles $\mathbf{q}'$
end

Fig. 5. Implementation of $\mathcal{F}^{PrepQ}$ that outputs $\mathbf{q}', \tilde{\mathbf{q}}$ from $\mathbf{q}$, Fig. 7 shows an illustration of $\mathcal{F}^{PrepQ}$ with $\mathbf{q}$.

by computing $\tilde{\mathbf{w}}[m] = \mathbf{h}[\tilde{\mathbf{t}}[m]]$ for all $1 \leq m \leq \bar{n}$. Note that $\mathbf{h}[\tilde{\mathbf{t}}[m]]$ is a valid assignment since $\mathbf{h}$ and $\tilde{\mathbf{t}}$ have the same range $[1, \bar{t}]$, where $\bar{t} = \hat{t}d$. We stress that even though $\mathcal{A}$ learns the permutation of $\tilde{\mathbf{q}}$ from $\mathbf{h}$, no knowledge about the feature being accessed is leaked since $\mathcal{A}$ does not hold $\tilde{\mathbf{q}}$. Finally, $\mathcal{A}$ sends an index r along with $[\![\tilde{\mathbf{w}}]\!]$ to $\mathcal{P}_k$ such that $\tilde{\mathbf{t}}[r] = \mathbf{t}[i]$. Since $\tilde{\mathbf{t}}$ is obtained by randomly shuffling $\mathbf{t}$, sending r in plain leaks no information as r is also random. $\mathcal{B}$ meanwhile sends $[\![\tilde{\mathbf{q}}]\!]$ to $\mathcal{P}_k$, who obtain a random feature s by jointly revealing $[\![\tilde{\mathbf{w}}[r]]\!]$. Thus $\mathcal{P}_k$ securely obtains $\mathbf{q}'[j]$ by instead accessing $\tilde{\mathbf{q}}[s]$ without learning j. An implementation of Π^{SelQ} is shown in Fig. 6.

Correctness. We state that the protocol Π^{SelQ} is correct in the semi-honest security model if the feature selected using $\tilde{\mathbf{w}}$ on $\tilde{\mathbf{q}}$ correspond to the same feature in $\mathbf{q}'$. Thus to prove for correctness, we need to show that $\tilde{\mathbf{q}}[s]$ corresponds to $\mathbf{q}'[j]$. More precisely, we need to show that $\tilde{\mathbf{q}}[\tilde{\mathbf{w}}[r]]$ corresponds to $\mathbf{q}'[j]$. Since we know that $\tilde{\mathbf{w}}[r] := \mathbf{h}[\tilde{\mathbf{t}}[r]]$, and $\tilde{\mathbf{t}}[r] = \mathbf{t}[i]$, we have $\tilde{\mathbf{w}}[r] = \mathbf{h}[\mathbf{t}[i]]$ (see Sect. 4.3). Next, recall that $\mathbf{t}[i] := \omega_i$ and let us suppose that $\omega_i = j$, which implies that $\tilde{\mathbf{w}}[r] = \mathbf{h}[j]$. Thus, accessing $\tilde{\mathbf{q}}[\tilde{\mathbf{w}}[r]]$ is equivalent to accessing $\mathbf{q}'[j]$ since $\tilde{\mathbf{q}}[\mathbf{h}[j]] = \mathbf{q}'[j]$, hence proving for correctness.

Security. We assert that Π^{SelQ} is secure in the semi-honest security model and only provide a sketch-of-proof. First notice that the only interaction between the protocol participants, $\mathcal{A}$ and $\mathcal{B}$ is the exchange of $\mathbf{h}$. Since $\mathbf{h}$ is obtained by randomly shuffling $\mathbf{q}'$, it can be simulated by choosing a random permutation from $\mathbb{Z}^{\bar{t}}$. Next $\mathcal{A}$ computes and sends $[\![\tilde{\mathbf{w}}]\!]$, r to $\mathcal{P}_k$, whereas $\mathcal{B}$ sends $[\![\tilde{\mathbf{q}}]\!]$ to $\mathcal{P}_k$. $[\![\tilde{\mathbf{w}}]\!]$ and $[\![\tilde{\mathbf{q}}]\!]$ are secure by definition and r can be simulated by randomly sampling from $\mathbb{Z}^{\bar{t}}$ since r is obtained from a randomly shuffled $\tilde{\mathbf{t}}$. This shows that Π^{SelQ} is secure in the semi-honest security model.

Algorithm 4: Π^{SelQ}

Input of $\mathcal{A}$**:** $\tilde{\mathbf{t}} \in \mathbb{Z}^{\tilde{n}}$
Input of $\mathcal{B}$**:** $\tilde{\mathbf{q}} \in \mathbb{R}^{\tilde{t}}, \mathbf{q}' \in \mathbb{R}^{\tilde{t}}, \mathbf{h} \in \mathbb{Z}^{\tilde{t}}$
Computation by $\mathcal{B}$**:**
1 Compute $\mathbf{h}$ from $\tilde{\mathbf{q}}$ and $\mathbf{q}'$ ▷ Permutation order of $\tilde{\mathbf{q}}$
2 Compute $[\![\tilde{\mathbf{q}}]\!] = \mathsf{Share}(\tilde{\mathbf{q}})$
Input from $\mathcal{B}$ **to** $\mathcal{A}$**:** $\mathbf{h}$
Computation by $\mathcal{A}$**:**
3 Define $\tilde{\mathbf{w}} \in \mathbb{Z}^{\tilde{n}}$
4 **for** $1 \le m \le \tilde{n}$ **do**
5 | Set $\tilde{\mathbf{w}}[m] = \mathbf{h}[\tilde{\mathbf{t}}[m]]$
6 **end**
7 Compute $[\![\tilde{\mathbf{w}}]\!] = \mathsf{Share}(\tilde{\mathbf{w}})$
Input from $\mathcal{A}$ **to** $\mathcal{P}_k$**:** $[\![\tilde{\mathbf{w}}]\!], r$ where $\tilde{\mathbf{t}}[r] = \mathbf{t}[i]$
Input from $\mathcal{B}$ **to** $\mathcal{P}_k$**:** $[\![\tilde{\mathbf{q}}]\!]$
8 Define $j := \omega_i$ ▷ Query feature at x_i
Computation by $\mathcal{P}_k$**:**
9 Compute $s = \mathsf{Reveal}([\![\tilde{\mathbf{w}}[r]]\!])$
10 Obtain $[\![\tilde{\mathbf{q}}[s]]\!]$ ▷ $\tilde{\mathbf{q}}[s]$ corresponds to $\mathbf{q}'[j]$

Fig. 6. Protocol Π^{SelQ}, where $\mathcal{P}_k$ selects a feature j from $\mathbf{q}'$ by accessing a random index s in $\tilde{\mathbf{q}}$ with no knowledge of j. See Fig. 7 for a schematic representation.

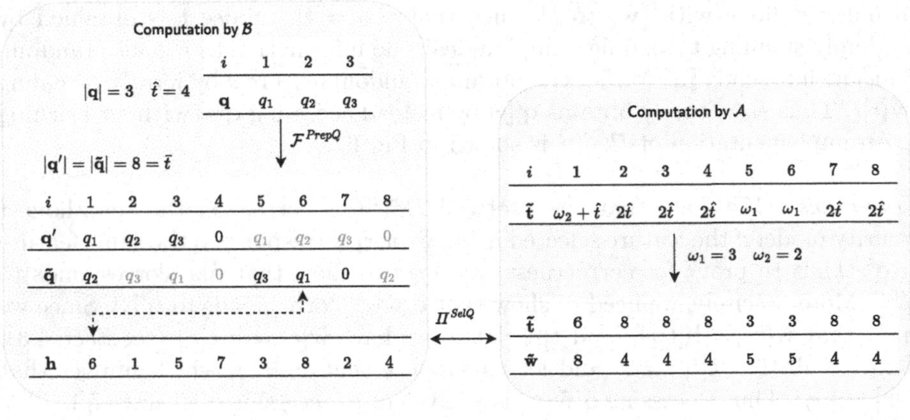

Fig. 7. Representation of shuffled query vector, $\tilde{\mathbf{q}}$ and secure query select vector $\tilde{\mathbf{w}}$ by applying $\mathcal{F}^{PrepQ}$ and Π^{SelQ}. As shown, $\mathcal{F}^{PrepQ}$ outputs $\mathbf{q}', \tilde{\mathbf{q}}$, and duplicated elements in $\mathbf{q}'$ are distinguished in gray. $\mathcal{A}$ and $\mathcal{B}$ run Π^{SelQ} (lines 1–6), based on which $\mathcal{B}$ obtains $\mathbf{h}$ and $\mathcal{A}$ computes $\tilde{\mathbf{w}}$ after receiving $\mathbf{h}$ from $\mathcal{B}$. Here $\mathbf{h}[1] = 6$, since $\mathbf{q}'[1] = q_1 = \tilde{\mathbf{q}}[6]$. Assuming $\omega_1 = 3$ and $\omega_2 = 2$, $\tilde{\mathbf{w}}[1] = 8$ since $\mathbf{h}[\tilde{\mathbf{t}}[1]] = \mathbf{h}[6] = 8$.

Evaluation Protocol. All the building blocks are now in place to describe our evaluation protocol Π^{Eval} which is an outsourced two-party protocol between the computing nodes $\mathcal{P}_0$ and $\mathcal{P}_1$. In this protocol, each $\mathcal{P}_k$ receives shares of $\mathcal{T}$ and $\mathbf{q}$ as an input from $\mathcal{A}$ and $\mathcal{B}$ respectively and evaluate $\mathcal{T}(q)$ using these shares. Let us suppose that $\mathcal{A}$ already holds $\tilde{\mathbf{x}}, \tilde{\mathbf{v}}, \tilde{\mathbf{d}}, \tilde{\mathbf{t}}, \tilde{\mathbf{f}}$ and $\tilde{\mathbf{c}}$ as described in Sect. 4.3 and that $\mathcal{B}$ holds $\tilde{\mathbf{q}}$ based on the steps described in Sect. 4.4. $\mathcal{A}$ and $\mathcal{B}$ then interact using Π^{SelQ} (lines 1–6 in Fig. 7) through which $\mathcal{A}$ obtains $\tilde{\mathbf{w}}$. Note that it is not necessary to run the rest of Π^{SelQ} since it corresponds to securely selecting a feature from $\tilde{\mathbf{q}}$. $\mathcal{A}$ then obtains a random r such that r corresponds to the index of root node (x_1) in $\tilde{\mathbf{v}}$, that is $\tilde{\mathbf{x}}[r] = \mathbf{x}[1]$. Following this, $\mathcal{A}$ creates the shares $[\![\tilde{\mathbf{v}}]\!], [\![\tilde{\mathbf{d}}]\!], [\![\tilde{\mathbf{f}}]\!], [\![\tilde{\mathbf{w}}]\!], [\![\tilde{\mathbf{c}}]\!]$ and likewise, $\mathcal{B}$ computes $[\![\tilde{\mathbf{q}}]\!]$. The parties then send their respective shares to $\mathcal{P}_k$. The above steps are performed prior to running Π^{Eval} and is referred to as the *preparation phase*. More concretely, this phase includes the execution of $\mathcal{F}^{PrepT}, \mathcal{F}^{Shuff}, \mathcal{F}^{PrepQ}$ and Π^{SelQ} (lines 1–6) including the creation of shares and the generation of necessary correlated randomness for running Π^{Eval}. Upon receiving the shares, $\mathcal{P}_k$ interactively participate in Π^{Eval}, obtain the class label $[\![\kappa]\!]$ as shares, and output their respective share of $[\![\kappa]\!]$ to $\mathcal{B}$. The execution of Π^{Eval} performed interactively by $\mathcal{P}_k$ is defined as the *evaluation phase* and its detailed implementation is shown in Fig. 8. The objective of Π^{Eval} is to traverse the tree by iteratively updating r based on the computation $r = \tilde{\mathbf{v}}[r] + g$ when represented in plain form (see Sect. 4.3 for a more detailed explanation). At the same time starting from $\kappa = 0$, κ is updated by computing $\kappa = \kappa + \tilde{\mathbf{c}}[r]$. After d such updates, r indexes the deepest node (at d) and thus summing κ over the traversal path will yield a κ_l corresponding to the classification label of leaf node x_l. A schematic representation of the entire PDTE protocol including the preparation and evaluation phases is shown in Fig. 9 and its computational complexity is shown in Table 1.

Correctness. We define the protocol Π^{Eval} to be correct if it outputs the correct class label corresponding to $\mathbf{q}$ on $\mathcal{T}$, more formally $\mathcal{T}(\mathbf{q}) \rightarrow \kappa_l$ where x_l is a leaf. As stated earlier Π^{Eval} evaluates $\mathcal{T}$ by iteratively updating $[\![r]\!]$, and for simplicity consider the case of updating r in plain form. That is, r is updated by computing $r = \tilde{\mathbf{v}}[r] + g$ (line 9 in Fig. 8). Here, g is obtained by computing $e \leftarrow \neg(\tilde{\mathbf{q}}[s] < \tilde{\mathbf{d}}[r])$, followed by $g \leftarrow e \oplus \tilde{\mathbf{f}}[r]$. The operation $(\tilde{\mathbf{q}}[s] < \tilde{\mathbf{d}}[r])$ compares the query feature ω_i with the threshold θ_i. This is because $\tilde{\mathbf{d}}[r] = \mathbf{d}[i] = \theta_i$ (see Sect. 4.3) and $\tilde{\mathbf{q}}[s] = \tilde{\mathbf{q}}[\mathbf{h}[\omega_i]] = \mathbf{q}'[\omega_i]$ (as we have shown in Sect. 4.4). Meanwhile, the operation $e \oplus \tilde{\mathbf{f}}[r]$ (line 7) inverts the randomly flipped decision path meaning that the correct path is selected. Note that for decision nodes, $g \rightarrow \{0, 1\}$, whereas for dummy and leaf nodes, $g \rightarrow 0$ always. The reasoning being that $\theta_i := 1$ and $\mathbf{q}[\omega_i] := 0$ for non-decision nodes (recall from Sect. 4.3 and 4.4). Lastly κ is summed up over the traversal path by computing $\kappa = \kappa + \tilde{\mathbf{c}}[r]$. Since Π^{Eval} runs for d iterations, there are d updates of $r = \tilde{\mathbf{v}}[r] + g$. After d such updates, r access a node at d and $\kappa = \kappa_l$ since there is only one leaf x_l in the traversal path. This is because $\kappa = 0 + \ldots \kappa_i + \ldots 0 = \kappa_l$, where $\kappa_i = 0$ for non-leaf nodes, $\kappa_i = \kappa_l$ for leaf nodes. Therefore, Π^{Eval} is correct since it outputs κ_l after d iterations.

Algorithm 5: Π^{Eval}

```
Input from 𝒜 to 𝒫_k: ⟦ṽ⟧, ⟦d̃⟧, ⟦w̃⟧, ⟦c̃⟧, ⟦f̃⟧ ∈ ℤ_p^n̄, r ∈ [1, n̄]
Input from ℬ to 𝒫_k: ⟦q̃⟧ ∈ ℤ_p^t̄
Computation by 𝒫_k:
Intialize ⟦κ⟧ ← 0
for 1 ≤ j ≤ d do
    Compute ⟦κ⟧ = ⟦κ⟧ + ⟦c̃[r]⟧                 ▷ Local computation
    Obtain ⟦s⟧ = ⟦w̃[r]⟧                        ▷ Local computation
    Compute s = Reveal(⟦s⟧)
    Compute ⟦e⟧ = LT(⟦q̃[s]⟧, ⟦d̃[r]⟧)
    Compute ⟦e⟧ = NOT(⟦e⟧)                      ▷ Local computation
    Compute ⟦g⟧ = XOR(⟦e⟧, ⟦f̃[r]⟧)
    Update ⟦r⟧ by ⟦r⟧ := ⟦ṽ[r]⟧ + ⟦g⟧           ▷ Local computation
    Compute r = Reveal(⟦r⟧)
end
Each 𝒫_k locally computes ⟦κ⟧ = ⟦κ⟧ + ⟦c̃[r]⟧   ▷ Node x̃_r at d
Output from 𝒫_k to ℬ: ⟦κ⟧ ∈ ℤ_p
```

Fig. 8. Implementation of Π^{Eval} which is instantiated by $\mathcal{A}$ and $\mathcal{B}$ sending their respective shares of $\tilde{\mathbf{v}}, \tilde{\mathbf{d}}, \tilde{\mathbf{w}}, \tilde{\mathbf{f}}, \tilde{\mathbf{c}}$ and $\tilde{\mathbf{q}}$ to $\mathcal{P}_k$, who then interactively run Π^{Eval} and output their respective shares $[\![\kappa]\!]$ to $\mathcal{B}$, which corresponds to the class label obtained by evaluating $\mathbf{q}$ on $\mathcal{T}$.

Security. We assert that Π^{Eval} is secure in the semi-honest security model and only provide a sketch of proof. First, let us consider what is revealed in the protocol for each query, namely the index variables r and s. Since s is used to access a randomly shuffled $\tilde{\mathbf{q}}$ for d iterations, s is revealed d times. Moreover, $|\tilde{\mathbf{q}}| = \bar{t}$ and $\tilde{\mathbf{q}}$ is randomly shuffled, and thus s can be simulated by sampling d elements without replacement from $\mathbb{Z}^{\bar{t}}$. However, this also implies that $\tilde{\mathbf{q}}$ is only secure for d accesses and a new $\tilde{\mathbf{q}}$ must be constructed for each new query. Likewise, r is obtained from a randomly shuffled look-up vector $\tilde{\mathbf{v}} \in \mathbb{Z}^{\bar{n}}$ and updated for d iterations. Elements of $\tilde{\mathbf{v}}$ point to nodes that are pairwise shuffled, and also shuffled within these pairs in case of decision nodes (see the discussion in Sect. 4.3). Thus r can be simulated by sampling d elements without replacement from $\mathbb{Z}^{\bar{n}}$. Since $\tilde{\mathbf{v}}$ is secure for d repeated accesses, revealing r leaks no information for *one* particular query. However similar to $\tilde{\mathbf{q}}$, a new $\tilde{\mathbf{v}}$ has to be obtained for each subsequent query since $\tilde{\mathbf{v}}$ cannot be reused. All other exchanges of the protocol are *shares* and are thus secure by definition. Hence, we can state that Π^{Eval} is secure in the semi-honest security model on each random instance of $\tilde{\mathbf{q}}$ and $\tilde{\mathbf{v}}$.

5 Experimental Evaluation

In this section, we discuss the performance of our PDTE protocol by analyzing its computational runtime and communication size. Following this, we compare our protocol with the existing methods of Kiss et al. and Ma et al. (sparse) using the same benchmark. We note that the protocol setup of Kiss et al. and Ma et al. does not feature computational nodes, does not assume the presence of a trusted initializer and is thus different from our proposed model both in terms of model

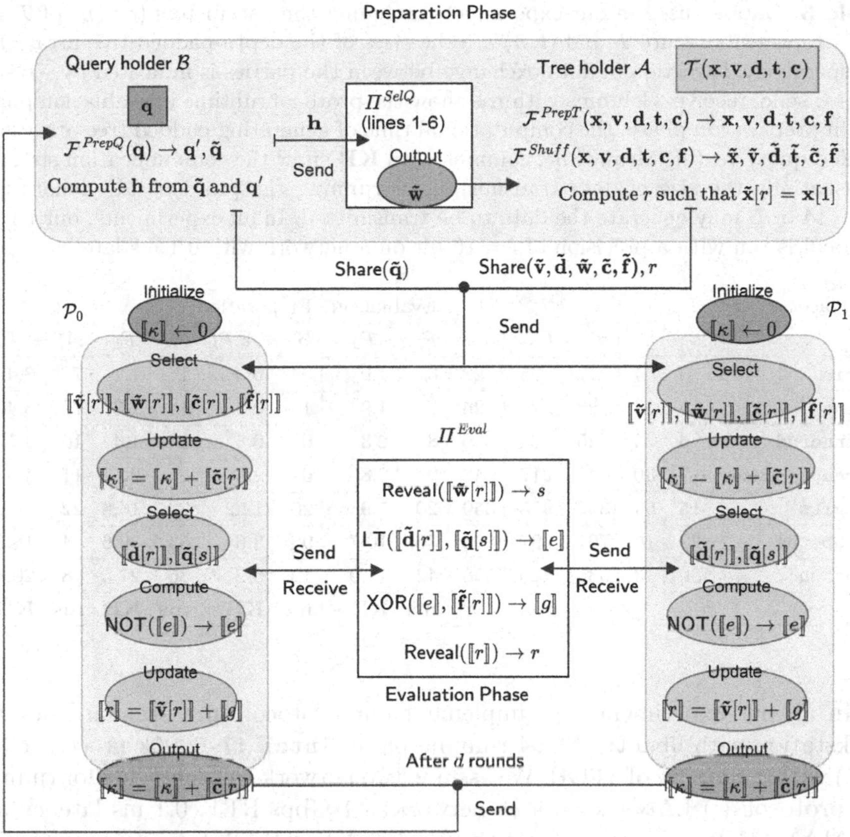

Fig. 9. Detailed overview of our entire PDTE protocol showing the interaction between the tree holder $\mathcal{A}$, query holder $\mathcal{B}$ and computing nodes $\mathcal{P}_k$. Only lines 1–6 of Π^{SelQ} (see Fig. 6) is run to obtain $\tilde{\mathbf{w}}$. Though not shown, it is assumed that the necessary correlated randomness for Π^{Eval} is generated by either one of $\mathcal{A}$ or $\mathcal{B}$ using the trusted initializer setting.

setup and security assumptions. In spite of this, we compare the computational runtime of the evaluation phase of our protocol (see Sect. 4.4) with their online phase since the number of parties interacting in these two phases is the same. As for the communication size, we compare the size during the data preparation phase of our protocol (see Sect. 4.4) with their offline phase, and the size during the evaluation phase of our protocol with their online phase since the aim is to benchmark the communication efficiency of our protocol.

Table 3. Dataset used in our experiments including the parameters (d, t, n) of $\mathcal{T}$ and $\mathbf{q}$. $\mathcal{T}^*$ represents secure $\mathcal{T}$ and $(\bar{t}, \bar{n})$ are the sizes of the depth-padded tree arrays and $\mathbf{q}$ respectively. Direction of data exchange between the parties is indicated by $\rightarrow$: send and $\leftrightarrow$: send/receive. Columns with **ms** show the protocol runtime in evaluation phase, and in preparation phase, the computational time of generating padded tree-arrays and padded query vector. Meanwhile, columns with **KB** show the communication size, and is essentially the size of data transmitted for running the protocol. $\mathcal{A}^*$ denote that either $\mathcal{A}$ or $\mathcal{B}$ may generate the data to be transmitted. In all experiments, our PDTA protocol is run with a precision of $l = 16$-bit on a network with 0.1 ms latency.

Dataset	$\mathcal{T}$			$\mathcal{T}^*$		Evaluation		Preparation					
	d	t	n	$\bar{t}$	$\bar{n}$	$\mathcal{P}_0 \leftrightarrow \mathcal{P}_1$		$\mathcal{B} \rightarrow \mathcal{A}, \mathcal{P}_k$		$\mathcal{A} \rightarrow \mathcal{P}_k$		$\mathcal{A}^* \rightarrow \mathcal{P}_k$	
iris	5	4	17	25	22	6	1.9	0	0.3	1	1.1	7	3.4
wine	5	13	23	70	26	7	1.9	1	0.8	1	1.3	7	3.4
linnerud	6	3	25	24	30	8	2.3	0	0.3	1	1.4	10	4.1
breast cancer	7	30	43	217	48	9	2.8	6	2.6	2	2.3	11	4.8
digits	15	64	337	975	350	20	5.9	26	12.2	22	16.8	22	10.2
diabetes	27	10	791	297	818	36	10.7	9	3.6	53	39.6	44	18.3
boston	30	13	535	420	568	42	11.9	12	5.2	36	27.5	48	20.3
						ms	**KB**	**ms**	**KB**	**ms**	**KB**	**ms**	**KB**

In all our experiments, we implement our protocol on a standard desktop workstation with `Ubuntu 22.04` running on an `Intel i7-6000k` processor (4.0 Ghz) with a memory of 64 GB. We assume two network environments for running our protocol: (i) LAN (Local area network) - 1 Gbps RTT, 0.1 ms latency and (ii) MAN (Metropolitan area network) - 100 Mbps RTT, 6 ms latency, similar to the setup of [42]. Our entire protocol is written in `C++` and only make use of `C++` standard libraries. We also note that the four participants of our protocol $(\mathcal{A}, \mathcal{B}, \mathcal{P}_0, \mathcal{P}_1)$ are simulated on the same workstation using four different process threads.

As was the case with prior works in [29,32], the performance of our protocol is evaluated using *real-world* datasets from UCI machine learning repository [21]. In all our experiments, a decision tree classification model is first trained using the `scikit-learn` library of `Python` [19] with default parameters. Since secret-sharing only uses integers, we handle real-valued numbers by multiplying with a constant and then rounding it to the nearest integer as suggested in [8,11]. The constant is adapted for a specific feature so that an appropriate precision is used during the comparison operation.

The dataset used in our experimental setup, in addition to the parameters of the trained decision tree model and the size of the depth-padded arrays is shown in Table 3. We report the communication size by saving the data exchanged during the protocol to a file and then measuring the file size. $\mathcal{A}$ acts as the trusted initializer in our experiments and thus generates the necessary correlated randomness required for LT, XOR subprotocols. This includes generating a total of $d \cdot l$-bit random numbers as *bitwise shares* and $d(l+2)$ pairs of BTs. In Table 3, we use $\mathcal{A}^* \rightarrow \mathcal{P}_k$ to denote the fact that either $\mathcal{A}$ or $\mathcal{B}$ can act as the trusted initializer.

The results in Table 3 are reported after averaging over 10 trials. Since we simulate the protocol participant as different threads running on the same machine, we simulate the network latency using `tc` utility of `Linux`. A precision of $l = 16$-bits is used in our experiments since we found it to be relatively accurate for most `UCI` datasets in Table 3. More concretely, we generate shares in an arithmetic field $\mathbb{Z}_p$ such that $p < 2^{16}$ and p is represented with 16-bits. A quick glance at the computational runtime from Table 3, shows that the runtime of our protocol is proportional to the depth of the tree. That is, the round complexity of our protocol is $\mathcal{O}(d)$ and hence our protocol is sublinear in tree size.

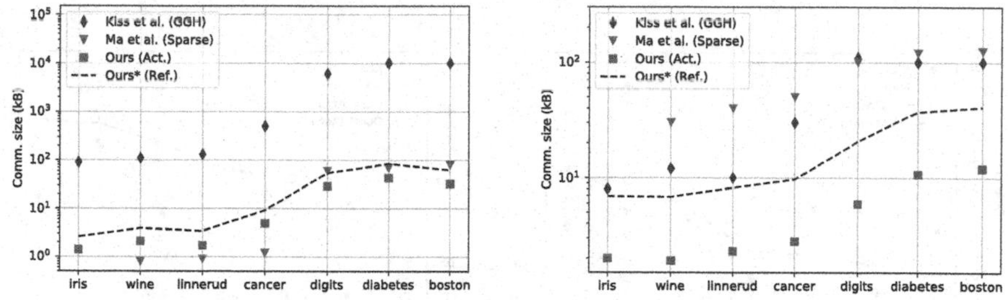

(a) Preparation phase (b) Evaluation phase

Fig. 10. Plots showing the communication cost of our protocol (in kB) compared to the methods of Kiss et al. [29] and Ma et al. [32]. The preparation phase of our PDTE protocol is compared with the offline phase of their protocol whereas the evaluation phase is compared with their online phase. We use a precision of $l = 16$ bits, and for reference, use dotted lines to show the trend with $l = 32$ bits.

5.1 Comparison with Other Methods

Here, we present a comparison of our approach with the evaluation methods of Kiss et al. [29] and Ma et al. [32] using the same datasets from Table 3. As mentioned in Sect. 4, the PDTE protocol of Kiss et al. use a combination of homomorphic encryption (HE) and garbled circuits (GC). The protocol of Ma et al. use GC and secret sharing, whereas ours is solely based on secret sharing. Figure 10 shows a plot comparing the communication size (in kB) of our protocol with the protocols of Kiss et al. and Ma et al. We would like to remark that the plots shown here are for references only since we did not implement the method of Ma et al. (Sparse) and Kiss et al. (GGH). We also note that Kiss et al. and Ma et al. exclude the cost of generating base OTs when reporting their offline phase results, and hence we exclude the cost of generating BTs and random numbers from the plot in Fig. 10(a). The communication cost associated with generating these correlated randomness can be referenced from Table 3 under $\mathcal{A}^* \rightarrow \mathcal{P}_k$.

A quick glance at the plot in Fig. 10(a) reveals that our protocol performs well for deeply rooted trees ($d > 14$), whereas the protocol of Ma et al. performs better for small sized trees. This is because in Ma et al.'s protocol, the communication size is $\approx 2ml + \log t$ whereas in our case it is $\approx 2(n + dt)$. Also note that in the preparation phase, the communication size of our protocol is independent of l when random number generation is excluded, since we share the arrays as arithmetic shares. Thus, despite having a slightly higher communication cost for small trees, our protocol has superior communication cost for deeply rooted trees due to our efficient depth padding strategy and our choice to operate using arithmetic shares only. Meanwhile, the plot in Fig. 10(b) shows that our protocol has significantly low bandwidth compared to both Kiss et al. and Ma et al. In fact, we see a reduction in communication size by a factor of ≈ 10 in the online phase since our protocol does not use public/symmetric key operations and thus transmits a lower number of bytes.

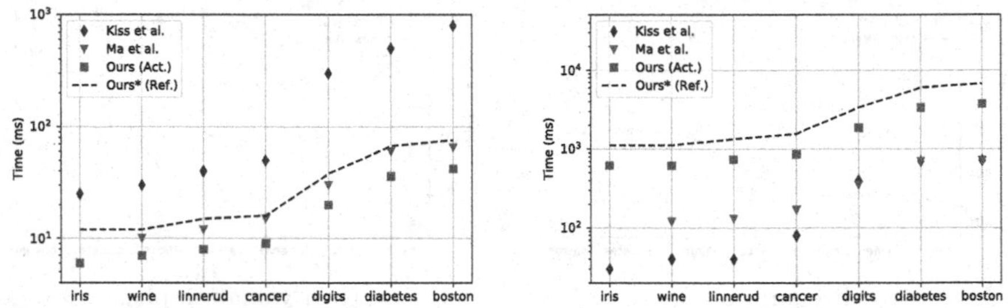

(a) LAN: 1Gbps/0.1 ms (b) MAN: 100Mbps/6 ms

Fig. 11. Plots showing the evaluation time (in ms) of our protocol compared to the methods of Kiss et al. [29] and Ma et al. [32] in the online phase on two different environment: Local Area Network (LAN) and Metropolitan Area Network (MAN). Here, the y–axis is in logarithmic scale and the protocol is run with a precision of $l = 16$ bits. As was the case in Fig. 10, we use dotted lines to show the trend with $l = 32$ bits.

The plots in Fig. 11 show the runtime in the evaluation phase of our protocol (in ms) compared to the methods of Kiss et al. and Ma et al. in their online phase. As was the case in Fig. 10, the plots here should not be used for a one-to-one comparison, since the runtime values of Kiss et al. and Ma et al. are estimated from the online runtime plot of Ma et al.'s paper. We use the same network settings as Ma et al. but would like to note that Ma et al. run with their experiments on a different computing environment compared to ours. As seen in Fig. 11, with a network latency of 0.1 ms, our protocol is faster than Ma et al.'s protocol (by a factor of 2 at $d = 30$), and thus is the best performing protocol since Ma et al.'s protocol in turn outperforms Kiss et al.'s (see Fig. 11(a)). On the other hand, at a network latency of 6ms, our protocol performs significantly worse than both Ma et al.'s and Kiss et al.'s protocol ($\approx$10x slower for small trees and $\approx$5x slower for deep trees as indicated in Fig. 11(b)). This because of the large number of interactions in the online phase of Garay et al.'s LT protocol [22] which we use in Π^{Eval}. Since we use a precision of $l = 16$, the LT protocol takes 16 rounds of interactions for each comparison operation and is thus significantly affected by network latency. This also suggest that a constant round LT protocol as suggested in [10, 37] can help us mitigate the effect of network latency in our current implementation.

6 Discussion

We have thus presented a two-party PDTE protocol based on an additive secret sharing scheme. The key feature of our protocol is that both the decision tree $\mathcal{T}$ and the query vector $\mathbf{q}$ are represented as arrays. We use a random shuffling algorithm to transform these arrays, traverse the tree by privately accessing a shuffled look-up vector and use the same approach to securely select query features. This helps us avoid public/symmetric key operations of OT based array indexing thereby reducing the computational cost of our protocol. We have showed that our implementation has low communication cost and achieves fast runtime at low network latency. However, our protocol is not competitive at higher network latency due to the larger number of interactions in the comparison functionality of our implementation. We now offer suggestions on how to improve our protocol and conclude with a discussion on potential areas of future research.

The most obvious area of improvement would be an implementation of the comparison functionality in our protocol in constant number of rounds. By replacing Garay et al.'s linear round LT protocol with a constant round protocol such as that of Nishide et al. [37], our PDTE protocol would also be competitive at higher network latency. There are however, drawbacks to this approach as Nishide et al.'s comparison protocol has relatively high communication cost in the offline phase [43] which would increase the offline communication cost of our protocol.

Lastly, at present we have designed our protocol for decision splits with numerical variables. Categorical variables were not considered in the design and future research should incorporate extending the protocol to handle categorical variables. This would require adding a private set intersection functionality (PSI) to our protocol and design split functions based on set membership test.

Acknowledgment. This work was supported in part by MEXT/JSPS KAKENHI Grant Number 19K12209 and 21H05052. The authors would like to thank Prof. Kunihiko Sadakane for his valuable comments during the design of the protocol.

References

1. Amazon: Amazon web services. https://aws.amazon.com/
2. Beaver, D.: Efficient multiparty protocols using circuit randomization. In: Feigenbaum, J. (ed.) CRYPTO 1991. LNCS, vol. 576, pp. 420–432. Springer, Heidelberg (1992). https://doi.org/10.1007/3-540-46766-1_34
3. Beaver, D.: Commodity-based cryptography. In: Proceedings of the Twenty-Ninth Annual ACM Symposium on Theory of Computing, pp. 446–455 (1997)

4. Beaver, D., Micali, S., Rogaway, P.: The round complexity of secure protocols. In: Proceedings of the Twenty-Second Annual ACM Symposium on Theory of Computing, pp. 503–513 (1990)
5. Ben-Or, M., Goldwasser, S., Wigderson, A.: Completeness theorems for non-cryptographic fault-tolerant distributed computation. In: Proceedings of the Twentieth Annual ACM Symposium on Theory of Computing, pp. 1–10. ACM (1988)
6. Bertilsson, M., Ingemarsson, I.: A construction of practical secret sharing schemes using linear block codes. In: Seberry, J., Zheng, Y. (eds.) AUSCRYPT 1992. LNCS, vol. 718, pp. 67–79. Springer, Heidelberg (1993). https://doi.org/10.1007/3-540-57220-1_53
7. Bogdanov, D., Jagomägis, R., Laur, S.: A universal toolkit for cryptographically secure privacy-preserving data mining. In: Chau, M., Wang, G.A., Yue, W.T., Chen, H. (eds.) PAISI 2012. LNCS, vol. 7299, pp. 112–126. Springer, Heidelberg (2012). https://doi.org/10.1007/978-3-642-30428-6_9
8. Bost, R., Popa, R.A., Tu, S., Goldwasser, S.: Machine learning classification over encrypted data. Cryptology ePrint Archive (2014)
9. Canetti, R.: Universally composable security: a new paradigm for cryptographic protocols. In: Proceedings 42nd IEEE Symposium on Foundations of Computer Science, pp. 136–145. IEEE (2001)
10. Catrina, O., de Hoogh, S.: Improved primitives for secure multiparty integer computation. In: Garay, J.A., De Prisco, R. (eds.) SCN 2010. LNCS, vol. 6280, pp. 182–199. Springer, Heidelberg (2010). https://doi.org/10.1007/978-3-642-15317-4_13
11. Catrina, O., Saxena, A.: Secure computation with fixed-point numbers. In: Sion, R. (ed.) FC 2010. LNCS, vol. 6052, pp. 35–50. Springer, Heidelberg (2010). https://doi.org/10.1007/978-3-642-14577-3_6
12. Chaum, D., Crépeau, C., Damgard, I.: Multiparty unconditionally secure protocols. In: Proceedings of the Twentieth Annual ACM Symposium on Theory of Computing, pp. 11–19 (1988)
13. Damgård, I., Fitzi, M., Kiltz, E., Nielsen, J.B., Toft, T.: Unconditionally secure constant-rounds multi-party computation for equality, comparison, bits and exponentiation. In: Halevi, S., Rabin, T. (eds.) TCC 2006. LNCS, vol. 3876, pp. 285–304. Springer, Heidelberg (2006). https://doi.org/10.1007/11681878_15
14. Damgård, I., Geisler, M., Krøigaard, M.: Efficient and secure comparison for on-line auctions. In: Pieprzyk, J., Ghodosi, H., Dawson, E. (eds.) ACISP 2007. LNCS, vol. 4586, pp. 416–430. Springer, Heidelberg (2007). https://doi.org/10.1007/978-3-540-73458-1_30
15. Damgård, I., Geisler, M., Krøigaard, M.: A correction to "efficient and secure comparison for on-line auctions. Cryptology EPrint Archive (2008)
16. Damgard, I., Geisler, M., Kroigard, M.: Homomorphic encryption and secure comparison. Int. J. Appl. Cryptography **1**(1), 22–31 (2008)
17. Damgård, I., Thorbek, R.: Non-interactive proofs for integer multiplication. In: Naor, M. (ed.) EUROCRYPT 2007. LNCS, vol. 4515, pp. 412–429. Springer, Heidelberg (2007). https://doi.org/10.1007/978-3-540-72540-4_24
18. De Cock, M., Dowsley, R., Horst, C., Katti, R., Nascimento, A.C., Poon, W.S., Truex, S.: Efficient and private scoring of decision trees, support vector machines and logistic regression models based on pre-computation. IEEE Trans. Dependable Secure Comput. **16**(2), 217–230 (2017)
19. learn developers, S.: Scikit-learn: Machine learning in Python. https://scikit-learn.org/stable/index.html

20. van Dijk, M.: A linear construction of secret sharing schemes. Des. Codes Cryptography **12**(2), 161–201 (1997)
21. Dua, D., Graff, C.: UCI machine learning repository (2017). http://archive.ics.uci.edu/ml
22. Garay, J., Schoenmakers, B., Villegas, J.: Practical and secure solutions for integer comparison. In: Okamoto, T., Wang, X. (eds.) PKC 2007. LNCS, vol. 4450, pp. 330–342. Springer, Heidelberg (2007). https://doi.org/10.1007/978-3-540-71677-8_22
23. Goldreich, O.: Foundations of cryptography: volume 2, basic applications. Cambridge University Press (2009)
24. Google: Google cloud. https://cloud.google.com/
25. Heikamp, K., Bajorath, J.: Support vector machines for drug discovery. Expert Opin. Drug Discov. **9**(1), 93–104 (2014)
26. Hoang, T., Ozkaptan, C.D., Yavuz, A.A., Guajardo, J., Nguyen, T.: S3oram: a computation-efficient and constant client bandwidth blowup oram with shamir secret sharing. In: Proceedings of the 2017 ACM SIGSAC Conference on Computer and Communications Security, pp. 491–505 (2017)
27. Ito, M., Saito, A., Nishizeki, T.: Secret sharing scheme realizing general access structure. Electron. Commun. Japan (Part III: Fundamental Electron. Sci.) **72**(9), 56–64 (1989)
28. Kamara, S., Mohassel, P., Raykova, M.: Outsourcing multi-party computation. Cryptology ePrint Archive (2011)
29. Kiss, Á., Naderpour, M., Liu, J., Asokan, N., Schneider, T.: Sok: modular and efficient private decision tree evaluation. Proc. Privacy Enhancing Technol. **2019**(2), 187–208 (2019)
30. Knuth, D.E.: The art of computer programming. volume 1: Fundamental algorithms. volume 2: Seminumerical algorithms. Bull. Amer. Math. Soc. (1997)
31. Kolesnikov, V., Schneider, T.: Improved garbled circuit: free XOR gates and applications. In: Aceto, L., Damgård, I., Goldberg, L.A., Halldórsson, M.M., Ingólfsdóttir, A., Walukiewicz, I. (eds.) ICALP 2008. LNCS, vol. 5126, pp. 486–498. Springer, Heidelberg (2008). https://doi.org/10.1007/978-3-540-70583-3_40
32. Ma, J.P., Tai, R.K., Zhao, Y., Chow, S.S.: Let's stride blindfolded in a forest: sublinear multi-client decision trees evaluation. In: NDSS (2021)
33. Maheswari, S., Pitchai, R.: Heart disease prediction system using decision tree and naive bayes algorithm. Current Med. Imaging **15**(8), 712–717 (2019)
34. Micali, S., Goldreich, O., Wigderson, A.: How to play any mental game. In: Proceedings of the Nineteenth ACM Symposium on Theory of Computing, STOC, pp. 218–229. ACM (1987)
35. Microsoft: Microsoft azure. https://azure.microsoft.com/
36. Mohassel, P., Orobets, O., Riva, B.: Efficient server-aided 2pc for mobile phones. Proc. Priv. Enhancing Technol. **2016**(2), 82–99 (2016)
37. Nishide, T., Ohta, K.: Multiparty computation for interval, equality, and comparison without bit-decomposition protocol. In: Okamoto, T., Wang, X. (eds.) PKC 2007. LNCS, vol. 4450, pp. 343–360. Springer, Heidelberg (2007). https://doi.org/10.1007/978-3-540-71677-8_23
38. Reistad, T.I., Toft, T.: Secret sharing comparison by transformation and rotation. In: Desmedt, Y. (ed.) ICITS 2007. LNCS, vol. 4883, pp. 169–180. Springer, Heidelberg (2009). https://doi.org/10.1007/978-3-642-10230-1_14
39. Shamir, A.: How to share a secret. Commun. ACM **22**(11), 612–613 (1979)

40. Sudo, H., Nuida, K., Shimizu, K.: An efficient private evaluation of a decision graph. In: Lee, K. (ed.) ICISC 2018. LNCS, vol. 11396, pp. 143–160. Springer, Cham (2019). https://doi.org/10.1007/978-3-030-12146-4_10
41. Tai, R.K.H., Ma, J.P.K., Zhao, Y., Chow, S.S.M.: Privacy-Preserving Decision Trees Evaluation via Linear Functions. In: Foley, S.N., Gollmann, D., Snekkenes, E. (eds.) ESORICS 2017. LNCS, vol. 10493, pp. 494–512. Springer, Cham (2017). https://doi.org/10.1007/978-3-319-66399-9_27
42. Tueno, A., Kerschbaum, F., Katzenbeisser, S.: Private evaluation of decision trees using sublinear cost. Proc. Priv. Enhancing Technol. **2019**(1), 266–286 (2019)
43. Veugen, T., Blom, F., de Hoogh, S.J., Erkin, Z.: Secure comparison protocols in the semi-honest model. IEEE J. Sel. Top. Sig. Process. **9**(7), 1217–1228 (2015)
44. Watanabe, T., Iwamura, K., Kaneda, K.: Secrecy multiplication based on a (k, n)-threshold secret-sharing scheme using only k servers. In: Computer Science and its Applications, pp. 107–112. Springer, Cham (2015)
45. Wu, D.J., Feng, T., Naehrig, M., Lauter, K.: Privately evaluating decision trees and random forests. Cryptology ePrint Archive (2015)
46. Xuan, P., Sun, C., Zhang, T., Ye, Y., Shen, T., Dong, Y.: Gradient boosting decision tree-based method for predicting interactions between target genes and drugs. Front. Genet. **10**, 459 (2019)
47. Yao, A.C.: Protocols for secure computations. In: 23rd Annual Symposium on Foundations of Computer Science (sfcs 1982), pp. 160–164. IEEE (1982)
48. Yao, A.C.C.: How to generate and exchange secrets. In: 27th Annual Symposium on Foundations of Computer Science (sfcs 1986), pp. 162–167. IEEE (1986)
49. Zahur, S., Rosulek, M., Evans, D.: Two Halves Make a Whole. In: Oswald, E., Fischlin, M. (eds.) EUROCRYPT 2015. LNCS, vol. 9057, pp. 220–250. Springer, Heidelberg (2015). https://doi.org/10.1007/978-3-662-46803-6_8
50. Zheng, Y., Duan, H., Wang, C.: Towards secure and efficient outsourcing of machine learning classification. In: European Symposium on Research in Computer Security, pp. 22–40. Springer (2019)

Reputation at Stake! A Trust Layer over Decentralized Ledger for Multiparty Computation and Reputation-Fair Lottery

Mario Larangeira[1,2(✉)]

[1] Department of Mathematical and Computing Science School of Computing, Tokyo Institute of Technology, Meguro, Japan
mario@c.titech.ac.jp
[2] Input Output Global (IOG), Tokyo, Japan
mario.larangeira@iohk.io

Abstract. This work introduces, to the best of our knowledge, the first stake based reputation and trust layer to proof of stake (PoS) system. Namely, we show that the delegation framework, introduced by Karakostas *et al.* (SCN'20) to provide a delegation framework, can be extended and repurposed to construct a trust layer over a PoS consensus protocol in addition to its original application. Furthermore, we show a concrete reputation system satisfying the positive results of (1) Asharov *et al.* (Asiacrypt'13), allowing the secure execution of multiparty protocols such as GMW (STOC' 87) and Damgard and Ishai (Crypto'05), and (2) Kleinrock *et al.* (Indocrypt'20), a Reputation-fair Lottery, thus, also, a Proof of Reputation system. More concretely, our devised layer is used to construct a concrete reputation system based on arbitrary stake distribution. In this layer groups of users can freely and dynamically "assign their respective trust" to members of a set of trustees, *i.e.* participants that offered themselves as receivers of such assignment. Furthermore, our work offers the advantage of providing a clear stake based criteria, verifiable in the ledger, and, therefore, naturally resistant to sybil attack, that the set of trustees indeed yields an honest majority. This setting provides a better situation than a simple assumption of honest majority, since it involves stake in a decentralized ledger, and the public verifiability of the reputation score via verification of the stake distribution.

Keywords: Ranking · Reputation · Trust · Proof-of-Stake · MPC

1 Introduction

To the best of our knowledge, this work is the first to introduce a concrete and practical distributed reputation layer for a PoS based blockchain. Given that trust between individuals and reputation are ubiquitous society, our protocol is relevant for modern life. Surprisingly, despite its fundamental role and numerous works in the literature, it seems there is still not a thorough solution that satisfactorily addresses it.

S.-H. Seo and H. Seo (Eds.): ICISC 2022, LNCS 13849, pp. 195–215, 2023.
https://doi.org/10.1007/978-3-031-29371-9_10

Technical Challenges. Although the straightforward practicality and deceivingly simplicity of the concept, reputation record has shown itself to be somewhat elusive to formal techniques intended to satisfactorily capture this concept, and properly embed it in a practical system free from manipulation and general enough to be used widely. It is natural to expect that such systems would eventually be securely incorporated into our lives via information systems that are increasingly permeating all aspects of our daily routine. For the moment, such a general system does not seem to exist. The explanation seems to rely on the technical challenges in pursuing such solution, and they can be broken down in three main areas in the available literature:

- eliciting feedback: Systems based on ranking crucially depend on the feedback of the system users. Briefly, a reputation framework needs to continuously gather and process the "opinion" from the parties;
- aggregating/displaying: The feedback from the user has to be aggregated in order to establish a comprehensible and meaningful value;
- distribution: Each player of such a system is subject to receive a "reputation" value, which others can consult or be used in decision making, in particular, it can be used in outlining general strategies.

Eliciting Feedback. In general, participants are entitled to decide whether to provide feedback or not. Therefore without proper incentive we may be led to the situation that we would have a highly biased view of the reputation of a particular target, since only parties willing to spread bad reputation, for some particular reason, would bother to interact with the system in order to feed with its opinion. The quality of the feedback is also subject to problems. Ideally, the desirable feedback are the honest ones, reporting bad or good behavior alike, however it is notoriously hard to obtain or verify. Furthermore, bad reports, if public, can even cause retaliation from the feedback target in future interactions. One approach to incentivize "good feedback", or at least "valid feedback", is to tie together some sort of stake to the participant providing such feedback.

Aggregating and Displaying. A highly popular technique to process feedback is simply associating a score with the target node, with respect to some service/interaction. In extreme cases, the nodes have only two options: "good" or "bad", *i.e.* 1 or −1. In this binary feedback scenario, reputation aggregators would apply a simple technique named *netfeedback*. Basically it is the simple sum of the feedbacks in order to provide a straightforward "good" or "bad" status, which, later, can be used to assemble a *ranking*, for the target nodes. This approach is widely deployed in major Internet websites, however it has clear setbacks, since it does not take into account the type of interaction which led to the reported score. More concretely, the target node which interacted with several other feedback providers but with respect with difference services/products.

Reputation Distribution. Once a reputation is established, as, for example, a simple score, a major challenge is to bind it with the parties and allow public availability, including compatibility with other systems. In an environment where users/identities can easily be created, participants with bad reputation can create new identities effectively erasing past history, and bad reputation, *i.e. whitewashing.* The newly created node would be free of the bad effects of its past actions. Here, once again some sort of relation with a stake, has the potential to minimize such erasure. A large amount of work was dedicated to minimizing such effects in game theory. A common strategy is to penalize the newcomer until it has enough history within the system. Previous work had shown that given the risk of *whitewashing*, the system as whole has to carry the burden in the form of penalties for every newcomer.

It is straightforward to understand that reputation systems are particularly needed when parties have a long term expectation of activities, *i.e.* a set of nodes is expected to keep interacting with each other in the long term. In the early mentioned main areas, if the problems are solved it paves the way to correctly capture feedback, process and distribute it, which is valuable in guiding future interactions. More importantly, they can fundamentally change the interactions by allowing parties to establish their own strategies for further interactions. For example, a reliable and available reputation system could be used to guide participants of a protocol to whom they would choose to interact in order to perform a joint protocol.

1.1 Related Work

An interesting overlap between reputation and multiparty computation was observed by Asharov *et al.* [1]. In particular, [1] points out that by observing the reputation of the protocol participants, in some cases, it is possible to guarantee an honest majority. It is important to remark that in the positive cases, a fair distributed computation can be performed and therefore such a scenario is highly desirable in numerous scenarios.

This early work adds to the rich and long literature of reputation and trust management [12], even in decentralized form [8,10]. In the set of decentralized reputation, Kleinrock *et al.* [17] proposed a new paradigm named Proof of Reputation, following roughly on the analogous idea of Proof of Stake (PoS) and Proof of Work (PoW). That is, proportionally to the stake, or computational work, a participant would be more frequently selected to issue the new block. Moreover, [17] introduces a new definition for *reputation-fair lottery* which is suitable for Proof of Reputation. Roughly, it states that given a vector of reputation scores for a set of participants, even the ones with the lowest reputation can still have a chance of being selected by the lottery, which differs from another work on, *i.e.* the Proof of Reputation by Biryukov *et al.* [3], that focuses on assuring a more even probability distribution for the lottery algorithm.

1.2 Our Work

We introduce, to the best of our knowledge, the first concrete and practical reputation system which can be deployed on a Delegated PoS blockchain protocol. The starting point of our work comes from the observation that the delegation of stake, as defined in [13], can be interpreted as *an assignment of trust*. In other words, when a stakeholder in the PoS environment delegates its stake to a *stake pool*, it is in fact, informing publicly that it trusts that entity. Hence, these special participants, or *trustees* as we later denote them, can publicly claim a higher reputation score by accumulating more votes, or assignments, of trust via a similar delegation method adapted from [13].

PoS Based Reputation Vector. We show that the framework proposed in [13] is general enough to be repurposed to a different context, *i.e.*, a trust layer. More concretely, when a participant wants to receive trust assignments from others, it would issue a certificate and publish it in the ledger $\mathcal{L}$. Similarly to what is already done with *stake pools* in [13]. The difference here is that such *registration certificates* contain a *context identification*, *i.e.* a string $ID_{context}$, which represents the context that the trust assigners trust that *trustee*. The string $ID_{context}$ is a unique identifier which can represent a particular service, product, company or a decentralized identity [18]. Therefore, by assigning trust, again, via delegation procedure similarly to the technique in [13], to the published certificate, a participant is publicly informing that it trusts the signer of that certificate with respect to that context. Needless to say, the trust assigning certificate should also contain the identifier $ID_{context}$. Hence it does not interfere with the critical PoS delegated consensus protocol, and also to allow multiple contexts. Relying on a PoS system has the advantage of the *honest stake majority* property which is a common security assumption of PoS systems. Furthermore, it also tackles a major technical challenge of reputation systems, namely, *aggregating and display*, since trust assigning and revocation are easy, and the PoS based ledger allows publicly verifiability.

In comparison to [17], our proposed reputation system is limited to PoS systems given the adaptation from [13]. On the other hand, [17] lacks the definition of a concrete reputation system (similarly with [1]), despite presenting concrete results, including a Nakamoto style fallback in case of flawed reputation ranking. Here, we concretely present a distributed reputation protocol by allowing the participants of the PoS system to freely, and publicly, show their trust, therefore allowing reputation to be created. Typically, the reputation of a set of participants, say $\mathcal{T}$, is a vector of (real) values between $[0, 1]$ of size $|\mathcal{T}|$, where the i-th position indicates the likelihood of the i-th player being honest. Hence reputation 1 means that the player is assured to behave honestly, or, depending on the context, has a perfectly good reputation.

In our model, given an unique context identifier, again, $ID_{context}$, participants can issue, and publish in the $\mathcal{L}$, certificates that tie together $ID_{context}$ and their respective verification keys. In this way, they are perceived by all the users of the PoS system as members of the pool of potential receivers of delegated trust, *e.g.* the set $\mathcal{T}$, in that particular *context*. Given that these certificates and verification keys are public, they can be widely advertised by their issuers outside of the protocol, *i.e.* in the real world. In this setting, any user of the entire PoS system, therefore a *stakeholder* which is a member of the set $\mathcal{U}$, such that $\mathcal{T} \subset \mathcal{U}$, can issue trust votes (delegation certificates in the jargon of [13]) also containing the context identifier $ID_{context}$. The reputation scores naturally arise by taking into account the stake associated with each trust assignment combined. For a fixed context identification string $ID_{context}$, each score of the reputation vector is the percentage of stake that each participant, in $\mathcal{T}$, was assigned with respect to the combination, that is, the summation, of all stake of the set $\mathcal{U}$.

Stake as Trust Weight. Assume, for example, that all participants in $\mathcal{U}$ are assigning trust with the identifier $ID_{context}$ for multiple trustees. Furthermore, assume also that each of them assigns trust for every player in $\mathcal{T}$. In this scenario, every reputation value in the vector is 1, since they received trust votes from every player in $\mathcal{U}$. Note that the participants can cast votes for different members of the $\mathcal{T}$ set at the same time, *i.e.* same context. The reputation percentage, *i.e.* score, is taken by considering how much a single address of $\mathcal{T}$ has harvest for its own, with respect to the summation of all the stake in the set $\mathcal{U}$, *i.e.* the players voting for that context. More concretely, the overall stake being used to vote is the summation of all $s_1, \ldots, s_{|\mathcal{U}|}$, the corresponding shares of the participants in $\mathcal{U}$, and the resulting reputation score for the i-th member of the $\mathcal{T}$ is $r_i = \frac{s_{\mathcal{U}_\mathcal{T}}}{s_1 + \cdots + s_\mathcal{U}}$, where $s_{\mathcal{U}_\mathcal{T}}$ is the summation of the stake of all assigners to the i-th trustee. Needless to say, although the system bases the "trust delegation" in the same fashion of [13], *i.e.* via certificates, this sort of purposely tailored delegation does not affect the stake delegation crucially important for the PoS consensus protocol. Given the context identification, it can be handled in isolation of the consensus.

This reputation system is compatible with the setting considered in [17]. More formally, each reputation value r_i is associated with a binary random variable H_i which tells if the i-th participant behaves honestly, thus $\Pr[H_i = 1] = r_i$. Differently from [1,17], our framework relies by design on the community of users interested in the context referred by the $ID_{context}$. Hence, ultimately, the reputation scores of our system reflect how the set of trust assigners, the set $\mathcal{U}$, perceives the members of the set $\mathcal{T}$. In other words, this perception can be subject to real world information.

Relying on the stake of the underlying PoS ledger when computing the reputation score has the "good" side effect to guarantee some accountability of the feedback, arguably increasing the quality of the resulting vector. Furthermore, it provides a more dynamic environment where the reputation can be verified with access to the ledger $\mathcal{L}$. On the other hand, our construction does not support negative feedback, *i.e.* -1 or "bad" as mentioned earlier in the technical challenge of modeling reputation. Our proposed system offers only a simple "trust association" which is already enough for numerous applications. Despite the limited functionality, regarding inclusion, our model supports easy addition of new participants, both as trust assigners and trustees, since any newcomer could generate a new certificate containing the context identifier, and, therefore, turning itself target of trust assignment.

Our proposed system addresses another drawback of handling reputation information. By relying on the underlying ledger also helps on the reputation distribution since all the trust assignments are public. In comparison to current and more common ranking reputation systems, our construction is not deterred to a particular silo as a company platform or database. It enjoys the advantages of distributed systems as long as the consensus security assumptions are valid, typically an honest majority of the stakes in the PoS paradigm. At the same time, by adopting specific context identifiers, groups of participants, for example, of the same market, can compare its own reputations by issuing certificates and publishing them in $\mathcal{L}$, thus competing by the trust delegation.

Public Perception. With our system honest users would assign trust to other honest participants which directly reflects the public perception. The main reason is that our framework allows participants to assign trust freely, dynamically and publicly in multiple contexts. However, our work does not advocate a notion of right reputation. In our setting the correct score reputation is as correct as the public perceives it. Moreover, in our setting, we consider that *trust is transitive.* In other words, if a participant assigns trust to another, it is assumed that the trustee will behave honestly, hence *transitive.* Our basic assumptions are:

- Honest participants assign trust only to honest participants;
- The majority of the combined stake of the assigners is honest.

We advocate that these two basic assumptions seem reasonable because while the latter can be assumed from the basic properties of the typical PoS ledgers [2, 7,15,16], the former can be assumed since the trust assignments could be revoked (similar to the regular delegation in [13]). Therefore, via information of the real world, it is expected that once, for a given context, the participants are not willing to associate their stake to a trustee any longer, they could revoke it. Leaving only honest trustees with assigned trust. Despite of being an optimistic view, this puts the reputation system in a better situation of contextualizing the reputation vector, in comparison to [1,17] which does not provide extra information on how the scores are obtained.

Our Contributions and Benefits of Stake Based Reputation. The concrete benefits of our novel design start by allowing us to revisit the works in [1,17] in the light of a stake based reputation system, and derive an alternative criteria, this time based on stake distribution, in order to obtain honest majority of players while executing multiparty computation and fair proof-of-reputation protocol. This brings immediate advantages, because the participants can verify if indeed the conditions are satisfied via stake distribution in $\mathcal{L}$.

We summarize our contributions as follows:

- extension of the framework from [13], by providing a functionality $\mathcal{F}_\mathcal{T}$ (arguing also the existence of a protocol that realizes it under Universal Composability Framework [4]) to allow assignment of trust among participants for multiple contexts;
- introduce a concrete reputation scheme $\mathsf{Rep}^m_\mathbb{S}$ based on $\mathcal{F}_\mathcal{T}$ and the stake distribution $\mathbb{S}$ of a set of participants $\mathcal{T}$ with size m, in a PoS ledger $\mathcal{L}$;

- revisit the work of [1] in the light of $\mathsf{Rep}_{\mathbb{S}}^{m}$, and show that the early mentioned basic assumptions yield an honest majority on the set $\mathcal{T}$ except with negligible probability, and therefore allows the secure execution of protocols [9] and [6];
- revisit the work of [17] in the light of $\mathsf{Rep}_{\mathbb{S}}^{m}$, showing that $\mathcal{T}$ yields an honest majority except with negligible probability, therefore $\mathcal{T}$ can be used to build a reputation-fair lottery algorithm, and consequently a proof-of-reputation system over $\mathcal{L}$.

A drawback of our work is that, in fact, the guarantees it provides in terms of honest majority relies heavily on the public perception. In other words, it relies on how much users assign their trust and that can mislead the fact that the trustee may not be *faithfully* honest. We argue that this is intrinsic to all reputation/trust systems. Furthermore, our framework allows a dynamic setting in which once an assigned trustee is identified as being dishonest, users can revoke their trust assignment in a publicly verifiable fashion via the ledger.

2 Basic Definitions

The trust in our model is closely tied to the stake, which will translate into an honest majority of users, therefore we need to review previous results for reputation vectors and basic lemmas as, for example, the Hoeffding Inequality used in [1]. We review of the proof of stake ledger $\mathcal{L}$, as it is given by the Kachina framework [14], and the delegation framework $\mathcal{F}_{\text{CoreWallet}}$, as given by [13] in Sects. 3 and 4, respectively.

2.1 Security with Reputation Vector

For completeness we briefly review the key definitions for secure computation with a reputation vector introduced in [1] which better suits our purposes. These definitions rely heavily on the standard definition available in the literature [4]. Let us start by reviewing the running time of the family of functionality and protocol. For a complete description we refer the reader to [1]. Moreover, in the next definitions, let PPT mean probabilistic polynomial-time with respect to the security parameter $\lambda \in \mathbb{N}$.

Definition 1. *Let $\mathcal{F} = \{f^m\}_{m\in\mathbb{N}}$ be an infinite family of functionalities, where f^m is an m-ary functionality. We say that $\mathcal{F}$ is a PPT family of functionalities if there exists a polynomial $p(\cdot)$ and a Turing machine M that on input λ and m outputs a circuit $C_{\lambda,m}$ in time at most $p(\lambda + m)$ such that for every input $x_1, \ldots, x_m$ it holds that $C_{\lambda,m}(x_1, \ldots, x_m) = f^{(m)}(1^\lambda, x_1, \ldots, x_m)$.*

Let the family of protocol π be defined analogously. That is, it is said to be **polynomial time** if the running time of all parties is upper bounded by a polynomial on $\lambda + m$. The next definition introduces the extra vector parameter $\mathbf{x} \in (\{0,1\}^*)^{m(\lambda)}$ corresponding to the reputation of the m participants defined as the function $m : \mathbb{N} \to \mathbb{N}$, for a varying number of participants.

Definition 2. *Let $m : \mathbb{N} \to \mathbb{N}$ be a function. We say that protocol π $t(\cdot)$-securely computes the functionality $\mathcal{F} = \{f^{m(\lambda)}\}_{\lambda \in \mathbb{N}}$ with respect to $m(\cdot)$, if for every PPT adversary $\mathcal{A}$, there exists a PPT simulator $\mathcal{S}$, such that for every PPT distinguisher D, there exist a negligible function $\mu(\cdot)$ such that for every $\lambda \in \mathbb{N}$, every $I \subseteq [m(\lambda)]$ with $|I| \leq t(m(\lambda))$, every reputation vector $\mathsf{x} \in (\{0,1\}^*)^{m(\lambda)}$ and $z \in \{0,1\}^*$, it holds that* $\big| \Pr\left[D(\mathsf{IDEAL}_{\mathcal{F},\mathcal{S}(z),I}(\lambda, m, \mathsf{x})) = 1\right] - \Pr\left[D(\mathsf{REAL}_{\pi,\mathcal{A}(z),I}(\lambda, m, \mathsf{x})) = 1\right] \big| \leq \mu(\lambda)$.

Lastly, assume Rep is the reputation system which provides $\mathsf{r}^m = (r_1^m, \ldots, r_m^m)$. Furthermore, we denote by $I \leftarrow \mathsf{r}^m$ the subset $I \subseteq [m]$ of parties chosen probabilistically where every $i \in I$ with probability $1 - r_i^m$, and the probabilistic choice of I is given to the distinguisher.

Definition 3. *Let m, Rep, $\mathcal{F}$ and π be as earlier mentioned. We say π securely computes $\mathcal{F}$ with respect to $(m(\cdot), \mathsf{Rep})$, if for every PPT adversary $\mathcal{A}$, there exists a PPT simulator $\mathcal{S}$, such that for every PPT distinguisher D, there exist a negligible function $\mu(\cdot)$ such that for every $\lambda \in \mathbb{N}$, every reputation vector $\mathsf{x} \in (\{0,1\}^*)^{m(\lambda)}$ and $z \in \{0,1\}^*$, it holds* $\big| \Pr_{I \leftarrow \mathsf{r}^{m(\lambda)}}\left[D(\mathsf{IDEAL}_{\mathcal{F},\mathcal{S}(z),I}(\lambda, m, \mathsf{x})) = 1\right] - \Pr_{I \leftarrow \mathsf{r}^{m(\lambda)}}\left[D(\mathsf{REAL}_{\pi,\mathcal{A}(z),I}(\lambda, m, \mathsf{x})) = 1\right] \big| \leq \mu(\lambda)$.

Feasibility Reputation. Similarly to [1], we focus on the relation between the honest majority of players performing a protocol, despite stating security assumptions in terms of stake. Namely, a major difference from our work is that we focus on the honest stake, whereas [1] focus on the majority in terms of the number of participants running the protocol. Although it is not immediately clear to establish the relation between stakes and number of players, for the moment we review Hoeffding Inequality [11], rather than the Chernoff bound, in order to relate to the summation on the individual reputation scores. Later, in Sect. 5, we formally clarify the relation between stakes and reputation by introducing a concrete reputation system. Concretely, given a family of reputations $\mathsf{Rep} = \{\mathsf{r}^{m(\lambda)}\}_{\lambda \in \mathbb{N}}$ for a number of participants $m = m(\lambda)$ being assigned trust from regular stakeholders, Hoeffding Inequality allows to state the average of the reputation should be greater than $1/2 + \omega\left(\sqrt{\frac{\log m}{m}}\right)$, or, equivalently, that the number of honest parties is greater than $m/2 + \omega\left(\sqrt{m \cdot \log m}\right)$, where ω is the standard small-omega notation.

Lemma 1 (The Hoeffding Inequality). *Let $X_1, \ldots, X_m$ be independent random variables, each ranging over the (real) interval $[0,1]$, and let $\mu = \frac{1}{m}$. Then let $E[\sum_{i=1}^m X_i]$ denote the expected value of the mean of these variables. Then*

$$\Pr\left[\left|\frac{\sum_{i=1}^m X_i}{m} - \mu \geq k\right|\right] \leq 2 \cdot e^{-2k^2 \cdot m}, \text{ for every } k > 0.$$

Like [1] and, as already outlined earlier, the random variables we consider only have the values 0 and 1, therefore we rely on a simpler version of the inequality. The following claim is proven in [1].

Claim. Let $m : \mathbb{N} \to \mathbb{N}$ be such that $O(\log m(\lambda)) = O(\log \lambda)$, let $\mathsf{Rep} = \{\mathsf{r}^{m(\lambda)}\}_{\lambda \in \mathbb{N}}$ be a family of reputation vectors, and let $m = m(\lambda)$. If it holds that

$$\sum_{i=1}^{m} r_i^m > \left\lfloor \frac{m}{2} \right\rfloor + \omega(\sqrt{m \cdot \log m}),$$

then there exist a negligible function $\mu(\lambda)$ such that for every λ

$$\Pr_{I \leftarrow \mathsf{r}^m}\left[|I| \geq \left\lfloor \frac{m}{2} \right\rfloor \right] < \mu(\lambda).$$

As we will see later, the existing frameworks, like ours, assume the existence of an EU-CMA signature scheme $\langle \mathsf{KeyGen}, \mathsf{Verify}, \mathsf{Sign} \rangle$.

3 The Proof of Stake Ledger

For our purposes, it suffices to assume that the consensus protocol progresses in a predefined number of rounds which composes a *time slot*, and each block is associated with a single slot. The parties are assumed to have semi-synchronous communication where messages sent by honest players are delivered upon a bounded number of rounds. Besides, we also assume the presence of a rushing adversary [4], which can actively corrupt parties. Regarding communication capabilities, we assume all the players have access to a diffusion (multicast) channel which can be built by standard flooding/gossip protocols.

Our protocol relies on the Kachina framework [14]. In particular we rely on its formulation of ledger due to its simplicity. Moreover it is designed as a global functionality, following the Global UC Framework [5], hence we will use the $\overline{\mathcal{G}}_{simpleLedger}$ functionality from Kachina [14], which we denote in this work by $\mathcal{L}$. The functionality is available in Fig. 1, where $\prec$ defines the prefix operation, *i.e.* $\Omega \prec \Omega'$ means the state Ω is included in Ω', and, for readability and consistency purposes, we rename *transaction* (τ) to *block* (b).

Global Ledger Functionality $\mathcal{L}$

The functionality keeps a state Ω and a mapping M of parties to states, both initially empty.

- When receiving a message (SUBMIT, b) from a party P, query $\mathcal{A}$ with (BLOCK, b).
- When receiving a message READ from a party P, return $M(P)$; if P is $\mathcal{A}$, it returns Ω.
- When receiving a message $(\mathsf{EXTEND}, \Omega')$ from $\mathcal{A}$, set $\Omega \leftarrow \Omega || \Omega'$.
- When receiving a message $(\mathsf{ADVANCE}, P, \Omega')$ from $\mathcal{A}$, if $M(P) \prec \Omega' \prec \Omega$ then set $M(P) \leftarrow \Omega'$.

Fig. 1. The Simple Global Ledger Ideal Functionality.

The functionality $\mathcal{L}$ is generic enough to abstract transactions and blocks, focusing on the ledger's properties. In general, that is enough for our purposes, however, for the sake of completeness and formality, we need to define, more concretely, the entries in the ledger.

Typically a transaction is the tuple $tx = (\Theta, \alpha_s, \alpha_r, v, f)$, where

1. $\alpha_s, \alpha_r \in \{0,1\}^*$ are the sender's and receiver's addresses respectively, for the tradable asset set Θ,
2. $v \in \mathbb{R}$ is the value transferred from α_s to α_r, and
3. $f \in \mathbb{R}$ is the fees of the transaction.

A block consists of an ordered list of transactions. In order to organize transaction in blocks, we assume a function $\mathsf{blockify}$ which, given a set of transactions and a chain, returns a block which can extend the chain.

4 The Stake Delegation Framework

In a nutshell [13] introduces a mechanism for issuing address strings which contain attributes. More concretely, their framework defines a core-wallet functionality $\mathcal{F}_{\text{CoreWallet}}$, representing the key management capabilities of a concrete wallet. That is, every PoS has an internal core which manages the private information with respect to that wallet, and therefore all its addresses, putting forth an *account*. For completeness the full description of $\mathcal{F}_{\text{CoreWallet}}$ is given by Figs. 2 and 3. Their framework introduces a predicative M for malleability of addresses and describes three types of addresses, *i.e. base*, *pointer* and *exile*, according to a list of attributes δ (which can contain cryptographic keys). We refer the reader to [13] for a complete discussion on the topic.

Stake Pool Registration and Delegation. The stake pools are identified by a registered staking key generated by accessing its internal $\mathcal{F}_{\text{CoreWallet}}$, to compute a new staking key $(\mathsf{vks}, \mathsf{sks})$ pair, respectively verification and secret keys, in order to issue a registration certificate (vks, m), where m is the pool's metadata. By accessing its internal functionality $\mathcal{F}_{\text{CoreWallet}}$, it receives back $((\mathsf{vks}, m), \sigma)$, where σ is the signature corresponding to sks of the tuple (vks, m). Next, it publishes in the ledger the registration certificate $\Sigma_{reg} = ((\mathsf{vks}, m), \sigma)$ via a regular transaction $tx = (\alpha_{reg}, \Sigma_{reg})$, where α_{reg} is the pool special address.

The stake delegation is achieved with certificates via a process similar to the staking pool registration described. A delegation certificate is a tuple $d = (\mathsf{vks}_s, \langle \mathsf{vks}_d, m \rangle)$. The first element is the staking key vks_s which assigns the rights of the stake to someone else, *i.e.* the owner, while the second is the staking key vks_d of the receiver of the rights, *i.e.* the delegate, while the third element is the certificate's metadata. In order to sign the delegation certificate, the participant accesses its internal $\mathcal{F}_{\text{CoreWallet}}$ and then publishes $\Sigma = (d, \sigma)$ on the ledger.

Functionality $\mathcal{F}^{M}_{\text{CoreWallet}}$ (First Part)

Initialization: Upon receiving (INIT, sid) from $P \in \mathbb{P}$, forward it to $\mathcal{S}$ and wait for (INITOK, sid). Then initialize the empty lists L_P of addresses and attribute lists and K_P of staking keys, and send (INITOK, sid) to P.
Wallet Recovery: Upon receiving (RECOVERWALLET, sid, i) from $P \in \mathbb{P}$, for the first i elements in L_P return (TAG, sid, δ_2).
Address Recovery: Upon receiving (RECOVERADDR, sid, α, i) from P, if (α, l) is one of the first i elements of L_P or $M(L_P, \text{"recover"}, \alpha) = 1$, return (RECOVEREDADDR, sid, α).
Address Generation: Upon receiving (GENERATEADDRESS, sid, aux) from $P \in \mathbb{P}$, forward it to $\mathcal{S}$. Upon receiving (ADDRESS, sid, α, l_α) from $\mathcal{S}$, parse l_α as $(\delta_1, \dots, \delta_g)$ and $\forall P' \in \mathbb{P}$ check if $\forall(\alpha', (\delta'_1, \dots, \delta'_g)) \in L_{P'}$ it holds that $\alpha \neq \alpha'$, $\delta'_2 \neq \delta_2$, and $\forall j \in [i, \dots, g] : \delta'_j \neq \delta_j$, *i.e.* the address, recovery tag, and private attributes are unique. If so, then:

- if $aux = (\text{"base"})$, check that $\forall(\alpha', (\delta'_1, \dots, \delta'_g)) \in L_P : \delta'_1 \neq \delta_1$,
- else if $aux = (\text{"pointer"}, \mathsf{vks})$, check that $\delta_1 = \mathsf{vks}$,
- else if $aux = (\text{"exile"})$, check that $\delta_1 = \bot$.

If the checks hold or P is corrupted, then insert (α, l_α) to L_P and return (ADDRESS, sid, α) to P. If $aux = (\text{"base"})$ also insert δ_1 to K_P and return (STAKINGKEY, sid, δ_1) to P.
Issue Transaction: Upon receiving (PAY, $sid, \Theta, \alpha_s, \alpha_r, m$) from $P \in \mathbb{P}$, if $\exists l_\alpha : (\alpha_s, l_\alpha) \in L_P$ forward it to $\mathcal{S}$. Upon receiving (TRANSACTION, sid, tx, σ) from $\mathcal{S}$, such that $tx = (\Theta, \alpha_s, \alpha_r, m)$, check if $\forall(tx', \sigma', b') \in \mathcal{T} : \sigma' \neq \sigma$, $(tx, \sigma, 0) \notin \mathcal{T}$, and $M(L_P, \text{"issue"}, \alpha_r) = 1$. If all checks hold, then insert $(tx, \sigma, 1)$ to $\mathcal{T}$ and return (TRANSACTION, sid, tx, σ).
Verify Transaction: Upon receiving (VERIFYPAY, sid, tx, σ) from $P \in \mathbb{P}$, with $tx = (\Theta, \alpha_s, \alpha_r, m)$ for a metadata string m, forward it to $\mathcal{S}$ and wait for a reply message (VERIFIEDPAY, sid, tx, σ, ϕ). Then:

- if $M(L_P, \text{"verify"}, \alpha_s) = 0$, set $f = 0$
- else if $(tx, \sigma, 1) \in \mathcal{T}$, set $f = 1$
- else, if P is not corrupted and $(tx, \sigma, 1) \notin \mathcal{T}$, set $f = 0$ and insert $(tx, \sigma, 0)$ to $\mathcal{T}$
- else, if $(\Theta, \alpha_s, \alpha_r, m, \sigma, b) \in \mathcal{T}$, set $f = b$
- else, set $f = \phi$.

Finally, send (VERIFIEDPAY, sid, tx, σ, f) to P.

Fig. 2. The first part of the full Core Wallet Functionality from [13].

Our trust platform, described in the body of the work, is based on similar ideas for delegation. In particular, we adapt the early mentioned $\mathcal{F}_{\text{CoreWallet}}$, by adding interfaces for special sort of delegation, *i.e.* the "trust assignment" (details on Sect. 5).

Functionality $\mathcal{F}^{M}_{\text{CoreWallet}}$ (Second Part)

Issue Staking: Upon receiving (STAKE, sid, stx) from P, such that $stx =$ (vks, m) for a metadata string m, forward the message to $\mathcal{S}$. Upon receiving (STAKED, sid, stx, σ) from $\mathcal{S}$, if $\forall(stx', \sigma', b') \in S : \sigma' \neq \sigma$, $(stx, \sigma, 0) \notin S$, and $\mathsf{vks} \in K_P$, add $(stx, \sigma, 1)$ to S and return (STAKED, sid, stx, σ) to P.
Verify Staking: Upon receiving (VERIFYSTAKE, sid, stx, σ) from $P \in \mathbb{P}$, forward it to $\mathcal{S}$ and wait for (VERIFIEDSTAKE, sid, stx, σ, ϕ), with $stx =$ (vks, m). Then find P_{s}, such that $\mathsf{vks} \in K_{P_{\mathsf{s}}}$, and:

- if $(stx, \sigma, 1) \in S$, set $f = 1$
- else if P_{s} is not corrupted and $(stx, \sigma, 1) \notin S$, set $f = 0$ and insert $(stx, \sigma, 0)$ to S
- else if exists an entry $(stx, \sigma, f') \in S$, set $f = f'$
- else set $f = \phi$ and insert (stx, σ, ϕ) to S.

Finally, return (VERIFIEDSTAKE, sid, stx, σ, f) to P.

Fig. 3. The second part of the full Core Wallet Functionality from [13].

5 Trust Layer over Proof of Stake Ledger

The basic setting we consider has two sets of participants, the regular ones $\mathcal{U}$ and the *trustees* $\mathcal{T}$, with varying sizes of, respectively, $n(\lambda)$ and $m(\lambda)$ for the trust *assigners* and the receivers of trust. Here we introduce a framework to deal with the assignment of trust, via the delegation of stake. That is, each participant $u \in \mathcal{U}$ controls an address α, such that it contains an amount of stake $\mathbb{S}(\alpha)$ as it is registered in a decentralized ledger $\mathcal{L}$. Our proposed reputation system $\mathsf{Rep}^{m}_{\mathbb{S}}$ takes into account the stake of all the trust assigners, say $\mathbb{S}(\alpha_{u_1}), \ldots, \mathbb{S}(\alpha_{u_n})$, to generate the reputation vector as they access $\mathcal{F}_{\mathcal{T}}$, our Trust Assignment Functionality. Before we define the Stake Reputation System $\mathsf{Rep}^{m}_{\mathbb{S}}$, we introduce $\mathcal{F}_{\mathcal{T}}$ in Fig. 4.

Trust Assignment Framework. From now we adapt the delegation and addressing framework of [13], and repurpose it in order to capture the "trust assignment" feature. In particular, we extend the functionality $\mathcal{F}_{\text{CoreWallet}}$ into the Trust Assignment Functionality $\mathcal{F}_{\mathcal{T}}$ by adding two new interfaces *Assign Trust* and *Verify Trust* which handle "trust transactions" ttx. We remark that $\mathcal{F}_{\mathcal{T}}$ contains the interfaces of $\mathcal{F}_{\text{CoreWallet}}$, however we left it out of the next definition for simplicity of the description. Furthermore, each regular participants u has verification keys vks_u which is used in the trust assignment.

For simplicity, let $\mathbb{P} = \mathcal{U} \cup \mathcal{T}$, the next functionality keeps a list $\mathbb{P}$ of both regular participants and trustees. Moreover, for each participant, it also keeps a list S of tuples (ttx, σ, f), respectively, a trust transaction string, a signature and the result of the signature verification. Lastly, for each participant P, it keeps lists K_P which contains the corresponding verification key vks.

Functionality $\mathcal{F}_T$

Assign Trust: Upon receiving (TRUST, sid, ttx) from P, such that $ttx = (\mathsf{vks}, m)$ for a metadata string m, forward the message to $\mathcal{S}$. Upon receiving the message (TRUSTED, sid, ttx, σ) from $\mathcal{S}$, if $\forall(ttx', \sigma', b') \in S$: $\sigma' \neq \sigma$, $(ttx, \sigma, 0) \notin S$, and $\mathsf{vks} \in K_P$, add $(ttx, \sigma, 1)$ to S and return (TRUSTED, sid, ttx, σ) to P.
Verify Trust: Upon receiving (VERIFYTRUST, sid, ttx, σ) from $P \in \mathbb{P}$, forward to $\mathcal{S}$ and wait for (VERIFIEDTRUST, sid, ttx, σ, ϕ), with $ttx = (\mathsf{vks}, m)$. Then find P_s, such that $\mathsf{vks} \in K_{P_s}$, and:

- if $(ttx, \sigma, 1) \in S$, set $f = 1$
- else if P_s is not corrupted and $(ttx, \sigma, 1) \notin S$, set $f = 0$ and insert $(ttx, \sigma, 0)$ to S
- else if exists an entry $(ttx, \sigma, f') \in S$, set $f = f'$
- else set $f = \phi$ and insert (ttx, σ, ϕ) to S.

Finally, return (VERIFIEDTRUSTED, sid, ttx, σ, f) to P.

Fig. 4. The trust interface which extends the delegation framework of [13].

Trustee Registration Certificate. We approach it, as follows: any trustee interested in receiving "trust" from regular participants generates a *Registration Certificate* Σ_{reg} and publishes it in the ledger $\mathcal{L}$ in similar fashion as outlined in Sect. 4 for stake pools. This certificate introduces the address whose keys are controlled by the trustee, say $\alpha_{\mathcal{T}_i}$, and it contains the metadata which is instantiated with an arbitrary string $ID_{context}$ of the choice of $\mathcal{T}_i$, that is $\mathcal{T}_i$ sets $m \leftarrow ID_{context}$. This string works as a unique identifier of the context in which $\mathcal{T}_i$ is expected to be assigned trust. In other words, $\mathcal{T}_i$ publishes the transaction $tx = (\alpha_{\mathcal{T}_i}, \Sigma_{reg})$, for $\Sigma_{reg} = ((\mathsf{vks}_{\mathcal{T}_i}, m), \sigma)$ where $\mathsf{vks}_{\mathcal{T}_i}$ is the verification key for $\mathcal{T}_i$. Other participants can issue similar certificates, and they also would be potential receivers of "trust" of regular participants.

Publicly Assigning Trust. The assignment is done via the issuing of "trust transactions" ttx, and then publishes a corresponding certificate in the ledger. A trust assigning certificate, is similar to the delegation certificate from Sect. 4, it is a tuple $d = (\mathsf{vks}_{\mathcal{U}_j}, \langle \mathsf{vks}_{\mathcal{T}_i}, m\rangle)$ with $m \leftarrow ID_{context}$, for a pre-existing Trustee Registration Certificate with metadata $m = ID_{context}$ to identify in which context $\mathcal{U}_j$ trusts $\mathcal{T}_i$. The first element is the verification key of the receiver of the trust assignment $\mathsf{vks}_{\mathcal{U}_j}$ which assigns trust, while the second is the verification key $\mathsf{vks}_{\mathcal{T}_i}$ of the receiver of the rights, *i.e.* the delegate, while the third element is the certificate's metadata which contains the identification of the context $ID_{context}$. In order to sign the delegation certificate, the $\mathcal{U}_j$ accesses $\mathcal{F}_T$ via the *Assign Trust* interface and then publishes $\Sigma = (d, \sigma)$ on the ledger. The trust assignment is publicly verifiable via the *Verify Trust* interface. Therefore we have the following definition.

Definition 4 (Trust Assignment). *It is said that the participant u assigns trust to $\mathcal{T}$ for a context ID when there is a Registration Certificate $\Sigma_{reg} = ((\mathsf{vks}_{\mathcal{T}}, ID), \sigma_{\mathcal{T}})$ published in the ledger $\mathcal{L}$, and u publishes the certificate $\Sigma_{trust} = (d_u, \sigma_u)$ such that $d_u = (\mathsf{vks}_u, \langle \mathsf{vks}_{\mathcal{T}}, ID\rangle)$.*

Protocol and Security. As mentioned earlier, the functionality $\mathcal{F}_{\mathcal{T}}$ is an extension of $\mathcal{F}_{\text{CoreWallet}}$ from [13]. Likewise, $\mathcal{F}_{\text{CoreWallet}}$, which has a corresponding protocol $\pi_{\text{CoreWallet}}$, we claim, without giving a concrete construction, that there is a corresponding protocol $\pi_{\mathcal{T}}$ which UC realizes $\mathcal{F}_{\mathcal{T}}$, given

- the signature scheme $\langle \mathsf{KeyGen}, \mathsf{Verify}, \mathsf{Sign}\rangle$ is Existential Unforgeability under Chosen Message Attack security (EUF-CMA);
- internal building blocks described in [13] and its security properties, *i.e.* RTagGen, HKeyGen, and GenAddr functions.

Presenting $\pi_{\mathcal{T}}$ and fully proving its security here would be tedious for the reader since it contains the basic technique of $\pi_{\text{CoreWallet}}$, thus we present the following theorem (without proof), assuming our claim that there is a protocol $\pi_{\mathcal{T}}$. Our next theorem states that $\pi_{\mathcal{T}}$ realizes $\mathcal{F}_{\mathcal{T}}$.

Theorem 1. *Let the protocol $\pi_{\mathcal{T}}$ be parameterized by a signature scheme be parameterized by a signat $\langle$KeyGen, Verify, Sign$\rangle$ and the* RTagGen, HKeyGen, *and* GenAddr *be functions. Then $\pi_{\mathcal{T}}$ securely realizes the ideal functionality $\mathcal{F}_{\mathcal{T}}$ if and only if Σ is EUF-CMA,* GenAddr *is collision resistant and attribute non-malleable,* RTagGen *is collision resistant, and* HKeyGen *is hierarchical for Σ.*

A proof for the earlier theorem derives very closely to the main theorem in [13] given that our adapted $\mathcal{F}_{\mathcal{T}}$ contains only minor changes to the original functionality definition. Therefore, as mentioned earlier, we skip a detailed proof.

Concrete Stake Based Reputation System. In order to concretely instantiate a stake based reputation system $\mathsf{Rep}^m_{\mathbb{S}}$, assume there are two sets $\mathcal{U}$ and $\mathcal{T}$, respectively the sets of regular participants and trustees, then assume there are n regular participants $u_1, \ldots, u_n$ who have respectively the following shares $\mathbb{S}(\alpha_1), \ldots, \mathbb{S}(\alpha_n)$ with respect to the ledger $\mathcal{L}$, for their respective addresses. Moreover, we assume that for a particular context (to be formally defined later), there are m *trustees* $\mathcal{T}_1, \ldots, \mathcal{T}_m$ which are targets of trust from the regular participants. Each single regular participant can publicly assign its own trust to multiple trustees.

Definition 5 (Stake based Reputation System). *Let $\mathbb{S}$ be the combination, the sum $\mathbb{S}(u_1) + \cdots + \mathbb{S}(u_n)$, of all the shares of participants. The reputation system $\mathsf{Rep}^m_{\mathbb{S}} = (r^m_1, \ldots, r^m_m)$ such that $r^m_i = \frac{\mathbb{S}(\mathcal{T}_i)}{\mathbb{S}}$, and $\mathbb{S}(\mathcal{T}_i)$ is the summation of the stake assigned to $\mathcal{T}_i$.*

Note that the earlier definition is handy because stakes are used to quantify the amount of trust assigned. Thus $\mathsf{Rep}^m_{\mathbb{S}}$ provides the percentile of how much stake a trustee receives as trust assigned with respect to all stake assigned for that context. Thus, once a participant u_i assigns trust to several trustees, its stake is taken into account only once in the total combination s, however it is taken multiple times on each value $\mathcal{T}_i$. We stress that with access to the functionalities $\mathcal{L}$ and $\mathcal{F}_\mathcal{T}$, respectively to verify the stakes of each address and the validity of the assignment of trust, any participant can compute the reputation vector, with respect to a context identification string $ID_{context}$.

Feasibility of Honest Majority with Respect to Stakes. Next, we take a closer look at $\mathsf{Rep}_\mathbb{S}^m$ and the guarantees it offers in order to provide an honest majority. Our approach is similar to the one in [1, Claim 3.2], which relates to the reputation values and the number of participants. In the terminology of our work, it is equivalent to the reputation values and the number of honest trustees. However, given our concrete reputation system $\mathsf{Rep}_\mathbb{S}^m$, we provide a lemma that relates the honest stake of the regular participants and the number of honest trustees. In the following, we slightly abuse the notation by denoting $\mathbb{S}(\mathcal{U})$ the combination, *i.e.* sum, of stakes in the set $\mathcal{U}$.

Lemma 2. *Let $m : \mathbb{N} \to \mathbb{N}$ be such that $O(\log m(\lambda)) = O(\log \lambda)$, let $\mathsf{Rep}_\mathbb{S}^m = \{\mathsf{r}^{m(\lambda)}\}_{\lambda \in \mathbb{N}}$ be a family of reputation vectors, $m = m(\lambda)$, and m trustees $\mathcal{T}_1, \ldots, \mathcal{T}_m$ and n regular participants $u_1, \ldots, u_n$. If the two following conditions hold*

- *given that all honest regular participants $\mathcal{U}_h \subseteq \mathcal{U}$ assign trust* only *to honest trustees $\mathcal{T}_i$;*
- *for the subset of honest regular participants $\mathcal{U}_h$, it holds that*

$$\frac{\mathbb{S}(\mathcal{U}_h)}{\mathbb{S}} > \left\lfloor \frac{m}{2} \right\rfloor + \omega(\sqrt{m \cdot \log m}),$$

then there exist a negligible function $\mu(\lambda)$ such that for every λ

$$\Pr_{I \leftarrow \mathsf{r}^m}\left[|I| \geq \left\lfloor \frac{m}{2} \right\rfloor\right] < \mu(\lambda).$$

Proof. Since all honest regular participants assign trust only to honest trustees as given by hypothesis, and the reputation system $\mathsf{Rep}_\mathbb{S}^m$ is defined as $r_i^m = \frac{\mathbb{S}(\mathcal{T}_i)}{\mathbb{S}}$ then

$$\sum_{i=1}^{m} r_i^m = |\mathcal{U}_h| \cdot \frac{\mathbb{S}(\mathcal{U}_h)}{\mathbb{S}} + (m - |\mathcal{U}_h|) \cdot \frac{\mathbb{S} - \mathbb{S}(\mathcal{U}_h)}{\mathbb{S}}.$$

Given the security assumption $\frac{\mathbb{S}(\mathcal{U}_h)}{\mathbb{S}} \geq \left\lfloor \frac{m}{2} \right\rfloor + \omega(\sqrt{m \cdot \log m})$, we infer that

$$\sum_{i=1}^{m} r_i^m \geq \left\lfloor \frac{m}{2} \right\rfloor + \omega(\sqrt{m \cdot \log m}).$$

The claim stated in Sect. 2.1 gives the proof.

6 Secure MPC and Reputation-Fair Lottery

Now we argue that our Lemma 2 translates the main positive results from [1] to the setting of PoS by considering the stakes of each participant, *i.e.* secure computation and subset with honest majority. Later, we also explore the consequences of the previous lemma with respect to [17].

6.1 Revisiting the Positive Results of [1]

Concretely, a set of parties willing to run a secure protocol that requires honest majority, like, for example, GMW [9], would need access to a ledger $\mathcal{L}$ and $\mathcal{F}_{\mathcal{T}}$, in order to compute the functionality $\mathcal{F}$. In order to present the next general theorem, likewise [1], we need to review a known fact.

Postulate. [1] *Let $\mathcal{F} = \{f^m\}_{m \in \mathbb{N}}$ be a functionality and let π denote the GMW protocol for $\mathcal{F}$. Then, for every polynomial $m(\cdot) : \mathbb{N} \rightarrow \mathbb{N}$, the protocol $\pi(m, \lambda)$ $\frac{m(\lambda)}{2}$- securely computes $\mathcal{F}$ with respect to $m(n)$.*

The earlier postulate is required by the following theorem.

Theorem 2. *Given the two sets of regular participants $\mathcal{U}$ and trustees $\mathcal{T}$ with access to a ledger $\mathcal{L}$ and a trust assignment functionality $\mathcal{F}_{\mathcal{T}}$, and $|T| = m$. Let $\mathcal{F} = \{f^m\}_{m \in \mathbb{N}}$ be a functionality, and assume $\pi = \{\pi(m, \lambda)\}$ be the GMW protocol as stated in the earlier Fact. Moreover assume $m(\cdot)$ is a function such that $O(\log m(\lambda)) = O(\log \lambda)$, let $m = m(\lambda)$ and $\mathsf{Rep}_{\mathbb{S}}^m$ be as given by Definition 5. If the two following conditions hold*

- *given that all honest regular participants $\mathcal{U}_h \subseteq \mathcal{U}$ assign trust* only *to honest trustees $\mathcal{T}_i$;*
- *for the subset of honest regular participants $\mathcal{U}_h$, it holds that*

$$\frac{\mathbb{S}(\mathcal{U}_h)}{\mathbb{S}} > \left\lfloor \frac{m}{2} \right\rfloor + \omega(\sqrt{m \cdot \log m}),$$

then π securely computes $\mathcal{F}$ with respect to $(m(\cdot), \mathsf{Rep}_{\mathbb{S}}^m)$.

As expected the proof of the theorem is immediate given the similarity with the equivalent result in [1]. The crucial observation for the proof is that our Lemma 2 guarantees honest majority, albeit considering the assignment of stake, with negligible probability in λ. Hence the ideal and real execution, as stated by Definition 3, are indistinguishable.

Subset Honest Majority. For completeness, we also state the result regarding finding a *subset honest majority* which is motivated by [6], which states that in order to achieve secure computation with complete fairness, it suffices to have a subset of participants that, with the except of negligible probability, contains an honest majority. In order to explore this subset, we slightly depart from our initial model by assuming a subset $T \subseteq \mathcal{U}$ which, in the setting of [6], would perform the computation. We emphasize that, given our framework with $\mathcal{L}$, $\mathcal{F}_{\mathcal{T}}$

and an arbitrary context, defined by the string $ID_{context}$, it is equivalent to say, basically, that the subset means that the regular participants $\mathcal{U}$ are issuing Registration Certificates and publishing them in $\mathcal{L}$ in order to receive trust from within members of the $\mathcal{U}$. Thus, from [6], as long as T contains an honest majority except with negligible probability, there is a protocol for $\mathcal{U}$ and a family of reputation vectors. In terms of stake, we can state the following.

Lemma 3. *Let $n(\cdot)$, $m(\cdot)$, $\mathcal{F}$, $\mathcal{U}$ and $\mathsf{Rep}^n_{\mathbb{S}}$ be defined as before. If there exists a negligible function $\mu(\cdot)$, such that*

- *for every λ there exists a subset $T_\lambda \subset \mathcal{U}$, with $|T_\lambda| = m$, for which*

$$\Pr_{I \leftarrow \mathsf{r}^{n(\lambda)}}\left[|T_\lambda \cap I| \leq \frac{|T_\lambda|}{2}\right] \leq \mu(\lambda),$$

- *given that all honest regular participants $\mathcal{U}_h \subseteq \mathcal{U}$, with $|\mathcal{U}| = n$, assign trust* only *to honest participants within $\mathcal{U}$;*
- *for the subset of honest regular participants $\mathcal{U}_h$, it holds that*

$$\frac{\mathbb{S}(\mathcal{U}_h)}{\mathbb{S}} > \left\lfloor \frac{m}{2} \right\rfloor + \omega(\sqrt{m \cdot \log m});$$

then there exists a (non-uniform) protocol π that securely computes *$\mathcal{F}$ with respect to $(m(\cdot), \mathsf{Rep}^n_{\mathbb{S}})$.*

The proof for this lemma is similar to the one from Theorem 2, therefore we skip it. Moreover, likewise [1] and as highlighted there, the subset T_λ may differ across the values of λ, which results in the claim that the protocol π is non-uniform.

Reputation Vector Criteria for $\mathsf{Rep}^n_{\mathbb{S}}$. The earlier Lemma 3 shows that given a subset of parties T it is possible to compute a functionality $\mathcal{F}$ with respect to $\mathsf{Rep}^n_{\mathbb{S}}$. However it says nothing regarding when $\mathsf{Rep}^n_{\mathbb{S}}$ gives a subset with an honest majority except with negligible probability. Here, once again due to the similarity of the proofs, in particular with the Lemma 2, we will skip them for the next lemmas.

Lemma 4. *Let $m(\cdot)$, $n(\cdot)$ and $\mathsf{Rep}^n_{\mathbb{S}}$ be defined as earlier. For every λ and subset $T_\lambda \subseteq \mathcal{U}$. If there is a series of subsets $\{T_\lambda\}_{\lambda \in \mathbb{N}}$, with $|T_\lambda| = m$, and*

- *all honest regular participants $\mathcal{U}_h \subseteq \mathcal{U}$, with $|\mathcal{U}| = n$, assign trust* only *to honest participants within $\mathcal{U}$, and $\Delta_{T_\lambda} \stackrel{def}{=} \frac{\mathbb{S}(\mathcal{U}_h)}{\mathbb{S}} - \frac{|T_\lambda|}{2}$, such that $\frac{(\Delta_{T_\lambda})^2}{|T_\lambda|} = \omega(\log \lambda)$;*
- *for the subset of honest regular participants $\mathcal{U}_h$, it holds that*

$$\frac{\mathbb{S}(\mathcal{U}_h)}{\mathbb{S}} > \left\lfloor \frac{m}{2} \right\rfloor + \omega(\sqrt{m \cdot \log m}),$$

then there exists a negligible function $\mu(\cdot)$ such that for every λ,

$$\Pr_{I \leftarrow \mathsf{r}^{n(\lambda)}}\left[|T_\lambda \cap I| \leq \frac{m}{2}\right] \leq \mu(\lambda).$$

Given the Lemmas 3 and 4, which, respectively, give us the existence of a suitable subset T, and a criteria for finding such subset, thus we can conclude, analogously to Theorem 2, but now for subsets, the following

Theorem 3. *Given the set of regular participants $\mathcal{U}$ with access to a ledger $\mathcal{L}$ and a trust assignment functionality $\mathcal{F}_T$. Let $\mathcal{F} = \{f^m\}_{m\in\mathbb{N}}$ be a functionality, $m(\cdot)$, $n(\cdot)$ and $\mathsf{Rep}^n_{\mathbb{S}}$ be defined as earlier. Now assume that the following conditions hold*

- *there is a series of subsets $\{T_\lambda\}_{\lambda\in\mathbb{N}}$, with $|T_\lambda| = m$, such that $\Delta_{T_\lambda} \stackrel{def}{=} \frac{\mathbb{S}(\mathcal{U}_h)}{\mathbb{S}} - \frac{m}{2}$ and $\frac{(\Delta_{T_\lambda})^2}{m} = \omega(\log\lambda)$;*
- *all honest regular participants $\mathcal{U}_h \subseteq \mathcal{U}$ assign trust* only *to honest participants within $\mathcal{U}$;*
- *for the subset of honest regular participants $\mathcal{U}_h$, it holds that*

$$\frac{\mathbb{S}(\mathcal{U}_h)}{\mathbb{S}} > \left\lfloor \frac{m}{2} \right\rfloor + \omega(\sqrt{m\cdot\log m}),$$

then there is (non-uniform) protocol π which securely computes *$\mathcal{F}$ with respect to $(m(\cdot), \mathsf{Rep}^n_{\mathbb{S}})$.*

Finding a Conservative Subset T via Stake. The generation of the subset T_λ or an equally valid subset given the non-uniformity of the protocol, is as straightforward as presented in [1]. The idea is to sort out the participants $\mathcal{U}$ in decreasing order of reputation, and then selecting the highest reputable members of the set. What differs from [1] is that, here, we rely primarily on the stakes of each member of the set as they are published on $\mathcal{L}$. Concretely, let $u_{i_1}, \ldots, u_{i_n}$ be the members of $\mathcal{U}$ sorted in decreasing order of reputation, as they were provided by $\mathsf{Rep}^n_{\mathbb{S}}$, and each respective stake $\mathbb{S}(u_{i_1}), \ldots, \mathbb{S}(u_{i_n})$ in $\mathcal{L}$. Then

1. for every $j = 1, \ldots, n$, compute $\Delta_j = \sum_{k=1}^{j} \frac{\mathbb{S}(u_{i_k})}{\mathbb{S}} - \lfloor \frac{j}{2} \rfloor$;
2. if j^* is the index such that $\frac{(\Delta_{j^*})^2}{j^*}$ is maximum over all indexes j, then output the set $T = \{i_1, \ldots, i_{j^*}\}$.

Roughly the above routine shows a conservative approach. That is, it *always* selects the highest reputation among the reputation vectors. Without a change in the reputation vector, the output of the selected T set remains the same.

6.2 Revisiting Reputation-Fair Lottery [17]

Given the early description for finding a subset T with the guarantees it contains an honest majority with high probability. However, as already mentioned, and also pointed out in [17], the earlier method for finding T is not suitable because members with low reputation score would not be selected. An alternative method was introduced by [17] and it is not based on the conservative approach from [1], but on partition of the candidate set, which in our case is $\mathcal{U}$. Each partition, or *tier*, $\mathcal{P}_i$ would aggregate users $u_j \in \mathcal{U}$ with similar reputation score, such that for a number of w tiers, $\mathcal{U} = \bigcup_{i=1}^{w} \mathcal{P}_i$. The procedure associates, for each set $\mathcal{P}_i$, a fixed number $\ell_i \in \mathbb{N}$ representing the number of participants to be picked in a random fashion on each sampling.

Given this setting, roughly, the procedure would progress in rounds. In the first round it randomly picks the set $\widehat{\mathcal{P}_1} \xleftarrow{\$} \mathcal{P}_1$ with $|\widehat{\mathcal{P}_1}| = \ell_1$, in the second round it randomly picks the set $\widehat{\mathcal{P}_2} \xleftarrow{\$} \mathcal{P}_1 \bigcup \mathcal{P}_2$, with $|\widehat{\mathcal{P}_2}| = \ell_2$, until $i = n$. It is not hard to understand the difference from the previous method, since this approach would even provide chances for participants with lower reputation scores, given that the tiers are sorted in decreasing order, *i.e.* members of $\mathcal{P}_n$ have the lowest reputation scores.

The authors in [17] formally showed that, with access to a reputation system Rep that presents the so called *feasibility* property, *i.e.* guarantee of an honest majority under right conditions, their introduced algorithm for lottery, say, $\mathsf{L}^{\mathsf{Rep}}$, which is based on partitioning the set $\mathcal{U}$ is *fair* for suitable definition of *reputation fairness* they provide. Given that the analogous *feasibility* property in our work is the Lemma 4, we have the following corollary.

Corollary 1. *Let $n(\cdot)$, $\mathcal{U}$ and $\mathsf{Rep}^n_{\mathbb{S}}$, with $|\mathcal{U}| = n$, be defined as before. For every λ, there is a series of subsets $\{T_\lambda\}_{\lambda \in \mathbb{N}}$ with $|T_\lambda| = m$. If the following hold*

- *all honest regular participants $\mathcal{U}_h \subseteq \mathcal{U}$, assign trust* only *to honest participants within $\mathcal{U}$, and $\Delta_{T_\lambda} \stackrel{def}{=} \frac{\mathbb{S}(\mathcal{U}_h)}{\mathbb{S}} - \frac{m}{2}$, such that $\frac{(\Delta_{T_\lambda})^2}{m} = \omega(\log \lambda)$;*
- *for the subset of honest regular participants $\mathcal{U}_h$, it holds that*

$$\frac{\mathbb{S}(\mathcal{U}_h)}{\mathbb{S}} > \left\lfloor \frac{m}{2} \right\rfloor + \omega(\sqrt{m \cdot \log m}),$$

then there is a lottery algorithm $\mathsf{L}^{(\cdot)}$, such that $\mathsf{L}^{\mathsf{Rep}^n_{\mathbb{S}}}$ is reputation-fair.

The proof of the corollary is immediate as one should notice that given the initial conditions, which are the same as in Lemma 4, the set $\mathcal{U}$ yields a subset with an honest majority which is the only requirement for the reputation system from Theorem 1 in [17]. Thus, $\mathsf{L}^{\mathsf{Rep}^n_{\mathbb{S}}}$ is reputation-fair as $\mathsf{L}^{(\cdot)}$ is the lottery algorithm given in [17].

7 Final Remarks

We have extended the Core Wallet Functionality from [13]. In addition to its regular stake delegation use, our proposed $\mathcal{F}_{\mathcal{T}}$ allows a participant of the PoS consensus protocol to "assign trust", without harming the ledger consensus protocol. The immediate consequence is that we could propose in this work the creation of a reputation system based on the stake of the "trust assigners". This concrete design of a reputation system allowed us to revisit the works of [1] and [17] which deals with the performing of relevant MPC protocols and the construction of proof of reputation protocol resistant to sybil attacks given the stake distribution underpinning the system, *i.e.* the PoS consensus protocol.

Our work is relevant because given the existing global PoS ledger in place, groups of users can gather and build reputation around a context of their choice. Furthermore, each honest participant, based on which of the other participants it trusts, can individually verify whether a certain group of players, say $\mathcal{T}$, who jointly received the trust assignments from a community of other players, yields an honest majority. This verification can be done just by simple checking of the ledger and verifying the stake distribution with respect to the trust assignments. This is an enhancement in comparison to [1,17]. Although these works do deal with reputation, they do not provide insights on how the reputation score is computed nor how it can be verified. Let alone to integrate them in concrete, and deployed, PoS ledgers.

A drawback of the work is that the guarantees of an honest majority are based on the public perception of honesty of the trustees, which can be misleading. However, given that the trust assignment of our construction is very dynamic and publicly verifiable, once a misbehavior trustee is identified, the trust assignment can be easily revoked by the users, which promotes accountability of actions by the trustees.

References

1. Asharov, G., Lindell, Y., Zarosim, H.: Fair and Efficient Secure Multiparty Computation with Reputation Systems. In: Sako, K., Sarkar, P. (eds.) ASIACRYPT 2013. LNCS, vol. 8270, pp. 201–220. Springer, Heidelberg (2013). https://doi.org/10.1007/978-3-642-42045-0_11
2. Badertscher, C., Gaži, P., Kiayias, A., Russell, A., Zikas, V.: Ouroboros genesis: composable proof-of-stake blockchains with dynamic availability. In: Proceedings of the 2018 ACM SIGSAC Conference on Computer and Communications Security, CCS 2018, pp. 913–930. ACM, New York (2018)
3. Biryukov, A., Feher, D., Khovratovich, D.: Guru: universal reputation module for distributed consensus protocols. Cryptology ePrint Archive, Report 2017/671 (2017). http://eprint.iacr.org/2017/671
4. Canetti, R.: Security and composition of multiparty cryptographic protocols. J. Cryptol. **13**(1), 143–202 (2000)
5. Canetti, R., Dodis, Y., Pass, R., Walfish, S.: Universally composable security with global setup. In: Vadhan, S.P. (ed.) TCC 2007. LNCS, vol. 4392, pp. 61–85. Springer, Heidelberg (2007). https://doi.org/10.1007/978-3-540-70936-7_4
6. Damgård, I., Ishai, Y.: Constant-round multiparty computation using a black-box pseudorandom generator. In: Shoup, V. (ed.) CRYPTO 2005. LNCS, vol. 3621, pp. 378–394. Springer, Heidelberg (2005). https://doi.org/10.1007/11535218_23
7. David, B., Gaži, P., Kiayias, A., Russell, A.: Ouroboros praos: an adaptively-secure, semi-synchronous proof-of-stake protocol. Cryptology ePrint Archive, Report 2017/573 (2017). http://eprint.iacr.org/2017/573
8. Dimitriou, T.: Decentralized reputation. Cryptology ePrint Archive, Report 2020/761 (2020). https://eprint.iacr.org/2020/761
9. Goldreich, O., Micali, S., Wigderson, A.: How to play any mental game or a completeness theorem for protocols with honest majority. In: Aho, A. (ed.) 19th ACM STOC, pp. 218–229. ACM Press, May 1987

10. Gutscher, A.: A trust model for an open, decentralized reputation system. In: Etalle, S., Marsh, S. (eds.) IFIPTM 2007. IIFIP, vol. 238, pp. 285–300. Springer, Boston, MA (2007). https://doi.org/10.1007/978-0-387-73655-6_19
11. Hoeffding, W.: Probability inequalities for sums of bounded random variables, pp. 409–426. Springer, New York (1994)
12. Josang, A., Ismail, R., Boyd, C.: A survey of trust and reputation systems for online service provision. Decis. Support Syst. **43**(2), 618–644 (2007)
13. Karakostas, D., Kiayias, A., Larangeira, M.: Account Management in Proof of Stake Ledgers. In: Galdi, C., Kolesnikov, V. (eds.) SCN 2020. LNCS, vol. 12238, pp. 3–23. Springer, Cham (2020). https://doi.org/10.1007/978-3-030-57990-6_1
14. Kerber, T., Kiayias, A., Kohlweiss, M.: Kachina - foundations of private smart contracts. In: 2021 2021 IEEE 34th Computer Security Foundations Symposium (CSF), pp. 47–62. IEEE Computer Society, Los Alamitos, June 2021
15. Kerber, T., Kiayias, A., Kohlweiss, M., Zikas, V.: Ouroboros crypsinous: privacy-preserving proof-of-stake. In: 2019 IEEE Symposium on Security and Privacy, pp. 157–174. IEEE Computer Society Press, May 2019
16. Kiayias, A., Russell, A., David, B., Oliynykov, R.: Ouroboros: A Provably Secure Proof-of-Stake Blockchain Protocol. In: Katz, J., Shacham, H. (eds.) CRYPTO 2017. LNCS, vol. 10401, pp. 357–388. Springer, Cham (2017). https://doi.org/10.1007/978-3-319-63688-7_12
17. Kleinrock, L., Ostrovsky, R., Zikas, V.: Proof-of-Reputation Blockchain with Nakamoto Fallback. In: Bhargavan, K., Oswald, E., Prabhakaran, M. (eds.) INDOCRYPT 2020. LNCS, vol. 12578, pp. 16–38. Springer, Cham (2020). https://doi.org/10.1007/978-3-030-65277-7_2
18. Wuille, P.: Decentralized identifiers (dids) v1.0 (2021). https://en.bitcoin.it/wiki/BIP_0032. Accessed 23 Feb 2021

Fault and Side-Channel Attack

Key-Recovery by Side-Channel Information on the Matrix-Vector Product in Code-Based Cryptosystems

Boly Seck[1,2(✉)], Pierre-Louis Cayrel[2], Idy Diop[1], Vlad-Florin Dragoi[4], Kalen Couzon[3], Brice Colombier[2], and Vincent Grosso[2]

[1] ESP, Laboratoire d'imagerie médicale et de Bio-informatique, Dakar, Senegal
seck.boly@ugb.edu.sn

[2] Univ Lyon, UJM-Saint-Etienne, CNRS, Laboratoire Hubert Curien UMR 5516, 42023 Saint-Etienne, France
{pierre.louis.cayrel,b.colombier,vincent.grosso}@univ-st-etienne.fr

[3] Univ de Versailles Saint-Quentin, Yvelines, France
kalen.couzon@ens.uvsq.fr

[4] Faculty of Exact Sciences, Aurel Vlaicu University, Arad, Romania
vlad.dragoi@uav.ro

Abstract. The modern security protocols in most of our systems rely primarily on three basic functions of asymmetric cryptography: public key encryption, digital signature, and key exchange. Today, we only do key exchange (TLS 1.3) with the ECDH protocol. The confidentiality is persistent because the session keys are discarded at the end and to certify this key exchange, we sign it with RSA or ECDSA. However, these cryptosystems are at least theoretically attackable in a quantum computer model. Thus the NIST PQC standardization process has given significant momentum to research on code-based public-key cryptosystems specifically. Their security is based on the hardness of the syndrome decoding problem. In this article, we first propose a new formalism of the matrix-vector product in based-code cryptography. Second, we present a chosen-ciphertext attack on the first step of Niederreiter decryption by solving the matrix-vector product problem with side-channel information. Finally, we put this result to recover secret information in code-based cryptosystems including some candidates for the extension of the NIST PQC normalization process.

Keywords: Code-based cryptography · Side-channel attack · Matrix-vector product problem · NIST PQC standardization

1 Introduction

In recent years, a lot of research has been done on quantum computers [14,17,32]. These are computers that exploit the phenomena of quantum mechanics to solve difficult mathematical problems in number theory, such as the Integer

S.-H. Seo and H. Seo (Eds.): ICISC 2022, LNCS 13849, pp. 219–234, 2023.
https://doi.org/10.1007/978-3-031-29371-9_6

Factorization Problem or the Discrete Logarithm Problem. Shor [28] proved that if large-scale quantum computers are built, they will be able to break most of the current asymmetric cryptography like RSA, ECDSA, and ECDH schemes. This would seriously compromise the confidentiality and integrity of all digital communications.

Since then, cryptographic community proposed alternative solutions which remain safe in the quantum era. These schemes are called post-quantum resistant. In 2016, the National Institute of Standards and Technology (NIST) made a call to the community to propose post-quantum secure solutions for standardization. The process consists of several rounds, and only some of the candidates in each round are chosen to enter the next round. The most popular approaches are those based on the search for low-weight words for lattice, the problem of decoding random codes, solving multivariate polynomial systems, isogenies, and hash functions [5,7]. Lattice-based cryptography has the reputation of being very efficient. Code-based cryptography using some codes is often considered to be already more mature and reliable such as McEliece [23] and Niederreiter [25] cryptosystems.

The majority of code-based post-quantum cryptosystems base their security on the classic hard problem in code-based cryptography: the binary Syndrome Decoding Problem (SDP). Informally, for a binary linear code $\mathcal{C}$ of length n and dimension k, having a parity-check matrix $\boldsymbol{H}$, the SDP is defined as follows: given $\boldsymbol{s} \in \mathbb{F}_2^{n-k}$, find a binary vector $\boldsymbol{x}$ having less than t values equal to one, such that $\boldsymbol{H}\boldsymbol{x} = \boldsymbol{s}$. The best algorithm to solve this problem in this original version is the Information Set Decoding (ISD) proposed by Prange [27]. The ISD techniques are considered the best strategy for message recovery. It consists, in randomly permuting the matrix $\boldsymbol{H}$ (denote $\boldsymbol{P}$ such a permutation) until the support of the permuted $\boldsymbol{x}$ is included in the set $\{0, \ldots, n-k-1\}$, *i.e.*, the set where the $\boldsymbol{HP}$ is in upper triangular form. It has been considerably improved since then [3,18,19,21,22,29], although the complexity remains exponential in t.

A recent possible solution to solve the syndrome decoding problem is to use Integer Linear Programming (ILP). The idea was first proposed by Feldman [11] and later improved by Feldman *et al.* [12]. Since the initial problem is nonlinear, some relaxation was proposed in order to decrease the complexity. Most recently, Cayrel *et al.* [9] showed that the SDP becomes considerably easier to solve if the syndrome is computed in $\mathbb{N}$. They perform a laser fault injection attack on the matrix-vector product when computing the syndrome in the encapsulation of *Classic McEliece*. This allows them by corrupting some specific instructions during this operation to have a syndrome in $\mathbb{N}$. To solve the syndrome decoding problem in $\mathbb{N}$, they propose to define the SDP as an ILP inspired by the ideas of Tanatmis *et al.* [33]. The complexity of recovering the secret message from the faulty syndrome is polynomial $\mathcal{O}(n^2)$ with an optimized version of their algorithm.

Afterwards, Colombier *et al.* [10] proposed to perform a message-recovery attack in *Classic McEliece* that relies on side-channel information only instead of laser fault injection in the previous work [9]. The latter depends on the very strong attacker model and does not apply to optimized implementations of the algorithm that make optimal usage of the machine words capacity. Improvements include the power consumption analysis that is sufficient to obtain an integer syndrome using machine learning techniques. To recover the secret message they use the computationally-efficient score function and known information-set decoding methods.

Contribution: In this work, a key-recovery chosen-ciphertext attack against code-based cryptosystems is performed. We analyze in particular the secret operation of matrix-vector multiplication in Niederreiter decryption using a physical attack. First, we will introduce a new formalism in code-based cryptography. Informally, for $\boldsymbol{z}$ in $\mathbb{F}_2^{n-k}$ of any weight, the Matrix-Vector Product Problem (MVPP) is defined as follows: given $\boldsymbol{z}^*$ in $\mathbb{N}^{n-k}$, find $\boldsymbol{S} \in \mathbb{F}_2^{(n-k)\times(n-k)}$ such that $\boldsymbol{S}\boldsymbol{z}^T = \boldsymbol{z}^*$. To get $\boldsymbol{z}^*$ in $\mathbb{N}^{n-k}$, we will use the same method of the power analysis attack in [10]. This method is based on side-channel analysis using random forests to recover $\boldsymbol{z}^*$ from the Hamming weight information obtained from the matrix-vector product in the first step of Niederreiter decryption. Second, we show that if we can construct the matrix $\boldsymbol{Z}^* = (\boldsymbol{z}_1^*, \cdots, \boldsymbol{z}_{n-k}^*)$ correctly, we can directly find the secret of the cryptosystem. We obtain directly the secret without solving the syndrome decoding problem unlike in [9,10] and this is applicable for most of the code-based cryptosystems.

Organization: The paper is organized as follows. In Sect. 2, we focus on code-based cryptosystems, and in particular on the results of the NIST PQC competition. Section 2.1 defines the new formalism in code-based cryptography, the Matrix-Vector Product Problem (MVPP). In Sect. 3, we present our attack on the matrix-vector product in Niederreiter decryption using a side-channel attack. Finally, we conclude this paper in Sect. 4.

2 Code-Based Cryptosystems

2.1 Encoding Theory

Notations. The following conventions and notations are used. A finite field is denoted by $\mathbb{F}$, and the ring of integers by $\mathbb{N}$. Vectors (column vectors) and matrices are written in bold, *e.g.*, a binary vector of length n is $\boldsymbol{x} \in \{0,1\}^n$, an $m \times n$ integer matrix is $\boldsymbol{A} = (a_{i,j})_{\substack{0\leq i\leq m-1\\ 0\leq j\leq n-1}} \in \mathcal{M}_{m,n}(\mathbb{N})$. $\boldsymbol{A}[i]$ denotes the i-th line of $\boldsymbol{A}$ and a row sub-matrix of $\boldsymbol{A}$ indexed by a set $I \subseteq \{0,\ldots,m-1\}$ is denoted by $\boldsymbol{A}_I, = (a_{i,j})_{\substack{i\in I\\ 0\leq j\leq n-1}}$. The same applies to column vectors, *i.e.*, $\boldsymbol{x}_I$ is the sub-vector induced by the set I on $\boldsymbol{x}$.

Error-Correcting Codes. An $[n,k]$ linear code $\mathcal{C}$ over $\mathbb{F}_q$ is a vector subspace of $\mathbb{F}_q^n$, where k, n are positive integers with $k < n$. The elements of $\mathcal{C}$ are called codewords. The support of a codeword $\mathsf{Supp}(\boldsymbol{c})$ is the set of non-zero positions of $\boldsymbol{c}$. We will represent a code either by its generator matrix $\boldsymbol{G} \in \mathbb{F}_q^{k\times n}$ such that its lines form a basis of the vector space $\mathcal{C}$, or by its parity-check matrix, $\boldsymbol{H} \in \mathbb{F}_q^{(n-k)\times n}$, where $\boldsymbol{H}\boldsymbol{G}^T = \boldsymbol{0}$ holds. One of the key elements of decoding is the use of metrics. In the Hamming metric, we consider codes with coefficients in $\mathbb{F}_q$ (generally, $\mathbb{F}_2$).

Definition 1 (Hamming metric). *Let $\boldsymbol{x} \in \mathbb{F}_2$, the Hamming weight $\mathsf{wt}(\boldsymbol{x})$ is the number of non null coordinates in $\boldsymbol{x}$, and the distance between two vectors $\boldsymbol{x}$ and $\boldsymbol{y}$ is the number of non null coordinates in $\mathsf{wt}(\boldsymbol{x}-\boldsymbol{y})$.*

The hardness of general decoding for a linear code is an $\mathcal{NP}$-complete problem in coding theory [4]. This is the syndrome decoding problem (SDP), which is the hard problem in code-based cryptography.

Definition 2 (Binary-SDP). *Let $\boldsymbol{H} \in \mathbb{F}_2^{(n-k)\times n}$, a vector $\boldsymbol{s} \in \mathbb{F}_2^{n-k}$ and $t \in \mathbb{N}$. The syndrome decoding problem is to find $\boldsymbol{x} \in \mathbb{F}_2^n$ such that $\boldsymbol{H}\boldsymbol{x}^T = \boldsymbol{s}$ and $\mathsf{wt}(\boldsymbol{x}) \leq t$.*

The best-known algorithms for solving this problem are all exponential in t. Except if the syndrome is computed in $\mathbb{N}$ instead of $\mathbb{F}_2$ [9].

Definition 3 ($\mathbb{N}$-SDP). *Let $\boldsymbol{H} \in \mathcal{M}_{n-k,n}(\mathbb{N})$, with $h_{i,j} \in \{0,1\}$ for all i,j, a vector $\boldsymbol{s} \in \mathbb{N}^{n-k}$ and $t \in \mathbb{N}^*$. The syndrome decoding problem in $\mathbb{N}$ is to find $\boldsymbol{x} \in \mathbb{N}^n$ with $x_i \in \{0,1\}$ such that $\boldsymbol{H}\boldsymbol{x}^T = \boldsymbol{s}$ and $\mathsf{wt}(\boldsymbol{x}) \leq t$.*

$\boldsymbol{H}$ and $\boldsymbol{x}$ are sampled in the same way as for the binary SDP, only the matrix-vector multiplication operation changes, and thus its result $\boldsymbol{s}$.

Thus we define the new problem on the matrix-vector product as follows,

Definition 4 (Binay-Matrix-Vector Product Problem (MVPP)). *Let $\boldsymbol{z} \in \mathbb{F}_2^{n-k}$ of any weight, a vector $\boldsymbol{z}^* \in \mathbb{N}^{n-k}$. The matrix-vector product problem is to find $\boldsymbol{S} \in \mathbb{F}^{(n-k)\times(n-k)}$ such that $\boldsymbol{S}\boldsymbol{z}^T = \boldsymbol{z}^*$.*

We can find $\boldsymbol{z}^*$ for side-channel information with power consumption analysis and then with a chosen-ciphertext attack we find $\boldsymbol{S}$.

2.2 NIST PQC Standardization - Results

On July 5, 2022, NIST released the first four winning algorithms from a campaign launched in 2016 to standardize post-quantum cryptographic algorithms. These future standards will be default options for selecting post-quantum algorithms in the majority of security products. Provided that these post-quantum algorithms are also combined with proven classical algorithms through hybrid mechanisms. The main goal of the process started by NIST is to replace three standards that are considered the most vulnerable to quantum attacks, *i.e.*, FIPS 186-4[1] (for digital signatures), NIST SP 800-56A[2], and NIST SP 800-56B[3](both for keys

[1] https://nvlpubs.nist.gov/nistpubs/FIPS/NIST.FIPS.186-4.pdf.
[2] https://nvlpubs.nist.gov/nistpubs/SpecialPublications/NIST.SP.800-56Ar2.pdf.
[3] https://nvlpubs.nist.gov/nistpubs/SpecialPublications/NIST.SP.800-56Br1.pdf.

establishment in public-key cryptography). For the first round of this competition, 69 candidates met the minimum criteria and the requirements imposed by NIST. 26 out of 69 were announced on January 30, 2019, for moving to the second round. Of these, 17 are public-key encryption and/or key-establishment schemes and 9 are digital signature schemes. In July 2020, NIST started the third round of this process where only seven finalists were admitted (four PKE/KEM and three signature schemes). In addition to the finalists, eight alternate candidates were selected.

The first four algorithms selected are a key establishment algorithm named CRYSTALS-Kyber; and three digital signature algorithms named CRYSTALS-Dilithium, FALCON, and SPHINCS+. The first three of these algorithms are based on structured lattices; the last one, SPHINCS+ is a hash-based signature scheme. These four algorithms will therefore be used as the basis for writing U.S. federal standards. The scope of the NIST announcement is international with strong involvement of the cryptography research community, which will make the future US standards also used as de facto international industry standards. Beside the four winners, an extension of the NIST PQC standardization campaign (4th round) is planned for four key establishment algorithms: BIKE [1], HQC [24], *Classic McEliece* [2] (all three based on error-correcting codes), and SIKE [16] (isogeny graphs-based). *Classic McEliece* was the first selected finalist as a key encapsulation mechanism, while BIKE and HQC were alternative candidates. The latter two use special codes to reduce the size of the public key, which is considered the main drawback of code-based cryptosystems.

Classic McEliece is a code-based scheme using binary Goppa codes, the same codes that McEliece originally proposed in [23]. During Round 2 the scheme merged with NTS-KEM, which was using the same codes. The Classic McEliece scheme uses the dual of McEliece's scheme, as proposed by Niederreiter [25], and tightly turns this OW-CPA PKE into an IND-CCA2 KEM.

BIKE (Bit Flipping Key Encapsulation) is a key encapsulation mechanism (KEM) based on quasi-cyclic codes with moderate density parity check matrices. The code structure in BIKE is public and allows to reduce the size of the public key. Bit flipping corrects errors by repeatedly flipping the input bits that, given the secret moderate-density parity checks, seem most likely to be errors.

HQC (Hamming Quasi-Cyclic) uses error-correcting codes built from Reed-Muller and Reed-Solomon. The public key includes a random $\boldsymbol{h}$ and $\boldsymbol{s} = \boldsymbol{x} + \boldsymbol{h} \cdot \boldsymbol{y}$, where $\boldsymbol{x}, \boldsymbol{y}$ are secretes and small Hamming weights. The ciphertext includes $\boldsymbol{u} = \boldsymbol{r}_1 + \boldsymbol{r}_2 \cdot \boldsymbol{h}$ and $\boldsymbol{v} = \mathbf{M} + \boldsymbol{s} \cdot \boldsymbol{r}_2 + \boldsymbol{e}$, where $\boldsymbol{r}_1, \boldsymbol{r}_2, \boldsymbol{e}$ are small Hamming weights and $\mathbf{M}$ is a message encoded using an error-correcting code. The receiver computes $\boldsymbol{v} - \boldsymbol{u} \cdot \boldsymbol{y} = \mathbf{M} + \boldsymbol{s} \cdot \boldsymbol{r}_2 + \boldsymbol{e} - \boldsymbol{u} \cdot \boldsymbol{y}$, which is close to $\mathbf{M}$ since $\boldsymbol{x}, \boldsymbol{y}, \boldsymbol{r}_1, \boldsymbol{r}_2, \boldsymbol{e}$ are small, and decodes the error-correcting code to recover $\mathbf{M}$.

SIKE (Supersingular Isogeny Key Encapsulation) is a key encapsulation mechanism based on the hard problem of pseudo-random walks in supersingular isogeny graphs. SIKE is a relatively new problem in the cryptographic arena and currently undergoing several attacks like its instantiation SIDH (Supersingular Isogeny Diffie-Hellman key exchange protocol) [8,13,20,34,35]. These are key recovery attacks, reduces of the level security, side-channel attacks, and fault injection.

Some of these algorithms could therefore later join the same standardization process as the four algorithms already selected. The final objective of NIST is indeed to be able to standardize a varied range of algorithms to cover a majority of use cases. Most of these constructions based on error-correcting codes use matrix-vector products in the decryption, as in Niederreiter's scheme (Table 1).

The goal of our attack is to find the secrete matrix $\boldsymbol{Q}$. But first, let's assume that we already have the result of the product $\boldsymbol{Q}^{-1}\boldsymbol{z}$ in $\mathbb{N}$ using the same technique as in [10].

Table 1. Niederreiter PKE scheme

$\mathsf{KeyGen}(n, k, t) = (\mathsf{pk}, \mathsf{sk})$
$\boldsymbol{H}$-parity-check of $\mathcal{C}$ that corrects t errors An $n \times n$ permutation matrix $\boldsymbol{P}$ An $(n-k) \times (n-k)$ invertible matrix $\boldsymbol{Q}$ Compute $\boldsymbol{H}_{\text{pub}} = \boldsymbol{QHP}$
$\mathsf{pk} = (\boldsymbol{H}_{\text{pub}}, t)$ $\mathsf{sk} = (\boldsymbol{Q}, \boldsymbol{H}, \boldsymbol{P})$
$\mathsf{Encrypt}(\boldsymbol{m}, \mathsf{pk}) = \boldsymbol{z}$
Encode $\boldsymbol{m} \rightarrow \boldsymbol{e}$ \\ error vector of $\mathsf{wt}(\boldsymbol{e}) = t$
$\boldsymbol{z} = \boldsymbol{H}_{\text{pub}}\boldsymbol{e}$
$\mathsf{Decrypt}(\boldsymbol{z}, \mathsf{sk}) = \boldsymbol{m}$
Compute $\boldsymbol{z}^* = \boldsymbol{Q}^{-1}\boldsymbol{z} = \boldsymbol{Sz}$ \\ target of our attack $\boldsymbol{z}^* = \boldsymbol{HPe}$ $\boldsymbol{e}^* = \mathcal{D}ecode(\boldsymbol{z}^*, \boldsymbol{H})$ Retrieve $\boldsymbol{m}$ from $\boldsymbol{P}^{-1}\boldsymbol{e}^*$

3 Our Attack and Results

3.1 On the Decryption of Niederreiter

Our attack on Niederreiter's decryption is now described. It consists in directly finding the secret matrix $\boldsymbol{Q}$. In the following, we note $\boldsymbol{S} = \boldsymbol{Q}^{-1} \in \mathbb{F}_2^{(n-k)\times(n-k)}$. We assume that, we can recover the result of the matrix-vector product $\boldsymbol{Sz}$ in $\mathbb{N}$ ($\boldsymbol{z}^* \in \mathbb{N}^{n-k}$) with side-channel information as in [10].

Profiled Side-Channel Measurements. We performed side-channel measurements during the computation of the product $\boldsymbol{Sz}$ in the Niederreiter decryption implementation. The vector $\boldsymbol{z}^*$ is computed as the matrix-vector product $\boldsymbol{Sz} = \boldsymbol{z}^*$. We have recorded a single trace that will be sufficient to form the training set for the profiled attack. This trace is composed of n samples and stored as a row vector. We chose the ciphertexts $\boldsymbol{z}_i$ in $\mathbb{F}_2^{(n-k)}$ linearly independent as the inputs of the matrix-vector product algorithm. In addition, we stored a second trace, used as a test set when training the classifier. For both traces, we also stored the Hamming weights of the intermediate value resulting from the matrix-vector product $\boldsymbol{Sz}_i$.

After the traces acquisition, we performed an adequate preprocessing for reducing the dimension (eight dimensions since there are nine possible values for the Hamming weight of a byte) of the data by Linear Discriminant Analysis (LDA) to make it easier to handle by the classifier. We chose the random forest algorithm, used previously for side-channel analysis with good results [15], to recover the Hamming weight of $\boldsymbol{z}^*$.

We obtained the Hamming weight of the intermediate value of the product $\boldsymbol{Sz}_i$, we derived the entries of $\boldsymbol{z}^*$ in $\mathbb{N}$ with 98.65% accuracy. Indeed, the Hamming distance between two consecutive intermediate values is exactly the number of 1's found in the bitwise AND between the row of the matrix $\boldsymbol{S}$ and the byte of the ciphertext $\boldsymbol{z}$. Computing the value of the integer $\boldsymbol{z}^*$ entry is equivalent to counting those ones, which in turn is equivalent to summing the Hamming distances between consecutive intermediate values (the absolute value of the difference of their Hamming weights). In our implementation ($n = 6,960$, $k = 5,413$ and $t = 119$), the Hamming distance between two consecutive intermediate values is small and satisfies the condition in [10, Equation (3)] to recover the entries of $\boldsymbol{z}^*$ in $\mathbb{N}$ with good accuracy (82% for Hamming distance).

Course of the Attack. We propose a chosen-ciphertext attack that essentially consists of 4 steps:

Step 1. We choose the ciphertexts or vectors $\boldsymbol{z}_i$ in $\mathbb{F}_2^{(n-k)}$ linearly independent. We therefore define a matrix $\boldsymbol{Z} = (\boldsymbol{z}_1, \cdots, \boldsymbol{z}_{n-k})$ which is invertible.

Step 2. For each vector $\boldsymbol{z}_i$ thanks to the side-channel attack, we have the vector $\boldsymbol{z}_i^* = \boldsymbol{Sz}_i$ in $\mathbb{N}$ (in reality we get the Hamming weight for each component). This gives us a new matrix $\boldsymbol{Z}^* = (\boldsymbol{z}_1^*, \cdots, \boldsymbol{z}_{n-k}^*)$.

Step 3. We solve a matrix system $\boldsymbol{SZ} = \boldsymbol{Z}^*$ with $\boldsymbol{S}$ the unknown matrix in $\mathbb{F}_2^{(n-k)\times(n-k)}$. Since $\boldsymbol{Z}$ is invertible, we multiply on the right-hand side by its inverse and we obtain

$$\boldsymbol{S} = \boldsymbol{Z}^* \boldsymbol{Z}^{-1}. \tag{1}$$

Then we just have to read the entries of the right matrix to get the values of $\boldsymbol{S}$ and thus the secret matrix $\boldsymbol{Q}$. A toy example is described in the Appendix A.

The attack as presented above allows to find the secret matrix directly. However, in Step 2, we can raise two questions:

1. Can we know if the matrix $\boldsymbol{Z}^*$ is not correct?

2. If so, how can we correct the errors and find the secret matrix $\boldsymbol{S}$?

We will discuss question 2 in Sect. 3.2. For the first point, we assume that in Step 2 we obtain the matrix $\boldsymbol{Z}^{**}$ instead of $\boldsymbol{Z}^{*}$. So we have

$$\boldsymbol{S}' = \boldsymbol{Z}^{**}\boldsymbol{Z}^{-1} \tag{2}$$

and

$$\boldsymbol{Z}^{**} = \boldsymbol{Z}^{*} + \boldsymbol{E}_r \tag{3}$$

where $\boldsymbol{E}_r$ is an error matrix.

How to distinguish $\boldsymbol{S}$ from $\boldsymbol{S}'$?

We know that $\boldsymbol{S}$ is an invertible matrix in $\mathbb{F}_2$. Thus it's enough to look directly at its coefficients and compute its determinant.

We have shown that our attack allows us to directly find the secret matrix $\boldsymbol{Q}$ in the case where there is no error in Step 2. Otherwise, we know how to detect it. We have two levels of optimization of this attack either minimize the risk of errors when recovering the matrix $\boldsymbol{Z}^{*}$ or reduce its coefficients modulo an integer number to speed up the computations. We can judiciously choose the $\boldsymbol{z}_i$ at step 1, for example, taking $\boldsymbol{z}_i$ of low Hamming weights allow a regularity of the words one "1" by block reduce considerably the risk of errors in the acquisition of traces. Moreover, in this case, we would have $\boldsymbol{Z} = \boldsymbol{I}_{n-k}$ and we obtain the secrete matrix $\boldsymbol{S}$ directly without computing $\boldsymbol{Z}^{-1}$. We can also suppose that the victim does not accept to decrypt $n-k$ ciphertexts for example, but with the choice of ciphertexts with low regular weights we avoid this problem.

We will now see how to correct the errors in the matrix $\boldsymbol{Z}^{*}$ and find the correct matrix $\boldsymbol{S}$.

3.2 Error Correction

In this section, we will provide an answer to question 2 and show that we can indeed find the matrix $\boldsymbol{S}$ in some cases. We consider the case where we have $\boldsymbol{E}_r$ in the matrix $\boldsymbol{Z}^{*}$ at Step 2, Eqs. (2) and (3). We consider two assumptions *h1* et *h2* about $\boldsymbol{E}_r$:

1. The matrix $\boldsymbol{E}_r$ has coefficients 0 or 1, (*h1*).
2. The matrix $\boldsymbol{E}_r$ has, at most, a 1 on each row, (*h2*).

These two assumptions are not restrictive, we will see that we can deduce the general case and we assume that the error can be controlled to some extent, i.e., $\boldsymbol{Z}^{**}$ does not differ "too much" from $\boldsymbol{Z}^{*}$.
According to the above assumptions, there exist two finite sets I and J such that:

$$\boldsymbol{E}_r = \sum_{(i,j)\in I\times J} \boldsymbol{E}_{i,j} \tag{4}$$

with $\boldsymbol{E}_{i,j}$ the square matrix of order $n-k$ where all coefficients are zero, except the one of row i and column j which is 1.

We will need the following lemma:

Lemma 1. *Let $1 \le a, b \le n$. Let $\boldsymbol{M} = (m_{i,j})$ be a square matrix of order $n-k$ then:*

$$\boldsymbol{E}_{a,b}\boldsymbol{M} = \begin{pmatrix} 0 & \cdots & 0 \\ 0 & \cdots & 0 \\ \vdots & \cdots & \vdots \\ m_{b,1} & \cdots & m_{b,n-k} \\ \vdots & \cdots & \vdots \\ 0 & \cdots & 0 \\ 0 & \cdots & 0 \end{pmatrix} \leftarrow a\text{-}th\ row$$

In other words: $[\boldsymbol{E}_{a,b}\boldsymbol{M}]_{i,j} = \begin{cases} 0 & \text{if } i \neq a \\ m_{b,j} & \text{if } i = a \end{cases}$

To find $\boldsymbol{S}$ despite the error in $\boldsymbol{Z}^*$. We have

$$\boldsymbol{S}\boldsymbol{Z} = \boldsymbol{Z}^* + \boldsymbol{E}_r = \boldsymbol{Z}^* + \sum_{(i,j)\in I\times J} \boldsymbol{E}_{i,j}$$

Hence

$$\boldsymbol{S} = \boldsymbol{Z}^*\boldsymbol{Z}^{-1} + \boldsymbol{E}_r\boldsymbol{Z}^{-1} = \boldsymbol{Z}^*\boldsymbol{Z}^{-1} + \sum_{(i,j)\in I\times J} (\boldsymbol{E}_{i,j}\boldsymbol{Z}^{-1})$$

From the above we deduce the following theorem:

Theorem 1. *For any $i \in [1, n-k]$, there exists $j \in [1, n-k]$ and $\varepsilon \in \{0, 1\}$ such that $\boldsymbol{Z}^{**}\boldsymbol{Z}^{-1}[i] - \varepsilon\boldsymbol{Z}^{-1}[j]$ is binary and $\boldsymbol{Z}^{**}\boldsymbol{Z}^{-1}[i] - \varepsilon\boldsymbol{Z}^{-1}[j] = \boldsymbol{S}[i]$.*

Proof. Let us suppose $|I \times J| = 1$, let $I \times J = (a, b)$. Then we have

$$\boldsymbol{S} = \boldsymbol{Z}^*\boldsymbol{Z}^{-1} + \boldsymbol{E}_{a,b}\boldsymbol{Z}^{-1}.$$

According to Lemma 1, only the line a of $\boldsymbol{E}_{a,b}\boldsymbol{Z}^{-1}$ is nonzero.

We deduce that for all $i \neq a$,

$$\boldsymbol{Z}^{**}\boldsymbol{Z}^{-1}[i] = \boldsymbol{S}[i].$$

It is, therefore, sufficient to take $\varepsilon = 0$ and any j.

According to Lemma 1,

$$\boldsymbol{E}_{a,b}\boldsymbol{Z}^{-1}[a] = \boldsymbol{Z}^{-1}[b]$$

and so it suffices to take $\varepsilon = 1$ and $j = b$.

Let $(a, b) \in I \times J$, $(c, d) \in (I \times J) \setminus (a, b)$ and if $|I \times J| \geq 2$, the hypothesis ($h2$) implies that $c \neq a$.

According to Lemma 1, we have

$$\boldsymbol{E}_{c,d}\boldsymbol{Z}^{-1}[a] = 0.$$

thus

$$Z^*Z^{-1}[a] + \sum_{(i,j)\in I\times J} (E_{i,j}Z^{-1}[a]) = Z^*Z^{-1}[a] + E_{a,b}Z^{-1}[a].$$

We thus have, on each line, at most one contribution. We deduce then

1. if $i \notin I$, then $Z^{**}Z^{-1}[i] = S[i]$, it is enough to take $\varepsilon = 0$ and any j.
2. if $i \in I$, then there exists j such that $(i,j) \in I \times J$, we have $Z^{**}Z^{-1}[i] = S[i] + Z^{-1}[j]$, so it is enough to take the j given previously and $\varepsilon = 1$.

We deduce that in some cases, it is possible to find S by the following Algorithm 1.

Algorithm 1. Finding S with errors in Z^*

1: We assume that we can determine the erroneous line(s) of S (for example, S is not binary).
2: Let L_i be an erroneous row of S, we subtract from L_i the rows of the matrix Z^{-1} and keep those that are binary.
3: We thus obtain a list of possible candidates for S and for each candidate matrix, we compute its determinant to check its invertibility in $\mathbb{F}_2$.
4: In particular, if this list is reduced to one element, we obtain S.

We will now lighten the assumptions by deleting (*h2*). According to Theorem 1, we can deduce the general case of our approach.

Corollary 1. *Let $i \in [1, n-k]$, let r_i be the Hamming weight of the vector $E_r[i]$, there exists a sequence $(j_k)_{1\leq k\leq r_i}$ of distinct pairwise elements and a sequence $(\varepsilon_k)_{1\leq k\leq r_i}$ such that*

$$Z^{**}Z^{-1}[i] - \sum Z^{**}Z^{-1}[i] - \sum_{k=1}^{r_i} \varepsilon_k Z^{-1}[j_k] \text{ is binary and } Z^{**}Z^{-1}[i] - \sum_{k=1}^{r_i} \varepsilon_k Z^{-1}[j_k] = S[i].$$

Proof. We use the same notations as before. We suppose that $|I \times J| \geq 2$ (if not, we are in the previous case). Let $(a,b) \in I \times J$.

We try to count the couples (a,t) with t in J. There are as many as the amount of "1" on the row $Er[a]$, in other words, there are r_a couples (a,t).

Let $G_a = \{\,(a,t) \mid t \in J\} = \{(a, j_1), (a, j_2), \cdots, (a, j_{r_a})\}$.

By Lemma 1, for all $c \neq a$ and $d \in J$, the a-th row of $E_{c,d}Z^{-1}$ is zero. We deduce that

$$S[a] = Z^{**}Z^{-1}[a] = Z^*Z^{-1}[a] + E_rZ^{-1}[a] = Z^*Z^{-1}[a] + \sum_{(i,j)\in I\times J} (E_{i,j}Z^{-1})[a]$$

$$= Z^*Z^{-1}[a] + \sum_{k=1}^{r_a} Z^{-1}[j_k].$$

Table 2. McEliece PKE scheme

$\mathsf{KeyGen}(n, k, t) = (\mathsf{pk}, \mathsf{sk})$
G-generator matrix of $\mathcal{C}$ that corrects t errors An $n \times n$ permutation matrix $\boldsymbol{P}$ An $k \times k$ invertible matrix $\boldsymbol{S}$ Compute $\boldsymbol{G}_{\text{pub}} = \boldsymbol{SGP}$
$\mathsf{pk} = (\boldsymbol{G}_{\text{pub}}, t)$ $\mathsf{sk} = (\boldsymbol{S}, \boldsymbol{G}, \boldsymbol{P})$
$\mathsf{Encrypt}(\boldsymbol{m}, \mathsf{pk}) = \boldsymbol{z}$
Encode $\boldsymbol{m} \rightarrow \boldsymbol{c} = \boldsymbol{m}\boldsymbol{G}_{\text{pub}}$
$\boldsymbol{z} = \boldsymbol{c} + \boldsymbol{e}$ \\ $\boldsymbol{e}$ is an error vector of $\mathsf{wt}(\boldsymbol{e}) = t$
$\mathsf{Decrypt}(\boldsymbol{z}, \mathsf{sk}) = \boldsymbol{m}$
Compute $\boldsymbol{z}^* = \boldsymbol{z}\boldsymbol{P}^{-1}$ $\boldsymbol{z}^* = \boldsymbol{mSG} + \boldsymbol{eP}^{-1}$ $\boldsymbol{m}^* = \mathcal{D}ecode(\boldsymbol{z}^*, \boldsymbol{G})$ Retrieve $\boldsymbol{m}$ from $\boldsymbol{m}^*\boldsymbol{S}^{-1}$

Thus we have the following result:

1. If $i \notin I$, then the sequence (ε_k) is null and it is enough to take any (j_k) and two by two distinct.
2. If $i \in I$, considering the set G_i defined above and according to what precedes, it is enough to take the sequence (ε_k) constant equal to 1 and the (j_k) given by G_i.

In the case where the matrix $\boldsymbol{E}_r$ has negative coefficients or is not binary, we can adapt Theorem 1. It is sufficient to allow the sequence ε_k to take the value -1 and to be able to subtract (or add) the same row several times.

We notice that, unlike in the previous case, we cannot give an algorithm to determine a list of possible candidates for the matrix $\boldsymbol{S}$. A similar approach as the one presented above would be too expensive. We do not know, a priori, the number of rows to remove from each erroneous row. Although correcting the error in the matrix $\boldsymbol{Z}^*$ at Step 2 is theoretically possible, it may be difficult in practice.

3.3 Comparison to Other Attacks

Recall that the goal of our attack is to find the secret matrix $\boldsymbol{Q}$ in the Niederreiter scheme. It has been shown in various previous works that it is possible to obtain secret information about the decryption in the McEliece scheme (Table 2). Falko Strenzke proposed in [30,31] two attacks on each of the two calls of the Extended Euclidean Algorithm (EEA) in McEliece decoding with the parameters $n = 2,048$ and $t = 50$. This vulnerability in the Patterson algorithm [26] in the error correction phase allows an attacker to gather information about the secret $n \times n$ permutation matrix $\boldsymbol{P}$ through a timing side channel.

The first attack [30] targets the second call of the EEA in the Patterson algorithm to determine the polynomials forming the error locator polynomial $\sigma(x)$. The polynomial of $deg(\sigma(x)) \leq t$ consists of two polynomials $a(x)$ and $b(x)$ whose degrees have a direct impact on the number of iterations of the EEA. This variation in the number of iterations implies a difference in the execution times and makes possible a timing attack. The attacker creates ciphertext (chosen-ciphertext attack) using random error vectors with Hamming weight $\mathsf{wt} = 4$ and then lets the decryption routine decrypt the ciphertext. It evaluates whether zero or one iteration occurred in the EEA. If an iteration has occurred, $deg(b(x)) = 1$, nothing is done, and if there are no iterations, $deg(b(x)) = 0$, the error vector is added as a new row of a matrix over $\mathbb{F}_2$ having n columns. Each time a row is added, a Gauss-Jordan elimination is performed and the rank is determined. Once the maximum rank is reached (here 2,036), the attack is completed with 7,848,229 ciphertexts. However, such an approach only recovers the secret permutation matrix $\boldsymbol{P}$ when the Hamming weight of error $\boldsymbol{e}$ is small (2 or 4).

The second attack [31] is based on the vulnerabilities that are present in the inversion of the error syndrome through the extended euclidean algorithm (first call in the Patterson algorithm). Strenzke showed the existence of a timing side channel vulnerability in the syndrome inversion that allows the attacker to gain knowledge of the zero-element of the secret support. It is based on the analysis of the key equation to deduce the relations between the degrees of the polynomials involved in it. As in the first attack, this approach only works for Hamming weights of 2, 4, or 6 of the error vector $\boldsymbol{e}$ to recover the secret permutation matrix $\boldsymbol{P}$. Despite the improvements in [6], the main problem with these two previous attacks is the number of cases (depending on the Hamming weight of $\boldsymbol{e}$) that can be exploited to find the secret.

In our attack, we have no constraints on the Hamming weights of the ciphertext (or error vector $\boldsymbol{e}$) to find the secret matrix $\boldsymbol{Q}$ in the case that we correctly construct the matrix $\boldsymbol{Z}^*$ with a random forest. Moreover, we attack the least complex step of Niederreiter decoding (first step). The Niederreiter PKE is slightly different from the McEliece PKE (Table 1 and Table 2). However, here

Table 3. Attacks to recover the secret matrix $\boldsymbol{P}$

Attack	Hamming weight	Number of ciphertexts	Target
Timing attacks of Strenzke	2, 4 or 6	7,848,229 in [30]	EEA in Patterson algorithm
Our attack against MVPP	no constraints	2,048	First step in McEliece's decryption

too, an error vector is chosen during the encryption and decryption features, and since these features are the prerequisites of our attack, it is also applicable to McEliece's PKE. Unlike the attack of Strenzke in [30] we only need 2,048 ciphertexts instead of 7,848,229 to find the secret $n \times n$ permutation matrix $\boldsymbol{P}$. The Table 3 give more details on the comparison with Strenzke's attacks to find the secret matrix $\boldsymbol{P}$.

4 Conclusion

This article presents a key-recovery attack against the Matrix-Vector Product Problem, which is a new formalism that we introduce in based-code cryptography. We have also shown that with a side-channel attack on this operation, we can recover secret information on based-code cryptosystems without solving the hardness of the binary syndrome decoding problem. In addition to the side-channel information, we performed a chosen-ciphertext attack, which, with careful choice of the ciphertexts, can find the secret matrix without errors. When noise (errors) is present during the attack, we have shown that in some cases it is possible to find the secret matrix. Our attack can be applied to code-based cryptosystems with matrix-vector product operations.

A Simple Version of Our Attack

Case 1: no Errors in $\boldsymbol{Z}^*$. Let the matrices $\boldsymbol{Z}$ invertible in $\mathbb{F}_2$ and $\boldsymbol{Z}^*$ in $\mathbb{N}$ respectively constructed in Step 1 and recovered in Step 2 of our attack. One chooses here $n - k = 3$, we have for instance

$$\boldsymbol{Z} = \begin{pmatrix} 1\,1\,1 \\ 1\,0\,1 \\ 1\,1\,0 \end{pmatrix}$$

its inverse

$$\boldsymbol{Z}^{-1} = \begin{pmatrix} -1 & 1 & 1 \\ 1 & -1 & 0 \\ 1 & 0 & -1 \end{pmatrix}$$

and

$$\boldsymbol{Z}^* = \begin{pmatrix} 2\,2\,1 \\ 1\,0\,1 \\ 2\,1\,2 \end{pmatrix}.$$

From the Eq. 1, $\boldsymbol{S} = \boldsymbol{Z}^*\boldsymbol{Z}^{-1}$, we find

$$\boldsymbol{S} = \begin{pmatrix} 1\,0\,1 \\ 0\,1\,0 \\ 1\,1\,0 \end{pmatrix}.$$

Case 2: Few Errors in $\boldsymbol{Z}^*$. We keep the same $\boldsymbol{Z}$, its inverse and $\boldsymbol{Z}^*$ matrices in **case 1**.

According to Eq. 3, $\boldsymbol{Z}^{**} = \boldsymbol{Z}^{*} + \boldsymbol{E}_r$, we have

$$\boldsymbol{E}_r = \begin{pmatrix} 1\,0\,0 \\ 0\,0\,0 \\ 0\,0\,0 \end{pmatrix}.$$

By performing the same operation as before, we obtain the following $\boldsymbol{S}'$ matrix according to Eq. 2

$$\boldsymbol{S}' = \begin{pmatrix} 0\,1\,2 \\ 0\,1\,0 \\ 1\,1\,0 \end{pmatrix}.$$

This matrix $\boldsymbol{S}'$ is not binary, so we deduce that the first row contains a fault. We then apply the Algorithm 1 of Sect. 3.2 to determine the list of possible candidates for the matrix $\boldsymbol{S}$

$$\boldsymbol{S}'[1] - \boldsymbol{Z}^{-1}[1] = [1\ \ 0\ \ 1]$$
$$\boldsymbol{S}'[1] - \boldsymbol{Z}^{-1}[2] = [-1\ \ 2\ \ 2]$$
$$\boldsymbol{S}'[1] - \boldsymbol{Z}^{-1}[3] = [-1\ \ 1\ \ 3].$$

Only the first case gives a binary vector, we deduce that $\boldsymbol{S}'[1] = \boldsymbol{S}[1] + \boldsymbol{Z}^{-1}[1]$ and we have directly $\boldsymbol{S}$.

Case 3: Errors in $\boldsymbol{Z}^{*}$. We consider the error matrix

$$\boldsymbol{E}_r = \begin{pmatrix} 0\,0\,0 \\ 0\,1\,0 \\ 0\,0\,0 \end{pmatrix}.$$

We then obtain the following matrix

$$\boldsymbol{S}' = \begin{pmatrix} 1\,0\,1 \\ 1\,0\,0 \\ 1\,1\,0 \end{pmatrix}.$$

Here the matrix is binary, moreover its determinant $det(\boldsymbol{S}') = 1$. In this case, we cannot detect that the matrix is not correct.

References

1. Aguilar Melchor, C., et al.: BIKE: bit flipping key encapsulation. In: NIST Post-Quantum Cryptography Standardization Project (Round 3) (2020)
2. Albrecht, M.R., et al.: Classic McEliece. In: NIST Post-Quantum Cryptography Standardization Project (Round 3) (2020). https://classic.mceliece.org
3. Becker, A., Joux, A., May, A., Meurer, A.: Decoding Random Binary Linear Codes in $2^{n/20}$: How $1 + 1 = 0$ Improves Information Set Decoding. In: Pointcheval, D., Johansson, T. (eds.) EUROCRYPT 2012. LNCS, vol. 7237, pp. 520–536. Springer, Heidelberg (2012). https://doi.org/10.1007/978-3-642-29011-4_31

4. Berlekamp, E.R., McEliece, R.J., van Tilborg, H.C.A.: On the inherent intractability of certain coding problems (Corresp.). IEEE Trans. Inf. Theory **24**(3), 384–386 (1978)
5. Bernstein, D.J., Lange, T.: Post-quantum cryptography. Nature **549**(7671), 188–194 (2017)
6. Bucerzan, D., Cayrel, P.-L., Dragoi, V., Richmond, T.: Improved timing attacks against the secret permutation in the McEliece PKC. Int. J. Comput. Commun. Control **12**(1), 7–25 (2016)
7. Buchmann, J.A., Butin, D., Göpfert, F., Petzoldt, A.: Post-quantum cryptography: state of the art. In: The New Codebreakers, pp. 88–108 (2016)
8. Castryck, W., Decru, T.: An efficient key recovery attack on SIDH (preliminary version). Cryptology ePrint Archive, Paper 2022/975 (2022). https://eprint.iacr.org/2022/975
9. Cayrel, P.-L., Colombier, B., Drăgoi, V.-F., Menu, A., Bossuet, L.: Message-recovery laser fault injection attack on the *Classic McEliece* cryptosystem. In: Canteaut, A., Standaert, F.-X. (eds.) EUROCRYPT 2021. LNCS, vol. 12697, pp. 438–467. Springer, Cham (2021). https://doi.org/10.1007/978-3-030-77886-6_15
10. Colombier, B., Drăgoi, V.-F., Cayrel, P.-L., Grosso, V.: Profiled side-channel attack on cryptosystems based on the binary syndrome decoding problem. IEEE Trans. Inf. Forensics Secur., 3407–3420 (2022). https://doi.org/10.1109/TIFS.2022.3198277
11. Feldman, J.: Decoding error-correcting codes via linear programming. Ph.D. thesis. Massachusetts Institute of Technology, Cambridge, MA USA (2003)
12. Feldman, J., Wainwright, M.J., Karger, D.R.: Using linear programming to Decode Binary linear codes. IEEE Trans. Inf. Theory **51**(3), 954–972 (2005)
13. Fouotsa, T.B., Petit, C.: A new adaptive attack on SIDH. In: Galbraith, S.D. (ed.) CT-RSA 2022. LNCS, vol. 13161, pp. 322–344. Springer, Cham (2022). https://doi.org/10.1007/978-3-030-95312-6_14
14. Gyongyosi, L., Imre, S.: A survey on quantum computing technology. Comput. Sci. Rev. **31**, 51–71 (2019)
15. Hettwer, B., Gehrer, S., Güneysu, T.: Applications of machine learning techniques in side-channel attacks: a survey. J. Cryptographic Eng. **10**(2), 135–162 (2020)
16. Jao, D., et al.: SIKE-Supersingular isogeny key encapsulation. In: NIST Round 3 (2020)
17. Larsen, M.V., Guo, X., Breum, C.R., Neergaard-Nielsen, J.S., Andersen, U.L.: Deterministic multi-mode gates on a scalable photonic quantum computing platform. Nature Phys. **17**(9), 1018–1023 (2021)
18. Lee, P.J., Brickell, E.F.: An observation on the security of McEliece's public-key cryptosystem. In: Barstow, D., et al. (eds.) EUROCRYPT 1988. LNCS, vol. 330, pp. 275–280. Springer, Heidelberg (1988)
19. Leon, J.S.: A probabilistic algorithm for computing minimum weights of large error-correcting codes. IEEE Trans. Inf. Theory **34**(5), 1354–1359 (1998)
20. Maino, L., Martindale, C.: An attack on SIDH with arbitrary starting curve. In: Cryptology ePrint Archive (2022)
21. May, A., Meurer, A., Thomae, E.: Decoding Random Linear Codes in $\tilde{\mathcal{O}}(2^{0.054n})$. In: Lee, D.H., Wang, X. (eds.) ASIACRYPT 2011. LNCS, vol. 7073, pp. 107–124. Springer, Heidelberg (2011). https://doi.org/10.1007/978-3-642-25385-0_6
22. May, A., Ozerov, I.: On Computing Nearest Neighbors with Applications to Decoding of Binary Linear Codes. In: Oswald, E., Fischlin, M. (eds.) EUROCRYPT 2015. LNCS, vol. 9056, pp. 203–228. Springer, Heidelberg (2015). https://doi.org/10.1007/978-3-662-46800-5_9

23. McEliece, R.J.: A public-key cryptosystem based on algebraic. Coding Thv. **4244**, 114–116 (1978)
24. Melchor, C.A., et al.: Hamming Quasi-Cyclic (HQC). NIST Post-Quantum Cryptography Standardization Project (Round 3) (2020)
25. Niederreiter, H.: Knapsack-type cryptosystems and algebraic coding theory. Prob. Contr. Inform. Theory **15**(2), 157–166 (1986)
26. Patterson, N.: The algebraic decoding of Goppa codes. IEEE Trans. Inf. Theory **21**(2), 203–207 (1975)
27. Prange, E.: The use of information sets in decoding cyclic codes. IRE Trans. Inf. Theory **8**(5), 5–9 (1962)
28. Shor, P.W.: Algorithms for quantum computation: discrete logarithms and factoring". In: Proceedings 35th Annual Symposium on Foundations of Computer Science, pp. 124–134. IEEE (1994)
29. Stern, J.: A method for finding codewords of small weight. In: Cohen, G., Wolfmann, J. (eds.) Coding Theory 1988. LNCS, vol. 388, pp. 106–113. Springer, Heidelberg (1989). https://doi.org/10.1007/BFb0019850
30. Strenzke, F.: A timing attack against the secret permutation in the McEliece PKC. In: Sendrier, N. (ed.) PQCrypto 2010. LNCS, vol. 6061, pp. 95–107. Springer, Heidelberg (2010). https://doi.org/10.1007/978-3-642-12929-2_8
31. Strenzke, F.: Timing attacks against the syndrome inversion in code-based cryptosystems. In: Gaborit, P. (ed.) PQCrypto 2013. LNCS, vol. 7932, pp. 217–230. Springer, Heidelberg (2013). https://doi.org/10.1007/978-3-642-38616-9_15
32. Takeda, S., Furusawa, A.: Toward large-scale fault-tolerant universal photonic quantum computing. APL Photonics **4**(6), 060902 (2019)
33. Tanatmis, A., Ruzika, S., Hamacher, H.W., Punekar, M., Kienle, F., Wehn, N.: A separation algorithm for improved LP-decoding of linear block codes. IEEE Trans. Inf. Theory **56**(7), 3277–3289 (2010)
34. Tasso, É., De Feo, L., El Mrabet, N., Pontié, S.: Resistance of Isogeny-Based Cryptographic Implementations to a Fault Attack. In: Bhasin, S., De Santis, F. (eds.) COSADE 2021. LNCS, vol. 12910, pp. 255–276. Springer, Cham (2021). https://doi.org/10.1007/978-3-030-89915-8_12
35. Zhang, F., et al.: Side-channel analysis and countermeasure design on ARM-based quantum-resistant SIKE. IEEE Trans. Comput. **69**(11), 1681–1693 (2010)

Differential Fault Attack on AES Using Maximum Four Bytes Faulty Ciphertexts

Jae-Won Huh[1] and Dong-Guk Han[1,2(✉)]

[1] Department of Financial Information Security, Kookmin University, Seoul, Republic of Korea
{gjwodnjs987,christa}@kookmin.ac.kr

[2] Department of Mathematics, Kookmin University, Seoul, Republic of Korea

Abstract. The Internet of Things connects various types of devices and hardware for the connection are built-in. Symmetric key-based encryption may be embedded in the chip according to the environment. Recently, security problems have increased since the development of IoT devices. In particular, as the use of these devices has increased dramatically, the possibility of accessing and stealing cryptographic devices is also increasing. According to such physical accessibility, the issue of side-channel analysis of the safety of IoT devices is increasing. Differential Fault Attack (DFA) is based on intentionally injecting a fault at a specific time in the process of the cryptographic operation in an embedded device with a chip to cause a malfunction desired by the attacker. The Piret & Quisquarter DFA (P&Q DFA) is a differential fault attack method proposed under the assumption that single-byte fault are injected into the input of the AES 9th round MixColumn. However, single-byte faults occur in an environment where actual faults are injected, and the fault ciphertext with faults of two or more bytes can be collected. This paper proposes an analysis technique that can utilize defective ciphertext data containing two to four byte faults by extending the existing P&Q DFA, and optimizing the table called D that needs to be calculated in advance. In addition, this paper presents the results of recovering four bytes of the 10-round key by applying it to the multi-byte faults data obtained through the electromagnetic wave fault injection attack experiment on real devices.

Keywords: Side-channel analysis · AES · Differential fault attack

1 Introduction

Side-channel analysis is a technique that acquires secret information through physical information such as power consumption, electromagnetic wave, and

This work was supported as part of Military Crypto Research Center (UD210027XD) funded by Defense Acquisition Program Administration (DAPA) and Agency for Defense Development (ADD).

S.-H. Seo and H. Seo (Eds.): ICISC 2022, LNCS 13849, pp. 235–245, 2023.
https://doi.org/10.1007/978-3-031-29371-9_12

sound generation, while an encryption algorithm is operating in an actual device [4]. With the recent development of IoT and smart devices, the technology is being applied and distributed widely to numerous devices. This situation makes it easier for a malicious attacker to access these devices, and a physical attack is also becoming possible naturally. Thus, in this environment, there is increasing interest in side-channel security. Differential fault attack (DFA) is a type of semi-invasive (SCA) that injects an unsupported voltage or current into a device containing an embedded processor, a strong electric or magnetic field, or a laser pulse at a specific point in time when it is operating. DFA was first proposed by Biham et al. for DES in 1997 [1]. After that, DFAs on various algorithms were studied [2,3], and various techniques for fault-injection were developed [5,7,8]. DFAs on AES have been studied. However, most of them have been directed to injecting a single byte fault into the Mixcolumns operation of a specific round of AES, and there are few studies have injected faults into multiple bytes.

Our Contributions. Our contributions are as follows:
- First, a method is proposed to reduce the amount of computation and memory when extending the Piret & Quisquarter DFA method for the AES to ciphertext targeting faults of four bytes or fewer. The proposed attack is based on a fault of fewer than four bytes, and shows that only a part of the data used in the full investigation for each of the two, three, and four-byte faults are used in the actual attack.

- Second, a multi-byte fault ciphertext can be obtained through an EM-FI attack on actual device and uses to verify the proposed method (Table 1).

Table 1. Notation for the whole process

Parameter	Description
rk_i^r	r^{th} round key i^{th} byte
SB^{-1}	Inverse Sbox operation
MC	Mixcolumn operation
C, C^f	Normal and fault ciphertexts
D	Mixcolumn differential table
Δ	Mixcolumn's output difference
$\oplus$	Bit exclusive or operation

Organization. The remainder of this paper is structured as follows. In Sect. 2, we introduce the Piret & Quisquarter DFA(P&Q DFA). Section 3 reported the methodology of the proposed DFA on AES. Section 4, evaluates the validity of the proposed attack with a EM-FI attack experiment for real device. Finally, the paper is concluded in Sect. 5.

2 Backgrounds

2.1 Differential Fault Analysis (DFA)

A DFA, a type of SCA, combines differential analysis with a fault injection attack. When the device is operating, the attack exploits on the difference information that results from injecting a fault in the middle. The actual difficulty of the attack is determined by the type of fault that occurs when performing the attack. They can be classified broadly into the following types:

- **Type 1 (capability of Attack Accuracy)**
  1. `Word Error[random value]`: The attacker can change one or more bytes to a random value.
  2. `Byte Error[random value]`: The attacker can change a single byte of a specific word into a random value.
  3. `Bit Flip`: The attacker can flip a single-bit of a specific word
- **Type 2 (capability of location tracking)**
  1. `Random Position`: Various position values that can produce the same result. The attacker cannot specify precisely where the fault was injected.
  2. `Deterministic position`: The attacker can pinpoint where the fault was injected by looking at the specific results.

A lower value indicates a stronger attacker assumption.

2.2 Piret & Quisquarter DFA(P&Q DFA)

Piret & Quisquarter DFA (P&Q DFA) is a differential fault attack technique proposed in 2003 for block cipher AES [6]. P&Q DFA is a method for inducing a change in a specific byte of the final ciphertext by inserting an input with a single byte error into the AES 9th round Mixcolumn, and recovering the AES secret key using the difference between the normal and fault ciphertext. Figure 1 shows that when a single byte error occurs in the AES 9th round Mixcolumn input, it can affect the difference between the final ciphertext and the specific bytes of the normal ciphertext (here, the 1st, 8th, 11th, and 14th). A basic P&Q DFA computes the following equation. The attacker calculates a four-byte output difference in table D that can occur when a single byte error is entered in the AES 9th round Mixcolumn input. D contains the following 4 X 255 elements, because there are four positions where a single byte fault can occur, and it is formed by considering all of them.

$$D = MC\,(\Delta\epsilon) = (\Delta_0, \Delta_1, \Delta_2, \Delta_3) \tag{1}$$

Form a 10th round key candidate list $L(rk_1^{10}, rk_{14}^{10}, rk_{10}^{10}, rk_8^{10})$ that satisfies the following equation.

$$\begin{cases} \Delta_0 = SB^{-1}(C_1 \oplus rk_1^{10}) \oplus SB^{-1}(C_1^{\lightning} \oplus rk_1^{10}) \\ \Delta_1 = SB^{-1}(C_{14} \oplus rk_{14}^{10}) \oplus SB^{-1}(C_{14}^{\lightning} \oplus rk_{14}^{10}) \\ \Delta_2 = SB^{-1}(C_{11} \oplus rk_{11}^{10}) \oplus SB^{-1}(C_{11}^{\lightning} \oplus rk_{11}^{10}) \\ \Delta_3 = SB^{-1}(C_8 \oplus rk_8^{10}) \oplus SB^{-1}(C_8^{\lightning} \oplus rk_8^{10}) \end{cases} \tag{2}$$

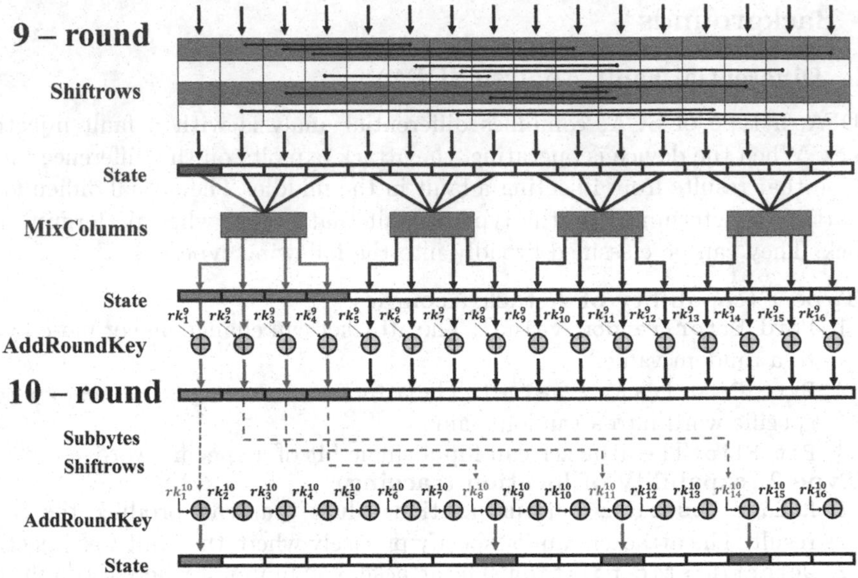

Fig. 1. Error propagation of the AES 9 round

The number of 10th round key candidates with a size of four bytes can be reduced to approximately 1000 using the difference between the normal and faulty ciphertext pairs. An attacker can recover four bytes of the 10th round key with a 98% probability using another faulty ciphertext.

Therefore, the entire 10th round key can be recovered if eight faulty ciphertexts are obtained for the 16-byte input of the Mixcolumn. The entire AES secret key can be recovered using this value.

3 Proposed Differential Fault Attack on AES for Multi-byte Fault

Figure 2 is a position where the value of a specific byte (1st, 8th, 11th, and 14th byte) can be changed for the final ciphertext of AES when an error is injected. Assume that the values of the 1st, 8th, 11th, and 14th byte values are different from the ciphertext obtained from the attacker through the fault injection attack compared to the normal ciphertext. An attacker cannot specify how many bytes the fault was injected with only the given faulty ciphertext. In other words, it is impossible to distinguish between a ciphertext resulting from the injection of a fault into a single byte and a ciphertext resulting from a fault injection into multiple bytes. In an actual attack environment, there may be differences in the parameters set by the attacker (e.g., the position where a fault is injected into the cryptographic device, strength to be injected, and time of injection. Depending on the parameters set, faults may not be injected or multi-byte errors may occur. The P&Q DFA produces a 4×255 sized difference table, assuming a single byte fault has occurred. However, a two-byte error can occur in six different positions. A three-byte error can occur in four positions, and in some cases, the entire byte can be affected. In addition, as the number of bytes affected by an error increases, the size of the difference table D increases. This section proposes an extended differential fault attack logic of P&Q DFA for multi-byte fault ciphertext by reflecting these characteristics. Each attack consists of four steps as follows:

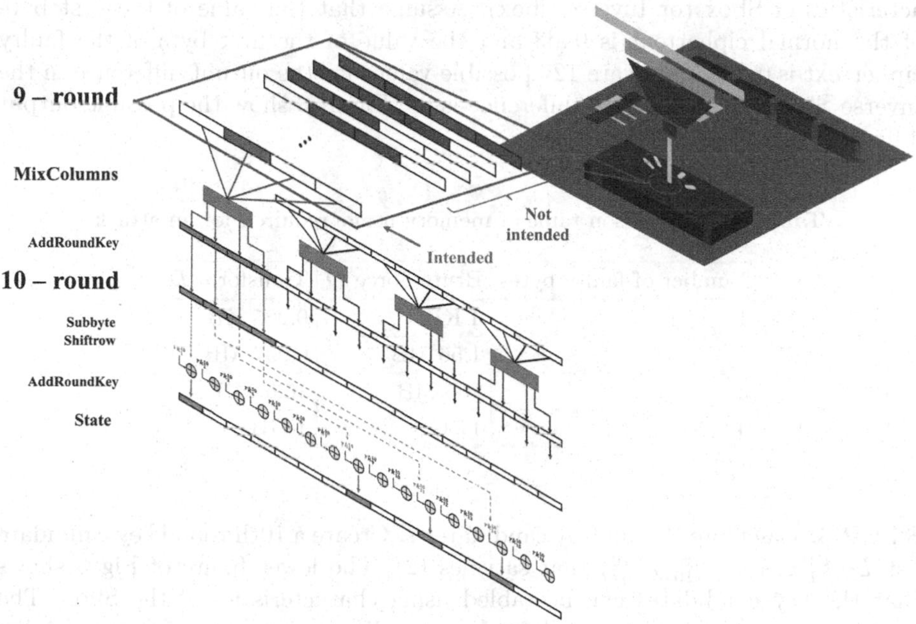

Fig. 2. AES 9th round Full differential path affecting specific bytes of ciphertext

3.1 Attacker's Assumption

The attacker can conduct encryption in the proposed DFA by obtaining a device with the AES operating with a fixed key. The attacker can induce a fault in which a random word is at a specific position during the operation and monitor pairs of the normal and fault ciphertext.

STEP 1. Calculating the Mixcolumn difference table D.

Mixcolumn operation is performed by changing all four bytes of the fixed value. The difference table is calculated with the results. This allows an attacker construct the normal and fault differential table D. The size of the D table produced by changing the Mixcolumn input by two, three, or four bytes is shown in step2.

STEP 2. Transforming D table

Table D used in the attack can be transformed due to the following characteristics of Sbox (or Inverse Sbox). Assume that the value of the first byte of the normal ciphertext is 0xd3 and the value of the first byte of the faulty ciphertext is 0xd0. There are 127 possible values for the output difference in the Inverse Sbox when the input difference is 03. Figure 3 show the possible output differences and key candidate pairs.

Table 2. Comparison table of memory usage required for an attack

Number of faulty bytes	Brute Force D	Transform D
1	4 KB	0.225 KB
2	1.56 MB	0.097 MB
3	265 MB	16.6 MB
4	17 GB	1 GB

STEP 3. Calculate Round Key candidates D Create a 10th round key candidate list $L(rk_1^{10}, rk_{14}^{10}, rk_{10}^{10}, rk_8^{10})$ that satisfies (2). The lower figure of Fig. 3 shows that the key candidates can be tabled using characteristics of the Sbox. The gray line indicates that the number of key candidates is four, and the remaining differences except for this value havecandidates. For example, only $k = 0 \times 48$, $0 \times 4b$ satisfies the following equation.

$$SB^{-1}(\texttt{0xd0} \oplus k) \oplus SB^{-1}(\texttt{0xd3} \oplus k) = \texttt{0xa}$$

That is, when the normal and fault ciphertext output difference is determined, the possible output difference of the inverse Sbox is determined, and the number of key candidates that can be obtained through the difference is two or four. An attacker can produce a set of four-byte key candidates using the key table produced from the normal and faulty ciphertext pair.

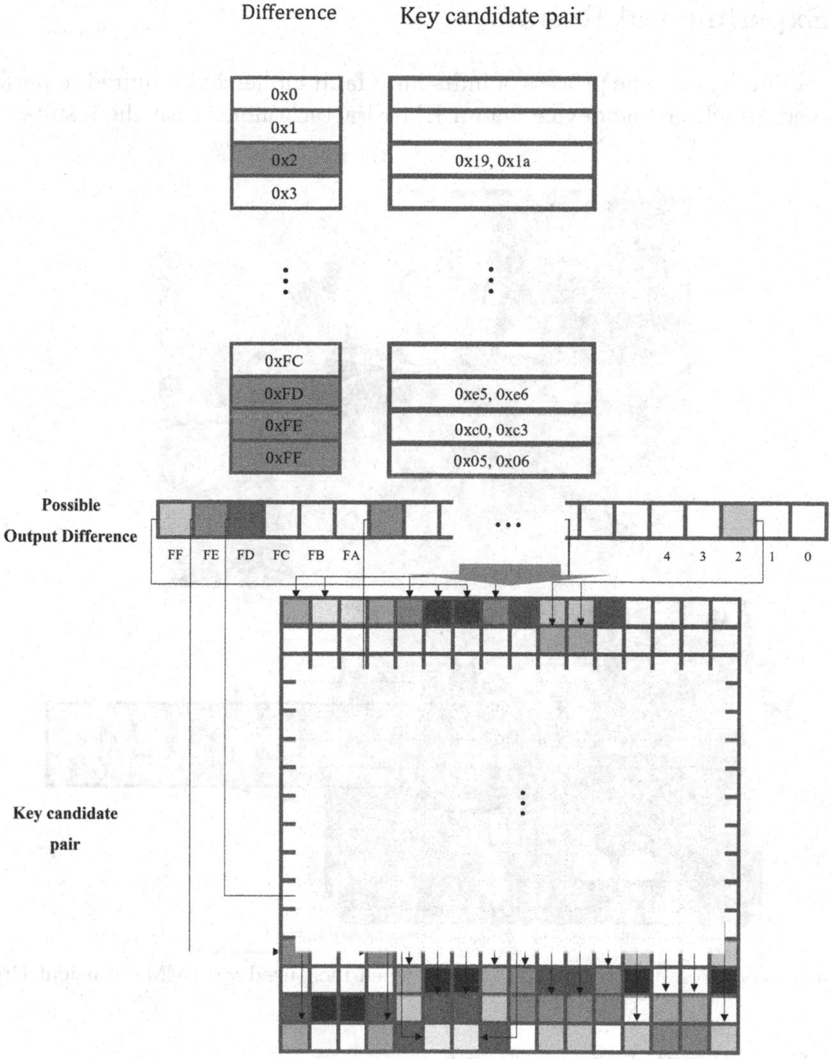

Fig. 3. Possible output difference and key candidate pairs

STEP 4. Confirm the secret key from key candidates
The size of the key candidate set can be reduced by also using the normal and fault ciphertext pairs. In the case of two-byte and three-byte faulty ciphertext, the number of key candidates decreases significantly. In the case of four bytes, however, the decrease in the number of key candidates is constant, and a much larger amount of fault ciphertext is required than in the previous case.

4 Experimental Results

This section reports the process of inducing a fault ciphertext required to perform proposed attack on the device via an EM-FI attack along with the results.

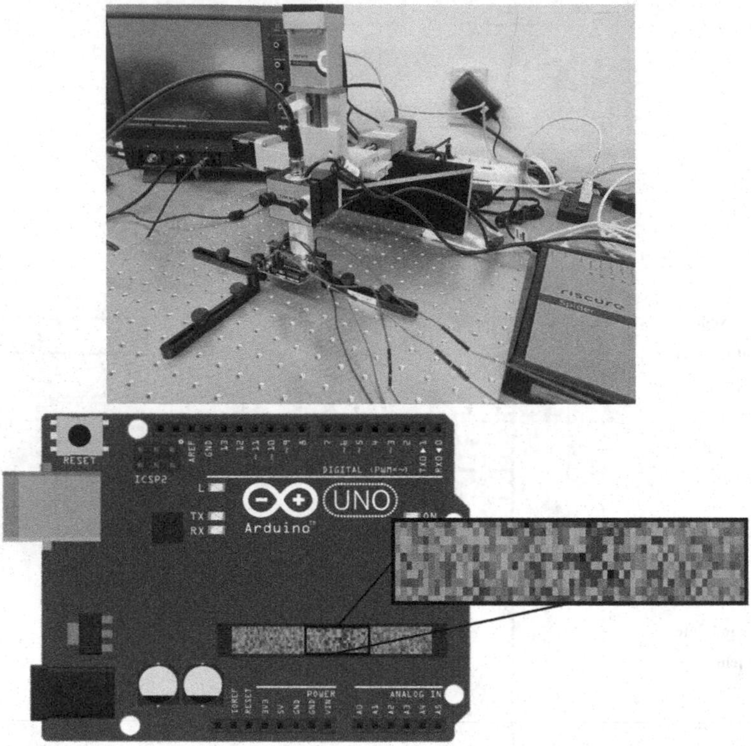

Fig. 4. Active area on Arduino Uno board when measured with EM Transient Probe

4.1 Experimental Environment

To inject a fault at the end of the shiftrow operation of the 9th round of AES, the point where may electromagnetic waves are emitted from the Arduino board while the shiftrow is operating was collected through EM Transient probe equipment. The position where many electromagnetic waves were emitted is the red area in Fig. 4, and the position was set as the EM-FI attack position. The experiment was conducted by gradually narrowing the area where the desired fault ciphertext occurred. The faulty ciphertexts can be retrieved if the attack is successful, as shown in Fig. 5. Compared to the normal ciphertext, ciphertext with different values of the 1st, 8th, 11th, and 14th bytes were filtered and used for the attack.

00 00 00 00 00 00 00 00 00 00 01 02 03 04 05 06	0D 78 91 47 D8 27 F8 49 E7 9F D4 8A 02 67 F0 88
00 00 00 00 00 00 00 00 00 00 01 02 03 04 05 06	0D 78 91 47 D8 27 F8 86 E7 9F 25 8A 02 7C F0 88
00 00 00 00 00 00 00 00 00 00 01 02 03 04 05 06	0D 78 91 47 D8 27 F8 86 E7 9F 25 8A 02 A3 F0 88
00 00 00 00 00 00 00 00 00 00 01 02 03 04 05 06	0D 78 91 47 D8 27 F8 8C E7 9F D0 8A 02 CF F0 88
00 00 00 00 00 00 00 00 00 00 01 02 03 04 05 06	0D 78 91 47 D8 27 F8 E7 E7 9F D0 8A 02 1E F0 88
00 00 00 00 00 00 00 00 00 00 01 02 03 04 05 06	0D 78 91 47 D8 27 F8 E7 E7 9F D0 8A 02 91 F0 88
00 00 00 00 00 00 00 00 00 00 01 02 03 04 05 06	18 78 03 47 D8 4F F8 86 E7 9F 54 8A 02 27 F0 88
00 00 00 00 00 00 00 00 00 00 01 02 03 04 05 06	18 78 03 47 D8 4F F8 E7 E7 9F D0 8A 02 DC F0 88
00 00 00 00 00 00 00 00 00 00 01 02 03 04 05 06	18 78 03 47 D8 4F F8 E7 E7 9F D0 8A 02 DC F0 88
00 00 00 00 00 00 00 00 00 00 01 02 03 04 05 06	18 78 03 47 D8 B4 F8 49 BD 9F D4 8A 02 85 F0 9E
00 00 00 00 00 00 00 00 00 00 01 02 03 04 05 06	18 78 37 47 D8 EF F8 E7 E7 9F D0 8A 02 DC F0 88
00 00 00 00 00 00 00 00 00 00 01 02 03 04 05 06	18 78 91 47 D8 27 F8 17 E7 9F 0D 8A 02 85 F0 88
00 00 00 00 00 00 00 00 00 00 01 02 03 04 05 06	18 78 91 47 D8 27 F8 17 E7 9F 0D 8A 02 85 F0 88
00 00 00 00 00 00 00 00 00 00 01 02 03 04 05 06	18 78 91 47 D8 27 F8 17 E7 9F 0D 8A 02 85 F0 88
00 00 00 00 00 00 00 00 00 00 01 02 03 04 05 06	18 78 91 47 D8 27 F8 1E E7 9F A5 8A 02 91 F0 88
00 00 00 00 00 00 00 00 00 00 01 02 03 04 05 06	18 78 91 47 D8 27 F8 2A E7 9F 50 8A 02 85 F0 88
00 00 00 00 00 00 00 00 00 00 01 02 03 04 05 06	18 78 91 47 D8 27 F8 2A E7 9F 50 8A 02 85 F0 88
00 00 00 00 00 00 00 00 00 00 01 02 03 04 05 06	18 78 91 47 D8 27 F8 2A E7 9F 50 8A 02 85 F0 88
00 00 00 00 00 00 00 00 00 00 01 02 03 04 05 06	18 78 91 47 D8 27 F8 2A E7 9F 50 8A 02 85 F0 88

four-byte fault ciphertext

Fig. 5. EM-FI result: four-byte faulty ciphertext

4.2 Experimental Results

When the first intended error occurred, there were 13127 normal ciphertexts, 4535 abnormal operations, and 338 erroneous ciphertexts, showing an error rate of about 1.87%. When the error injection strength is strong, it is confirmed that ciphertext affected by all 4 bytes can be generated. This can be seen in Table 3.

Table 3. Number of faulty ciphertext according to the number of erroneous bytes

Number of faulty bytes	1	2	3	4	Total
Number of faulty ciphertext	0	0	0	548	548

When the error injection strength is gradually weakened, it can be confirmed that the frequency of occurrence of a lot of 1-byte error ciphertext increases. This can be seen in Table 4.

However, it was confirmed that faulty ciphertexts of more than 2 bytes were still collected, and the location information and number of bytes could not be specified.

Table 4. Types of faulty ciphertext collected when error strength is weakened

Number of faulty bytes	1	2	3	4	Total
Number of faulty ciphertext	87	26	2	13	128

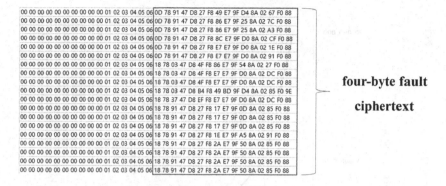

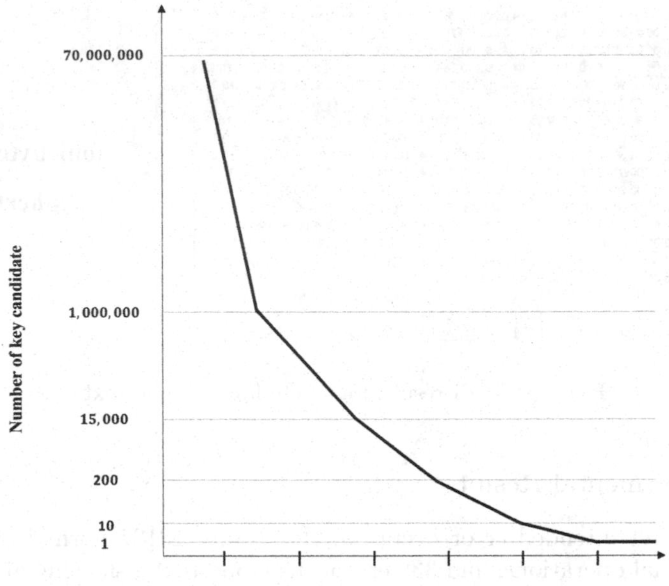

Fig. 6. Experimental Result three-byte fault ciphertext

As can be seen in Fig. 6, in the case of 3-byte faulty ciphertext, the number of key candidates rapidly decreases each time the faulty ciphertext is additionally compared, and the case of 2-byte shows a similar pattern. However, in the case of ciphertext affected by all 4 bytes, the reduction range is very small, and because of this, it was possible to reduce the key candidate to 1 through about 1500 erroneous ciphertext. The number of ciphertexts required for each byte is shown in Table 5.

Table 5. Number of pairs of normal and fault ciphertexts required for key recovery

Number of faulty bytes	2	3	4
Number of faulty ciphertext	3	6	1440

5 Conclusion

This paper proposed an attack that analyzes the key using only a part of the entire difference table when extending the existing P&Q DFA a fault of four bytes or less. Only the area used for the actual attack (approximately 1/16 of the total table) is extracted from the entire table when the I/O differential characteristic of Sbox is used. In addition, the type and number of candidate keys can be calculated once the difference used in the attack is determined. With this information, a set of key candidates can be generated from only table references given a pair of normal and faulty ciphertext. With the proposed methodology, four bytes of the 10th round key were recovered with two, three, and four-byte faulty ciphertext obtained after performing an EM-FI attack on the Arduino Uno.

Future studied will analyze the frequency band of electromagnetic waves emitted from the target device with other EM-MI equipment. In addition, the effect of an attack will be assessed using an electromagnetic wave similar to the frequency band of the electromagnetic wave collected by EM transient probe on the performance of fault injection attack.

References

1. Biham, E., Shamir, A.: Differential fault analysis of secret key cryptosystems. In: Kaliski, B.S. (ed.) CRYPTO 1997. LNCS, vol. 1294, pp. 513–525. Springer, Heidelberg (1997). https://doi.org/10.1007/BFb0052259
2. Floissac, N., L'Hyver, Y.: From AES-128 to AES-192 and aes-256, how to adapt differential fault analysis attacks on key expansion. In: Breveglieri, L., Guilley, S., Koren, I., Naccache, D., Takahashi, J. (eds.) 2011 Workshop on Fault Diagnosis and Tolerance in Cryptography, FDTC 2011, Tokyo, Japan, September 29, 2011, pp. 43–53. IEEE Computer Society (2011). https://doi.org/10.1109/FDTC.2011.15
3. Han, L., Wu, N., Ge, F., Zhou, F., Wen, J., Qing, P.: Differential fault attack for the iterative operation of aes-192 key expansion. In: 2020 IEEE 20th International Conference on Communication Technology (ICCT), pp. 1156–1160. IEEE (2020)
4. Kocher, P.C.: Timing attacks on implementations of Diffie-Hellman, RSA, DSS, and other systems. In: Koblitz, N. (ed.) CRYPTO 1996. LNCS, vol. 1109, pp. 104–113. Springer, Heidelberg (1996). https://doi.org/10.1007/3-540-68697-5_9
5. Lim, H., Lee, J., Han, D.G.: Novel fault injection attack without artificial trigger, vol. 10, p. 3849. Multidisciplinary Digital Publishing Institute (2020)
6. Piret, G., Quisquater, J.-J.: A differential fault attack technique against SPN structures, with application to the AES and Khazad. In: Walter, C.D., Koç, Ç.K., Paar, C. (eds.) CHES 2003. LNCS, vol. 2779, pp. 77–88. Springer, Heidelberg (2003). https://doi.org/10.1007/978-3-540-45238-6_7
7. Roscian, C., Dutertre, J., Tria, A.: Frontside laser fault injection on cryptosystems - application to the aes' last round. In: 2013 IEEE International Symposium on Hardware-Oriented Security and Trust, HOST 2013, Austin, TX, USA, 2–3 June 2013, pp. 119–124. IEEE Computer Society (2013). https://doi.org/10.1109/HST.2013.6581576
8. Seaborn, M., Dullien, T.: Exploiting the dram rowhammer bug to gain kernel privileges. **15**, 71 (2015)

Efficient Implementation

A Performance Evaluation of IPsec with Post-Quantum Cryptography

Seungyeon Bae, Yousung Chang, Hyeongjin Park, Minseo Kim, and Youngjoo Shin(✉)

School of Cybersecurity, Korea University, Seoul, South Korea
{bsybsy012,lisachangys,be2overflow,ichbinminseo,syoungjoo}@korea.ac.kr

Abstract. As Post-Quantum Cryptography (PQC) incurs higher costs in some metrics compared to conventional cryptosystems, performance evaluation to determine the trade-offs on circumstantial usage is essential. In this paper, we provide state-of-the-art performance evaluation results of PQC algorithms in the IPsec protocol. Specifically, we perform a deep dive into the performance of PQC-integrated IKEv2 in terms of the execution speed of each IKEv2 stage and packet size according to various PQC algorithms and their security levels. The evaluation is conducted with our implementation, constructed upon strongSwan, the most popular open-source IPsec implementation. As only the latest, but unstable version of strongSwan supports PQC, it is not straightforward to integrate the existing PQC implementations into strongSwan. We propose a well-established method to integrate PQC algorithmhe code base of strongSwan. Our evaluation targets a variety of PQC KEM algorithms, including NIST Round 3 finalists (i.e., Kyber, NTRU, and Saber) and algorithms developed in Korea and China. The performance evaluation shows the trade-offs between the security level and performance for individual PQC algorithms in the IPsec protocol.

Keywords: Post-quantum cryptography · IPsec · Internet key exchange version 2 · Benchmark

1 Introduction

With the underlying development of quantum computing research, the birth of movie-like robust and unstoppable quantum computers is becoming a reality [1]. The existence of Shor's and Grover's algorithms initiated the threat to the real-world conventional cryptosystem [2]. The two uprising cryptographic attacks are agile and clever enough to break through the classical public key algorithms. As a result of the continuous threats by the quantum computing-aided code-breakers, the effort in the realm of Post-Quantum Cryptography (PQC) has become vital [3].

Accordingly, NIST announced the outline and the call for PQC standardization submission in 2016 [4]. The breathtaking measurements concluded the standardizing mechanism to be CRYSTALS-Kyber for the public-key encryption

S.-H. Seo and H. Seo (Eds.): ICISC 2022, LNCS 13849, pp. 249–266, 2023.
https://doi.org/10.1007/978-3-031-29371-9_13

algorithm and key-encapsulation mechanism (KEM) in 2022 [5]. The excessive growth of quantum computers is also considered a threat to the confidentiality and integrity of digital communication in numerous Asian and European countries. China has launched rounds of domestic cryptographic competitions to determine the utmost cryptographic schemes within the country [6]. The lattice-based LAC, and AKCN, algorithms were enlisted as possible standardizing PQC candidates as a result of the competition. Similarly, Korea and European Union members operate national cybersecurity institutions to find promising quantum-resistant algorithms.

Unlike the existing cryptosystem in secure network protocols (e.g., TLS and IPsec), applying PQCs to those protocols may provide an inefficient trade-off between security and performance. Some metrics cause higher computational costs, additional storage requirements, or larger network bandwidth. To enhance the balance between security and performance, executing practical measurements to evaluate PQC algorithms is critical to efficiently replace the existing cryptosystem with PQC. There are many studies on performance evaluations for PQC-integrated TLS protocols [7,8]. However, there are few works on evaluation for the case of applying PQC to IPsec, a secure Internet protocol standardized by IETF, in the literature.

In this paper, we present the state-of-the-art performance measurement results for PQC algorithms integrated into the IPsec protocol. Specifically, we provide extensive measurements of the key exchange performance of PQC-integrated IKEv2 in terms of the execution speed (i.e., the latency) of each IKEv2 stage and packet size according to different PQC algorithms and their security levels. To assess how a PQC algorithm affects the individual IKEv2 stages, we further evaluate the execution performance of each KEM operation (e.g., key generation, encapsulation, and decapsulation) in the IPsec implementation. We aim to evaluate each algorithm's security level and performance level in the PQC-integrated IPsec environment through performance measurements. The charted values suggest the trade-offs between the security and the performance context of embedded algorithms variant by their security level. Our evaluation results may help users to choose the algorithm based on their circumstances.

We construct our implementation for the performance evaluation. The implementation is built upon strongSwan, one of the most popular open-source IPsec implementations that support PQC integration. As only the latest but unstable version of strongSwan provides a framework for the integration, there are some challenging issues in integrating the existing PQC implementations into the code base of strongSwan. We overcome the issues by analyzing the source code of strongSwan as well as liboqs, the related library for an open-source implementation of PQC algorithms. Based on the analysis, we provide a precise and well-established method to integrate general PQC algorithms into strongSwan's IPsec implementation. The proposed method may ease the migration from the conventional public-key cryptosystems to the PQC to encourage users to deploy quantum-safe secure network protocols.

Targets for our evaluation include a variety of PQC KEM algorithms, such as NIST Round 3 finalists (i.e., Kyber, NTRU, and Saber) and algorithms developed in Korea and China. The performance evaluation provides users with insights into the trade-offs between the security level and performance for individual PQC algorithms in the IPsec protocol.

The main contributions of our work are as follows:

- To the best of our knowledge, we provide the first performance evaluation results of various PQC algorithms, such as CRYSTALS-Kyber, NTRU, Saber, RLizard, LAC, and AKCN, in the IPsec protocol.
- We present a well-established method to integrate general PQC algorithms into an open-source IPsec implementation.
- We extensively measure the performance and security of each algorithm with varying security levels to determine the feasibility of the cryptosystem depending on circumstances. The measurements encompass KEM operations: key generation, encapsulation, and decapsulation and include the key exchange stages from the IKEv2: `IKE_SA_INIT`, `CREATE_CHILD_SA`, and Additional Key Exchange.

The remaining of this paper is structured as follows. In Sect. 2, we introduce readers to the general outlook of PQC, IKEv2 and hybrid key exchange. Section 3 underscores related work to the current project. and Sect. 4 explains the methodology to combine IPsec, particularly with IKEv2 and PQC. In Sect. 5, we provide our evaluation for the performance of PQC algorithms. Lastly, Sect. 6 concludes our work.

2 Background

In this section, we briefly overview the correlating mechanisms of PQC and IKEv2, which are the main considerations of the study.

2.1 Post-quantum Cryptography

The purpose of PQC is to resist quantum computing-aided code-breaking attacks by leveraging hard mathematical problems that even quantum computers cannot easily solve. The PQC schemes compromise into five distinct families: code-based, lattice-based, hash-based, multivariate, and supersingular elliptic curve isogeny cryptography [9]. Each category determines unique mathematical structure and properties of cryptographic algorithms. The underlying attributes cause a significant difference in the efficiency, computing time, security level, and other elements that define each security scheme.

For the study, we select lattice-based schemes as they comprise the majority of the existing PQC algorithms. Lattice-based schemes have smaller key sizes, unlike some code-based and multivariate schemes that have larger public key sizes [10]. Therefore, the lattice-based schemes provide practical security counter measurements against potential attacks from quantum computers.

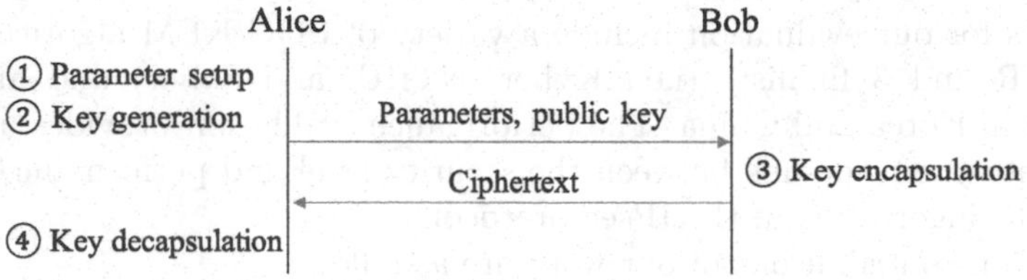

Fig. 1. General KEM procedure

KEM is a scheme that allows two entities to share an ephemeral key. The procedure for KEM instructs as follows.

1. Parameter setup: Generate the parameters.
2. Key generation: Generate the public and secret key with the created parameters.
3. Key encapsulation: Create ciphertext by encrypting a shared key through the generated public key.
4. Key decapsulation: Obtain the shared key by decrypting the ciphertext with the generated secret key.

This step is performed by sharing the generated parameters, public key, and ciphertext between the two hosts, as shown in Fig. 1.

As CRYSTALS-Kyber [11], NTRU [12], and Saber [13] are the lattice-based KEM schemes that are nominated as NIST Round 3 finalists; we scrutinized their behavior when interacting with IKEv2 networking protocol. Other than NIST finalist candidates, the cryptographic schemes developed in Asian countries, including LAC [14] and AKCN [15] from China, and RLizard [16] from Korea are selected based on their recognition in their nations.

2.2 Internet Key Exchange Version 2

Internet key exchange version 2 (IKEv2) [17] is a component of IPsec used to perform mutual authentication and establish and maintain secure associations (SAs) [17]. IKEv2 consists of several steps, but we only deal with steps that contain key exchange, where PQC KEM operations are used. The demonstration of the IKEv2 negotiation steps is shown in Fig. 2.

The first step in IKEv2's key exchange process, `IKE_SA_INIT`, is the initial exchange in which peers establish a secure channel. In order to perform the `IKE_SA_INIT`, the initiator transmits the SA proposal (SA_i), key exchange payload (KE_i), and nonce (N_i). The responder selects the SA (SA_r) from the SA proposal received from the initiator and transmits key exchange payload (KE_r) and nonce (N_r).

Thereafter, both peers deploy the selected SA and the shared key (SK) generated by the key exchange. Once the `IKE_SA_INIT` procedure is completed, further exchanges are encrypted with SK.

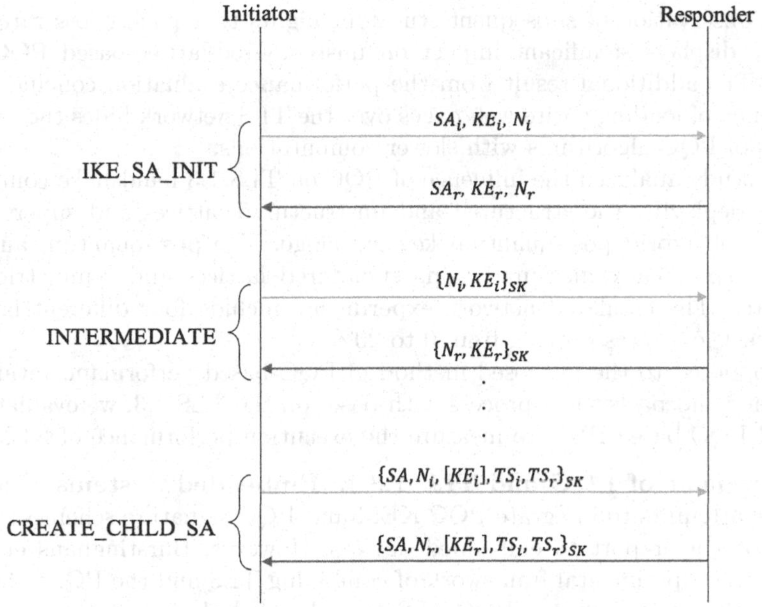

Fig. 2. IKEv2 Key Exchange

For each additional key exchange that has agreed to an IKE_SA_INIT exchange, the initiator and responder proceed to an INTERMEDIATE phase [18]. In this phase, the initiator sends key exchange data (KE_i) with a nonce (N_i) in a payload encrypted with SK. After receiving the encrypted payload, the responder sends the key exchange payload (KE_r) and nonce (N_r) back. When the INTERMEDIATE stage is completed, both sides need to update their key material for subsequent communication.

The CREATE_CHILD_SA is performed for additional child SAs are required or either IKE SAs or child SAs need to be rekeyed. The CREATE_CHILD_SA sends an additional SA and traffic selector payload (TS_i and TS_r) to create a new child SA. If necessary, the key exchange data (KE_i and KE_r) are optionally used for additional key negotiation.

3 Related Work

In this section, we discuss previous studies related to our work.

Evaluation of PQC Implementations in TLS. Paquin et al. [7] proposed the integration strategy of PQC into TLS using an emulated network setting. The testbed of the experiment independently controls latency and packet loss rate to examine the performance impact of various PQC primitives on established TLS connection.

The observation of subsequent study highlights that packet loss rate above 3 to 5% displays significant impact on unstructured-lattice-based PQC algorithms. The additional result from the performance evaluation concluded that the latency of loading entire web pages over the TLS network hides the essential impacts of PQC algorithms with slower computations.

The study analyzed the influence of PQC on TLS 1.3 handshake completion time by deploying the structured and unstructured lattices and supersingular isogenies of hybrid post-quantum key exchange. The post-quantum authentication is specifically measured using structured lattices and symmetric-based signatures. The emulated network experiments include four different latencies and packet loss rates ranging from 0 to 20%.

As opposed to the proposed method of PQC-based performance evaluation on latency and packet loss process with bases on the TLS 1.3, we evaluated the selected PQC-based IPsec to measure the execution performance of KEM.

Measurement of PQC and TLS 1.3 in Embedded Systems. There are multiple attempts to integrate PQC KEM and PQC signature schemes into the TLS protocol or port to embedded devices. However, Bürstinghaus et al. [8] provide the experimental framework of combining TLS and the PQC scheme to evaluate the performance of PQC-TLS on embedded platforms.

The evaluation further compares the performance of PQC cipher suite to the classical TLS variant using elliptic curve cryptography (ECC). As a result, the study demonstrates that PQC key establishment performs better in TLS on embedded devices than ECC variants. On the contrary, the SPHINCS+ signature is challenged with signature size and signing time, which affects the use of embedded systems to act as PQC-TLS.

Our study highlights the strategy for measuring the KEM and IKEv2 schemes under the condition of PQC-IPsec. Proudly, to the best of our knowledge, such a perspective of the experiment is the novel approach to evaluating the performance of the PQC to a specific network protocol.

4 Implementation

In this section, we present our implementation to evaluate the performance of PQC in IPsec and determine the trade-offs on different target PQC algorithms. Our implementation is basically constructed upon strongSwan [19], one of the most popular open-source IPsec implementations that support the integration of PQC algorithms into the IPsec protocol. Although the latest version of strongSwan already includes several PQC algorithms, such as the NIST Round 3 finalists [4], in its code base, it still lacks broad support for various algorithms yet. Hence, some challenging engineering efforts are necessary to integrate the existing PQC implementations into strongSwan. We present in detail our method to integrate general PQC algorithms into the current version of strongSwan.

Source Code Structure. We first analyze the source code of strongSwan with version 6.0dr14 [20], which is the latest version that supports PQC. As that

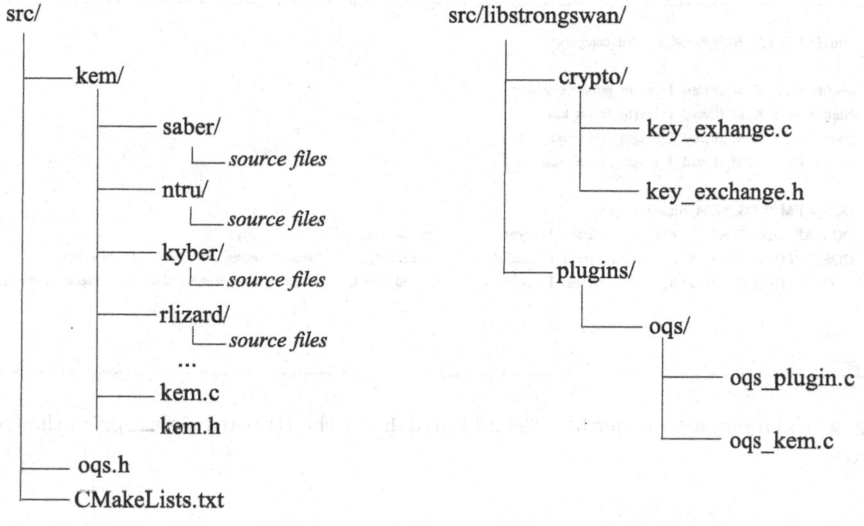

(a) OQS library (b) strongSwan

Fig. 3. The structure of strongSwan with OQS library

version of strongSwan internally utilizes liboqs, an Open Quantum Safe (OQS) library [21] for PQC algorithms, we also analyze the source code of liboqs with version 0.7.1 [22].

Figure 3 shows the hierarchical structure of the source code of strongSwan and the related library. The strongSwan has an oqs plugin (i.e., `oqs_kem.c` in the `oqs` directory) in its code base, which provides links to the OQS library. The actual PQC implementations are located in the code base of an OQS library. For KEM algorithms, each header and source file for individual algorithms is located in the `kem` directory (e.g., `kem/rlizard` for the RLizard algorithm). Every header file is included by `kem.h` for integrating the algorithm to liboqs.

Integration to Liboqs. We first initiated the integration by embedding PQC algorithms to liboqs, then implement the following cryptosystems to the IKEv2 protocols through the strongSwan's plugin. According to the architecture of strongSwan, the initial integration of any algorithm must occur with liboqs first. The following procedure is the steps to combine a new PQC algorithm using liboqs.

Step 1. Modify the source code of the new PQC algorithm to match the function and the parameter names to the liboqs format. As shown in Fig. 3, define the name of the new PQC algorithm to add it to the `kem.h` header file and declare the function name to map it to the name of the algorithm, which is defined in the header file, in the `kem.c` source file.

```
...
1  #ifdef OQS_ENABLE_KEM_Rlizard_category1
2
3  #define OQS_KEM_rlizard_1_length_public_key 4096
4  #define OQS_KEM_rlizard_1_length_secret_key 1152
5  #define OQS_KEM_rlizard_1_length_ciphertext 2080
6  #define OQS_KEM_rlizard_1_length_shared_secret 32
7
8  OQS_KEM *OQS_KEM_rlizard_1_new(void);
9  OQS_API OQS_STATUS OQS_KEM_rlizard_1_keypair(uint8_t *public_key, uint8_t *secret_key);
10 OQS_API OQS_STATUS OQS_KEM_rlizard_1_encaps(uint8_t *ciphertext, uint8_t *shared_secret, const uint8_t *public_key);
11 OQS_API OQS_STATUS OQS_KEM_rlizard_1_decaps(uint8_t *shared_secret, const uint8_t *ciphertext, const uint8_t *secret_key);
12
13 #endif
...
```

Fig. 4. Example of a header file, `kem_rlizard.h`, for the RLizard algorithm in the OQS library

Step 2. Specify the parameter size for public key, secret key, ciphertext, and shared secret newly added algorithms by following the format of liboqs, as shown in Lines 3-6 in Fig. 4. Then modify the functions' name of the newly added algorithm according to the format of the liboqs API as shown in Lines 8-11 in Fig. 4.

Step 3. Then, add the source code path to `CMakeLists.txt` so that the source code of the new PQC algorithm can be added to the liboqs build process.

Step 4. Build liboqs as a shared library. After completing the steps, the newly added algorithm can be retrieved through generic KEM functions (`keypair`, `encaps`, and `decaps`) in the liboqs.

Integration to StrongSwan. The new PQC algorithm has been integrated to the liboqs through the above steps. Now we need to register the modified liboqs in the strongSwan's oqs plugin to use the new algorithm in strongSwan; the detailed procedure is described as follows:

Step 1. Declare a new keyword to identify the new PQC algorithm (e.g., `KE_RLIZARD_L1` for the RLizard algorithm), and the corresponding short keyword (e.g., `rlizard1`) in `key_exchange.c` of strongSwan (Fig. 3).

Step 2. Assign a new Transform ID, which is an unique ID that identifies a PQC algorithm in IPsec packets, for the new algorithm.

Step 3. Declare onto the `oqs_plugin.c` source file to load the strongSwan plugin with the declared keyword for the PQC algorithm.

Step 4. Declare onto the `oqs_kem.c` source file to map the new PQC algorithm from liboqs with the declared keyword.

After completing the above steps, the users of strongSwan are given a chance to select the PQC algorithm for SA proposal through a short keyword (declared in Step 1.) that maps the declared keyword in `key_exchange.c`. Beside the algorithms presented in this work, our procedure suggests that other PQC-KEM algorithms can also be integrated with strongSwan as well.

5 Measurements and Evaluation

In this section, we evaluate the performance of the PQC algorithm embedded to the IPsec protocol in terms of the speed of KEM and IKEv2 along with the IKEv2 packet size.

5.1 Experimental Setup

For the experiment, we settled an environment for machines to communicate in IPsec with a host-to-host mode. The first machine acting as an IPsec initiator is equipped with AMD Ryzen 5 5600X 6-core processor(3.7 GHz) with 16GB RAM. Another machine acting as an IPsec responder is equipped with is AMD Ryzen 9 3950X 16-core processor(3.5 GHz) with 16GB RAM.

Both machines are connected via 100Mbps ethernet in LAN environment, operate on the Ubuntu 20.04 LTS, built around the host-host IPsec VPN environment with the strongSwan 6.0dr14 and liboqs 0.7.1. Therewith, the IPsec environment is built using strongSwan and liboqs, including new PQCs throughout the method introduced in Sect. 4.

All the algorithm source codes used in the performance evaluation are obtained from the PQC website of the NIST Computer Security Resource Center (CSRC) [23].

5.2 Measurements

We measure the performance of CRYSTALS-Kyber, NTRU, and Saber from the NIST's finalist candidates, RLizard from Korea, and LAC and AKCN from China depending on their security level.

In our study, KEM, IKEv2, and packet size are used as performance evaluation metrics. In addition, we use strongSwan to measure the performance of each KEM operation and specify the performance of each operation in detail. The IKEv2 evaluation metric indicates IPsec performance when the PQC algorithm is used as the key exchange algorithm.

Table 1 presents the parameter set and security level [24] for individual algorithm. The security level employed for our experiment is the announced security standard level from NIST's security requirements for cryptographic modules. NIST describes four qualitative security levels (Level 1, Level 3, Level 4, and Level 5) for exhaustive key retrieval. Each security level has a different security strength. Level 1 should be as hard to break as AES-128, Level 3 should be as hard to break as AES-192. And Level 4 should be as hard to break as SHA-384, Level 5 should be as hard to break as AES-256.

We compare individual algorithms to evaluate the trade-offs between the security level and performance of these algorithms. The research strive for the optimized implementation rather than the reference version of the implementation. To assess the individual cryptographic schemes, three performance metrics are deployed as essential measurements:

- The execution speed of KEM operations: key generation, encapsulation and decapsulation.
- The latency of IKEv2 stages: `IKE_SA_INIT`, `CREATE_CHILD_SA`, and Additional Key Exchange.
- The packet size of IKEv2 messages for `IKE_SA_INIT`, `CREATE_CHILD_SA`, and Additional Key Exchange.

We utilize `gettimeofday()` function to measure the speed of key generation (i.e., `OQS_KEM_keypair()` in `kem.c`), encapsulation (i.e., `OQS_KEM_encaps()`), and decapsulation (i.e., `OQS_KEM_decaps()`) with a resolution of microseconds. The measurements for the latency of IKEv2 messages are also achieved by observing the processing time of `IKE_SA_INIT`, `CREATE_CHILD_SA`, and Additional Key Exchange with the task manager of the IKEv2 protocol in the strongSwan daemon. In addition, we also measure the size of the IPsec initiator's sending and

Table 1. The parameters of PQC algorithms

Algorithm	Security level	Size (bytes)			
		Public key	Secret key	Ciphertext	Shared secret
Kyber512	1	800	1,632	768	32
Kyber768	3	1,184	2,400	1,088	32
Kyber1024	5	1,568	3,168	1,568	32
NTRU-HPS-2048509	1	699	935	699	32
NTRU-HPS-2048607	3	930	1,234	930	32
NTRU-HPS-4096821	5	1,230	1,590	1,230	32
LightSaber	1	672	1,568	736	32
Saber	3	992	2,304	1,088	32
FireSaber	5	1,312	3,040	1,472	32
RLizard-category1	1	4,096	1,152	2,080	32
RLizard-category3	3	4,096	1,152	4,144	48
RLizard-category5	5	8,192	2,304	8,256	64
LAC-128	1	544	1,056	1,024	32
LAC-192	3	1,056	2,080	1,536	48
LAC-256	5	1,056	2,080	2,048	64
AKCN-MLWE	4	992	288	1,120	32
AKCN-SEC	5	1,696	1,664	2,083	95

receiving packets by investigating the daemon's debugging log. We repeated experiments with individual IPsec connections 1,000 times and then averaged the measurement results to obtain the above metrics.

5.3 Evaluation

The complete measurement results of the performance of PQC algorithms are presented in Table 2 in Appendix. The general trend of the measurement denotes that the increase in the security level represent the decrease in KEM and IKEv2 speed and the increase in the packet size. In this section, we focus on analyzing the results in relation to the performance metrics and investigate the changes in performance outcomes on the security level of each algorithm.

Analysis on the Performance of KEM. Although mainly interested in the performance of IKEv2 for each PQC algorithm, we first analyze the execution time of KEM in IPsec, as it solely represents the performance of the algorithms.

We introduce the performance results concerning the speed (i.e., the execution time) measurement on three KEM operations: key generation, key encapsulation, and key decapsulation in Fig. 5. The overall result depicts that all algorithms performs within 150µs for key generation, 237µs for key encapsulation and 222µs within key decapsulation. The fastest key generation and key decapsulation is performed by Kyber512, and the fastest key encapsulation is performed by NTRU-HPS-2048509. The slowest algorithm to perform key generation is NTRU-HPS-4096821, key encapsulation is AKCN-SEC, and key decapsulation is LAC-256.

As the security level increases, Kyber and Saber equally experience about 40% latency at all stages. For NTRU, the increase in the key generation is twice as large as key encapsulation and key decapsulation. RLizard shows that the execution time of key generation and key encapsulation is approximately twice as large as when the security level increases from Level 3 to Level 5 than from Level 1 to Level 3. The key decapsulation stage depicts a similar increase. When LAC performs key generation, it shows minor changes when the security level increases from Level 3 to Level 5. However, when the security level increases from Level 1 to Level 3, there is a 130% increase. Based on the security level 1, the key encapsulation and key decapsulation depicts 100% increase in the security level, which is simailar to key generation. A significant increase is depicted in AKCN from security level 4 to 5. For a key generation, the increase is by 36%, key encapsulation by 93%, and key decapsulation by 129%.

Analysis on the Performance of IKEv2. We evaluate the latency of IKEv2 key exchanges for IKE_SA_INIT, CREATE_CHILD_SA, and Additional Key Exchange. The metrics of our study examines the performance of key exchange mechanism for each targeted PQC algorithms within IPsec.

Figure 6 presents the measurements of latency for each IKEv2 messages. The result represents that the speed of KEM corresponds to the performance of IKEv2 as it includes the key exchange phase in every stage. Unlike measuring KEM, the noise may occur when measuring the performance of IKEv2 due to

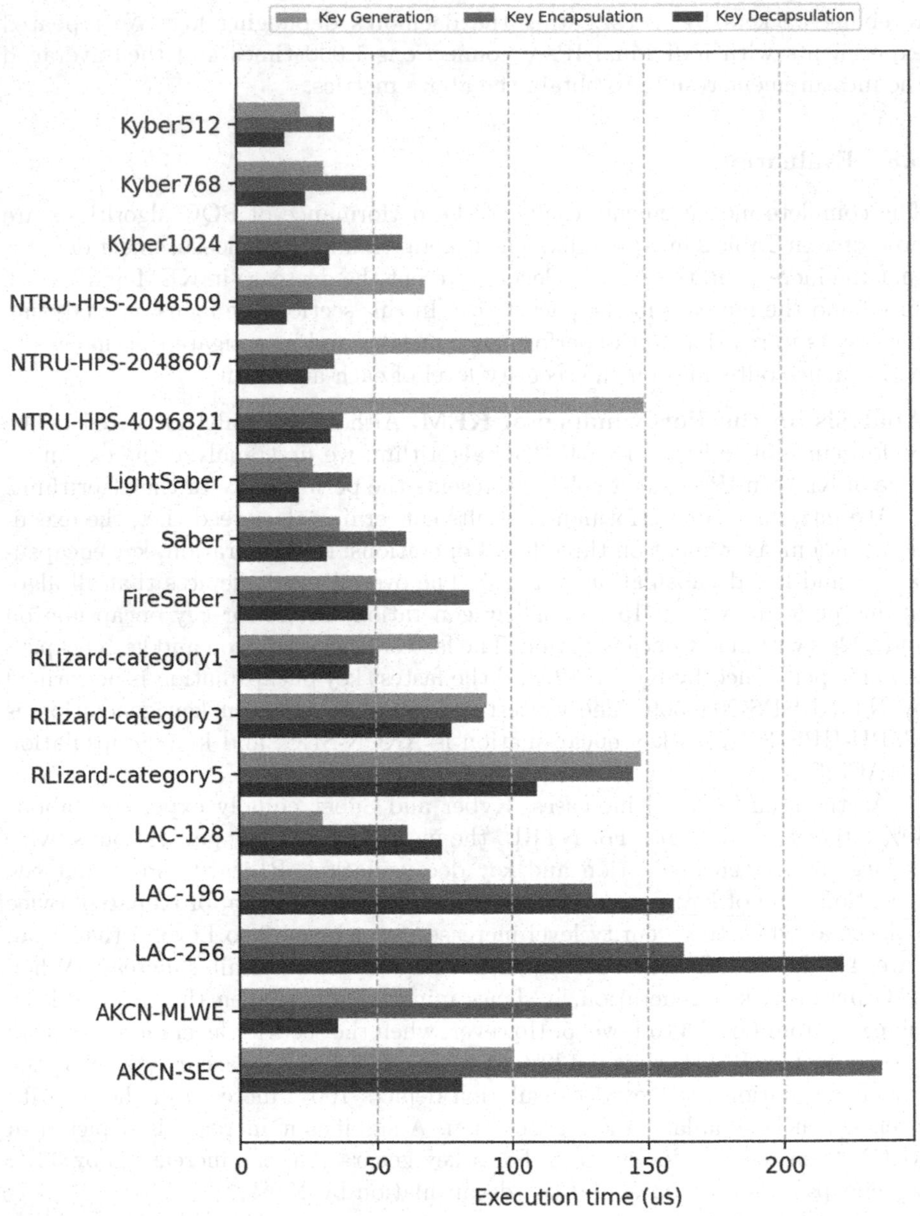

Fig. 5. Average execution time for each KEM operation

the network environment. Therefore, the presence of error should be in consideration. The latency of all KEM stages for three different IKEv2: the numbers for `IKE_SA_INIT` are between 1109µs and 3040µs; for `CREATE_CHILD_SA`, the perfor-

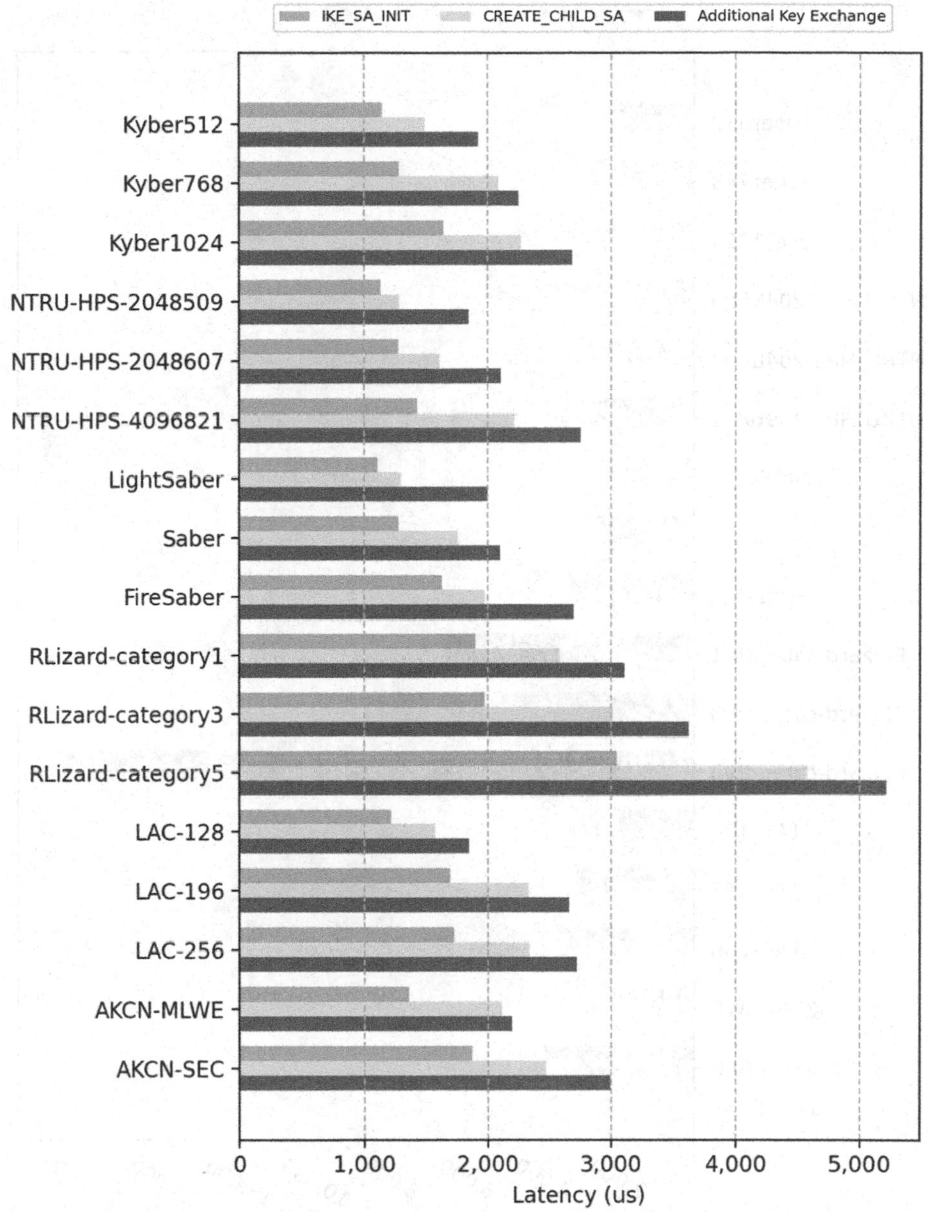

Fig. 6. Average latency for each IKEv2 stage

mance is within 1495μs and 5329μs, then finally, for Additional Key Exchange, the numbers range from 1849μs to 5209μs.

The fastest IKE_SA_INIT performance at security level 1 is the LightSaber algorithm, for CREATE_CHILD_SA is Kyber512, and for Additional Key Exchange

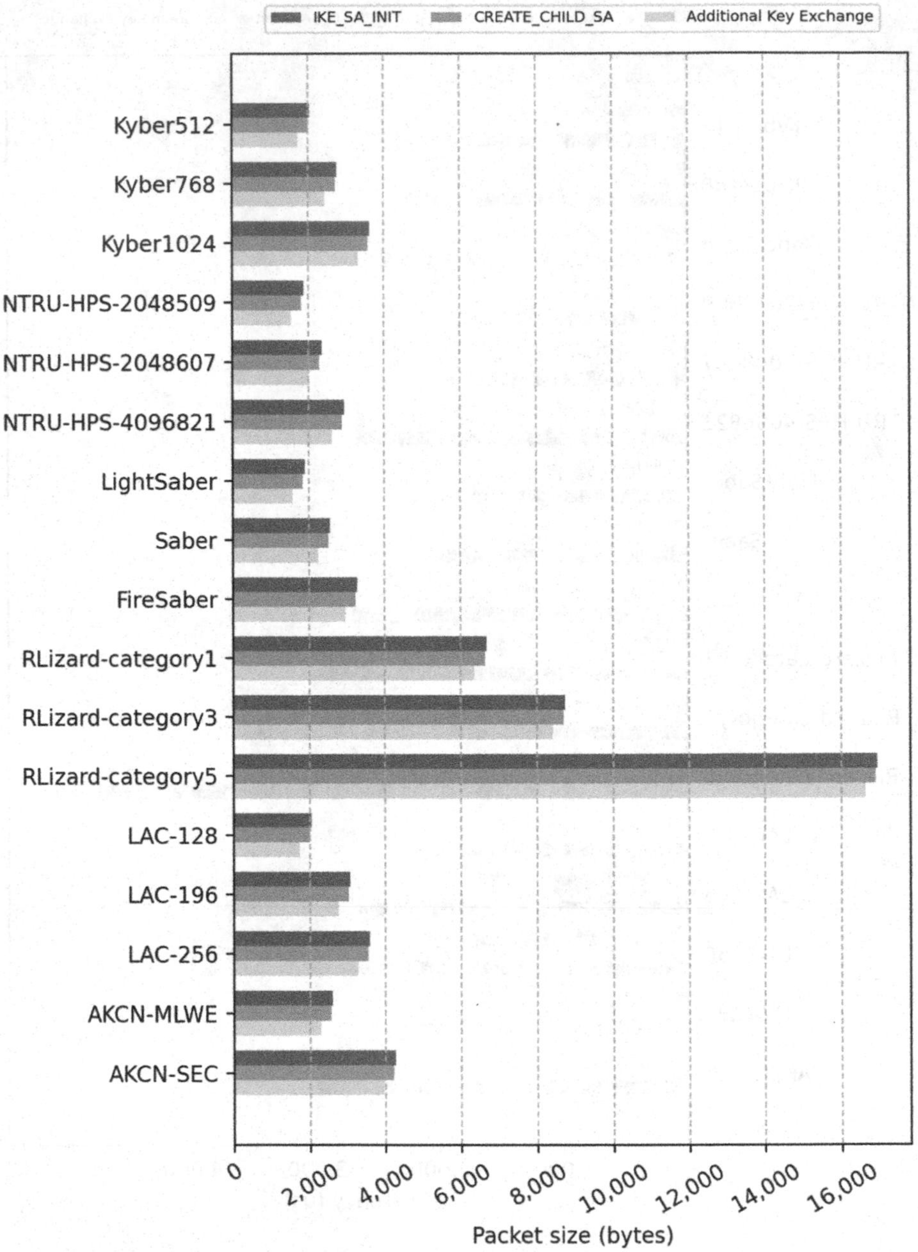

Fig. 7. Total packet size for each IKEv2 packet

is LAC-129. The shortest latency for IKE_SA_INIT and CREATE_CHILD_SA at security level 3 is NTRU-HPS-2048607 and Saber for the Additional Key Exchange. The fastest completion of IKE_SA_INIT in security level 5 is NTRU-HPS-4096821, then Kyber1024 demonstrates the highest performance for CREATE_CHILD_SA and Additional Key Exchange. As the security level increases, CRYSTALS-Kyber, NTRU, and Saber show an equal increase in latency in all three stages of KEM. Even though the increase in latency ranges from 140μs to a maximum of 650μs, we conclude that the increase is relatively equal considering the margin of error caused by the network environment. RLizard demonstrates a significant degradation in performance as the latency outreaches 1000μs when the security level elevates from Level 3 to Level 5. On the other hand, the elevation for latency in security level 1 to 3 is insignificant as it is similar to the KEM performance. Unlike RLizard, LAC demonstrates the elevation in latency from 480μs to 800μs when the security level increases from Level 1 to Level 3. However, the latency inclines by 100μs when the security level raises from Level 3 to Level 5. AKCN causes a latency of 500μs to 800μs when the security level increases from Level 4 to Level 5.

The IKEv2 latency results are closely related to the sum of execution time of KEM operations: key generation, key encapsulation, and key decapsulation. Although the execution time for KEM is shorter than the IKEv2, our experiment confirms that the IKEv2 stage introduces greater latency. For example, even though NTRU-HPS-4096821 takes a longer KEM execution time than RLizard-category1, RLizard-category1 denotes greater latency in IKE_SA_INIT, CREATE_CHILD_SA, and Additional Key Exchange compared NTRU-HPS-4096821. It is because the process is affected by the parameter set size. The overall network latency is provoked by the increase in the parameter set size and the packet size. The scrutiny of evaluating the packet size results continues in the section below.

Analysis on the IKEv2 Packet Size. Finally, we analyze the size of IPsec packets of each IKEv2 stage. The increase in the set parameter, key size, ciphertext size, shared secret, and shared secret corresponds with the increase in the security level. Such an increase in various aspects of parameter set size directly influences the performance of IKEv2. In addition to the influence of parameter set size on the speed of IKEv2, the packet size is also affected by the parameter set size. In particular, the public key must be included in the key exchange packet payload from the initiator to the responder, and the ciphertext must be in the packet payload from the responder to the initiator. Therefore, we measure the sending and the receiving packet size of two hosts to observe the overhead corresponding to the increase of the security level. Figure 7 highlights the measurement results of packet sizes for individual IKEv2 stages. Note that the measured packet size includes all headers except the key exchange payload and the measurement results are the combination of sending and the receiving packet size.

When the security level increases, the packet size increase by about 400 bytes to about 900 bytes for CRYSTALS-Kyber, NTRU, and Saber. Since the inclination of the public key and the secret key size is about 300 to 500 bytes, the increase in the packet size on the elevation of security level is insignificant.

With RLizard, about 2,000 bytes of overhead occurs with security level 1 and 3. However, about 8,000 bytes of overhead occurs between the security level of 3 and 5, which is about 4 times more than security level 1 and 3. The significant difference occurs when the security level for RLizard increases from Level 1 to Level 3, the public key size remains the same, and the ciphertext size increase by about 2,000 bytes. Nonetheless, when the security level elevates from Level 3 to Level 5, the public key and the ciphertext size individually increase by about 4,000 bytes.

Further with LAC, the increase in overhead occurs by 1,100 bytes from security level 1 to level 3. In contrast, only about 100 bytes of difference occurred with security level 3 and 5. For instance with the LAC algorithm, the difference in the public key size for security level 5 to 3 is 1,000, and the increase in the ciphertext is only 100 bytes.

AKCN-SEC carries a packet size that is 1,600 bytes larger than AKCN-MLWE. AKCN also displays an increase reflecting the public key and ciphertext sizes. About 700 bytes of the increase occurred with the public key size, and about 900 bytes of ciphertext size increased.

6 Conclusion

As quantum computers develop, the conventional public key cryptosystems are easily broken. Accordingly, a post-quantum cryptographic algorithm that is secure from quantum computers has emerged. However, PQC needs to be rigorously evaluated for its practicability before being deployed to the real world.

In this paper, we conducted performance evaluation of various PQC algorithms under the IPsec-secured networking environment. For this, we integrated the existing PQC implementations into strongSwan, the most popular open-source IPsec implementation. After that, we performed extensive performance evaluations on PQC-integrated IKEv2 of the IPsec protocol, targeting NIST Round 3, Korea, and China PQC-KEM algorithms. We measured KEM operation execution time, IKEv2 stage-specific average latency and packet size of each algorithm as performance metrics. The benchmarking result, which shows a trade-off between the security level and the performance, provides an useful guideline to those who want to implement the IPsec protocol combined with PQC. We believe that our study has contributed to the evaluation of the performance of IPsec with PQC.

Acknowledgements. This work was supported by Institute of Information & communications Technology Planning & Evaluation (IITP) grant funded by the Korea government(MSIT) (No.2019-0-00533, Research on CPU vulnerability detection and validation). This work is the result of commissioned research project supported by the affiliated institute of ETRI[2022-123].

Appendix

Table 2. The evaluation of algorithms

Algorithm	PQC KEM (µs)			Evaluation time (µs)			Evaluation packet size (bytes)		
	Key Generation	Key Encapsulation	Key Decapsulation	IKE_SA_INIT	CREATE_CHILD_SA	Additional Key Exchange	IKE_SA_INIT	CREATE_CHILD_SA	Additional Key Exchange
Kyber512	23.22	35.61	17.56	1,144.67	1,495.56	1,923.20	2,057	2,016	1,744
Kyber768	31.50	47.35	24.97	1,284.48	2,089.01	2,254.63	2,761	2,720	2,448
Kyber1024	37.89	60.51	33.61	1,646.72	2,270.73	2,684.87	3,625	3,584	3,312
NTRU-HPS-2048509	68.63	27.55	17.98	1,135.28	1,283.96	1,850.93	1,887	1,824	1,568
NTRU-HPS-2048607	108.22	35.09	25.52	1,278.26	1,617.81	2,109.77	2,349	2,304	2,032
NTRU-HPS-4096821	149.39	38.41	33.68	1,434.04	2,220.45	2,757.17	2,949	2,880	2,624
LightSaber	27.21	41.47	21.98	1,109.26	1,297.67	1,999.48	1,897	1,856	1,584
Saber	36.81	61.35	32.03	1,279.06	1,765.10	2,100.41	2,569	2,528	2,256
FireSaber	50.08	84.81	47.27	1,637.19	1,976.33	2,700.67	3,273	3,232	2,960
RLizard-category1	72.89	50.80	40.01	1,901.64	2,586.32	3,104.66	6,665	6,624	6,352
RLizard-category3	90.99	89.89	77.72	1,974.20	3,013.36	3,620.43	8,729	8,688	8,416
RLizard-category5	147.70	144.91	109.49	3,040.21	4,584.53	5,209.32	16,937	16,896	16,624
LAC-128	30.11	61.36	74.08	1,218.41	1,580.02	1,849.32	2,057	2,016	1,744
LAC-196	69.80	129.71	159.35	1,698.61	2,331.11	2,662.70	3,081	3,040	2,768
LAC-256	70.24	163.09	221.99	1,729.74	2,337.28	2,721.12	3,593	3,552	3,280
AKCN-MLWE	63.16	121.89	35.46	1,361.99	2,115.69	2,196.70	2,601	2,560	2,288
AKCN-SEC	100.73	236.02	81.32	1,877.65	2,473.04	2,994.95	4,268	4,224	3,952

References

1. Steane, A.: Quantum computing. Rep. Prog. Phys. **61**(2), 117 (1998)
2. Shor, P.W.: Algorithms for quantum computation: discrete logarithms and factoring. In: Proceedings 35th Annual Symposium on Foundations of Computer Science, pp. 124–134. IEEE (1994)
3. Sikeridis, D., Kampanakis, P., Devetsikiotis, M.: Post-quantum authentication in TLS 1.3: a performance study. Cryptology ePrint Archive (2020)
4. Alagic, G., et al.: Status report on the second round of the NIST post-quantum cryptography standardization process. US Department of Commerce, NIST (2020)
5. Alagic, G., et al.: Status report on the third round of the NIST post-quantum cryptography standardization process. Tech. rep, NIST (2022)
6. Ding, J., Steinwandt, R. (eds.): PQCrypto 2019. LNCS, vol. 11505. Springer, Cham (2019). https://doi.org/10.1007/978-3-030-25510-7
7. Paul, S., Kuzovkova, Y., Lahr, N., Niederhagen, R.: Mixed certificate chains for the transition to post-quantum authentication in TLS 1.3. In: Proceedings of the 17th ACM Asia Conference on Computer and Communications Security, pp. 727–740 (2022)

8. Bürstinghaus-Steinbach, K., Krauß, C., Niederhagen, R., Schneider, M.: Post-quantum TLS on embedded systems: integrating and evaluating Kyber and SPHINCS+ with mbed TLS. In: Proceedings of the 15th ACM Asia Conference on Computer and Communications Security, pp. 841–852 (2020)
9. Beullens, W., et al.: Post-quantum cryptography: current state and quantum mitigation. ENISA (2021)
10. Nejatollahi, H., Dutt, N., Ray, S., Regazzoni, F., Banerjee, I., Cammarota, R.: Post-quantum lattice-based cryptography implementations: a survey. ACM Comput. Surv. (CSUR) **51**(6), 1–41 (2019)
11. Bos, J., et al.: Crystals-Kyber: a CCA-secure module-lattice-based KEM. In: 2018 IEEE European Symposium on Security and Privacy (EuroS&P), pp. 353–367. IEEE (2018)
12. Hoffstein, J., Pipher, J., Silverman, J.H.: NTRU: a ring-based public key cryptosystem. In: Buhler, J.P. (ed.) ANTS 1998. LNCS, vol. 1423, pp. 267–288. Springer, Heidelberg (1998). https://doi.org/10.1007/BFb0054868
13. D'Anvers, J.-P., Karmakar, A., Sinha Roy, S., Vercauteren, F.: Saber: module-LWR based key exchange, CPA-secure encryption and CCA-secure KEM. In: Joux, A., Nitaj, A., Rachidi, T. (eds.) AFRICACRYPT 2018. LNCS, vol. 10831, pp. 282–305. Springer, Cham (2018). https://doi.org/10.1007/978-3-319-89339-6_16
14. Lu, X., et al.: Lac: Practical ring-LWE based public-key encryption with byte-level modulus. Cryptology ePrint Archive (2018)
15. Jin, Z., Shen, S., Zhao, Y.: Compact and flexible KEM from ideal lattice. IEEE Trans. Inf. Theory **68**(6), 3829–3840 (2022)
16. Lee, J., Kim, D., Lee, H., Lee, Y., Cheon, J.H.: Rlizard: post-quantum key encapsulation mechanism for IoT devices. IEEE Access **7**, 2080–2091 (2018)
17. Kaufman, C., Hoffman, P., Nir, Y., Eronen, P., Kivinen, T.: Internet key exchange protocol version 2 (ikev2). Tech. rep, IETF (2014)
18. Bindel, N., Brendel, J., Fischlin, M., Goncalves, B., Stebila, D.: Hybrid key encapsulation mechanisms and authenticated key exchange. In: Ding, J., Steinwandt, R. (eds.) PQCrypto 2019. LNCS, vol. 11505, pp. 206–226. Springer, Cham (2019). https://doi.org/10.1007/978-3-030-25510-7_12
19. Andreas-Steffen: strongswan documentation. Tech. rep., strongSec GmbH (2021). https://docs.strongswan.org/docs/5.9/index.html
20. strongswan 6.0dr14. https://github.com/strongswan/strongswan/tree/6.0dr14
21. Stebila, D., Mosca, M.: Post-quantum key exchange for the internet and the open quantum safe project. In: Avanzi, R., Heys, H. (eds.) SAC 2016. LNCS, vol. 10532, pp. 14–37. Springer, Cham (2017). https://doi.org/10.1007/978-3-319-69453-5_2
22. Liboqs 0.7.1. https://github.com/open-quantum-safe/liboqs/tree/0.7.1
23. Chen, L., et al.: Report on post-quantum cryptography, vol. 12. NIST (2016)
24. Chen, L., Moody, D., Liu, Y.: NIST post-quantum cryptography standardization. Transition **800**, 131A (2017)

An Ultrafast Cryptographically Secure Pseudorandom Number Generator

Jianliang Zheng[1(✉)] and Jie Li[2]

[1] Red Bitbox, New York, USA
zheng@redbbx.com

[2] Farmingdale State College, State University of New York, Farmingdale, NY 11735, USA
jie.li@farmingdale.edu

Abstract. An ultrafast cryptographically secure pseudorandom number generator, referred to as MaD4, is presented in this paper. MaD4 maintains a small byte-oriented state, whose transition follows a pseudorandom permutation, and a large integer-oriented state, whose transition follows a pseudorandom mapping. The byte-oriented state is initialized from a secret key and then further used to bootstrap and initialize the integer-oriented state. After initialization, both states evolve, with the byte-oriented state serving as a source of entropy and periodically reseeding the integer-oriented state. The combination of slow byte-oriented operations and fast integer-oriented operations renders a nice balance between quality and speed. MaD4 generates high quality pseudorandom numbers as attested by standard statistical testing tools and runs at a speed close to half clock cycle per byte on an Intel Core i7 processor. With a large state space of 10520 bits, MaD4 has an expected period length around 1.00e+1783. It is designed to resist various known cryptographic attacks and withstand state compromise extension attacks as well.

Keywords: Pseudorandom number generator · Pseudorandom permutation · Pseudorandom mapping · Unpredictability · Cryptanalysis · High performance

1 Introduction

Random numbers and pseudorandom numbers have broad applications and they are of paramount importance in cryptography. Keystreams, keys, seeds, salts, and challenges used in various cryptosystems are all assumed to be random. A pseudorandom number generator (PRNG) targeting secure applications should have several properties. First of all, it must be secure. A basic requirement is that there is no polynomial-time algorithm that can be used to deduce the internal state or the seed from the output sequence. A cryptographically secure pseudorandom number generator (CSPRNG) should also withstand state compromise extensions. Second and obviously, a PRNG should be able to generate high quality pseudorandom numbers. Although, in a strict sense, generating high

S.-H. Seo and H. Seo (Eds.): ICISC 2022, LNCS 13849, pp. 267–291, 2023.
https://doi.org/10.1007/978-3-031-29371-9_14

quality pseudorandom numbers subsumes being secure, these two features are often addressed separately and will be so treated in this paper. The quality of pseudorandom number generation is usually measured by the difficulty of distinguishing the generated pseudorandom sequence from a truly random one. Last, high speed is another desirable feature, especially for those PRNGs designed for high performance computing such as data encryption in cloud computing.

So far many PRNGs have been developed, but dedicated high performance high quality PRNGs are still in demand, particularly in the cryptographic category. In light of this, we propose a new CSPRNG in this paper. This generator, referred to as MaD4, demonstrates a new design paradigm for high speed and high quality pseudorandom number generators. At the core of this paradigm is a two-layer approach, which closely combines a slow byte-oriented layer with a fast integer-oriented layer. The first layer maintains a small byte-oriented state (BOS), whose transition follows a pseudorandom permutation, and the second layer maintains a large integer-oriented state (IOS), whose transition follows a pseudorandom mapping. The byte-oriented state is first initialized from a seed or key[1] and the integer-oriented state is then bootstrapped and initialized through the byte-oriented state. After initialization, both states evolve, with the byte-oriented state serving as a source of entropy and periodically reseeding the integer-oriented state. The slow-start strategy of the first layer ensures high quality initialization, which shows to have an avalanche effect that meets the strict avalanche criterion (SAC) [32]. The second layer takes advantages of modern 64-bit platforms and uses integer operations for high speed pseudorandom number generation.

The combination of slow byte operations and fast integer operations renders a nice balance between quality and speed. MaD4 generates high quality pseudorandom numbers as attested by standard statistical testing tools and runs at a speed close to half clock cycle per byte on a typical Intel Core i7 personal computer, which is several times faster than any CSPRNGs we know. It has a state space of 10520 bits and an expected period length around 10^{1783}. MaD4 is designed with various cryptanalytic attacks in mind and our security analysis shows it has strong resistance against attacks that range from those special attacks mounted against the popular stream cipher RC4 [29] to other well-known attacks such as time-memory tradeoff attacks, guess-and-determine attacks, algebraic attacks, distinguishing attacks, differential attacks, and side channel attacks. It can also withstand state compromise extension attacks due to the use of non-invertible pseudorandom mappings and the design that the byte-oriented state serves as an unpredictable source of entropy and periodically reseeds the integer-oriented state during pseudorandom number generation. While MaD4 is not based on computationally hard problems, it is practically impossible to go backwards, either from the observed stream of pseudorandom numbers to the internal state or from a compromised state to its previous states or the stream of pseudorandom numbers generated before the state is compromised. For its excellent statistical property, ultrafast speed, and strong resistance against various attacks, MaD4

[1] Seed and key are used interchangeably in this paper.

is well suited for high speed pseudorandom number generation, pervasive data encryption, and a range of other cryptographic applications.

The rest of this paper is structured as follows. In Sect. 2, we introduce a simple byte-oriented PRNG that is used as a building block of MaD4. In Sect. 3, we describe the algorithm of MaD4 in detail. In Sect. 4, we analyze the period of MaD4. Next, in Sect. 5, we present the security analysis. Then, in Sects. 6 and 7, we give the statistical testing results and performance testing results respectively. Finally, in Sect. 8, we conclude the paper with a summary.

2 A Building Block

In this section we first give a brief review of MARC [35] and then describe an iteration reduced version of MARC, which is used as a building block of MaD4. All algorithms given in this section and next section will be described using pseudo code and the following notations are used:

Notation	Usage
`#`	starting a comment line
`++`	increment (x++ is same as $x = x + 1$)
`%`	modulo
`<<`	left logical bitwise shift
`>>`	right logical bitwise shift
`&`	bitwise AND
`|`	bitwise OR
`^`	bitwise XOR
`[]`	array subscripting (subscript starts from 0)

Hexadecimal numbers are prefixed by "0x" and all variables and constants are unsigned integers in little endian.

2.1 MARC

MARC is a variant of stream cipher RC4 [29]. While retaining the simplicity of RC4, MARC enhances the security of RC4 by modifying its key scheduling algorithm (KSA) and improves the performance by modifying its pseudorandom generation algorithm (PRGA). It supports a key up to 64 bytes. Its internal state consists of a 256-byte state table S and three 8-bit indices i, j, and k. The KSA and PRGA of MARC are shown in Listing 1. The KSA first initializes the state table S to an identity permutation as RC4 KSA does. It then enhances the security of RC4 KSA by increasing the number of iterations from 256 to $256 + 256 + 64 = 576$ and during each iteration using a left rotation operation among $S[i]$, $S[j]$, and $S[k]$ (i.e., $tmp = S[i]$, $S[i] = S[j]$, $S[j] = S[k]$, $S[k] = tmp$) instead of a swap operation between $S[i]$ and $S[j]$ to shuffle the state table S. The PRGA reuses the values of indices j and k from the KSA and sets the initial value of index i to the sum of indices j and k. It then iterates as many times as needed and during each iteration shuffles the state table S using a swap operation as RC4 PRGA does. It outputs four bytes during each iteration.

Listing 1. MARC Pseudorandom Number Generator

```
1   ## addition (+) and increment (++) operations   ##
2   ## are performed modulo 256; except variable r,  ##
3   ## which is a 16-bit unsigned integer, all other ##
4   ## variables are 8-bit unsigned integers.        ##
5   ## % means modulo; ∧ means bitwise XOR.          ##
6
7   # Key Scheduling Algorithm (KSA)
8   for r from 0 to 255
9       S[r] = r
10  endfor
11  i = 0
12  j = 0
13  k = 0
14  for r from 0 to 575
15      j = j + S[i] + key[r % keylength]
16      k = k ∧ j
17      left_rotate(S[i], S[j], S[k])
18      i++
19  endfor
20
21  # Pseudorandom Generation Algorithm (PRGA)
22  # (j and k are from KSA)
23  i = j + k
24  while GeneratingOutput
25      i++
26      j = j + S[i]
27      k = k ∧ j
28      swap(S[i], S[j])
29      m = S[j] + S[k]
30      n = S[i] + S[j]
31      output S[m]
32      output S[n]
33      output S[m ∧ j]
34      output S[n ∧ k]
35  endwhile
```

2.2   MARC-bb: MARC as a Building Block

As a byte-oriented PRNG, MARC does not take advantage of modern 64-bit platforms. However, it can be used as a building block to construct more advanced
PRNGs. In MaD4, we use an iteration-reduced version of MARC, referred to
as MARC-bb (bb stands for building block), for key scheduling, state initialization, and reseeding. The only difference between MARC-bb and MARC is
that MARC-bb KSA iterates 320 times instead of 576 times. The reason we
choose MARC-bb over MARC is that MARC-bb KSA already has an avalanche
effect that meets the strict avalanche criterion (SAC) [32] (details given in Subsect. 2.3) and the additional 256 iterations implemented in MARC KSA are
mainly for increasing the security margin, which is achieved in MaD4 through
the additional shuffling introduced after the key scheduling (details given in
Subsect. 3.3).

2.3 Avalanche Effect of MARC-bb KSA

We study the avalanche effect of MARC-bb KSA in this subsection. Avalanche effect measures the diffusion efficiency of a system, e.g., a hash function, a PRNG, or a block cipher. It shows how the output changes when the input is changed slightly. The strict avalanche criterion (SAC) [32] is satisfied if each output bit changes with a probability of 0.5 whenever a single input bit is complemented. We investigate the avalanche effect as follows:

1. Randomly select a key of 64 bytes (worst case for diffusion in MARC-bb KSA), denoted by K1.
2. Get the following variants of K1:
   (a) K2 = 1's complement of K1
   (b) K3 = reverse of K2 (i.e., reverse the bits of K2 and assign the result to K3)
   (c) K4 = 1's complement of K3
   If K2 and K3 are the same (i.e., the input is symmetric), then K3 and K4 are not used.
3. For each selected key or its variant, flip one bit of it each time (starting from the most significant bit) and compare the output of the flipped version with the output of its unflipped version. This step is also referred to as one experiment.
4. Repeat step 1, 2, 3 until the number of flippings, denoted by N, reaches a specified number, for example 10^5. Because we do not stop until all the bits of a key or its variant are flipped and the key length is 512 bits, the actual number of flippings will be a multiple of 512. For an expected number 10^5, the actual number of flippings is $N =$ ceiling $(10^5/512) \times 512 = 100352$.

Once enough number of experiments are carried out, we conduct a chi-square goodness-of-fit test. Our test goal is to accept or reject the null hypothesis $\mathcal{H}_0$ that, for the flippings of input bits, the flippings of output bits follow a binomial distribution.

Let $S = (s_0, s_1, ..., s_{L-1})$ represent the output, where$L$ is the bit length of the output. For the flipping of each input bit, we calculate the Hamming distance H between the flipped version S' and the unflipped version S as:

$$H = \sum_{i=0}^{L-1} (s_i^{'} \wedge s_i)$$

Let H_j denote the Hamming distance corresponding to the j-th experiment (i.e., the j-th flipping of input bits). The number of times that exactly m output bits are flipped is

$$Count_m = \sum_{j=1}^{N} \delta_{mH_j} \quad m = 0, 1, 2, ..., L$$

where N is the number of experiments and δ_{mH_j} is the Kronecker delta. Then we compute the chi-square value

$$\chi^2 = \sum_{m=0}^{L} \frac{(Count_m - NP_m)^2}{NP_m} \tag{1}$$

where P_m is the theoretical probability that m output bits are flipped for a binomial distribution, calculated as,

$$P_m = \binom{L}{m} \times \frac{1}{2^L} = \frac{L!}{m!(L-m)!} \times \frac{1}{2^L}$$

The critical value of the chi-square distribution with the degrees of freedom ($d.o.f.$), v, can be computed as (see [16]):

$$C.V. = v + \sqrt{2v}x_p + \frac{2}{3}x_p^2 - \frac{2}{3} + O(\frac{1}{\sqrt{v}})$$

where $x_p = 2.33$ for our chosen significance level $\alpha = 0.01$. Finally we compare the chi-square statistic with the critical value to determine whether to accept or reject the null hypothesis $\mathcal{H}_0$.

Table 1. Chi-Square Statistic Testing Results for MARC-bb Key Scheduling

Algorithm	Input size (bytes)	Output size (bytes)	$d.o.f.$	$C.V.$ ($\alpha = 0.01$)	χ^2	Reject $\mathcal{H}_0$?
MD5	64	16	128	168.233	49.527	No
SHA-1		20	160	204.633	66.401	No
SHA-256		32	256	311.674	77.629	No
SHA3-256		32	256	311.674	80.472	No
MARC-bb		32	256	311.674	79.463	No
		256*	2047	2199.06	238.36	No
RC4		256*	2047	2199.06	4.56×10^{55}	Yes
RC4 (+64 iterations)		256*	2047	2199.06	1.87×10^{16}	Yes
RC4 (+256 iterations)		256*	2047	2199.06	244.29	No

*We use 2047 bits out of the total 2048 output bits, because for swap operations the number of flippings is always an even number if the entire state table is used.

The chi-square test results are shown in Table 1. The test results for RC4 and hash functions MD5, SHA-1, SHA-256, and SHA3-256 are also provided for comparison. Each χ^2 value is the average result of 10 runs, with each run containing $N = 100352$ experiments. The results show that MARC-bb KSA has a similar avalanche effect as hash functions MD5, SHA-1, SHA-256, and SHA3-256. It satisfies the strict avalanche criterion. Each χ^2 value is far less than the corresponding critical value at the 0.01 significance level, suggesting that the null hypothesis cannot be rejected and the observed distribution has a close match with the expected binomial distribution. The distributions of the original RC4 and revised RC4 with additional 64 iterations do not agree with the expected binomial distribution. But more shuffling, e.g., with additional 256 iterations, helps to improve the avalanche effect of RC4 key scheduling.

3 Algorithm Details

In this section we present the algorithm details of MaD4, including data structure, key scheduling, state initialization, and pseudorandom number generation. The functional model of MaD4 is illustrated in Fig. 1. MaD4 uses MARC-bb for key scheduling, state initialization, and reseeding. The pseudorandom generation algorithm includes a *generate function* to generate pseudorandom numbers, an *update function* to update the internal state, and a *reseed function* to provide new entropies. The details of this model are discussed in the following subsections.

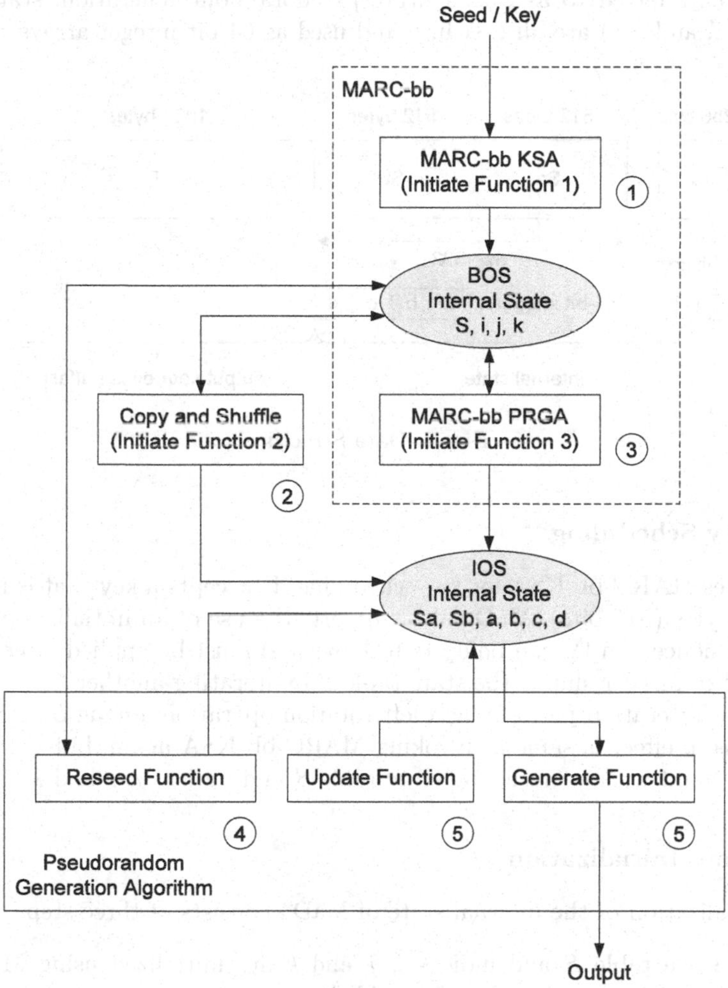

Fig. 1. Functional Model

3.1 Data Structure

MaD4 maintains a data structure shown in Fig. 2, which comprises one 256-byte state table (denoted by S), two 512-byte state tables (denoted by Sa and Sb), three 8-bit indices (denoted by i, j, and k), four 64-bit integers (denoted by a, b, c, and d), and one 1024-byte output sequence buffer (denoted by T). State tables S, Sa, Sb, indices i, j, k, and integers a, b, c, d construct the internal state of MaD4. T is used for buffering pseudorandom numbers generated from the internal state. In some functions, the concatenation of Sa and Sb is used as a large 1024-byte state table, referred to as Sw, or cast into a 32-bit integer array of size 256, referred to as $S32$. During pseudorandom generation, state tables (Sa, Sb, T, and Sw) are all cast into and used as 64-bit integer arrays.

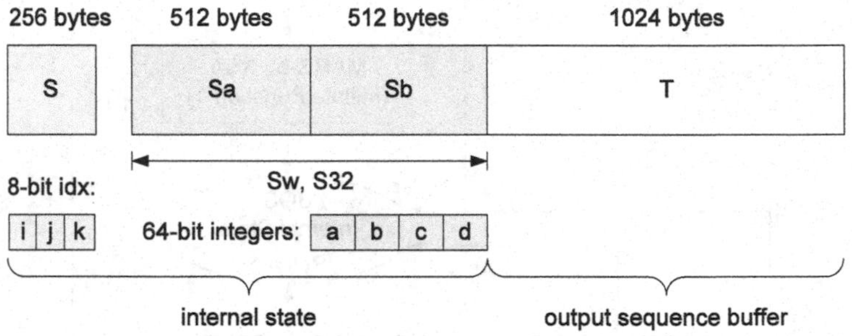

Fig. 2. Data Structure

3.2 Key Scheduling

MaD4 uses MARC-bb KSA for key scheduling. It accepts a key that is no larger than 64 bytes (512 bits). MaD4 also supports the use of an initialization vector (IV) or a nonce. An IV can be up to 64 bytes and must be applied after the key. It is used to further shuffle the state table S by iterating another 320 times and during each iteration performing a left rotation operation among $S[i]$, $S[j]$, and $S[k]$. This in effect is same as invoking MARC-bb KSA again, but with the IV as the key and without resetting state table S and indices i, j, and k.

3.3 State Initialization

The initialization of the internal state of MaD4 consists of three steps.

1. First, state table S and indices i, j, and k are initialized using MARC-bb KSA with a key (and an IV, if provided).
2. Next, state table S and indices i, j, and k are used to initialize state tables Sa and Sb, by repeating the following *copy-and-shuffle* process.
   (a) Copy $S[0]$, $S[1]$, ..., $S[255]$ to $Sa[0]$, $Sa[1]$, ..., $Sa[255]$;

Listing 2. Initialization Shuffling Algorithm (ISA)

```
# addition (+) and increment (++) operations
# are performed modulo 256
for r from 0 to 255
    i++
    j = j + S[i]
    k = k ∧ j
    left_rotate(S[i], S[j], S[k])
endfor
```

(b) Shuffle S according to the Initialization Shuffling Algorithm (ISA) shown in Listing 2 (the ISA shuffles the 256-byte state table S to generate a new permutation);
(c) Copy $S[0]$, $S[1]$, ..., $S[255]$ to $Sa[256]$, $Sa[257]$, ..., $Sa[511]$;
(d) Repeat ISA;
(e) Copy $S[0]$, $S[1]$, ..., $S[255]$ to $Sb[0]$, $Sb[1]$, ..., $Sb[255]$;
(f) Repeat ISA;
(g) Copy $S[0]$, $S[1]$, ..., $S[255]$ to $Sb[256]$, $Sb[257]$, ..., $Sb[511]$;
(h) Repeat ISA.

3. Last, 32 pseudorandom bytes are generated using MARC-bb PRGA. These 32 bytes are converted into four 64-bit integers using little endian and assigned to integers a, b, c, and d.

Now the internal state is initialized and contains five permutations of {0, 1, ..., 255}, three initialized 8-bit indices, and four initialized 64-bit integers.

3.4 Pseudorandom Number Generation

The pseudorandom generation algorithm is shown in Listing 3. MaD4 uses 64-bit operations for pseudorandom number generation. Initially, the output sequence buffer T is marked as empty. During each round of pseudorandom number generation, 128 64-bit integers or 1024 bytes are generated and stored in the output sequence buffer. When a pseudorandom number generation request is received, the output sequence buffer is checked. If it is not empty, the data stored in it are used to serve the need. After all the data in the buffer are consumed, MaD4 refreshes the buffer by generating new pseudorandom numbers. During each generation round, the algorithm iterates 64 times and generates two 64-bit integers during each iteration.

The internal state of MaD4 is functionally divided into two parts. State table S and indices i, j, and k form the byte-oriented state (BOS) since they are used as bytes in all the operations. State tables Sa, Sb and integers a, b, c, d construct the integer-oriented state (IOS) since they are used in 64-bit integer format in most operations. The BOS serves as a source of entropy to the IOS. Before each generation round, 32 pseudorandom bytes are obtained from the BOS using the

Listing 3. One Round of Pseudorandom Number Generation

```
## additions are performed modulo ##
## 0x10000000000000000           ##

# declare a byte array of size 64
byte x[64]

# cast the byte array into 64-bit integer array
x[64] => x64[8]

# reseed
(e, f, g, h) = reseed(S32)

# update a, b, c, and d
a = a + e
b = b + f
c = c + g
d = d + h

# populate array x (through x64)
M = 0x7878787878787878
N = 0x0405060700010203
x64[0] = (a & M) | N
x64[1] = (b & M) | N
x64[2] = (c & M) | N
x64[3] = (d & M) | N
x64[4] = ((a >> 1) & M) | N
x64[5] = ((b >> 1) & M) | N
x64[6] = ((c >> 1) & M) | N
x64[7] = ((d >> 1) & M) | N

# generate pseudorandom numbers and update internal state
for r from 0 to 63
    a = a << 1
    b = b >> 1
    a = a + (e ∧ Sw[x[r]])
    b = b + (f ∧ Sw[x[r]∧0x78])
    c = c + (g ∧ Sa[r])
    d = d + (h ∧ Sb[r])
    T[2r] = c ∧ (a + d)
    T[2r+1] = d ∧ (b + c)
    Sw[x[r]] = a + b
endfor
```

reseed function given in Listing 4. These 32 bytes are converted into four 64-bit intermediate variables *e*, *f*, *g*, and *h* using little endian. The reseed function is similar to MARC-bb PRGA except that the 32-bit integer array $S32$ is shuffled, i.e., four elements in $S32$ are left rotated during each of the eight iterations. The four integers *e*, *f*, *g*, and *h* are then used to update *a*, *b*, *c*, and *d*. It is worth noting that, while MaD4 is presented as a deterministic CSPRNG in this paper, it can be used as a non-deterministic CSPRNG as well by introducing additional non-deterministic and/or true random sources during reseeding. Those additional entropy inputs make MaD4 behave like a true random number generator (TRNG).

Listing 4. Reseed Function

```
# function reseed(S32)
for r from 0 to 7
    i++
    j = j + S[i]
    k = k ∧ j
    swap(S[i], S[j])
    m = S[j] + S[k]
    n = S[i] + S[j]
    left_rotate(S32[i], S32[j], S32[k], S32[n])
    output S[m]
    output S[n]
    output S[m ∧ j]
    output S[n ∧ k]
endfor
```

Variable x is a byte array of size 64, used as indices to access state tables for indirection operation. It is computed from the updated a, b, c, d, and two constants M and N. Each byte of x has a value falling in the range [0, 127] and any two bytes with a distance less than 8 have distinct values. The combination of $Sw[x[r]]$, $Sw[x[r]\wedge 0x78]$, $Sa[r]$, and $Sb[r]$ introduces pseudorandom indirect access and at the same time guarantees all state table integers get involved during each generation round. The way we choose these four state table integers during each iteration deserves some explanations. First note that both $Sw[x[r]]$ and $Sw[x[r]\wedge 0x78]$ can access either state table Sa or state table Sb but they can never access the same state table, which also means each state table has the same chance to be accessed by them. The use of constants M and N results in a special feature – the four state table integers $Sw[x[r]]$, $Sw[x[r]\wedge 0x78]$, $Sa[r]$, and $Sb[r]$ are distinct and they are also different from any of the four state table integers used in the previous 3 or next 3 iterations. By distinct and different, we mean they point to different state table integers, which do not necessarily but with a high probability have different values. One can verify this feature by observing the following facts: $Sw[x[r]]$ and $Sw[x[r]\wedge 0x78]$ are distinct; so are $Sa[r]$ and $Sb[r]$; the lower three bits of $x[r]$ and $x[r]\wedge 0x78$ come from N and cycle through the values 4, 5, 6, 7, 0, 1, 2, 3; while those of r cycle through the values 0, 1, 2, 3, 4, 5, 6, 7. This is demonstrated in Table 2.

Table 2. State Table Access During Pseudorandom Number Generation

State table integer	Subscript	State table accessed	Subscript values (last 3 bits)
$Sw[x[r]]$	$x[r]$	Sy ($y = a$ or b)	4, 5, 6, 7, 0, 1, 2, 3, ...
$Sw[x[r]\wedge 0x78]$	$x[r]\wedge 0x78$	Sz ($z = a$ or b, $z \neq y$)	4, 5, 6, 7, 0, 1, 2, 3, ...
$Sa[r]$	r	Sa	0, 1, 2, 3, 4, 5, 6, 7, ...
$Sb[r]$	r	Sb	0, 1, 2, 3, 4, 5, 6, 7, ...

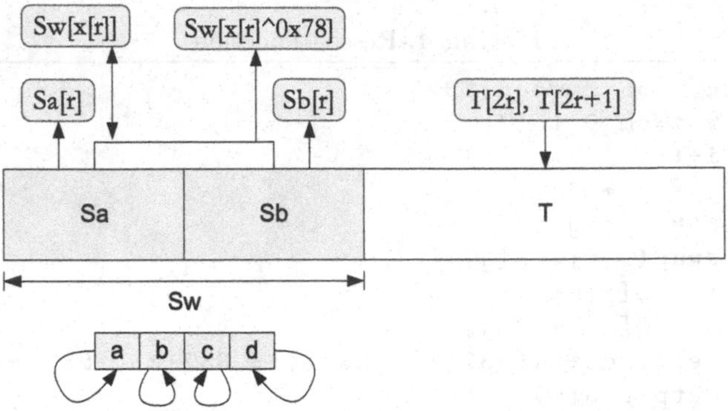

Fig. 3. Data Flow in One Iteration of PRGA

Figure 3 summarizes the data flow during one iteration in pseudorandom number generation, with detailed interactions among different elements omitted.

For efficiency and simplicity, only a few types of operations are used. They are bitwise AND, bitwise OR, bitwise XOR, addition, left logical bitwise shift, and right logical bitwise shift, each taking only one clock cycle for most processors when operands are immediate constants or register variables [12]. All four integers a, b, c, and d are updated during each iteration. Besides that, one element from state table Sa or Sb is also updated via $Sw[x[r]]$ during each iteration. In other words, nearly half of Sa and Sb is updated during each generation round or on average each state table element has a 50% chance to get updated. Is it fast enough to update half of Sa and Sb during each generation round? The answer is "yes". Due to the shift operations, the value of a is determined by the most recent 64 values of $Sw[x[r]]$ (and e) and the value of b is largely determined by the most recent 64 values of $Sw[x[r]\wedge 0\text{x}78]$ (and f). On the other hand, c and d are permanently affected by any state table element that has been involved in the computation of their values. This means the update of a single state table element can completely change the evolution path of c and d.

4 State Transition and Period

The internal state of MaD4 consists of a byte-oriented state whose transition follows a pseudorandom permutation and an integer-oriented state whose transition follows a pseudorandom mapping. For the 256-byte state table S, the number of possible permutations is $N = 256! \approx 2^{1684}$. This gives an average period around $N/2 = 2^{1683}$. The index i is used as a loop counter and has a cycle of 2^8. The transition of index j or k roughly follows a pseudorandom mapping and has a cycle around $2^{8/2} = 2^4$. Therefore the expected period of the byte-oriented state is $2^{1683+8+4+4} = 2^{1699}$. The integer-oriented state consists of the 1024-byte state table S_w and the four 64-bit integers a, b, c, and d. Its transition follows a pseudorandom mapping. This gives an expected period of $2^{(1024\times 8+4\times 64)/2} = 2^{4224}$. So the overall expected period of MaD4 is $2^{1699+4224} = 2^{5923} \approx 1.00 \times 10^{1783}$.

Aside from the average period length, another metric of practical interest is the lower bound of the period length. Some stream ciphers and pseudorandom number generators provide a hard lower bound of period length through the use of a counter [8,10,15]. MaD4 does not use a counter and theoretically any period length is possible, but it is unlikely to hit a short period length in practice due to the huge number of internal states. For an n-bit state, the probability that the period length is equal to or smaller than k can be computed as

$$\begin{aligned} P_{\leq k} &= 1 - P_{>k} \\ &= 1 - \left(\frac{2^n-1}{2^n}\right)\left(\frac{2^n-2}{2^n}\right)\cdots\left(\frac{2^n-k}{2^n}\right) \\ &< 1 - \left[\left(\frac{2^n-k}{2^n}\right)\right]^k \\ &= 1 - \left(1 + \frac{-k}{2^n}\right)^k \\ &= 1 - \sum_{j=0}^{k} \binom{k}{j}\left(\frac{-k}{2^n}\right)^j \end{aligned}$$

where

$$\binom{k}{j} = \frac{k!}{j!(k-j)!}$$

is the binomial coefficient. For $1 \lll k \lll 2^{n/2}$, it follows that

$$\begin{aligned} P_{\leq k} &< 1 - \sum_{j=0}^{k} \binom{k}{j}\left(\frac{-k}{2^n}\right)^j \\ &= 1 - \left[1 + \binom{k}{1}\left(\frac{-k}{2^n}\right) + \binom{k}{2}\left(\frac{-k}{2^n}\right)^2 + \cdots\right] \\ &< \binom{k}{1}\left(\frac{k}{2^n}\right) \\ &= \frac{k^2}{2^n} \end{aligned} \tag{2}$$

Table 3 gives some "small" period lengths of MaD4 and their associated probabilities computed using Eq. (2). Note that, MaD4 has a state of 10520 bits, but the 2048-bit state table S is a permutation of $\{0, 1, ..., 255\}$, which gives a total $256! \approx 2^{1684}$ states instead of 2^{2048} states. Therefore we need to substitute 10156 instead of 10520 for n in Eq. (2) when computing the probabilities.

5 Security Analysis

5.1 Resistance Against Known Attacks

In this subsection, we analyze the security of MaD4 in the context of known attacks.

Table 3. Period Lengths and Associated Probabilities

Period length	$\leq 2^{64}$	$\leq 2^{128}$	$\leq 2^{256}$
Probability	$< 2^{-10028}$ $\approx 1.87 \times 10^{-3019}$	$< 2^{-9900}$ $\approx 6.35 \times 10^{-2981}$	$< 2^{-9644}$ $\approx 7.36 \times 10^{-2904}$

Time-Memory Tradeoff Attacks. Time-memory tradeoff attacks rely on precomputation to reduce the effort needed for recovering the internal state and/or secret key [6]. This type of attacks proceed as follows: assume that the PRNG is in a certain state and calculate a number of output bits and put the pair (output, state) in a sorted list; after enough pairs are calculated and stored, try to match a received output sequence with the saved output sequences; if the match is successful, then with some likelihood the internal state or partial of it may be determined, which may further lead to the recovery of the secret key. The parameters in a time-memory tradeoff attack are time (T), memory (M), and amount of output data (D). In general $T \times M^2 \times D^2 = S^2$, where S is the state space of the PRNG and $D^2 \leq T$. The precomputation time P is computed as $P = S/D$. The design strength of MaD4 is 512 bits. For the brute-force equivalent attack with $T = 2^{512}$ and $D \leq \sqrt{T} = 2^{256}$, $M = S/D/\sqrt{T} \geq 2^{10156}/2^{256}/2^{256} = 2^{9644}$. The lower bound on memory for the attack is 2^{9644} bits, which is simply impractical.

Guessing Attacks. The strategy for this type of attacks is to guess a small part of the internal state and then deduce the remaining part. This is particularly powerful when applied to a word-based PRNG because a word-based PRNG has a relatively small number of internal words and any word guessed has a good chance to participate in the computation of next iteration if the algorithm is not designed with caution. The consequence is that more and more words get revealed and the PRNG is eventually broken. MaD4 is designed to resist this type of attacks.

To be successful, an attacker must be able to do two things, namely, be able to efficiently verify his guessing (guess and verify) and be able to determine more unknowns based on his guessing (guess and determine). In MaD4, by knowing the value of $T[2r]$ at a certain moment, an attacker can guess two of the three integers (a, c, and d) and then compute the third integer. Since he also knows $T[2r{+}1]$, he can further compute the value of b. The attacker needs to guess 128 bits to figure out the values of all four integers a, b, c, and d. Once the attacker knows a and b, he can compute $Sw[x[r]] = a + b$. To know $x[r]$ and therefore identify which integer is to be updated, he needs to guess another 4 bits (out of the 7 bits, the lower 3 bits are known apriori). So the attacker needs to guess 132 bits (128 bits if he chooses not to know $x[r]$) in total during the first iteration of guessing.

During the second iteration, the attacker needs to guess 128 bits like in the first iteration to figure out the new values of a, b, c, and d, and then another 128 bits to figure out the values of two of e, f, g, and h (and also two of the four state table integers $Sw[x[r]]$, $Sw[x[r]\wedge 0x78]$, $Sa[r]$, and $Sb[r]$). Note that since the attacker only needs to find out two values (one must be c or d) so as to know all the values of a, b, c, and d during each iteration, it is not necessary for him to find out all the values of e, f, g, and h. Also notice that the second 128 bits guessing is based on the design that the four state table integers $Sw[x[r]]$, $Sw[x[r]\wedge 0x78]$, $Sa[r]$, and $Sb[r]$ are distinct and they are also different from any of the four state table integers used in the previous iteration. If two integers, for example $Sw[x[r]]$ and $Sa[r]$, are identical, then the attacker only needs to guess 64 bits instead of 128 bits. If a state table integer used in the previous iteration, for example the already known $Sw[x[r]]$, can appear in the next iteration, then the 128 bits guessing is also reduced to 64 bits. Here we have ignored the relatively small cost that is needed to make two integers point to the same state table integer (a probability of $\frac{1}{128} = 2^{-7}$ or a cost of 7 bits) or make a state table integer used in the previous iteration appear in the next iteration (a probability of $2 \times \frac{1}{128} = 2^{-6}$ or a cost of 6 bits; the coefficient 2 comes from that each of the two state table integers whose values need to be determined can take the known value).

During the third iteration, the attacker still needs to find out the new values of two of the four integers a, b, c, and d. To achieve this, he needs to know the values of two of the four state table integers $Sw[x[r]]$, $Sw[x[r]\wedge 0x78]$, $Sa[r]$, and $Sb[r]$. This requires to guess another 128 bits. Note that even though the attacker already knows the values of five distinct state table integers, one during the first iteration and four during the second iteration, none of them can reappear during the third iteration. Since none of the state table integers accessed during the first three iterations can reappear in the fourth iteration, the attacker still needs to guess 128 bits during the fourth iteration.

The first four iterations require at least $128 + 2 \times 128 + 128 + 128 = 640$ bits of work, which is far more than our design strength 512 bits. The above attack is not unique and different attack strategies can be taken, but none is likely to be more efficient than the above one. The above analysis only covers one generation round. Between each two generation rounds, the attacker has to deal with the 32 pseudorandom bytes obtained from state table S, otherwise he will not be able to track the values he has already guessed and determined. So the cost to completely break MaD4 through guessing attacks is far more than that of a brute force attack. To conclude this subsection, we also want to point out that it is infeasible to break the 64-bit integers into smaller units so as to reduce the attack cost. If the smaller units, say bytes, can be computed independently, then the attack cost will be significantly reduced. This is because each 64 bits can be reduced to, for example, eight 8 bits, which is equivalent to 11 bits only ($8 \times 2^8 = 2^{11}$).

Distinguishing Attacks. As its name suggests, a distinguishing attack tries to distinguish the output sequence of a PRNG from a truly random sequence. Distinguishing attacks are low-cost and powerful attacks. For a distinguishing attack to be successful, it is usually sufficient to find a bias, a correlation, or some non-uniform distribution in the internal state and/or the output sequence. As such, being resistant to distinguishing attacks is a fundamental requirement for a CSPRNG and has been taken into account in a general sense throughout the design and testing of MaD4. In this subsection, we look into a few specific distinguishing attacks and examine the security of MaD4 against them.

All statistical testing tools are designed for detecting this problem in the design of various pseudorandom number generators and ciphers. Passing statistical tests, however, does not necessarily mean a pseudorandom number generator or cipher is immune to distinguishing attacks. A sequence not distinguishable from a truly random sequence by statistical testing tools may still be revealed as not random by distinguishing attacks. This is particularly true when considering that distinguishing attacks often explore specific design details that are not considered by general purpose testing tools.

One way to launch a distinguishing attack against a PRNG is to explore the algebraic structure of the PRNG and try to demonstrate that it can be (partially) described by some algebraic equations, thereby proving it is not random. Although similar techniques are used, a distinguishing attack does not try to completely solve the algebraic equations as an algebraic attack does. It suffices to show that those equations are satisfied with a non-trivially high probability that cannot happen with a truly random sequence. There are only two values in $\mathbb{F}_2$ and therefore each equation is satisfied with a probability of 0.5 for a truly random sequence. For a successful algebraic attack, each equation is satisfied with a probability of 1. For a successful distinguishing attack, each equation should be satisfied with a probability that is non-trivially higher than 0.5 or, equivalently, the number of equations that are satisfied should be non-trivially larger than half of the total number of equations.

The degree of equations, denoted as d, that makes algebraic attacks more efficient than a k-bit brute force search for an n-bit internal state can be numerically evaluated using the following inequality:

$$\left(\frac{n!}{d!(n-d)!}\right)^{2.3727} < 2^k$$

Our analysis shows the degree of equations derived for one round of pseudorandom generation in MaD4 is 256 and the degree for a feasible algebraic attack must be less than 19 according to the above inequality (analysis details are omitted due to page limit). This big difference indicates MaD4 has a strong resistance to both algebraic attacks and distinguishing attacks based on similar techniques.

Another distinguishing attack technique that targets stream ciphers using linear masking was proposed by Coppersmith et al. and applied to SNOW 1.0 [11]. Stream ciphers (also PRNGs) usually include some nonlinear process in their design. The nonlinear process resembles a block cipher and its states are deemed uncorrelated if they are far away in time. Linear masking tries to mask the correlation among states close in time. It masks those states using independent parts of a linear process. The basic idea of the attack is to find some linear combination of the linear process that vanishes. When this same combination is applied to the output stream, the linear process would vanish. This way the attacker is left with the nonlinear process only, for which he can further look for a characteristic that can be distinguished from randomness. Distinguishing attacks have also been mounted for other stream ciphers that use linear masking, including SNOW 2.0 and Sosemanu, [19,26,31]. MaD4 does not use linear masking, thus rendering this type of distinguishing attacks irrelevant.

Differential Attacks. Differential cryptanalysis tries to track the relationship between differences in input and differences in the corresponding output of a cryptosystem. A special differential cryptanalysis called impossible differential cryptanalysis exploits differences that are impossible (i.e., having a probability of 0) instead of differences that have a probability higher than what can be expected from a random transformation. Differential attacks are of particular concern and have long since been the subject of intensive research for block ciphers and other cryptosystems whose process depends on the input plaintext.

Differential cryptanalysis can be used to track how differences of keys and/or IVs propagate and affect the internal state and the output sequence of a PRNG. This has been demonstrated in several attacks on RC4 [5,13,22]. All these attacks have exploited the relatively simple key scheduling algorithm and pseudorandom generation algorithm of RC4. As shown in Subsect. 2.3, MaD4 significantly improves the avalanche effect by using a more complex key scheduling algorithm than RC4. This makes it more difficult to track the relationship between the input key and the internal state. Compared with RC4, MaD4 also performs some additional state initialization and uses a more complex pseudorandom generation algorithm, which further enhance its resistance against differential attacks.

Other Attacks. We have also analyzed the security of MaD4 against other attacks, including special attacks against RC4, algebraic attacks, and side channel attacks, but cannot include the results here due to page limit.

5.2 Next-Bit Test and State Compromise Extensions

Besides those requirements set for an ordinary PRNG, a CSPRNG also needs to meet some additional requirements, that is, satisfying the "next-bit test" and withstanding "state compromise extensions". In this subsection we address these two requirements.

Next-Bit Test. Given the first k bits of a random sequence, if there is no polynomial-time algorithm that can predict the $(k+1)$-th bit with a probability of success significantly greater than $1/2$, then the random sequence is said to pass the next-bit test [7]. A more general test is Yao's test [34], which tests whether a random sequence is distinguishable from a truly random sequence by any polynomial-time algorithm. Obviously next-bit test is only a special case of Yao's test and passing next-bit test is a necessary condition for passing Yao's test.

However, Yao proved that passing next-bit test is also a sufficient condition for passing Yao's test. The significance of Yao's work is that it reduces randomness test to a single test, i.e., next-bit test.

It is important to notice that the next-bit test is a theoretical test due to the fact that it needs to be conducted against every polynomial-time algorithm, which is impossible in practice. Although some next-bit tests have been developed [14,17,28,30], they are only based on a few specific prediction algorithms and passing them is far from enough to conclude a PRNG passes the next-bit test. Those tests have more values for research than for practical use.

Since it is impossible to implement a perfect next-bit test, no PRNG can prove it passes the next-bit test in the strict sense given in [34]. A common practice is to relax the requirement by replacing *all polynomial-time algorithms* with *(most) known polynomial-time algorithms.* This less strict requirement can be addressed from several respects:

1. Several standard statistical test suites have been developed. They include many tests designed for distinguishing a pseudorandom sequence from a truly random sequence. We tested MaD4 using those statistical test suites and the results will be given in Sect. 6.
2. Standard statistical test suites are developed with no knowledge of a specific PRNG, which means they do not address the next-bit test issue with respect to the PRNG algorithm itself. An attacker can use the PRNG algorithm itself to predict or even compute the next bit if he knows part or all of the internal state. How to prevent an attacker from using the PRNG algorithm itself to predict the next bit is addressed by the requirement that a CSPRNG should be able to withstand state compromise extensions. We will discuss MaD4's this capability in next subsection.
3. A third group of polynomial-time algorithms are those used in various known attacks. Being resistant to known attacks is a necessary condition for passing the next-bit test. For MaD4, this has largely been addressed in Sect. 5.
4. There are always unknown attacks and new attacks can keep on emerging. As such, a CSPRNG should be routinely revisited and, if necessary, revised.

State Compromise Extensions. A state compromise extension attack attempts to recover unknown outputs and/or internal states of a PRNG by using the knowledge of the internal state of the PRNG at some time. A formal requirement defined in terms of backtracking resistance and prediction resistance is given in NIST special publication 800-90A [1]:

- *Backtracking Resistance* – Backtracking resistance is provided relative to time T if there is assurance that an adversary who has knowledge of the internal state of a PRNG at some time subsequent to time T would be unable to distinguish between observations of ideal random bitstrings and (previously unseen) bitstrings that were output by the PRNG prior to time T.
- *Prediction Resistance* – Prediction resistance is provided relative to time T if there is assurance that an adversary who has knowledge of the internal state

of the PRNG at some time prior to T would be unable to distinguish between observations of ideal random bitstrings and bitstrings output by the PRNG at or subsequent to time T.

The above definition means that a CSPRNG should withstand both distinguishing attacks and state recovery attacks in both backward and forward directions in the case the internal state is compromised at some time. Since distinguishing attacks are easier than state recovery attacks, being resistant to this type of attacks means a higher requirement for the designer of the generator.

While MaD4 is not based on computationally hard problems, it is practically impossible to go backwards, either from the observed stream of pseudorandom numbers to the internal state or from a compromised state to its previous states or the stream of pseudorandom numbers generated before the state is compromised. State compromise extension attacks are likely to happen if state initialization does not provide sufficient entropy. Many attacks mounted against RC4 exploit the weakness of RC4's key scheduling. MaD4 uses a more advanced KSA that meets the strict avalanche criterion. State compromise extension attacks can also happen when the internal state is leaked out or compromised by attacks. Since it is impossible to guarantee that occasional compromises of the internal state cannot happen, a CSPRNG should be designed to resist state compromise extension attacks.

One difference between RC4 and MaD4 is that RC4 uses pseudorandom permutations for state transition and MaD4 uses both pseudorandom permutations and pseudorandom mappings for state transition. Pseudorandom permutations are invertible and it requires no efforts to go from a state to its previous state. For example, RC4's state transition is done through the following code:

```
i++
j = j + S[i]
swap(S[i], S[j])
```

If the internal state (j plus S) completely leaks out or is compromised, one can easily go back by reversing the algorithm, that is,

```
swap(S[i], S[j])
j = j - S[i]
i--
```

It is possible to recover the entire internal state of RC4 within a minute by launching a cache timing attack against it [9]. So state compromise extensions are real threats to RC4 and, for this reason, RC4 cannot be used as a CSPRNG.

Pseudorandom mappings are non-invertible and therefore have a better backtracking resistance. Knowing the internal state of MaD4 at a point in time does not enable one to compute its previous state. During each of the 64 iterations of the generation round of MaD4, all four state integers a, b, c, and d are updated. Another state table integer $Sw[x[r]]$ is also updated. The update of those integers involves the old values of those integers, the byte array x, and the intermediate variable e, f, g, and h. Therefore it is impossibleto directly compute the old values from the current known values. Knowing the output pseudorandom sequence additionally does not help much either, since each output integer is computed from many internal integers and the computation involves indirect access (via $Sw[x[r]]$ and $Sw[x[r] \wedge 0x78]$), which is nonlinear. It is also worth noting that, to go back to the previous state, one must find out the byte array x and the four intermediate variables e, f, g, and h, which are computed at the beginning of the generation round, that is, they are computed from some state that is far before the previous state one is trying to recover. In principle, this issue can be solved by constructing and resolving a system of equations. But neither the construction nor the resolution of such a system of equations would be easy, if not impossible, due to the special design of the pseudorandom generation algorithm of MaD4.

Prediction resistance can only be achieved when at least some part of the internal state or some entropy input is kept unknown or unpredictable from attackers. Knowing the whole internal state does enable one to compute the future states. This is likely to happen when an attacker gains physical access to the internal state. It is often assumed that one or more unpredictable sources of entropies are available to a CSPRNG. In other words, it is a reasonable assumption that at least some information (e.g., a seed, part of the internal state, etc.) is not leaked out. In our case, we assume at least one part of the internal state is not compromised. The internal state of MaD4 is functionally divided into two parts. A specific implementation should take this into consideration and maintain the two parts of the internal state in such a way that they are unlikely to be compromised (e.g., through physical access) at the same time. Prediction resistance can also be achieved by periodically querying some non-deterministic random sources and using them as unpredictable sources of entropies. One such implementation can be found in [21]. It converts MaD4 into a non-deterministic pseudorandom generator that behaves like a true random number generator.

6 Statistical Testing

A couple of statistical testing tools have been developed, among which are the most widely used NIST statistical test suite [27], Diehard battery of tests [23], and TestU01 batteries of tests [18]. We tested MaD4 using these three statistical test suites and the results are summarized in this section.

6.1 NIST Statistical Test Suite

The NIST tests are based on hypothesis testing. Each test is formulated to test a specific null hypothesis, i.e., a specific sequence of zeroes and ones is random. A probability value (*P-value*) is computed for each test, which summarizes the strength of the evidence against the null hypothesis. The probability that the null hypothesis for randomness is rejected for a random sequence is called the level of significance (α) of the test. If *P-value* $\geq \alpha$, then the null hypothesis is accepted; i.e., the sequence appears to be random. If *P-value* $< \alpha$, then the null hypothesis is rejected; i.e., the sequence appears to be non-random. We tested 1000 random sequences, each containing one million bits (125 KB). The significance level (α) is set to 0.01 in all tests. MaD4 passed the NIST statistical tests.

6.2 Diehard Battery of Tests

Most of the tests in Diehard return a *P-value*, which should be uniform on [0,1) if the input file contains truly independent random bits. A *P-value* near 0 or 1 indicates deviation from true randomness. This is in contrast with NIST tests, where a bigger *P-value* indicates better randomness. The new Diehard release contains 17 tests, including some "tough" tests [24]. The tests are divided into two groups based on the minimum random sequence size that is needed by each test. For the first group, we tested 50 random sequences, each containing 2176 million bits (272 MB). For the second group, we tested 100 random sequences, each containing 96 million bits (12 MB). MaD4 passed the Diehard battery of tests.

6.3 TestU01 Batteries of Tests

TestU01 is the most comprehensive statistical test suite that is publicly available so far. Six pre-defined batteries of tests are available in TestU01. TestU01 requires much more (pseudo-)random numbers than the NIST and Diehard suites. It takes many hours to run all the 6 batteries on our machine. MaD4 cleared the 6 TestU01 batteries of tests.

7 Performance Testing

Table 4. Pseudorandom Number Generation Speed (cycle/byte)

Generator	Sequence size (KB)				
	1	10	100	1000	10000
RC4	5.87	3.88	3.80	3.81	3.83
HC-128	18.50	3.17	1.52	1.35	1.34
Rabbit	6.65	5.36	5.25	5.23	5.24
Salsa20	6.51	5.94	5.84	5.83	5.90
Sosemanuk	13.60	3.13	2.02	1.91	1.90
ChaCha8	7.22	2.80	2.35	2.30	2.30
ChaCha12	8.11	3.79	3.34	3.29	3.29
ChaCha20	10.09	5.77	5.31	5.27	5.28
MaD4	12.65	1.74	0.63	0.51	0.50

Table 5. Data Encryption Speed (cycle/byte)

Cipher	Sequence size (KB)				
	1	10	100	1000	10000
RC4	5.89	3.90	3.82	3.83	3.85
HC-128	19.25	3.50	1.84	1.67	1.66
Rabbit	6.70	5.57	5.41	5.31	5.34
Salsa20	9.41	8.74	8.63	8.60	8.71
Sosemanuk	14.83	4.50	3.43	3.32	3.32
ChaCha8	7.76	3.26	2.76	2.71	2.70
ChaCha12	9.16	4.36	3.85	3.80	3.81
ChaCha20	11.14	6.53	6.02	5.97	6.00
AES-128	30.97	12.29	10.42	10.23	10.27
AES-192	32.70	13.99	12.11	11.93	12.01
AES-256	34.37	15.69	13.82	13.63	13.66
AES-NI-128	3.82	3.23	3.18	3.17	3.17
AES-NI-192	4.23	3.65	3.59	3.59	3.59
AES-NI-256	4.48	4.05	4.01	4.00	4.00
MaD4	12.67	1.78	0.69	0.58	0.56

In this section, we present the performance testing results for MaD4, including both pseudorandom number generation speed and data encryption speed. The testing results for RC4, the four software-efficient finalists of eStream [2,3,8,33], the ChaCha stream cipher [4], and Advanced Encryption Standard (AES) [25] are also included for comparison[2].

The testing is done for a software implementation using C programming language. The C implementation closely follows the pseudo code given in Sect. 2 and Sect. 3. There are no special optimizations done at the source code level except that register variables are used to minimize memory access whenever possible. Most modern compilers are smart enough and know more about code generation than the developer [20]. They can perform various optimizations to generate more compact and/or faster code, including constant folding, dead code elimination, inline expansion or macro expansion, strength reduction, loop optimization, code re-ordering for maximum pipeline throughput and cache effects, and many more. Therefore we leave optimizations largely to the compiler.

All implementations are compiled using Microsoft Visual C/C++ 64-bit Optimizing Compiler Version 19 with option /O2 (optimized for maximum speed) and tested on an Intel Core i7-7500U 2.7 GHz personal computer with 128 KB L1 cache, 512 KB L2 cache, and 4 MB L3 cache. For each sequence size, we run each executable 100 times and get the average value of the top 5 speeds. The reason we exclude low speeds in our calculation is that the measured cycles may contain contributions from some system processes that we cannot stop and the small cycles more likely reflect the actual performance. The testing does not involve any file I/O operations. The data given here are more for relative comparison than for benchmarking, which would require more comprehensive testing on different platforms. For the same reason, we refrain from using the commercial Intel C/C++ compiler, which has the potential to generate faster executables than Microsoft Visual C/C++ compiler on Intel platforms.

The testing results for pseudorandom number generation are given in Table 4. MaD4 does not perform better than other PRNGs for short sequences of 1 KB due to its relatively heavy state initialization. MaD4 is significantly faster than other PRNGs for long sequences and is 2.4 to 2.7 times as fast as the second fastest HC-128 when the sequence size is 100 KB or more.

The testing results for data encryption are given in Table 5. All stream ciphers are faster than the software implementation of block cipher AES (specifically, the optimized software implementation from OpenSSL). MaD4 is the fastest cipher and is about 18 to 24 times as fast as AES for long sequences. Notice, however, the Intel AES New Instructions (AES-NI) achieve a speedup of 3.2 to 3.4 times, which makes AES comparable to most stream ciphers.

[2] The Electronic Code Book (ECB) mode is used in the performance testing of AES. This is not a recommended mode due to its security weaknesses, but it is the simplest and the fastest mode, which enables us to find the upper limit of the speed of AES.

8 Conclusion

A new design paradigm is introduced and used to construct a cryptographically secure pseudorandom number generator in this paper. The key of this paradigm is the close combination of slow byte-oriented operations that are used for initialization and reseeding and fast integer-oriented operations that are used for pseudorandom number generation. The state space of the generator is accordingly divided into a small byte-oriented state, whose transition follows a pseudorandom permutation, and a large integer-oriented state, whose transition follows a pseudorandom mapping. The byte-oriented state is first initialized through a key scheduling process as usual. The integer-oriented state is then bootstrapped and initialized through the byte-oriented state. After initialization, the byte-oriented state serves as a source of entropy and periodically reseeds the integer-oriented state. The effectiveness of this new design paradigm is well demonstrated through the construction of MaD4, the new cryptographically secure pseudorandom number generator presented in this paper. MaD4 excels in several respects:

- **high quality key scheduling and initialization.** It has an avalanche effect that meets the strict avalanche criterion.
- **high quality pseudorandom number generation.** It clears all the NIST statistical tests, the new Diehard battery of tests, and the most stringent TestU01 batteries of tests.
- **high speed.** It reaches a speed close to half clock cycle per byte on a typical Intel Core i7 personal computer, which is several times faster than any existing cryptographically secure pseudorandom number generator that we are aware of. When used as a stream cipher, it is about 18 to 24 times as fast as AES and 6 to 7 times as fast as AES-NI.
- **cryptographically secure.** It resists various known cryptographic attacks and withstands state compromise extension attacks as well.

It can be used in a wide range of cryptographic applications, including those having stringent requirements for security, randomness, and speed.

References

1. Barker, E., Kelsey, J.: Recommendation for Random Number Generation Using Deterministic Random Bit Generators. National Institute of Standards and Technology (2012). NIST Special Publication 800-90A
2. Berbain, C., et al.: SOSEMANUK, a fast software-oriented stream cipher. In: Robshaw, M., Billet, O. (eds.) New Stream Cipher Designs. LNCS, vol. 4986, pp. 98–118. Springer, Heidelberg (2008). https://doi.org/10.1007/978-3-540-68351-3_9
3. Bernstein, D.J.: Salsa20/8 and Salsa20/12. eSTREAM, ECRYPT Stream Cipher Project (2006)
4. Bernstein, D.J., et al.: Chacha, a variant of salsa20. In: Workshop Record of SASC, vol. 8, pp. 3–5 (2008)
5. Biham, E., Dunkelman, O.: Differential cryptanalysis in stream ciphers. IACR Cryptology ePrint Archive 2007, p. 218 (2007)

6. Biryukov, A., Shamir, A.: Cryptanalytic time/memory/data tradeoffs for stream ciphers. In: Okamoto, T. (ed.) ASIACRYPT 2000. LNCS, vol. 1976, pp. 1–13. Springer, Heidelberg (2000). https://doi.org/10.1007/3-540-44448-3_1
7. Blum, M., Micali, S.: How to generate cryptographically strong sequences of pseudo random bits. In: Foundations of Computer Science, 1982, 23rd Annual Symposium on Foundations of Computer Science, pp. 112–117. IEEE (1982)
8. Boesgaard, M., Vesterager, M., Christensen, T., Zenner, E.: The stream cipher Rabbit. ECRYPT Stream Cipher Project Report 6 (2005)
9. Chardin, T., Fouque, P.-A., Leresteux, D.: Cache timing analysis of RC4. In: Lopez, J., Tsudik, G. (eds.) ACNS 2011. LNCS, vol. 6715, pp. 110–129. Springer, Heidelberg (2011). https://doi.org/10.1007/978-3-642-21554-4_7
10. Chen, K., et al.: Dragon: a fast word based stream cipher. In: Park, C., Chee, S. (eds.) ICISC 2004. LNCS, vol. 3506, pp. 33–50. Springer, Heidelberg (2005). https://doi.org/10.1007/11496618_5
11. Coppersmith, D., Halevi, S., Jutla, C.: Cryptanalysis of stream ciphers with linear masking. In: Yung, M. (ed.) CRYPTO 2002. LNCS, vol. 2442, pp. 515–532. Springer, Heidelberg (2002). https://doi.org/10.1007/3-540-45708-9_33
12. Fog, A.: Instruction tables: lists of instruction latencies, throughputs and micro-operation breakdowns for Intel, AMD and VIA CPUs. Copenhagen University College of Engineering (2011). http://www.agner.org/optimize/instruction_tables.pdf
13. Grosul, A.L., Wallach, D.S.: A related-key cryptanalysis of RC4. Technical report TR-00-358, Department of Computer Science, Rice University (2000)
14. Hernandez, J., Sierra, J., Mex-Perera, C., Borrajo, D., Ribagorda, A., Isasi, P.: Using the general next bit predictor like an evaluation criteria. In: Proceedings of NESSIE Workshop (2000)
15. Jenkins, R.J.: ISAAC. In: Gollmann, D. (ed.) FSE 1996. LNCS, vol. 1039, pp. 41–49. Springer, Heidelberg (1996). https://doi.org/10.1007/3-540-60865-6_41
16. Knuth, D.E.: The Art of Computer Programming: Seminumerical Algorithms, 3rd edn, vol. 2. Addison Wesley Longman, Boston (1998)
17. Lavasani, A., Eghlidos, T.: Practical next bit test for evaluating pseudorandom sequences. Electr. Eng. **16**(1), 19–33 (2009)
18. L'Ecuyer, P., Simard, R.: Testu01: a C library for empirical testing of random number generators. ACM Trans. Math. Softw. (TOMS) **33**(4), 22 (2007)
19. Lee, J.-K., Lee, D.H., Park, S.: Cryptanalysis of Sosemanuk and SNOW 2.0 using linear masks. In: Pieprzyk, J. (ed.) ASIACRYPT 2008. LNCS, vol. 5350, pp. 524–538. Springer, Heidelberg (2008). https://doi.org/10.1007/978-3-540-89255-7_32
20. Leitner, F.: Source code optimization (2009). http://www.linux-kongress.org/2009/slides/compiler_survey_felix_von_leitner.pdf
21. Li, J.: Ultrafast pseudorandom number generation using pseudorandom permutations and mappings. Dissertation, City University of New York, ProQuest/UMI (2013). publication No. 3601931
22. Mantin, I.: A practical attack on the fixed RC4 in the WEP mode. In: Roy, B. (ed.) ASIACRYPT 2005. LNCS, vol. 3788, pp. 395–411. Springer, Heidelberg (2005). https://doi.org/10.1007/11593447_21
23. Marsaglia, G.: The Marsaglia random number CDROM including the Diehard battery of tests of randomness (1995). New version http://www.csis.hku.hk/diehard/
24. Marsaglia, G., Tsang, W.W.: Some difficult-to-pass tests of randomness. J. Stat. Softw. **7**(3), 1–9 (2002)
25. National Institute of Standards and Technology: Advanced encryption standard (AES) (2001). Federal Information Processing Standards Publication 197

26. Nyberg, K., Wallén, J.: Improved linear distinguishers for SNOW 2.0. In: Robshaw, M. (ed.) FSE 2006. LNCS, vol. 4047, pp. 144–162. Springer, Heidelberg (2006). https://doi.org/10.1007/11799313_10
27. Rukhin, A., Soto, J., Nechvatal, J., et al.: A Statistical Test Suite for Random and Pseudorandom Number Generators for Cryptographic Applications. National Institute of Standards and Technology (2001). NIST special publication 800–22
28. Sadeghiyan, B., Mohajeri, J.: A new universal test for bit strings. In: Pieprzyk, J., Seberry, J. (eds.) ACISP 1996. LNCS, vol. 1172, pp. 311–319. Springer, Heidelberg (1996). https://doi.org/10.1007/BFb0023309
29. Schneier, B.: Applied Cryptography. Protocols, Algorithms, and Source Code in C. Wiley, New York (1996)
30. Schrift, A.W., Shamir, A.: Universal tests for nonuniform distributions. J. Cryptol. **6**(3), 119–133 (1993). https://doi.org/10.1007/BF00198461
31. Watanabe, D., Biryukov, A., De Cannière, C.: A distinguishing attack of SNOW 2.0 with linear masking method. In: Matsui, M., Zuccherato, R.J. (eds.) SAC 2003. LNCS, vol. 3006, pp. 222–233. Springer, Heidelberg (2004). https://doi.org/10.1007/978-3-540-24654-1_16
32. Webster, A.F., Tavares, S.E.: On the design of S-boxes. In: Williams, H.C. (ed.) CRYPTO 1985. LNCS, vol. 218, pp. 523–534. Springer, Heidelberg (1986). https://doi.org/10.1007/3-540-39799-X_41
33. Wu, H.: The stream cipher HC-128. In: Robshaw, M., Billet, O. (eds.) New Stream Cipher Designs. LNCS, vol. 4986, pp. 39–47. Springer, Heidelberg (2008). https://doi.org/10.1007/978-3-540-68351-3_4
34. Yao, A.C.: Theory and application of trapdoor functions. In: Foundations of Computer Science, 1982, 23rd Annual Symposium on Foundations of Computer Science, pp. 80–91. IEEE (1982)
35. Zheng, J., Li, J.: MARC: modified ARC4. In: Garcia-Alfaro, J., Cuppens, F., Cuppens-Boulahia, N., Miri, A., Tawbi, N. (eds.) FPS 2012. LNCS, vol. 7743, pp. 33–44. Springer, Heidelberg (2013). https://doi.org/10.1007/978-3-642-37119-6_3

Time-Efficient Finite Field Microarchitecture Design for Curve448 and Ed448 on Cortex-M4

Mila Anastasova[1(✉)], Reza Azarderakhsh[1(✉)], Mehran Mozaffari Kermani[2], and Lubjana Beshaj[3]

[1] Computer and Electrical Engineering and Computer Science Department, I-SENSE at Florida Atlantic University, Boca Raton, FL, USA
{manastasova2017,razarderakhsh}@fau.edu

[2] Computer Engineering and Science Department, University of South Florida, Tampa, FL, USA
mehran2@usf.edu

[3] United States Military Academy West Point, West Point, NY, USA
lubjana.beshaj@westpoint.edu

Abstract. The elliptic curve family of schemes has the lowest computational latency, memory use, energy consumption, and bandwidth requirements, making it the most preferred public key method for adoption into network protocols. Being suitable for embedded devices and applicable for key exchange and authentication, ECC is assuming a prominent position in the field of IoT cryptography. The attractive properties of the relatively new curve Curve448 contribute to its inclusion in the TLS1.3 protocol and pique the interest of academics and engineers aiming at studying and optimizing the schemes. When addressing low-end IoT devices, however, the literature indicates little work on these curves. In this paper, we present an efficient design for both protocols based on Montgomery curve Curve448 and its birationally equivalent Edwards curve Ed448 used for key agreement and digital signature algorithm, specifically the X448 function and the Ed448 DSA, relying on efficient low-level arithmetic operations targeting the ARM-based Cortex-M4 platform. Our design performs point multiplication, the base of the Elliptic Curve Diffie-Hellman (ECDH), in 3,2KCCs, resulting in more than 48% improvement compared to the best previous work based on Curve448, and performs sign and verify, the main operations of the Edwards-curves Digital Signature Algorithm (EdDSA), in 6,038KCCs and 7,404KCCs, showing a speedup of around 11% compared to the counterparts. We present novel modular multiplication and squaring architectures reaching ~25% and ~35% faster runtime than the previous best-reported results, respectively, based on Curve448 key exchange counterparts, and ~13% and ~25% better latency results than the Ed448-based digital signature counterparts targeting Cortex-M4 platform.

Keywords: Elliptic Curve Cryptography · Curve448 · Elliptic Curve Diffie-Hellman (ECDH) · Edwards-Curve Digital Signature Algorithm (EdDSA) · Cortex-M4

S.-H. Seo and H. Seo (Eds.): ICISC 2022, LNCS 13849, pp. 292–314, 2023.
https://doi.org/10.1007/978-3-031-29371-9_15

1 Introduction

The use of Public Key Cryptography, often known as PKC, protects the confidentiality of data by ensuring its secure transmission through an unsecured channel, such as the internet, relying on hard mathematical problems to protect the privacy of the information. The NP-hard factorization and (Elliptic Curve) Discrete Logarithm Problems (DLP) are the foundations upon which traditional cryptosystems are constructed. Elliptic Curve Cryptography (ECC), which is entrenched in the complexity of solving ECDLP, delivers high-security levels while demonstrating minimal computational latency and small key sizes in comparison to other classical cryptosystems. As a consequence, ECC-based cryptoschemes are essential for network protocols, as they are frequently used for key agreement and digital signature algorithms. Despite the minimal resource requirements of ECC schemes, public key cryptography remains challenging to implement and deploy on low-end real-time devices which feature scarce memory, limited battery life, and restricted bandwidth.

The continuous advancement of technology leads to its integration into daily life activities, producing the vast universe of the Internet of Things (IoT), which implies an improved standard of living. The widespread usage of real-time embedded systems over the last several decades has created a demand for efficient cryptographic scheme implementation on resource-constrained devices. The specifications of the ARMv7-based Cortex-M4 processor, suitable for cost-conscious and power-constrained development, position the platform among the most widely used embedded devices in the IoT market. This is the reason why the National Institute of Standards and Technology (NIST) [1] selected it as a target platform for evaluating the performance of the cryptographic primitives.

The classical cryptosystems, believed to be robust against today's computers, are, however, shown to be vulnerable to quantum attacks as presented by *Shor* in [2]. The hard mathematical problems underpinning classical schemes could be broken in polynomial time, rather than exponential, when a large-scale quantum computer is developed. Although the availability of such a class of quantum computers cannot be predicted, the need for quantum-robust encryption prompted NIST to initialize a Post-Quantum (PQ) standardization process in 2016. The newly proposed PQ primitives are being evaluated and optimized during the standardization effort. The use of stand-alone post-quantum primitives in network protocols, however, is not in accordance with industry and government standards; hence, hybrid systems based on classical and PQ algorithms are the primary focus of cryptography researchers for transitioning from classical- to PQ- robust environment, thus, the optimal implementation of classical schemes such as ECDH and EdDSA, focus of this work, remains critical for the performance of cryptographic network protocols.

ECC is a critical component of the majority of cryptographic libraries. Yet, in recent years, certain NIST curves have been a subject of further investment and analysis, rising concerns about their security. Due to the resolved backdoor issues associated with existing NIST curves introduced in [3], the recently proposed Montgomery curves Curve25519 and Curve448 and their birationally equivalent (un)twisted Edwards curves Ed25519 and Ed448 have been widely used and recommended by NIST. Providing 128- and 224-bit security, the curves are suitable for implementing key agreement and digital signature protocols. As a result, they have been included in the TLS1.3 version of the widely used Transport Layer Security protocol from 2018. The interest in the curves leads to several target-specific optimizations, resulting in better performance and energy outcomes. Due to its low calculation latency and reduced resource requirements, several research teams are concentrating on Curve25519 and Ed25519 on different systems, according to the literature. To the best of our knowledge, Curve448 and Ed448 have not yet been explored in such depth, particularly on low-end devices, due to the challenging implementation of long-integer finite field arithmetic on such resource-constrained targets. In this work, we present a new performance record of the key exchange protocol based on Curve448 and the digital signature algorithm based on Ed448 targeting low-end embedded devices based on ARM Cortex-M4 platform.

1.1 Related Work

The implementation of cryptographic primitives on low-end IoT devices is a challenge, especially when designing public key cryptography, due to the enormous resource needs of such schemes. This is why academics and engineers are focusing on the ideal development of asymmetric schemes for embedded devices, where ECC has been the dominant choice when addressing resource-constrained devices due to its efficiency and low bandwidth needs.

Bernstein introduced the new-generation elliptic curve Curve25519 and its birationally equivalent twisted Edwards curve Ed25519 in [4] and [5], respectively, to achieve a high level of security and optimal performance outcomes for the Elliptic Curve Diffie-Hellman (ECDH) key agreement and the Edwards-curves Digital Signature Algorithm (EdDSA). Some of the most recent work on Curve25519 and Ed25519 is presented in [6–8] aimed at optimizing the finite field and group computations on high-end platforms. Time-efficient implementation of Curve25519 arithmetic targeting embedded devices is presented in [9–11] based on optimal register utilization and careful instruction scheduling. Another research focus is the optimization on hardware presented in [12–14]. Extensive study on side-channel protection of the scheme is also present in the literature [15–17].

Curve448 along with its birationally equivalent untwisted Edwards curve Ed448, proposed by *Hamburg* in [18], offers higher security level than the discussed Curve25519. The optimizations for Curve448, however, to the best of our knowledge, have not been as exhaustive, specifically when targeting low-ended devices with scarce resources due to the higher security level and thus more computationally intensive arithmetic operations.

Recent enhancements to the 224-bit secure ECDH/EdDSA over Curve448 targeting Haswell and the Skylake microarchitectures are presented in [19] where *Oliveira et al.* present an optimal fixed-point multiplication strategy based on precomputation of constant values derived from the fixed point and its multiples.

Later, in [20], *Seo* presents an optimized implementation of Curve448 arithmetic targeting low-end 8-bit AVR and 16-bit MSP processors, where the main contribution consists of the adoption of two- and three-level subtractive Karatsuba method for the execution of the multi-precision multiplication and squaring subroutines. *Faz-Hernandez et al.* present speed optimizations of the Curve448 in [6] targeting the Intel AVX2 vector instruction set, reaching 10–30% of performance improvements for key agreement and digital signature cryptographic schemes. Finally *Seo et al.* present the first implementation of Curve448 ECDH targeting the low-end embedded platform ARM Cortex-M4 [21] and *Anastasova et al.* show optimal target-specific implementation of EdDSA algorithm based on Ed448 [22].

The Elliptic Curve Cryptography has a pyramid-like layered structure, where the computation of high-layer group operations is based on low-layer finite field arithmetic. The pyramidal structure enables high-level improvements aimed at breaking speed records for group operations. The low-level arithmetic computations, the topic of this study, result in an overall acceleration of the ECC primitives, with the platform characteristics dictating the optimization tactics used to create the architecture. The primary challenge when implementing Curve448 and Ed448 field arithmetic is that the operands frequently exceed the available CPU resources, particularly on low-end platforms. Due to the unavoidable necessity for safe and efficient cryptographic protocols, the ECC architectural design undergoes continual research and optimization efforts on both high- and low-level enhancements.

The high-level improvements include representing the curve elements in projective coordinates rather than affine coordinates to minimize the number of costly arithmetic operations required for scalar-point multiplication. Montgomery ladder [23], significantly lowers the latency of ECC-based protocols by combining Montgomery's doubling formulae with Montgomery's differential-addition formulas and enables the use of Y-only coordinate calculations.

Several efforts to optimize low-level field arithmetic operations are documented in the literature, with optimal execution strategies resulting in record performance of the cryptographic protocols. Due to the complexity of the long-integer operations' execution flow, there is no implementation option that can be considered ideal. Indeed, different platforms offer a diversity of capabilities, each of which facilitates a specific set of instructions, hence favors the deployment of a specific multi-precision approach. The adaptation of Product Scanning (PS) or Operand Scanning (OS) methodologies, with a focus on long-integer optimal solutions, for low-end devices, has been rigorously investigated and tested. The literature also proposes combination of multi-precision strategies to provide further performance improvements.

In [24] *Hutter et al.* present the first implementation of Operand Caching (OC) multiplication technique which outperforms the previous best hybrid implementation architectures. Based on the OC strategy, *Seo et al.* present in [25] and [26] optimized variant of the multi-precision arithmetic where the execution flow of the inner loop is re-arranged to optimally re-use common operands between previous and new partial products reporting significant speedup results. Optimization of long-integer multiplication and squaring techniques based on the Cortex-M4 platform is presented by *Seo et al.* in [27], where the authors propose Refined-OC multiplication technique based on increased number of cached limbs in the register bank of the processor. The article offers optimal field operations independently of the post-quantum nature of the target protocol since classical ECC techniques, as well as the post-quantum Supersingular Isogeny Key Encapsulation (SIKE) mechanism, are defined over large finite fields and so operate on big integers, thus, implement the same lowest layer arithmetic for the performance of the high layer group operations. Further work on the finite field operations of the elliptic curve-based PQ protocol is presented in [27–30] targeting specifically the ARM Cortex-M4 platform.

Literature indicates that little effort has been spent optimizing 448-bit integer finite field arithmetic for the entry-level ARM-based Cortex-M4 architecture. Multiple research teams are implementing and enhancing the lowest layer of ECC primitives. Using a novel architecture for finite field arithmetic, we extend this study by demonstrating a new performance benchmark for Curve448 and Ed448. [21] and [22] show the most relevant research based on Curve448 that focuses on low-end RISC devices. In this paper, we extend this area of research by introducing a novel method for long-integer operations and compare its performance to that of prior work. In addition, the long-integer implementation subroutines are an excellent fit for the PQ protocol SIKE.

1.2 Contributions

In this work, we demonstrate novel implementation techniques for accelerating the execution of the Curve448- and Ed448-based key derivation and digital signature protocols. Our contributions include the following:

1. We present a novel design for the underlying finite field operations multi-precision multiplication and squaring targeting the ARM Cortex-M4 platform. We observe a speedup of 25% and 35%, respectively for modular multiplication and squaring functions when compared to the Curve448-based key exchange protocol counterparts in [21] and 13% and 24% when compared to the previously best-reported results for the Ed448-based digital signature algorithm presented in [22].
2. We present the first handcrafted assembly implementation of multi-precision squaring procedure with the goal of improving Curve448 and Ed448 for the ARMv7-M architecture. Both multi-precision multiplication and squaring are implemented using a novel architecture in which we combine multiplication techniques. We allocate a fixed number of registers for storing words from A and lower the number of registers for storing operand B's limbs, where we compute current and successive column-wise partial results. Thus, we present the first multi-precision multiplication architecture, combining product- and operand-scanning techniques in the inner multiplication loop execution flow.

Algorithm 1. Montgomery ladder

Input: $P = (X_P : Z_P)$, $k = \sum_{i=0}^{l-1} k_i 2^i$ where $k_{l-1} = 1$
Output: $R = k \cdot P$
$R \leftarrow (X_R, Z_R) = (1, 0)$
$Q \leftarrow (X_Q, Z_Q) = (X_P, 1)$
for $(i = 447; i >= 0; i - -)$ **do**
  if $k_i = 0$ **then**
    $(R, Q) = \mathit{ladderstep}(X_P, R, Q)$
  else
    $(Q, R) = \mathit{ladderstep}(X_P, Q, R)$
  end if
end for
return $x_R = X_R / Z_R$

3. We present a speedup of around 48% and 11% for the X448 and Ed448 DSA protocols, compared to the best previously reported results in [21] and [22], respectively on the target platform when running on STM32F407VG discovery board @24MHz to avoid zero wait state and to disregard memory controller stalls.
4. We evaluate and analyze the proposed design's performance by conducting benchmarking experiments at 24MHz, which presents the exact number of clock cycles on the target platform regardless of the microcontroller's specifications, and 168MHz, which boosts the performance of the STM32F407VG board to obtain real-world values.

The rest of the paper is organized as follows. In Sect. 2 we present an overview of the mathematical concepts underlying X448 and Ed448 DSA protocols and summarize the main features of the target architecture. Section 3 presents the proposed finite field arithmetic architecture and overviews the performance results of the newly implemented functions. In Sect. 4 we perform latency evaluation of the entire protocols after integrating our new function implementations. Finally, we conclude our work in Sect. 5.

2 Preliminaries

This section provides an overview of the mathematical ideas underpinning the Curve448 and Ed448 key exchange and digital signature protocols. We discuss both protocols and illustrate their execution flow, as well as the primary properties of the target platform.

2.1 ECC Mathematical Background

A Montgomery Elliptic Curve Curve448 over a finite field $\mathbb{F}_p$ is defined by the solutions of the equation:

$$E_M / \mathbb{F}_p : v^2 \equiv u^3 + Au^2 + u$$

Algorithm 2. Montgomery ladder step

Input: x_P, $R = (X_R, Z_R)$, $Q = (X_Q, Z_Q)$
Output: $P_{PD} = 2 \cdot R$, $P_{PA} = R + Q$
1: $X_{PD} = (X_R - Z_R)^2 \cdot (X_R + Z_R)^2$
2: $Z_{PD} = 4X_R Z_R \cdot (X_R^2 + 39081 X_R Z_R + Z_R^2)$
3: $X_{PA} = 4(X_R X_Q - Z_R Z_Q)^2$
4: $Z_{PA} = 4x_p(X_R Z_Q - Z_R X_Q)^2$
5: **return** $P_{PD} = (X_{PD}, Z_{PD})$, $P_{PA} = (X_{PA}, Z_{PA})$

where the value of A is defined as 156326 and $p = 2^{448} - 2^{224} - 1$. Montgomery curves have their birationally analogue Edwards curves, where Curve448 can be represented by the solutions to the equation:

$$E_{Ed}/\mathbb{F}_p : ax^2 + y^2 = 1 + dx^2y^2$$

with $d = -39081$ and $a = 1$ since the value of the prime number is congruent to $3 mod 4$ and thus the curve is untwisted Edwards curve called Ed448. The elements of Curve448 are represented by two coordinated $(u, v) \in \mathbb{F}_p \times \mathbb{F}_p$. The birational map to project a point from Montgomery to Edwards curve is as follow:

$$(u, v) = ((y - 1)/(y + 1), sqrt(156324) * u/x)$$

where to map the point back to Montgomery curve the next formula is applied:

$$(x, y) = (sqrt(156324) * u/v, (1 + u)/(1 - u))$$

Elliptic Curve Cryptography's nature is based on the difficulty of solving the Elliptic Curve Discrete Logarithm Problem (ECDLP). Executing scalar-point multiplications with the point $P = [k] \cdot Q$ results in the addition of point Q with itself k times, where the value of k is difficult to resolve given P and Q.

Point multiplication requires several point additions and point doublings, where various techniques can be applied to obtain the resulting coordinates such as Double-And-Add (and its constant time variants) or Montgomery ladder Algorithm 1, where the latter requires p steps of combined point addition (PA) and point doubling (PD) function (referred to as Montgomery ladder step) offering better performance results.

To further increase the speed of the scalar-point multiplication, the point is transformed from affine (x, y) to projective representation (X, Y, Z) with $x, y = (X \cdot Z^{-1}, Y \cdot Z^{-1})$, which relaxes group operations by reducing the number of costly operations such as modular inversions. Algorithm 2 illustrates the Montgomery ladder step, a more thorough illustration of the execution steps for point addition and point doubling unified formula.

The usage of Montgomery ladder enables the computing of time-efficient $X-$only formulae in which the Y coordinate is not required for point multiplication computations and is restored once the method is done, which results

Algorithm 3. X448 algorithm. G represents the value of the base point

Alice		**Bob**
$sk_A \in_R \mathbb{Z}/\mathbb{F}_p$		$sk_B \in_R \mathbb{Z}/\mathbb{F}_p$
$pk_A = [sk_A] \cdot G$		$pk_B = [sk_B] \cdot G$
	exchange	
	$pk_A \longleftrightarrow pk_B$	
$ss_A = [sk_A] \cdot pk_B$		$ss_B = [sk_B] \cdot pk_A$
$ss_A = [sk_A] \cdot sk_B \cdot G$	$ss_A = ss_B$	$ss_B = [sk_B] \cdot sk_A \cdot G$

in further speed optimizations and it represents the method deployed in most implementations, including this work.

2.2 X448

Elliptic Curve Diffie-Hellman (ECDH) protocol implementation enables communication parties to agree on a shared secret that is later utilized in low-cost symmetric encryption schemes. To execute ECDH over a finite field using Curve448 requires both computing parties to generate secret key values represented by a long-integer value. Later on, each must apply the scalar-point multiplication function X448 depending on the scalar value of their secret key and a public base point G, for instance using the Montgomery ladder Algorithm 1. The newly computed points, representing the public keys of each party, are exchanged and another point multiplication is computed, applying their own secret key scalar value and the received point public key value. Algorithm 3 provides a representation of the ECDH algorithm in detail.

Following the execution of the two-point multiplications, as presented in Algorithm 3, both parties can ensure the privacy of their communication via efficient symmetric encryption scheme. The symmetric key is being derived through the equivalent values of the shared secrets and is then being used to encrypt data based on symmetric algorithm such as AES.

2.3 Ed448

The digital signature algorithm is mainly used to verify that the communication was sent by the intended recipient. The Edwards-Curve Digital Signature Algorithm (EdDSA) is defined in three phases - Key Generation, Sign and Verify. Ed448 DSA has a thorough explanation of these procedures, which may be found in Algorithm 4. The key generation uses a seed value to produce a secret key and its respective public key that are generated using a eXtendable Output Function (XOF) SHAKE256 (denoted with capital letter H in Algorithm 4) and scalar-point multiplication function. After running the signing function, it returns a signature $R||S$ generated based on the secret key and the message value. Finally,

Algorithm 4. Ed448 algorithm [31]. H denotes $SHAKE256$. L represents the order of Ed448 curve. G represents the value of the base point

Key Generation
Input: $seed$
Output: $(p, s), pk_A$
1. $sk_A \in_R^{seed} \mathbb{Z}/\mathbb{F}_p$
2. $(p, s) \leftarrow H(sk_A)$
3. $pk_A \leftarrow encode([s] \cdot G)$
Return $(p, s), pk_A$

Sign
Input: $pk_A, (p, s), M$
Output: $sign \equiv R||S$
1. $r \leftarrow (H(p||M))(modL)$
2. $R \leftarrow encode([r] \cdot G)$
3. $k \leftarrow (H(R||pk_A||M))(modL)$
4. $S \leftarrow encode((r + k * s)(modL))$
Return $R||S$

Verify
Input: $pk_A, M, R||S$
Output: $true/fasle$
1. $k \leftarrow H(R||pk_A||M)(modL)$
2. $A \leftarrow decode(pk_A)$
Return $[S] \cdot G == R + [k] \cdot A$

the verification is executed based on the public key and the message value and returns success upon the correctness of the equation $[S] \cdot G == R + [k] \cdot A$.

As noted, the scalar multiplication subroutine is forming the basis of both - elliptic curve based key agreement and digital signature algorithms, thus, its optimization is the main focus of this work. A new design and a performance record of the multi-precision multiplication and squaring, the base operations of point multiplication, are described later in the paper and the timing results of both cryptographic primitives are reported based on the proposed finite field arithmetic design.

2.4 Target Architecture

The ARM Cortex-M4 processor's Reduced Instruction Set Computer (RISC) architecture delivers a set of basic yet powerful instructions that are devoid of structural hazards and data dependence delays. This is why it is in such great demand in the realm of IoT and real-time systems. Furthermore, NIST recommended ARMv7-M Cortex-M4-based STM32F407VG discovery board microcontroller for low-end device performance assessment, featuring 192KB of RAM and

Table 1. ARMv7-M ISA [32] for memory access and MAC instructions

Instruction	Functionality	Latency (CC)
(V)LDR/ (V)STR	$R_n \leftarrow$ memory memory $\leftarrow R_n$ $S_n \leftarrow$ memory memory $\leftarrow S_n$	2
VMOV	$R_n \leftarrow S_m$ $S_m \leftarrow R_n$	1
UMULL	Rd_1, $Rd_2 \leftarrow R_n \times R_m$	1
UMAAL	Rd_1, $Rd_2 \leftarrow R_n \times R_m + Rd_1 + Rd_2$	1

1MB of flash memory, thus, it represents the board chosen by NIST for performance evaluation of the cryptographic algorithms and is, therefore, the target platform of this article.

The limited register set of just 16 32-bit General-Purpose Registers (GPRs) R0-R15 where two of them are reserved for the Stack Pointer SP and the Program Counter PC and are not accessible by the programmer, converts the implementation of multi-precision arithmetic operations into a challenging task. The ARMv7-M architecture offers another 32-bit Floating-Point Registers (FPRs) S0–S31. The transition of register values between the two register banks is ensured to be instant via the powerful VMOV instruction. The single clock cycle instruction latency, specific for the ARMv7-M 3-stage pipeline, has as only exception the memory access LDR/STR instructions where if not properly scheduled they can induce an additional clock cycle before another instruction can be processed. The nature of the long-integer arithmetic does not always allow to schedule the instructions, thus, to avoid stalling the pipeline. To maximize the performance of a hand-crafted assembly code, a thorough structure of the instruction flow and an in-depth examination of the Instruction Set Architecture (ISA) Table 1 are required. The precise order of the instruction flow is a combinatoric problem which requires careful analysis and deployment to provide the most optimal execution path.

The ARMv7-M ISA supports powerful multiplication instructions, referred to as Multiply ACcumulate (MAC), ensuring the execution of 32 × 32-bit multiplication, resulting in a 64-bit long value. The simple long multiply UMULL instruction offers an accumulative variant UMAAL executing another two 32-bit accumulative additions. The single clock cycle latency of the MAC instruction considerably improves the performance of long integer multi-precision multiplication and squaring subroutines when utilized correctly as presented in this work.

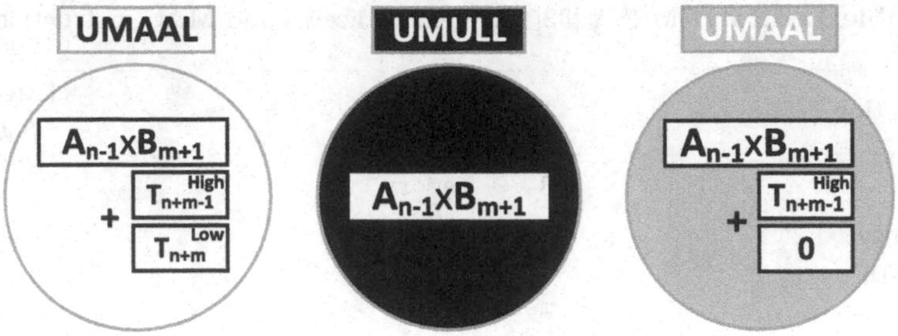

Fig. 1. Instruction set notation in dot format for the rhombus representation of the arithmetic operations multiplication and squaring.

3 Proposed Design for Field Arithmetic

3.1 Notation

The proposed architecture for multi-precision multiplication and squaring may be presented in a variety of ways, the most visually appealing of which is through the use of a rhombus representation. The implementation of finite field procedures needs distinct instruction sequences, which we represent with dots on the rhombus figures.

We utilize a different pattern of dots to a different color of dots, as shown in Fig. 1, to denote various MAC instructions. The white color dot indicates the execution of Unsigned Multiply with double Accumulate Long `UMAAL` where the multiplication of two 32-bit registers is performed, resulting in a 64-bit value accumulated with the content of the destination registers as two 32-bit numbers. The black dot represents an Unsigned MULtiply Long `UMUUL` with the destination registers containing the result's low and high 32-bits. Finally, the implementation of the multi-precision squaring routine requires the accumulation of a single 32-bit value to the 64-bit multiplication result, thus, we use the `UMAAL` and zero out one of the accumulated values. We denote the use of this instruction by a gray dot on the rhombus schemes.

For our implementation, we refer to the previous multi-precision strategies, such as Product-Scanning (PS), Operand-Scanning (OS) and Refined Operand-Caching techniques (R-OC). OS method is predicated on the concept of reusing a single limb from one operand while employing the whole set of limbs from the second operand. In particular, each calculation step should accumulate the previously stored partial result limb with a single partial result value. The computation of a partial result limb in each iteration can be represented as $T_i = T_i + A_k B_{i-k}$ with k being the iteration count. Finally, the product limb $R_i = T_i$ when the iteration count equals the result index being computed. Therefore, the computation of R_4 requires the execution of 5 iterations, where in each iteration one partial result is being computed and accumulated to the current partial result value.

The PS method is based on computing the entire set of accumulative partial multiplication results at once, allowing to obtain the final result, and, thus, not re-load any partial product values. Therefore, for the computation of the result limb R_i all partial multiplications would be computed and accumulated, i.e. $R_i = \sum_{k=0}^{i} A_k B_{i-k}$. Both techniques are the base of the modern multi-precision multiplication strategies and are combined, depending on the characteristics of the target device, to offer optimal performance results.

One such combination among PS and OS is the so called Operand Caching (and its variants), where the multiplication implementation is split into different sections, referred as rows, and each row consists of straightforward implementation of the product scanning multiplication technique. The size of the row represents the number of consecutive accumulated partial results computed in each iteration. Each row, thus, produces *row-size* number of accumulated partial results. The rows among them employ the OS approach, wherein the previously computed partial result is accumulated with the newly computed partial value at each iteration. The multi-precision multiplication design is also referred to as a combination of two loops - inner and outer multiplication loop. The OC deploys PS in the inner loop, i.e. the computations inside the scope of the rows. The outer loop in OC implements OS method which is applied among the different rows. The size of the row is one of the factors to determine the variant of the OC multiplication method, where the latest and most efficient variant of the OC targeting the Cortex-M4 platform is the Refined-OC (R-OC) method with row size equal to four.

The use of one or another multi-precision multiplication approach to enhance performance is entirely dependent on the platform being targeted. Large processors, for instance, have a large register set bank, so they can store more operand limbs and favor the PS technique. In addition, modern processors feature instant memory access instructions, therefore, multiple operand re-loading is inexpensive. However, the usage of low-end devices, such as the intended ARM Cortex-M4 chip, makes long-integer computations difficult due to register bank constraints and expensive memory accesses. We disclose the obtained speedup for the provided arithmetic and the performance record after incorporating our design into the ECDH and EdDSA cryptographic algorithms in this paper.

3.2 Multi-precision Multiplication

The design and implementation of the multi-precision multiplication subroutines are extremely important for the efficiency of the cryptographic protocols when based on long-integer values. The nature of the multi-precision multiplication places it into the most frequently invoked routines in Elliptic Curve and Isogeny-based protocols. Additionally, due to the high computational cost of these procedures, optimizing them results in an overall speedup of the protocols. This is why several academics have concentrated their efforts on optimizing it for various platforms.

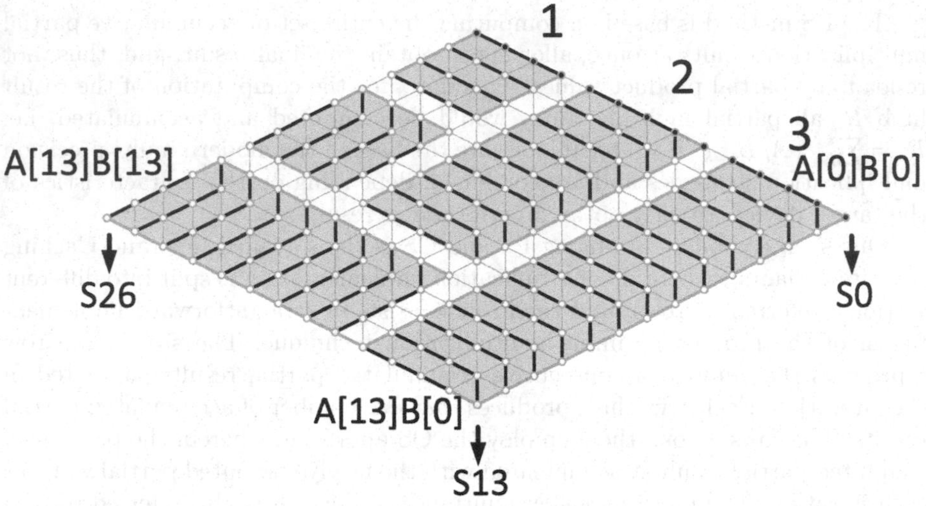

Fig. 2. Proposed architecture for 448-bit multi-precision multiplication. Black lines denote inner loop execution flow.

In this paper, we present a novel multi-precision multiplication approach, demonstrating a speed record on the target platform.

We illustrate our architecture in detail in Fig. 2, where the diagonal lines in the rhombus indicate the operands A and B and the dots represent the word-level operand partial operations. Numerous studies in the literature focus on the combinatorics of this topic with the goal of optimizing the performance outcomes of this function. The primary multiplication approaches are frequently used in high-level implementation designs that include product- or operand-scanning. However, owing to resource limits, a single application of one of the multiplication algorithms is not practical. Additionally, both have some significant downsides. To be more precise, the former requires numerous accesses to the value of the (partial) product in order to compute the result, whereas the latter requires continual reloading of the operand words in the accessible register set. Which approach is the most optimal is entirely dependent on the technical requirements of the target platform.

To optimize multiplication performance, the authors in [24,25,27,33] provide designs that combine the two major approaches to take use of the benefits of each one, namely the Hybrid, Operand Caching, Consecutive Operand Caching, and Refined-Operand Caching (R-OC) multi-precision multiplication. The methods already proposed in the literature apply one of the major techniques to the outer multiplication loop and one to the inner loop. The primary goal of routine optimization for low-end devices is to minimize memory accesses, since it can cause additional stalls when no cache memory is available, which is frequently the case with embedded low-cost devices. The R-OC, the most efficient multiplication in the literature, method's concept is to load operands into the register set and

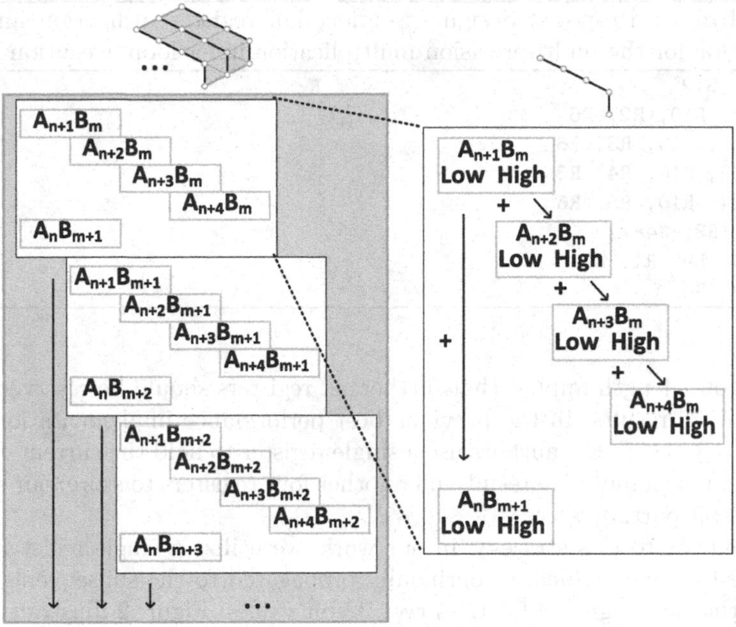

Fig. 3. Proposed design, register utilization and carry propagation for the multi-precision multiplication outer (left) and inner (right) loop execution flow.

reuse the operands' values. To do so, the authors in [27] introduce a method for storing four words of both operands in the instant memory units, thus, increase the size of the inner loop (i.e., row size) to four 32 × 32-bit multiplications. This technique optimizes the memory accesses by reusing the four loaded limbs from the second operand, when the growing operand index is switched (i.e., at the middle of the inner loop).

In this work, we present a novel technique for multi-precision multiplication, with an emphasis on increasing row (inner loop) size and hence decreasing memory accesses for partial value accumulation. To accomplish this aim of creating rows of size five, we reserve five registers for the value of operand A, and three registers for operand B (further detail of the register utilization is provided in Fig. 3). In our approach, two partial results are computed for the current column of calculation and one multiplication is performed for the subsequent three columns. This reduces register requirement for the storage of the second operand. Therefore, we maximize the available registers and increase the row size to five 32-bit multiplications per iteration, as there are sufficient free registers for the partial column-wise results. A close view of the inner loop operations is shown in Fig. 3, where it is presented that each step computes a single partial column value, stores it into memory and keeps another four columns partial values in the register set.

Algorithm 5. Proposed design (pseudocode), register utilization and carry propagation for the multi-precision multiplication inner loop execution flow.

```
VMOV R0, S12                  // R12
UMAAL R0, R10, R2, R6         // a6b6
UMAAL R11, R10, R3, R6        // a7b6
UMAAL R12, R10, R4, R6        // a8b6
UMAAL R14, R10, R5, R6        // a9b6
LDR R7, [R8, #4*7]            // b7
UMAAL R0, R9, R1, R7          // a5b7
VMOV S12, R0                  // R12
```

The row's length implies that further six registers should be reserved for the 32-bit partial results. In the previous best performance implementation design (i.e., R-OC) in [27], the authors use a single register to hold the current column's lower 32-bit accumulative result and another four registers to store four separate upper 32-bit partial values.

In contrast to this strategy, in our work, we utilize a single register for the upper 32-bit value, which is continually propagated to the subsequent column, and another five registers for the lower 32-bit values. Figure 2 illustrates graphically our architecture design with each inner loop iteration denoted by a black line. A more detailed view is shown in Fig. 3 and a pseudocode is presented in Algorithm 5, where one register R_{n+1+m} stores the low results of $A_{n+1}B_m$ accumulated to A_nB_{m+1}, R_{n+2+m} stores low $A_{n+2}B_m$, R_{n+3+m} stores low $A_{n+3}B_m$, R_{n+4+m} stores low $A_{n+4}B_m$ and R_{n+5+m} stores high $A_{n+4}B_m$ result, which has accumulated all previously created upper 32 bits (carry propagation).

To our knowledge, this new combination of product scanning and operand scanning approaches in the inner loop of multi-precision multiplication is introduced for the first time in the literature. As described in Fig. 3, this hybrid-inner loop design enables a reduction in the number of words allotted for operand B to only two. We reserve three to minimize the cost of reloading operands in the midst of the multiplication; consequently, we require just two more reloads per row above R-OC. By utilizing the register set optimally and following the new instruction flow, we optimize the R-OC approach by raising the row widths, which lowers access to partial results for accumulation.

3.3 Multi-precision Squaring

Due to the high invocation ratio of the multi-precision squaring routine, its performance optimization benefits the overall execution time and resource requirements of Curve448- and Ed448-based key exchange and digital signature algorithm protocols. In this work, we propose and implement the first multi-precision squaring procedure in hand-crafted assembly target-specific ARMv7 architecture code for the finite field of length 448 bits.

Due to the fact that the bottom portion of the rhombus representation mirrors the top part, the software design of the squaring benefits from the

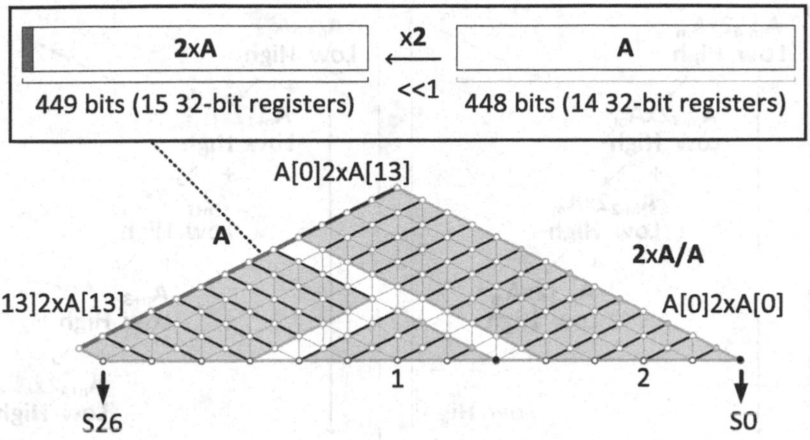

Fig. 4. Proposed architecture for 448-bit multi-precision multiplication with 14th index word for the doubled operand value (red line). (Color figure online)

duplication of some of the partial result values, and so can produce higher performance results than multi-precision multiplication. Since the result of $A_n A_m$ equals the result of $A_m A_n$ the accumulation of bottom and top rhombus sides may be implemented by doubling one of both values. The computation for the rhombus diagonal consists of operands with coinciding indexes (e.g. $A_k A_k$), as seen in Fig. 4 where they are marked with a red line. Their partial outcomes occur just once and are hence not duplicated. Additionally, because only one operand is involved in the operation, loading the operand words into the register set is eased. Numerous teams have worked in the literature to exploit these aspects of the subroutine and optimize the output for low-end target systems. There has been no software implementation of multi-precision squaring for the Curve448 and Ed448 protocols; hence, this work covers this gap by offering the first and most optimal design of 448-bit multi-precision squaring on the Cortex-M4 platform in comparison to other similar research.

Scott et al. provide one of the first attempts for multi-precision squaring function aiming low-end devices in [34]. The authors propose a carry catcher approach with an additional number of registers dedicated to storing and accumulating the generated carry. Later, *Lee et al.* propose lazy doubling method in [35] the authors, where each computed column is doubled and then accumulated to the non-doubled values. While this approach is the closest similar to our novel design, it does not produce ideal results due to the numerous result doublings and accumulations required.

In this work, we propose a new design for the implementation of finite field long-integer squaring. Our implementation's inner loop is based on the operand scanning mechanism. The rationale for picking this method is the enormous amount of free registers available due to the routine's single operand nature. Our primary goal is to raise the row size. For our design, we used the

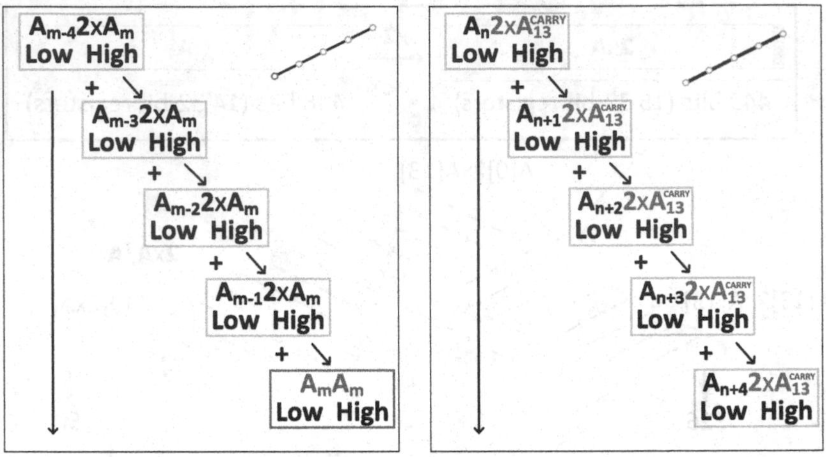

Fig. 5. Proposed design, register utilization and carry propagation for the multi-precision squaring with coinciding indexes of the operand (left) and with the carry word produced after doubling the operand (right).

double-operand approach presented in [27]. Additionally, we use the improved execution flow described in [29], which decreases the row number.

We should note that due to the exact fit of the prime number consisting of 448-bits into 14 32-bit value registers, the doubling the operand A may produce a carry. The carry bit specifies whether the doubled value of A is 448 or 449 bits. Thus, we simulate an additional word with index 14 of the duplicated A to obtain accurate results. We draw a red line through the word with index 14 of the doubled A in Fig. 4 and regard it as a regular limb of 2xA.

A thorough depiction of the implemented design is shown in Fig. 5 which illustrates the execution flow of one inner step iteration. On the left is a representation of the 32-bit partial multiplication of four doubled operand words with the original A. As with multiplication, the carry is kept in a single register and is propagated across subsequent short multiplications through the MAC UMAAL instruction. The right side of Fig. 5 depicts the execution flow when the 2xA is utilized. As it could be noticed, there is not much difference with the rest of the iterations, except that the value of the carry A_{13} is dynamically computed during the execution of the program.

3.4 Side-Channel Implications

Side-channel analysis (SCA) attack uses data leakage based on timing, power consumption, or electromagnetism information to recover secret information about the communication parties.

In this work, we propose new constant-time implementation of the multi-precision multiplication and squaring architectures for our Curve448-based key agreement and digital signature algorithms. Our subroutines' designs do not contain conditional execution flow, thus, are robust against timing attacks.

A question that can emerge is based on the fact that multiplication and squaring deploy different architectures and, therefore, show different latencies. This, however, should not present an issues in terms of information leakage since we deploy Montgomery ladder point multiplication design, where in each Montgomery ladder step one point doubling and one point addition are executed, independently of the secret key bit values. The sequence of multi-precision multiplication/squaring is known and is the same in each Montgomery ladder step. We should note again that this work is focused on the multi-precision modular operations, not on the group operations. Thus, our proposed design is not directly dependent on the users' secret information, but rather forms part of the multiple executions of the Montgomery ladder step.

3.5 Implementation Results

The next section compares the implemented multi-precision multiplication and squaring methods to their literature counterparts.

We present the execution time of low-level finite field arithmetic operations and the speedup obtained by integrating them into group operations. We base our experiment results on the STM32F407VG microcontroller running at 24MHz in order to remove memory controller stalls and deliver more exact findings that remain relatively similar on any ARMv7-M-based board.

We compare our work with the best-known counterparts in the literature targeting the same platform for Curve448- and Ed448-based algorithms and we present the latency results in number of clock cycles in Table 2. In this work, we achieve 25% of improvement compared to [21] for finite field multiplication when integrating our new multi-precision designs. Additionally we observe another 35% of speedup after introducing the first 448-bit modular squaring subroutine. The low-level arithmetic optimization leads to a 31% speedup for the inversion routine.

The group operations point addition and point doubling show 49% of performance improvement for the execution of the point doubling and addition. Our design is based on the execution of Montgomery ladder step where the doubling and addition are performed by the subroutine. After integrating the low-level finite field arithmetic along with the Montgomery ladder point multiplication strategy we observe more than 48% improvement for the execution of point multiplication.

The work on Ed448 we compare with the recently published work [22] where we achieve 13.1% and 24.5% latency speedup for the execution of the multiplication and squaring routine. Sequentially, we observe around 24% better results for the execution of the inversion and another 13.5% for the execution of the Montgomery ladder step. Finally, we observe 12% better performance for the Montgomery ladder based scalar multiplication routine.

Table 2. Finite field operations for Curve448/Ed448 targeting ARMv7-M

Ref.	Arithmetic performance evaluation					
	Fp			Group		
	Mul	Sqr	Inv	Add	Double	Multiply
	Curve448					
Seo et al.[a]	821	821	363,485	6,566	6,567	6,218,135
This work	**613**	**532**	**247,707**	**6,640(total)**		**3,220,682**
	25.33%	35.20%	31.85%	49.44%		48.21%
	Ed448					
Anastasova et al.[b]	705	705	325,997	8,465(total)		3,703,755
This work	**613**	**532**	**247,934**	**7,323(total)**		**3,259,379**
	13.05%	24.54%	23.95%	13.49%		12.00%

Refer to: [a][21], [b][22]

In the following section, we perform a more exhaustive report of the overall elliptic curve based key agreement and digital signature algorithms latencies when integrating our new low-level architecture designs.

4 Performance Evaluation

The next section analyzes the acquired findings in terms of performance. We report on the latency of our designs when they are executed on the STM32F407VG discovery board, which features a Cortex-M4 CPU. We run our results at 24MHz to assure a zero-wait condition and hence eliminate memory control unit stalls. Additionally, we report our results when the Curve448 ECDH key exchange and Ed448 DSA protocols are run at 168MHz in order to simulate a real-world scenario on the given microcontroller. Note that the high frequency measurement is extremely reliant on the target platform and varies between devices based on the memory control unit's clock speed.

We base our results on the version `gcc-arm-none-eabi-10.3-2021.07` cross-compiler setting the `-O3` optimization flag for optimized performance results. We compare our work with Curve25519- and Curve448-based implementations where we note that the results presented for Curve25519 are significantly better than our results due to the size of the prime number and thus the minimal length of the operands.

We provide the performance findings in Table 3 in terms of clock cycles $\times 10^3$. We notice that we obtain $\sim 3.6\times$ slower results for Curve448 in comparison to the Curve25519 results reported in [10] targeting the same platform. However, we should note that the Curve448 offers a much higher security level, in particular, 224-bit compared to 128-bit of Curve25519. We present more than $22\times$ better results for executing scalar-point multiplication X448 function than the work presented in [10]. However, we find that the limited resources available on their

Table 3. Curve 25519 and Curve448 key exchange and digital signature computation latency performance on IoT platforms

Work	Platform	Freq. [MHz]	X448	Ed448 KeyGen	Ed448 sign	Ed448 verify
Curve25519[a]	Cortex-M4	84	894	390	544	1,331
Curve448[b]	AVR	32	103,229	–	–	–
	MSP	25	73,478	–	–	–
Curve448[c]	Cortex-M4	24	6,218	–	–	–
		168	6,286	–	–	–
Ed448[d]	Cortex-M4	24	–	4,069	6,571	8,452
		168	–	4,195	6,699	8,659
This work	Cortex-M4	24	**3,221**	**3,536**	**6,038**	**7,404**
		168	**3,975**	**4,282**	**6,787**	**8,854**

Refer to: [a][10], [b][20], [c][21], [d][22]

low-end target systems necessitate more extensive outcome improvements. Thus, a portion of the reason for the enormous latency discrepancy is due to the target restrictions experienced by the writers on such low-end architecture device.

We compare the best performance results on the target platform, as provided by *Seo et al.* in [21] and *Anastasova et al.* in [22], by assessing the X448 point multiplication function and the Ed448 DSA key generation, sign, and verify functions. We mark around 48.2% and 36.8% of speedup when comparing our optimized X448 design running at 24 MHz and 168 MHz, respectively. The gains realized are a result of the novel arithmetic architecture introduced in this study. Thus, we report the execution of point multiplication in $3,221 \times 10^3$CCs. We also report a speedup of 13.1%, 8.1%, and 12.4% compared to the most recent literature equivalents while analyzing Ed448 EdDSA on the STM32F407 discovery board. We note that our implementation design shows a 1.4% of latency increase when running the digital signature procedures at the maximum platform frequency of 168 MHz. This is due to the floating-point register set being utilized as a storage unit rather than memory. This change, however, is negligible and is mostly due to the board's increased speed, a scenario that may not exist with other microcontrollers with different features.

5 Conclusion

In this work, we present a novel design for time-efficient finite field arithmetic over Curve448 and its birationally equivalent Ed448, where the pyramid-like structure of the protocols, results in an overall speedup of the key derivation and digital signature protocols based on the Montgomery and Edwards representation of Curve448. We describe an optimum multi-precision multiplication architecture and the first hybrid implementation of operand and product scanning techniques in the multiplication routine's inner loop. Additionally, we provide the first multi-precision squaring technique for 448-bit finite field arithmetic, where the carry of the operand doubling is represented as a new word and utilized to compute the right final value.

Acknowledgements. We would like to thank the reviewers for their comments. This work is supported in parts by research grants from NSF awards 214796 and 2101085.

References

1. National Institute of Standards and Technology: Security Requirements for Cryptographic Modules. Technical report, Federal Information Processing Standards Publications (FIPS PUBS) 140-2, Change Notice 2 December 03, 2002, U.S. Department of Commerce, Washington, D.C. (2001)
2. Shor, P.W.: Polynomial-time algorithms for prime factorization and discrete logarithms on a quantum computer. SIAM Rev. **41**(2), 303–332 (1999)
3. Bernstein, D.J., Lange, T.: Security dangers of the NIST curves. In: Invited talk. International State of the Art Cryptography Workshop, Athens, Greece (2013)
4. Bernstein, D.J.: Curve25519: New Diffie-Hellman speed records. In: Yung, M., Dodis, Y., Kiayias, A., Malkin, T. (eds.) PKC 2006. LNCS, vol. 3958, pp. 207–228. Springer, Heidelberg (2006). https://doi.org/10.1007/11745853_14
5. Bernstein, D.J., Duif, N., Lange, T., Schwabe, P., Yang, B.-Y.: High-speed high-security signatures. In: Preneel, B., Takagi, T. (eds.) CHES 2011. LNCS, vol. 6917, pp. 124–142. Springer, Heidelberg (2011). https://doi.org/10.1007/978-3-642-23951-9_9
6. Faz-Hernández, A., López, J., Dahab, R.: High-performance implementation of elliptic curve cryptography using vector instructions. ACM Trans. Math. Softw. (TOMS) **45**(3), 1–35 (2019)
7. Hisil, H., Egrice, B., Yassi, M.: Fast 4 way vectorized ladder for the complete set of montgomery curves. Cryptology ePrint Archive (2020)
8. Nath, K., Sarkar, P.: Security and efficiency trade-offs for elliptic curve Diffie-Hellman at the 128-bit and 224-bit security levels. J. Cryptogr. Eng. 1–15 (2021)
9. Düll, M., et al.: High-speed Curve25519 on 8-bit, 16-bit, and 32-bit microcontrollers. Des. Codes Cryptogr. **77**, 493–514 (2015). https://doi.org/10.1007/s10623-015-0087-1
10. Fujii, H., Aranha, D.F.: Curve25519 for the Cortex-M4 and beyond. In: Lange, T., Dunkelman, O. (eds.) LATINCRYPT 2017. LNCS, vol. 11368, pp. 109–127. Springer, Cham (2019). https://doi.org/10.1007/978-3-030-25283-0_6
11. Ullah, S., Zahilah, R.: Curve25519 based lightweight end-to-end encryption in resource constrained autonomous 8-bit IoT devices. Cybersecurity **4**(1), 1–13 (2021). https://doi.org/10.1186/s42400-021-00078-6
12. Turan, F., Verbauwhede, I.: Compact and flexible FPGA implementation of Ed25519 and X25519. ACM Trans. Embed. Comput. Syst. (TECS) **18**(3), 1–21 (2019)
13. Niasar, M.B., El Khatib, R., Azarderakhsh, R., Mozaffari-Kermani, M.: Fast, small, and area-time efficient architectures for key-exchange on Curve25519. In: 2020 IEEE 27th Symposium on Computer Arithmetic (ARITH), pp. 72–79. IEEE (2020)
14. Bisheh-Niasar, M., Azarderakhsh, R., Mozaffari-Kermani, M.: Cryptographic accelerators for digital signature based on Ed25519. IEEE Trans. Very Large Scale Integr. (VLSI) Syst. **29**(7), 1297–1305 (2021)

15. De Santis, F., Sigl, G.: Towards side-channel protected X25519 on ARM Cortex-M4 processors. In: Proceedings of Software Performance Enhancement for Encryption and Decryption, and Benchmarking, Utrecht, The Netherlands, pp. 19–21 (2016)
16. Liu, Z., Longa, P., Pereira, G.C.C.F., Reparaz, O., Seo, H.: FourQ on embedded devices with strong countermeasures against side-channel attacks. In: Fischer, W., Homma, N. (eds.) CHES 2017. LNCS, vol. 10529, pp. 665–686. Springer, Cham (2017). https://doi.org/10.1007/978-3-319-66787-4_32
17. Weissbart, L., Chmielewski, Ł, Picek, S., Batina, L.: Systematic side-channel analysis of Curve25519 with machine learning. J. Hardw. Syst. Secur. **4**(4), 314–328 (2020)
18. Hamburg, M.: Ed448-Goldilocks, a new elliptic curve. Cryptology ePrint Archive (2015)
19. Oliveira, T., López, J., Hışıl, H., Faz-Hernández, A., Rodríguez-Henríquez, F.: How to (pre-)compute a ladder. In: Adams, C., Camenisch, J. (eds.) SAC 2017. LNCS, vol. 10719, pp. 172–191. Springer, Cham (2018). https://doi.org/10.1007/978-3-319-72565-9_9
20. Seo, H.: Compact implementations of Curve Ed448 on low-end IoT platforms. ETRI J. **41**(6), 863–872 (2019)
21. Seo, H., Azarderakhsh, R.: Curve448 on 32-bit ARM Cortex-M4. In: Hong, D. (ed.) ICISC 2020. LNCS, vol. 12593, pp. 125–139. Springer, Cham (2021). https://doi.org/10.1007/978-3-030-68890-5_7
22. Anastasova, M., Bisheh-Niasar, M., Seo, H., Azarderakhsh, R., Kermani, M.M.: Efficient and side-channel resistant design of high-security Ed448 on ARM Cortex-M4. In: 2022 IEEE International Symposium on Hardware Oriented Security and Trust (HOST), pp. 93–96, IEEE (2022)
23. Montgomery, P.L.: Speeding the Pollard and elliptic curve methods of factorization. Math. Comput. **48**(177), 243–264 (1987)
24. Hutter, M., Wenger, E.: Fast multi-precision multiplication for public-key cryptography on embedded microprocessors. In: Preneel, B., Takagi, T. (eds.) CHES 2011. LNCS, vol. 6917, pp. 459–474. Springer, Heidelberg (2011). https://doi.org/10.1007/978-3-642-23951-9_30
25. Seo, H., Kim, H.: Multi-precision multiplication for public-key cryptography on embedded microprocessors. In: Lee, D.H., Yung, M. (eds.) WISA 2012. LNCS, vol. 7690, pp. 55–67. Springer, Heidelberg (2012). https://doi.org/10.1007/978-3-642-35416-8_5
26. Seo, H., Kim, H.: Consecutive operand-caching method for multiprecision multiplication. J. Inf. Commun. Converg. Eng. **13**(1), 27–35 (2015)
27. Seo, H., Anastasova, M., Jalali, A., Azarderakhsh, R.: Supersingular isogeny key encapsulation (SIKE) round 2 on ARM Cortex-M4. IEEE Trans. Comput. **70**(10), 1705–1718 (2020)
28. Seo, H.: Memory efficient implementation of modular multiplication for 32-bit ARM Cortex-M4. Appl. Sci. **10**(4), 1539 (2020)
29. Anastasova, M., Azarderakhsh, R., Kermani, M.M.: Fast strategies for the implementation of SIKE round 3 on ARM Cortex-M4. IEEE Trans. Circuits Syst. I Regul. Pap. **68**(10), 4129–4141 (2021)
30. Anastasova, M., Bisheh-Niasar, M., Azarderakhsh, R., Kermani, M.M.: Compressed SIKE round 3 on ARM Cortex-M4. In: Garcia-Alfaro, J., Li, S., Poovendran, R., Debar, H., Yung, M. (eds.) SecureComm 2021. LNICST, vol. 399, pp. 441–457. Springer, Cham (2021). https://doi.org/10.1007/978-3-030-90022-9_24
31. Josefsson, S., Liusvaara, I.: Edwards-curve digital signature algorithm (EdDSA). RFC 8032, January 2017

32. ARM: Cortex-M4 ISA. https://developer.arm.com/documentation/100166/0001. Accessed 1 May 2022
33. Gura, N., Patel, A., Wander, A., Eberle, H., Shantz, S.C.: Comparing elliptic curve cryptography and RSA on 8-bit CPUs. In: Joye, M., Quisquater, J.-J. (eds.) CHES 2004. LNCS, vol. 3156, pp. 119–132. Springer, Heidelberg (2004). https://doi.org/10.1007/978-3-540-28632-5_9
34. Scott, M., Szczechowiak, P.: Optimizing multiprecision multiplication for public key cryptography. Cryptology ePrint Archive (2007)
35. Lee, Y., Kim, I.-H., Park, Y.: Improved multi-precision squaring for low-end RISC microcontrollers. J. Syst. Softw. **86**(1), 60–71 (2013)

Signature Schemes

Pointcheval-Sanders Signature-Based Synchronized Aggregate Signature

Masayuki Tezuka[1(✉)] and Keisuke Tanaka[2]

[1] National Institute of Technology, Tsuruoka College, Yamagata, Japan
tezuka.m@tsuruoka-nct.ac.jp
[2] Tokyo Institute of Technology, Tokyo, Japan
keisuke@is.titech.ac.jp

Abstract. Synchronized aggregate signature is a special type of signature that all signers have a synchronized time period and allows aggregating signatures which are generated in the same period. This signature has a wide range of applications for systems that have a natural reporting period such as log and sensor data, or blockchain protocol.

In CT-RSA 2016, Pointcheval and Sanders proposed the new randomizable signature scheme. Since this signature scheme is based on type-3 pairing, this signature achieves a short signature size and efficient signature verification.

In this paper, we design the Pointchcval-Sanders signature-based synchronized aggregate signature scheme and prove its security under the generalized Pointcheval-Sanders assumption in the random oracle model. Our scheme offers the most efficient aggregate signature verification among synchronized aggregate signature schemes based on bilinear groups.

Keywords: Synchronized aggregate signature · Pointcheval-Sanders signature · Bilinear groups

1 Introduction

1.1 Background

Aggregate Signature. Aggregate signature originally introduced by Boneh, Gentry, Lynn, and Shacham [6] allows anyone to compress many signatures produced by different signers on different messages into a short aggregate signature. The size of an aggregate signature size is the same as any signature. By verifying an aggregate signature, we can check the validity of all those individual signatures which are compressed into an aggregate signature.

These attractive features are useful for the internet of things (IoT) system to reduce the storage space for signatures and realize efficient verification of

A part of this work was supported by JST CREST JP-MJCR2113, JSPS KAKENHI JP21H04879, and the technology promotion association of Tsuruoka KOSEN.

S.-H. Seo and H. Seo (Eds.): ICISC 2022, LNCS 13849, pp. 317–336, 2023.
https://doi.org/10.1007/978-3-031-29371-9_16

signatures. An aggregate signature scheme is expected to be used in a wide range of applications such as Border Gateway Protocol (BGP) routing [4], certificate chain compression [6], bundling software updates [2], sensor network data [2], or blockchain protocol [23].

Currently, only three aggregate signature scheme constructions are known. The first construction by Boneh et al. [6] is based on bilinear maps. This scheme can aggregate signatures as well as already aggregated signatures (i.e., full aggregation) in any order. The security of this scheme is proven under the co-computational Diffie-Hellman (co-CDH) assumption in the random oracle model (ROM). However, their scheme has a drawback in that the verification cost of an aggregate signature is expensive. Concretely, the number of pairing operations in verification for an aggregate signature is proportional to the number of signatures compressed into the aggregate signature.

The other schemes are constructed in the standard model (without the ROM). The second scheme by Hohenberger, Sahai, and Waters [22] is based on multilinear maps. The third scheme by Hohenberger, Koppula, and Waters [21] is an indistinguishability obfuscation (iO) based construction. Since constructing aggregate signature schemes from standard computational assumptions without ROM is a difficult task, several variants of aggregate signature with restricted aggregation have been proposed.

Synchronized Aggregate Signature. One variant of aggregate signature is synchronized aggregate signature. The concept of this signature was proposed by Gentry and Ramzan [16]. They constructed an identity-based aggregate signature that is based on the computational Diffie-Hellman (CDH) assumption in the ROM.

After their seminal work, Ahn, Green, and Hohenberger [2] revisited their model and proposed a synchronized aggregate signature. In this scheme, all of the signers have a synchronized time period. For each time period, each signer can sign a message at most once and signatures generated in the same time period only can be compressed into an aggregate signature. Even though a synchronized aggregate signature scheme has restrictions described above, it is still useful for systems that have a natural reporting period. (e.g. log data [2], sensor data [2], blockchain protocols [23])

So far, several synchronized aggregate signature schemes were proposed. Ahn, Green, and Hohenberger [2] gave a pairing-based synchronized aggregate signature scheme based on the CDH assumption without the ROM. Moreover, they also gave an efficient pairing-based synchronized aggregate signature scheme whose security is proven under the CDH assumption in the ROM.

Lee, Lee, and Yung [26] gave a synchronized aggregate signature scheme based on the Camenisch-Lysyanskaya (CL) signature scheme [9]. The security of this scheme relies on an interactive assumption called Lysyanskaya-Rivest-Sahai-Wolf (LRSW) assumption [30] in the ROM. Tezuka and Tanaka [40] revisited their security analysis result and improved it by showing the security based on a non-interactive assumption called the modified 1-strong Diffie-Hellman-2 (1-MSDH-2) assumption [33] in the ROM.

As for a pairing-free scheme, Hohenberger and Waters [23] proposed the synchronized aggregate signature scheme based on the RSA assumption without the ROM.

Motivation: Efficient Synchronized Aggregate Signature. In pairing-based synchronized aggregate signature schemes, the scheme by Lee et al. [26] is the most efficient synchronized aggregate signature scheme. Their scheme offers the smallest number of pairing operations (3 pairing operations) in an aggregate signature verification (See Fig. 1). From the viewpoint of the efficiency of aggregate signature verification, it is desirable to construct a synchronized aggregate signature scheme with fewer pairing operations for aggregate signature verification.

1.2 Our Result

Our Result. In this paper, we give a new synchronized aggregate signature scheme based on the Pointcheval-Sanders (PS) signature scheme [32]. The security of our scheme can be proven under the generalized Pointcheval-Sanders (GPS) assumption [24] in the ROM.

In general, compared to the computation cost of multiplication for elliptic curve points, the computation of pairing is more costly. To clarify the advantages of our synchronized aggregate scheme, we compare our scheme with other schemes (See Fig. 1).

Comparison with Other Schemes. The scheme BGLS [6] is a full-aggregate signature scheme that offers optimal public-key size and aggregate signature size. A full-aggregate signature scheme can be used as a synchronized aggregate signature scheme, with the following trivial modifications. A message m is changed to a message-period pair (m, t). Aggregation of signatures is only allowed for signatures that are signed in the same time period t. However, if we use BGLS as a synchronized aggregate signature scheme, $n + 1$ pairing operations are needed for verifying an aggregate signature where n is the number of aggregated original signatures.

The scheme $\mathsf{SAS}_{\mathsf{AGH1}}$ [2] is a synchronized aggregate signature scheme in the standard model. In $\mathsf{SAS}_{\mathsf{AGH1}}$, message space is $\ell \times k$-bits message space. (k chunks of ℓ-bits strings). If we set $k = 1$ in $\mathsf{SAS}_{\mathsf{AGH1}}$, $k + 3 = 4$ pairing operations is needed for verifying an aggregate signature.

The $\mathsf{SAS}_{\mathsf{AGH2}}$ [2] and $\mathsf{SAS}_{\mathsf{LLY}}$ [26] are synchronized aggregate signature schemes in the random oracle model. In both schemes, a public key is composed of 1 group element. $\mathsf{SAS}_{\mathsf{AGH2}}$ needs 4 paring operations and $\mathsf{SAS}_{\mathsf{LLY}}$ needs 3 paring operations for verifying an aggregate signature, respectively. Although a public key of our scheme is composed of 2 group elements, our scheme only needs 2 paring operations for verifying an aggregate signature.

Thus, compared with existing paring-based synchronized aggregate signature schemes, our scheme offers the fewest paring operations in a verification of an aggregate signature. Our scheme offers the most efficient aggregate signature

Scheme	Assumption	*pp* size	pk size	Agg size	Agg Ver (Pairing op)	Pairing type	CertKey model
$\mathsf{AS}_{\mathsf{BGLS}}$† [6] §3	co-CDH + ROM	$O(1)$	1	2	$n+1$	Type-2	✓
$\mathsf{SAS}_{\mathsf{AGH1}}$ [2] §4	CDH	$O(k)$	1	3	$k+3$	Type-3	✓
$\mathsf{SAS}_{\mathsf{AGH2}}$ [2] §A	CDH + ROM	$O(1)$	1	3	4	Type-3	✓
$\mathsf{SAS}_{\mathsf{LLY}}$ [26]	1-MSDH-2 + ROM	$O(1)$	1	2	3	Type-1	✓
$\mathsf{SAS}_{\mathsf{Ours}}$ §4.3	GPS + ROM	$O(1)$	2	2	2	Type-3	✓

Fig. 1. Comparison with pairing-based synchronized aggregate signature schemes. In the column of "Assumption", "ROM" represents the random oracle model. In the columns of "pp size", "pk size", "Agg size" represent the number of elements in a public parameter pp, a public key pk, and an aggregate signature, respectively. In the column of "Agg Ver (Pairing op)" represents the number of pairing operations in the verification of an aggregate signature. In the column of "CertKey model ", "✓" represents that the EUF-CMA security of the corresponding scheme is proven in the certified-key model. In $\mathsf{AS}_{\mathsf{BGLS}}$, n represents the number of original signatures which are aggregated into an aggregate signature. $\mathsf{AS}_{\mathsf{BGLS}}$ can be used as a synchronized aggregate signature scheme, with the following trivial modifications. A message m is changed to a message-period pair (m, t). Aggregation of signature is only allowed for signatures that are signed in the same time period t. An aggregate signature of $\mathsf{AS}_{\mathsf{BGLS}}$ is composed 1 element, but in other synchronized aggregate signature schemes, information of time period t is included in an aggregate signature. For fair comparison to other synchronized aggregate signature schemes, we include t into an aggregate signature and count the number of elements in an aggregate signature as 2. Security of $\mathsf{AS}_{\mathsf{BGLS}}$ simply can be proven under the co-CDH assumption in the ROM under the aggregation restriction that signatures for the same message cannot be aggregated. Without this aggregation restriction, $\mathsf{AS}_{\mathsf{BGLS}}$ can be used as a multi-signature, however, it falls victim to the rogue key attack which is known as a notorious attack for multi-signature schemes [5]. In synchronized aggregate signature has a restriction that each signer issues a signature one-time for each period, but it allows aggregating signatures on the same message. To prevent the rogue key attack, we should pose the certified-key model for $\mathsf{AS}_{\mathsf{BGLS}}$. In $\mathsf{SAS}_{\mathsf{AGH1}}$ has a $\ell \times k$-bits message space (k chunks of ℓ-bits message).

verification among synchronized aggregate signature schemes based on bilinear groups.

1.3 Technical Overview

How to Construct Our Signature Scheme. The core idea of our construction is based on the combination of randomizable signature, the "public-key sharing technique" and the "randomness re-use technique" [28]. These technique are used to construct variants of aggregate signatures scheme [11,26,28,37].

Lee et al. [26] used these techniques to construct a synchronized aggregate signatures scheme based on the CL signature scheme which is a randomizable signature scheme. The security of these schemes can be proven by the security of the original (CL) signature scheme.

Problem in Security Proof. However, it is not clear that it is possible to design a PS signature-based synchronized aggregate signature scheme with provable security. Since existing CL signature-based synchronized aggregate signature scheme $\mathsf{SAS}_{\mathsf{LLY}}$ [26] is given in only type-1 pairing, a type-3 pairing variant of CL signature-based synchronized aggregate signature scheme is not known.

Our first attempt is to apply the public-key sharing technique and the randomness re-use technique to the PS signature scheme which is also a randomizable signature scheme. In fact, we obtain the PS signature-based synchronized signature scheme but we fail to prove our scheme from the EUF-CMA security of the original (PS) signature scheme.

Now, we briefly explain the reason why the security proof technique in [26] fails in our scheme. In $\mathsf{SAS}_{\mathsf{LLY}}$, a group element of a public-key and group elements of signature belong to the same group $\mathbb{G}$. This fact allows signature simulation in the security proof of $\mathsf{SAS}_{\mathsf{LLY}}$ scheme. In the security proof of $\mathsf{SAS}_{\mathsf{LLY}}$, by using the programmability of the random oracle model, a signature is generated by computing multiplications of public-key.

By contrast, in our construction, group elements of signature and a group element of signature belong to different groups (See Fig. 7). Group elements of a public-key $(\widetilde{X}, \widetilde{Y})$ belong to the group $\widetilde{\mathbb{G}}$ and a group element of signature B belongs to the group $\mathbb{G}$. If we try to generate a signature by multiplying public-key elements $\widetilde{X}$ and $\widetilde{Y}$, the result of the multiplication does not belong to $\mathbb{G}$. Thus, the security proof technique by [26] cannot be applied to our scheme.

Our Approach for Security Proof. To prove the security of our scheme, we use the generalized PS (GPS) assumption [24] which is a variant of the PS assumption [32]. These assumptions are classified into interactive assumptions. The interactive assumption is that the computational problem is difficult for all probabilistic polynomial time adversary which tries to solve the problem even if oracle queries that are related to the problem are allowed.

Briefly, the difference between the PS assumption and the GPS assumption is equipped oracles (See Assumption 1 and Assumption 2). The GPS assumption is obtained by changing the oracle equipped with the PS assumption as follows. We divide the computation of the equipped oracle in the PS assumption into 2 computation steps and replace the equipped oracle with 2 oracles that compute each step. By using 2 oracles in the GPS assumption, we prove the security of our scheme under the GPS assumption in the random oracle model.

1.4 Related Works

Variants of Aggregate Signature. An aggregate signature can be categorized into various types from the point of view of aggregation restriction. The full aggregate signature proposed by Boneh et al. [6] allows any user to aggregate signatures generated by different signers. Moreover, this scheme allows us to aggregate individual signatures as well as already aggregated signatures in any order.

Lysyanskaya, Micali, Reyzin, and Shacham [29] proposed sequential aggregate signature. This signature scheme allows a signer to add his signature to an aggregate signature in sequential order.

Synchronized aggregate signature scheme [2,16] allows signers to generate at most one signature for each period and aggregate signatures generated in the same period into an aggregate signature.

Chalkias, Garillot, Kondi, and Nikolaenko [10] proposed the notion of half-aggregation. Half-aggregation allows compressing signatures into an aggregate signature that has half size of the total signature size.

Hartung, Kaidel, Koch, Koch, and Rup [20] proposed fault-tolerant aggregate signature. In this signature, as long as the number of invalid signatures aggregated does not exceed a certain bound, a verification algorithm can determine a subset of all messages belonging to an aggregate that were signed correctly.

Goyal and Vaikuntanathan [19] proposed locally verifiable aggregate signature. In this scheme, given an aggregate signature corresponding to the set of M of n messages, a local verification algorithm can check whether a particular message m is in the set M. Moreover, the runtime of a local verification algorithm is independent of N and the local verification algorithm can be run without knowledge of the entire set M.

Pointcheval-Sanders Signature. The Pointcheval-Sanders (PS) signature scheme [32] is a randomizable signature scheme that allows anyone to refresh a valid signature σ on a message m to a new valid signature σ' on the same message m. Compared to the Camenisch-Lysyanskaya signature scheme [9] which is also a randomizable signature scheme, this scheme offers a short signature size.

Security of this signature scheme was proven under the interactive assumption called the PS assumption [32]. In [33], Pointcheval and Sanders introduced the non-interactive assumption called the modified q-strong Diffie-Hellman-1 (q-MSDH-1) assumption. They proved the weak-EUF-CMA security of the PS signature scheme from the q-MSDH-1 assumption.

The PS signature scheme (the PS assumption) and its variant are important starting points to construct signature schemes with functionalities. (e.g. sequential aggregate signature [31,32], redactable signature [31,34], threshold signature [3], group signature [13,24,25,35,36], threshold group signature [8], multi-signature [8], updatable signature [12]) Moreover, relationships between the PS signature and the structure-preserving signature have been studied.

Gardafi [18] introduced the notion of a partially structure-preserving signature. In a structure-preserving signature scheme [1], all the messages, signatures, and public keys are group elements. Partially-preserving signature is the same with the exception that the message space is $\mathbb{Z}_p^n$ where n is an integer and p is a prime. They further proposed the notion of linear-massage strongly partially structure-preserving signature where the message is embedded in a linear manner. This signature class includes the CL signature scheme and the PS signature scheme. They proved some impossibility results and lower bound results for a linear-massage strongly partially structure-preserving signature and gave a generic transformation from a linear-massage strongly partially structure-preserving signature scheme to a structure-preserving signature scheme.

In recent work by Sedaghat, Slamanig, Kohlweiss, Preneel [38], they introduced the notion of a message-indexed structure-preserving signature which is a variant of a structure-preserving signature whose message is parameterized by a message indexing function. They gave a message-indexed structure-preserving signature scheme whose construction is inspired by the PS signature scheme and the structure-signature scheme by Ghadafi [17]. Moreover, they proposed a notion of a structure-preserving threshold signature and gave a construction based on a message-indexed structure-preserving signature scheme.

1.5 Road Map

In Sect. 2, we recall pairing groups and a digital signature. In Sect. 3, we review synchronized aggregate signature scheme and its security. In Sect. 4, we review the PS signature scheme, provide a high-level idea of our construction, and give our synchronized aggregate signature and prove its security.

2 Preliminaries

In this section, we introduce notations and review pairing groups and the Pointcheval Sanders assumption. Then, we review a digital signature scheme.

Notations. Let 1^λ be the security parameter. A function f is negligible in k if $f(k) \leq 2^{-\omega(\log k)}$. For a positive integer n, we define $[n] := \{1, \ldots, n\}$. For a finite set S, $s \xleftarrow{\$} S$ represents that an element s is chosen from S uniformly at random. For a group $\mathbb{G}$, we define $\mathbb{G}^* := \mathbb{G} \backslash \{1_{\mathbb{G}}\}$. For an algorithm A, $y \leftarrow \mathsf{A}(x)$ denotes that the algorithm A outputs y on input x. We abbreviate probabilistic polynomial time as PPT.

2.1 Bilinear Group

A pairing group is a tuple $\mathcal{BG} = (p, \mathbb{G}, \widetilde{\mathbb{G}}, \mathbb{G}_T, e)$ where $\mathbb{G}$, $\widetilde{\mathbb{G}}$ and $\mathbb{G}_T$ are cyclic group of prime order p and $e : \mathbb{G} \times \widetilde{\mathbb{G}} \rightarrow \mathbb{G}_T$ is an efficient computable, non-degenerating bilinear map. (i.e., e satisfies the following properties.)

1. For all $X \in \mathbb{G}$, $\widetilde{Y} \in \widetilde{\mathbb{G}}$ and $a, b \in \mathbb{Z}_p$, then $e(X^a, \widetilde{Y}^b) = e(X, \widetilde{Y})^{ab}$.
2. For all $G \in \mathbb{G}^*$, $\widetilde{G} \in \widetilde{\mathbb{G}}^*$, $e(G, \widetilde{G}) \neq 1_{\mathbb{G}_T}$.

Type-3 pairing groups [15] are pairing groups which satisfy $\mathbb{G} \neq \widetilde{\mathbb{G}}$ and there is no efficiently computable homomophism from $\widetilde{\mathbb{G}}$ to $\mathbb{G}$.

We introduce a type-3 bilinear group generator. A type-3 bilinear group generator BG is an algorithm that takes as an input a security parameter 1^λ. Then, it returns the descriptions of an asymmetric pairing $\mathcal{BG} = (p, \mathbb{G}, \widetilde{\mathbb{G}}, \mathbb{G}_T, e)$ where p is a λ-bits prime.

Pointcheval and Sanders [32] introduced the interactive assumption called Pointcheval-Sanders (PS) assumption. This assumption holds in the generic group model [39].

Assumption 1 (PS Assumption [32]**).** *Let* BG *be a type-3 bilinear group generator and* A *be a PPT algorithm. The Pointcheval-Sanders (PS) assumption over* BG *is defined by the game* $\mathsf{PS}_{\mathsf{BG}}$ *in Fig. 2.*

GAME $\mathsf{PS}^{\mathsf{A}}_{\mathsf{BG}}(\lambda)$:
$Q \leftarrow \{\}$, $\mathcal{BG} = (p, \mathbb{G}, \widetilde{\mathbb{G}}, \mathbb{G}_T, e) \leftarrow \mathsf{BG}(1^\lambda)$, $G \xleftarrow{\$} \mathbb{G}^*$, $\widetilde{G} \xleftarrow{\$} \widetilde{\mathbb{G}}^*$,
$x, y \xleftarrow{\$} \mathbb{Z}_p^*$, $\widetilde{X} \leftarrow \widetilde{G}^x$, $\widetilde{Y} \leftarrow \widetilde{G}^y$, $(A^*, B^*, m^*) \leftarrow \mathsf{A}^{\mathcal{O}_{x,y}(\cdot)}(\mathcal{BG}, G^*, \widetilde{G}^*, \widetilde{X}, \widetilde{Y})$
If $m^* \notin Q \wedge A^* \neq 1_{\mathbb{G}} \wedge B^* = (A^*)^{x+m^* \cdot y}$, return 1. Otherwise, return 0
$\mathcal{O}_{x,y}(m)$:
$Q \leftarrow Q \cup \{m\}$, $A \xleftarrow{\$} \mathbb{G}^*$, return $(A, A^{x+m \cdot y})$

Fig. 2. The game $\mathsf{PS}^{\mathsf{A}}_{\mathsf{BG}}$.

The advantage of an adversary A *in the game* $\mathsf{PS}_{\mathsf{BG}}$ *is defined by* $\mathsf{Adv}^{\mathsf{PS}}_{\mathsf{BG},\mathsf{A}}(\lambda) := \Pr[1 \Leftarrow \mathsf{PS}^{\mathsf{A}}_{\mathsf{BG}}(\lambda)]$. *We say that the PS assumption holds if* $\mathsf{Adv}^{\mathsf{PS}}_{\mathsf{BG},\mathsf{A}}(\lambda)$ *is negligible in* λ *for all PPT adversaries* A.

Kim, Lee, Abdalla, and Park proposed the generalized Pointcheval-Sanders (GPS) assumption [24]. This assumption is a modification of the PS assumption in that the oracle $\mathcal{O}_{x,y}(\cdot)$ in the PS assumption is divided into the following two oracles. $\mathcal{O}_0^{\mathsf{GPS}}$ samples a group element A and $\mathcal{O}_1^{\mathsf{GPS}}$ computes $B \leftarrow A^{x+m \cdot y}$ where (A, m) is given to $\mathcal{O}_1^{\mathsf{GPS}}$ as an input.

Assumption 2 (GPS Assumption [24]**).** *Let* BG *be a type-3 bilinear group generator and* A *be a PPT algorithm. The generalized Pointcheval-Sanders (GPS) assumption over* BG *is defined by the game* $\mathsf{GPS}_{\mathsf{BG}}$ *in Fig. 3.*

The advantage of an adversary A *in the game* $\mathsf{GPS}_{\mathsf{BG}}$ *is defined by* $\mathsf{Adv}^{\mathsf{GPS}}_{\mathsf{BG},\mathsf{A}}(\lambda) := \Pr[1 \Leftarrow \mathsf{GPS}^{\mathsf{A}}_{\mathsf{BG}}(\lambda)]$. *We say that the GPS assumption holds if* $\mathsf{Adv}^{\mathsf{GPS}}_{\mathsf{BG},\mathsf{A}}(\lambda)$ *is negligible in* λ *for all PPT adversaries* A.

Kim et al. [24] proved that the GPS assumption holds in the generic group model. Moreover, Kim, Sanders, Abdalla, and Park [25] analyzed the relationship among the PS assumption, the GPS assumption, and the symmetric discrete logarithm assumption. More precisely, from their result, the following facts are clarified.

- If the GPS assumption holds, the PS assumption holds.
- If the symmetric discrete logarithm assumption holds, the GPS assumption holds in the algebraic group model [14].

GAME $\mathsf{GPS}^{\mathsf{A}}_{\mathsf{BG}}(\lambda)$:

$Q_0, Q_1 \leftarrow \{\}, \mathcal{BG} = (p, \mathbb{G}, \widetilde{\mathbb{G}}, \mathbb{G}_T, e) \leftarrow \mathsf{BG}(1^\lambda), G \xleftarrow{\$} \mathbb{G}^*, \widetilde{G} \xleftarrow{\$} \widetilde{\mathbb{G}}^*,$

$x, y \xleftarrow{\$} \mathbb{Z}_p^*, \widetilde{X} \leftarrow \widetilde{G}^x, \widetilde{Y} \leftarrow \widetilde{G}^y, (A^*, B^*, m^*) \leftarrow \mathsf{A}^{\mathcal{O}_0^{\mathsf{GPS}}(), \mathcal{O}_1^{\mathsf{GPS}}(\cdot,\cdot)}(\mathcal{BG}, G, \widetilde{G}, \widetilde{X}, \widetilde{Y})$

If $(\cdot, m^*) \notin Q_1 \wedge A^* \neq 1_{\mathbb{G}} \wedge B^* = (A^*)^{x+m^* \cdot y}$, return 1. Otherwise, return 0

$\mathcal{O}_0^{\mathsf{GPS}}()$:

$A \xleftarrow{\$} \mathbb{G}^*, Q_0 \leftarrow Q_0 \cup \{A\}$, return A

$\mathcal{O}_1^{\mathsf{GPS}}(A, m \in \mathbb{Z}_p)$:

If $(A \notin Q_0 \vee (A, \cdot) \in Q_1)$, return $\perp$.

$B \leftarrow A^{x+m \cdot y}, Q_1 \leftarrow Q_1 \cup \{(A, m)\}$, return B.

Fig. 3. The game $\mathsf{GPS}^{\mathsf{A}}_{\mathsf{BG}}$.

2.2 Digital Signature Scheme

We review a digital signature scheme and its security notion.

Definition 1 (Digital Signature Scheme). *A digital signature scheme* DS *consists of following four algorithms* (Setup, KGen, Sign, Verify).

- Setup(1^λ) : *A setup algorithm takes as an input a security parameter* 1^λ. *It returns the public parameter* pp. *In this work, we assume that* pp *defines a message space and represents this space by* $\mathcal{M}_{\mathsf{pp}}$. *We omit a public parameter* pp *in the input of all algorithms except for* KGen.
- KGen(pp) : *A key-generation algorithm takes as an input a public parameter* pp. *It returns a public key* pk *and a secret key* sk.
- Sign(sk, m) : *A signing algorithm takes as an input a secret key* sk *and a message* m. *It returns a signature* σ.
- Verify(pk, m, σ) : *A verification algorithm takes as an input a public key* pk, *a message* m, *and a signature* σ. *It returns a bit* $b \in \{0, 1\}$.

Correctness. DS *satisfies correctness if for all* $\lambda \in \mathbb{N}$, pp $\leftarrow$ Setup(1^λ) *for all* $m \in \mathcal{M}_{\mathsf{pp}}$, (pk, sk) $\leftarrow$ KGen(pp), *and* $\sigma \leftarrow$ Sign(sk, m), Verify(pk, m, σ) $= 1$ *holds.*

We review a security notion called the existentially unforgeable under chosen message attacks (EUF-CMA) security for digital signature.

Definition 2 (EUF-CMA Security). *The existentially unforgeable under chosen message attacks (EUF-CMA) security of a digital signature scheme* DS *is defined as Fig. 4.*

The advantage of an adversary A *for the EUF-CMA security game is defined by* $\mathsf{Adv}^{\mathit{EUF\text{-}CMA}}_{\mathsf{DS,A}} := \Pr[\mathit{EUF\text{-}CMA}^{\mathsf{DS}}_{\mathsf{A}} \Rightarrow 1]$. DS *satisfies EUF-CMA security if for all PPT adversaries* A, $\mathsf{Adv}^{\mathit{EUF\text{-}CMA}}_{\mathsf{DS,A}}$ *is negligible in* λ.

3 Synchronized Aggregate Signature

In this section, we review a synchronized aggregate signature scheme and it security model.

GAME $\text{EUF-CMA}_{\text{A}}^{\text{DS}}$:
$Q \leftarrow \{\}$, $\text{pp} \leftarrow \text{Setup}(1^\lambda)$, $(\text{pk}, \text{sk}) \leftarrow \text{KGen}(\text{pp})$, $(m^*, \sigma^*) \leftarrow \text{A}^{\mathcal{O}^{\text{Sign}}(\cdot)}(\text{pp}, \text{pk})$
If $\text{Verify}(\text{pk}, m^*, \sigma^*) = 1 \wedge m^* \notin Q$, return 1. Otherwise return 0.

Oracle $\mathcal{O}^{\text{Sign}}(m)$:
$Q \leftarrow Q \cup \{m\}$, $\sigma \leftarrow \text{Sign}(\text{sk}, m)$, return σ.

Fig. 4. The EUF-CMA security game $\text{EUF-CMA}_{\text{A}}^{\text{DS}}$.

3.1 Synchronized Aggregate Signature Scheme

An aggregate signature [6] allows us to compress an arbitrary number of individual signatures into a short aggregate signature. A synchronized aggregate signature [2] is a variant of aggregate signature that all signers have a synchronized time clock or has an access to the public current time period. For each time period t, each signer can sign a message at most once and anyone can aggregate signatures generated by different signers in the same period t. A generated aggregate signature is the same size as an individual signature.

Now, we review a definition of a synchronized aggregate signature.

Definition 3 (Synchronized Aggregate Signature Scheme [2,16]**).** *A synchronized aggregate signature scheme* SAS *for a bounded number of periods is a tuple of algorithms* (Setup, KGen, Sign, Verify, Agg, AVer).

- $\text{Setup}(1^\lambda, 1^T)$: *A setup algorithm takes as an input a security parameter* λ *and the time period bound* T. *It returns the public parameter* pp. *We assume that* pp *defines the message space* $\mathcal{M}_{\text{pp}}$. *We omit a public parameter* pp *in the input of all algorithms except for* KGen.
- $\text{KGen}(\text{pp})$: *A key-generation algorithm takes as an input a public parameter* pp. *It returns a public key* pk *and a secret key* sk.
- $\text{Sign}(\text{sk}, t, m)$: *A signing algorithm takes as an input a secret key* sk, *a time period* $t \leq T$, *and a message* m. *It returns a signature* σ. *We assume that the information of time period* t *is contained in a signature* σ.
- $\text{Verify}(\text{pk}, m, \sigma)$: *A verification algorithm takes as an input a public key* pk, *a message* m, *and a signature* σ. *It returns a bit* $b \in \{0, 1\}$.
- $\text{Agg}((\text{pk}_i, m_i, \sigma_i)_{i \in [\ell]})$: *An aggregation algorithm takes as an input a list of tuple* $(\text{pk}_i, m_i, \sigma_i)_{i \in [\ell]}$. *It return either an aggregate signature* Σ *or* $\perp$. *We assume that the information of time period* t *is contained in an aggregate signature* Σ.
- $\text{AVer}((\text{pk}_i, m_i)_{i \in [\ell]}, \Sigma)$: *An aggregate signature verification algorithm takes as an input a list of tuple* $(\text{pk}_i, m_i)_{i \in [\ell]}$ *and an aggregate signature* Σ. *It returns a bit* $b \in \{0, 1\}$.

Correctness. SAS *satisfies correctness if for all* $\lambda \in \mathbb{N}$, $T \in \mathbb{N}$, $\text{pp} \leftarrow \text{Setup}(1^\lambda, 1^T)$, *for any finite sequence of key pairs* $(\text{pk}_1, \text{sk}_1), \ldots (\text{pk}_\ell, \text{sk}_\ell) \leftarrow \text{KGen}(\text{pp})$ *where* pk_i *are all distinct, for any time period* $t \leq T$, *for any* *sequence of messages* $(m_1, \ldots m_\ell) \in \mathcal{M}_{pp}^{\ell}$, $\sigma_i \leftarrow \mathsf{Sign}(\mathsf{sk}_i, t, m_i)$ *for* $i \in [\ell]$, $\Sigma \leftarrow \mathsf{Agg}((\mathsf{pk}_i, m_i, \sigma_i)_{i\in[\ell]})$, *we have*

$$\mathsf{Verify}(\mathsf{pk}_i, m_i, \sigma_i) = 1 \text{ for all } i \in [\ell] \wedge \mathsf{AVer}((\mathsf{pk}_i, m_i)_{i\in[\ell]}, \Sigma) = 1.$$

3.2 Security for Synchronized Aggregate Signature

We review a security model called the existentially unforgeable under chosen message attacks (EUF-CMA) security in the certified-key model.

Gentry and Ramzan [16] introduced the existentially unforgeable under chosen message attacks (EUF-CMA) security for synchronized aggregate signature. In this security model, a public parameter pp and a challenge public key pk^* are given to an adversary which tries to forge an aggregate signature without secret key sk^*. For each period t, the adversary allows to access signing oracle $\mathcal{O}^{\mathsf{Sign}}$ and obtain a signature for an arbitrary message. This security guarantees that it is hard for an adversary to forge an aggregate signature that is valid and non-trivial. Gentry and Ramzan [16] constructed an identity-based synchronized aggregate signature scheme.

Ahn, Green, and Hohenberger [2] introduced the certified-key model for a synchronized aggregate signature. In this model, signers must prove that a tuple of keys $(\mathsf{pk}, \mathsf{sk})$ is generated honestly by an algorithm KGen. To prove the honest generation of a public key pk, the signer (adversaries for EUF-CMA) must submit a tuple $(\mathsf{pk}, \mathsf{sk})$ to the certification oracle $\mathcal{O}^{\mathsf{Cert}}$. Now, we review the EUF-CMA security in the certified-key model.

Definition 4 (EUF-CMA Security in the Certified-Key Model [2,26]**).** *The existentially unforgeable under chosen message attacks (EUF-CMA) security of a synchronized aggregate signature scheme* SAS *in the certified-key model is defined as Fig. 5.*

The advantage of an adversary A *for the EUF-CMA security game in the certified-key model is defined by* $\mathsf{Adv}_{\mathsf{SAS},\mathsf{A}}^{\mathit{EUF\text{-}CMA}} := \Pr[\mathit{EUF\text{-}CMA}_{\mathsf{A}}^{\mathsf{SAS}} \Rightarrow 1]$. SAS *satisfies EUF-CMA security in the certified-key model if for all PPT adversaries* A, $\mathsf{Adv}_{\mathsf{SAS},\mathsf{A}}^{\mathit{EUF\text{-}CMA}}$ *is negligible in* λ.

4 PS Signature-Based Synchronized Aggregate Signature

In this section, we review the Pointcheval-Sanders (PS) signature scheme [32]. Then, we give a high-level idea of our synchronized aggregate signature scheme from the PS signature scheme and give our synchronized aggregate signature scheme. Finally, we prove the security of our scheme from the EUF-CMA security of the PS signature scheme in the ROM.

4.1 Pointcheval-Sanders Signature Scheme [32]

Pointcheval and Sanders [32] proposed a short randomizable signature scheme. We review the single-message Pointcheval-Sanders (PS) signature scheme

GAME $\mathsf{EUF\text{-}CMA}_{\mathsf{A}}^{\mathsf{SAS}}$:
$Q \leftarrow \{\}$, $L \leftarrow \{\}$, $t \leftarrow 1$, $\mathsf{pp} \leftarrow \mathsf{Setup}(1^\lambda)$, $(\mathsf{pk}^*, \mathsf{sk}^*) \leftarrow \mathsf{KGen}(\mathsf{pp})$,
$((\mathsf{pk}_i^*, m_i^*)_{i\in[\ell^*]}, \Sigma^*) \leftarrow \mathsf{A}^{\mathcal{O}^{\mathsf{Cert}}(\cdot,\cdot), \mathcal{O}^{\mathsf{Sign}}(\cdot,\cdot)}(\mathsf{pp}, \mathsf{pk}^*)$
If $(\mathsf{SAS.AVer}((\mathsf{pk}_i^*, m_i^*)_{i\in[\ell^*]}, \Sigma^*) = 1)$
$\wedge$ (for all $i \in [\ell^*]$ such that $\mathsf{pk}_j^* \neq \mathsf{pk}^*$, $\mathsf{pk}_j^* \in L$)
$\wedge$ ($\mathsf{pk}_{j^*}^* = \mathsf{pk}^* \wedge m_{j^*}^* \notin Q$ for some $j^* \in [\ell^*]$), return 1.
Otherwise return 0.

Oracle $\mathcal{O}^{\mathsf{Cert}}(\mathsf{pk}, \mathsf{sk})$:
If the key pair $(\mathsf{pk}, \mathsf{sk})$ is valid, $L \leftarrow L \cup \{\mathsf{pk}\}$ and return "accept".
Otherwise, return "reject".
Oracle $\mathcal{O}^{\mathsf{Sign}}(\mathbf{inst}, m)$:
If $\mathbf{inst} = \mathbf{skip}$, $t \leftarrow t + 1$.
Otherwise, $Q \leftarrow Q \cup \{m\}$, $\sigma \leftarrow \mathsf{SAS.Sign}(\mathsf{sk}^*, t, m)$, $t \leftarrow t + 1$, return σ.

Fig. 5. The EUF-CMA security game in the certified-key model $\mathsf{EUF\text{-}CMA}_{\mathsf{A}}^{\mathsf{SAS}}$.

$\mathsf{Setup}_{\mathsf{PS}}(1^\lambda)$:
$\mathcal{BG} = (p, \mathbb{G}, \widetilde{\mathbb{G}}, \mathbb{G}_T, e) \leftarrow \mathsf{BG}(1^\lambda)$, return $\mathsf{pp} \leftarrow \mathcal{BG}$.
$\mathsf{KGen}_{\mathsf{PS}}(\mathsf{pp})$:
$\widetilde{G} \xleftarrow{\$} \widetilde{\mathbb{G}}^*$, $x, y \xleftarrow{\$} \mathbb{Z}_p^*$, $\widetilde{X} \leftarrow \widetilde{G}^x$, $\widetilde{Y} \leftarrow \widetilde{G}^y$, return $(\mathsf{pk}, \mathsf{sk}) \leftarrow ((\widetilde{G}, \widetilde{X}, \widetilde{Y}), (x, y))$.
$\mathsf{Sign}_{\mathsf{PS}}(\mathsf{sk} = (x, y), m)$:
$A \xleftarrow{\$} \mathbb{G}^*$, $B \leftarrow A^{x+m\cdot y}$, return $\sigma \leftarrow (A, B)$.
$\mathsf{Verify}_{\mathsf{PS}}(\mathsf{pk} = (\widetilde{G}, \widetilde{X}, \widetilde{Y}), m, \sigma = (A, B))$:
If $A \neq 1_{\mathbb{G}} \wedge e(A, \widetilde{X}\widetilde{Y}^m) = e(B, \widetilde{G})$, return 1. Otherwise return 0.

Fig. 6. The single-message PS signature scheme $\mathsf{DS}_{\mathsf{PS}}$.

$\mathsf{DS}_{\mathsf{PS}} = (\mathsf{Setup}_{\mathsf{PS}}, \mathsf{KGen}_{\mathsf{PS}}, \mathsf{Sign}_{\mathsf{PS}}, \mathsf{Verify}_{\mathsf{PS}})$. The construction of their scheme is described in Fig. 6.

Theorem 1 [32]. *If the Pointcheval-Sanders (PS) assumption holds,* $\mathsf{DS}_{\mathsf{PS}}$ *satisfies the EUF-CMA security.*

4.2 High-Level Idea of Our Construction

We give a high-level idea of our synchronized-aggregate signature construction from the PS signature scheme $\mathsf{DS}_{\mathsf{PS}}$. Let $(\mathsf{pk}_i, \mathsf{sk}_i) = ((\widetilde{G}_i, \widetilde{X}_i, \widetilde{Y}_i), (x_i, y_i))$ be a key pair of the signer i in $\mathsf{DS}_{\mathsf{PS}}$. The signature σ_i on a message m_i signed by sk_i is formed as $\sigma_i = (A_i, B_i = A_i^{x_i+m_i\cdot y_i})$ where $A_i \xleftarrow{\$} \mathbb{G}^*$.

To construct our synchronized-aggregate signature, we apply the "public-key sharing technique" and the "randomness re-use technique" [28]. These techniques are used to construct variants of aggregate signatures [11,26,28,37,40]. We explain how to apply these techniques to $\mathsf{DS}_{\mathsf{PS}}$.

First, we consider applying the "public-key sharing technique". In this technique, one of element in public key of underlying scheme is replaced by the public parameter. We change pk_i as $(\widetilde{X}_i, \widetilde{Y}_i)$ and force signers to use same $\widetilde{G}_i$. That is, we include $\widetilde{G} = \widetilde{G}_i$ into the public parameter of the scheme.

Second, we consider applying the "randomness re-use technique". This technique forces all signers to use the same randomness to sign a message. If all of signer share same A_i, a signature σ on a message m_i by each signer i is formed as $(A, B_i = A^{x_i + m_i \cdot y_i})$. Then, we can compress signatures $\{\sigma_i\}_{i \in [\ell]}$ into an aggregate signature $\Sigma = (A, \prod_{i \in [\ell]} B_i = A^{\sum_{i \in [\ell]} (x_i + m_i \cdot y_i)})$.

To share the same randomness A to all signers for each time period t, we change A to $H_1(t)$ where $H_1 : [T] \rightarrow \mathbb{G}^*$ is a hash function. Hashing the time as group element has been used to construct variants of aggregate signature schemes [26,27]. Moreover, to prove the security, we modify m_i to $H_2(t, m_i)$ where $H_2 : [T] \times \{0,1\}^* \rightarrow \mathbb{Z}_p$ is a hash function.

4.3 Our Synchronized Aggregate Signature Scheme

We describe our synchronized aggregate signature scheme $\mathsf{SAS}_{\mathsf{Ours}} = (\mathsf{Setup}_{\mathsf{Ours}}, \mathsf{KGen}_{\mathsf{Ours}}, \mathsf{Sign}_{\mathsf{Ours}}, \mathsf{Verify}_{\mathsf{Ours}}, \mathsf{Agg}_{\mathsf{Ours}}, \mathsf{AVer}_{\mathsf{Ours}})$. The construction of our synchronized aggregate signature scheme is described in Fig. 7.

$\mathsf{Setup}_{\mathsf{Ours}}(1^\lambda, 1^T)$:
- $\mathcal{BG} = (p, \mathbb{G}, \widetilde{\mathbb{G}}, \mathbb{G}_T, e) \leftarrow \mathsf{BG}(1^\lambda)$, $\widetilde{G} \xleftarrow{\$} \widetilde{\mathbb{G}}^*$.
- Choose hash functions: $H_1 : [T] \rightarrow \mathbb{G}^*$, $H_2 : [T] \times \{0,1\}^* \rightarrow \mathbb{Z}_p$.
- Return $\mathsf{pp} \leftarrow (\mathcal{BG}, \widetilde{G}, H_1, H_2)$.

$\mathsf{KGen}_{\mathsf{Ours}}(\mathsf{pp})$:
- $x, y \xleftarrow{\$} \mathbb{Z}_p^*$, $\widetilde{X} \leftarrow \widetilde{G}^x$, $\widetilde{Y} \leftarrow \widetilde{G}^y$, return $(\mathsf{pk}, \mathsf{sk}) \leftarrow ((\widetilde{X}, \widetilde{Y}), (x, y))$.

$\mathsf{Sign}_{\mathsf{Ours}}(\mathsf{sk} = (x, y), t, m)$:
- $m' \leftarrow H_2(t, m)$, $B \leftarrow H_1(t)^{x + m' \cdot y}$, return (B, t).

$\mathsf{Verify}_{\mathsf{Ours}}(\mathsf{pk} = (\widetilde{X}, \widetilde{Y}), m, \sigma)$:
- $m' \leftarrow H_2(t, m)$, parse σ as (B, t).
- If $e(H_1(t), \widetilde{X}\widetilde{Y}^{m'}) = e(B, \widetilde{G})$, return 1. Otherwise return 0.

$\mathsf{Agg}_{\mathsf{Ours}}((\mathsf{pk}_i, m_i, \sigma_i)_{i \in [\ell]})$:
- For $i = 1$ to ℓ, parse σ_i as (B_i, t_i).
- If there exists $i \in \{2, \ldots, \ell\}$ such that $t_i \neq t_1$, return $\perp$.
- If there exists $(i, j) \in [\ell] \times [\ell]$ such that $i \neq j \wedge \mathsf{pk}_i = \mathsf{pk}_j$, return $\perp$.
- If there exists $i \in [\ell]$ suth that $\mathsf{Verify}_{\mathsf{Ours}}(\mathsf{pk}_i, m_i, \sigma_i) \neq 0$, return $\perp$.
- $B' \leftarrow \prod_{i=1}^{\ell} B_i$, return $\Sigma \leftarrow (B', t)$.

$\mathsf{AVer}_{\mathsf{Ours}}((\mathsf{pk}_i, m_i)_{i \in [\ell]}, \Sigma)$:
- There exists $(i, j) \in [\ell] \times [\ell]$ such that $i \neq j \wedge \mathsf{pk}_i = \mathsf{pk}_j$, return 0.
- For $i = 1$ to ℓ, $m'_i \leftarrow H_2(t, m_i)$.
- Parse Σ as (B', t).
- If $e(H_1(t), (\prod_{i=1}^{\ell} \widetilde{X}_i \widetilde{Y}_i^{m'_i})) = e(B', \widetilde{G})$, return 1. Otherwise return 0.

Fig. 7. Our synchronized aggregate signature scheme $\mathsf{SAS}_{\mathsf{Ours}}$.

Correctness. We confirm the correctness of our scheme $\mathsf{SAS}_{\mathsf{Ours}}$. Let $\mathsf{pp} \leftarrow \mathsf{Setup}_{\mathsf{Ours}}(1^\lambda, 1^T)$, $t \in [T]$, $(\mathsf{pk}_i, \mathsf{sk}_i) \leftarrow \mathsf{KGen}_{\mathsf{Ours}}(\mathsf{pp})$ for $i \in [\ell]$ and $\sigma_i \leftarrow \mathsf{Sign}_{\mathsf{Ours}}(\mathsf{sk}_i, t, m_i)$ for $i \in [\ell]$ where pk_i are all distinct. First, we check the correctness of a non-aggregated signature. For each $i \in [\ell]$, $B_i = H_1(t)^{x_i + H_2(t,m_i)\cdot y_i}$ holds where $\sigma_i = (B_i, t)$ and $\mathsf{sk}_i = (x_i, y_i)$. By these fact, $e(H_1(t), \widetilde{X}_i\widetilde{Y}_i^{H_2(t,m_i)}) = e(B_i, \widetilde{G})$ holds where $\mathsf{pk}_i = (\widetilde{X}_i, \widetilde{Y}_i)$. Thus, we can see that the correctness of a non-aggregated signature σ_i holds.

Next, we check the correctness of an aggregate signature. Let $\Sigma = (B', t) \leftarrow \mathsf{Agg}_{\mathsf{Ours}}((\mathsf{pk}_i, m_i, \sigma_i)_{i \in [\ell]})$. Then, $B' = \prod_{i=1}^{\ell} B_i = \prod_{i=1}^{\ell}(H_1(t)^{x_i + H_2(t,m_i)\cdot y_i}) = H_1(t)^{\sum_{i=1}^{\ell}(x_i + H_2(t,m_i)\cdot y_i)}$ holds. By these fact, $e(H_1(t), \prod_{i=1}^{\ell}(\widetilde{X}_i\widetilde{Y}_i^{H_2(t,m_i)})) = e(H_1(t), \widetilde{G}^{\sum_{i=1}^{\ell}(x_i + H_2(t,m_i)\cdot y_i)}) = e(B_i, \widetilde{G})$ holds. Thus, we can see that the correctness of aggregate signature Σ holds.

4.4 Security Analysis

As explained in Sect. 1.3, security proof technique by Lee et al. [26] cannot be applicable. Instead, we prove the EUF-CMA security of our scheme $\mathsf{SAS}_{\mathsf{Ours}}$ from the GSP assumption.

Theorem 2. *Let H_1, H_2 be a hash function of $\mathsf{SAS}_{\mathsf{Ours}}$ in Fig. 6 and T is a polynomial in λ. If the GPS assumption holds and H_1, H_2 are modeled as the random oracle, our scheme $\mathsf{SAS}_{\mathsf{Ours}}$ satisfies the EUF-CMA security in the certified-key model.*

Proof. Let A be an EUF-CMA security game adversary of the $\mathsf{SAS}_{\mathsf{Ours}}$ scheme with q_{H_2} hash queries to $\mathcal{O}^{H_2}$. We construct an adversary B for the GPS security game of $\mathsf{BG}_{\mathsf{GPS}}$ by using A. The construction of B is given in Fig. 8.

We confirm that if B does not abort, B simulates the EUF-CMA game for $\mathsf{SAS}_{\mathsf{Ours}}$. Now, we discuss the distribution of $\mathsf{pp}*$, pk^*, output of oracles $\mathcal{O}^{\mathsf{Cert}}$, $\mathcal{O}^{H_1}$, $\mathcal{O}^{H_2}$, and $\mathcal{O}^{\mathsf{Sign}}$

- **Distribution of pp^* and pk^*:** It is clear that B simulates pp and pk in the EUF-CMA game for the $\mathsf{SAS}_{\mathsf{Ours}}$.
- **Output of $\mathcal{O}^{\mathsf{Cert}}$:** It is clear that B simulates $\mathcal{O}^{\mathsf{Cert}}$ in the EUF-CMA game for the $\mathsf{SAS}_{\mathsf{Ours}}$ in the certified-key model.
- **Output of $\mathcal{O}^{H_1}$:** In the original game, hash values of H_1 are chosen from $\mathbb{G}^*$ uniformly at random. In the simulation of B, the hash value $H(t_i)$ is set by $A_i \leftarrow \mathcal{O}_0^{\mathsf{GPS}}$. Since $\mathcal{O}_0^{\mathsf{GPS}}$ samples A_i from $\mathbb{G}^*$ uniformly at random, B perfectly simulates $\mathcal{O}^{H_1}$.
- **Output of $\mathcal{O}^{H_2}$:** It is clear that B simulates $\mathcal{O}^{H_2}$.
- **Output of $\mathcal{O}^{\mathsf{Sign}}$:** In the simulation of B, by the programming of $\mathcal{O}^{H_1}$ and $\mathcal{O}^{H_2}$, $H_1(t) = A$ and $H_2(t, m_j) = m'_{(t,j)}$ hold. If $B \neq \perp$, $\mathcal{O}_1^{\mathsf{GPS}}(A, m'_{(t,j)})$ returns $B = A^x \cdot A^{m'_{(t,j)}\cdot y} = H_1(t)^{x + H_2(t,m_j)\cdot y}$. Thus if B does not abort, B simulate $\mathcal{O}^{\mathsf{Sign}}$.

$\mathsf{B}^{\mathcal{O}_0^{\mathsf{GPS}}(),\mathcal{O}_1^{\mathsf{GPS}}(\cdot,\cdot)}(\mathcal{BG}, G, \widetilde{G}, \widetilde{X}^*, \widetilde{Y}^*)$

$\mathbb{T}_1 \leftarrow \{\}$, $\mathbb{T}_2 \leftarrow \{\}$, $Q \leftarrow \{\}$, $C \leftarrow \{\}$, $L \leftarrow \{\}$, $K \leftarrow \{\}$,

$\mathsf{pp}^* \leftarrow (\mathcal{BG}, \widetilde{G})$, $\mathsf{pk}^* \leftarrow (\widetilde{X}^*, \widetilde{Y}^*)$, $t \leftarrow 1$

$((\mathsf{pk}_i^*, m_i^*)_{i\in[\ell^*]}, \Sigma^*) \leftarrow \mathsf{A}^{\mathcal{O}^{\mathsf{Cert}}(\cdot,\cdot),\mathcal{O}^{H_1}(\cdot),\mathcal{O}^{H_2}(\cdot,\cdot),\mathcal{O}^{\mathsf{Sign}}(\cdot,\cdot)}(\mathsf{pp}^*, \mathsf{pk}^*)$

If $\mathsf{AVer}_{\mathsf{Ours}}((\mathsf{pk}_i^*, m_i^*)_{i\in[\ell^*]}, \Sigma^*) \neq 1$, then abort.

If there exists $j \in [\ell^*]$ such that $\mathsf{pk}_j^* \neq \mathsf{pk}^* \wedge \mathsf{pk}_j^* \notin L$, then abort.

If there is no $j^* \in [\ell^*]$ such that $\mathsf{pk}_{j^*}^* = \mathsf{pk}^* \wedge m_{j^*}^* \notin Q$, then abort.

Set $j^* \in [\ell^*]$ such that $\mathsf{pk}_{j^*}^* = \mathsf{pk}^* \wedge m_{j^*}^* \notin Q$, $\Sigma^* \leftarrow (B^{*\prime}, t^*)$.

$m_{j^*}^{*}{}' \leftarrow H_2(t^*, m_{j^*}^*)$

If $m_{j^*}^{*}{}' \in C$, then abort.

Retrive $(x_i, y_i) \leftarrow \mathsf{sk}_i^*$ of pk_i^* from K for $i \in [\ell^*]\backslash\{j^*\}$.

$A' \leftarrow H_1(t^*)$, $m_i' \leftarrow H_2(t^*, m_i^*)$ for $i \in [\ell^*]\backslash\{j^*\}$,

$B' \leftarrow B^{*\prime} \cdot \left(A'^{\sum_{i\in[\ell^*]\backslash\{j^*\}}(x_i+m_i'\cdot y_i)}\right)^{-1}$.

Return $(m_{j^*}^*, A', B')$.

$\mathcal{O}^{\mathsf{Cert}}(\mathsf{pk} = (\widetilde{X}, \widetilde{Y}), \mathsf{sk} = (x, y))$:

If $(\widetilde{X} = \widetilde{G}^x) \wedge (\widetilde{Y} = \widetilde{G}^y)$, $L \leftarrow L \cup \{\mathsf{pk}\}$, $K \leftarrow K \cup \{(\mathsf{pk}, \mathsf{sk})\}$, return "**accept**".

Otherwise return "**reject**".

$\mathcal{O}^{H_1}(t_i)$:

If there is an entry (t_i, A_i) for some $A_i \in \mathbb{G}^*$ in $\mathbb{T}_1$, return A_i.

$A_i \leftarrow \mathcal{O}_0^{\mathsf{GPS}}()$, $\mathbb{T}_1 \leftarrow \mathbb{T}_1 \cup \{(t_i, A_i)\}$, return A_i.

$\mathcal{O}^{H_2}(t_i, m_j)$:

If there is an entry $(t_i, m_j, m'_{(t_i,j)})$ for some $m'_{(t_i,j)} \in \mathbb{Z}_p$ in $\mathbb{T}_2$, return $m'_{(t_i,j)}$.

$m'_{(t_i,j)} \xleftarrow{\$} \mathbb{Z}_p$, $\mathbb{T}_2 \leftarrow \mathbb{T}_2 \cup \{(t_i, m_j, m'_{(t_i,j)})\}$, return $m'_{(t_i,j)}$.

$\mathcal{O}^{\mathsf{Sign}}(\text{"inst"}, m_j)$:

$t \notin [T]$, return $\perp$.

If "**inst**" = "**skip**", $t \leftarrow t + 1$.

If "**inst**" = "**sign**",

If there is no entry $(t, \cdot)$ in $\mathbb{T}_1$, run $\mathcal{O}^{H_1}(t)$.

If there is no entry $(t, m_j, \cdot)$ in $\mathbb{T}_2$, run $\mathcal{O}^{H_2}(t, m_j)$.

Retrieve entries (t, A) and $(t, m_j, m'_{(t,j)})$ from $\mathbb{T}_1$ and $\mathbb{T}_2$, respectively.

$B \leftarrow \mathcal{O}_1^{\mathsf{GPS}}(A, m'_{(t,j)})$.

If $B = \perp$, abort the simulation.

$Q \leftarrow Q \cup \{m_j\}$, $C \leftarrow C \cup \{m'_{(t,j)}\}$, return $\sigma \leftarrow (B, t)$, $t \leftarrow t + 1$.

Fig. 8. The reduction B.

From the above discussion, we can see that B does not abort, B can simulate the EUF-CMA game for $\mathsf{SAS}_{\mathsf{Ours}}$.

Second, we confirm that if A successfully output a valid forgery $((\mathsf{pk}_i^*, m_i^*)_{i\in[\ell^*]}, \Sigma^*)$ of $\mathsf{SAS}_{\mathsf{Ours}}$, B can extract a solution for the GPS problem. Let $((\mathsf{pk}_i^*, m_i^*)_{i\in[\ell^*]}, \Sigma^*)$ be a valid forgery output by A. Then there exists

$j^* \in [\ell^*]$ such that $\mathsf{pk}^*_{j^*} = \mathsf{pk}^*$. By the verification of $\mathsf{AVer}_{\mathsf{Ours}}$,

$$e(H_1(t^*), (\prod_{i=1}^{\ell} \widetilde{X}_i \widetilde{Y}_i^{H_2(t^*, m_i^*)})) = e(B^{*\prime}, \widetilde{G})$$

holds. If B does not abort in the procedure $\boxed{\text{If } m_{j^*}^{*}{}' \in C, \text{ then abort.}}$ in Fig. 8, $m_{j^*}^{*}{}' \in C$ has not been queried to $\mathcal{O}_1^{\mathsf{GPS}}$.

We can see that $B^{*\prime} = A'^{\sum_{i=1}^{\ell^*}(x_i^* + y_i^* \cdot m_i^{*\prime})}$ holds where $(x_i, y_i) = \mathsf{sk}_i^*$ is a secret key corresponding to pk_i^*. In the certified-key model, since B knows all $\{\mathsf{sk}_i^*\}_{i \in [\ell^*] \setminus \{j^*\}}$, B can compute the following.

$$B' = A'^{x_{j^*} + m'_{j^*} \cdot y_{j^*}} = B^{*\prime} \cdot \left(A'^{\sum_{i \in [\ell^*] \setminus \{j^*\}}(x_i + m'_i \cdot y_i)}\right)^{-1}$$

Therefore, if B does not abort, and B a solution $(m_{j^*}^{*}{}', A', B')$ for the GPS problem.

We analyze the probability that B succeeds in forging a signature of PS. First, we consider the probability that B aborts at the simulation of signatures. B aborts the simulation of $\mathcal{O}^{\mathsf{Sign}}$ if B queries same A at least twice for $\mathcal{O}_1^{\mathsf{GPS}}(A, m'_{(t,j)})$. To give an upper bound of this probability, it is sufficient to consider the probability that collision is found in H_1. We can bound the probability that B fails simulating a signature for each signing query by $q_s/|\mathbb{G}^*| = q_s/(p-1)$ where q_s is the number of queries to $\mathcal{O}^{\mathsf{Sign}}$ from A. By taking union bound, the probability that B fails simulating signatures through the EUF-CMA game is upper bounded by $q_s^2/(p-1)$

Next, we consider the probability that B aborts at $\boxed{\text{If } m_{j^*}^{*}{}' \in C, \text{ then abort.}}$ in Fig. 8. This probability can be bounded by the probability that a collision is found in H_2. We can bound this probability by $q_{H_2}/|\mathbb{Z}_p| = q_{H_2}/p$ where q_{H_2} is the number of queries to $\mathcal{O}^{H_2}$.

Finally, we summarize the above discussion. Let $\mathsf{Adv}^{\mathsf{EUF\text{-}CMA}}_{\mathsf{SAS}_{\mathsf{Ours}},\mathsf{A}}$ be the advantage of the EUF-CMA game for the $\mathsf{SAS}_{\mathsf{Ours}}$ scheme of A. The advantage of the GPS game B is

$$\mathsf{Adv}^{\mathsf{GPS}}_{\mathsf{BG},\mathsf{A}} \geq \mathsf{Adv}^{\mathsf{EUF\text{-}CMA}}_{\mathsf{SAS}_{\mathsf{Ours}},\mathsf{A}} - \frac{q_s^2}{p-1} - \frac{q_{H_2}}{p}.$$

Therefore, we can conclude Theorem 2. □

5 Conclusion

In this paper, we construct the PS signature-based synchronized aggregate signature scheme which offers the most efficient aggregate signature verification among existing synchronized aggregate signature schemes. As for the security proof of our scheme, since the reduction technique by Lee et al. [26], could not be applied in the security proof of our scheme, we prove its security by using the GPS assumption in the ROM as a new approach.

If we apply the public-key sharing technique and the randomness re-use technique to the CL signature scheme on type-3 pairing, we will obtain the CL signature-based synchronized aggregate signature scheme on type-3 pairing. However, as with our PS signature-based synchronized aggregate signature scheme, group elements of a public key and group element in a signature belong to different groups $\widetilde{\mathbb{G}}$ and $\mathbb{G}$ respectively, the reduction technique by Lee et al. [26], would not be applied. Fortunately, similar to the GPS assumption, the generalized LRSW (GLRSW) assumption [7] that is a variant of the LRSW assumption [30] was proposed. We leave a future task to confirm whether our reduction technique can be applied to the CL signature-based synchronized aggregate signature scheme on type-3 pairing and prove its security from the GLRSW assumption.

References

1. Abe, M., Fuchsbauer, G., Groth, J., Haralambiev, K., Ohkubo, M.: Structure-preserving signatures and commitments to group elements. In: Rabin, T. (ed.) CRYPTO 2010. LNCS, vol. 6223, pp. 209–236. Springer, Heidelberg (2010). https://doi.org/10.1007/978-3-642-14623-7_12
2. Ahn, J.H., Green, M., Hohenberger, S.: Synchronized aggregate signatures: new definitions, constructions and applications. In: Proceedings of the 17th ACM Conference on Computer and Communications Security, CCS 2010, Chicago, Illinois, USA, 4–8 October 2010, pp. 473–484 (2010)
3. Aranha, D.F., Dalskov, A., Escudero, D., Orlandi, C.: Improved threshold signatures, proactive secret sharing, and input certification from LSS isomorphisms. In: Longa, P., Ràfols, C. (eds.) LATINCRYPT 2021. LNCS, vol. 12912, pp. 382–404. Springer, Cham (2021). https://doi.org/10.1007/978-3-030-88238-9_19
4. Boldyreva, A., Gentry, C., O'Neill, A., Yum, D.H.: Ordered multisignatures and identity-based sequential aggregate signatures, with applications to secure routing. In: Proceedings of the 2007 ACM Conference on Computer and Communications Security, CCS 2007, Alexandria, Virginia, USA, 28–31 October 2007, pp. 276–285 (2007)
5. Boneh, D., Drijvers, M., Neven, G.: Compact multi-signatures for smaller blockchains. In: Peyrin, T., Galbraith, S. (eds.) ASIACRYPT 2018. LNCS, vol. 11273, pp. 435–464. Springer, Cham (2018). https://doi.org/10.1007/978-3-030-03329-3_15
6. Boneh, D., Gentry, C., Lynn, B., Shacham, H.: Aggregate and verifiably encrypted signatures from bilinear maps. In: Biham, E. (ed.) EUROCRYPT 2003. LNCS, vol. 2656, pp. 416–432. Springer, Heidelberg (2003). https://doi.org/10.1007/3-540-39200-9_26
7. Camenisch, J., Chen, L., Drijvers, M., Lehmann, A., Novick, D., Urian, R.: One TPM to bind them all: fixing TPM 2.0 for provably secure anonymous attestation. In: 2017 IEEE Symposium on Security and Privacy, SP 2017, San Jose, CA, USA, 22–26 May 2017, pp. 901–920. IEEE Computer Society (2017)
8. Camenisch, J., Drijvers, M., Lehmann, A., Neven, G., Towa, P.: Short threshold dynamic group signatures. In: Galdi, C., Kolesnikov, V. (eds.) SCN 2020. LNCS, vol. 12238, pp. 401–423. Springer, Cham (2020). https://doi.org/10.1007/978-3-030-57990-6_20

9. Camenisch, J., Lysyanskaya, A.: Signature schemes and anonymous credentials from bilinear maps. In: Franklin, M. (ed.) CRYPTO 2004. LNCS, vol. 3152, pp. 56–72. Springer, Heidelberg (2004). https://doi.org/10.1007/978-3-540-28628-8_4
10. Chalkias, K., Garillot, F., Kondi, Y., Nikolaenko, V.: Non-interactive half-aggregation of EdDSA and variants of Schnorr signatures. In: Paterson, K.G. (ed.) CT-RSA 2021. LNCS, vol. 12704, pp. 577–608. Springer, Cham (2021). https://doi.org/10.1007/978-3-030-75539-3_24
11. Chatterjee, S., Kabaleeshwaran, R.: From rerandomizability to sequential aggregation: efficient signature schemes based on SXDH assumption. In: Liu, J.K., Cui, H. (eds.) ACISP 2020. LNCS, vol. 12248, pp. 183–203. Springer, Cham (2020). https://doi.org/10.1007/978-3-030-55304-3_10
12. Cini, V., Ramacher, S., Slamanig, D., Striecks, C., Tairi, E.: Updatable signatures and message authentication codes. In: Garay, J.A. (ed.) PKC 2021. LNCS, vol. 12710, pp. 691–723. Springer, Cham (2021). https://doi.org/10.1007/978-3-030-75245-3_25
13. Clarisse, R., Sanders, O.: Group signature without random oracles from randomizable signatures. In: Nguyen, K., Wu, W., Lam, K.Y., Wang, H. (eds.) ProvSec 2020. LNCS, vol. 12505, pp. 3–23. Springer, Cham (2020). https://doi.org/10.1007/978-3-030-62576-4_1
14. Fuchsbauer, G., Kiltz, E., Loss, J.: The algebraic group model and its applications. In: Shacham, H., Boldyreva, A. (eds.) CRYPTO 2018. LNCS, vol. 10992, pp. 33–62. Springer, Cham (2018). https://doi.org/10.1007/978-3-319-96881-0_2
15. Galbraith, S.D., Paterson, K.G., Smart, N.P.: Pairings for cryptographers. Discrete Appl. Math. **156**(16), 3113–3121 (2008)
16. Gentry, C., Ramzan, Z.: Identity-based aggregate signatures. In: Yung, M., Dodis, Y., Kiayias, A., Malkin, T. (eds.) PKC 2006. LNCS, vol. 3958, pp. 257–273. Springer, Heidelberg (2006). https://doi.org/10.1007/11745853_17
17. Ghadafi, E.: Short structure-preserving signatures. In: Sako, K. (ed.) CT-RSA 2016. LNCS, vol. 9610, pp. 305–321. Springer, Cham (2016). https://doi.org/10.1007/978-3-319-29485-8_18
18. Ghadafi, E.: Partially structure-preserving signatures: lower bounds, constructions and more. In: Sako, K., Tippenhauer, N.O. (eds.) ACNS 2021. LNCS, vol. 12726, pp. 284–312. Springer, Cham (2021). https://doi.org/10.1007/978-3-030-78372-3_11
19. Goyal, R., Vaikuntanathan, V.: Locally verifiable signature and key aggregation. In: Dodis, Y., Shrimpton, T. (eds.) CRYPTO 2022, Part II. LNCS, vol. 13508, pp. 761–791. Springer, Cham (2022). https://doi.org/10.1007/978-3-031-15979-4_26
20. Hartung, G., Kaidel, B., Koch, A., Koch, J., Rupp, A.: Fault-tolerant aggregate signatures. In: Cheng, C.-M., Chung, K.-M., Persiano, G., Yang, B.-Y. (eds.) PKC 2016. LNCS, vol. 9614, pp. 331–356. Springer, Heidelberg (2016). https://doi.org/10.1007/978-3-662-49384-7_13
21. Hohenberger, S., Koppula, V., Waters, B.: Universal signature aggregators. In: Oswald, E., Fischlin, M. (eds.) EUROCRYPT 2015. LNCS, vol. 9057, pp. 3–34. Springer, Heidelberg (2015). https://doi.org/10.1007/978-3-662-46803-6_1
22. Hohenberger, S., Sahai, A., Waters, B.: Full domain hash from (leveled) multilinear maps and identity-based aggregate signatures. In: Canetti, R., Garay, J.A. (eds.) CRYPTO 2013. LNCS, vol. 8042, pp. 494–512. Springer, Heidelberg (2013). https://doi.org/10.1007/978-3-642-40041-4_27
23. Hohenberger, S., Waters, B.: Synchronized aggregate signatures from the RSA assumption. In: Nielsen, J.B., Rijmen, V. (eds.) EUROCRYPT 2018. LNCS, vol.

10821, pp. 197–229. Springer, Cham (2018). https://doi.org/10.1007/978-3-319-78375-8_7
24. Kim, H., Lee, Y., Abdalla, M., Park, J.H.: Practical dynamic group signature with efficient concurrent joins and batch verifications. J. Inf. Secur. Appl. **63**, 103003 (2021)
25. Kim, H., Sanders, O., Abdalla, M., Park, J.H.: Practical dynamic group signatures without knowledge extractors. Cryptology ePrint Archive, Paper 2021/351 (2021). https://eprint.iacr.org/2021/351
26. Lee, K., Lee, D.H., Yung, M.: Aggregating CL-signatures revisited: extended functionality and better efficiency. In: Sadeghi, A.-R. (ed.) FC 2013. LNCS, vol. 7859, pp. 171–188. Springer, Heidelberg (2013). https://doi.org/10.1007/978-3-642-39884-1_14
27. Leontiadis, I., Elkhiyaoui, K., Önen, M., Molva, R.: PUDA – privacy and unforgeability for data aggregation. In: Reiter, M., Naccache, D. (eds.) CANS 2015. LNCS, vol. 9476, pp. 3–18. Springer, Cham (2015). https://doi.org/10.1007/978-3-319-26823-1_1
28. Lu, S., Ostrovsky, R., Sahai, A., Shacham, H., Waters, B.: Sequential aggregate signatures and multisignatures without random oracles. In: Vaudenay, S. (ed.) EUROCRYPT 2006. LNCS, vol. 4004, pp. 465–485. Springer, Heidelberg (2006). https://doi.org/10.1007/11761679_28
29. Lysyanskaya, A., Micali, S., Reyzin, L., Shacham, H.: Sequential aggregate signatures from trapdoor permutations. In: Cachin, C., Camenisch, J.L. (eds.) EUROCRYPT 2004. LNCS, vol. 3027, pp. 74–90. Springer, Heidelberg (2004). https://doi.org/10.1007/978-3-540-24676-3_5
30. Lysyanskaya, A., Rivest, R.L., Sahai, A., Wolf, S.: Pseudonym systems. In: Heys, H., Adams, C. (eds.) SAC 1999. LNCS, vol. 1758, pp. 184–199. Springer, Heidelberg (2000). https://doi.org/10.1007/3-540-46513-8_14
31. McDonald, K.L.: The landscape of pointcheval-sanders signatures: mapping to polynomial-based signatures and beyond. Cryptology ePrint Archive, Paper 2020/450 (2020). https://eprint.iacr.org/2020/450
32. Pointcheval, D., Sanders, O.: Short randomizable signatures. In: Sako, K. (ed.) CT-RSA 2016. LNCS, vol. 9610, pp. 111–126. Springer, Cham (2016). https://doi.org/10.1007/978-3-319-29485-8_7
33. Pointcheval, D., Sanders, O.: Reassessing security of randomizable signatures. In: Smart, N.P. (ed.) CT-RSA 2018. LNCS, vol. 10808, pp. 319–338. Springer, Cham (2018). https://doi.org/10.1007/978-3-319-76953-0_17
34. Sanders, O.: Efficient redactable signature and application to anonymous credentials. In: Kiayias, A., Kohlweiss, M., Wallden, P., Zikas, V. (eds.) PKC 2020. LNCS, vol. 12111, pp. 628–656. Springer, Cham (2020). https://doi.org/10.1007/978-3-030-45388-6_22
35. Sanders, O.: Improving revocation for group signature with redactable signature. In: Garay, J.A. (ed.) PKC 2021. LNCS, vol. 12710, pp. 301–330. Springer, Cham (2021). https://doi.org/10.1007/978-3-030-75245-3_12
36. Sanders, O., Traoré, J.: EPID with malicious revocation. In: Paterson, K.G. (ed.) CT-RSA 2021. LNCS, vol. 12704, pp. 177–200. Springer, Cham (2021). https://doi.org/10.1007/978-3-030-75539-3_8
37. Schröder, D.: How to aggregate the CL signature scheme. In: Atluri, V., Diaz, C. (eds.) ESORICS 2011. LNCS, vol. 6879, pp. 298–314. Springer, Heidelberg (2011). https://doi.org/10.1007/978-3-642-23822-2_17

38. Sedaghat, M., Slamanig, D., Kohlweiss, M., Preneel, B.: Structure-preserving threshold signatures. Cryptology ePrint Archive, Paper 2022/839 (2022). https://eprint.iacr.org/2022/839
39. Shoup, V.: Lower bounds for discrete logarithms and related problems. In: Fumy, W. (ed.) EUROCRYPT 1997. LNCS, vol. 1233, pp. 256–266. Springer, Heidelberg (1997). https://doi.org/10.1007/3-540-69053-0_18
40. Tezuka, M., Tanaka, K.: Improved security proof for the Camenisch-Lysyanskaya signature-based synchronized aggregate signature scheme. In: Liu, J.K., Cui, H. (eds.) ACISP 2020. LNCS, vol. 12248, pp. 225–243. Springer, Cham (2020). https://doi.org/10.1007/978-3-030-55304-3_12

Trapdoor Sanitizable and Redactable Signatures with Unlinkability, Invisibility and Strong Context-Hiding

Masahito Ishizaka(✉), Kazuhide Fukushima, and Shinsaku Kiyomoto

KDDI Research, Inc., Saitama, Japan
{xma-ishizaka,ka-fukushima,sh-kiyomoto}@kddi.com

Abstract. In trapdoor sanitizable signatures (TSS) (ACNS'08), a signer can partially delegate its signing ability to someone. When signing a message, the signer chooses its sanitizable parts. Each signature is associated with a trapdoor, enabling any entity arbitrarily to modify the sanitizable parts while retaining validity of the signature. In previous TSS, the sanitizable parts are permanently sanitizable. We formalize *sanitization-controllable* TSS, where the sanitizable parts can be partially (and irreversibly) changed into fixed. We formally define its security notions, including *unlinkablity* (any sanitized signature and its trapdoor cannot be linked to their original ones), *invisibility* (each signature leaks no information about its sanitizable parts) and *strong context-hiding (SCH)* (any sanitized signature and its trapdoor distribute like fresh ones). We propose a generic transformation from a *downgrade controllable* downgradable affine MAC (DAMAC), which is a generalization of DAMAC (CT-RSA'19). Our TSS scheme is the first TSS scheme satisfying unlinkability or invisibility. In redactable signatures (ICISC'01), we can partially black out a signed message. We formalize *disclosure-controllable* trapdoor redactable signatures (TRS). We propose a generic transformation from a sanitization-controllable TSS. Our TRS scheme is the first unlinkable and disclosure-controllable (T)RS scheme.

Keywords: Trapdoor Sanitizable Signatures · Trapdoor Redactable Signatures · Downgradable Affine Message Authentication Codes · Unlinkability · Invisibility · Strong Context-Hiding

1 Introduction

1.1 Background and Related Works

Sanitizable Signatures. In the ordinary digital signature, if a single bit of a signed message is altered, its signature loses its validity. In sanitizable signatures (SS) [6], a special entity called sanitizer is able to partially modify a message while retaining validity of the signature. Specifically, a message consists of multiple sub-messages in a form like $m = (m_1, \cdots, m_n)$ for some $n \in \mathbb{N}$. A signer, when

S.-H. Seo and H. Seo (Eds.): ICISC 2022, LNCS 13849, pp. 337–362, 2023.
https://doi.org/10.1007/978-3-031-29371-9_17

signing a message m, chooses a public-key pk_z of sanitizer and a set $\mathbb{T} \subseteq [1, n]$ of indices for sanitizable sub-messages in m. The sanitizer (with the secret-key sk_z for pk_z) can change any sub-message m_i s.t. $i \in \mathbb{T}$ into any binary string. As security requirements for SS, the followings have been formalized [17,18,20][1].

Unforgeability. The most standard security requirement for digital signature. Informally, no outsider can forge a correct signature.
Immutability. No sanitizer can modify other than the modifiable parts.
Privacy. Any sanitized signature includes no information about the original message.
Transparency. From a signature, we cannot correctly guess whether the signer or sanitizer has generated it.
Unlinkability. Any sanitized signature includes no information about either the original message or signature.
Invisibility. Any signature includes no information about the sanitizable parts.

In the first work on SS [6], they proposed a scheme based on chameleon hash function. The first unlinkable (resp. invisible) SS scheme was proposed in [18] (resp. [20]). Recently, the first unlinkable and invisible SS scheme, based on non-accountable SS (NASS) and verifiable ring signatures, was proposed in [19].

Trapdoor SS. In trapdoor SS [21], a specific sanitizer is not designated. Each sanitizable signature is associated with a trapdoor which enables any entity to sanitize the signature. Canard et al. [21] proposed a generic construction based on identity-based chameleon hash function [27]. Yum et al. [38] formalized unforgeability, privacy and transparency for TSS, and proved their simple generic transformation from ordinary digital signature are secure.

In TSS, even after a signer generate a signature, the signer can designate a single or multiple sanitizers. A trapdoor given to the sanitizer might need to be encrypted. If we use (ciphertext-policy) attribute-based encryption [11], a trapdoor can be distributed to anyone whose attributes satisfy a policy. If we use *anonymous* identity-based encryption [16], the signer can anonymously delegate her signing ability to someone with an identity. If we use the ordinary public-key encryption (PKE), that can be a NASS appeared in [19][2].

P-Homomorphic Signatures. In P-homomorphic signatures (P-HS) [5] for a predicate P, from a signature on a message m, we can derive a randomized signature on another message $\overline{m}$ s.t. $1 \leftarrow P(m, \overline{m})$. Ahn et al. [5] defined unforgeability and a strong notion of privacy, named *strong context hiding* (SCH), meaning that any signature derived from an honestly generated one distributes like a fresh one.

[1] In transparent SS, it is unknown whether signer or sanitizer generated the signature. In some applications, *accountability* is required. Specifically, any signer can prove the fact that she has (or has not) generated the signature. As related security requirements, *signer-accountability* and *sanitizer-accountability* have been defined [17].

[2] Verifying whether invisibility and unlinkability of the underlying TSS are inherited by the NASS is an open problem.

Attrapadung et al. [7] defined a stronger notion, called *complete* context hiding (CCH), requiring that any signature derived from any correct one (which might have been dishonestly generated) distributes like a fresh one.

Homomorphic signature for subset predicate (HSSP) is a subclass of P-HS. Each message is a set. From a signature on a set m, a new signature on any of its subsets $\overline{m} \subseteq m$ can be derived. In [5] (resp. [7]), unforgeable and SCH-secure (resp. CCH-secure) scheme was proposed.

Redactable Signatures. Redactable signatures [35] is also a subclass of P-HS. Each message m consists of some sub-messages in a form like $m = (m_1, \cdots, m_n)$. Each (non-blacked-out) sub-message can be blacked-out (or redacted). Steinfeld et al. [35] proposed a simple generic construction based on message commitment and ordinary digital signature. A signer, when firstly signing a message, chooses a set of indices for its redactable sub-messages, named *content extraction access structure* (CEAS). However, in their scheme, CEAS is eternally fixed and visible from verifier. A property that any redactable sub-message can irreversibly change into non-redactable was named *(consecutive) disclosure-controllability* [33], and disclosure-controllable schemes have been proposed, e.g. [24,32–34].

Any HSSP scheme can be transformed into a RS scheme. A signature on a list $m = (m_1, \cdots, m_n)$ for RS is a signature on a set $S = \{i||m_i\}_{i=1}^{n}$ for HSSP. Redacting a sub-message m_i is excluding $i||m_i$ from S. Note that the HSSP schemes [5,7] lead to SCH and CCH secure RS schemes, respectively.

The other sub-classes of P-HS include quotable signatures [5,8], linearly homomorphic signatures [5,8], append-only signatures (AOS) [25] and history-hiding AOS [10,31].

Downgradable Affine MAC. Affine MAC (AMAC) [14] is an algebraic MAC with a group description $(\mathbb{G}, p, g)$, where $\mathbb{G}$ is a group, p is a prime and g is a generator of $\mathbb{G}$. For $\boldsymbol{a} \in \mathbb{Z}_p^n$, let $[\boldsymbol{a}]$ denote $(g^{a_1}, \cdots, g^{a_n})^\top \in \mathbb{G}^n$. A tag $\tau = ([\boldsymbol{t}], [u])$ on $m \in \mathcal{M}$ consists of a randomness $[\boldsymbol{t}] \in \mathbb{G}^n$ and a message-depending $[u] \in \mathbb{G}$, satisfying $\boldsymbol{t} := \boldsymbol{B}\boldsymbol{s} \in \mathbb{Z}_p^n$ and $u := \sum_{i=0}^{l} f_i(m)\boldsymbol{x}_i^\top \boldsymbol{t} + \sum_{i=0}^{l'} f_i'(m)x_i \in \mathbb{Z}_p$, where $f_i, f_i' : \mathcal{M} \to \mathbb{Z}_p$ are public functions, $\boldsymbol{B} \in \mathbb{Z}_p^{n \times n'}$, $\boldsymbol{x}_i \in \mathbb{Z}_p^n$ and $x_i \in \mathbb{Z}_p$ are from the secret-key sk_{MAC}, and $\boldsymbol{s} \xleftarrow{\$} \mathbb{Z}_p^{n'}$[3]. Pseudo-randomness, a security notion related to unforgeability, guarantees that no PPT adversary, who arbitrarily chooses m^* then receives $([h]_1, [\boldsymbol{h}_0]_1, [h_1]_T)$, can distinguish the case (I) where they have been honestly generated, i.e., $h \xleftarrow{\$} \mathbb{Z}_p$, $\boldsymbol{h}_0 := \sum_{i=0}^{l} f_i(m^*)\boldsymbol{x}_i h$ and $h_1 := \sum_{i=0}^{l'} f_i'(m^*)x_i h$, from the case (II) where they have been randomly generated. Note that the adversary can adaptively use tag-generation oracle, which takes $m \neq m^*$ then returns a tag on it. They proposed two AMAC schemes, one of which based on a hash-proof system (HPS) [22] is pseudo-random under k-Linear assumption.

Blazy et al. [14] showed that an AMAC with message-length $l \in \mathbb{N}$ can be transformed into an anonymous identity-based KEM (AIBKEM) with

[3] $\xleftarrow{\$}$ means that we select an element uniformly at random from a space.

identity-length l. A key-issuing authority randomly generates sk_{MAC} for the AMAC and perfectly-hiding commitments $\{Z_i\}$ (resp. $\{\boldsymbol{z}_i\}$) to $\{\boldsymbol{x}_i\}$ (resp. $\{x_i\}$). A secret-key for an identity id is identical to a Bellare-Goldwasser (BG) signature [9]. Specifically, it consists of an AMAC tag $([\boldsymbol{t}]_2, [u]_2)$ on a message id and a non-interactive zero knowledge proof $[\boldsymbol{u}]_2$ w.r.t. the commitments, which proves the tag has been correctly generated. Key-encapsulation and key-decapsulation are a randomized verification of the NIZK proof. They proved that its adaptive security is tightly reduced to the pseudo-randomness of the AMAC.

In delegatable AMAC (DlgAMAC) [14], each message is hierarchical. A tagged message can be transformed into any of its descendants. Its pseudo-randomness is a natural extension from the one for AMAC, where the tag-generation oracle returns not only a tag but also related elements used to *delegate* and *re-randomize* it. They showed that the HPS-based AMAC is delegatable. Their anonymous HIBKEM based on DlgAMAC is a natural extension from the AMAC-based AIBKEM. Each secret-key for a hierarchical ID consists of a BG-signature on the ID and elements for delegating and re-randomizing it.

Downgradable AMAC (DAMAC) [13] is also an AMAC with tag-delegatability. Any tagged message can be downgraded. In other words, any bit 1 can be changed into 0. They proposed (anonymous) downgradable IBKEM (DIBKEM) based on DAMAC. In DIBKEM, each user secret-key, associated with an identity, can be downgraded. They also proposed generic transformations from DIBKEM to HIBKEM, wildcarded IBKEM [2,12] and wicked IBKEM [3].

1.2 Our Contributions

In this work, we formally define *downgrade-controllable* DAMAC (DCDAMAC) and prove that a natural extension from the delegatable AMAC in [14] satisfies the definition. We formally define *sanitization-controllable* TSS (SCTSS) and propose a generic construction based on the DCDAMAC. Moreover, we propose a generic transformation of *disclosure-controllable* trapdoor RS from SCTSS.

1. Downgrade-Controllable DAMAC. In the DAMAC [13], any bit 1 (in a tagged message) is permanently downgradable. In downgrade-controllable DAMAC (DCDAMAC), a generalization of the original DAMAC, any downgradable bit 1 can be irreversibly changed into non-downgradable (or fixed). As security requirements, we define pseudo-randomness and strong context-hiding (SCH).

The pseudo-randomness notion is a weakened version of the natural extension from the one for delegatable AMAC [14]. Firstly, pseudo-randomness of $[\boldsymbol{h}_0]_1$ is not considered. Secondly, the oracles (incl. a oracle for tag-generation) cannot be used after the challenge instance is issued. Like the SCH for P-HS [5], SCH for DCDAMAC means that any tag downgraded from another tag distributes identically to a fresh tag directly-generated by the secret-key sk_{MAC}. We prove that any scheme (satisfying a definition for DCDAMAC) is unconditionally SCH.

2. Sanitization-Controllable TSS. A message is simply a binary string of length $l \in \mathbb{N}$. A TSS scheme consists of 4 polynomial-time algorithms, namely key-generation, signing (`Sig`), sanitization (`Sanit`) and verification. A signer, when signing a message $m \in \{0,1\}^l$, chooses a set of indices $\mathbb{T} \subseteq [1,l]$ for its sanitizable bits. When a signature is generated in `Sig` or `Sanit`, its trapdoor is simultaneously generated[4]. We assume that each trapdoor explicitly includes the set $\mathbb{T}$ so that any sanitizer knows it. The sanitizer can alter the set $\mathbb{T}$ to any $\overline{\mathbb{T}} \subseteq \mathbb{T}$.

Our TSS is a subclass of P-HS (or P-trapdoor HS). As a security requirement, we define SCH for TSS. Informally, it guarantees that any pair of signature and trapdoor, generated from an honestly-generated one, distributes like a fresh one. Other than SCH, we formally define (existential) unforgeability, privacy, transparency, unlinkability and invisibility. Among the security notions, we prove that some implications hold. Especially, SCH is an important (or useful) notion because it directly implies transparency and unlinkability, and *simplifies* unforgeability and invisibility. The details will be in Subsect. 4.2.

We propose a generic construction based on DCDAMAC. We *implicitly* consider the downgrade controllable version of the DIBKEM based on DAMAC [13]. We know that a user secret-key in an encryption system can function as a signature, e.g., the transformation from HIBE to hierarchical identity-based signatures [26], the transformation from (CP-)ABE to HSSP [5]. Our TSS scheme is a transformation from the implicit downgrade-controllable DIBKEM (DCDIBKEM) based on DCDAMAC. Either signature or trapdoor on $(m, \mathbb{T})$ is a user secret-key for the DCDIBKEM scheme. For instance, a signature is a secret-key for an $ID = m \in \{0,1\}^l$ with no downgradability. Verifying a signature is generating a test ciphertext then decrypting it by the signature. A trapdoor td is a secret-key for the DCDIBKEM scheme associated with an $ID' = F(m, \mathbb{T})$ and a set $\mathbb{T}$. Informally, the function F changes every downgradable bit 0 in m into 1. Our proof for its unforgeability is an extension of the proof for the security (indistinguishability) of the HIBKEM based on delegatable AMAC [14]. Its SCH security is directly implied by the SCH security of the underlying DCDAMAC.

We prove that the existing TSS schemes [21,38] are neither unlinkable nor invisible. Thus, our scheme is the first one satisfying unlinkability or invisibility.

3. Disclosure-Controllable TRS. In DCTRS, message space is simply $\{0,1,*\}^l$, where $*$ denotes a redacted (or blacked-out) bit. The set $\mathbb{T} \subseteq [1,l]$ for m denotes a set of indices for redactable bits in m. Since every redactable bit has not been redacted yet, $\mathbb{T}$ is naturally a subset of $\mathbb{I}_0(m) \cup \mathbb{I}_1(m)$[5]. We require the same security as TSS. The same implications as TSS hold for TRS.

The technique for our transformation from (SC)TSS to (DC)TRS is similar to the transformation from DIBKEM to wildcarded IBKEM in [13]. We use a TSS scheme with message length $2l$. A message $m \in \{0,1,*\}^l$ for the TRS is deterministically changed into a message $m' \in \{0,1\}^{2l}$ for the TSS. The i-th bit of m determines the $2i-1$ and $2i$ bits of m' as follows. Formally, $(m'[2i-1], m'[2i])$ are set to $(0,1)$ if $m[i] = 0$, $(1,0)$ if $m[i] = 1$, or $(0,0)$ if $m[i] = *$. The set $\mathbb{T} \subseteq [1,l]$

---

[4] In the previous model [21], there is a trapdoor-generation algorithm, enabling the signer to generate a trapdoor from a signature using her signing-key.

[5] In this paper, $\mathbb{I}_b(a)$ denotes a set of indices for all bits with value b in a.

is also deterministically changed into $\mathbb{T}' \subseteq [1, 2l]$ based on m. For all $i \in \mathbb{T}$, in $(m'[2i-1], m'[2i]) \in \{(0,1),(1,0)\}$, only element with value 1 is sanitizable.

Disclosure-controllable RS schemes have been proposed in [24,32–34]. Either one cannot be unlinkable since there exist eternally-fixed elements in each signature, e.g., committed values [24,33], document ID [32]. The SCH-secure HSSP schemes [5,7] can lead to unlinkable RS schemes. However, either one is not disclosure-controllable. Our TRS scheme is the first unlinkable and disclosure-controllable (T)RS scheme.

1.3 Paper Organization

In Sect. 2, some notations and matrix Diffie-Hellman assumption are introduced. In Sect. 3, syntax and security notions for (DC)DAMAC are defined. A secure DAMAC scheme is also given. In Sect. 4, syntax and security notions for TSS are defined. In Sect. 5, we propose a generic transformation from (DC)DAMAC to (SC)TSS and prove that it satisfies our security notions. In Sect. 6, we propose a generic transformation from (SC)TSS to (DC)TRS. We compare our TSS and TRS schemes with existing schemes in these sections.

2 Preliminaries

Notations. 1^λ (for $\lambda \in \mathbb{N}$) denotes a security parameter. PPTA means probabilistic polynomial-time algorithm. We say that a function $f : \mathbb{N} \to \mathbb{R}$ is negligible if $\forall c \in \mathbb{N}, \exists x_0 \in \mathbb{N}$ s.t. $\forall x \geq x_0$, $f(x) \leq x^{-c}$. For a binary string $x \in \{0,1\}^n$, $x[i] \in \{0,1\}$ for $i \in [1,n]$ denotes the value of its i-th bit. For a string $x \in \mathbb{X}^n$, e.g., $\mathbb{X}$ is $\{0,1\}$ or $\{0,1,*\}$, $\mathbb{I}_b(x)$ for $b \in \mathbb{X}$ denotes the set $\{i \in [1,n]$ s.t. $x[i] = b\}$. For $x, y \in \{0,1\}^n$, the relation $x \preceq y$ holds if $\bigwedge_{i\in[1,n]} x[i] = 1 \implies y[i] = 1$. For $x, y \in \{0,1\}^n$ and a set $\mathbb{J} \subseteq \mathbb{I}_1(y)$, the relation $x \preceq_{\mathbb{J}} y$ holds if $\bigwedge_{i\in[1,n]\setminus\mathbb{J}} x[i] = y[i] \bigwedge_{i\in\mathbb{J}} x[i] = 1 \implies y[i] = 1$. $a \xleftarrow{\$} A$ means that we extract an element a uniformly at random from a set A. For a matrix $A \in \mathbb{N}^{(k+1)\times k}$, $\bar{A} \in \mathbb{N}^{k\times k}$ denotes the square matrix composed of the upper k rows of A, and $\underline{A} \in \mathbb{N}^{1\times k}$ denotes the lowest row of A.

Matrix Diffie-Hellman Assumption. Let $\mathcal{G}_{BG}$ denote a generator of asymmetric bilinear pairing. Let $\lambda \in \mathbb{N}$. $\mathcal{G}_{BG}$ takes 1^λ, then generates $(p, \mathbb{G}_1, \mathbb{G}_2, \mathbb{G}_T, e, g_1, g_2)$. p is a prime of length λ. $(\mathbb{G}_1, \mathbb{G}_2, \mathbb{G}_T)$ are multiplicative groups of order p. g_1 and g_2 are generators of $\mathbb{G}_1$ and $\mathbb{G}_2$, respectively. $e : \mathbb{G}_1 \times \mathbb{G}_2 \to \mathbb{G}_T$ is an asymmetric function, computable in polynomial time and satisfying both of the following conditions: (i) Bilinearity: For every $a, b \in \mathbb{Z}_p$, $e(g_1^a, g_2^b) = e(g_1, g_2)^{ab}$. (ii) Non-degeneracy: $e(g_1, g_2) \neq 1_{\mathbb{G}_T}$, where $1_{\mathbb{G}_T}$ denotes the unit element of $\mathbb{G}_T$.

Note that $g_T := e(g_1, g_2)$ is a generator of $\mathbb{G}_T$. For $s \in \{1, 2, T\}$ and $a \in \mathbb{Z}_p$, $[a]_s$ denotes $g_s^a \in \mathbb{G}_s$. Generally, for $s \in \{1, 2, T\}$ and a matrix $A \in \mathbb{Z}_p^{n\times m}$ whose (i,j)-th element is $a_{ij} \in \mathbb{Z}_p$, $[A]_s \in \mathbb{G}^{n\times m}$ denotes a matrix whose (i,j)-th element is $g_s^{a_{ij}} \in \mathbb{G}_s$. Obviously, from $[a]_s$ and an integer $x \in \mathbb{Z}_p$, $[xa]_s \in \mathbb{G}_s$ is efficiently computable. From $[a]_1$ and $[b]_2$ (for $b \in \mathbb{Z}_p$), $[ab]_T$ is also efficiently computable. Note that for $\boldsymbol{a}, \boldsymbol{b} \in \mathbb{Z}_p^n$, $[\boldsymbol{a}^\top \boldsymbol{b}]_T = e([\boldsymbol{a}]_1, [\boldsymbol{b}]_2) = e([\boldsymbol{b}]_1, [\boldsymbol{a}]_2)$.

Based on [14,22,28], we define matrix Diffie-Hellman assumption.

Definition 1. *Let $l, k \in \mathbb{N}$ s.t. $l > k$. We call a set $\mathcal{D}_{l,k}$ a matrix distribution if it consists of matrices in $\mathbb{Z}_p^{l \times k}$ of full rank k and extracting an element from it uniformly at random can be efficiently done. W.l.o.g., we assume that the upper k rows of $A \xleftarrow{\$} \mathcal{D}_{l,k}$ form an invertible matrix.*

Definition 2. *Let $\mathcal{D}_{l,k}$ be a matrix distribution. Let $s \in \{1, 2, T\}$. $\mathcal{D}_{l,k}$-matrix (decisional) Diffie-Hellman (MDDH) assumption holds relative to $\mathcal{G}_{BG}$ in group $\mathbb{G}_s$, if for every PPT $\mathcal{A}$, its advantage $\mathtt{Adv}_{\mathcal{A},\mathcal{G}_{BG},\mathbb{G}_s}^{\mathcal{D}_{l,k}\text{-}\mathtt{MDDH}}(\lambda) := |\Pr[1 \leftarrow \mathcal{A}(gd, [A]_s, [A\boldsymbol{w}]_s)] - \Pr[1 \leftarrow \mathcal{A}(gd, [A]_s, [\boldsymbol{u}]_s)]|$ is negligible, where $gd := (p, \mathbb{G}_1, \mathbb{G}_2, \mathbb{G}_T, e, g_1, g_2) \leftarrow \mathcal{G}_{BG}(1^\lambda)$, $A \xleftarrow{\$} \mathcal{D}_{l,k}$, $\boldsymbol{w} \xleftarrow{\$} \mathbb{Z}_p^k$ and $\boldsymbol{u} \xleftarrow{\$} \mathbb{Z}_p^l$.*

Corollary 1 is directly obtained from *Lemma 4* in [29].

Corollary 1. *For any prime p and $n \in \mathbb{N}$, $\Pr[\mathtt{rank}(S) \neq n \mid S \xleftarrow{\$} \mathbb{Z}_p^{n \times n}] \leq \frac{1}{p-1}$.*

3 Downgradable Affine MAC (DAMAC)

A randomized message authentication code (MAC) consists of following 3 polynomial-time algorithms. Key-generation $\mathtt{Gen}_{\mathrm{MAC}}$ takes a system parameter *par*, then generates a secret-key sk_{MAC}. Tag-generation $\mathtt{Tag}$ takes sk_{MAC} and a message, then generates a tag. Tag-verification $\mathtt{Ver}$ takes sk_{MAC}, a message and a tag, then deterministically returns 1 (*accept*) or 0 (*reject*).

3.1 Our Model

Affine MAC (AMAC) [14] over $\mathbb{Z}_p^n$ are group-based MAC with an algebraic structure. In delegatable AMAC (DlgAMAC) [14], a message is hierarchical. From a tag on a message, we can produce a valid tag on any of its descendant message. Downgradable AMAC (DAMAC) [13] is also an AMAC with tag-delegatability. Given a tag on a message $\{0, 1\}^l$, we can *downgrade* any bit 1 in m into 0. Note that any bit 1 can be permanently downgradable.

We define *(consecutively) downgrade-controllable* DAMAC[6]. Any downgradable bit 1 can be irreversibly changed into non-downgradable (or fixed). The downgrade-controllability is required for the DAMAC-based trapdoor SS (TSS) in Sect. 5 to be *sanitization-controllable*, and for the TSS-based trapdoor RS in Sect. 6 to be disclosure-controllable. The following definition is an extension from the one for DlgAMAC [14].

Definition 3 (DAMAC). *We say that a MAC system $\Sigma_{\mathrm{MAC}} = \{\mathtt{Gen}_{MAC}, \mathtt{Tag}, \mathtt{Down}, \mathtt{Ver}\}$ is downgradable over $\mathbb{Z}_p^{n \times n'}$ if it satisfies the following conditions.*

[6] The name of (consecutive) downgrade-controllability comes from (consecutive) disclosure-controllability for redactable signatures [33].

- ***Key-Generation*** $\text{Gen}_{MAC}(par)$*: It takes a public parameter par including integers n, n', l and a description $(p, \mathbb{G}_1, \mathbb{G}_2, \mathbb{G}_T, e, g_1, g_2)$ for bilinear groups, then returns sk_{MAC}. We parse sk_{MAC} as $(B, \boldsymbol{x}_0, \boldsymbol{x}_1, \cdots, \boldsymbol{x}_l, x)$, where $B \in \mathbb{Z}_p^{n\times n'}$, $\boldsymbol{x}_i \in \mathbb{Z}_p^n$ and $x \in \mathbb{Z}_p$. Message space is $\mathcal{M} = \{0,1\}^l$.*
- ***Tag-Generation*** $\text{Tag}(sk_{\mathrm{MAC}}, m \in \mathcal{M}, \mathbb{J} \subseteq \mathbb{I}_1(m))$[7]*: It chooses $\boldsymbol{s} \xleftarrow{\$} \mathbb{Z}_p^{n'}$ and $S \xleftarrow{\$} \mathbb{Z}_p^{n'\times n'}$. It computes*
  - $\boldsymbol{t} := B\boldsymbol{s} \in \mathbb{Z}_p^n$, $T := BS \in \mathbb{Z}_p^{n\times n'}$,
  - $u := \sum_{i=0}^{l} f_i(m)\boldsymbol{x}_i^\top \boldsymbol{t} + x \in \mathbb{Z}_p$, $\boldsymbol{w} := \sum_{i=0}^{l} f_i(m)\boldsymbol{x}_i^\top T \in \mathbb{Z}_p^{1\times n'}$, *and*
  - $d_i := h_i(m)\boldsymbol{x}_i^\top \boldsymbol{t} \in \mathbb{Z}_p$ *and* $\boldsymbol{e}_i := h_i(m)\boldsymbol{x}_i^\top T \in \mathbb{Z}_p^{1\times n'}$ *for all* $i \in \mathbb{J}$,

  where $f_i : \mathcal{M} \to \mathbb{Z}_p$ for $i \in [0,l]$ and $h_i : \mathcal{M} \to \mathbb{Z}_p$ for $i \in \mathbb{J}$ are public functions. For every $m \in \{0,1\}^l$, every $\mathbb{J} \subseteq \mathbb{I}_1(m)$, every $\overline{m} \in \{0,1\}^l$ and every $\overline{\mathbb{J}} \subseteq \mathbb{I}_1(\overline{m})$ s.t. $\overline{m} \preceq_{\mathbb{J}} m \wedge \overline{\mathbb{J}} \subseteq \mathbb{J}$, they satisfy both of the following conditions.
  - *For every $i \in [0,l]$,*

$$f_i(\overline{m}) = \begin{cases} f_i(m) & (\text{if } i = 0 \vee \overline{m}[i] = m[i]), \\ f_i(m) - h_i(m) & (\text{otherwise}). \end{cases}$$

  - *For every $i \in \overline{\mathbb{J}}$, $h_i(\overline{m}) = h_i(m)$.*

  It returns $\tau := ([\boldsymbol{t}]_2, [u]_2, [T]_2, [\boldsymbol{w}]_2, \mathbb{J}, \{[d_i]_2, [\boldsymbol{e}_i]_2 \mid i \in \mathbb{J}\})$. Core of the tag is $([\boldsymbol{t}]_2, [u]_2) \in \mathbb{G}_2^n \times \mathbb{G}_2$. The former is randomness. It uniquely determines the latter under sk_{MAC}. The other elements are used to rerandomize and downgrade the core part.
- ***Downgrade*** $\text{Down}(m \in \mathcal{M}, \tau, \overline{m} \in \mathcal{M}, \overline{\mathbb{J}} \subseteq \mathbb{I}_1(\overline{m}))$ *(see footnote 7): It parses τ as $([\boldsymbol{t}]_2, [u]_2, [T]_2, [\boldsymbol{w}]_2, \mathbb{J}, \{[d_i]_2, [\boldsymbol{e}_i]_2 \mid i \in \mathbb{J}\})$. It returns $\perp$ if $\overline{m} \not\preceq_{\mathbb{J}} m \vee \overline{\mathbb{J}} \not\subseteq \mathbb{J}$. It computes the followings*[8]*.*
  - $\overline{\boldsymbol{s}} \xleftarrow{\$} \mathbb{Z}_p^{n'}$, $\overline{S} \xleftarrow{\$} \mathbb{Z}_p^{n'\times n'}$. $[\overline{\boldsymbol{t}}]_2 := [\boldsymbol{t} + T\overline{S}\overline{\boldsymbol{s}}]_2$, $[\overline{T}]_2 := [T\overline{S}]_2$.
  - $[\overline{\boldsymbol{e}}_i]_2 := [\boldsymbol{e}_i\overline{S}]_2$ *and* $[\overline{d}_i]_2 := [d_i + \boldsymbol{e}_i\overline{S}\overline{\boldsymbol{s}}]_2$ *for all* $i \in \overline{\mathbb{J}}$.
  - $[\overline{\boldsymbol{w}}]_2 := \left[\boldsymbol{w}\overline{S} - \sum_{i\in\mathbb{I}_1(m)\cap\mathbb{I}_0(\overline{m})} \overline{\boldsymbol{e}}_i\right]_2$, $[\overline{u}]_2 := \left[u + \boldsymbol{w}\overline{S}\overline{\boldsymbol{s}} - \sum_{i\in\mathbb{I}_1(m)\cap\mathbb{I}_0(\overline{m})} \overline{d}_i\right]_2$.

  It returns $\overline{\tau} := ([\overline{\boldsymbol{t}}]_2, [\overline{u}]_2, [\overline{T}]_2, [\overline{\boldsymbol{w}}]_2, \overline{\mathbb{J}}, \{[\overline{d}_i]_2, [\overline{\boldsymbol{e}}_i]_2 \mid i \in \overline{\mathbb{J}}\})$.
- ***Verification*** $\text{Ver}(sk_{\mathrm{MAC}}, m, \tau)$*: It parses τ as $([\boldsymbol{t}]_2, [u]_2, \cdots)$. It returns 1 if it holds that $[u]_2 = \left[\sum_{i=0}^{l} f_i(m)\boldsymbol{x}_i^\top \boldsymbol{t} + x\right]_2$, or 0 otherwise.*

We require every DAMAC scheme to be correct. A DAMAC scheme is correct if $\forall par \in \{0,1\}^*$ (incl. $l, n, n' \in \mathbb{N}$), $\forall sk_{\mathrm{MAC}} = (B, \boldsymbol{x}_0, \cdots, \boldsymbol{x}_l, x) \leftarrow \text{Gen}_{\mathrm{MAC}}(par)$, $\forall m \in \mathcal{M}, \forall \mathbb{J} \subseteq \mathbb{I}_1(m), \forall \tau \leftarrow \text{Tag}(sk_{\mathrm{MAC}}, m, \mathbb{J}), \forall \overline{m} \in \mathcal{M}$ s.t. $\overline{m} \preceq_{\mathbb{J}} m, \forall \overline{\mathbb{J}} \subseteq \mathbb{I}_1(\overline{m})$ s.t. $\overline{\mathbb{J}} \subseteq \mathbb{J}, \forall \overline{\tau} \leftarrow \text{Down}(m, \tau, \overline{m}, \overline{\mathbb{J}}), 1 \leftarrow \text{Ver}(sk_{\mathrm{MAC}}, \overline{m}, \overline{\tau})$. Definition 3 implies correctness. We prove the following theorem in the full version of this paper.

Theorem 1. *Any DAMAC scheme satisfying Definition 3 is correct.*

[7] To make the inner-randomnesses explicit, we sometimes use notations like $\tau \leftarrow \text{Tag}(sk_{\mathrm{MAC}}, m, \mathbb{J}; \boldsymbol{s}, S)$ and $\overline{\tau} \leftarrow \text{Down}(m, \tau, \overline{m}, \overline{\mathbb{J}}; \overline{\boldsymbol{s}}, \overline{S})$.

[8] If the original tag has been honestly generated by Tag or Down, it holds that $\overline{\boldsymbol{e}}_i = h_i(\overline{m})\boldsymbol{x}_i^\top \overline{T}$, $\overline{d}_i = h_i(\overline{m})\boldsymbol{x}_i^\top \overline{\boldsymbol{t}}$, $\overline{\boldsymbol{w}} = \sum_{i=0}^{l} f_i(\overline{m})\boldsymbol{x}_i^\top \overline{T}$ and $\overline{u} = \sum_{i=0}^{l} f_i(\overline{m})\boldsymbol{x}_i^\top \overline{\boldsymbol{t}} + x$.

Security. We define strong context-hiding and pseudo-randomness.

Strong context-hiding (SCH) [5] was originally introduced as a strong privacy notion for P-homomorphic signatures [5]. We will define SCH for TSS and TRS in later sections. Here, we define it for DAMAC. It intuitively means that any tag generated by Down distributes like a fresh tag generated by Tag.

Definition 4 (SCH). *A DAMAC scheme Σ_{DAMAC} is statistically SCH if $\forall par \in \{0,1\}^*$ (incl. $l, n, n' \in \mathbb{N}$), $\forall sk_{\mathrm{MAC}} = (B, \boldsymbol{x}_0, \cdots, \boldsymbol{x}_l, x) \leftarrow \mathtt{Gen}_{MAC}(par)$, $\forall m \in \mathcal{M}$, $\forall \mathbb{J} \subseteq \mathbb{I}_1(m)$, $\forall \overline{m} \in \mathcal{M}$ s.t. $\overline{m} \preceq_{\mathbb{J}} m$, $\forall \overline{\mathbb{J}} \subseteq \mathbb{I}_1(\overline{m})$ s.t. $\overline{\mathbb{J}} \subseteq \mathbb{J}$, $\forall$ probabilistic algorithm $\mathcal{A}$, its advantage $\boldsymbol{Adv}^{SCH}_{\Sigma_{\mathrm{DAMAC}},\mathcal{A},par,l,n,n'}(\lambda)$ defined as*

$$\Big|\Pr\left[1 \leftarrow \mathcal{A}(sk_{\mathrm{MAC}}, \tau, \overline{\tau}) \,\middle|\, \tau \leftarrow \mathtt{Tag}(sk_{\mathrm{MAC}}, m, \mathbb{J}), \overline{\tau} \leftarrow \mathtt{Down}(m, \tau, \overline{m}, \overline{\mathbb{J}})\right]$$
$$- \Pr\left[1 \leftarrow \mathcal{A}(sk_{\mathrm{MAC}}, \tau, \overline{\tau}) \,\middle|\, \tau \leftarrow \mathtt{Tag}(sk_{\mathrm{MAC}}, m, \mathbb{J}), \overline{\tau} \leftarrow \mathtt{Tag}(sk_{\mathrm{MAC}}, \overline{m}, \overline{\mathbb{J}})\right]\Big|$$

is negligible. It is perfectly SCH if the advantage is 0[9].

Definition 3 implies SCH. We prove the following theorem in the full paper.

Theorem 2. *Any DAMAC scheme satisfying Definition 3 is SCH. Formally, for any probabilistic algorithm $\mathcal{A}$, $\boldsymbol{Adv}^{SCH}_{\Sigma_{\mathrm{DAMAC}},\mathcal{A},par}(\lambda) \leq \frac{4}{p-1}$.*

As (delegatable) AMAC [14], we define pseudo-randomness for DAMAC. We define two notions, namely PR-CMA1 and PR-CMA1′.

For PR-CMA1, we define two experiments $\boldsymbol{Expt}^{\texttt{PR-CMA1}}_{\Sigma_{\mathrm{DAMAC}},\mathcal{A},b}$ with $b \in \{0,1\}$ for a PPT adversary $\mathcal{A}$. In these experiments, every part surrounded by a grey box is ignored. $\mathcal{A}$ can adaptively use three oracles. $\mathcal{A}$ can make $\mathfrak{Tag}$ produce a tag on a message. $\mathcal{A}$ can make $\mathfrak{Down}$ downgrade a tag generated on $\mathfrak{Tag}$ or $\mathfrak{Down}$. On $\mathfrak{Tag}$ or $\mathfrak{Down}$, $\mathcal{A}$ cannot get the whole tag, but only its *core* part, i.e., $[\boldsymbol{t}]_2$ and $[u]_2$. $\mathcal{A}$ can make $\mathfrak{Reveal}$ reveal any of the hidden tags. Finally, $\mathcal{A}$ chooses a target m^*, then gets $([h]_1, [\boldsymbol{h}_0]_1, [h_1]_1)$, where $h \xleftarrow{\$} \mathbb{Z}_p$ and $\boldsymbol{h}_0 := \sum_i f_i(m^*)\boldsymbol{x}_i h$. $\mathcal{A}$ has to guess whether h_1 is hx or random on $\mathbb{Z}_p$. If $\mathcal{A}$ has a correct tag on m^*, she can correctly guess that[10]. Because of that, we require that no tag on m^* has been generated on $\mathfrak{Tag}$ or $\mathfrak{Down}$, and no tag on a message downgradable into m^* has been revealed on $\mathfrak{Reveal}$.

PR-CMA1 is not a natural extension from the one for AMAC (DlgAMAC) [14], but weaker. Firstly, pseudo-randomness of $[\boldsymbol{h}_0]_1$ is not considered. Secondly, the three oracles cannot be used after the challenge instance is issued[11].

PR-CMA1′ is weaker than PR-CMA1. We define two experiments $\boldsymbol{Expt}^{\texttt{PR-CMA1}'}_{\Sigma_{\mathrm{DAMAC}},\mathcal{A},b}$ with $b \in \{0,1\}$. It is the same as the counterpart experiment for PR-CMA1, i.e., $\boldsymbol{Expt}^{\texttt{PR-CMA1}}_{\Sigma_{\mathrm{DAMAC}},\mathcal{A},b}$, except for the gray part. In short, $\mathcal{A}$ cannot use $\mathfrak{Down}$.

[9] When we say that a DAMAC system is SCH-secure, that means the *statistical* one.
[10] Let $([\boldsymbol{t}^*]_2, [u^*]_2, \cdots)$ denote the tag on m^*. She can correctly guess that by verifying whether $e([h]_1, [u^*]_2) = e([\boldsymbol{h}_0]_1, [\boldsymbol{t}^*]_2) \cdot e([h_1]_1, [1]_2)$ holds.
[11] The name PR-CMA1 comes from IND-CCA1 for public-key encryption.

$\boldsymbol{Expt}^{\text{PR-CMA1}}_{\Sigma_{\text{DAMAC}},\mathcal{A},b}(par)$: // $\boldsymbol{Expt}^{\text{PR-CMA1}'}_{\Sigma_{\text{DAMAC}},\mathcal{A},b}$

$sk_{\text{MAC}} \leftarrow \text{Gen}_{\text{MAC}}(par)$. Parse sk_{MAC} as $(B, \boldsymbol{x}_0, \cdots, \boldsymbol{x}_l, x)$.

$(m^* \in \{0,1\}^l, st) \leftarrow \mathcal{A}_0^{\mathfrak{Tag},\mathfrak{Down},\mathfrak{Reveal}}(par)$.

- $\mathfrak{Tag}(m \in \{0,1\}^l, \mathbb{J} \subseteq \mathbb{I}_1(m))$:
  - $\tau \leftarrow \text{Tag}(sk_{\text{MAC}}, m, \mathbb{J})$. Parse τ as $([\boldsymbol{t}]_2, [u]_2, [T]_2, [\boldsymbol{w}]_2, \mathbb{J}, \{[d_i]_2, [\boldsymbol{e}_i]_2 \mid i \in \mathbb{J}\})$.
  - $\mathbb{Q} := \mathbb{Q} \cup \{(m, \mathbb{J}, \tau)\}$. **Rtrn** $([\boldsymbol{t}]_2, [u]_2)$.
- $\mathfrak{Down}(m \in \{0,1\}^l, \mathbb{J} \subseteq \mathbb{I}_1(m), [\boldsymbol{t}]_2 \in \mathbb{G}_2^n, [u]_2 \in \mathbb{G}_2, \overline{m} \in \{0,1\}^l, \overline{\mathbb{J}} \subseteq \mathbb{I}_1(\overline{m}))$:
  - **Rtrn** $\perp$. **Rtrn** $\perp$ if $\overline{m} \not\preceq_{\mathbb{J}} m \vee \overline{\mathbb{J}} \not\subseteq \mathbb{J}$.
  - **Rtrn** $\perp$ if $\nexists\tau$ such that $(m, \mathbb{J}, \tau) \in \mathbb{Q}$ and being parsed as $([\boldsymbol{t}]_2, [u]_2, [T]_2, [\boldsymbol{w}]_2, \mathbb{J}, \{[d_i]_2, [\boldsymbol{e}_i]_2 \mid i \in \mathbb{J}\})$ for some $T, \boldsymbol{w}, d_i$ and $\boldsymbol{e}_i$.
  - $\overline{\tau} \leftarrow \text{Down}(m, \tau, \overline{m}, \overline{\mathbb{J}})$. Parse $\overline{\tau}$ as $([\overline{\boldsymbol{t}}]_2, [\overline{u}]_2, [\overline{T}]_2, [\overline{\boldsymbol{w}}]_2, \overline{\mathbb{J}}, \{[\overline{d_i}]_2, [\overline{\boldsymbol{e}_i}]_2 \mid i \in \overline{\mathbb{J}}\})$.
  - $\mathbb{Q} := \mathbb{Q} \cup \{(\overline{m}, \overline{\mathbb{J}}, \overline{\tau})\}$. **Rtrn** $([\overline{\boldsymbol{t}}]_2, [\overline{u}]_2)$.
- $\mathfrak{Reveal}(m \in \{0,1\}^l, \mathbb{J} \subseteq \mathbb{I}_1(m), [\boldsymbol{t}]_2 \in \mathbb{G}_2^n, [u]_2 \in \mathbb{G}_2)$:
  - **Rtrn** $\perp$ if $\nexists\tau$ such that $(m, \mathbb{J}, \tau) \in \mathbb{Q}$ and being parsed as $([\boldsymbol{t}]_2, [u]_2, [T]_2, [\boldsymbol{w}]_2, \mathbb{J}, \{[d_i]_2, [\boldsymbol{e}_i]_2 \mid i \in \mathbb{J}\})$ for some $T, \boldsymbol{w}, d_i$ and $\boldsymbol{e}_i$.
  - $\mathbb{Q}_r := \mathbb{Q}_r \cup \{(m, \mathbb{J})\}$. **Rtrn** τ.

Abrt if $(m^*, \cdot, \cdot) \in \mathbb{Q} \vee \exists (m, \mathbb{J}) \in \mathbb{Q}_r$ s.t. $m^* \preceq_{\mathbb{J}} m$.

$h \xleftarrow{\$} \mathbb{Z}_p$, $\boldsymbol{h}_0 := \sum_{i=0}^{l} f_i(m^*)\boldsymbol{x}_i h$. If $b = 0$, $h_1 := xh$. If $b = 1$, $h_1 \xleftarrow{\$} \mathbb{Z}_p$.

Rtrn $b' \leftarrow \mathcal{A}_1(st, [h]_1, [\boldsymbol{h}_0]_1, [h_1]_1)$.

Definition 5 (PR-CMA1). *A DAMAC system is PR-CMA1 if* $\forall\lambda \in \mathbb{N}$, $\forall par \in \{0,1\}^*$, $\forall$ *PPT* $\mathcal{A}$, *its advantage* $\boldsymbol{Adv}^{\text{PR-CMA1}}_{\Sigma_{\text{DAMAC}},\mathcal{A},par}(\lambda)$ *defined as* $|\sum_{b=0}^{1}(-1)^b \Pr[1 \leftarrow \boldsymbol{Expt}^{\text{PR-CMA1}}_{\Sigma_{\text{DAMAC}},\mathcal{A},b}(par)]|$ *is negligible.*

Analogously, PR-CMA1′ is defined. Theorem 3 is proven in the full paper.

Theorem 3. *A DAMAC scheme* Σ_{DAMAC} *is PR-CMA1 if it is PR-CMA1′ and SCH. Formally, for any PPTA* $\mathcal{A}$, *there exist a probabilistic algorithm* $\mathcal{B}_1$ *and a PPTA* $\mathcal{B}_2$ *such that* $\boldsymbol{Adv}^{\text{PR-CMA1}}_{\Sigma_{\text{DAMAC}},\mathcal{A},par}(\lambda) \leq 2q_d \cdot \boldsymbol{Adv}^{\text{SCH}}_{\Sigma_{\text{DAMAC}},\mathcal{A},par}(\lambda) + \boldsymbol{Adv}^{\text{PR-CMA1}'}_{\Sigma_{\text{DAMAC}},\mathcal{A},par}(\lambda)$, *where* $q_d \in \mathbb{N}$ *denotes total number that* $\mathcal{A}$ *uses the oracle* $\mathfrak{Down}$.

3.2 Construction

The DAMAC scheme Π_{DAMAC} is essentially the same as the AMAC scheme based on hash-proof system in [14].

$\text{Gen}_{\text{MAC}}(par)$: $B \xleftarrow{\$} \mathcal{D}_{n,n'}$, $\boldsymbol{x}_0, \cdots, \boldsymbol{x}_l \xleftarrow{\$} \mathbb{Z}_p^n$, $x \xleftarrow{\$} \mathbb{Z}_p$. **Rtrn** $sk_{\text{MAC}} := (B, \boldsymbol{x}_0, \cdots, \boldsymbol{x}_l, x)$.

$\text{Tag}(sk_{\text{MAC}}, m \in \{0,1\}^l, \mathbb{J} \subseteq \mathbb{I}_1(m))$:

$\boldsymbol{s} \xleftarrow{\$} \mathbb{Z}_p^{n'}$, $S \xleftarrow{\$} \mathbb{Z}_p^{n' \times n'}$. $\boldsymbol{t} := B\boldsymbol{s} \in \mathbb{Z}_p^n$, $T := BS \in \mathbb{Z}_p^{n \times n'}$.

$u := (\boldsymbol{x}_0^\top + \sum_{i \in \mathbb{I}_1(m)} \boldsymbol{x}_i^\top)\boldsymbol{t} + x \in \mathbb{Z}_p$. $\boldsymbol{w} := (\boldsymbol{x}_0^\top + \sum_{i \in \mathbb{I}_1(m)} \boldsymbol{x}_i^\top)T \in \mathbb{Z}_p^{1 \times n'}$.

For all $i \in \mathbb{J}$, $d_i := \boldsymbol{x}_i^\top \boldsymbol{t} \in \mathbb{Z}_p$ and $\boldsymbol{e}_i := \boldsymbol{x}_i^\top T \in \mathbb{Z}_p^{1 \times n'}$.

Rtrn $\tau := ([\boldsymbol{t}]_2, [u]_2, [T]_2, [\boldsymbol{w}]_2, \mathbb{J}, \{[d_i]_2, [\boldsymbol{e}_i]_2 \mid i \in \mathbb{J}\})$.

$\texttt{Down}\,(m \in \{0,1\}^l, \tau, \overline{m} \in \{0,1\}^l, \overline{\mathbb{J}} \subseteq \mathbb{I}_1(\overline{m}))$:
Parse τ as $([\boldsymbol{t}]_2, [u]_2, [T]_2, [\boldsymbol{w}]_2, \mathbb{J}, \{[d_i]_2, [\boldsymbol{e}_i]_2 \mid i \in \mathbb{J}\})$. **Rtrn** $\perp$ if $\overline{m} \not\preceq_{\mathbb{J}} m \vee \overline{\mathbb{J}} \not\subseteq \mathbb{J}$.
$\overline{\boldsymbol{s}} \xleftarrow{\$} \mathbb{Z}_p^{n'}$, $\overline{S} \xleftarrow{\$} \mathbb{Z}_p^{n' \times n'}$. $\left[\overline{\boldsymbol{t}}\right]_2 := \left[\boldsymbol{t} + T\overline{S}\overline{\boldsymbol{s}}\right]_2$, $\left[\overline{T}\right]_2 := \left[T\overline{S}\right]_2$.
$[\overline{\boldsymbol{e}}_i]_2 := \left[\boldsymbol{e}_i\overline{S}\right]_2$ and $\left[\overline{d}_i\right]_2 := \left[d_i + \boldsymbol{e}_i\overline{S}\overline{\boldsymbol{s}}\right]_2$ for all $i \in \overline{\mathbb{J}}$.
$[\overline{\boldsymbol{w}}]_2 := \left[\boldsymbol{w}\overline{S} - \sum_{i \in \mathbb{J} \cap \mathbb{I}_0(\overline{m})} \overline{\boldsymbol{e}}_i\right]_2$, $[\overline{u}]_2 := \left[u + \boldsymbol{w}\overline{S}\overline{\boldsymbol{s}} - \sum_{i \in \mathbb{J} \cap \mathbb{I}_0(\overline{m})} \overline{d}_i\right]_2$.
Rtrn $\overline{\tau} := (\left[\overline{\boldsymbol{t}}\right]_2, [\overline{u}]_2, \left[\overline{T}\right]_2, [\overline{\boldsymbol{w}}]_2, \overline{\mathbb{J}}, \{\left[\overline{d}_i\right]_2, [\overline{\boldsymbol{e}}_i]_2 \mid i \in \overline{\mathbb{J}}\})$.

$\texttt{Ver}\,(sk_{\text{MAC}}, m \in \{0,1\}^l, \tau)$:
Parse sk_{MAC} as $(B, \boldsymbol{x}_0, \cdots, \boldsymbol{x}_l, x)$. Parse τ as $([\boldsymbol{t}]_2, [u]_2, \cdots)$.
Rtrn 1 if $[u]_2 = \left[(\boldsymbol{x}_0^\top + \sum_{i=1}^{l} m[i]\boldsymbol{x}_i^\top)\boldsymbol{t} + x\right]_2$. **Rtrn** 0, otherwise.

It satisfies Definition 3. Note that for every $m \in \{0,1\}^l$ and every $i \in [0,l]$, $f_i(m) = 1$ if $i = 0 \vee m[i] = 1$) or $f_i(m) = 0$ otherwise, and $h_i(m) = 1$ if $m[i] = 1$. By Theorem 1 and Theorem 2, it is correct and SCH.

Theorem 4 guarantees that the DAMAC is PR-CMA1′ under the MDDH assumption. A proof of the theorem is given in the full paper. We modify the proof of a theorem for pseudo-randomness of the delegatable AMAC scheme [14].

Theorem 4. *The DAMAC scheme is PR-CMA1′ if the $\mathcal{D}_{n,n'}$-MDDH assumption w.r.t. $\mathcal{G}_{BG}$ and $\mathbb{G}_2$ holds. Formally, for any PPTA $\mathcal{A}$, there exists a PPTA $\mathcal{B}$ s.t.* $\mathit{Adv}_{\Pi_{\text{DAMAC}},\mathcal{A}}^{\text{PR-CMA1}'}(\lambda) \leq \frac{1}{p^n} + \frac{1}{p^{n-n'}} + \mathit{Adv}_{\mathcal{B},\mathcal{G}_{BG},\mathbb{G}_2}^{\mathcal{D}_{n,n'}\text{-MDDH}}(\lambda)$.

Since the scheme is SCH, by Theorem 3, it is PR-CMA1.

4 Trapdoor Sanitizable Signatures (TSS)

In the ordinary digital signature, any signed message cannot be modified. Sanitizable signatures (SS) [6] allows an entity called sanitizer to partially modify the message while retaining validity of the signature. In SS, the signer chooses a public-key of a sanitizer. The sanitizer can modify the message using her secret-key. In trapdoor SS (TSS) [21], each signed message is associated with a *trapdoor*. Any entity who knows the trapdoor can modify the message.

4.1 Our Model

Syntax. TSS consists of following four polynomial time algorithms. KGen, Sig and Sanit are probabilistic and Ver are deterministic. In the original model [21], each message consists of multiple sub-messages with unbounded length. In our model, each message is simply a binary string with constant length $l \in \mathbb{N}$.

Key-generation KGen: Let $l \in \mathbb{N}$ denote bit length of a message. It generates a key-pair of a signer. Formally, it takes 1^λ and l, then outputs a key-pair (pk, sk). $[(pk, sk) \leftarrow \texttt{KGen}(1^\lambda, l)]$

Signing $\texttt{Sig}$**:** It generates a signature on a message. Formally, it takes a secret-key sk, a message $m \in \{0,1\}^l$ and a set $\mathbb{T} \subseteq [1,l]$ of indices for its modifiable bits, then outputs a signature σ and a trapdoor td. We require that the set $\mathbb{T}$ is uniquely identified by the trapdoor td, e.g., explicitly included in td. $[(\sigma, td) \leftarrow \texttt{Sig}(sk, m, \mathbb{T})]$

Sanitizing $\texttt{Sanit}$**:** It modifies a signed message into another. Formally, it takes a public-key pk, a message m, a signature σ, a trapdoor td, a modified message $\overline{m}$ and a modified set $\overline{\mathbb{T}} \subseteq \mathbb{T}$, then outputs a signature $\overline{\sigma}$ and a trapdoor $\overline{td}$. $[(\overline{\sigma}, \overline{td}) \leftarrow \texttt{Sanit}(pk, m, \sigma, td, \overline{m}, \overline{\mathbb{T}})]$

Verification $\texttt{Ver}$**:** It verifies a signature. It takes a public-key pk, a message m and a signature σ, then returns 1 or 0. $[1/0 \leftarrow \texttt{Ver}(pk, m, \sigma)]$

A relation must hold between an original and modified message. We define the relation algorithm $R_{\mathtt{s}}$ for TSS as follows.

Definition 6 (TSS Relation). *$m, \overline{m} \in \{0,1\}^l$ are arbitral messages. $\mathbb{T} \subseteq [1,l]$ is an arbitral set of indices for modifiable bits.*

$$R_{\mathtt{s}}(m, \overline{m}, \mathbb{T}) := \begin{cases} 1 & (\textit{if } \bigwedge_{i \in [1,l]} [\overline{m}[i] \neq m[i] \implies i \in \mathbb{T}]) \\ 0 & (\textit{otherwise}) \end{cases}$$

We require every TSS scheme to be correct. We say that a TSS scheme is correct, if $\forall \lambda \in \mathbb{N}$, $\forall l \in \mathbb{N}$, $\forall (pk, sk) \leftarrow \texttt{KGen}(1^\lambda, l)$, $\forall m \in \{0,1\}^l$, $\forall \mathbb{T} \subseteq [1,l]$, $\forall (\sigma, td) \leftarrow \texttt{Sig}(sk, m, \mathbb{T})$, $\forall \overline{m} \in \{0,1\}^l$ s.t. $1 \leftarrow R_{\mathtt{s}}(m, \overline{m}, \mathbb{T})$, $\forall \overline{\mathbb{T}} \subseteq \mathbb{T}$, $\forall (\overline{\sigma}, \overline{td}) \leftarrow \texttt{Sanit}(pk, m, \sigma, td, \overline{m}, \overline{\mathbb{T}})$, $1 \leftarrow \texttt{Ver}(pk, m, \sigma)$ and $1 \leftarrow \texttt{Ver}(pk, \overline{m}, \overline{\sigma})$.

Comparison with [21,38]. In our model, a trapdoor is generated simultaneously with a signature. In the original model [21,38], there is an algorithm which generates a trapdoor from a signature using the signing-key. Its usefulness is limited. If someone demands a trapdoor associated with a signature, the signer only needs to ignore the signature and generate a fresh signature and its trapdoor on the same message and set of indices for modifiable bits. Moreover, our model differs in the following three respects. First, $\texttt{Sanit}$ is probabilistic. As we explain later, this property is necessary to achieve unlinkability. Because the sanitization algorithms of the schemes [21,38] are not probabilistic[12], they cannot be unlinkable. Second, a signature and its trapdoor can be re-randomized. This is done by running $\texttt{Sanit}$ with $(\overline{m}, \overline{\mathbb{T}}) = (m, \mathbb{T})$. Third, a set of indices for modifiable bits can be *consecutively downsizable*. We call this property *(consecutive) sanitization-controllability*. This is done by running $\texttt{Sanit}$ with $\overline{m}(= m)$ and $\overline{\mathbb{T}}(\subset \mathbb{T})$. In the original model, each trapdoor and set of indices for modifiable bits are permanently fixed.

4.2 Security Definitions

As security notions for SS, for instance, unforgeability, privacy, transparency, unlinkability and invisibility have been defined [17,18,20]. Yum et al. [38] have

[12] Precisely, they are deterministic and *semi*-probabilistic, respectively.

defined only the first three notions for TSS. In this work, we define all of them and strong context-hiding (SCH) for TSS. These notions are categorized into two groups *search*-type and *distinction*-type based on their problems the adversary solves. The former includes unforgeability and the latter the others.

Search-Type Notion. One of the standard security notions for the ordinary digital signature is (weak) existential unforgeability against chosen messages attacks, shortly wEUF-CMA. We define two notions for TSS, wEUF-CMA and wEUF-CMA′. The former is a naive extension from the one for the ordinary digital signature, and the latter is a slight *downgrade* of the former.

In the following experiment for wEUF-CMA, a PPT adversary $\mathcal{A}$ can adaptively use three oracles. Signing oracle $\mathfrak{Sig}$ takes a message m and a set $\mathbb{T}$. A signature σ and its trapdoor td are generated. Here, only σ is revealed. Sanitization oracle $\mathfrak{Sanit}$ is used when $\mathcal{A}$ wants to sanitize the signature generated on $\mathfrak{Sig}$. The (trapdoor-)revelation oracle $\mathfrak{Reveal}$ is used when $\mathcal{A}$ wants to get the hidden trapdoor generated on $\mathfrak{Sig}$ or $\mathfrak{Sanit}$. Finally, $\mathcal{A}$ outputs a forgery σ^* on a target message m^*. Since this notion is *weak* existential unforgeability, m^* must not be the one queried to $\mathfrak{Sig}$ or $\mathfrak{Sanit}$. Naturally, the message must not be obtained by modifying a message whose trapdoor has been revealed on $\mathfrak{Reveal}$.

$\boldsymbol{Expt}^{\texttt{wEUF-CMA}}_{\Sigma_{\text{TSS}},\mathcal{A}}(1^\lambda, l)$: // $\boldsymbol{Expt}^{\texttt{wEUF-CMA}'}_{\Sigma_{\text{TSS}},\mathcal{A}}$.

1. $(pk, sk) \leftarrow \texttt{KGen}(1^\lambda, l)$. $(\sigma^*, m^*) \leftarrow \mathcal{A}^{\mathfrak{Sig},\mathfrak{Sanit},\mathfrak{Reveal}}(pk)$.

- -

- $\mathfrak{Sig}(m, \mathbb{T})$: $(\sigma, td) \leftarrow \texttt{Sig}(sk, m, \mathbb{T})$. $\mathbb{Q} := \mathbb{Q} \cup \{(m, \mathbb{T}, \sigma, td)\}$. **Rtrn** σ.
- $\mathfrak{Sanit}(m, \sigma, \overline{m}, \overline{\mathbb{T}})$:
  Rtrn $\perp$. **Rtrn** $\perp$ if $\nexists(\mathbb{T}, td)$ s.t. $(m, \mathbb{T}, \sigma, td) \in \mathbb{Q} \wedge 1 \leftarrow R_s(m, \overline{m}, \mathbb{T}) \wedge \overline{\mathbb{T}} \subseteq \mathbb{T}$.
  $(\overline{\sigma}, \overline{td}) \leftarrow \texttt{Sanit}(pk, m, \sigma, td, \overline{m}, \overline{\mathbb{T}})$. $\mathbb{Q} := \mathbb{Q} \cup \{(\overline{m}, \overline{\mathbb{T}}, \overline{\sigma}, \overline{td})\}$. **Rtrn** $\overline{\sigma}$.
- $\mathfrak{Reveal}(m, \mathbb{T}, \sigma)$:
  Rtrn $\perp$ if $\nexists td$ s.t. $(m, \mathbb{T}, \sigma, td) \in \mathbb{Q}$. $\mathbb{Q}_r := \mathbb{Q}_r \cup \{(m, \mathbb{T})\}$. **Rtrn** td.

- -

2. **Rtrn** 1 if $1 \leftarrow \texttt{Ver}(pk, m^*, \sigma^*) \bigwedge_{(m,\mathbb{T}) \in \mathbb{Q}_r} 0 \leftarrow R_s(m, m^*, \mathbb{T}) \bigwedge (m^*, \cdot, \cdot, \cdot) \notin \mathbb{Q}$.
3. **Rtrn** 0.

Definition 7 (wEUF-CMA). *A TSS scheme Σ_{TSS} is wEUF-CMA, if for any $\lambda \in \mathbb{N}$, any $l \in \mathbb{N}$ and any PPT $\mathcal{A}$, its advantage $\boldsymbol{Adv}^{\textit{wEUF-CMA}}_{\Sigma_{\text{TSS}},\mathcal{A},l}(\lambda)$ defined as* $\Pr[1 \leftarrow \boldsymbol{Expt}^{\textit{wEUF-CMA}}_{\Sigma_{\text{TSS}},\mathcal{A}}(1^\lambda, l)]$ *is negligible.*

In wEUF-CMA′, the sanitization oracle cannot be used. This notion is defined analogously to wEUF-CMA. As we prove later in Theorem 5, the two notions are equivalent if the TSS scheme is SCH.

Distinction-Type Notions. We define (i) transparency, (ii) privacy, (iii) unlinkability, (iv) invisibility and (v) SCH.

For the notions, we commonly define two experiments, namely $\boldsymbol{Expt}_0$ and $\boldsymbol{Expt}_1$. They require that no probabilistic algorithm (with unbounded computational time) $\mathcal{A}$ can distinguish the two experiments statistically or perfectly.

Informally, (i) *transparency* (TRN) means that we cannot correctly guess that a signature is generated by Sig or Sanit. In $\boldsymbol{Expt}_1$, on the oracle of $\mathfrak{Sanit}/\mathfrak{Sig}$, we generate the signature $\overline{\sigma}$ directly by Sig. In $\boldsymbol{Expt}_0$, we firstly generate a signature σ on m, then $\overline{\sigma}$ from it by Sanit. Note that sk is directly given to $\mathcal{A}$.

$\boldsymbol{Expt}^{\mathtt{TRN}}_{\Sigma_{\mathrm{TSS}},\mathcal{A},b}(1^\lambda, l)$: // $b \in \{0, \mathbf{1}\}$.
1. $(pk, sk) \leftarrow \mathtt{KGen}(1^\lambda, l)$. **Rtrn** $b' \leftarrow \mathcal{A}^{\mathfrak{Sanit}/\mathfrak{Sig}}(pk, sk)$.

- $\mathfrak{Sanit}/\mathfrak{Sig}(m, \mathbb{T}, \overline{m}, \overline{\mathbb{T}})$:
  Rtrn $\perp$ if $0 \leftarrow R_s(m, \overline{m}, \mathbb{T}) \vee \overline{\mathbb{T}} \not\subseteq \mathbb{T}$.
  $(\sigma, td) \leftarrow \mathtt{Sig}(sk, m, \mathbb{T})$. $(\overline{\sigma}, \overline{td}) \leftarrow \mathtt{Sanit}(pk, m, \sigma, td, \overline{m}, \overline{\mathbb{T}})$.
  $(\overline{\sigma}, \overline{td}) \leftarrow \mathtt{Sig}(sk, \overline{m}, \overline{\mathbb{T}})$. **Rtrn** $(\overline{\sigma}, \overline{td})$.

Definition 8 (TRN). *A scheme Σ_{TSS} is statistically TRN if for any $\lambda \in \mathbb{N}$, any $l \in \mathbb{N}$ and any probabilistic algorithm $\mathcal{A}$, its advantage $\mathbf{Adv}^{\mathit{TRN}}_{\Sigma_{\mathrm{TSS}},\mathcal{A},l}(\lambda)$ defined as $|\sum_{b=0}^{1}(-1)^b \Pr[1 \leftarrow \boldsymbol{Expt}^{\mathit{TRN}}_{\Sigma_{\mathrm{TSS}},\mathcal{A},b}(1^\lambda, l)]|$ is negligible. It is perfectly TRN if the advantage is 0*[13].

Intuitively, (ii) *privacy* (PRV) means that from a sanitized signature on a modified message we cannot get any information about the original message. PRV is defined analogously to TRN, cf. Definition 8.

$\boldsymbol{Expt}^{\mathtt{PRV}}_{\Sigma_{\mathrm{TSS}},\mathcal{A},b}(1^\lambda, l)$: // $b \in \{0, 1\}$.
1. $(pk, sk) \leftarrow \mathtt{KGen}(1^\lambda, l)$. **Rtrn** $b' \leftarrow \mathcal{A}^{\mathfrak{SigSanitLR}}(pk, sk)$.

- $\mathfrak{SigSanitLR}(m_0, m_1, \mathbb{T}_0, \mathbb{T}_1, \overline{m}, \overline{\mathbb{T}})$:
  Rtrn $\perp$ if $\exists \beta \in \{0, 1\}$ s.t. $0 \leftarrow R_s(m_\beta, \overline{m}, \mathbb{T}_\beta) \vee \overline{\mathbb{T}} \not\subseteq \mathbb{T}_\beta$.
  $(\sigma, td) \leftarrow \mathtt{Sig}(sk, m_b, \mathbb{T}_b)$. $(\overline{\sigma}, \overline{td}) \leftarrow \mathtt{Sanit}(pk, m_b, \sigma, td, \overline{m}, \overline{\mathbb{T}})$. **Rtrn** $(\overline{\sigma}, \overline{td})$.

(iii) *Unlinkability* (UNL) is a stronger notion than PRV. Intuitively, it means that from a sanitized signature we cannot get any information about not only the original message but also the original signature. For a TSS scheme, its sanitization algorithm must be probabilistic to be UNL. No scheme, such that a sanitized signature is (partially) determined by the original signature, can be UNL, e.g., the ones [21,38]. UNL is also defined analogously to TRN, cf. Definition 8.

$\boldsymbol{Expt}^{\mathtt{UNL}}_{\Sigma_{\mathrm{TSS}},\mathcal{A},b}(1^\lambda, l)$: // $b \in \{0, 1\}$.
1. $(pk, sk) \leftarrow \mathtt{KGen}(1^\lambda, l)$. **Rtrn** $b' \leftarrow \mathcal{A}^{\mathfrak{Sig},\mathfrak{Sanit},\mathfrak{SanitLR}}(pk, sk)$.

- $\mathfrak{Sig}(m, \mathbb{T})$: $(\sigma, td) \leftarrow \mathtt{Sig}(sk, m, \mathbb{T})$. $\mathbb{Q} := \mathbb{Q} \cup \{(m, \mathbb{T}, \sigma, td)\}$. **Rtrn** (σ, td).
- $\mathfrak{Sanit}(m, \mathbb{T}, \sigma, td, \overline{m}, \overline{\mathbb{T}})$:
  Rtrn $\perp$ if $(m, \mathbb{T}, \sigma, td) \notin \mathbb{Q} \vee \overline{\mathbb{T}} \not\subseteq \mathbb{T}$.
  $(\overline{\sigma}, \overline{td}) \leftarrow \mathtt{Sanit}(pk, m, \sigma, td, \overline{m}, \overline{\mathbb{T}})$. $\mathbb{Q} := \mathbb{Q} \cup \{(\overline{m}, \overline{\mathbb{T}}, \overline{\sigma}, \overline{td})\}$. **Rtrn** $(\overline{\sigma}, \overline{td})$.
- $\mathfrak{SanitLR}(m_0, \mathbb{T}_0, \sigma_0, td_0, m_1, \mathbb{T}_1, \sigma_1, td_1, \overline{m}, \overline{\mathbb{T}})$:

---

[13] Let $\mathtt{Z} \in \{\mathtt{TRN}, \mathtt{PRV}, \mathtt{UNL}, \mathtt{INV}, \mathtt{SCH}, \mathtt{INV}', \mathtt{INV}^\dagger\}$. When we shortly say that a scheme is Z-secure, that means it is statistically Z-secure..

Rtrn $\perp$ if $\exists\beta \in \{0,1\}$ s.t. $(m_\beta, \mathbb{T}_\beta, \sigma_\beta, td_\beta) \notin \mathbb{Q} \vee 0 \leftarrow R_s(m_\beta, \overline{m}, \mathbb{T}_\beta) \vee \overline{\mathbb{T}} \not\subseteq \mathbb{T}_\beta$.
$(\overline{\sigma}, \overline{td}) \leftarrow \mathtt{Sanit}(pk, m_b, \sigma_b, td_b, \overline{m}, \overline{\mathbb{T}})$. $\mathbb{Q} := \mathbb{Q} \cup \{(\overline{m}, \overline{\mathbb{T}}, \overline{\sigma}, \overline{td})\}$. **Rtrn** $(\overline{\sigma}, \overline{td})$.

Intuitively, (iv) *invisibility* (INV) means that from a signature we get no information about its set of indices for modifiable bits $\mathbb{T}$. More precisely, it means that *only* from a signature we can get no information about its set of indices for modifiable bits because our model has assumed that the set can be uniquely identified by the trapdoor.

We define two notions for invisibility, namely INV and INV′.

We define two experiments for INV. The latter one $\boldsymbol{Expt}_1$ is associated with three simulation algorithms {SimKGen, SimSig, SimSanit}. $\mathcal{A}$ can adaptively use two oracles $\mathfrak{SimSig}$ and $\mathfrak{SimSanit}$. In $\boldsymbol{Expt}_0$, on $\mathfrak{SimSig}$, a signature and its trapdoor on $(m, \mathbb{T})$ are honestly generated by Sig. In $\boldsymbol{Expt}_1$, they are generated by the simulated signing algorithm SimSig which is not given $\mathbb{T}$ as input. If both of the signatures are indistinguishable, that means no information about $\mathbb{T}$ is included in an honestly generated signature.

$\boldsymbol{Expt}^{\mathtt{INV}}_{\Sigma_{\mathrm{TSS}},\mathcal{A},b}(1^\lambda, l)$: // $b \in \{0, 1\}$.
$(pk, sk) \leftarrow \mathtt{KGen}(1^\lambda, l)$. $(pk, sk'(\ni sk)) \leftarrow \mathtt{SimKGen}(1^\lambda, l)$.
Rtrn $b' \leftarrow \mathcal{A}^{\mathfrak{SimSig},\mathfrak{SimSanit}}(pk, sk)$.

- $\mathfrak{SimSig}(m, \mathbb{T})$:
$(\sigma, td) \leftarrow \mathtt{Sig}(sk, m, \mathbb{T})$. $\sigma \leftarrow \mathtt{SimSig}(sk', m)$. $td := 0$.
$\mathbb{Q} := \mathbb{Q} \cup \{(m, \mathbb{T}, \sigma, td)\}$. **Rtrn** σ.
- $\mathfrak{SimSanit}(m, \sigma, \overline{m}, \overline{\mathbb{T}})$:
Rtrn $\perp$ if $\nexists(\mathbb{T}, td)$ s.t. $(m, \mathbb{T}, \sigma, td) \in \mathbb{Q} \bigwedge 1 \leftarrow R_s(m, \overline{m}, \mathbb{T}) \bigwedge \overline{\mathbb{T}} \subseteq \mathbb{T}$.
$(\overline{\sigma}, \overline{td}) \leftarrow \mathtt{Sanit}(pk, m, \sigma, td, \overline{m}, \overline{\mathbb{T}})$. $\overline{\sigma} \leftarrow \mathtt{SimSanit}(sk', m, \sigma, \overline{m})$. $\overline{td} := 0$.
$\mathbb{Q} := \mathbb{Q} \cup \{(\overline{m}, \overline{\mathbb{T}}, \overline{\sigma}, \overline{td})\}$. **Rtrn** $\overline{\sigma}$.

Definition 9 (INV). *A scheme Σ_{TSS} is statistically INV if for any $\lambda \in \mathbb{N}$, any $l \in \mathbb{N}$ and any probabilistic algorithm $\mathcal{A}$, there exist simulation algorithms* {SimKGen, SimSig, SimSanit} *such that $\mathcal{A}$'s advantage $\boldsymbol{Adv}^{\mathtt{INV}}_{\Sigma_{\mathrm{TSS}},\mathcal{A},l}(\lambda)$ defined as $|\sum_{b=0}^{1}(-1)^b \Pr[1 \leftarrow \boldsymbol{Expt}^{\mathtt{INV}}_{\Sigma_{\mathrm{TSS}},\mathcal{A},b}(1^\lambda, l)]|$ is negligible. It is perfectly INV if the advantage is 0(see footnote 13).*

The two experiments for INV′ are the same as INV except that the (simulated) sanitization oracle $\mathfrak{SimSanit}$ cannot be used. This notion is defined as Definition 9. As we prove in Theorem 5, the two notions are equivalent if the scheme is SCH.

In P-homomorphic signatures (P-HS) [5] for a predicate P, from a signature on a message m, we can derive a correct signature on any message $\overline{m}$ such that $1 \leftarrow P(m, \overline{m})$. Obviously, TSS is a sub-class of P-HS[14]. As a strong notion of privacy for P-HS, Ahn et al. [1] defined strong context-hiding (SCH) (SCH), which informally says that any signature derived from another one is indistinguishable from a fresh signature directly generated by the signing-key. We define SCH for TSS as follows.

[14] Precisely, we should probably say that TSS is a sub-class of *P-trapdoor* HS.

Definition 10 (SCH). *A TSS scheme Σ_{TSS} is statistically* SCH *if for any $\lambda \in \mathbb{N}$, any $l \in \mathbb{N}$, any $(pk, sk) \leftarrow \mathtt{KGen}(1^\lambda, l)$, any $m, \overline{m} \in \{0,1\}^l$, any $\mathbb{T}, \overline{\mathbb{T}} \subseteq [1, l]$ such that $1 \leftarrow R_{\mathsf{s}}(m, \overline{m}, \mathbb{T}) \wedge \overline{\mathbb{T}} \subseteq \mathbb{T}$ and any probabilistic algorithm $\mathcal{A}$, its advantage $Adv^{SCH}_{\Sigma_{\mathrm{TSS}},\mathcal{A},l}(\lambda)$ defined as*

$$\Big|\Pr\Big[1 \leftarrow \mathcal{A}(sk, \sigma, td, \overline{\sigma}, \overline{td}) \Big| (\sigma, td) \leftarrow \mathtt{Sig}(sk, m, \mathbb{T}), (\overline{\sigma}, \overline{td}) \leftarrow \mathtt{Sanit}(pk, m, \sigma, td, \overline{\sigma}, \overline{\mathbb{T}})\Big]$$
$$- \Pr\Big[1 \leftarrow \mathcal{A}(sk, \sigma, td, \overline{\sigma}, \overline{td}) \Big| (\sigma, td) \leftarrow \mathtt{Sig}(sk, m, \mathbb{T}), (\overline{\sigma}, \overline{td}) \leftarrow \mathtt{Sig}(sk, \overline{m}, \overline{\mathbb{T}})\Big]\Big|$$

is negligible. It is perfectly SCH *if the advantage is* 0 *(see footnote 13).*

Relations among the Security Notions. The following six implications hold.

Theorem 5. *For any TSS scheme, (1)* wEUF-CMA′ $\bigwedge$ SCH *implies* wEUF-CMA*, (2)* INV′ $\bigwedge$ SCH *implies* INV*, (3)* TRN *implies* PRV*, (4)* UNL *implies* PRV*, (5)* SCH *implies* TRN*, and (6)* SCH *implies* UNL*. Note that any of the implications hold in either of the statistical and perfect formalizations.*

The theorem is formally proven in Sect. A.

The relations are visualized in Fig. 1. Note that TRN does not imply UNL because there exists a counterexample which is TRN but not UNL, e.g. the scheme by Yum et al. [38] as we will prove in Subsect. 5.2. We can prove that UNL does not imply TRN by presenting a simple counterexample. Let Σ denote a scheme satisfying UNL. Another Σ' is basically the same as Σ, but Sanit always adds a special symbol (like $\star$) somewhere in a signature. Any user can correctly guess the generator based on it. Thus, Σ' is not TRN. Obviously, Σ' is still UNL.

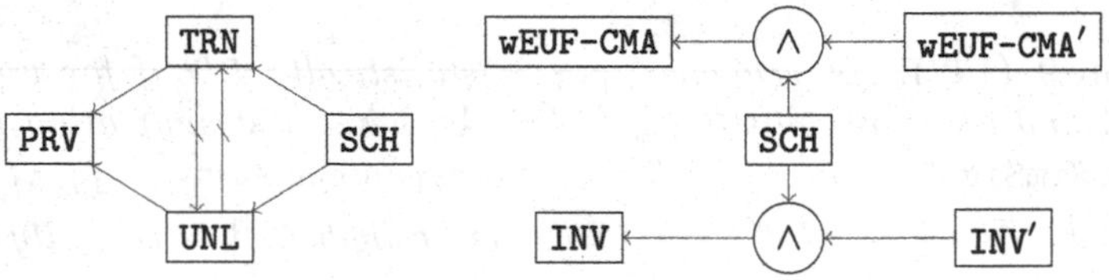

Fig. 1. Relations among security notions for TSS. Normal arrow (→) indicates a (combinational) implication result. Negated arrow (↛) indicates a separation result. (Color figure online)

5 Our TSS Scheme

5.1 Contruction

Downgradable IBE (DIBE) [13] is a generalization of hierarchical IBE [15]. Each secret-key is associated with an ID. The ID can be *downgraded*, which means that any bit 1 can be changed into 0. We can propose *downgrade-controllable* DIBE (DCDIBE). For each bit 1, we can decide *downgradable* or *fixed.* Blazy et al. [13]

proposed a DIBE scheme based on DAMAC (w/o downgrade-controllability), which is an extension of the HIBE scheme based on delegatable AMAC [14]. We believe that the same approach effectively works for DCDIBE. We *implicitly* construct a DCDIBE scheme based on (downgrade-controllable) DAMAC.

We have known that a user secret-key in an encryption system can function as a signature, e.g., the transformation from HIBE to hierarchical identity-based signatures [26], the transformation from (CP-)ABE to HSSP [5]. Our TSS scheme is a transformation from the *implicit* DCDIBE scheme.

Each signature or trapdoor on $(m, \mathbb{T})$ is a user secret-key for the DCDIBE scheme. For instance, each signature is a secret-key for an $ID = m \in \{0,1\}^l$ with no downgradability. We verify it as the HIBE-to-HIBS transformation. Thus, we generate a test ciphertext then decrypt it by the signature. Each trapdoor td is a secret-key for the DCDIBE scheme associated with an $ID' = F(m, \mathbb{T})$ and a set $\mathbb{T}$. Informally, the function F changes every downgradable bit 0 in m into 1.

In `Sig` and `Sanit`, we firstly generate a trapdoor then a signature. In `Sig`, we firstly generate a trapdoor td (using sk), then a signature σ by td. Likewise, in `Sanit`, we firstly generate a trapdoor $\overline{td}$ (using the *original* td), then a signature $\overline{\sigma}$ by $\overline{td}$. Figure 2 depicts a simple case where we, given a signature on $m = 0101$ with $\mathbb{T} = \{3, 4\}$, modify the message into $\overline{m} = 0100$ with $\overline{\mathbb{T}} = \{4\}$.

Our TSS scheme Ω_{TSS} is formally described as follows.

$\texttt{KGen}(1^\lambda, l)$:

$A \xleftarrow{\$} \mathbb{D}_{n'+1,n'}$. $sk_{\text{MAC}} \leftarrow \texttt{Gen}_{\text{MAC}}(1^\lambda, l)$. Parse sk_{MAC} as $(B, \boldsymbol{x}_0, \cdots, \boldsymbol{x}_l, x)$.

$\boldsymbol{y} \xleftarrow{\$} \mathbb{Z}_p^{1\times n'}$, $\boldsymbol{z} := (\boldsymbol{y} \mid x) A \in \mathbb{Z}_p^{1\times n'}$.

For all $i \in [0, l]$, $Y_i \xleftarrow{\$} \mathbb{Z}_p^{n\times n'}$ and $Z_i := (Y_i \mid \boldsymbol{x}_i) A \in \mathbb{Z}_p^{n\times n'}$.

$pk := ([A]_1, \{[Z_i]_1 \mid i \in [0, l]\}, [\boldsymbol{z}]_1)$. $sk := (sk_{\text{MAC}}, \{Y_i \mid i \in [0, l]\}, \boldsymbol{y})$. **Rtrn** (pk, sk).

$\texttt{Sig}(sk, m, \mathbb{T})$:

$m' \leftarrow F(m, \mathbb{T})$.

$\tau' \leftarrow \texttt{Tag}(sk_{\text{MAC}}, m', \mathbb{T})$. Parse τ' as $([\boldsymbol{t}']_2, [u']_2, [T']_2, [\boldsymbol{w}']_2, \mathbb{T}, \{[\boldsymbol{d}_i']_2, [\boldsymbol{e}_i']_2 \mid i \in \mathbb{T}\})$.

$\boldsymbol{u}' := \sum_{i=0}^{l} f_i(m') Y_i{}^\top \boldsymbol{t}' + \boldsymbol{y}^\top \in \mathbb{Z}_p^{n'}$. $W' := \sum_{i=0}^{l} f_i(m') Y_i{}^\top T' \in \mathbb{Z}_p^{n'\times n'}$.

For all $i \in \mathbb{T}$, $\boldsymbol{d}_i' := h_i(m') Y_i{}^\top \boldsymbol{t}'$ and $E_i' := h_i(m') Y_i{}^\top T'$.

$td := (\tau', [\boldsymbol{u}']_2, [W']_2, \{[\boldsymbol{d}_i']_2, [E_i']_2 \mid i \in \mathbb{T}\})$. $\sigma \leftarrow \texttt{Derive}(m', td, m, \emptyset)$. **Rtrn** (σ, td).

$F(m \in \{0,1\}^l, \mathbb{T} \subseteq [1, l])$:

$m' := m$. For all $i \in \mathbb{T}$ s.t. $m[i] = 0$, $m'[i] := 1$. **Rtrn** m'.

$\texttt{Derive}(m' \in \{0,1\}^l, td', m \in \{0,1\}^l, \mathbb{T} \subseteq \mathbb{I}_1(m))$:

Parse td' as $(\tau', [\boldsymbol{u}']_2, [W']_2, \{[\boldsymbol{d}_i']_2, [E_i']_2 \mid i \in \mathbb{T}'\})$ for some $\mathbb{T}' \subseteq \mathbb{I}_1(m')$.

Parse τ' as $([\boldsymbol{t}']_2, [u']_2, [T']_2, [\boldsymbol{w}']_2, \mathbb{T}', \{[\boldsymbol{d}_i']_2, [\boldsymbol{e}_i']_2 \mid i \in \mathbb{T}'\})$.

$\tau \leftarrow \texttt{Down}(m', \tau', m, \mathbb{T}; \boldsymbol{s}, S)$, where $\boldsymbol{s} \xleftarrow{\$} \mathbb{Z}_p^{n'}$ and $S \xleftarrow{\$} \mathbb{Z}_p^{n'\times n'}$.

Parse τ as $([\boldsymbol{t}]_2, [u]_2, [T]_2, [\boldsymbol{w}]_2, \mathbb{T}, \{[\boldsymbol{d}_i]_2, [\boldsymbol{e}_i]_2 \mid i \in \mathbb{T}\})$.

For all $i \in \mathbb{T}'$, $[E_i]_2 := [E_i' S]_2$ and $[\boldsymbol{d}_i]_2 := [\boldsymbol{d}_i' + E_i' S \boldsymbol{s}]_2$.

$[W]_2 := \left[W'S - \sum_{i \in \mathbb{I}_1(m') \cap \mathbb{I}_0(m)} E_i\right]_2$. $[\boldsymbol{u}]_2 := \left[\boldsymbol{u}' + W' S \boldsymbol{s} - \sum_{i \in \mathbb{I}_1(m') \cap \mathbb{I}_0(m)} \boldsymbol{d}_i\right]_2$

$\tau := ([\boldsymbol{t}]_2, [u]_2, [T]_2, [\boldsymbol{w}]_2, \mathbb{T}, \{[\boldsymbol{d}_i]_2, [\boldsymbol{e}_i]_2 \mid i \in \mathbb{T}\})$.

$td := (\tau, [\boldsymbol{u}]_2, [W]_2, \{[\boldsymbol{d}_i]_2, [E_i]_2 \mid i \in \mathbb{T}\})$. **Rtrn** td.

$\texttt{Sanit}(pk, m, \sigma, td, \overline{m}, \mathbb{T})$:

Rtrn $\perp$ if $0 \leftarrow \texttt{Ver}(pk, m, \sigma)$.

Parse td as $(\tau', [\boldsymbol{u}']_2, [W']_2, \{[\boldsymbol{d}_i']_2, [E_i']_2 \mid i \in \mathbb{T}\})$ for some $\mathbb{T}$.

Parse τ' as $([\boldsymbol{t}']_2, [u']_2, [T']_2, [\boldsymbol{w}']_2, \mathbb{T}, \{[\boldsymbol{d}_i']_2, [\boldsymbol{e}_i']_2 \mid i \in \mathbb{T}\})$.

Rtrn $\perp$ if $\overline{\mathbb{T}} \not\subseteq \mathbb{T} \vee 0 \leftarrow R_{\mathrm{s}}(m, \overline{m}, \mathbb{T})$.
$m' \leftarrow F(m, \mathbb{T})$. $\overline{m}' \leftarrow F(\overline{m}, \overline{\mathbb{T}})$.
$\overline{td} \leftarrow \mathtt{Derive}(m', td, \overline{m}', \overline{\mathbb{T}})$. $\overline{\sigma} \leftarrow \mathtt{Derive}(\overline{m}', \overline{td}, \overline{m}, \emptyset)$. **Rtrn** $(\overline{\sigma}, \overline{td})$.

$\mathtt{Ver}(pk, m, \sigma)$:
Parse σ as $(\tau, [\boldsymbol{u}]_2, \cdots)$. Parse τ as $([\boldsymbol{t}]_2, [u]_2, \cdots)$.
$\boldsymbol{r} \xleftarrow{\$} \mathbb{Z}_p^{n'}$. $[\boldsymbol{v}_0]_1 := [A\boldsymbol{r}]_1 \in \mathbb{G}^{n'+1}$. $[v]_1 := [\boldsymbol{z}\boldsymbol{r}]_1 \in \mathbb{G}$. $[\boldsymbol{v}_1]_1 := \left[\sum_{i=0}^{l} f_i(m) Z_i \boldsymbol{r}\right]_1 \in \mathbb{G}^n$.
Rtrn 1 if $e\left([\boldsymbol{v}_0]_1, \begin{bmatrix} \boldsymbol{u} \\ u \end{bmatrix}_2\right) \cdot e\left([\boldsymbol{v}_1]_1, [\boldsymbol{t}]_2\right)^{-1} = e\left([v]_1, [1]_2\right)$. **Rtrn** 0 otherwise.

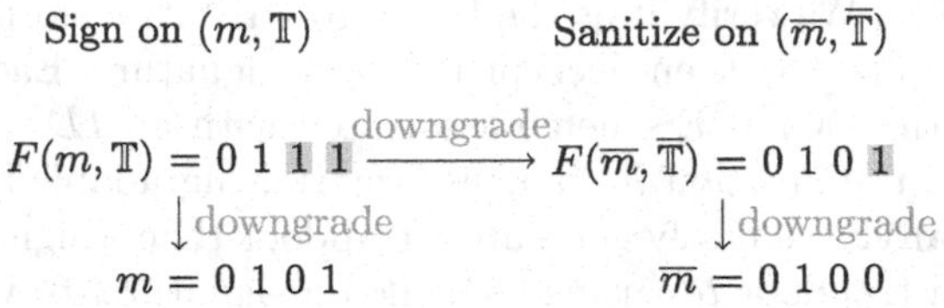

Fig. 2. A simple example of sanitization in our TSS scheme. The grey ( ) box indicates downgradable bits.

For correctness and security, we give the following four theorems. They are formally proven in the full paper.

Theorem 6. *The TSS scheme is correct if Σ_{DAMAC} satisfies Definition 3.*

Theorem 7. *The TSS scheme is SCH if Σ_{DAMAC} is SCH.*

Theorem 8. *The TSS scheme is perfectly PRV and perfectly INV′.*

Theorem 9. *The TSS scheme is wEUF-CMA′ if the MDDH assumption relative to $\mathcal{G}_{BG}$ in group $\mathbb{G}_1$ holds and Σ_{DAMAC} is PR-CMA1′ and SCH.*

5.2 Security Analysis of Existing Two TSS Schemes

We check whether existing two TSS schemes are secure under our definitions.

The first one is a TSS scheme by Canard et al. [21]. It uses identity-based chameleon hash function (IBCH) and digital signature, and adopts *(IB)CH-then-Sign* approach. A signing-key consists of a master secret-key msk of the IBCH and a signing-key sk of the digital signature. She signs a message $m = (m_1, \cdots, m_n)$ with $\mathbb{T} \subseteq [1, n]$ as follows. For every $i \in \mathbb{T}$, she computes the hash value h_i of the sub-message m_i under an identity m and randomness r_i. She sets $\hat{m}_i := h_i$. On the other hand, for every $i \in [1, n] \setminus \mathbb{T}$, she simply sets $\hat{m}_i := m_i$. Next, she computes the hash value h of m under an identity m and randomness r. Then, she generates a signature $\hat{\sigma}$ on $\hat{m}_1 || \cdots || \hat{m}_n || h$ using sk. Finally, the signature σ consists of $(\hat{\sigma}, \{h_i, r_i \mid i \in \mathbb{T}\}, h, r)$. Its trapdoor td is an IBCH secret-key for the identity m generated from msk. We have proven that the TSS scheme is neither INV nor PRV, which implies that it is neither TRN, UNL nor SCH because of Theorem 5. Their proofs are simple, which are given in the full paper.

The second one is a generic scheme based on an ordinary signature scheme proposed by Yum et al. [38]. A key-pair of a signer is a key-pair (vk, sk) of the underlying signature scheme. To sign a message $m = (m_1, \cdots, m_n)$ for $\mathbb{T} \subseteq [1, n]$, the signer generates a new key-pair $(\hat{vk}, \hat{sk})$, then makes a message $\hat{m} := ||_{i=1}^{n} \hat{m}_i$, where $\hat{m}_i$ is set to a special symbol (e.g. $\star$) if $i \in \mathbb{T}$, or m_i itself otherwise. The signature consists of $(\hat{vk}, \sigma_0, \sigma_1)$, where σ_0 is a signature on a message $\hat{vk}||\hat{m}$ generated by sk, and σ_1 is a signature on $\hat{vk}||\hat{m}||m$ generated by $\hat{sk}$. Its trapdoor is $\hat{sk}$. We have proven that the TSS scheme is perfectly TRN, which implies that it is perfectly PRV. We have also proven that it is neither INV nor UNL, which implies that it is not SCH. Their proofs are simple, which are given in the full paper.

Our DAMAC-based TSS scheme is perfectly PRV, and (statistically) TRN, UNL, INV and SCH. We obtain Table 1. Our scheme is the first one which has been rigorously proven to achieve either UNL, INV or SCH. We do not compare the schemes in terms of existential unforgeability because its definitions are different in each work. We emphasize that our definition is stronger in the sense that the sanitization-controllability is considered.

Table 1. Comparing our TSS scheme with existing TSS schemes in terms of security. Stat. (Perf.) means statistical (resp. perfect).

Generic const.	TRN	PRV	UNL	INV	SCH	Building blocks
CLM08 [21]	✗	✗	✗	✗	✗	IBCH, Digital Signature
YSL10 [38]	Perf.	Perf.	✗	✗	✗	Digital Signature
Ours	Stat.	Perf.	Stat.	Stat.	Stat.	DAMAC

6 Trapdoor Redactable Signatures (TRS)

Redactable signatures (RS) [35] is a subclass of P-homomorphic signatures [5]. Any signed message can be partially blacked out while maintaining validity of the signature. Unlike (T) SS, alteration is not allowed. In this section, we formally define *trapdoor* RS (TRS), and propose a generic transformation from TSS.

6.1 Our TRS Model

Message space is simply $\{0, 1, *\}^l$ for some integer l, where $*$ denotes a blacked-out bit. Like TSS, it consists of four algorithms {KGen, Sig, Redact, Ver}. Sig takes a message $m \in \{0, 1, *\}^l$ and a set of indices for redactable bits $\mathbb{T} \subseteq \mathbb{I}_0(m) \cup \mathbb{I}_1(m)$. Redact takes a signature on a message m, a redacted message $\overline{m} \in \{0, 1, *\}$ and a set $\overline{\mathbb{T}} \subseteq \mathbb{I}_0(\overline{m}) \cup \mathbb{I}_1(\overline{m})$. The redacted message must satisfy the TRS relation.

Definition 11 (TRS Relation). *$m, \overline{m} \in \{0,1,*\}^l$ are arbitral messages. $\mathbb{T} \subseteq \mathbb{I}_0(m) \cup \mathbb{I}_1(m)$ is an arbitral set of indices for redactable bits.*

$$R_{\mathrm{r}}(m, \overline{m}, \mathbb{T}) := \begin{cases} 1 & (\textit{if } \bigwedge_{i \in [1,l]} [\overline{m}[i] \neq m[i] \implies i \in \mathbb{T} \wedge \overline{m}[i] = *]) \\ 0 & (\textit{otherwise}) \end{cases}$$

We define the same security notions as TSS. To avoid the redundancy, we do not formally describe the security experiments. Among the security notions for TRS, the same implications as TSS hold, c.f. Theorem 5.

$$\begin{array}{ccc} m = 0\,1 * \boxed{0}\,\boxed{1} * & \xrightarrow{\text{transform}} & m' = 01\ 10\ 00\ 01\ 10\ 00 \\ \downarrow \text{redact} & & \downarrow \text{sanitize} \\ \overline{m} = 0\,1 * \boxed{0} * * & \xrightarrow{\text{transform}} & \overline{m}' = 01\ 10\ 00\ 01\ 00\ 00 \end{array}$$

Fig. 3. Redacting $m = 01*01*$ with $\mathbb{T} = \{4, 5\}$ into $\overline{m} = 01*0**$ with $\overline{\mathbb{T}} = \{4\}$ in our TRS scheme. The normal ($\square$) and grey ($\blacksquare$) boxes indicate redactable and sanitizable bits, respectively.

6.2 A Generic Tranformation from TSS

Its technique is similar to the transformation from DIBKEM to wildcarded IBKEM [13]. We use a TSS scheme of message length $2l$. A TRS message $m \in \{0,1,*\}^l$ and a set of indices $\mathbb{T} \subseteq \mathbb{I}_0(m) \cup \mathbb{I}_1(m)$ are transformed into a TSS message $m' \in \{0,1\}^{2l}$ and a set $\mathbb{T}' \subseteq [1, 2l]$ as follows: For each $i \in [1, l]$, $(m'[2i-1], m'[2i])$ are set to $(0, 1)$ if $m[i] = 0$, $(1, 0)$ if $m[i] = 1$, or $(0, 0)$ if $m[i] = *$. $\mathbb{T}'$ is set to $\bigcup_{i \in \mathbb{T} \text{ s.t. } m[i]=0} \{2i\} \bigcup_{i \in \mathbb{T} \text{ s.t. } m[i]=1} \{2i-1\}$.

Figure 3 visualizes a redaction example in our TRS scheme. The TRS scheme is a functionally-restricted TSS scheme with message length $2l$. Thus, for every security notion, the notion of the TRS scheme is straightforwardly implied by the one of the TSS scheme.

Theorem 10. *For any $Z \in$ {wEUF-CMA′, wEUF-CMA, TRN, PRV, UNL, INV′, INV, SCH}, the TRS scheme is Z-secure, if the underlying TSS scheme is Z-secure.*

6.3 Comparison with Existing RS Constructions

Disclosure-controllable RS schemes have been proposed in [24, 32–34]. Either one cannot be unlinkable since there exist eternally-fixed elements in a signature, e.g., committed values [24, 33], document ID [32]. The homomorphic signatures for subset predicates (HSSP) schemes [5, 7] can lead to unlinkable RS schemes.

In HSSP, a message is a set. From a signature on a set M, we can obtain a signature on any subset $M' \subseteq M$. Any HSSP scheme can be transformed into a RS scheme. A RS signature on a message $m = (m_1, \cdots, m_n)$ is an HSSP signature on a set $\bigcup_{i=1}^{n} \{i || m_i\}$. Redacting m_i is excluding $i || m_i$ from the set.

Ahn et al. [5] proposed a transformation from attribute-based encryption (ABE) [11] (with specific properties) into HSSP. Each HSSP signature on a set M is a user secret-key associated with the same set M of the ABE. The ABE scheme must satisfy *key-delegatability*[15] and *key-re-randomizability*[16]. As schemes satisfying the properties, [11,30,37] are picked. Since any of them is perfectly key-re-randomizable, it derives an HSSP scheme with perfect SCH.

Table 2. Comparing our TRS scheme with existing SCH-secure RS schemes. Note: Selec., Adap., Stand., GG, BG, SGD, dBDH, Comp. and DC mean selective, adaptive, standard (model), generic group (model), subgroup decision (problem), decisional bilinear Diffie-Hellman, bilinear groups, composite and disclosure-controllability, respectively.

(T)RS schemes	Privacy	Unlinkability	Context-hiding	Unforgeability			Order of BG	TRS	DC	Invisibility
				Level	Model	Assump.				
ABC+12 [5]w. [11]	Perf. PRV	Perf. UNL	Perf. SCH	Adap.	GG	–	Prime	–	–	–
ABC+12 [5]w. [30]	Perf. PRV	Perf. UNL	Perf. SCH	Adap.	Stand.	SGD	Comp.	–	–	–
ABC+12 [5]w. [37]	Perf. PRV	Perf. UNL	Perf. SCH	Selec.	Stand.	dBDH	Prime	–	–	–
ALP12 [7]	Perf. PRV	Perf. sUNL	Perf. CCH	Adap.	Stand.	q-type	Prime	–	–	–
Ours	Perf. PRV	Stat. UNL	Stat. SCH	Adap.	Stand.	k-Lin.	Prime	✓	✓	Stat. INV

Attrapadung et al. [7] defined *complete* CH (CCH) for P-HS. CCH is stronger than SCH. CCH guarantees that any signature derived from any correct signature (which might have been dishonestly generated) distributes like a fresh signature. Their CCH-secure concrete HSSP scheme is based on two (structure-preserving) signature schemes [4,36] and Groth-Sahai NIWI proof [23].

Remind that, in TSS and TRS, SCH implies UNL, cf. Theorem 5. The same implication must hold for the (ordinary) RS. Thus, the HSSP scheme [5] leads to a RS scheme with perfect SCH and perfect UNL. In the experiments for UNL, every signature queried to $\mathfrak{SanitLR}$ must be one which was (honestly) generated on $\mathfrak{Sig}$, $\mathfrak{Sanit}$ or $\mathfrak{SanitLR}$. We slightly strengthen the experiments for UNL by forcing $\mathfrak{SanitLR}$ to accept any correct signature as input. Let sUNL denote the stronger unlinkability notion defined with the new experiments. It must be obvious that sUNL (for RS) is implied by CCH (for RS). Hence, the HSSP scheme by Attrapadung et al. derives a RS scheme with perfect CCH and perfect sUNL.

The above RS schemes are compared with our DAMAC-based TRS scheme in Table 2. Any RS scheme derived from [5,7] is neither trapdoor RS nor disclosure-controllable, implying it cannot be invisible[17]. Thus, our TRS scheme is not only the first (T)RS scheme which is UNL and disclosure-controllable, but also the first one which is adaptively unforgeable under a static assumption in the standard model based on prime-order bilinear groups.

[15] From a secret-key for a set, we can derive a secret-key for any of its subsets.

[16] The derived secret-key is re-randomized and distributes like a *fresh* secret-key.

[17] This is because that invisibility is a notion meaningful only for disclosure-controllable TRS (or sanitization-controllable TSS) schemes.

A Proof of Theorem 5 (on Six Implications among the Security Notions of TSS)

Each implication holds in either of the statistical and perfect formalizations. For instance, if a TSS scheme is statistically (resp. perfectly) TRN, then it is statistically (resp. perfectly) PRV. In this subsection, we prove only the statistical implications. The perfect ones can be proven analogously.

(1) wEUF-CMA′ $\wedge$ SCH $\Longrightarrow$ wEUF-CMA. Let $\boldsymbol{Expt}_0$ denote the standard wEUF-CMA experiment, i.e., $\boldsymbol{Expt}^{\texttt{wEUF-CMA}}_{\Sigma_{\mathrm{TSS}},\mathcal{A},l}$. Let $q_{\mathsf{z}} \in \mathbb{N}$ denote number that $\mathcal{A}$ uses the sanitizing oracle $\mathfrak{Sanit}$. We introduce some experiments. For $i \in [1, q_{\mathsf{z}}]$, $\boldsymbol{Expt}_i$ is identical to $\boldsymbol{Expt}_{i-1}$ except that on the i-th query to $\mathfrak{Sanit}$ the signature $\overline{\sigma}$ is generated directly by the signing algorithm Sig but not by the sanitizing algorithm Sanit. Let W_i denote the event where $\boldsymbol{Expt}_i$ outputs 1. We obtain $\mathtt{Adv}^{\texttt{wEUF-CMA}}_{\Sigma_{\mathrm{TSS}},\mathcal{A},l}(\lambda) = \Pr[W_0] \leq \sum_{i=1}^{q_{\mathsf{z}}} |\Pr[W_{i-1}] - \Pr[W_i]| + \Pr[W_{q_{\mathsf{z}}}] \leq q_{\mathsf{z}} \cdot \mathtt{Adv}^{\texttt{SCH}}_{\Sigma_{\mathrm{TSS}},\mathcal{B}_1,l}(\lambda) + \mathtt{Adv}^{\texttt{wEUF-CMA}'}_{\Sigma_{\mathrm{TSS}},\mathcal{B}_2,l}(\lambda)$. The last inequality is because of the following two statements. We omit their proofs because they are straightforward.

- For any $i \in [1, q_{\mathsf{z}}]$, there exists a PPTA $\mathcal{B}_1$, $|\Pr[W_{i-1}] - \Pr[W_i]| \leq \mathtt{Adv}^{\texttt{SCH}}_{\Sigma_{\mathrm{TSS}},\mathcal{B}_1,l}(\lambda)$.
- There exists a PPTA $\mathcal{B}_2$, $\Pr[W_{q_{\mathsf{z}}}] \leq \mathtt{Adv}^{\texttt{wEUF-CMA}'}_{\Sigma_{\mathrm{TSS}},\mathcal{B}_2,l}(\lambda)$.

□

(2) INV′ $\wedge$ SCH $\Longrightarrow$ INV. This proof is basically the same as the proof of the first implication (1), which is omitted because of the page restriction. □

(3) TRN $\Longrightarrow$ PRV. We temporarily introduce an experiment $\boldsymbol{Expt}_{temp}$. The experiment is the same as the standard PRV experiment w.r.t. Σ_{TSS} parameterized by $b \in \{0, 1\}$, i.e., $\boldsymbol{Expt}^{\texttt{PRV}}_{\Sigma_{\mathrm{TSS}},\mathcal{A},b}$, except that the signature $\overline{\sigma}$ and its trapdoor $\overline{td}$ on $\mathfrak{SigSanitLR}$ are directly generated by the signing algorithm Sig. The experiment is formally described as follows.

$\boldsymbol{Expt}_{temp}(1^\lambda, l)$:
  $(pk, sk) \leftarrow \mathtt{KGen}(1^\lambda, l)$. **Rtrn** $b' \leftarrow \mathcal{A}^{\mathfrak{SigSanitLR}}(pk, sk)$.

- -

- $\mathfrak{SigSanitLR}(m_0, m_1, \mathbb{T}, \overline{m}, \overline{\mathbb{T}})$:
  Rtrn $\perp$ if $\overline{\mathbb{T}} \not\subseteq \mathbb{T} \vee \exists \beta \in \{0, 1\}$ s.t. $0 \leftarrow R_{\mathsf{s}}(m_\beta, \overline{m}, \mathbb{T})$.
  $(\overline{\sigma}, \overline{td}) \leftarrow \mathtt{Sig}(sk, \overline{m}, \overline{\mathbb{T}})$. **Rtrn** $(\overline{\sigma}, \overline{td})$.

Let W_0 (resp. W_1, W_{temp}) denote the event where $\boldsymbol{Expt}^{\texttt{PRV}}_{\Sigma_{\mathrm{TSS}},\mathcal{A},0}$ (resp. $\boldsymbol{Expt}^{\texttt{PRV}}_{\Sigma_{\mathrm{TSS}},\mathcal{A},0}$, $\boldsymbol{Expt}_{temp}$) outputs 1. By the triangle inequality, we obtain $\mathtt{Adv}^{\texttt{PRV}}_{\Sigma_{\mathrm{TSS}},\mathcal{A},l} = |\Pr[W_0] - \Pr[W_1]| \leq |\Pr[W_0] - \Pr[W_{temp}]| + |\Pr[W_{temp}] - \Pr[W_1]|$. Obviously, if we can prove that $\forall b \in \{0, 1\}$, $\exists$ a PPT simulator $\mathcal{B}_b$ s.t. $|\Pr[W_b] - \Pr[W_{temp}]| = \mathtt{Adv}^{\texttt{TRN}}_{\Sigma_{\mathrm{TSS}},\mathcal{B}_b,l}(\lambda)$, then the proof of the theorem is done. The simulator $\mathcal{B}_b$ uses $\mathcal{A}$ which tries to distinguish $\boldsymbol{Expt}^{\texttt{PRV}}_{\Sigma_{\mathrm{TSS}},\mathcal{A},b}$ from $\boldsymbol{Expt}_{temp}$ as a sub-routine to distinguish the TRN experiments. $\mathcal{B}_b$ behaves as follows.

$\mathcal{B}_b^{\mathfrak{Sanit}/\mathfrak{Sig}'}(pk, sk)$: // $(pk, sk) \leftarrow \mathtt{KGen}(1^\lambda, l)$.
Rtrn $b' \leftarrow \mathcal{A}^{\mathfrak{SigSanitLR}}(pk, sk)$.

- -

- $\mathfrak{SigSanitLR}(m_0, m_1, \mathbb{T}, \overline{m}, \overline{\mathbb{T}})$:
  Rtrn $\perp$ if $\overline{\mathbb{T}} \not\subseteq \mathbb{T} \vee \exists \beta \in \{0,1\}$ s.t. $0 \leftarrow R_s(m_\beta, \overline{m}, \mathbb{T})$.
  $(\overline{\sigma}, \overline{td}) \leftarrow \mathfrak{Sanit}/\mathfrak{Sig}'(m_b, \mathbb{T}, \overline{m}, \overline{\mathbb{T}})$. **Rtrn** $(\overline{\sigma}, \overline{td})$.

Firstly, let us consider the case where the TRN experiment is the first one parameterized by 0, i.e., $\boldsymbol{Expt}^{\mathtt{TRN}}_{\Sigma_{\mathrm{TSS}},\mathcal{B}_b,0}$. In this case, $\mathcal{B}_b$ unconsciously perfectly simulates the PRV experiment, i.e., $\boldsymbol{Expt}^{\mathtt{PRV}}_{\Sigma_{\mathrm{TSS}},\mathcal{A},b}$, to $\mathcal{A}$. Since $\mathcal{B}_b$ directly outputs what $\mathcal{A}$ outputs, it holds that $\Pr[W_b] = \Pr[1 \leftarrow \boldsymbol{Expt}^{\mathtt{TRN}}_{\Sigma_{\mathrm{TSS}},\mathcal{B}_b,0}(1^\lambda, l)]$. Secondly, let us consider the case where the TRN experiment is the second one parameterized by 1, i.e., $\boldsymbol{Expt}^{\mathtt{TRN}}_{\Sigma_{\mathrm{TSS}},\mathcal{B}_b,1}$. In this case, $\mathcal{B}_b$ perfectly simulates $\boldsymbol{Expt}_{temp}$ to $\mathcal{A}$. It holds that $\Pr[W_{temp}] = \Pr[1 \leftarrow \boldsymbol{Expt}^{\mathtt{TRN}}_{\Sigma_{\mathrm{TSS}},\mathcal{B}_b,1}(1^\lambda, l)]$. □

(4) UNL $\Longrightarrow$ PRV. The standard PRV experiment parameterized by $b \in \{0,1\}$ is denoted by $\boldsymbol{Expt}_b$. Let W_b denote the event where $\boldsymbol{Expt}_b$ outputs 1. We prove that there exists a PPT simulator $\mathcal{B}$ such that $\mathtt{Adv}^{\mathtt{PRV}}_{\Sigma_{\mathrm{TSS}},\mathcal{A},l}(\lambda) = |\Pr[W_0] - \Pr[W_1]| = \mathtt{Adv}^{\mathtt{UNL}}_{\Sigma_{\mathrm{TSS}},\mathcal{B},l}(\lambda)$. The simulator $\mathcal{B}$ uses $\mathcal{A}$ which tries to distinguish the PRV experiments as a sub-routine to distinguish the UNL experiments.

$\mathcal{B}^{\mathfrak{Sig}',\mathfrak{Sanit}',\mathfrak{SanitLR}'}(pk, sk)$: // $(pk, sk) \leftarrow \mathtt{KGen}(1^\lambda, l)$.
Rtrn $b' \leftarrow \mathcal{A}^{\mathfrak{SigSanitLR}}(pk, sk)$.

- -

- $\mathfrak{SigSanitLR}(m_0, m_1, \mathbb{T}, \overline{m}, \overline{\mathbb{T}})$:
  Rtrn $\perp$ if $\overline{\mathbb{T}} \not\subseteq \mathbb{T} \vee \exists \beta \in \{0,1\}$ s.t. $0 \leftarrow R_s(m_\beta, \overline{m}, \mathbb{T})$.
  $(\sigma_0, td_0) \leftarrow \mathfrak{Sig}'(sk, m_0, \mathbb{T})$. $(\sigma_1, td_1) \leftarrow \mathfrak{Sig}'(sk, m_1, \mathbb{T})$.
  $(\overline{\sigma}, \overline{td}) \leftarrow \mathfrak{SanitLR}'(m_0, \mathbb{T}, \sigma_0, td_0, m_1, \mathbb{T}, \sigma_1, td_1, \overline{m}, \overline{\mathbb{T}})$. **Rtrn** $(\overline{\sigma}, \overline{td})$.

If the UNL experiment is $\boldsymbol{Expt}^{\mathtt{UNL}}_{\Sigma_{\mathrm{TSS}},\mathcal{B},0}$, then $\mathcal{B}$ perfectly simulates $\boldsymbol{Expt}^{\mathtt{PRV}}_{\Sigma_{\mathrm{TSS}},\mathcal{A},0}$ to $\mathcal{A}$. Since $\mathcal{B}$ directly outputs what $\mathcal{A}$ outputs, $\Pr[W_0] = \Pr[1 \leftarrow \boldsymbol{Expt}^{\mathtt{UNL}}_{\Sigma_{\mathrm{TSS}},\mathcal{B},0}(1^\lambda, l)]$. Analogously, we obtain $\Pr[W_1] = \Pr[1 \leftarrow \boldsymbol{Expt}^{\mathtt{UNL}}_{\Sigma_{\mathrm{TSS}},\mathcal{B},1}(1^\lambda, l)]$. □

(5) SCH $\Longrightarrow$ TRN. In this proof, $q_{\mathsf{zs}} \in \mathbb{N}$ denotes total number that $\mathcal{A}$ uses the oracle of $\mathfrak{Sanit}/\mathfrak{Sig}$. For each $i \in [0, q_{\mathsf{zs}}]$, we define an experiment $\boldsymbol{Expt}_i$. $\boldsymbol{Expt}_0$ is identical to the standard TRN experiment parameterized by $b = 0$. For $i \in [1, q_{\mathsf{zs}}]$, $\boldsymbol{Expt}_i$ is identical to $\boldsymbol{Expt}_{i-1}$ except that on the i-th query to $\mathfrak{Sanit}/\mathfrak{Sig}$ a pair $(\overline{\sigma}, \overline{td})$ of signature and trapdoor is directly generated by the algorithm of Sig, i.e., $(\overline{\sigma}, \overline{td}) \leftarrow \mathtt{Sig}(sk, \overline{m}, \overline{\mathbb{T}})$. Obviously, $\boldsymbol{Expt}_{q_{\mathsf{zs}}}$ is identical to the standard TRN experiment parameterized by $b = 1$. We obtain $\mathtt{Adv}^{\mathtt{TRN}}_{\Sigma_{\mathrm{TSS}},\mathcal{A},l}(\lambda) = |\Pr[1 \leftarrow \boldsymbol{Expt}_0(1^\lambda, l)] - \Pr[1 \leftarrow \boldsymbol{Expt}_{q_{\mathsf{zs}}}(1^\lambda, l)]| \leq \sum_{i=1}^{q_{\mathsf{zs}}} |\Pr[1 \leftarrow \boldsymbol{Expt}_{i-1}(1^\lambda, l)] - \Pr[1 \leftarrow \boldsymbol{Expt}_i(1^\lambda, l)]| \leq q_{\mathsf{zs}} \cdot \mathtt{Adv}^{\mathtt{SCH}}_{\Sigma_{\mathrm{TSS}},\mathcal{B},l}(\lambda)$. The last transformation is because of the fact that for every i there exists a probabilistic algorithm $\mathcal{B}$ s.t. $|\Pr[1 \leftarrow \boldsymbol{Expt}_{i-1}(1^\lambda, l)] - \Pr[1 \leftarrow \boldsymbol{Expt}_i(1^\lambda, l)]| \leq \mathtt{Adv}^{\mathtt{SCH}}_{\Sigma_{\mathrm{TSS}},\mathcal{B},l}(\lambda)$. We omit its proof because it is straightforward. □

(6) SCH $\Longrightarrow$ UNL. In this proof, the standard UNL experiment parameterized by $b \in \{0,1\}$ is shortly denoted by $\boldsymbol{Expt}_{b,0}$. Let $q_{\mathsf{z}}, q'_{\mathsf{z}} \in \mathbb{N}$ denote total number

that $\mathcal{A}$ uses the oracles of $\mathfrak{Sanit}$ and $\mathfrak{SanitLR}$, respectively. For $i \in [1, q_z + q_z']$, $\boldsymbol{Expt}_{b,i}$ denotes an experiment which is the same as $\boldsymbol{Expt}_{b,i-1}$ except that on the i-th query to $\mathfrak{Sanit}$ or $\mathfrak{SanitLR}$ a sanitized signature $\overline{\sigma}$ and its trapdoor $\overline{td}$ are directly generated by $\mathtt{Sig}$. For $b \in \{0,1\}$, $i \in [0, q_z + q_z']$, $W_{b,i}$ denotes the event where $\boldsymbol{Expt}_{b,i}$ outputs 1. We obtain $\mathtt{Adv}^{\mathtt{UNL}}_{\Sigma_{\mathrm{TSS}},\mathcal{A},l}(\lambda) = |\Pr[W_{0,0}] - \Pr[W_{1,0}]| \leq \sum_{b=0}^{1} \sum_{i=1}^{q_z+q_z'} |\Pr[W_{b,i-1}] - \Pr[W_{b,i}]| \leq 2(q_z + q_z') \cdot \mathtt{Adv}^{\mathtt{SCH}}_{\Sigma_{\mathrm{TSS}},\mathcal{B},l}(\lambda)$. We used the following statement, which can be proven straightforwardly.

- For each $b \in \{0,1\}$ and each $i \in [1, q_z + q_z']$, there exists a probabilistic algorithm $\mathcal{B}$ s.t. $|\Pr[W_{b,i-1}] - \Pr[W_{b,i}]| \leq \mathtt{Adv}^{\mathtt{SCH}}_{\Sigma_{\mathrm{TSS}},\mathcal{B},l}(\lambda)$.

□

References

1. Abdalla, M., et al.: Wildcarded identity-based encryption. J. Cryptol. **24**(1), 42–82 (2011)
2. Abdalla, M., Catalano, D., Dent, A.W., Malone-Lee, J., Neven, G., Smart, N.P.: Identity-based encryption gone wild. In: Bugliesi, M., Preneel, B., Sassone, V., Wegener, I. (eds.) ICALP 2006. LNCS, vol. 4052, pp. 300–311. Springer, Heidelberg (2006). https://doi.org/10.1007/11787006_26
3. Abdalla, M., Kiltz, E., Neven, G.: Generalized key delegation for hierarchical identity-based encryption. In: Biskup, J., López, J. (eds.) ESORICS 2007. LNCS, vol. 4734, pp. 139–154. Springer, Heidelberg (2007). https://doi.org/10.1007/978-3-540-74835-9_10
4. Abe, M., Fuchsbauer, G., Groth, J., Haralambiev, K., Ohkubo, M.: Structure-preserving signatures and commitments to group elements. In: Rabin, T. (ed.) CRYPTO 2010. LNCS, vol. 6223, pp. 209–236. Springer, Heidelberg (2010). https://doi.org/10.1007/978-3-642-14623-7_12
5. Ahn, J.H., Boneh, D., Camenisch, J., Hohenberger, S., shelat, A., Waters, B.: Computing on authenticated data. In: Cramer, R. (ed.) TCC 2012. LNCS, vol. 7194, pp. 1–20. Springer, Heidelberg (2012). https://doi.org/10.1007/978-3-642-28914-9_1
6. Ateniese, G., Chou, D.H., de Medeiros, B., Tsudik, G.: Sanitizable signatures. In: di Vimercati, S.C., Syverson, P., Gollmann, D. (eds.) ESORICS 2005. LNCS, vol. 3679, pp. 159–177. Springer, Heidelberg (2005). https://doi.org/10.1007/11555827_10
7. Attrapadung, N., Libert, B., Peters, T.: Computing on authenticated data: new privacy definitions and constructions. In: Wang, X., Sako, K. (eds.) ASIACRYPT 2012. LNCS, vol. 7658, pp. 367–385. Springer, Heidelberg (2012). https://doi.org/10.1007/978-3-642-34961-4_23
8. Attrapadung, N., Libert, B., Peters, T.: Efficient completely context-hiding quotable and linearly homomorphic signatures. In: Kurosawa, K., Hanaoka, G. (eds.) PKC 2013. LNCS, vol. 7778, pp. 386–404. Springer, Heidelberg (2013). https://doi.org/10.1007/978-3-642-36362-7_24
9. Bellare, M., Goldwasser, S.: New paradigms for digital signatures and message authentication based on non-interactive zero knowledge proofs. In: Brassard, G. (ed.) CRYPTO 1989. LNCS, vol. 435, pp. 194–211. Springer, New York (1990). https://doi.org/10.1007/0-387-34805-0_19

10. Bethencourt, J., Boneh, D., Waters, B.: Cryptographic methods for storing ballots on a voting machine. In: NDSS 2007, pp. 209–222 (2007)
11. Bethencourt, J., Sahai, A., Waters, B.: Ciphertext-policy attribute-based encryption. In: IEEE SP 2007, pp. 321–334. IEEE (2007)
12. Birkett, J., Dent, A.W., Neven, G., Schuldt, J.C.N.: Efficient chosen-ciphertext secure identity-based encryption with wildcards. In: Pieprzyk, J., Ghodosi, H., Dawson, E. (eds.) ACISP 2007. LNCS, vol. 4586, pp. 274–292. Springer, Heidelberg (2007). https://doi.org/10.1007/978-3-540-73458-1_21
13. Blazy, O., Germouty, P., Phan, D.H.: Downgradable identity-based encryption and applications. In: Matsui, M. (ed.) CT-RSA 2019. LNCS, vol. 11405, pp. 44–61. Springer, Cham (2019). https://doi.org/10.1007/978-3-030-12612-4_3
14. Blazy, O., Kiltz, E., Pan, J.: (Hierarchical) identity-based encryption from affine message authentication. In: Garay, J.A., Gennaro, R. (eds.) CRYPTO 2014. LNCS, vol. 8616, pp. 408–425. Springer, Heidelberg (2014). https://doi.org/10.1007/978-3-662-44371-2_23
15. Boneh, D., Boyen, X., Goh, E.-J.: Hierarchical identity based encryption with constant size ciphertext. In: Cramer, R. (ed.) EUROCRYPT 2005. LNCS, vol. 3494, pp. 440–456. Springer, Heidelberg (2005). https://doi.org/10.1007/11426639_26
16. Boyen, X., Waters, B.: Anonymous hierarchical identity-based encryption (without random oracles). In: Dwork, C. (ed.) CRYPTO 2006. LNCS, vol. 4117, pp. 290–307. Springer, Heidelberg (2006). https://doi.org/10.1007/11818175_17
17. Brzuska, C., et al.: Security of sanitizable signatures revisited. In: Jarecki, S., Tsudik, G. (eds.) PKC 2009. LNCS, vol. 5443, pp. 317–336. Springer, Heidelberg (2009). https://doi.org/10.1007/978-3-642-00468-1_18
18. Brzuska, C., Fischlin, M., Lehmann, A., Schröder, D.: Unlinkability of sanitizable signatures. In: Nguyen, P.Q., Pointcheval, D. (eds.) PKC 2010. LNCS, vol. 6056, pp. 444–461. Springer, Heidelberg (2010). https://doi.org/10.1007/978-3-642-13013-7_26
19. Bultel, X., Lafourcade, P., Lai, R.W.F., Malavolta, G., Schröder, D., Thyagarajan, S.A.K.: Efficient invisible and unlinkable sanitizable signatures. In: Lin, D., Sako, K. (eds.) PKC 2019. LNCS, vol. 11442, pp. 159–189. Springer, Cham (2019). https://doi.org/10.1007/978-3-030-17253-4_6
20. Camenisch, J., Derler, D., Krenn, S., Pöhls, H.C., Samelin, K., Slamanig, D.: Chameleon-hashes with ephemeral trapdoors. In: Fehr, S. (ed.) PKC 2017. LNCS, vol. 10175, pp. 152–182. Springer, Heidelberg (2017). https://doi.org/10.1007/978-3-662-54388-7_6
21. Canard, S., Laguillaumie, F., Milhau, M.: *Trapdoor* sanitizable signatures and their application to content protection. In: Bellovin, S.M., Gennaro, R., Keromytis, A., Yung, M. (eds.) ACNS 2008. LNCS, vol. 5037, pp. 258–276. Springer, Heidelberg (2008). https://doi.org/10.1007/978-3-540-68914-0_16
22. Escala, A., Herold, G., Kiltz, E., Ràfols, C., Villar, J.: An algebraic framework for Diffie-Hellman assumptions. In: Canetti, R., Garay, J.A. (eds.) CRYPTO 2013. LNCS, vol. 8043, pp. 129–147. Springer, Heidelberg (2013). https://doi.org/10.1007/978-3-642-40084-1_8
23. Groth, J., Sahai, A.: Efficient non-interactive proof systems for bilinear groups. In: Smart, N. (ed.) EUROCRYPT 2008. LNCS, vol. 4965, pp. 415–432. Springer, Heidelberg (2008). https://doi.org/10.1007/978-3-540-78967-3_24
24. Haber, S., et al.: Efficient signature schemes supporting redaction, pseudonymization, and data deidentification. In: AsiaCCS 2008, pp. 353–362. ACM (2008)

25. Kiltz, E., Mityagin, A., Panjwani, S., Raghavan, B.: Append-only signatures. In: Caires, L., Italiano, G.F., Monteiro, L., Palamidessi, C., Yung, M. (eds.) ICALP 2005. LNCS, vol. 3580, pp. 434–445. Springer, Heidelberg (2005). https://doi.org/10.1007/11523468_36
26. Kiltz, E., Neven, G.: Identity-based signatures. Identity-Based Cryptogr. **2**(31), 75 (2009)
27. Krawczyk, H., Rabin, T.: Chameleon hashing and signatures. In: NDSS 2000, pp. 143–154 (2000)
28. Langrehr, R., Pan, J.: Tightly secure hierarchical identity-based encryption. In: Lin, D., Sako, K. (eds.) PKC 2019. LNCS, vol. 11442, pp. 436–465. Springer, Cham (2019). https://doi.org/10.1007/978-3-030-17253-4_15
29. Langrehr, R., Pan, J.: Hierarchical identity-based encryption with tight multi-challenge security. In: Kiayias, A., Kohlweiss, M., Wallden, P., Zikas, V. (eds.) PKC 2020. LNCS, vol. 12110, pp. 153–183. Springer, Cham (2020). https://doi.org/10.1007/978-3-030-45374-9_6
30. Lewko, A., Okamoto, T., Sahai, A., Takashima, K., Waters, B.: Fully secure functional encryption: attribute-based encryption and (hierarchical) inner product encryption. In: Gilbert, H. (ed.) EUROCRYPT 2010. LNCS, vol. 6110, pp. 62–91. Springer, Heidelberg (2010). https://doi.org/10.1007/978-3-642-13190-5_4
31. Libert, B., Joye, M., Yung, M., Peters, T.: Secure efficient history-hiding append-only signatures in the standard model. In: Katz, J. (ed.) PKC 2015. LNCS, vol. 9020, pp. 450–473. Springer, Heidelberg (2015). https://doi.org/10.1007/978-3-662-46447-2_20
32. Miyazaki, K., Hanaoka, G., Imai, H.: Digitally signed document sanitizing scheme based on bilinear maps. In: AsiaCCS 2006, pp. 343–354. ACM (2006)
33. Miyazaki, K., et al.: Digitally signed document sanitizing scheme with disclosure condition control. IEICE Trans. **88-A**(1), 239–246 (2005)
34. Samelin, K., Pöhls, H.C., Bilzhause, A., Posegga, J., de Meer, H.: Redactable signatures for independent removal of structure and content. In: Ryan, M.D., Smyth, B., Wang, G. (eds.) ISPEC 2012. LNCS, vol. 7232, pp. 17–33. Springer, Heidelberg (2012). https://doi.org/10.1007/978-3-642-29101-2_2
35. Steinfeld, R., Bull, L., Zheng, Y.: Content extraction signatures. In: Kim, K. (ed.) ICISC 2001. LNCS, vol. 2288, pp. 285–304. Springer, Heidelberg (2002). https://doi.org/10.1007/3-540-45861-1_22
36. Waters, B.: Efficient identity-based encryption without random oracles. In: Cramer, R. (ed.) EUROCRYPT 2005. LNCS, vol. 3494, pp. 114–127. Springer, Heidelberg (2005). https://doi.org/10.1007/11426639_7
37. Waters, B.: Ciphertext-policy attribute-based encryption: an expressive, efficient, and provably secure realization. In: Catalano, D., Fazio, N., Gennaro, R., Nicolosi, A. (eds.) PKC 2011. LNCS, vol. 6571, pp. 53–70. Springer, Heidelberg (2011). https://doi.org/10.1007/978-3-642-19379-8_4
38. Yum, D.H., Seo, J.W., Lee, P.J.: Trapdoor sanitizable signatures made easy. In: Zhou, J., Yung, M. (eds.) ACNS 2010. LNCS, vol. 6123, pp. 53–68. Springer, Heidelberg (2010). https://doi.org/10.1007/978-3-642-13708-2_4

Group Testing Aggregate Signatures with Soundness

Shingo Sato[1(✉)], Junji Shikata[1,2], and Tsutomu Matsumoto[1,2]

[1] Institute of Advanced Sciences, Yokohama National University, Yokohama, Japan
{sato-shingo-zk,shikata-junji-rb,tsutomu}@ynu.ac.jp
[2] Graduate School of Environment and Information Sciences, Yokohama National University, Yokohama, Japan

Abstract. In this paper, we comprehensively study group testing aggregate signatures that have functionality of both keyless aggregation of multiple signatures and identifying an invalid message from the aggregate signature, in order to reduce a total amount of signature-size for lots of messages. Our contribution is (i) to formalize strong security notions including soundness for group testing aggregate signatures by taking into account related work such as fault-tolerant aggregate signatures and non-interactive aggregate MACs with detecting functionality (i.e., symmetric case); (ii) to construct group testing aggregate signatures from aggregate signatures in a generic and comprehensive way; and (iii) to present an aggregate signature scheme which we can apply to our generic construction of group testing aggregate signatures with the formalized security.

Keywords: Aggregate signature · Digital signature · Group testing

1 Introduction

Background and Related Work. Digital signature is a fundamental and important primitive in modern cryptography, and it has a wide range of applications that require integrity of data. In the era of IoT (Internet of Things), it is important to ensure integrity of data gathered from many and various IoT devices, however, it is often the case where a total amount of size of signatures for checking validity of big data is too large. An aggregate signature scheme allows any user to compress multiple signatures into a short signature (called an aggregate signature) and can reduce signature-size on an insecure channel. Thus, there are many applications such as sensor network data (with IoT), secure BGP protocols, and block chain protocols. From this viewpoint, we study techniques for the purpose of reducing a total amount of signature-size for many and various data, in particular, techniques of compressing (or aggregating) multiple signatures on data.

For the purpose mentioned above, Boneh et al. [3] proposed aggregate signatures and proposed a pairing-based scheme in the random oracle model (ROM). Assuming the weaker security model (i.e., certified-key model) in which signers have to prove knowledge of the secret key at key-registration, Rückert and

S.-H. Seo and H. Seo (Eds.): ICISC 2022, LNCS 13849, pp. 363–381, 2023.
https://doi.org/10.1007/978-3-031-29371-9_18

Schröder gave an aggregate signature scheme using multilinear maps in the standard model [21]. Gentry and Ramzan dealt with the identity-based setting so that not only signature-size but also verification key-size can be reduced, and then proposed an identity-based aggregate signature scheme (with pairing) in the ROM [10]. Hohenberger, Sahai, and Waters presented (identity-based) aggregate signature schemes using multilinear maps in the standard model [13].

Hartung et al. [11] introduced the notion of fault-tolerant aggregate signatures, that has functionality of both compressing multiple signatures and identifying an invalid message from the aggregate signature, and they proposed a generic construction starting from any aggregate signature scheme and cover-free family. However, their scheme does not guarantee the property of identifying valid and invalid message-signature pairs correctly, if an adversary generates message-signature pairs so that the aggregate signature scheme incorrectly identifies these pairs. Hence, in this paper, we deal with this by formalizing a security notion *identifiability*.

Regarding aggregate authentication in the symmetric key setting, Katz and Lindell introduced the notion of aggregate message authentication code (AMAC) that can compress MAC-tags on multiple messages into a short aggregate tag, and they proposed a generic construction using any MAC scheme [15]. Minematsu studied a MAC scheme with combinatorial group testing [7], and this can be seen as an AMAC with keyed aggregation, which has the functionality of identifying an invalid message from the aggregate tag [17]. Hirose and Shikata proposed AMAC that has the functionality of both compressing multiple MAC-tags into a short aggregate tag and identifying an invalid message from the aggregate tag [12]. In [12], the model considers keyless aggregation like in [15], and the scheme is constructed from non-adaptive group testing in addition to the underlying MAC scheme in a generic way. Related work by applying non-adaptive group testing in symmetric-key cryptography includes [18,19,22]. In addition, Sato and Shikata [23,24] consider an interactive version of [12], and they constructed the interactive protocol from adaptive group testing in addition to the underlying MAC.

Contribution. In this paper, we comprehensively study aggregate signatures with detecting functionality (called group testing aggregate signatures), that have functionality of both keyless aggregation of multiple signatures and identifying an invalid message from the aggregate signature, in order to reduce a total amount of signature-size for lots of messages. The goal of this paper is to provide a group testing aggregate signature scheme which achieves strong security notions considering related work mentioned above, especially for [11,12,23,24]. To this end, we formalize the model and security notions for (non-adaptive) group testing aggregate signatures. In addition, we present construction methodology for group testing aggregate signatures with the formalized security in a generic and comprehensive way. Details on our contribution are as follows.

I. In Sect. 2.2, we revisit the security of conventional aggregate signatures and introduce a new security notion called *soundness*. We deal with this property in order to extend a security notion called *identifiability* (concretely, ident-soundness

Table 1. Comparison of GT-ASIG schemes: Soundness and Weak-Soundness mean ident-soundness and ident-weak-soundness (see Definition 9), respectively. ROM means the random oracle model. Standard model means the model without random oracles. (M)CDH means the (multilinear) computational Diffie-Hellman assumption. ℓ (resp. d) is the total number of messages (resp. the maximum number of invalid messages). $|\sigma|$ is the bit-length of the signature generated by the signing algorithm of an aggregate signature scheme. $|r|$ is the bit-length of the randomness used by the aggregation algorithm of our aggregate signature scheme with soundness.

Scheme	Identifiability Soundness ?	Standard Model?	Assumption	Total aggregate Signature-Size
$\text{HKKKR}_{\text{BGLS}}$	Weak-Soundness	ROM	CDH	$O(d^2 \log \ell)\|\sigma\|$
$\text{HKKKR}_{\text{HSW}}$	Weak-Soundness	✓	MCDH	$O(d^2 \log \ell)\|\sigma\|$
Our GT-ASIG	✓	ROM	CDH	$O(d^2 \log \ell)(\|\sigma\| + \|r\|)$

defined in Sect. 2.3) for group testing aggregate signatures. In addition, the soundness property is also useful to achieve the functionality of batch verification [1,5,9].

II. In Sect. 2.3, we propose a formal model and security formalization of non-adaptive group testing aggregate signatures (GT-ASIG) that have functionality of both keyless aggregation of multiple signatures and identifying an invalid message from the aggregate signature. A similar functionality was proposed in fault-tolerant aggregate signatures in [11], however, the functionality of fault tolerant aggregate signatures guarantees that valid messages must be regarded as valid from the aggregate signature even if some fault occurs, just like the property of error-correcting codes. On the other hand, GT-ASIG in this paper guarantees that, from the aggregate signature, (i) valid messages must be regarded as valid (ident-completeness); and (ii) invalid messages must be regarded as invalid (ident-soundness), even in presence of malicious adversary in the chosen-key security model of [3]. Namely, *identifiability* consists of ident-completeness and ident-soundness; and ident-soundness can be weakened as ident-weak-soundness. To formalize these security notions, we take into account the similar notion in the symmetric-key setting in [12].

III. In Sect. 3, we propose a generic construction for GT-ASIG starting from an aggregate signature scheme, and we show that the resulting GT-ASIG meets unforgeability, ident-completeness, and ident-soundness (resp. unforgeability, ident-completeness, and ident-weak-soundness) if the underlying aggregate signature scheme fulfills both unforgeability and soundness in Definition 5 (resp. only unforgeability). Furthermore, we present an aggregate signature scheme satisfying both unforgeability and soundness, in order to obtain a concrete GT-ASIG scheme satisfying the formalized security notions including ident-soundness. This aggregate signature scheme is given by modifying the aggregate signature scheme of [3]. Hence, we can obtain the first GT-ASIG scheme satisfying all the formalized security notions: unforgeability, ident-completeness, and ident-soundness.

Comparison of GT-ASIG Schemes. We compare our work with the existing one [11] since a fault-tolerant aggregate signatures can be seen as a GT-ASIG. Table 1 shows this comparison. $\text{HKKKR}_{\mathsf{BGLS}}$ (resp. $\text{HKKKR}_{\mathsf{HSW}}$) means the fault-tolerant aggregate signature scheme constructed by applying the aggregate signature scheme of [3] (resp. [13]) to the generic construction of [11]. Our GT-ASIG means the GT-ASIG scheme obtained by applying our aggregate signature scheme with soundness (proposed in Sect. 3.2) to our generic construction of GT-ASIG.

From Table 1, the main advantage of our scheme is to achieve a stronger security notion (i.e., ident-soundness) by just adding randomness as a component of an aggregate signature. In addition, ours does not need any additional computational assumption. The disadvantage of ours is to achieve security under the ROM while $\text{HKKKR}_{\mathsf{HSW}}$ is secure under the standard model. However, the computational assumption of $\text{HKKKR}_{\mathsf{HSW}}$ is stronger. In addition, we achieve the goal in this paper since our scheme satisfies a stronger security notion compared to the existing ones.

2 Preliminaries

Notation. In this paper, we use the following notation: For a positive integer n, let $[n] := \{1, \dots, n\}$. For a function $f : \mathbb{N} \to \mathbb{R}$, if $f(\lambda) = o(\lambda^{-c})$ for arbitrary positive c, then f is negligible in λ, and we write $\mathsf{negl}(\lambda)$. A probability is overwhelming if it is $1 - \mathsf{negl}(\lambda)$. *Probabilistic polynomial-time* is abbreviated as PPT.

Sets and Sequences. For n values $x_1, \dots, x_n$ and a subset $I \subseteq [n]$ of indexes, let $(x_i)_{i \in I}$ be a sequence of elements whose indexes are in I, and let $\{x_i\}_{i \in I}$ be a set of elements whose indexes are in I.

Vectors and Matrices. For a vector $\boldsymbol{x}$ with dimension n, let x_i be the i-th entry ($i \in [n]$). For a $m \times n$ matrix $\boldsymbol{X}$, let $x_{i,j}$ be the entry at the i-th row and the j-th column ($i \in [m]$, $j \in [n]$).

In addition, we describe definitions of several cryptographic primitives.

2.1 Group Testing Protocol

The first paper about group testing is published by Dorfman [6]. Group testing (e.g., [7]) is a method to detect positive items called *defectives* among many whole items with a small number of tests than the trivial individual testing for each item. The applications of group testing include screening blood samples for detecting a disease, and detecting clones which have a particular DNA sequence.

The group testing techniques are classified into two types: the first type means the testing techniques by non-adaptive strategies, called non-adaptive group testing [8,20,25], and the second type means the techniques by adaptive strategies, called adaptive group testing (or called sequential group testing) [6, 8,14,16]. Suppose that there are totally ℓ items of which there are (at most) d

defectives. In non-adaptive group testing, we need to know d beforehand and to select all the subsets of ℓ items to be tested without knowing the results of other tests. On the other hand, in adaptive group testing, we do tests several times such that we can select a subset of items to be tested after observing the result of the previous test. In this paper, we focus on non-adaptive group testing. This is because non-adaptive group testing can run all tests simultaneously, since all test-designs are determined in advance. On the other hand, adaptive group testing cannot execute all tests at the same time, since each test-design depends on the result of the previous test. To sum up, non-adaptive group testing is much better than adaptive one, in terms of time-complexity.

Non-adaptive group testing is typically designed by providing a d-disjunct matrix, a d-cover-free family, or a d-separable matrix (e.g., see [7]). And, a non-adaptive group testing protocol with u tests for ℓ items is represented by a $u \times \ell$ binary matrix, and the (i, j)-th element of the matrix is equal to 1 if and only if the i-th test is executed to the j-th item. Among such matrices for representing non-adaptive group testing, a disjunct matrix (or cover-free family) is well studied in combinatorics and bioinformatics, and it is defined as follows.

Definition 1 (d-disjunct). *A matrix $\boldsymbol{G} = [\boldsymbol{g}_1, \ldots, \boldsymbol{g}_\ell] \in \{0,1\}^{u \times \ell}$ is d-disjunct if for any d columns $\boldsymbol{g}_{s_1}, \ldots, \boldsymbol{g}_{s_d}$ and every $\bar{\boldsymbol{g}} \in \{\boldsymbol{g}_1, \ldots, \boldsymbol{g}_\ell\} \backslash \{\boldsymbol{g}_{s_1}, \ldots, \boldsymbol{g}_{s_d}\}$ $(s_1, \ldots, s_d \in [\ell])$, there exists $z \in [u]$ such that $v_z < \bar{g}_z$, where let $\boldsymbol{v} = \bigvee_{i=1}^{d} \boldsymbol{g}_{s_i}$, and $\bigvee$ is the bitwise-OR.*

By using a d-disjunct matrix, a non-adaptive group testing protocol can efficiently detect at most d positive items (defectives). We simply describe the process of group testing protocol with a d-disjunct matrix $\boldsymbol{G} \in \{0,1\}^{u \times \ell}$ as follows: Let $S_i(\boldsymbol{G}) = \{j \mid j \in [\ell] \wedge g_{i,j} = 1\}$ for $i \in [u]$ and $\boldsymbol{G} \in \{0,1\}^{u \times \ell}$. We assume that if multiple items including at least one positive item (defective) are compressed, the test outcome of the compressed item shows positive, and otherwise the test outcome shows negative.

1. Let $J \leftarrow \{1, 2, \ldots, \ell\}$ be a set of indexes of all items.
2. For each $i \in [u]$, compress items with indexes in $S_i(\boldsymbol{G})$.
3. For each $i \in [u]$, set $J \leftarrow J \backslash S_i(\boldsymbol{G})$ if the test result of the i-th compressed item shows negative.
4. Output J, which is the set of all defectives' indexes due to the d-disjunct property of $\boldsymbol{G}$.

In this paper, we mainly deal with non-adaptive group testing based on disjunct matrices and its application to GT-ASIG introduced in Sect. 2.3, however, other types of non-adaptive group testing such as separable matrices can be applied to GT-ASIG in a similar way. We note that the number of tests required in non-adaptive group testing using d-disjunct matrices is $O(d^2 \log \ell)$ (see [7]), and it is expected that the number of signatures can be reduced to $O(d^2 \log \ell)$ in GT-ASIG instead of checking ℓ signatures.

2.2 Aggregate Signatures

In this section, we describe the definitions of aggregate signatures and introduce a new security notion called *soundness*.

Definition 2. *An aggregate signature scheme consists of five polynomial-time algorithms* $(\mathsf{KGen}, \mathsf{Sign}, \mathsf{Vrfy}, \mathsf{Agg}, \mathsf{AVrfy})$*: For a security parameter* λ*, let* $\mathcal{M} = \mathcal{M}(\lambda)$ *be a message space.*

- $(\mathsf{pk}, \mathsf{sk}) \leftarrow \mathsf{KGen}(1^\lambda)$*: The randomized algorithm* KGen *takes as input a security parameter* 1^λ*, and it outputs a public key* pk *and a secret key* sk*.*
- $\sigma \leftarrow \mathsf{Sign}(\mathsf{sk}, \mathsf{m})$*: The randomized or deterministic algorithm* Sign *takes as input a secret key* sk *and a message* $\mathsf{m} \in \mathcal{M}$*, and it outputs a signature* σ*.*
- $1/0 \leftarrow \mathsf{Vrfy}(\mathsf{pk}, \mathsf{m}, \sigma)$*: The deterministic algorithm* Vrfy *takes as input a public key* pk*, a message* $\mathsf{m} \in \mathcal{M}$*, and a signature* σ*, and it outputs* 1 *or* 0*.*
- $\widehat{\sigma} \leftarrow \mathsf{Agg}((\mathsf{pk}_1, \mathsf{m}_1, \sigma_1), \ldots, (\mathsf{pk}_\ell, \mathsf{m}_\ell, \sigma_\ell))$*: The randomized or deterministic algorithm* Agg *takes as input a tuple* $(\mathsf{pk}_1, \mathsf{m}_1, \sigma_1), \ldots, (\mathsf{pk}_\ell, \mathsf{m}_\ell, \sigma_\ell)$ *of triplets of public keys, messages and signatures, and it outputs an aggregate signature* $\widehat{\sigma}$*.*
- $1/0 \leftarrow \mathsf{AVrfy}((\mathsf{pk}_1, \mathsf{m}_1), \ldots, (\mathsf{pk}_\ell, \mathsf{m}_\ell), \widehat{\sigma})$*: The deterministic algorithm* AVrfy *takes as input a tuple* $(\mathsf{pk}_1, \mathsf{m}_1), \ldots, (\mathsf{pk}_\ell, \mathsf{m}_\ell)$ *of pairs of public keys and messages, and an aggregate signature* $\widehat{\sigma}$*, and it outputs* 1 *or* 0*.*

Definition 3 (Correctness). *An aggregate signature scheme* $\mathsf{ASIG} = (\mathsf{KGen}, \mathsf{Sign}, \mathsf{Vrfy}, \mathsf{Agg}, \mathsf{AVrfy})$ *meets* correctness *if the following holds:*

- *For every* $(\mathsf{pk}, \mathsf{sk}) \leftarrow \mathsf{KGen}(1^\lambda)$ *and every* $\mathsf{m} \in \mathcal{M}$*, it holds that* $\mathsf{Vrfy}(\mathsf{pk}, \mathsf{m}, \sigma) = 1$ *with overwhelming probability, where* $\sigma \leftarrow \mathsf{Sign}(\mathsf{sk}, \mathsf{m})$*.*
- *For any* $\ell = \mathsf{poly}(\lambda)$*, every* $(\mathsf{pk}_1, \mathsf{sk}_1) \leftarrow \mathsf{KGen}(1^\lambda), \ldots, (\mathsf{pk}_\ell, \mathsf{sk}_\ell) \leftarrow \mathsf{KGen}(1^\lambda)$*, and every* $\mathsf{m}_1, \ldots, \mathsf{m}_\ell \in \mathcal{M}$*, it holds that* $\mathsf{AVrfy}((\mathsf{pk}_1, \mathsf{m}_1), \ldots, (\mathsf{pk}_\ell, \mathsf{m}_\ell), \widehat{\sigma}) = 1$ *with overwhelming probability, where* $\widehat{\sigma} \leftarrow \mathsf{Agg}((\mathsf{pk}_1, \mathsf{m}_1, \sigma_1), \ldots, (\mathsf{pk}_\ell, \mathsf{m}_\ell, \sigma_\ell))$ *and* $\sigma_i \leftarrow \mathsf{Sign}(\mathsf{sk}_i, \mathsf{m}_i)$ *for all* $i \in [\ell]$*.*

Following [3], we describe the definition of *existential unforgeability against chosen message attacks*, denoted by EUF-CMA security.

Definition 4 (EUF-CMA security). *An aggregate signature scheme* $\mathsf{ASIG} = (\mathsf{KGen}, \mathsf{Sign}, \mathsf{Vrfy}, \mathsf{Agg}, \mathsf{AVrfy})$ *satisfies* EUF-CMA *security if for any PPT adversary* A *against* ASIG*, the advantage* $\mathsf{Adv}^{\text{euf-cma}}_{\mathsf{ASIG},\mathsf{A}}(\lambda) := \Pr[\mathsf{A} \text{ wins}]$ *is negligible in* λ*.* $[\mathsf{A} \text{ wins}]$ *is the event that* A *wins in the following game:*

Setup. *The challenger generates* $(\mathsf{pk}^*, \mathsf{sk}^*) \leftarrow \mathsf{KGen}(1^\lambda)$ *and sets* $\mathcal{Q} \leftarrow \emptyset$*. It gives* pk^* *to* A*.*

Queries. *Given a signing-query* $\mathsf{m} \in \mathcal{M}$*, the signing oracle* SIGN *returns* $\sigma \leftarrow \mathsf{Sign}(\mathsf{sk}^*, \mathsf{m})$ *and sets* $\mathcal{Q} \leftarrow \mathcal{Q} \cup \{\mathsf{m}\}$*.*

Output. A *outputs a forgery* $((\mathsf{pk}_1, \mathsf{m}_1), \ldots, (\mathsf{pk}_\ell, \mathsf{m}_\ell), \widehat{\sigma})$*.* A *wins if* $\mathsf{AVrfy}((\mathsf{pk}_1, \mathsf{m}_1), \ldots, (\mathsf{pk}_\ell, \mathsf{m}_\ell), \widehat{\sigma}) = 1$ *and* $\mathsf{m}_z \notin \mathcal{Q}$ *hold, where* $z \in [\ell]$ *is an index such that* $\mathsf{pk}_z = \mathsf{pk}^*$*.*

Soundness and its Relation to Unforgeability. We introduce a new security notion called soundness, denoted by asig-soundness, of aggregate signatures. The functionality of aggregate signatures is to compress multiple signatures of multiple messages, and we would expect that all the pairs of the messages and signatures are valid if the compressed signature (i.e., aggregate signature) is valid. However, the aggregate signature scheme in [3] does not guarantee this property, and there is an invalid pair of a message and a signature though the compressed signature is valid (see the explanation after Proposition 2). The notion of soundness prevents such a case, and asig-soundness achieves what we expect explained above[1].

Definition 5 (asig-soundness). *An aggregate signature scheme* $\mathsf{ASIG} = (\mathsf{KGen}, \mathsf{Sign}, \mathsf{Vrfy}, \mathsf{Agg}, \mathsf{AVrfy})$ *satisfies* asig-soundness *if for any PPT adversary* A *against* ASIG, *the advantage* $\mathsf{Adv}^{\text{asig-sound}}_{\mathsf{ASIG},\mathsf{A}}(\lambda) := \Pr[\mathsf{A}\ wins]$ *is negligible in* λ. $[\mathsf{A}\ wins]$ *is the event that* A *wins in the following game:*

Setup. *The challenger generates* $(\mathsf{pk}^*, \mathsf{sk}^*) \leftarrow \mathsf{KGen}(1^\lambda)$ *and gives* pk^* *to* A.
Queries. *Given a signing-query* $\mathsf{m} \in \mathcal{M}$, *signing oracle* SIGN *returns* $\sigma \leftarrow \mathsf{Sign}(\mathsf{sk}^*, \mathsf{m})$.
Output. A *outputs* $((\mathsf{pk}_1, \mathsf{m}_1, \sigma_1), \ldots, (\mathsf{pk}_\ell, \mathsf{m}_\ell, \sigma_\ell))$. *Then, the challenger computes* $\widehat{\sigma} \leftarrow \mathsf{Agg}((\mathsf{pk}_1, \mathsf{m}_1, \sigma_1), \ldots, (\mathsf{pk}_\ell, \mathsf{m}_\ell, \sigma_\ell))$. A *wins if* $\mathsf{AVrfy}((\mathsf{pk}_1, \mathsf{m}_1), \ldots, (\mathsf{pk}_\ell, \mathsf{m}_\ell), \widehat{\sigma}) = 1$ *and* $\mathsf{Vrfy}(\mathsf{pk}_z, \mathsf{m}_z, \sigma_z) = 0$ *hold, where* $z \in [\ell]$ *is an index such that* $\mathsf{pk}_z = \mathsf{pk}^*$.

We show that the two security notions EUF-CMA security and asig-soundness are separated (i.e., one of the two does not imply the other). First, EUF-CMA security does not imply asig-soundness, since it is shown that the scheme $\mathsf{ASIG}_{\mathsf{BGLS}}$ of [3] satisfies EUF-CMA security but does not meet asig-soundness (in the description of $\mathsf{ASIG}_{\mathsf{BGLS}}$ in Sect. 3.2, we show how to break this scheme in the asig-soundness game).

Second, asig-soundness security does not imply EUF-CMA security. We consider an aggregate signature scheme satisfying asig-soundness that is the same as the scheme $\mathsf{ASIG}^{snd}_{\mathsf{BGLS}}$ given in Sect. 3.2 except that the underlying aggregate signature scheme is insecure in the EUF-CMA security game. It is clear that an adversary can generate a forgery of this scheme by making a forgery for pk^*. In addition, we will see that the asig-soundness of that scheme does not follow from the EUF-CMA security of the underlying aggregate signature scheme by Theorem 3. Hence, the above scheme does not satisfy EUF-CMA security though it meets asig-soundness.

[1] We should notice the difference between asig-soundness and batch verification, as follows: In the asig-soundness game, the adversary is allowed to generate key-pairs except for the key-pair generated by the challenger, while batch verification requires all key-pairs to be generated according to the key generation algorithm. See [5] on details of the definition of batch verification.

2.3 Group Testing Aggregate Signatures

In this section, we introduce the syntax and security formalization of group testing aggregate signatures (GT-ASIG schemes for short) that fulfill functionality of both keyless aggregation of multiple signatures and identifying an invalid message from the aggregate signature.

Definition 6. *A GT-ASIG*[2] *consists of five polynomial-time algorithms* (KGen, Sign, Vrfy, GTAgg, GTVrfy) *associated with a set* $\mathcal{G}$ *consisting of d-disjunct matrices, where the size (i.e., the number of rows or the number of columns) of the matrices in* $\mathcal{G}$ *may be different from each other in general: For a security parameter* λ*, let* $\mathcal{M} = \mathcal{M}(\lambda)$ *be a message space.*

Key Generation $(\mathsf{pk}, \mathsf{sk}) \leftarrow \mathsf{KGen}(1^\lambda)$*: The randomized algorithm* KGen *takes as input a security parameter* 1^λ*, and it outputs a public key* pk *and a secret key* sk.

Signing $\sigma \leftarrow \mathsf{Sign}(\mathsf{sk}, \mathsf{m})$*: The randomized or deterministic algorithm* Sign *takes as input a secret key* sk *and a message* $\mathsf{m} \in \mathcal{M}$*, and it outputs a signature* σ.

Verification $1/0 \leftarrow \mathsf{Vrfy}(\mathsf{pk}, \mathsf{m}, \sigma)$*: The deterministic algorithm* Vrfy *takes as input a public key* pk*, a message* $\mathsf{m} \in \mathcal{M}$*, and a signature* σ*, and it outputs* 1 *or* 0.

Group Testing Aggregation $(\widehat{\sigma}_1, \ldots, \widehat{\sigma}_u) \leftarrow \mathsf{GTAgg}(\boldsymbol{G}, (\mathsf{pk}_i, \mathsf{m}_i, \sigma_i)_{i\in[\ell]})$*: The randomized or deterministic algorithm* GTAgg *takes as input a d-disjunct matrix* $\boldsymbol{G} \in \{0,1\}^{u\times\ell} \cap \mathcal{G}$*, a tuple* $((\mathsf{pk}_1, \mathsf{m}_1, \sigma_1), \ldots, (\mathsf{pk}_\ell, \mathsf{m}_\ell, \sigma_\ell))$ *of triplets of public keys, messages, and signatures, and it outputs a tuple* $(\widehat{\sigma}_1, \ldots, \widehat{\sigma}_u)$ *of aggregate signatures.*

Group Testing Verification $J \leftarrow \mathsf{GTVrfy}(\boldsymbol{G}, ((\mathsf{pk}_1, \mathsf{m}_1), \ldots, (\mathsf{pk}_\ell, \mathsf{m}_\ell)), (\widehat{\sigma}_1, \ldots, \widehat{\sigma}_u))$*: The deterministic algorithm* GTVrfy *takes as input a d-disjunct matrix* $\boldsymbol{G} \in \{0,1\}^{u\times\ell} \cap \mathcal{G}$*, a tuple* $((\mathsf{pk}_1, \mathsf{m}_1), \ldots, (\mathsf{pk}_\ell, \mathsf{m}_\ell))$ *of pairs of public keys and messages, and a tuple* $(\widehat{\sigma}_1, \ldots, \widehat{\sigma}_u)$ *of aggregate signatures, and it outputs a set* J *of (invalid) pairs of public keys and messages*[3].

A D-ASIG scheme is required to meet correctness, as follows.

Definition 7 (Correctness). *A GT-ASIG scheme* GT-ASig = (KGen, Sign, Vrfy, GTAgg, GTVrfy) *satisfies* correctness *if the following conditions hold:*

- *For every* $(\mathsf{pk}, \mathsf{sk}) \leftarrow \mathsf{KGen}(1^\lambda)$ *and every* $\mathsf{m} \in \mathcal{M}$*, it holds that* $\mathsf{Vrfy}(\mathsf{pk}, \mathsf{m}, \sigma) = 1$ *with overwhelming probability, where* $\sigma \leftarrow \mathsf{Sign}(\mathsf{sk}, \mathsf{m})$.

---

[2] One may wonder if the detecting functionality of GT-ASIGs can be achieved by cryptographic methodology, rather than combinatorial methodology (i.e., group testing with d-disjunct matrices). However, to the best of our knowledge, the property of d-disjunct matrices is necessary to achieve the non-interactive detecting functionality, in a practical way. As described in **Conclusion**, constructing an aggregate signature scheme with this functionality (in a practical way) is important as future work in this research.

[3] $J = \emptyset$ means that the given pairs of public keys and signed messages are all valid.

– *For every d-disjunct matrix* $\boldsymbol{G} \in \{0,1\}^{u \times \ell} \cap \mathcal{G}$, *every* $(\mathsf{pk}_1, \mathsf{sk}_1) \leftarrow \mathsf{KGen}(1^\lambda)$, $\ldots, (\mathsf{pk}_\ell, \mathsf{sk}_\ell) \leftarrow \mathsf{KGen}(1^\lambda)$, *and every* $\mathsf{m}_1, \ldots, \mathsf{m}_\ell \in \mathcal{M}$, *it holds that* $\mathsf{GTVrfy}(\boldsymbol{G}, ((\mathsf{pk}_1, \mathsf{m}_1), \ldots, (\mathsf{pk}_\ell, \mathsf{m}_\ell)), (\widehat{\sigma}_1, \ldots, \widehat{\sigma}_\ell)) = \emptyset$ *with overwhelming probability, where* $(\widehat{\sigma}_1, \ldots, \widehat{\sigma}_\ell) \leftarrow \mathsf{GTAgg}(\boldsymbol{G}, ((\mathsf{pk}_1, \mathsf{m}_1, \sigma_1), \ldots, (\mathsf{pk}_\ell, \mathsf{m}_\ell, \sigma_\ell)))$ *and* $\sigma_i \leftarrow \mathsf{Sign}(\mathsf{pk}_i, \mathsf{m}_i)$ *for all* $i \in [\ell]$.

We define the security notions of GT-ASIG: EUF-CMA security and identifiablity. EUF-CMA security is formalized as in [11]:

Definition 8 (EUF-CMA **security**). *A GT-ASIG scheme* GT-ASig = (KGen, Sign, Vrfy, GTAgg, GTVrfy) *satisfies* EUF-CMA *security for any PPT adversary* A *against* GT-ASig, *the advantage* $\mathsf{Adv}^{\mathsf{euf\text{-}cma}}_{\mathsf{GT\text{-}ASig},\mathsf{A}}(\lambda) := \Pr[\mathsf{A}\ wins]$ *is negligible in* λ. [A *wins*] *is the event that* A *wins in the following game:*

Setup. *The challenger generates a key-pair* $(\mathsf{pk}^*, \mathsf{sk}^*) \leftarrow \mathsf{KGen}(1^\lambda)$ *and sets* $\mathcal{Q} \leftarrow \emptyset$. *It gives* pk^* *to* A.

Queries. *Given a signing-query* $\mathsf{m} \in \mathcal{Q}$, *signing oracle* SIGN *returns* $\sigma \leftarrow \mathsf{Sign}(\mathsf{sk}^*, \mathsf{m})$ *and sets* $\mathcal{Q} \leftarrow \mathcal{Q} \cup \{\mathsf{m}\}$.

Output. A *outputs a forgery* $(\boldsymbol{G}, ((\mathsf{pk}_1, \mathsf{m}_1), \ldots, (\mathsf{pk}_\ell, \mathsf{m}_\ell)), (\widehat{\sigma}_1, \ldots, \widehat{\sigma}_u))$. *The challenger computes* $J \leftarrow \mathsf{GTVrfy}(\boldsymbol{G}, ((\mathsf{pk}_1, \mathsf{m}_1), \ldots, (\mathsf{pk}_\ell, \mathsf{m}_\ell)), (\widehat{\sigma}_1, \ldots, \widehat{\sigma}_u))$. A *wins if* $(\mathsf{pk}_z, \mathsf{m}_z) \notin J$ *and* $\mathsf{m}_z \notin \mathcal{Q}$ *hold, where* $z \in [\ell]$ *is an index such that* $\mathsf{pk}_z = \mathsf{pk}^*$.

Identifiablity guarantees that, from the aggregate signature, (i) valid messages must be regarded as valid (ident-completeness); and (ii) invalid messages must be regarded as invalid (ident-soundness), in the chosen-key security model introduced in [3]. This notion is formalized as follows.

Definition 9 (Identifiability). *Regarding the* identifiability *of GT-ASIG scheme* GT-ASig = (KGen, Sign, Vrfy, GTAgg, GTVrfy), *the two notions* ident-completeness *and* ident-soundness *are defined. Let* A *be a d-dishonest PPT adversary against* GT-ASig, *where a PPT adversary* A *against* GT-ASig *is d-dishonest if it outputs* $(\boldsymbol{G}, (\mathsf{pk}_1, \mathsf{m}_1, \sigma_1), \ldots, (\mathsf{pk}_\ell, \mathsf{m}_\ell, \sigma_\ell))$ *such that* $|\{(\mathsf{pk}_i, \mathsf{m}_i) \mid i \in [\ell] \wedge \mathsf{Vrfy}(\mathsf{pk}_i, \mathsf{m}_i, \sigma_i) = 0\}| \leq d$, *in the following security game:*

Setup. *The challenger generates a key-pair* $(\mathsf{pk}^*, \mathsf{sk}^*) \leftarrow \mathsf{KGen}(1^\lambda)$ *and sets* $\mathcal{Q} \leftarrow \emptyset$. *It gives* pk^* *to* A.

Queries. *Given a sign-query* $\mathsf{m} \in \mathcal{Q}$, *signing oracle* SIGN *returns* $\sigma \leftarrow \mathsf{Sign}(\mathsf{sk}^*, \mathsf{m})$ *and sets* $\mathcal{Q} \leftarrow \mathcal{Q} \cup \{\mathsf{m}\}$.

Output. A *outputs* $(\boldsymbol{G}, (\mathsf{pk}_1, \mathsf{m}_1, \sigma_1), \ldots, (\mathsf{pk}_\ell, \mathsf{m}_\ell, \sigma_\ell))$. *The challenger computes* $(\widehat{\sigma}_1, \ldots, \widehat{\sigma}_u) \leftarrow \mathsf{GTAgg}(\boldsymbol{G}, ((\mathsf{pk}_1, \mathsf{m}_1, \sigma_1), \ldots, (\mathsf{pk}_\ell, \mathsf{m}_\ell, \sigma_\ell)))$ *and* $J \leftarrow \mathsf{GTVrfy}(\boldsymbol{G}, ((\mathsf{pk}_1, \mathsf{m}_1), \ldots, (\mathsf{pk}_\ell, \mathsf{m}_\ell)), (\widehat{\sigma}_1, \ldots, \widehat{\sigma}_u))$.

Ident-completeness *and* ident-soundness *are defined as follows: For a set* $\{(\mathsf{pk}_1, \mathsf{m}_1, \sigma_1), \ldots, (\mathsf{pk}_\ell, \mathsf{m}_\ell, \sigma_\ell)\}$, *let* $D = \{(\mathsf{pk}_i, \mathsf{m}_i) \mid i \in [\ell] \wedge \mathsf{Vrfy}(\mathsf{pk}_i, \mathsf{m}_i, \sigma_i) = 0\}$, *and* $\bar{D} = \{(\mathsf{pk}_i, \mathsf{m}_i) \mid i \in [\ell] \wedge \mathsf{Vrfy}(\mathsf{pk}_i, \mathsf{m}_i, \sigma_i) = 1\}$. *Let* $z \in [\ell]$ *be an index such that* $\mathsf{pk}_z = \mathsf{pk}^*$.

Completeness: $\mathsf{GT\text{-}ASig}$ *satisfies* $\mathsf{ident\text{-}completeness}$ *against d-dishonest adversaries, if for any d-dishonest PPT adversary* A *against* $\mathsf{GT\text{-}ASig}$*, the advantage* $\mathsf{Adv}^{\mathrm{complete}}_{\mathsf{GT\text{-}ASig},\mathsf{A}}(\lambda) := \Pr\left[(\mathsf{pk}_z, \mathsf{m}_z) \in \bar{D} \cap J\right]$ *is negligible in* λ.

Soundness: $\mathsf{GT\text{-}ASig}$ *satisfies* $\mathsf{ident\text{-}soundness}$ *against d-dishonest adversaries, if for any d-dishonest PPT adversary* A *against* $\mathsf{GT\text{-}ASig}$*, the advantage* $\mathsf{Adv}^{\mathrm{sound}}_{\mathsf{GT\text{-}ASig},\mathsf{A}}(\lambda) := \Pr\left[(\mathsf{pk}_z, \mathsf{m}_z) \in D \backslash J\right]$ *is negligible in* λ.

In addition, a weak variant $\mathsf{ident\text{-}weak\text{-}soundness}$ *of* $\mathsf{ident\text{-}soundness}$ *is defined in the same way as* $\mathsf{ident\text{-}soundness}$ *except that the advantage of a d-dishonest PPT adversary* A *against* $\mathsf{GT\text{-}ASig}$ *is defined as* $\mathsf{Adv}^{\mathrm{w\text{-}sound}}_{\mathsf{GT\text{-}ASig},\mathsf{A}}(\lambda) := \Pr\left[(\mathsf{pk}_z, \mathsf{m}_z) \in D' \backslash J\right]$*, where* $D' = \{(\mathsf{pk}_{\gamma(i)}, \mathsf{m}_i) \mid i \in [\ell] \wedge \mathsf{Vrfy}(\mathsf{pk}_i, \mathsf{m}_i, \sigma_i) = 0 \wedge \mathsf{m}_i \notin \mathcal{Q}\}$.

For the relations among EUF-CMA security, ident-soundness, and ident-weak-soundness, we show the implications, "EUF-CMA security $\Rightarrow$ ident-weak-soundness" and "ident-soundness $\Rightarrow$ ident-weak-soundness", and the separations, "EUF-CMA $\not\Rightarrow$ ident-soundness" and "EUF-CMA $\not\Leftarrow$ ident-soundness". The separations can be shown similarly as those of aggregate signatures in Sect. 2.2, and the following proposition shows the implication "EUF-CMA $\Rightarrow$ ident-weak-soundness".

Proposition 1. *Let d be an arbitrary positive integer. If a GT-ASIG scheme* $\mathsf{GT\text{-}ASig}$ *meets* EUF-CMA *security, it also satisfies* ident-weak-soundness *against d-dishonest adversaries.*

Proof. By using a d-dishonest PPT adversary A against ident-weak-soundness, we construct a PPT algorithm F^{euf} breaking EUF-CMA security, as follows: It takes as input a public key pk^* of $\mathsf{GT\text{-}ASig}$ and gives pk^* to A. By using the given signing oracle, F^{euf} simulates the oracle access of A in the straightforward way. When A outputs $(\boldsymbol{G}, (\mathsf{pk}_1, \mathsf{m}_1, \sigma_1), \ldots, (\mathsf{pk}_\ell, \mathsf{m}_\ell, \sigma_\ell))$, F^{euf} computes $(\widehat{\sigma}_1, \ldots, \widehat{\sigma}_u) \leftarrow \mathsf{GTAgg}(\boldsymbol{G}, ((\mathsf{pk}_1, \mathsf{m}_1, \sigma_1), \ldots, (\mathsf{pk}_\ell, \mathsf{m}_\ell, \sigma_\ell)))$, and outputs $(\boldsymbol{G}, ((\mathsf{pk}_1, \mathsf{m}_1), \ldots, (\mathsf{pk}_\ell, \mathsf{m}_\ell)), (\widehat{\sigma}_1, \ldots, \widehat{\sigma}_u))$.

If the output of A fulfills $(\mathsf{pk}_z, \mathsf{m}_z) \in \{(\mathsf{pk}_i, \mathsf{m}_i) \mid i \in [\ell] \wedge \mathsf{Vrfy}(\mathsf{pk}_i, \mathsf{m}_i, \sigma_i) = 0 \wedge \mathsf{m}_i \notin \mathcal{Q}\} \backslash J$ for some $z \in [\ell]$ such that $\mathsf{pk}_z = \mathsf{pk}^*$, then the output of F^{euf} is a forgery of EUF-CMA security game since $(\mathsf{pk}_z, \mathsf{m}_z) \notin J$ and $\mathsf{m}_z \notin \mathcal{Q}$ hold. Thus, we obtain $\mathsf{Adv}^{\mathrm{w\text{-}sound}}_{\mathsf{GT\text{-}ASig},\mathsf{A}}(\lambda) \leq \mathsf{Adv}^{\mathrm{euf\text{-}cma}}_{\mathsf{GT\text{-}ASig},\mathsf{F}^{euf}}(\lambda)$. □

3 Proposed (Group Testing) Aggregate Signatures

In this section, we propose a generic construction of GT-ASIG starting from an aggregate signature scheme, and an aggregate signature scheme with asig-soundness, which we can apply to the proposed GT-ASIG scheme with all the formalized security notions including ident-soundness.

3.1 GT-ASIG from Aggregate Signatures

We propose a generic construction of GT-ASIG and prove that the resulting GT-ASIG scheme satisfies EUF-CMA security, ident-completeness, and ident-soundness (resp. EUF-CMA security, ident-completeness, and ident-weak-soundness) if the underlying aggregate signature fulfills EUF-CMA security and asig-soundness (resp. only EUF-CMA security). This indicates that the security notion asig-soundness of aggregate signatures is extended to the ident-soundness of GT-ASIG.

Our construction GT-ASig = (KGen, Sign, Vrfy, GTAgg, GTVrfy) is as follows: Let ASIG = (KGen^{asig}, Sign^{asig}, Vrfy^{asig}, Agg^{asig}, AVrfy^{asig}) be an aggregate signature scheme. For $\boldsymbol{G} \in \{0,1\}^{u\times\ell}$ and $i \in [u]$, let $S_i(\boldsymbol{G}) = \{j \mid j \in [\ell] \wedge g_{i,j} = 1\}$.

- KGen, Sign, and Vrfy are the same as KGen^{asig}, Sign^{asig}, and Vrfy^{asig}, respectively.
- $(\widehat{\sigma}_1,\ldots,\widehat{\sigma}_u) \leftarrow \mathsf{GTAgg}(\boldsymbol{G}, ((\mathsf{pk}_1,\mathsf{m}_1,\sigma_1),\ldots,(\mathsf{pk}_\ell,\mathsf{m}_\ell,\sigma_\ell)))$: For each $i \in [u]$, generate $\widehat{\sigma}_i \leftarrow \mathsf{Agg}^{asig}((\mathsf{pk}_k,\mathsf{m}_k,\sigma_k)_{k\in S_i(\boldsymbol{G})})$. Output $(\widehat{\sigma}_1,\ldots,\widehat{\sigma}_u)$.
- $J \leftarrow \mathsf{GTVrfy}(\boldsymbol{G}, ((\mathsf{pk}_1,\mathsf{m}_1),\ldots,(\mathsf{pk}_\ell,\mathsf{m}_\ell)), (\widehat{\sigma}_1,\ldots,\widehat{\sigma}_u))$: Set $J \leftarrow \{(\mathsf{pk}_1,\mathsf{m}_1),\ldots,(\mathsf{pk}_\ell,\mathsf{m}_\ell)\}$. For each $i \in [u]$, if $\mathsf{AVrfy}^{asig}((\mathsf{pk}_k,\mathsf{m}_k)_{k\in S_i(\boldsymbol{G})},\widehat{\sigma}_i) = 1$ holds, then set $J \leftarrow J\setminus\{(\mathsf{pk}_k,\mathsf{m}_k)\}_{k\in S_i(\boldsymbol{G})}$. Then, output J.

Theorem 1. *If an aggregate signature scheme* ASIG *meets* EUF-CMA *security, then the resulting GT-ASIG scheme* GT-ASig *satisfies* EUF-CMA *security.*

Proof. To prove the theorem, we construct a PPT algorithm F^{asig} breaking the EUF-CMA security of ASIG, as follows: F^{asig} is given the public key pk^* of ASIG. In **Setup** phase, it sets $\mathcal{Q} \leftarrow \emptyset$ and gives pk^* to A. The SIGN oracle is simulated by using the given signing oracle in the EUF-CMA security game of ASIG. When A outputs $(\boldsymbol{G}, ((\mathsf{pk}_1,\mathsf{m}_1),\ldots,(\mathsf{pk}_\ell,\mathsf{m}_\ell)), (\widehat{\sigma}_1,\ldots,\widehat{\sigma}_u))$, then F^{asig} computes $J \leftarrow \mathsf{GTVrfy}(\boldsymbol{G}, ((\mathsf{pk}_1,\mathsf{m}_1),\ldots,(\mathsf{pk}_\ell,\mathsf{m}_\ell)), (\widehat{\sigma}_1,\ldots,\widehat{\sigma}_u))$. If there exits an index $z \in [\ell]$ such that $\mathsf{pk}_z = \mathsf{pk}^*$, $(\mathsf{pk}_z,\mathsf{m}_z) \notin J$, and $\mathsf{m}_z \notin \mathcal{Q}$, then it checks whether there exits $i \in [u]$ such that $z \in S_i(\boldsymbol{G})$ and $\mathsf{AVrfy}^{asig}((\mathsf{pk}_k,\mathsf{m}_k)_{k\in S_i(\boldsymbol{G})},\widehat{\sigma}_i) = 1$. If there exists such an index, then F^{asig} outputs $(\mathsf{pk}_k,\mathsf{m}_k)_{k\in S_i(\boldsymbol{G})}$ and $\widehat{\sigma}_i$. Otherwise, it aborts.

If A outputs a valid forgery $(\boldsymbol{G}, ((\mathsf{pk}_1,\mathsf{m}_1),\ldots,(\mathsf{pk}_\ell,\mathsf{m}_\ell)), (\widehat{\sigma}_1,\ldots,\widehat{\sigma}_u))$, then there exist the above indexes $z \in [\ell]$ and $i \in [u]$ such that $\mathsf{m}_z \notin \mathcal{Q}$ and $\mathsf{AVrfy}^{asig}((\mathsf{pk}_k,\mathsf{m}_k)_{k\in S_i(\boldsymbol{G})},\widehat{\sigma}_i) = 1$, due to the winning condition of A (i.e., $\mathsf{m}_z \notin \mathcal{Q}$ and $(\mathsf{pk}_z,\mathsf{m}_z) \notin J$). Thus, the output of F^{asig} is a valid forgery of ASIG, and we obtain $\mathsf{Adv}^{\text{euf-cma}}_{\text{GT-ASig},\mathsf{A}}(\lambda) \leq \mathsf{Adv}^{\text{euf-cma}}_{\text{ASIG},\mathsf{F}^{asig}}(\lambda)$. □

Theorem 2. *For* identifiability, *the GT-ASIG scheme* GT-ASig *constructed from an aggregate signature scheme* ASIG *satisfies the following: Let d be an arbitrary positive integer.*

(i) If $\boldsymbol{G} \in \{0,1\}^{u\times\ell}$ is a d-disjunct matrix, and ASIG *meets* correctness, *then* GT-ASig *satisfies* ident-completeness *against d-dishonest adversaries.*
(ii) If $\boldsymbol{G} \in \{0,1\}^{u\times\ell}$ is a matrix such that $u \leq \ell$ and every column vector of $\boldsymbol{G}$ is non-zero, and ASIG *meets* EUF-CMA *security, then* GT-ASig *satisfies* ident-weak-soundness *against d-dishonest adversaries.*

(iii) If $\boldsymbol{G} \in \{0,1\}^{u\times\ell}$ is a matrix such that $u \le \ell$ and every column vector of $\boldsymbol{G}$ is non-zero, and ASIG *meets* asig-soundness*, then* GT-ASig *satisfies* ident-soundness *against d-dishonest adversaries.*

Proof. First, we prove that GT-ASig satisfies ident-completeness. For the output $(\boldsymbol{G},(\mathsf{pk}_1,\mathsf{m}_1,\sigma_1),\ldots,(\mathsf{pk}_\ell,\mathsf{m}_\ell,\sigma_\ell))$ of a d-dishonest PPT adversary A, let $(\widehat{\sigma}_1,\ldots,\widehat{\sigma}_u) \leftarrow \mathsf{GTAgg}(\boldsymbol{G},((\mathsf{pk}_1,\mathsf{m}_1,\sigma_1),\ldots,(\mathsf{pk}_\ell,\mathsf{m}_1,\sigma_\ell)))$ be a tuple of aggregate signatures. For any valid pair $(\mathsf{pk}_v,\mathsf{m}_v)$ such that $\mathsf{Vrfy}^{asig}(\mathsf{pk}_v,\mathsf{m}_v,\sigma_v)=1$ $(v \in [\ell])$, there exists a valid pair $((\mathsf{pk}_k,\mathsf{m}_k)_{k\in S_i(\boldsymbol{G})},\widehat{\sigma}_i)$ such that $v \in S_i(\boldsymbol{G})$ and $\mathsf{Vrfy}^{asig}((\mathsf{pk}_k,\mathsf{m}_k)_{k\in S_i(\boldsymbol{G})},\widehat{\sigma}_i)=1$. This reason is as follows: Without loss of generality, we assume that at most d invalid pairs are fixed. Due to the d-disjunct property of $\boldsymbol{G}$, for any column corresponding to a valid pair, there exists the i-th entry of the column $(i \in [u])$, such that the entry is 1, but all i-th entries of columns corresponding to invalid ones are 0. That is, the i-th aggregate signature is valid. Hence, the d-disjunct property guarantees that for any valid pair, there exists an aggregate signature on only valid ones including the valid pair. In addition, the correctness of ASIG guarantees that all aggregate signatures on valid messages are accepted by Vrfy^{asig} algorithm with overwhelming probability. Hence, we have $\mathsf{Adv}^{\text{complete}}_{\mathsf{GT\text{-}ASig},\mathsf{A}}(\lambda) \le \mathsf{negl}(\lambda)$. In addition, it is clear that $\mathsf{Adv}^{\text{w-sound}}_{\mathsf{GT\text{-}ASig},\mathsf{A}}(\lambda) \le \mathsf{Adv}^{\text{euf-cma}}_{\mathsf{ASIG},\mathsf{F}^{asig}}(\lambda)$ holds by combining Proposition 1 and Theorem 1.

Next, we prove that GT-ASig satisfies ident-soundness. By using A which breaks the ident-soundness of GT-ASig, we construct a PPT algorithm S^{snd} which breaks asig-soundness, as follows: S^{snd} takes as input a public key pk^* of ASIG, and gives pk^* to A. By using the given signing oracle, it can simulate the SIGN oracle in the ident-soundness game. When A outputs $(\boldsymbol{G},(\mathsf{pk}_1,\mathsf{m}_1,\sigma_1),\ldots,(\mathsf{pk}_\ell,\mathsf{m}_\ell,\sigma_\ell))$, S^{snd} computes $(\widehat{\sigma}_1,\ldots,\widehat{\sigma}_u) \leftarrow \mathsf{GTAgg}(\boldsymbol{G},(\mathsf{pk}_1,\mathsf{m}_1,\sigma_1),\ldots,(\mathsf{pk}_\ell,\mathsf{m}_\ell,\sigma_\ell))$ and $J \leftarrow \mathsf{GTVrfy}(\boldsymbol{G},((\mathsf{pk}_1,\mathsf{m}_1),\ldots,(\mathsf{pk}_\ell,\mathsf{m}_\ell)),(\widehat{\sigma}_1,\ldots,\widehat{\sigma}_u))$. Then, it finds a pair $(z,i) \in [\ell]\times[u]$ of indexes such that $\mathsf{pk}_z = \mathsf{pk}^*$, $z \in S_i(\boldsymbol{G})$, $\mathsf{AVrfy}^{asig}((\mathsf{pk}_k,\mathsf{m}_k)_{k\in S_i(\boldsymbol{G})},\widehat{\sigma}_i) = 1$, and $\mathsf{Vrfy}^{asig}(\mathsf{pk}_z,\mathsf{m}_z,\sigma_z) = 0$. If there exits such a pair, it outputs $(\mathsf{pk}_k,\mathsf{m}_k,\sigma_k)_{k\in S_i(\boldsymbol{G})}$. Otherwise, it aborts.

If A succeeds in generating $(\boldsymbol{G},(\mathsf{pk}_1,\mathsf{m}_1,\sigma_1),\ldots,(\mathsf{pk}_\ell,\mathsf{m}_\ell,\sigma_\ell))$ which meets the winning condition in the ident-soundness game, then $(\mathsf{pk}_z,\mathsf{m}_z) \in D\backslash J$ holds for $z \in [\ell]$ such that $\mathsf{pk}_z = \mathsf{pk}^*$. There exists an index $i \in [u]$ such that $z \in S_i(\boldsymbol{G})$ and $\mathsf{AVrfy}^{asig}((\mathsf{pk}_k,\mathsf{m}_k)_{k\in S_i(\boldsymbol{G})},\widehat{\sigma}_i)=1$, due to $(\mathsf{pk}_z,\mathsf{m}_z) \notin J$. In addition, $\mathsf{AVrfy}^{asig}(\mathsf{pk}_z,\mathsf{m}_z,\sigma_z)=0$ also holds due to $(\mathsf{pk}_z,\mathsf{m}_z) \in D$. Hence, the output $(\mathsf{pk}_k,\mathsf{m}_k,\sigma_k)_{k\in S_i(\boldsymbol{G})}$ of S^{snd} fulfills the winning condition in the asig-soundness game, and we have $\mathsf{Adv}^{\text{sound}}_{\mathsf{GT\text{-}ASig},\mathsf{A}}(\lambda) \le \mathsf{Adv}^{\text{asig-sound}}_{\mathsf{ASIG},\mathsf{S}^{snd}}(\lambda)$. □

3.2 Aggregate Signatures with Soundness

In this section, we describe the aggregate signature scheme of [3] and then propose its variant satisfying asig-soundness. We are focusing on this scheme [3] because the other schemes are secure under the non-standard assumption or need some constraint (e.g., sequential aggregation and synchronized aggregation) for aggregating signatures.

Aggregate Signature Scheme in [3]. The aggregate signature scheme $\mathsf{ASIG_{BGLS}} = (\mathsf{KGen}, \mathsf{Sign}, \mathsf{Vrfy}, \mathsf{Agg}, \mathsf{AVrfy})$ of [3] is as follows: For a security parameter λ, set the following parameters: let $\{0,1\}^*$ be a message space. Let G_1, G_2 be the base groups with a prime order p, g_1 and g_2 be generators of G_1 and G_2, respectively. Let ϕ be the computable isomorphism from G_2 to G_1, and $e : G_1 \times G_2 \to G_T$ be the bilinear map with the target group G_T. Let $H : \{0,1\}^* \to G_1$ be a random oracle.

- $(\mathsf{pk}, \mathsf{sk}) \leftarrow \mathsf{KGen}(1^\lambda)$: Choose $x \xleftarrow{\$} \mathbb{Z}_p$ and compute $v \leftarrow g_2^x \in G_2$. Output $\mathsf{pk} = v$ and $\mathsf{sk} = x$.
- $\sigma \leftarrow \mathsf{Sign}(\mathsf{sk}, \mathsf{m})$: Output $\sigma \leftarrow h^x \in G_1$, where $h \leftarrow H(\mathsf{m}) \in G_1$.
- $1/0 \leftarrow \mathsf{Vrfy}(\mathsf{pk}, \mathsf{m}, \sigma)$: Output 1 if $e(\sigma, g_2) = e(H(\mathsf{m}), v)$ holds, where $\mathsf{pk} = v$. Output 0 otherwise.
- $\widehat{\sigma} \leftarrow \mathsf{Agg}((\mathsf{pk}_1, \mathsf{m}_1, \sigma_1), \ldots, (\mathsf{pk}_\ell, \mathsf{m}_\ell, \sigma_\ell))$: Output $\widehat{\sigma} \leftarrow \prod_{i=1}^{\ell} \sigma_i \in G_1$.
- $1/0 \leftarrow \mathsf{AVrfy}((\mathsf{pk}_1, \mathsf{m}_1), \ldots, (\mathsf{pk}_\ell, \mathsf{m}_\ell), \widehat{\sigma})$: Let $\mathsf{pk}_i = v_i$ for all $i \in [\ell]$. Output 1 if $e(\widehat{\sigma}, g_2) = \prod_{i=1}^{\ell} e(H(\mathsf{m}_i), v_i)$ holds, and all $\mathsf{m}_1, \ldots, \mathsf{m}_\ell$ are distinct. Output 0 otherwise.

The computational problems related to this scheme are given in Appendix A. Regarding its security, the following proposition was proven in [3].

Proposition 2. ([3, Theorem 1]). *If (G_1, G_2) is a bilinear group pair for co-Diffie-Hellman, then* $\mathsf{ASIG_{BGLS}}$ *satisfies* EUF-CMA *security.*

Furthermore, we can show that $\mathsf{ASIG_{BGLS}}$ does not satisfy asig-soundness as follows: An adversary has $((\mathsf{pk}_1, \mathsf{m}_1, \sigma_1), \ldots, (\mathsf{pk}_\ell, \mathsf{m}_\ell, \sigma_\ell))$ such that $\sigma_1 = H(\mathsf{m}_1)^{x_1}$, $\sigma_2 = H(\mathsf{m}_2)^{x_2}$, $\sigma_3 = H(\mathsf{m}_3)^{x_3}, \ldots, \sigma_\ell = H(\mathsf{m}_\ell)^{x_\ell}$, where $\mathsf{sk}_1 = x_1$, $\mathsf{sk}_2 = x_2, \ldots, \mathsf{sk}_\ell = x_\ell$, by accessing SIGN oracle and generating key-pairs by itself. And, it outputs $((\mathsf{pk}_1, \mathsf{m}_1, \sigma_1'), (\mathsf{pk}_2, \mathsf{m}_2, \sigma_2'), (\mathsf{pk}_3, \mathsf{m}_3, \sigma_3), \ldots, (\mathsf{pk}_\ell, \mathsf{m}_\ell, \sigma_\ell))$ such that $\sigma_1' = H(\mathsf{m}_1)^{x_1} v$, $\sigma_2' = H(\mathsf{m}_2)^{x_2} v^{-1}$, $\sigma_3 = H(\mathsf{m}_3)^{x_3}, \ldots, \sigma_\ell = H(\mathsf{m}_\ell)^{x_\ell}$, where $v \neq 1$. Then, the Vrfy algorithm of $\mathsf{ASIG_{BGLS}}$ accepts this output, since $e(\sigma_1'\sigma_2' \prod_{i=3}^{\ell} \sigma_i, g_2) = e(\prod_{i=1}^{\ell} \sigma_i, g_2)$ holds. Although the triplets $(\mathsf{pk}_1, \mathsf{m}_1, \sigma_1')$, $(\mathsf{pk}_2, \mathsf{m}_2, \sigma_2')$ are invalid, $\widehat{\sigma}' := \sigma_1'\sigma_2' \prod_{i=3}^{\ell} \sigma_i$ is a valid aggregate signature on $((\mathsf{pk}_1, \mathsf{m}_1), \ldots, (\mathsf{pk}_\ell, \mathsf{m}_\ell))$. Hence, the output satisfies the winning condition in the asig-soundness game.

Aggregate Signatures Satisfying asig-soundness. We propose a direct construction satisfying asig-soundness, which is based on the aggregate signature scheme $\mathsf{ASIG_{BGLS}}$. The idea to achieve asig-soundness is as follows: Given message-signature pairs $(\mathsf{m}_1, \sigma_1), \ldots, (\mathsf{m}_\ell, \sigma_\ell)$ of $\mathsf{ASIG_{BGLS}}$, the aggregation algorithm of our scheme chooses $(\delta_1, \ldots, \delta_\ell) \in \mathbb{Z}_p^\ell$ uniformly at random and computes $\widehat{\sigma}' \leftarrow \prod_{i=1}^{\ell} \sigma_i^{\delta_i} \in G_1$, and sets $(\delta_1, \ldots, \delta_\ell, \widehat{\sigma}')$ as an aggregate signature. When verifying messages $(\mathsf{m}_1, \ldots, \mathsf{m}_\ell)$ and this aggregate signature, the verifier checks if $e(\widehat{\sigma}', g_2) = \prod_{i=1}^{\ell} e(H(\mathsf{m}_i), \mathsf{pk}_i^{\delta_i})$. An adversary needs to guess $(\delta_1, \ldots, \delta_\ell)$ if it tries to break the asig-soundness of $\mathsf{ASIG_{BGLS}}$. Notice that our concrete aggregation algorithm computes $(\delta_1, \ldots, \delta_\ell) \leftarrow \widehat{H}(r)$ (where $\widehat{H}$ is a random oracle, and

r is randomness) and sets $(r, \widehat{\sigma}')$ as an aggregate signature, so that the aggregate signature-size does not depend on the number of signers linearly.

Then, we assume the adversary against the asig-soundness of this scheme, which does the following:

1. Generate $(\mathsf{pk}_1, \mathsf{m}_1, \sigma_1), \ldots, (\mathsf{pk}_\ell, \mathsf{m}_\ell, \sigma_\ell)$, and $(\delta_1, \ldots, \delta_\ell) = \widehat{H}(r)$ by using the given signing oracle and random oracle.
2. Compute $\sigma_1^* \leftarrow \sigma_1 \cdot v^{\delta_2}$ and $\sigma_2^* \leftarrow \sigma_2 \cdot v^{-\delta_1}$ (where $v \neq 1$) in the same way as the above attack against $\mathsf{ASIG}_{\mathsf{BGLS}}$.
3. Output $(\mathsf{pk}_1, \mathsf{m}_1, \sigma_1^*), (\mathsf{pk}_2, \mathsf{m}_2, \sigma_2^*), (\mathsf{pk}_3, \mathsf{m}_3, \sigma_3), \ldots, (\mathsf{pk}_\ell, \mathsf{m}_\ell, \sigma_\ell)$.

Even though there exists this adversary, our scheme prevents this attack, since the challenger chooses fresh randomness r^* in order to generate a new aggregate signature $(r^*, \widehat{\sigma}'^*)$ (see the **Output** phase in Definition 5). Namely, the randomness r^* chosen by the challenger is different from r chosen by the adversary (i.e., $H(r) \neq H(r^*)$), with overwhelming probability. Hence, it is clear that $(r^*, \widehat{\sigma}'^*)$ is an invalid aggregate signature, and the attack fails in the asig-soundness game.

We construct the proposed aggregate signature scheme $\mathsf{ASIG}^{snd}_{\mathsf{BGLS}} = (\mathsf{KGen}, \mathsf{Sign}, \mathsf{Vrfy}, \mathsf{Agg}, \mathsf{AVrfy})$. The system parameters and the algorithms $(\mathsf{KGen}, \mathsf{Sign}, \mathsf{Vrfy})$ of this scheme are the same as those of $\mathsf{ASIG}_{\mathsf{BGLS}}$. The Agg and AVrfy algorithms are described as follows: Let $\{0,1\}^\kappa$ be a randomness space with $\kappa = \mathsf{poly}(\lambda)$. Let $\widehat{H} : \{0,1\}^\kappa \times \{0,1\}^* \to \mathbb{Z}_p^\ell$ be a random oracle.

- $\widehat{\sigma} \leftarrow \mathsf{Agg}((\mathsf{pk}_1, \mathsf{m}_1, \sigma_1), \ldots, (\mathsf{pk}_\ell, \mathsf{m}_\ell, \sigma_\ell))$:
  1. Sample $r \xleftarrow{\$} \{0,1\}^\kappa$.
  2. Compute $(\delta_1, \ldots, \delta_\ell) \leftarrow \widehat{H}(r, \mathsf{pk}_1, \ldots, \mathsf{pk}_\ell, \mathsf{m}_1, \ldots, \mathsf{m}_\ell)$.
  3. Compute $\widehat{\sigma}' \leftarrow \prod_{i=1}^{\ell} \sigma_i^{\delta_i} \in G_1$.
  4. Output $\widehat{\sigma} \leftarrow (r, \widehat{\sigma}')$.
- $1/0 \leftarrow \mathsf{AVrfy}((\mathsf{pk}_1, \mathsf{m}_1), \ldots, (\mathsf{pk}_\ell, \mathsf{m}_\ell), \widehat{\sigma})$:
  1. Parse $\widehat{\sigma} = (r, \widehat{\sigma}')$.
  2. Compute $(\delta_1, \ldots, \delta_\ell) \leftarrow \widehat{H}(r, \mathsf{pk}_1, \ldots, \mathsf{pk}_\ell, \mathsf{m}_1, \ldots, \mathsf{m}_\ell)$.
  3. Output 1 if $e(\widehat{\sigma}', g_2) = \prod_{i=1}^{\ell} e(H(\mathsf{m}_i), v_i^{\delta_i})$ holds, and all $\mathsf{m}_1, \ldots, \mathsf{m}_\ell$ are distinct, where $\mathsf{pk}_i = v_i$ for $i \in [\ell]$. Output 0 otherwise.

We should notice that this scheme is different from the existing multi-/aggregate signatures based on [4] (e.g., [2,3]). As we explained beforehand, our key-idea of achieving asig-soundness is to choose fresh randomness r when compressing signatures, while the existing schemes (e.g., [2,3]) do not employ such an idea.

We show that the proposed scheme satisfies correctness. The first condition of the correctness holds clearly. The second condition also holds because if $(r, \widehat{\sigma}')$ is a valid aggregate signature (where $(\delta_1, \ldots, \delta_\ell) \leftarrow \widehat{H}(r, \mathsf{pk}_1, \ldots, \mathsf{pk}_\ell, \mathsf{m}_1, \ldots, \mathsf{m}_\ell)$ and $\widehat{\sigma}' = \prod_{i=1}^{\ell} \sigma_i^{\delta_i} = \prod_{i=1}^{\ell} H(\mathsf{m}_i)^{x_i \delta_i}$), then we have

$$
\begin{aligned}
e(\widehat{\sigma}', g_2) &= e(\prod_{i=1}^{\ell} H(\mathsf{m}_i)^{x_i \delta_i}, g_2) \\
&= \prod_{i=1}^{\ell} e(H(\mathsf{m}_i), g_2)^{x_i \delta_i} \\
&= \prod_{i=1}^{\ell} e(H(\mathsf{m}_i), g_2^{x_i \delta_i}) = \prod_{i=1}^{\ell} e(H(\mathsf{m}_i), v_i^{\delta_i}).
\end{aligned}
$$

Hence, $\mathsf{ASIG}^{snd}_{\mathsf{BGLS}}$ satisfies correctness.

Regarding the security of $\mathsf{ASIG}^{snd}_{\mathsf{BGLS}}$, we can prove that this scheme satisfies EUF-CMA security, in the same way as the proof of Theorem 1 in [3]. Notice that the unforgeability of $\mathsf{ASIG}^{snd}_{\mathsf{BGLS}}$ is ensured in the chosen-key model (Definition 4). This is because the AVrfy algorithm checks whether the given messages $\mathsf{m}_1, \ldots, \mathsf{m}_\ell$ are all distinct, in the same way as the $\mathsf{ASIG}_{\mathsf{BGLS}}$ scheme. Namely, it is unnecessary to use zero-knowledge proofs or disclose secret keys.

Regarding the asig-soundness of $\mathsf{ASIG}^{snd}_{\mathsf{BGLS}}$, the following theorem holds.

Theorem 3. *The aggregate signature scheme* $\mathsf{ASIG}^{snd}_{\mathsf{BGLS}}$ *satisfies* asig-soundness *in the random oracle model.*

Proof. Let A be a PPT adversary against $\mathsf{ASIG}^{snd}_{\mathsf{BGLS}}$. Let $((\mathsf{pk}_1, \mathsf{m}_1, \sigma_1), \ldots, (\mathsf{pk}_\ell, \mathsf{m}_\ell, \sigma_\ell))$ be the A's output in the asig-soundness game, and let $(r, \widehat{\sigma}') \leftarrow \mathsf{Agg}((\mathsf{pk}_1, \mathsf{m}_1, \sigma_1), \ldots, (\mathsf{pk}_\ell, \mathsf{m}_\ell, \sigma_\ell))$ be an aggregate signature computed from the A's output. Then, due to the winning condition of A, $e(\widehat{\sigma}', g_2) = \prod_{i=1}^{\ell} e(H(\mathsf{m}_i), v_i^{\delta_i})$ holds, but $e(H(\mathsf{m}_z)^{x_z}, g_2) \neq e(H(\mathsf{m}_z), g_2^{x_z})$ holds for $z \in [\ell]$ such that $\mathsf{pk}_z = \mathsf{pk}^*$, where $\mathsf{pk}_z = v_z = g_2^{x_z}$.

Let $\sigma_i = g_1^{c_i}$ for some $c_i \in \mathbb{Z}_p$, and $H(\mathsf{m}_i) = g_1^{c'_i}$ for some $c'_i \in \mathbb{Z}_p$. Then, we can write $e(\widehat{\sigma}', g_2) = \prod_{i=1}^{\ell} e(\sigma_i, g_2)^{\delta_i} = e(g_1, g_2)^{\sum_{i=1}^{\ell} c_i \delta_i}$ and $\prod_{i=1}^{\ell} e(H(\mathsf{m}_i), v_i^{\delta_i}) = \prod_{i=1}^{\ell} e(g_1, g_2)^{c'_i x_i \delta_i} = e(g_1, g_2)^{\sum_{i=1}^{\ell} c'_i x_i \delta_i}$. Thus, if AVrfy accepts the given pairs $((\mathsf{pk}_1, \mathsf{m}_1), \ldots, (\mathsf{pk}_\ell, \mathsf{m}_\ell))$ and $(r, \widehat{\sigma}')$ (i.e., $e(\widehat{\sigma}', g_2) = \prod_{i=1}^{\ell} e(H(\mathsf{m}_i), v_i^{\delta_i})$), then we have

$$
e(g_1, g_2)^{\sum_{i=1}^{\ell} c_i \delta_i} = e(g_1, g_2)^{\sum_{i=1}^{\ell} c'_i x_i \delta_i} \Leftrightarrow \sum_{i=1}^{\ell} c_i \delta_i - \sum_{i=1}^{\ell} c'_i x_i \delta_i \equiv 0 \pmod{p}.
$$

By letting $\beta_i = c_i - c'_i x_i$, it holds that $\sum_{i=1}^{\ell} \beta_i \delta_i \equiv 0 \pmod{p}$. Due to the winning condition of A, $\beta_z \neq 0$ holds for $z \in [\ell]$ such that $\mathsf{pk}_z = \mathsf{pk}^*$. In addition, since p is a prime, there exists γ_z such that $\beta_z \gamma_z \equiv 1 \pmod{p}$. Hence, we have $\delta_z \equiv -\gamma_z \sum_{i \in [\ell] \text{ s.t. } i \neq z} \beta_i \delta_i \pmod{p}$. Since $(\delta_1, \ldots, \delta_\ell) = \widehat{H}(r, \mathsf{pk}_1, \ldots, \mathsf{pk}_\ell, \mathsf{m}_1, \ldots, \mathsf{m}_\ell)$, the probability of choosing r such that $\delta_z \equiv -\gamma_z \sum_{i \in [\ell] \text{ s.t. } i \neq z} \beta_i \delta_i \pmod{p}$ is at most $2^{-\kappa}$. Hence, if $\mathsf{Vrfy}(\mathsf{pk}_z, \mathsf{m}_z, \sigma_z) = 0$, the probability that A guesses r such that $\mathsf{AVrfy}((\mathsf{pk}_1, \mathsf{m}_1), \ldots, (\mathsf{pk}_\ell, \mathsf{m}_\ell), (r, \widehat{\sigma}')) = 1$ is at most $2^{-\kappa}$, and we obtain $\mathsf{Adv}^{\text{asig-sound}}_{\mathsf{ASIG}^{snd}_{\mathsf{BGLS}}, \mathsf{A}}(\lambda) \leq 2^{-\kappa}$. □

4 Conclusion

In this paper, we comprehensively studied group testing aggregate signatures (GT-ASIG) that had functionality of both keyless aggregation of multiple signatures and identifying an invalid message from the aggregate signature, in order to reduce a total amount of signature-size for lots of messages. Specifically, we formalized the model and security notions for group testing aggregate signatures, and we provided construction methodology from aggregate signatures in a generic and comprehensive way. Furthermore, we proposed an aggregate signature scheme which we could apply to this construction methodology.

As explained in [11], aggregate signatures have interesting applications including sensor networks, secure logging, and authenticating software. We would like to expect that aggregate signatures with detecting functionality would be useful primitives for such applications in the era of IoT.

Regarding future work, it is important to consider a wider class of aggregate signatures with the non-interactive detecting functionality. Namely, it is meaningful to achieve the detecting functionality of GT-ASIG, without using combinatorial methods (i.e., group testing with d-disjunct matrices), though we formalized the notion of this aggregate signature by using d-disjunct matrices (Definition 6). Hence, constructing such an aggregate signature scheme without combinatorial methodology is future work in this research.

Acknowledgements. This paper is in part based on results obtained from a project, JPNP16007, commissioned by the New Energy and Industrial Technology Development Organization (NEDO). In addition, this work was in part supported by JSPS KAKENHI Grant Numbers JP22K19773, JP21H03395. The authors would like to thank the anonymous referees for their helpful comments.

Appendix A: Bilinear Groups for Co-Diffie-Hellman

We define bilinear groups for co-Diffie-Hellman, which are used in the aggregate signature scheme of [3]. The following notation is used: G_1, G_2, and G_T are multiplicative cyclic groups of prime order p. g_1 and g_2 are generators of G_1 and G_2, respectively. $\phi : G_2 \rightarrow G_1$ is an isomorphism with $\phi(g_2) = g_1$. $e : G_1 \times G_2 \rightarrow G_T$ is a bilinear map. Then, Co-computational Diffie-Hellman (co-CDH) problem, co-decision Diffie-Hellman (co-DDH) problem, and co-Gap Diffie-Hellman (co-GDH) group pairs are defined.

Definition 10 (co-CDH **and** co-DDH **problems**).

co-CDH. *Given* $g_2, g_2^a \in G_2$ *and* $h \in G_1$*, compute* $h^a \in G_1$
co-DDH. *Given* $g_2, g_2^a \in G_2$ *and* $h, h^b \in G_1$*, determine if* $a = b$ *or not.*

In [4], it is known that in the case of $G_1 = G_2$ and $g_1 = g_2$, there are reductions from co-CDH and co-DDH to the standard CDH and DDH problems, respectively.

Next, co-Gap Diffie-Hellman (co-GDH) group pairs are defined, as follows.

Definition 11 (Decision Group Pair). *The pair (G_1, G_2) of two groups is a decision group pair for co-Diffie-Hellman if the group action on G_1, the group action on G_2, and the map ϕ from G_2 to G_1 can be computed in one time unit, and co-decision Diffie-Hellman on (G_1, G_2) can be solved in one time unit.*

Definition 12 (Co-GDH Group Pair). *Suppose two groups G_1, G_2 are selected by following a security parameter λ. The advantage of a PPT algorithm* A *solving the* co-CDH *problem in groups G_1, G_2 is defined as* $\mathsf{Adv}_{\mathsf{A}}^{\text{co-cdh}}(\lambda) := \Pr[\mathsf{A}(g_2, g_2^a, h) \to h^a \mid a \xleftarrow{\$} \mathbb{Z}_p, h \xleftarrow{\$} G_1]$. *The pair (G_1, G_2) is a* co-GDH *group pair if the pair is a decision group pair for co-Diffie-Hellman, and* $\mathsf{Adv}_{\mathsf{A}}^{\text{co-cdh}}(\lambda) \leq \mathsf{negl}(\lambda)$ *holds for any PPT algorithm* A.

We define bilinear group pairs for co-Diffie-Hellman, which are used in the aggregate signature scheme of [3].

Definition 13 (Bilinear Group Pair for co-Diffie-Hellman). *Suppose two groups G_1, G_2 are selected by following a security parameter λ. The pair (G_1, G_2) is a bilinear group pair if the group action on either can be computed in one time unit, the map ϕ from G_2 to G_1 can be computed in one time unit, a bilinear map e is computable in one time unit. Furthermore, the pair (G_1, G_2) is a bilinear group pair for co-Diffie-Hellman if it is a bilinear group pair and* $\mathsf{Adv}_{\mathsf{A}}^{\text{co-cdh}}(\lambda) \leq \mathsf{negl}(\lambda)$ *holds for any PPT algorithm* A.

References

1. Bellare, M., Garay, J.A., Rabin, T.: Fast batch verification for modular exponentiation and digital signatures. In: EUROCRYPT. LNCS, vol. 1403, pp. 236–250. Springer (1998)
2. Boneh, D., Drijvers, M., Neven, G.: Compact Multi-signatures for Smaller Blockchains. In: Peyrin, T., Galbraith, S. (eds.) ASIACRYPT 2018. LNCS, vol. 11273, pp. 435–464. Springer, Cham (2018). https://doi.org/10.1007/978-3-030-03329-3_15
3. Boneh, D., Gentry, C., Lynn, B., Shacham, H.: Aggregate and Verifiably Encrypted Signatures from Bilinear Maps. In: Biham, E. (ed.) EUROCRYPT 2003. LNCS, vol. 2656, pp. 416–432. Springer, Heidelberg (2003). https://doi.org/10.1007/3-540-39200-9_26
4. Boneh, D., Lynn, B., Shacham, H.: Short signatures from the weil pairing. J. Cryptology **17**(4), 297–319 (2004)
5. Camenisch, J., Hohenberger, S., Pedersen, M.Ø.: Batch Verification of Short Signatures. In: Naor, M. (ed.) EUROCRYPT 2007. LNCS, vol. 4515, pp. 246–263. Springer, Heidelberg (2007). https://doi.org/10.1007/978-3-540-72540-4_14
6. Dorfman, R.: The detection of defective members of large populations. Ann. Math. Stat. **14**(4), 436–440 (1943)
7. Du, D.Z., Hwang, F.K.: Combinatorial Group Testing and Its Applications. Series on Applied Mathematics, 2nd edn. vol. 12. World Scientific (2000)
8. Eppstein, D., Goodrich, M.T., Hirschberg, D.S.: Improved combinatorial group testing algorithms for real-world problem sizes. SIAM J. Comput. **36**(5), 1360–1375 (2007)

9. Ferrara, A.L., Green, M., Hohenberger, S., Pedersen, M.Ø.: Practical short signature batch verification. In: Fischlin, M. (ed.) CT-RSA 2009. LNCS, vol. 5473, pp. 309–324. Springer, Heidelberg (2009). https://doi.org/10.1007/978-3-642-00862-7_21
10. Gentry, C., Ramzan, Z.: Identity-based aggregate signatures. In: Yung, M., Dodis, Y., Kiayias, A., Malkin, T. (eds.) PKC 2006. LNCS, vol. 3958, pp. 257–273. Springer, Heidelberg (2006). https://doi.org/10.1007/11745853_17
11. Hartung, G., Kaidel, B., Koch, A., Koch, J., Rupp, A.: Fault-tolerant aggregate signatures. In: Cheng, C.-M., Chung, K.-M., Persiano, G., Yang, B.-Y. (eds.) PKC 2016. LNCS, vol. 9614, pp. 331–356. Springer, Heidelberg (2016). https://doi.org/10.1007/978-3-662-49384-7_13
12. Hirose, S., Shikata, J.: Aggregate message authentication code capable of non-adaptive group-testing. IEEE Access **8**, 216116–216126 (2020)
13. Hohenberger, S., Sahai, A., Waters, B.: Full domain hash from (leveled) multilinear maps and identity-based aggregate signatures. In: Canetti, R., Garay, J.A. (eds.) CRYPTO 2013. LNCS, vol. 8042, pp. 494–512. Springer, Heidelberg (2013). https://doi.org/10.1007/978-3-642-40041-4_27
14. Hwang, F.K.: A method for detecting all defective members in a population by group testing. J. Am. Stat. Assoc. **67**(339), 605–608 (1972)
15. Katz, J., Lindell, A.Y.: Aggregate message authentication codes. In: Malkin, T. (ed.) CT-RSA 2008. LNCS, vol. 4964, pp. 155–169. Springer, Heidelberg (2008). https://doi.org/10.1007/978-3-540-79263-5_10
16. Li, C.H.: A sequential method for screening experimental variables. J. Am. Stat. Assoc. **57**(298), 455–477 (1962)
17. Minematsu, K.: Efficient message authentication codes with combinatorial group testing. In: Pernul, G., Ryan, P.Y.A., Weippl, E. (eds.) ESORICS 2015. LNCS, vol. 9326, pp. 185–202. Springer, Cham (2015). https://doi.org/10.1007/978-3-319-24174-6_10
18. Minematsu, K., Kamiya, N.: Symmetric-key corruption detection: when XoR-macs meet combinatorial group testing. In: Sako, K., Schneider, S., Ryan, P.Y.A. (eds.) ESORICS 2019. LNCS, vol. 11735, pp. 595–615. Springer, Cham (2019). https://doi.org/10.1007/978-3-030-29959-0_29
19. Ogawa, Y., Sato, S., Shikata, J., Imai, H.: Aggregate message authentication codes with detecting functionality from biorthogonal codes. In: 2020 IEEE International Symposium on Information Theory (ISIT 2020). IEEE (2020)
20. Porat, E., Rothschild, A.: Explicit non-adaptive combinatorial group testing schemes. In: Aceto, L., Damgård, I., Goldberg, L.A., Halldórsson, M.M., Ingólfsdóttir, A., Walukiewicz, I. (eds.) ICALP 2008. LNCS, vol. 5125, pp. 748–759. Springer, Heidelberg (2008). https://doi.org/10.1007/978-3-540-70575-8_61
21. Rückert, M., Schröder, D.: Aggregate and verifiably encrypted signatures from multilinear maps without random oracles. In: Park, J.H., Chen, H.-H., Atiquzzaman, M., Lee, C., Kim, T., Yeo, S.-S. (eds.) ISA 2009. LNCS, vol. 5576, pp. 750–759. Springer, Heidelberg (2009). https://doi.org/10.1007/978-3-642-02617-1_76
22. Sato, S., Hirose, S., Shikata, J.: Sequential aggregate MACs with detecting functionality revisited. In: Liu, J.K., Huang, X. (eds.) NSS 2019. LNCS, vol. 11928, pp. 387–407. Springer, Cham (2019). https://doi.org/10.1007/978-3-030-36938-5_23
23. Sato, S., Shikata, J.: Interactive aggregate message authentication scheme with detecting functionality. In: Barolli, L., Takizawa, M., Xhafa, F., Enokido, T. (eds.) AINA 2019. AISC, vol. 926, pp. 1316–1328. Springer, Cham (2020). https://doi.org/10.1007/978-3-030-15032-7_110

24. Sato, S., Shikata, J.: Interactive aggregate message authentication equipped with detecting functionality from adaptive group testing. In: Cryptology ePrint Archive. IACR, October 2020
25. Thierry-Mieg, N.: A new pooling strategy for high-throughput screening: the shifted transversal design. BMC Bioinform. **7**, 28 (2006)

Attribute-Based Signatures for Range of Inner Product and Its Applications

Masahito Ishizaka(✉) and Kazuhide Fukushima

KDDI Research, Inc., Saitama, Japan
{xma-ishizaka,ka-fukushima}@kddi.com

Abstract. In attribute-based signatures (ABS) for inner products, the digital signature analogue of attribute-based encryption for inner products (Katz et al., EuroCrypt'08), a signing-key (resp. signature) is labeled with an n-dimensional vector $\mathbf{x} \in \mathbb{Z}_p^n$ (resp. $\mathbf{y} \in \mathbb{Z}_p^n$) for a prime p, and the signing succeeds iff their inner product is zero, i.e., $\langle \mathbf{x}, \mathbf{y} \rangle = 0 \pmod p$. We generalize it to ABS for *range* of inner product (ARIP), requiring the inner product to be within an arbitrarily-chosen range $[L, R]$. As security notions, we define adaptive unforgeablity and perfect signer-privacy. The latter means that any signature reveals no more information about $\mathbf{x}$ than $\langle \mathbf{x}, \mathbf{y} \rangle \in [L, R]$. We propose two efficient schemes, secure under some Diffie-Hellman type assumptions in the standard model, based on non-interactive proof and linearly homomorphic signatures. The 2nd (resp. 1st) scheme is independent of the parameter n in secret-key size (resp. signature size and verification cost). We show that ARIP has many applications, e.g., ABS for range evaluation of polynomials/weighted averages, fuzzy identity-based signatures, time-specific signatures, ABS for range of Hamming/Euclidean distance and ABS for hyperellipsoid predicates.

Keywords: Attribute-based signatures for range of inner product · Adaptive unforgeablity · Signer-privacy · Symmetric bilinear groups of prime order

1 Introduction

Attribute-Based Encryption (ABE) for Inner Products. In ABE for inner products [16], n-dimensional vector $\mathbf{x} \in \mathbb{Z}_p^n$ (resp. $\mathbf{y} \in \mathbb{Z}_p^n$) for a prime p is associated with secret-key (resp. ciphertext). The decryption succeeds iff $\langle \mathbf{x}, \mathbf{y} \rangle = 0 \pmod p$. It can be generically transformed into various ABE primitives, e.g., (anonymous) identity-based encryption (IBE), hidden-vector encryption (HVE) [10], the dual variant of HVE (= wildcarded IBE [1]), ABE for evaluation of polynomials/weighted averages, ABE for CNF and DNF formulas, and ABE for exact thresholds. Let us consider a generalized primitive, named ABE for arbitrarily-chosen inner product (ACIP), enabling a signer to choose a value of inner product $a \in \mathbb{Z}_p$. Obviously, ABE for ACIP with n dimensions can be transformed from the usual ABE for inner products with $n + 1$ dimensions[1].

[1] The $(n+1)$-th elements of $\mathbf{x}, \mathbf{y} \in \mathbb{Z}_p^{n+1}$ are set to 1 and $-a \pmod p$, respectively.

S.-H. Seo and H. Seo (Eds.): ICISC 2022, LNCS 13849, pp. 382–407, 2023.
https://doi.org/10.1007/978-3-031-29371-9_19

Attribute-Based Signatures (ABS) for Inner Products (AIP). AIP is the signature analogue of the ABE for inner products. The signing succeeds iff $\langle \mathbf{x}, \mathbf{y} \rangle = 0 \pmod{p}$. A signer-privacy guarantees that any signature leaks no more information about $\mathbf{x}$ than $\langle \mathbf{x}, \mathbf{y} \rangle = 0$. It has many applications, e.g., identity-based signatures (IBS), hidden-vector signatures (HVS) (= the signature analogue of HVE), the dual variant of HVS, ABS for evaluation of polynomials/weighted averages, ABS for CNF and DNF formulas, and ABS for exact thresholds.

ABS for Range of Inner Product (ARIP). We generalize a specific value of inner product to a *range* of values. A range $[L, R]$ with $L, R \in \mathbb{Z}_p$ is associated with a signature. If the inner product is within the range, the signing succeeds. The encryption analogue of ARIP, named ABE for range of inner product, can be transformed from ABE for ACIP in a simple manner, where for each integer $i \in [L, R]$, the encryptor generates a ciphertext C_i whose inner product is set to i^2. The same transformation is not directly applicable to ARIP since the signer-privacy requires the real inner product $\langle \mathbf{x}, \mathbf{y} \rangle$ to be hidden. The ABS scheme by Sakai et al. [26] supporting any circuit as signer-predicate can be an ARIP scheme by properly configuring the circuit. A vector $\mathbf{x} \in \mathbb{Z}_p^n$ is transformed into a binary attribute $x \in \{0,1\}^{n\lambda}$. In their ABS scheme, at signature generation, a signer generates a commitment of the non-interactive witness indistinguishable proof (NIWI) system by Groth and Sahai (GS) [11] for each bit $x[i] \in \{0,1\}$ of x. Thus, at least, its signature length linearly increases with n.

Contribution of this work is threefold. First, we formally define the syntax and security of ARIP. Second, we propose two efficient ARIP schemes based on NIWI and linearly homomorphic signatures (LHS)[3] [9], one of which is independent of n in signature length. Third, we show that ARIP has various applications.

Formalization of ARIP. As the security requirements, we define adaptive existential unforgeability [20,26] and perfect signer-privacy [7]. The latter guarantees that any signature leaks no information about $\mathbf{x} \in \mathbb{Z}_p^n$ of the signer. Its definition is simulatability-based, which requires us to prove that any signature which should be generated using a specific revealed secret-key associated with a vector $\mathbf{x} \in \mathbb{Z}_p$ is simulatable even if without knowing the secret-key.

Our Efficient ARIP Schemes. We propose two efficient ARIP schemes, based on symmetric bilinear pairing groups of prime order, and secure under the computational Diffie-Hellman (CDH), flexible CDH (flexCDH) [6] and decisional linear (DLIN) assumptions. The 2nd (resp. 1st) scheme is independent of n in secret-key size (resp. signature size and verification cost). They are originally a generic

[2] A drawback of this simple approach is low efficiency. Ciphertext length and encryption cost linearly increase with the maximal cardinality of the range $[L, R]$, which is p if $L, R \in \mathbb{Z}_p$ or T if $L, R \in [0, T-1]$ for $T \in \mathbb{N}$.

[3] In LHS, any signature on a message of vector $\boldsymbol{v} \in \mathbb{Z}_p^n$ is labeled with a tag $\tau \in \{0,1\}^*$. Any entity collecting l signatures $\sigma_1, \cdots, \sigma_l$ with the same tag τ on $\boldsymbol{v}_1, \cdots, \boldsymbol{v}_l \in \mathbb{Z}_p^n$ can derive a new $\overline{\sigma}$ on any linear combination $\overline{\boldsymbol{v}} = \sum_{i=1}^{l} \beta_i \cdot \boldsymbol{v}_i \in \mathbb{Z}_p^n$ with $\beta_i \in \mathbb{Z}_p$.

construction based on NIWI and LHS, which is instantiated from the GS NIWI system and a simplified variant of the LHS scheme by Attrapadung, Libert and Peters (ALP) [6].

The generic construction behind our 1st scheme is as follows. For a secret-key $sk_{\mathbf{x}}$ for $\mathbf{x} \in \mathbb{Z}_p^n$, we generate $n+4$ number of vectors $\{\boldsymbol{v}_i\}_{i=1}^{n+4}$. Each $\boldsymbol{v}_i \in \mathbb{Z}_p^{n+5}$ is set to $x_i | \boldsymbol{e}_i$ if $i \in [1, n]$, or $0 | \boldsymbol{e}_i$ otherwise, where $\boldsymbol{e}_i \in \mathbb{Z}_p^{n+4}$ is the i-th unit vector. Then, randomly choose a tag $\tau \in \{0,1\}^N$ and generate $n+4$ signatures $\sigma_1, \cdots, \sigma_{n+4}$ of the LHS on the vectors $\boldsymbol{v}_1, \cdots, \boldsymbol{v}_{n+4}$ under the tag τ. $sk_{\mathbf{x}}$ consists of all of the signatures. To sign a message $M \in \mathbb{Z}_p$ under a vector $\mathbf{y} \in \mathbb{Z}_p^n$ and a range $[L, R] \subseteq \mathbb{Z}_p$, we set $n+4$ number of weight coefficients $\beta_1, \cdots, \beta_{n+4}$ as $\beta_i := y_i$ for each $i \in [1, n]$, and $(\beta_{n+1}, \beta_{n+2}, \beta_{n+3}, \beta_{n+4}) := (L, R, M, 1)$. Then, derive a new signature $\overline{\sigma}$ on the linear combination $\overline{\boldsymbol{v}} := \sum_{i=1}^{n+4} \beta_i \boldsymbol{v}_i$. Note that $\overline{\boldsymbol{v}}$ is in the form of $(\langle \mathbf{x}, \mathbf{y} \rangle \pmod p), y_1, \cdots, y_n, L, R, M, 1)$. Finally, under the witness of $\langle \mathbf{x}, \mathbf{y} \rangle$, τ and $\overline{\sigma}$, generate an NIWI proof π that both of the following two conditions are satisfied, namely (1) *$\overline{\sigma}$ is a correct LHS signature on $\overline{\boldsymbol{v}}$ under τ*, and (2) $\langle \mathbf{x}, \mathbf{y} \rangle \in [L, R]$. In the GS NIWI system, the prover computes a commitment for each variable, then generates proofs that the variables satisfy a pairing-product equation in a form of $\prod_{i=1}^{m} e(\mathcal{A}_i, \mathcal{X}_i) \cdot \prod_{i=1}^{m} \prod_{j=1}^{m} e(\mathcal{X}_i, \mathcal{X}_j)^{a_{ij}} = t_T$, where $\mathcal{X}_i \in \mathbb{G}$ are variables and $\mathcal{A}_i \in \mathbb{G}$, $a_{ij} \in \mathbb{Z}_p$ and $t_T \in \mathbb{G}_T$ are constants. Actually, the verification algorithm of the simplified variant of ALP LHS scheme consists of only two such equations. Thus, proving for the 1st condition (1) is non-problematic. To prove for the 2nd condition (2), we adopt the tree-based range membership technique used for efficient time-specific encryption/signatures constructions [14,23].

In our 2nd scheme, each secret-key $sk_{\mathbf{x}}$ consists of only four LHS signatures $\sigma_1, \cdots, \sigma_4$ on vectors $\boldsymbol{v}_1, \cdots, \boldsymbol{v}_4$. Each $\boldsymbol{v}_i \in \mathbb{Z}_p^{n+4}$ is set to $(x_1, \cdots, x_n) | \boldsymbol{e}_i$ if $i = 1$, or $(0, \cdots, 0) | \boldsymbol{e}_i$ otherwise, where $\boldsymbol{e}_i \in \mathbb{Z}_p^4$ is the i-th unit vector. At signature generation, we derive a signature $\overline{\sigma}$ on $\overline{\boldsymbol{v}} := \sum_{i=1}^{4} \beta_i \boldsymbol{v}_i$, where $(\beta_1, \beta_2, \beta_3, \beta_4) := (1, L, R, M)$. Note that $\overline{\boldsymbol{v}} = (x_1, \cdots, x_n, 1, L, R, M) \in \mathbb{Z}_p^{n+4}$. Finally, under the witness of $\langle \mathbf{x}, \mathbf{y} \rangle$, τ, $\overline{\sigma}$ and $\mathbf{x}$, generate an NIWI proof that all of the following three conditions are satisfied, namely (1) *$\overline{\sigma}$ is a correct LHS signature on $\overline{\boldsymbol{v}}$ under τ*, (2) $\langle \mathbf{x}, \mathbf{y} \rangle \in [L, R]$ and (3) $\langle \mathbf{x}, \mathbf{y} \rangle = \sum_{i=1}^{n} x_i \cdot y_i \pmod p$.

Applications of ARIP. Since ARIP is a generalization of AIP, any ABS primitive which can be transformed from AIP, can also be transformed from ARIP. And not only that, for some of such primitives, ARIP can transform into more generalized primitives. The first example is ABS for *range* evaluation of polynomials (AREP), which is a generalization of the ABS for evaluation of polynomial. In AREP, each signature is labeled with a polynomial $f : \mathbb{Z}_p \to \{0,1\}$ and a range $[L, R] \subseteq \mathbb{Z}_p$. A secret-key with $x \in \mathbb{Z}_p$ correctly signs iff $f(x) \in [L, R] \pmod p$. Another example is ABS for *range* evaluation of weighted average (resp. fuzzy identity-based signatures), which is a generalization of the ABS for evaluation of weighted averages (resp. the ABS for exact thresholds). Moreover, ARIP can be transformed into the following (original) ABS, namely time-specific signatures

[14,23], ABS for range of Hamming/Euclidean distance, and ABS for hypersphere/hyperellipsoid predicates. For the details, refer to Sect. 5.

Further Related Work. The idea of ABS was proposed by Maji et al. [19,20]. They proposed a generic construction, supporting monotone span programs as predicate, based on a non-interactive proof system and a digital signature scheme. Okamoto and Takashima [22] proposed an ABS scheme supporting non-monotone span programs as predicate based on the technique of dual pairing vector spaces. Sakai et al. [26] proposed an ABS scheme supporting arbitral circuits as predicate, built from the GS proof [11] and the structure-preserving signatures by Kiltz et al. [17]. Sakai et al. [27] proposed key-policy ABS for any deterministic Turing machines as predicate. Zhang et al. [29] proposed an ABS scheme for inner products, secure under a lattice assumption of Short Integer Solution problem in the random oracle model. In ABE for *non-zero* inner products [16], unlike ABE for inner products [16], the decryption succeeds iff the inner product is non-zero. A lot of secure schemes based on bilinear maps [3,4,21] or lattice assumptions [15] have been proposed. Phuong et al. [24] proposed a secure construction of edit distance based encryption (EdDBE). In EdDBE, each secret-key (resp. ciphertext) is associated with an alphabet string A (resp. an alphabet string A' and a threshold value t). The decryption succeeds iff the edit distance (aka. Levenshtein distance) between A and A' is smaller than t. Guo et al. [12] proposed the notion of Euclidean distance based encryption (EuDBE). In EuDBE, each secret-key (resp. ciphertext) is associated with a vector $\boldsymbol{x} = (x_1, \cdots, x_n) \in \mathbb{R}^n$ (resp. a vector $\boldsymbol{y} = (y_1, \cdots, y_n) \subset \mathbb{R}^n$ and a threshold $t \in \mathbb{R}$) with a real number space $\mathbb{R}$. The decryption succeeds iff the Euclidean distance between $\boldsymbol{x}$ and $\boldsymbol{y}$ is smaller than t[4]. They proposed a generic EuDBE construction from any ABE for inner products [16].

Paper Organization. In Sect. 2, we explain some notations and define the CDH, FlexCDH and DLIN assumptions. In Sect. 3, we define the syntax and security of ABS for a general predicate f and ARIP. In Sect. 4, we propose two ARIP schemes and its optimized versions in terms of efficiency. In Sect. 5, we explain that ARIP has many applications. In Sect. 6, we summarize the paper, then discuss possible functional developments of ARIP.

2 Preliminaries

Notations. For $\lambda \in \mathbb{N}$, 1^λ denotes a security parameter. A function $f : \mathbb{N} \rightarrow \mathbb{R}$ is negligible if for every $c \in \mathbb{N}$, there exists $x_0 \in \mathbb{N}$ s.t. for every $x \geq x_0$, $f(x) \leq x^{-c}$. Given a binary string $x \in \{0,1\}^L$, for every $i \in [0, L-1]$, let $x[i] \in \{0,1\}$ denote its i-th bit. PPTA means probabilistic polynomial time algorithm. For a set A, $a \xleftarrow{U} A$ means that an element a is chosen uniformly at random from A.

[4] The EuDBE is similar to the encryption analogue of our ABS for range of Euclidean distance, but more functionally-restricted than it, because in the latter, not only the upper bound R (of the Euclidean distance) but also the lower bound L can be chosen.

Symmetric Bilinear Pairing on Groups with Prime Order. $\mathcal{G}$ takes a security parameter 1^λ with $\lambda \in \mathbb{N}$ and outputs a group description $(p, \mathbb{G}, \mathbb{G}_T, e, g)$. p is a prime with length λ. $\mathbb{G}$ and $\mathbb{G}_T$ are multiplicative groups with order p. g is a generator of $\mathbb{G}$. $e : \mathbb{G} \times \mathbb{G} \to \mathbb{G}_T$ is an efficiently-computable function which satisfies both of the following conditions.

Bilinearity. For any $a, b \in \mathbb{Z}_p$, $e(g^a, g^b) = e(g, g)^{ab}$

Non-degeneracy. $e(g, g) \neq 1_{\mathbb{G}_T}$, where $1_{\mathbb{G}_T}$ denotes the unit element of $\mathbb{G}_T$.

Assumptions. We define the three computational hardness assumptions.

Definition 1. *The computational Diffie-Hellman (CDH) assumption holds on the group* $\mathbb{G}$ *if for every PPT* $\mathcal{A}$, $\mathit{Adv}^{\mathit{CDH}}_{\mathcal{A},\mathbb{G}}(\lambda) := \Pr[g^{ab} \leftarrow \mathcal{A}(g, g^a, g^b)]$ *with* $a, b \overset{\mathrm{U}}{\longleftarrow} \mathbb{Z}_p$, *is negligible.*

Definition 2. *The flexible CDH (FlexCDH) assumption [6] holds on the group* $\mathbb{G}$ *if for every PPT* $\mathcal{A}$, $\mathit{Adv}^{\mathit{FlexCDH}}_{\mathcal{A},\mathbb{G}}(\lambda) := \Pr[(g^\mu, g^{a\cdot\mu}, g^{ab\cdot\mu}) \leftarrow \mathcal{A}(g, g^a, g^b)]$ *with* $a, b \overset{\mathrm{U}}{\longleftarrow} \mathbb{Z}_p$ *and* $\mu \neq 0$, *is negligible.*

Definition 3. *The decisional linear (DLIN) assumption holds on the group* $\mathbb{G}$ *if for every PPT* $\mathcal{A}$, $\mathit{Adv}^{\mathit{DLIN}}_{\mathcal{A},\mathbb{G}}(\lambda) := |\Pr[1 \leftarrow \mathcal{A}(g^a, g^b, g^{ab}, g^{bd}, g^{c+d})]| - \Pr[1 \leftarrow \mathcal{A}(g^a, g^b, g^{ab}, g^{bd}, g^z)]$ *with* $a, b, c, d, z \overset{\mathrm{U}}{\longleftarrow} \mathbb{Z}_p$, *is negligible.*

3 ABS for Range of Inner-Product (ARIP)

We define general ABS for predicate f in the first subsection, then show that ARIP is a concrete example of the general ABS in the second subsection.

3.1 General ABS for Predicate f

General ABS for predicate $f : \{0,1\}^* \to \{0,1\}$ in $\mathcal{F}$ consists of the following four polynomial-time algorithms. `Ver` is deterministic and the others are probabilistic.

Setup `Setup`**:** It takes a security parameter 1^λ for $\lambda \in \mathbb{N}$, then outputs a public parameter pp and master-key mk. Let $\mathcal{M}$ denote the message space. Note that the other algorithms implicitly take pp as input. $[(pp, mk) \leftarrow \mathtt{Setup}(1^\lambda)]$

Key-Generation `KGen`**:** It takes mk and an attribute $x \in \{0,1\}^*$, then outputs a secret-key sk. $[sk \leftarrow \mathtt{KGen}(mk, x)]$

Signing `Sig`**:** It takes a secret-key sk, a message $M \in \mathcal{M}$, a predicate $f \in \mathcal{F}$, then outputs a signature σ. $[\sigma \leftarrow \mathtt{Sig}(sk, M, f)]$

Verification `Ver`**:** It takes a signature σ, a message $M \in \mathcal{M}$, a predicate $f \in \mathcal{F}$, then outputs 1 or 0. $[1/0 \leftarrow \mathtt{Ver}(\sigma, M, f)]$

Every ABS scheme must be correct. Informally the property means that every correctly generated signature is accepted. Formally the property is defined as follows. An ABS scheme is correct if $\forall\lambda \in \mathbb{N}$, $\forall(pp, mk) \leftarrow \mathtt{Setup}(1^\lambda)$,

$\forall x \in \{0,1\}^*$, $\forall sk \leftarrow \mathtt{KGen}(mk, x)$, $\forall M \in \mathcal{M}$, $\forall f \in \mathcal{F}$ s.t. $1 \leftarrow f(x)$, $\forall \sigma \leftarrow \mathtt{Sig}(sk, M, f)$, $1 \leftarrow \mathtt{Ver}(\sigma, M, f)$ holds.

As security for ABS, we require unforgeability and signer-privacy. As a notion of unforgeability, we define *(weak) existential unforgeability against adaptively-chosen messages and predicate attack* (EUF-CMA). For a PPT algorithm $\mathcal{A}$, we consider the following experiment.

$\boldsymbol{Expt}^{\mathtt{EUF\text{-}CMA}}_{\Sigma_{\mathrm{ABS}},\mathcal{A}}(1^\lambda)$:
  1. $(pp, mk) \leftarrow \mathtt{Setup}(1^\lambda)$. $(\sigma^*, M^* \in \mathcal{M}, f^* \in \mathcal{F}) \leftarrow \mathcal{A}^{\mathfrak{Reveal},\mathfrak{Sign}}(pp)$.

- -

  - $\mathfrak{Reveal}(x \in \{0,1\}^*)$: $sk \leftarrow \mathtt{KGen}(mk, x)$. $Q := Q \cup \{x\}$. **Rtrn** sk.
  - $\mathfrak{Sign}(x \in \{0,1\}^*, M \in \mathcal{M}, f \in \mathcal{F})$:
    $sk \leftarrow \mathtt{KGen}(mk, x)$. $\sigma \leftarrow \mathtt{Sig}(sk, M, f)$. $Q' := Q' \cup \{(M, f, \sigma)\}$. **Rtrn** σ.

- -

  2. **Rtrn** 1 if
    (1) $1 \leftarrow \mathtt{Ver}(\sigma^*, M^*, y^*)$, (2) $\forall x \in Q, 0 \leftarrow f^*(x)$ and (3) $(M^*, f^*, \cdot) \notin Q'$.
  3. **Rtrn** 0.

Definition 4. *An ABS scheme Σ_{ABS} is EUF-CMA if for every $\lambda \in \mathbb{N}$ and every PPT $\mathcal{A}$, $\mathcal{A}$'s advantage $\boldsymbol{Adv}^{\mathit{EUF\text{-}CMA}}_{\Sigma_{\mathrm{ABS}},\mathcal{A}}(\lambda) := \Pr[1 \leftarrow \boldsymbol{Expt}^{\mathit{EUF\text{-}CMA}}_{\Sigma_{\mathrm{ABS}},\mathcal{A}}(1^\lambda)]$ is negligible.*

As a notion of signer-privacy, we define perfect signer-privacy (PRV). For a probabilistic algorithm $\mathcal{A}$, we consider the following two experiments.

$\boldsymbol{Expt}^{\mathtt{PRV}}_{\Sigma_{\mathrm{ABS}},\mathcal{A},0}(1^\lambda)$: // $\boldsymbol{Expt}^{\mathtt{PRV}}_{\Sigma_{\mathrm{ABS}},\mathcal{A},1}$
  $(pp, mk) \leftarrow \mathtt{Setup}(1^\lambda)$. $(pp, mk, \mu) \leftarrow \mathtt{SimSetup}(1^\lambda)$.
  Rtrn $b' \leftarrow \mathcal{A}^{\mathfrak{Reveal},\mathfrak{Sign}}(pp, mk)$.

- -

  - $\mathfrak{Reveal}(x \in \{0,1\}^*)$:
    $sk \leftarrow \mathtt{KGen}(mk, x)$. $sk \leftarrow \mathtt{SimKGen}(mk, \mu, x)$. $Q := Q \cup \{(x, sk)\}$. **Rtrn** sk.
  - $\mathfrak{Sign}(x \in \{0,1\}^*, sk, M \in \mathcal{M}, f \in \mathcal{F})$:
    Rtrn $\perp$ if $(x, sk) \notin Q \vee 0 \leftarrow f(x)$. $\sigma \leftarrow \mathtt{Sig}(sk, M, f)$.
    $\sigma \leftarrow \mathtt{SimSig}(mk, \mu, M, f)$. **Rtrn** σ.

The latter is associated with 3 polynomial-time algorithms {SimSetup, SimKGen, SimSig}. The grey parts are considered in the latter, but ignored in the former.

Definition 5. *An ABS scheme Σ_{ABS} is perfectly signer-private (PRV) if for every $\lambda \in \mathbb{N}$ and every probabilistic algorithm $\mathcal{A}$, there exist polynomial-time algorithms {SimSetup, SimKGen, SimSig} such that $\mathcal{A}$'s advantage $\boldsymbol{Adv}^{\mathit{PRV}}_{\Sigma_{\mathrm{ABS}},\mathcal{A}}(\lambda) := |\sum_{b=0}^{1}(-1)^b \Pr[1 \leftarrow \boldsymbol{Expt}^{\mathit{PRV}}_{\Sigma_{\mathrm{ABS}},\mathcal{A},b}(1^\lambda)]|$ is 0.*

3.2 ARIP

ARIP is a sub-class of the general ABS for predicate f. p denotes a prime number of bit length λ. $n \in \mathbf{poly}(\lambda)$ is an integer. An attribute $x \in \{0,1\}^*$ in the general ABS is changed into an n-dimensional vector $\mathbf{x} \in \mathbb{Z}_p^n$ in ARIP. A predicate $f \in \mathcal{F}$ is associated with an n-dimensional vector $\mathbf{y} \in \mathbb{Z}_p^n$ and a range $[L, R]$ with $L, R \in \mathbb{Z}_p$. We parse $\mathbf{x}$ (resp. $\mathbf{y}$) as $(x_1, \cdots, x_n)$ (resp. $(y_1, \cdots, y_n)$). The predicate outputs 1 if (and only if) $\langle \mathbf{x}, \mathbf{y} \rangle (:= \sum_{i=1}^{n} x_i \cdot y_i) \in [L, R] \pmod p$.

4 Our ARIP Schemes

Non-Interactive Witness-Indistinguishable Proof (NIWI). An NIWI system by Groth and Sahai (GS) [11], based on a group $\mathbb{G}$ whose order is a prime p, is secure under the DLIN assumption. The CRS consists of 3 vectors $\vec{f}_1, \vec{f}_2, \vec{f}_3 \in \mathbb{G}^3$, where $\vec{f}_1 = (f_1, 1, g)$, $\vec{f}_2 = (1, f_2, g)$ and $f_1, f_2 \in \mathbb{G}$. A commitment $\vec{C}$ to a group element $X \in \mathbb{G}$ is given as $\vec{C} := (1, 1, X) \cdot \vec{f}_1^r \cdot \vec{f}_2^s \cdot \vec{f}_3^t$, where $r, s, t \xleftarrow{U} \mathbb{Z}_p$. The CRS is in one of the following two settings, (1) perfect soundness setting and (2) perfect witness-indistinguishability (WI) setting. The CRS in the former setting satisfies $\vec{f}_3 = \vec{f}_1^{\xi_1} \cdot \vec{f}_2^{\xi_2}$ with $\xi_1, \xi_2 \in \mathbb{Z}_p$. From any commitment $\vec{C} = (f_1^{r+\xi_1 t}, f_2^{s+\xi_2 t}, X \cdot g^{r+s+t(\xi_1+\xi_2)})$ distributing as a Boneh-Boyen-Shacham (BBS) ciphertext [8], the committed variable X is extracted by using $\beta_1 = \log_g(f_1)$ and $\beta_2 = \log_g(f_2)$. In the latter setting, where the element $\vec{f}_3$ is chosen outside the span of $\vec{f}_1$ and $\vec{f}_2$, any commitment is perfectly hiding. In the GS NIWI system, the prover can efficiently prove that committed variables satisfy a paring-product equation in the form of $\prod_{i=1}^{m} e(\mathcal{A}_i, \mathcal{X}_i) \cdot \prod_{i=1}^{m} \prod_{j=1}^{m} e(\mathcal{X}_i, \mathcal{X}_j)^{a_{ij}} = t_T$ for variables $\mathcal{X}_i \in \mathbb{G}$ and constants $\mathcal{A}_i \in \mathbb{G}$, $a_{ij} \in \mathbb{Z}_p$ and $t_T \in \mathbb{G}_T$.

Linearly Homomorphic Signatures (LHS) [9]. In LHS, each signature on a message of vector $\boldsymbol{v} \in \mathbb{Z}_p^n$ is labeled with a tag $\tau \in \{0,1\}^N$. Any entity collecting l number of signatures $\sigma_1, \cdots, \sigma_l$ labeled with the same tag τ on messages $\boldsymbol{v}_1, \cdots, \boldsymbol{v}_l \in \mathbb{Z}_p^n$ can derive a new signature $\overline{\sigma}$ on any linear combination $\overline{\boldsymbol{v}} = \sum_{i=1}^{l} \beta_i \cdot \boldsymbol{v}_i \in \mathbb{Z}_p^n$ with $\beta_i \in \mathbb{Z}_p$. The unforgeability security informally means that no PPT adversary, given q number of signatures $\{\sigma_i\}_{i=1}^q$ with $q \in \mathbf{poly}(\lambda)$ on arbitrarily and adaptively chosen vectors $\{\boldsymbol{v}_i\}_{i=1}^q$ with tags $\{\tau_i\}_{i=1}^q$, can find a correct signature on a vector $\boldsymbol{v}^* \notin V_{\tau^*}$ on a tag τ^* with a non-negligible probability, where V_{τ^*} denotes the subspace spanned by all of the vectors $\boldsymbol{v}_i$ s.t. $\tau_i = \tau^*$. Attrapadung, Libert and Peters (ALP) [6] proposed unforgeable and complete context-hiding (CCH) secure scheme, based on the CDH and FlexCDH assumptions. The CCH notion [5] and a weaker notion called strong context-hiding (SCH) [2] are unlinkability-related notions, which guarantee that any derived signature (from some of the other signatures) distributes identically to a fresh signature directly generated by the signing-key. Our ARIP schemes do not need these unlinkablity notions. We consider the following simplified variant of the ALP LHS scheme lacking CCH security. The verification-key includes group elements $g, v, \{g_i\}_{i=1}^n, u'$ and $\{u_i\}_{i=0}^{N-1}$. The signing-key is $\alpha \in \mathbb{Z}_p$. A signature on $\boldsymbol{v} \in \mathbb{Z}_p^n$ under a tag $\tau \in \{0,1\}^N$ distributes as $((\prod_{i=1}^n g_i^{v_i} v^s)^\alpha H_{\mathbb{G}}(\tau)^r, g^r, g^s, g^{s \cdot \alpha})$ with randomnesses $r, s \xleftarrow{U} \mathbb{Z}_p$, where $H_{\mathbb{G}}(\tau) = u' \prod_{i=0}^{N-1} u_i^{\tau[i]}$. The simplified variant of the ALP LHS scheme is formally described in Sect. A.

4.1 Our First ARIP Scheme

Generic Construction Based on NIWI and LHS. A secret-key $sk_{\mathbf{x}}$ for $\mathbf{x} \in \mathbb{Z}_p^n$ consists of a tag $\tau \in \{0,1\}^N$ for $N \in \mathbb{N}$ and $n+4$ signatures $\{\sigma_i\}_{i=1}^{n+4}$ of LHS. The tag is uniform-randomly chosen for each secret-key. The LHS signature σ_i

is on a vector $\boldsymbol{v}_i \in \mathbb{Z}_p^{n+5}$. Each vector $\boldsymbol{v}_i$ is set to $x_i|\boldsymbol{e}_i$ if $i \in [1,n]$, or $0|\boldsymbol{e}_i$ otherwise, where $\boldsymbol{e}_i \in \mathbb{Z}_p^{n+4}$ is the i-th unit vector. The signer with $sk_{\mathbf{x}}$ signs a message $M \in \mathbb{Z}_p$ under a vector $\mathbf{y} \in \mathbb{Z}_p^n$ and a range $[L,R]$ with $L,R \in \mathbb{Z}_p$ as follows. Compute the weights $\beta_1,\cdots,\beta_{n+4} \in \mathbb{Z}_p$ as follows. β_i for $i \in [1,n]$ is set to y_i. β_i for $i \in [n+1,n+4]$ is set to L, R, M, and 1, respectively. Derive an LHS signature $\overline{\sigma}$ on the weighted vector $\overline{\boldsymbol{v}} := \sum_{i=1}^{n+4} \beta_i \cdot \boldsymbol{v}_i = (\langle \mathbf{x},\mathbf{y}\rangle \pmod p), y_1, \cdots, y_n, L, R, M, 1) \in \mathbb{Z}_p^{n+5}$. Finally, using $\langle \mathbf{x},\mathbf{y}\rangle$, τ and $\overline{\sigma}$ as witness, generate NIWI proofs that both of the following two conditions are satisfied, namely (a) *$\overline{\sigma}$ is a correct signature on the vector $\overline{\boldsymbol{v}}$ under the tag τ* and (b) $\langle \mathbf{x},\mathbf{y}\rangle \in [L,R]$. Since the verification algorithm of the simplified variant of the ALP LHS scheme consists of only two pairing-product equations, generating GS proofs for the first condition (a) is non-problematic. For the second condition (b), we adopt the tree-based range membership technique used for the efficient constructions of time-specific encryption/signatures [14,23].

Formal Description. For any $X \in \mathbb{G}$, $\iota(X)$ denotes $(1,1,X) \in \mathbb{G}^3$. For any $X \in \mathbb{G}_T$, $\iota_{\mathbb{G}_T}(X)$ denotes the 3×3 matrix which has X as the $(3,3)$-th element and $1_{\mathbb{G}_T}$ as any of the other elements. For any $h, g_1, g_2, g_3 \in \mathbb{G}$, $E(h,(g_1,g_2,g_3))$ denotes $(e(h,g_1), e(h,g_2), e(h,g_3)) \in \mathbb{G}_T^3$. For any $\vec{X} = (X_1,X_2,X_3) \in \mathbb{G}^3$ and $\vec{Y} = (Y_1,Y_2,Y_3) \in \mathbb{G}^3$, $F(\vec{X},\vec{Y}) := \tilde{F}(\vec{X},\vec{Y})^{1/2} \cdot \tilde{F}(\vec{Y},\vec{X})^{1/2} \in \mathbb{G}_T^{3\times 3}$, where $\tilde{F}(\vec{X},\vec{Y}) \in \mathbb{G}_T^{3\times 3}$ contains $e(X_i,Y_j)$ as the (i,j)-th element for all $i,j \in \{1,2,3\}$.

`Setup`$(1^\lambda, n)$: Choose bilinear groups $(\mathbb{G},\mathbb{G}_T)$ whose order is a prime p of bit length λ. Choose $\alpha \xleftarrow{U} \mathbb{Z}_p$. Let $g, v, g_1, \cdots, g_{n+5}, u', u_0, \cdots, u_{N-1} \xleftarrow{U} \mathbb{G}$ with $N \in \mathbb{N}$. $H_{\mathbb{G}}$ is a function which takes $\tau \in \{0,1\}^N$ then outputs $u' \prod_{i=0}^{N-1} u_i^{\tau[i]} \in \mathbb{G}$. Generate a GS CRS $\boldsymbol{f} = (\vec{f}_1, \vec{f}_2, \vec{f}_3)$ for the perfect WI setting as $\vec{f}_1 := (f_1, 1, g)$, $\vec{f}_2 := (1, f_2, g)$ and $\vec{f}_3 := \vec{f}_1^{\xi_1} \cdot \vec{f}_2^{\xi_2} \cdot (1,1,g)^{-1}$, where $f_1, f_2 \xleftarrow{U} \mathbb{G}$, $\xi_1, \xi_2 \xleftarrow{U} \mathbb{Z}_p$. Finally, output (pp, mk), where $pp := (\mathbb{G}, \mathbb{G}_T, g, g^\alpha, v, \{g_i\}_{i=1}^{n+5}, u', \{u_i\}_{i=0}^{N-1}, \boldsymbol{f})$ and $mk := \alpha$.

`KGen`$(mk, \mathbf{x})$: Choose a tag $\tau \xleftarrow{U} \{0,1\}^N$. Generate $n+4$ vectors $\boldsymbol{v}_1, \cdots, \boldsymbol{v}_{n+4} \subset \mathbb{Z}_p^{n+5}$. Each vector $\boldsymbol{v}_i = (v_{i,1}, \cdots, v_{i,n+5}) \in \mathbb{Z}_p^{n+5}$ is set to $x_i|\boldsymbol{e}_i$ if $i \in [1,n]$, or $0|\boldsymbol{e}_i$ otherwise. Compute an ALP signature $(\sigma_{i,1}, \sigma_{i,2}, \sigma_{i,3}, \sigma_{i,4})$ on $\boldsymbol{v}_i$, where $\sigma_{i,1} := (\prod_{j=1}^{n+5} g_i^{v_{i,j}} v^{s_i})^\alpha H_{\mathbb{G}}(\tau)^{r_i}$, $\sigma_{i,2} := g^{r_i}$, $\sigma_{i,3} := g^{s_i}$ and $\sigma_{i,4} := g^{\alpha \cdot s_i}$ with $r_i, s_i \xleftarrow{U} \mathbb{Z}_p$. Finally, output the secret-key $sk := (\mathbf{x}, \tau, \{\{\sigma_{i,j}\}_{j=1}^4\}_{i=1}^{n+4})$.

`Sig`$(sk, M, \mathbf{y}, L, R)$: Conduct the following 5 steps first.

1. Calculate the inner product $d := \langle \mathbf{x},\mathbf{y}\rangle \pmod p$. Assume that $d \in [L,R]$.
2. Choose $\overline{r} \xleftarrow{U} \mathbb{Z}_p$. For each $i \in [1,n]$, $\beta_i := y_i$. Set $(\beta_{n+1}, \beta_{n+2}, \beta_{n+3}, \beta_{n+4}) := (L, R, M, 1)$.
3. Compute $\overline{\sigma}_1 := \prod_{i=1}^{n+4} \sigma_{i,1}^{\beta_i} \cdot H_{\mathbb{G}}(\tau)^{\overline{r}}$, $\overline{\sigma}_2 := \prod_{i=1}^{n+4} \sigma_{i,2}^{\beta_i} \cdot g^{\overline{r}}$, $\overline{\sigma}_3 := \prod_{i=1}^{n+4} \sigma_{i,3}^{\beta_i}$ and $\overline{\sigma}_4 := \prod_{i=1}^{n+4} \sigma_{i,4}^{\beta_i}$. Note that if sk is a correct secret-key with inner-randomness $\{r_j, s_j\}_{j=1}^{n+4}$, the computed ALP signature distributes as

$$\left(\left\{g_1^{\langle \mathbf{x},\mathbf{y}\rangle}\prod_{i=1}^{n} g_{i+1}^{y_i}\cdot g_{n+2}^{L}\cdot g_{n+3}^{R}\cdot g_{n+4}^{M}\cdot g_{n+5}\cdot v^{\sum_{j=1}^{n+4} y_j s_j}\right\}^{\alpha} H_{\mathbb{G}}(\tau)^{\sum_j y_j r_j+\overline{r}},\right.$$
$$\left. g^{\sum_j y_j r_j+\overline{r}}, g^{\sum_j y_j s_j}, g^{\alpha\sum_j y_j s_j}\right). \quad (1)$$

4. Compute the GS commitments for all of the following variables in $\mathbb{G}$.
   (a) $g^{\tau[i]}$ and $g^{1-\tau[i]}$ (for all $i \in [0, N-1]$)
   (b) $H_{\mathbb{G}}(\tau)$
   (c) $g_1^{d[i]}$ and $g_1^{1-d[i]}$ (for all $i \in [0, \lambda-1]$)
   (d) g_1^d
   (e) $\overline{\sigma}_1, \overline{\sigma}_3$ and $\overline{\sigma}_4$

   Let the commitments be denoted by $\vec{C}_{\tau[i]}$, $\vec{C}_{1-\tau[i]}$, $\vec{C}_{H_{\mathbb{G}}(\tau)}$, $\vec{C}_{d[i]}$, $\vec{C}_{1-d[i]}$, $\vec{C}_d$, $\vec{C}_{\overline{\sigma}_1}$, $\vec{C}_{\overline{\sigma}_3}$, $\vec{C}_{\overline{\sigma}_4} \in \mathbb{G}^3$ respectively. The GS commitment $\vec{C}_X$ for a variable $X \in \mathbb{G}$ is computed as $\iota(X)\cdot \vec{f}_1^{\,r}\cdot \vec{f}_2^{\,s}\cdot \vec{f}_3^{\,t}$, where $r, s, t \xleftarrow{U} \mathbb{Z}_p$.
5. Compute the GS proofs that the variables satisfy the following relations.
   [a] $e(g^{\tau[i]}, g^{1-\tau[i]}) = 1_{\mathbb{G}_T}$ and $e(g^{\tau[i]}, g)\cdot e(g^{1-\tau[i]}, g) = e(g, g)$ (for all $i \in [0, N-1]$)
   [b] $e(H_{\mathbb{G}}(\tau), g) = e(u', g)\prod_{i=0}^{N-1} e(u_i, g^{\tau[i]})$
   [c] $e(g_1^{d[i]}, g_1^{1-d[i]}) = 1_{\mathbb{G}_T}$ and $e(g_1^{d[i]}, g_1)\cdot e(g_1^{1-d[i]}, g_1) = e(g_1, g_1)$ (for all $i \in [0, \lambda-1]$)
   [d] $e(g_1^d, g) = \prod_{i=0}^{\lambda-1} e(g_1^{d[i]}, g^{2^i})$
   [e] $e(\overline{\sigma}_1, g) = e(g_1^d, g^\alpha)\cdot e(\prod_{i=1}^{n+4} g_{i+1}^{y_i}, g^\alpha)\cdot e(v, \overline{\sigma}_4)\cdot e(H_{\mathbb{G}}(\tau), \overline{\sigma}_2)$
   [f] $e(\overline{\sigma}_3, g^\alpha) = e(g, \overline{\sigma}_4)$

   The relations [a] guarantee that the variable $\tau[i]$ used in the committed variables $g^{\tau[i]}$ and $g^{1-\tau[i]}$ is one bit value. Likewise, the ones [c] guarantee that the variable $d[i]$ is one bit value. The above GS proofs are categorized into two groups, namely type-1 (resp. type-2) proofs consisting of 3 (resp. 9) elements in $\mathbb{G}$. Specifically, the proofs for the relations with the grey background are type-2, and the others are type-1. Let the proofs be denoted by $\vec{\pi}_{\tau[i]} \in \mathbb{G}^9$, $\vec{\pi}'_{\tau[i]} \in \mathbb{G}^3$, $\vec{\pi}_{H_{\mathbb{G}}(\tau)} \in \mathbb{G}^3$, $\vec{\pi}_{d[i]} \in \mathbb{G}^9$, $\vec{\pi}'_{d[i]} \in \mathbb{G}^3$, $\vec{\pi}_d \in \mathbb{G}^3$, $\vec{\pi}_{\overline{\sigma}_1} \in \mathbb{G}^3$, $\vec{\pi}_{\overline{\sigma}_3} \in \mathbb{G}^3$, respectively.

What remains is proving that $d \in [L, R]$.

Consider a complete binary tree with p leaf nodes. The root node is associated with the null value. Any non-leaf node associated with a binary value $a \in \{0,1\}^{\leq\lambda}$ has two subordinates associated with $a||0$ and $a||1$ respectively. The p leaf n are associated with $0, 1, \cdots, p-1$ from left to right.

We derive a set of intermediate nodes Θ which *covers* two leaf nodes L and R. For an intermediate node with $\theta \in \{0,1\}^{\leq\lambda}$, $\mathbf{LEAVES}_\theta$ denotes a set of leaf nodes, each of which is descendant of the node with θ. The covering set Θ consists of nodes with $\theta \in \{0,1\}^{\leq\lambda}$ such that (1) *the union set of* $\mathbf{LEAVES}_\theta$ *for all* $\theta \in \Theta$ *is identical to the set of leaf nodes for* $[L, R]$, and (2) *the cardinality of* Θ, *i.e.*, $|\Theta|$, *is the minimum*[5]. Parse Θ as $\{\theta \in \{0,1\}^{\leq\lambda}\}$. For each θ, we define a Boolean variable $A_\theta \in \{0,1\}$ as follows.

[5] Note that $|\Theta|$ is maximized when $[L, R] = [1, p-2]$ and becomes $2\lambda - 2$.

$[A_\theta :]$ *Be* 1 *if the leaf node with* $d \in \{0,1\}^\lambda$ *is descendant of the leaf node with* $\theta \in \{0,1\}^{\le\lambda}$. *Be* 0 *otherwise.*

Note that if $d \in [L, R]$, there must exist (at most) one node $\theta^* \in \Theta$ which has the leaf node d as descendant. The highest $|\theta^*|$ bits of d are identical to θ^*. For each $\theta \in \Theta$ and $j \in [1, |\theta|]$, we define two Boolean variables $A_{\theta,j}, A'_{\theta,j} \in \{0,1\}$ as follows.

$[A_{\theta,j} :]$ *Be* 1 *if the* j*-th highest bit of* $d \in \{0,1\}^\lambda$ *is identical to the one of* $\theta \in \{0,1\}^{\le\lambda}$, *i.e.,* $d[\lambda - j] = \theta[|\theta| - j]$. *Be* 0 *otherwise.*
$[A'_{\theta,j} :]$ *Be* 1 *if all of the* j *highest bits of* $d \in \{0,1\}^\lambda$ *are identical to the ones of* $\theta \in \{0,1\}^{\le\lambda}$, *i.e.,* $d[\lambda - k] = \theta[|\theta| - k]$ *for all* $k \in [1, j]$. *Be* 0 *otherwise. Obviously,* $A'_{\theta,|\theta|} = A_\theta$.

Finally, conduct the following two steps.

1. Compute the GS commitments for all of the following variables in $\mathbb{G}$.
   (f) $g_1^{A_\theta}$ (for all $\theta \in \Theta$)
   (g) $g_1^{A_{\theta,j}}$ and $g_1^{A'_{\theta,j}}$ (for all $\theta \in \Theta$ and $j \in [1, |\theta|]$)
   Let the commitments be denoted by $\vec{C}_{A_\theta}, \vec{C}_{A_{\theta,j}}, \vec{C'}_{A_{\theta,j}} \in \mathbb{G}^3$.
2. Compute the GS proofs that the above variables satisfy the followings.
   [g] $e(g_1^{A_{\theta,j}}, g) = \begin{cases} e(g_1^{d[\lambda-j]}, g) & (\text{if } \theta[|\theta| - j] = 1) \\ e(g_1^{1-d[\lambda-j]}, g) & (\text{otherwise}) \end{cases}$
   (for all $\theta \in \Theta$ and $j \in [1, |\theta|]$)
   [h] $e(g_1^{A'_{\theta,1}}, g_1) = e(g_1^{A_{\theta,1}}, g_1)$ (for all $\theta \subset \Theta$)
   [i] $e(g_1^{A'_{\theta,j}}, g_1) = e(g_1^{A'_{\theta,j-1}}, g_1^{A_{\theta,j}})$ (for all $\theta \in \Theta$ and $j \in [2, |\theta|]$)
   [j] $\prod_{\theta\in\Theta} e(g_1^{A'_{\theta,|\theta|}}, g) = e(g_1, g)$
   Let the computed GS proofs be denoted by $\pi_{A_{\theta,j}} \in \mathbb{G}^3$, $\vec{\pi}'_{A_{\theta,1}} \in \mathbb{G}^3$, $\vec{\pi}'_{A_{\theta,j}} \in \mathbb{G}^9$ and $\pi_A \in \mathbb{G}^3$ respectively.

The signature σ consists of all of the GS commitments and proofs, and the second ALP signature element $\overline{\sigma}_2 \in \mathbb{G}$.

$\texttt{Ver}(\sigma, M, \mathbf{y}, L, R)$: Each GS proof $\pi \in \mathbb{G}^3$ (resp. $\vec{\pi} \in \mathbb{G}^9$), composed of 3 (resp. 9) elements in $\mathbb{G}$, is parsed as (π_1, π_2, π_3) (resp. $(\vec{\pi}_1, \vec{\pi}_2, \vec{\pi}_3)$ with $\vec{\pi}_i \in \mathbb{G}^3$). Output 1 if all of the following equations are satisfied.

1. $F(\vec{C}_{\tau[i]}, \vec{C}_{1-\tau[i]}) = \iota_{\mathbb{G}_T}(1_{\mathbb{G}_T}) \cdot \prod_{k=1}^3 F(\vec{\pi}_{\tau[i],k}, \vec{f}_k)$ (for all $i \in [0, N-1]$)
2. $E(g, \vec{C}_{\tau[i]}) \cdot E(g, \vec{C}_{1-\tau[i]}) = E(g, \iota(g)) \cdot \prod_{k=1}^3 E(\pi'_{\tau[i],k}, \vec{f}_k)$ (for all $i \in [0, N-1]$)
3. $E(g, \vec{C}_{H_{\mathbb{G}}(\tau)}) = E(u', \iota(g)) \cdot \prod_{i=0}^{N-1} E(u_i, \vec{C}_{\tau[i]}) \cdot \prod_{k=1}^3 E(\pi_{H_{\mathbb{G}}(\tau),k}, \vec{f}_k)$
4. $F(\vec{C}_{d[i]}, \vec{C}_{1-d[i]}) = \iota_{\mathbb{G}_T}(1_{\mathbb{G}_T}) \cdot \prod_{k=1}^3 F(\vec{\pi}_{d[i],k}, \vec{f}_k)$ (for all $i \in [0, \lambda-1]$)
5. $E(g, \vec{C}_{d[i]}) = E(g, \iota(g)) \cdot E(g, \vec{C}_{1-d[i]}) \cdot \prod_{k=1}^3 E(\pi'_{d[i],k}, \vec{f}_k)$ (for all $i \in [0, \lambda-1]$)

6. $E(g, \vec{C}_d) = \prod_{i=0}^{\lambda-1} E(g^{2^i}, \vec{C}_{d[i]}) \cdot \prod_{k=1}^{3} E(\pi_{d,k}, \vec{f}_k)$
7. $E(g, \vec{C}_{\overline{\sigma}_1}) = E(g^\alpha, \vec{C}_d) \cdot E(\prod_{i=1}^{n+4} g_{i+1}^{y_i}, \iota(g^\alpha)) \cdot E(v, \vec{C}_{\overline{\sigma}_4}) \cdot E(\overline{\sigma}_2, \vec{C}_{H_{\mathbb{G}}(\tau)}) \cdot \prod_{k=1}^{3} E(\pi_{\overline{\sigma}_1,k}, \vec{f}_k)$
8. $E(g^\alpha, \vec{C}_{\overline{\sigma}_3}) = E(g, \vec{C}_{\overline{\sigma}_4}) \cdot \prod_{k=1}^{3} E(\pi_{\overline{\sigma}_3,k}, \vec{f}_k)$
9. $E(g, \vec{C}_{A_{\theta,j}}) = \begin{cases} E(g, \vec{C}_{d[\lambda-j]}) \cdot \prod_{k=1}^{3} E(\pi_{A_{\theta,j},k}, \vec{f}_k) & (\text{if } \theta[|\theta|-j]=1) \\ E(g, \vec{C}_{1-d[\lambda-j]}) \cdot \prod_{k=1}^{3} E(\pi_{A_{\theta,j},k}, \vec{f}_k) & (\text{otherwise}) \end{cases}$
   (for all $\theta \in \Theta$ and $j \in [1, |\theta|]$)
10. $E(g_1, \vec{C}'_{A_{\theta,1}}) = E(g_1, \vec{C}_{A_{\theta,1}}) \cdot \prod_{k=1}^{3} E(\pi'_{A_{\theta,1},k}, \vec{f}_k)$
    (for all $\theta \in \Theta$)
11. $F(\iota(g_1), \vec{C}'_{A_{\theta,j}}) = F(\vec{C}'_{A_{\theta,j-1}}, \vec{C}_{A_{\theta,j}}) \cdot \prod_{k=1}^{3} F(\vec{\pi}'_{A_{\theta,j},k}, \vec{f}_k)$
    (for all $\theta \in \Theta$ and $j \in [2, |\theta|]$)
12. $\prod_{\theta \in \Theta} E(g, \vec{C}'_{A_{\theta,|\theta|}}) = E(g_1, \iota(g)) \cdot \prod_{k=1}^{3} E(\pi_{A,k}, \vec{f}_k)$

Output 0 otherwise.

Unforgeability. We present the following theorem.

Theorem 1. *Our 1st ARIP scheme is* EUF-CMA *if the DLIN, CDH and FlexCDH assumptions hold in the group* $\mathbb{G}$.

Proof. To prove the theorem, we define the following 5 experiments.

Expt$_0$: The standard EUF-CMA experiment for the ARIP scheme.
Expt$_1$: The same as ***Expt***$_0$ except that it aborts when we choose a tag on the key-revelation or signing oracle, the tag matches a tag previously chosen.
Expt$_2$: The same as ***Expt***$_1$ except that the ALP signature $(\overline{\sigma}_1, \overline{\sigma}_2, \overline{\sigma}_3, \overline{\sigma}_4)$ used on the signing oracle $\mathfrak{Sign}$ is directly generated by the master-key $mk(=\alpha)$ as follows: $(\{g_1^{\langle \mathbf{x},\mathbf{y}\rangle} \prod_{i=1}^{n} g_{i+1}^{y_i} \cdot g_{n+2}^{L} \cdot g_{n+3}^{R} \cdot g_{n+4}^{M} \cdot g_{n+5} \cdot v^s\}^\alpha \cdot H_{\mathbb{G}}(\tau)^r, g^r, g^s, g^{\alpha s})$, where $r, s \xleftarrow{U} \mathbb{Z}_p$ and $\tau \xleftarrow{U} \{0,1\}^N$.
Expt$_3$: The same as ***Expt***$_2$ except that the GS CRS $\boldsymbol{f} = (\vec{f}_1, \vec{f}_2, \vec{f}_3)$ is generated as a perfectly sound one. Specifically, $\vec{f}_1 := (f_1, 1, g)$, $\vec{f}_2 := (1, f_2, g)$ and $\vec{f}_3 := \vec{f}_1^{\xi_1} \cdot \vec{f}_2^{\xi_2}$, where $f_1 := g^{\phi_1}$, $f_2 := g^{\phi_2}$ and $\phi_1, \phi_2, \xi_1, \xi_2 \xleftarrow{U} \mathbb{Z}_p$. Note that in this experiment and the next experiment ***Expt***$_4$, all GS commitments are perfectly binding ones. We use the BBS decryption keys (ϕ_1, ϕ_2) to extract all of the hidden variables from the GS commitments in the forged signature σ^*. Since the GS proofs in σ^* are perfectly sound, the extracted variables satisfy all of the relations [a], [b], $\cdots$, [j]. Hereafter, some of the extracted variables are denoted by $\tau^* \in \{0,1\}^N$, $d^* \in \mathbb{Z}_p$, $\overline{\sigma}_1^*, \overline{\sigma}_3^*, \overline{\sigma}_4^* \in \mathbb{G}$. Let $\overline{\sigma}_2^* \in \mathbb{G}$ denote the 2nd ALP signature element included in σ^*.
Expt$_4$: The same as ***Expt***$_3$ except that it aborts if the tag τ^* matches none of the tags chosen on the key-revelation or signing oracle.

W_i denotes the event where ***Expt***$_i$ outputs 1. We obtain $\mathtt{Adv}_{\Sigma_{\mathrm{ARIP}},\mathcal{A},n}^{\mathtt{EUF\text{-}CMA}}(\lambda) = \Pr[W_0] \le \sum_{i=1}^{4} |\Pr[W_{i-1}] - \Pr[W_i]| + \Pr[W_4] \le q(q-1)/2^{N+1} + \mathtt{Adv}_{\mathcal{B}_1,\mathbb{G}}^{\mathtt{DLIN}}(\lambda) + 4q(N+1)(\mathtt{Adv}_{\mathcal{B}_2,\mathbb{G}}^{\mathtt{CDH}}(\lambda) + \mathtt{Adv}_{\mathcal{B}_3,\mathbb{G}}^{\mathtt{FlexCDH}}(\lambda) + 2/p)$, where $q \in \mathbb{N}$ is number that $\mathcal{A}$

uses the key-revelation and signing oracles. The last inequality is because of the following lemmas. We omit the proof of Lemma 3. As said in [5,6,18], $\boldsymbol{Expt}_2$ and $\boldsymbol{Expt}_3$ are indistinguishable under the DLIN assumption. □

Lemma 1. $|\Pr[W_0] - \Pr[W_1]| \leq q(q-1)/2^{N+1}$.

Proof. For $i \in [1, q]$, τ_i denotes the tag chosen on the i-th key-revelation or signing oracle. E_i denotes the event where τ_i is the first tag which matches one of the tags previously chosen. $\boldsymbol{Expt}_0$ and $\boldsymbol{Expt}_1$ are identical except for the case where an event from $E_2, \cdots, E_q$ occurs. Thus, we obtain $|\Pr[W_0] - \Pr[W_1]| \leq \Pr[\bigvee_{i=2}^{q} E_i] \leq \sum_{i=2}^{q} \Pr[E_i]$. We derive an upper bound for $\Pr[E_i]$. A denotes the event where no one from $\tau_1, \cdots, \tau_{i-1}$ matches another. B denotes the event where τ_i matches one of $\tau_1, \cdots, \tau_{i-1}$. Obviously, $\Pr[E_i] = \Pr[A] \cdot \Pr[B \mid A] \leq \Pr[B \mid A] = \frac{i-1}{2^N}$. Hence, $|\Pr[W_0] - \Pr[W_1]| \leq \frac{1}{2^N} + \cdots + \frac{q-1}{2^N} = \frac{1}{2^N} \cdot \frac{q(q-1)}{2} = \frac{q(q-1)}{2^{N+1}}$. □

Lemma 2. $|\Pr[W_1] - \Pr[W_2]| = 0$.

Proof. In $\boldsymbol{Expt}_1$, on the signing oracle, a secret-key $sk_{\mathbf{x}}$ for $\mathbf{x} \in \mathbb{Z}_p^n$ is generated. Parse $sk_{\mathbf{x}}$ as $(\mathbf{x}, \tau, \{\{\sigma_{ij}\}_{j=1}^{4}\}_{i=1}^{n+4})$. For each $i \in [1, n+4]$, $r_i, s_i \in \mathbb{Z}_p$ denote the randomness used for the ALP signature $\{\sigma_{ij}\}_{j=1}^{4}$. Using $sk_{\mathbf{x}}$, we generate a signature σ on M associated with $\mathbf{y} \in \mathbb{Z}_p^n$ and $L, R \in \mathbb{Z}_p$. Let $\overline{\sigma} = (\overline{\sigma}_1, \overline{\sigma}_2, \overline{\sigma}_3, \overline{\sigma}_4)$ denote the ALP signature generated during the generation of σ. $\overline{\sigma}$ is expressed as follows, where $\overline{r} \xleftarrow{\mathrm{U}} \mathbb{Z}_p$. $\overline{\sigma}_1 = (g_1^{\langle \mathbf{x}, \mathbf{y} \rangle} \cdot \prod_{i=1}^{n} g_{i+1}^{y_i} \cdot g_{n+2}^{L} \cdot g_{n+3}^{R} \cdot g_{n+4}^{M} \cdot g_{n+5} \cdot v^{\sum_{i=1}^{n+4} y_i s_i})^{\alpha} \cdot H_{\mathbb{G}}(\tau)^{\sum_{i=1}^{n+4} y_i r_i + \overline{r}}$, $\overline{\sigma}_2 = g^{\sum_{i=1}^{n+4} y_i r_i + \overline{r}}$, $\overline{\sigma}_3 = g^{\sum_{i=1}^{n+4} y_i s_i}$ and $\sigma_4 = g^{(\sum_{i=1}^{n+4} y_i s_i)\alpha}$. Since any information about $\{r_i, s_i\}_{i=1}^{n+4}$ is not revealed to $\mathcal{A}$, both $\sum_{i=1}^{n+4} y_i r_i$ and $\sum_{i=1}^{n+4} y_i s_i$ distribute uniformly at random in $\mathbb{Z}_p$. Hence, $\overline{\sigma}$ in $\boldsymbol{Expt}_1$ distributes identically to the one in $\boldsymbol{Expt}_2$. □

Lemma 3. *There is a PPTA $\mathcal{B}_1$ s.t.* $|\Pr[W_2] - \Pr[W_3]| \leq \boldsymbol{Adv}_{\mathcal{B}_1,\mathbb{G}}^{\boldsymbol{DLIN}}(\lambda)$.

Lemma 4. *There is a PPTA $\mathcal{B}_2$ s.t.* $|\Pr[W_3] - \Pr[W_4]| \leq 4q(N+1)(\boldsymbol{Adv}_{\mathcal{B}_2,\mathbb{G}}^{\boldsymbol{CDH}}(\lambda) + 1/p)$.

Proof. E denotes the event where $\mathcal{A}$ makes $\boldsymbol{Expt}_3$ output 1. F denotes the event where $\mathcal{A}$ makes $\boldsymbol{Expt}_4$ abort. By a basic theorem, $\Pr[E] - \Pr[E \wedge \neg F] = \Pr[E \wedge F]$. Since $\Pr[E] = \Pr[W_3]$ and $\Pr[E \wedge \neg F] = \Pr[W_4]$, we obtain $|\Pr[W_3] - \Pr[W_4]| = \Pr[E \wedge F]$. Assume that $\mathcal{A}$ is a PPTA which makes the event $E \wedge F$ occur with a non-negligible probability. Let $\mathcal{B}_2$ be a PPTA who attempts to solve the CDH problem by using $\mathcal{A}$. $\mathcal{B}_2$ behaves as follows.

Receive (g, g^a, g^b) as an instance of the CDH problem. Set $l := 2q$. Choose uniformly at random an integer k satisfying $0 \leq k \leq N$. Assume that $l(N+1) \leq p$. Set $g^{\alpha} := g^a$. Choose $\kappa_v, \kappa_1, \delta_1, \cdots, \kappa_{n+5}, \delta_{n+5} \xleftarrow{\mathrm{U}} \mathbb{Z}_p$. Set $v := g^{\kappa_v}$ and $g_i := (g^b)^{\kappa_i} g^{\delta_i}$ for $i \in [1, n+5]$. Choose $x', x_0, \cdots, x_{N-1} \xleftarrow{\mathrm{U}} \mathbb{Z}_l$ and $y', y_0, \cdots, y_{N-1} \xleftarrow{\mathrm{U}} \mathbb{Z}_p$. For a tag $\tau \in \{0,1\}^N$, define two functions $F, J : \{0,1\}^N \to \mathbb{Z}_p$ as $F(\tau) := x' + \sum_{i=0}^{N-1} x_i \cdot \tau[i] - lk$ and $J(\tau) := y' + \sum_{i=0}^{N-1} y_i \cdot \tau[i]$.

Set $u' := (g^b)^{-lk+x'} \cdot g^{y'}$ and $u_i := (g^b)^{x_i} \cdot g^{y_i}$ for $i \in [0, N-1]$. It holds that $u' \prod_{i=0}^{N-1} u_i^{\tau[i]} = (g^b)^{-lk+x'+\sum_{i=0}^{N-1} x_i \cdot \tau[i]} \cdot g^{y'+\sum_{i=0}^{N-1} y_i \cdot \tau[i]} = (g^b)^{F(\tau)} \cdot g^{J(\tau)}$. Generate the GS CRS $\boldsymbol{f} = (\vec{f}_1, \vec{f}_2, \vec{f}_3)$ as perfectly sound one. Set $pp := (\mathbb{G}, \mathbb{G}_T, g, g^\alpha, v, \{g_i\}_{i=1}^{n+5}, u', \{u_i\}_{i=0}^{N-1}, \boldsymbol{f})$ and send it to $\mathcal{A}$. When $\mathcal{A}$ issues a query to the key-revelation or signing oracle, $\mathcal{B}_2$ behaves as follows.

Key-Revelation $\mathfrak{Reveal}(\mathbf{x})$**:** Let $\tau \xleftarrow{U} \{0,1\}^N$. Consider the following two cases, (1) $F(\tau) \neq 0 \pmod{l}$ and (2) $F(\tau) = 0 \pmod{l}$. If the case (2) occurs, abort the simulation. If the case (1) occurs, continue as follows. Since we have assumed that $l(N+1) < p$ and $0 \leq k \leq N$, it holds that $F(\tau) = 0 \pmod{p} \implies F(\tau) = 0 \pmod{l}$ for any τ. Its contraposition is that $F(\tau) \neq 0 \pmod{l} \implies F(\tau) \neq 0 \pmod{p}$ for any τ.

Choose $r \xleftarrow{U} \mathbb{Z}_p$. Compute $(d_1, d_2) := ((g^\alpha)^{-\frac{J(\tau)}{F(\tau)}} (u' \prod_{i=0}^{N-1} u_i^{\tau[i]})^r, (g^\alpha)^{-\frac{1}{F(\tau)}} g^r)$. Let $\tilde{r} := r - \alpha / F(\tau)$. Obviously, $d_2 = g^{\tilde{r}}$. It holds that $d_1 = (g^b)^\alpha H_{\mathbb{G}}(\tau)^{\tilde{r}}$ since $d_1 = (g^b)^\alpha \{(g^b)^{F(\tau)} g^{J(\tau)}\}^{-\frac{\alpha}{F(\tau)}} \{(g^b)^{F(\tau)} g^{J(\tau)}\}^r = (g^b)^\alpha H_{\mathbb{G}}(\tau)^{r - \frac{\alpha}{F(\tau)}}$.

Generate $n+4$ vectors $\boldsymbol{v}_1, \cdots, \boldsymbol{v}_{n+4} \in \mathbb{Z}_p^{n+5}$ in the normal manner. For each $i \in [1, n+4]$, generate an ALP signature $(\sigma_{i,1}, \sigma_{i,2}, \sigma_{i,3}, \sigma_{i,4})$ as

$$\left(d_1^{\sum_{j=1}^{n+5} \kappa_j v_{ij}} (g^\alpha)^{s_i \kappa_v + \sum_{j=1}^{n+5} \delta_j v_{ij}} H_{\mathbb{G}}(\tau)^{r_i}, d_2^{\sum_{j=1}^{n+5} \kappa_j v_{ij}} g^{r_i}, g^{s_i}, (g^\alpha)^{s_i} \right),$$

where $r_i, s_i \xleftarrow{U} \mathbb{Z}_p$. Let $\hat{r}_i := \tilde{r} \sum_{j=1}^{n+5} \kappa_j v_{ij} + r_i$. Obviously, $\sigma_{i,2} = g^{\hat{r}_i}$. It holds that $\sigma_{i,1} = (\prod_{j=1}^{n+5} g_j^{v_{ij}} v^{s_i})^\alpha H_{\mathbb{G}}(\tau)^{\hat{r}_i}$ since

$$\begin{aligned} \sigma_{i,1} &= (g^{b\alpha})^{\sum_{j=1}^{n+5} \kappa_j v_{ij}} \cdot H_{\mathbb{G}}(\tau)^{\tilde{r} \sum_{j=1}^{n+5} \kappa_j v_{ij} + r_i} \cdot (g^\alpha)^{s_i \kappa_v + \sum_{j=1}^{n+5} \delta_j v_{ij}} \\ &= \{(g^b)^{\sum_{j=1}^{n+5} \kappa_j v_{ij}} g^{s_i \kappa_v + \sum_{j=1}^{n+5} \delta_j v_{ij}}\}^\alpha H_{\mathbb{G}}(\tau)^{\hat{r}_i} \\ &= \left[\prod_{j=1}^{n+5} \{(g^b)^{\kappa_j} g^{\delta_j}\}^{v_{ij}} g^{s_i \kappa_v} \right]^\alpha H_{\mathbb{G}}(\tau)^{\hat{r}_i}. \end{aligned}$$

Finally, return $sk_{\mathbf{x}} := (\mathbf{x}, \tau, \{\{\sigma_{ij}\}_{j=1}^4\}_{i=1}^{n+4})$ to $\mathcal{A}$.

Signing $\mathfrak{Sign}(\mathbf{x}, M, \mathbf{y}, L, R)$**:** Compute $d := \langle \mathbf{x}, \mathbf{y} \rangle \pmod{p}$. Choose $\tau \xleftarrow{U} \{0,1\}^L$. If $F(\tau) = 0 \pmod{l}$, abort the simulation. Else if $F(\tau) \neq 0 \pmod{l}$, as the key-revelation oracle, $\mathcal{B}_2$ derives the variables (d_1, d_2), then an ALP signature $(\overline{\sigma}_1, \overline{\sigma}_2, \overline{\sigma}_3, \overline{\sigma}_4)$ on the vector $\overline{\boldsymbol{v}} = (d, y_1, \cdots, y_n, L, R, M, 1)$. In the normal manner, compute all of the GS commitments and proofs. Return a signature σ, composed of all of the GS commitments/proofs and $\overline{\sigma}_2$, to $\mathcal{A}$.

$\mathcal{B}_2$ receives a forged signature σ^* from $\mathcal{A}$. Set $\boldsymbol{v}^* := (d^*, y_1^*, \cdots, y_n^*, L^*, R^*, M^*, 1) \in \mathbb{Z}_p^{n+5}$. Parse it as $(v_1^*, \cdots, v_{n+5}^*)$. The ALP signature $(\overline{\sigma}_1^*, \overline{\sigma}_2^*, \overline{\sigma}_3^*, \overline{\sigma}_4^*)$ extracted from the forged signature σ^* satisfies that $\overline{\sigma}_1^* = (\prod_{i=1}^{n+5} g_i^{v_i^*} v^{s^*})^\alpha H_{\mathbb{G}}(\tau^*)^{r^*}$, $\overline{\sigma}_2^* = g^{r^*}$, $\overline{\sigma}_3^* = g^{s^*}$ and $\overline{\sigma}_4^* = g^{s^* \cdot \alpha}$ for some $r^*, s^* \in \mathbb{Z}_p$.

We assume that it holds $\kappa_{n+5} \neq -\sum_{i=1}^{n+4} \kappa_i v_i^*$ (mod p), which implies $\sum_{i=1}^{n+5} \kappa_i v_i^* \neq 0$ (mod p). Since κ_{n+5} has not been used yet from $\mathcal{A}$'s viewpoint and κ_{n+5} has been chosen uniformly at random from $\mathbb{Z}_p$, the probability that $\kappa_{n+5} = -\sum_{i=1}^{n+4} \kappa_i v_i^*$ (mod p) is at most $1/p$. Hence, this assumption is reasonable.

Compute (ω_1^*, ω_2^*) as

$$\left(\left\{\frac{\overline{\sigma}_1^*}{(\overline{\sigma}_4^*)^{\kappa_v}(g^\alpha)^{\sum_{i=1}^{n+5} \delta_i v_i^*}}\right\}^{1/\sum_{i=1}^{n+5} \kappa_i v_i^*}, \{\overline{\sigma}_2^*\}^{1/\sum_{i=1}^{n+5} \kappa_i v_i^*}\right).$$

Let $\tilde{r}^* := r^*/\sum_{i=1}^{n+5} \kappa_i v_i^*$. Obviously, $\omega_2^* = g^{\tilde{r}^*}$. It holds $\omega_1^* = g^{ab} H_{\mathbb{G}}(\tau^*)^{\tilde{r}^*}$ since

$$\begin{aligned}
\omega_1^* &= \left\{\frac{(\prod_{i=1}^{n+5} g_i^{v_i^*} v^{s^*})^\alpha H_{\mathbb{G}}(\tau^*)^{r^*}}{(g^\alpha)^{s^*\kappa_v + \sum_{i=1}^{n+5} \delta_i v_i^*}}\right\}^{1/\sum_{i=1}^{n+5} \kappa_i v_i^*} \\
&= \left[\frac{\{\prod_{i=1}^{n+5} (g^{b\kappa_i} g^{\delta_i})^{v_i^*} g^{s^*\kappa_v}\}^\alpha H_{\mathbb{G}}(\tau^*)^{r^*}}{(g^\alpha)^{s^*\kappa_v + \sum_{i=1}^{n+5} \delta_i v_i^*}}\right]^{1/\sum_{i=1}^{n+5} \kappa_i v_i^*} \\
&= \left\{(g^{b\alpha})^{\sum_{i=1}^{n+5} \kappa_i v_i^*} H_{\mathbb{G}}(\tau^*)^{r^*}\right\}^{1/\sum_{i=1}^{n+5} \kappa_i v_i^*} = g^{ab} H_{\mathbb{G}}(\tau^*)^{r^*/\sum_{i=1}^{n+5} \kappa_i v_i^*}.
\end{aligned}$$

Consider the following two cases, (1) $F(\tau^*) = 0$ (mod p) and (2) $F(\tau^*) \neq 0$ (mod p). If the second case occurs, abort the simulation. If the first occurs, $\mathcal{B}_2$ outputs $\frac{\omega_1^*}{(\omega_2^*)^{J(\tau^*)}}$, which is equivalent to $\frac{g^{ab} H_{\mathbb{G}}(\tau^*)^{\tilde{r}^*}}{(g^{\tilde{r}^*})^{J(\tau^*)}} = g^{ab}$ because $H_{\mathbb{G}}(\tau^*) = (g^b)^{F(\tau^*)} g^{J(\tau^*)} = g^{J(\tau^*)}$, as the correct answer to the CDH problem.

Consider a situation where $\mathcal{B}_2$ has not aborted and $\mathcal{A}$ has made $E \wedge F$ occur. Except for the case where $\kappa_{n+5} = \sum_{i=1}^{n+4} \kappa_i v_i^*$ (mod p) which occurs with the probability $1/p$ at most, $\mathcal{B}_2$ outputs the correct answer for the CDH problem. Thus, it holds $\Pr[E \wedge F \wedge \neg\mathsf{abort}] - \mathtt{Adv}_{\mathcal{B}_2,\mathbb{G}}^{\mathtt{CDH}}(\lambda) \leq 1/p$, where abort is the event where $\mathcal{B}_2$ aborts the simulation. The first term is equivalent to $\Pr[\neg\mathsf{abort}] \cdot \Pr[E \wedge F \mid \neg\mathsf{abort}] = \Pr[\neg\mathsf{abort}] \cdot \Pr[E \wedge F]$. We obtain $\Pr[E \wedge F] \leq \frac{1}{\Pr[\neg\mathsf{abort}]}(\mathtt{Adv}_{\mathcal{B}_2,\mathbb{G}}^{\mathtt{CDH}}(\lambda) + \frac{1}{p})$. In the same manner as [28], the lower bound of $\Pr[\neg\mathsf{abort}]$ is derived, i.e., $\frac{1}{4q(N+1)}$. Details of the derivation are described the full version of this paper [13]. □

Lemma 5. *There is a PPTA $\mathcal{B}_3$ s.t.* $\Pr[W_4] \leq 4q(N+1)(\mathit{Adv}_{\mathcal{B}_3,\mathbb{G}}^{\mathit{FlexCDH}}(\lambda) + 1/p)$.

Proof. Assume that $\mathcal{A}$ is a PPT algorithm which makes $\boldsymbol{Expt}_4$ outputs 1 with a non-negligible probability. Let $\mathcal{B}_3$ be a PPT simulator who attempts to solve the FlexCDH problem by using $\mathcal{A}$.

Receive (g, g^a, g^b) as an instance of the FlexCDH problem. As the proof of Lemma 4, compute the variables $l, k, \kappa_1, \delta_1, \cdots, \kappa_{n+5}, \delta_{n+5}, x', x_0, y_0, \cdots, x_{N-1}, y_{N-1}$ and $\boldsymbol{f}$, and define the functions F and J.

Set $g^\alpha := g^a$, $v := g^b$, $g_i := (g^b)^{\kappa_i} g^{\delta_i}$, $u' := (g^a)^{-lk+x'} \cdot g^{y'}$ and $u_i := (g^a)^{x_i} \cdot g^{y_i}$ for $i \in [0, N-1]$. It holds that $u' \prod_{i=0}^{N-1} u_i^{\tau[i]} = (g^a)^{F(\tau)} \cdot g^{J(\tau)}$.

Set $pp := (\mathbb{G}, \mathbb{G}_T, g, g^\alpha, v, \{g_i\}_{i=1}^{n+5}, u', \{u_i\}_{i=0}^{N-1}, \boldsymbol{f})$ and send it to $\mathcal{A}$. When $\mathcal{A}$ issues a query to the key-revelation or signing oracle, $\mathcal{B}_3$ behaves as follows.

Key-Revelation $\mathfrak{Reveal}(\mathbf{x})$: Choose $\tau \in \{0,1\}^N$. Generate the $n+4$ vectors $\boldsymbol{v}_1, \cdots, \boldsymbol{v}_{n+4} \in \mathbb{Z}_p^{n+5}$ in the normal way. As the proof of the previous lemma, consider the following two cases.

(1) $F(\tau) \neq 0 \pmod{l}$**:** For each $i \in [1, n+4]$, generate an ALP signature $(\sigma_{i,1}, \sigma_{i,2}, \sigma_{i,3}, \sigma_{i,4})$ as

$$\left((g^\alpha)^{\sum_{j=1}^{n+5} \delta_j v_{ij}} (g^b)^{-\frac{J(\tau)(\sum_{j=1}^{n+5} \kappa_j v_{ij} + s_i)}{F(\tau)}} H_{\mathbb{G}}(\tau)^{r_i}, (g^b)^{-\frac{\sum_j \kappa_j v_{ij} + s_i}{F(\tau)}} g^{r_i}, g^{s_i}, g^{\alpha \cdot s_i} \right),$$

where $r_i, s_i \xleftarrow{\text{U}} \mathbb{Z}_p$. Let $\tilde{r}_i := r_i - b\frac{\sum_{j=1}^{n} \kappa_j v_{ij} + s_i}{F(\tau)}$. Obviously, $\sigma_{i,2} = g^{\tilde{r}_i}$. The ALP signature correctly distributes since

$$\left(\prod_{j=1}^{n+5} g_j^{v_{ij}} v^{s_i} \right)^\alpha H_{\mathbb{G}}(\tau)^{\tilde{r}_i} = \left[\prod_{j=1}^{n+5} (g^{b \cdot \kappa_j} g^{\delta_j})^{v_{ij}} g^{b \cdot s_i} \right]^\alpha H_{\mathbb{G}}(\tau)^{r_i - b\frac{\sum_{j=1}^{n} \kappa_j v_{ij} + s_i}{F(\tau)}}$$

$$= \cancel{\{(g^b)^{\sum_{j=1}^{n+5} \kappa_j v_{ij} + s_i}\}^\alpha} \cdot (g^{\sum_{j=1}^{n+5} \delta_j v_{ij}})^\alpha \cdot H_{\mathbb{G}}(\tau)^{r_i} \cdot \cancel{(g^\alpha)^{-b(\sum_{j=1}^{n+5} \kappa_j v_{ij} + s_i)}}$$
$$\cdot g^{-b\frac{J(\tau)}{F(\tau)}(\sum_{j=1}^{n+5} \kappa_j v_{ij} + s_i)}$$

is equivalent to the above $\sigma_{i,1}$.

(2) $F(\tau) = 0 \pmod{l}$**:** Immediately abort the simulation if this condition has already been satisfied by a tag previously chosen on the key-revelation or signing oracle. For each $i \in [1, n+4]$, choose $r_i \xleftarrow{\text{U}} \mathbb{Z}_p$, set $s_i := -\sum_{j=1}^{n+5} \kappa_j v_{ij}$, then generate an ALP signature $(\sigma_{i,1}, \sigma_{i,2}, \sigma_{i,3}, \sigma_{i,4})$ as $((g^a)^{\sum_{j=1}^{n+5} \delta_j v_{ij}} H_{\mathbb{G}}(\tau)^{r_i}, g^{r_i}, g^{s_i}, (g^\alpha)^{s_i})$. Since the vectors $\{\boldsymbol{v}_i\}_{i=1}^{n+4}$ are linearly independent and any of $\{\kappa_i\}_{i=1}^{n+5}$ has been chosen randomly from $\mathbb{Z}_p$, any of $\{s_i\}_{i=1}^{n+4}$ distributes randomly in $\mathbb{Z}_p$. The ALP signature correctly distributes since $(\prod_{j=1}^{n+5} g_j^{v_{ij}} \cdot v^{s_i})^\alpha \cdot H_{\mathbb{G}}(\tau)^{r_i} = [\prod_{j=1}^{n+5} \{(g^b)^{\kappa_i} g^{\delta_i}\}^{v_{ij}} \cdot (g^b)^{-\sum_{j=1}^{n+5} \kappa_j v_{ij}}]^\alpha \cdot H_{\mathbb{G}}(\tau)^{r_i}$ is equivalent to the above $\sigma_{i,1}$.

Finally, return $sk_{\mathbf{x}} := (\mathbf{x}, \tau, \{\{\sigma_{ij}\}_{j=1}^{4}\}_{i=1}^{n+4})$ to $\mathcal{A}$.

Signing $\mathfrak{Sign}(\mathbf{x}, M, \mathbf{y}, L, R)$: Compute $d := \langle \mathbf{x}, \mathbf{y} \rangle \pmod{p}$. Choose $\tau \xleftarrow{\text{U}} \{0,1\}^N$. As the key-revelation oracle, consider the mutually exclusive two cases w.r.t. $F(\tau) \in \mathbb{Z}_p$, and in each case compute an ALP signature $(\overline{\sigma}_1, \overline{\sigma}_2, \overline{\sigma}_3, \overline{\sigma}_4)$ on the message $\overline{\boldsymbol{v}} = (d, y_1, \cdots, y_n, L, R, M, 1)$. In the normal manner, compute all of the GS commitments and proofs. Return a signature σ, composed of all of the GS commitments/proofs and $\overline{\sigma}_2$, to $\mathcal{A}$.

$\mathcal{B}_3$ receives a forged signature σ^* from $\mathcal{A}$. Consider the following two cases, namely (1) $F(\tau^*) = 0 \pmod{p}$ and (2) $F(\tau^*) \neq 0 \pmod{p}$. If the case (2) occurs, abort the simulation. If the case (1) occurs, compute the following three variables, namely $\xi_1 := \overline{\sigma}_3^* \cdot g^{\sum_{j=1}^{n+5} \kappa_j v_j^*}$, $\xi_2 := \overline{\sigma}_4^* \cdot (g^\alpha)^{\sum_{j=1}^{n+5} \kappa_j v_j^*}$ and $\xi_3 := \overline{\sigma}_1^* \cdot (\overline{\sigma}_2^*)^{-J(\tau^*)} \cdot (g^\alpha)^{\sum_{j=1}^{n+5} \delta_j v_j^*}$.

Let $\hat{s}^* := s^* + \sum_{j=1}^{n+5} \kappa_j v_j^*$. Obviously, $\xi_1 := g^{\hat{s}^*}$ and $\xi_2 := g^{a\hat{s}^*}$. It holds that $\xi_3 = [\prod_{i=1}^{n+5}\{(g^b)^{\kappa_i} \cancel{g^{\delta_i}}\}^{v_i^*} \cdot (g^b)^{s^*}]^\alpha \cdot \cancel{H_{\mathbb{G}}(\tau^*)^{r^*}} \cancel{(g^{r^*})^{-J(\tau^*)}} \cdot \cancel{(g^\alpha)^{-\sum_{j=1}^{n+5}\delta_j v_i^*}} = (g^{ab})^{s^* + \sum_{j=1}^{n+5}\kappa_j v_j^*} = g^{ab\hat{s}^*}$.

Thus, (ξ_1, ξ_2, ξ_3) is the correct answer to the FlexCDH problem under an assumption that it holds $\hat{s}^* \neq 0 \pmod p \Leftrightarrow s^* \neq -\sum_{j=1}^{n+5}\kappa_j v_j^* \pmod p$. This assumption is reasonable since the probability $\Pr[s^* = -\sum_{j=1}^{n+5}\kappa_j v_j^* \pmod p]$ is at most $1/p$. As the proof of the previous lemma, we obtain $\Pr[1 \leftarrow \boldsymbol{Expt}_4(1^\lambda, n)] \leq 4q(N+1)(\mathtt{Adv}_{\mathcal{B}_3,\mathbb{G}}^{\mathtt{FlexCDH}}(\lambda) + \frac{1}{p})$. □

Signer-Privacy. We present the following theorem.

Theorem 2. *Our 1st ARIP scheme is perfectly signer-private.*

Proof. $\boldsymbol{Expt}_1$ is associated with the three simulation algorithms `SimSetup`, `SimKGen` and `SimSig`. The first two are the same as the original ones of our scheme[6]. `SimSig` is defined as follows.

`SimSig`$(mk, M, \mathbf{y}, L, R)$**:** Arbitrarily choose an attribute $\mathbf{x}^* \in \mathbb{Z}_p^n$ s.t. $\langle \mathbf{x}^*, \mathbf{y}\rangle \pmod p \in [L, R]$. Choose $\tau^* \xleftarrow{U} \{0,1\}^N$. Generate an ALP signature $(\overline{\sigma}_1, \overline{\sigma}_2, \overline{\sigma}_3, \overline{\sigma}_4)$ as $(\{g_1^{\langle \mathbf{x}^*, \mathbf{y}\rangle} \cdot \prod_{i=1}^n g_{i+1}^{y_i} \cdot g_{n+2}^L \cdot g_{n+3}^R \cdot g_{n+4}^M \cdot g_{n+5} \cdot v^s\}^\alpha \cdot H_{\mathbb{G}}(\tau^*)^r, g^r, g^s, g^{\alpha s})$, where $r, s \xleftarrow{U} \mathbb{Z}_p$. As the original signing algorithm, generate all of the GS commitments and proofs. Return a signature, composed of all of the GS commitments/proofs and $\overline{\sigma}_2$.

In $\boldsymbol{Expt}_0$, an ALP signature used to generate a signature on the signing oracle distributes as (1). Its second element $\overline{\sigma}_2$ distributes identically to the one in $\boldsymbol{Expt}_1$ because of $\overline{r} \xleftarrow{U} \mathbb{Z}_p$. Even though the adversary $\mathcal{A}$ knows of directly $\mathbf{x}, \tau$ and indirectly $\{s_i\}_{i=1}^n$, because of the perfect WI of the GS NIWI system, all of the GS commitments (incl. the ones related to $\langle \mathbf{x}, \mathbf{y}\rangle, \tau, \overline{\sigma}_1, \overline{\sigma}_3, \overline{\sigma}_4$) and proofs distribute identically to the ones in $\boldsymbol{Expt}_1$. □

4.2 Efficiency Analysis

We analyze efficiency of our 1st ARIP scheme. Precisely, we calculate (1) bit length of a secret-key, (2) bit length of a signature, and (3) computational cost of signature verification.

(1) Size of Secret-Key. Let $|g|$ denote bit length of an element in $\mathbb{G}$. Obviously, bit length of a secret-key is expressed as $|sk| = N + 4(n+4)|g|$.[7]

---

[6] The auxiliary variable μ has no information, i.e., $\mu = \_$.

[7] Note that bit length of $\mathbf{x} \in \mathbb{Z}_p^n$ is ignored here.

(2) Size of Signature. Each signature consists of 3 types of element, namely the ALP signature element $\overline{\sigma}_2$, GS commitments, and GS proofs. If we denote the bit length of the 3 types of element by s_1, s_2, s_3 respectively, bit length of a signature is $|\sigma| = s_1 + s_2 + s_3$. Obviously, $s_1 = |g|$. Total number of the GS commitments is $\underset{(b),(d),(e)}{\underline{5}} + \underset{(a)}{\underline{2N}} + \underset{(c)}{\underline{2\lambda}} + \underset{(f)}{\underline{|\Theta|}} + \underset{(g)}{\underline{2\sum_{\theta\in\Theta}|\theta|}}$. Note that the blue alphabet below each number indicates the alphabet assigned to each committed variable in the signing algorithm of our ARIP scheme. Both of the two terms $|\Theta|$ and $\sum_{\theta\in\Theta}|\theta|$ are maximized when $[L, R] = [1, p-2]$ and become $2\lambda-2$ and $(2+3+\cdots+\lambda)\times 2 = \lambda^2 + \lambda - 2$ respectively. As a result, total number of the GS commitments is upper bounded by $2N + 6\lambda + 2\lambda^2 - 1$, which is asymptotically $\mathcal{O}(N + \lambda^2)$. Since each GS commitment consists of 3 group elements, $s_2 = \mathcal{O}(N + \lambda^2)|g|$. Total number of the type-1 (resp. type-2) GS proofs is $4 + N + \lambda + \sum_{\theta\in\Theta}|\theta| + 2$ (resp. $N + \lambda + \sum_{\theta\in\Theta}(|\theta| - 1)$), either of which is asymptotically $\mathcal{O}(N + \lambda^2)$. Since a type-1 (resp. type-2) GS proof consists of 3 (resp. 9) group elements, $s_1 = \mathcal{O}(N + \lambda^2)|g|$. Hence, $|\sigma| = \mathcal{O}(N + \lambda^2)|g|$.

(3) Cost of Verification. We derive total number of multiplication and exponentiation on the group $\mathbb{G}_T$ and calculation of the paring function e. In verification, a verifier checks whether all of the 12 equations hold or not. The verifier conducts following 4 types of calculation, namely (a) *calculation of the function* E, (b) *calculation of* F, (c) *multiplication of two vectors in* $\mathbb{G}_T^3$ *outputted by* E, and (d) *multiplication of two matrices in* $\mathbb{G}_T^{3\times 3}$ *outputted by* F. They require the following number of multiplication, exponentiation and pairing, respectively, (a) $(0, 0, 3)$, (b) $(9, 9, 9)$, (c) $(3, 0, 0)$, and (d) $(9, 0, 0)$. Total number of the 4 types of calculation executed in one verification is derived as follows.

- $N_a := \underset{2}{\underline{5N}} + \underset{3}{\underline{5 + N}} + \underset{5}{\underline{5\lambda}} + \underset{6}{\underline{4 + \lambda}} + \underset{7}{\underline{8}} + \underset{8}{\underline{5}} + \underset{9}{\underline{\sum_{\theta\in\Theta}\sum_{j=1}^{|\theta|} 5}} + \underset{10}{\underline{5|\Theta|}} + \underset{12}{\underline{|\Theta| + 4}}$
  $= L + 6\lambda + 26 + 6|\Theta| + \sum_{\theta\in\Theta}\sum_{j=1}^{|\theta|} 5$
- $N_b := \underset{1}{\underline{4N}} + \underset{4}{\underline{4\lambda}} + \underset{11}{\underline{\sum_{\theta\in\Theta}\sum_{j=2}^{|\theta|} 5}}$
- $N_c := \underset{2}{\underline{4N}} + \underset{3}{\underline{N + 3}} + \underset{5}{\underline{4\lambda}} + \underset{6}{\underline{\lambda + 2}} + \underset{7}{\underline{6}} + \underset{8}{\underline{3}} + \underset{9}{\underline{\sum_{\theta\in\Theta}\sum_{j=1}^{|\theta|} 3}} + \underset{10}{\underline{3|\Theta|}} + \underset{12}{\underline{|\Theta| - 1 + 3}}$
  $= 5N + 5\lambda + 16 + 4|\Theta| + \sum_{\theta\in\Theta}\sum_{j=1}^{|\theta|} 3$
- $N_d := \underset{1}{\underline{3N}} + \underset{4}{\underline{3\lambda}} + \underset{11}{\underline{\sum_{\theta\in\Theta}\sum_{j\in[2,|\theta|]} 3}}$

Note that the blue number below each number indicates the identification number assigned to each equation verified in the verification algorithm of our ARIP scheme. Each of them is asymptotically $\mathcal{O}(N + \lambda^2)$. Each of number of multiplication, number of exponentiation and number of pairing per one verification is the linear summation of N_a, N_b, N_c and N_d with coefficients of integers from 0 to 9. Thus, $\mathcal{O}(N + \lambda^2)$.

As a result we obtain the 1st entry in Table 1. The 2nd, 3rd and 4th entries are for the other our schemes explained in later subsections.

4.3 Efficiency Optimization

The prime p is exponentially large in λ. In some applications of ARIP, it is possible that for every vectors $\mathbf{x}, \mathbf{y} \in \mathbb{Z}_p$, their inner product $\langle \mathbf{x}, \mathbf{y} \rangle$ is upper-bounded by $T-1$ for an integer $T \in \mathbf{poly}(\lambda)$ s.t. $T \ll p$. In this case, our 1st scheme (in Subsect. 4.1) can be optimized in terms of efficiency.

Table 1. Efficiency of our ARIP schemes.

Our schemes	Size of secret-key $\lvert sk \rvert$	Size of signature $\lvert \sigma \rvert$	Cost of verification		
			# of Mul.	# of Exp.	# of Pair.
The 1st one (Subsect. 4.1)	$N + (4n+16)\lvert g \rvert$	$\mathcal{O}(N+\lambda^2)\lvert g \rvert$	$\mathcal{O}(N+\lambda^2)$		
→ Its optimization (Subsect. 4.3)	$N + (4n+16)\lvert g \rvert$	$\mathcal{O}(N+\log^2 T)\lvert g \rvert$	$\mathcal{O}(N+\log^2 T)$		
The 2nd one (Subsect. 4.4)	$N + 16\lvert g \rvert$	$\mathcal{O}(N+\lambda^2+n)\lvert g \rvert$	$\mathcal{O}(N+\lambda^2+n)$		
→ Its optimization	$N + 16\lvert g \rvert$	$\mathcal{O}(N+\log^2 T+n)\lvert g \rvert$	$\mathcal{O}(N+\log^2 T+n)$		

The inner product $d := \langle \mathbf{x}, \mathbf{y} \rangle \in [0, T-1]$ is $\log T \in \mathbb{N}$ bit. Since for every $i \in [\log T, \lambda-1]$, $d[i]$ (= the i-th bit of d) must be 0, we do not need to generate the GS commitments $\vec{C}_{d[i]}, \vec{C}_{1-d[i]} \in \mathbb{G}^3$ and the related GS proofs $\vec{\pi}_{d[i]}, \vec{\pi}'_{d[i]} \in \mathbb{G}^3$. The complete binary tree used to prove that $d \in [L, R]$ has only T leaf nodes associated with 0 to $T-1$ from left to right. Both cardinality of the set Θ (consisting of nodes covering all of the leaf nodes from L to R) and $\sum_{\theta \in \Theta} |\theta|$ are maximized when $[L, R] = [1, \log T - 2]$ and become $2\log T - 2$ and $\log T^2 + \log T - 2$. As a result we obtain the 2nd entry in Table 1.

4.4 Our 2nd ARIP Scheme with Constant-Size Secret-Keys

We propose another scheme that a trade-off relationship in terms of efficiency holds with our 1st scheme. Its secret-key length is independent of n. In return, any of its signature length and verification cost linearly increases with n.

A secret-key $sk_{\mathbf{x}}$ consists of only four ALP signatures $\sigma_1, \cdots, \sigma_4$ on vectors $\boldsymbol{v}_1, \cdots, \boldsymbol{v}_4 \in \mathbb{Z}_p^{n+4}$. The vector $\boldsymbol{v}_i$ is $(x_1, \cdots, x_n) \| \boldsymbol{e}_i$ if $i = 1$, or $(0, \cdots, 0) \| \boldsymbol{e}_i$ otherwise, where $\boldsymbol{e}_i$ is the i-th unit vector in $\mathbb{Z}_p^4$. At signature generation, the signer derives an ALP LHS signature $\overline{\sigma}$ on $\overline{\boldsymbol{v}} := \sum_{i=1}^4 \beta_i \cdot \boldsymbol{v}_i$, where $(\beta_1, \beta_2, \beta_3, \beta_4) := (1, L, R, M)$. Note that $\overline{\boldsymbol{v}} = (x_1, \cdots, x_n, 1, L, R, M) \in \mathbb{Z}_p^{n+4}$. The signer has to compute GS commitments for $x_1, \cdots, x_n \in \mathbb{Z}_p$ and $d (:= \langle \mathbf{x}, \mathbf{y} \rangle) \in \mathbb{Z}_p$ then prove that d is genuinely the inner product of $\mathbf{x}$ and $\mathbf{y}$. Actually, the signer computes GS commitments for g^{x_i} and $g_i^{x_i}$ for all $i \in [1, n]$. Then, the signer computes GS proofs for the following relations, namely $e(g^{x_i}, g_i) = e(g, g_i^{x_i})$ for all $i \in [1, n]$ and $e(g_1^d, g) = \prod_{i=1}^n e(g^{x_i}, g_1^{y_i})$. Moreover, the relation [e] (in our 1st scheme) is modified into $e(\overline{\sigma}_1, g) = e(\prod_{i=1}^n g_i^{x_i}, g^\alpha) \cdot e(\prod_{i=1}^4 g_{i+n}^{\beta_i}, g^\alpha) \cdot e(v, \overline{\sigma}_4) \cdot e(H_{\mathbb{G}}(\tau), \overline{\sigma}_2)$. The formal description of our 2nd scheme is given in Subsect. B.

Theorem 3. *Our 2nd ARIP scheme is* EUF-CMA *if the DLIN, CDH and Flex-CDH assumptions hold in the group* $\mathbb{G}$ *and perfectly signer-private.*

5 Applications of ARIP

Katz et al. [16] showed that attribute-based encryption (ABE) for inner products[8] can be transformed into various ABE primitives, namely (anonymous) identity-based encryption (IBE), hidden-vector encryption (HVE), the dual version of HVE (= wildcarded IBE [1]), ABE for evaluation of polynomials/weighted averages/CNF and DNF formulas, and ABE for exact thresholds. Based on the same techniques, its digital signature analogue named ABS for inner products can be transformed into identity-based signatures (IBS), hidden-vector signatures (HVS), the dual of HVS (= wildcarded IBS), ABS for evaluation of polynomials/weighted averages/CNF and DNF formulas, and ABS for exact thresholds. Since ARIP is a generalization of the ABS for inner products, it can be transformed into more generalized (or powerful) ABS primitives as follows.

(1) ABS for Range Evaluation of Polynomials (AREP): Assume that the polynomial is univariate. AREP is a sub-class of the general ABS in Subsect. 3.1. The attribute $x \in \{0,1\}^*$ in the general ABS is changed into a single variable $x \in \mathbb{Z}_p$ in AREP. The predicate f_{AREP}, associated with a d-dimensional polynomial ϕ with coefficients $a_d, \cdots, a_0 \in \mathbb{Z}_p$ and a range $[L, R]$ with $L, R \in \mathbb{Z}_p$, is defined as

$$f_{\mathrm{AREP}}(x) := \begin{cases} 1 & (\text{If } \phi(x) := \sum_{i=0}^{d} a_i \cdot x^i \in [L, R] \pmod p) \\ 0 & (\text{Otherwise}). \end{cases}$$

An AREP scheme is transformed from any ARIP scheme of $d+1$ dimensions. The vector $\mathbf{x} \in \mathbb{Z}_p^{d+1}$ in ARIP is changed into $(x^d, x^{d-1}, \cdots, x, 1)$. The vector $\mathbf{y} \in \mathbb{Z}_p^{d+1}$ in ARIP is $(a_d, a_{d-1}, \cdots, a_1, a_0)$. The AREP scheme is correct because if $\phi(x) = \sum_{i=0}^{d} a_i \cdot x^i \in [L, R]$ implies $\langle \mathbf{x}, \mathbf{y} \rangle \in [L, R]$. Even if the polynomial is multivariate with t variables, the transformation still works. In this case, we need an ARIP scheme of $(d^t + 1)$ dimensions.

(2) ABS for Range Evaluation of Weighted Average (AREWA): The attribute x consists of t variables $x_1, \cdots, x_t \in \mathbb{Z}_p$. The predicate f_{AREWA}, associated with t coefficients $a_1, \cdots, a_t \in \mathbb{Z}_p$ and a range $[L, R]$ for $L, R \in \mathbb{Z}_p$, is defined as follows: $f_{\mathrm{AREWA}}(x_1, \cdots, x_t)$ outputs 1 if $\sum_{i=1}^{t} a_i \cdot x_i \in [L, R] \pmod p$, or 0 otherwise.
An AREWA scheme is transformed from an ARIP scheme of $n = t$ dimensions. The vector $\mathbf{x} \in \mathbb{Z}_p^t$ (resp. $\mathbf{y} \in \mathbb{Z}_p^t$) in ARIP is $(x_1, \cdots, x_t)$ (resp. $(a_1, \cdots, a_t)$). The AREWA scheme obviously satisfies the correctness.

(3) Fuzzy IBS (FIBS): This is a generalization of the ABS for exact thresholds. Let A be $\{1, \cdots, l\}$ for $l \in \mathbb{N}$. The attribute x is a set of attributes $S \subseteq A$. The predicate f_{FIBS}, associated with a set of attributes $S' \subseteq A$ and a range $[L, R]$ for $0 \leq L \leq R \leq l$, is defined as follows: $f_{\mathrm{FIBS}}(S)$ outputs 1 if $|S \cap S'| \in [L, R]$, or 0 otherwise[9].

[8] Like ARIP, vectors $\mathbf{x}, \mathbf{y}$ are associated with secret-key and ciphertext respectively. The decryption succeeds if the inner product is 0.

[9] This FIBS is a further generalization of the signature analogue of FIBE [25] since the upper bound R of the overlapped attributes can be set.

Table 2. Efficiency of existing and our TSS schemes.

TSS schemes	$\|pp\|$	$\|mk\|$	$\|sk\|$	$\|\sigma\|$	Assumptions
FSS-based [14]	$(2\log T + m + 3)\cdot(\|g\| + \|\tilde{g}\|)$	$\|g\|$	$\mathcal{O}(\log T)\|g\|$	$(2\log T + 2)\|g\|$	co-CDH
WIBRS-based [14]	$\mathcal{O}(\log T)\|\tilde{g}\|$	$\mathcal{O}(\log T)\|g\|$	$\mathcal{O}(1)(\|g\| + \|\tilde{g}\|)$	$\mathcal{O}(\log^2 T)\cdot(\|g\| + \|\tilde{g}\|)$	SXDH
Ours 1	$(N + 9)\|g\|$	λ	$(N + 20)\|g\|$	$\mathcal{O}(N + \log^2 T)\|g\|$	CDH,FlexCDH,DLIN
Ours 2	$(N + 8)\|g\|$	λ	$(N + 16)\|g\|$	$\mathcal{O}(N + \log^2 T)\|g\|$	CDH,FlexCDH,DLIN

Note: Both of the FSS-based and WIBRS-based schemes [14] use an asymmetric bilinear map $e : \mathbb{G} \times \tilde{\mathbb{G}} \to \mathbb{G}_T$. $|g|$ (resp. $|\tilde{g}|$) denotes bit length of an element in $\mathbb{G}$ (resp. $\tilde{\mathbb{G}}$). For the FSS-based scheme, $m \in \mathbb{N}$ denotes bit length of a message. SXDH means Symmetric External Diffie-Hellman.

An FIBS scheme is transformed from an ARIP scheme with $n = l$ dimensions. For the vector $\mathbf{x} \in \mathbb{Z}_p^l$, its i-th element x_i is set to 1 if $i \in S$ or 0 otherwise. For the vector $\mathbf{y} \in \mathbb{Z}_p^l$, y_i is 1 if $i \in S'$ or 0 otherwise. The FIBS scheme is correct since $\langle \mathbf{x}, \mathbf{y} \rangle = |S \cap S'|$.

Additionally, we present the following 4 applications.

(4) **Time-Specific Signatures (TSS)** [14,23]**:** TSS is a sub-class of the ABS. The attribute $x \in \{0,1\}^*$ is a time-period $t \in [0, T-1]$ for an integer $T \in \mathbb{N}$. The predicate f_{TSS}, associated with a range $[L, R]$ with $L, R \in [0, T-1]$, is defined as follows: $f_{\text{TSS}}(t)$ is set to 1 if $t \in [L, R]$, or 0 otherwise.
We use an ARIP scheme of 1 dimension. The scalar $x_1 \in \mathbb{Z}_p$ in ARIP is t. The scalar $y_1 \in \mathbb{Z}_p$ in ARIP is always 1. The TSS scheme is correct because $t \in [L, R]$ implies $\langle \mathbf{x}, \mathbf{y} \rangle = x_1 \cdot y_1 = t \in [L, R]$.
In [23], TSS was firstly mentioned and its secure construction was presented as a open problem. In [14], the authors formally defined TSS and proposed two secure schemes based on forward-secure signatures (FSS) and wildcarded identity-based ring signatures (WIBRS), respectively. In Table 2, their TSS schemes [14] and ours are compared in terms of efficiency and security assumptions. Ours 1 (resp. Ours 2) is the TSS scheme obtained by instantiating the optimized variant of our 1st (resp. 2nd) ARIP scheme. Ours are the first ones whose $|pp|$, $|mk|$ and $|sk|$ are independent of the parameter T.

(5) **ABS for Range of Hamming Distance (ARHD):** A signer with a (binary) string $x \in \{0,1\}^l$ can sign a message under a string $y \in \{0,1\}^l$ iff the Hamming distance between x and y is within a range $[L, R]$. The attribute x in the ABS is a string $x \in \{0,1\}^l$. The predicate f_{ARHD} is defined as follows: $f_{\text{ARHD}}(x)$ outputs 1 if $\mathbf{HD}(x, y) := \sum_{i=0}^{l-1} |x[i] - y[i]| \in [L, R]$, or 0 otherwise. We use an ARIP scheme of $2l$ dimensions. The strings $x, y \in \{0,1\}^l$ are changed into $\mathbf{x}, \mathbf{y} \in \mathbb{Z}_p^{2l}$ as follows. For each $i \in [0, l-1]$, (x_{2i+1}, x_{2i+2}) (resp. (y_{2i+1}, y_{2i+2})) is set to $(0, 1)$ (resp. $(1, 0)$) if $x[i] = 0$, or $(1, 0)$ (resp. $(0, 1)$) otherwise. Obviously, $x_{2i+1} \cdot y_{2i+1} + x_{2i+2} \cdot y_{2i+2}$ is 1 if $x[i] \neq y[i]$, or 0 otherwise. The ARHD scheme is correct because $\langle \mathbf{x}, \mathbf{y} \rangle = \mathbf{HD}(x, y)$.

(6) **ABS for Range of Euclidean Distance (ARED):** A signer with a vector $\overrightarrow{X} \in \mathbb{Z}_p^n$ declares another vector $\overrightarrow{Y} \in \mathbb{Z}_p^n$ and a range $[L, R]$. If the Euclidean distance between the two vectors is within the range, the signing

succeeds. The predicate f_{ARED} is defined as follows: $f_{\text{ARED}}(\vec{X})$ outputs 1 if $\mathbf{ED}(\vec{X}, \vec{Y}) := \sqrt{\sum_{i=1}^{n}(X_i - Y_i)^2} \in [L, R]$, or 0 otherwise.
An ARIP scheme with $n+2$ dimensions is available. The vectors $\vec{X}, \vec{Y} \in \mathbb{Z}_p^n$ for ARED are transformed into $\mathbf{x}, \mathbf{y} \in \mathbb{Z}_p^{n+2}$ as follows.
- $x_i := X_i$ for all $i \in [1, n]$. $(x_{n+1}, x_{n+2}) := (\sum_{i=1}^{n} X_i^2, 1)$.
- $y_i := -2Y_i$ for all $i \in [1, n]$. $(y_{n+1}, y_{n+2}) := (1, \sum_{i=1}^{n} Y_i^2)$.

The range $[L, R]$ for ARED is extended into $[L^2, R^2] \subseteq \mathbb{Z}_p$ for ARIP. The ARED scheme is correct since it holds $\langle \mathbf{x}, \mathbf{y} \rangle = \sum_{i=1}^{2n+1} x_i \cdot y_i = \sum_{i=1}^{n} X_i^2 - 2X_iY_i + Y_i^2 = \sum_{i=1}^{n}(X_i - Y_i)^2 = \mathbf{ED}(\vec{X}, \vec{Y})^2$, which implies $\mathbf{ED}(\vec{X}, \vec{Y}) \in [L, R] \Leftrightarrow \langle \mathbf{x}, \mathbf{y} \rangle (= \mathbf{ED}(\vec{X}, \vec{Y})^2) \in [L^2, R^2]$.

(7) ABS for Hyperellipsoid Predicates (AHEP): An n-dimensional hypersphere is a set of points (or vectors) whose Euclidean distance to the central point is constant. Let us consider a special type of ABS, where a secret-key is associated with a vector $\vec{X} \in \mathbb{Z}_p^n$, a signature is associated with a hypersphere with center $\vec{Y} \in \mathbb{Z}_p^n$ and radius $a \in \mathbb{Z}_p$ and the signing succeeds iff the vector $\vec{X}$ is inside of the hypersphere, named ABS for hypersphere predicates (AHSP). Obviously, AHSP is transformed from ARED defined above.
AHEP is a generalization of AHSP. The hypersphere is generalized to the hyperellipsoid. The predicate f_{AHEP} is defined as follows: $f_{\text{AHEP}}(\vec{X})$ outputs 1 if $\sum_{i=1}^{n}(X_i - Y_i)^2/a_i^2 \leq 1$, or 0 otherwise, where $\vec{Y} \in \mathbb{Z}_p^n$ is the center and $a_i \in \mathbb{Z}_p$ is the radius in the i-th axis.
An AHEP scheme is transformed from an ARIP scheme with $2n+1$ dimensions. For $i \in [1, n]$, let $\delta_i := (\prod_{j=1}^{n} a_j^2)/a_i^2$. The vectors $\vec{X}, \vec{Y} \in \mathbb{Z}_p^n$ for AHEP are transformed into $\mathbf{x}, \mathbf{y} \in \mathbb{Z}_p^{2n+1}$ as follows.
- $(x_{2i-1}, x_{2i}) := (X_i^2, X_i)$ for all $i \in [1, n]$. $x_{2n+1} := 1$.
- $(y_{2i-1}, y_{2i}) := (\delta_i, -2\delta_i Y_i)$ for all $i \in [1, n]$. $y_{2n+1} := \sum_{i=1}^{n} \delta_i Y_i^2$.

The range $[L, R]$ for ARIP is set to $[0, \prod_{i=1}^{n} a_i^2] \subseteq \mathbb{Z}_p$. The AHEP scheme is correct since $\langle \mathbf{x}, \mathbf{y} \rangle = \sum_{i=1}^{2n+1} x_i \cdot y_i = \sum_{i=1}^{n} \delta_i (X_i - Y_i)^2 = \sum_{i=1}^{n} \frac{\prod_{j=1}^{n} a_j^2}{a_i^2}(X_i - Y_i)^2 \in [0, \sum_{j=1}^{n} a_j^2] \Leftrightarrow \sum_{i=1}^{n}(X_i - Y_i)^2/a_i^2 \in [0, 1]$.

6 Conclusion

We formally defined ARIP and proposed two efficient schemes secure under standard assumptions, i.e., the CDH, FlexCDH and DLIN assumptions, in the standard model, based on the GS NIWI system [11] and a simplified variant of the ALP LHS scheme [6]. The 2nd (resp. 1st) scheme is independent of the number of dimensions $n \in \mathbf{poly}(\lambda)$ in secret-key length (resp. signature length and verification cost). We also optimized their efficiency for the case where each possible variable for $x_i, y_i, L, R, \langle \mathbf{x}, \mathbf{y} \rangle \in \mathbb{Z}_p$ is upper-bounded by $T-1$ with $T \ll p$. We showed that ARIP can be generically transformed into various ABS. Since this work is the first research on ARIP, ARIP can develop in many directions. Some of the examples are given below.

***Key-Policy* ARIP (KPARIP):** A range $[L, R]$ is associated with each secret-key (but not signature). The transformations from ARIP to various ABS (in Sect. 5) work for KPARIP. Specifically, KPARIP can be transformed into the key-policy analogues of AREP, AREWA, TSS, ARHD, ARED and AHEP.

***Multi-Vectorial* ARIP:** Each secret-key has l number of n-dimensional vectors $\mathbf{x}_1, \cdots, \mathbf{x}_l \in \mathbb{Z}_p^n$. Each signature has l number of n-dimensional vectors $\mathbf{y}_1, \cdots, \mathbf{y}_l \in \mathbb{Z}_p^n$ and ranges $[L_1, R_1], \cdots, [L_l, R_l] \subseteq \mathbb{Z}_p$, and a Boolean formula $f : \underbrace{\{0,1\} \times \cdots \times \{0,1\}}_{l} \to \{0,1\}$. For each $i \in [1, l]$, a Boolean variable z_i is set to 1 if $\langle \mathbf{x}_i, \mathbf{y}_i \rangle \in [L_i, R_i]$, or 0 otherwise. If $f(z_1, \cdots, z_l) = 1$, the signing succeeds. For the form of f, we have various options, e.g., AND, OR or Threshold function, CNF or DNF formula, and a general circuit.

Attribute-Based *Encryption* for Range of Inner-Product: The transformations from ARIP to various ABS (in Sect. 5) also work for the encryption analogue of ARIP. Specifically, it can be transformed into the encryption analogues of AREP, AREWA, TSS, ARHD, ARED and AHEP.

A The Simplified Variant of the ALP LHS Scheme [6]

Syntax of LHS. An LHS scheme consists of the following 4 polynomial-time algorithms. Note that `Setup` and `Sig` are probabilistic, `Ver` is deterministic and `Derive` is (possibly) probabilistic.

Key-Generation `KGen`**:** It takes a security parameter 1^λ for $\lambda \in \mathbb{N}$ and an integer $n \in \mathbb{N}$, being polynomial in λ, that indicates the dimension of a vector to be signed, then outputs a key-pair (pk, sk).
$[(pk, sk) \leftarrow \mathtt{KGen}(1^\lambda, n)]$

Signing `Sig`**:** It takes the secret-key sk, a tag (called a file identifier in [5]) $\tau \in \{0,1\}^*$ and a vector $\boldsymbol{v} \in \mathbb{Z}_p^n$ to be signed, then outputs a signature σ.
$[\sigma \leftarrow \mathtt{Sig}(sk, \tau, \boldsymbol{v})]$

Derivation `Derive`**:** It takes the public-key pk, a tag $\tau \in \{0,1\}^*$ and l triples $\{\boldsymbol{v}_i, \sigma_i, \beta_i\}_{i=1}^l$, consisting of a vector $\boldsymbol{v}_i \in \mathbb{Z}_p^n$, a signature σ_i and a weight β_i, then outputs a signature $\overline{\sigma}$ on the weighted vector $\overline{\boldsymbol{v}} := \sum_{i=1}^l \beta_i \cdot \boldsymbol{v}_i \in \mathbb{Z}_p^n$.
$[\overline{\sigma} \leftarrow \mathtt{Derive}(pk, \tau, \{\boldsymbol{v}_i, \sigma_i, \beta_i\}_{i=1}^l)]$

Verification `Ver`**:** It takes the public-key pk, a tag $\tau \in \{0,1\}^*$, a vector $\boldsymbol{v} \in \mathbb{Z}_p^n$ and a signature σ, then outputs a verification result 1 or 0.
$[1/0 \leftarrow \mathtt{Ver}(pk, \tau, \boldsymbol{v}, \sigma)]$

We require every LHS scheme to be correct. An LHS scheme is correct if for every $\lambda \in \mathbb{N}$, every $n \in \mathbf{poly}(\lambda)$ and every $(pk, sk) \leftarrow \mathtt{KGen}(1^\lambda, n)$, both of the following conditions hold, namely (a) *For every tag* $\tau \in \{0,1\}^*$ *and every vector* $\boldsymbol{v} \in \mathbb{Z}_p^n$, *it holds that* $1 \leftarrow \mathtt{Ver}(pk, \tau, \boldsymbol{v}, \mathtt{Sig}(sk, \tau, \boldsymbol{v}))$. and (b) *For every tag* $\tau \in \{0,1\}^*$, *every integer* $l \in \mathbb{N}$ *and every* l *triples* $\{\boldsymbol{v}_i \in \mathbb{Z}_p^n, \sigma_i, \beta_i \in \mathbb{Z}_p\}_{i=1}^l$ *such that* $1 \leftarrow \mathtt{Ver}(pk, \tau, \boldsymbol{v}_i, \sigma_i)$ *for all* i, *it holds that* $1 \leftarrow \mathtt{Ver}(pk, \tau, \sum_{i=1}^l \beta_i \boldsymbol{v}_i, \mathtt{Derive}(pk, \tau, \{\boldsymbol{v}_i, \sigma_i, \beta_i\}_{i=1}^l))$.

The Simplified ALP LHS Scheme. It is described as follows.

KGen($1^\lambda, n$): Choose bilinear groups $(\mathbb{G}, \mathbb{G}_T)$ whose order is a prime p of bit length λ. Choose $\alpha \overset{U}{\leftarrow} \mathbb{Z}_p$. Let $g, v, g_1, \cdots, g_n \overset{U}{\leftarrow} \mathbb{G}$. Let $u', u_0, \cdots, u_{N-1} \overset{U}{\leftarrow} \mathbb{G}$ for an integer $N \in \mathbb{N}$. Let $H_{\mathbb{G}}$ be a function which takes $\tau \in \{0,1\}^N$ as input, then outputs $u' \prod_{i=0}^{N-1} u_i^{\tau[i]} \in \mathbb{G}$. Output (pk, sk), where $pk := (\mathbb{G}, \mathbb{G}_T, g, g^\alpha, v, \{g_i\}_{i=1}^n, u', \{u_i\}_{i=0}^{N-1})$ and $sk := \alpha$.

Sig($sk, \tau \in \{0,1\}^N, \boldsymbol{v} \in \mathbb{Z}_p^n$): Parse $\boldsymbol{v}$ as $(v_1, \cdots, v_n)$. Choose $r, s \overset{U}{\leftarrow} \mathbb{Z}_p$. Compute $(\sigma_1, \sigma_2, \sigma_3, \sigma_4) := ((\prod_{j=1}^n g_i^{v_i} v^s)^\alpha H_{\mathbb{G}}(\tau)^r, g^r, g^s, g^{\alpha \cdot s})$. Output $\sigma := (\boldsymbol{v}, \tau, \sigma_1, \sigma_2, \sigma_3, \sigma_4)$.

Derive($pk, \tau \in \{0,1\}^N, \{\boldsymbol{v}_i \in \mathbb{Z}_p^n, \sigma_i, \beta_i \in \mathbb{Z}_p\}$): Parse σ_i as $(\boldsymbol{v}, \tau, \sigma_{i,1}, \sigma_{i,2}, \sigma_{i,3}, \sigma_{i,4})$. Choose $\overline{r} \overset{U}{\leftarrow} \mathbb{Z}_p$. Compute $(\overline{\sigma}_1, \overline{\sigma}_2, \overline{\sigma}_3, \overline{\sigma}_4) := (\prod_{i=1}^l \sigma_{i,1}^{\beta_i} \cdot H_{\mathbb{G}}(\tau)^{\overline{r}}, \prod_{i=1}^l \sigma_{i,2}^{\beta_i} \cdot g^{\overline{r}}, \prod_{i=1}^l \sigma_{i,3}^{\beta_i}, \prod_{i=1}^l \sigma_{i,4}^{\beta_i})$. Output $\overline{\sigma} := (\sum_{i=1}^l \beta_i \cdot \boldsymbol{v}_i, \tau, \overline{\sigma}_1, \overline{\sigma}_2, \overline{\sigma}_3, \overline{\sigma}_4)$.

Ver($pk, \tau \in \{0,1\}^N, \boldsymbol{v} \in \mathbb{Z}_p^n, \sigma$): Parse $\boldsymbol{v} \in \mathbb{Z}_p^n$ as $(v_1, \cdots, v_n)$. Parse σ as $(\boldsymbol{v}, \tau, \sigma_1, \sigma_2, \sigma_3, \sigma_4)$. Output 1 if both of the following two conditions hold, namely (a) $e(g, \sigma_1) = e(\prod_{i=1}^n g_i^{v_i}, g^\alpha) \cdot e(v, \sigma_4) \cdot e(H_{\mathbb{G}}(\tau), \sigma_2)$ and (b) $e(g^\alpha, \sigma_2) = (g, \sigma_4)$. Output 0 otherwise.

B Our 2nd ARIP Scheme

Setup($1^\lambda, n$): The same as the one of our 1st ARIP scheme except that number of the variables $\{g_i\}_{i=1}^{n+5}$ is reduced to $n+4$.

KGen($mk, \mathbf{x}$): Parse $\mathbf{x}$ as $(x_1, \cdots, x_n)$. Choose a tag $\tau \overset{U}{\leftarrow} \{0,1\}^N$. Generate 4 vectors $\boldsymbol{v}_1, \cdots, \boldsymbol{v}_4 \in \mathbb{Z}_p^{n+4}$. For each $i \in [1,4]$, generate a vector $\boldsymbol{v}_i \in \mathbb{Z}_p^{n+4}$ as follows. $\boldsymbol{v}_1 := (x_1, \cdots, x_n)|\boldsymbol{e}_1$ and $\boldsymbol{v}_i := (0, \cdots, 0)|\boldsymbol{e}_i$ for each $i \in \{2,3,4\}$. For each vector $\boldsymbol{v}_i = (v_{i,1}, v_{i,2}, \cdots, v_{i,n+4}) \in \mathbb{Z}_p^{n+4}$, compute an ALP signature on the vector $\boldsymbol{v}_i$ as $(\sigma_{i,1}, \sigma_{i,2}, \sigma_{i,3}, \sigma_{i,4}) := ((\prod_{j=1}^{n+4} g_i^{v_{i,j}} v^{s_i})^\alpha H_{\mathbb{G}}(\tau)^{r_i}, g^{r_i}, g^{s_i}, g^{\alpha \cdot s_i})$, where $r_i, s_i \overset{U}{\leftarrow} \mathbb{Z}_p$. Finally, output the secret-key $sk := (\mathbf{x}, \tau, \{\{\sigma_{i,j}\}_{j=1}^4\}_{i=1}^4)$.

Sig($sk, M, \mathbf{y}, L, R$): Parse sk as $(\mathbf{x}, \tau, \{\{\sigma_{i,j}\}_{j=1}^4\}_{i=1}^4)$. Parse $\mathbf{y}$ as $(y_1, \cdots, y_n)$. To generate a signature σ, conduct the following five steps first.

1. Set $d := \langle \mathbf{x}, \mathbf{y} \rangle \pmod p$. Assume that $d \in [L, R]$.
2. Choose $\overline{r} \overset{U}{\leftarrow} \mathbb{Z}_p$. Set $(\beta_1, \beta_2, \beta_3, \beta_4) := (1, L, R, M)$.
3. Compute $\overline{\sigma}_1 := \prod_{i=1}^4 \sigma_{i,1}^{y_i} \cdot H_{\mathbb{G}}(\tau)^{\overline{r}}$, $\overline{\sigma}_2 := \prod_{i=1}^4 \sigma_{i,2}^{y_i} \cdot g^{\overline{r}}$, $\overline{\sigma}_3 := \prod_{i=1}^4 \sigma_{i,3}^{y_i}$ and $\overline{\sigma}_4 := \prod_{i=1}^4 \sigma_{i,4}^{y_i}$. Note that if sk is a correct secret-key with inner-randomness $\{r_j, s_j\}_{j=1}^4$, the computed ALP signature distributes as $(\{\prod_{i=1}^n g_i^{x_i} \cdot g_{n+1} \cdot g_{n+2}^L \cdot g_{n+3}^R \cdot g_{n+4}^M \cdot v^{\sum_{j=1}^4 \beta_j s_j}\}^\alpha H_{\mathbb{G}}(\tau)^{\sum_j \beta_j r_j + \overline{r}}, g^{\sum_j \beta_j r_j + \overline{r}}, g^{\sum_j \beta_j s_j}, g^{\alpha \sum_j \beta_j s_j})$.
4. As our 1st ARIP scheme, compute the GS commitments for all of the variables (a), $\cdots$, (e). Additionally, compute the commitments for all of the following variables.

– g^{x_i} and $g_i^{x_i}$ (for all $i \in [1, n]$)

Let the commitments be denoted by $\vec{C}_{x_i}, \vec{C'}_{x_i} \in \mathbb{G}^3$, respectively.

5. As our 1st ARIP scheme, compute the GS proofs for all of the relations [a], $\cdots$, [f] except for the relation [e] which is modified as follows.

   [e'] $e(\overline{\sigma}_1, g) = e(\prod_{i=1}^n g_i^{x_i} \cdot \prod_{i=1}^4 g_{i+n}^{y_i}, g^\alpha) \cdot e(v, \overline{\sigma}_4) \cdot e(H_{\mathbb{G}}(\tau), \overline{\sigma}_2)$

   Additionally, compute the GS proofs for all of the following relations.
   – $e(g^{x_i}, g_i) = e(g, g_i^{x_i})$ (for all $i \in [1, n]$)
   – $e(g_1^d, g) = \prod_{i=1}^n e(g^{x_i}, g_1^{y_i})$

Let the proofs be denoted by $\vec{\pi}_{x_i}, \vec{\pi}_{\mathtt{ip}} \in \mathbb{G}^3$, respectively.

As our 1st ARIP scheme, generate the GS commitments/proofs for the fact that $d \in [L, R]$.

The signature σ consists of all of the GS commitments and proofs generated so far, and the second ALP signature element $\overline{\sigma}_2 \in \mathbb{G}$.

$\mathtt{Ver}(\sigma, M, \mathbf{y}, L, R)$: As our 1st ARIP scheme, verify the 12 equations except for the 7th equation which is modified as follows.

7'. $E(g, \vec{C}_{\overline{\sigma}_1}) = \prod_{i=1}^n E(g^\alpha, \vec{C'}_{x_i}) \cdot E(\prod_{i=1}^4 g_{i+n}^{y_i}, \iota(g^\alpha)) E(v, \vec{C}_{\overline{\sigma}_4}) \cdot E(\overline{\sigma}_2, \vec{C}_{H_{\mathbb{G}}(\tau)}) \cdot \prod_{k=1}^3 E(\pi_{\overline{\sigma}_1,k}, \vec{f}_k)$

Additionally, verify the following 13rd and 14th equations.

13. $E(g_i, \vec{C}_{x_i}) = E(g, \vec{C'}_{x_i}) \cdot \prod_{k=1}^3 E(\pi_{x_i,k}, \vec{f}_k)$ (for all $i \in [1, n]$)
14. $E(g, \vec{C}_d) = \prod_{i=1}^n E(g_1^{y_i}, \vec{C}_{x_i}) \cdot \prod_{k=1}^3 E(\pi_{\mathtt{ip},k}, \vec{f}_k)$

References

1. Abdalla, M., et al.: Wildcarded identity-based encryption. J. Cryptol. **24**(1), 42–82 (2011)
2. Ahn, J.H., Boneh, D., Camenisch, J., Hohenberger, S., shelat, A., Waters, B.: Computing on authenticated data. In: Cramer, R. (ed.) TCC 2012. LNCS, vol. 7194, pp. 1–20. Springer, Heidelberg (2012). https://doi.org/10.1007/978-3-642-28914-9_1
3. Attrapadung, N., Libert, B.: Functional encryption for inner product: achieving constant-size ciphertexts with adaptive security or support for negation. In: Nguyen, P.Q., Pointcheval, D. (eds.) PKC 2010. LNCS, vol. 6056, pp. 384–402. Springer, Heidelberg (2010). https://doi.org/10.1007/978-3-642-13013-7_23
4. Attrapadung, N., Libert, B., de Panafieu, E.: Expressive key-policy attribute-based encryption with constant-size ciphertexts. In: Catalano, D., Fazio, N., Gennaro, R., Nicolosi, A. (eds.) PKC 2011. LNCS, vol. 6571, pp. 90–108. Springer, Heidelberg (2011). https://doi.org/10.1007/978-3-642-19379-8_6
5. Attrapadung, N., Libert, B., Peters, T.: Computing on authenticated data: new privacy definitions and constructions. In: Wang, X., Sako, K. (eds.) ASIACRYPT 2012. LNCS, vol. 7658, pp. 367–385. Springer, Heidelberg (2012). https://doi.org/10.1007/978-3-642-34961-4_23

6. Attrapadung, N., Libert, B., Peters, T.: Efficient completely context-hiding quotable and linearly homomorphic signatures. In: Kurosawa, K., Hanaoka, G. (eds.) PKC 2013. LNCS, vol. 7778, pp. 386–404. Springer, Heidelberg (2013). https://doi.org/10.1007/978-3-642-36362-7_24
7. Blömer, J., Eidens, F., Juhnke, J.: Enhanced security of attribute-based signatures. In: Camenisch, J., Papadimitratos, P. (eds.) CANS 2018. LNCS, vol. 11124, pp. 235–255. Springer, Cham (2018). https://doi.org/10.1007/978-3-030-00434-7_12
8. Boneh, D., Boyen, X., Shacham, H.: Short group signatures. In: Franklin, M. (ed.) CRYPTO 2004. LNCS, vol. 3152, pp. 41–55. Springer, Heidelberg (2004). https://doi.org/10.1007/978-3-540-28628-8_3
9. Boneh, D., Freeman, D., Katz, J., Waters, B.: Signing a linear subspace: signature schemes for network coding. In: Jarecki, S., Tsudik, G. (eds.) PKC 2009. LNCS, vol. 5443, pp. 68–87. Springer, Heidelberg (2009). https://doi.org/10.1007/978-3-642-00468-1_5
10. Boneh, D., Waters, B.: Conjunctive, subset, and range queries on encrypted data. In: Vadhan, S.P. (ed.) TCC 2007. LNCS, vol. 4392, pp. 535–554. Springer, Heidelberg (2007). https://doi.org/10.1007/978-3-540-70936-7_29
11. Groth, J., Sahai, A.: Efficient non-interactive proof systems for bilinear groups. In: Smart, N. (ed.) EUROCRYPT 2008. LNCS, vol. 4965, pp. 415–432. Springer, Heidelberg (2008). https://doi.org/10.1007/978-3-540-78967-3_24
12. Guo, F., Susilo, W., Mu, Y.: Distance-based encryption: how to embed fuzziness in biometric-based encryption. IEEE Trans. Inf. Forensics Secur. **11**(2), 247–257 (2015)
13. Ishizaka, M., Fukushima, K.: Attribute-based signatures for range of inner product and its applications. Cryptology ePrint Archive: Report 2022/8131 (2022)
14. Ishizaka, M., Kiyomoto, S.: Time-specific signatures. In: Susilo, W., Deng, R.H., Guo, F., Li, Y., Intan, R. (eds.) ISC 2020. LNCS, vol. 12472, pp. 20–38. Springer, Cham (2020). https://doi.org/10.1007/978-3-030-62974-8_2
15. Katsumata, S., Yamada, S.: Non-zero inner product encryption schemes from various assumptions: LWE, DDH and DCR. In: Lin, D., Sako, K. (eds.) PKC 2019. LNCS, vol. 11443, pp. 158–188. Springer, Cham (2019). https://doi.org/10.1007/978-3-030-17259-6_6
16. Katz, J., Sahai, A., Waters, B.: Predicate encryption supporting disjunctions, polynomial equations, and inner products. In: Smart, N. (ed.) EUROCRYPT 2008. LNCS, vol. 4965, pp. 146–162. Springer, Heidelberg (2008). https://doi.org/10.1007/978-3-540-78967-3_9
17. Kiltz, E., Pan, J., Wee, H.: Structure-preserving signatures from standard assumptions, revisited. In: Gennaro, R., Robshaw, M. (eds.) CRYPTO 2015. LNCS, vol. 9216, pp. 275–295. Springer, Heidelberg (2015). https://doi.org/10.1007/978-3-662-48000-7_14
18. Libert, B., Joye, M., Yung, M., Peters, T.: Secure efficient history-hiding append-only signatures in the standard model. In: Katz, J. (ed.) PKC 2015. LNCS, vol. 9020, pp. 450–473. Springer, Heidelberg (2015). https://doi.org/10.1007/978-3-662-46447-2_20
19. Maji, H.K., Prabhakaran, M., Rosulek, M.: Attribute-based signatures: achieving attribute-privacy and collusion-resistance. Cryptology ePrint Archive: Report 2008/394 (2008)
20. Maji, H.K., Prabhakaran, M., Rosulek, M.: Attribute-based signatures. In: Kiayias, A. (ed.) CT-RSA 2011. LNCS, vol. 6558, pp. 376–392. Springer, Heidelberg (2011). https://doi.org/10.1007/978-3-642-19074-2_24

21. Okamoto, T., Takashima, K.: Fully secure functional encryption with general relations from the decisional linear assumption. In: Rabin, T. (ed.) CRYPTO 2010. LNCS, vol. 6223, pp. 191–208. Springer, Heidelberg (2010). https://doi.org/10.1007/978-3-642-14623-7_11
22. Okamoto, T., Takashima, K.: Efficient attribute-based signatures for non-monotone predicates in the standard model. In: Catalano, D., Fazio, N., Gennaro, R., Nicolosi, A. (eds.) PKC 2011. LNCS, vol. 6571, pp. 35–52. Springer, Heidelberg (2011). https://doi.org/10.1007/978-3-642-19379-8_3
23. Paterson, K.G., Quaglia, E.A.: Time-specific encryption. In: Garay, J.A., De Prisco, R. (eds.) SCN 2010. LNCS, vol. 6280, pp. 1–16. Springer, Heidelberg (2010). https://doi.org/10.1007/978-3-642-15317-4_1
24. Phuong, T.V.X., Yang, G., Susilo, W., Liang, K.: Edit distance based encryption and its application. In: Liu, J.K., Steinfeld, R. (eds.) ACISP 2016. LNCS, vol. 9723, pp. 103–119. Springer, Cham (2016). https://doi.org/10.1007/978-3-319-40367-0_7
25. Sahai, A., Waters, B.: Fuzzy identity-based encryption. In: Cramer, R. (ed.) EUROCRYPT 2005. LNCS, vol. 3494, pp. 457–473. Springer, Heidelberg (2005). https://doi.org/10.1007/11426639_27
26. Sakai, Y., Attrapadung, N., Hanaoka, G.: Attribute-based signatures for circuits from bilinear map. In: Cheng, C.-M., Chung, K.-M., Persiano, G., Yang, B.-Y. (eds.) PKC 2016. LNCS, vol. 9614, pp. 283–300. Springer, Heidelberg (2016). https://doi.org/10.1007/978-3-662-49384-7_11
27. Sakai, Y., Katsumata, S., Attrapadung, N., Hanaoka, G.: Attribute-based signatures for unbounded languages from standard assumptions. In: Peyrin, T., Galbraith, S. (eds.) ASIACRYPT 2018. LNCS, vol. 11273, pp. 493–522. Springer, Cham (2018). https://doi.org/10.1007/978-3-030-03329-3_17
28. Waters, B.: Efficient identity-based encryption without random oracles. In: Cramer, R. (ed.) EUROCRYPT 2005. LNCS, vol. 3494, pp. 114–127. Springer, Heidelberg (2005). https://doi.org/10.1007/11426639_7
29. Zhang, Y., Liu, X., Hu, Y., Zhang, Q., Jia, H.: Attribute-based signatures for inner-product predicate from lattices. In: Vaidya, J., Zhang, X., Li, J. (eds.) CSS 2019. LNCS, vol. 11982, pp. 173–185. Springer, Cham (2019). https://doi.org/10.1007/978-3-030-37337-5_14

Identity-based Interactive Aggregate Signatures from Lattices

Shingo Sato[1(✉)] and Junji Shikata[1,2]

[1] Institute of Advanced Sciences, Yokohama National University, Yokohama, Japan
{sato-shingo-zk,shikata-junji-rb}@ynu.ac.jp
[2] Graduate School of Environment and Information Sciences, Yokohama National University, Yokohama, Japan

Abstract. Aggregate signature allows users to compress multiple signatures into a short signature (called an aggregate signature), and can reduce a total amount of signature-size on a channel. In particular, identity-based aggregate signature can reduce not only total signature-size but also total verification key-size, because it is possible to check the validity of multiple messages and an aggregate signature by using signers' IDs, instead of verification keys. Furthermore, we focus on lattice-based constructions as post-quantum cryptography, due to recent advancement of quantum computers. In this paper, we propose the first identity-based interactive aggregate signature scheme from lattices. The security of our scheme is based on a standard lattice assumption, and its aggregate signature-size is logarithmic in the number of signatures.

Keywords: Identity-based aggregate signatures · Interactive aggregation · Lattice-based cryptography

1 Introduction

1.1 Background

Digital signature is a fundamental and important primitive in cryptography and provides a wide range of applications. Due to advancement of IoT (Internet of Things) and blockchain technologies, data-integrity is important when gathering data from many and various devices through an insecure channel. In these applications, a total amount of signature-size for checking validity of data is too large, since a lot of data is sent through a channel. Hence, in recent years, it has been necessary to reduce such total size. Aggregate signature is useful because this cryptographic technique can compress multiple signatures into a short signature (called an aggregate signature) and reduce a total amount of signature-size on an insecure channel. Thus, there are many applications such as sensor networks, blockchain protocols, secure BGP protocols, and more. However, the verifier of an aggregate signature scheme needs to obtain verification keys of signers and store these keys in order to check the validity of multiple messages and an aggregate signature. Thus, there are many situations where we have to be concerned

S.-H. Seo and H. Seo (Eds.): ICISC 2022, LNCS 13849, pp. 408–432, 2023.
https://doi.org/10.1007/978-3-031-29371-9_20

about a total amount of key-size, even though total signature-size can be reduced. Identity-based aggregate signature (IBAS) allows users to verify messages and an aggregate signature by using signers' IDs, instead of verification keys. Hence, IBAS can reduce both total key-size and total signature-size, and we focus on this cryptography.

On the other hand, we consider lattice-based aggregate signatures because lattice-based cryptography is resistant to attacks using quantum computers, and many lattice-based cryptosystems have been researched as promising post-quantum cryptography. There are several (identity-based) lattice-based aggregate signature schemes [8,9,11,27]. Doröz et al. proposed an aggregate signature scheme based on a non-standard lattice problem whose hardness is based on an average-case lattice problem [11]. Boneh and Kim proposed an aggregate one-time signature scheme and an interactive aggregate signature scheme which generates an aggregate signature by using interactive process among signers, and these schemes are based on (Ring-)SIS assumption [8]. Boudgoust and Roux-Langlois proposed a non-interactive aggregate signature scheme from module-lattices [9]. Li et al. presented an IBAS scheme based on NTRU [27].

Related Work. Boneh et al. introduced the notion of aggregate signatures and proposed a pairing-based scheme secure in the random oracle model (ROM) [7]. Rückert and Schröder presented an aggregate signature scheme using multilinear maps in the standard model [39], and its security is guaranteed under the certified-key model in which signers have to prove knowledge of their signing keys at key-registration,. Gentry and Ramzan introduced the notion of IBASs so that a total amount of signatures and verification keys can be reduced. They proposed an IBAS scheme (with pairing) secure in the ROM [17]. Hohenberger, Sahai, and Waters presented (identity-based) aggregate signature schemes using multilinear maps in the standard model [22]. Ahn, Green, and Hohenberger proposed pairing-based synchronized aggregate signature schemes in the standard model or the ROM, which aggregates signatures embedded a shared value [1]. Hohenberger and Waters proposed a synchronized aggregate signature scheme without using pairing, and its security is based on the RSA assumption [23]. In addition, there are other variants of aggregate signatures as follows: Sequential aggregate signatures [6,10,13,15,26,28,29,35] and fault-tolerant (sequential) aggregate signatures [18,19].

1.2 Contribution

Our goal is to propose an identity-based interactive aggregate signature (IBIAS) scheme secure in a weak lattice assumption.

We construct an IBAS scheme so that we can reduce both key-size and signature-size on a channel. Furthermore, we focus on interactive aggregation and security in a weak assumption, owing to problems of existing lattice-based (identity-based) aggregate signature schemes [8,9,11,27]. First, we consider interactive aggregation so that we can construct an IBAS scheme whose aggregate signature-size does not depend on the number of signatures linearly.

The aggregate signature-sizes of the existing lattice-based non-interactive aggregate signature schemes [9,11] linearly grow with the number of signatures. In the same way as the interactive aggregate signature of [8], it is possible to construct an aggregate signature scheme whose aggregate signature-size is at most logarithmic in such a number. Second, the existing IBAS scheme [27] is based on the (modified) NTRU cryptosystem [21,40], though its aggregate signature-size logarithmically depends on the number of signatures. This scheme uses a non-standard assumption, rather than standard assumptions such as *learning with errors* (LWE) and *small integer solution* (SIS) whose hardness is based on the worst-case hardness of lattice approximation problems [34,37]. Furthermore, it is impossible to construct an IBIAS scheme from the interactive aggregate signature scheme [8], in a straightforward way. For these reasons, we aim at proposing an IBIAS scheme secure under a standard lattice assumption. Details on our contribution are as follows:

- First, we construct an identity-based signature (IBS) scheme from lattices, which is secure in the ROM. Our IBIAS scheme is based on this scheme. Although there are existing lattice-based IBS schemes [36,38], it is difficult to convert these ones into IB(I)AS schemes (for details on this, see Sect. 3). Thus, we present an SIS-based IBS suitable for constructing an IBIAS scheme. As another advantage of our IBS scheme, it is possible to convert this scheme into an IBAS scheme with non-interaction (see Appendix B). There are some applications for which non-interactive aggregation is more desirable though its aggregate signature-size linearly grows with the number of signatures.
- Second, we propose our IBIAS scheme constructed from our IBS scheme. The interactive aggregation algorithm of this scheme is based on that of the interactive aggregate signature scheme of [8]. Notice that, unlike aggregate signature schemes, there is no rogue-key attack for IB(I)ASs since no verification/signing key-pair is generated. Thus, we do not have to add other assumptions or security models (e.g., knowledge of secret keys model) in order to prevent such an attack.

As the result, we can obtain the first IBIAS scheme based on the SIS assumption and achieve our goal in this paper. We should notice that it is possible to convert this scheme to the one based on structured lattice assumptions such as ring-SIS [32] or module-SIS [25] assumption, in the straightforward way. For simplicity, we give a security proof for the plain SIS-based scheme, in this paper.

Technical Overview. One may think of constructing an IB(I)AS scheme from an (interactive) aggregate signature scheme, in the same way as a generic IBS construction from two signature schemes [24]. However, we cannot use this construction to construct the objective IB(I)AS scheme. Concretely, a signature of this generic construction consists of a verification key vk and two signatures (σ_1, σ_2) of the underlying (aggregate) signature schemes. When aggregating such signatures, it is possible to compress the two components (σ_1, σ_2). However, it is impossible to aggregate vk. Hence, its aggregate signature-size linearly grows with the number of signatures.

As described beforehand, we employ interactive aggregation so that the aggregate signature-size of our scheme does not linearly depend on the number of signatures. In order to use interactive aggregation, its (aggregate) signing protocol utilizes Fiat-Shamir with aborts [30,31], in the same way as the scheme of [8]. In our scheme, the secret key of the underlying identification scheme corresponds to the signing key for a signer-ID. In order to generate such a key, we utilize a lattice trapdoor and its algorithms [16,33]. To analyze its security, we first construct a new IBS, and then propose an IBIAS scheme from this IBS.

2 Preliminaries

In this paper, we use the following notation: For a positive integer n, let $[n] := \{1,\ldots,n\}$. For n values $x_1,\ldots,x_n$ and a subset $\mathcal{I} \subseteq [n]$, let $(x_i)_{i\in\mathcal{I}}$ be a sequence of values whose indexes are included in $\mathcal{I}$ and let $\{x_i\}_{i\in\mathcal{I}}$ be a set of values whose indexes are included in $\mathcal{I}$. For a vector $\boldsymbol{x}$, let x_i be the i-th entry. For a vector $\boldsymbol{v} = [v_1,\ldots,v_n]^\top \in \mathbb{R}^n$, let $\|\boldsymbol{v}\|_p = (\sum_{i=1}^n |v_i|^p)^{1/p}$ be the ℓ_p-norm. In particular, let $\|\boldsymbol{v}\| = \sqrt{v_1^2+\cdots+v_n^2}$ be the Euclidean norm (the ℓ_2-norm). For a matrix $\boldsymbol{U} \in \mathbb{Z}^{k\times m}$, let $\widetilde{\boldsymbol{U}}$ be the result of applying Gram-Schmidt orthogonalization to the columns of $\boldsymbol{U}$. For a matrix $\boldsymbol{U} = [\boldsymbol{u}_1,\ldots,\boldsymbol{u}_m]$, let $\|\boldsymbol{U}\| := \max_{i\in[m]} \|\boldsymbol{u}_i\|$. For two sets S_1, S_2, fix an element $e_1 \in S_1$, and then we write $(e_1,\cdot) \notin S_1 \times S_2$ if $(e_1, e_2) \notin S_1 \times S_2$ for any $e_2 \in S_2$. For a function $f : \mathbb{N} \to \mathbb{R}$, f is negligible in λ if $f(\lambda) = o(\lambda^{-c})$ for any constant $c > 0$ and sufficiently large $\lambda \in \mathbb{N}$. Then, we write $f(\lambda) = \mathsf{negl}(\lambda)$. A probability is an overwhelming probability if $1 - \mathsf{negl}(\lambda)$. "Probabilistic polynomial-time" is abbreviated as PPT. For a positive integer λ, let $\mathsf{poly}(\lambda)$ be a universal polynomial of λ. For a probabilistic algorithm $\mathcal{A}$, $y \leftarrow \mathcal{A}(x; r)$ means that $\mathcal{A}$ on input x outputs y by using randomness r.

Let X, Y be two random variables over a finite field $\mathcal{D}$, and let $\Delta(X;Y) = \frac{1}{2}\sum_{s\in\mathcal{D}} |\Pr[X = s] - \Pr[Y = s]|$ be the statistical distance between X and Y. Let $U_{\mathcal{D}}$ be a uniformly random variable over $\mathcal{D}$, and we say that X is δ-uniform over $\mathcal{D}$ if $\Delta(X; U_{\mathcal{D}}) \le \delta$. For a parameter λ, $X = X(\lambda)$, and $Y = Y(\lambda)$, we say that X and Y are statistically close if $\Delta(X;Y)$ is negligible in λ.

Furthermore, let L be a subset of $\mathbb{Z}^m$. For a vector $\boldsymbol{c} \in \mathbb{R}^m$ and a positive parameter $\delta \in \mathbb{R}$, the continuous normal distribution over $\mathbb{R}^m$ is defined as the function $\rho^m_{c,\delta}(\boldsymbol{x}) = \left(\frac{1}{\sqrt{2\pi\delta^2}}\right)^m \exp\left(-\frac{\|\boldsymbol{x}-\boldsymbol{c}\|^2}{2\delta^2}\right)$. In addition, $\rho^m_{c,\delta}(\mathbb{Z}^m) = \sum_{\boldsymbol{x}\in\mathbb{Z}^m} \rho^m_{c,\delta}(\boldsymbol{x})$ is defined. For a center $\boldsymbol{c} \in \mathbb{Z}^m$, and a parameter $\delta \in \mathbb{R}^+$, the discrete Normal distribution over $\mathbb{Z}^m$ is defined as $D^m_{c,\delta}(\boldsymbol{y}) = \frac{\rho^m_{c,\delta}(\boldsymbol{y})}{\rho^m_{c,\delta}(\mathbb{Z}^m)}$. In the case $\boldsymbol{c} = \boldsymbol{0}$, we write $\rho^m_\delta(\boldsymbol{x}) = \rho^m_{\boldsymbol{0},\delta}(\boldsymbol{x})$, $D^m_\delta(\boldsymbol{x}) = D^m_{\boldsymbol{0},\delta}(\boldsymbol{x})$ for $\boldsymbol{x} \in \mathbb{Z}^m$.

2.1 Identity-Based Signatures

In this section, we describe the syntax and security definitions of identity-based signatures (IBSs).

Definition 1 (IBS). *An IBS scheme consists of four polynomial-time algorithms* (Setup, KeyGen, Sign, Vrfy)*: For a security parameter λ, let $\mathcal{ID} = \mathcal{ID}(\lambda)$ be an identity space and let $\mathcal{M} = \mathcal{M}(\lambda)$ be a message space.*

- $(\mathsf{pp}, \mathsf{msk}) \leftarrow \mathsf{Setup}(1^\lambda)$*: The randomized algorithm* Setup *takes as input a security parameter 1^λ and outputs a public parameter* pp *and a master secret key* msk.
- $\mathsf{sk}_{\mathsf{id}} \leftarrow \mathsf{KeyGen}(\mathsf{pp}, \mathsf{msk}, \mathsf{id})$*: The randomized algorithm* KeyGen *takes as input a public parameter* pp*, a master secret key* msk*, and an ID* $\mathsf{id} \in \mathcal{ID}$*, and it outputs a secret key* $\mathsf{sk}_{\mathsf{id}}$ *of* id.
- $\sigma \leftarrow \mathsf{Sign}(\mathsf{pp}, \mathsf{sk}_{\mathsf{id}}, \mu)$*: The randomized or deterministic algorithm* Sign *takes as input a public parameter* pp*, a secret key* $\mathsf{sk}_{\mathsf{id}}$*, and a message $\mu \in \mathcal{M}$, and it outputs a signature σ.*
- $1/0 \leftarrow \mathsf{Vrfy}(\mathsf{pp}, \mathsf{id}, \mu, \sigma)$*: The deterministic algorithm* Vrfy *takes as input a public parameter* pp*, an ID* $\mathsf{id} \in \mathcal{ID}$*, a message $\mu \in \mathcal{M}$, and a signature σ, and it outputs* 1 *(accept) or* 0 *(reject).*

An IBS scheme is required to be *correct*, as follows:

Definition 2 (Correctness). *An IBS scheme* $\mathsf{IBS} = (\mathsf{Setup}, \mathsf{KeyGen}, \mathsf{Sign}, \mathsf{Vrfy})$ *is* correct *if for every* $(\mathsf{pp}, \mathsf{msk}) \leftarrow \mathsf{Setup}(1^\lambda)$*, every* $\mathsf{id} \in \mathcal{ID}$*, every* $\mathsf{sk}_{\mathsf{id}} \leftarrow \mathsf{KeyGen}(\mathsf{pp}, \mathsf{msk}, \mathsf{id})$*, and every $\mu \in \mathcal{M}$, it holds that* $\mathsf{Vrfy}(\mathsf{pp}, \mathsf{id}, \mu, \sigma) = 1$ *with overwhelming probability, where* $\sigma \leftarrow \mathsf{Sign}(\mathsf{pp}, \mathsf{sk}_{\mathsf{id}}, \mu)$.

Following [4,14], we describe the definition of *unforgeability*, as a security notion of IBSs.

Definition 3 (Unforgeability). *An IBS scheme* $\mathsf{IBS} = (\mathsf{Setup}, \mathsf{KeyGen}, \mathsf{Sign}, \mathsf{Vrfy})$ *is* unforgeable *if for any PPT adversary $\mathcal{A}$, its advantage* $\mathsf{Adv}^{\mathrm{unforge}}_{\mathsf{IBS},\mathcal{A}}(\lambda) := \Pr[\mathcal{A}\ wins]$ *is negligible in λ. $[\mathcal{A}$ wins$]$ is the event that $\mathcal{A}$ wins in the following game:*

Setup. *The challenger generates* $(\mathsf{pp}, \mathsf{msk}) \leftarrow \mathsf{Setup}(1^\lambda)$*, gives* pp *to $\mathcal{A}$, and sets* $\mathsf{L}_K \leftarrow \emptyset$, $\mathsf{L}_S \leftarrow \emptyset$.

Queries. *$\mathcal{A}$ is given access to the following oracles:*

- *The key generation oracle* O_{KG}*: Given a key generation query* $\mathsf{id} \in \mathcal{ID}$*, it returns* $\mathsf{sk}_{\mathsf{id}} \leftarrow \mathsf{KeyGen}(\mathsf{pp}, \mathsf{msk}, \mathsf{id})$ *and sets* $\mathsf{L}_K \leftarrow \mathsf{L}_K \cup \{\mathsf{id}\}$*. $\mathcal{A}$ is not allowed to submit the same* id *to* O_{KG} *twice.*
- *The signing oracle* $\mathsf{O}_{\mathsf{SIGN}}$*: Given a signing-query* $(\mathsf{id}, \mu) \in \mathcal{ID} \times \mathcal{M}$*,* $\mathsf{O}_{\mathsf{SIGN}}$ *obtains* $\mathsf{sk}_{\mathsf{id}} \leftarrow \mathsf{KeyGen}(\mathsf{pp}, \mathsf{msk}, \mathsf{id})$ *by invoking* $\mathsf{O}_{\mathsf{KG}}(\mathsf{id})$*, returns* $\sigma \leftarrow \mathsf{Sign}(\mathsf{pp}, \mathsf{sk}_{\mathsf{id}}, \mu)$*, and sets* $\mathsf{L}_S \leftarrow \mathsf{L}_S \cup \{(\mathsf{id}, \mu)\}$.

Output. *$\mathcal{A}$ outputs* $((\mathsf{id}^*, \mu^*), \sigma^*)$*. $\mathcal{A}$ wins if it holds that* $\mathsf{Vrfy}(\mathsf{pp}, \mathsf{id}^*, \mu^*, \sigma^*) = 1$*,* $\mathsf{id}^* \notin \mathsf{L}_K$*, and* $(\mathsf{id}^*, \mu^*) \notin \mathsf{L}_S$.

2.2 Identity-based Interactive Aggregate Signatures

In this section, we describe the definitions of identity-based interactive aggregate signatures (IBIASs). Because there is no existing definition of IBIASs, we formalize this syntax and security notion by following the definitions of IBSs [4,14] and interactive aggregate signatures [8] (see Appendix A regarding the definition of interactive aggregate signatures).

Definition 4 (IBIAS). *An IBIAS scheme consists of four polynomial-time algorithms* $(\mathsf{Setup}, \mathsf{KeyGen}, \mathsf{Sign}^{\leftrightarrow}, \mathsf{Vrfy})$*: For a security parameter* λ*, let* $\mathcal{ID} = \mathcal{ID}(\lambda)$ *be an identity space and let* $\mathcal{M} = \mathcal{M}(\lambda)$ *be a message space.*

- $(\mathsf{pp}, \mathsf{msk}) \leftarrow \mathsf{Setup}(1^\lambda)$*: The randomized algorithm* Setup *takes as input a security parameter* 1^λ *and outputs a public parameter* pp *and a master secret key* msk.
- $\mathsf{sk}_{\mathsf{id}} \leftarrow \mathsf{KeyGen}(\mathsf{pp}, \mathsf{msk}, \mathsf{id})$*: The randomized algorithm* KeyGen *algorithm takes as input a public parameter* pp*, a master secret key* msk*, and an ID* $\mathsf{id} \in \mathcal{ID}$*, and it outputs a signing key* $\mathsf{sk}_{\mathsf{id}}$.
- $\widehat{\sigma}/0 \leftarrow \mathsf{Sign}^{\leftrightarrow}\langle(\mathsf{pp}, \mathsf{sk}_{\mathsf{id}_i}, \mu_i)_{i\in[\ell]}\rangle$*: The interactive protocol* $\mathsf{Sign}^{\leftrightarrow}$ *is run by a set of signers.*

  Start of the Protocol: *For each* $i \in [\ell]$*, the signer* $\mathsf{id}_i \in \mathcal{ID}$ *has a public parameter* pp*, a signing key* $\mathsf{sk}_{\mathsf{id}_i}$*, and a message* μ_i.

  End of the Protocol: *For each* $i \in [\ell]$*, the signer* $\mathsf{id}_i \in \mathcal{ID}$ *has an aggregate signature* $\widehat{\sigma}$ *on* $(\mathsf{id}_{i'}, \mu_{i'})_{i'\in[\ell]}$*, or* 0 *(reject)*[1].
- $1/0 \leftarrow \mathsf{Vrfy}(\mathsf{pp}, (\mathsf{id}_i, \mu_i)_{i\in[\ell]}, \widehat{\sigma})$*: The deterministic algorithm* Vrfy *takes as input a public parameter* pp*, a set of IDs and messages* $(\mathsf{id}_i, \mu_i)_{i\in[\ell]}$*, and an aggregate signature* $\widehat{\sigma}$*, and it outputs* 1 *(accept) or* 0 *(reject).*

Regarding the correctness of IBIASs, we should notice the following, in the same way as [8]: Since $\mathsf{Sign}^{\leftrightarrow}$ of an IBIAS scheme is not a single signing algorithm (i.e., $\mathsf{Sign}^{\leftrightarrow}$ is a protocol), we allow this signing protocol to successfully generate a valid signature with constant probability. By parallel (or sequential) repetition, it is possible to convert this protocol into a protocol which successfully generates a valid signature with overwhelming probability.

Then, an IBIAS scheme is required to be *correct* and *compact*, as follows:

Definition 5 (Correctness). *An IBIAS scheme* $\mathsf{IBIAS} = (\mathsf{Setup}, \mathsf{KeyGen}, \mathsf{Sign}^{\leftrightarrow}, \mathsf{Vrfy})$ *is* correct *if for every* $(\mathsf{pp}, \mathsf{msk}) \leftarrow \mathsf{Setup}(\lambda)$*, every* $\{\mathsf{sk}_{\mathsf{id}_i} \leftarrow \mathsf{KeyGen}(\mathsf{pp}, \mathsf{msk}, \mathsf{id}_i)\}_{i\in[\ell]}$ *(*$\{\mathsf{id}_i\}_{i\in[\ell]} \subseteq \mathcal{ID}$*), every* $\mu_1, \ldots, \mu_\ell \in \mathcal{M}$*, there exists some positive constant* $C \in \mathbb{Z}$ *such that* $\mathsf{Vrfy}(\mathsf{pp}, (\mathsf{id}_i, \mu_i)_{i\in[\ell]}, \widehat{\sigma}) = 1$ *holds with constant probability* $1/C$*, where* $\widehat{\sigma} \leftarrow \mathsf{Sign}^{\leftrightarrow}\langle(\mathsf{pp}, \mathsf{sk}_{\mathsf{id}_i}, \mu_i)_{i\in[\ell]}\rangle$.

Definition 6 (Compactness). *An IBIAS scheme* $\mathsf{IBIAS} = (\mathsf{Setup}, \mathsf{KeyGen}, \mathsf{Sign}^{\leftrightarrow}, \mathsf{Vrfy})$ *is* compact *if for every* $(\mathsf{pp}, \mathsf{msk}) \leftarrow \mathsf{Setup}(\lambda)$*, every* $\{\mathsf{sk}_{\mathsf{id}_i} \leftarrow \mathsf{KeyGen}(\mathsf{pp}, \mathsf{msk}, \mathsf{id}_i)\}_{i\in[\ell]}$ *(*$\{\mathsf{id}_i\}_{i\in[\ell]} \subseteq \mathcal{ID}$*), every* $\mu_1, \ldots, \mu_\ell \in \mathcal{M}$*, it holds that* $|\widehat{\sigma}| \leq \mathsf{poly}(\lambda, \log \ell)$*, where* $\widehat{\sigma} \leftarrow \mathsf{Sign}^{\leftrightarrow}\langle(\mathsf{pp}, \mathsf{sk}_{\mathsf{id}_i}, \mu_i)_{i\in[\ell]}\rangle$.

As a security notion of IBIASs, we define *unforgeability.* In the security game of this security notion, the adversary against an IBIAS scheme is given access to the signing oracle. This oracle on input ID-message pairs executes the signing

[1] In the $\mathsf{Sign}^{\leftrightarrow}$ protocol, each signer can compute an aggregate signature, rather than generating such a signature by using an aggregation algorithm.

protocol $\mathsf{Sign}^{\leftrightarrow}$ and behaves as signers whose keys are not revealed by the key generation oracle. In this execution, the adversary behaves as the other signers. Then, this adversary is allowed to pause the signing protocol and initiate a new one at any point in the security game. Hence, multiple parallel executions of the signing protocol can be performed by the adversary in the security game.

Definition 7 (Unforgeability). *An IBIAS scheme* $\mathsf{IBIAS} = (\mathsf{Setup}, \mathsf{KeyGen}, \mathsf{Sign}^{\leftrightarrow}, \mathsf{Vrfy})$ *is* unforgeable *if for any PPT adversary $\mathcal{A}$ against* IBIAS, *its advantage* $\mathsf{Adv}^{\text{unforge}}_{\mathsf{IBIAS},\mathcal{A}}(\lambda) := \Pr[\mathcal{A}\ wins]$ *is negligible in λ, where $[\mathcal{A}\ wins]$ is the event that $\mathcal{A}$ wins in the following security game:*

Setup. *The challenger generates* $(\mathsf{pp}, \mathsf{msk}) \leftarrow \mathsf{Setup}(1^\lambda)$ *and gives* pp *to the adversary $\mathcal{A}$. The challenger sets the lists* $\mathsf{L}_K \leftarrow \emptyset$ *and* $\mathsf{L}_S \leftarrow \emptyset$.

Queries. *$\mathcal{A}$ is given access to the following oracles:*

- *The key generation oracle* O_{KG}*: Given a key generation query* $\mathsf{id} \in \mathcal{ID}$, O_{KG} *computes* $\mathsf{sk}_{\mathsf{id}} \leftarrow \mathsf{KeyGen}(\mathsf{pp}, \mathsf{msk}, \mathsf{id})$, *returns* $\mathsf{sk}_{\mathsf{id}}$, *and sets* $\mathsf{L}_K \leftarrow \mathsf{L}_K \cup \{\mathsf{id}\}$. *Then, $\mathcal{A}$ is not allowed to submit the same* id *to* O_{KG} *twice.*
- *The signing oracle* $\mathsf{O}_{\mathsf{SIGN}}$*: Given a signing-query* $(\mathsf{id}_i, \mu_i)_{i\in[\ell]}$, $\mathsf{O}_{\mathsf{SIGN}}$ *does the following:*
  1. *$\mathcal{A}$ and* $\mathsf{O}_{\mathsf{SIGN}}$ *execute* $\widehat{\sigma}' \leftarrow \mathsf{Sign}^{\leftrightarrow}\langle(\mathsf{pp}, \mathsf{id}_i, \mu_i)_{i\in[\ell]}\rangle$, *where* $\mathsf{O}_{\mathsf{SIGN}}$ *behaves as signers* $\mathsf{id} \in \{\mathsf{id}_i\}_{i\in[\ell]}$ *such that* $\mathsf{id} \notin \mathsf{L}_K$, *and $\mathcal{A}$ behaves as the other signers* $\bar{\mathsf{id}} \in \{\mathsf{id}_i\}_{i\in[\ell]}$ *(i.e.,* $\bar{\mathsf{id}} \in \mathsf{L}_K$*).*
  2. *If* $\widehat{\sigma}' \neq 0$, $\mathsf{O}_{\mathsf{SIGN}}$ *sets* $\mathsf{L}_S \leftarrow \mathsf{L}_S \cup \{(\mathsf{id}_i, \mu_i)\}_{i\in[\ell]}$

Output. *$\mathcal{A}$ outputs* $((\mathsf{id}_i^*, \mu_i^*)_{i\in[\ell]}, \widehat{\sigma}^*)$. *$\mathcal{A}$ wins if* $\mathsf{AggVrfy}(\mathsf{pp}, (\mathsf{id}_i, \mu_i)_{i\in[\ell]}, \widehat{\sigma}) = 1$ *holds, and there exists* $j \in [\ell]$ *such that* $\mathsf{id}_j^* \notin \mathsf{L}_K$ *and* $(\mathsf{id}_j^*, \mu_j^*) \notin \mathsf{L}_S$.

2.3 Lattices

In this paper, we consider the following integer lattices:

Definition 8. *Let n, m be positive integers and q be a prime. For a matrix* $\boldsymbol{A} \in \mathbb{Z}_q^{n\times m}$ *and a vector* $\boldsymbol{u} \in \mathbb{Z}_q^n$, *the following lattices are defined:* $\Lambda_q^{\perp}(\boldsymbol{A}) := \{\boldsymbol{e} \in \mathbb{Z}^m \mid \boldsymbol{A}\boldsymbol{e} = \boldsymbol{0} \pmod q\}, \Lambda_q^{\boldsymbol{u}}(\boldsymbol{A}) := \{\boldsymbol{e} \in \mathbb{Z}^m \mid \boldsymbol{A}\boldsymbol{e} = \boldsymbol{u} \pmod q\}$. *In addition, for a positive integer k and a matrix* $\boldsymbol{U} \in \mathbb{Z}_q^{n\times k}$, *let* $\Lambda_q^{\boldsymbol{U}}(\boldsymbol{A}) := \{\boldsymbol{E} \in \mathbb{Z}^{m\times k} \mid \boldsymbol{A}\boldsymbol{E} = \boldsymbol{U} \pmod q\}$.

We describe the definition of *Small Integer Solution* (SIS) which is at least as hard as worst-case lattice approximation problems [34].

Definition 9 ($\mathsf{SIS}_{n,m,q,\beta}$). *Let n, m be positive integers, q be a prime, and β be a positive real number. Given* $\boldsymbol{A} \xleftarrow{\$} \mathbb{Z}_q^{n\times m}$, $\mathsf{SIS}_{n,m,q,\beta}$ *is to find a vector* $\boldsymbol{x} \in \mathbb{Z}^m\backslash\{\boldsymbol{0}\}$ *such that* $\boldsymbol{A}\boldsymbol{x} = \boldsymbol{0}$ *and* $\|\boldsymbol{x}\| \leq \beta$. *In addition, the* $\mathsf{SIS}_{n,m,q,\beta}$ *assumption holds if for any PPT algorithm $\mathcal{S}$, it holds that*

$$\Pr\left[\boldsymbol{A}\boldsymbol{x} = \boldsymbol{0} \wedge \|\boldsymbol{x}\| \leq \beta \wedge \boldsymbol{x} \neq \boldsymbol{0} \mid \boldsymbol{A} \xleftarrow{\$} \mathbb{Z}_q^{n\times m}; \boldsymbol{x} \leftarrow \mathcal{S}(\boldsymbol{A})\right] \leq \mathsf{negl}(\lambda).$$

Furthermore, it is proven that there exist the following algorithms:

Lemma 1 ([2,3,16,33]). *For a security parameter λ, let $n = n(\lambda)$ be a positive integer, $q = q(\lambda)$ be a prime, $m = \Theta(n \log q)$ be a positive integer. Then, there exist the following polynomial-time algorithms:*

- $(\boldsymbol{A}, \boldsymbol{S_A}) \leftarrow \mathsf{TrapGen}(n, m, q)$: *A randomized algorithm which outputs a full-rank matrix $\boldsymbol{A} \in \mathbb{Z}_q^{n\times m}$ and a basis $\boldsymbol{S_A} \in \mathbb{Z}^{m\times m}$ for $\Lambda_q^{\perp}(\boldsymbol{A})$ such that $\boldsymbol{A}$ is* $\mathsf{negl}(n)$*-uniform and $\|\widetilde{\boldsymbol{S_A}}\| = O(\sqrt{n \log q})$, with overwhelming probability.*
- $\boldsymbol{X} \leftarrow \mathsf{SampleD}(\boldsymbol{A}, \boldsymbol{S_A}, \boldsymbol{U}, \gamma)$: *A randomized algorithm which takes as input a matrix $\boldsymbol{A} \in \mathbb{Z}_q^{n\times m}$, a basis $\boldsymbol{S_A} \in \mathbb{Z}^{m\times m}$ for $\Lambda_q^{\perp}(\boldsymbol{A})$, a matrix $\boldsymbol{U} \in \mathbb{Z}_q^{n\times k}$, and a positive integer $\gamma \geq \|\widetilde{\boldsymbol{S_A}}\| \cdot \omega(\sqrt{\log m})$, and then outputs $\boldsymbol{X} \in \mathbb{Z}^{m\times k}$ sampled from a distribution which is statistically close to $D^{m\times k}_{\Lambda_q^{\boldsymbol{U}}(\boldsymbol{A}),\gamma}$.*

In order to construct our IBS and IBIAS schemes, we use the two polynomial-time algorithms $\mathsf{TrapGen}, \mathsf{SampleD}$.

3 Our IBS Scheme from Lattices

3.1 Construction

We construct a lattice-based IBS scheme so that we can construct an IBIAS scheme. Although there are several lattice-based IBS constructions [36,38], we cannot convert these ones into IB(I)AS schemes, straightforwardly. These constructions use Hash-and-Sign paradigm [16] when generating a signature on an ID and a message. Aggregating these signatures seems difficult. Concretely, the signer in these schemes generates a signature vector $\sigma_{\mathsf{id},\mu}$, and the verifier checks whether $\boldsymbol{A}_{\mathsf{id},\mu} \cdot \sigma_{\mathsf{id},\mu} = \boldsymbol{y}$ and $\|\sigma_{\mathsf{id},\mu}\| \leq \beta_S$, where $\boldsymbol{A}_{\mathsf{id},\mu}$ is a matrix generated when producing a signature on an ID id and a message μ, $\boldsymbol{y}$ is a public vector, and $\beta_S \in \mathbb{R}$ is a public value. When these signatures $\sigma_{\mathsf{id}_1,\mu_1}, \ldots, \sigma_{\mathsf{id}_\ell,\mu_\ell}$ are compressed into $\widehat{\sigma} \leftarrow \sum_{i\in[\ell]} \sigma_{\mathsf{id}_i,\mu_i}$, the above verification procedure does not work, since the corresponding matrices $\boldsymbol{A}_{\mathsf{id}_1,\mu_1}, \ldots, \boldsymbol{A}_{\mathsf{id}_\ell,\mu_\ell}$ are distinct. Therefore, we do not use those IBS schemes and consider a new construction.

The idea to construct our IBS is to utilize Fiat-Shamir with aborts [12,30,31] and a lattice trapdoor [16,33] in order to generate the signing key of an ID. In fact, the existing lattice-based aggregate signature schemes [8,9,11] employ Fiat-Shamir with aborts [12,30,31], rather than Hash-and-Sign. Hence, our IBS scheme is based on the lattice-based signature scheme [31] constructed from Fiat-Shamir with aborts, and we chose this scheme because this is suitable for constructing an IBS scheme. To generate the signing key for each ID, we utilize a lattice trapdoor and its algorithms [16,33], and this signing key corresponds to the secret key of the underlying identification scheme used in [31].

Our IBS scheme $\mathsf{IBS} = (\mathsf{Setup}, \mathsf{KeyGen}, \mathsf{Sign}, \mathsf{Vrfy})$ is constructed as follows: For a security parameter λ, we define the following parameters: Let $n = n(\lambda)$, $m = m(\lambda)$, $k = k(\lambda)$, $\gamma = \gamma(\lambda)$, $\delta = \delta(\lambda)$, $\kappa = \kappa(\lambda)$, $M = M(\lambda)$ be positive integers, $q = q(\lambda)$ be a prime, and $\eta = \eta(\lambda)$ be a positive real number. We define $\mathcal{ID} = \{0,1\}^\lambda$ as an ID space and $\mathcal{M} = \{0,1\}^*$ as a message space. In addition, let $\mathcal{D}_{H_1} := \{\boldsymbol{v} \mid \boldsymbol{v} \in \{-1,0,1\}^k \wedge \|\boldsymbol{v}\|_1 \leq \kappa\}$, and let $H_0 : \mathcal{ID} \rightarrow \mathbb{Z}_q^{n\times k}$,

$H_1 : \{0,1\}^* \to \mathcal{D}_{H_1}$ be cryptographic hash functions. In this scheme, we use the algorithms TrapGen, SampleD defined in Lemma 1.

- $(\mathsf{pp}, \mathsf{msk}) \leftarrow \mathsf{Setup}(1^\lambda)$:
  1. Generate $(\boldsymbol{A}, \boldsymbol{S_A}) \leftarrow \mathsf{TrapGen}(n, m, q)$.
  2. Output $\mathsf{pp} = \boldsymbol{A} \in \mathbb{Z}_q^{n \times m}$ and $\mathsf{msk} = \boldsymbol{S_A} \in \mathbb{Z}^{m \times m}$.
- $\mathsf{sk_{id}} \leftarrow \mathsf{KeyGen}(\mathsf{pp}, \mathsf{msk}, \mathsf{id})$:
  1. Let $\mathsf{pp} = \boldsymbol{A}$ and $\mathsf{msk} = \boldsymbol{S_A}$.
  2. Compute $\boldsymbol{S}_{\mathsf{id}} \leftarrow \mathsf{SampleD}(\boldsymbol{A}, \boldsymbol{S_A}, H_0(\mathsf{id}), \gamma)$ (such that $\boldsymbol{S}_{\mathsf{id}} \leftarrow D_\gamma^{m \times k}$ and $\boldsymbol{A}\boldsymbol{S}_{\mathsf{id}} = H_0(\mathsf{id}) \pmod q$).
  3. Output $\mathsf{sk_{id}} = \boldsymbol{S}_{\mathsf{id}} \in \mathbb{Z}^{m \times k}$.
- $\sigma \leftarrow \mathsf{Sign}(\mathsf{pp}, \mathsf{sk_{id}}, \mu)$:
  1. Let $\mathsf{pp} = \boldsymbol{A}$ and $\mathsf{sk_{id}} = \boldsymbol{S}_{\mathsf{id}}$.
  2. Choose $\boldsymbol{y} \leftarrow D_\delta^m$.
  3. Compute $\boldsymbol{c} \leftarrow H_1(\boldsymbol{A}\boldsymbol{y} \bmod q, \mathsf{id}, \mu)$.
  4. Compute $\boldsymbol{z} \leftarrow \boldsymbol{y} + \boldsymbol{S}_{\mathsf{id}}\boldsymbol{c} \in \mathbb{Z}^m$.
  5. Output $\sigma = (\boldsymbol{c}, \boldsymbol{z})$ with probability $\min\left(\frac{D_\delta^m(\boldsymbol{z})}{M \cdot D^m_{\boldsymbol{S}_{\mathsf{id}}\boldsymbol{c},\delta}(\boldsymbol{z})}, 1\right)$.
- $1/0 \leftarrow \mathsf{Vrfy}(\mathsf{pp}, \mathsf{id}, \mu, \sigma)$:
  1. Parse $\sigma = (\boldsymbol{c}, \boldsymbol{z})$.
  2. Output 1 if $H_1(\boldsymbol{A}\boldsymbol{z} - H_0(\mathsf{id})\boldsymbol{c} \bmod q, \mathsf{id}, \mu) = \boldsymbol{c} \wedge \|\boldsymbol{z}\| \leq \eta\delta\sqrt{m}$. Otherwise, output 0.

Parameter Setting. In order to show the correctness of IBS, we can set the following parameters: For a security parameter λ, let $n \gg \lambda$ be a lattice parameter, and let C_0, C_1 be positive constants. Due to Lemma 1, we set a prime $q = \mathsf{poly}(n)^2$, $m \geq 3n \log q$, $\gamma \geq C_0\sqrt{m} \cdot \omega(\sqrt{\log m})^2$. In addition, in order to prove the security of IBS, we need to set the parameters m, γ s.t. $m > \lambda + n\log q / \log(2\lambda\gamma + 1)$ due to the condition of [31, Lemma 5.2]. Based on [31], we set the parameters $k = O(n)$, κ s.t. $2^\kappa \geq \binom{n}{\kappa}2^{O(\lambda)}$, $\delta = C_1\gamma\kappa$, $\eta = O(1)$ s.t. $\eta\delta \geq (\lambda\delta + \lambda\gamma\kappa)$, $M = \exp(C_1\gamma\kappa\sqrt{m}/\delta + (\gamma\kappa\sqrt{m}/2\delta)^2)$.

Lemma 2 (Correctness). *The IBS scheme* IBS *is* correct, *under the parameters of* IBS.

Proof. For every $\mathsf{id} \in \mathcal{ID}$ and every $\mu \in \mathcal{M}$, let $(\mathsf{pp}, \mathsf{msk}) \leftarrow \mathsf{Setup}(1^\lambda)$, let $\mathsf{sk_{id}} \leftarrow \mathsf{KeyGen}(\mathsf{pp}, \mathsf{msk}, \mathsf{id})$, and let $\sigma = (\boldsymbol{c}, \boldsymbol{z}) \leftarrow \mathsf{Sign}(\mathsf{pp}, \mathsf{sk_{id}}, \mu)$. Under the parameters n, q, m, γ, the Setup and KeyGen algorithms are run correctly, due to Lemma 1. Thus, we can assume that the keys $\mathsf{pp}, \mathsf{msk}, \mathsf{sk}_{\mathsf{id}_i}$ are generated correctly.

We show that the Vrfy algorithm accepts the signature σ. Regarding the first condition of Vrfy, we have

$$\begin{aligned} H_1(\boldsymbol{A}\boldsymbol{z} - H_0(\mathsf{id})\boldsymbol{c} \bmod q, \mathsf{id}, \mu) &= H_1(\boldsymbol{A}(\boldsymbol{y} + \boldsymbol{S}_{\mathsf{id}}\boldsymbol{c}) - \boldsymbol{A}\boldsymbol{S}_{\mathsf{id}}\boldsymbol{c} \bmod q, \mathsf{id}, \mu) \\ &= H_1(\boldsymbol{A}\boldsymbol{y} \bmod q, \mathsf{id}, \mu) = \boldsymbol{c}. \end{aligned}$$

[2] For a security reduction from lattice assumptions [34], q should be larger than $\beta \cdot \mathsf{poly}(n)$, where $\beta = 2(\delta\eta + \gamma\kappa)\sqrt{m}$.

Next, we show that the second condition of Vrfy holds. Due to [31, Lemma 4.4] and Lemma 1, we have $\|\boldsymbol{y}\| \leq \lambda\delta\sqrt{m}$ and $\|\boldsymbol{S}_{\mathsf{id}}\| \leq \lambda\gamma\sqrt{m}$, with at least probability $1 - \lambda^m e^{(1-\lambda^2)m/2}$. In addition, $\|\boldsymbol{c}\|_1 \leq \kappa$, owing to the definition of H_1. Hence, we have $\|\boldsymbol{z}\| = \|\boldsymbol{y} + \boldsymbol{S}_{\mathsf{id}}\boldsymbol{c}\| \leq \lambda\delta\sqrt{m} + \lambda\gamma\kappa\sqrt{m} \leq \eta\delta\sqrt{m}$.

Therefore, the both conditions of Vrfy hold, and we complete the proof. □

3.2 Security Analysis

Theorem 1 shows the security of our proposed IBS scheme IBS, and we give the proof of this theorem.

Theorem 1 (Unforgeability). *If the* $\mathsf{SIS}_{n,m,q,\beta}$ *assumption holds for* $\beta = 2(\delta\eta + \gamma\kappa)\sqrt{m}$, *then the IBS scheme* IBS *is* unforgeable *in the random oracle model.*

Proof. Let $\mathcal{A}$ be a PPT adversary against IBS. Let Q_K, Q_S, Q_0, and Q_1 be the numbers of queries submitted to O_{KG}, $\mathsf{O}_{\mathsf{SIGN}}$, H_0, and H_1 oracles, respectively. In addition, let T_0 be a table of query-response pairs issued to the H_0 oracle. In order to prove Theorem 1, we consider the security games $\mathsf{Hybrid}_0, \ldots, \mathsf{Hybrid}_5$.

Hybrid_0**:** This game is the same as the ordinary security game of IBSs.

Hybrid_1**:** This game is the same as Hybrid_0 except that the H_0 and O_{KG} oracles are modified as follows: At the beginning of the security game, the challenger sets a table $\mathsf{T}_0 \leftarrow \emptyset$.

$H_0(\mathsf{id})$:
1. H_0 returns $\boldsymbol{T}_{\mathsf{id}}$ if $\mathsf{T}_0[\mathsf{id}] = (\boldsymbol{T}_{\mathsf{id}}, \boldsymbol{S}_{\mathsf{id}}) \in \mathbb{Z}_q^{n\times k} \times \mathbb{Z}^{m\times k}$ (i.e., $\mathsf{T}_0[\mathsf{id}] \neq \emptyset$).
2. If $\mathsf{T}_0[\mathsf{id}] = \emptyset$, then H_0 chooses $\boldsymbol{S}_{\mathsf{id}} \leftarrow D_\gamma^{m\times k}$ and computes $\boldsymbol{T}_{\mathsf{id}} \leftarrow \boldsymbol{A}\boldsymbol{S}_{\mathsf{id}} \in \mathbb{Z}_q^{n\times k}$. It returns $\boldsymbol{T}_{\mathsf{id}}$ and sets $\mathsf{T}_0[\mathsf{id}] \leftarrow (\boldsymbol{T}_{\mathsf{id}}, \boldsymbol{S}_{\mathsf{id}})$.

$\mathsf{O}_{\mathsf{KG}}(\mathsf{id})$:
1. If $\mathsf{T}_0[\mathsf{id}] = (\boldsymbol{T}_{\mathsf{id}}, \boldsymbol{S}_{\mathsf{id}}) \in \mathbb{Z}_q^{n\times k} \times \mathbb{Z}^{m\times k}$, then O_{KG} returns $\boldsymbol{S}_{\mathsf{id}}$ and sets $\mathsf{L}_K \leftarrow \mathsf{L}_K \cup \{\mathsf{id}\}$.
2. If $\mathsf{T}_0[\mathsf{id}] = \emptyset$, then O_{KG} chooses $\boldsymbol{S}_{\mathsf{id}} \leftarrow D_\gamma^{m\times k}$ and computes $\boldsymbol{T}_{\mathsf{id}} \leftarrow \boldsymbol{A}\boldsymbol{S}_{\mathsf{id}} \in \mathbb{Z}_q^{n\times k}$. It returns $\boldsymbol{S}_{\mathsf{id}}$ and sets $\mathsf{L}_K \leftarrow \mathsf{L}_K \cup \{\mathsf{id}\}$, $\mathsf{T}_0[\mathsf{id}] \leftarrow (\boldsymbol{T}_{\mathsf{id}}, \boldsymbol{S}_{\mathsf{id}})$.

Hybrid_2**:** This game is the same as Hybrid_1 except that $\boldsymbol{A}$ generated by TrapGen is replaced with a matrix chosen from $\mathbb{Z}_q^{n\times m}$ uniformly at random.

Hybrid_3**:** This game is the same as Hybrid_2 except that the challenger aborts if $H_0(\mathsf{id}^*)$ is not defined (i.e., $\mathsf{T}_0[\mathsf{id}^*] = \emptyset$).

Hybrid_4**:** This game is the same as Hybrid_3 except that the $\mathsf{O}_{\mathsf{SIGN}}$ oracle is modified as follows:
1. Choose $\boldsymbol{y} \leftarrow D_\delta^m$.
2. Choose $\boldsymbol{c} \xleftarrow{\$} \mathcal{D}_{H_1}$.
3. Compute $\boldsymbol{z} \leftarrow \boldsymbol{y} + \boldsymbol{S}_{\mathsf{id}}\boldsymbol{c}$.
4. Do the following with probability $\min\left(\frac{D_\delta^m(\boldsymbol{z})}{M\cdot D^m_{\boldsymbol{S}_{\mathsf{id}}\boldsymbol{c},\delta}(\boldsymbol{z})}, 1\right)$:
   (a) Return $\sigma = (\boldsymbol{c}, \boldsymbol{z})$.

(b) Program $H_1(\boldsymbol{Az} - H_0(\mathsf{id})\boldsymbol{c}, \mathsf{id}, \mu) = \boldsymbol{c}$.

Hybrid$_5$: This game is the same as Hybrid$_4$ except that the $\mathsf{O_{SIGN}}$ oracle is modified as follows:

1. Choose $\boldsymbol{c} \xleftarrow{\$} \mathcal{D}_{H_1}$.
2. Choose $\boldsymbol{z} \leftarrow D_\delta^m$.
3. Do the following with probability $1/M$:
   (a) Output $\sigma = (\boldsymbol{c}, \boldsymbol{z})$.
   (b) Program $H_1(\boldsymbol{Az} - H_0(\mathsf{id})\boldsymbol{c}, \mathsf{id}, \mu) = \boldsymbol{c}$.

In addition, for $i \in \{0, \ldots, 5\}$, let W_i be the event that $\mathcal{A}$ wins in Hybrid$_i$. We estimate the upper bound of $|\Pr[W_{i-1}] - \Pr[W_i]|$ for $i \in \{1, \ldots, 5\}$.

Proof of $|\Pr[W_0] - \Pr[W_1]| \leq \mathsf{negl}(\lambda)$: The output $\boldsymbol{T}_{\mathsf{id}} = \boldsymbol{AS}_{\mathsf{id}} \in \mathbb{Z}_q^{n\times k}$ of H_0 is independent of a query id and statistically close to a uniformly random value in $\mathbb{Z}_q^{n\times k}$ due to the leftover hash lemma [20]. Thus, $\mathcal{A}$ cannot distinguish Hybrid$_0$ and Hybrid$_1$ statistically.

Proof of $|\Pr[W_1] - \Pr[W_2]| \leq \mathsf{negl}(\lambda)$: Due to Lemma 1, the matrices $\boldsymbol{A}$ in Hybrid$_1$ and Hybrid$_2$ are distributed statistically. In addition, $\mathsf{O_{SIGN}}$ does not have to use the trapdoor $\boldsymbol{S_A}$ to generate a secret key of an ID, in both games. Hence, $\mathcal{A}$ cannot distinguish these security games.

Proof of $|\Pr[W_2] - \Pr[W_3]| \leq 2^{-nk\lceil \log q \rceil}$: The challenger aborts if $\mathcal{A}$ predicts the value of $H_0(\mathsf{id}^*)$ without querying id^* to H_0. The probability of predicting the value $H_0(\mathsf{id}^*)$ is at most $2^{-nk\lceil \log q \rceil}$. Thus, the probability of distinguishing between Hybrid$_2$ and Hybrid$_3$ is at most $2^{-nk\lceil \log q \rceil}$.

Proof of $|\Pr[W_3] - \Pr[W_4]| \leq Q_S(Q_1 + Q_S)2^{-n+1}$: The difference between Hybrid$_3$ and Hybrid$_4$ is that the H_1 oracle chooses $\boldsymbol{c} \in \mathcal{D}_{H_1}$ uniformly at random and programs $H_1(\boldsymbol{Az} - H_0(\mathsf{id})\boldsymbol{c}, \mathsf{id}, \mu) = H_1(\boldsymbol{Ay}, \mathsf{id}, \mu)$. Since the number of queries issued to H_1 is at most $Q_1 + Q_S$, H_1 programs $Q_1 + Q_S$ values $(\boldsymbol{Ay}, \mathsf{id}, \mu)$. In addition, when $\mathsf{O_{SIGN}}$ is called, $(\boldsymbol{Ay}, \mathsf{id}, \mu)$ is defined with at most probability 2^{-n+1}. When $\mathsf{O_{SIGN}}$ is invoked each time, the probability of getting a collision is at most $(Q_1 + Q_S)2^{-n+1}$. Hence, when Q_S queries are issued to $\mathsf{O_{SIGN}}$, the adversary distinguishes Hybrid$_3$ and Hybrid$_4$ by getting a collision each time, with at most probability $Q_S(Q_1 + Q_S)2^{-n+1}$.

Proof of $|\Pr[W_4] - \Pr[W_5]| \leq Q_S \cdot 2^{-\omega(\log m)}/M$: By applying the rejection sampling lemma [31, Theorem 4.6], it is shown that the probability of distinguishing Hybrid$_4$ and Hybrid$_5$ is at most $Q_S \cdot 2^{-\omega(\log m)}/M$.

Finally, we show that $\epsilon = \Pr[W_5]$ is negligible if the $\mathsf{SIS}_{n,m,q,\beta}$ assumption holds. To do this, we construct a PPT algorithm $\mathcal{F}$ solving $\mathsf{SIS}_{n,m,q,\beta}$, as follows: Given an $\mathsf{SIS}_{n,m,q,\beta}$ instance $\boldsymbol{A} \in \mathbb{Z}_q^{n\times m}$, responses $\boldsymbol{r}_1, \ldots, \boldsymbol{r}_{Q_1+Q_S} \xleftarrow{\$} \mathcal{D}_{H_1}$ of H_1, randomness $\rho_\mathcal{A}, \rho_\mathcal{F}$ used in $\mathcal{A}$ and $\mathcal{F}$ respectively, $\mathcal{F}$ runs $\mathcal{A}$ by giving $\mathsf{pp} = \boldsymbol{A}$ and $\rho_\mathcal{A}$. Then, $\mathsf{O_{KG}}$, $\mathsf{O_{SIGN}}$, H_0, and H_1 are simulated in the same way as Hybrid$_5$, and $(\boldsymbol{r}_i)_{i\in[Q_1+Q_S]}$ are used as the responses of H_1. Finally, $\mathcal{A}$ outputs a forgery $(\mathsf{id}^*, \mu^*, (\boldsymbol{c}^*, \boldsymbol{z}^*))$ and halts. $\|\boldsymbol{z}^*\| \leq \eta\delta\sqrt{m}$ and $H_1(\boldsymbol{Az}^* - H_0(\mathsf{id}^*)\boldsymbol{c}^*, \mathsf{id}^*, \mu^*) = \boldsymbol{c}^*$ holds with probability ϵ.

If $\mathcal{A}$ does not issue any query to H_1, or $\boldsymbol{w}^* = \boldsymbol{A}\boldsymbol{z}^* - H_0(\mathsf{id}^*)\boldsymbol{c}^*$ has never been programmed, then $\boldsymbol{c}^*$ such that $\boldsymbol{c}^* = H_1(\boldsymbol{w}^*, \mathsf{id}^*, \mu^*)$ is predicted with at most probability $1/|\mathcal{D}_{H_1}|$. Thus, $\mathcal{A}$ succeeds in generating a forgery $(\boldsymbol{c}^*, \boldsymbol{z}^*)$ such that $\boldsymbol{c}^* \in \{\boldsymbol{r}_i\}_{i\in[Q_1+Q_S]}$, with at least probability $\epsilon - 1/|\mathcal{D}_{H_1}|$.

We show that it is possible to extract a solution to the $\mathsf{SIS}_{n,m,q,\beta}$ instance $\boldsymbol{A}$, by using the $\mathcal{A}$'s forgery. We consider $\boldsymbol{c}^* = \boldsymbol{r}_J$, where $\boldsymbol{r}_J$ is the response of the J-th query issued to H_1 $(J \in [Q_1 + Q_S])$. First, we consider the case where $\boldsymbol{c}^* = \boldsymbol{r}_J$ is set by the $\mathsf{O_{SIGN}}$ oracle. For any $\mathsf{id} \in \mathcal{ID}$, let $\boldsymbol{T}_{\mathsf{id}} = H_0(\mathsf{id})$. In addition, we assume that $\mathcal{A}$ queries $(\widetilde{\mathsf{id}}, \widetilde{\mu}) \in \mathcal{ID}\times\mathcal{M}$ to H_1, and $H_1(\boldsymbol{A}\widetilde{\boldsymbol{z}} - \boldsymbol{T}_{\widetilde{\mathsf{id}}}c^*, \widetilde{\mathsf{id}}, \widetilde{\mu}) = \boldsymbol{c}^*$ is set. If $(\boldsymbol{c}^*, \boldsymbol{z}^*)$ satisfies the winning condition of the security game, it holds that $H_1(\boldsymbol{A}\widetilde{\boldsymbol{z}} - \boldsymbol{T}_{\widetilde{\mathsf{id}}}c^*, \widetilde{\mathsf{id}}, \widetilde{\mu}) = H_1(\boldsymbol{A}\boldsymbol{z}^* - \boldsymbol{T}_{\mathsf{id}^*}\boldsymbol{c}^*, \mathsf{id}^*, \mu^*)$. Since $(\widetilde{\mathsf{id}}, \widetilde{\mu}) \neq (\mathsf{id}^*, \mu^*)$ holds due to the winning condition, $\mathcal{A}$ succeeds in finding the preimage of $\boldsymbol{r}_J$. This success probability is negligible under the random oracle model.

Next, we consider the case where $\boldsymbol{c}^* = \boldsymbol{r}_J$ is set by H_1. In this case, $\mathcal{F}$ records the $\mathcal{A}$'s output $(\mathsf{id}^*, \mu^*, \sigma^* = (\boldsymbol{r}_J, \boldsymbol{z}^*))$. Then, given the matrix $\boldsymbol{A}$, the randomness $\rho_{\mathcal{A}}, \rho_{\mathcal{F}}$, and a new sequence $(\boldsymbol{r}_1, \ldots, \boldsymbol{r}_{J-1}, \boldsymbol{r}'_J, \ldots, \boldsymbol{r}'_{Q_1+Q_S})$ for fresh randomness $\boldsymbol{r}'_J, \ldots, \boldsymbol{r}'_{Q_1+Q_S} \xleftarrow{\$} \mathcal{D}_{H_1}$, $\mathcal{F}$ runs $\mathcal{A}$ by giving $\boldsymbol{A}$ and $\rho_{\mathcal{A}}$. Owing to the forking lemma [5, Lemma 1], $\boldsymbol{r}'_J \neq \boldsymbol{r}_J$ holds, and $\mathcal{A}$ generates a forgery by using $\boldsymbol{r}'_J$, with at least probability

$$\left(\epsilon - \frac{1}{|\mathcal{D}_{H_1}|}\right)\left(\frac{\epsilon - 1/|\mathcal{D}_{H_1}|}{Q_1 + Q_S} - \frac{1}{|\mathcal{D}_{H_1}|}\right).$$

With this probability, $\mathcal{A}$ outputs a forgery $\sigma' = (\boldsymbol{r}'_J, \boldsymbol{z}')$ on (id^*, μ^*). Then, by letting $\boldsymbol{c}^* = \boldsymbol{r}_J$, $\boldsymbol{c}' = \boldsymbol{r}'_J$, we have $\boldsymbol{A}(\boldsymbol{z}^* - \boldsymbol{z}' + \boldsymbol{S}_{\mathsf{id}^*}\boldsymbol{c}' - \boldsymbol{S}_{\mathsf{id}^*}\boldsymbol{c}^*) = \boldsymbol{0}$.

Due to $\|\boldsymbol{z}^*\|, \|\boldsymbol{z}'\| \leq \eta\delta\sqrt{m}$ and $\|\boldsymbol{S}_{\mathsf{id}^*}\boldsymbol{c}^*\|, \|\boldsymbol{S}_{\mathsf{id}^*}\boldsymbol{c}'\| \leq \gamma\kappa\sqrt{m}$, it holds that $\|\boldsymbol{z}^* - \boldsymbol{z}' + \boldsymbol{S}_{\mathsf{id}^*}\boldsymbol{c}' - \boldsymbol{S}_{\mathsf{id}^*}\boldsymbol{c}^*\| \leq 2(\eta\delta + \gamma\kappa)\sqrt{m}$. In addition, we show $\boldsymbol{z}^* - \boldsymbol{z}' + \boldsymbol{S}_{\mathsf{id}^*}\boldsymbol{c}' - \boldsymbol{S}_{\mathsf{id}^*}\boldsymbol{c}^* \neq \boldsymbol{0}$. Due to the proof of [31, Lemma 5.2] and the parameters based on the condition of this lemma, there exists a signing key $\boldsymbol{S}'_{\mathsf{id}^*}$ such that all column vectors except for one column are the same as those of $\boldsymbol{S}_{\mathsf{id}^*}$ and $\boldsymbol{A}\boldsymbol{S}_{\mathsf{id}^*} = \boldsymbol{A}\boldsymbol{S}'_{\mathsf{id}^*}$, with overwhelming probability. Then, if $\boldsymbol{z}^* - \boldsymbol{z}' + \boldsymbol{S}_{\mathsf{id}^*}(\boldsymbol{c}' - \boldsymbol{c}^*) = \boldsymbol{0}$, we have $\boldsymbol{z}^* - \boldsymbol{z}' + \boldsymbol{S}'_{\mathsf{id}^*}(\boldsymbol{c}' - \boldsymbol{c}^*) \neq \boldsymbol{0}$. When simulating the $\mathsf{O_{SIGN}}$ oracle, $\mathcal{A}$ cannot distinguish $\boldsymbol{S}_{\mathsf{id}^*}$ and $\boldsymbol{S}'_{\mathsf{id}^*}$ since these keys are not used. Hence, we obtain a solution to an $\mathsf{SIS}_{n,m,q,\beta}$ instance with at least probability $1/2$ since both keys are chosen with equal probability. Therefore, the probability of solving $\mathsf{SIS}_{n,m,q,\beta}$ is at least

$$\frac{1}{2}\left(\epsilon - \frac{1}{|\mathcal{D}_{H_1}|}\right)\left(\frac{\epsilon - 1/|\mathcal{D}_{H_1}|}{Q_1 + Q_S} - \frac{1}{|\mathcal{D}_{H_1}|}\right).$$

From the discussion above, the proof is completed. □

4 Our IBIAS Scheme from Lattices

4.1 Construction

We construct a lattice-based IBIAS scheme by combining the interactive aggregate signature scheme of [8] and our IBS scheme. As described in Sect. 1.2, we do not need to consider rogue-key attacks since an IBIAS scheme does not generate any verification/secret key-pair. Hence, it is possible to construct an IBIAS scheme without any additional security model and computational assumption.

Our IBIAS scheme $\mathsf{IBIAS} = (\mathsf{Setup}, \mathsf{KeyGen}, \mathsf{Sign}^{\leftrightarrow}, \mathsf{Vrfy})$ is constructed as follows: For a security parameter λ, we set positive integers $n = n(\lambda)$, $m = m(\lambda)$, $k = k(\lambda)$, $\gamma = \gamma(\lambda)$, $\delta = \delta(\lambda)$, $\kappa = \kappa(\lambda)$, a prime $q = q(\lambda)$, and a positive real number $\eta = \eta(\lambda)$. Let $\mathcal{ID} = \mathcal{ID}(\lambda)$ be an ID space and let $\mathcal{M} = \{0,1\}^*$ be a message space. We define two sets $\mathcal{D}_{H_1} = \{0,1\}^{\mathsf{poly}(\lambda)}$, $\mathcal{D}_{H_2} = \{\boldsymbol{v} \mid \boldsymbol{v} \in \{-1,0,1\}^k \wedge \|\boldsymbol{v}\|_1 \leq \kappa\}$. Let $H_0 : \mathcal{ID} \to \mathbb{Z}_q^n$, $H_1 : \mathbb{Z}_q^n \to \mathcal{D}_{H_1}$, and $H_2 : \{0,1\}^* \to \mathcal{D}_{H_2}$ be cryptographic hash functions. We use the algorithms $\mathsf{TrapGen}$, $\mathsf{SampleD}$ defined in Lemma 1.

- $(\mathsf{pp}, \mathsf{msk}) \leftarrow \mathsf{Setup}(1^\lambda)$:
  1. Generate $(\boldsymbol{A}, \boldsymbol{S_A}) \leftarrow \mathsf{TrapGen}(n, q, m)$.
  2. Output $\mathsf{pp} = \boldsymbol{A} \in \mathbb{Z}_q^{n\times m}$ and $\mathsf{msk} = \boldsymbol{S_A} \in \mathbb{Z}^{m\times m}$.
- $\mathsf{sk}_{\mathsf{id}} \leftarrow \mathsf{KeyGen}(\mathsf{pp}, \mathsf{msk}, \mathsf{id})$:
  1. Let $\mathsf{pp} = \boldsymbol{A}$ and $\mathsf{msk} = \boldsymbol{S_A}$.
  2. Compute $\boldsymbol{S}_{\mathsf{id}} \leftarrow \mathsf{SampleD}(\boldsymbol{A}, \boldsymbol{S_A}, H_0(\mathsf{id}), \gamma)$.
  3. Output $\mathsf{sk}_{\mathsf{id}} = \boldsymbol{S}_{\mathsf{id}} \in \mathbb{Z}^{m\times k}$.
- $\widehat{\sigma}/0 \leftarrow \mathsf{Sign}^{\leftrightarrow}\langle(\mathsf{pp}, \mathsf{sk}_{\mathsf{id}_i}, \mu_i)_{i\in[\ell]}\rangle$: Let $\mathsf{pp} = \boldsymbol{A}$ and $\mathsf{sk}_{\mathsf{id}_i} = \boldsymbol{S}_{\mathsf{id}_i}$.

  Round 1. Each signer id_j chooses $\boldsymbol{y}_j \leftarrow D_\delta^m$ and computes $\boldsymbol{w}_j \leftarrow \boldsymbol{A}\boldsymbol{y}_j \in \mathbb{Z}_q^n$. And then, it computes $h_j \leftarrow H_1(\boldsymbol{w}_j)$ and sends h_j to the cosigners.

  Round 2. After receiving $(h_i)_{i\in[\ell]\setminus\{j\}}$, id_j sends $\boldsymbol{w}_j$ to the cosigners.

  Round 3. After each signer id_j receives $(\boldsymbol{w}_i)_{i\in[\ell]\setminus\{j\}}$, it does the following:
  1. For all $i \in [\ell]$, check whether $h_i = H_1(\boldsymbol{w}_i)$. If there exists $i \in [\ell]$ such that $h_i \neq H_1(\boldsymbol{w}_i)$, return 0 to the cosigners.
  2. Compute $\widehat{\boldsymbol{w}} \leftarrow \sum_{i\in[\ell]} \boldsymbol{w}_i$ and $\boldsymbol{c}_j \leftarrow H_2(\mathsf{id}_j, \widehat{\boldsymbol{w}}, (\mathsf{id}_i)_{i\in[\ell]}, \mu_j)$.
  3. Compute $\boldsymbol{z}_j \leftarrow \boldsymbol{y}_j + \boldsymbol{S}_{\mathsf{id}_j}\boldsymbol{c}_j$.
  4. Send $\boldsymbol{z}_j$ to the cosigners with probability $\min\left(\frac{\ell-1}{\ell}\frac{D_\delta^m(\boldsymbol{z}_j)}{D^m_{\boldsymbol{S}_{\mathsf{id}_j}\boldsymbol{c}_j,\delta}(\boldsymbol{z}_j)}, 1\right)$.

  If there exists a signer which sends 0 during the execution of the protocol $\mathsf{Sign}^{\leftrightarrow}$, then this protocol halts. Otherwise, each signer id_j holds $\widehat{\boldsymbol{w}}$ and $\{\boldsymbol{z}_i\}_{i\in[\ell]}$. Then it computes $\widehat{\boldsymbol{z}} \leftarrow \sum_{i\in[\ell]} \boldsymbol{z}_i$ and holds $\widehat{\sigma} = (\widehat{\boldsymbol{w}}, \widehat{\boldsymbol{z}})$.
- $1/0 \leftarrow \mathsf{Vrfy}(\mathsf{pp}, (\mathsf{id}_i, \mu_i)_{i\in[\ell]}, \widehat{\sigma})$:
  1. Parse $\widehat{\sigma} = (\widehat{\boldsymbol{w}}, \widehat{\boldsymbol{z}})$.
  2. For $i \in [\ell]$, compute $\boldsymbol{c}_i \leftarrow H_2(\mathsf{id}_i, \widehat{\boldsymbol{w}}, (\mathsf{id}_{i'})_{i'\in[\ell]}, \mu_i)$.
  3. Compute $\widehat{\boldsymbol{v}} \leftarrow \sum_{i\in[\ell]} H_0(\mathsf{id}_i) \cdot \boldsymbol{c}_i$.
  4. Output 1 if $\boldsymbol{A}\widehat{\boldsymbol{z}} = \widehat{\boldsymbol{v}} + \widehat{\boldsymbol{w}} \bmod q$ and $\|\boldsymbol{z}\| \leq \eta\delta\ell\sqrt{m}$. Otherwise, output 0.

Parameter Setting. In order to satisfy the correctness and compactness of IBIAS, we can set the following parameters: Let $n \gg \lambda$ be a positive integer, and let C_0 be a positive constant. Due to Lemma 1, let $q = \mathsf{poly}(n)$ be a prime, and $m \geq 3n\log q$ be a positive integer. In addition, in order to prove the security of IBIAS, we need to set the parameters m, γ s.t. $m > \lambda + n\log q/\log(2\lambda\gamma + 1)$ due to the condition of [31, Lemma 5.2]. In the same way as our propose scheme IBS, we set the parameters $k = O(n)$, κ s.t. $2^\kappa \geq \binom{n}{\kappa}2^{O(\lambda)}$, $\delta = C_0\gamma\kappa$, and $\eta = O(1)$ s.t. $\eta\delta \geq (\lambda\delta + \lambda\gamma\kappa)\ell$.

Then, the following lemmas show the correctness and compactness of IBIAS.

Lemma 3 (Correctness). *The IBIAS scheme* IBIAS *is* correct, *under the parameters of* IBIAS.

Proof. We assume $\ell = \mathsf{poly}(\lambda)$. For every $\mathsf{id}_1, \ldots, \mathsf{id}_\ell \in \mathcal{ID}$ and every $\mu_1, \ldots, \mu_\ell \in \mathcal{M}$, let $(\mathsf{pp}, \mathsf{msk}) \leftarrow \mathsf{Setup}(1^\lambda)$, let $\mathsf{sk}_{\mathsf{id}_i} \leftarrow \mathsf{KeyGen}(\mathsf{pp}, \mathsf{msk}, \mathsf{id})$, and let $\widehat{\sigma} = (\widehat{\boldsymbol{w}}, \widehat{\boldsymbol{z}}) \leftarrow \mathsf{Sign}^{\leftrightarrow}\langle(\mathsf{pp}, \mathsf{sk}_{\mathsf{id}_i}, \mu_i)_{i\in[\ell]}\rangle$. Then, it is shown that the keys pp, msk, $\mathsf{sk}_{\mathsf{id}_i}$ are generated correctly, in the same way as the proof of Lemma 5.

We show that the Vrfy algorithm accepts the aggregate signature $\widehat{\sigma}$. Regarding the first condition of Vrfy, it holds that

$$\boldsymbol{A}\widehat{\boldsymbol{z}} = \boldsymbol{A}\sum_{i\in[\ell]} (\boldsymbol{y}_i + \boldsymbol{S}_{\mathsf{id}_i}\boldsymbol{c}_i) = \sum_{i\in[\ell]} \boldsymbol{A}\boldsymbol{y}_i + \sum_{i\in[\ell]} \boldsymbol{A}\boldsymbol{S}_{\mathsf{id}_i}\boldsymbol{c}_i = \sum_{i\in[\ell]} \boldsymbol{w}_i + \sum_{i\in[\ell]} H_0(\mathsf{id}_i)\boldsymbol{c}_i.$$

Since $\widehat{\boldsymbol{w}} - \sum_{i\in[\ell]} \boldsymbol{w}_i$ and $\widehat{\boldsymbol{v}} = \sum_{i\in[\ell]} H_0(\mathsf{id}_i)\boldsymbol{c}_i$, we have $\boldsymbol{A}\widehat{\boldsymbol{z}} = \widehat{\boldsymbol{w}} + \widehat{\boldsymbol{v}}$.

Next, we show that $\widehat{\sigma}$ also fulfills the second condition of Vrfy. Due to [31, Lemma 4.4] and Lemma 1, we have $\|\boldsymbol{y}_i\| \leq \lambda\delta\sqrt{m}$, $\|\boldsymbol{S}_{\mathsf{id}_i}\| \leq \lambda\gamma\sqrt{m}$, with at least probability $1 - \lambda^m e^{(1-\lambda^2)m/2}$. In addition, we have $\|\boldsymbol{c}_i\|_1 \leq \kappa$ due to the definition of H_2. As for the second condition of Vrfy, we have

$$\|\widehat{\boldsymbol{z}}\| \leq \ell \cdot \max_{i\in[\ell]} \|\boldsymbol{z}_i\| = \ell \cdot \max_{i\in[\ell]} \|\boldsymbol{y}_i + \boldsymbol{S}_{\mathsf{id}_i}\boldsymbol{c}_i\| \leq \ell\left(\lambda\delta\sqrt{m} + \lambda\gamma\kappa\sqrt{m}\right) \leq \eta\delta\ell\sqrt{m}.$$

Finally, we show that the probability that $\mathsf{Sign}^{\leftrightarrow}$ generates a valid $\widehat{\sigma} \neq 0$ is at least $1 - \mathsf{negl}(\lambda)$. Each signer id_i sends $\boldsymbol{z}_i$ to the cosigners with probability $\min\left(\frac{\ell-1}{\ell}\frac{D_\delta^m(\boldsymbol{z}_j)}{D^m_{\boldsymbol{S}_{\mathsf{id}_j}\boldsymbol{c}_j,\delta}(\boldsymbol{z}_j)}, 1\right)$. Due to the rejection sampling lemma [8, Lemma 6.6], this probability is close to the probability $(\ell-1)/\ell$. Hence, the probability that all signers do not reject the protocol $\mathsf{Sign}^{\leftrightarrow}$ is $\left(\frac{\ell-1}{\ell}\right)^\ell = O(1)$, and $\mathsf{Sign}^{\leftrightarrow}$ works with constant probability.

From the above discussions, the proof of the correctness is completed. □

Lemma 4 (Compactness). *The IBIAS scheme* IBIAS *is* compact, *under the parameters of* IBIAS.

Proof. The proof of Lemma 4 is similar to that of Lemma 3. For every $\mathsf{id}_1, \ldots, \mathsf{id}_\ell \in \mathcal{ID}$ and every $\mu_1, \ldots, \mu_\ell \in \mathcal{M}$, let $(\mathsf{pp}, \mathsf{msk}) \leftarrow \mathsf{Setup}(1^\lambda)$, let $\mathsf{sk}_{\mathsf{id}_i} \leftarrow \mathsf{KeyGen}(\mathsf{pp}, \mathsf{msk}, \mathsf{id})$, and let $\widehat{\sigma} = (\widehat{\boldsymbol{w}}, \widehat{\boldsymbol{z}}) \leftarrow \mathsf{Sign}^{\leftrightarrow}\langle(\mathsf{pp}, \mathsf{sk}_{\mathsf{id}_i}, \mu_i)_{i\in[\ell]}\rangle$.

In the same way as the proof of 3, it is shown that the size of each element of $\widehat{\boldsymbol{z}}$ is at most $\ell(\lambda\delta + \lambda\gamma\kappa)$ with overwhelming probability. Thus, the bit-length of $\widehat{\boldsymbol{z}}$ is at most $m\lceil\log\left(\ell(\lambda\delta + \lambda\gamma\kappa)\right)\rceil$ (i.e., at most $\mathsf{poly}(\lambda, \log\ell)$). In addition, it is clear that the bit-length of $\widehat{\boldsymbol{w}}$ is $n\lceil\log q\rceil$.

Therefore, the bit-length of $\widehat{\sigma}$ is at most $\mathsf{poly}(\lambda, \log\ell)$. □

4.2 Security Analysis

We give the security proof of our IBIAS scheme IBIAS. Theorem 2 shows the security of this scheme.

Theorem 2 (Unforgeability). *If the* $\mathsf{SIS}_{n,m,q,\beta}$ *assumption holds for* $\beta = 2(\eta\delta + \gamma\kappa)\ell\sqrt{m}$, *the IBIAS scheme* IBIAS *is* unforgeable *in the random oracle model.*

Proof. Let $\mathcal{A}$ be a PPT adversary against IBIAS. Let Q_K, Q_S, Q_0, Q_1, and Q_2 be the numbers of queries issued to $\mathsf{O_{KG}}$, $\mathsf{O_{SIGN}}^{\leftrightarrow}$, H_0, H_1, and H_2, respectively. Let T_0, T_1, and $(\mathsf{T}_2^{(\widehat{\boldsymbol{w}})}, \mathsf{T}_2^{(\mathsf{id})})$ be the tables of query-response pairs issued to the H_0, H_1, and H_2 oracles, respectively. In order to prove Theorem 2, we consider the security games $\mathsf{Hybrid}_0, \ldots, \mathsf{Hybrid}_5$.

Hybrid_0: This game is the ordinary security game of IBIASs.

Hybrid_1: This game is the same as Hybrid_0 except that the H_0, H_1, and $\mathsf{O_{KG}}$ oracles are modified in the following way: At the beginning of the security game, the challenger sets the tables $\mathsf{T}_0 \leftarrow \emptyset$ and $\mathsf{T}_1 \leftarrow \emptyset$.

$H_0(\mathsf{id})$:

1. If $\mathsf{T}_0[\mathsf{id}] = (\boldsymbol{T}_{\mathsf{id}}, \boldsymbol{S}_{\mathsf{id}}) \in \mathbb{Z}_q^{n\times k} \times \mathbb{Z}^{m\times k}$, then H_0 returns $\boldsymbol{T}_{\mathsf{id}}$.
2. If $\mathsf{T}_0[\mathsf{id}] = \emptyset$, then H_0 chooses $\boldsymbol{S}_{\mathsf{id}} \leftarrow D_\gamma^{m\times k}$ and computes $\boldsymbol{T}_{\mathsf{id}} \leftarrow \boldsymbol{A}\boldsymbol{S}_{\mathsf{id}} \in \mathbb{Z}_q^{n\times k}$. And then, it returns $\boldsymbol{T}_{\mathsf{id}}$ and sets $\mathsf{T}_0[\mathsf{id}] \leftarrow (\boldsymbol{T}_{\mathsf{id}}, \boldsymbol{S}_{\mathsf{id}})$.

$H_1(\boldsymbol{w})$: If $\mathsf{T}_1[\boldsymbol{w}] = h (\neq \emptyset)$, then H_1 returns h. If $\mathsf{T}_1[\boldsymbol{w}] = \emptyset$, it samples $h \xleftarrow{\$} \mathcal{D}_{H_1}$, returns h, and sets $\mathsf{T}_1[\boldsymbol{w}] \leftarrow h$.

$\mathsf{O_{KG}}(\mathsf{id})$:

1. If $\mathsf{T}_0[\mathsf{id}] = (\boldsymbol{T}_{\mathsf{id}}, \boldsymbol{S}_{\mathsf{id}})$, then $\mathsf{O_{KG}}$ returns $\boldsymbol{S}_{\mathsf{id}}$ and sets $\mathsf{L}_K \leftarrow \mathsf{L}_K \cup \{\mathsf{id}\}$.
2. If $\mathsf{T}_0[\mathsf{id}] = \emptyset$, it samples $\boldsymbol{S}_{\mathsf{id}} \leftarrow D_\gamma^{m\times k}$ and computes $\boldsymbol{T}_{\mathsf{id}} \leftarrow \boldsymbol{A}\boldsymbol{S}_{\mathsf{id}} \in \mathbb{Z}_q^{n\times k}$. And then it returns $\boldsymbol{S}_{\mathsf{id}}$ and sets $\mathsf{L}_K \leftarrow \mathsf{L}_K \cup \{\mathsf{id}\}$, $\mathsf{T}_0[\mathsf{id}] \leftarrow (\boldsymbol{T}_{\mathsf{id}}, \boldsymbol{S}_{\mathsf{id}})$.

Hybrid_2: This game is the same as Hybrid_1 except that $\boldsymbol{A}$ generated by TrapGen is replaced with a uniformly random $\boldsymbol{A} \in \mathbb{Z}_q^{n\times m}$.

Hybrid_3: This game is the same as Hybrid_2 except that the challenger aborts if for $(\mathsf{id}_i^*)_{i\in[\ell]}$, there exists $j \in [\ell]$ such that $\mathsf{T}_0[\mathsf{id}_j^*] = \emptyset$.

Hybrid_4: This game is the same as Hybrid_3 except that the procedures of the oracles $H_2, \mathsf{O_{SIGN}}^{\leftrightarrow}$ and the **Output** phase are modified as follows: At the beginning of the game, the challenger sets $\mathsf{T}_2^{(\mathsf{id})} \leftarrow \emptyset$, $\mathsf{T}_2^{(\boldsymbol{w})} \leftarrow \emptyset$, and $\mathsf{ctr} \leftarrow 0$ where ctr is used to assign an index to each query issued to H_2. In addition, $\boldsymbol{r}_1, \ldots, \boldsymbol{r}_{Q_2+\ell\cdot Q_S} \xleftarrow{\$} \mathcal{D}_{H_2}$ are used as the responses of H_2.

$H_2(\mathsf{id}, \widehat{\boldsymbol{w}}, (\mathsf{id}_{i'})_{i'\in[\ell]}, \mu)$:

1. If $\mathsf{T}_2^{(\mathsf{id})}[\mathsf{id}] = \emptyset$, then H_2 sets $\mathsf{T}_2^{(\mathsf{id})}[\mathsf{id}] \leftarrow 1$.
2. If $\mathsf{T}_2^{(\widehat{\boldsymbol{w}})}[\mathsf{id}, \widehat{\boldsymbol{w}}, (\mathsf{id}_{i'})_{i'\in[\ell]}, \mu] = \emptyset$, then H_2 chooses $\boldsymbol{c} \xleftarrow{\$} \mathcal{D}_{H_2}$ and sets $\mathsf{ctr} \leftarrow \mathsf{ctr} + 1$, $\mathsf{T}_2^{(\widehat{\boldsymbol{w}})}[\mathsf{id}, \widehat{\boldsymbol{w}}, (\mathsf{id}_{i'})_{i'\in[\ell]}, \mu] \leftarrow \boldsymbol{r}_{\mathsf{ctr}}$.
3. If $\mathsf{T}_2^{(\widehat{\boldsymbol{w}})}[\mathsf{id}, \widehat{\boldsymbol{w}}, (\mathsf{id}_{i'})_{i'\in[\ell]}, \mu] = \boldsymbol{c} (\neq \emptyset)$, then it returns $\boldsymbol{c}$.

$\mathsf{O_{SIGN}}^{\leftrightarrow}((\mathsf{id}_i, \mu_i)_{i\in[\ell]})$: For $j \in [\ell]$ such that $\mathsf{id}_j \notin \mathsf{L}_K$, $\mathsf{O_{SIGN}}$ simulates the procedure of id_j, in the following way:

Round 1.

1. If $\mathsf{T}_2^{(\mathsf{id})}[\mathsf{id}_j] = \emptyset$, then set $\mathsf{T}_2^{(\mathsf{id})}[\mathsf{id}_j] \leftarrow 1$.
2. Let $\mathsf{ctr} \leftarrow \mathsf{ctr} + 1$, $\boldsymbol{c}_j \leftarrow \boldsymbol{r}_{\mathsf{ctr}}$.

3. Choose $\boldsymbol{y}_j \leftarrow D_\delta^m$ and compute $\boldsymbol{w}_j \leftarrow \boldsymbol{A}\boldsymbol{y}_j \bmod q$. If $\mathsf{T}_1[\boldsymbol{w}_j] = \emptyset$, choose $h_j \xleftarrow{\$} \mathcal{D}_{H_1}$ and set $\mathsf{T}_1[\boldsymbol{w}_j] \leftarrow h_j$. Send the defined h_j to the cosigners.

Round 2. After receiving $(h_i)_{i \in [\ell] \setminus \{j\}}$ from the cosigners, do the following:

1. Abort if there is no $\boldsymbol{w} \in \mathbb{Z}_q^n$ such that $\mathsf{T}_1[\boldsymbol{w}] = h_i$ for some $i \in [\ell] \setminus \{j\}$. Let Abort_1 be the event that this condition holds.
2. Abort if for some $i \in [\ell] \setminus \{j\}$, there exist distinct vectors $\boldsymbol{w}, \boldsymbol{w}'$ such that $\mathsf{T}_1[\boldsymbol{w}] = \mathsf{T}_1[\boldsymbol{w}'] = h_i (\neq \emptyset)$. Let Abort_2 be the event that this condition holds.
3. For all $i \in [\ell]$, find $\boldsymbol{w}_i$ such that $\mathsf{T}_1[\boldsymbol{w}_i] = h_i$ and compute $\widehat{\boldsymbol{w}} \leftarrow \sum_{i \in [\ell]} \boldsymbol{w}_i \in \mathbb{Z}_q^n$. Abort if there exists $i \in [\ell]$ such that $\mathsf{T}_2^{(\widehat{\boldsymbol{w}})}[\mathsf{id}_i, \widehat{\boldsymbol{w}}, (\mathsf{id}_{i'})_{i' \in [\ell]}, \mu_i] \neq \emptyset$. Let Abort_3 be the event that this condition holds.
4. Set $\mathsf{ctr} \leftarrow \mathsf{ctr} + 1$ and $\mathsf{T}_2^{(\widehat{\boldsymbol{w}})}[\mathsf{id}_j, \widehat{\boldsymbol{w}}, (\mathsf{id}_{i'})_{i' \in [\ell]}, \mu_j] \leftarrow \boldsymbol{r}_{\mathsf{ctr}}$. Send $\boldsymbol{w}_j$ to the cosigners.

Round 3. After receiving $(\boldsymbol{w}_i)_{i \in [\ell] \setminus \{j\}}$ from the cosigners, do the following:

1. For all $i \in [\ell]$, check if $\mathsf{T}_1[\boldsymbol{w}_i] = h_i$. Return 0 to $\mathcal{A}$ if there exists some $i \in [\ell]$ such that $\mathsf{T}_1[\boldsymbol{w}_i] \neq h_i$.
2. Compute $\boldsymbol{z}_j \leftarrow \boldsymbol{y}_j + \boldsymbol{S}_{\mathsf{id}_j} \boldsymbol{c}_j$. Send $\boldsymbol{z}_j$ to the cosigners with probability $\min\left(\frac{\ell-1}{\ell} \frac{D_\delta^m(\boldsymbol{z}_j)}{D^m_{\boldsymbol{S}_{\mathsf{id}_j}\boldsymbol{c}_j, \delta}(\boldsymbol{z}_j)}, 1\right)$.

The other procedure of this security game is the same as that of Hybrid_3.

Output: $\mathcal{A}$ outputs $(\mathsf{id}_i^*, \mu_i^*)_{i \in [\ell]}$ and a signature $\widehat{\sigma}^* = (\widehat{\boldsymbol{w}}^*, \widehat{\boldsymbol{z}}^*)$. The challenger aborts if $\mathsf{T}_2^{(\mathsf{id})}[\mathsf{id}_i^*] = \emptyset$ for some $i \in [\ell]$. Let Abort_4 be the event this condition holds. After checking this, the procedure of this security game is the same as that of Hybrid_3.

Hybrid_5: This game is the same as Hybrid_4 except that $\mathsf{O}_{\mathsf{SIGN}}^{\leftrightarrow}$ is modified as follows: For $j \in [\ell]$ such that $\mathsf{id}_j \notin \mathsf{L}_K$, $\mathsf{O}_{\mathsf{SIGN}}$ simulates the procedure of id_j, in the following way:

Round 1.

1. If $\mathsf{T}_2^{(\mathsf{id})}[\mathsf{id}_j] = \emptyset$, then set $\mathsf{T}_2^{(\mathsf{id})}[\mathsf{id}_j] \leftarrow 1$.
2. Set $\mathsf{ctr} \leftarrow \mathsf{ctr} + 1$, $\boldsymbol{c}_j \leftarrow \boldsymbol{r}_{\mathsf{ctr}}$.
3. Choose $\boldsymbol{z}_j \leftarrow D_\delta^m$ and set $\boldsymbol{w}_j \leftarrow \boldsymbol{A}\boldsymbol{z}_j - H_0(\mathsf{id}_j)\boldsymbol{c}_j$.
4. Program $h_j = H_1(\boldsymbol{w}_j)$ and send h_j to the cosigners.

Round 2. After receiving $(h_i)_{i \in [\ell] \setminus \{j\}}$, do the following:

1. Abort if there is no $\boldsymbol{w} \in \mathbb{Z}_q^n$ such that $\mathsf{T}_1[\boldsymbol{w}] = h_i$ for some $i \in [\ell] \setminus \{j\}$. Let Abort_1 be the event that this condition holds.
2. Abort if for some $i \in [\ell] \setminus \{j\}$, there exist two distinct vectors $\boldsymbol{w}, \boldsymbol{w}'$ such that $\mathsf{T}_1[\boldsymbol{w}] = \mathsf{T}_1[\boldsymbol{w}'] = h_i (\neq \emptyset)$ is defined. Let Abort_2 be the event that this condition holds.
3. For all $i \in [\ell]$, find $\boldsymbol{w}_i$ such that $\mathsf{T}_1[\boldsymbol{w}_i] = h_i$, and compute $\widehat{\boldsymbol{w}} \leftarrow \sum_{i \in [\ell]} \boldsymbol{w}_i$.

4. Send $\boldsymbol{w}_j$ to the cosigners.

Round 3. After receiving $(\boldsymbol{w}_i)_{i\in[\ell]\setminus\{j\}}$ from the cosigners, do the following:

1. Return 0 if $\mathsf{T}_1[\boldsymbol{w}_i] \neq h_i$ for some $i \in [\ell]$.
2. Compute $\boldsymbol{z}_j \leftarrow \boldsymbol{y}_j + \boldsymbol{S}_{\mathsf{id}_j^*}\boldsymbol{c}_j$. Send $\boldsymbol{z}_j$ to the cosigners with probability $\frac{\ell-1}{\ell}$.

The other procedure of this security game is the same as that of Hybrid_4.

For $i \in \{0, 1, \ldots, 5\}$, let W_i be the event that $\mathcal{A}$ wins in Hybrid_i. We estimate the upper bound of $|\Pr[W_{i-1}] - \Pr[W_i]|$ for each $i \in [5]$.

In the same way as the proof of Theorem 1, we have the following:

- $|\Pr[W_0] - \Pr[W_1]| \leq \mathsf{negl}(\lambda)$ holds due to the leftover hash lemma [20].
- $|\Pr[W_1] - \Pr[W_2]| \leq \mathsf{negl}(\lambda)$ holds due to Lemma 1.
- $|\Pr[W_2] - \Pr[W_3]| \leq 2^{-nk\lceil \log q \rceil}$ holds due to the unpredictability of preimage of the random oracle H_0.

Proof of $|\Pr[W_3] - \Pr[W_4]| \leq \mathsf{negl}(\lambda)$: We estimate the upper bound of the probability that the abort event Abort_i occurs in Hybrid_4 for $i \in [4]$.

Abort_1 occurs when $\mathcal{A}$ succeeds in guessing the preimage $\boldsymbol{w}$ of H_1. The challenger checks if this event happens ℓ times. Hence, we have $\Pr[\mathsf{Abort}_1] \leq \ell \cdot Q_S/|\mathcal{D}_{H_1}|$.

Abort_2 occurs when $\mathcal{A}$ finds a collision of H_1. $\mathcal{A}$ issues at most Q_1 queries to H_1, and the challenger issues at most $\ell \cdot Q_S$ queries to H_1. Hence, we have $\Pr[\mathsf{Abort}_2] \leq (Q_1 + \ell \cdot Q_S)/|\mathcal{D}_{H_1}|$.

Abort_3 occurs when $\mathcal{A}$ queries $\widehat{w}$ beforehand. Due to the leftover hash lemma, the statistical distance between $\boldsymbol{w}_i = \boldsymbol{A}\boldsymbol{y}_i$ ($i \in [\ell]$) and a uniformly random value over $\mathbb{Z}_q^n$ is at most n/q^n. Since $\mathcal{A}$ submits at most Q_S queries to $\mathsf{O}_{\mathsf{SIGN}}$, we have $2n\ell Q_S/q^n$.

Abort_4 occurs when $\mathcal{A}$ succeeds in guessing the output of H_2. For each id_i^*, the probability that this happens is at most $1/|\mathcal{D}_{H_2}|$. $\mathcal{A}$ generates a forgery on ℓ ID-message pairs. Hence, we have $\Pr[\mathsf{Abort}_4] \leq \ell/|\mathcal{D}_{H_2}|$.

Hence, the probability of distinguishing the two games is negligible.

Proof of $|\Pr[W_4] - \Pr[W_5]| \leq \frac{\ell-1}{\ell} \cdot Q_S \cdot 2^{-\omega(\log n)}$: Due to the rejection sampling lemma [8, Lemma 6.6] in the setting of $\mathbb{Z}^{n\times n}$ (rather than the ring setting $\mathbb{Z}[X]/(X^n + 1)$ in this lemma), the probability of distinguishing Hybrid_4 and Hybrid_5 is at most $\frac{\ell-1}{\ell} \cdot Q_S \cdot 2^{-\omega(\log n)}$.

Finally, we prove that $\epsilon = \Pr[W_5]$ is negligible if the $\mathsf{SIS}_{n,m,q,\beta}$ assumption holds. In order to do this, we construct a PPT algorithm $\mathcal{F}$ solving $\mathsf{SIS}_{n,m,q,\beta}$. $\mathcal{F}$ is given the following values: An $\mathsf{SIS}_{n,m,q,\beta}$ instance $\boldsymbol{A} \in \mathbb{Z}_q^{n\times m}$, random responses $\boldsymbol{r}_1, \ldots, \boldsymbol{r}_{Q_2+\ell\cdot Q_S} \in \mathcal{D}_{H_2}$ of H_2, and randomness $\rho_{\mathcal{A}}, \rho_{\mathcal{F}}$ used for running $\mathcal{A}$ and $\mathcal{F}$, respectively. At the beginning of the security game, $\mathcal{F}$ gives $\mathsf{pp} = \boldsymbol{A}$ and $\rho_{\mathcal{A}}$ to $\mathcal{A}$. Without using a secret key, $\mathcal{F}$ simulates the H_0, H_1, H_2, O_{KG}, and $\mathsf{O}_{\mathsf{SIGN}}^{\leftrightarrow}$ oracle in the same way as Hybrid_5. When $\mathcal{A}$ outputs $(\mathsf{id}_i^*, \mu_i^*)_{i\in[\ell]}$ and $\widehat{\sigma}^* = (\widehat{\boldsymbol{w}}^*, \widehat{\boldsymbol{z}}^*)$ as a forgery. Then $\mathcal{F}$ finds indexes $j \in [\ell]$ and $J \in [Q_2+\ell\cdot Q_S]$ such that $\mathsf{id}_j^* \notin \mathsf{L}_K$, $(\mathsf{id}_j^*, \mu_j^*) \notin \mathsf{L}_S$, and $\mathsf{T}_2^{(\widehat{w})}[\mathsf{id}_j^*, \widehat{\boldsymbol{w}}^*, (\mathsf{id}_{i'}^*)_{i'\in[\ell]}, \mu_j^*] = \boldsymbol{r}_J$. $\mathcal{F}$ runs $\mathcal{A}$

again, when it takes as input the instance $\boldsymbol{A}$, the same randomness $\rho_{\mathcal{A}}, \rho_{\mathcal{F}}$, and a new sequence $\boldsymbol{r}_1, \ldots, \boldsymbol{r}_{J-1}, \boldsymbol{r}'_J, \ldots, \boldsymbol{r}'_{Q_2+\ell\cdot Q_S}$ of randomness for uniformly random $\boldsymbol{r}'_J, \ldots, \boldsymbol{r}'_{Q_2+\ell\cdot Q_S} \in \mathcal{D}_{H_2}$. In the same way as the previous execution, $\mathcal{F}$ simulates the environment of $\mathcal{A}$. Due to the forking lemma [5, Lemma 1], $\mathcal{A}$ outputs $(\widehat{\boldsymbol{w}}', \widehat{\boldsymbol{z}}')$ on $(\mathsf{id}_i^*, \mu_i^*)_{i\in[\ell]}$, by using $\boldsymbol{r}'_J = H_2(\mathsf{id}_j^*, \widehat{\boldsymbol{w}}', (\mathsf{id}_{i'}^*)_{i'\in[\ell]}, \mu_j^*)$ for the indexes $(j, J) \in [\ell] \times [Q_2 + \ell \cdot Q_S]$. Then, $\mathcal{F}$ obtains the two forgeries $(\widehat{\boldsymbol{w}}^*, \widehat{\boldsymbol{z}}^*), (\widehat{\boldsymbol{w}}', \widehat{\boldsymbol{z}}')$ with at least probability

$$\epsilon\left(\frac{\epsilon}{Q_2 + \ell\cdot Q_S} - \frac{1}{|\mathcal{D}_{H_2}|}\right).$$

We show that $\widehat{\boldsymbol{z}} - \widehat{\boldsymbol{z}}' - \boldsymbol{S}_{\mathsf{id}_j^*}(\boldsymbol{r}_J - \boldsymbol{r}'_J)$ obtained by the two executions is a solution to the $\mathsf{SIS}_{n,m,q,\beta}$ instance $\boldsymbol{A}$. Since the two forgeries $(\widehat{\boldsymbol{w}}, \widehat{\boldsymbol{z}}), (\widehat{\boldsymbol{w}}', \widehat{\boldsymbol{z}}')$ are valid, we have $\boldsymbol{A}\widehat{\boldsymbol{z}}^* = \sum_{i\in[\ell]} H_0(\mathsf{id}_i^*)\boldsymbol{c}_i^* + \widehat{\boldsymbol{w}}^*$, $\boldsymbol{A}\widehat{\boldsymbol{z}}' = \sum_{i\in[\ell]} H_0(\mathsf{id}_i^*)\boldsymbol{c}'_i + \widehat{\boldsymbol{w}}'$.

Since all values of H_2 except for the J-th one in the two executions of $\mathcal{A}$ are equal, we have

$$\boldsymbol{A}(\widehat{\boldsymbol{z}}^* - \widehat{\boldsymbol{z}}') = \sum_{i\in[\ell]} (H_0(\mathsf{id}_i^*)\boldsymbol{c}_i^* - H_0(\mathsf{id}_i^*)\boldsymbol{c}'_i) - (\widehat{\boldsymbol{w}}^* - \widehat{\boldsymbol{w}}') = \boldsymbol{A}\boldsymbol{S}_{\mathsf{id}_j^*}(\boldsymbol{c}_J^* - \boldsymbol{c}'_J).$$

From this equation, it holds that $\boldsymbol{A}(\widehat{\boldsymbol{z}}^* - \widehat{\boldsymbol{z}}' - \boldsymbol{S}_{\mathsf{id}_j^*}(\boldsymbol{c}_J^* - \boldsymbol{c}'_J)) = \boldsymbol{0}$. Then, we have the vector $\widehat{\boldsymbol{z}}^* - \widehat{\boldsymbol{z}}' - \boldsymbol{S}_{\mathsf{id}_j^*}(\boldsymbol{c}_J^* - \boldsymbol{c}'_J)$ whose norm is at most $2(\eta\delta + \gamma\kappa)\ell\sqrt{m}$, with overwhelming probability. In addition, it is shown that this vector is non-zero since the secret key $\boldsymbol{S}_{\mathsf{id}_j^*}$ is independent of the view of $\mathcal{A}$ in the same way as the proof of Theorem 1. Hence, we obtain a solution $\widehat{\boldsymbol{z}}^* - \widehat{\boldsymbol{z}}' - \boldsymbol{S}_{\mathsf{id}_j^*}(\boldsymbol{c}_J^* - \boldsymbol{c}'_J)$ of $\mathsf{SIS}_{n,m,q,\beta}$ with at least probability

$$\frac{\epsilon}{2}\left(\frac{\epsilon}{Q_2 + \ell\cdot Q_S} - \frac{1}{|\mathcal{D}_{H_2}|}\right).$$

From the discussion above, the proof is completed. □

5 Conclusion

Our goal is to propose an IBIAS scheme based on a standard lattice assumption. To this end, we presented an SIS-based IBS scheme because there is no existing IBS construction suitable for constructing an IB(I)AS scheme. Then, we proposed an SIS-based IBIAS scheme based on our IBS, and its aggregate signature-size is at most logarithmic in the number of signatures by interactive aggregation. Therefore, we obtained the objective IBIAS scheme and achieved our goal.

Acknowledgements. This research was conducted under a contract of "Research and development on new generation cryptography for secure wireless communication services" among "Research and Development for Expansion of Radio Wave Resources (JPJ000254)", which was supported by the Ministry of Internal Affairs and Communications, Japan. The authors would like to thank the anonymous referees for their helpful comments.

Appendix A: Syntax and Security Definition of Interactive Aggregate Signatures

Following [8], we describe the definition of interactive aggregate signatures (IASs).

Definition 10 (IAS). *An IAS scheme consists of polynomial-time algorithms* $(\mathsf{Setup}, \mathsf{KeyGen}, \mathsf{Sign}^{\leftrightarrow}, \mathsf{Vrfy})$*: For a security parameter* λ*, let* $\mathcal{M} = \mathcal{M}(\lambda)$ *be a message space.*

- $\mathsf{pp} \leftarrow \mathsf{Setup}(1^\lambda)$*: The randomized algorithm* Setup *takes as input a security parameter* 1^λ *and outputs a pubic parameter* pp.
- $(\mathsf{pk}, \mathsf{sk}) \leftarrow \mathsf{KeyGen}(\mathsf{pp})$*: The randomized algorithm* KeyGen *takes as input a public parameter* pp *and outputs a public key* pk *and a secret key* sk.
- $\widehat{\sigma}/0 \leftarrow \mathsf{Sign}^{\leftrightarrow}\langle(\mathsf{PK}, \mathsf{sk}_i, \mu_i)_{i\in[\ell]}\rangle$*: The interactive protocol* $\mathsf{Sign}^{\leftrightarrow}$ *is run by a set of signers.*
  Start of the Protocol: *Each signer* $i \in [\ell]$ *has a sequence of public keys* $\mathsf{PK} = (\mathsf{pk}_{i'})_{i'\in[\ell]}$*, a signing key* sk_i*, and a message* μ_i*.*
  End of the Protocol: *Each signer* $i \in [\ell]$ *has an aggregate signature* $\widehat{\sigma}$ *on* $(\mathsf{pk}_{i'}, \mu_{i'})_{i'\in[\ell]}$*, or* 0 *(reject).*
- $1/0 \leftarrow \mathsf{Vrfy}((\mathsf{pk}_i, \mu_i)_{i\in[\ell]}, \widehat{\sigma})$*: The deterministic algorithm* Vrfy *takes as input a set of public keys and messages* $(\mathsf{pk}_i, \mu_i)_{i\in[\ell]}$*, and an aggregate signature* $\widehat{\sigma}$*, and it outputs* 1 *(accept) or* 0 *(reject).*

We require an IAS scheme to be *correct* and *compact*, as follows:

Definition 11 (Correctness). *An IAS scheme* $\mathsf{IAS} = (\mathsf{Setup}, \mathsf{KeyGen}, \mathsf{Sign}^{\leftrightarrow}, \mathsf{Vrfy})$ *is* correct *if for every* $\mathsf{pp} \leftarrow \mathsf{Setup}(1^\lambda)$*, every* $\{(\mathsf{pk}_i, \mathsf{sk}_i) \leftarrow \mathsf{KeyGen}(\mathsf{pp})\}_{i\in[\ell]}$ *and every* $\mu_1, \ldots, \mu_\ell \in \mathcal{M}$*, there exists some positive constant* $C \in \mathbb{Z}$ *such that* $\mathsf{Vrfy}((\mathsf{pk}_i, \mu_i)_{i\in[\ell]}, \widehat{\sigma}) = 1$ *holds with at least probability* $1/C$*, where* $\widehat{\sigma} \leftarrow \mathsf{Sign}^{\leftrightarrow}\langle(\mathsf{PK}, \mathsf{sk}_i, \mu_i)_{i\in[\ell]}\rangle$ *and* $\mathsf{PK} = (\mathsf{pk}_{i'})_{i'\in[\ell]}$*.*

Definition 12 (Compactness). *An IAS scheme* $\mathsf{IAS} = (\mathsf{Setup}, \mathsf{KeyGen}, \mathsf{Sign}^{\leftrightarrow}, \mathsf{Vrfy})$ *is* compact *if for every* $\mathsf{pp} \leftarrow \mathsf{Setup}(1^\lambda)$*, every* $\{(\mathsf{pk}_i, \mathsf{sk}_i) \leftarrow \mathsf{KeyGen}(\mathsf{pp})\}_{i\in[\ell]}$ *and every* $\mu_1, \ldots, \mu_\ell \in \mathcal{M}$*, it holds that* $|\widehat{\sigma}| \leq \mathsf{poly}(\lambda, \log \ell)$*, where* $\widehat{\sigma} \leftarrow \mathsf{Sign}^{\leftrightarrow}\langle(\mathsf{PK}, \mathsf{sk}_i, \mu_i)_{i\in[\ell]}\rangle$ *and* $\mathsf{PK} = (\mathsf{pk}_{i'})_{i'\in[\ell]}$*.*

As a security notion of IASs, *unforgeability* is defined, as follows:

Definition 13 (Unforgeability). *An IAS scheme* $\mathsf{IAS} = (\mathsf{Setup}, \mathsf{KeyGen}, \mathsf{Sign}^{\leftrightarrow}, \mathsf{Vrfy})$ *is* unforgeable *if for any PPT adversary* $\mathcal{A}$ *against* IAS*, its advantage* $\mathsf{Adv}^{\mathrm{unforge}}_{\mathsf{IAS},\mathcal{A}}(\lambda) := \Pr[\mathcal{A} \text{ wins}]$ *is negligible in* λ*.* $[\mathcal{A}$ *wins*$]$ *is the event that* $\mathcal{A}$ *wins in the following security game:*

Setup. *The challenger generates* $\mathsf{pp} \leftarrow \mathsf{Setup}(1^\lambda)$ *and* $(\mathsf{pk}^*, \mathsf{sk}^*) \leftarrow \mathsf{KeyGen}(\mathsf{pp})$ *and gives* $(\mathsf{pp}, \mathsf{pk}^*)$ *to* $\mathcal{A}$*. It initializes a list* $\mathsf{L}_S \leftarrow \emptyset$*.*

Queries. $\mathcal{A}$ *is allowed to access the following oracle:*

- *The signing oracle* $\mathsf{O}_{\mathsf{SIGN}}$*: Given a signing-query* $\mathsf{PK} = (\mathsf{pk}_{i'})_{i'\in[\ell]}$ *and* $(\mu_{i'})_{i'\in[\ell]}$ *(where* $\mathsf{pk}_j = \mathsf{pk}^*$ *for some* $j \in [\ell]$*),* $\mathsf{O}_{\mathsf{SIGN}}$ *does the following:*

1. *$\mathcal{A}$ and* $\mathsf{O_{SIGN}}$ *execute* $\widehat{\sigma} \leftarrow \mathsf{Sign}^{\leftrightarrow}\langle(\mathsf{PK}, \mathsf{sk}_i, \mu_i)_{i\in[\ell]}\rangle$*, where* $\mathsf{O_{SIGN}}$ *behaves as the signer with* pk^**, and* $\mathcal{A}$ *behaves as the other signers.*
2. *If* $\widehat{\sigma} \neq 0$*,* $\mathsf{O_{SIGN}}$ *sets* $\mathsf{L}_S \leftarrow \mathsf{L}_S \cup \{(\mathsf{pk}_{i'}, \mu_{i'})\}_{i'\in[\ell]}$*.*

Output. *$\mathcal{A}$ outputs* $\mathsf{PK}^* = (\mathsf{pk}^*_{i'})_{i'\in[\ell]}$*,* $(\mu^*_{i'})_{i'\in[\ell]}$*, and* $\widehat{\sigma}^*$*. $\mathcal{A}$ wins if it holds that* $\mathsf{Vrfy}((\mathsf{pk}^*_{i'}, \mu^*_{i'})_{i'\in[\ell]}, \widehat{\sigma}^*) = 1$*, and* $\mathsf{pk}^*_i = \mathsf{pk}^* \wedge (\mathsf{pk}^*_i, \mu^*_i) \notin \mathsf{L}_S$ *for some* $i \in [\ell]$*.*

Appendix B: Identity-Based Non-Interactive Aggregate Signatures from Lattices

In this section, we describe the definition of identity-based non-interactive aggregate signatures (IBASs) and present a lattice-based IBAS scheme constructed from our IBS scheme.

Appendix B.1: Syntax and Security Definition of IBAS

Definition 14 (IBAS). *An IBAS scheme consists of six polynomial-time algorithms* $(\mathsf{Setup}, \mathsf{KeyGen}, \mathsf{Sign}, \mathsf{Vrfy}, \mathsf{Agg}, \mathsf{AggVrfy})$*: For a security parameter λ, let $\mathcal{ID} = \mathcal{ID}(\lambda)$ be an ID space and let $\mathcal{M} = \mathcal{M}(\lambda)$ be a message space.*

- $(\mathsf{pp}, \mathsf{msk}) \leftarrow \mathsf{Setup}(1^\lambda)$*: The randomized algorithm* Setup *takes as input a security parameter* 1^λ *and outputs a public parameter* pp *and a master secret key* msk*.*
- $\mathsf{sk_{id}} \leftarrow \mathsf{KeyGen}(\mathsf{pp}, \mathsf{msk}, \mathsf{id})$*: The randomized algorithm* KeyGen *takes as input a public parameter* pp*, a master secret key* msk*, and an ID* $\mathsf{id} \in \mathcal{ID}$*, and it outputs a signing key* $\mathsf{sk_{id}}$*.*
- $\sigma \leftarrow \mathsf{Sign}(\mathsf{pp}, \mathsf{sk_{id}}, \mu)$*: The randomized or deterministic algorithm* Sign *takes as input a public parameter* pp*, a signing key* $\mathsf{sk_{id}}$*, and a message* $\mu \in \mathcal{M}$*, and it outputs a signature* σ*.*
- $1/0 \leftarrow \mathsf{Vrfy}(\mathsf{pp}, \mathsf{id}, \mu, \sigma)$*: The deterministic algorithm* Vrfy *takes as input a public parameter* pp*, an ID* $\mathsf{id} \in \mathcal{ID}$*, a message* $\mu \in \mathcal{M}$*, and a signature* σ*, and it outputs* 1 *(accept) or* 0 *(reject).*
- $\widehat{\sigma} \leftarrow \mathsf{Agg}((\mathsf{id}_i, \mu_i, \sigma_i)_{i\in[\ell]})$*: The randomized or deterministic algorithm* Agg *takes as input triplets* $(\mathsf{id}_i, \mu_i, \sigma_i)_{i\in[\ell]}$ *of IDs, messages, and signatures and outputs an aggregate signature* $\widehat{\sigma}$*.*
- $1/0 \leftarrow \mathsf{AggVrfy}(\mathsf{pp}, (\mathsf{id}_i, \mu_i)_{i\in[\ell]}, \widehat{\sigma})$*: The deterministic algorithm* $\mathsf{AggVrfy}$ *takes as input a public parameter* pp*, pairs* $(\mathsf{id}_i, \mu_i)_{i\in[\ell]}$ *of IDs and messages, and an aggregate signature* $\widehat{\sigma}$*, and it outputs* 1 *(accept) or* 0 *(reject).*

An IBAS scheme is required to be *correct* and *compact*, as follows:

Definition 15 (Correctness). *An IBAS scheme* $\mathsf{IBAS} = (\mathsf{Setup}, \mathsf{KeyGen}, \mathsf{Sign}, \mathsf{Vrfy}, \mathsf{Agg}, \mathsf{AggVrfy})$ *is* correct *if the following holds:*

- *For every* $(\mathsf{pp}, \mathsf{msk}) \leftarrow \mathsf{Setup}(1^\lambda)$*, every* $\mathsf{id} \in \mathcal{ID}$*, every* $\mathsf{sk_{id}} \leftarrow \mathsf{KeyGen}(\mathsf{pp}, \mathsf{msk}, \mathsf{id})$*, and every* $\mu \in \mathcal{M}$*, it holds that* $\mathsf{Vrfy}(\mathsf{pp}, \mathsf{id}, \mu, \sigma) = 1$*, where* $\sigma \leftarrow \mathsf{Sign}(\mathsf{pp}, \mathsf{sk_{id}}, \mu)$*.*

– *For every* $(\mathsf{pp}, \mathsf{msk}) \leftarrow \mathsf{Setup}(1^\lambda)$, *every* $\{\mathsf{sk}_{\mathsf{id}_i} \leftarrow \mathsf{KeyGen}(\mathsf{pp}, \mathsf{msk}, \mathsf{id}_i)\}_{i \in [\ell]}$ ($\{\mathsf{id}_i\}_{i \in [\ell]} \subseteq \mathcal{ID}$), *and every* $\mu_1, \ldots, \mu_\ell \in \mathcal{M}$, *it holds that* $\mathsf{AggVrfy}(\mathsf{pp}, (\mathsf{id}_i, \mu_i)_{i \in [\ell]}, \widehat{\sigma}) = 1$, *where for* $i \in [\ell]$, $\sigma_i \leftarrow \mathsf{Sign}(\mathsf{pp}, \mathsf{sk}_{\mathsf{id}_i}, \mu_i)$ *and* $\widehat{\sigma} \leftarrow \mathsf{Agg}((\mathsf{id}_i, \mu_i, \sigma_i)_{i \in [\ell]})$.

Definition 16 (Compactness). *An IBAS scheme* $\mathsf{IBAS} = (\mathsf{Setup}, \mathsf{KeyGen}, \mathsf{Sign}, \mathsf{Vrfy}, \mathsf{Agg}, \mathsf{AggVrfy})$ *is* compact *if for every* $(\mathsf{pp}, \mathsf{msk}) \leftarrow \mathsf{Setup}(\lambda)$, *every* $\{\mathsf{sk}_{\mathsf{id}_i} \leftarrow \mathsf{KeyGen}(\mathsf{pp}, \mathsf{msk}, \mathsf{id}_i)\}_{i \in [\ell]}$ ($\{\mathsf{id}_i\}_{i \in [\ell]} \subseteq \mathcal{ID}$), *every* $\mu_1, \ldots, \mu_\ell \in \mathcal{M}$, *it holds that* $|\widehat{\sigma}| \leq \mathsf{poly}(\lambda, \log \ell)$, *where* $\widehat{\sigma} \leftarrow \mathsf{Agg}((\mathsf{id}_i, \mu_i, \sigma_i)_{i \in [\ell]})$, *and* $\sigma_i \leftarrow \mathsf{Sign}(\mathsf{pp}, \mathsf{sk}_{\mathsf{id}_i}, \mu_i)$ *for* $i \in [\ell]$.

We describe the definition of *unforgeability* as a security notion of IBASs.

Definition 17 (Unforgeability). *An IBAS scheme* $\mathsf{IBAS} = (\mathsf{Setup}, \mathsf{KeyGen}, \mathsf{Sign}, \mathsf{Vrfy}, \mathsf{Agg}, \mathsf{AggVrfy})$ *is* unforgeable *if for any PPT adversary* $\mathcal{A}$ *against* IBAS, *its advantage* $\mathsf{Adv}^{\mathsf{unforge}}_{\mathsf{IBAS},\mathcal{A}}(\lambda) := \Pr[\mathcal{A} \text{ wins}]$ *is negligible in* λ. $[\mathcal{A}$ *wins*$]$ *is the event that* $\mathcal{A}$ *wins in the following security game:*

Setup. *The challenger generates* $(\mathsf{pp}, \mathsf{msk}) \leftarrow \mathsf{Setup}(1^\lambda)$ *and gives* pp *to* $\mathcal{A}$. *It initializes two lists* $\mathsf{L}_K \leftarrow \emptyset$, $\mathsf{L}_S \leftarrow \emptyset$.

Queries. $\mathcal{A}$ *is allowed to access the following oracles:*

- *The key generation oracle* O_{KG}: *Given a key generation query* $\mathsf{id} \in \mathcal{ID}$, O_{KG} *returns* $\mathsf{sk}_{\mathsf{id}} \leftarrow \mathsf{KeyGen}(\mathsf{pp}, \mathsf{msk}, \mathsf{id})$ *and sets* $\mathsf{L}_K \leftarrow \mathsf{L} \cup \{\mathsf{id}\}$. *Then,* $\mathcal{A}$ *is not allowed to submit the same* id *to* O_{KG} *twice.*
- *The signing oracle* $\mathsf{O}_{\mathsf{SIGN}}$: *Give a signing-query* (id, μ), $\mathsf{O}_{\mathsf{SIGN}}$ *obtains* $\mathsf{sk}_{\mathsf{id}}$ *by using* O_{KG} *and computes* $\mathsf{sk}_{\mathsf{id}} \leftarrow \mathsf{KeyGen}(\mathsf{pp}, \mathsf{msk}, \mathsf{id})$, *returns* $\sigma \leftarrow \mathsf{Sign}(\mathsf{pp}, \mathsf{sk}_{\mathsf{id}}, \mu)$, *and sets* $\mathsf{L}_S \leftarrow \mathsf{L}_S \cup \{(\mathsf{id}, \mu)\}$.

Output. $\mathcal{A}$ *outputs* $((\mathsf{id}_i^*, \mu_i^*)_{i \in [\ell]}, \widehat{\sigma})$. $\mathcal{A}$ *wins if* $\mathsf{AggVrfy}(\mathsf{pp}, (\mathsf{id}_i^*, \mu^*)_{i \in [\ell]}) = 1$ *holds and there exists some* $j \in [\ell]$ *such that* $\mathsf{id}_j^* \notin \mathsf{L}_K$ *and* $(\mathsf{id}_j^*, \mu_j^*) \notin \mathsf{L}_S$.

Appendix B.2: Construction from Our IBS scheme

We describe an IBAS scheme based on our IBS scheme. Although its aggregate signature-size linearly depends on the number of signatures, it is possible to aggregate multiple signatures without interactive process. Thus, such aggregation is useful in a situation where it is required to reduce the time-complexity of generating an aggregate signature.

The IBAS scheme $\mathsf{IBAS} = (\mathsf{Setup}, \mathsf{KeyGen}, \mathsf{Sign}, \mathsf{Vrfy}, \mathsf{Agg}, \mathsf{AggVrfy})$ is constructed as follows: For a security parameter, let $n = n(\lambda)$, $m = m(\lambda)$, $k = k(\lambda)$, $\gamma = \gamma(\lambda)$, $\delta = \delta(\lambda)$, $\kappa = \kappa(\lambda)$, $M = M(\lambda)$ be positive integers, $q = q(\lambda)$ be a prime, and $\eta = \eta(\lambda)$ be a positive real number. We define $\mathcal{ID} = \{0,1\}^\lambda$ as an ID space and $\mathcal{M} = \{0,1\}^*$ as a message space. In addition, let $\mathcal{D}_{H_1} := \{\boldsymbol{v} \mid \boldsymbol{v} \in \{-1,0,1\}^k \wedge \|\boldsymbol{v}\|_1 \leq \kappa\}$, and let $H_0 : \mathcal{ID} \rightarrow \mathbb{Z}_q^{n \times k}$, $H_1 : \{0,1\}^* \rightarrow \mathcal{D}_{H_1}$ be cryptographic hash functions. This scheme uses the algorithms $\mathsf{TrapGen}$, $\mathsf{SampleD}$ in Lemma 1.

Because the Setup and KeyGen of this scheme are the same as those of the IBS scheme IBS in Sect. 3, we omit to describe these algorithms.

- $\sigma \leftarrow \mathsf{Sign}(\mathsf{pp}, \mathsf{sk}_{\mathsf{id}}, \mu)$:
  1. Let $\mathsf{pp} = \boldsymbol{A}$ and $\mathsf{sk}_{\mathsf{id}} = \boldsymbol{S}_{\mathsf{id}}$.
  2. Choose $\boldsymbol{y} \leftarrow D_\delta^m$.
  3. Compute $\boldsymbol{w} \leftarrow \boldsymbol{A}\boldsymbol{y} \in \mathbb{Z}_q^n$.
  4. Compute $\boldsymbol{c} \leftarrow H_1(\boldsymbol{w}, \mathsf{id}, \mu)$.
  5. Compute $\boldsymbol{z} \leftarrow \boldsymbol{y} + \boldsymbol{S}_{\mathsf{id}}\boldsymbol{c} \in \mathbb{Z}^m$.
  6. Output $\sigma = (\boldsymbol{w}, \boldsymbol{z})$ with probability $\min\left(\frac{D_\delta^m(\boldsymbol{z})}{M \cdot D^m_{\boldsymbol{S}_{\mathsf{id}}\boldsymbol{c},\delta}(\boldsymbol{z})}, 1\right)$.
- $1/0 \leftarrow \mathsf{Vrfy}(\mathsf{pp}, \mathsf{id}, \mu, \sigma)$:
  1. Parse $\sigma = (\boldsymbol{w}, \boldsymbol{z})$.
  2. Compute $\boldsymbol{c} \leftarrow H_1(\boldsymbol{w}, \mathsf{id}, \mu)$.
  3. Output 1 if $\|\boldsymbol{z}\| \leq \eta\delta\sqrt{m} \wedge \boldsymbol{A}\boldsymbol{z} = \boldsymbol{w} + H_0(\mathsf{id}) \cdot \boldsymbol{c} \bmod q$. Output 0 otherwise.
- $\widehat{\sigma} \leftarrow \mathsf{Agg}((\mathsf{id}_i, \mu_i, \sigma_i)_{i \in [\ell]})$:
  1. Parse $\sigma_i = (\boldsymbol{w}_i, \boldsymbol{z}_i)$ for $i \in [\ell]$.
  2. Compute $\widehat{\boldsymbol{z}} \leftarrow \sum_{i \in [\ell]} \boldsymbol{z}_i$.
  3. Output $\widehat{\sigma} = ((\boldsymbol{w}_i)_{i \in [\ell]}, \widehat{\boldsymbol{z}})$.
- $1/0 \leftarrow \mathsf{AggVrfy}(\mathsf{pp}, (\mathsf{id}_i, \mu_i)_{i \in [\ell]}, \widehat{\sigma})$:
  1. Parse $\widehat{\sigma} = ((\boldsymbol{w}_i)_{i \in [\ell]}, \widehat{\boldsymbol{z}})$.
  2. Compute $\boldsymbol{c}_i \leftarrow H_1(\boldsymbol{w}_i, \mathsf{id}_i, \mu_i)$ for $i \in [\ell]$.
  3. Compute $\widehat{\boldsymbol{w}} \leftarrow \sum_{i \in [\ell]} \boldsymbol{w}_i$.
  4. Output 1 if $\boldsymbol{A}\widehat{\boldsymbol{z}} = \widehat{\boldsymbol{w}} + \sum_{i \in [\ell]} H_0(\mathsf{id}_i) \cdot \boldsymbol{c}_i \bmod q$ and $\|\widehat{\boldsymbol{z}}\| \leq \eta\delta\ell\sqrt{m}$. Output 0 otherwise.

Parameter Setting. To satisfy correctness, we can set the following parameters: For a security parameter λ, let $n \gg \lambda$ be a lattice parameter, let $q = \mathsf{poly}(\lambda)$ be a prime, and let C_0, C_1 be positive constants. Due to Lemma 1, we set $m \geq 3n \log q$, $\gamma \geq C_0\sqrt{m} \cdot \omega(\sqrt{\log m})^2$. In addition, in order to prove the security of IBAS, we need to set the parameters m, γ s.t. $m > \lambda + n \log q / \log(2\lambda\gamma + 1)$ due to the condition of [31, Lemma 5.2]. We set the parameters $k = O(n)$, κ s.t. $2^\kappa \geq \binom{n}{\kappa} 2^{O(\lambda)}$, $\delta = C_1\gamma\kappa\sqrt{m}$, $\eta = O(1)$ s.t. $\eta\delta \geq (\lambda\delta + \lambda\gamma\kappa)\ell$, and $M = \exp(C_1\gamma\kappa\sqrt{m}/\delta + (\gamma\kappa\sqrt{m}/2\delta)^2)$.

Then, Lemma 5 shows the correctness of IBAS. In this paper, we omit to describe this proof because this lemma can be proven in the same way as the proof of Lemma 3.

Lemma 5 (Correctness). *The IBAS scheme* IBAS *is* correct, *under the parameters of* IBAS.

In addition, it is clear that IBAS is non-compact. However, it is shown that the bit-length of $\widehat{\boldsymbol{z}}$ is at most $m\lceil \log(\ell(\lambda\delta + \lambda\gamma\kappa)) \rceil$, in the same way as the proof of Lemma 4. Thus, the bit-length of its aggregate signature is shorter than that of the naive aggregation $(\sigma_1, \ldots, \sigma_\ell) \leftarrow \mathsf{Agg}((\mathsf{id}_i, \mu_i, \sigma_i)_{i \in [\ell]})$.

Furthermore, the following theorem shows the security of our scheme IBAS.

Theorem 3 (Unforgeability). *If the* $\mathsf{SIS}_{n,m,q,\beta}$ *assumption holds for* $\beta = 2(\eta\delta + \gamma\kappa)\ell\sqrt{m}$, *then the IBAS scheme* IBAS *is* unforgeable *in the random oracle model.*

The proof of Theorem 3 is similar to that of Theorem 2. Regarding this proof, see the full version of this paper.

References

1. Ahn, J.H., Green, M., Hohenberger, S.: Synchronized aggregate signatures: new definitions, constructions and applications. In: ACM Conference on Computer and Communications Security. ACM, pp. 473–484 (2010)
2. Ajtai, Miklós: Generating Hard Instances of the Short Basis Problem. In: Wiedermann, Jirí, van Emde Boas, Peter, Nielsen, Mogens (eds.) ICALP 1999. LNCS, vol. 1644, pp. 1–9. Springer, Heidelberg (1999). https://doi.org/10.1007/3-540-48523-6_1
3. Alwen, J., Peikert, C.: Generating shorter bases for hard random lattices. In: STACS. LIPIcs Schloss Dagstuhl - Leibniz-Zentrum für Informatik, Germany. 3, pp. 75–86. (2009)
4. Bellare, M., Namprempre, C., Neven, G.: Security proofs for identity-based identification and signature schemes. J. Cryptol. **22**(1), 1–61 (2009)
5. Bellare, M., Neven, G.: Multi-signatures in the plain public-key model and a general forking lemma. In: CCS. ACM, pp. 390–399 (2006)
6. Boldyreva, A., Gentry, C., O'Neill, A., Yum, D.H.: Ordered multisignatures and identity-based sequential aggregate signatures, with applications to secure routing. In: ACM Conference on Computer and Communications Security. ACM, pp. 276–285 (2007)
7. Boneh, D., Gentry, C., Lynn, B., Shacham, H.: Aggregate and Verifiably Encrypted Signatures from Bilinear Maps. In: Biham, E. (ed.) EUROCRYPT 2003. LNCS, vol. 2656, pp. 416–432. Springer, Heidelberg (2003). https://doi.org/10.1007/3-540-39200-9_26
8. Boneh, D., Kim, S.: One-time and interactive aggregate signatures from lattices. https://crypto.stanford.edu/ skim13/agg_ots.pdf (2020)
9. Boudgoust, K., Roux-Langlois, A.: Compressed linear aggregate signatures based on module lattices. IACR Cryptol. ePrint Arch., p. 263 (2021)
10. Brogle, K., Goldberg, S., Reyzin, L.: Sequential Aggregate Signatures with Lazy Verification from Trapdoor Permutations. In: Wang, X., Sako, K. (eds.) ASIACRYPT 2012. LNCS, vol. 7658, pp. 644–662. Springer, Heidelberg (2012). https://doi.org/10.1007/978-3-642-34961-4_39
11. Doröz, Y., Hoffstein, J., Silverman, J.H., Sunar, B.: MMSAT: a scheme for multimessage multiuser signature aggregation. IACR Cryptol. ePrint Arch., p. 520 (2020)
12. Fiat, Amos, Shamir, Adi: How To Prove Yourself: Practical Solutions to Identification and Signature Problems. In: Odlyzko, Andrew M.. (ed.) CRYPTO 1986. LNCS, vol. 263, pp. 186–194. Springer, Heidelberg (1987). https://doi.org/10.1007/3-540-47721-7_12
13. Fischlin, M., Lehmann, A., Schröder, D.: History-Free Sequential Aggregate Signatures. In: Visconti, I., De Prisco, R. (eds.) SCN 2012. LNCS, vol. 7485, pp. 113–130. Springer, Heidelberg (2012). https://doi.org/10.1007/978-3-642-32928-9_7
14. Galindo, D., Garcia, F.D.: A Schnorr-Like Lightweight Identity-Based Signature Scheme. In: Preneel, B. (ed.) AFRICACRYPT 2009. LNCS, vol. 5580, pp. 135–148. Springer, Heidelberg (2009). https://doi.org/10.1007/978-3-642-02384-2_9
15. Gentry, C., O'Neill, A., Reyzin, L.: A Unified Framework for Trapdoor-Permutation-Based Sequential Aggregate Signatures. In: Abdalla, M., Dahab, R. (eds.) PKC 2018. LNCS, vol. 10770, pp. 34–57. Springer, Cham (2018). https://doi.org/10.1007/978-3-319-76581-5_2

16. Gentry, C., Peikert, C., Vaikuntanathan, V.: Trapdoors for hard lattices and new cryptographic constructions. In: STOC. ACM, pp. 197–206 (2008)
17. Gentry, C., Ramzan, Z.: Identity-Based Aggregate Signatures. In: Yung, M., Dodis, Y., Kiayias, A., Malkin, T. (eds.) PKC 2006. LNCS, vol. 3958, pp. 257–273. Springer, Heidelberg (2006). https://doi.org/10.1007/11745853_17
18. Hartung, G., Kaidel, B., Koch, A., Koch, J., Hartmann, D.: Practical and Robust Secure Logging from Fault-Tolerant Sequential Aggregate Signatures. In: Okamoto, T., Yu, Y., Au, M.H., Li, Y. (eds.) ProvSec 2017. LNCS, vol. 10592, pp. 87–106. Springer, Cham (2017). https://doi.org/10.1007/978-3-319-68637-0_6
19. Hartung, Gunnar, Kaidel, Björn., Koch, Alexander, Koch, Jessica, Rupp, Andy: Fault-Tolerant Aggregate Signatures. In: Cheng, Chen-Mou., Chung, Kai-Min., Persiano, Giuseppe, Yang, Bo-Yin. (eds.) PKC 2016. LNCS, vol. 9614, pp. 331–356. Springer, Heidelberg (2016). https://doi.org/10.1007/978-3-662-49384-7_13
20. Håstad, J., Impagliazzo, R., Levin, L.A., Luby, M.: A pseudorandom generator from any one-way function. SIAM J. Comput. **28**(4), 1364–1396 (1999)
21. Hoffstein, Jeffrey, Pipher, Jill, Silverman, Joseph H..: NTRU: A ring-based public key cryptosystem. In: Buhler, Joe P.. (ed.) ANTS 1998. LNCS, vol. 1423, pp. 267–288. Springer, Heidelberg (1998). https://doi.org/10.1007/BFb0054868
22. Hohenberger, S., Sahai, A., Waters, B.: Full Domain Hash from (Leveled) Multilinear Maps and Identity-Based Aggregate Signatures. In: Canetti, R., Garay, J.A. (eds.) CRYPTO 2013. LNCS, vol. 8042, pp. 494–512. Springer, Heidelberg (2013). https://doi.org/10.1007/978-3-642-40041-4_27
23. Hohenberger, S., Waters, B.: Synchronized Aggregate Signatures from the RSA Assumption. In: Nielsen, J.B., Rijmen, V. (eds.) EUROCRYPT 2018. LNCS, vol. 10821, pp. 197–229. Springer, Cham (2018). https://doi.org/10.1007/978-3-319-78375-8_7
24. Kiltz, E., Neven, G.: Identity-based signatures. In: Identity-Based Cryptography, Cryptology and Information Security Series. IOS Press. 2, pp. 31–44. (2009)
25. Langlois, A., Stehlé, D.: Worst-case to average-case reductions for module lattices. Des. Codes Cryptogr. **75**(3), 565–599 (2015)
26. Lee, K., Lee, D.H., Yung, M.: Sequential Aggregate Signatures Made Shorter. In: Jacobson, M., Locasto, M., Mohassel, P., Safavi-Naini, R. (eds.) ACNS 2013. LNCS, vol. 7954, pp. 202–217. Springer, Heidelberg (2013). https://doi.org/10.1007/978-3-642-38980-1_13
27. Li, Q., Luo, M., Hsu, C., Wang, L., He, D.: A quantum secure and noninteractive identity-based aggregate signature protocol from lattices. IEEE Syst. J., **16**(3), 4816-4826 (2021)
28. Lu, S., Ostrovsky, R., Sahai, A., Shacham, H., Waters, B.: Sequential Aggregate Signatures and Multisignatures Without Random Oracles. In: Vaudenay, S. (ed.) EUROCRYPT 2006. LNCS, vol. 4004, pp. 465–485. Springer, Heidelberg (2006). https://doi.org/10.1007/11761679_28
29. Lysyanskaya, A., Micali, S., Reyzin, L., Shacham, H.: Sequential Aggregate Signatures from Trapdoor Permutations. In: Cachin, C., Camenisch, J.L. (eds.) EUROCRYPT 2004. LNCS, vol. 3027, pp. 74–90. Springer, Heidelberg (2004). https://doi.org/10.1007/978-3-540-24676-3_5
30. Lyubashevsky, V.: Fiat-Shamir with Aborts: Applications to Lattice and Factoring-Based Signatures. In: Matsui, M. (ed.) ASIACRYPT 2009. LNCS, vol. 5912, pp. 598–616. Springer, Heidelberg (2009). https://doi.org/10.1007/978-3-642-10366-7_35

31. Lyubashevsky, V.: Lattice Signatures without Trapdoors. In: Pointcheval, D., Johansson, T. (eds.) EUROCRYPT 2012. LNCS, vol. 7237, pp. 738–755. Springer, Heidelberg (2012). https://doi.org/10.1007/978-3-642-29011-4_43
32. Lyubashevsky, V., Peikert, C., Regev, O.: On Ideal Lattices and Learning with Errors over Rings. In: Gilbert, H. (ed.) EUROCRYPT 2010. LNCS, vol. 6110, pp. 1–23. Springer, Heidelberg (2010). https://doi.org/10.1007/978-3-642-13190-5_1
33. Micciancio, D., Peikert, C.: Trapdoors for Lattices: Simpler, Tighter, Faster, Smaller. In: Pointcheval, D., Johansson, T. (eds.) EUROCRYPT 2012. LNCS, vol. 7237, pp. 700–718. Springer, Heidelberg (2012). https://doi.org/10.1007/978-3-642-29011-4_41
34. Micciancio, D., Regev, O.: Worst-case to average-case reductions based on gaussian measures. SIAM J. Comput. **37**(1), 267–302 (2007)
35. Neven, G.: Efficient Sequential Aggregate Signed Data. In: Smart, N. (ed.) EUROCRYPT 2008. LNCS, vol. 4965, pp. 52–69. Springer, Heidelberg (2008). https://doi.org/10.1007/978-3-540-78967-3_4
36. Pan, J., Wagner, B.: Short Identity-Based Signatures with Tight Security from Lattices. In: Cheon, J.H., Tillich, J.-P. (eds.) PQCrypto 2021 2021. LNCS, vol. 12841, pp. 360–379. Springer, Cham (2021). https://doi.org/10.1007/978-3-030-81293-5_19
37. Regev, O.: On lattices, learning with errors, random linear codes, and cryptography. J. ACM **56**(6), 34–40 (2009)
38. Rückert, M.: Strongly Unforgeable Signatures and Hierarchical Identity-Based Signatures from Lattices without Random Oracles. In: Sendrier, N. (ed.) PQCrypto 2010. LNCS, vol. 6061, pp. 182–200. Springer, Heidelberg (2010). https://doi.org/10.1007/978-3-642-12929-2_14
39. Rückert, M., Schröder, D.: Aggregate and Verifiably Encrypted Signatures from Multilinear Maps without Random Oracles. In: Park, J.H., Chen, H.-H., Atiquzzaman, M., Lee, C., Kim, T., Yeo, S.-S. (eds.) ISA 2009. LNCS, vol. 5576, pp. 750–759. Springer, Heidelberg (2009). https://doi.org/10.1007/978-3-642-02617-1_76
40. Stehlé, D., Steinfeld, R.: Making NTRU as Secure as Worst-Case Problems over Ideal Lattices. In: Paterson, K.G. (ed.) EUROCRYPT 2011. LNCS, vol. 6632, pp. 27–47. Springer, Heidelberg (2011). https://doi.org/10.1007/978-3-642-20465-4_4

Post-quantum Cryptography

Analysis of (U,U+V)-code Problem with Gramian over Binary and Ternary Fields

Ichiro Iwata(✉), Yusuke Yoshida, and Keisuke Tanaka

Tokyo Institute of Technology, Tokyo, Japan
iwata.i.aa@m.titech.ac.jp, yoshida.yusuke@c.titech.ac.jp,
keisuke@is.titech.ac.jp

Abstract. Debris-Alazard, Sendrier, and Tillich proposed SURF, which is a code-based signature scheme and enjoys efficient signature generation and verification (eprint in 2017). The security of this scheme is based on two problems: one is DOOM (Decoding One Out of Many), and the other is the plain (U,U+V)-code problem over $\mathbb{F}_2$. There are many studies on the former one but few studies on the latter one. Later the security of SURF was broken because the hardness of the plain (U,U+V)-code problem does not hold with considering a notion of the hull.

Then Debris-Alazard et al. proposed Wave as a successor of SURF, which is known as one of the most promising quantum-resistant signature schemes (ASIACRYPT 2019). Wave is based on similar problems used in SURF. Wave uses DOOM and the normalized generalized (U,U+V)-code problem over $\mathbb{F}_3$.

In this paper, we utilize a notion of the Gramian (the determinant of the Gram matrices) of public keys and analyze the plain (U,U+V)-code problem over $\mathbb{F}_2$. For this purpose, we compute the asymptotic probability distribution of Gramians of random matrices. Furthermore, we also show a way to analyze the normalized generalized (U,U+V)-code problem over $\mathbb{F}_2$. Finally, we apply our analysis to the normalized generalized (U,U+V)-code problem over $\mathbb{F}_3$. By our analysis with Gramian, SURF is completely broken, however, Wave is not directly threatened.

Keywords: Code-based cryptography · Digital signature scheme · (U,U+V)-code problem · Gramian

1 Introduction

1.1 Code-Based Signature Schemes

Digital signature plays a significant role in modern cryptographic applications and recently it becomes necessary to be quantum-resistant. To build secure digital signature schemes, first, we have to find quantum-resistant cryptographic problems.

Decoding a linear code is counted as one of those problems and cryptosystems based on this problem are called code-based. Recently, NIST announced the first

S.-H. Seo and H. Seo (Eds.): ICISC 2022, LNCS 13849, pp. 435–449, 2023.
https://doi.org/10.1007/978-3-031-29371-9_21

three quantum-resistant digital signature schemes for standardization. Two of them are based on lattices while the other is based on hash functions. A code-based digital signature scheme was proposed as a candidate [7], but unfortunately not selected. It is still an important problem to build a secure code-based digital signature scheme.

Courtois, Finiasz, and Sendrier gave the first code-based digital signature scheme [3]. Its security depends on two problems; one is distinguishing Goppa codes from random codes and the other is decoding a linear code. However, it was later discovered that the former problem is not as hard as originally thought. As a result, the unpractical size of public keys is required for practical security level. Later its variant was proposed [10] but failed [13].

Aragon, Blazy, Gaborit, Hauteville, and Zémor proposed a new code-based digital signature scheme recently, whose name is Durandal [1]. By adopting Lyubashevsky's approach [11], this scheme enjoys small sizes of signatures and public keys. Durandal is based on a novel assumption, namely PSSI+ (Product Spaces Subspaces Indistinguishability). However, this assumption is not studied adequately and this scheme could leak the secret key information [6].

Debris-Alazard, Sendrier, and Tillich proposed a code-based signature scheme SURF, which enjoys efficient signature generation and verification [4]. This scheme is based on the GPV construction, which is an improved hash-and-sign digital signature scheme with trapdoor functions [8]. SURF is based on two problems: one is DOOM (Decoding One Out of Many) and the other is the plain (U,U+V)-code problem over $\mathbb{F}_2$.

First, DOOM is a kind of a decoding problem as follows:

> Given $\mathbf{H} \in \mathbb{F}_2^{(n-k)\times n}, \mathbf{s}_1, \ldots, \mathbf{s}_q \in \mathbb{F}_2^{n-k}$ and a sufficiently small w $(\leq n)$, find $(\mathbf{e}, i)$ such that $|\mathbf{e}| = w$ and $\mathbf{He}^t = \mathbf{s}_i^t$.

There are many studies on DOOM and its related problems [2,14,15].

Second, given linear codes U and V, we define a (U,U+V)-code as follows:

$$\{(\mathbf{u}, \mathbf{u}+\mathbf{v}) : \mathbf{u} \in U, \mathbf{v} \in V\}.$$

The plain (U,U+V)-code problem is a decisional problem such that deciding whether a linear code is a permuted (U,U+V)-code or a random code. This problem can be converted into the problem of distinguishing a parity check matrix of a permuted (U,U+V)-code from a random matrix. The parity check matrix is denoted by

$$\mathbf{SHP} = \mathbf{S}\begin{pmatrix} \mathbf{H}_U & \mathbf{O} \\ \mathbf{H}_V & \mathbf{H}_V \end{pmatrix}\mathbf{P}$$

where $\mathbf{S}$ is an invertible matrix, $\mathbf{P}$ is a permutation matrix, $\mathbf{H}_U$, $\mathbf{H}_V$ are parity check matrices of U and V, and $\mathbf{O}$ is the zero matrix.

In summary, the main idea of SURF is to use the following code-based function:

$$\begin{aligned} f_{\mathbf{H},w} : S_w &\to \mathbb{F}_2^{n-k} \\ \mathbf{e} &\mapsto \mathbf{eH}^t \end{aligned}$$

for $\mathbf{H} \in \mathbb{F}_2^{(n-k)\times n}$, a sufficiently small w ($\leq n$) and $S_w = \{\mathbf{x} \in \mathbb{F}_2^n : |\mathbf{x}| = w\}$. Generally, this function is one way as far as $\mathbf{H}$ is random due to the DOOM problem, and in some cases invertible when $\mathbf{H}$ has a particular structure, for example, $\mathbf{H}$ is a parity check matrix of a (U,U+V)-code. Here $\mathbf{SHP}$ is random due to the plain (U,U+V)-code problem, therefore $f_{\mathbf{SHP},w}$ can be considered as a trapdoor function where $\mathbf{S}$, $\mathbf{H}$ and $\mathbf{P}$ are the trapdoors. We obtain a signature of a message m as $f_{\mathbf{SHP},w}^{-1}(h(m))$ with a hash function h.

Unfortunately, the security of SURF was broken because the hardness of the plain (U,U+V)-code problem does not hold with considering the hull of the code [5]. For a linear code C, the hull of C is defined by the intersection of C itself and its dual code. Generally, the dimension of the hull of a random code is not always 0, but that of a permuted (U,U+V)-code is 0 with an overwhelming probability. Hence if we compute the dimension of the hull of a code, then we can decide whether a permuted (U,U+V)-code or a random code. They showed an attack on SURF.

After that, Debris-Alazard, Sendrier, and Tillich proposed Wave [6] as a successor of SURF. Wave works over $\mathbb{F}_3$, unlike SURF works over $\mathbb{F}_2$. Therefore the security of Wave is based on the normalized generalized (U,U+V)-code problem over $\mathbb{F}_3$ instead of the plain (U,U+V)-code problem over $\mathbb{F}_2$. Given linear codes U and V, the normalized generalized (U,U+V)-code is as follows:

$$\{(\mathbf{a}\odot\mathbf{u}+\mathbf{b}\odot\mathbf{v}, \mathbf{c}\odot\mathbf{u}+\mathbf{d}\odot\mathbf{v}) : \mathbf{u}\in U, \mathbf{v}\in V\}$$

where $\odot$ denotes Hadamard product and $\mathbf{a}, \mathbf{b}, \mathbf{c}$, and $\mathbf{d}$ are random vectors which satisfy

$$\forall i \in \{1,\ldots,n/2\}, \quad and \quad a_i c_i \neq 0 \quad a_i d_i - b_i c_i = 1.$$

The normalized generalized (U,U+V)-code problem is a decisional problem such that deciding whether a linear code is a permuted normalized generalized (U,U+V)-code or a random code. As far as we know, there are few studies on this problem, and no efficient attack against this problem is found.

1.2 Our Contribution

First, we utilize a notion of the Gramian as an indicator for distinguishing the plain (U,U+V)-code problem. By considering the Gramian in case of $\mathbf{H}_{pk} = \mathbf{SH}_{sk}\mathbf{P}$, the effect of the randomizing matrices $\mathbf{S}$ and $\mathbf{P}$ is canceled and we obtain the Gramian of a secret key matrix $\mathbf{H}_{sk}$ such that

$$\det(\mathbf{H}_{pk}\mathbf{H}_{pk}^t) = \det(\mathbf{H}_{sk}\mathbf{H}_{sk}^t).$$

We prove that if we instantiate $\mathbf{H}_{sk}$ with a parity check matrix of (U,U+V)-code, then we obtain $\det(\mathbf{H}_{sk}\mathbf{H}_{sk}^t) = 0$.

Second, we estimate the distribution of the Gramian of random matrices. In other words, for each $a \in \mathbb{F}_q$, we would like to know

$$\Pr[\det(\mathbf{H}\mathbf{H}^t) = a \mid \mathbf{H} \in \mathbb{F}_q^{m\times n}].$$

Though this distribution seems to be common but has never been analyzed mathematically. Hence we show an asymptotical formula, and conclude that this probability approaches around 0.42 in case of $q = 2$ and $a = 1$ as n increases. With such an analysis, we can construct a polynomial-time algorithm that distinguishes the plain (U,U+V)-code problem over $\mathbb{F}_2$.

Third, we deal with the normalized generalized (U,U+V)-code problem over $\mathbb{F}_2$. In this problem, we have to consider the additional secret variables. However, we prove that this problem is distinguished as well.

Finally, we apply our analysis to the normalized generalized (U,U+V)-code problem over $\mathbb{F}_3$ which Wave is based on. By our analysis with Gramian, SURF is completely broken, however, Wave is not directly threatened.

2 Preliminaries

2.1 Vectors and Matrices

For a prime number q, we denote the finite field with q elements by $\mathbb{F}_q$ for example $\mathbb{F}_3$ denotes $\{0, 1, -1\}$. Vectors are denoted by small bold letters (such as $\mathbf{a}$) and matrices by capital bold letters (such as $\mathbf{A}$).

Vectors are in row notation. Let $\mathbf{u}, \mathbf{v}$ be two vectors in $\mathbb{F}_q^n$. $(\mathbf{u}, \mathbf{v}) \in \mathbb{F}_q$ denotes their inner product. $\mathbf{u} \odot \mathbf{v} \in \mathbb{F}_q^n$ denotes their Hadamard product such that $(u_1v_1, \ldots, u_nv_n)$. The Hamming weight of $\mathbf{u}$ is denoted by $|\mathbf{u}|$. For a vector $\mathbf{a} \in \mathbb{F}_q^n$, $\mathbf{Diag}(\mathbf{a})$ denotes the diagonal matrix $\mathbf{A} \in \mathbb{F}_q^{n\times n}$ with its entries given by $\mathbf{a}$, i.e. for all $i, j \in \{1, \ldots, n\}$, $\mathbf{A}(i, i) = a_i$ and $\mathbf{A}(i, j) = 0$ for $i \neq j$.

denotes the identity matrix and $\mathbf{O}$ denotes the zero matrices. For $\mathbf{X} \in \mathbb{F}_q^{m\times n}$, $\mathbf{X}^t \in \mathbb{F}_q^{n\times m}$ denotes the transpose of $\mathbf{X}$. We also define $\dim(V)$ as the dimension of a linear space V and $\text{rank}(\mathbf{X})$ as the dimension of the vector space generated by the columns of $\mathbf{X}$.

We define a notion of permutations and their signatures for the definition of the determinant. S_n denotes the set which is consisted of all permutations of the set $\{1, \ldots, n\}$. If σ is achieved by interchanging two entries an odd/even number of times, σ is called odd/even. The signature of σ is defined to be $+1$ if σ is even and -1 if σ is odd, and which is denoted by $\text{sgn}(\sigma)$. Given $\mathbf{A} \in \mathbb{F}_q^{n\times n}$, the determinant of $\mathbf{A}$ is defined as follows:

$$\det(\mathbf{A}) \triangleq \sum_{\sigma\in S_n} \left(\text{sgn}(\sigma) \prod_{i=1}^{n} a_{i,\sigma(i)} \right).$$

Furthermore, we refer to a couple of well-known elementary linear algebraic results.

Remark 1. For $\mathbf{A} \in \mathbb{F}_q^{m\times n}$, let $\mathbf{B} \in \mathbb{F}_q^{n\times n}$ and $\mathbf{C} \in \mathbb{F}_q^{m\times m}$ be full rank matrices. Then we have $\text{rank}(\mathbf{AB}) = \text{rank}(\mathbf{CA}) = \text{rank}(\mathbf{A})$.

Remark 2. For $\mathbf{A} \in \mathbb{F}_q^{m\times n}$, $\mathbf{B} \in \mathbb{F}_q^{n\times m}$ and $m = n$, $\det(\mathbf{AB}) = \det(\mathbf{A})\det(\mathbf{B})$. However, in case of $m \neq n$, $\det(\mathbf{AB})$ is not necessarily $\det(\mathbf{A})\det(\mathbf{B})$.

Remark 3. For $\mathbf{S} \in \mathbb{F}_q^{n \times n}$, $\det(\mathbf{S}) = \det(\mathbf{S}^t)$. In addition, we have $\det(\mathbf{S}\mathbf{S}^t) = \det(\mathbf{S})^2$ by Remark 2.

2.2 Coding Theory

A linear code of length n and dimension k is denoted by $[n,k]$-code, which is defined as a linear subspace V with dimension k of the vector space $\mathbb{F}_q^n$.

In the following, let C be an $[n,k]$-code. $C^\perp$ denotes the dual of C which is defined as:

$$\{\mathbf{h} \in \mathbb{F}_q^n : \forall \mathbf{c} \in C (\mathbf{c}, \mathbf{h}) = 0\}.$$

We denote hull(C) as a vector space such that $C \cap C^\perp$.

2.3 (U,U+V)-codes and Problems

Given linear codes U and V of length $n/2$, we define a (U,U+V)-code as

$$\{(\mathbf{u}, \mathbf{u}+\mathbf{v}) : \mathbf{u} \in U, \mathbf{v} \in V\}.$$

The plain (U,U+V)-code problem is defined as deciding whether a certain linear code is a permuted (U,U+V)-code or a random code.

This problem over $\mathbb{F}_2$ is equivalent to the following problem in the light of a parity check matrix.

Problem 1 (The plain (U,U+V)-code problem over $\mathbb{F}_2$). For a random non-singular matrix $\mathbf{S} \in \mathbb{F}_2^{m \times m}$, a random permutation matrix $\mathbf{P} \in \mathbb{F}_2^{n \times n}$ and $\mathbf{H}_{sk} \in \mathbb{F}_2^{m \times n}$ given by

$$\begin{pmatrix} \mathbf{H}_U & \mathbf{O} \\ \mathbf{H}_V & \mathbf{H}_V \end{pmatrix}$$

where $\mathbf{H}_U \in \mathbb{F}_2^{l \times (n/2)}, \mathbf{H}_V \in \mathbb{F}_2^{m \times (n/2)} (l < m)$ are random, distinguish $\mathbf{H}_{pk} \triangleq \mathbf{S}\mathbf{H}_{sk}\mathbf{P}$ from a random matrix $\mathbf{H}_{rand} \in \mathbb{F}_2^{m \times n}$.

Remark 4. The notations above such that $\mathbf{H}_{pk}$ and $\mathbf{H}_{sk}$ imply that $\mathbf{H}_{pk}$ is used as a public key and $\mathbf{H}_{sk}$ is used as a secret key.

Also, we define a normalized generalized (U,U+V)-code as

$$\{(\mathbf{a} \odot \mathbf{u} + \mathbf{b} \odot \mathbf{v}, \mathbf{c} \odot \mathbf{u} + \mathbf{d} \odot \mathbf{v}) : \mathbf{u} \in U, \mathbf{v} \in V\}$$

where $\mathbf{a}, \mathbf{b}, \mathbf{c}$ and $\mathbf{d} \in \mathbb{F}_q^{n/2}$ are some random vectors which satisfy the following conditions:

$$\forall i \in \{1, \ldots, n/2\}, \quad and \quad a_i c_i \neq 0 \quad a_i d_i - b_i c_i = 1.$$

The normalized generalized (U,U+V)-code problem is defined as deciding whether a certain linear code is a permuted normalized generalized (U,U+V)-code or a random code.

This problem is equivalent to the following problem in the light of a parity check matrix.

Problem 2 (The normalized generalized (U,U+V)-code problem). Let n be an even integer and let $\mathbf{a}, \mathbf{b}, \mathbf{c}$ and $\mathbf{d} \in \mathbb{F}_q^{n/2}$ be some random vectors which satisfy the following conditions:

$$\forall i \in \{1, \ldots, n/2\}, \quad and \quad a_i c_i \neq 0 \quad a_i d_i - b_i c_i = 1.$$

In addition, we take $\mathbf{H}_U \in \mathbb{F}_q^{l \times (n/2)}$ and $\mathbf{H}_V \in \mathbb{F}_q^{m \times (n/2)}$ at random and define $\mathbf{H}_{sk} \in \mathbb{F}_q^{m \times n}$ as follows:

$$\mathbf{H}_{sk} \triangleq \begin{pmatrix} \mathbf{H}_U \mathbf{D} & -\mathbf{H}_U \mathbf{B} \\ -\mathbf{H}_V \mathbf{C} & \mathbf{H}_V \mathbf{A} \end{pmatrix}$$

where $\mathbf{A} \triangleq \mathbf{Diag}(\mathbf{a}), \mathbf{B} \triangleq \mathbf{Diag}(\mathbf{b}), \mathbf{C} \triangleq \mathbf{Diag}(\mathbf{c})$, and $\mathbf{D} \triangleq \mathbf{Diag}(\mathbf{d})$.

Then for a random non-singular matrix $\mathbf{S} \in \mathbb{F}_q^{m \times m}$ and a random permutation matrix $\mathbf{P} \in \mathbb{F}_q^{n \times n}$, distinguish $\mathbf{H}_{pk} \triangleq \mathbf{S}\mathbf{H}_{sk}\mathbf{P} \in \mathbb{F}_q^{m \times n}$ from a random matrix $\mathbf{H}_{rand} \in \mathbb{F}_q^{m \times n}$.

3 Gramian

We define a notion of the Gramian and prove some useful properties. In this section, K denotes $\mathbb{F}_2$ or $\mathbb{F}_3$.

3.1 Basic Formulae

Definition 1. *Given* $\mathbf{H} \in \mathbb{F}_q^{m \times n}$, *the Gramian (the determinant of Gram matrix) of* $\mathbf{H}$ *is defined by* $\det(\mathbf{H}\mathbf{H}^t)$.

Lemma 1. *For any non-singular matrix* $\mathbf{S} \in K^{n \times n}$, *the Gramian of* $\mathbf{S}$ *equals to* 1.

Proof. When $K = \mathbb{F}_2$, $\det(\mathbf{S}) = 1$. When $K = \mathbb{F}_3$, $\det(\mathbf{S}) = 1$ or -1. In any case, we obtain $\det(\mathbf{S}\mathbf{S}^t) = \det(\mathbf{S})^2 = 1$ by Remark 3.

Remark 5. In case of K is not $\mathbb{F}_2$ or $\mathbb{F}_3$, this lemma does not hold.

Theorem 1. *Suppose that* $\mathbf{S} \in K^{m \times m}, \mathbf{H}_{sk} \in K^{m \times n}, \mathbf{P} \in K^{n \times n}$, *and* $\mathbf{H}_{pk} \triangleq \mathbf{S}\mathbf{H}_{sk}\mathbf{P}$, *where* $\mathbf{S}$ *is a non-singular matrix and* $\mathbf{P}$ *is a permutation matrix. Then we have*

$$\det(\mathbf{H}_{pk}\mathbf{H}_{pk}^t) = \det(\mathbf{H}_{sk}\mathbf{H}_{sk}^t).$$

Proof. By Remark 2, Lemma 1 and a well-known fact that $\mathbf{P}\mathbf{P}^t = \mathbf{I}$ for any permutation matrix $\mathbf{P}$, we can obtain:

$$\begin{aligned} \det(\mathbf{H}_{pk}\mathbf{H}_{pk}^t) &= \det((\mathbf{S}\mathbf{H}_{sk}\mathbf{P})(\mathbf{P}^t\mathbf{H}_{sk}^t\mathbf{S}^t)) \\ &= \det(\mathbf{S}\mathbf{H}_{sk}(\mathbf{P}\mathbf{P}^t)\mathbf{H}_{sk}^t\mathbf{S}^t) \\ &= \det(\mathbf{S})\det(\mathbf{H}_{sk}\mathbf{H}_{sk}^t)\det(\mathbf{S}^t) \\ &= \det(\mathbf{S}\mathbf{S}^t)\det(\mathbf{H}_{sk}\mathbf{H}_{sk}^t) \\ &= \det(\mathbf{H}_{sk}\mathbf{H}_{sk}^t). \end{aligned}$$

We also have the following theorem:

Theorem 2. *Let the notations be the same as above, then we have*

$$\mathrm{rank}(\mathbf{H}_{pk}\mathbf{H}_{pk}^t) = \mathrm{rank}(\mathbf{H}_{sk}\mathbf{H}_{sk}^t).$$

Proof. By Remark 1, we can obtain as above:

$$\begin{aligned}\mathrm{rank}(\mathbf{H}_{pk}\mathbf{H}_{pk}^t) &= \mathrm{rank}((\mathbf{S}\mathbf{H}_{sk}\mathbf{P})(\mathbf{P}^t\mathbf{H}_{sk}^t\mathbf{S}^t)) \\ &= \mathrm{rank}(\mathbf{S}\mathbf{H}_{sk}(\mathbf{P}\mathbf{P}^t)\mathbf{H}_{sk}^t\mathbf{S}^t) \\ &= \mathrm{rank}(\mathbf{S}(\mathbf{H}_{sk}\mathbf{H}_{sk}^t)\mathbf{S}^t) \\ &= \mathrm{rank}(\mathbf{H}_{sk}\mathbf{H}_{sk}^t).\end{aligned}$$

3.2 Distribution of Gramian

As far as we know, the distribution of the Gramian of random matrices is not studied adequately. Here we show an asymptotic analysis over $\mathbb{F}_2$ as follows:

Theorem 3. *For a random matrix $\mathbf{A} \in \mathbb{F}_2^{m\times n}$, the probability that the Gramian of A equals to 1 approaches the following proportion asymptotically as n increases:*

$$\Pr\left[\det(\mathbf{A}\mathbf{A}^t) = 1\right] \xrightarrow[n\to\infty]{} \left(1-\frac{1}{2}\right)\left(1-\frac{1}{2^3}\right)\left(1-\frac{1}{2^5}\right)\cdots\left(1-\frac{1}{2^{\ m \text{ or } m-1}}\right).$$

Proof. We prove this theorem by demonstrating that $\mathbf{A}\mathbf{A}^t$ approaches a random symmetric matrix asymptotically. In this proof, vectors are column notation. We can write

$$\mathbf{A} = \begin{pmatrix}\mathbf{v}_1 \\ \vdots \\ \mathbf{v}_m\end{pmatrix}$$

where $\mathbf{v}_1, \cdots, \mathbf{v}_m \in \mathbb{F}_2^n$ and

$$\det(\mathbf{A}\mathbf{A}^t) = \det\begin{pmatrix}(\mathbf{v}_1,\mathbf{v}_1) & (\mathbf{v}_1,\mathbf{v}_2) & \cdots & (\mathbf{v}_1,\mathbf{v}_m) \\ (\mathbf{v}_2,\mathbf{v}_1) & (\mathbf{v}_2,\mathbf{v}_2) & \cdots & (\mathbf{v}_2,\mathbf{v}_m) \\ \vdots & & & \\ (\mathbf{v}_m,\mathbf{v}_1) & (\mathbf{v}_m,\mathbf{v}_2) & \cdots & (\mathbf{v}_m,\mathbf{v}_m)\end{pmatrix}.$$

First, we prove the following lemma:

Lemma 2. *For arbitarary $i, j \in \{1, \ldots, m\}$,*

$$\Pr\left[(\mathbf{v}_i,\mathbf{v}_j) = 1\right] = \begin{cases}\dfrac{1}{2} & i = j \\ \dfrac{1}{2} - \dfrac{1}{2^{n+1}} & i \neq j\end{cases}$$

Proof. When $i = j$, it is easy to show that $(\mathbf{v}_i, \mathbf{v}_i) = |\mathbf{v}_i| \mod 2$. Then we obtain:

$$\begin{aligned}
\Pr[(\mathbf{v}_i, \mathbf{v}_i) = 1] &= \frac{\{\mathbf{v}_i : |\mathbf{v}_i| = 1 \mod 2\}}{2^n} \\
&= \frac{\sum_{\text{i : odd number}} \binom{n}{i}}{2^n} \\
&= \frac{2^{n-1}}{2^n} \\
&= \frac{1}{2}.
\end{aligned}$$

When $i \neq j$, we divide the problem into whether $\mathbf{v}_i = \mathbf{0}$ or $\mathbf{v}_i \neq \mathbf{0}$. In the former case, $(\mathbf{v}_i, \mathbf{v}_j)$ definitely equals to 0. In the latter case, the elements of $\mathbf{v}_i$ contains at least one 1 and let such a set of indices of $\mathbf{v}_i$ be Λ. Then we have $(\mathbf{v}_i, \mathbf{v}_j) = |\mathbf{v}_{j\Lambda}|$ where $\mathbf{v}_{j\Lambda}$ denotes a vector whose elements are $\mathbf{v}_j$ on Λ. Therefore for a certain $\mathbf{v}_i \neq \mathbf{0}$ and λ which denotes the number of elements of Λ,

$$\begin{aligned}
\Pr[(\mathbf{v}_i, \mathbf{v}_j) = 1] &= \frac{\{\mathbf{v}_{j\Lambda} : |\mathbf{v}_{j\Lambda}| = 1 \mod 2\}}{2^\lambda} \\
&= \frac{\sum_{\text{i : odd number}} \binom{\lambda}{i}}{2^\lambda} \\
&= \frac{2^{\lambda-1}}{2^\lambda} \\
&= \frac{1}{2}.
\end{aligned}$$

Hence we obtain:

$$\begin{aligned}
\Pr[(\mathbf{v}_i, \mathbf{v}_j) = 1] &= \Pr[\mathbf{v}_i \neq \mathbf{0}] \cdot \frac{1}{2} \\
&= (1 - \frac{1}{2^n}) \cdot \frac{1}{2} \\
&= \frac{1}{2} - \frac{1}{2^{n+1}}.
\end{aligned}$$

□

By this lemma, all of the elements of $\mathbf{AA}^t$ approach to $\frac{1}{2}$ asymptotically as n increases.

Second, we consider the independence of the elements. Here we remark on their pairwise independence. Without loss of generality, we would like to prove the following three patterns where i, j, k are different indices:

$$\Pr[(v_i,v_i)=1\cap(v_j,v_j)=1]\xrightarrow[n\to\infty]{}\Pr[(v_i,v_i)=1]\cdot\Pr[(v_j,v_j)=1] \quad (1)$$
$$\Pr[(v_i,v_i)=1\cap(v_i,v_j)=1]\xrightarrow[n\to\infty]{}\Pr[(v_i,v_i)=1]\cdot\Pr[(v_i,v_j)=1] \quad (2)$$
$$\Pr[(v_i,v_j)=1\cap(v_i,v_k)=1]\xrightarrow[n\to\infty]{}\Pr[(v_i,v_j)=1]\cdot\Pr[(v_i,v_k)=1]. \quad (3)$$

By the above lemma, the right sides of (1) to (3) approach $\frac{1}{4}$ asymptotically. We can check easily the left side of (1) equals $\frac{1}{4}$. As for (2), we have v_i has odd number 1s from the first condition of the left side. From the second condition, the probability of $(v_i,v_j)=1$ is $\frac{1}{2}$, so the left side probability equals to $\frac{1}{4}$. As for (3), considering the above lemma as well, we obtain the left side probability equals to $\frac{1}{4}(1-\frac{1}{2^n})$.

Finally, we refer to a kind of counting symmetric matrices theorem. MacWilliams showed the following [12]:

Theorem 4. *Let $N(t,r)$ denote the number of symmetric matrices of size $t\times t$, rank r, with entries in a finite field $GF(q)$, $q=p^n$.*

$$N(t,2s)=\prod_{i=1}^{s}\frac{q^{2i}}{q^{2i}-1}\cdot\prod_{i=0}^{2s-1}(q^{t-i}-1) \qquad (2s\le t),$$
$$N(t,2s+1)=\prod_{i=1}^{s}\frac{q^{2i}}{q^{2i}-1}\cdot\prod_{i=0}^{2s}(q^{t-i}-1) \qquad (2s+1\le t).$$

By this theorem,

$$\begin{aligned}
&\Pr\left[\det(\mathbf{X})=1 \mid \mathbf{X}\in\mathbb{F}_2^{2s\times 2s}\text{ is symmetric matrix}\right]\\
&=\frac{N(2s,2s)}{2\cdot 2^2\cdot\dots\cdot 2^{2s-1}\cdot 2^{2s}}\\
&=\frac{2^2\cdot 2^4\cdot\dots\cdot 2^{2s-2}\cdot 2^{2s}}{(2^2--1)(2^4--1)(2^{2s-2}-1)(2^{2s}-1)}\\
&\quad\cdot\frac{(2^{2s}-1)(2^{2s-1}-1)\cdots(2^2--1)(2--1)}{2\cdot 2^2\cdot\dots\cdot 2^{2s-1}\cdot 2^{2s}}\\
&=\frac{(2^{2s-1}-1)(2^{2s-3}-1)\cdots(2^3--1)(2--1)}{2^{2s-1}\cdot 2^{2s-3}\cdot\dots\cdot 2^3\cdot 2}\\
&=\left(1-\frac{1}{2}\right)\left(1-\frac{1}{2^3}\right)\cdots\left(1-\frac{1}{2^{2s-3}}\right)\left(1-\frac{1}{2^{2s-1}}\right),
\end{aligned}$$

and we obtain the following equation as well:

$$\begin{aligned}
&\Pr\left[\det(\mathbf{X})=1 \mid \mathbf{X}\in\mathbb{F}_2^{2s+1\times 2s+1}\text{ is symmetric matrix}\right]\\
&=\left(1-\frac{1}{2}\right)\left(1-\frac{1}{2^3}\right)\cdots\left(1-\frac{1}{2^{2s-1}}\right)\left(1-\frac{1}{2^{2s+1}}\right).
\end{aligned}$$

This concludes the proof.

We would also like to mention the well-known theorem as follows:

Theorem 5.

$$|\{\mathbf{X} \in \mathbb{F}_q^{m\times m} \mid \mathbf{X} \textit{ is invertible}\}| = (q^m - q^{m-1}) \cdots (q^m - 1).$$

By this theorem, for $\mathbf{A} \in \mathbb{F}_2^{m\times m}$, the probability distribution of the Gramian of A equals to the following proportion:

$$\begin{aligned}\Pr\left[\det(\mathbf{A}\mathbf{A}^t) = 1\right] &= \Pr\left[\det(\mathbf{A}) = 1\right] \\ &= \frac{(2^m - 2^{m-1})\cdots(2^m - 1)}{(2^m)^m} \\ &= \left(1 - \frac{1}{2}\right)\left(1 - \frac{1}{2^2}\right)\cdots\left(1 - \frac{1}{2^m}\right).\end{aligned}$$

Let $G(m,n)$ be $\Pr\left[\det(\mathbf{A}\mathbf{A}^t) = 1 | \mathbf{A} \in \mathbb{F}_q^{m\times n}\right]$. We conduct some experiments in order to estimate $G(10,n)$ for $n = 10, 12, 14, 16, 18$ and $G(100,n)$ for $n = 100, 102, 104, 106, 108$. We compute the average of the determinants of one million random matrices for each (m,n).

The results of Table 1 and Fig. 1 for $G(10,n)$ and of Table 2 and Fig. 2 for $G(100,n)$ are on the next page. It shows that they converge to around 0.42 quickly. We use these results in the following section.

Table 1. $G(10,n)$

N	10	12	14	16	18	∞
Theoretic	0.28907	-	-	-	-	0.41969
Experimental	0.28907	0.38533	0.41099	0.41751	0.41915	-

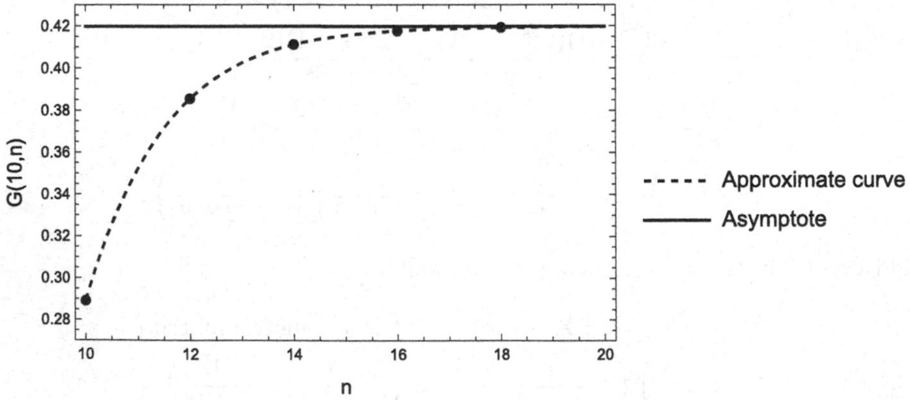

Fig. 1. $G(10,n)$

Table 2. $G(100, n)$

N	100	102	104	106	108	∞
Theoretic	0.28878	–	–	–	–	0.41942
Experimental	0.28878	0.38505	0.41072	0.41724	0.41887	–

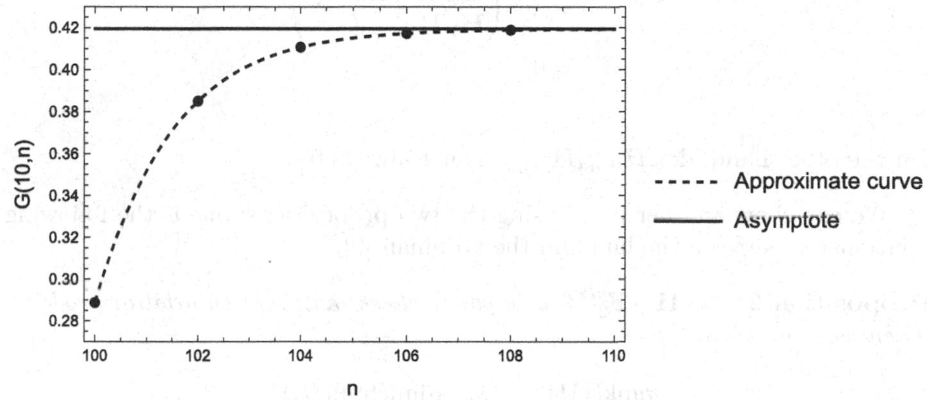

Fig. 2. $G(100, n)$

4 The Plain (U,U+V)-code Problem over $\mathbb{F}_2$.

Debris-Alazard et al. analyze SURF with a notion of the hull [5]. Here, we produce another analysis with the Gramian.

Proposition 1. *For any block matrix* $\mathbf{X} \in \mathbb{F}_q^{(l+m)\times(l+m)}$ *given by*

$$\left(\begin{array}{c|c} \mathbf{A} & \mathbf{B} \\ \hline \mathbf{C} & \mathbf{O} \end{array}\right)$$

where $\mathbf{A} \in \mathbb{F}_q^{l\times l}, \mathbf{B} \in \mathbb{F}_q^{l\times m}$ *and* $\mathbf{C} \in \mathbb{F}_q^{m\times l}$, $\det(\mathbf{X})$ *equals to* 0 *in case of* $l < m$.

Proof. By the pigeonhole principle, for any $\sigma \in S_{l+m}$, $\{\sigma(l+1), \ldots, \sigma(l+m)\}$ contains at least one element of $\{l+1, \ldots, l+m\}$. For such an element $\sigma(i)$, we have $x_{i,\sigma(i)} = 0$. Hence, the definition of the determinant shows that all additive terms in the expansion of $\det(\mathbf{X})$ equal 0, and the sum of those is as well.

Theorem 6. *There exists an algorithm that solves the plain (U,U+V)-code problem in polynomial time.*

Proof. By Theorem 1 and Proposition 1, we have

$$\begin{aligned}\det(\mathbf{H}_{pk}\mathbf{H}_{pk}^t) &= \det(\mathbf{H}_{sk}\mathbf{H}_{sk}^t)\\ &= \det\left(\begin{pmatrix}\mathbf{H}_U & \mathbf{O}\\ \mathbf{H}_V & \mathbf{H}_V\end{pmatrix}\begin{pmatrix}\mathbf{H}_U^t & \mathbf{H}_V^t\\ \mathbf{O} & \mathbf{H}_V^t\end{pmatrix}\right)\\ &= \det\begin{pmatrix}\mathbf{H}_U\mathbf{H}_U^t & \mathbf{H}_U\mathbf{H}_V^t\\ \mathbf{H}_V\mathbf{H}_U^t & \mathbf{O}\end{pmatrix}\\ &= 0.\end{aligned}$$

On the other hand, $\det(\mathbf{H}_{rand}\mathbf{H}_{rand}^t)$ is not always 0.

We can show another proof using the two propositions: one is the following relationship between the hull and the Gramian [9].

Proposition 2. *Let* $\mathbf{H} \in \mathbb{F}_2^{m\times n}$ *be a parity check matrix of an arbitrary code* C. *Then we can obtain:*

$$\mathrm{rank}(\mathbf{H}\mathbf{H}^t) = m - \dim(\mathrm{hull}(C)).$$

The other is the proposition of the original analysis of SURF [5]:

Proposition 3. *For* $\mathbf{H}_U \in \mathbb{F}_2^{l\times(n/2)}$ *and* $\mathbf{H}_V \in \mathbb{F}_2^{m\times(n/2)}$, *let* $\mathbf{H}_{sk} \in \mathbb{F}_2^{m\times n}$ *be same as problem 1 and* $l \leq m$. *If* $\mathbf{H}_{sk}$ *is a parity check matrix of an arbitrary code* C, *then we have with probability* $1 - O(2^{l-m})$

$$\dim(\mathrm{hull}(C)) = m - l.$$

Proof (Theorem 6) By Theorem 2 and the two propositions above, we have

$$\begin{aligned}\mathrm{rank}(\mathbf{H}_{pk}\mathbf{H}_{pk}^t) &= \mathrm{rank}(\mathbf{H}_{sk}\mathbf{H}_{sk}^t)\\ &= m - \dim(\mathrm{hull}(C))\\ &= l \quad < m.\end{aligned}$$

Then we have $\det(\mathbf{H}_{pk}\mathbf{H}_{pk}^t) = 0$.

5 The Normalized Generalized (U,U+V)-code Problem over $\mathbb{F}_2$

In the binary case ($q = 2$), since $a_i c_i \neq 0$, we obtain $a_i = 1$ and $c_i = 1$ and $d_i - b_i = 1$. Thus, we have $\mathbf{A} = \mathbf{C} = \mathbf{I}$ and $\mathbf{B} + \mathbf{D} = \mathbf{I}$. In addition, since $\mathbf{B}$ and $\mathbf{D}$ are binary diagonal matrices, we also have $\mathbf{B}^2 = \mathbf{B}$ and $\mathbf{D}^2 = \mathbf{D}$. Hence, we obtain:

$$\begin{aligned}\det(\mathbf{H}_{pk}\mathbf{H}_{pk}^t) &= \det(\mathbf{H}_{sk}\mathbf{H}_{sk}^t)\\ &= \det\left(\begin{pmatrix}\mathbf{H}_U\mathbf{D} & \mathbf{H}_U\mathbf{B}\\ \mathbf{H}_V & \mathbf{H}_V\end{pmatrix}\begin{pmatrix}\mathbf{D}\mathbf{H}_U^t & \mathbf{H}_V^t\\ \mathbf{B}\mathbf{H}_U^t & \mathbf{H}_V^t\end{pmatrix}\right)\\ &= \det\begin{pmatrix}\mathbf{H}_U(\mathbf{D}+\mathbf{B})\mathbf{H}_U^t & \mathbf{H}_U(\mathbf{D}+\mathbf{B})\mathbf{H}_V^t\\ \mathbf{H}_V(\mathbf{D}+\mathbf{B})\mathbf{H}_U^t & \mathbf{O}\end{pmatrix}\\ &= \det\begin{pmatrix}\mathbf{H}_U\mathbf{H}_U^t & \mathbf{H}_U\mathbf{H}_V^t\\ \mathbf{H}_V\mathbf{H}_U^t & \mathbf{O}\end{pmatrix}\\ &= 0.\end{aligned}$$

Therefore, we reach the following theorem by Theorem 6:

Theorem 7. *There exists an algorithm that solves the normalized generalized (U,U+V)-code problem over $\mathbb{F}_2$ in polynomial time.*

6 Ternary Case

The security proof of Wave depends on two problems [6]. One is DOOM (Decoding One Out of Many) and the other is the normalized generalized (U,U+V)-code problem over $\mathbb{F}_3$. Our analysis with the Gramian does not seem to be efficient as the previous section, since the determinant does not vanish and even four secret variables $\mathbf{A}, \mathbf{B}, \mathbf{C}$, and $\mathbf{D}$ remain as follows:

$$\begin{aligned}\det(\mathbf{H}_{pk}\mathbf{H}_{pk}^t) &= \det(\mathbf{H}_{sk}\mathbf{H}_{sk}^t)\\ &= \det\left(\begin{pmatrix}\mathbf{H}_U\mathbf{D} & -\mathbf{H}_U\mathbf{B}\\ -\mathbf{H}_V\mathbf{C} & \mathbf{H}_V\mathbf{A}\end{pmatrix}\begin{pmatrix}\mathbf{D}\mathbf{H}_U^t & -\mathbf{C}\mathbf{H}_V^t\\ -\mathbf{B}\mathbf{H}_U^t & \mathbf{A}\mathbf{H}_V^t\end{pmatrix}\right)\\ &= \det\begin{pmatrix}\mathbf{H}_U(\mathbf{D}^2+\mathbf{B}^2)\mathbf{H}_U^t & -\mathbf{H}_U(\mathbf{A}\mathbf{B}+\mathbf{C}\mathbf{D})\mathbf{H}_V^t\\ -\mathbf{H}_V(\mathbf{A}\mathbf{B}+\mathbf{C}\mathbf{D})\mathbf{H}_U^t & \mathbf{H}_V(\mathbf{A}^2+\mathbf{C}^2)\mathbf{H}_V^t\end{pmatrix}.\end{aligned}$$

If we can reduce the number of secret variables, then we could reduce the number of secret keys. We can transform this into a simpler one by the following theorem:

Theorem 8. *Let a matrix $\boldsymbol{\Delta}$ be $-(\mathbf{AB}+\mathbf{CD})$. Then we obtain:*

$$\det(\mathbf{H}_{pk}\mathbf{H}_{pk}^t) = \det\begin{pmatrix}-\mathbf{H}_U(\boldsymbol{\Delta}^2+\mathbf{I})\mathbf{H}_U^t & \mathbf{H}_U\boldsymbol{\Delta}\mathbf{H}_V^t\\ \mathbf{H}_V\boldsymbol{\Delta}\mathbf{H}_U^t & -\mathbf{H}_V\mathbf{H}_V^t\end{pmatrix}.$$

Proof. In the ternary case ($q = 3$), among all $81 (= 3^4)$ tuples of (a_i, b_i, c_i, d_i), there are only 12 tuples which satisfies $a_i c_i \neq 0$ and $a_i d_i - b_i c_i = 1$. Table 3 shows these tuples and additional 3 values corresponding to $\mathbf{A}^2+\mathbf{C}^2$, $\mathbf{AB}+\mathbf{CD}$ and $\mathbf{D}^2+\mathbf{B}^2$.

From this table, we can easily check $a_i^2+c_i^2 = -1$ and $-(-(a_i b_i + c_i d_i))^2 - 1 = b_i^2 + d_i^2$. Hence we can obtain $\mathbf{A}^2+\mathbf{C}^2 = -\mathbf{I}$ and $-\boldsymbol{\Delta}^2 - \mathbf{I} = \mathbf{D}^2+\mathbf{B}^2$, then this concludes the proof.

Table 3. Tuples of (a_i, b_i, c_i, d_i)

a_i	b_i	c_i	d_i	$a_i^2 + c_i^2$	$-(a_i b_i + c_i d_i)$	$b_i^2 + d_i^2$
1	0	1	1	-1	-1	1
1	1	1	-1	-1	0	-1
1	-1	1	0	-1	1	1
1	0	-1	1	-1	1	1
1	1	-1	0	-1	-1	1
1	-1	-1	-1	-1	0	-1
-1	0	1	-1	-1	1	1
-1	1	1	1	-1	0	-1
-1	-1	1	0	-1	-1	1
-1	0	-1	-1	-1	-1	1
-1	1	-1	0	-1	1	1
-1	-1	-1	1	-1	0	-1

By this theorem, we can reduce the number of random variables. However, the Gramian cannot be computed simply. By our analysis with Gramian, SURF is completely broken, however, Wave is not directly threatened.

7 Conclusion

In this work, we have introduced another view on the (U,U+V)-code problem. However, our approaches with the Gramian can be used only over binary or ternary fields, because concerning integer fields larger than 3, the squared determinant of randomizing matrix S does not always vanish. Wave can be instantiated with such large integer fields like $\mathbb{F}_5$ and $\mathbb{F}_7$, so this remains an important problem.

We have shown the distribution of random Gramians only asymptotically. Hence deducing a formula of this value is an open problem. This problem is interesting not only cryptographically. In mathematics, random matrices over $\mathbb{R}$ and $\mathbb{C}$ are studied well whereas those over finite fields are not studied adequately. Therefore our proposed problem is important for mathematics.

Acknowledgements. A part of this work was supported by JST CREST JPMJCR2113 and JSPS KAKENHI JP21H04879.

References

1. Aragon, N., Blazy, O., Gaborit, P., Hauteville, A., Zémor, G.: Durandal: A Rank Metric Based Signature Scheme. In: Ishai, Y., Rijmen, V. (eds.) EUROCRYPT 2019. LNCS, vol. 11478, pp. 728–758. Springer, Cham (2019). https://doi.org/10.1007/978-3-030-17659-4_25

2. Bricout, Rémi., Chailloux, André, Debris-Alazard, Thomas, Lequesne, Matthieu: Ternary Syndrome Decoding with Large Weight. In: Paterson, Kenneth G.., Stebila, Douglas (eds.) SAC 2019. LNCS, vol. 11959, pp. 437–466. Springer, Cham (2020). https://doi.org/10.1007/978-3-030-38471-5_18
3. Courtois, N.T., Finiasz, M., Sendrier, N.: How to Achieve a McEliece-Based Digital Signature Scheme. In: Boyd, C. (ed.) ASIACRYPT 2001. LNCS, vol. 2248, pp. 157–174. Springer, Heidelberg (2001). https://doi.org/10.1007/3-540-45682-1_10
4. Debris-Alazard, T., Sendrier, N., Tillich, J.: A new signature scheme based on (u—u+v) codes. Cryptology ePrint Archive, Paper 2017/662 (2017). https://eprint.iacr.org/2017/662
5. Debris-Alazard, T., Sendrier, N., Tillich, J.: The problem with the surf scheme. https://csrc.nist.gov/projects/post-quantum-cryptography/round-1-submissions (2017). https://csrc.nist.gov/projects/post-quantum-cryptography/round-1-submissions
6. Debris-Alazard, T., Sendrier, N., Tillich, J.-P.: Wave: A New Family of Trapdoor One-Way Preimage Sampleable Functions Based on Codes. In: Galbraith, S.D., Moriai, S. (eds.) ASIACRYPT 2019. LNCS, vol. 11921, pp. 21–51. Springer, Cham (2019). https://doi.org/10.1007/978-3-030-34578-5_2
7. Fukushima, K., Roy, P.S., Xu, R., Kiyomoto, S., Morozov, K., Takagi, T.: Racoss. first round submission to the NIST post-quantum cryptography call (2017). https://eprint.iacr.org/2017/662
8. Gentry, C., Peikert, C., Vaikuntanathan, V.: Trapdoors for hard lattices and new cryptographic constructions. In: Dwork, C. (ed.) In: Proceedings of the 40th Annual ACM Symposium on Theory of Computing, Victoria, British Columbia, Canada, pp. 197–206. ACM (2008)
9. Guenda, K., Jitman, S., Gulliver, T.A.: Constructions of good entanglement-assisted quantum error correcting codes. Des. Codes Cryptogr. **86**(1), 121–136 (2018)
10. Kabatianskii, G.., Krouk, E.., Smeets, B..: A digital signature scheme based on random error-correcting codes. In: Darnell, Michael (ed.) Cryptography and Coding 1997. LNCS, vol. 1355, pp. 161–167. Springer, Heidelberg (1997). https://doi.org/10.1007/BFb0024461
11. Lyubashevsky, V.: Fiat-Shamir with Aborts: Applications to Lattice and Factoring-Based Signatures. In: Matsui, M. (ed.) ASIACRYPT 2009. LNCS, vol. 5912, pp. 598–616. Springer, Heidelberg (2009). https://doi.org/10.1007/978-3-642-10366-7_35
12. MacWilliams, J.: Orthogonal matrices over finite fields. The American Mathematical Monthly 76(2), 152–164 (1969). http://www.jstor.org/stable/2317262
13. Otmani, Ayoub, Tillich, Jean-Pierre.: An Efficient Attack on All Concrete KKS Proposals. In: Yang, Bo-Yin. (ed.) PQCrypto 2011. LNCS, vol. 7071, pp. 98–116. Springer, Heidelberg (2011). https://doi.org/10.1007/978-3-642-25405-5_7
14. Sendrier, Nicolas: Decoding One Out of Many. In: Yang, Bo-Yin. (ed.) PQCrypto 2011. LNCS, vol. 7071, pp. 51–67. Springer, Heidelberg (2011). https://doi.org/10.1007/978-3-642-25405-5_4
15. Wagner, D.: A Generalized Birthday Problem. In: Yung, M. (ed.) CRYPTO 2002. LNCS, vol. 2442, pp. 288–304. Springer, Heidelberg (2002). https://doi.org/10.1007/3-540-45708-9_19

A Message Recovery Attack on LWE/LWR-Based PKE/KEMs Using Amplitude-Modulated EM Emanations

Ruize Wang(✉), Kalle Ngo, and Elena Dubrova

KTH Royal Institute of Technology, Stockholm, Sweden
{ruize,kngo,dubrova}@kth.se

Abstract. Creating a good deep learning model is an art which requires expertise in deep learning and a large set of labeled data for training neural networks. Neither is readily available. In this paper, we introduce a method that enables us to recover messages of LWE/LWR-based PKE/KEMs using simple multilayer perceptron (MLP) models trained on a small dataset. The core idea is to extend the attack dataset so that at least one of its traces has the ground truth label to which the models are biased towards. We demonstrate the effectiveness of the presented method on the examples of CRYSTALS-Kyber and Saber algorithms implemented in ARM Cortex-M4 CPU on nRF52832 system-on-chip supporting Bluetooth 5.2. We use amplitude-modulated EM emanations which are typically weaker and noisier than power or near-field EM side channels, and thus more difficult to exploit.

Keywords: Public-key cryptography · Post-quantum cryptography · CRYSTALS-Kyber · Saber · LWE/LWR-based KEM · Side-channel attack · EM analysis

1 Introduction

Amplitude-modulated electromagnetic (EM) emanations are a type of side channels which occur in mixed-signal chips with an on-board antenna. As a result of various coupling effects, signals from computations in the digital part of the chip may be modulated by the CPU clock signal, leak to the analog part of the chip, modulated again by the radio-frequency block, and eventually transmitted by the antenna.

Side-channel attacks based on amplitude-modulated EM emanations are more stealthy than power or near-field EM attacks because the signal transmitted by the on-chip antenna escapes hardware-level countermeasures like decoupling capacitors (used to smooth sharp changes in power supply voltage) and Faraday shields (used to block EM fields). Furthermore, since amplitude-modulated EM emanations are intertwined into the carrier signal, they can be captured at a considerably farther distance than the near-field EM side channels. For example, in [6], a successful attack on AES on 15 m distance from the device under attack was demonstrated.

S.-H. Seo and H. Seo (Eds.): ICISC 2022, LNCS 13849, pp. 450–471, 2023.
https://doi.org/10.1007/978-3-031-29371-9_22

However, amplitude-modulated EM emanations are weaker and typically noisier than power or near-field EM side channels, and thus more difficult to exploit. They require expensive equipment to capture and typically need post-processing e.g. by averaging multiple repeated measurements to increase the signal-to-noise ratio. For example, 500 and 1000 measurements representing the same encryption were averaged in the attacks on AES presented in [7] and [6], respectively.

Such excessive repetitions are undesirable in profiling deep learning (DL)-based side-channel attacks because they increase the size of training and attack sets by the corresponding factor. While the attack set is typically small, the training set is large. Minimizing the size of the latter is particularly important in the attacks on public key encryption algorithms since, in this case, the device under attack can be used for profiling [17] (since the public key is known). Profiling on the device under attack eliminates the problem of intra-device variability and maximizes the prediction accuracy of DL models. If the size of the secret to be recovered is large, achieving high prediction accuracy is crucial. For example, the messages of CRYSTALS-Kyber, which has been recently selected by the NIST as a new public-key encryption and key-establishment algorithm to be standardized [14], are 256-bit. So, the byte prediction accuracy should be at least 0.98 to ensure $0.98^{32} = 0.52$ message recovery probability. It is very difficult to achieve 0.98 byte prediction accuracy unless the model is trained on traces from the device under attack [17].

However, if attackers wish to use the device under attack for profiling, they face the problem of training DL models on a small dataset, since the access time to the device under attack is typically limited. Training a good model on a small dataset is not easy, especially if the number of classes to be distinguished is large, e.g. 256 classes in a byte classification with one-hot encoding. In such cases, training on a small dataset usually results in biased models which predict different classes non-uniformly. It has been observed that some labels might be strongly preferred [5].

Our contributions: In this paper, we introduce a new message recovery method, called *multi-bit error injection*, that enables us to extract messages of LWE/LWR-based PKE/KEM algorithms from amplitude-modulated EM side channels using biased DL models trained on a small dataset.

To recover the message m encrypted into a ciphertext c, we extend the attack set from a single trace captured with c as input to 256 traces captured with c_e as inputs, for all $e \in \{0, 1, \ldots, 255\}$. The ciphertexts c_e are constructed so that they decrypt to messages m_e in which the error e is injected into each byte of m. The errors are injected using the bit-flipping technique from [21]. By flipping all possible combinations of multiple bits of each byte, we create an attack set in which, for each byte, at least one trace has the ground truth label to which the models are biased towards. This makes it possible to utilize weak and noisy amplitude-modulated EM side channels. In its essence, the multi-bit error injection method converts a traditional non-differential side-channel attack into a differential one, as shown in Fig. 1. Since the attack set is several orders of

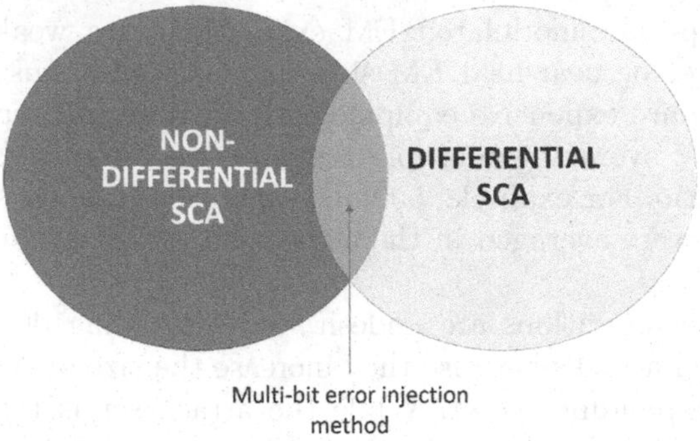

Fig. 1. The proposed multi-bit error injection method converts a non-differential side-channel attack (SCA) into a differential one.

magnitude smaller than the training set, the total number of traces required for a successful attack is minimized. This is important for attacks that do profiling on the device under attack.

We demonstrate the effectiveness of the multi-bit error injection method on the examples of CRYSTALS-Kyber and Saber algorithms implemented in ARM Cortex-M4 CPU on nRF52832 system-on-chip supporting Bluetooth 5.2.

Our experiments show that, for both algorithms, we can recover messages from the profiling device without enumeration. We need enumeration up to 2^{32} to recover messages from a different device.

A successful message recovery trivially implies the session key recovery. Furthermore, by recovering messages for chosen ciphertexts constructed using known methods, e.g. [17,21,22,24], the secret key can be recovered as well. We demonstrate the secret key recovery on the example of Saber.

Paper Organization: The rest of this paper is organized as follows. Section 2 describes previous work related to the side-channel analysis of LWE/LWR-based PKE/KEM algorithms. Section 3 gives background on CRYSTALS-Kyber and Saber algorithms and known vulnerabilities of their implementations. Section 4 presents the experimental setup. Sections 5 and 6 describe how we train neural networks and perform message recovery. Experimental results are summarized in Sect. 7. Section 8 concludes the paper.

2 Previous Work

Since the launch of NIST PQC standardization process in 2016 [19], timing, power and near field EM side-channel attacks on software and hardware implementations of NIST PQC candidates have received considerable attention.

In [25], a message recovery attack using a single power trace from an unprotected encapsulation part of several lattice-based round 3 candidates was presented. In [22], near field EM message recovery attacks on some round 3 candidates were described. In [12], timing attacks were considered.

In [21], near field EM secret key recovery attacks on unprotected implementations of three LWE/LWR-based NIST PQC finalists were presented. It was shown how masked implementations can be broken by attacking each share individually. In [17], message and secret key recovery attacks on a first-order masked implementation of Saber KEM through DL-based power analysis were demonstrated. In this attack, the DL models recover messages directly, without explicitly extracting random masks. In [18], it was shown that it is possible to recover Saber secret key even if masking is complemented with shuffling. In [27], power/near field EM secret key recovery attacks targeting the execution of the re-encryption on some round 3 candidates was described. In [2], side-channel attacks on two implementations of masked polynomial comparison, applied to Kyber, are presented. In [32], secret key recovery attack on a reference implementation of Kyber-512 by simple power analysis with chosen ciphertexts was demonstrated. In [24] another secret key recovery attack on Kyber using near field EM was presented.

The resistance of NIST PQC finalists to amplitude-modulated EM emanations has been investigated much less compared to timing, power and near-field EM side-channels. The first attack on Saber KEM has been presented in [29]. This attack uses the same C implementation of Saber KEM and the same target device as in our experiments. The C implementation is compiled with the optimization level `-O0` (no optimization). Using amplitude-modulated EM emanations during the PKE decryption step of decapsulation, each bit of a message is recovered from the profiling device with probability 0.91 on average. Thus, the probability to recover a complete message is small, only $0.91^{256} = 0.33 \cdot 10^{-12}$. In contrast, for the optimization level `-O0`, the method presented in this paper can recover messages with the probability 1 from the profiling device and with the probability 0.74 from a different device. We also show successful results for `-O3` optimization level (the highest) for both, Saber and CRYSTALS-Kyber algorithms.

The presented method makes use of the bit-flip technique introduced in [21] for breaking implementations of LWE/LWR-based PKE/KEMs protected by the shuffling countermeasure. In [21], single message bits are flipped in order to quantify the effect of the change on the message Hamming weight (HW). The decrease/increase of the HW implies that the original message bit has the value 1/0. Note that the purpose of flipping bits in [21] is quite different from the one in the presented method. We inject multi-bit errors to match the modified message bytes with labels preferred by the DL models.

3 Background

This section briefly CRYSTALS-Kyber and Saber algorithms and vulnerabilities discovered in their implementations so far. More detailed specifications can be found in [23] and [8].

CPA-PKE.KeyGen()

$seed_{\mathbf{A}} \leftarrow \mathcal{U}(\{0,1\}^{256})$

$\mathbf{A} \leftarrow \mathcal{U}(R_q^{l\times l}; seed_{\mathbf{A}})$

$\mathbf{s}, \mathbf{e} \leftarrow \beta_\mu(R_q^{l\times 1})$

$\mathbf{b} = \mathbf{A} \times \mathbf{s} + \mathbf{e}$

return $(pk := (seed_{\mathbf{A}}, \mathbf{b}), sk := \mathbf{s})$

CPA-PKE.Dec($\mathbf{s}, c = (\mathbf{u}, v)$)

$x' = v - \mathbf{s} \times \mathbf{u}$

$m' = \mathsf{decode}(x')$

return m'

CPA-PKE.Enc($pk = (seed_{\mathbf{A}}, \mathbf{b}), m, r$)

$\mathbf{A} \leftarrow \mathcal{U}(R_q^{l\times l}; seed_{\mathbf{A}})$

$\mathbf{s}', \mathbf{e}' \leftarrow \beta_\mu(R_q^{l\times 1}; r)$

$e'' \leftarrow \beta_\mu(R_q^{1\times 1}; r)$

$\mathbf{u} = \mathbf{A} \times \mathbf{s}' + \mathbf{e}'$

$v = \mathbf{b} \times \mathbf{s}' + \mathsf{encode}(m) + e''$

return $c := (\mathbf{u}, v)$

Fig. 2. Pseudocode of CPA-PKE algorithms.

CCA-KEM.KeyGen()

$z \leftarrow \mathcal{U}(\{0,1\}^{256})$

$(pk, \mathbf{s}) =$ CPA-PKE.KeyGen()

$sk = (\mathbf{s}, pk, \mathcal{H}(pk), z)$

return (pk, sk)

CCA-KEM.Encaps(pk)

$m \leftarrow \mathcal{U}(\{0,1\}^{256})$

$m = \mathcal{H}(m)$

$(\hat{K}, r) = \mathcal{G}(m, \mathcal{H}(pk))$

$c =$ CPA-PKE.Enc(pk, m, r)

$K = \mathsf{KDF}(\hat{K}, \mathcal{H}(c))$

return (c, K)

CCA-KEM.Decaps($sk = (\mathbf{s}, pk, \mathcal{H}(pk), z), c$)

$m' =$ CPA-PKE.Dec($\mathbf{s}, c$)

$(\hat{K}', r') = \mathcal{G}(m', \mathcal{H}(pk))$

$c' =$ CPA-PKE.Enc(pk, m', r')

if $c = c'$ **then**

  return $K = \mathsf{KDF}(\hat{K}, \mathcal{H}(c))$

else

  return $K = \mathsf{KDF}(z, \mathcal{H}(c))$

end if

Fig. 3. Pseudocode of CCA-KEM algorithms.

3.1 LWE/LWR Based CCA-secure KEMs

CRYSTALS-Kyber [23] and Saber [8] are CCA-secure key encapsulation mechanisms which apply the Fujisaki-Okamoto transform [9] on CPA-secure public key encryption schemes. The security of CRYSTALS-Kyber relies on the hardness of Module Learning With Error (Mod-LWE) problem. The security of Saber relies on the hardness of (Mod-LWR) problem.

Figure 2 and 3 show pseudocodes of CPA-PKE and CCA-KEM algorithms, respectively. CPA-PKE contains three algorithms: key generation, CPA-PKE.KeyGen; encryption, CPA-PKE.Enc; and decryption, CPA-PKE.Dec. CCA-KEM also contains three algorithms: key generation, CCA-KEM.KeyGen; encapsulation, CCA-KEM.Encaps; and decapsulation, CCA-KEM.Decaps.

Let $\mathbb{Z}_q$ be the ring of integers modulo a positive integer q and R_q be the quotient ring $\mathbb{Z}_q[X]/(X^n + 1)$. Both Saber and Kyber work with vectors of ring elements in R_q^l, where l is an integer representing the security level between 2 and 4. In this paper we focus on the security level $l = 3$

```
void POL2MSG(uint16_t *v, char *m)
for (j = 0; j < BYTES; j++) do
    m[j] = 0;
    for (i = 0; i < 8; i++) do
        m[j] = m[j]|(v[8*j+i]<<i);
    end for
end for
```

```
void poly_tomsg(char *msg, poly *a)
for (i = 0; i < BYTES; i++) do
    msg[i] = 0;
    for (j = 0; j < 8; j++) do
        t=(((a->coeffs[8*i+j]<<1)
          +KYBER_Q/2)/KYBER_Q)&1;
        msg[i] |= t<<j;
    end for
end for
```

Fig. 4. C code of POL2MSG() procedure of Saber.PKE.Dec [1] (left) and poly_tomsg() procedure of Kyber.PKE.Dec [3] (right). The lines marked in red show the location of vulnerabilities. (Color figure online)

The term $x \leftarrow \chi(S)$ denotes sampling x from a distribution χ over a set S. The uniform distribution is denoted by $\mathcal{U}$. The centered binomial distribution with parameter μ is denoted by β_μ. The term $\beta_\mu(R_q^{l\times k}; r)$ induces a matrix in $R_q^{l\times k}$ in which the coefficients of polynomials of R_q are sampled deterministically from β_μ using seed r.

The functions $\mathcal{G}$ and $\mathcal{H}$ are SHA3-512 and SHA3-256 hash functions, respectively. The KDF represents key derivation function. The operation "×" denotes the polynomial multiplication in R_q. The encode function encodes each message byte into a corresponding polynomial coefficient in R_q, while the inverse function decode maps each polynomial coefficient in R_q into a message byte.

3.2 Known Vulnerabilities

Several vulnerabilities have been discovered in the implementations of LWE/LWR-based PKE/KEMs, including incremental storage vulnerability [21], weakness of re-encryption operation in Fujisaki-Okamoto transform [27] and weakness of polynomial multiplication [16]. For CRYSTALS-Kyber, secret key information has also been extracted through Barrentt reduction procedure [15,26].

The previous amplitude-modulated EM emanation-based side channel attack presented in [29] exploited the vulnerability of POL2MSG() message packing procedure of the Saber implementation [1] shown in Fig. 4 to recover messages with the average bit accuracy of 0.91. This accuracy is not sufficient to extract complete messages with a high probability.

In this paper, we show that the same vulnerability can be exploited more effectively with the help of the new message recovery method. To demonstrate the generality of the method, we also apply it to CRYSTALS-Kyber. Figure 4 shows the location of vulnerability in the poly_tomsg() message packing procedure of the CRYSTALS-Kyber implementation [3] which we exploit.

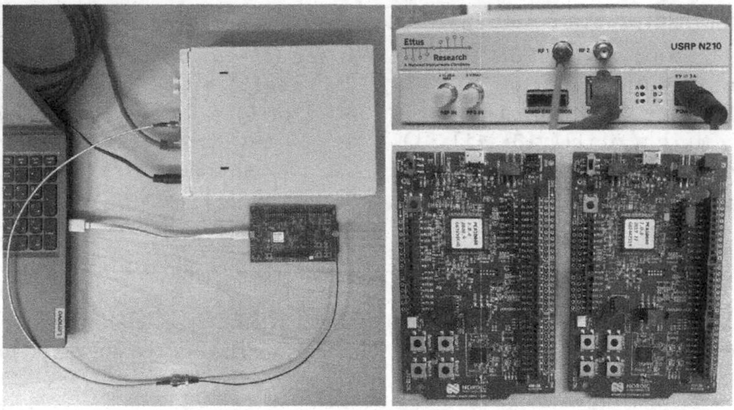

Fig. 5. Equipment for acquiring amplitude-modulated EM emissions.

4 Trace Acquisition

This section describes how we capture amplitude-modulated EM emanations, pre-process resulting traces, and select intervals of interest.

4.1 Experimental Setup

The equipment used in our experiments is shown in Fig. 5. The target device is an nRF52832 chip mounted on a Nordic Semiconductors nRF52 DK development board. The chip supports Bluetooth 5.2 with a data transmission rate of 2Mbps. The option `nRF5_SDK_14.2.0_17b948a` is used for the radio setup.

The 32-bits ARM Cortex-M4 CPU contained in nRF52832 is programmed to the C implementation of Saber from [1] and CRYSTALS-Kyber from [3] without any countermeasures against power/EM analysis. The C implementations are complied using `gcc-arm-none-eabi-8-2018-q4-major` with two different optimization options: `-O0` (no optimization) and `-O3` (the highest). The CPU runs at 64MHz.

The receiver is an Ettus Research USRP N210 software defined radio (SDR). The center receiving frequency is set to $2f_{clock} + f_{\text{Bluetooth}} = 2.528\text{GHz}$, where $f_{\text{Bluetooth}} = 2.4\text{GHz}$ is the Bluetooth channel center frequency and $f_{clock} =$ 64MHz is the frequency of the CPU clock.

The signals are sampled with the sampling frequency of 25MHz, which is the maximum sampling frequency of USRP N210 SDR 25MHz (limited by interface). This implies that we sample $25/64 = 0.39$ points per clock cycle. The signals are transmitted from the target device to the receiver through an SMA coaxial cable.

Note that, in order to make a fair comparison with the amplitude modulated EM-based side-channel attack on Saber from [29], we use the same target device, the same equipment for trace acquisition, and the same implementation of Saber as in [29]. In this way, we can demonstrate that the improvement in the success probability is due to the new method for message recovery rather than other factors. Also note that the implementation of Saber [1] used in the attack of [29] is not the latest version any longer. In the latest version [13], `POL2MSG()` procedure is called `POLmsg2BS()`. The presented message recovery method is equally applicable to the latest version because `POLmsg2BS()` also has a vulnerability, as shown in [20].

4.2 Trace Pre-processing

Amplitude-modulated EM emanations are very noisy and thus need to be pre-processed to increase the signal-to-noise (SNR) ratio. Similarly to [29], we pre-process all traces by averaging 100 repeated measurements. This improves the SNR by a factor of ten, $\sqrt{100} = 10$.

In our experiments, we carry out the attacks on both, the profiling device and a different device, shown in Fig. 5. To reduce the negative effect of intra-device variability in the latter case, we apply two scaling methods: *min-max scaling* and *standardization* (also known as *variance scaling* [33]).

Let $\mathbb{R}$ denote the set of real numbers. Given a set of traces $\boldsymbol{\mathcal{T}}$ with elements of type $\mathcal{T} = (\tau_1, \ldots, \tau_w) \in \mathbb{R}^w$, each trace $\mathcal{T} \in \boldsymbol{\mathcal{T}}$ is scaled to $\mathcal{T}' = (\tau'_1, \ldots, \tau'_w) \in \mathbb{R}^w$ such that

$$\tau'_i = \begin{cases} \dfrac{\tau_i - \tau_{min}}{\tau_{min} - \tau_{max}}, & \text{for min-max scaling} \\[2ex] \dfrac{\tau_i - \mu_i}{\sigma_i}, & \text{for standardization,} \end{cases}$$

where τ_{min} and τ_{max} are the minimum and the maximum data points in $\mathcal{T}$, and μ_i and σ_i are the mean and standard deviation of traces in $\boldsymbol{\mathcal{T}}$ at the ith trace point, for all $i \in \{1, \ldots, w\}$.

4.3 Selecting Intervals of Interest

To exploit the vulnerability of `POL2MSG()` procedure of Saber, we first locate the part of traces representing the execution of `POL2MSG()` during the decapsulation of the message. The message is computed at the step 1 of CCA-KEM.Decaps() in Fig. 3, when the ciphertext c is decrypted by CPA-PKE.Dec().

According to the C implementation of `POL2MSG()` shown in Fig. 4, we expect to see 32 similarly looking patterns representing the packing of each block of eight message bits into a byte. The top part of Fig. 6(a) shows a segment of trace containing `POL2MSG()` procedures. The top part of Fig. 6(b) shows a zoomed-in view of the first four message bytes in `POL2MSG()`.

Once the approximate position of `POL2MSG()` is determined, the precise intervals are located by test vector leakage assessment (TVLA) method [11], which applies Welch's t-test [31] to compare the means of two sets of measurements. For each byte $i \in \{0, 1 \ldots, 31\}$, we partition the measurements $\boldsymbol{\mathcal{T}}$ into two sets, $\boldsymbol{\mathcal{T}}_0$

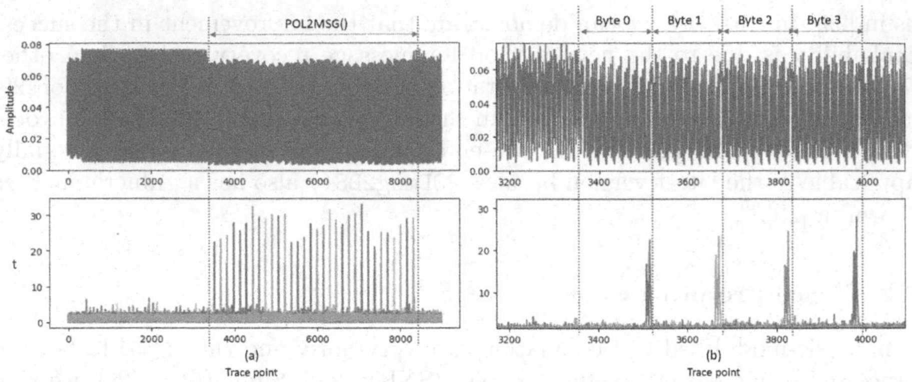

Fig. 6. (a) A trace representing the execution of `POL2MSG()` procedure of Saber (top) and t-test results for 32 message bytes (bottom) for 30K traces; (b) A zoomed-in view on the first four message bytes of `POL2MSG()`.

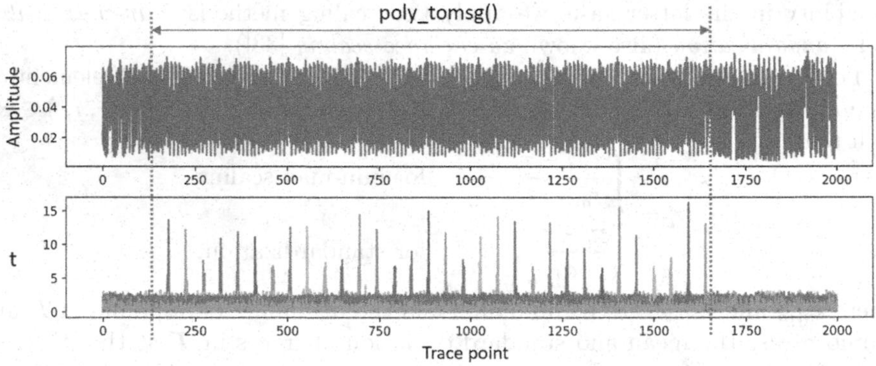

Fig. 7. A trace representing the execution of `poly_tomsg()` procedure of CRYSTALS-Kyber (top) and t-test results for 32 message bytes (bottom) for 30K traces.

and $\boldsymbol{\mathcal{T}}_1$, containing traces in which the message byte, $m_j[i]$, has a value smaller than 128, or larger than 128, respectively:

$$\boldsymbol{\mathcal{T}}_0 = \{\mathcal{T}_j \in \boldsymbol{\mathcal{T}} \mid m_j[i] < 128\},$$
$$\boldsymbol{\mathcal{T}}_1 = \{\mathcal{T}_j \in \boldsymbol{\mathcal{T}} \mid m_j[i] > 128\},$$

for all $j \in \{1, \ldots, |\boldsymbol{\mathcal{T}}|\}$, where $m_j[i]$ is ith byte of the message m in trace $\mathcal{T}_j$.

The bottom part of Fig. 6(a) shows the results of the t-test carried out on a set of 30K traces with random messages and random keys. Each trace in the set is an average of 100 repeated measurements. We can clearly see 32 peaks corresponding to the processing of 32 message bytes by `POL2MSG()` procedure.

In the zoomed-in view of Fig. 6(b) bottom, we can see that the t-test peaks are located at the end of the interval of the corresponding byte. This is expected since, according to the implementation of `POL2MSG()`, the packed message byte is stored in memory after the inner `for`-loop is completed (see line 4 of `POL2MSG()` in Fig. 4). The intervals of traces denoted by "Byte 0" etc. in Fig 6(b) are used for training of the neural networks at the profiling stage.

The selection of the intervals of interest for CRYSTALS-Kyber is done similarly. Figure 7 shows a trace representing the execution of `poly_tomsg()` procedure of CRYSTALS-Kyber and t-test results for all message bytes.

5 Profiling Stage

This section describes how we train neural networks at the profiling stage.

Let $\mathbb{I}$ denote the set of real numbers within the interval [0,1], $\mathbb{I} := \{x \in \mathbb{R} \mid 0 \leq x \leq 1\}$.

We use w-point segments of traces containing the execution of the ith message byte by `POL2MSG()`/`poly_tomsg()` to train neural networks of type $\mathcal{N}_i : \mathbb{R}^w \rightarrow \mathbb{I}^{256}$ which predict the value of the ith message byte, for all $i \in \{0, 1, \ldots, 31\}$. The set of training traces, $\boldsymbol{\mathcal{T}}_T$, is captured for random messages and random keys. Message byte values are used as labels for traces. Using the Hamming weight of bytes as labels is less effective in our experience.

Table 1 shows the architecture of neural networks in our experiments. The network's input size is $w = 160$ and $w = 20$ points for the Saber `-O0` and `-O3` implementations, respectively, and $w = 50$ for the CRYSTALS-Kyber `-O3` implementation.

During training, we use *Nadam* optimizer with the learning rate of 0.0001 and numerical stability constant *epsilon*=1e-8. Categorical cross-entropy is used as a loss function to evaluate the network classification error. The number of epoch is set to 100 with a batch size 128. The dropout rate is set to 0.2. 10% traces are used for validation. Only the model with the highest validation accuracy is saved.

Note that, in principle, the profiling can also be done using templates, as in the near field EM-based template attack of [21]. However, due to the high noise level of amplitude-modulated EM side channels, using templates for profiling of amplitude-modulated EM side-channel attacks is at least an order of magnitude less effective than the DL-based approach [30].

6 Attack Stage

In this section, we present the new message recovery method and describe how the session and secret keys can be derived from the recovered messages.

Table 1. The architecture of MLPs used for message recovery. The input size is $w = 160, 20$ and 50 for Saber -00, Saber -03 and Kyber -03 implementations, respectively.

Layer (Type)	Output Shape	Parameter #
Input	w	0
BatchNormalization1	w	$4w$
Dense1 (ReLU)	512	82432
Dense2 (ReLU)	256	131328
Dense3 (ReLU)	256	65792
Dropout1	256	0
Output (Softmax)	256	65792

6.1 Multi-bit Error Injection Method

Let $m = (m[0], m[1], \ldots, m[31])$ be a message to be recovered, where $m[i]$ is the ith message byte, and $c = (\mathbf{u}, v)$ be a properly generated ciphertext which contains m.

We create 255 modified versions of c, denoted by c_e, such that CPA-PKE.Dec() decrypts c_e to

$$m_e = (m[0] \oplus e, m[1] \oplus e, \ldots, m[31] \oplus e), \tag{1}$$

where $e \in \{1, 2, \ldots, 255\}$ is the error. The same error is injected into all message bytes in parallel. The original ciphertext c corresponds to the error-free case, $c = c_0$.

The modified ciphertexts c_e are created by changing the coefficients of v so that, for every message byte $i \in \{0, 1, \ldots, 31\}$, all bits of $m[i]$ in which the 8-bit binary expansion of e has the value 1 are flipped. To flip a message bit j, the value of the center of the integer ring $\mathbb{Z}_q$ is subtracted from the jth coefficient of v, for any $j \in \{0, 1, \ldots, 255\}$. Since the message polynomial is only additively hidden within v (see line 5 of CPA-PKE.Enc()), this results in a ciphertext decrypting to a message equal to the original message m with the jth bit flipped [21].

Next we acquire 256 attack traces $\boldsymbol{\mathcal{T}}_A = \{\mathcal{T}_0, \mathcal{T}_1, \ldots, \mathcal{T}_{255}\}$ captured during the decapsulation of the chiphertext c_e by the device under attack, for all $e \in \{0, 1, \ldots, 255\}$. For each message byte $i \in \{0, 1, \ldots, 31\}$, the w-point segments containing the processing of $m[i]$ by the message packing procedure are located in $\boldsymbol{\mathcal{T}}_A$ and extracted. The extracted trace segments are given as input to the MLP model $\mathcal{N}_i$ trained at the profiling stage.

For each $\mathcal{T}_e \in \boldsymbol{\mathcal{T}}_A$, the model $\mathcal{N}_i$ outputs a score vector $S_{i,e} = \mathcal{N}_i(\mathcal{T}_e)$ in which the value of the lth element, $S_{i,e}[l]$, is the probability that $m_e[i] = l$ in $\mathcal{T}_e$, for $l, e \in \{0, \ldots, 255\}$.

The most likely label for $m[i]$ among 256 candidates is decided as:

$$\tilde{l} = \underset{l \in \{0,1,\ldots,255\}}{\arg\max} \left(\prod_{e=0}^{255} S_{i,e}[l \oplus e]\right).$$

If $\tilde{l} = m[i]$, the classification is successful. The condition $\tilde{l} = m[i]$ can be verified by checking if the rank of the message byte i, $rank_i$, is zero.

Since we inject all possible multi-bit errors into each message byte $i \in \{0, 1, \ldots, 31\}$, for every i, the ground truth labels of 256 traces of $\mathcal{T}_A$ are mutually disjoint. Therefore, at least one of the traces of $\mathcal{T}_A$ has the label preferred by the model $\mathcal{N}_i$ for every i.

6.2 Session Key Recovery

Given a properly generated ciphertext c, the session key can be trivially extracted by first recovering the message m contained in c from 256 traces using the presented method. Then, the session key is computed as $K = \mathsf{KDF}(\hat{K}', c)$ where $(\hat{K}', r') = \mathcal{G}(m, \mathcal{H}(pk))$ (see lines 3 and 5 of CCA-KEM.Encaps()).

6.3 Secret Key Recovery

It is known that the secret key of LWE/LWR-based PKE/KEM algorithms can be derived from messages recovered from chosen ciphertexts. Many different methods for choosing the ciphertexts have been presented in the past, including [17,21,22,24]. In the experimental results section, we illustrate the secret key recovery using the ciphertext construction method from [17].

7 Experimental Results

In the experiments, we use two nRF52832 devices, D_P and D_A, shown in Fig. 5. D_P is used for capturing training traces for the profiling stage. Both D_P and D_A are used for capturing test traces for the attack stage. All training and test traces are pre-processed by averaging 100 repeated measurements.

7.1 Bias in Neural Networks

In this section, we demonstrate that multi-class neural networks which are trained on a small dataset may be strongly biased towards certain classes in their predictions. This phenomenon has been observed in previous side-channel attacks, e.g. [5].

We trained an MLP model $\mathcal{N}_0$ with the architecture listed in Table 1 on 30K traces with random messages (with 10% left for validation). The model was trained on the segment of `POL2MSG()` procedure of Saber corresponding to the processing of the first message byte, $m[0]$.

After training, we tested $\mathcal{N}_0$ on 3K traces from the same device captured for random messages. Each prediction was done based on a single trace (single-trace attack). Figure 8 illustrates the results. The top plot shows the distribution of ground truth labels in the 3K attack set. We can see that the labels are more or less uniform. The bottom plot shows the distribution of labels predicted by $\mathcal{N}_0$. There is a strong bias towards one label, 128, which is predicted correctly with

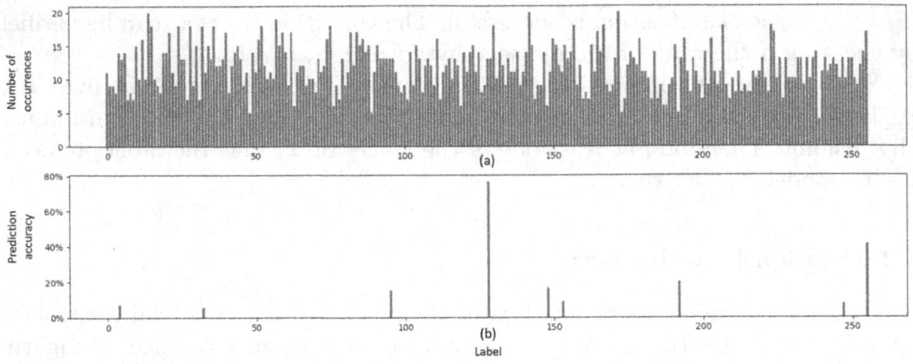

Fig. 8. The distribution of (a) ground truth labels and (b) labels predicted by a model $\mathcal{N}_0$ trained on a 30K trace set. Average results of a single-trace attack on Saber -O0 implementation on D_P for 3K traces with random messages.

75% probability. In the rest of the section, we call such labels *preferred.* We can also see that, the majority of labels, 96.5%, are predicted with 0% probability. We refer to them as *non-preferred.*

We believe that the strong bias of $\mathcal{N}_0$ is due to the fact that the 256-class model was trained on a small dataset in which each class appears only roughly 100 times. This does not seem sufficient. For a comparison, in the single-trace attack on Saber presented in [17], using power side channels, a 1.6M dataset was used for training 2-class MLP models which achieve 0.997% message bit prediction accuracy. In their training dataset, each class from $\{0, 1\}$ appears 0.8M times. This is four orders of magnitude larger compared to the number of occurrences of each class from $\{0, 1, \ldots, 255\}$ in the 30K dataset in our experiment. Another reason can be that MLP models are quite simple. More complex DL models, e.g. transformers [28], may achieve better results [4].

The key idea of the presented method is that, instead of increasing the training set by several orders of magnitude to get unbiased models, we increase the attack set 256 times and achieve high prediction accuracy with biased models. Since the the attack set is several orders of magnitude smaller than the training set, the presented method minimizes the total number of training plus attack traces required for a successful attack.

One can ask if a similar improvement in the success rate can be achieved by a repetition attack which uses 256 traces with the *same* ciphertext c. Figure 9(a) and 9(b) show that the repetition method is not as good as the presented method. For both methods, we used the model $\mathcal{N}_0$ from the previous experiment for predicting labels in two scenarios:

1. The ground truth label of a trace in the attack set captured with c as input is a preferred label of $\mathcal{N}_0$ (blue plot).

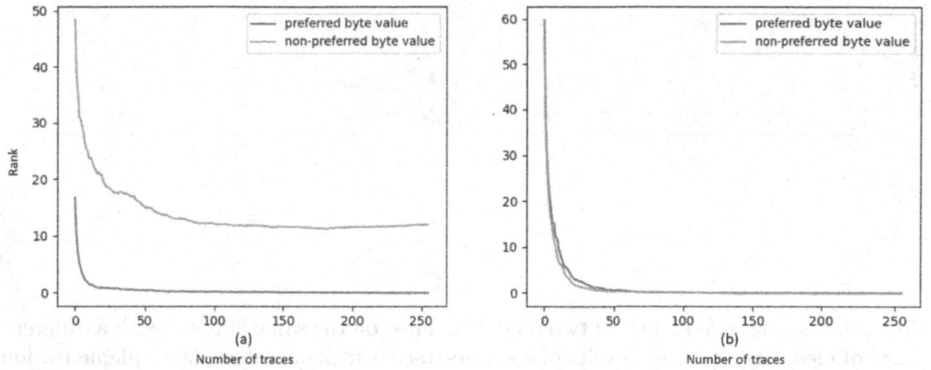

Fig. 9. (a).The rank of $m[0]$ in a repetition attack using 256 traces with the same ciphertext. (b).The rank of $m[0]$ in an attack using 256 traces of the presented method. (Color figure online)

2. The ground truth label of a trace in the attack set captured with c as input is a non-preferred label of $\mathcal{N}_0$ (orange plot).

From Fig. 9(a) we can see that, in the repetition attack, $\mathcal{N}_0$ successfully recovers the former and fails to recover the latter. Contrary, Fig. 9(b) shows that, in the attack using the presented method, $\mathcal{N}_0$ successfully recovers labels in both cases. This is not surprising since the injected errors assure that at least one of the 256 traces in the attack set has a label preferred by the model.

7.2 Message Recovery Attack

In this section, we evaluate the effects of scaling, ensemble learning, repetitions, and optimization level on the success rate of the presented message recovery attack.

Scaling. First, we quantify the impact of different scaling methods.

At the profiling stage, we captured from the profiling device, D_P, implementing Saber -O0 a set of 30K traces with random messages, $\mathcal{T}_T$. Then we scaled $\mathcal{T}_T$ using two different methods: min-max normalization and standardization. Using the profiling strategy described in Sect. 5, for each message byte $i \in \{0, 1, \ldots, 31\}$, we trained models $\mathcal{N}_i$ on each of these three training sets.

At the attack stage, we selected at random five different messages and computed the corresponding ciphertexts using the public key of the device under attack, D_A. These five ciphertexts, together with their 255 mutiple-bit error injected versions, were applied as inputs to D_A to capture the set of attack traces, $\mathcal{T}_A$. The set $\mathcal{T}_A$ was scaled using the same two methods as $\mathcal{T}_T$.

Table 2 lists the average empirical probabilities of recovering a message byte from $\mathcal{T}_A$ for each of the five messages. We calculate the probabilities as $p_i = \frac{1}{1+rank_i}$, where $i \in \{0, 1, \ldots, 31\}$ is the byte number.

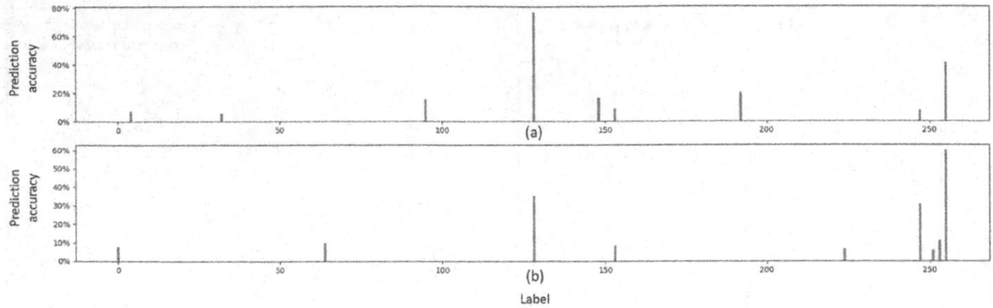

Fig. 10. The preferred labels of two models trained on the same 30K set with a different order of elements. Average results of a single-trace attack on Saber -O0 implementation on D_P for 3K traces with random messages.

Table 2. The impact of scaling on the success rate of message recovery from Saber -O0 implementation on D_A.

Scaling method	Message					Avg. byte probability
	1	2	3	4	5	
No scaling	0.6652	0.8135	0.6865	0.6647	0.7891	0.7238
Min-max normalization	0.7649	0.8412	0.7781	0.7315	0.8576	0.7947
Standardization	0.8958	0.9271	0.8698	0.9167	0.9323	0.9083

We can see that both min-max normalization and standardization improve the message byte recovery probability. For the standardization, the average probability is by 18.45% larger than the one for non-scaled traces. In the rest of experiments, we use traces scaled with the standardization method.

Ensemble Learning. Ensemble learning is a well-known technique which helps improving prediction accuracy if the models make independent errors [10]. It has been shown useful in previous message recovery attacks on LWE/LWR-Based PKE/KEMs [18]. In this section, we evaluate its effect on the MBF method.

Since we randomly shuffle traces in a training set for each training session and set aside 10% of the set for validation, at each training session the models are trained on a slightly different set. In addition, data in the beginning of the training set seem to have a higher impact on the model than the data at the end. Due to these and other factors, two models trained on the same dataset may have different preferred labels, as illustrated in Fig. 10. It shows the results of a single-trace attack for two models trained on the same 30K set captured from Saber. We can see that some of their preferred labels are different. This implies that the models may be making different errors on the same attack set and, hence, the ensemble approach might be beneficial.

To verify the latter, we used the same 30K training set to train 10 different models for each message byte $i \in \{0, 1, \ldots, 31\}$ and used an ensemble of k of these

Table 3. The impact of ensemble learning on the success rate of message recovery from Saber `-O0` implementation on D_A.

Number of models, k	1	2	3	4	5
Average byte probability	0.9083	0.9370	0.9469	0.9573	0.9458
Number of models, k	6	7	8	9	10
Average byte probability	0.9385	0.9448	0.9510	0.9510	0.9417

Table 4. The impact of number of repetitions, N, on the the success rate of message recovery from Saber `-O0` implementation on D_A.

N	Message					Avg. byte probability	Avg. message probability
	1	2	3	4	5		
1	0.9688	0.9844	0.9323	0.9375	0.9635	0.9573	0.2475
2	0.9844	0.9688	1.0000	0.9531	1.0000	0.9813	0.5459
3	1.0000	0.9688	1.0000	0.9844	1.0000	0.9906	0.7401

Table 5. The impact of number of repetitions, N, on the the success rate of message recovery from Saber `-O0` implementation on D_P.

N	Message					Avg. byte probability	Avg. message probability
	1	2	3	4	5		
1	0.9688	1.0000	1.0000	0.9844	0.9844	0.9875	0.6691
2	1.0000	1.0000	1.0000	1.0000	1.0000	1.0000	1.0000
3	1.0000	1.0000	1.0000	1.0000	1.0000	1.0000	1.0000

models to recover the bytes using the presented method. Table 3 summarizes the results. We can see that combining four models into an ensemble is the best choice. In the rest of experiments, we use an ensemble of four models.

Repetitions. Finally, we investigate if the probability of message recovery can be further improved if each trace in the attack set is captured with N repetitions.

Table 4 shows the results for $N = 1, 2$ and 3 for the case when the device under attack is different from the profiling device. We can see that, by raising the degree of repetition N to 3, we can boost the average probability of recovering a message byte to 0.9906 and hence the likelihood of recovering the complete message to 0.7401. We believe that, by raising N, the latter can be further improved.

Table 5 presents similar results for the case when the device under attack is the same as the profiling device. We can see that, in this case, the probability of recovering the message is 1 for $N \geq 2$. We show both tables to emphasize the significant impact of intra-device variability and justify the advantage of profiling on the device under attack (and hence the need for minimizing the training set).

Table 6. Maximum t-test scores for all message bytes.

Byte	0	1	2	3	4	5	6	7	8	9	10
Saber -O0	22.5	23.4	24.4	27.9	25.7	27.7	32.6	29.5	29.1	30.2	29.8
Saber -O3	7.2	5.3	7.2	6.1	6.4	4.3	7.1	5.9	6.2	3.8	6.4
Kyber -O3	13.7	12.2	7.6	10.9	11.9	11.1	6.8	12.6	12.7	7.3	7.7
Byte	11	12	13	14	15	16	17	18	19	20	21
Saber -O0	30.4	22.4	22.5	23.7	27.6	26.0	27.2	31.6	28.8	27.5	29.9
Saber -O3	5.6	6.6	5.8	7.0	7.1	5.8	5.6	6.2	6.0	6.8	6.3
Kyber -O3	14.5	12.3	6.8	9.0	15.0	11.8	7.8	11.2	14.1	13.4	6.7
Byte	22	23	24	25	26	27	28	29	30	31	Avg
Saber -O0	30.6	33.1	25.5	21.1	25.1	25.1	23.7	27.4	29.0	29.2	27.2
Saber -O3	6.4	7.9	6.8	5.7	6.9	6.2	6.2	5.3	5.1	8.9	6.3
Kyber -O3	13.2	9.3	9.4	6.5	15.5	11.3	6.7	8.1	16.3	13.1	10.8

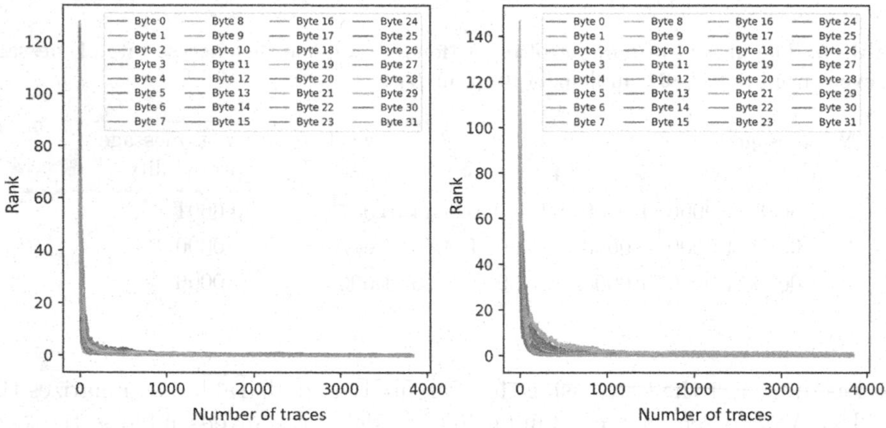

Fig. 11. The ranks of message bytes in an attack on Saber -O3 (left) and Kyber -O3 (right) implementations on D_A using an ensemble of four models and 15 repetitions.

Higher Optimization Level. All previous experiments are performed on the implementation of Saber compiled with -O0 optimization level to allow for a comparison with the attack of [29] which uses that implementation. In this section, we show the results for the implementations of Saber and CRYSTALS-Kyber compiled with the highest optimization level, -O3. Typically -O3 optimization level is the most difficult one to break by side-channel analysis [25].

Table 6 compares the leakage of all three implementations in terms of the maximum t-test scores. We can see that, on average, the leakage from the -O3 implementation of Saber is 4.3 times weaker than the one from the -O0.

Table 7. The mapping of message bits into secret key coefficients of Saber [17].

Coef. of **s**	The message bit value for the pair (k_1, k_0)							
	(186,0)	(293,7)	(311,7)	(615,2)	(613,2)	(890,4)	(903,4)	(199,0)
−4	0	1	1	1	1	0	0	0
−3	1	1	1	0	0	0	0	1
−2	1	0	0	1	1	0	0	1
−1	0	0	0	0	0	0	0	0
0	0	1	1	0	0	1	1	0
1	0	0	0	1	1	1	1	0
2	1	0	0	0	0	1	1	1
3	1	1	1	1	1	1	1	1
4	1	1	0	1	0	0	1	0

For both Saber and CRYSTALS-Kyber, we trained models $\mathcal{N}_i$ for each message byte $i \in \{0, 1, \ldots, 31\}$ using the same size of the training set, 30K, captured from D_P and the same training strategy as in the experiments with `-O0` optimization level. Figure 11 shows the ranks of all message bytes recovered using an ensemble of four models from 256 traces captured from a different device, D_A, with 15 repetitions.

Even though the leakage from `-O3` implementations is much weaker than the one from `-O0`, by using a higher degree of repetition, $N = 15$, we can recover messages successfully. For Saber, the ranks of all bytes reach 0 (average byte accuracy = 1). For CRYSTALS-Kyber, the ranks of all but one byte reach 0 (average byte accuracy = 0.9844). The remaining byte (byte 29) has the rank 1. Therefore, by using enumeration up to 2^{32}, complete messages can be recovered.

7.3 Secret Key Recovery Attack

In this section we show how the secret key of Saber can be derived from messages recovered from the ciphertexts chosen using the method of [17]. Although the method of [17] uses twice as many ciphertexts as the methods of [21,22], it can correct errors in the recovered messages, which is a great advantage.

In the method of [17], the coefficients of the secret key of Saber are mapped into the codewords of an $[8, 4, 4]_2$ extended Hamming code. The method uses 24 ciphertexts to recover all secret key coefficients (768 in total). They are constructed as $c_i = (\mathbf{u}, v)$ where $v = k_0 \sum_{j=0}^{255} x^j$ and

$$\mathbf{u} = \begin{cases} (k_1, 0, 0) \in R_p^{3\times 1} \text{ for } i = \{1, \ldots, 8\}, \\ (0, k_1, 0) \in R_p^{3\times 1} \text{ for } i = \{9, \ldots, 16\}, \\ (0, 0, k_1) \in R_p^{3\times 1} \text{ for } i = \{17, \ldots, 24\}, \end{cases}$$

where the pairs (k_0, k_1) are defined by the mapping Table 7.

Table 8. The statistic on different types of errors in 768 secret key coefficients recovered from Saber -OO implementations on D_A using N repetitions.

	# Correct predictions		# Errors	
N	No errors	Errors corrected by ECC	Detected errors	Undetected errors
1	665	84	17	2
2	744	22	2	0
3	758	10	0	0
4	766	2	0	0
5	766	2	0	0

We used the presented method to recover 24 messages contained in the chosen ciphertexts from traces captured from Saber -OO implementations on D_A using N repetitions, for $N = \{1, 2, 3, 4, 5\}$. To evaluate the attack, we group possible outcomes into four cases:

1. *No errors:* The recovered coefficient matches the ground truth key coefficient.
2. *Errors corrected by the ECC:* There is exactly one error in the eight message bits. This error is corrected by the ECC.
3. *Detected errors:* ECC detects more than one errors in the eight message bits and this combination of bits is not in Table 7. These errors are detected by the ECC.
4. *Undetected errors:* The combination of the eight message bits is in Table 7, but the recovered coefficient does not match the ground truth secret key coefficient.

The case (4) implies a failed secret key recovery because any number of wrong coefficients makes the recovered key useless. The errors in case (3) may be fixed by enumeration if their number is small, since the location of the error is known. The complexity of enumeration is 9^n, where n is the number of detected errors. Table 8 lists the statistic on the number of occurrences of each of the four cases for different degrees of repetitions N.

For $N = 1$, there are 2 undetected errors, so the attack fails. For $N = 2$, there are no undetected errors and only 81 enumerations are required to find the secret key. Therefore, the attack is successful. For $N \geq 3$, the secret key can be recovered without any enumeration.

8 Conclusion

We presented the first side-channel attack which can successfully recover messages of CRYSTALS-Kyber and Saber algorithms from their software implementations using amplitude-modulated EM emanations. The previous amplitude-modulated EM emanation-based attack on LWE/LWR-Based PKE/KEMs [29] was not able to recover complete messages with a sufficiently high probability.

The presented message recovery method is not limited to LWE/LWR-Based PKE/KEMs. In principle, is applicable to any cryptographic algorithm whose sensitive variables can be manipulated in a controlled manner through input data. It is also applicable to any type of side channels, but seems to be most valuable when the leakage is weak.

Acknowledgements. This work was supported in part by the Swedish Civil Contingencies Agency (Grant No. 2020-11632) and the Swedish Research Council (Grant No. 2018-04482).

References

1. Beirendonck, M.V., D'anvers, J.P., Karmakar, A., Balasch, J., Verbauwhede, I.: A side-channel-resistant implementation of Saber. ACM J. Emerg. Technol. Comput. Syst. (JETC) **17**(2), 1–26 (2021)
2. Bhasin, S., D'Anvers, J.P., Heinz, D., Pöppelmann, T., Beirendonck, M.V.: Attacking and defending masked polynomial comparison for lattice-based cryptography. Cryptology ePrint Archive, Paper 2021/104 (2021), https://eprint.iacr.org/2021/104
3. Bos, J., et al.: CRYSTALS-Kyber: a CCA-secure module-lattice-based KEM. In: 2018 IEEE European Symposium on Security and Privacy (EuroS&P), pp. 353–367. IEEE (2018)
4. Brisfors, M.: Advanced Side-Channel Analysis of USIMs, Bluetooth SoCs and MCUs. Master's thesis, School of Electrical Engineering and Computer Science, KTH (2021)
5. Brisfors, M., Forsmark, S.: Deep learning side-channel attacks on AES. Bachelor's thesis, School of Electrical Engineering and Computer Science, KTH (2019)
6. Camurati, G., Francillon, A., Standaert, F.X.: Understanding screaming channels: from a detailed analysis to improved attacks. IACR Trans. Crypt. Hardware Embed. Syst., pp. 358–401 (2020)
7. Camurati, G., Poeplau, S., Muench, M., Hayes, T., Francillon, A.: Screaming channels: when electromagnetic side channels meet radio transceivers. In: Proceedings of the 2018 ACM SIGSAC Conference on Computer and Communications Security, pp. 163–177 (2018)
8. D'Anvers, J., et al.: Saber algorithm specifications and supporting documentation (2020). https://www.esat.kuleuven.be/cosic/pqcrypto/saber/files/saberspecround3.pdf
9. Fujisaki, E., Okamoto, T.: Secure integration of asymmetric and symmetric encryption schemes. J. Cryptol. **26**(1), 80–101 (2011). https://doi.org/10.1007/s00145-011-9114-1
10. Goodfellow, I., Bengio, Y., Courville, A.: Deep learning. MIT Press (2016). http://www.deeplearningbook.org
11. Goodwill, G., Jun, B., Jaffe, J., Rohatgi, P.: A testing methodology for side-channel resistance validation. In: NIST Non-Invasive Attack Testing Workshop (2011)
12. Guo, Q., Johansson, T., Nilsson, A.: A key-recovery timing attack on post-quantum primitives using the fujisaki-okamoto transformation and its application on FrodoKEM. In: Micciancio, D., Ristenpart, T. (eds.) CRYPTO 2020. LNCS, vol. 12171, pp. 359–386. Springer, Cham (2020). https://doi.org/10.1007/978-3-030-56880-1_13

13. Kundu, S., D'Anvers, J.P., Beirendonck, M.V., Karmakar, A., Verbauwhede, I.: Higher-order masked Saber. Cryptology ePrint Archive, Paper 2022/389 (2022). https://eprint.iacr.org/2022/389
14. Moody, D.: Status report on the third round of the NIST post-quantum cryptography standardization process. Nistir 8309, pp. 1–27 (2022). https://nvlpubs.nist.gov/nistpubs/ir/2022/NIST.IR.8413.pdf
15. Mu, J., et al.: A voltage template attack on the modular polynomial subtraction in Kyber. In: 2022 27th Asia and South Pacific Design Automation Conference (ASP-DAC), pp. 672–677. IEEE (2022)
16. Mujdei, C., Beckers, A., Mera, J.M.B., Karmakar, A., Wouters, L., Verbauwhede, I.: Side-channel analysis of lattice-based post-quantum cryptography: exploiting polynomial multiplication. Cryptology ePrint Archive, Paper 2022/474 (2022). https://eprint.iacr.org/2022/474
17. Ngo, K., Dubrova, E., Guo, Q., Johansson, T.: A side-channel attack on a masked IND-CCA secure Saber KEM implementation. IACR Trans. Crypt. Hardware Embed. Syst., pp. 676–707 (2021)
18. Ngo, K., Dubrova, E., Johansson, T.: Breaking masked and shuffled CCA secure Saber KEM by power analysis. In: Proceedings of the 5th Workshop on Attacks and Solutions in Hardware Security, pp. 51–61 (2021)
19. NIST: Submission requirements and evaluation criteria for the post-quantum cryptography standardization process (2016). https://csrc.nist.gov/CSRC/media/Projects/Post-Quantum-Cryptography/documents/call-for-proposals-final-dec-2016.pdf
20. Paulsrud, N.: A side channel attack on a higher-order masked software implementation of Saber. Master's thesis, School of Electrical Engineering and Computer Science, KTH (2022)
21. Ravi, P., Bhasin, S., Roy, S.S., Chattopadhyay, A.: On exploiting message leakage in (few) NIST PQC candidates for practical message recovery attacks. IEEE Trans. Inf. Forensics Secur. (2021)
22. Ravi, P., Roy, S.S., Chattopadhyay, A., Bhasin, S.: Generic side-channel attacks on CCA-secure lattice-based PKE and KEMs. IACR Trans. Crypt. Hardware Embed. Syst. **2020**(3), 307–335 (2020)
23. Schwabe, P., et al.: CRYSTALS-Kyber algorithm specifications and supporting documentation (2020). https://pq-crystals.org/kyber/data/kyber-specification-round3-20210131.pdf
24. Shen, M., Cheng, C., Zhang, X., Guo, Q., Jiang, T.: Find the bad apples: an efficient method for perfect key recovery under imperfect SCA oracles - a case study of Kyber. Cryptology ePrint Archive, Paper 2022/563 (2022). https://eprint.iacr.org/2022/563
25. Sim, B.Y., et al.: Single-trace attacks on message encoding in lattice-based KEMs. IEEE Access **8**, 183175–183191 (2020)
26. Sim, B.Y., Park, A., Han, D.G.: Chosen-ciphertext clustering attack on CRYSTALS-KYBER using the side-channel leakage of Barrett reduction. IEEE Internet of Things J. (2022)
27. Ueno, R., Xagawa, K., Tanaka, Y., Ito, A., Takahashi, J., Homma, N.: Curse of re-encryption: a generic power/EM analysis on post-quantum KEMs. IACR Trans. Crypt. Hardware Embed. Syst., pp. 296–322 (2022)
28. Vaswani, A., et al.: Attention is all you need. CoRR abs/1706.03762 (2017). http://arxiv.org/abs/1706.03762

29. Wang, R., Ngo, K., Dubrova, E.: Side-channel analysis of Saber KEM using amplitude-modulated EM emanations. In: Proceedings of the Euromicro DSD/SEAA (2022)
30. Wang, R., Wang, H., Dubrova, E.: Far field EM side-channel attack on AES using deep learning. In: Proceedings of the 4th ACM Workshop on Attacks and Solutions in Hardware Security, pp. 35–44 (2020)
31. Welch, B.L.: The generalization of 'Student's' problem when several different population variances are involved. Biometrika **34**(1–2), 28–35 (1947)
32. Xu, Z., Pemberton, O.M., Roy, S.S., Oswald, D., Yao, W., Zheng, Z.: Magnifying side-channel leakage of lattice-based cryptosystems with chosen ciphertexts: the case study of Kyber. IEEE Trans. Comput. (2021)
33. Zheng, A., Casari, A.: Feature engineering for machine learning: principles and techniques for data scientists. O'Reilly Media, Inc. (2018)

Preimage Sampling in the Higher-bit Approximate Setting with a Non-spherical Gaussian Sampler

Anaëlle Le Dévéhat[1], Shingo Hasegawa[2(✉)], and Hiroki Shizuya[2]

[1] Inria & Laboratoire CNRS LIX, École Polytechnique, Institut Polytechnique de Paris, Palaiseau, France
anaelle.le-devehat@inria.fr

[2] Graduate School of Information Sciences, Tohoku University, Sendai, Japan
{shingo.hasegawa.b7,hiroki.shizuya.c1}@tohoku.ac.jp

Abstract. Approximate lattice trapdoors are introduced to improve the efficiency of lattice-based hash-and-sign signature. There are two improvements of the approximate setting for such schemes. The first is to use a non-spherical Gaussian sampler, and the second is the higher-bit approximate setting.

In this paper we consider further improvements of the approximate setting, namely we combine the higher-bit approximate setting with the use of a non-spherical Gaussian sampler. We assess the effectiveness of this approach by doing an analysis with a proof-of-concept implementation. We observe that our construction brings several improvements, especially in the public key size and signature size. Moreover, an exhaustive search for parameter sets make us aware of new parameters choices which lead to better results in the higher-bit approximate setting than those of previous work.

Keywords: Approximate lattice trapdoor · Higher-bit approximation · Non-spherical gaussian sampler

1 Introduction

Our work takes place as the threat of quantum computing grows quickly in regard to modern cryptographic constructions. Peter Shor work in 1994 [20] put forward the need for efficient post-quantum secure cryptography as, for instance, a quantum computer can easily break factoring-based cryptography in polynomial time of the security parameter. Post-quantum standardization has become a wide field of research since the understanding of this threat.

In this work, we focus on lattice-based cryptography, which is considered as one of the most promising candidate of post-quantum cryptography. Several lattice-based problems are believed to be hard against attacks even for quantum adversaries. Moreover, Ajtai's breakthrough work [2] in 1996 demonstrates strong worst-case to average-case reductions on lattices problems which is necessary for cryptography.

S.-H. Seo and H. Seo (Eds.): ICISC 2022, LNCS 13849, pp. 472–490, 2023.
https://doi.org/10.1007/978-3-031-29371-9_23

Lattice-based cryptography appears as a good alternative to modern cryptography since it enjoys several advantages. Its constructions are simple and rather elegant while enjoying strong security. Indeed, several candidates for the NIST standardization process are lattice-based schemes. Lattices and their algebraic structure were shown to bring improvements in efficiency [11,16], and, in the last decades, several different cryptographic primitives have been studied. This versatility is obtained by using lattice-based problems such as the learning with errors (LWE) problem [19]. For instances, fully homomorphic encryption [9], public-key encryption [11,14], attribute-based encryption and (hierarchical) identity-based encryption [1,6] have been explored.

We focus on lattice-based signatures among lattice-based cryptographic schemes. The first provably secure lattice-based signature is the signature scheme introduced by Gentry, Peikert and Vaikuntanathan [10]. Their scheme is based on the "hash-and-sign" construction and its security is proven in the random oracle model. Another line of lattice-based signatures is started by Lyubashevsky [15] based on the Fiat-Shamir transformation and the rejection sampling method. Thus there are two research lines of constructing lattice-based signature.

At present time, the best candidates in NIST PQC standardization procedure are based on the Fiat-Shamir transformation and the rejection sampling method [8]. On the other hand, in the hash-and-sign line of work, the schemes seem to be rather inefficient. This is because hash-and-sign type lattice signatures aim to sample a solution of the Ajtai's function, and it involves the use of a Gaussian sampler. The efficiency of using a Gaussian sampler depends on the quality of the *lattice trapdoor*, thus the follow-up works such as [18] consider simpler or smaller trapdoors to improve both security and efficiency when it is used in the hash-and-sign signatures.

1.1 Related Works

This paper considers a lattice-based hash-and-sign signature, thus we follow the GPV line of work. It is based on Ajtai's one-way function and lattice trapdoors [3]. At first, a trapdoor $\boldsymbol{S}$ would be a basis of short lattice vectors which verifies $\boldsymbol{AS} = \boldsymbol{0} \pmod q$ for some assigned public matrix $\boldsymbol{A} \in \mathbb{Z}_q^{n\times m}$. The knowledge of $\boldsymbol{S}$ allows one to sample some short preimage of $\boldsymbol{0}$ by $\boldsymbol{A}$. However, this method was rather inefficient and unpractical. In 2012, Micciancio and Peikert proposed their elegant $\boldsymbol{G}$-trapdoor construction [18] for "hash-and-sign" signature. This new kind of trapdoors enables faster and shorter signatures. This construction was modified into an approximate version defined as $\boldsymbol{F}$-trapdoors by Chen, Genise and Mukherjee [7]. To construct such an approximate setting, they also had to define an approximate version of the ISIS problem. Using $\boldsymbol{F}$-trapdoors instead of $\boldsymbol{G}$-trapdoors is interesting in terms of memory storage which is the main downside of such signatures schemes when compared to other NIST PQC standardization process [4,8].

In light of this memory size problem, two optimization methods for cryptosystems based on $\boldsymbol{F}$-trapdoors were studied in 2021. The first work by Jia, Hu and Tang [12] replaces the spherical Gaussian sampler used in the approximate preimage sampling algorithm from [7] by a non-spherical Gaussian sampler.

This modification allows more precision in the perturbation used in the Gaussian sampler. As a result, shorter approximate preimages are obtained.

The second optimization method is a bitwise modification by Le Dévéhat, Shizuya and Hasegawa [13] on the original $\boldsymbol{F}$-trapdoors construction. In their works, the authors introduced the higher-bit version of the approximate problem. In this newly defined problem, the approximate setting is used to discard all low-weighted bits in the matrix $\boldsymbol{A} \in \mathbb{Z}_q^{n\times m}$ which defines Ajtai's function. They showed that this bitwise modification can lead to better sizes in both the public matrix and sampled approximate preimage.

1.2 Our Contribution

This paper considers the combination of two methods which aim to optimize cryptosystems using the $\boldsymbol{F}$-trapdoors construction and algorithms [7]. We combine the higher-bit approximate setting method from [13] with the use of a non-spherical Gaussian sampler as in [12]. We assess and study the relevance of using the higher-bit approximate setting on the hash-and-sign signature construction from [12]. Then resulting public key belongs to $\mathbb{Z}_{\frac{q}{b^d}}^{n\times m}$ rather than $\mathbb{Z}_q^{n\times m}$, where $q = b^k$ and $d < k$. This is a direct consequence of employing the higher-bit approximate ISIS problem as the underlying hardness problem. Moreover, the signature is in $\mathbb{Z}_{\frac{q}{b^d}}^m$ rather than $\mathbb{Z}_q^m$. Our combination of these two methods enables some experimental improvement in public key and signature sizes and we obtain better theoretical results and length bounds than those observed in [13].

We seek the best possible parameter set through an exhaustive search. We analyse all our results and obtain a parameters choice which brings us significantly smaller key sizes than in [12]. Moreover, we generalize this parameter set as a better choice in the higher-bit approximate setting and construction from [13].

2 Preliminaries

We denote the set of reals by $\mathbb{R}$, the set of integers by $\mathbb{Z}$ and the set of naturals by $\mathbb{N}$, respectively. $\mathbb{Z}_q$ is the quotient ring $\mathbb{Z}/q\mathbb{Z}$. We write $x \leftarrow U(S)$ when x is sampled uniformly at random from the set S. We say that a function ϵ is *negligible* in λ if for any polynomial μ, there exists a natural λ_0 such that $\epsilon(\lambda) < 1/\mu(\lambda)$ for $\lambda > \lambda_0$.

Let X, Y be distributions over a finite set D, which is a set of strings of length λ. The statistical distance between X and Y is defined by $\Delta(X, Y) = \frac{1}{2}\sum_{w\in D}|X(w) - Y(w)|$. We say the distributions X and Y are statistically indistinguishable if $\Delta(X, Y) \leq \epsilon$ for a negligible function ϵ, and we write $X \approx_s Y$.

A vector $\boldsymbol{v}$ is supposed to be in column form and represented in lower-case bold letters. A matrix $\boldsymbol{A}$ is represented in upper-case bold letters. For a vector $\boldsymbol{v}$, v_i denotes the i-th component of $\boldsymbol{v}$. In a similar manner, $a_{i,j}$ denotes the

i-th component of the j-th column of a matrix $\boldsymbol{A}$. We employ the l_p-norm of a vector $\boldsymbol{v}$ defined as $\|\boldsymbol{v}\|_p := (\sum v_i^p)^{1/p}$. The l_p-norm of a matrix is the l_p-norm of its longest column, i.e. $\|\boldsymbol{A}\|_p := \max \|\boldsymbol{a}_i\|_p$. We basically use l_2-norm. A short vector is a vector whose norm is small but not necessarily its dimension.

If a symmetric matrix $\boldsymbol{\Sigma} \in \mathbb{R}^{n \times n}$ verifies that for all $\boldsymbol{x} \in \mathbb{R}^n$, $\boldsymbol{x}^t \boldsymbol{\Sigma} \boldsymbol{x} > 0$ (≥ 0) then $\boldsymbol{\Sigma}$ is positive (semi)-definite. For two positive (semi)-definite matrices $\boldsymbol{\Sigma}_1$ and $\boldsymbol{\Sigma}_2$, we write $\boldsymbol{\Sigma}_1 > \boldsymbol{\Sigma}_2$ ($\geq$) if $\boldsymbol{\Sigma}_1 - \boldsymbol{\Sigma}_2$ is positive (semi)-definite. $\sqrt{\boldsymbol{\Sigma}}$ designates any full rank matrix $\boldsymbol{T}$ such that $\boldsymbol{\Sigma} = \boldsymbol{T}\boldsymbol{T}^t$.

2.1 Lattices

A lattice Λ of dimension m and rank $k \leq m$ is a discrete additive subgroup of $\mathbb{R}^m$. It is generated by all linear combinations with integer coefficients of k linearly independent basis vectors $\boldsymbol{B} = \{\boldsymbol{b}_1, ..., \boldsymbol{b}_k\}$. The *span* span$(\boldsymbol{A})$ of a matrix $\boldsymbol{A}$ is generated by all linear combinations with *real* coefficients of the column vectors of $\boldsymbol{A}$. The span of a lattice Λ is span(Λ) = span$(\boldsymbol{B})$ for any basis $\boldsymbol{B}$ of Λ.

q-ary integer lattices are of great cryptographic interest. For positive integers $m, n \in \mathbb{N}$, $q \geq 2$, set $\boldsymbol{u} \in \mathbb{Z}_q^n$ and $\boldsymbol{A} \in \mathbb{Z}_q^{n \times m}$. Then the m-dimensional full rank q-ary lattices are defined as follows.

$$\Lambda^{\perp}(\boldsymbol{A}) = \Lambda_q^{\perp}(\boldsymbol{A}) := \{\boldsymbol{x} \in \mathbb{Z}^m : \boldsymbol{A}\boldsymbol{x} = \boldsymbol{0} \pmod{q}\},$$
$$\Lambda_u^{\perp}(\boldsymbol{A}) := \{\boldsymbol{x} \in \mathbb{Z}^m : \boldsymbol{A}\boldsymbol{x} = \boldsymbol{u} \pmod{q}\}.$$

We will often use vectors obtained when sampling in q-ary lattices. The sampled vectors will usually follow either a spherical or non-spherical Gaussian distribution over a lattice Λ.

Definition 1 (Gaussian function [7]**).** *For any $s > 0$, the Gaussian function ρ_s on $\mathbb{R}^n$ with parameter s is defined as*

$$\rho_s(\boldsymbol{x}) = e^{-\pi||\boldsymbol{x}||^2/s^2} \quad \textit{for} \quad \boldsymbol{x} \in \mathbb{R}^n.$$

Definition 2 (Discrete Gaussian distribution [7]**).** *For any $\mathbf{c} \in \mathbb{R}^n$, real $s > 0$, and n-dimensional lattice Λ, the discrete Gaussian distribution $D_{\Lambda+\mathbf{c},s}$ is defined as*

$$D_{\Lambda+\mathbf{c},s}(\boldsymbol{x}) = \frac{\rho_s(\boldsymbol{x})}{\rho_s(\Lambda + \mathbf{c})} \quad \textit{for} \quad \boldsymbol{x} \in \Lambda + \mathbf{c},$$

$$\textit{where} \quad \rho_s(\Lambda + \mathbf{c}) = \sum_{a \in \Lambda + c} \rho_s(\boldsymbol{a}).$$

When s and $\mathbf{c}$ are omitted, they are taken to be 1 and $\mathbf{0}$, respectively.

Definition 3 (Non-spherical Gaussian function [7]**).** *For any semi-definite matrix $\boldsymbol{\Sigma} = \boldsymbol{T}\boldsymbol{T}^t$, the non-spherical Gaussian function $\rho_{\boldsymbol{T}} = \rho_{\sqrt{\boldsymbol{\Sigma}}}$ is defined as*

$$\rho_{\boldsymbol{T}}(\boldsymbol{x}) = e^{-\pi \boldsymbol{x}^t \boldsymbol{\Sigma}^+ \boldsymbol{x}} \quad \textit{for} \quad \boldsymbol{x} \in \operatorname{span}(\boldsymbol{T}) = \operatorname{span}(\boldsymbol{\Sigma}),$$

and $\rho_{\boldsymbol{T}}(\boldsymbol{x}) = 0$ for all $\boldsymbol{x} \notin$ span$(\boldsymbol{\Sigma})$.

Definition 4 (Generalized Discrete Gaussian distribution [7]**).** *For any* $\boldsymbol{c} \in \mathbb{R}^n$*, any positive semi-definite matrix* $\boldsymbol{\Sigma}$*, and n-dimensional lattice* Λ *such that* $(\Lambda + \boldsymbol{c}) \cap \operatorname{span}(\boldsymbol{\Sigma})$ *is non-empty, the generalized discrete Gaussian distribution* $D_{\Lambda+\boldsymbol{c},\sqrt{\boldsymbol{\Sigma}}}$ *is defined as*

$$D_{\Lambda+\boldsymbol{c},\sqrt{\boldsymbol{\Sigma}}}(\boldsymbol{x}) = \frac{\rho_{\sqrt{\boldsymbol{\Sigma}}}(\boldsymbol{x})}{\rho_{\sqrt{\boldsymbol{\Sigma}}}(\Lambda + \boldsymbol{c})} \quad \text{for} \quad \boldsymbol{x} \in \Lambda + \boldsymbol{c},$$

$$\text{where} \quad \rho_{\sqrt{\boldsymbol{\Sigma}}}(\Lambda + \boldsymbol{c}) = \sum_{\boldsymbol{a} \in \Lambda + \boldsymbol{c}} \rho_{\sqrt{\boldsymbol{\Sigma}}}(\boldsymbol{a}).$$

In this work, the smoothing parameter is used to set parameters.

Definition 5 (Smoothing parameter [17]**).** *For any lattice* Λ *and positive real* $\epsilon > 0$*, the smoothing parameter* $\eta_\epsilon(\Lambda)$ *is the smallest real* $s > 0$ *such that* $\rho_{1/s}(\Lambda^* \backslash \{\mathbf{0}\}) \leq \epsilon$.

Definition 6 ([7]**).** *For a positive semi-definite matrix* $\boldsymbol{\Sigma} = \boldsymbol{T}\boldsymbol{T}^t$, $\epsilon > 0$*, and a lattice* Λ *with* $\operatorname{span}(\Lambda) \subseteq \operatorname{span}(\boldsymbol{\Sigma})$*, we say* $\eta_\epsilon(\Lambda) \leq \sqrt{\boldsymbol{\Sigma}}$ *if* $\eta_\epsilon(\boldsymbol{T}^+\Lambda) \leq 1$.

The following lemma provides us an upper bound on objects sampled from a spherical Gaussian distribution.

Lemma 1 ([5]**).** *Let* $\Lambda \in \mathbb{R}^n$ *be a lattice and* $r \geq \eta_\epsilon(\Lambda)$ *for some* $\epsilon \in [0, 1[$*. For any* $\boldsymbol{c} \in \operatorname{span}(\Lambda)$*, we have*

$$\Pr[\|\boldsymbol{x}\| \geq r\sqrt{n} \mid \boldsymbol{x} \leftarrow D_{\Lambda+\boldsymbol{c},r}] \leq 2^{-n}.\frac{1+\epsilon}{1-\epsilon}.$$

2.2 Lattice Problems

We recall definitions of some lattice problems. Security often relies on the one-wayness of one or both of the following two functions. The one-wayness of these functions is closely related to the SIS and LWE problems.

Definition 7 (Ajtai's function [2]**).** *Let* $\boldsymbol{A} \in \mathbb{Z}_q^{n \times m}$*. Ajtai's function* $f_{\boldsymbol{A}}$ *is defined as*

$$f_{\boldsymbol{A}}(\boldsymbol{x}) = \boldsymbol{A}\boldsymbol{x} \bmod q \quad \text{for} \quad \boldsymbol{x} \in \mathbb{R}^m.$$

Definition 8. *Let* $\boldsymbol{A} \in \mathbb{Z}_q^{n \times m}$*. For some short error vector* $\boldsymbol{e} \in \mathbb{R}^m$*, the function* $g_{\boldsymbol{A}}$ *is defined as*

$$g_{\boldsymbol{A}}(\boldsymbol{s}, \boldsymbol{e}) = \boldsymbol{s}^t\boldsymbol{A} + \boldsymbol{e}^t \bmod q \quad \text{for} \quad \boldsymbol{s} \in \mathbb{R}^n.$$

The short integer solution (SIS) problem considers a short root of Ajtai's function. The inhomogeneous short integer solution (ISIS) problem is a variant of the SIS problem.

Definition 9 (Short integer solution (SIS) [2]). *Let $n, m \in \mathbb{N}$, $q \in \mathbb{Z}$ and $\beta \in \mathbb{R}$. For given $\boldsymbol{A} \in \mathbb{Z}_q^{n\times m}$, the short integer solution (SIS) problem $\mathrm{SIS}_{n,m,q,\beta}$ asks a non-zero vector $\boldsymbol{x} \in \mathbb{Z}^m$ such that $\|\boldsymbol{x}\| \leq \beta$, and*

$$\boldsymbol{A}\boldsymbol{x} = \boldsymbol{0} \pmod q$$

Definition 10 (Inhomogeneous short integer solution (ISIS)). *Let $n, m \in \mathbb{N}$, $q \in \mathbb{Z}$ and $\beta \in \mathbb{R}$. For given $\boldsymbol{A} \in \mathbb{Z}_q^{n\times m}$ and $\boldsymbol{y} \in \mathbb{Z}_q^n$, the inhomogeneous short integer solution (ISIS) problem $\mathrm{ISIS}_{n,m,q,\beta}$ asks a vector $\boldsymbol{x} \in \mathbb{Z}^m$ such that $\|\boldsymbol{x}\| \leq \beta$, and*

$$\boldsymbol{A}\boldsymbol{x} = \boldsymbol{y} \pmod q$$

We recall the definition of the learning with errors (LWE) problem. It can be seen as the dual of SIS problem.

Definition 11 (Learning with errors (LWE) [19]). *For $n, m \in \mathbb{N}$ and modulus $q \geq 2$, let $\theta, \pi, \chi \subseteq \mathbb{Z}_q$ be distributions. An LWE sample is obtained from sampling secret vector $\boldsymbol{s} \leftarrow \theta^n$, public matrix $\boldsymbol{A} \leftarrow \pi^{n\times m}$, and error vector $\boldsymbol{e} \leftarrow \chi^m$, and outputting $(\boldsymbol{A}, \boldsymbol{y}^t := \boldsymbol{s}^t\boldsymbol{A} + \boldsymbol{e}^t \pmod q)$.*

We say that an algorithm solves $\mathrm{LWE}_{n,m,q,\theta,\pi,\chi}$ if it distinguishes an LWE sample from a random sample distributed as $\pi^{n\times m} \times U(\mathbb{Z}_q^m)$ with probability greater than 1/2 plus non-negligible.

Chen, Genise and Mukherjee [7] introduced a relaxed notion of the ISIS problem. It allows for a little error in the solution. They also defined an *approximate trapdoor* for a public matrix $\boldsymbol{A} \in \mathbb{Z}_q^{n\times m}$ as a string that allows one to solve efficiently the approximate version of ISIS problem with respect to the matrix $\boldsymbol{A}$.

Definition 12 (Approximate ISIS (AISIS) [7]). *Let $n, m \in \mathbb{N}$, $q \in \mathbb{Z}$ and $\alpha, \beta \in \mathbb{R}$. For given $\boldsymbol{A} \in \mathbb{Z}_q^{n\times m}$ and $\boldsymbol{y} \in \mathbb{Z}_q^n$, the approximate inhomogeneous short integer solution (AISIS) problem $\mathrm{AISIS}_{n,m,q,\alpha,\beta}$ asks a vector $\boldsymbol{x} \in \mathbb{Z}^m$ such that $\|\boldsymbol{x}\| \leq \beta$ and*

$$\boldsymbol{A}\boldsymbol{x} = \boldsymbol{y} + \boldsymbol{z} \pmod q,$$

for some $\boldsymbol{z} \in \mathbb{Z}^n$ satisfying $\|\boldsymbol{z}\| \leq \alpha$.

2.3 F-trapdoor [7]

The approximate trapdoor method of [7] is based on the gadget-based trapdoor generation and preimage sampling algorithms of Micciancio and Peikert [18]. In [7], the authors introduced a new gadget matrix $\boldsymbol{F}$ which is obtained from the $\boldsymbol{G}$-gadget matrix [18] by dropping the l lower-orders entries. Let $b \geq 2$ an integer. b defines the base used in decomposition. q is the modulus so that $k = \lceil \log_b q \rceil$. The gadget matrix $\boldsymbol{F}$ is constructed so as to sample a short approximate preimage from $\Lambda_u^\perp(\boldsymbol{F})$ easily. First, the approximate gadget-vector is set as $\boldsymbol{f}^t :=$

$(b^l, b^{l+1}, ..., b^{k-1})^t \in \mathbb{Z}_q^{(k-l)}$. Then the approximate gadget matrix $\boldsymbol{F}$ is defined as $\boldsymbol{F} := \boldsymbol{I}_n \otimes \boldsymbol{f}^t \in \mathbb{Z}_q^{(n \times w)}$, where the number of columns of $\boldsymbol{F}$ is $w = n(k-l)$. Also, the numbers of columns in $\boldsymbol{A}$ as defined below is $m = 2n + w$. The public matrix $\boldsymbol{A}$ is defined as

$$\boldsymbol{A} = [\bar{\boldsymbol{A}} | \boldsymbol{F} - \bar{\boldsymbol{A}}\boldsymbol{R}] \in \mathbb{Z}_q^{n \times m} \quad \text{with} \quad \bar{\boldsymbol{A}} = [\boldsymbol{I}_n, \hat{\boldsymbol{A}}] \in \mathbb{Z}_q^{n \times 2n},$$

where $\boldsymbol{R}$ is a secret trapdoor matrix with small random entries, and $\hat{\boldsymbol{A}}$ is sampled from $U(\mathbb{Z}_q^{n \times n})$. $\boldsymbol{R}$ is sampled from the distribution $\chi^{2n \times w}$ where $\chi \subseteq \mathbb{Z}$ is chosen to be a distribution such that $\mathrm{LWE}_{n,n,q,\chi,U(\mathbb{Z}_q),\chi}$ is hard. Then, $\boldsymbol{A}$ can be pseudorandom.

When we want to compute a short approximate preimage of $\boldsymbol{u}$, we use the trapdoor $\boldsymbol{R}$ which enables us mapping short approximate coset representatives of $\Lambda_{\boldsymbol{u}}^{\perp}(\boldsymbol{F})$ to short approximate coset representatives of $\Lambda_{\boldsymbol{u}}^{\perp}(\boldsymbol{A})$ by using the relation

$$\boldsymbol{A} \begin{bmatrix} \boldsymbol{R} \\ \boldsymbol{I} \end{bmatrix} = \boldsymbol{F}.$$

However, this relation would leak information about the secret trapdoor $\boldsymbol{R}$. Thus, the perturbation-based Gaussian sampler technique of [18] is employed to avoid such a situation. The covariance of the perturbation $\boldsymbol{p}$ is defined by the positive semi-definite matrix

$$\boldsymbol{\Sigma}_p = s^2 \boldsymbol{I}_m - \sigma^2 \begin{bmatrix} \boldsymbol{R}\boldsymbol{R}^t & \boldsymbol{R} \\ \boldsymbol{R}^t & \boldsymbol{I} \end{bmatrix},$$

where σ is at least $\eta_\epsilon(\Lambda^{\perp}(\boldsymbol{G}))$ and s is a parameter. This perturbation can be computed as $\boldsymbol{p} \leftarrow D_{\mathbb{Z}^m, \sqrt{\boldsymbol{\Sigma}_p}}$.

To sample from $\Lambda_{\boldsymbol{u}}^{\perp}(\boldsymbol{A})$ in an approximate manner, we first set $\boldsymbol{v} = \boldsymbol{u} - \boldsymbol{A}\boldsymbol{p}$ and sample a vector $\boldsymbol{z}$ from the distribution $D_{\Lambda_{\boldsymbol{v}}^{\perp}(\boldsymbol{F}),\sigma}$. The approximate preimage is set as

$$\boldsymbol{y} = \boldsymbol{p} + \begin{bmatrix} \boldsymbol{R} \\ \boldsymbol{I} \end{bmatrix} \boldsymbol{z}.$$

2.4 Higher-bit Approximate Setting [13]

Building on the approximate setting defined in [7], Le Dévéhat, Shizuya and Hasegawa [13] introduced the notion of the higher-bit approximate ISIS problem. The intuitive idea is to discard low-weighted bits in the public matrix $\boldsymbol{A}$. Then, we can reduce its size while increasing a little bit the error on the sampled preimage $\boldsymbol{y}$. We briefly recall required notions and notations.

Let $b \geq 2$ be the base used in decomposition and $q \in \mathbb{Z}$ is the modulus such that $k = \lceil \log_b q \rceil$. Let d be an integer such that $0 \leq d < k$. d is chosen as the turning point exponent between high order and low order bits.

Definition 13 (Decomposition in base b **[13]).** *Let* $z \in \mathbb{Z}_q$*. The* decomposition in base b of z *is the elements* $\{\alpha_{z,r}\}_{r=0}^{k-1}$ *in* $[0, b-1]$ *such that*

$$z = \sum_{r=0}^{k-1} \alpha_{z,r} b^r.$$

Definition 14 (HighBits and LowBits functions [13]). *For* $z \in \mathbb{Z}_q$*, the* HighBits function *and the* LowBits function *are defined as*

$$\mathsf{HighBits}_d(z) = \sum_{r=d}^{k-1} \alpha_{z,r} b^r \quad and \quad \mathsf{LowBits}_d(z) = \sum_{r=0}^{d-1} \alpha_{z,r} b^r.$$

We extend these definition from integers to vectors and matrices.

Definition 15 (HighBits and LowBits functions extended [13]). *For a vector* $\boldsymbol{y} \in \mathbb{Z}_q^n$*,*

$$\boldsymbol{y}^H = \mathsf{HighBits}_d(y_i) \quad and \quad \boldsymbol{y}^L = \mathsf{LowBits}_d(y_i) \quad (0 \le i < n),$$

and for a matirix $\boldsymbol{A} \in \mathbb{Z}_q^{n \times m}$*,*

$$\boldsymbol{A}^H = \mathsf{HighBits}_d(a_{i,j}) \quad and \quad \boldsymbol{A}^L = \mathsf{LowBits}_d(a_{i,j}) \quad (0 \le i < n, 0 \le j < m).$$

We write $\boldsymbol{A}^H = \mathsf{HighBits}_d(\boldsymbol{A})$ to mean $\boldsymbol{A}^H = \mathsf{HighBits}_d(a_{i,j})$ with $\boldsymbol{A} = (a_{i,j})$. The lower-bit case and the case for vectors are also defined in a same manner.

By using the definitions above, The higher-bit version of ISIS is defined as follows.

Definition 16 (Higher-bit AISIS (HAISIS) [13]). *Let* $n, m \in \mathbb{N}$*,* $q \in \mathbb{Z}$*,* $\alpha, \beta \in \mathbb{R}$ *and* $d \in \mathbb{N}$ *with* $d < \lceil \log_b q \rceil$*. For given* $\boldsymbol{A} \in \mathbb{Z}_{\frac{q}{b^d}}^{n \times m}$ *and* $\boldsymbol{y} \in \mathbb{Z}_q^n$*, the higher-bit approximate inhomogeneous short integer solution (HAISIS) problem* $\mathrm{HAISIS}_{n,m,q,d,\alpha,\beta}$ *asks a vector* $\boldsymbol{x} \in \mathbb{Z}^m$ *such that* $\|\boldsymbol{x}\| \le \beta$ *and*

$$b^d \boldsymbol{A}\boldsymbol{x} = \boldsymbol{y} + \boldsymbol{z} \pmod{q},$$

for some $\boldsymbol{z} \in \mathbb{Z}^n$ *satisfying* $\|\boldsymbol{z}\| \le \alpha$*.*

The higher-bit approximate ISIS problem is as hard as the standard ISIS from the following lemma.

Lemma 2 ([13]).

$$\mathrm{ISIS}_{n,n+m,q,\beta} \ge_p \mathrm{HAISIS}_{n,m,q,d,\alpha+\beta,\beta},$$
$$\mathrm{HAISIS}_{n,m,q,d,\alpha,\beta} \ge_p \mathrm{ISIS}_{n,n+m,q,\alpha+(\sqrt{n}b^d+1)\beta}.$$

We now consider the higher-bit version of the approximate gadget matrix $\boldsymbol{F}$. For the public matrix $\boldsymbol{A} = [\bar{\boldsymbol{A}}|\boldsymbol{F} - \bar{\boldsymbol{A}}\boldsymbol{R}]$, the new high-weighted matrix $\boldsymbol{A}^{new}$ is obtained by

$$\boldsymbol{A}^{new} = \frac{\boldsymbol{A}^H}{b^d}, \quad \text{where} \quad \boldsymbol{A}^H = [\bar{\boldsymbol{A}}^H|(\boldsymbol{F} - \bar{\boldsymbol{A}}\boldsymbol{R})^H].$$

This modification implies a rather simple optimization on the sampled preimage set as

$$\boldsymbol{y}^{new} = \boldsymbol{y} \bmod b^{k-d}.$$

This modification saves memory storage in both the public matrix and sampled preimage at the cost of an increased approximation.

2.5 Non-Spherical Gaussian [12]

In Subsect. 2.3, we have seen the perturbation-based Gaussian samplers. The perturbation is defined by the matrix $\boldsymbol{\Sigma_p}$ as

$$\boldsymbol{\Sigma}_p := s^2\boldsymbol{I}_m - \sigma^2 \begin{bmatrix} \boldsymbol{R}\boldsymbol{R}^t & \boldsymbol{R} \\ \boldsymbol{R}^t & \boldsymbol{I} \end{bmatrix}.$$

The output distribution of samplers is to be a spherical Gaussian. In order to correctly sample such perturbation, the matrix $\boldsymbol{\Sigma_p}$ needs to be positive semi-definite. In the setting of a spherical Gaussian sampler, this implies a condition on the parameter s of the resulting distribution such as

$$s \geq \sigma s_1\left(\begin{bmatrix} \boldsymbol{R} \\ \boldsymbol{I} \end{bmatrix}\right),$$

where $s_1(\cdot)$ denotes the largest singular value of its input matrix. The observation made in [12] is that we are trying to hide the information leaking from the distribution of $\begin{bmatrix} \boldsymbol{R} \\ \boldsymbol{I} \end{bmatrix} \boldsymbol{z}$ during the preimage sampling procedure. However, the linear transformation $\begin{bmatrix} \boldsymbol{R} \\ \boldsymbol{I} \end{bmatrix}$ distorts much more the top $2n$ entries in $\boldsymbol{z}$ than the bottom kn entries. In regards with this, it is "unnecessary" to apply the same correction on the top and bottom entries. In [12], this uneven distortion is taken into account as they changes the perturbation to

$$\boldsymbol{\Sigma}_p := \begin{bmatrix} \bar{s}^2\boldsymbol{I}_{2n} & \\ & \tilde{s}^2\boldsymbol{I}_{kn} \end{bmatrix} - \sigma^2 \begin{bmatrix} \boldsymbol{R}\boldsymbol{R}^t & \boldsymbol{R} \\ \boldsymbol{R}^t & \boldsymbol{I} \end{bmatrix}, \quad \text{where} \quad \bar{s} >> \tilde{s}.$$

The conditions required so that $\boldsymbol{\Sigma_p}$ is positive semi-definite are less restrictive. Thus, we can have a smaller $\tilde{s}$ than $\bar{s}$ which results in a smaller sampled preimage than with a spherical Gaussian sampler.

3 Higher-bit Approximate Lattice Trapdoor with Non-Spherical Gaussian

We would like to assess the impact of the higher-bit approximate setting when combined with the optimization of [12] which considers the non-spherical Gaussian distribution. We first show that the $\boldsymbol{F}$-trapdoor construction instantiated with a non-spherical Gaussian sampler can be adapted in the higher-bit setting just as it was done for the normal $\boldsymbol{F}$-trapdoor construction in [13].

3.1 Modification in the Public Matrix

Let $\boldsymbol{F}$ be an approximate gadget matrix defined as in Subsect. 2.3 with the base b and the parameter l. As mentioned above, we use the decomposition in base b and the modulus q and $k = \lceil \log_b q \rceil$. Let d be an integer such that $0 \leq d \leq l$.

According to [13], we modify the public matrix $\boldsymbol{A}$ of [12] by discarding its low-weighted bits. Namely,

$$\boldsymbol{A}^{new} = \frac{\boldsymbol{A}^H}{b^d}, \quad \text{where} \quad \boldsymbol{A}^H = [\bar{\boldsymbol{A}}^H | \boldsymbol{F} + (-\bar{\boldsymbol{A}}\boldsymbol{R})^H].$$

Note that $\boldsymbol{R}$ is the approximate trapdoor associated with the Ajtai's Function defined by $\boldsymbol{A}$ and $\boldsymbol{A}^{new}$ is in $\mathbb{Z}_{\frac{q}{b^d}}^{n \times m}$.

To sample a preimage of $f_{\boldsymbol{A}^{new}}$, we use the perturbation based non-spherical Gaussian sampler on $f_{\boldsymbol{A}}$. Compared to [13], we use the perturbation matrix $\boldsymbol{\Sigma}_p$ considered in Subsect. 2.5.

Repercussion on the Sizes and Underlying Problem Hardness. The use of the higher-bit setting is expected to imply a trade-off between an improvement in the sizes of objects and a lower hardness of the underlying problems which will lead to lower security in cryptosystems. The optimization in [12] reduces the size of sampled preimage. It achieves a win-win scenario as it provides a shorter approximate preimage which implies better security. In light of this, we are interested in whether the use of a non-spherical Gaussian sampler could lessen the impact of the trade-off observed in [13].

3.2 Higher-bit Version Algorithms with Non-Spherical Gaussian

In this subsection, We propose our approximate trapdoor generation algorithm HB.JHT.App.TrapGen and approximate preimage sampling algorithm HB.JHT.App.Samp. HB.JHT.App.TrapGen is the same as the approximate trapdoor generation algorithm HighBits.Approx.TrapGen of [13]. HB.JHT.App.Samp use the non-spherical Gaussian sampler JHT.Approx.Samp from [12], instead of a spherical Gaussian sampler as done in [13]. Our method allows us to sample an approximate preimage $\boldsymbol{y} \in \mathbb{Z}_{\frac{q}{b^d}}^m$ for higher-bit Ajtai's function defined by $\boldsymbol{A}$ with approximate trapdoor $\boldsymbol{R}$. We denote by $\boldsymbol{A}_0$ the original matrix which is generated by the approximate trapdoor generation algorithm from the $\boldsymbol{F}$-trapdoors construction. The description of algorithms is given in Fig. 1.

Algorithm 1 HighBits.Approx.TrapGen$_\chi$[13]

Input: Security parameter λ
Output: A pair $(\boldsymbol{A},\boldsymbol{R}) \in \mathbb{Z}_{\frac{q}{b^d}}^{n\times m} \times \mathbb{Z}^{2n\times w}$ of a public matrix and a approximate trapdoor, a matrix $\boldsymbol{A}_0^L \in \mathbb{Z}_{b^d}^{n\times m}$
1: $(\boldsymbol{A}_0,\boldsymbol{R}) \leftarrow$ Approx.TrapGen$_\chi(\lambda)$ {Algorithm from [7]}
2: $\boldsymbol{A}_0^H$ = HighBits$_d(\boldsymbol{A}_0)$
3: $\boldsymbol{A}_0^L$ = LowBits$_d(\boldsymbol{A}_0)$
4: $\boldsymbol{A} = \frac{\boldsymbol{A}_0{}^H}{b^d}$
5: **return** $((\boldsymbol{A},\boldsymbol{R}),\boldsymbol{A}_0^L)$

Algorithm 2 HB.JHT.App.Samp

Input: $(\boldsymbol{A},\boldsymbol{A}_0^L,\boldsymbol{R},\boldsymbol{u},\bar{s},\tilde{s})$
Output: An approximate preimage $\boldsymbol{y} \in \mathbb{Z}_{\frac{q}{b^d}}^m$ of $\boldsymbol{u} \in \mathbb{Z}_q^n$
1: $\boldsymbol{y}_0$ = JHT.Approx.Samp$(b^d\boldsymbol{A} + \boldsymbol{A}_0^L,\boldsymbol{R},\boldsymbol{u},\bar{s},\tilde{s})$ {Algorithm from [12]}
2: $\boldsymbol{y}$ = LowBits$_{k-d}(\boldsymbol{y}_0)$
3: **return** $\boldsymbol{y}$

Fig. 1. Pseudocode for the higher-bit version approximate trapdoor generation and non-spherical Gaussian approximate preimage sampling algorithm. The distribution χ is chosen so that $\mathrm{LWE}_{n,n,q,\chi,U(\mathbb{Z}_q),\chi}$ is hard. For the sake of optimization in Algorithm 2, we need to set $q = b^k$.

$\bar{s}$ and $\tilde{s}$ parameters choices. We choose these parameters as defined in "mode 2" from [12]. That is to say we want to maximize optimization in storage as this is the main focus of this work. Thus, we set

$$\bar{s}^2 = \left(1 + \frac{k-l}{2}\right)\sigma^2 s_1(\boldsymbol{R})^2 \quad and \quad \tilde{s}^2 = \left(1 + \frac{2}{k-l}\right)\sigma^2.$$

Also, as described in Subsect. 2.5, the perturbation matrix $\boldsymbol{\Sigma}_p$ is set as

$$\boldsymbol{\Sigma}_p := \begin{bmatrix} \bar{s}^2\boldsymbol{I}_{2n} & \\ & \tilde{s}^2\boldsymbol{I}_{kn} \end{bmatrix} - \sigma^2 \begin{bmatrix} \boldsymbol{R}\boldsymbol{R}^t & \boldsymbol{R} \\ \boldsymbol{R}^t & \boldsymbol{I} \end{bmatrix}.$$

Algorithm 1. The algorithm first generates a public matrix $\boldsymbol{A}_0$ with an approximate trapdoor $\boldsymbol{R}$. Then the algorithm computes the high-bit approximated matrix $\boldsymbol{A}$ from $\boldsymbol{A}_0$. Note that this algorithm outputs an auxiliary output $\boldsymbol{A}_0^L$ which is used by the approximate preimage sampling algorithm

Algorithm 2. The algorithm samples an approximate preimage $\boldsymbol{y} \in \mathbb{Z}_{\frac{q}{b^d}}^m$ of $\boldsymbol{u} \in \mathbb{Z}_q^n$ by the higher-bit Ajtai's function $\boldsymbol{A} \in \mathbb{Z}_{\frac{q}{b^d}}^{n\times m}$. First, we sample an approximate preimage $\boldsymbol{y}_0 \in \mathbb{Z}_q^m$ of the Ajtai's function defined by $\boldsymbol{A}_0$ using the algorithm from [12]. Then we discard all d highest-weighted bit from $\boldsymbol{y}_0$ to get $\boldsymbol{y}$. Note that we have $b^d\boldsymbol{A}\boldsymbol{y} = b^d\boldsymbol{A}\boldsymbol{y}_0 \pmod q$ by Theorem 1 of [13].

Error Term. We define the error $\boldsymbol{e} \in \mathbb{Z}_q^n$ as $\boldsymbol{e} = \boldsymbol{u} - b^d \boldsymbol{A}\boldsymbol{y} \bmod q$. $\boldsymbol{e}_0$ is the error term induced by $\boldsymbol{y}_0$, i.e. $\boldsymbol{e}_0 = \boldsymbol{u} - \boldsymbol{A}_0\boldsymbol{y}_0 \bmod q$. For these terms $\boldsymbol{e}$ and $\boldsymbol{e}_0$, the following holds as in [13].

$$\boldsymbol{e} = \boldsymbol{e}_0 + \boldsymbol{e}_{new} \pmod q, \quad \text{where} \quad \boldsymbol{e}_{new} = \boldsymbol{A}_0^L \boldsymbol{y}_0 \bmod q.$$

3.3 Distributions of Modified Algorithms

For public matrices output by HighBits.Approx.TrapGen, the following lemma is known.

Lemma 3 ([13]). *Let* $((\boldsymbol{A}, \boldsymbol{R}), \boldsymbol{A}_0^L) \leftarrow \mathsf{HighBits.Approx.TrapGen}_\chi$. *Assume that* $\mathrm{LWE}_{n,n,q,\chi,U(\mathbb{Z}_q),\chi}$ *is hard. Then* $\boldsymbol{A}$ *and* $\boldsymbol{A}_0^L$ *are pseudorandom.*

We next estimate the resulting distribution of sampled preimage. We recall the following lemma which states the distribution of the sampled preimage.

Lemma 4 ([12]). *Let* $\Sigma = \bar{s}^2 \boldsymbol{I}_{2n} \otimes \tilde{s}^2 \boldsymbol{I}_{kn}$. *Let* D_0 *and* D_1 *be the distributions defined as*

$$\begin{aligned} D_0 = \{(\boldsymbol{A}, \boldsymbol{y}, \boldsymbol{u}, \boldsymbol{e}) | \boldsymbol{u} \leftarrow U(\mathbb{Z}_q^n), \boldsymbol{y} \leftarrow \mathsf{JHT.Approx.Samp}(\boldsymbol{A}, \boldsymbol{A}_0^L, \boldsymbol{R}, \boldsymbol{u}, \bar{s}, \tilde{s}), \\ \boldsymbol{e} = \boldsymbol{u} - \boldsymbol{A}\boldsymbol{y} \bmod q\}, \\ D_1 = \{(\boldsymbol{A}, \boldsymbol{y}, \boldsymbol{u}, \boldsymbol{e}) | \boldsymbol{y} \leftarrow D_{\mathbb{Z}^m, \sqrt{\Sigma}}, \boldsymbol{e} \leftarrow D_{\mathbb{Z}^n, \sigma\sqrt{(b^{2l}-1)/(b^2-1)}}, \\ \boldsymbol{u} = \boldsymbol{A}\boldsymbol{y} + \boldsymbol{e} \bmod q\}. \end{aligned}$$

Then D_0 *and* D_1 *are statistically indistinguishable.*

Thus, using Lemma 4, we are able to deduce the distributions in our new higher-bit approximate setting with non-spherical Gaussian sampler.

Theorem 1. *Let* $\Sigma = \bar{s}^2 \boldsymbol{I}_{2n} \otimes \tilde{s}^2 \boldsymbol{I}_{kn}$. *Let* $((\boldsymbol{A}, \boldsymbol{R}), \boldsymbol{A}_0^L) \leftarrow \mathsf{HighBits.Approx.TrapGen}_\chi$. *Let* D_0 *and* D_1 *be the distributions defined as*

$$\begin{aligned} D_0 = \{(\boldsymbol{A}, \boldsymbol{y}, \boldsymbol{u}, \boldsymbol{e}) | \boldsymbol{u} \leftarrow U(\mathbb{Z}_q^n), \boldsymbol{y} \leftarrow \mathsf{JHT.Approx.Samp}(\boldsymbol{A}, \boldsymbol{A}_0^L, \boldsymbol{R}, \boldsymbol{u}, \bar{s}, \tilde{s}), \\ \boldsymbol{e} = \boldsymbol{u} - b^d \boldsymbol{A}\boldsymbol{y} \bmod q\}, \\ D_1 = \{(\boldsymbol{A}, \boldsymbol{y}, \boldsymbol{u}, \boldsymbol{e}) | \boldsymbol{y}_0 \leftarrow D_{\mathbb{Z}^m, \sqrt{\Sigma}}, \boldsymbol{e}_0 \leftarrow D_{\mathbb{Z}^n, \sigma\sqrt{(b^{2l}-1)/(b^2-1)}}, \\ \boldsymbol{y} = \mathsf{LowBits}_{k-d}(\boldsymbol{y}_0), \boldsymbol{e} = \boldsymbol{e}_0 + \boldsymbol{A}_0^L \boldsymbol{y}_0 \bmod q, \\ \boldsymbol{u} = b^d \boldsymbol{A}\boldsymbol{y} + \boldsymbol{e} \bmod q\}. \end{aligned}$$

Then, D_0 *and* D_1 *are statistically indistinguishable for any* $\sigma \geq \sqrt{b^2+1}w(\sqrt{\log n})$.

The proof of Theorem 1 proceeds in a similar manner as in Theorem 4 in [13]. It will be given in the full paper.

Lengths Bounds. Theorem 1 provides us with length bounds on a preimage $\boldsymbol{y}$ and an error term $\boldsymbol{e}$. This is summarized in Table 1. For the sake of comparison, we included the length bounds of the constructions from [13] and [12].

Table 1. The length bounds for $\boldsymbol{y}$ and $\boldsymbol{e}$.

	This work Non-spherical Gaussian in higher-bit approximate setting	[13] Spherical Gaussian in higher-bit approximate setting	[12] Non-spherical Gaussian in approximate setting
preimage $\boldsymbol{y}$	$\bar{s}\sqrt{2n} + \tilde{s}\sqrt{kn}$	$s\sqrt{m}$	$\bar{s}\sqrt{2n} + \tilde{s}\sqrt{kn}$
error term $\boldsymbol{e}$	$b^l\sigma\sqrt{n} + nb^d(\bar{s}\sqrt{2} + \tilde{s}\sqrt{k})$	$b^l\sigma\sqrt{n} + \sqrt{nm}b^d s$	$b^l\sigma\sqrt{n}$

We can conclude that, from a theoretical point of view, combining the higher-bit approximate setting [13] with a non-spherical Gaussian sampler [12] leads to better lengths bounds on the objects we use than when using a spherical Gaussian sampler. Thus we obtain a better theoretical security and storage space for the sampled preimage. When we compare our construction with the one in [12], the length bound on the error is increased. This is the direct consequence of using the higher-bit setting. On the other hand, we should obtain better key sizes in our hash-and-sign construction. We will show it by experiments later.

4 Hash-and-Sign Signature

We now propose a hash-and-sign signature scheme instantiated with the algorithms in Fig. 1. We set $k = \lceil \log_b q \rceil$, and d is the turning point exponent for the higher-bit form. Let $\sigma, \bar{s}, \tilde{s} \in \mathbb{R}^+$ be the discrete Gaussian widths of the distributions over the cosets of $\Lambda_q^{\perp}(\boldsymbol{G})$ [18] and $\Lambda_q^{\perp}(\boldsymbol{A}_0)$ [7], respectively. We choose a distribution χ to sample $\boldsymbol{R}$ so that $\mathrm{LWE}_{n,n,q,\chi,U(\mathbb{Z}_q),\chi}$ is hard.

4.1 Construction

Construction 1 *Let* HB.JHT.App.TrapGen *and* HB.JHT.App.Samp *be as given in Fig. 1. A hash function* $H = \{H_\lambda : \{0,1\}^* \to \mathbb{Z}_q^n\}$ *is modeled as a random oracle. The signature scheme* $\Pi =$ (Gen, Sig, Ver) *is constructed as follows.*

- $\mathsf{Gen}(1^\lambda)$ *: The key-generation algorithm samples* $\boldsymbol{A} \in \mathbb{Z}_{\frac{q}{b^d}}^{n \times m}$ *together with its approximate trapdoor* $\boldsymbol{R}$ *and the matrix* $\boldsymbol{A}_0^L \in \mathbb{Z}_{b^d}^{n \times m}$ *from* HighBits.Approx. $\mathsf{TrapGen}_\chi(\lambda)$*. It outputs* $\boldsymbol{A}$ *as the verification key,* $(\boldsymbol{A}_0^L, \boldsymbol{R})$ *as the secret signing key.*
- $\mathsf{Sig}(\boldsymbol{A}, (\boldsymbol{A}_0^L, \boldsymbol{R}), \boldsymbol{m})$ *: The signing algorithm checks if the message-signature pair* $(\boldsymbol{m}, \boldsymbol{y}_m)$ *has been produced before. If so, it outputs* $\boldsymbol{y}_m$ *as the signature of* $\boldsymbol{m}$*. Otherwise, it computes* $\boldsymbol{u} = H(\boldsymbol{m})$*, and samples an approximate preimage* $\boldsymbol{y}_m \leftarrow \mathsf{HB.JHT.App.Samp}(\boldsymbol{A}, \boldsymbol{A}_0^L, \boldsymbol{R}, \boldsymbol{u}, \bar{s}, \tilde{s})$*. It outputs* $\boldsymbol{y}_m$ *as the signature and stores* $(\boldsymbol{m}, \boldsymbol{y}_m)$ *in the signature list.*
- $\mathsf{Ver}(\boldsymbol{A}, \boldsymbol{m}, \boldsymbol{y})$ *: The verification algorithm checks if* $\|\boldsymbol{y}\| \leq \beta$ *and* $\|b^d \boldsymbol{A}\boldsymbol{y} - H(\boldsymbol{m})\| \leq \alpha$*. If so, it outputs accept; otherwise, it outputs reject.*

4.2 Correctness

Theorem 2. *The signature scheme in Construction 1 is correct.*

Proof. Fix $\beta = \bar{s}\sqrt{2n}+\tilde{s}\sqrt{kn}$ and $\alpha = b^l\sigma\sqrt{n}+nb^d(\bar{s}\sqrt{2}+\tilde{s}\sqrt{k})$. Let $\boldsymbol{m} \in \{0,1\}^*$ be a message. We take $(\boldsymbol{A},(\boldsymbol{A}_0^L,\boldsymbol{R})) \leftarrow \mathsf{Gen}(1^\lambda)$. Then, we produce a signature $\boldsymbol{y} \in \mathbb{Z}_{\frac{q}{b^d}}^m$ for $\boldsymbol{m}$ by taking $\boldsymbol{y} \leftarrow \mathsf{Sig}(\boldsymbol{A},(\boldsymbol{A}_0^L,\boldsymbol{R}),\boldsymbol{m})$. We check whether the verifier accepts the signature for $\boldsymbol{m}$.

The signature is smaller than the original preimage $\boldsymbol{y}_0$ sampled by a non-spherical Gaussian distribution of parameters $\bar{s},\tilde{s}$. Let $\boldsymbol{y}_{0,2n}$ be the vector of the $2n$ first entries in $\boldsymbol{y}_0$ and $\boldsymbol{y}_{0,kn}$ be the vector of the kn last entries in $\boldsymbol{y}_0$, respectively. Then, we have

$$||\boldsymbol{y}|| \le ||\boldsymbol{y}_0|| \le ||\boldsymbol{y}_{0,2n}+\boldsymbol{y}_{0,kn}|| \le ||\boldsymbol{y}_{0,2n}||+||\boldsymbol{y}_{0,kn}|| \le \bar{s}\sqrt{2n}+\tilde{s}\sqrt{kn},$$

with overwhelming probability by Lemma 1. Thus the first condition $||\boldsymbol{y}|| \le \beta$ is satisfied.

Moreover,

$$\begin{aligned} ||b^d\boldsymbol{A}\boldsymbol{y}-H(\boldsymbol{m})|| &= ||H(\boldsymbol{m})-\boldsymbol{e}-H(\boldsymbol{m})|| \\ &= ||\boldsymbol{e}|| = ||\boldsymbol{e_0}+\boldsymbol{e_{new}}|| \\ &\le ||\boldsymbol{e_0}||+||\boldsymbol{e_{new}}|| \\ &\le ||\boldsymbol{e_0}||+||\boldsymbol{A}_0^L\boldsymbol{y}_0|| \\ &\le ||\boldsymbol{e_0}||+||\boldsymbol{A}_0^L||\cdot||\boldsymbol{y}_0||. \end{aligned}$$

By Lemma 1 and 4, we have $||\boldsymbol{e_0}|| \le b^l\sigma\sqrt{n}$. Since $\boldsymbol{A}_0^L$ is in a "low-bits" form, $||\boldsymbol{A}_0^L|| \le \sqrt{n}b^d$ follows. Then,

$$||b^d\boldsymbol{A}\boldsymbol{y}-H(\boldsymbol{m})|| \le b^l\sigma\sqrt{n}+nb^d(\bar{s}\sqrt{2}+\tilde{s}\sqrt{k}) = \alpha.$$

The second condition $||b^d\boldsymbol{A}\boldsymbol{y}-H(\boldsymbol{m})|| \le \alpha$ is satisfied.

Construction 1 is correct with overwhelming probability by the appropriate settings of the parameters and definitions of our algorithms.

4.3 Security

Theorem 3. *Construction 1 is strongly existentially unforgeable under a chosen-message attack in the random oracle model under the assumption that both* $\mathrm{SIS}_{n,n+m,q,2(\alpha+(\sqrt{n}b^d+1)\beta)}$ *problem and* $\mathrm{LWE}_{n,n,q,\chi,U(\mathbb{Z}_q),\chi}$ *problem are hard.*

The proof proceeds in a similar manner of hash-and-sign signatures [7,13]. It will be given in the full paper.

5 Implementation and Analysis

We aim to find the best concrete parameters which could achieve high security and low storage sizes simultaneously. We note that the resulting parameters might be different than the ones recommended in [12] or [13]. As a result of our experiments, we will assess the impact of the higher-bit approximation on the work of [12]. Thus, we test different parameter sets and estimate which parameter set derives better results than [12] for signature schemes.

We follow the implementation used in [13] which was built from the implementation by [7]. It has been adapted for a non-spherical Gaussian sampler. We realized an exhaustive search and we obtained 1245 experiment results each with a different parameters set. We make a comparison between all of these results in terms of security and storage to find the best choices.

5.1 Non-Spherical Gaussian Sampler with Higher-bit Approximate Setting

Combining the higher-bit approximate setting with the construction from [12] brings a lot of improvement to their results, especially in the size of public keys. This is displayed in Fig. 2 where the first two columns are the best results obtained by [12] and the rest fours are ours. For the sake of this comparison, we show the results with the exact same parameter sets. However, we note that we get even better results with the parameters showed in last two columns in our setting. This confirms the improvements brought by using the higher-bit approximate setting. Indeed, even though our construction suffers from a little drop in security, the savings in storage sizes are striking, especially when compared with our best parameters sets.

Actually, using this new parameters sets, we get better results than both [13] and [12]. Even though we do not obtain the same levels of security as in [12], we are able to decrease consequently the public key size.

Adapting the higher-bit approximate setting with the use of a non-spherical Gaussian sampler decreases the security when compared to the original scheme of [7] as it employs two optimization methods. However, fortunately, it turns out that we are able to achieve 155.4-bit security with public key sizes of 3.84kB and signature size of 4.4kb. A possible explanation for these results relies on the fact that using the higher-bit approximate setting allows for some bigger parameters. Namely, our construction allows us to use a a slightly bigger l than compared to [12] as shown in Fig. 2. In the approximate setting [12], the use of a big parameter l would decrease the security since the approximation error grows bigger. However, in our construction, the error occurred in the trapdoor is counterbalanced by having a smaller approximate preimage size which brings

	Construction from [12]	Construction from [12]	Construction 1	Construction 1	Construction 1	Construction 1
n	1024	1024	1024	1024	512	1024
$k = \lceil \log_b q \rceil$	9	18	9	18	16	16
b	4	2	4	2	2	2
l	5	10	5	10	11	11
d	-	-	5	10	11	11
τ	Unknown	Unknown	2.8	2.8	2.6	2.8
$\bar{s}$	27343.3	23894.3	6902.3	6039.8	2694	4350.1
$\tilde{s}$	25.2	12.5	16.0	7.9	7.9	8.4
m	6144	10240	6144	10240	3584	7168
$\|\|y\|\|_2$	536010	462876	12732.6	16752.4	1107.4	1544.0
$\|\|e\|\|_2$	173254	184505	2448537.1	2394955.5	430599.2	603592.8
PK (kB)	**11.25**	**20.25**	**5.12**	**9.22**	**1.92**	**3.84**
Sig (kB)	**5.75**	**6.73**	**5.50**	**8.43**	**2.19**	**4.4**
LWE	218.0	218.0	192.7	192.7	104.7	192.7
AISIS	**168.82**	**171.1**	**140.5**	**140.8**	**75.0**	**155.4**

Fig. 2. Comparison of parameters choices and Gaussian samplers. n and m are parameters for lattice settings. b, k and l are parameters as in the $\boldsymbol{F}$-trapdoor construction. d is the turning point exponent between high order and low order bits. s is the Gaussian parameter of our Gaussian sampler. τ is the Gaussian width of the secret matrix $\boldsymbol{R}$. $||y||$ and $||e||$ are the norms of the preimage and error terms. The size of public keys and signatures are measured in kB. LWE and AISIS refers to the security levels of breaking the associated problems.

better security. That is the reason why we chose parameter sets in the higher-bit approximate setting which differs from the ones in [12]. Thus, our results show some new choices of parameters that work well with the higher-bit approximate setting.

5.2 New Parameters Sets for Higher-bit Approximate Setting with Spherical Gaussian Sampler

We also show that these parameters sets for non-spherical Gaussian sampler with the higher-bit approximate setting brings better results even for the original higher-bit approximate setting by [13] which works with a spherical Gaussian sampler. The experiments results are summarized in Fig. 3.

From Fig. 3, we can see that for the same security parameter n, our new parameters sets achieve the same or better security, i.e., 75-bit security for $n = 512$ and 155-bit security for $n = 1024$, with smaller public key size and signature size. These results improve the trade-off between the original approximate trapdoor technique of [7] and the higher-bit approximate setting [13].

	$\boldsymbol{F}$-trapdoor [7]	$\boldsymbol{F}$-trapdoor [7]	[13]	[13]	New parameter set for [13]	New parameter set for [13]
n	512	1024	512	1024	512	1024
$k = \lceil \log_b q \rceil$	8	9	8	9	16	16
b	4	4	4	4	2	2
l	4	5	4	5	11	11
d	-	-	4	5	11	11
τ	2.6	2.8	2.6	2.8	2.6	2.8
s	2505.6	3733.1	2494.5	3741.7	1453.0	2163.9
m	3072	6144	3072	6144	3584	7168
$\|\|y\|\|_2$	138326.9	296473.0	8273.1	11534.9	1072.2	1535.5
$\|\|e\|\|_2$	19793.8	1502259.7	433381.2	2422789.0	428806.9	607601.6
PK (kB)	5.12	11.52	2.56	5.12	**1.92**	**3.84**
Sig (kB)	4.5	9.4	3.09	6.14	**2.25**	**4.5**
LWE	104.7	192.7	104.7	192.7	104.7	192.7
AISIS	87.8	183.7	75.0	140.5	**75.0**	**155.4**

Fig. 3. New parameters sets for the higher-bit approximate setting with the spherical Gaussian sampler. n and m are parameters for lattice settings. b, k and l are parameters as in the $\boldsymbol{F}$-trapdoor construction. d is the turning point exponent between high order and low order bits. s is the Gaussian parameter of our Gaussian sampler. τ is the Gaussian width of the secret matrix $\boldsymbol{R}$. $||y||$ and $||e||$ are the norms of the preimage and error terms. The size of public keys and signatures are measured in kB. LWE and AISIS refers to the security levels of breaking the associated problems.

6 Concluding Remarks

In this paper we have considered further improvement in approximate lattice trapdoors. Our approach is to combine the higher-bit approximate setting with the use of a non-spherical Gaussian sampler. We have estimated the impact of our proposed algorithm by using a proof-of-concept implementation. Although our construction suffers from a little drop in security, we get better public key size and signature size than previous works. Moreover, as part of our result, we find new parameters choices which lead to better results in the higher-bit approximate setting even with a spherical Gaussian sampler.

We finally note about the impact of a non-spherical Gaussian sampler with the higher-bit approximation setting. By the implementation results, the impact on the results observed with our proof-of-concept implementation does not look much big, however we have got better theoretical length bounds on the signature and error terms when compared with a spherical Gaussian sampler in Table 1. This fact suggests that there might be a possibility of further improvement in algorithms and implementations. It is an interesting question to explore.

Acknowledgement. This work has benefited from state aid managed by the National Research Agency under the France 2030 Plan bearing the reference ANR-22-PETQ-0006.

References

1. Agrawal, S., Boneh, D., Boyen, X.: Efficient lattice (H)IBE in the standard model. In: Gilbert, H. (ed.) EUROCRYPT 2010. LNCS, vol. 6110, pp. 553–572. Springer, Heidelberg (2010). https://doi.org/10.1007/978-3-642-13190-5_28
2. Ajtai, M.: Generating hard instances of lattice problems (extended abstract). In: Proceedings of the Twenty-Eighth Annual ACM Symposium on Theory of Computing, pp. 99–108. STOC 1996, Association for Computing Machinery, New York, NY, USA (1996). https://doi.org/10.1145/237814.237838
3. Ajtai, M.: Generating hard instances of the short basis problem. In: Wiedermann, J., van Emde Boas, P., Nielsen, M. (eds.) ICALP 1999. LNCS, vol. 1644, pp. 1–9. Springer, Heidelberg (1999). https://doi.org/10.1007/3-540-48523-6_1
4. Alkim, E., Barreto, P.S.L.M., Bindel, N., Krämer, J., Longa, P., Ricardini, J.E.: The lattice-based digital signature scheme qTESLA. In: Conti, M., Zhou, J., Casalicchio, E., Spognardi, A. (eds.) ACNS 2020. LNCS, vol. 12146, pp. 441–460. Springer, Cham (2020). https://doi.org/10.1007/978-3-030-57808-4_22
5. Banaszczyk, W.: New bounds in some transference theorems in the geometry of numbers. Math. Annalen **296**(4), 625–636 (1993). http://eudml.org/doc/165105
6. Cash, D., Hofheinz, D., Kiltz, E., Peikert, C.: Bonsai trees, or how to delegate a lattice basis. In: Gilbert, H. (ed.) EUROCRYPT 2010. LNCS, vol. 6110, pp. 523–552. Springer, Heidelberg (2010). https://doi.org/10.1007/978-3-642-13190-5_27
7. Chen, Y., Genise, N., Mukherjee, P.: Approximate trapdoors for lattices and smaller hash-and-sign signatures. In: Galbraith, S.D., Moriai, S. (eds.) ASIACRYPT 2019. LNCS, vol. 11923, pp. 3–32. Springer, Cham (2019). https://doi.org/10.1007/978-3-030-34618-8_1
8. Ducas, L., et al.: Crystals-dilithium: a lattice-based digital signature scheme. IACR Trans. Crypt. Hardware Embed. Syst. **2018**(1), 238–268 (2018). https://doi.org/10.13154/tches.v2018.i1.238-268. https://tches.iacr.org/index.php/TCHES/article/view/839
9. Gentry, C.: Fully homomorphic encryption using ideal lattices. In: Proceedings of the Forty-First Annual ACM Symposium on Theory of Computing. p. 169–178. STOC 2009, Association for Computing Machinery, New York, NY, USA (2009). https://doi.org/10.1145/1536414.1536440
10. Gentry, C., Peikert, C., Vaikuntanathan, V.: Trapdoors for hard lattices and new cryptographic constructions. In: Proceedings of the Fortieth Annual ACM Symposium on Theory of Computing, pp. 197–206. STOC 2008, Association for Computing Machinery, New York, NY, USA (2008). https://doi.org/10.1145/1374376.1374407
11. Hoffstein, J., Pipher, J., Silverman, J.H.: NTRU: a ring-based public key cryptosystem. In: Buhler, J.P. (ed.) ANTS 1998. LNCS, vol. 1423, pp. 267–288. Springer, Heidelberg (1998). https://doi.org/10.1007/BFb0054868
12. Jia, H., Hu, Y., Tang, C.: Lattice-based hash-and-sign signatures using approximate trapdoor, revisited. IET Inf. Secur. **16**(1), 41–50 (2022). https://doi.org/10.1049/ise2.12039. https://ietresearch.onlinelibrary.wiley.com/doi/abs/10.1049/ise2.12039
13. Le Dévéhat, A., Shizuya, H., Hasegawa, S.: On the higher-bit version of approximate inhomogeneous short integer solution problem. In: Conti, M., Stevens, M., Krenn, S. (eds.) CANS 2021. LNCS, vol. 13099, pp. 253–272. Springer, Cham (2021). https://doi.org/10.1007/978-3-030-92548-2_14

14. Lindner, R., Peikert, C.: Better key sizes (and attacks) for LWE-based encryption. In: Kiayias, A. (ed.) CT-RSA 2011. LNCS, vol. 6558, pp. 319–339. Springer, Heidelberg (2011). https://doi.org/10.1007/978-3-642-19074-2_21
15. Lyubashevsky, V.: Fiat-Shamir with aborts: applications to lattice and factoring-based signatures. In: Matsui, M. (ed.) ASIACRYPT 2009. LNCS, vol. 5912, pp. 598–616. Springer, Heidelberg (2009). https://doi.org/10.1007/978-3-642-10366-7_35
16. Micciancio, D.: Generalized compact knapsacks, cyclic lattices, and efficient one-way functions from worst-case complexity assumptions. In: The 43rd Annual IEEE Symposium on Foundations of Computer Science, 2002. Proceedings, pp. 356–365 (2002). https://doi.org/10.1109/SFCS.2002.1181960
17. Micciancio, D., Regev, O.: Worst-case to average-case reductions based on Gaussian measures. In: 45th Annual IEEE Symposium on Foundations of Computer Science, pp. 372–381 (2004). https://doi.org/10.1109/FOCS.2004.72
18. Micciancio, D., Peikert, C.: Trapdoors for lattices: simpler, tighter, faster, smaller. In: Pointcheval, D., Johansson, T. (eds.) EUROCRYPT 2012. LNCS, vol. 7237, pp. 700–718. Springer, Heidelberg (2012). https://doi.org/10.1007/978-3-642-29011-4_41
19. Regev, O.: On lattices, learning with errors, random linear codes, and cryptography. J. ACM **56**(6), 84–93 (2009). https://doi.org/10.1145/1568318.1568324
20. Shor, P.: Algorithms for quantum computation: discrete logarithms and factoring. In: Proceedings 35th Annual Symposium on Foundations of Computer Science, pp. 124–134 (1994). https://doi.org/10.1109/SFCS.1994.365700

WOTSwana: A Generalized $\mathcal{S}_{\text{leeve}}$ Construction for Multiple Proofs of Ownership

David Chaum[1], Mario Larangeira[2(✉)], and Mario Yaksetig[1]

[1] xx network, Cayman Islands, UK
{david,mario,will}@xx.network

[2] Tokyo Institute of Technology and IOG, Tokyo, Japan
mario@c.titech.ac.jp, mario.larangeira@iohk.io

Abstract. The $\mathcal{S}_{\text{leeve}}$ construction proposed by Chaum et al. (ACNS'21) introduces an extra security layer for digital wallets by allowing users to generate a "back up key" securely nested inside the secret key of a signature scheme, *i.e.*, ECDSA. The "back up key", which is secret, can be used to issue a "proof of ownership", *i.e.*, only the real owner of this secret key can generate a *single* proof, which is based on the WOTS+ signature scheme. The authors of $\mathcal{S}_{\text{leeve}}$ proposed the formal technique for a *single* proof of ownership, and only informally outlined a construction to generalize it to multiple proofs. This work identifies that their proposed construction presents drawbacks, *i.e.*, varying of signature size and signing/verifying computation complexity, limitation of linear construction, etc. Therefore we introduce *WOTSwana*, a generalization of $\mathcal{S}_{\text{leeve}}$, which is, more concretely, a more general scheme, *i.e.* an extra security layer that generates *multiple* proofs of ownership, and put forth a thorough formalization of two constructions: (1) one given by a linear concatenation of numerous WOTS+ private/public keys, and (2) a construction based on tree like structure, *i.e.*, an underneath Merkle tree whose leaves are WOTS+ private/public key pairs. Furthermore, we present the security analysis for multiple proofs of ownership, showcasing that this work addresses the early mentioned drawbacks of the original construction. In particular, we extend the original security definition for $\mathcal{S}_{\text{leeve}}$. Finally, we illustrate an alternative application of our construction, by discussing the creation of an encrypted group chat messaging application.

Keywords: Hash-based Signatures · Post-Quantum Cryptography · ECDSA

1 Introduction

The ECDSA based wallets have been target to intensive exposure given its wide use in cryptopocurrencies, *e.g.*, Bitcoin [21], Ethereum [24] and Ouroboros [2,12, 16], which has driven the research community to channel its efforts to propose

This work was supported by JSPS KAKENHI Grant Number JP21K11882.

S.-H. Seo and H. Seo (Eds.): ICISC 2022, LNCS 13849, pp. 491–511, 2023.
https://doi.org/10.1007/978-3-031-29371-9_24

new attacks to the signature scheme/wallets [1,23]. The solution proposed by Chaum et al. [7], *i.e.* $\mathcal{S}_{\text{leeve}}$, is a signature based new cryptographic primitive designed to mitigate damages during massive leaks of private information of wallets. In a nutshell, the construction in [7] allows the rightful user to prove its ownership in the face of its secret key becoming public. Important to note, that proving the knowledge of the correct secret key, via zero knowledge protocols for example, is of no use as, potentially, anyone could generate such a proof during a massive leak. The main technique of $\mathcal{S}_{\text{leeve}}$ is to leverage the regular ECDSA scheme by having a nested "back up key" to generate the proof of ownership, or even to fully discard the ECDSA scheme for a (post-quantum) signature scheme; a hash based signature scheme.

The Single Proof of Ownership of $\mathcal{S}_{\text{leeve}}$. The most significant novelty of [7] is the introduction of a *second layer of security* by allowing the user to verify the correct ownership of the leaked keys, which would be impossible otherwise. However this feature, as fully presented in [7], is rather limited given that only *a single* proof can be issued. The main construction relies on a variant of the WOTS+ [15], therefore it can be used only once. The authors of [7] mitigate it by presenting the sketch of a general construction which concatenates several instances of the WOTS+ like scheme in order to generate multiple proofs. Unfortunately, the description is rather informal and the construction seemingly introduces an unusual feature: the signature has varying size and sign/verification times depending on how many proofs of ownership were previously issued.

By closer inspection of their described construction, one would realize that the varying time and size of the proofs are due to the level of the linear sequence of WOTS+ like *ladders*, *i.e.*, sequence of hash function executions. Given that each proof generation uses one instance of the signature, the issuer has to keep the state, *i.e.* the "height" position, in the sequence of ladders and add it to the signature. Moreover the presented security analysis does not cover the case that the adversary can sample several proof of ownership in order to come up with a forgery. Their security proofs focus on the single proof case.

Related Works. The work by Chaum et al. [7] seems to be unique in the sense that introduces a novel strategy in adding extra layer of security to wallets. It, for example, sharply contrasts with hot/cold wallet strategies used before, as for example [9,11,14]. A follow up work by Chaum et al. [6] introduces a much more robust security analysis. Whereas the original construction relies on the L-Tree data structure, as it was introduced by Hülsing [15], the work in [6] updates the original Sleeve construction to support Tweakable Hash functions as introduced by Bernstein et al. [3]. The latter puts forth a more module design and therefore it is more desirable approach, which is use in our constructions.

Our Contribution. This work tackles the early mentioned limitations of [7]. That is, we introduce the first generalization of $\mathcal{S}_{\text{leeve}}$ by proposing two constructions for "multiple generations of proof of ownership": the linear and the tree constructions. The main difference between them is how the $\mathcal{S}_{\text{leeve}}$ back up key is kept underneath the ECDSA secret key. We recall the $\mathcal{S}_{\text{leeve}}$ introduces an extra key, the early mentioned "back up key", in the key generation algorithm in addition to the verification and secret keys. Whereas the verification and secret key are used as a regular signature key pair, the back up key remains secret and is only used when issuing the proof of ownership.

Novel Constructions. The proof of ownership of the original $\mathcal{S}_{\text{leeve}}$ is a variant of the WOTS+ signature scheme [15] by Hülsing, named Extended WOTS+ (eWOTS+). Briefly, the proof generated by [7] is an eWOTS+ signature, whose the single respective private key is kept nested into the ECDSA secret key, *i.e.*, thus used as the "back up key". This work reviews this design and proposes *Wotswana* with two constructions: (1) a linear construction, under a similar design to the one outlined in [7], and (2) a tree based construction, *i.e.*, the nested key pairs are kept under a Merkle Tree nested inside the ECDSA secret key. Both constructions rely on the regular WOTS+ signature scheme, instead of the eWOTS+.

In our (1) *linear construction*, blocks of WOTS+ keys are concatenated linearly. Briefly, the "deepest" WOTS+ verification key is used to derive the next WOTS+ secret key, up to the point that the uppermost WOTS+ verification key is converted into the ECDSA secret/verification key pair. This construction naturally extends the original [7] by adding more underlying WOTS+ key pairs as the set of backup keys to be used to issue proofs of ownership. Providing varying verification/generation time complexity as the outlined construction of [7]. The (2) *tree construction* does not compose the early described "sequence" of WOTS+ blocks. Instead, it organizes them as leaves of a Merkle Tree, such that the root of the tree is converted into the ECDSA key pair. This design provides the advantage that, although both constructions keep a state, *i.e.*, the WOTS+ pair to be used for the proof of ownership, the tree construction does not require the verification routine to transverse the whole structure (as in (1) linear construction). For comparison, we remark that while verifying the linear construction proof of ownership, the routine transverses the linear structure from the point in the structure upwards until the ECDSA verification key. The Merkle Tree structure prevents that in the tree based construction. Furthermore, our linear and tree based constructions rely on the original WOTS+ construction, instead of eWOTS+ from [7], because they are based on Tweakable Hash Functions (while [7] relies on L-Trees [10]). This brings the advantage of using a more well established signature scheme.

Multiple Proofs and Fallback. Furthermore we extend the original proof of ownership [7] security definition which is suitable for *only* a single proof. Concretely, our proposed security definition allows the adversary to have access to a "proof generation oracle". Therefore, for a given Wotswana scheme with capability of t proofs of ownership, the adversary can query the oracle for at most $t - 1$ proofs, before attempting to generate a forgery of its own. Yet we highlight that while the original constructions reveal the ECDSA secret in order to prove ownership, our constructions keep the full secret-key undisclosed even after numerous proofs of ownership generations.

Our construction does not rely on any type of publishing on public data structures (e.g., a blockchain). This allows for a cleaner and more secure design that takes place completely off-chain during the key generation phase of the users. For example, if users posted a signed hash of the secret key using the fallback key instead, there is the risk of a block producer taking advantage of the miner extractable value (MEV) and front-running these different transactions and posting such data with a malicious signature instead. As a result, solutions that rely on posting on a public board, require indistinguishability assumptions of the underlying and potentially different post-quantum signature schemes. It is a conservative approach to avoid that sort of additional assumption. We highlight that our system is front-running resistant in a setting where there is an ongoing proof-of-ownership stage (e.g., traditional transactions are halted). Therefore, a miner extracting the user's private key from a proof-of-ownership signature should not be able to steal the user's money.

The motivation for this design is to allow users to rollover to a quantum-secure blockchain—using the fallback key—and then use the multiple proofs-of-ownership as a main mechanism to perform transactions in the new chain. Therefore, the construction can potentially act as a replacement for hash-based signature schemes such as SPHINCS [3] or XMSS [5] as it results in constant-sized signatures at the cost of linear verification time. The chain, however, can feature potential improvements as it can act as a state-keeping layer.

We also carried out a formal method analysis of Wotswana using Verifpal [17, 19]. Our formal analysis shows that our design preserves the confidentiality of the underlying keys.

In summary our contributions are:

- **Two Wotswana Constructions:** Sect. 3 presents the two designs , the *linear* and the *tree* constructions. Both keep a state, meaning how many proofs of ownership were issued. However the main difference is how the WOTS+ keys are kept internally. Namely, in linear or tree fashion;
- **Security Analysis:** Sect. 4 introduces the security analysis of our protocol with respect to the Key Derivation Function (KDF), the component used in our construction to internally concatenate WOTS+ blocks, and our two constructions for Wotswana;
- **Formal Methods:** Next, in Sect. 5, after a brief description of the main tool used, *i.e.*, Verifpal, we describe our proposed model for the Wotswana Protocol. We end our formal methods approach by discussion the interpretation of our results;
- **Application:** Finally, Sect. 6 discusses Encrypted Group Chat as an application for Wotswana. In particular, we discuss the applicability of multiple proofs of ownership.

2 Preliminaries

It is convenient to quickly review the WOTS+ signature construction from [15], the Tweakable Hash proposal from [3], the original $\mathcal{S}_{\text{leeve}}$ definitions [7], and the definitions for Key Derivation Function (KDF) [8,20] used in our constructions. We also denote Probabilistic Polynomial Time algorithms as PPT.

2.1 The WOTS+ Signature Scheme

Here we review the original WOTS+ signature scheme. The Wotswana later constructions, linear and tree, rely on the standard WOTS+ construction.

Definition 1 (Family of Functions). *Given the security and the Winternitz parameters, respectively,* $\lambda \in \mathbb{N}$ *and* $w \in \mathbb{N}, w > 1$, *let a family of functions* $\mathcal{H}_\lambda$ *be* $\{h_k : \{0,1\}^\lambda \rightarrow \{0,1\}^\lambda | k \in \mathcal{K}_\lambda\}$ *with key space* $\mathcal{K}_\lambda$.

Definition 2 (Chaining Function). *Given a family of functions* $\mathcal{H}_\lambda$, $x \in \{0,1\}^\lambda$, *an iteration counter* $i \in \mathbb{N}$, *a key* $k \in \mathcal{K}_\lambda$, *for* j λ*−bit strings* $\mathbf{r} = (r_1, \ldots, r_j) \in \{0,1\}^{\lambda \times j}$ *with* $j \geq i$, *then we have the chaining function as follows*

$$c_k^i(\mathbf{r}, x) = \begin{cases} h_k(c_k^{i-1}(\mathbf{r}, x) \oplus r_i), & 1 \leq i \leq j; \\ x, & i = 0. \end{cases}$$

We rely on the same setting from [15], that is this work assumes the chaining function uses a family of functions $\mathcal{F}_n : \{f_k : \{0,1\}^n \rightarrow \{0,1\}^n | k \in \mathcal{K}_n\}$ with a key space $\mathcal{K}_n$. Additionally, we review the notation for the subset of randomness vector $\mathbf{r} = (r_1, \ldots, r_\ell)$, and denote by $\mathbf{r}_{a,b}$ the subset of $(r_a, \ldots, r_b)$.

Definition 3 (*W-OTS*$^+$). *Given the security parameter* λ, *a chaining function* c, *and* $k \leftarrow \mathcal{K}$ *from the key space* $\mathcal{K}$, *the W-OTS*$^+$ *signature scheme is the tuple* $(\mathsf{Gen}_W, \mathsf{Sign}_W, \mathsf{Verify}_W)$, *defined as in Table 1.*

The Security of WOTS+. The standard security notion for digital signature schemes is existential unforgeability under adaptive chosen message attacks (EU-CMA) which is defined using the following experiment. By DSS(1^λ), we denote the digital signature scheme (DSS) with security parameter λ, then we model the security by defining the security experiment $\mathsf{Exp}_{\mathsf{DSS}(1^\lambda)}^{\mathsf{EU\text{-}CMA}}(\mathcal{A})$, as follows:

Experiment $\mathsf{Exp}_{\mathsf{DSS}(1^\lambda)}^{\mathsf{EU\text{-}CMA}}(\mathcal{A})$

$(\mathsf{sk}, \mathsf{pk}) \longleftarrow \mathsf{keygen}(1^\lambda)$
$(M^*, \sigma^*) \longleftarrow \mathcal{A}^{\mathsf{Sign}(sk,\cdot)}(\mathsf{pk})$
Let $\{M_i, \sigma_i\}_1^q$ be the query-answer pairs of $\mathsf{Sign}(sk, \cdot)$
Return 1 iff $\mathsf{Verify}(pk, M^*, \sigma^*) = 1$ and $M^* \notin \{M_i\}_1{}^q$

We define the success probability of the adversary $\mathcal{A}$ in the above EU-CMA experiment as $\mathsf{Succ}_{\mathsf{DSS}(1^\lambda)}^{\mathsf{EU\text{-}CMA}}(\mathcal{A}) = \Pr[\mathsf{Exp}_{\mathsf{DSS}(1^\lambda)}^{\mathsf{EU\text{-}CMA}}(\mathcal{A}) = 1]$.

Definition 4 (EU-CMA). *For a polynomial poly*$(\cdot)$, *let* $\lambda, t, q \in \mathbb{N}, t, q = poly(\lambda)$, *DSS a digital signature scheme. It is said the DSS is EU-CMA-secure, if the maximum success probability* $\mathsf{InSec}^{EU\text{-}CMA}(DSS(1^\lambda); t, q)$ *of all possibly probabilistic adversaries* $\mathcal{A}$, *running in time* $\leq t$, *making at most* q *queries to Sign in the above experiment, is negligible in* λ, $\mathsf{InSec}^{EU\text{-}CMA}(DSS(1^\lambda); t, q) = max\,\{\mathsf{Succ}_{\mathsf{DSS}(1^\lambda)}^{\mathsf{EU\text{-}CMA}}(\mathcal{A})\} = negl(\lambda)$.

Table 1. The main idea of the W-OTS$^+$ construction is to create "ladders" of hash function executions, via the Chaining Function $c_k^i(\cdot,\cdot)$, from the secret keys sk_i to the verification keys vk_i.

$\mathsf{Gen}_W^k(1^\lambda)$	$\mathsf{Sign}_W^k(\mathsf{m},\mathsf{sk})$
Pick $(\ell+w-1)$ λ-bit strings r_i	Compute $\mathsf{m} \rightarrow (\mathsf{m}_1,\ldots,\mathsf{m}_{\ell_1})$,
Set $\mathsf{sk}_i \leftarrow r_i$, for $1 \le i \le \ell$	for $\mathsf{m}_i \in \{0,\ldots,w-1\}$
Set $\mathsf{sk} = (\mathsf{sk}_1,\ldots,\mathsf{sk}_\ell)$	Compute checksum $C = \sum_{i=1}^{\ell_1}(w-1-\mathsf{m}_i)$,
Set $\mathbf{r} = (r_{\ell+1},\ldots,r_{\ell+w-1})$	and its base w representation $(C_1,\ldots,C_{\ell_2})$,
Set $\mathsf{vk}_0 = (\mathbf{r},k)$	for $C_i \in \{0,\ldots,w-1\}$
Set $\mathsf{vk}_i = c_k^{w-1}(\mathbf{r},\mathsf{sk}_i)$, $1 \le i \le \ell$	Parse $B = \mathsf{m}\|C$ as $(b_1,\ldots,b_{\ell_1+\ell_2})$
Set $\mathsf{vk} = (\mathsf{vk}_0,\mathsf{vk}_1,\ldots,\mathsf{vk}_\ell)$	Set $\sigma_i = c_k^{b_i}(\mathbf{r},\mathsf{sk}_i)$, for $1 \le i \le \ell_1+\ell_2$
Return $(\mathsf{sk},\mathsf{vk})$	Return $\sigma = (\sigma_1,\ldots,\sigma_{\ell_1+\ell_2})$

$\mathsf{Verify}_W^k(\mathsf{m},\mathsf{vk},\sigma)$
Compute $\mathsf{m} \rightarrow (\mathsf{m}_1,\ldots,\mathsf{m}_{\ell_1})$,
for $\mathsf{m}_i \in \{0,\ldots,w-1\}$
Compute checksum $C = \sum_{i=1}^{\ell_1}(w-1-\mathsf{m}_i)$,
and the base w representation $(C_1,\ldots,C_{\ell_2})$,
for $C_i \in \{0,\ldots,w-1\}$
Parse $B = \mathsf{m}\|C$ as $(b_1,\ldots,b_{\ell_1+\ell_2})$
Return 1, if the following equations hold
$\mathsf{vk}_0 = (\mathbf{r},k)$
$\mathsf{vk}_i = c_k^{w-1-b_i}(\mathbf{r}_{b_i+1,w-1},\sigma_i)$ for $1 \le i \le \ell_1+\ell_2$

2.2 Tweakable Hash Functions

Tweakable hash functions allow for a better abstraction of hash-based signature scheme description. By decoupling the computations of hash chains, hash trees, and nodes, protocol designers can separate the analysis of the high-level construction from exactly how the computation is done. Therefore abstracting the computation away in hash-based schemes only requires analyzing the hashing construction. The standard definition is as follows.

Definition 5 (Tweakable Hash Function). *For a security parameter λ and a polynomial $n(\lambda)$, a tweakable hash function has three inputs: a public parameter $P \in \mathcal{P}$, a tweak $T \in \mathcal{T}$ and a message $M \in \{0,1\}^\alpha$. The hash produces an output digest $\mathcal{MD} \in \{0,1\}^{n(\lambda)}$: Let $\mathcal{P}$ the public parameters space, $\mathcal{T}$ the tweak space, and $n, \alpha \in \mathbb{N}$. A Tweakable Hash Function is an efficient function mapping an α-bit message M to an n-bit hash value* MD *using a function key called public parameter $P \in \mathcal{P}$ and a tweak $T \in \mathcal{T}$. Therefore, we have* $\mathsf{Th} : \mathcal{P} \times \mathcal{T} \times \{0,1\}^\alpha \rightarrow \{0,1\}^{n(\lambda)}, \quad \mathsf{MD} \leftarrow \mathsf{Th}(P,T,M)$.

For later sections, we may omit the security parameter out of polynomial $n(\lambda)$.

A tweakable hash function takes public parameters P and context information in the form of a tweak T in addition to the message. The public parameters might be thought of as a function key or index. The tweak might be interpreted as a nonce. We use the term public parameter for the function key to emphasize that it is intended to be public.

2.3 The Security of $\mathcal{S}_{\text{leeve}}$

The $\mathcal{S}_{\text{leeve}}$ primitive is composed by the tuple $(\mathsf{Gen}_{\pi_{\mathcal{S}_{\text{leeve}}}}, \mathsf{Sign}, \mathsf{Verify}, \mathsf{Proof}, \mathsf{Verify\text{-}Proof})$. The generation algorithm outputs the pairs of keys, vk and sk, and the backup key bk. The first pair is the regular verification key, used for verifying a signature, and the secret-key used for issuing a signature. While the last key is used to issue the *Proof of Ownership* $\pi_{\mathcal{S}_{\text{leeve}}}$, with respect to vk as follows.

Definition 6 ($\mathcal{S}_{leeve}$[7]). *A fallback scheme* $\mathcal{S}_{leeve} = (\mathsf{Gen}_{\pi_{\mathcal{S}_{leeve}}}, \mathsf{Sign}, \mathsf{Verify}, \mathsf{Proof}, \mathsf{Verify\text{-}Proof})$ *is a set of PPT algorithms:*

- $\mathsf{Gen}_{\pi_{\mathcal{S}_{leeve}}}(1^{\lambda})$ *on input of a security parameter* λ *outputs a private signing key* sk, *a public verification key* vk *and the back up key* bk;
- $\mathsf{Sign}\ (\mathsf{sk}, \mathsf{m})$ *outputs a signature* σ *under* sk *for a message* m *using the designated main signature scheme, in our example this is an ECDSA signature;*
- $\mathsf{Verify}\ (\mathsf{vk}, \sigma, \mathsf{m})$ *outputs* 1 *iff* σ *is a valid signature on* m *under* vk;
- $\mathsf{Proof}(\mathsf{bk}, c)$ *on input of the backup information* bk *and the challenge* c, *it outputs the ownership proof* $\pi_{\mathcal{S}_{leeve}}$. *In our example, this is a WOTS+ signature on the challenge* c *using the fallback key* bk;
- $\mathsf{Verify\text{-}Proof}(\mathsf{vk}, \mathsf{sk}, \pi_{\mathcal{S}_{leeve}}, c)$ *is a deterministic algorithm that on input of a public-key* vk, *secret-key* sk, *a ownership proof* $\pi_{\mathcal{S}_{leeve}}$ *and a challenge* c, *it outputs either* 0, *for an invalid proof, or* 1 *for a valid one.*

The two main security properties of $\mathcal{S}_{\text{leeve}}$ are (1) the capability of issuing a proof to confirm the ownership of the secret key, even in the face of a massive leakage, when the secret key becomes public, and (2) the capability to smoothly switch to another signature scheme, namely a quantum resistant one. Briefly, we formally review both properties.

Definition 7 (Single Proof of Ownership[7]). *For any PPT algorithm* $\mathcal{A}$ *and security parameter* λ, *it holds* $\Pr[(\mathsf{vk}, \mathsf{sk}, \mathsf{bk}) \leftarrow \mathsf{Gen}_{\pi_{\mathcal{S}_{leeve}}}(1^{\lambda}) : (c^*, \pi^*_{\mathcal{S}_{leeve}}) \leftarrow \mathcal{A}(\mathsf{sk}, \mathsf{vk}) \wedge \mathsf{Verify\text{-}Proof}(\mathsf{vk}, \mathsf{sk}, \pi^*_{\mathcal{S}_{leeve}}, c^*) = 1] < negl(\lambda)$ *for all the probabilities are computed over the random coins of the generation and proof verification algorithms and the adversary.*

Definition 8 (Fallback[7]). *We say that the scheme* $(\mathsf{Gen}_{\pi_{\mathcal{S}_{leeve}}}, \mathsf{Sign}, \mathsf{Verify})$, *with secret and verification key respectively* sk *and* vk *such that* $\mathsf{Gen}_{\pi_{\mathcal{S}_{leeve}}}(1^{\lambda}) \rightarrow$

(vk, sk, bk), *has fallback if there are sign and verification algorithms* $\mathsf{Sign}_{\pi_{S_{leeve}}}$ *and* $\mathsf{Verify}_{\pi_{S_{leeve}}}$ *such that* sk *and* bk *can be used as verification and secret keys respectively, along with* $\mathsf{Sign}_{\pi_{S_{leeve}}}$ *and* $\mathsf{Verify}_{\pi_{S_{leeve}}}$ *as fully independent signature scheme.*

2.4 Key Derivation Functions

The Key Derivation Function KDF [8,20] is a cryptographic component that takes as input an initial source of entropy, or initial keying material, and allows for the derivation of one (or more) cryptographically secure key values. This input is not necessarily uniformly distributed and the adversary may have partial knowledge of such input. The adversary, however, should not be able to distinguish an output from a random uniform string of the same length, and a KDF output should not leak information on any of the other generated bits. We note that these KDF output values are not necessarily exclusive for secret key derivation and may optionally be made public depending on the cryptographic use case.

Definition 9 (KDF[20]). *A* KDF *accepts as input four arguments: a value* σ *sampled from a source of keying material, a length value* ℓ*, a salt value* r *defined over a set of possible salt values, and a context variable* c*. The latter two values are both optional. As a result, these values can either be null, or assigned a constant value. In this setting, the source of keying material* Σ *is a two-valued probability distribution* (σ, α) *generated by an efficient probabilistic algorithm. The resulting* KDF *output is a string of* ℓ *bits.*

In this model, the adversary $\mathcal{A}$ should be given the value pair (σ, α) to model the "partial knowledge" of the input entropy. Later in our constructions we rely on the use of $\mathsf{KDF}(\sigma, \ell, r, c)$, for fixed values of ℓ and c. In particular, we fix $r = null$. Hence, we drop two arguments in the later descriptions of the Wotswana by denoting the KDF as a two-value function $\mathsf{KDF}(\sigma, c) = \mathsf{KDF}(\sigma, \ell_{fix}, null, c)$, for a fixed length ℓ_{fix}.

Definition 10 (KDF One-wayness). *A* KDF *is* $(t_{\mathcal{A}}, q, \epsilon)$*-one-way secure if no adversary* $\mathcal{A}$ *running in time* $t_{\mathcal{A}}$ *and making at most* q *queries produces the input entropy* Σ*, when given the output value* σ *and the partial knowledge* α*, with probability* $p > \frac{q}{2^n} + \epsilon$*, where* n *is the length of the input entropy* $|\Sigma|$*.*

3 The WOTSwana Versions

We present two constructions; a linear and a tree based construction. While the former the WOTS+ ladders are concatenated in a *linear* fashion. Each new back up key has nested another one inside "deeper" in the linear structure. The verification of each new signature includes the generation of the previous back up key. The latter construction, *i.e.* the tree based, does not have this feature as each new back up key is located in a different branch. Figure 1 illustrates a simplified outline of both constructions.

3.1 The Linear Construction

Here we introduce a construction for the generation of t proofs of ownership. The main idea is to concatenate t blocks of a variant of the WOTS+ signature. Additionally, we review the notation for the subset of the randomness vector $\mathbf{r} = (r_1, \ldots, r_\ell)$. We denote by $\mathbf{r}_{a,b}$ the subset of $(r_a, \ldots, r_b)$, and our constructions to be presented next rely on the KDF [8,20].

The Auxiliary Blocks: Ladder and Block. Given the security parameter λ, a chaining function c, and $k \leftarrow \mathcal{K}$ from the key space $\mathcal{K}$, Table 2 defines the auxiliary procedures, namely *Ladder* and *Block*. The former is used to derive the new internal "internal public key" $(\mathsf{v}_0, \mathsf{v}_1, \ldots, \mathsf{v}_\ell)$ from the "internal secret key" $(\mathsf{sk}_1, \ldots, \mathsf{sk}_\ell)$. While the latter uses the former, as an internal routine, to derive the secret key to the new "internal secret key", *i.e.* the key one level above in the linear structure. These auxiliary routines are used in the linear and tree based constructions in further sections.

Table 2. The Ladder procedure performs the sequence of the hashes, *i.e.* the "ladders", from the secret key, in order to output a intermediate key, *i.e.* similar to WOTS+ public key. The *Block* procedure concatenates each of the secret key generation block to the next one.

$Ladder_w^k(\mathsf{sk}_1, \ldots, \mathsf{sk}_\ell)$	$Block_w^{P,T,k}(\mathsf{sk}_1, \ldots, \mathsf{sk}_\ell)$
Set $r_p \leftarrow \mathsf{KDF}(\mathsf{sk}_1 \| \ldots \| \mathsf{sk}_\ell, p), 1 \le p \le w-1$	$Ladder_w^k(\mathsf{sk}_1, \ldots, \mathsf{sk}_\ell) \rightarrow (\mathsf{v}_0, \mathsf{v}_1, \ldots, \mathsf{v}_\ell)$
Set $\mathbf{r} = (r_1, \ldots, r_{w-1})$	Set $\mathsf{v} \leftarrow (\mathsf{v}_0, \mathsf{v}_1, \ldots, \mathsf{v}_\ell)$
Set $\mathsf{v}_0 = (\mathbf{r}, k)$	Set $\mathsf{seed} = \mathsf{Th}(P \| T \| \mathsf{v})$
Set $\mathsf{v}_i = c_k^{w-1}(\mathbf{r}, \mathsf{sk}_i), 1 \le i \le \ell$	Set $\mathsf{sk}'_i \leftarrow \mathsf{KDF}(\mathsf{seed}, i), 1 \le i \le \ell$
Return $\mathsf{v} = (\mathsf{v}_0, \mathsf{v}_1, \ldots, \mathsf{v}_\ell)$	Return $(\mathsf{sk}'_1, \ldots, \mathsf{sk}'_\ell)$

From now we present the three main algorithms for key generation, and proof generation and verification for both constructions: Linear-Gen, Linear-Proof, in Table 3, and Linear-Verify-Proof in Table 4.

Table 3. The generation procedure selects the random secret key $(\mathsf{sk}_1^{(t)}, \ldots, \mathsf{sk}_\ell^{(t)})$, and interactively, by executing *Ladder* and *Block* algorithms, creates t signatures while keeping the tweaks in the list $\mathbb{T}$. The generation of the proofs works by traversing the linear construction for each new proof of ownership from t to 1.

$\mathsf{Linear\text{-}Gen}_w^{k,t}(\lambda)$	$\mathsf{Linear\text{-}Proof}_w^{k,t,\mathsf{st}}(c, \mathsf{bk})$
Pick $P \xleftarrow{\$} \{0,1\}^{n(\lambda)}$, $\mathcal{X} \xleftarrow{\$} \{0,1\}^{n(\lambda)}$	Parse $\mathsf{bk} \rightarrow (\mathbb{T}[\mathsf{st}], \mathsf{bk}_1^{(t)}, \ldots, \mathsf{bk}_\ell^{(t)})$
Pick $\mathbb{T}[t] \xleftarrow{\$} \{0,1\}^{n(\lambda)}$, random value a	Set $r_p \leftarrow \mathsf{KDF}(\mathsf{bk}_1^{(t)} \Vert \ldots \Vert \mathsf{bk}_\ell^{(t)} \Vert p), 1 \le p \le w-1$
Set $\mathsf{bk}_i^{(t)} \xleftarrow{\$} \{0,1\}^{n(\lambda)}, 1 \le i \le \ell$	Set $\mathbf{r} = (r_1, \ldots, r_{w-1})$
For $t \ge i \ge 2$	For $t \ge i \ge \mathsf{st}$
$\quad(\mathsf{bk}_1^{(i-1)}, \ldots, \mathsf{bk}_\ell^{(i-1)})$	$\quad\mathbb{T}[i-1] \leftarrow \mathsf{KDF}(\mathbb{T}[i], i)$
$\quad\leftarrow Block_w^{P,\mathbb{T}[i],k}(\mathsf{bk}_1^{(i)}, \ldots, \mathsf{bk}_\ell^{(i)})$	$\quad(\mathsf{bk}_1^{(i-1)}, \ldots, \mathsf{bk}_\ell^{(i-1)})$
$\quad\mathbb{T}[i-1] \leftarrow \mathsf{KDF}(\mathbb{T}[i], i)$	$\qquad\leftarrow Block_w^{P,\mathbb{T}[i],k}(\mathsf{bk}_1^{(i)}, \ldots, \mathsf{bk}_\ell^{(i)})$
Set $(\mathsf{bk}_1^{(1)}, \ldots, \mathsf{bk}_\ell^{(1)})$	Compute $c \rightarrow (c_1, \ldots, c_{\ell_1})$,
$\quad\leftarrow Block_w^{P,\mathbb{T}[2],k}(\mathsf{bk}_1^{(2)}, \ldots, \mathsf{bk}_\ell^{(2)})$	$\qquad$for $c_i \in \{0, \ldots, w-1\}$
Set $\mathsf{v}^{(1)} \leftarrow Ladder(\mathsf{bk}_1^{(1)}, \ldots, \mathsf{bk}_\ell^{(1)})$	Compute checksum $C = \sum_{i=1}^{\ell_1}(w-1-c_i)$,
Set $W = \mathsf{Th}(P \Vert \mathbb{T}[1] \Vert \mathsf{v}^{(1)})$	$\quad$and its base w representation $(C_1, \ldots, C_{\ell_2})$
Set $\mathsf{sk} = a \cdot \mathsf{Th}(P \Vert \mathcal{X} \Vert W)$	Parse $B = c \Vert C$ as $(b_1, \ldots, b_{\ell_1+\ell_2})$, $\ell = \ell_1 + \ell_2$
Set $\mathsf{vk} \leftarrow g^{\mathsf{sk}}$	Set $\sigma_i = c_k^{b_i}(\mathbf{r}, \mathsf{sk}_i)$, $1 \le i \le \ell$
Set $\mathsf{bk} \leftarrow (\mathbb{T}[t], \mathsf{bk}_1^{(t)}, \ldots, \mathsf{bk}_\ell^{(t)})$	Set $\sigma_0 \leftarrow (\mathbb{T}[\mathsf{st}], st, \mathbf{r}, k), h \leftarrow g^a$
Return $(\mathsf{bk}, \mathsf{sk}, \mathsf{vk})$	Return $\pi_{\mathcal{S}_{\text{leeve}}} = (\sigma_0, \sigma_1, \ldots, \sigma_\ell, h)$

Table 4. The intuition of the verification procedure is that given the state st, *i.e.* the height in the linear structure, and execute the list of hashes and generation through the ladders up until the verification key on the upmost position.

$\mathsf{Linear\text{-}Verify\text{-}Proof}_w^{k,t,\mathsf{st}}(\mathsf{vk}, \pi_{\mathcal{S}_{\text{leeve}}}, c)$
Parse $\pi_{\mathcal{S}_{\text{leeve}}} \rightarrow (T, st, \mathbf{r}, k, \sigma_1, \ldots, \sigma_\ell, h)$
Compute $c \rightarrow (c_1, \ldots, c_{\ell_1})$, $c_i \in \{0, \ldots, w-1\}$
Compute checksum $C = \sum_{i=1}^{\ell_1}(w-1-c_i)$,
$\quad$and its base w representation $(C_1, \ldots, C_{\ell_2})$
Parse $B = \mathsf{c} \Vert C$ as $(b_1, \ldots, b_{\ell_1+\ell_2})$ and $\ell = \ell_1 + \ell_2$
Set $\mathsf{v}_0 = (\mathbf{r}, k)$
Set $\mathsf{v}_i = c_k^{w-1-b_i}(\sigma_i, \mathbf{r}_{b_i+1,w-1})$, $1 \le i \le \ell$
Set $\mathsf{v} = (\mathsf{v}_0, \ldots, \mathsf{v}_\ell)$
For $st \ge j > 1$
$\quad W^{(j)} = \mathsf{Th}(P \Vert T \Vert \mathsf{v}^{(j)})$
$\quad$Set $(\mathsf{bk}_1^{(j)}, \ldots, \mathsf{bk}_\ell^{(j)}) \leftarrow \mathsf{KDF}(W^{(j)}, i)$, $1 \le i \le \ell$
$\quad$Set $T \leftarrow \mathsf{KDF}(T, j)$
$\quad$Set $\mathsf{v}^{(j-1)} \leftarrow Ladder(\mathsf{bk}_1^{(j)}, \ldots, \mathsf{bk}_\ell^{(j)})$
$W^{(1)} = \mathsf{Th}(P \Vert T \Vert \mathsf{v}^{(1)})$
$\mathsf{sk}' = \mathsf{Th}(P \Vert \mathcal{X} \Vert W^{(1)})$
If $\mathsf{vk} = h^{\mathsf{sk}'}$: Output 1
Else: Output 0

3.2 The Tree Construction

The next construction (Tables 5 and 6) makes use of Merkle Tree, which is described as (MT.Gen, MT.Proof, MT.Verify). That is, given 2^t strings $s^{(1)}, \dots, s^{(2^t)}$, the root generation is given by $\mathsf{MT.Gen}(s^{(1)}, \dots, s^{(2^t)}) = \mathsf{M}$, such that for any $s^{(i)}$, $\mathsf{MT.Proof}(\mathsf{M}, s^{(i)}) = \pi_{\mathsf{M}}^{(i)}$. The generated proof $\pi^{(i)}$, can be verified as the verification $\mathsf{MT.Verify}(\mathsf{M}, s^{(i)}, \pi_{\mathsf{M}}^{(i)}) = 1$. The proof fails to verify if the output is $\mathsf{MT.Verify}(\mathsf{M}, s^{(i)}, \pi_{\mathsf{M}}^{(i)}) = 0$.

Table 5. Differently from the linear construction, the sets of values for each back up key $(\mathsf{bk}_1^{(i)}, \dots, c_\ell^{(i)})$ in a Merkle Tree whose root is given by its root M. The root of the Merkle-tree M is a component of the signature, therefore it is only revealed when generating a proof of ownership. Namely, it is not disclosed while using the ECDSA signature.

$\mathsf{Tree\text{-}Gen}_w^{k,t}(\lambda)$	$\mathsf{Tree\text{-}Proof}_w^{k,\mathsf{st}}(c, \mathsf{bk})$
Pick $P \xleftarrow{\$} \{0,1\}^{n(\lambda)}$, random value a	Parse $\mathsf{bk} \rightarrow (\mathsf{M}, u, \dots, (\mathsf{bk}_1^{(\mathsf{st})}, \dots, \mathsf{bk}_\ell^{(\mathsf{st})}), \dots)$
For $1 \leq i \leq t$	Set $r_p \leftarrow \mathsf{KDF}(\mathsf{bk}_1^{(\mathsf{st})} \| \dots \| \mathsf{bk}_\ell^{(\mathsf{st})}, p), 1 \leq p \leq w-1$
Pick $\mathsf{bk}_j^{(i)} \xleftarrow{\$} \{0,1\}^{n(\lambda)}, 1 \leq j \leq \ell$	Set $\mathbf{r} = (r_1, \dots, r_{w-1})$
Set $T \leftarrow \mathsf{KDF}(\mathsf{bk}_1^{(i)} \| \dots \| \mathsf{bk}_\ell^{(i)}, i)$	Set $(\mathsf{y}_1^{(\mathsf{st})}, \dots, \mathsf{y}_\ell^{(\mathsf{st})}) \leftarrow Block_w^{P,T,k}(\mathsf{bk}_1^{(\mathsf{st})}, \dots, \mathsf{bk}_\ell^{(\mathsf{st})})$
Set $(\mathsf{y}_1^{(i)}, \dots, \mathsf{y}_\ell^{(i)})$	Set $\mathsf{v}^{(\mathsf{st})} \leftarrow Ladder(\mathsf{y}_1^{(\mathsf{st})}, \dots, \mathsf{y}_\ell^{(\mathsf{st})})$
$\leftarrow Block_w^{P,T,k}(\mathsf{bk}_1^{(i)}, \dots, \mathsf{bk}_\ell^{(i)})$	Set $T \leftarrow \mathsf{KDF}(\mathsf{y}_1^{(\mathsf{st})} \| \dots \| \mathsf{y}_\ell^{(\mathsf{st})}, \mathsf{st})$
Set $\mathsf{v}^{(i)} \leftarrow Ladder(\mathsf{y}_i^{(i)}, \dots, \mathsf{y}_\ell^{(i)})$	Set $W = \mathsf{Th}(P \| T \| \mathsf{v}^{(\mathsf{st})})$
Set $W^{(i)} = \mathsf{Th}(P \| T \| \mathsf{v}^{(i)})$	Set $\mathsf{MT.Proof}(W, \mathsf{M}) = \pi_{\mathsf{M}}$
Set $\mathsf{M} = \mathsf{MT.Gen}(W^{(1)}, \dots, W^{(t)})$	Compute $c \rightarrow (c_1, \dots, c_{\ell_1})$, for $c_i \in \{0, \dots, w-1\}$
Pick $u \xleftarrow{\$} \{0,1\}^{n(\lambda)}$	Compute checksum $C = \sum_{i=1}^{\ell_1}(w - 1 - c_i)$
Set $\mathsf{sk} \leftarrow a \cdot \mathsf{Th}(P \| \mathsf{M} \| u)$	and its base w representation $(C_1, \dots, C_{\ell_2})$
Set $\mathsf{vk} \leftarrow g^{\mathsf{sk}}$	Parse $B = c \| C$ as $(b_1, \dots, b_{\ell_1+\ell_2})$ and $\ell = \ell_1 + \ell_2$
Set $\mathsf{bk} \leftarrow (\mathsf{M}, u, (\mathsf{bk}_1^{(1)}, \dots, \mathsf{bk}_\ell^{(1)}),$	Set $\sigma_i = c_k^{b_i}(\mathbf{r}, \mathsf{bk}_i)$, for $1 \leq i \leq \ell$
$\dots, (\mathsf{bk}_1^{(t)}, \dots, \mathsf{bk}_\ell^{(t)}))$	Set $\sigma_0 \leftarrow (\mathsf{M}, u, \pi_{\mathsf{M}}, \mathsf{st}, \mathbf{r}, k)$, $h \leftarrow g^a$
Return $(\mathsf{bk}, \mathsf{sk}, \mathsf{vk})$	Return $\pi_{\mathcal{S}_{\mathrm{leeve}}} = (\sigma_0, \sigma_1, \dots, \sigma_\ell, h)$

4 Security Analysis

We assume an adversary attempting to forge a single WOTSwana proof-of-ownership, hence this section discusses the unforgeability of such proofs for our linear and tree based constructions, respectively Sects. 4.2 and 4.3. Given that both constructions allow multiple proofs, we start by defining an extended security game, in comparison to the one reviewed in Sect. 2.3, where we model the adversary accessing multiple proofs before issuing its forgery. Next we prove the security of our constructions in the light of such a security game.

Table 6. The verification of the proof of ownership $\pi_{\mathcal{S}_{\text{leeve}}}$ depends directly on a two-step verification: (1) the used back up key is part of the Merkle Tree given in the proof, and (2) and the obtained public key vk is correct.

$\mathsf{Tree\text{-}Verify\text{-}Proof}_w^{k,\mathsf{st}}(\mathsf{vk}, \pi_{\mathcal{S}_{\text{leeve}}}, c)$
Parse $\pi_{\mathcal{S}_{\text{leeve}}} \rightarrow (\sigma_0, \sigma_1, \ldots, \sigma_\ell, h)$
Parse $\sigma_0 \rightarrow (\mathsf{M}, u, \pi_\mathsf{M}, \mathsf{st}, \mathbf{r}, k)$
Compute $c \rightarrow (c_1, \ldots, c_{\ell_1})$, $c_i \in \{0, \ldots, w-1\}$
Compute checksum $C = \sum_{i=1}^{\ell_1}(w - 1 - c_i)$,
and its base w representation $(C_1, \ldots, C_{\ell_2})$
Parse $B = c\|C$ as $(b_1, \ldots, b_{\ell_1+\ell_2})$ and $\ell = \ell_1 + \ell_2$
Set $y_i = c_k^{w-1-b_i}(\mathbf{r}_{b_i+1,w-1}, \sigma_i)$, $1 \leq i \leq \ell$
Compute $(\mathsf{v}_0, \ldots, \mathsf{v}_\ell) \leftarrow \mathit{Ladder}(y_1, \ldots, y_\ell)$
Set $T \leftarrow \mathsf{KDF}(\mathsf{v}_0\|\ldots\|\mathsf{v}_\ell, \mathsf{st})$
Compute $W = \mathsf{Th}(P\|T\|(\mathsf{v}_0, \ldots, \mathsf{v}_\ell))$
If the following equations hold, return 1
$\mathsf{MT.Verify}(\mathsf{M}, W, \pi_\mathsf{M}) = 1$
$\mathsf{vk} = h^{\mathsf{Th}(P\|\mathsf{M}\|u)}$

4.1 The Extended Security Definition for WOTSwana

The next definition provide the adversary with access to the Ownership Proof Oracle $\mathcal{O}_{\mathsf{Proof}}(\mathsf{bk}, \cdot)$, since the original scheme has the capacity of only a *single* proof, extending it to multiple ones. The adversary can sample up to $t-1$ proofs by querying the oracle with challenges c_i of its choice, assuming the scheme with capacity of t proofs of ownership.

Definition 11 (Multiple Proofs of Ownership). *For any PPT $\mathcal{A}$, which can query the Ownership Proof Oracle $\mathcal{O}_{\mathsf{Proof}}(\mathsf{bk}, \cdot)$ for challenge-proofs pairs $(c_i, \pi^i_{\mathcal{S}_{leeve}})$, and a list of queried pairs $\mathcal{C}$ initially empty, on a polynomial number of queries, it holds*

$$\Pr[(\mathsf{vk}, \mathsf{sk}, \mathsf{bk}) \leftarrow \mathsf{Gen}_{\pi_{\mathcal{S}_{leeve}}}(1^\lambda) : (c^*, \pi^*_{\mathcal{S}_{leeve}}) \leftarrow \mathcal{A}^{\mathcal{O}_{\mathsf{Proof}}(\mathsf{bk},\cdot)}(\mathsf{sk}, \mathsf{vk})$$
$$\wedge (c^*, \pi^*_{\mathcal{S}_{leeve}}) \notin \mathcal{C} \wedge \mathsf{Verify\text{-}Proof}(\mathsf{vk}, \mathsf{sk}, \pi^*_{\mathcal{S}_{leeve}}, c^*) = 1] < negl(\lambda)$$

for all the probabilities are computed over the random coins of the generation and proof verification algorithms and the adversary.

4.2 The Unforgeability of the (Linear) Proof of Ownership

To produce a forgery and subvert the security of our construction, $\mathcal{A}$ may attempt to explore different attack vectors. For example, $\mathcal{A}$ may attempt to invert the used KDF, find a collision in the used tweakable hash function $\mathsf{Th}(\cdot)$,

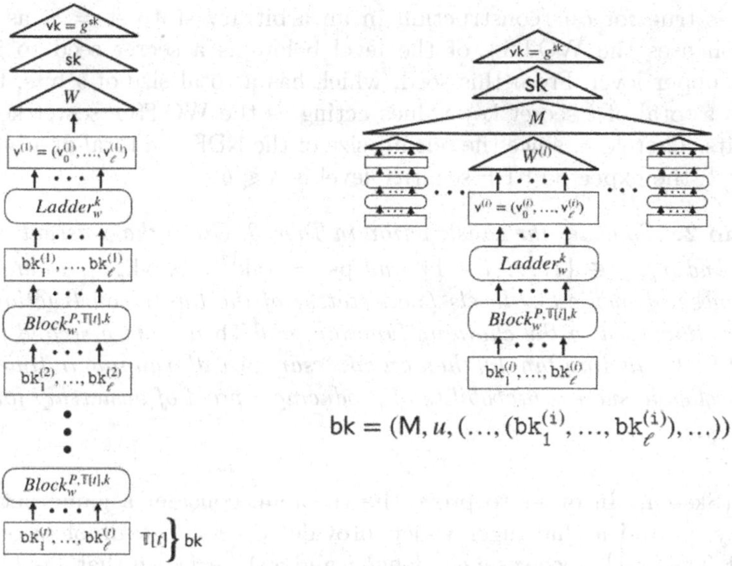

Fig. 1. Outline of the linear (left) and the tree (right) based constructions of WOTSwana. Note that the linear constructions back up key is the lowest part of the data structure. Whereas the tree based construction, the back up key is given by the Merkle Tree root M, the random value u and the each individual WOTS+ key $\mathtt{bk}^{(i)} = (\mathtt{bk}_1^{(i)}, \ldots, \mathtt{bk}_\ell^{(i)})$.

break the unforgeability of the used signature scheme (i.e., WOTS+), or even forge a proof of inclusion for the Merkle tree used in the construction. These scenarios represent the different attack vectors we identified and model in this section.

Theorem 1. *Consider the construction in Table 3, and assume a secure* KDF, *as in Definition 10, is used as in the Block and Ladder routines, given by Table 2 with security parameter λ and a b-bit long string as seed, then a PPT adversary $\mathcal{A}$, with running in time at most $t_{\mathcal{A}}$, produces a forged proof of ownership for any state $\mathtt{st} = j$ with success probability at most $\epsilon \leq 1/2^b$ by performing an exhaustive search over all possible seed values.*

Proof: (Sketch.) We consider that the security of a key derivation function is measured by the amount of work required to distinguish the output of the KDF from a truly uniformly distributed bit string of the same length, under the assumption that the seed is the only unknown input to the KDF. We know that the security upper bound for the subversion of the KDF is defined by the exhaustive search over all the possible seed values, which can be recovered in (at least) 2^b attempts, where b is the bit-length of the seed. This bound holds if the output key is sufficiently long (*i.e.*, no less than b bits).

This is true for our construction in an arbitrary state $\mathsf{st} = j$, as the key generation uses the WOTS+ of the level below as a secret seed to generate the next upper level. From this seed, which has a total size of b bits, the KDF produces a total of ℓ secret key values acting as the WOTS+ secret keys, each with b bits. Therefore, since the output size of the KDF is a total of a bit stream of size $\ell \cdot b$, the expected KDF security level is $\lambda \leqslant b$. □

Theorem 2. *Consider the construction in Table 3. Given the consecutive public-key* pk_j *and* σ_j, $j \in \{1, \ldots, t-1\}$ *and* $\mathsf{pk}_j = (\mathsf{vk}_1^{(j)}, \ldots, \mathsf{vk}_\ell^{(j)})$*, where* t *is the total number of public-key levels (*i.e., *states) of the linear construction. If* $\mathcal{H}_n$ *is the function used in the chaining function, and* Th *is from a second preimage resistant hash-function family, then an adversary* $\mathcal{A}$ *with running in time at most* $t_{\mathcal{A}}$ *has negligible success probability of producing a proof of ownership forgery for any level* j.

Proof: (Sketch.) In order to prove the theorem, consider a game between an adversary $\mathcal{A}$, and a challenger which provides access to a proof of ownership oracle $\mathcal{O}$. The oracle receives a challenge c and a state j such that $j \in \{1, \ldots, t-1\}$, and returns a proof of ownership $\pi_{S_{\text{leeve}}}$ and the WOTS+ verification key internally generated by the *Ladder* procedure of Table 2, *i.e.* $(\mathsf{vk}_0, \mathsf{vk}_1, \ldots, \mathsf{vk}_\ell)$. The adversary goal is to output a proof of ownership forgery $\pi'_{S_{\text{leeve}}}$ for an arbitrary challenge of its choice $c_\prime$.

Since WOTS+ uses a family of functions $\mathcal{F}_n : \{f_k : \{0,1\}^n \rightarrow \{0,1\}^n | k \in \mathcal{K}_n\}$ with a key space $\mathcal{K}_n$, and we know from [15] that, to attack the EU-CMA property, an adversary $\mathcal{A}$ must break the security level λ_1, such that $\lambda_1 \geqslant n - \log_2(w^2\ell + w)$, given the WOTS+ parameter w.

Assume $\mathcal{A}$ succeeds. Then $\mathcal{A}$ produces a forgery for the challenge c' such that $c \neq c'$, for previously queried challenges. Then $\mathcal{A}$ breaks the unforgeability of the WOTS+ scheme, which is considered infeasible as long as the scheme is instantiated with an appropriate security parameter.

Alternatively, $\mathcal{A}$ may attempt to subvert the underlying tweakable hash function Th used for public-key compression and find a different set of top ladder values or verification keys that result in a public-key collision. Therefore, to successfully perform this attack, $\mathcal{A}$ must find a colliding set of verification keys $(\mathsf{vk}'_1, \ldots, \mathsf{vk}'_\ell) \neq (\mathsf{vk}_1, \ldots, \mathsf{vk}_\ell)$ and a potentially different tweak T', such that $\mathsf{Th}(P \,||\, T' \,||\, \mathsf{vk}'_1, \ldots, \mathsf{vk}'_\ell) = \mathsf{Th}(P \,||\, T \,||\, \mathsf{vk}_1, \ldots, \mathsf{vk}_\ell)$. We know from [3] that to find the described collision, $\mathcal{A}$ must break the second-preimage resistance property of Th. This break corresponds to an amount of work of $\lambda_2 = 2^n$, where n is the digest output of the used tweakable hash function. As a result, the security level λ of our construction against an attacker attempting to produce a forgery is equivalent to the attack that requires the less amount of work. Consequently, $\lambda = \min\{\lambda_1, \lambda_2\}$.

We note that, however, previous proofs-of-ownership are trivially forgeable, as the public key of the level j is used as a seed for the secret key generation of the level $j-1$. □

Theorem 3. *The adversary $\mathcal{A}$ running in time at most $t_{\mathcal{A}}$, that issues arbitrary challenges c_j, and receives consecutive public-key and proofs of ownership* $(\mathsf{pk}_j, \pi_{\mathcal{S}_{leeve}}{}^{(j)})$*,* $j \in \{1, \ldots, t-1\}$ *and* $\mathsf{pk}_j = (\mathsf{vk}_1^{(j)}, \ldots, \mathsf{vk}_\ell^{(j)})$*, has negligible probability of producing a proof of ownership forgery for any of the unrevealed levels $j + \delta$, s.t. $\delta \geq 1$, if both $\mathcal{H}_n$ and Th are from a second preimage resistant hash-function family.*

Proof: (Sketch.) We start by highlighting that this proof is an extension of the previous proof where $\mathcal{A}$ queries the oracle for a proof of ownership on an arbitrary challenge using the key of index $j \in \{1, \ldots, h\}$. In this setting, however, the oracle $\mathcal{O}$ receives a set of consecutive index queries and challenge pairs (j, c_j), and releases the corresponding proofs $\pi_{\mathcal{S}_{\text{leeve}}}^{(j)}$ for each of the queried levels. The previous proof is easily applicable to this stronger adversarial setting, where $\mathcal{A}$ starts by setting the index to query to the first level of the construction ($j = 1$), creates a challenge of their choosing, and sends it to the oracle. Upon every response from the oracle, $\mathcal{A}$ successively increments the index j by 1, creates a new challenge for that index, and sends the challenge/index pair to the $\mathcal{O}$. To succeed, $\mathcal{A}$ must produce a forgery of the proof-of-ownership for level $j + 1$.

In this case, $\mathcal{A}$ must perform the exact same work and subvert the described security level λ. Initially, the reader may expect that the release of different key material associated with different indexes could provide $\mathcal{A}$ with additional knowledge or even additional attack vectors (e.g., multi-target attacks). The used primitives, however, are instantiated in a manner that is resistant against multi-target attacks and therefore require the adversary to actually break the second preimage of the used functions. □

4.3 Attacking the Tree Construction

The previous proofs are not exclusive to the linear construction and also apply to the tree construction as the main introduction in the latter approach is the use of a tree to aggregate string values. We now review the security of the added data structure.

Theorem 4. *Given a merkle root, a string, and a proof of inclusion* $(\mathsf{M}, s^{(i)}, \pi_{\mathsf{M}}^{(i)})$ *for a specific level $i \in \{1, \ldots, t\}$, the adversary has negligible probability of producing a proof forgery $\pi_{\mathsf{M}}'^{(i)}$ for the tree construction, if the hash function used for Merkle Tree generation is from a second preimage resistant hash function family.*

Proof: (Sketch.) In this setting, $\mathcal{A}$ attempts to prove inclusion of a value that is not in the original Merkle tree data structure generated by the signer. Since the algorithm $\mathsf{MT.Verify}(\mathsf{M}, s^{(i)}, \pi_{\mathsf{M}}^{(i)}) = 0$ if a proof $\pi_{\mathsf{M}}^{(i)}$ fails to verify, and the value M is fixed upon the generation of the key material, $\mathcal{A}$ must produce a value $s'^{(i)} \neq s^{(i)}$ and use the algorithm $\mathsf{MT.Proof}(\mathsf{M}, s^{(i)})$ to generate a colliding

$\pi_{\mathsf{M}}^{(i)}$. Alternatively, $\mathcal{A}$ may attempt to generate a different tree with a different set of values that results in a tree with the same Merkle root. Both settings are equivalent to finding a different second preimage, such that the malicious values result in a collision with the initial signer generated values. □

5 Formal Methods Analysis

In this section, we define the Verifpal [17,19] model used to analyze Wotswana along with the description of some of the technical challenges inherent to the model development process. The purpose of this section is to confirm the early analytical proofs of the construction and verify whether or not both approaches for security analyses provide the same results.

5.1 Verifpal and Modeling Challenges

Verifpal is a software that allows for the verification of the security of cryptographic protocols and is particularly oriented towards real-world practitioners attempting to integrate formal verification into their line of work. Moreover, this tool supports advanced security properties such as forward secrecy or key compromise impersonation. We note that Verifpal has been used to verify security properties of widely deployed tools, such as Signal [18] and TLS 1.3 [4].

Challenges to Modelling Wotswana in Verifpal. Symbolic model protocol verifiers, typically face a problem when analysing complex protocols: the space of the user states and different combinations of variables the verifier must assess, quickly becomes too large for the verifier to terminate in a reasonable time. Verifpal attempts to optimize for this challenge by separating the analysis into a number of stages in which it gradually allows the increasing modification of states. The different variable combinations quickly becoming too large is a challenge we faced while a ladder, where each level contains a WOTS+ keypair, and the tool constantly issued memory fault errors when starting to perform the hash ladder iterations for the key generation processed. These memory errors resulted in the stopping of the verification process in a faulty manner. Additionally, we highlight the lack of existence of the *XOR* logical function in the verification tool, which leads to initial design attempts with a slightly changed variant of the chaining function used in WOTS+.

Verifpal Model of Wotswana. To avoid the memory fault issues derived from iterating different attack scenarios involving a high number of hash function calls, we model a simpler Lamport signature scheme instead of WOTS+. For simplicity of the model and readability of the code, we simulate a setting with only two ladder levels, each containing a hash-based key pair. This code, containing the Verifpal model, is open-sourced and published in [25].

Participants. We model two participants: a signer and a verifier. The signer generates an initial Lamport keypair $(\mathsf{sk}, \mathsf{pk})$ to sign a single bit $b \in \{0, 1\}$. Upon generating this first hash-based key pair, the signer compresses the first public key value using the tweakable hash function and then uses a hash-based key derivation function (HKDF) to generate the second Lamport keypair. This HKDF receives the first Lamport public key, now compressed into a single value, as key material to be expanded and outputs a second Lamport keypair. This second public key is also compressed using a tweakable hash function. For consistency with the protocol specification from this work, we compress the Lamport public keys using a tweakable hash function. We note, however, that this step is purely for readability as the main purpose of using tweakable hash functions in Wotswana is to mitigate multi-target attacks, which are out of scope of the results produced by the tool.

Attacker Model and Message Flow. We assume the Dolev-Yao model [13] where the adversary is in charge of delivering the messages. Therefore, all the transmitted messages go through the adversary first or are in fact delivered by $\mathcal{A}$. In our model, the signer starts by sending to the verifier the following values: a signature on a 1 bit from one level lower than the top one, and a public key for verification. We note that all the public key values transmitted between both parties are authenticated using the guarded constant feature from Verifpal, which allows the model to ensure that the public key used to verify the signature is authenticated. Therefore, man-in-the-middle or impersonation attacks are out of the scope of the analysis. We consider this approach as the scheme is designed to be used in a blockchain setting where the public keys are openly available on the distributed ledger.

We assume that after signing a message, and submitting the signature to the network, the signer exposes the next public key on the ladder to inform the network of what the next verification key is. This exposure is achieved using the *leaks* command present in the Verifpal tool, which fully exposes a variable to the adversary. The goal of this step is to simulate the adversary $\mathcal{A}$ from the security game described in the formal security proof, where $\mathcal{A}$ cannot invert a hash function, yet is capable of looking at messages sent to the network before anyone else.

5.2 Modelling Results

After performing these steps, we run four confidentiality queries and request the tool to perform an analysis on whether or not the adversary can break the confidentiality of the two individual Lamport secret keys $(\mathsf{sk}_0, \mathsf{sk}_1)$ for each of the ladder levels. The tool output a positive result for two of these confidentiality queries. Therefore, the adversary can fully obtain the secret key values for the top Lamport key pair and produce forgeries on additional messages. The lower two secret values, however, remain confidential. Therefore, the adversary $\mathcal{A}$ is not expected to be able to produce a forgery with the necessary key, which matches our results obtained in the security proof.

In summary, Verifpal returned that there is no breach in the confidentiality of any of the secret key variables that must remain private for the construction to achieve its security goals, thus outputting a formal positive result about our design. We note that this formal methods analysis does not find attacks involving structural weaknesses of the used cryptographic primitives. For example, the use of a hash function with a small security parameter is not in the scope of the attack model of the tool. Therefore, implementations of this construction must take into account and appropriate choice of security parameters.

6 Use Case: Encrypted Group Chat

We now expose an alternative use-case for this work, namely an approach where secure messaging apps can use our construction to achieve constant-sized messaging in an encrypted group chat setting, while preserving fundamental security properties for secure messaging (e.g., deniability). We start by exposing the main existing approaches along with its associated communication complexity. Finally, we showcase a Wotswana -based encrypted group chat.

Trivial Client Fan-Out. One scheme is for Bob to encrypt the message with every participant's key. In a group chat with 30 other participants, Bob sends the message 30 times, encrypting each message for the intended reader. An advantage of client-side fan-out is that it reuses the same protocol used for two-person conversations. This approach, however, quickly becomes prohibitive if the group is big or the network bandwidth is small.

Improved Client Fan-Out. Alternatively, Bob can encrypt a message for a global group chat shared key and attach an authentication tag (i.e., MAC) for each of the group participants. In a group chat with 30 other participants, Bob sends one message and 30 tags for the intended readers. We call this scheme "improved client fan-out" as it improves on the communication complexity of the trivial fan-out approach. An advantage of this approach is the bandwidth savings as this only results in the linearly increasing of the number of sent authentication tags and constant-sized number of messages, which in this case is only one.

Signed Server Fan-Out. A final possible approach is for Bob to encrypt a single message for a global group chat shared key along with a digital signature. In a group chat with 30 other participants, Bob sends a single message along with one digital signature for the server, which then fans out the same message for the total set of 30 participants. This scheme can be called "signed server fan-out". This approach can even feature an optimization where the server does not fan out and instead simply relays the message to a message fetching service. Later in time, clients in this group chat can contact this fetching service and obtain the corresponding message(s) associated with this group chat.

FFS-Based Encrypted Group Chat. We now discuss the approach that relies on forward-forgeable signatures [22] to achieve linear complexity and preserve deniability. Bob encrypts a single message for a global group chat shared key and attaches a single forward-forgeable digital signature. In a group chat with 30 other participants, Bob sends a single message along with one FFS for the server, which then fans out the same message for the total set of 30 participants. This scheme can be called "FFS-based group chat" and features a potentially optimal communication complexity as the sender simply sends a single message, regardless of the total number of participants in the group, which results in bandwidth savings and, unlike the previous approach, preserves the deniability property as for each newly signed message or a specific time window, Bob removes the non-repudiation property of the previously sent message. Therefore, Bob is able to deny sending specific group messages. Table 7 illustrates a communication complexity comparison of the different approaches.

Table 7. Communication complexity comparison for the different approaches. Where $|\sigma|$, $|t|$ and $|m|$ are the sizes of signatures, tags and message, and N is the number of group participants.

Group Chat Approach	Communication Complexity
Trivial Client fan-out	$\mathcal{O}((N-1)\cdot(\lvert m\rvert+\lvert t\rvert))$
Improved Client fan-out	$\mathcal{O}(\lvert m\rvert+(N-1)\cdot\lvert t\rvert)$
Signed Server fan-out	$\mathcal{O}(\lvert m\rvert+\lvert\sigma\rvert)$
Wotswana-based [This Work]	$\mathcal{O}(\lvert m\rvert+\lvert\sigma'\rvert)$

7 Conclusion

The recently introduced $\mathcal{S}_{\text{leeve}}$ primitive adds an extra layer of security for cryptocurrency wallets. It is specifically designed to provide means for the users to assure the ownership of the cryptographic keys in the event of a massive leak. A wallet with the $\mathcal{S}_{\text{leeve}}$ design provides the user with a *back up key* which can be used to generate a single proof of ownership; a clear limitation of the original design.

This work extends the security guarantees of $\mathcal{S}_{\text{leeve}}$ by introducing a new design named Wotswana, and its main feature is the capability of issuing multiples proofs of ownership. This novel capability naturally extends the original security definition for $\mathcal{S}_{\text{leeve}}$. Furthermore, we propose two constructions for Wotswana and in both cases the back up keys provided by the Sleeve design are kept two types of data structures: (1) a linear and (2) a binary tree.

Finally, we prove the security of both constructions given an extended security notion adapted from the single proof of ownership, *i.e.* multiple proofs of ownership. Moreover we analyse the security of our constructions based on formal methods, *i.e.* Verifpal. We introduced practical use cases for our design and initiated the process of contacting development groups to analyze the possibility of integrating this construction into some of their services. We hope this design helps the community, and raises awareness about the importance of preparing for the eventual integration of quantum secure solutions in commercial applications.

References

1. Aranha, D.F., Novaes, F.R., Takahashi, A., Tibouchi, M., Yarom, Y.: Ladderleak: Breaking ECDSA with less than one bit of nonce leakage. In Proceedings of the 2020 ACM SIGSAC Conference on Computer and Communications Security, CCS 2020, New York, NY, USA, pp. 225–242. Association for Computing Machinery (2020)
2. Badertscher, C., Gazi, P., Kiayias, A., Russell, A., Zikas, V.: Ouroboros genesis: composable proof-of-stake blockchains with dynamic availability. In: Lie, D., Mannan, M., Backes, M., Wang, X.F. (eds.) ACM CCS 2018: 25th Conference on Computer and Communications Security, Toronto, ON, Canada, October 15–19, pp. 913–930. ACM Press (2018)
3. Bernstein, D.J., Hülsing, A., Kölbl, S., Niederhagen, R., Rijneveld, J., Schwabe, P.: The SPHINCS$^+$ signature framework. In: Cavallaro, L., Kinder, J., Wang, X.F., Katz, J. (eds.), ACM CCS 2019: 26th Conference on Computer and Communications Security, 11–15 November 2019, pp. 2129–2146. ACM Press (2019)
4. Bhargavan, K., Blanchet, B., Kobeissi, N.: Verified models and reference implementations for the tls 1.3 standard candidate. In: 2017 IEEE Symposium on Security and Privacy (SP), pp. 483–502 (2017)
5. Buchmann, J., Dahmen, E., Hülsing, A.: XMSS - a practical forward secure signature scheme based on minimal security assumptions. In: Yang, B.-Y. (ed.) PQCrypto 2011. LNCS, vol. 7071, pp. 117–129. Springer, Heidelberg (2011). https://doi.org/10.1007/978-3-642-25405-5_8
6. Chaum, D., Larangeira, M., Yaksetig, M.: Tweakable sleeve: a novel sleeve construction based on tweakable hash functions. In: The 3rd International Conference on Mathematical Research for Blockchain Economy (MARBLE) (2022)
7. Chaum, D., Larangeira, M., Yaksetig, M., Carter, W.: Wots+ up my sleeve! a hidden secure fallback for cryptocurrency wallets. In: International Conference on Applied Cryptography and Network Security, pp. 195–219. Springer (2021)
8. Chen, L.: Recommendation for key derivation using pseudorandom functions-revision 1. NIST special publication (2021). Accessed 20 Feb 2022
9. Courtois, N.T., Emirdag, P., Valsorda, F.: Private key recovery combination attacks: on extreme fragility of popular bitcoin key management, wallet and cold storage solutions in presence of poor RNG events. Cryptology ePrint Archive, Report 2014/848 (2014). http://eprint.iacr.org/2014/848
10. Dahmen, E., Okeya, K., Takagi, T., Vuillaume, C.: Digital signatures out of second-preimage resistant hash functions. In: Buchmann, J., Ding, J. (eds.) PQCrypto 2008. LNCS, vol. 5299, pp. 109–123. Springer, Heidelberg (2008). https://doi.org/10.1007/978-3-540-88403-3_8
11. Das, P., Faust, S., Loss, J.: A formal treatment of deterministic wallets. In: Cavallaro, L., Kinder, J., Wang, X.F., Katz, J. (eds.) ACM CCS 2019: 26th Conference on Computer and Communications Security, 11–15 November 2019, pp. 651–668. ACM Press (2019)
12. David, B., Gaži, P., Kiayias, A., Russell, A.: Ouroboros Praos: an adaptively-secure, semi-synchronous proof-of-stake blockchain. In: Nielsen, J.B., Rijmen, V. (eds.) EUROCRYPT 2018. LNCS, vol. 10821, pp. 66–98. Springer, Cham (2018). https://doi.org/10.1007/978-3-319-78375-8_3
13. Dolev, D., Yao, A.: On the security of public key protocols. IEEE Trans. Inf. Theory **29**(2), 198–208 (1983)

14. Fan, C.-I., Tseng, Y.-F., Su, H.-P., Hsu, R.-H., Kikuchi, H.: Secure hierarchical bitcoin wallet scheme against privilege escalation attacks. Int. J. Inf. Secur. **19**, 245–255 (2019)
15. Hülsing, A.: W-OTS+ – shorter signatures for hash-based signature schemes. In: Youssef, A., Nitaj, A., Hassanien, A.E. (eds.) AFRICACRYPT 2013. LNCS, vol. 7918, pp. 173–188. Springer, Heidelberg (2013). https://doi.org/10.1007/978-3-642-38553-7_10
16. Kiayias, A., Russell, A., David, B., Oliynykov, R.: Ouroboros: a provably secure proof-of-stake blockchain protocol. In: Katz, J., Shacham, H. (eds.) CRYPTO 2017. LNCS, vol. 10401, pp. 357–388. Springer, Cham (2017). https://doi.org/10.1007/978-3-319-63688-7_12
17. Kobeissi, N.: Verifpal: Cryptographic Protocol Analysis for Students and Engineers (2021). https://verifpal.com. Accessed 05 Mar 2022
18. Kobeissi, N., Bhargavan, K., Blanchet, B.: Automated verification for secure messaging protocols and their implementations: a symbolic and computational approach. In: 2017 IEEE European Symposium on Security and Privacy (EuroS P), pp. 435–450 (2017)
19. Kobeissi, N., Nicolas, G., Tiwari, M.: Verifpal: cryptographic protocol analysis for the real world. In: Proceedings of the 2020 ACM SIGSAC Conference on Cloud Computing Security Workshop, CCSW 2020, New York, NY, USA, 2020, pp. 159. Association for Computing Machinery (2020)
20. Krawczyk, H.: Cryptographic extraction and key derivation: the HKDF scheme. In: Rabin, T. (ed.) CRYPTO 2010. LNCS, vol. 6223, pp. 631–648. Springer, Heidelberg (2010). https://doi.org/10.1007/978-3-642-14623-7_34
21. Nakamoto, S.: Bitcoin: a peer-to-peer electronic cash system (2009)
22. Specter, M.A., Park, S., Green, M.: Keyforge: non-attributable email from forward-forgeable signatures. In: Bailey, M., Greenstadt, R. (eds.) 30th USENIX Security Symposium, USENIX Security 2021, August 11–13, 2021, pp. 1755–1773. USENIX Association (2021)
23. Trinity attack incident part 1: Summary and next steps. https://blog.iota.org/trinity-attack-incident-part-1-summary-and-next-steps-8c7ccc4d81e8. Accessed 22 Sept 2020
24. Wood, G.: Ethereum: A secure decentralised generalised transaction ledger. Ethereum Project Yellow Paper **151**, 1–32 (2014)
25. xx network. Wotswana verifpal model. https://github.com/xx-labs/wotswana

Author Index

S.-H. Seo and H. Seo (Eds.): ICISC 2022, LNCS 13849, pp. 513–514, 2023.
https://doi.org/10.1007/978-3-031-29371-9